Educational Research

Sixth Edition

SAGE was founded in 1965 by Sara Miller McCune to support the dissemination of usable knowledge by publishing innovative and high-quality research and teaching content. Today, we publish over 900 journals, including those of more than 400 learned societies, more than 800 new books per year, and a growing range of library products including archives, data, case studies, reports, and video. SAGE remains majority-owned by our founder, and after Sara's lifetime will become owned by a charitable trust that secures our continued independence.

Los Angeles | London | New Delhi | Singapore | Washington DC | Melbourne

Educational Research

Quantitative, Qualitative, and Mixed Approaches

Sixth Edition

R. Burke Johnson
University of South Alabama

Larry Christensen
University of South Alabama

Los Angeles | London | New Delhi
Singapore | Washington DC | Melbourne

FOR INFORMATION:

SAGE Publications, Inc.
2455 Teller Road
Thousand Oaks, California 91320
E-mail: order@sagepub.com

SAGE Publications Ltd.
1 Oliver's Yard
55 City Road
London, EC1Y 1SP
United Kingdom

SAGE Publications India Pvt. Ltd.
B 1/I 1 Mohan Cooperative Industrial Area
Mathura Road, New Delhi 110 044
India

SAGE Publications Asia-Pacific Pte. Ltd.
3 Church Street
#10-04 Samsung Hub
Singapore 049483

Acquisitions Editor: Terri Accomazzo
Development Editor: Jessica Miller
eLearning Editor: Robert Higgins
Editorial Assistant: Erik Helton
Production Editor: Kelly DeRosa
Copy Editor: Christina West
Typesetter: C&M Digitals (P) Ltd.
Proofreader: Theresa Kay
Indexer: Jeanne Busemeyer
Cover Designer: Scott Van Atta
Marketing Manager: Kara Kindstrom

Printed in the United States of America

Names: Johnson, Burke, author. | Christensen, Larry B., 1941- author.

Title: Educational research : quantitative, qualitative, and mixed approaches / R. Burke Johnson, University of South Alabama, Larry Christensen, University of South Alabama.

Description: Sixth edition. | Thousand Oaks, California : SAGE Publications, Inc., 2016. | Includes bibliographical references and index.

Identifiers: LCCN 2016013693 | ISBN 978-1-4833-9160-1 (hardcover : alk. paper)

Subjects: LCSH: Education research.

Classification: LCC LB1028 .J59 2016 | DDC 370.72—dc23 LC record available at https://lccn.loc.gov/2016013693

This book is printed on acid-free paper.

18 19 20 9 8 7 6 5 4 3 2

Brief Contents

Detailed Contents

PREFACE

Welcome to the sixth edition of *Educational Research: Quantitative, Qualitative, and Mixed Approaches.* This text is written for the introductory research methods course that is required in most colleges in the United States. *We assume no prior knowledge of research methods on the part of our readers.* Our book can be used as a first text for undergraduate- or graduate-level courses. Instructors should be able to cover the material in one semester. Instructors also can choose to emphasize some material over the other.

PURPOSE

We had several purposes in writing this textbook. The first was a desire to write an introductory research methods book that was accurate and up-to-date. We come from interdisciplinary backgrounds and have attempted to incorporate our respective insights into this book. Dr. Johnson is an educational research methodologist and program evaluator, with additional graduate training in psychology, public policy, and sociology; Dr. Christensen is a psychological research methodologist and the author of a highly successful book titled *Experimental Methodology* (now in its 12th edition under the revised title *Research Methods, Design, and Analysis*). We have kept up with the changes taking place in the field of research methods in our disciplines, and we continue to incorporate the latest information in this textbook, including references that allow interested readers to further examine original sources.

Second, we have tried to write a research methods textbook that takes an evenhanded approach to the different types of educational research. Whereas many texts emphasize one method at the expense of others, we believe that *all major approaches to research discussed in this text have merit* when they are employed carefully and properly. We show the strengths and appropriateness of each method and demonstrate how the experts in each area conduct high-quality research and how they view their approach to research.

Third, we have tried to make our textbook highly readable and to make learning about research fun. Believe it or not, learning about research methods can be exciting. We are excited about research methods, and we share our enthusiasm with you without losing the necessary rigor.

Finally, we have tried to enable readers to become critical *consumers* of research and *users* of research. We suspect that most readers of this text will be called on at some point in their careers to summarize research literature, write a research proposal, construct a questionnaire, or test an idea empirically. *Educational Research,* sixth edition, will help prepare you for these activities and will help you become adept at reading, understanding, critiquing, and building on published empirical research articles.

ORGANIZATION OF THE BOOK

We have organized the sixth edition of *Educational Research* to follow the major components or steps involved in the research process.

Part I. Introduction

In this section we introduce you to the field of educational research. We begin by defining *science* in an inclusive way and explaining the general research process. We discuss inductive and deductive reasoning, and we describe the exploratory (knowledge-generation) and confirmatory (knowledge-testing) components of the research wheel. We outline some general areas of research, such as basic research, applied research, action research, evaluation research, and orientational research. We examine the three major research paradigms: (1) quantitative research, (2) qualitative research, and (3) mixed research. Last, we include a new chapter on *action research* to engage students in thinking about and applying the ideas discussed in this book. Each of the remaining 19 chapters ends with a section titled "Action Research Reflection"—the purpose of this section is to help students reflect on the chapter material and relate it to their lives and places of work.

Part II. Planning the Research Study

In this section we carefully explain how to come up with a research idea, conduct a review of the research literature, write research questions and hypotheses, and organize and write a research proposal. We also explain the importance of ethics in educational research and how to write an informed consent form. Upon completion of this section, students will be ready to begin writing a research proposal.

Part III. Foundations of Research

In Part III we cover concepts that researchers must master before fully understanding or conducting a research study. We begin with an introduction to measurement. Without reliable and valid measurement, nothing else really matters because poor data quality cannot be fixed. Next we discuss the *six major methods of data collection*: tests, questionnaires, interviews, focus groups, observations, and constructed and secondary or existing data. We then explain the procedures for selecting samples of people to participate in a research study. Finally, we discuss the importance of research validity (or trustworthiness or legitimation) in quantitative, qualitative, and mixed research, showing the primary threats to good research and providing specific techniques used to prevent mistakes.

Part IV. Selecting a Research Method

In Part IV we provide extensive discussion of the major methods of research or "research methods" and demonstrate how to match the appropriate research design with various research questions. We divide Part IV into three sections. In Section A we explain the five major approaches to quantitative research—strong experimental research, quasi-experimental research, weak experimental research, single-case research, and nonexperimental quantitative research. In Section B we explain the five major approaches to qualitative research—narrative inquiry, case study research, phenomenology, ethnography, and grounded theory. In Section C we explain mixed methods research, which includes many approaches and possibilities.

Part V. Analyzing the Data

In this section we provide two chapters on quantitative data analysis (descriptive and inferential statistics) and one chapter on how to analyze qualitative and mixed research data.

Part VI. Writing the Research Report

In this final part, we explain how to prepare research manuscripts in a format that can be submitted to an academic journal for publication. We explain how to use the guidelines from the sixth edition of the *Publication Manual of the American Psychological Association* (2010), the guidelines required by the vast majority of journals in education and psychology.

Features of the Text

We have included several features in the sixth edition of *Educational Research* to make the task of learning about research easier for students.

In addition to **opening vignettes** that connect research with current events, each chapter begins with a list of **objectives** to get students thinking about what they are going to learn.

Within the chapters, several learning aids assist with reviewing key concepts. These include margin definitions of all the **key terms**, multiple **examples** of concepts from published research studies, **review questions** at the end of major sections, and margin **icons** to connect the reader to journal articles and tools and tips provided at the book's companion website.

Each chapter ends with a full **chapter summary**, a list of the key terms used in the chapter, **discussion questions**, **research exercises**, relevant **Internet sites**, and **recommended reading**.

New to the Sixth Edition

While keeping the vast majority of the book intact for long-term users, we have made multiple changes in the sixth edition to better reflect the latest advances in educational research and to improve the student learning experience. The following are of particular note:

- Removed the chapter on historical research to shorten the book. This chapter is now available in custom editions for instructors who would like to continue covering this potentially useful material.
- Many professors have their students write a research proposal in the introductory research course. Therefore, most chapters now include an exercise at the end called **Proposal**

Exercises. The purpose of these exercises is to help students relate the chapter material to writing a research proposal.

- Chapter 1: Included an additional objective of educational research, specifically "understanding" as in subjective understanding, which is at the core of qualitative research.
- Chapter 2: Included a little more emphasis on controlling for extraneous variables in non-experimental quantitative research.
- Chapter 4: Included new sections on literature review, problem statement, purpose statement, and research questions for mixed methods research. Also added brief discussion of meta-synthesis (the qualitative version of meta-analysis). Added extension and generating a new theory to Table 4.1.
- Chapter 7: Added short discussion of consequential validity.
- Chapter 9: Added new sections on Technology and Tests, Technology and Questionnaires, Technology and Interviews, Technology and Focus Groups, and added a new comparative table on Modes of Questionnaire and Interview Data Collection.
- Chapter 10: Revised definition of event sampling, and for mixed methods sampling relation, a nonparallel relation has been added to make the list exhaustive; therefore, there are now 10 mixed sampling designs.
- Chapter 11: Added two new types of validity/legitimation for mixed methods research, specifically pragmatic legitimation and integration legitimation; emphasized that a good synonym for internal validity is "causal validity" and for external validity is "generalizing validity"; emphasized that some threats to internal validity are only for single-group designs and that others affect multigroup designs. Emphasized that random assignment is an excellent way to eliminate the threats for multi-group designs. Deleted Figure 11.4 because the material is covered in the chapter on sampling; removed much of the material on operationalism (except a short discussion of operationalizing a construct) because it was dated; idiographic causation is now called "idiographic or local or singular causation" to emphasize what it is about directly in its name; interpretative validity is now called "interpretative or emic validity" to emphasize what it is about and avoid confusion. The types of mixed methods validity are now called types of mixed methods *legitimation* to emphasize the use of the term "legitimation" in mixed methods research.
- Chapter 12: Separated the discussion of random assignment from the discussion of matching and in Figure 12.3 (previously the emphasis was on using these jointly under the heading of matching); added definition of single-blind procedure; gave a more positive overall assessment of repeated-measures designs.
- Chapter 14: Emphasized, a little more, the need (and how) to control for extraneous variables in nonexperimental quantitative research. Intervening variable is now called "intervening or mediating variable" to emphasize the synonyms.
- Chapter 15: Added definition of within-case analysis, to provide a contrast with cross-case analysis. Sample size for grounded theory, in Table 15.2, now reads "20–30 people or collect data until theoretical saturation is reached." Also, the definition of a case study is slightly improved.
- Chapter 16: Added a continuum for emphases of phenomenology, including the following categories: particularistic experiences, group-level experiences, and transcendental experiences.
- Chapter 17: Exhibit 17.2 (A Multiple-Dimension Approach to Mixed Design) has been rewritten; changed "weaknesses" to "limitations" in Tables 17.1, 17.2, and 17.4.
- Chapter 20: Added discussion of first-stage and second-stage coding; added brief section on qualitative subgroup analysis; added a section on joint displays in mixed methods research; added a chapter appendix discussing 13 additional kinds of coding as a resource for the interested beginning or advanced qualitative data analyst.

- Chapter 21: Added headings for the mixed methods Result section in a research report.
- Glossary: Added definitions of consequential validity, first-stage coding, meta-synthesis, pragmatic legitimation, integration legitimation, qualitative subgroup analysis, second-stage coding, single-blind procedure, understanding, and within-case analysis; edited definitions of event sampling, reflexivity, and case study research.

Digital Resources for Instructors and Students

Additional digital resources further support and enhance the learning goals of the sixth edition of *Educational Research: Quantitative, Qualitative, and Mixed Approaches*. These digital resources include the following:

Password-Protected Instructor Teaching Site

edge.sagepub.com/rbjohnson6e

This password-protected site offers instructors a variety of resources that supplement the book material, including the following:

- A **test bank** offers a large and diverse set of test questions and answers for each chapter of the book. Multiple-choice and true/false questions are included for every chapter to aid instructors in assessing students' progress and understanding.
- **PowerPoint presentations** are designed to assist with lecture and review, highlighting essential content, features, and artwork from the book.
- Carefully selected, web-based **video resources** feature relevant content for use in independent and classroom-based exploration of key topics.
- **Teaching tips** are designed to help instructors conceptualize their overall teaching plan for each chapter.
- **Lecture notes** summarize key concepts on a chapter-by-chapter basis to assist in preparing for lecture and class discussion.
- Lively and stimulating ideas for **class activities** in and out of the classroom are provided. These are designed to reinforce active learning.
- Links to relevant **web resources** direct instructors to additional tools for further research on important chapter topics.
- Downloadable versions of the tables, figures, and worksheets are provided.
- The authors have provided **suggested answers to the review questions** that are found throughout each chapter.
- **Sample syllabi** for quarter, semester, and online courses are provided.

Open-Access Student Study Site

edge.sagepub.com/rbjohnson6e

This web-based student study site provides a variety of additional resources to enhance students' understanding of the book's content and take their learning one step further. The site includes the following:

- **Lecture notes** are here for students to print out and bring to class.
- **Self-quizzes** allow students to independently assess their progress in learning course material.

- **eFlashcards** are study tools that reinforce student understanding and learning of the key terms and concepts outlined in the chapters.
- Carefully selected, web-based **video links** feature relevant content for use in independent and classroom-based exploration of key topics.
- Links to relevant **web resources** direct students to additional tools for further research on important chapter topics.

Book Icons

Below are several icons you will find throughout the text, which will guide you to additional materials found on the student study site.

Interactive and expandable **concept maps** for each chapter. These clickable, downward-branching maps present each chapter's content in a hierarchical structure so that students can visualize the relationships among different concepts.

Full-text **SAGE research articles** are presented for each chapter so that students can read published examples the key topics covered.

Author-created **tools and tips** provide information on a variety of subjects and include helpful web resources, writing tips, and an SPSS data set.

NOTE TO STUDENTS

You are probably wondering how best to study research methods. When studying, first and foremost, use the book's companion website, which has been developed to help you learn the material. As you read the book, we suggest that you begin each chapter by reading the learning objectives and the chapter summary. This will give you an overview of the material. Then look at the chapter concept map included at the book's companion website. This will give you the "big picture." Next, read the chapter carefully. After finishing the chapter, answer the study questions and make sure you understand each concept shown in the concept map. Also, read the lecture provided at the companion website, where we touch on most of the major points of each chapter; this will be quick reading after having read the chapter. To get practice doing research and to learn by doing, complete at least one of the research exercises at the end of each chapter and consider completing the action research activities. As you prepare for tests, make sure that you know the definitions of all the key terms because these are the building blocks and the vocabulary of the research "language." Don't get lost in the details! Continue to use the concept maps to remind yourself of the big picture. Finally, read as many of the empirical research articles as you can, because one of the best ways to learn how to understand, design, and conduct educational research is to read many high-quality, published research articles in your research area. If you do these things, you can become an expert consumer and producer of research, as well as get an A in your class!

NOTE TO INSTRUCTORS

To help keep the length and price of the textbook low for students, we have placed the many supporting empirical research articles on the companion website (rather than including them in the textbook). Your students can easily print out these articles. Also, you will find many helpful teaching tips and materials at the Instructor Teaching Site described above. You also will find the student companion website useful, especially the lectures and the concept maps. One effective in-class teaching strategy would be to connect to the concept maps (via the Internet) during class and discuss these in class. Another strategy is to have your students print out the lectures and then discuss the lectures in class. Yet another strategy is to use the PowerPoint presentations provided at the Instructor Teaching Site. Please note that we have removed the chapter on historical research from this edition, to help shorten the book. If you want this chapter, however, it is available in custom editions. This text also works very well in online courses; the lectures on the companion website were developed by Burke Johnson specifically for his online research course. Our goal is to provide you with the most up-to-date and useful book and the best set of supplements available. Please contact us if you have any questions or suggestions.

COMMENTS

We hope that you (students and instructors) will send your comments to us so that we can continually improve our textbook and the companion website. You can contact us at the following email address: bjohnson@southalabama.edu (Burke Johnson).

Acknowledgments

First and foremost, Burke Johnson would like to thank his wife, Dr. Lisa A. Turner, for putting up with the long days and for being the first reviewer of everything he wrote. Second, we offer our sincere and special thanks to Terri Accomazzo (our editor), Jessica Miller (our development editor), Erik Helton (editorial assistant), and Robert Higgins (digital content editor). Thanks also go to our outstanding copy editor, Christina West, and our production editor, Kelly DeRosa, who meticulously worked with us to get the manuscript into its "perfect" final form. In short, we thank the entire SAGE team for their professionalism, friendliness, emphasis on high-quality work, and openness to innovation—everyone at SAGE was always ready to provide ideas and help when it was needed.

We also offer our gratitude and thanks to our students and to our expert reviewers for their many insights and useful comments. Our reviewers are as follows:

First edition reviewers:

Amy Gillet, University of Wisconsin–Stout

Bill Gilley, University of South Alabama

Bryan Griffin, Georgia Southern University

Beverly A. Joyce, Dowling College

Robert W. Lissitz, University of Maryland at College Park

Joe Newman, University of South Alabama

Doris L. Prater, University of Houston–Clear Lake

Joan Quilling, University of Missouri–Columbia

Thomas A. Romberg, University of Wisconsin

Bikas Sinha, Indian Statistical Institute, Calcutta, India

Paul Westmeyer, The University of Texas at San Antonio

Second edition reviewers:

Kathy Green, University of Denver

Tony Onwuegbuzie, University of South Florida

Shaireen Rasheed, Long Island University

Vemelle Tyler, University of South Carolina–Aiken

Daniel Weigel, Southern Oklahoma State University

Third edition reviewers:

Don Dillman, Washington State University

Jim Van Haneghan, University of South Alabama

Jason D. Baker, Regent University

Ronald S. Beebe, Cleveland State University

Dorinda J. Gallant, The Ohio State University

John Hanes, Regent University

John A. Huss, Northern Kentucky University

David R. Kovach, The University of Toledo

Vincent Rinaldo, Niagara University

Sandra L. Stein, Rider University

Wilford A. Weber, University of Houston

Fourth edition reviewers:

Jeff Lorentz, University of Houston–Clear Lake

Rebecca S. Lake, National Louis University

E. Lea Witta, University of Central Florida

David R. Kovach, University of Toledo

Jamie Branam Kridler, East Tennessee State University

Fifth edition reviewers:

Diane Bagwell, University of West Florida

Denetta Dowler, West Virginia University

Cynthia L. Jew, California Lutheran University

Shlomo S. Sawilowsky, Wayne State University

Jennifer Veltsos, Minnesota State University

Lihshing Leigh Wang, University of Cincinnati

Timothy G. Ford, University of Louisiana–Monroe

Misty M. Ginicola, Southern Connecticut State University

John Huss, Northern Kentucky University

Sara C. Lawrence, Texas A&M University–Texarkana

S. Kim MacGregor, Louisiana State University

Patrice D. Petroff, Queens University of Charlotte

Elizabeth Ann Rivet, Bay Path College

Sixth edition reviewers:

Patricia L. Hardré, University of Oklahoma

Joel M. Hicks, Northwestern State University

R. Stewart Mayers, Southeastern Oklahoma State University

Edward Schultz, Midwestern State University

Susan M. Bartel, Maryville University of Saint Louis

Jane Beese, Youngstown State University

Krishna Bista, University of Louisiana at Monroe

Camille L. Bryant, Columbus State University

Ronald F. Dugan, The College of Saint Rose

Lydia Kyei-Blankson, Illinois State University

Patricia A. Lutz, Kutztown University

Benjamin C. Ngwudike, Jackson State University

Graham B. Stead, Cleveland State University

PART I

Introduction

Chapter 1

Introduction to Educational Research

LEARNING OBJECTIVES

After reading this chapter, you should be able to

- Explain the importance of educational research.
- List at least five areas of educational research.
- Explain the difference between basic and applied research.
- Describe evaluation research, action research, and orientational research.
- Discuss the different sources of knowledge.
- Explain the scientific approach to knowledge generation.
- Explain how to determine the quality of a theory or explanation.
- List the six objectives of educational research and provide an example of each.

Visit the Student Study Site for an interactive concept map.

RESEARCH IN REAL LIFE Research Aids Decision Making

istock/Savas Keskiner

In June 2002, New York governor George Pataki signed a state law giving New York City mayor Michael Bloomberg control of that city's public school system. Most observers agree that this is a school system desperately in need of reform. The 1,100 schools within this system educate 1.1 million kids. However, using the word *educate* would seem to be somewhat of a misnomer because only about half of the city's public school students finish high school in 4 years. Only 40 percent of third- through eighth-grade students score at an acceptable level in reading, and only 34 percent do so in math. About 100 of the 1,100 schools are classified by the state as failing, and another 300 are almost as bad. Clearly, something needs to be done.

While campaigning for mayor, Michael Bloomberg had many ideas, one of which was to establish an unpaid board of education that functioned like a corporate board, providing fiscal oversight and expertise. This idea was approved by new legislation and was a radical departure from the old board of education, which was responsible for day-to-day management decisions, including even routine contracting and procurement decisions.

Bloomberg needs to do a lot more than just reconstitute the board of education because no single panacea will fix all of the problems facing the New York City school system. There is no shortage of ideas to assist Bloomberg in this process. Coles (2002) wrote an article in the *City Journal* giving his opinion as to what should be done. He stated that Bloomberg should choose a chancellor from outside the system so that he or she would not be constrained by existing relationships or vested interests. A uniform core curriculum should be established that would focus on basic skills, particularly in the elementary and middle schools. Social promotion should end. Finally, the best teachers should be rewarded, contended Coles, because fully 40% of the city's teachers had failed the basic teacher certification test.

Given differing opinions about what should be done with a school system such as New York City's, which ideas do you think should be implemented? Which ones would provide the best return on capital expenditures and best help students? Obviously, there are many differing philosophies and many differing opinions. However, we contend that policymakers will benefit if they examine the findings of educational research studies that compare the outcomes resulting from implementing different ideas and approaches. This will help eliminate personal bias and vested interests in particular approaches by providing strong evidence of what really works best. In short, research provides an effective and evidentiary way to sort out and resolve differing ideas and opinions on educational issues. Perhaps our most important goal in writing this book is to convince you that it is important and helpful to add the examination and conduct of research to your list of ingredients to use when making decisions about education.

Welcome to the world of educational research! Research has been conducted in virtually every area in the field of education. In fact, the research techniques described in this book are used all over the world to help people in many fields advance their knowledge and solve problems. The search for better and better answers to important questions will probably always continue. In this book, we discuss the way in which research is conducted in an attempt to provide answers to important questions. We hope you will enjoy learning about research, and we hope it opens up new ways of thinking for you.

As you read this book, you will learn how to think about research, how to evaluate the quality of published research reports, and how to conduct research on your own. In a sense, you will also be learning a new *language*, the language of researchers, because researchers use a specialized language or jargon. But remember, don't be afraid of new words. The words used in this book have definitions that represent ideas you can understand, and you have been learning new words and ideas all of your life. On the lighter side, perhaps you can use some of the new words to impress your friends. In sum, we welcome you to the world of research and hope that you will enjoy it. Because this is likely to be a required course for you, we begin by discussing a few reasons for taking a course on educational research methods.

WHY STUDY EDUCATIONAL RESEARCH?

You might have asked, "Why do I have to take a class on educational research?" First of all, research can be more interesting than you might think, and we hope that in time you will find the material and the ways of thinking not only interesting but also beneficial. Second, throughout this book, you will be learning critical thinking skills. Rather than assuming that what is written in a book or what someone says is "fact" or undeniable "truth," you can use the techniques that you will learn for evaluating arguments. In all cases, the question is one of evidence. As a start, we suggest that you take the word *proof* and eliminate it from your vocabulary this semester or quarter when you talk about research results. Proof exists in the realms of mathematics and deductive logic, but in science and research, the best we can do is to provide evidence. Sometimes the evidence is very convincing; at other times, it might not be. You must use your critical thinking skills to judge the available evidence on any given topic. These critical thinking skills will be helpful in your studies and professional work as long as you live. Learning about research methods should help sharpen your critical thinking skills.

Another important reason to study research is to help you better understand discussions of research you hear and see in the media, such as on television and radio, on the Internet, or at professional meetings. Examples of research in our society abound. For example, when you watch a television program, what comes between those short segments of actual programming? Commercials! Do you ever wonder about those "research studies" that claim to "prove" that one laundry detergent is better than another? As you know, the purpose of commercials is to influence what you buy. Advertisers spend millions of dollars each year on marketing research to understand your thinking and behavior. If you watch a sporting event, you will likely see commercials for beer, cars, trucks, food, and tennis shoes. If you watch soap operas in the afternoon, you are likely to see very different commercials. The reason for this variation is that advertisers generally know who is watching what programs at which times. The commercials are developed to appeal to viewers' ways of thinking about what is fun, exciting, and important. And did you know that every major presidential candidate has a research consultant who tries to identify the most effective ways to get your vote and win the election? The point is that other people study you all the time and, in this book, you will learn about the techniques they use. Understanding these techniques should help you be more aware of their efforts.

You will learn here that not all research is created equal. That is, some research studies are more defensible than others. You will learn how to ask the right questions about research studies, and you will find out when to put confidence in a set of research findings. You will learn to ask questions such as these: Was the study an experiment, or was it nonexperimental? Were control groups included in the design? Did the researcher randomly assign participants to the different comparison groups? How did the researchers control for the influence of extraneous variables? How were the participants in the research selected? Did the researcher use techniques that help reduce the effects of human bias?

One day you might need to examine the research on a topic and make an informed judgment about what course of action to take or to recommend to someone else. Therefore, it is important that you understand how to review and evaluate research. Understanding research terminology, the characteristics of the different types of research, and how research can be designed to provide solid evidence will allow you to evaluate research results critically and make informed decisions based on research literatures. A **research literature** is the set of published research studies on a particular topic. A fundamental point to remember is that you should always place more confidence in a research finding when several different researchers in different places and settings have found the same result. You should never treat a single research study as the final word on any topic.

- **Research literature** Set of published research studies on a particular topic

On a practical level, understanding research techniques might even help you in your career as a student and as a professional teacher, counselor, or coach. Perhaps one day you will be asked to write a proposal to obtain a grant or conduct a research study on your own. If you study the contents of this book, you will learn how to design and conduct a defensible study, and you will learn about the different sections in a research grant proposal. You will learn how to construct a questionnaire and how to write a proposal. Furthermore, if you look at the bibliographies in the books you use in your other education courses, you will see that many of these references are research studies. After learning about research, you will be able to go back and evaluate the research studies on which your textbooks are based. In other words, you will not have to accept something as true just because someone said it was true. You might find that an article with what you believe to be a questionable finding is based on highly questionable research strategies.

REVIEW QUESTION

1.1 Why should we study educational research?

Areas of Educational Research

To give you a feel for educational research, let's look at some of the areas of research in education. In Table 1.1 you will find a list of the major divisions and the special interest areas in the American Educational Research Association (AERA). (The AERA website is at http://aera.net.) The AERA is the largest and most prestigious research association in the field of education, and it has approximately 25,000 members. It is composed of university professors from all areas of education; governmental employees; teachers; and professionals from educational think tanks, consulting firms, and testing companies. Each year, approximately 11,000 of these members and many nonmembers attend a national conference sponsored by the AERA, where many attendees present the results of their latest research.

You can see in Table 1.1 that education is a broad field that includes many research areas. Do you see any areas of research in Table 1.1 that seem especially interesting? If you are writing a research paper, you might pick one of these as your starting point. The areas of research listed in Table 1.1 are still fairly general, however. To see the specific areas and topics of current interest to educational researchers, go to the library and browse through the education journals.

TABLE 1.1 Divisions and Special Interest Groups in the American Educational Research Association, 2012–2013*

Major Divisions in the AERA	
Division A: Administration, Organization, & Leadership	Division G: Social Context of Education
Division B: Curriculum Studies	Division H: Research, Evaluation, & Assessment in Schools
Division C: Learning & Instruction	Division I: Education in the Professions
Division D: Measurement & Research Methodology	Division J: Postsecondary Education
Division E: Counseling & Human Development	Division K: Teaching & Teacher Education
Division F: History & Historiography	Division L: Educational Policy & Politics
Special Interest Groups in the AERA (called SIGs)	
Academic Audit Research in Teacher Education	Mixed Methods Research
Action Research	Moral Development and Education
Adolescence and Youth Development	Motivation in Education
Adult Literacy and Adult Education	Multicultural/Multiethnic Education: Research, Theory, and Practice
Advanced Studies of National Databases	Multilevel Modeling
Advanced Technologies for Learning	Multiple Linear Regression: The General Linear Model
Applied Research in Virtual Environments for Learning	Music Education
Arts and Inquiry in the Visual and Performing Arts in Education	NAEP Studies
Arts and Learning	Narrative Research
Arts-Based Educational Research	Online Teaching and Learning
Associates for Research on Private Education	Organizational Theory
Bilingual Education Research	Out-of-School Time
Biographical and Documentary Research	Paulo Freire, Critical Pedagogy, and Emancipation
Brain, Neurosciences, and Education	Peace Education
Career and Technical Education	Philosophical Studies in Education
Caribbean and African Studies in Education	Politics of Education
Catholic Education	Portfolios and Reflection in Teaching and Teacher Education
Chaos & Complexity Theories	Postcolonial Studies and Education
Charter School Research and Evaluation	Problem-Based Education
Classroom Assessment	Professional Development School Research
Classroom Management	Professional Licensure and Certification
Classroom Observation	Professors of Educational Research
Cognition and Assessment	Qualitative Research
Communication of Research	Queer Studies
Computer and Internet Applications in Education	Rasch Measurement
Conflict Resolution and Violence Prevention	Religion and Education
Confucianism, Taoism, and Education	Research Focus on Black Education
Constructivist Theory, Research, and Practice	Research Focus on Education and Sport
Cooperative Learning: Theory, Research, and Practice	Research in Mathematics Education
Critical Educators for Social Justice	

Critical Examination of Race, Ethnicity, Class, and Gender in Education
Critical Issues in Curriculum and Cultural Studies
Critical Perspectives on Early Childhood Education
Cultural Historical Research
Democratic Citizenship in Education
Design and Technology
Dewey Studies
Disability Studies in Education
Districts in Research and Reform
Doctoral Education across the Disciplines
Early Education and Child Development
Education and Philanthropy
Education and Student Development in Cities
Education, Health, and Human Services Linkages
Educational Change
Educational Statisticians
Environmental Education
Faculty Teaching, Evaluation, and Development
Family, School, Community Partnerships
Fiscal Issues, Policy, and Education Finance
Foucault and Contemporary Theory in Education
Grassroots Community & Youth Organizing for Education Reform
Hispanic Research Issues
Holistic Education
Inclusion & Accommodation in Educational Assessment
Indigenous Peoples of the Americas
Indigenous Peoples of the Pacific
Informal Learning Environments Research
Instructional Technology
International Studies
Invitational Learning
Ivan Illich
Language and Social Processes
Large Scale Assessment
Law and Education
Leadership for School Improvement
Leadership for Social Justice
Learning and Teaching in Educational Leadership
Learning Environments
Learning Sciences
Literature
Lives of Teachers
Longitudinal Studies
Marxian Analysis of Society, Schools, and Education
Measurement and Assessment in Higher Education
Media, Culture and Curriculum
Mentorship and Mentoring Practices
Middle-Level Education Research
Research in Reading and Literacy
Research on Evaluation
Research on Giftedness, Creativity, and Talent
Research on Learning and Instruction in Physical Education
Research on Teacher Induction
Research on the Education of Asian and Pacific Americans
Research on the Education of Deaf Persons
Research on the Superintendency
Research on Women and Education
Research Use
Research, Education, Information and School Libraries
Rural Education
Safe Schools and Communities
School Choice
School Community, Climate and Culture
School Effectiveness and School Improvement
School Indicators, Profiles, and Accountability
School Turnaround and Reform
School/University Collaborative Research
Science Teaching and Learning
Second Language Research
Self-Study of Teacher Education Practices
Semiotics in Education
Service-Learning & Experiential Education
Social and Emotional Learning
Social Studies Research
Sociology of Education
Special Education Research
Spirituality and Education
Stress and Coping in Education
Structural Equation Modeling
Studying and Self-Regulated Learning
Supervision and Instructional Leadership
Survey Research in Education
Systems Thinking in Education
Talent Development of Students Placed at Risk
Teacher as Researcher
Teacher's Work/Teachers Unions
Teaching Educational Psychology
Teaching History
Technology as an Agent of Change in Teaching and Learning
Technology, Instruction, Cognition and Learning
Test Validity Research and Evaluation
Tracking and Detracking
Urban Learning, Teaching and Research
Vocabulary
Workplace Learning
Writing and Literacies

*For more information about any of these divisions or special interest groups, go to the AERA website at http://aera.net.

Examples of Educational Research

- **Abstract** Brief summary of what is in an article

The majority of journal articles in education include an abstract on the front page of the article. An **abstract** is a brief summary of what is included in the article. We have reproduced the abstracts of several research articles here so that you can get a feel for what is done in an actual research study. Abstracts are helpful because they are short and include the main ideas of the study. You can often decide whether you want to read a journal article by first reading its abstract. We recommend that you read some full-length research articles as soon as possible to see some full examples of educational research. Throughout this book, we will be putting an icon in the margin telling you to go to the companion website to examine a relevant journal article. You can see the journal article icon right now in the margin. The next time you see it, it will be referring you to a full-length article to download at your convenience.

See Student Study Site for journal articles.

For the moment, just examine the following three abstracts and see if you can determine (a) the purpose of the study, (b) how the researchers studied the phenomenon, and (c) what the major results were.

I. The Development of a Goal to Become a Teacher, by Paul A. Schutz (University of Georgia), Kristen C. Croder (University of Georgia), and Victoria E. White (University of North Carolina at Greensboro), 2001, from *Journal of Educational Psychology*, *93*(2), pp. 299–308.

The purpose of this project was to investigate how the goal of becoming a teacher emerges. The study used interviews to develop goal histories for 8 preservice teachers. There tended to be 4 sources of influence for their goal to become a teacher: (a) family influences, (b) teacher influences, (c) peer influences, and (d) teaching experiences. The categories developed from the interviews to describe the types of influences those sources provided were (a) suggesting that the person become a teacher, (b) encouraging the person to become a teacher, (c) modeling teacher behavior, (d) exposing the person to teaching experiences, and (e) discouraging the person from becoming a teacher. In addition, influences such as critical incidents, emotions, and social-historical factors, such as the status and pay of teachers, were prominent in the goal histories of the participants. Finally, the results of the study are discussed within the context of goals and self-directed behavior.

II. Getting Tough? The Impact of High School Graduation Exams, by Brian A. Jacob at John F. Kennedy School of Government, Harvard University, 2001, from *Educational Evaluation and Policy Analysis*, *23*(3), pp. 99–121.

The impact of high school graduation exams on student achievement and dropout rates is examined. Using data from the National Educational Longitudinal Survey (NELS), this analysis is able to control for prior student achievement and a variety of other student, school, and state characteristics. It was found that graduation tests have no significant impact on 12th-grade math or reading achievement. These results are robust with a variety of specification checks. Although graduation tests have no appreciable effect on the probability of dropping out for the average student, they increase the probability of dropping out among the lowest ability students. These results suggest that policymakers would be well advised to rethink current test policies.

III. Giving Voice to High School Students: Pressure and Boredom, Ya Know What I'm Saying? by Edwin Farrell, George Peguero, Rashed Lindsey, and Ronald White, 1988, from *American Education Research Journal*, *25*(4), pp. 489–502.

> The concerns of students identified as at-risk of dropping out of school in an urban setting were studied using innovative ethnographic methods. Students from the subject population were hired to act as collaborators rather than informants and to collect taped dialogues between themselves and their peers. As collaborators, they also participated in the analysis of data and contributed to identifying the research questions of the inquiry. Data indicated that pressure and boredom were most often mentioned as negative factors in the lives of the students, with pressure emanating from social forces outside of school but contributing to boredom inside.

General Kinds of Research

In this section we introduce you to some of the general kinds of research conducted by educational researchers (see Table 1.2). Although these general research types can overlap at times, they have different purposes and are intended for different audiences.

TABLE 1.2 Summary of General Kinds of Research

Kind of Research	*Key Characteristics*
Basic research	Focuses on generating fundamental knowledge.
Applied research	Focuses on real-world questions and applications.
Evaluation research	Focuses on determining the worth, merit, or quality of intervention programs.
Action research	Focuses on solving local problems that practitioners face.
Orientational research	Focuses on reducing inequality and giving voice to the disadvantaged.

Basic and Applied Research

Research studies can be placed along a continuum with the words *basic research* at one end and the words *applied research* at the other end. The word *mixed* can be placed in the center to represent research that has characteristics of both basic and applied research. Basic research and applied research are typically conducted by researchers at universities. Basic research and applied research are also conducted by researchers working for think tanks, corporations, government agencies, and foundations. The primary outlet for basic and applied research is academic and professional research journals.

Basic research is aimed at generating fundamental knowledge and theoretical understanding about basic human and other natural processes. An example of basic research is a study examining the effect of priming in memory. Priming is "an enhancement of the processing of a stimulus as a function of prior exposure" (Anderson, 1995, p. 459). Assume that a researcher asks you to name a fruit and you say, "Pineapple." Then on the second trial, the researcher either asks you to name another type of fruit or asks you to name a type of dog. Which response do you think you could provide more quickly? It turns out that research participants could name another type of fruit faster than they could name a type of dog when they were asked to name a type of fruit first (Loftus, cited in Anderson). The naming of the fruit on the first trial primed the research participants' mental processing to

Basic research Research aimed at generating fundamental knowledge and theoretical understanding about basic human and other natural processes

name another fruit. It is believed that priming operates because the first exposure activates the complex of neurons in long-term memory, where the concept is being stored. Basic research is usually conducted by using the most rigorous research methods (e.g., experimental) under tightly controlled laboratory conditions. The primary audience includes the other researchers in the research area. The key purpose of basic research is to develop a solid foundation of reliable and fundamental knowledge and theory on which future research can be built.

- **Applied research** Research focused on answering practical questions to provide relatively immediate solutions

At the other end of the continuum is applied research. **Applied research** focuses on answering real-world, practical questions to provide relatively immediate solutions. Topics for applied research are often driven by current problems in education and by policymakers' concerns. Applied research is often conducted in more natural settings (i.e., more realistic or real-world settings) than basic research. An applied research study might focus on the effects of retaining low-performing elementary school students in their present grade level or on the relative effectiveness of two approaches to counseling (e.g., behavior therapy versus cognitive therapy). In the former, the results would potentially have practical implications for education policy; in the latter, the results would potentially have implications for practicing counselors. The primary audiences for applied research are other applied researchers (who read the results in educational research journals) as well as policymakers, directors, and managers of programs who also read research journals. Applied research often leads to the development of interventions and programs aimed at improving societal conditions, which leads us to the next type of research.

Evaluation Research

See Journal Article 1.1 on the Student Study Site.

- **Evaluation** Determining the worth, merit, or quality of an evaluation object

When interventions and social or educational programs aimed at improving various conditions are implemented, evaluation research is often carried out to determine how well the programs work in real-world settings and to show how they might be improved. Evaluation research, or, more simply, **evaluation**, specifically involves determining the worth, merit, or quality of an evaluation object, such as an educational program. Evaluation requires evaluators to make value judgments about evaluation objects (e.g., Program XYZ is a good program, and it should be continued; Program ABC is a bad program, and it should be discontinued). An evaluation object (also called the *evaluand*) is the thing being evaluated: a program, a person, or a product (Guba & Lincoln, 1981; Scriven, 1967; Worthen, Sanders, & Fitzpatrick, 1997). An educational program might be an afterschool program for students with behavioral problems or a new curriculum at school. A person might be your new school district superintendent. A product might be a new textbook or a new piece of equipment that a school is considering purchasing.

- **Formative evaluation** Evaluation focused on improving the evaluation object

- **Summative evaluation** Evaluation focused on determining the overall effectiveness and usefulness of the evaluation object

Evaluation traditionally is subdivided into two types according to the purpose of the evaluation. When the primary purpose of an evaluation is to lead to judgments about how a program can be improved, it is called a **formative evaluation**. Formative evaluation information helps program developers and support staff design, implement, and improve their program so that it works well. When the primary purpose of an evaluation is to lead to judgments about whether a program is effective and whether it should be continued, it is called a **summative evaluation**. Summative evaluation information is important for policymakers and others who commission programs when they make funding decisions and when they have to make choices about which competing programs will be supported and which will be eliminated.

It is currently popular to divide evaluation into five areas or types (e.g., Rossi, Lipsey, & Freeman, 2004), each of which is based on a fundamental evaluation question:

1. Needs assessment: Is there a need for this type of program?
2. Theory assessment: Is this program conceptualized in a way that it should work?
3. Implementation assessment: Was this program implemented properly and according to the program plan?
4. Impact assessment: Did this program have an impact on its intended targets?
5. Efficiency assessment: Is this program cost-effective?

As you can see, evaluation can provide important information to educators. On the basis of the evidence collected and the recommendations made, program evaluators provide an important voice in decision making about educational and other social programs.

Action Research

In Chapter 3, we devote an entire chapter to action research. Therefore, for the moment, we just want to get the basic idea and a definition into your thinking. **Action research** is focused on solving specific problems that local practitioners face in their schools and communities (Lewin, 1946; Stringer, 2013). It views your classroom or other work environment as the place to conduct research. Action research is based on the idea that having a "researcher attitude" is helpful in dealing with your complex and changing environments. This attitude involves continuously identifying new problems that you want to work on and trying new strategies and actions to see what improves your situation. Many practitioners find action research helpful because it helps them to integrate theory and research with practice. We hope all of our readers of this book will take the attitude of the "action researcher" as they go about their professional careers (i.e., think about how research can help you improve your practices and conduct research sometimes to empirically test your ideas).

- **Action research** Applied research focused on solving practitioners' local problems

Orientational Research

The last general type of research, called **orientational research**, focuses on collecting information to help a researcher advance a specific ideological or political position or orientation that he or she believes will improve some part of our society (e.g., Sandoval, 2000; L. T. Smith, 2008). Orientational research also focuses on "giving voice" and increased power to the disadvantaged in society. Orientational researchers are concerned about such issues as social discrimination and the inequitable distribution of power and wealth in society. Although all orientational researchers are concerned with *reducing* inequality of some form, there are several variants of orientational research. The most common areas of focus are class stratification (i.e., income and wealth inequality), gender inequality, racial and ethnic inequality, sexual orientation inequality, and international inequality (i.e., rich and poor nations).

- **Orientational research** Research explicitly done for the purpose of advancing an ideological position or orientation

All researchers are ideological to some degree (e.g., in their selection of their research topics, in the recommendations they make), but orientational researchers make their ideology and political agendas very explicit. Orientational research is sometimes called *critical theory research* (Anyon, 2009). This is appropriate because these researchers often

See Journal Article 1.2 on the Student Study Site.

are critical of "mainstream research," which they argue supports the current power structure in society. If orientational research sounds interesting, you will find a wealth of information on the web (using search terms such as *critical theory*, *ethnic studies*, *feminism*, *postcolonialism*, and *queer theory*).

REVIEW QUESTIONS

1.2 What are the definitions of the five general kinds of research?

1.3 Why is it important that both basic and applied research be done?

1.4 What is the difference between formative and summative evaluation?

1.5 What is the key question associated with each of the following forms of evaluation: needs assessment, theory assessment, implementation assessment, impact assessment, and efficiency assessment?

Sources of Knowledge

Take a moment now to consider how you have learned about the world around you. Try to identify the source or sources of one of your particular beliefs (e.g., parents, friends, books, tradition, culture, thinking, experiences). For example, consider your political party identification (i.e., Democrat, Republican, independent, or something else). Political scientists have shown that college students' party identification can often be predicted by their parents' party identification. How does your party identification compare with that of your parents? Obviously, many additional influences affect party identification. Can you identify some of them?

In this section, we examine the primary ways in which people relate to the world and how they generate knowledge. The study of knowledge—including its nature, how it is gained or generated, how it is warranted, and the standards that are used to judge its adequacy—is known as **epistemology**. Epistemology sometimes is called the "theory of knowledge." We group the sources of knowledge into the primary areas discussed in the field of epistemology.

- **Epistemology** The theory of knowledge and its justification

Experience

- **Empiricism** The idea that knowledge comes from experience

- **Empirical statement** A statement based on observation, experiment, or experience

Empiricism is the idea that all knowledge comes from experience. We learn by observing, and when we observe, we rely on our sensory perception. Each day of our lives, we look, feel, hear, smell, and taste so that we can understand our surroundings. According to the philosophical doctrine of empiricism, what we observe with our senses is said to be *true*. John Locke (1632–1704), a proponent of this idea, said that our mind at birth is a *tabula rasa*, a blank slate ready to be written on by our environment. Throughout our lives, our slate is filled up with knowledge based on our experiences. The statement "I know the car is blue because I saw it" is an example of an **empirical statement**: a statement based on observation, experiment, or experience. *Empirical* is a fancy word meaning "based on observation, experiment, or experience." The word *empirical* denotes that a statement is capable of being verified or disproved by observation, experiment, or experience. In the next paragraph, we try to trace some of the sources of experiences you might have had during your lifetime.

Throughout our lives, we participate in and learn about the world around us. We interact with people and generate our personal knowledge. In the beginning, we are born at a certain time, in a certain place, into a specific family that uses a specific language. When we are young, our family is the most important source of our knowledge, our attitudes, and our values. As we grow older, other people and social institutions around us—including our peers, our religion, our schools (and libraries), our economy, our government, and the various media we are exposed to or seek out—influence us more and more. We learn the customs, beliefs, and traditions of the people around us. As we learn "how things are," we construct our personal knowledge and viewpoints about our worlds. Over time, many of our actions and beliefs become automatic and unquestioned.

Reasoning

Rationalism is the philosophical idea that reason is the primary source of knowledge. One famous rationalist philosopher was René Descartes (1596–1650). Reason involves thinking about something and developing an understanding of it through reasoning. In its strong form, rationalism means that many truths are knowable independent of observation. In its weaker form, rationalism simply refers to our use of reason in developing understandings about the world. Deductive reasoning and inductive reasoning are the two major kinds of reasoning.

- **Rationalism** The philosophical idea that reason is the primary source of knowledge

Deductive reasoning is the process of drawing a conclusion that is necessarily true if the premises are true. One form of deductive reasoning is the syllogism. Here is an example:

- **Deductive reasoning** The process of drawing a conclusion that is necessarily true if the premises are true

Major Premise: All schoolteachers are mortal.

Minor Premise: John is a schoolteacher.

Conclusion: Therefore, John is mortal.

According to this deductive argument, John *necessarily* is a mortal. Keep in mind, however, that reasoning like this depends on the validity of the premises. Just try replacing the word *mortal* with the word *Martian;* you then conclude that John is a Martian. Deductive reasoning is useful as we reason about things in our world, but we must always make sure that our premises are true, and we must use valid argument forms. We need to be careful about what we assume when we draw our conclusions.

Inductive reasoning is the form of reasoning in which the premises "provide good reasons, but not conclusive reasons to accept the conclusion" (Salmon, 2007, p. 79). We engage in inductive reasoning frequently in our everyday lives when we observe many specific instances of some phenomenon and draw conclusions about it. For example, you have certainly observed all of your life that the sun appears every morning (except on cloudy days). On the basis of your observations, you probably feel comfortable concluding that the sun will make its appearance again tomorrow (if it is not cloudy). In this case, you are indeed likely to be correct. But notice that, when you use inductive reasoning, you are using a

- **Inductive reasoning** The process of drawing a conclusion that is "probably" true

- **Probabilistic** Stating what is likely to occur, not what will necessarily occur

probabilistic form of reasoning. That is, you are stating what is likely to occur, not what will necessarily occur. Because of this, you are taking a risk (albeit a very small risk in this case) because induction involves making conclusions that go beyond the evidence in the premises (e.g., going from some to more, from the examined to the unexamined, from the observed to the unobserved). This is not necessarily a problem, but you should be aware that it could be one if you expect certainty in your conclusions.

- **Problem of induction** The future might not resemble the past

The famous philosopher named David Hume (1711–1776) pointed out what is called the **problem of induction**: Although something might have happened many times in the past, it is still possible that it will not happen in the future. In short, *the future might not resemble the past.* Let's say that every cat you have ever seen had a tail. Using inductive reasoning, you might be led to conclude that all cats have tails. You can see the problem here: One day you might run across a Manx cat, which has no tail. The point is that inductive reasoning is useful in helping us come up with useful conclusions, predictions, and generalizations about the world; however, we must remember that we have not *proven* these to be true. Induction only provides statements of probability.

REVIEW QUESTIONS

1.6 What are the different sources of knowledge? Which ones are especially important for educational research?

1.7 What is the key difference between inductive reasoning and deductive reasoning?

The Scientific Approach to Knowledge Generation

Although the word *science* has become a hot-button or loaded word in some circles, the root of the word is the Latin *scientia*, which simply means "knowledge." We define *science* in this book in a way that is inclusive of the different approaches to educational research. We define it as an approach to the generation of knowledge that holds empirical data in high regard and follows certain norms and practices that developed over time because of their usefulness. Many of these norms and effective practices are explained in this book.

- **Science** An approach for the generation of knowledge

Science includes any systematic or carefully done actions that are carried out to answer research questions or meet other needs of a developing research domain (e.g., describing things, exploring, experimenting, explaining, predicting). Science often involves the application of a scientific method; however, as philosophers and historians of science have pointed out, science includes many methods and activities that are carried out by researchers as they attempt to generate scientific knowledge. Science does not accept at face value taken-for-granted knowledge (i.e., things that we assume to be true); instead, it uncovers and justifies descriptions and explanations of people, groups, and the world around us. In this book, we generally treat the term *science* (as just defined) and the term *research* as synonyms.

Dynamics of Science

Over time, science results in an accumulation of specific findings, theories, and other knowledge. In this sense, science is said to be progressive. When researchers conduct new research studies, they try to build on and extend current research theories and results. Sir Isaac Newton expressed it well when he said, "We stand on the shoulders of giants." Newton's point was that researchers do not and cannot start completely from scratch, and Newton knew that he was no exception to this rule. In short, researchers usually build on past findings and understandings.

At the same time, science is dynamic and open to new ideas and theories that show promise. Different researchers approach research differently, and they often describe, explain, and interpret things in different though often complementary ways. New ideas emerge. As new ideas are generated and evidence is obtained, results are presented at conferences and are published in monographs, books, and journals so that other members of the research community can examine them. Before findings are published in journals, the studies are usually evaluated by a group of experts, called referees, to make sure there are no major flaws and that the procedures are defensible. Researchers are usually required to report exactly how they conducted their research so that other researchers can evaluate the procedures or even replicate the study. Once published, research findings are openly discussed and are critically evaluated by members of the research community. Overall, we can say that science is a never-ending process that includes rational thinking, reliance on empirical observation, constant peer evaluation and critique, and—very importantly—active creativity and attempts at discovery.

Basic Assumptions of Science

Educational researchers must make a few general assumptions so that they can go about their daily business of doing research. Most practicing researchers do not think much about these philosophical assumptions as they carry out their daily research activities; nonetheless, it is helpful to examine some of them. The most common assumptions are summarized in Table 1.3.

TABLE 1.3 Summary of Common Assumptions Made by Educational Researchers

1. There is a world that can be studied. This can include studying the inner worlds of individuals.
2. Some of the world is unique, some of it is regular or patterned or predictable, and much of it is dynamic and complex.
3. The unique, the regular, and the complex in the world all can be examined and studied by researchers.
4. Researchers should try to follow certain agreed-on norms and practices.
5. It is possible to distinguish between more and less plausible claims and between good and poor research.
6. Science cannot provide answers to all questions.

- **Psychological factors** Individual-level factors
- **Social psychological factors** Factors relating individuals to other individuals and to social groups

First, at the most basic level, educational researchers assume that there is a world that can be studied. In education, this includes studying many phenomena that are internal to people (e.g., attitudes, values, beliefs, lived experiences), as well as many broader phenomena or institutions that are either connected to people or external to them (e.g., schools, cultures, and physical environments). Educational researchers study how the following factors relate to educational issues: **psychological factors** (e.g., characteristics of individuals and individual-level phenomena), **social psychological factors**

- **Sociological factors** Group- and society-level factors

(e.g., examining how individuals interact and relate to one another and how groups and individuals affect one another), and **sociological factors** (e.g., examining how groups form and change; documenting the characteristics of groups; studying intergroup relations; and studying group-level phenomena, such as cultural, social, political, familial, and economic institutions).

Second, researchers assume that part of the world is unique, part of the world is regular or patterned or predictable, and much of the world is dynamic (i.e., changing) and complex (e.g., involving many pieces or factors). One important task of educational research is to document the stories and experiences of particular people and groups. Another important task is to identify the predictable part of the world in order to generate findings that will apply to more than one person, group, kind of person, context, or situation. As you can imagine, conducting research would be very difficult if we had to do so on every single individual! To see an example of regularity in the world, the next time you go to your research class, note the seats that you and a few people around you are sitting in. When your class meets again, see whether you and the others you observed sit in the same seats as during the previous meeting. You will probably notice that many of the people sit in the same seats. Why is this? This happens because humans are to some degree predictable. Understanding the predictable part of the world allows researchers to generalize and apply their findings beyond the people and places used in their particular studies.

Third, the unique, the regular, and the complex in the world can be examined and studied by researchers. In other words, "discoverability" exists in our world (i.e., it is possible to document the unique, discover the regularity in human behavior, and, in time, better understand many of the complexities of human behavior). This does not mean that the task of discovering the nature of educational phenomena is simple. For example, although significant progress has been made, we still do not know all of the causes of many learning disabilities. Research must continue, and over time, we hope to find more and more pieces to the puzzles we are trying to solve. One day we hope we will be able to solve many educational problems.

The fourth assumption is that researchers should follow certain agreed-on norms and practices. A few of these are the selection of educational and social problems in need of attention, collection of empirical data, open discussion of findings, integrity, honesty, competence, systematic inquiry, empathic neutrality and respect toward research participants, a healthy skepticism toward results and explanations, a sense of curiosity and openness to discovery, the active search for negative evidence (e.g., instances that do not fit your emerging or current explanation of a phenomenon), the careful examination of alternative explanations for your findings, and an adherence to the principle of evidence. One of this book's authors (Johnson) likes to tell his students that a researcher is a lot like the slogan on Missouri's license plates: "The Show Me State." If you have a claim to make, then "show me the evidence, please!" A good researcher tries to collect and assemble high-quality evidence and expects other researchers to do the same. Obviously, it is all but impossible for a researcher to follow fully all of the ideals listed here. Furthermore, because science is a human activity, it is also affected by social and power relationships among researchers and society (Kuhn, 1962; Lincoln & Guba, 2000). That's why it is so important that researchers strive to follow the norms we have listed.

The fifth assumption is that it is possible to distinguish between more and less plausible claims and between good and poor research. For example, through empirical research, we can choose between competing theories by determining which theory best fits the data. We can also judge the quality of a research study by examining the research strategies used and the evidence that is provided for each of the conclusions drawn by a researcher. We say that high-quality research is more trustworthy or more valid than low-quality research. We will explain throughout this textbook how to identify and carry out research that is trustworthy, valid, credible, and, therefore, defensible.

The sixth assumption made by researchers is that science cannot provide answers to all questions. For example, science cannot answer philosophical questions such as what the meaning of life is, what virtue is, or what beauty is. Science cannot settle issues of which position is morally correct (e.g., human cloning versus no human cloning; pro-choice versus pro-life in the abortion debate) or politically correct (e.g., Republican or Democrat) and cannot explain ideas such as the difference between good and evil in the world or the veracity of claims about the existence of life after death. As you can see, many important questions simply lie outside the domain of science and empirical research.

Scientific Methods

Science is not a perfectly orderly process (Kuhn, 1962). It is a dynamic process that includes countless activities. However, several of the key features of science are (1) making empirical observations, (2) generating and testing **hypotheses** (predictions or educated guesses), (3) generating or constructing and testing or justifying **theories** (explanations or explanatory systems), and (4) attempting to predict and influence the world to make it a better place to live (American Association for the Advancement of Science, 1990). Although the conduct of research is clearly not a perfectly orderly process and is composed of many activities, it still is helpful to start with some commonly used *scientific methods.*

- **Hypothesis** A prediction or educated guess
- **Theory** An explanation or explanatory system that discusses how a phenomenon operates and why it operates as it does

We distinguish two major scientific methods here: the exploratory method and the confirmatory method. (Several additional methods are listed under Research Exercise 3 at the end of this chapter.) Although both of these methods use empirical data, their purpose is different. The basic **exploratory method** includes three steps. First, the researcher starts by making observations. Second, the researcher studies the observations and searches for patterns (i.e., a statement of what is occurring). Third, the researcher makes a tentative conclusion or a generalization about the pattern or how some aspect of the world operates. The basic **confirmatory method** also includes three steps. First, the researcher states a hypothesis, which is frequently based on existing theory (i.e., currently available scientific explanations). Second, the researcher collects data to be used to test the hypothesis empirically. Third, the researcher decides tentatively to accept or reject the hypothesis on the basis of the data.

- **Exploratory method** A bottom-up or theory-generation approach to research
- **Confirmatory method** A top-down or theory-testing approach to research

The exploratory method can be thought of as a *bottom-up approach* because it emphasizes starting with particular data and observations and discovering what is occurring more generally (i.e., movement from data to patterns to theory). This exploratory method is sometimes called the *inductive method* because it moves from the "particular to the general." On the other hand, the confirmatory method can be thought of as a *top-down approach* because it emphasizes the process of starting with a general theory and testing it with particular data (i.e., movement from theory to hypothesis to data). This confirmatory method is sometimes called the *deductive method* because it moves from the "general to the particular."

The exploratory method is the theory-*generation* approach: It follows a "logic of discovery" that says to look at your world and try to generate ideas and construct theories about how it operates. The confirmatory method is the traditional theory-*testing* approach: It follows a "logic of justification" that says always to test your theories and hypotheses with new data to see if they are justified. New knowledge is generated using the exploratory or inductive method, and this tentative knowledge is tested or justified using the confirmatory or deductive method. The bottom line is this: The exploratory scientific method focuses on theory discovery, generation, and construction, and the confirmatory scientific method focuses on theory testing or justification.

Although we have talked about two separate scientific methods (the exploratory method and the confirmatory method), it is important to understand that researchers use both of these methods in practice. As you can see in Figure 1.1, the use of the methods follows a cyclical process. One researcher might focus on the theory-testing process, and another researcher might focus on theory generation, but both researchers will usually go through the full cycle many, many times as they think about and carry out their research programs over time. In fact, **quantitative researchers** (i.e., educational researchers who like "hard" quantitative data, such as standardized test results, and focus on hypothesis testing) and **qualitative researchers** (i.e., educational researchers who like to explore educational issues using qualitative data, such as open-ended interviews that provide data based on the participants' perspectives and their actual words) both go through the full research cycle, but they emphasize different parts. Quantitative researchers emphasize movement from theory to hypotheses to data to conclusions (i.e., the "logic of justification"), and qualitative researchers emphasize movement directly from observations and data to descriptions and patterns and, *sometimes*, to theory generation (i.e., the "logic of discovery").

- **Quantitative researcher** A researcher who focuses on testing theories and hypotheses using quantitative data to see if they are confirmed or not
- **Qualitative researcher** A researcher who focuses on the exploration, description, and sometimes generation and construction of theories using qualitative data

Theory

The exploratory and confirmatory methods both involve the concept of theory (i.e., explanation). The term *theory* as used in this book most simply refers to an explanation or an explanatory system that discusses *how* a phenomenon operates and *why* it operates as it does. Theory often refers to a generalization or set of generalizations that are used

FIGURE 1.1 The research wheel

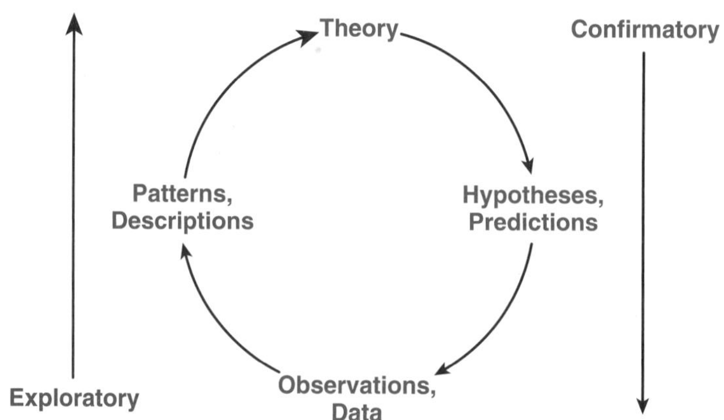

systematically to explain some phenomenon. In other words, a well-developed theory explains how something operates in general (i.e., for many people), and it enables one to move beyond the findings of any single research study. Using a well-developed theory, you should be able to explain a phenomenon, make sense of it, and make useful predictions. When you need to judge the quality of a theory or explanation, you should try to answer the nine questions listed in Table 1.4. We now define and briefly elaborate on the *criterion of falsifiability* and the *rule of parsimony.*

TABLE 1.4 How to Evaluate the Quality of a Theory or Explanation

1. Is the theory or explanation logical and coherent?
2. Is it clear and parsimonious?
3. Does it fit the available data?
4. Does it provide testable claims?
5. Have theory-based predictions been tested and supported?
6. Has it survived numerous attempts by researchers to identify problems with it or to falsify it?
7. Does it work better than competing or rival theories or explanations?
8. Is it general enough to apply to more than one place, situation, or person?
9. Can practitioners use it to control or influence things in the world (e.g., a good theory of teaching helps teachers to influence student learning positively; a good theory of counseling helps counselors to influence their clients' mental health positively)?

Sir Karl Popper (1902–1994), who was one of the most famous philosophers of science of the 20th century, contended that the most important criterion used to judge theories is the **criterion of falsifiability** (Popper, 1965, 1974, 1934/1985). The criterion of falsifiability is "the property of a statement or theory that it is capable of being refuted by experience" (Blackburn, 1994, p. 135). If someone said, "I don't care what the results of my research study are because I'm going to conclude that my theory is supported, no matter what," then that person would obviously not be doing the kind of research that could ever reject or falsify a theory. There must be two sorts of possible outcomes for empirical research: (a) outcomes that would support the theory (that would "confirm" the theory) and (b) outcomes that would not support the theory (that would "not confirm" the theory and over many tests would be used to reject or falsify the theory). Then you conduct your research to find out which type of outcome occurs. In practice, researchers do not give up on promising theories based on a single negative test, but if a theory fails many times, then the theory will be abandoned. The criterion of falsifiability also says that we should not selectively search for confirming evidence for our beliefs and explanations and then stop with that so-called evidence. Good researchers carefully search for and examine any negative evidence that operates against their beliefs, research conclusions, and theoretical explanations.

Criterion of falsifiability The property that statements and theories should be testable and refutable

Another criterion for evaluating theories is called the **rule of parsimony**. A theory is parsimonious when it is simple, concise, and succinct. If two competing theories explain and predict a phenomenon equally well, then the more parsimonious theory is to be preferred according to the rule of parsimony. In other words, simple theories are preferred over highly complex ones, other things being equal.

Rule of parsimony Preferring the most simple theory that works

Now let's briefly examine an educational theory to give you an idea of what a relatively well-developed theory looks like. According to *expectation theory*, teachers' expectations about their students affect their behavior toward their students, which in turn affects their students' behavior. The theory is based on the self-fulfilling prophecy (Merton, 1948). Robert Rosenthal and Lenore Jacobson (1968) studied the effects of teachers' expectations and found that students whom teachers expected to perform well had higher increases in IQ than did other students. These authors labeled this the *Pygmalion effect.* Rosenthal also found that "those children in whom intellectual growth was expected were described as having a significantly better chance of becoming successful in the future, as significantly more interesting, curious, and happy" (Rosenthal, 1991, p. 6). Students who had IQ increases but had not been expected to have increases by the teachers were not viewed more favorably by the teachers. These results suggest that teacher expectations can sometimes affect student performance. Note, however, that recent research has suggested that the power of expectations is not as great as had originally been concluded (Goldenberg, 1992). Nonetheless, the theory of expectations is a useful idea.

There are many theories in education. A few are attribution theory, constructivism, labeling theory, Kohlberg's theory of moral development, operant conditioning, proximal development, rational emotive therapy, site-based management, situated learning, and social learning theory. If you want to find out more about any of these theories, just go to the library (or, using your computer, go to http://www.eric.ed.gov) and conduct a search using ERIC or one of the other computerized search tools, which are discussed in Chapter 4. You can also find nice descriptions of many educational and psychological theories at http://www.instructionaldesign.org/theories/.

Keep in mind as you read research articles that you will not always find the word *theory* in the article because often a well-developed or *explicit theory* will not be available to the researcher, or the researcher might not have a fancy name for his or her theory. In this case, you can view the authors' explanations of their findings as the theory. Remember that some theories are highly developed and others are very brief or not well developed. When we use the word *theory* in this book, you might replace it with the word *explanation* until you get used to the idea that *theory* most simply means "explanation."

The Principle of Evidence

Many beginning students believe that science and research are processes in which researchers constantly prove what is true. You might be surprised to learn that researchers rarely use the word *prove* when discussing their research findings. In fact, as we mentioned earlier, we recommend that you eliminate the word *prove* from your vocabulary when you are talking about research because most researchers hold knowledge to be ultimately tentative (D. C. Phillips & Burbules, 2000; Shadish, Cook, & Campbell, 2002). They recognize that principles that are believed to be true today might change eventually; some of today's findings will later be found to be partially true or even patently false. What we obtain in research is scientific "evidence." It is essential that you understand this idea. An important educational methodologist, the late Fred Kerlinger (1986), made this point very clearly:

> The interpretation of research data culminates in conditional probabilistic statements of the "If p, then q" kind. We enrich such statements by qualifying them in some such way as: If p, then q, under conditions r, s, and t. *Let us flatly assert that nothing can be "proved" scientifically.*

> *All one can do is to bring evidence to bear that such-and-such a proposition is true.* Proof is a deductive matter, and experimental methods of inquiry are not methods of proof [emphasis added]. (p. 145)

Here is the way the American Association for the Advancement of Science (1990) put it:

> Science is a process for producing knowledge. The process depends on making careful observations of phenomena and on inventing theories for making sense out of those observations. Change in knowledge is inevitable because new observations may challenge prevailing theories. No matter how well one theory explains a set of observations, it is possible that another theory may fit just as well or better, or may fit a still wider range of observations. In science, the testing and improving and occasional discarding of theories, whether new or old, go on all the time. (p. 2)

As you learn more about research, keep these points in mind. It is also important to understand that you should never place too much weight on a single research study. **Replication** by other researchers (i.e., research examining the same variables with different people and in different ways) should make you more confident about a research finding because the resulting evidence is much stronger. But even in the face of replication, strong evidence rather than proof is all that is obtained because we always leave open the possibility that future researchers will come up with new theories and new conclusions.

- **Replication** Research examining the same variables with different people

Whenever you are tempted to use the word *prove*, stop and think and remind yourself about the fundamental nature of educational research. For now, whenever you want to use the word *proof*, just use the word *evidence* instead. Sometimes I (Johnson) like to tell my students that proof is what television commercials claim for their products' performance, but in research the best we can do is to obtain *evidence*. During a presidential election in the 1990s, a campaign manager kept a slogan posted in the campaign office that read, "It's the economy, stupid!" to keep the staff focused on the economic performance of the current administration as the primary campaign issue. In research our slogan goes like this: "It's about evidence, not proof!" We call this idea the **principle of evidence**.

- **Principle of evidence** The philosophical idea that empirical research provides evidence, not proof

REVIEW QUESTIONS

1.8 Describe the two forms of the scientific method and explain why both are important.

1.9 Explain why researchers do not use the word *proof* when they write up the results of their empirical research in journal articles.

1.10 What criteria can you use to determine the quality of a theory or an explanation?

1.11 What does the principle of evidence state?

Objectives of Educational Research

Discussions of science and empirical research often focus on the importance of explanation. However, several additional objectives are also important if the field of educational research is to continue to operate effectively and to progress. The first objective is **exploration**, or attempting to learn about and generate ideas about phenomena. Exploration is especially

- **Exploration** Attempting to generate ideas about phenomena

important in the early phases of research because researchers must generate ideas about phenomena before additional research can progress. To determine whether exploration was the objective of a particular research study, answer the following questions:

1. Were the researchers studying a phenomenon or some aspect of a phenomenon about which little was previously known?
2. Did the researchers choose to ignore previous research or explanations so that they could study a phenomenon without any preconceived notions?
3. Were the researchers trying to "discover" important factors or "generate" new ideas for further research?

If you answer yes to any of these questions, then the researchers were probably operating in the exploratory mode of research.

As is implied in the second and third questions, exploration does not always have to be done in the early phases of research. Sometimes researchers might want to enter the field without fixed or preconceived notions about what they are studying so that they can explore a phenomenon in a new way and so that they can avoid being biased or blinded by previous findings or theories. The article mentioned earlier in this chapter (in the section "Examples of Educational Research") titled "Giving Voice to High School Students" was exploratory because the researchers tried to uncover what at-risk students thought was important in their lives, why the students acted in the ways they did, and how the students viewed various formal and informal groups (e.g., teachers). The researchers tried to describe the at-risk adolescents' beliefs and circumstances to explain why they acted as they did. One finding was that some at-risk students formed subcultures that were in conflict with the teachers' culture; that is, the groups differed on such criteria as values, beliefs, and activities that were considered appropriate. These differences made it difficult for the teachers and the students to communicate, which resulted in student apathy and boredom in the classroom. For another example in which the objective was exploratory, you can reread the abstract of the article mentioned in the same section titled "The Development of a Goal to Become a Teacher."

Exploration sometimes is focused on describing the nature of something that previously was unknown; it also is used when the researcher tries to understand the specifics of some phenomenon or some situation to develop tentative hypotheses or generalizations about it. Exploration is similar to basic descriptive activities in that it often includes description. However, attempts are also frequently made in exploratory research to generate preliminary explanations or theories about how and why a phenomenon operates as it does.

■ **Description** Attempting to describe the characteristics of a phenomenon

The second objective is **description**, or attempting to describe the characteristics of a phenomenon. To determine whether description was the main objective of a particular research study, answer the following questions:

1. Were the researchers primarily describing a phenomenon?
2. Were the researchers documenting the characteristics of some phenomenon?

Description is one of the most basic activities in research. It might simply involve observing a phenomenon and recording what one sees. For example, a seasoned teacher might observe the behavior of a student teacher and take notes. At other times, description might rely on the use of quantitative measuring instruments such as standardized tests. For example, a researcher might want to measure the intangible construct called intelligence quotient, or IQ. To do this, the researcher must rely on some type of test that has been constructed specifically for this purpose. At other times, description might involve reporting attitudes and opinions about certain issues. For an example, see the September 1996 issue of *Phi Delta Kappan*, which reports national attitudes toward education each year. The study is conducted by the Gallup Organization and is commissioned by the education honor society Phi Delta Kappa (1996). Two questions and their responses are shown in Table 1.5.

TABLE 1.5 Items From Phi Delta Kappa/Gallup Poll (September 1996)

Question: Would you favor or oppose a requirement for high school graduation that all students in the local public schools perform some kind of community service?

	National Totals %	*No Children in School %*	*Public School Parents %*	*Nonpublic School Parents %*
Favor	66	66	67	75
Oppose	32	32	32	25
Don't know	2	2	1	*

Question: Just your impression, do you think that the national dropout rate of students in high school is higher today than it was twenty-five years ago, lower today, or about the same as it was twenty-five years ago?

	National Totals %	*No Children in School %*	*Public School Parents %*	*Nonpublic School Parents %*
Higher	64	62	66	73
Lower	15	15	15	8
About the same	18	19	17	16
Don't know	3	4	2	3

*Less than one half of 1 percent.

The third objective is **understanding**, or, more specifically, *subjective* understanding. This is the goal of what is called, in the remainder of this book, "qualitative research," which is the kind of research that seeks to go into particular places with particular individuals and learn about their unique world from their perspectives. You might go into peoples' places as a participant observer, or interview them and have them tell you what their culture means to them and what life is like for them as individuals and members of their group. For example, you might interview members of a Hopi Native American group in Arizona, USA, to learn what it's like in their place as a member of their group (e.g., what's important to them, what games they play, their educational practices and learning, their religious practices, their political activities, their family structure[s], their jobs, and their shared cultural values and beliefs). If you conduct qualitative research well, you end up with *understanding*.

- **Understanding** Attempting to understand the subjective viewpoints of particular people and particular groups

The fourth objective is **explanation**, or attempting to show how and why a phenomenon operates as it does. According to many writers, this is the key purpose of science.

- **Explanation** Attempting to show how and why a phenomenon operates as it does

To determine whether explanation was the primary objective of a particular research study, answer the following questions:

1. Were the researchers trying to develop or test a theory about a phenomenon to explain how and why it operates as it does?
2. Were the researchers trying to explain how certain phenomena operate by identifying the factors that produce change in them? More specifically, were the researchers studying cause-and-effect relationships?

If the answer to either of these questions is yes, then the researchers' primary objective is probably explanation. The objective of the majority of educational research is explanation. An example of a research study focusing on explanation is a study titled "Are Effects of Small Classes Cumulative?" by Nye, Hedges, and Konstantopoulos (2001). In that study, the researchers were interested in determining the effect of class size on student performance. They found that smaller classes in Grades 1 through 3 resulted in improved reading and mathematics achievement scores and that the effect continues to occur over time. The study used a strong experimental design that provided relatively solid evidence about cause and effect. In a study like this, the cause (i.e., smaller class sizes) is used to explain the effect (i.e., improved achievement scores). For another example in which the objective was explanation, see the article mentioned earlier (in the section "Examples of Educational Research") entitled "Getting Tough? The Impact of High School Graduation Exams."

- **Prediction** Attempting to predict or forecast a phenomenon

The fifth objective is **prediction**, or attempting to predict or forecast a phenomenon. To determine whether prediction was the primary objective of a particular research study, answer the following question: Did the researchers conduct the research so that they could predict or forecast some event in the future? A researcher is able to make a prediction when certain information that is known in advance can be used to determine what will happen at a later point in time. Sometimes predictions can also be made from research studies in which the primary focus is on explanation. That is, when researchers determine cause-and-effect operations (explanations), they can use this information to form predictions.

One research study in which the focus was on prediction was conducted by Fuertes, Sedlacek, and Liu (1994). These researchers conducted a 10-year research study and found that Asian American university students' academic performance and retention could be predicted by using the Scholastic Assessment Test (SAT) and another instrument called the Noncognitive Questionnaire. The strongest predictor of the students' GPAs was their SAT math scores. Other useful predictors (from the Noncognitive Questionnaire) were community service, realistic self-appraisal, academic self-concept, nontraditional knowledge, and handling racism. The strongest predictors of enrollment (i.e., retention) were self-concept, realistic self-appraisal, and SAT math score.

- **Influence** Attempting to apply research to make certain outcomes occur

The sixth objective is called control or **influence**, or attempting to apply research to make certain outcomes occur. This objective refers to the application of research knowledge rather than the generation of research knowledge. It refers to the application of previous research to control various aspects of the world. Here you should ask the following questions:

1. Were the researchers applying research knowledge to make something useful happen in the world?
2. Were the researchers checking a "demonstration program" to see if it works in practice?

The ultimate objective of most social, behavioral, and educational research is improvement of the world or social betterment. Therefore, influence is important. For teachers, influence involves things like helping students learn more than they previously knew, helping children with special needs, and preventing negative outcomes such as dropping out of school or disruptive behavior in the classroom. For counselors, influence might involve helping clients overcome psychological problems such as depression, personality disorders, and dysfunctional behaviors.

As you work through this book and learn about the different methods of research, you will be learning more about these objectives. At this point, you should be able to examine a research article and determine what the researcher's objectives were. Don't be surprised if there appears to be more than one objective. That is not at all uncommon. You should also be aware that researchers often use the terms *descriptive research*, *exploratory research*, *explanatory research*, and *predictive research*. When they do this, they are simply describing the primary objective of the research.

REVIEW QUESTIONS

1.12 What are the six main objectives of science? (Hint: The first letters form the acronym EDUEPI.)

1.13 Why is each of the six main objectives of science important?

Overview of This Book

We have organized your textbook to follow the general steps involved in the research process. In Part I we introduce you to the kinds of educational research and the process and assumptions of research. In Part II we show how to come up with a research idea and how to plan a research study. In Part III we introduce some concepts required to design and conduct a good study. In Part IV we discuss the major methods of research. In Part V we show how to analyze data resulting from a research study. In Part VI we explain how to write a research manuscript.

To master the material fully, you will need to take advantage of some of the application exercises provided in the book and on the companion website because they will give you some practice applying the material. As you start to review for exams, you can test your overall knowledge of the material by taking the practice quizzes on the companion website and by answering the chapter study questions. You can also print the definitions of the terms given in the chapters. Don't look at the answers in the book or on the companion website until you have stated your own answers; then compare and identify your areas of strength and weakness. Use the concept maps on the companion website to keep what you learn organized in terms of the big picture and its parts.

We also strongly recommend that you read some examples of published research to see full-length examples of how research is done. Throughout the text, we provide references to many published research articles that you can examine. Furthermore, *we have provided downloadable copies of 71 journal articles on the companion website that you can print out and read and discuss in class.* You can start right now by going to the companion website and printing the article entitled "Gifted Dropouts: The Who and the

Why." Reading or carefully examining this article will give you a concrete example of educational research.

See Journal Article 1.3 on the Student Study Site.

Our practical conclusion for this chapter is clear: Anyone can learn the material in this book if he or she works hard at it, and that means that *you* can do it! We hope to show you that learning about research can actually be fun. Good luck, and *don't forget to use the many learning tools that are available at the companion website to make your learning experience easier and more productive.*

SUMMARY

It is important that educators and counselors be research literate because of the importance of research in education and our society. By learning about research, you will be able to find published research articles that are relevant for your profession, evaluate those research articles, and propose and conduct research studies on your own if the need ever arises in your career (e.g., perhaps one day your principal or manager will ask you to conduct a survey or to write a grant proposal). Educational researchers generate evidence about educational phenomena by collecting empirical data and using the exploratory and confirmatory scientific methods. We also explained that six general objectives of research are to explore, to describe, to understand, to explain, to predict, and to influence or control things in our world. When reading research articles, you should determine the primary objective researchers had when they conducted their research studies. In the next chapter, we will finish our introduction to educational research by describing the key features of the three major research paradigms: quantitative research, qualitative research, and mixed research.

KEY TERMS

abstract (p. 8)
action research (p. 11)
applied research (p. 10)
basic research (p. 9)
confirmatory method (p. 17)
criterion of falsifiability (p. 19)
deductive reasoning (p. 13)
description (p. 22)
empirical statement (p. 12)
empiricism (p. 12)
epistemology (p. 12)
evaluation (p. 10)
explanation (p. 23)
exploration (p. 21)
exploratory method (p. 17)
formative evaluation (p. 10)
hypothesis (p. 17)
inductive reasoning (p. 13)
influence (p. 24)
orientational research (p. 11)
prediction (p. 24)
principle of evidence (p. 21)
probabilistic (p. 14)
problem of induction (p. 14)
psychological factors (p. 15)
qualitative researcher (p. 18)
quantitative researcher (p. 18)
rationalism (p. 13)
replication (p. 21)
research literature (p. 5)
rule of parsimony (p. 19)
science (p. 14)
social psychological factors (p. 15)
sociological factors (p. 16)
summative evaluation (p. 10)
theory (p. 17)
understanding (p. 23)

DISCUSSION QUESTIONS

1. Which of the following do you think is the most important kind of research: basic, applied, evaluation, action, or critical theory research? Why?
2. Why is it asserted in this chapter that one does not obtain necessary or final *proof* in educational research?

3. How does the presentation of exploratory and confirmatory scientific methods fit with your prior understanding of the methods of scientific research?
4. What is a research finding that you have heard (e.g., on the news or in another class) and wondered about?

RESEARCH EXERCISES

1. We have put a Research Methods Questionnaire on the book's companion website under Chapter 1 bonus materials. Fill it out and test your prior knowledge about research methods.
2. Search on the web for more information on some of the terms that you found most interesting in the chapter. For example, you might want to search for more material on critical theory, inductive reasoning, program evaluation, or epistemology.
3. In this chapter we distinguished between the exploratory and confirmatory methods of science. As we mentioned, however, researchers use many approaches to gain knowledge. As an exercise, find the needed information on the web and summarize (in a two-page paper) one of these scientific methods: inference to best explanation, Mill's methods, abductive reasoning, analogical reasoning, deductive-nomothetic model, hypothetico-deductive model, inductive methods, or deductive methods.
4. Take a moment, right now, to examine what is available at the companion website that goes with this book. Here are some of the many features you will find: lectures, concept maps, answers to the review questions, quizzes, web resources, chapter supplements, and more. If you think of something else that will help you learn the material in your book, please email us and let us know because we are always adding new features to the companion website. Our email addresses are bjohnson@southalabama.edu and lchriste@southalabama.edu.

RELEVANT INTERNET SITES

Action Research Special Interest Group
http://www.aera.net/SIG002/ActionResearchSIG2/tabid/11391/Default.aspx

American Educational Research Association
http://www.aera.net

American Evaluation Association (program evaluation)
http://www.eval.org

Center for Philosophy of Science
http://www.pitt.edu/~pittcntr/About/links.htm

The Evaluation Center at Western Michigan University (program evaluation)
http://www.wmich.edu/evalctr/

STUDENT STUDY SITE

Visit the Student Study Site at **edge.sagepub.com/rbjohnson6e** for these additional learning tools:

Video Links
Self-Quizzes
eFlashcards
Lecture Notes
Full-Text SAGE Journal Articles
Interactive Concept Maps
Web Resources

RECOMMENDED READING

Chilisa, B. (2011). *Indigenous research methods.* Los Angeles, CA: SAGE.
Davidson, E. J. (2005). *Evaluation methodology basics: The nuts and bolts of sound evaluation.* Thousand Oaks, CA: SAGE.
Harding, S. (Ed.). (2004). *The feminist standpoint theory reader.* New York, NY: Routledge.
Kirkpatrick, D. L. (2006). *Evaluating training programs: The four levels.* San Francisco, CA: Berrett-Koehler.
Phillips, D. C., & Burbules, N. C. (2000). *Postpositivism and educational research.* New York, NY: Rowman & Littlefield.
Reason, P., & Bradbury, H. (Eds.). (2006). *Handbook of action research: Concise paperback edition.* Thousand Oaks, CA: SAGE.
Sandoval, C. (2000). *Methodology of the oppressed.* Minneapolis: University of Minnesota Press.

Chapter 2

Quantitative, Qualitative, and Mixed Research

LEARNING OBJECTIVES

After reading this chapter, you should be able to

- Describe the characteristics of quantitative research.
- List and explain the different types of variables used in quantitative research.
- Explain the difference between experimental and nonexperimental quantitative research.
- Explain the concept of a correlation coefficient.
- Describe the characteristics of qualitative research.
- List and explain the differences among the different types of qualitative research introduced in this chapter.
- Describe the characteristics of mixed research.
- Explain when each of the three major research paradigms (quantitative, qualitative, and mixed) would be appropriate to use.

Visit the Student Study Site for an interactive concept map.

RESEARCH IN REAL LIFE Paradigms and Perspectives

istock/Percy9058

This chapter is about the three major research paradigms in educational research. Each of these paradigms tends to bring a slightly different view or perspective to what we study. It seems appropriate to start this chapter with an age-old poem (written by the Persian poet/philosopher Rumi) that tells us that different perspectives can all have truth value and that, when we put those perspectives together, we can come away with a fuller picture of what we are studying. We use the poem to support our view of the importance of using all three major research paradigms in educational research.

Elephant in the Dark

Some Hindus have an elephant to show.
No one here has ever seen an elephant.
They bring it at night to a dark room.
One by one, we go in the dark and come out
saying how we experience the animal.
One of us happens to touch the trunk.
"A water-pipe kind of creature."
Another, the ear. "A very strong, always moving
back and forth, fan-animal."
Another, the leg. "I find it still,
like a column on a temple."
Another touches the curved back.
"A leathery throne."
Another, the cleverest, feels the tusk.
"A rounded sword made of porcelain."
He's proud of his description.
Each of us touches one place
and understands the whole in that way.
The palm and the fingers feeling in the dark are
how the senses explore the reality of the elephant.
If each of us held a candle there,
and if we went in together,
we could see it.

Source: From Jelaluddin Rumi, *The Essential Rumi*, trans. & ed. by Coleman Barks, 1995, San Francisco, CA: Castle Books, 1995. p. 252. © Coleman Barks.

A **research paradigm** is a worldview or perspective about research held by a community of researchers that is based on a set of shared assumptions, concepts, values, and practices. More simply, it is an approach to thinking about and doing research and, therefore, producing knowledge. In this chapter we introduce you to the three major educational research paradigms or approaches: *quantitative research*, *qualitative research*, and *mixed research*. Mixed research also is commonly called *mixed methods research*, but we use the simpler term *mixed research*. Not only is the label *mixed research* simpler than the label *mixed methods research*, but it also is more accurate because the quantitative, qualitative, and mixed research debates are about much more than just methods. Quantitative research was the generally accepted research paradigm in educational research until the early 1980s, when the "paradigm wars" between advocates of quantitative and qualitative research reached a new peak (Guba, 1990; Tashakkori & Teddlie, 1998). During the 1980s, many quantitative and qualitative researchers argued that their approach was superior. Some of these researchers were "purists," in the sense that they argued that the two approaches could not be used together because of differences in the worldviews or philosophies associated with the two approaches.

■ **Research paradigm** A worldview or perspective held by a community of researchers that is based on a set of shared assumptions, concepts, values, and practices

This either-or position (i.e., one must use quantitative or qualitative research but not both) is called the **incompatibility thesis**. The problem with the incompatibility thesis is its failure to recognize that creative and *thoughtful* mixing of assumptions, ideas, and methods can be very helpful and offers a third paradigm. The mixing of ideas and approaches has been present throughout history because mixing or combining builds upon what we know and offers new ways to understand and study our world. In short, in addition to quantitative and quantitative research, mixed research offers an exciting way of conducting educational research.

■ **Incompatibility thesis** The proposition that one cannot mix quantitative and qualitative research

Exhibit 2.1 shows one of the leading figures in the paradigm dialogue that had become a worldwide phenomenon by the 1990s and continues to play an important part in educational research today.

■ **EXHIBIT 2.1** Egon G. Guba (1924–2008)

During the 1970s, 1980s, and early 1990s, Egon Guba helped initiate the "paradigm dialogue" between quantitative research and the "new" research paradigm of qualitative research. Guba emphasized that research paradigms are characterized by their distinctive **ontology**—"What is the nature of the knowable? Or what is the nature of reality?"; **epistemology**—"What is the relationship between the knower (the inquirer) and the known (or knowable)?" or What is the paradigm's theory of knowledge; and **methodology**—"How should the inquirer go about finding out knowledge?" or, more specifically, What methods should be used in research? (quotes are from Guba, 1990). Later, two more dimensions of paradigms were added: **axiology**—What is the role of values in the inquiry process? and **rhetoric**—What kind of language and communication should be used in writing and discussing research? The differences among quantitative, qualitative, and mixed research on these and additional dimensions are found in Table 2.1 and in the section "Characteristics of the Three Research Paradigms." Guba was author of many important books, chapters, and articles on qualitative research and evaluation (e.g., Guba; Guba & Lincoln, 1989, 1992; Lincoln & Guba, 1985).

(Continued)

(Continued)

Exhibit definitions:

- Ontology—the branch of philosophy dealing with the nature of reality and truth
- Epistemology—the branch of philosophy dealing with knowledge and its justification
- Methodology—the identification, study, and justification of research methods
- Axiology—the branch of philosophy dealing with values and ethics
- Rhetoric—the art or science of language and oral and written communication and argument

■ **Pragmatism** The philosophical position that what works in particular situations is what is important and justified or "valid"

Starting in the 1990s, many researchers rejected the incompatibility thesis and started advocating the pragmatic position that says that both quantitative and qualitative research are very important and often should be thoughtfully mixed in single research studies. According to **pragmatism**, what is ultimately important and justified or "valid" is what solves our problems and what works in particular situations in practice and what promotes social justice. Pragmatism is focused on the ends that we value. According to pragmatism, your research design should be planned and conducted based on what will best help you answer your research questions; the result is *pragmatic knowledge.* Pragmatism says that theories or programs or actions that are demonstrated to work for particular groups of people are the ones that we should view as currently being the most valid for those people. We specifically call our version of pragmatism "*dialectical* pragmatism" because a philosophy for mixed research should carefully listen to ideas, assumptions, and approaches found in qualitative and quantitative research and in any other relevant domain (e.g., perspectives found in different academic disciplines, viewpoints of different stakeholder and social groups). The word *dialectical* is intended to imply a dynamic back-and-forth listening to multiple perspectives and multiple forms of data. Although mixed research is still the "new kid on the block," the list of researchers identifying with this approach is increasing rapidly.

You can see in Figure 2.1 that the three major research approaches can be viewed as falling on a research continuum with qualitative research on the left side, quantitative research on the right side, and mixed research in the center of the continuum. In other words, research can be *fully qualitative* or mixed with an emphasis on qualitative, *fully quantitative* or mixed with an emphasis on quantitative, or *mixed* with an equal emphasis on qualitative and quantitative. A particular research study would fall at a particular point on the continuum.

We now compare the characteristics or tenets of the three research paradigms in their pure forms. Later in the chapter, we will introduce you to some ideas and terminology associated with each of the research paradigms.

■ **FIGURE 2.1** The research continuum

Characteristics of the Three Research Paradigms

Pure **quantitative research** relies on the collection of quantitative data (i.e., numerical data) and follows the other characteristics of the quantitative research paradigm shown in Table 2.1. Pure **qualitative research** relies on the collection of qualitative data (i.e., nonnumerical data such as words and pictures) and follows the other characteristics of the qualitative research paradigm shown in Table 2.1. **Mixed research** involves the mixing of quantitative and qualitative research methods, approaches, or other paradigm characteristics. The exact mixture that is considered appropriate will depend on the research questions and the situational and practical issues facing a researcher. All three research paradigms are important as we attempt to solve the manifold and complex problems facing us in the field of education. Take a moment now to examine Table 2.1 and then read the following discussion of the key differences among the three approaches.

- **Quantitative research** Research that relies primarily on the collection of quantitative data
- **Qualitative research** Research that relies primarily on the collection of qualitative data
- **Mixed research** Research that involves the mixing of quantitative and qualitative methods or other paradigm characteristics

First, the quantitative research approach primarily follows the confirmatory scientific method (discussed in Chapter 1) because its focus is on hypothesis testing and theory testing. Quantitative researchers consider it to be of primary importance to state one's hypotheses and then test those hypotheses with empirical data to see if they are supported. On the other hand, qualitative research primarily follows the exploratory scientific method (also discussed in Chapter 1). Qualitative research is used to describe what is seen locally and sometimes to come up with or generate new hypotheses and theories. Qualitative research is used when little is known about a topic or phenomenon and when one wants to discover or learn more about it. It is commonly used to understand people's experiences and to express their perspectives. Researchers advocating mixed research argue that it is important to use both the exploratory and the confirmatory methods in one's research (Johnson & Onwuegbuzie, 2004).

Most researchers use inductive *and* deductive reasoning when they conduct research. For example, they use inductive reasoning when they search for patterns in their particular data, when they make generalizations (e.g., from samples to populations), and when they make inferences as to the best explanation. Ultimately, the logic of confirmation is inductive because we do not get conclusive proof from empirical research (see principle of evidence in Chapter 1). Researchers use deductive reasoning when they deduce from their hypotheses the observable consequences that should occur with new empirical data *if* their hypotheses are true. Researchers also use deductive reasoning if they conclude that a theory is false. If they draw this conclusion, they will then move on to generate and test new ideas and new theories.

Quantitative and qualitative research are also distinguished by different views of human behavior. In quantitative research, it is assumed that cognition and behavior are highly predictable and explainable. Traditionally, the assumption of **determinism**, which means that all events are fully determined by one or more causes, was made in quantitative research (Salmon, 2007). For example, the process by which children learn to read is determined by one or more causes. Because quantitative research has not identified any universal or unerring laws of human behavior, most contemporary quantitative researchers search for **probabilistic causes** (Humphreys, 1989). A probabilistic statement might go like this: "Adolescents who become involved with drugs and alcohol are more likely to drop out of high school than are adolescents who do not become involved with drugs and alcohol." The point is that most

- **Determinism** Assumption that all events have causes
- **Probabilistic causes** Causes that usually produce an outcome

TABLE 2.1 Emphases of Quantitative, Mixed, and Qualitative Research

	Quantitative Research	*Mixed Research*	*Qualitative Research*
Scientific method	Confirmatory or "top-down"—the researcher *tests* hypotheses and theory with data	Confirmatory and exploratory	Exploratory or "bottom-up"—The researcher *generates* or *constructs* knowledge, hypotheses, and grounded theory from data collected during fieldwork
Ontology (i.e., nature of reality/ truth)	Objective, material, structural, agreed-upon	Pluralism; appreciation of objective, subjective, and intersubjective realities and their interrelations	Subjective, mental, personal, and constructed
Epistemology (i.e., theory of knowledge)	Scientific realism; search for Truth; justification by empirical confirmation of hypotheses; universal scientific standards	Dialectical pluralism; pragmatic justification (what works for whom in specific contexts); mixture of universal (e.g., *always* be ethical) and community-specific needs-based standards	Relativism; individual and group justification; varying standards
View of human thought and behavior	Regular and predictable	Dynamic, complex, and partially predictable—multiple influences include environment/nurture, biology/nature, freewill/agency, and chance/fortuity	Situational, social, contextual, personal, and unpredictable
Most common research objectives	Quantitative/numerical description, causal explanation, and prediction	Multiple objectives; provide complex and fuller explanation and understanding; understand multiple perspectives	Qualitative/subjective description, empathetic understanding, and exploration
Interest	Identify general scientific laws; inform national policy	Connect theory and practice; understand multiple causation, nomothetic (i.e., general) causation, and idiographic (i.e., particular, individual) causation; connect national and local interests and policy	Understand and appreciate particular groups and individuals; inform local policy
"Focus"	Narrow-angle lens, testing specific hypotheses	Multilens focus	Wide-angle and "deep-angle" lens, examining the breadth and depth of phenomena to learn more about them
Nature of observation	Study behavior under controlled conditions; isolate the causal effect of single variables	Study multiple contexts, perspectives, or conditions; study multiple factors as they operate together	Study groups and individuals in natural settings; attempt to understand insiders' views, meanings, and perspectives
Form of data collected	Collect quantitative data based on precise measurement using structured and validated data-collection instruments	Collect multiple kinds of data	Collect qualitative data such as in-depth interviews, participant observations, field notes, and open-ended questions. The researcher is the primary data-collection instrument
Nature of data	Variables	Mixture of variables, words, categories, and images	Words, images, categories
Data analysis	Identify statistical relationships among variables	Quantitative and qualitative analysis used separately and in combination	Use descriptive data; search for patterns, themes, and holistic features; and appreciate difference/variation

	Quantitative Research	*Mixed Research*	*Qualitative Research*
Results	Generalizable findings providing representation of objective outsider viewpoint of populations	Provision of "subjective insider" and "objective outsider" viewpoints; presentation and integration of multiple dimensions and perspectives	Particularistic findings; provision of insider viewpoints
Form of final report	Formal statistical report (e.g., with correlations, comparisons of means, and reporting of statistical significance of findings)	Mixture of numbers and narrative	Less formal narrative report with contextual description and direct quotations from research participants

quantitative researchers try to identify cause-and-effect relationships that enable them to make probabilistic predictions and generalizations.

On the other hand, qualitative researchers often view human behavior as being fluid, dynamic, and changing over time and place, and they usually are *not interested in generalizing* beyond the particular people who are studied. In qualitative research, different groups are said to construct their different realities or perspectives, and these social constructions, reciprocally, influence how they "see" or understand their worlds, what they see as normal and abnormal, and how they should act.

Mixed researchers see positive value in both the quantitative *and* the qualitative views of human behavior. They view the use of only quantitative research or only qualitative research as limiting and incomplete for many research problems. As can be seen by examining the middle column in Table 2.1, mixed researchers use a combination of quantitative and qualitative concepts and approaches to understand the world more fully.

Quantitative research often uses what might be called a "narrow-angle lens" because the focus is on only one or a few causal factors at the same time. Quantitative researchers attempt to hold constant the factors that are not being studied. This is often accomplished under laboratory conditions in which an experimenter randomly assigns participants to groups, manipulates only one factor, and then examines the outcome. For example, a researcher might first randomly assign research volunteers to two groups. Random assignment makes the two groups very similar. Then the researcher might expose one group to a new teaching method and another group to a different teaching method, treating the two groups similarly during the study except for the research-manipulated difference in teaching method. The researcher then examines which group learns the most and attributes the difference in learning to the teaching method received. The researcher is able to make a causal attribution because the two groups were similar at the start of the experiment and the only factor they differed on was which teaching method they received.

Qualitative research uses a wide- and deep-angle lens, examining human choice and behavior as it occurs naturally in all of its detail. Qualitative researchers do not want to intervene in the natural flow of behavior. Qualitative researchers study behavior naturalistically and holistically. They try to understand multiple dimensions and layers of reality, such as the types of people in a group, how they think, how they interact, what kinds of agreements or norms are present, and how these dimensions come together holistically to describe the group. For example, perhaps a qualitative researcher wants to study the social climate and culture of a highly successful school. The researcher would spend a great deal of time studying the many aspects of the school to come up with an analysis of how the school operates and for whom and why it is successful. Depending on the research questions, a researcher using the mixed approach would spend part of his or her time in each of the different focus modes, moving back and forth between wide-angle, narrow-angle, and deep-angle viewpoints.

Quantitative researchers attempt to operate under the assumption of objectivity. They assume that there is a reality to be observed and that rational observers who look at the same phenomenon will basically agree on its existence and its characteristics. They try to remain as neutral or value-free as they can, and they attempt to avoid human bias whenever possible. In a sense, quantitative researchers attempt to study the phenomena that are of interest to them "from a distance." For example, standardized questionnaires and other quantitative measuring tools are often used to measure carefully what is observed. In experiments, researchers frequently use random assignment to place participants into different groups to eliminate the possibility of human bias while constructing the comparison groups. In judging results, statistical criteria are used to form many conclusions.

Qualitative researchers generally contend that "reality is socially constructed" (e.g., Guba & Lincoln, 1989). For example, social behavior follows socially constructed norms. Language also has an important influence on our views of the world. For example, it has been suggested that the Inuit "see" many types of snow, whereas the average American probably only sees a few types. Inuits' local languages might allow them to see distinctions that you do not notice; this idea is known as the **linguistic-relativity hypothesis**.

- **Linguistic-relativity hypothesis** The idea that people see and understand the world through the lens of their local language and their thoughts are bound by their language

Qualitative researchers argue that it is important to "get close" to their objects of study through participant observation so that they can experience for themselves the subjective dimensions of the phenomena they study. In qualitative research, the researcher is said to be the "instrument of data collection." Rather than using a standardized instrument or measuring device, the qualitative researcher asks the questions, collects the data, makes interpretations, and records what is observed. The qualitative researcher constantly tries to understand the people he or she is observing from the participants' or "natives'" or "actors'" viewpoints. This is the concept of "empathetic understanding." The famous sociologist Max Weber, writing in the early 20th century, called this idea of *understanding* something from the *other* person's viewpoint ***verstehen*** (M. Weber, 1968). This is expressed in an American idiom as "putting yourself into someone else's shoes." It is important to remember that qualitative research is focused on understanding the "insider's perspective" of people and their cultures and this requires direct personal and often participatory contact.

- ***Verstehen*** A method of empathetic understanding of others' viewpoints, meanings, intentions, and cultural beliefs

According to mixed research, it is important to understand the *subjective* (individual), *intersubjective* (language-based, discursive, cultural), and *objective* (material and causal) realities in our world. Although it is important not to influence or bias what you are observing, it also is important to understand the insiders' meanings and viewpoints. For example, if you were studying the culture of the snake-handling churches in the area where Alabama, Tennessee, and Georgia come together, it might be helpful to collect quantitative data by having the church members fill out standardized instruments measuring their personality and demographic characteristics. It would also be essential to collect qualitative data through in-depth personal interviews and close observations of the members to gain a better understanding (from the insiders' perspectives) of the snake-handling culture. In short, the mixing of methods would add very useful and complementary information.

Quantitative research generally reduces measurement to numbers. In survey research, for example, attitudes are usually measured by using *rating scales*. The following 5-point agreement scale is an example:

Strongly Disagree	Disagree	Neutral	Agree	Strongly Agree
1	2	3	4	5

The interviewer or questionnaire provides a statement, and the respondents reply with one of the five allowable response categories. After all respondents have provided their answers, the researcher typically calculates and reports an average for the group of respondents. Let us say, for example, that a researcher asks a group of teachers for their degree of agreement with the following statement: "Teachers need more training in the area of child psychopathology." The researcher might then calculate the average response for the whole group, which might be 4.15 based on a 5-point scale. The researcher might also determine whether the ratings vary by years of teaching experience. Perhaps the average agreement for new teachers is 4.5, and the average for teachers with 5 or more years of experience is 3.9. As you might guess, quantitative data are usually analyzed by using statistical analysis programs on a computer.

On the other hand, qualitative researchers do not usually collect data in the form of numbers. Rather, they conduct observations and in-depth interviews, and the data are usually in the form of words. For example, a qualitative researcher might conduct a focus group discussion with six or seven new teachers to discuss the adequacy of their undergraduate educational programs in preparing them to deal with real-world problems that they face in schools. The facilitator of the focus group would probably videotape the group and tape-record what was said. Later, the recording would be transcribed into words, which would then be analyzed by using the techniques of qualitative data analysis (see Chapter 20). Also, when a qualitative researcher enters the field and makes observations, the researcher will write down what he or she sees, as well as relevant insights and thoughts. The data are again in the form of words. During qualitative data analysis, the researcher will try to identify categories that describe what happened, as well as general themes appearing again and again in the data. The mixed research approach would use a variety of data collection and analysis approaches.

Finally, qualitative, mixed, and quantitative research reports tend to differ. Quantitative reports are commonly reported in journal articles ranging from 5 to 15 pages. The reports include many numbers and results of statistical significance testing (to be explained later). In contrast, qualitative research reports are generally longer, and they are written in narrative form, describing what was found, especially from the insider perspectives of the people in the group being studied. This report is more interpretative, as the researcher attempts to understand and portray the lives and experiences and language of the research participants. Qualitative journal articles are frequently 20–25 pages long, and the results of qualitative research are often published in the form of books or monographs rather than journal articles. Mixed research might follow the quantitative style or the qualitative style or, more frequently, might use a mixture of the styles.

REVIEW QUESTIONS

2.1 What are the key features of quantitative and qualitative research?

2.2 What are the key features of mixed methods research?

QUANTITATIVE RESEARCH METHODS: EXPERIMENTAL AND NONEXPERIMENTAL RESEARCH

You now know some of the characteristics of quantitative, qualitative, and mixed research. We next introduce some of the different methods of quantitative research. Before we do that, however, you need to know about variables, because quantitative researchers usually describe the world by using variables and they attempt to explain and predict aspects of the world by demonstrating the relationships among variables. You can see a summary of the types of variables in Table 2.2.

TABLE 2.2 Common Types of Variables Classified by Level of Measurement and by Role of Variable

Variable Type	*Key Characteristic*	*Example*
Level of Measurement		
Categorical variable	A variable that is made up of different types or categories of a phenomenon	The variable *gender* is made up of the categories of male and female.
Quantitative variable	A variable that varies in degree or amount of a phenomenon	The variable *annual income* varies from zero income to a very high income level.
Role Taken by the Variable		
Independent variable (symbolized as IV)	A variable that is presumed to cause changes to occur in another variable; a causal variable	Amount of studying (IV) affects test grades (DV).
Dependent variable (symbolized as DV)	A variable that changes because of another variable; the effect or outcome variable	Amount of studying (IV) affects test grades (DV).
Mediating variable (also called an intervening variable)	A variable that comes in between other variables, helping to delineate the process through which variables affect one another	Amount of studying (IV) leads to input and organization of knowledge in long-term memory (mediating variable), which affects test grades (DV).
Moderator variable	A variable that delineates how a relationship of interest changes under different conditions or circumstances	Perhaps the relationship between studying (IV) and test grades (DV) changes according to the different levels of use of a drug such as Ritalin (moderator).
Extraneous variable	A variable that may compete with the independent variable in explaining an outcome	Perhaps an observed relationship between coffee drinking (IV) and cancer (DV) is actually due to smoking cigarettes.

Variables

A **variable** is a condition or characteristic that can take on different values or categories. A much-studied educational variable is intelligence, which varies from low to high for different people. Age is another variable that varies from low to high (e.g., from 1 minute old to 130 years old or so). Another variable is gender, which is either male or female. To better understand the concept of a variable, it is helpful to compare it with a constant, its opposite. A **constant** is a single value or category of a variable. Here's the idea: The variable *gender* is a marker for two constants: male and female. The category (i.e., constant) *male* is a marker for only one thing; it is one of the two constants forming the variable called gender. *Gender* varies, but *male* does not vary. Therefore, *gender* is a variable, and *male* is a constant. In the case of the variable *age*, all of the ages make up the values (i.e., constants) of the variable, and each value (e.g., 13 years old) is a constant. If you are still having a hard time with the distinction between a variable and a constant, think of it like this: A variable is like a *set* of things, and a constant is *one* of those things.

- **Variable** A condition or characteristic that can take on different values or categories
- **Constant** A single value or category of a variable

The variables that we just used, age and gender, are actually different types of variables. Age is a quantitative variable, and gender is a categorical variable. A **quantitative variable** is a variable that varies in degree or amount. It usually involves numbers. A **categorical variable** is a variable that varies in type or kind. It usually involves different groups. Age takes on numbers (e.g., number of years old), and gender takes on two types or kinds (male and female). Now consider the variable *annual income.* How does it vary? It varies in amount, ranging from no income at all to some very large amount of income. Therefore, income is a quantitative variable. If you think about how much money you made last year, you can determine your value on the variable annual income. Now think about the variable religion. How does this variable vary? It varies in kind or type. For instance, it can take on any of the categories standing for the different world religions (e.g., Christianity, Judaism, Islam). For practice identifying quantitative and categorical variables, take a look at the examples in Table 2.3.

- **Quantitative variable** A variable that varies in degree or amount
- **Categorical variable** A variable that varies by type or kind

TABLE 2.3 Examples of Quantitative and Categorical Variables

Quantitative Variables	*Categorical Variables*
Height	Gender
Weight	Religion
Temperature	Ethnicity
Annual income	Method of therapy
Most aptitude tests	College major
Most achievement tests	Political party identification
School size	Type of school
Class size	Marital status of parents
Self-esteem level	Student retention (retained or not)
Grade point average	Type of teacher expectation

(Continued)

■ **TABLE 2.3** (Continued)

Quantitative Variables	*Categorical Variables*
Teacher-pupil ratio	Native language
Time spent on homework	Teaching method
Age	Personality type
Anxiety level	Learning style
Job satisfaction score	Type of feedback
Number of behavioral outbursts	Computer use (or not)
Reading performance	Type of reading instruction
Spelling accuracy	Inclusion (or not)
Number of performance errors	Problem-solving strategy used
Rate of cognitive processing	Memory strategy used
Dropout rate	Social class

■ **Independent variable** A variable that is presumed to cause a change in another variable

■ **Dependent variable** A variable that is presumed to be influenced by one or more independent variables

■ **Cause-and-effect relationship** Relationship in which one variable affects another variable

Yet another categorization scheme for variables is to speak of independent and dependent variables. An **independent variable** is a variable that is presumed to cause a change to occur in another variable. Sometimes the independent variable is manipulated by the researcher (i.e., the researcher determines the value of the independent variable); at other times, the independent variable is studied by the researcher but is not directly manipulated (i.e., the researcher studies what happens when an independent variable changes naturally). The independent variable is an antecedent variable because it must come before another variable if it is to produce a change in it. A **dependent variable** is the variable that is presumed to be influenced by one or more independent variables. The dependent variable is the variable that is "dependent on" the independent (i.e., antecedent) variable(s). A **cause-and-effect relationship** between an independent variable and a dependent variable is present when changes in the independent variable tend to cause changes in the dependent variable. Sometimes researchers call the dependent variable an *outcome variable* or a *response variable* because it is used to measure the effect of one or more independent variables.

Here is a simple example of a cause-and-effect relationship. Think about the US Surgeon General's warning printed on cigarette packages: "Smoking Causes Lung Cancer, Heart Disease, Emphysema, and May Complicate Pregnancy." Can you identify the independent and dependent variables in this relationship? It is smoking that is presumed to cause lung cancer and several other diseases. (You should be aware that extensive research beyond simply observing that smoking and lung cancer were associated was conducted to establish that the link between smoking and cancer was causal.) In this example, *smoking* is the independent variable (the values corresponding to the number of cigarettes smoked a day), and *presence of lung cancer* is the dependent variable (the values being *lung cancer present* and *lung cancer not present*).

As shorthand, we can use *IV* to stand for independent variable and *DV* to stand for dependent variable. We also sometimes use an arrow: IV → DV. The arrow → means "tends to cause changes in" or "affects." In words, this says that the researcher believes "changes in the independent variable tend to cause changes in the dependent variable." In the smoking example, we write Smoking → Onset of Lung Cancer.

Another type of variable is an **intervening variable** (also commonly called a *mediating* or *mediator variable*). An intervening or **mediating variable** occurs between two other variables in a causal chain (Kenny, Kashy, & Bolger, 1998). In the case X → Y, we have only an independent variable and a dependent variable. In the case X → I → Y, we have an intervening variable (I) occurring between the two other variables. In the case of smoking, perhaps an intervening variable is the development of damaged lung cells. In other words, smoking tends to lead to the development of damaged lung cells, which tends to lead to lung cancer. It is helpful to identify intervening variables because these variables may help explain the process by which an independent variable leads to changes in a dependent variable.

■ **Intervening or mediating variable** A variable that occurs between two other variables in a causal chain

As another example, let *X* stand for teaching approach (perhaps the levels of this variable are lecture method and cooperative group method), and let *Y* stand for test score on class exam (varying from 0 to 100 percent correct). Research may show that X → Y; that is, test scores depend on which teaching approach is used. In this case, an intervening variable might be student motivation (varying from low motivation to high motivation). Therefore, the full causal chain is X → I → Y, where *X* is teaching approach, *I* is student motivation, and *Y* is students' test scores; that is, teaching method → student motivation → student test scores.

The next type of variable is a moderator variable. A **moderator variable** is a variable that changes (i.e., moderates) the relationship between other variables. It's a variable that delineates how a relationship changes under different conditions or contexts or for different kinds of people. For example, you might analyze a set of research data and find little or no difference between the performance scores of students who are taught by using the lecture approach and the scores of students who are taught by using the cooperative learning approach. On further analysis, however, you might learn that cooperative learning works better for extroverted students and that lecture works better for introverted students. In this example, personality type is a moderator variable: The relationship between teaching approach and performance scores depends on the personality type of the student. One thing we commonly find in research on teaching is that what works well depends on the type of student. As you can see, it is helpful to know the important moderator variables so that you can adjust your teaching accordingly.

■ **Moderator variable** A variable that changes the relationship between other variables

Experimental Research

The purpose of experimental research is to determine cause-and-effect relationships. The experimental research method enables us to identify causal relationships because it allows us to observe, under controlled conditions, the effects of systematically changing one or more variables. Specifically, in **experimental research**, the researcher *manipulates* the independent variable, actively intervening in the world, and then observes what happens. Thus, **manipulation**, an intervention studied by an experimenter, is the key defining characteristic of experimental research. The use of manipulation in studying cause-and-effect relationships is based on the activity theory of causation (Collingwood, 1940; Cook & Shadish, 1994). Active manipulation is involved only in experimental research. Because of this (and because of experimental control), experimental research provides the strongest evidence of all the research methods about the existence of cause-and-effect relationships.

■ **Experimental research** Research in which the researcher manipulates the independent variable and is interested in showing cause and effect

■ **Manipulation** An intervention studied by an experimenter

In a simple experiment, a researcher will systematically vary an independent variable and assess its effects on a dependent variable. For example, perhaps an educational researcher wants to determine the effect of a new teaching approach on reading achievement. The researcher could perform the new teaching approach with one group of participants and perform the traditional teaching approach with another group of participants. After the treatment, the experimenter would determine which group showed the greater amount of learning (reading achievement). If the group receiving the new teaching approach showed the greater gain, then the researcher would tentatively conclude that the new approach is better than the traditional approach.

Although the type of experiment just described is sometimes done, there is a potential problem with it. What if the two groups of students differed on variables, such as vocabulary, reading ability, and/or age? More specifically, what if the students in the new teaching approach group happened to be older, had better vocabularies, and were better readers than the students in the traditional teaching approach group? Furthermore, suppose the students with better vocabularies, who were older, and who were better readers also tended to learn more quickly than other students. If this were the case, then it is likely that the students in the new teaching approach group would have learned faster regardless of the teaching approach. In this example, the variables *age*, *vocabulary*, and *reading ability* are called extraneous variables.

▪ **Extraneous variable** A variable that may compete with the independent variable in explaining the outcome

Extraneous variables are variables other than the independent variable of interest (e.g., teaching approach) that may be related to the outcome. When extraneous variables are not controlled for or dealt with in some way, an outside reviewer of the research study may come up with competing explanations for the research findings. The reviewer might argue that the outcome is due to a particular extraneous variable rather than to the independent variable. These competing explanations for the relationship between an independent and a dependent variable are sometimes called *alternative explanations* or *rival hypotheses.* In our example, the researcher cannot know whether the students in the new teaching approach performed better because of the teaching approach or because they had better vocabularies, were older, or were better readers. All these factors are said to be *confounded*; that is, these factors are entangled with the independent variable, and the researcher can't state which is the most important factor. Sometimes we use the term **confounding variables** to refer to extraneous variables that were not controlled for by the researcher and are the reason a particular result occurred.

▪ **Confounding variable** An extraneous variable that was not controlled for and is the reason a particular "confounded" result is observed

Because the presence of extraneous variables makes the interpretation of research findings difficult, the effective researcher attempts to control them whenever possible. The best way to control for extraneous variables in an experiment like the one above is to randomly assign research participants to the groups to be compared. Random assignment helps ensure that the people in the groups to be compared are similar before the intervention or manipulation. For example, if the researcher wants to randomly assign 30 people to two groups, then the researcher might put 30 slips of paper, each with one name on it, into a hat and randomly pull out 15 slips. The 15 names that are pulled out will become one of the two groups, and the 15 names remaining in the hat will become the other group. When this is done, the only differences between the groups will be due to chance. In other words, the people in the groups will be *similar* at the start of the experiment. After making the groups similar, the researcher administers the levels of the independent variable, making the groups different only on this variable. Perhaps teaching method is the independent variable, and the levels are cooperative learning and lecture. The administration of the independent variable, or manipulation, would involve exposing one group to cooperative learning and the other group to lecture. Then if the two groups become different after the manipulation, the researcher can conclude that the difference was due to the independent variable.

In summary, (1) the experimenter uses random assignment to *make the groups similar*; (2) the experimenter does something different with the groups; and (3) if the groups then become different, the experimenter concludes that the difference was due to what the experimenter did (i.e., it was due to the independent variable). In later chapters, we will introduce you to additional methods that are used to control for extraneous variables when one is not able to use random assignment. For now, remember that random assignment to groups is the most effective way to make the groups similar and therefore control for extraneous variables.

See Journal Article 2.1 on the Student Study Site.

Nonexperimental Research

In **nonexperimental research**, there is *no manipulation* of an independent variable. There also is no random assignment to groups by the researcher. As a result of these two deficiencies, evidence gathered in support of cause-and-effect relationships in nonexperimental research is more limited and much weaker than evidence gathered in experimental research (especially experimental research designs that include random assignment). If you want to study cause and effect, you should try to conduct an experiment, but sometimes this is not feasible. When important causal research questions need to be answered and an experiment cannot be done, research must still be conducted. In research, we try to do the best we can, and sometimes this means that we must use weaker research methods. For example, during the 1960s, extensive research linking cigarette smoking to lung cancer was conducted. Experimental research with humans was not possible because it would have been unethical. Therefore, in addition to experimental research with laboratory animals, medical researchers relied on nonexperimental research methods for their extensive study of humans.

- **Nonexperimental research** Research in which the independent variable is not manipulated and there is no random assignment to groups

One type of nonexperimental research is sometimes called *causal-comparative research.* In **causal-comparative research**, the researcher studies the relationship between one or more categorical independent variables and one or more quantitative dependent variables. In the most basic case, there are a single categorical independent variable and a single quantitative dependent variable. Because the independent variable is categorical (e.g., males vs. females, parents vs. nonparents, or public school teachers vs. private school teachers), the different groups' average scores on a dependent variable are compared to determine whether a relationship is present between the independent and dependent variables. For example, if the independent variable is *student retention* (and the categories of the variable are *retained in the first grade* and *not retained in the first grade*) and the dependent variable is *level of achievement*, then the retained students' average achievement would be compared to the nonretained students' average achievement. (Which group do you think would have higher achievements on average: the retained or the nonretained students?) But remember that you must always worry about extraneous/confounding variables. In this case we might want to statistically control (discussed later in book) for prior achievement, parental support, quality of school, quality of teacher, and any other extraneous variable that is believed to affect the dependent variable and systematically vary with the independent variable. Can you think of any other extraneous variables in this case?

- **Causal-comparative research** A form of nonexperimental research in which the primary independent variable of interest is a categorical variable

To design a basic nonexperimental study with a categorical variable as an exercise, look at Table 2.3 and find a categorical variable that can serve as your independent variable (i.e., one that you would not manipulate) and a quantitative variable that can be your dependent variable. As an example, we can select *retention* as the independent variable and *self-esteem* as a dependent variable. We hypothesize that student retention (retained vs. nonretained) has an influence on self-esteem. More specifically, we predict that, on average, retained students will have lower self-esteem than nonretained students. We would have to go to a school and collect data if we actually wanted to conduct a research study to see whether there is any support for this hypothesis.

Another nonexperimental research method is called correlational research. As in causal-comparative research, there is no manipulation of an independent variable. In **correlational research**, the researcher studies the relationship between one or more quantitative independent variables and one or more quantitative dependent variables; in correlational research, the independent and dependent variables are quantitative. In this chapter, we introduce the basic case in which the researcher has a single quantitative independent variable and a single quantitative dependent variable. To understand how to study the relationship between two variables when both variables are quantitative, you need a basic understanding of a correlation coefficient.

- **Correlational research** A form of nonexperimental research in which the primary independent variable of interest is a quantitative variable

A **correlation coefficient** is a numerical index that provides information about the strength and direction of the relationship between two variables. It provides information about how two variables are associated. More specifically, a correlation coefficient is a number that can range from −1 to 1, with zero standing for no correlation at all. If the number is greater than zero, there is a positive correlation. If the number is less than zero, there is a negative correlation. If the number is equal to zero, then there is no correlation between the two variables being correlated. If the number is equal to +1.00 or equal to −1.00, the correlation is called perfect; that is, it is as strong as possible. Now we provide an explanation of these points.

- **Correlation coefficient** A numerical index that indicates the strength and direction of the relationship between two variables

A **positive correlation** is present when scores on two variables tend to move in the same direction. For example, consider the variables high school GPA and SAT (the college entrance exam). How do you think scores on these two variables are related? A diagram of this relationship is shown in Figure 2.2a. As you can see there, the students who have high GPAs tend also to have high scores on the SAT, and students who have low GPAs tend to have low scores on the SAT. That's the relationship. We say that GPA and SAT are positively correlated because as SAT scores increase, GPAs also tend to increase (i.e., the variables move in the same direction). Because of this relationship, researchers can use SAT scores to help make predictions about GPAs. However, because the correlation is not perfect, the prediction is also far from perfect.

- **Positive correlation** The situation when scores on two variables tend to move in the same direction

A **negative correlation** is present when the scores on two variables tend to move in opposite directions—as one variable goes up, the other tends to go down, and vice versa. For example, consider these variables: amount of daily cholesterol consumption and life expectancy. How do you think these variables are related? Do you think the relationship meets the definition of a negative correlation? A diagram of this relationship is shown in Figure 2.2b. You can see that as daily cholesterol consumption increases, life expectancy tends to decrease. That is, the variables move in opposite directions. Therefore, researchers can use information about cholesterol consumption to help predict life expectancies. High values on one variable are associated with low values on the other variable, and vice versa. This is what we mean by a negative correlation.

- **Negative correlation** The situation when scores on two variables tend to move in opposite directions

FIGURE 2.2 Examples of positive and negative correlation

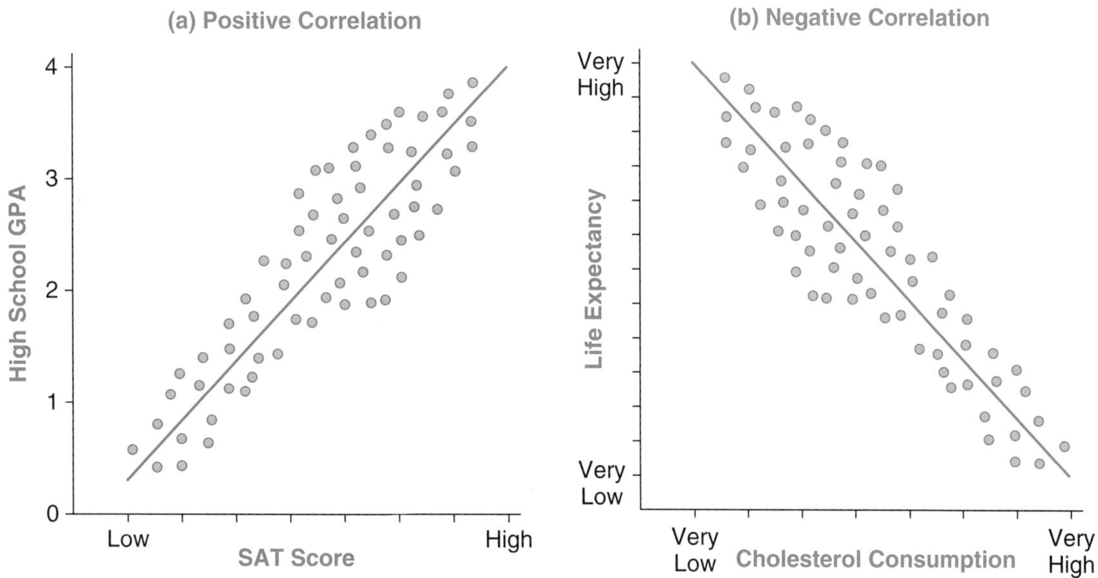

At this point, you know the difference between a positive correlation (the variables move in the same direction) and a negative correlation (the variables move in opposite directions). There is, however, one more point about a correlation coefficient that you need to know. In addition to the direction of a correlation (positive or negative), we are interested in the strength of the correlation. By *strength*, we mean "How strong is the relationship?" Remember this point: Zero means no relationship at all, and +1.00 and –1.00 mean that the relationship is as strong as possible.

The higher the number (the negative sign is ignored), the stronger the relationship is. For example, if you have a correlation of –.5, then ignore the negative sign and you have.5, which shows the strength of the correlation. Therefore, a correlation of –.5 and a correlation of +.5 have the same strength. The only difference between the two is the direction of the relationship (–.5 is a negative correlation, and +.5 is a positive correlation). When you are interested in its strength, it does not matter whether a correlation is positive or negative. The strength of a correlation operates like this: Zero stands for no correlation at all (i.e., it is the smallest possible strength), and +1.00 and –1.00 are both as strong as a correlation can ever be. That is, +1.00 and –1.00 are equally strong; in research jargon, we say that both +1.00 and –1.00 are *perfect correlations.* The only difference between +1.00 and –1.00 is the direction of the relationship, not the strength. You can see some diagrams of correlations of different strengths and directions in Figure 2.3.

If you found the previous paragraph a little hard to understand, here is a different way to determine how strong a correlation is. Simply check to see how far away the number is from zero. The farther the number is from zero, the stronger the correlation is. A correlation of .9 is stronger than a correlation of .2 because it is farther from zero. Likewise, a correlation of –.9 is stronger than a correlation of –.2 because it, too, is farther from zero. Now for a trick question: Which correlation do you believe is stronger: –.90 or +.80? The answer is –.90 because –.90 is farther from zero than +.80. (I think you've got it!)

FIGURE 2.3 Correlations of different strengths and directions

(a) Perfect Correlations

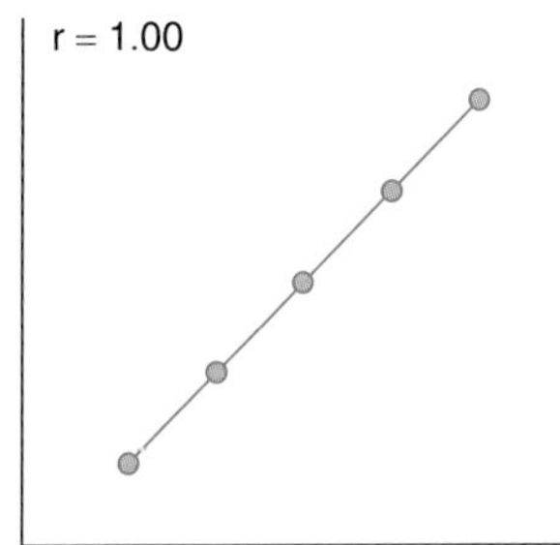

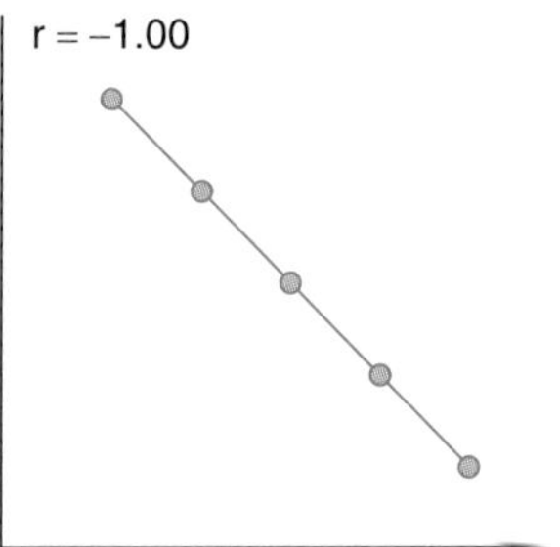

(b) Large or Strong Correlations

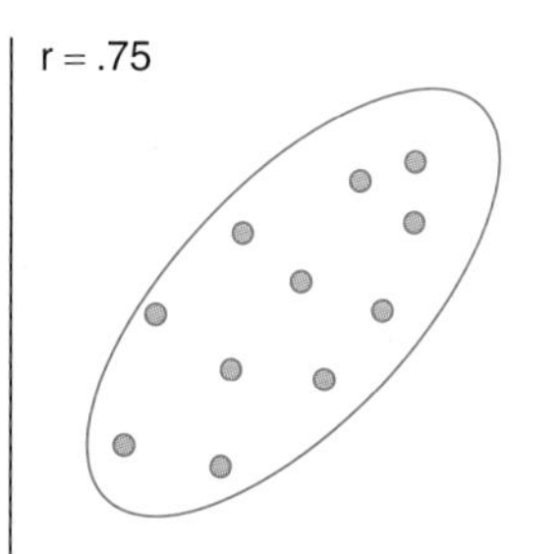

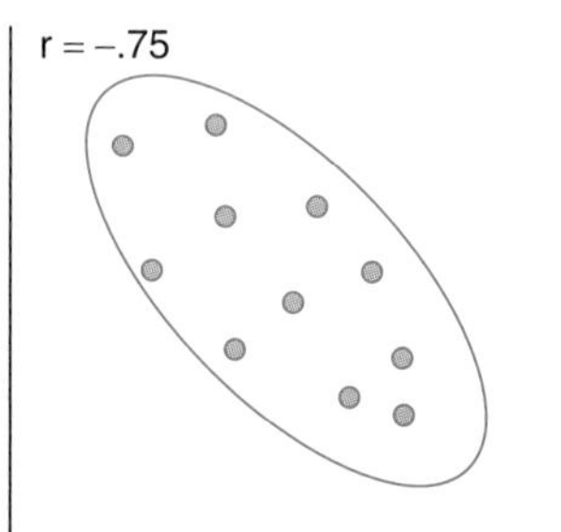

(c) Small or Weak Correlations

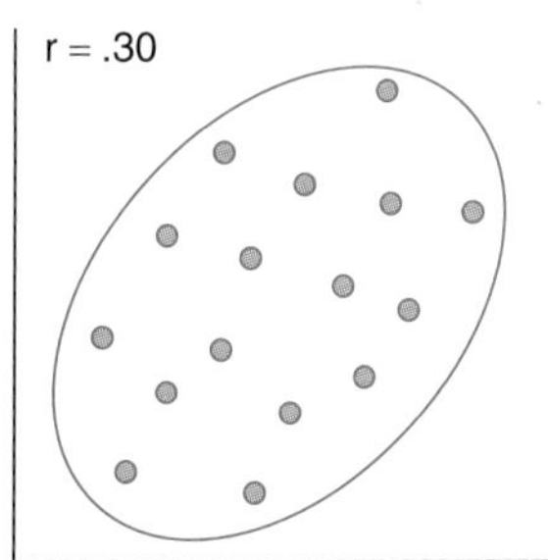

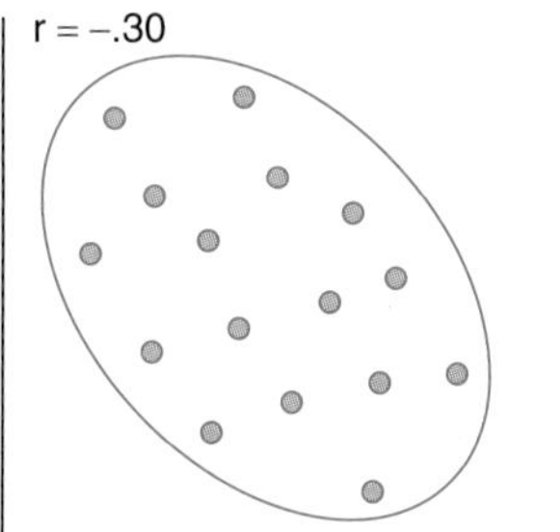

(d) No Correlation

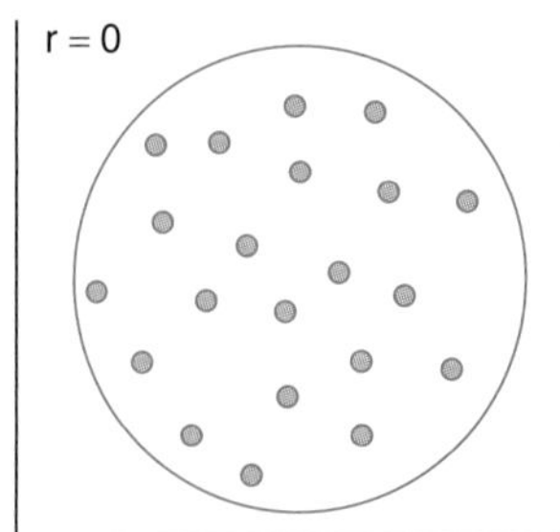

This is only a brief introduction to the idea of a correlation coefficient. You will become more comfortable with the concept the more you use it, and we will be using the concept often in later chapters. For now, you should clearly understand that you can have positive and negative correlations or no correlation at all and that some correlations are stronger than other correlations. You have learned more already than you thought you would, haven't you?

In the most basic form of correlational research, the researcher examines the correlation between two quantitative variables, and oftentimes researchers attempt to statistically control for worrisome extraneous variables in the study (explained in Chapter 14 under the heading "Statistical Control"). For a simple example, perhaps an educational psychologist has a theory stating that global self-esteem (which is a relatively stable personality trait) should predict class performance. More specifically, the educational psychologist predicts that students entering a particular history class with high self-esteem will tend to do better than students entering the class with low self-esteem, and vice versa. To test this hypothesis, the researcher could collect the relevant data and calculate the correlation between self-esteem and performance on the class examinations. We would expect a positive correlation (i.e., the higher the self-esteem, the higher the performance on the history exam). In our hypothetical example, let's say that the correlation was +.5. That is a medium-size positive correlation, and it would support our hypothesis of a positive correlation.

In our example of self-esteem and class performance, however, the researcher would be able to say virtually nothing about cause and effect based on the correlation of .5. All that one can claim is that there is a predictive relationship between self-esteem and class performance: The higher the self-esteem, the higher class performance tends to be. This is the same problem that we experienced in the basic case of causal-comparative research in which there is one independent variable and one dependent variable and no control variables (i.e., ability to make a claim of *causation*). In our correlation example of self-esteem and class performance, some worrisome extraneous variables that would need to be "controlled for" are prior achievement, intelligence, self-efficacy, motivation, and any other extraneous variables that worry *you*.

There are three key problems with the basic (two-variable and no controls) cases of correlational and causal-comparative research described in this chapter:

1. There is no manipulation of the independent variable by the researcher.
2. It can be difficult to determine the temporal order of the variables (i.e., which of the variables occurs first).
3. There are usually too many other reasons why we might observe the relationship (i.e., the correlation or the difference between groups); that is, there are usually too many extraneous variables that are left unexplained and act as rival or alternative explanations for why something occurs in the world. (Note: In good research, the researcher identifies plausible extraneous/confounding variables, measures them, and controls for them using techniques discussed later in this book [e.g., statistical control and matching discussed in Chapter 14].)

Remember this important point: *You must not jump to a conclusion about cause and effect in a nonexperimental research study* in which the researcher has examined only the relationship between two variables, such as examining a correlation coefficient in correlational research or comparing two group means in causal-comparative research. Simply finding a relationship between self-esteem and class performance (correlational research) or between gender and class performance (causal-comparative research) is *not* sufficient evidence for concluding that the relationship is causal. Therefore, *you* must not jump to that conclusion. We will discuss the issue of cause and effect more in later chapters. Note that we have hinted at a way to improve the simple cases of nonexperimental research—attempt to control for worrisome extraneous variables. Even when you control for variables in nonexperimental research, however, the evidence is still much weaker that the evidence of causation provided by experimental research. For now, make sure you remember this key point: *Experimental research with random assignment is the single best research method for determining cause-and-effect relationships, and nonexperimental research methods are much weaker.*

See Journal Article 2.2 on the Student Study Site.

REVIEW QUESTIONS

2.3 What is the difference between a categorical variable and a quantitative variable? Think of an example of each.

2.4 Why is experimental research more effective than nonexperimental research when a researcher is interested in studying cause and effect?

2.5 What are the three main problems with the simple cases of causal-comparative and correlational research?

2.6 What are two variables that you believe are positively correlated?

2.7 What are two variables that you believe are negatively correlated?

QUALITATIVE RESEARCH METHODS

As you saw in Table 2.1, qualitative research is based on qualitative data and tends to follow the exploratory mode of the scientific method. In this book, we will be discussing five specific types of qualitative research: phenomenology, ethnography, narrative inquiry, case study research, and grounded theory research. Chapters 15 and 16 provide detailed discussions of these five kinds of research; now we introduce you to the key ideas of each of these research methods to foreshadow our later, in-depth discussions of these methods.

Phenomenology

- **Phenomenology** A form of qualitative research in which the researcher attempts to understand how one or more individuals experience a particular phenomenon

The first major type of qualitative research is **phenomenology**. When conducting a phenomenological research study, a researcher attempts to understand how one or more individuals *experience* a phenomenon. For example, you might conduct a phenomenological study of elementary school students who have lost a parent to describe the elements and whole of the experience of parental loss. The key element of a phenomenological research study is that the researcher attempts to understand how people experience a phenomenon from each person's own perspective. Your goal is to enter the inner world of each participant to understand his or her perspective and experience. Phenomenological researchers have studied many phenomena, such as what it is like to participate in a religious group that handles serpents as part of the worship service (Williamson, Pollio, & Hood, 2000), the experience of grief (Bailley, Dunham, & Kral, 2000), the experience of learning to become a music teacher (Devries, 2000), the experience of living with alcoholism (B. A. Smith, 1998), the meaning of age for young and old adults (Adams-Price, Henley, & Hale, 1998), and elementary school children's experiences of stress (Omizo & Omizo, 1990).

See Journal Article 2.3 on the Student Study Site.

Ethnography

Ethnography is one of the most popular approaches to qualitative research in education. The word **ethnography** literally means "writing about people." When ethnographers conduct research, they are interested in describing the **culture** of a group of people and learning what it is like to be a member of the group from the perspective of the members of that group. That is, they are interested in documenting things like the shared attitudes, values, norms, practices, patterns of interaction, perspectives, and language of a group of people. They may also be interested in the material things that the group members produce or use, such as clothing styles, ethnic foods, and architectural styles. Ethnographers try to use **holistic descriptions**; that is, they try to describe how the members of a group interact and how they come together to make up the group as a whole. In other words, the group is more than just the sum of its parts. Just a few of the many groups that ethnographers have studied recently are panhandlers living on the streets of Washington, D.C. (Lankenau, 1999), men with mental retardation living in a group home (Croft, 1999), black and white sorority members (Berkowitz & Padavic, 1999), students in a US history class (Keedy, Fleming, Gentry, & Wheat, 1998), sixth-grade students in science classes (Solot & Arluke, 1997), karaoke bar performers (Drew, 1997), Puerto Rican American parents with children in special education (Harry, 1992), and a group of Native American students who had dropped out of school (Deyhle, 1992). In all of these studies, the researchers were interested in describing some aspect of the culture of the people in the study.

- **Ethnography** A form of qualitative research focused on discovering and describing the culture of a group of people
- **Culture** The shared attitudes, values, norms, practices, patterns of interaction, perspectives, and language of a group of people
- **Holistic description** The description of how members of a group interact and how they come together to make up the group as a whole
- **Narrative inquiry** The study of life experiences as a storied phenomenon

Narrative Inquiry

In **narrative inquiry**, participants tell stories of their lived experiences, and then, in relational ways, researchers inquire into and about the experiences. Researchers might share with a participant similar experiences that they have had. In contrast to phenomenology, where the goal is to describe the essence of the experience of a phenomenon, the narrative researcher works with the participant to discern the individual storied experience through narrative threads, narrative tensions, plotlines, narrative coherences, and/or silences and composes a narrative account of the participant's storied experience. Narrative inquirers also inquire into the institutional, social, cultural, familial, and linguistic narratives in which each participant's experiences are embedded and that shape the individual's experience. Multiple data sources, such as conversations, field notes, memory box items, photographs, and field notes, among others, are also used.

What all narrative inquiry has in common is that it is the study of experience as a storied phenomenon. For example, in *Composing Lives in Transition* (Clandinin, Steeves, & Caine, 2013), narrative inquirers inquired into the stories told by 11 youth who had left school before graduating. The researchers attended to how the stories each youth told of their experience of leaving school early shaped their life and how their life shaped their leaving of school. For example, in "A Narrative Account of Skye" (Lessard in Clandinin et al.) is a compelling account of a young woman's experiences of composing her life in different places, times, and relationships as she attends school and leaves school early.

Case Study Research

■ **Case study research** A form of qualitative research that focuses on providing a detailed account of one or more cases

In **case study research**, the researcher provides a detailed account of one or more cases. Although case study research usually relies on qualitative data, multiple methods are also used. Case study research can be used to address exploratory, descriptive, and explanatory research questions (Stake, 1995; Yin, 1994). Case study research is more varied than phenomenology, which focuses on individuals' experience of some phenomenon; ethnography, which focuses on some aspect of culture; or grounded theory, which focuses on developing an explanatory theory. What all pure case studies have in common, however, is a focus on each case as a whole unit (i.e., case study research is holistic) as it exists in its real-life context. For example, in "Building Learning Organizations in Engineering Cultures," Ford, Voyer, and Wilkinson (2000) examined how a specific organization changed over time into a learning organization. Although their focus was on a single case, other organizations might be able to learn from the experiences of Ford and colleagues. In "The Journey Through College of Seven Gifted Females: Influences on Their Career Related Decisions," Grant (2000) examined in detail the personal, social, and academic experiences of seven people. After analyzing each case, Grant made cross-case comparisons, searching for similarities and differences.

Grounded Theory

■ **Grounded theory research** A qualitative approach to generating and developing a theory from the data that the researcher collects

Grounded theory research is a qualitative approach to generating and developing a theory from the data you collect in a research study. You will recall from Chapter 1 that a theory is an explanation of how and why something operates. We will explain the details of grounded theory in Chapter 16; for now, remember that grounded theory is an inductive approach for generating theories or explanations. One example of a grounded theory is found in "An Analysis of Factors That Contribute to Parent-School Conflict in Special Education" by Lake and Billingsley (2000). Lake and Billingsley wanted to explain why conflict takes place between the parents of children in special education programs and school officials. The researchers conducted in-depth interviews (lasting an average of 1 hour) with parents, principals, special education program directors, and mediators. They identified several factors as contributing to the escalation of parent-school conflict. The primary or core factor was a discrepancy in views about the child's needs. The other factors were lack of knowledge (e.g., lack of problem-solving knowledge), disagreements over service delivery, the presence of constraints (e.g., the lack of funds to deliver services), differences in how a child is valued, unilateral use of power, poor communication, and lack of trust. In addition to discussing what factors lead to conflict, the authors discussed how conflict can be reduced and how it can be prevented. The authors generated a tentative explanation about conflict based on their data. To strengthen their explanation, they would need to develop their theory further and test it with new empirical data (which would result in a mixed research approach).

2.8 What are the different types of qualitative research, and what is the defining feature of each of these?

Mixed Research (or Mixed Methods Research)

In mixed research, the researcher uses a mixture or combination of quantitative and qualitative methods, approaches, or concepts in a single research study or in a set of related studies. The qualitative and quantitative parts of a research study might be conducted concurrently (conducting both parts at roughly the same time) or sequentially (conducting one part first and the other second) to address a research question or a set of related questions. For example, let's say that you are interested in studying the phenomenon of living with dyslexia for high school students. You might decide first to conduct a qualitative (exploratory) component of your research study by conducting open-ended or unstructured interviews with 10 or 20 high school students who have dyslexia so that you can directly hear from these students in their own words what it is like to live with dyslexia. On the basis of the data from this phase of your overall study and from your reading of the current research literature, you construct a closed-ended and more structured questionnaire. Next, in the quantitative phase of your study, you ask another group of high school students with dyslexia to rate how descriptive each of the characteristics on the structured questionnaire is of them. For this quantitative phase of your study, you might select a sample of students with dyslexia from several high schools and have these students fill out your questionnaire. You then analyze your questionnaire data and write up your "integrated" findings from the qualitative and quantitative parts of your research study. In this example, the qualitative phase was used to explore the words, categories, and dimensions to include in a structured questionnaire. Then you started testing (or validating) how well the questionnaire operated in the quantitative phase. Together, the qualitative and quantitative approaches produced a superior questionnaire.

The Advantages of Mixed Research

We view the use of multiple perspectives, theories, and research methods as a strength in educational research. In fact, we view the quantitative and qualitative research methods as complementary. When mixing research or when you read and evaluate research that involved mixing, be sure to consider the **fundamental principle of mixed research**, which says that it is wise to collect multiple sets of data using different research methods, epistemologies, and approaches in such a way that the resulting mixture or combination has multiple (convergent and divergent) and complementary strengths and nonoverlapping weaknesses (Johnson & Turner, 2003). The idea of multiple means that your research can include more than one purpose or a creative mixture of purposes. The idea of **complementary strengths** here means that the whole in a mixed research study is greater than the sum of the parts. The mixed approach helps improve research because the different research approaches provide different sorts of knowledge and they have different strengths and different weaknesses.

By combining two (or more) research methods with different strengths and weaknesses in a research study, you can make it less likely that you will miss something important or make a mistake. The famous qualitative researchers Lincoln and Guba (1985) explained this idea using the metaphor of fish nets. Perhaps a fisherman has several fishing nets, each with one or more holes. To come up with one good net, the fisherman decides to overlap the different fishing nets, forming one overall net. All the nets have holes in them; however, when the nets are put together, there will probably

- **Fundamental principle of mixed research** Advises researchers to thoughtfully and strategically mix or combine qualitative and quantitative research methods, approaches, procedures, concepts, and other paradigm characteristics in a way that produces an overall design with multiple (convergent and divergent) and complementary (broadly viewed) strengths and nonoverlapping weaknesses

- **Complementary strengths** Idea that the whole is greater than the sum of its parts

no longer be a hole in the overall net. In the case of research methods, an experimental research study might demonstrate causality well, but it might be limited in realism because of the confines of the research laboratory. On the other hand, an ethnographic research study might not demonstrate causality especially well, but it can be done in the field, which enables a researcher to observe behavior as it naturally takes place and therefore increases realism. When both methods are used, causality is strong, and realism is no longer a big problem. Although it is sometimes not practical to use more than one research method or strategy in a single research study, you should be aware of the potential benefit of using multiple methods and strategies. Furthermore, even if a researcher does not use multiple approaches or methods in a single research study, the relevant set of published research studies will usually include research based on several different research methods. The research literature is therefore mixed method. As a result, the mixed method (or mixed fishing net) advantage will be gained in the overall area of research.

REVIEW QUESTION

2.9 What is mixed research, and what is an example of this kind of research?

OUR RESEARCH TYPOLOGY

See Journal Article 2.4 on the Student Study Site.

The forms of research that we have covered in this chapter are shown in Figure 2.4. We will discuss each of these types of research in later chapters. It is important to understand that all of the major types of research that we discuss in this textbook have value! It is not uncommon for an educational researcher to use several different types of research at different times. A researcher should always select the appropriate research method on the basis of a consideration of the research question(s) of interest, the objective(s) of the research, time and cost constraints, available populations, the possibility (or not) of the manipulation of an independent variable, and the availability of data. Sometimes a researcher will use more than one research approach within a single study. However, even if researchers never used more than one method in a single study, published research literature would still tend to include articles based on different approaches and methods because of the diversity of the researchers working in the area.

FIGURE 2.4 Research typology (Later chapters will add a third level to this typology.)

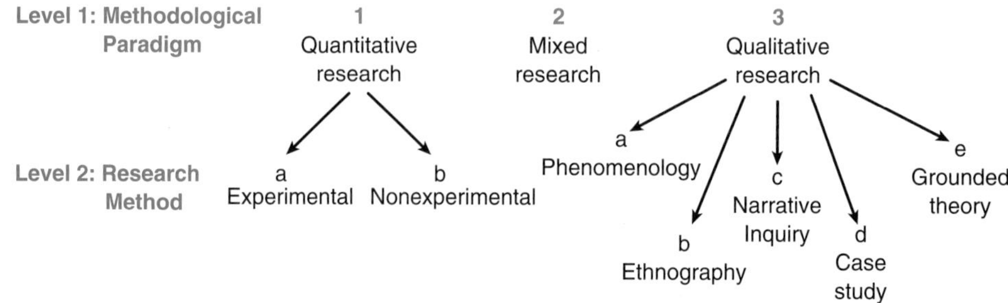

When a research finding has been demonstrated by using more than one type of research, one can place more confidence in it. We say that a finding has been *corroborated* if the same result is found by using different types of research. Conversely, if different data sources or types of research result in conflicting information, then additional research will be needed to explore the nature of the phenomenon more completely and to determine the source of conflict. That is, if different types of research result in different findings, then the researcher should study the phenomenon in more depth to determine the exact reason for the conflicting findings. The world is a complex and ever-changing place. As we study it, it is helpful to be equipped with the best methods and approaches currently available. You will probably find that some methods and approaches we discuss will fit your style or personality better than others. However, we hope that you will keep an open mind as you learn about all of the kinds of research. All the research methods can be useful if used properly.

REVIEW QUESTION

2.10 What are the three methodological paradigms in education, and what are the major types of research in each of these paradigms? (Hint: See Figure 2.4.)

SUMMARY

The three major research traditions in educational research are qualitative research, quantitative research, and mixed research. All three of these traditions are important and have value. Qualitative research tends to use the exploratory scientific method to generate theory and understand particular people, places, and groups (e.g., in case studies, ethnography, phenomenology, and historical research). Qualitative researchers typically are not interested in making generalizations. An exception to this lack of interest in generalizing is found in the grounded theory approach to qualitative research. Qualitative research is discovery oriented and is conducted in natural settings. On the other hand, quantitative research is typically done under more tightly controlled conditions and tends to use the confirmatory scientific method, focusing on hypothesis testing and theory testing. Quantitative researchers hope to find common patterns in thought and behavior and to generalize broadly. Mixed research involves mixing and combining qualitative and quantitative research in single research studies. It is based on the philosophy of pragmatism (i.e., solving problems and determining what works should be considered important in answering research questions). In this chapter, two quantitative research types or methods were introduced (experimental and nonexperimental research), five types of qualitative research were introduced (phenomenology, ethnography, case study, narrative research, and grounded theory), and mixed research (which mixes or combines qualitative and quantitative research approaches in single research studies) was introduced. In later chapters, we elaborate on each part of the research typology shown in Figure 2.4.

KEY TERMS

axiology (p. 31)
case study research (p. 50)
categorical variable (p. 39)
causal-comparative research (p. 43)
cause-and-effect relationship (p. 40)
complementary strengths (p. 51)
confounding variable (p. 42)
constant (p. 39)
correlation coefficient (p. 44)
correlational research (p. 44)
culture (p. 49)
dependent variable (p. 40)
determinism (p. 33)
epistemology (p. 31)
ethnography (p. 49)

experimental research (p. 41)
extraneous variable (p. 42)
fundamental principle of mixed research (p. 51)
grounded theory research (p. 50)
holistic description (p. 49)
incompatibility thesis (p. 31)
independent variable (p. 40)
intervening variable (p. 41)
linguistic-relativity hypothesis (p. 36)
manipulation (p. 41)
mediating variable (p. 41)
methodology (p. 31)
mixed research (p. 33)
moderator variable (p. 41)
narrative inquiry (p. 49)
negative correlation (p. 44)
nonexperimental research (p. 43)
ontology (p. 31)
phenomenology (p. 48)
positive correlation (p. 44)
pragmatism (p. 32)
probabilistic causes (p. 33)
qualitative research (p. 33)
quantitative research (p. 33)
quantitative variable (p. 39)
research paradigm (p. 31)
rhetoric (p. 31)
variable (p. 39)
verstehen (p. 36)

DISCUSSION QUESTIONS

1. Which of the three research/methodological paradigms do you like the most? Explain why.
2. If you find a statistical relationship between two variables (e.g., income and education, or gender and grades, or time spent studying and grades) in a nonexperimental research study, should you confidently conclude that one variable is the *cause* of the other variable?
3. What is an example of a positive correlation? What is an example of a negative correlation?
4. Following are several research questions. For each, list the research method that you believe would be most appropriate to use in answering the question.
   a. How do individuals experience the phenomenon of being one of only a few minority students in a predominantly homogeneous high school?
   b. What is the effect of a new teaching technique on elementary school students' arithmetic performance?
   c. Does cognitive therapy or behavioral therapy work better for treating childhood depression?
   d. What is the culture of the band at a high school in your local community?
   e. What is the relationship between the GRE and student performance in graduate school?
   f. Do males and females have different performance levels in high school English classes?
   g. Does the student-to-teacher ratio have an effect on elementary students' level of performance in the classroom?
   h. Do students perform better on an academic test when they are exposed to a cooperative learning style or a lecture style of teaching?

RESEARCH EXERCISES

1. Go to this book's companion website or to a database on the website of your university library and locate a qualitative research article, a quantitative research article, or a mixed methods research article. Briefly summarize the purpose of the research and the methodology (i.e., how it attempted to answer the research questions). Explain why you classified your article as a qualitative, a quantitative, or a mixed research study.

2. Read the quantitative research study on the companion website (article 1.3) and write a two-page (typed, double-spaced) summary of the article. Organize your paper into the following three sections:

    (1) Purpose: What was the research study about? What did the researchers hope to learn?

    (2) Methods: How did the researchers carry out their research study? What did they actually do?

    (3) Results: What were the key findings of the research study? Don't worry about the technical jargon in the research article. Just try to understand and clearly communicate its main ideas.

3. Read the qualitative research study on the companion website (article 1.2) and write a two-page summary of the article. Organize your paper into the three sections described in Exercise 2 (purpose, methods, and results).

4. Read the mixed research study on the companion website (article 1.1) and write a two-page summary of the article. Organize your paper into the three sections described in Exercise 2 (purpose, methods, and results).

RELEVANT INTERNET SITES

Quantitative research–oriented book materials and links

Go to the *Research Methods, Design, and Analysis* textbook website (under the Website Gallery section). Make sure that you use the resources available for the 12th edition.
http://www.pearsonhighered.com/educator/product/Research-Methods-Design-and-Analysis/9780205961252.page

Qual Page: Resources for Qualitative Research
http://www.qualitativeresearch.uga.edu/QualPage/

Pearson Correlation Coefficient Calculator
http://www.socscistatistics.com/tests/pearson/Default.aspx

Mixed Methods International Research Association
http://MMIRA.org

Mixed Methods Network for Behavioral, Social, and Health Sciences
https://www.linkedin.com/groups/1888486/profile

STUDENT STUDY SITE

Visit the Student Study Site at **edge.sagepub.com/rbjohnson6e** for these additional learning tools:

- Video Links
- Self-Quizzes
- eFlashcards
- Lecture Notes
- Full-Text SAGE Journal Articles
- Interactive Concept Maps
- Web Resources

RECOMMENDED READING

Baron, R. M., & Kenny, D. A. (1986). The moderator-mediator variable distinction in social psychological research: Conceptual, strategic, and statistical considerations. *Journal of Personality and Social Psychology*, *51*(6), 1173–1182.

Christensen, L. B., Johnson, R. B., & Turner, L. A. (2014). *Research methods, design, and analysis* (12th ed.). Boston, NJ: Pearson.

Hesse-Biber, S. N., & Johnson, R. B. (Eds.). (2014). *Oxford handbook of multimethod and mixed methods research inquiry*. New York, NY: Oxford.

Johnson, R. B. (2001). Toward a new classification of nonexperimental quantitative research. *Educational Researcher*, 30(2), 3–13.

Johnson, R. B., & Onwuegbuzie, A. J. (2004). Mixed methods research: A research paradigm whose time has come. *Educational Researcher*, *33*(7), 14–26.

Johnson, R. B., Onwuegbuzie, A. J., & Turner, L. A. (2007). Toward a definition of mixed methods research. *Journal of Mixed Methods Research*, *1*, 112–133.

Patton, M. Q. (2014). *Qualitative research and evaluation methods* (4th ed.). Thousand Oaks, CA: SAGE.

Pedhazur, E. J., & Schmelkin, L. P. (1991). *Measurement, design, and analysis: An integrated approach*. Hillsdale, NJ: Erlbaum.

Tashakkori, A., & Teddlie, C. (Eds.). (2010). *Handbook of mixed methods in the social and behavioral sciences*. Thousand Oaks, CA: SAGE.

Chapter 3

Action Research for Lifelong Learning

LEARNING OBJECTIVES

After reading this chapter, you should be able to

- Define action research and describe its origins.
- Contrast the different types of action research.
- Describe Lewin's change theory.
- Describe Dewey's approach to inquiry.
- Explain the Cycle of Action Research.
- Compare the strengths and weaknesses of action research.
- State a problem at your workplace that can be addressed via action research.

Visit the Student Study Site for an interactive concept map.

RESEARCH IN REAL LIFE Solving a Problem at Your School

istock/monkeybusinessimages

Constructive discipline for misbehaving school students is an important and often poorly addressed task that teachers and administrators face. Losen and Skiba (2010) reported, in *Suspended Education: Urban Middle Schools in Crisis,* that middle schools have recently increased their use of out-of-school suspension as a means to punish a host of offenses. Although out-of-school suspension may be needed in cases of serious misconduct, analysis of suspension data from 18 large school districts showed that out-of-school suspension is frequently used for nonviolent offenses. The data also revealed strong racial and gender differences in the use of out-of-school suspensions. African Americans were suspended at higher rates than other groups, and males were suspended at higher rates than females. In fact, in two districts, the suspension rate for African American males was greater than 50%. Unfortunately, out-of-school suspension brings several unwanted by-products. Suspended students miss instructional time, they often are left unsupervised during their time away from school, and they may feel that the school does not want them and does not care about them. These "by-products" are known predictors of greater school difficulties. Zero tolerance does not work very well. Principals who supported zero tolerance tended to make greater use of out-of-school suspension.

How does the local school you are most familiar with deal with disruptive students? When do school authorities use out-of-school suspension? Does the administration track the effectiveness of its procedures? Can you think of an innovative method that should be tried at your local school? Action research will prepare you to address these kinds of questions and help you think about how to conduct your own research study.

Defining Action Research

- **Action research** Studies that focus on solving practitioners' local problems
- **Action research attitude** Valuing and thinking like a practitioner and researcher in your job and life

In Chapter 1 you learned that **action research** is focused on solving specific problems that local practitioners face in their schools and communities (Lewin, 1946; Stringer, 2013). Action research is a combination of research and action. It generates local knowledge, and it often results in changes in practices. Action research is used to try out new strategies and practices, and the researcher carefully measures and observes the outcomes and consequences of these actions.

You have the **action research attitude** when *you* take on the attitude of a practitioner *and* a researcher and you think about how you can improve your workplace, try new strategies, and determine the consequences. The idea is for you to identify problems you face and act in ways that can help "fix" those problems and observe whether your "fix" has worked. This attitude asks you to be both reflective and forward thinking and to be a good observer. If you become an action researcher, you can continually develop theories (your understandings, explanations, predictions), test your theory, and integrate your theory with practice. You should generate and test your theory but also inform your theory based on what you find in the published research literature. Action research starts with you and your place of work, and it is used to address what you believe is important to address. The purpose of this chapter is to help you begin your journey toward becoming an "action researcher."

Origins of Action Research

See Journal Article 3.1 on the Student Study Site.

There is no perfect starting point for the origin or founding of action research, but almost all action research historians consider Kurt Lewin (1890–1947) to be the founder. This is because Lewin first coined the term *action research* and he practiced applied social research during the 1930s and 1940s until his untimely death in 1947. Kurt Lewin was also a great social psychologist. He is often considered the father of academic social psychology in the United States. Lewin tried to link theory with practice, and he spent his career attempting to solve social problems. He sometimes worked at the local level but attempted to move up to city, state, and national levels whenever possible. Lewin wanted to connect national problems with local problems. For example, racism, sexism, anti-Semitism, and poverty are both local and national problems.

Lewin emphasized that research and theory be connected and should lead to action, specifically social improvement. Throughout his career, Lewin emphasized the importance of connecting theory and practice and developing theories that work. According to his friend and colleague Dorwin Cartwright (1978), Lewin famously said, "There is nothing so practical as a good theory." This quote has been reproduced in perhaps a hundred books because of its simplicity and its power to guide us. We all strive for practical theory.

When considering change in a community, in an organization (e.g., a school), or in a smaller place (e.g., in a classroom or even an individual), Lewin's **force field theory** is helpful. According to this theory, where we are right now and what we routinely do in our lives tends not to change very much. Why? We are in what Lewin called a *quasi-stationary equilibrium* that is the result of multiple dynamic forces operating upon us. Put more simply, in our equilibrium state, the forces for change (**driving forces**) and the forces against change (**restraining forces**) are about equal. That's why we don't change much, and that's why things don't change much in our places of work, such as our schools and our classrooms.

Types of driving and restraining forces include (a) *physical* forces (e.g., physical abilities, school buildings, technology), (b) *psychological* forces (e.g., our desire for change or our resistance to personal change because of habit, personality, beliefs, or fear), (c) *group* forces (e.g., school cultures, community cultures, parental values and beliefs, social and group institutions, and social attitudes such as stereotypes of groups of people), and (d) any other forces that affect us (e.g., gravity!). You can conduct a **force field analysis** by identifying the forces that are pushing for change (e.g., vision for something better than the status quo, desire to try something new in your classroom) and identifying the forces that are resisting change in the status quo (e.g., politics, power, custom, tradition). In your current equilibrium state, you will probably find that these two sets of forces are about equal. So how can you change or produce change in others? Answer: Reduce resisting forces and increase driving forces. It sounds easy, but as you know, it's not!

According to **Lewin's change theory**, systematic change follows three phases: *unfreezing* (i.e., identifying and removing the resisting forces), *changing* (i.e., creating an unbalance of forces such that the driving forces are greater relative to the resisting forces, for example,

- **Force field theory** Explanation of action and inaction as resulting from driving and restraining forces
- **Driving forces** Forces pushing for changes from the current state
- **Restraining forces** Forces resisting change and supporting the status quo
- **Force field analysis** Identifying and understanding the driving and restraining forces present in a situation
- **Lewin's change theory** A detailed theory of change that includes a three-step process for planned changes in human settings

implementing your new classroom management system), and *refreezing* (i.e., reaching a new equilibrium state, e.g., making the new classroom management system the new and expected way of doing things). What do you think is the hardest: unfreezing, changing, or refreezing? It's usually unfreezing (i.e., getting people to be open to new ways of doing things, realizing that their current beliefs and behaviors are problematic, and making the decision to act rather than being content with the status quo). Lewin's change theory and force field concepts are combined into Lewin's overall theory depicted in Figure 3.1.

FIGURE 3.1 Lewin's force field analysis and three stages of change. If you make it to stage 3, that becomes your new beginning point for future change.

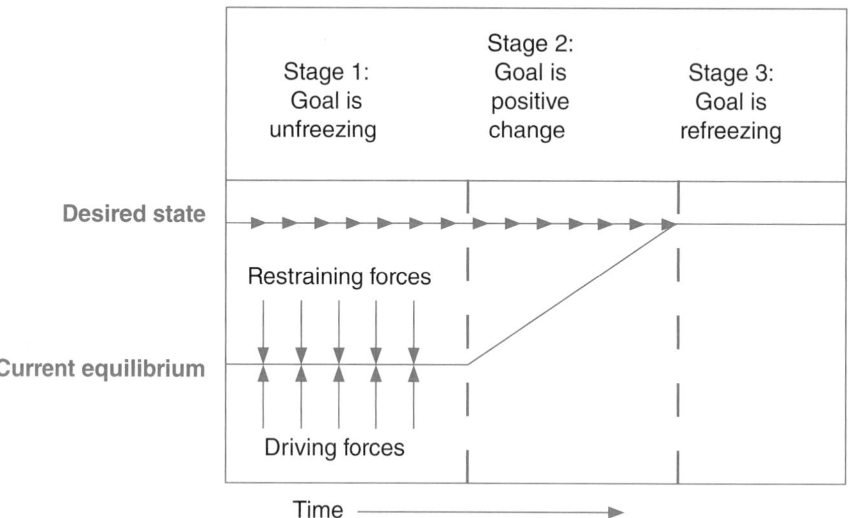

Another major influence on action research, especially in education, was the work of John Dewey (1859–1952). Dewey was an educator, a philosopher, and a psychologist. His career spanned many decades, beginning in the 1880s and continuing until his death at age 92 in 1952. In the late 19th century, he critiqued stimulus-response (S-R) psychology that viewed human behavior as merely the result of stimuli and responses pairings (and punishment and reinforcement). Instead, Dewey in 1896 was the earliest advocate for S-O-R psychology. He inserted the *thinking* and *acting* organism (O) into the observed stimulus response relationship. In the early 20th century and continuing for many decades, S-R psychology became the dominant learning paradigm in education and psychology. It became known as behaviorism, and B. F. Skinner (1904–1990) was one of its most prolific advocates and theorists. As you probably know, cognitivism, constructivism, neuropsychology, and additional specialized paradigms have now been added to behaviorism as schools of thought in educational psychology. Today, we have many approaches to draw upon. Interestingly, however, there is a resurgence of interest in the works of John Dewey.

Dewey believed that the thinking human organism is always embedded in and part of a dynamic, local, and complex ecology. According to his transactional theory, we are not separate from our environments but are part of our environments. Our environments affect us and we affect our environments, continuously. Dewey argued that humans are adaptive organisms, continuously trying to improve their world. Dewey also was one of the original American philosophical *pragmatists* who said that humans (a) observe the consequences of our actions, (b) determine what works in what situations, and (c) act in ways to produce what we value and improve our world. Although Dewey was worried that many people had not been raised to think for themselves and to fully participate in a deliberative/thoughtful democracy, *he believed that education was the cure*. Our freedom increases and we become better citizens when education empowers us (and our students) to think intelligently. Dewey had great faith in the power of education to improve society.

Psychologically speaking, Dewey believed that people are problem solvers. As individuals, we will find ourselves in problematic situations and experience *doubt*. When we experience doubt, we start thinking and planning ways to *act* that will bring us into a more satisfactory condition of equilibrium between our beliefs and our environment. Very much like a scientist, we identify a problem, we think and hypothesize about likely outcomes of new actions, we act, we examine the consequences, and we continue this process until we get back to our normal and preferred state of equilibrium.

Dewey had great faith in the method of scientific experimentation that he thought had been successful in the mature/hard sciences (e.g., biology, physics, chemistry). Dewey talked about scientific experimentation often, but he brought it down to the level of daily life. He emphasized that *every person can engage in experimentation in the workplace and in daily life* (i.e., experiments were not just for scientists in universities). Dewey believed that all humans could be "intelligent" and that intelligent humans were active participants in their environments, trying new approaches to find what works and to make their schools, communities, and society better.

For Dewey, the scientific method was just another name for *inquiry*. Inquiry is something individuals have been doing since the beginning of time. They do it to move themselves from doubt toward belief—specifically toward beliefs that work. Because Dewey thought that each of us should try new approaches to problematic situations to determine what works better, he sometimes referred to himself as an *instrumentalist*. In philosophy, Dewey is one of the three classical American pragmatists (the other two are Charles Sanders Peirce and William James). Although Dewey was an instrumentalist for learning and meaning as tested in our actions (i.e., he wanted to learn what actions and meanings worked best in our experiences), he also viewed values as central to inquiry. For Dewey, our values always guide us, and we learn what values are most important in particular situations through inquiry. Dewey's pragmatism was a values-based pragmatism.

David Hildebrand (2008), a philosopher and Dewey scholar, has described **Deweyan inquiry** as following five phases. The phases are a slight simplification of Dewey's writings, but they are directly based on two books written by Dewey: (1) *How We Think*, published in 1933, and (2) *Logic: The Theory of Inquiry*, published in 1938(b). In case you didn't realize it, Dewey's writings were far ahead of his time. Many current concepts and approaches in education were suggested by Dewey almost 100 years ago! You can find many of his insights about education in his *Democracy and Education* (1916) and his *Experience and Education* (1938a). Dewey was 78 years old when he wrote *Experience and Education*. Here are Dewey's five phases of inquiry (paraphrased by Hildebrand):

▪ **Deweyan inquiry** Problem solving that relies on reflection, observation, and experimentation

(1) An indeterminate situation in which a difficulty is felt—"Something's wrong . . . "

(2) The institution of a problem; its location and definition—"The problem seems to be . . . "

(3) Hypothesis of a possible solution—"Maybe what I should do is . . . "

(4) Reasoning out of the bearings of the suggestion—"Doing that would mean . . . "

(5) Active experimental or observational testing of the hypothesis—"Let's try this and see what happens . . . " (pp. 53–56)

One can move back and forth between phases as well as move through the phases linearly. Dewey emphasized that there is no end to the process of inquiry, and *this is exactly the same emphasis that you will find in action research.*

You might wonder whether, according to Dewey, "we obtain truth in educational research." His answer was yes and no. According to Dewey, we obtain provisional or working truths *that are always subject to updating and improvement.* He believed that we do not find final, eternal, or universal truths (e.g., that a certain educational strategy works best in all places, situations, and times). For Dewey, what works in schools has a strong, bottom-up, and local flavor that emphasizes context. You work in a particular place—in a particular context—and, according to Dewey, you will need to continually determine what works there and try to improve it.

REVIEW QUESTION

3.1 What are the roots and early vision from which action research emerged?

BASIC SCIENTIFIC RESEARCH VERSUS ACTION RESEARCH

We have pointed out that action research is a combination of research *and* action. However, it also is helpful to contrast action research with more basic scientific research. Action research falls on the applied end of the basic-versus-applied research continuum described in Chapter 1. Furthermore, in basic or regular scientific research, the primary goal is to *produce knowledge.* Application of the knowledge is important, but the primary purpose is to produce scientific knowledge. Another goal of regular educational research is to find principles that work broadly, that generalize, and that can be used in multiple places. In contrast, action research has in common with qualitative research a focus on the local and the particular, rather than on the national and the general.

You learned in Chapter 2 that both quantitative research (focused on the general and on testing theories) *and* qualitative research (focused on the particular and on generating/developing theories) are important for education science. We believe that mixed methods research is especially important because it brings together the insights of both quantitative and qualitative research. We also believe that education will be served well by bringing together national and local experts, as well as both academic researchers and local practitioners. Our ideas are depicted in Figure 3.2. National education policy should emphasize that we help our students to think intelligently (in Dewey's sense). This requires that we empower students to become lifelong thinkers and learners and contributors to their community and society.

In Figure 3.2, we show that the *enterprise of education science* needs both producers of general/theoretical knowledge *and* producers of local/particularistic knowledge (Johnson & Stefurak, 2013). On the one hand, the top-down arrow shows that local practice should be informed by academic research about best practices; **translational research** is important for this endeavor by translating scientific research into easily understood language and procedures of practice. On the other hand, the bottom-up arrow shows that "best practices" also should be informed by what practitioners find works well at the local level. Each of these two levels needs to learn from the other, sometimes collaboratively (e.g., when university researchers and local teacher researchers work together).

- **Translational research** Studies focused on converting scientific research into easily understood language and procedures

The model in Figure 3.2 is centered on the importance of values. A few key *values* that we recommend are the importance of learning from others, active listening, tolerance, diversity, and deliberative democracy. We further recommend the traditional and important *quantitative research values* of explanation and prediction and the *qualitative research values* of understanding local meanings. If national and local knowledge producers can work together, then, through many cycles or iterations of the model, educational science can become a *learning system* that operates in top-down and bottom-up directions and continually learns and improves.

FIGURE 3.2 Circle of knowledge for the enterprise of education science

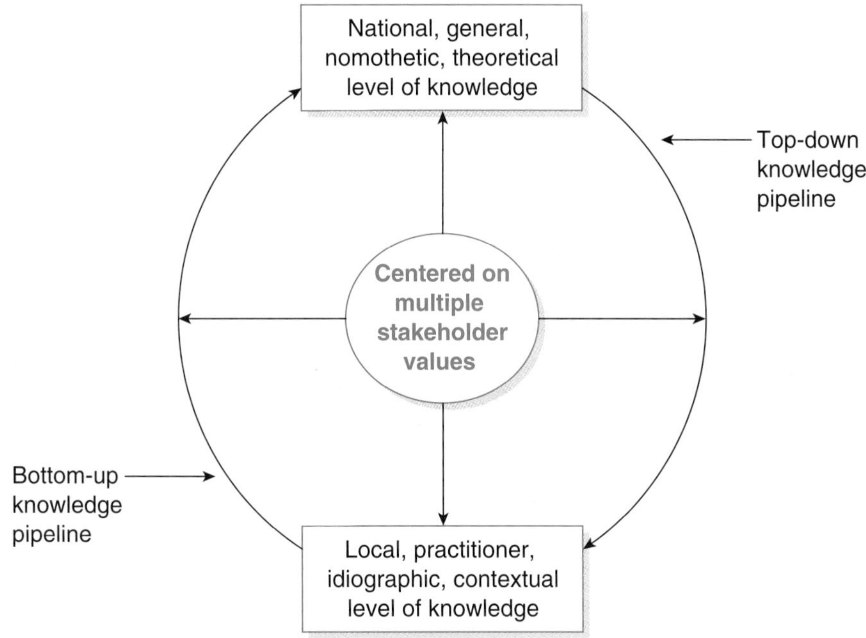

A key point here is that action research usually operates at the local (bottom) level in Figure 3.2. Action research looks for what works well in particular places and contexts. It helps teachers and practitioners to solve the problems they face, but this research should over time be disseminated to the more general level (e.g., universities, government, national and international journals) so that the local knowledge can be integrated into more general theory. This improved theory will incorporate what are called *contextual*

contingencies (or *moderator variables* as explained in Table 2.2 in Chapter 2 on page 38). In other words, this theory will show what can be done broadly but also when and how it might need to be adapted for it to work in particular situations.

Again, a key idea of action research is for you to conduct research in your place of work. When you find strategies and principles that work, you should share them with others in journals, professional associations, and universities. That's how local practice can inform broader practice and policy.

See Journal Article 3.2 on the Student Study Site.

In the next section we introduce you to some different types of action research. You might select one type for your practice, or you can construct your own *mixed* type by selecting features from the different types. You might find that the type you like the most depends on your situational needs.

REVIEW QUESTION

3.2 What kind of knowledge does action research produce?

Types of Action Research

The types of AR we discuss now are not mutually exclusive. They do, however, have different emphases. We take a "mixed view" of action research. That is, we think it is fine for an action researcher to select from and mix the various types we discuss below. The AR types focus on slightly different kinds of research questions, and a complex research question might require a combination of AR types.

We view action research as a local form of research, producing local knowledge, but that knowledge can and should work its way up and inform the entire field of education. You should "dialogue" with the multiple types of AR discussed next, dialogue with multiple research approaches (discussed in the remainder of this book), and dialogue with any relevant person or literature that you believe will be helpful for your research study. Your research might focus on your classroom and professional development, but your work is part of a larger social ecological system. Others might be affected by your research, and they might be interested in your research results. Therefore, consider involving others through collaboration and participation.

- **Participatory action research** Studies in which team members jointly frame and conduct research, producing knowledge about a shared problem

The first specific type of action research is **participatory action research** (PAR), which emphasizes that multiple parties or stakeholders with an interest in the research topic and project must work together as a research team in conducting the action research study. You would be just one member in such a team and would have to relinquish some power. PAR is conducted by teachers, administrators, counselors, coaches, and other professionals to solve very specific problems. Sometimes PAR members collaborate with university-based researchers; when this is done, those researchers also must give up power. The strategy is to work in a complementary way such that each person contributes to the whole. Some examples are a principal studying teacher burnout and dissatisfaction in a local school context, a group of teachers studying classroom discipline problems in their classrooms, teachers and administrators studying the lack of parental involvement with their school's PTA, and a teacher studying problems of a particular child in his or her classroom.

Participatory research breaks down the traditional distinction between objective researchers and their research subjects. Participatory research can vary in degree. In its full form, research participants frame and write the research questions, collect the data, analyze and interpret the data, and write reports or present the data in additional ways (presentations, meetings, word of mouth). If you want your research to be used by others, you need to take dissemination of results seriously and get the findings into the hands of everyone who has a stake in the results and is potentially interested. When participants are involved in a research study, they are likely to remember the results and share the results with others. A key point of participatory action research is *involvement* of participants in conduct of the research and its dissemination.

A published example of PAR is in an article titled "Seeking Renewal, Finding Community: Participatory Action Research in Teacher Education" by Draper et al. (2011). In this study, 11 education professors at Brigham Young University collaborated over 4 years by examining and attempting to improve their practices. They cycled many times through identifying problems, trying out possible solutions, observing and collecting data, reflecting on the results, and deciding what to do next. They reported that their sense of self changed (improved) over time, their views of their subject material changed, they engaged with their students and the community more, they improved their approach to teaching, and they changed their views about research. Participatory/collaborative research worked well for them. We were surprised that the professors did not more *directly* include student and community participants in their study, which would have increased the amount of participation. Nonetheless, they all shared their experiences, participated, gave each other equal power, dialogued with each other and with students and parents and community members, learned, and improved their practices.

See Journal Article 3.3 on the Student Study Site.

Another type of action research is **critical action research** (CAR). CAR is similar to participatory action research, and the terms are sometimes used interchangeably. However, CAR places more emphasis on the political possibilities of action research and emphasizes the empowerment of those with little power in their communities and society. In education, one "father" of this kind of action research is Paulo Freire, who wrote the famous book titled *Pedagogy of the Oppressed* (1968/1970). Freire wanted to use education to free the disadvantaged from what he called oppression.

- **Critical action research** An openly transparent form of ideology-driven research designed to emancipate and reduce oppression of disadvantaged groups in society

The word *critical* in critical action research signifies the addition of an ideological element to the research; it is a type of what we called, in Chapter 1, orientational research (see page 11). In addition to being participatory, as in PAR, CAR attempts to take an emancipatory stance, it strives for immediate social change, and it emphasizes increasing *social justice* (i.e., reduction of social inequalities resulting from societal norms such as sexism, racism, etc.). The key point is that CAR studies focus on reduction of inequality of income and wealth and/or reduction of some form of discrimination (gender, race, ethnicity, disability). CAR studies often include attempts at "consciousness raising" of the individuals and groups that have minimal power in society.

An example of CAR is a study by Lindsay Mack (2012) titled "Does Every Student Have a Voice? Critical Action Research on Equitable Classroom Participation Practices." The study was conducted in a multicultural ESL (English as a second language) classroom, and one goal was to produce equal classroom participation by students regardless of their national, cultural, or linguistic group. The teacher had observed that her Asian students were quiet during class discussions, and her immediate goal was to increase their comfort and participation levels.

Lack of participation can also mean a lack of voice and power and a lack of social justice in the classroom. To determine the multiple causes of participation, the teacher started by having students fill out a questionnaire. Then the teacher interviewed students to learn their reasons and understand their perspectives. Her active intervention was to share these results and to put students in groups to discuss and make suggestions for change. From this activity, the teacher and her students constructed a new set of classroom policies. The teacher found initial positive results, but you can see that this study would naturally lead into another cycle of data collection to determine the effectiveness of the new policies. Action research tends to be cyclical or ongoing because as you reflect on your findings, you will usually want to plan another round of intervention and data collection.

- **Feminist action research** Studies that provide a feminist lens to help eliminate various forms of sexism and empower women in society

One type of critical action research, which has many similarities with critical action research as just described, is **feminist action research** (FAR). The focus is on viewing the world through a feminist lens, eliminating binary (either/or) thinking, raising consciousness about women's issues, and adding women's voices to conversations that are typically controlled by white men. Ultimately, the goal is to improve the lives of women in society, including their psychological health, their cultural power, the prestige of their contributions to society, and their material wealth. Other kinds of critical action research focus on inequalities in society due to other individual/group characteristics, such as inequalities based on race, ethnicity, physical or mental disability, sexual orientation—you can add to this list as needed.

- **Action science** The science of practice, with the aim of making theories in use explicit and producing a learning organization

The next type of action research, **action science** (AS), was founded by Chris Argyris and Donald Schön. Its focus is on research in organizations. What makes AS different from other forms of action research (e.g., PAR, CAR) is that it (a) places more emphasis on traditional scientific rigor and (b) emphasizes that you try to make your organization a learning organization in which people work together and grow over time. Action science encourages rigorous experimentation, and it builds on Lewin's idea that the best way to understand human behavior is to try to change it. You can think of action science as a *science of practice*. In the words of Argyris, Putnam, and McLain Smith (1985):

> Action science is centrally concerned with the practice of intervention. It is by reflecting on this practice that we hope to contribute to an understanding of how knowledge claims can be tested and justified in practice and of how such inquiry is similar to and different from mainstream science. (p. 35)

- **Learning organization** Organization in which members work together and grow over time, continually improving the organization as a whole

Action science researchers hope to build learning organizations. The concept of a **learning organization** came from Chris Argyris and Donald Schön (e.g., Argyris & Schön, 1978, 1996). If you are in a leadership role, you should attempt to build an organization whose members continually learn, develop, and grow. They together produce an organization as a whole that continually improves at what it does and continually adapts to its changing environment. The idea of a learning organization has been extended by Argyris's student Peter Senge in *The Fifth Discipline: The Art and Practice of the Learning Organization* (Senge, 2006) and *Schools That Learn: A Fifth Discipline Fieldbook for Educators, Parents, and Everyone Who Cares About Education* (Senge et al., 2012). Here is the concept in the words of Senge (2006):

> The tools and ideas presented in this book [*The Fifth Discipline*] are for destroying the illusion that the world is created of separate, unrelated forces. When we give up this illusion—we can then build "learning organizations," where people continually expand their capacity to create

> the results they truly desire, where new and expansive patterns of thinking are nurtured, where collective aspiration is set free, and where people are continually learning how to learn together. (p. 3)

We encourage you to search the Internet and learn more (especially if you are in leadership) about a learning organization and its five major characteristics (Senge, 2006).[1]

Action scientists argue that to produce change in organizational members, we need to determine their **espoused theory** (i.e., individuals' stated reasons for their actions) and especially their **theory in use** (i.e., individuals' operative but often tacit or unconscious mental models that can be inferred from their actions). The former refers to what we say we do and the latter refers to what we actually do. We need to determine why people act as they do, including their conscious reasons, as well as their tacit mental models. Schön wrote entire books on how to become a reflective practitioner (Schön, 1983, 1987), which asks you to carefully reflect on your actions and what theory it expresses.

Action science also asks us to examine single-loop and double-loop learning within organizations. **Single-loop learning** focuses on finding an efficient solution to a small problem. This is good, but unfortunately it often leads to a short-term solution. Many interventions work for a while but ultimately fail because they do not solve the larger and deeper organizational problem. **Double-loop learning** critically examines and challenges our deep assumptions, values, realities, and reasons for actions and learns how the problem relates to the larger system. The deeper underlying causes are identified. Double-loop learning transforms us and our organization's worldview and practice into a better, wiser, more-successful-in-the-long-run organization in which all members and the organization continually learn and grow. Ultimately, it is double-loop learning that leads to a learning organization.

The next type of action research is **appreciative inquiry** or AI (Cooperrider & Whitney, 2005; Cooperrider, Whitney, & Stavros, 2008). This type of research focuses on finding the best in ourselves and in others and working together to achieve a jointly constructed and shared purpose, vision, and goal. AI focuses on the positives rather than the negatives, based on the theory that this practice will bring out the best in everyone. Cooperrider, Whitney, and Stavros defined AI as

> the cooperative search for the best in people, their organization, and the world around them. It involves the systematic discovery of what gives a system 'life' when the system is most effective and capable in economic, ecological, and human terms. (p. 433)

AI follows four phases (called the four Ds):

1. *Discovery*. You identify (via focus groups and interviews) and appreciate the strengths present in the organization and discover the organization's potential.
2. *Dream*. A cross section of members meet and create a results-oriented vision for the organization; it is co-created, shared, revised, and agreed upon.
3. *Design*. Members collaborate and determine how the organization will need to be structured to achieve its vision.
4. *Destiny*. Members and teams creatively work together to enact the new design/structure and sustain its momentum over time.

- **Espoused theory** The theory or explanation we provide for our actions
- **Theory in use** The theory or explanation that explains what we actually do
- **Single-loop learning** "Fixing" a small problem to get the immediately desired result
- **Double-loop learning** Learning how a problem relates to the system it resides in so that a more satisfying solution can be found
- **Appreciative inquiry** Finding the best in organization members and working with them to achieve a jointly constructed and shared purpose, vision, and goal

The learning organization and AI are both transformative theories (attempting to transform organizations), but the former emphasizes continual learning and the later emphasizes building on its strengths. One day, you might conduct an AI study in your school or any other place that you spend much time. If you could do this in your school, it would make it a more positive working environment. For one example, see Calabrese et al. (2010).

The key point is that AI is the kind of action research in which you would collect your colleagues' stories about what has worked well and form these together into a plan of action to create the kind of organization that you and your colleagues have dreamed about.

- **Individual action research** Action research that is planned, designed, and conducted by one primary person, such as a teacher
- **Collaborative action research** An action research study in which a team designs and enacts research on one part of an organization
- **Systemwide action research** An action research study in which all organization members work to produce systemwide change

The last way of classifying action research in education is according to its scope. Action research can be individual, collaborative, or systemwide. In **individual action research** (or individual teacher AR or individual coach or counselor AR), the research question is decided by the individual researcher, and the research study is conducted by the individual researcher. In this case, an individual teacher might try a different classroom management approach in the classroom and observe the outcome. The immediate audience for this research is the individual who is addressing a problem she or he faces and wants to find a "better way" (e.g., Bourke, 2008; Capobianco & Lehman, 2006).

In **collaborative action research**, a team of researchers, usually bringing different but complementary strengths to the team, work together in developing the research questions and designing and conducting the research study. Each makes important contributions to the project. An example of this was the Draper et al. (2011) study examined earlier in this chapter.

In schoolwide or **systemwide action research**, the focus is on changing something large, such as an entire school or even an entire school district. For example, the entire faculty at one school might work together on identifying a problem and determining what actions will solve this system problem, or representatives from different schools might work together on solving a problem for the entire school system (e.g., Clark, Lee, Goodman, & Yacco, 2008). Systemwide AR has the largest scope of the three types, collaborative AR has the second largest, and individual AR has the smallest scope. When you are starting your first action research study, you will probably want to act alone or work with a small team to solve a fairly small/local problem.

REVIEW QUESTION

3.3 What one-sentence descriptor describes the emphasis of each of the kinds of action research discussed in this section of the chapter?

The Cycle of Action Research

Figure 3.3 depicts the process of action research as a cycle of reflect, plan, act, and observe (RPAO). Depending on the situation, an action researcher might start at the reflection phase, another at the planning phase, another at the action phase, and yet others at the observation phase. It depends on where you are, and most of us go through this cycle many times. In other words, you can enter the cycle at any point. For example, acting (at your workplace), observing outcomes, reflecting, and planning are all fine starting points. This cyclical process is similar to Dewey's idea that we need to learn and grow over our lifetime. He grounded his work in what he called a *philosophy of experience*.

■ **FIGURE 3.3** Action research is a dynamic cycle. You can enter at any point (e.g., observing, reflecting, planning, or acting); you can circle back to earlier phases; and after a full cycle is completed, a new cycle will usually begin. The goal is continuous improvement.

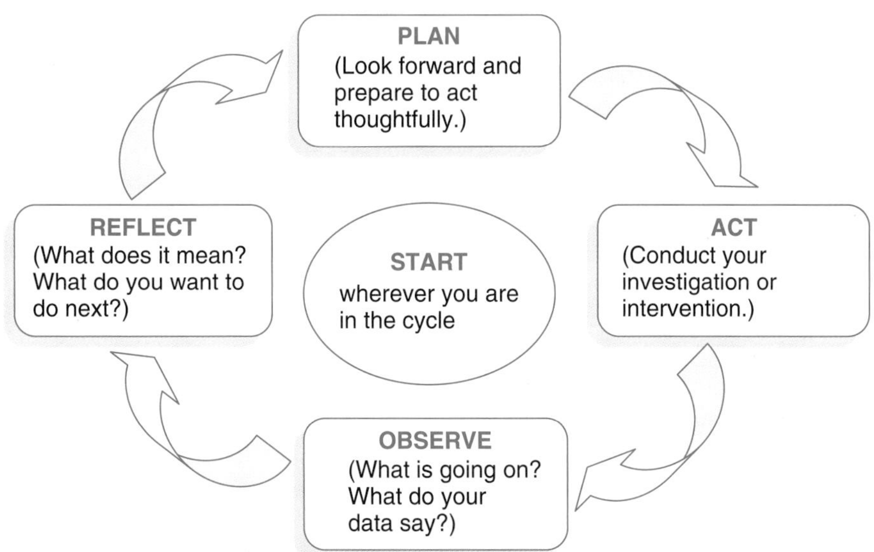

Where are you in your experience? Regardless, you (and all of us) should strive to become what Schön called a reflective practitioner. We need to be self-reflective, we need to think about what we do and why, and we need to become intelligent observers of our actions and the outcomes. Not only is the action research cycle continuous, but you also can circle back to earlier phases within a cycle (e.g., cycle back and forth between reflection and planning or between observing and reflecting). When you finish a full cycle, you will typically enter into another cycle as you think about and try to improve on what you have already accomplished (or not accomplished). Many action research projects require multiple cycles in which you plan and try something small, observe and reflect (e.g., make a formative evaluation and adjust your theory), and then plan a new cycle of improvement. In education, we often call this process *lifelong learning*; in the business world, it is often called *continuous quality improvement*.

If you conduct an action research study, you will need to diagnose the specific problem you are facing and conduct a thorough literature review to see if a useful answer already exists that you can try out in your context/setting. You will then plan and carry out your own action research study (i.e., collect data to help answer your question) in your environment with your students or clients. The goal is to help solve your local problem. A key element, again, is for you to be a reflective practitioner—to continually reflect on your actions, outcomes, and any other factors. As a result of this reflection, at some point you will be ready to plan your own systematic study.

An example of a basic individual action research study is seen in Patricia Anguiano's (2001) short article titled "A First-Year Teacher's Plan to Reduce Misbehavior in the Classroom." Patricia, a new third-grade teacher, realized that misbehavior was taking time away from instruction. She reviewed the literature and identified some strategies she should try.

The strategies she selected were eye contact, physical proximity to the student, "withitness," and overlapping. (*Withitness* is a term used in education to refer to teacher awareness of what is happening in all places in the classroom at all times.) She developed four research questions: (1) What strategies are effective in reducing misbehavior during direct instruction? (2) What strategies are effective in reducing misbehavior during transitions? (3) What strategies are effective in reducing misbehavior during recess? (4) What are the most effective strategies overall? She collected pretest baseline data using (a) a survey of misbehavior the students self-reported and (b) teacher-recorded data on observed misbehaviors. During the intervention, she also kept a journal. After the intervention, she surveyed the students again. She found that misbehaviors had decreased and the students also noted the decrease. As misbehavior decreased, instruction time increased. This was a very small individual study, but it was a good start for Anguiano, who reported that she learned a lot about herself and how she could become a better teacher.

- **Planning phase** Articulation of the action research project plan

Now, let's more closely examine the **planning phase** of the AR cycle. In this phase, you try to articulate what it is about your situation that needs improvement. What is inadequate? What do you want to know more about? What do you want to try to see if it works? You will need to translate your concern into research questions, identify a likely remedy, and write your action plan. What actions will change your situation? Remember to consult the research literature to see what has worked for others, seek advice from people who have been successful with the problem, and discuss ideas with your colleagues. Ask a **critical friend** to carefully observe your practice and make suggestions for improvement.

- **Critical friend** A person whom you trust to be open, honest, and constructively critical of your work

Two popular types of action research methods are exploratory/descriptive methods and experimental/intervention methods. You might even do both, starting with an exploratory/descriptive design in your first AR cycle and following up with an experimental/intervention AR cycle.

For example, you might plan to first conduct an exploratory/descriptive study (e.g., a needs assessment, a study of attitudes, a fact-finding investigation) to help you better understand your situation, its context, the people involved and their attitudes, and the characteristics of the social system. You could plan to conduct a survey of all the teachers in your grade or your subject area; you might also survey parents and students. You could include administrators for yet another perspective. You will learn a lot by examining multiple perspectives. The survey research study could be your first action research study. Plan it (plan), conduct it (act), examine the results (observe), and think about what the results mean and what you should do next (reflect).

After conducting your survey action research study, your reflection might suggest that you should plan an intervention. In this second AR cycle, you might construct a specific and answerable research question about what might improve your teaching or your curriculum. You could plan a small experiment or intervention in which you act in a new way and observe the consequences. Using Lewin's change theory, you should identify the driving forces and the restraining forces. Also, think about how your actions will affect the people around you who are part of the larger social/school system.

- **Who does what, when chart** A useful chart showing what is to occur during the study

A key outcome of the planning phase is writing down who does what and when they do it. (We call this a "**who does what, when chart**.") You also must make sure the project members are trained so that they know how to conduct their activities. Before you act, think about what the outcomes might be; state your hypotheses. Plan to observe and measure attitudes and behavior before and after your experiment. Finally, make sure that your plan is feasible and ethical. In action research, this is called your **action plan**; it's your detailed plan of who does what when, and how they are to do it.

- **Action plan** A synonym for the research proposal that is used by action researchers

The next phase in the AR cycle (i.e., after planning) is the **action phase**. This could be a needs assessment or an exploratory and descriptive study of the different people and positions in your system. Or your action might be to conduct an experiment, like Anguiano's described earlier. Trying new actions is important in action research. This key idea is articulated in Kurt Lewin's famous principle of action that goes like this: *If you want truly to understand something, try to change it.* If you want to truly understand your classroom, your clients, your work situation, your school, or anything else, think about how you can change it and then try to change it. You will need to use measurement techniques and one of the research designs that we discuss later in this book to determine the effects of your action. When you conduct your experiment, stick to your plan and record any deviations. You are probably a beginning researcher. Therefore, you should start by conducting a small experiment or pilot study. Then you can recycle (through the action research cycle) to a larger and more rigorous research study.

- **Action phase** Step in the action research cycle in which one conducts an exploratory-descriptive study or an experimental-intervention study

Next in the AR cycle is the **observe phase**, when you determine what happens. That is, you should collect data through one or more of the major methods of data collection that we discuss in Chapters 7, 8, and 9 (i.e., tests, questionnaires, interviews, focus groups, observation, existing or constructed data). A key point to know now is that you will (a) collect quantitative data to measure what you are interested in studying and (b) collect qualitative data to help you understand the meanings of what takes place and to hear what your participants think in their own words. It is a good idea to use more than one source of evidence and use more than one method of data collection. Doing so will provide you with more complete information about your planned action and its impact. You need to measure and listen to different perspectives and different vantage points regarding your action. In addition to collecting data on what you expect to happen (i.e., your objectives or hypotheses), you should be on the lookout for any unanticipated outcomes; the father of modern evaluation, Michael Scriven, called this *goal-free evaluation*, which simply means to look for outcomes that were not included in your research or program objectives. In short, look for what you expected and what you did not expect. Often quantitative methods are used to examine the objectives, while qualitative methods are used to understand the objectives and outcomes in a deeper way and to explore for other unanticipated outcomes.

- **Observe phase** A step in the action research cycle in which one collects data and obtains evidence about the success of actions

Following observation in the AR cycle is the **reflection phase**. You now think about your data and the results, make sense of them, and reflect on what they mean. What conclusions should you draw and, perhaps, what should be done next? Did your intervention work? What worked and what didn't work? Consider the multiple perspectives. Can your intervention be improved so that it will work better next time? This is like the *formative evaluation* approach described in Chapter 1. What do you need to change in your theory or explanation? Revise your action theory as needed and consider testing your revised theory in another action research cycle. This is how continual theory development and theory testing operates in education science. You generate a theory, test it, revise it, test it again, and continually improve it.

- **Reflection phase** Step in the action research cycle in which one thinks about the results, considers strategies for improvement, and begins future planning

After you conduct a few individual action research studies, you should shift into larger studies, such as a participatory study of your entire school. Action research is especially useful when you and many of your coworkers are all interested in conducting the research.

Collaboratively, you can brainstorm, learn from each other's ideas and each other's work, self-reflect with critical and creative eyes, and try to form an action research culture in your school. Most problems are not fully solved through a single research study. Many larger school districts have departments that are set up to facilitate and conduct research about their local schools. You might find that many teachers and administrators whom you know are familiar with action research.

The last key point in this section is that self-reflection is something that you should do throughout your career: Do it every day; do it from moment to moment. It will serve you well to become a reflective practitioner, regardless of your job. You should also be reflective in your other life activities. No matter what you do, learn to be reflective and try to become better. In short, try to become a lifelong learner.

REVIEW QUESTION

3.4 How does the action research cycle operate, and why is it a never-ending process?

STRENGTHS AND WEAKNESSES OF ACTION RESEARCH

We have presented action research as a positive activity, and it is. Perhaps its biggest strength is that it helps to produce lifelong learners who produce local knowledge that can be shared with the larger enterprise of education (see Figure 3.2 again). Here is a list of the major strengths of action research:

- Can be conducted by local practitioners.
- Produces lifelong learners.
- Integrates theory and practice.
- Is committed to democratic social change.
- Empowers practitioners to contribute to knowledge.
- Describes the complexities of local situations.
- Improves practice at the local level.

We would be remiss if we did not inform you about the major weaknesses of action research. Perhaps its biggest weakness is that it sometimes ignores more basic research literature and, oftentimes, relies on weaker methods and validity strategies than does regular scientific research. Here is a list of the major weaknesses of action research:

- Often involves a small-scale study that produces a limited and delimited amount of information and knowledge.
- Produces small-scale results that are difficult to generalize to different and larger contexts.
- Tends to have less scientific objectivity compared to regular education science.
- Is often based on weaker research designs, compared to regular education science.
- Does not lend itself to making strong general statements of cause and effect.
- Often lacks rigor in terms of traditional measurement and research validity criteria.
- Presents difficulties for institutional review boards (IRBs), which evaluate the ethical practice of the research, because multiple people might be involved and the researcher cannot foresee many possible actions because of the study's fluid nature and continual development.

Action Research Journaling

Action research is an excellent way to develop the attitude of a researcher: It is what John Dewey hoped every teacher would do in his or her own life, and it is what Dewey hoped teachers would instill in their students' minds and abilities. We recommend that you start working now on your reflective journal as you read the rest of this book. You will need to think about (i.e., reflect on) what you learn in each of the remaining chapters, and you should try to relate that material to your individual improvement and professional practice. To become a better practitioner and researcher, you will need to record your thinking/reflections as you read this book in an **action research journal**. Stop at the drugstore on your way home from work today and purchase a notebook. This can become *your* systematic place to record your reflections about the book material, about who you are, about how you should go about your work, and—most importantly—about how you can become better at what you do. To facilitate your *growth* as a teacher, a coach, a counselor, or whatever, we will ask you in each of the remaining chapters to reflect on how the chapter material can help you to become an action researcher and lifelong learner. In short, the purpose of your action research journal is to help you to make the material relevant to your career and your life. As an aside, *this also will help you on your tests*, because it is through reflection that you will learn the material at a much deeper level! Try to relate the material to your life.

- **Action research journal** A place where one records learnings and reflections

You have already read Chapters 1 and 2. Therefore, you need to catch up. Start now by reviewing and thinking about the material in Chapter 1. One key idea in Chapter 1, we believe, is that people like you can learn to think like a researcher. Action researchers are interested in science as a way to help their practice and contribute to the relevant research literature. Action researchers are "practical scientists."

Here are some starting reflection questions for Chapter 1:

1. How might you start viewing science broadly as something that can be useful in your everyday life and professional practice (e.g., as an "action science")?
2. What insights and questions did you have as you read Chapters 1 and 2? (If you didn't have any, try to think of some now!)
3. What do education scientists do? What do education practitioners do? Why are they important for each other? Remember that action researchers attempt to connect science and practice.

It is also time to reflect on Chapter 2, to get caught up in your AR journal. Take a moment to look back and think about Chapter 2. Action researchers typically follow the mixed research paradigm because they like to select what works best from both qualitative and quantitative research. Answer these questions in your journal (realizing that over the semester, your answers might change):

1. What research paradigm(s) do you like to operate from (qualitative, quantitative, mixed)? Why?
2. What philosophical and practical assumptions do you think you tend to operate from?
   a. What do you mean by the word *reality*, and do you think that reality is singular (universal truths) or plural (particular domain specific truths)? (These are some of your *ontological assumptions*, that is, your assumptions about reality.)

b. Do you think there is one best way to gain knowledge or multiple ways, and what do you mean by "warranted or justified knowledge"? (These are some of your *epistemological assumptions*, that is, your assumptions about what knowledge is and when you can claim to have knowledge.)

c. What research methods discussed in Chapter 2 do you think might be useful for learning about your world? (This is one of your *methodological assumptions*, that is, your beliefs about what methods you prefer to use and believe are effective.)

We know this is deep stuff, but self-reflection can be a deep look into your "self." Don't be afraid; go for it.

Last, add some reflections to your journal about the material in this chapter. Here are some questions to get you started:

1. What are some benefits of taking an "action research attitude" about your work?
2. What do you think about the circle of knowledge shown in Figure 3.2? Specifically, consider the suggestion that education science needs to provide knowledge to the local level, but it also needs to listen to knowledge produced by people at the local level of practice.
3. What type of action research do you like and why?
4. If you were to conduct an action research study this semester, what are your initial thoughts about what you would do it on?

Here is a list of a few action research ideas to help you get started thinking about an action research project that you would like to conduct this semester or about a research study that you would like to propose to conduct:

- How can I increase my students' intrinsic motivation to read?
- How can I increase my students' self-efficacy for giving in-class presentations?
- How can I get students in social cliques ("insiders") to care for and respect other students ("outsiders")?
- What are teachers' and administrators' views of the characteristics of a "good teacher," and how can these be merged?
- How can I get students to increase their care for and interaction with students who have special needs?
- How can I get my students more engaged in mathematics (or reading or history)?
- How can I tailor my class so that low- and high-achieving students are progressing?
- How can I increase parental participation in students' homework?
- How can I increase staff participation in school activities?
- How can I improve the school culture at my school?
- What are students', teachers', parents', and administrators' views about the purposes of school, and how can I increase communication among these groups?

ACTION RESEARCH IN THE REMAINING CHAPTERS OF THIS BOOK

In this book, we focus on how to conduct high-quality quantitative, qualitative, and mixed methods research that can be published in journals. We also hope to empower you to become an action researcher in your day-to-day life! To facilitate your growth as a researcher, we include a short section at the end of each of the remaining chapters to help you relate to the chapter material in a meaningful way. Our goal is to make the material practical in your own life and workplace. In short, we hope to train you to think like a research scientist and like an action research scientist. Both of these approaches will be helpful in your career. Keeping an action research journal will help you to prepare better for your tests, because you will have thought more deeply and more practically about the material in each chapter.

SUMMARY

Action research is conducted by professionals (often in collaboration with others) to improve problem situations they face. Action research arose from the ideas, theories, and philosophy of Kurt Lewin and John Dewey. Lewin's key ideas are found in his *force-field theory* (we are subject to driving and restraining forces) and his *change theory* (change is a three-stage process of unfreezing, changing, and refreezing). Dewey emphasized a scientific/experimenting form of *inquiry* and a *philosophy of experience* (we are embedded in local contexts and situations, and we must continually try to improve our situations through continual inquiry and personal growth throughout our lifetimes). We listed the five steps in Dewey's process of inquiry, and we compared basic scientific research (focused on general knowledge) and action research (focused on local knowledge). Our circle of education science showed that both of these sources of knowledge need to "learn" from the other in a continuous feedback system.

We contrasted the following types or kinds of action research, with each having its own special emphasis: *participatory action research* (conducted in teams where everyone participates in the study), *critical action research* (emphasizes empowerment of the less advantaged in society), *feminist action research* (focused on providing a feminist lens), *action science* (focused on producing learning organizations), and *appreciative inquiry* (focused on identifying the strengths in an organization and producing an effort to work together for a shared purpose). We also distinguished action research by its scope; you can think of these types as following a continuum from more micro to more macro. They include *individual action research* (designed and conducted by an individual), *collaborative action research* (designed and conducted by a team), and *system or schoolwide action research* (designed, conducted, and focused on macro or large system changes).

The *cycle of action research* includes four phases: reflection, planning, acting, and observing. You can enter the cycle at any point, you can circle back to earlier phases within the overall cycle, and the end of a full cycle becomes the starting point for your next cycle as you continually focus on improvement.

Action research is a way of life, and we hope this chapter motivates and helps you to obtain the *action research attitude*—a commitment to continuous improvement in what you do and lifelong learning.

KEY TERMS

action phase (p. 71)
action plan (p. 71)
action research (p. 58)
action research attitude (p. 58)
action research journal (p. 73)
action science (p. 66)
appreciative inquiry (p. 67)
collaborative action research (p. 68)
critical action research (p. 65)
critical friend (p. 70)
Deweyan inquiry (p. 61)
double-loop learning (p. 67)
driving forces (p. 59)
espoused theory (p. 67)
feminist action research (p. 66)
force field analysis (p. 59)
force field theory (p. 59)
individual action research (p. 68)
learning organization (p. 66)
Lewin's change theory (p. 59)
observe phase (p. 71)

participatory action research (p. 64)
planning phase (p. 70)
reflection phase (p. 71)
restraining forces (p. 59)
single-loop learning (p. 67)
systemwide action research (p. 68)
theory in use (p. 67)
translational research (p. 63)
who does what, when chart (p. 70)

DISCUSSION QUESTIONS

1. What type of action research do you like the most and why?
2. What type of action research do you like the least and why?
3. What are some problems that you could address by conducting an action research study in your place of work?

RESEARCH EXERCISES

1. In the section above entitled "Action Research Journaling," we provided some questions for you to answer about Chapter 1. Think about these and write your thoughts and answers in your action research journal.
2. In the section above entitled "Action Research Journaling," we provided some questions for you to answer about Chapter 2. Think about these and write your thoughts and answers in your action research journal.
3. In the section above entitled "Action Research Journaling," we provided some questions for you to answer about this chapter. Think about these and write your thoughts and answers in your action research journal.
4. Identify two action research studies published in journals that look interesting. What kind of AR study was it? How did the researchers conduct the AR study? What were the findings? Do you think their findings will be useful in a practical sense? How so?

RELEVANT INTERNET SITES

The following link has free copies (pdf files) of many of Dewey's books: http://onlinebooks.library.upenn.edu. Just click on the "Authors" link under "Books Online," type "John Dewey" in the "Author" box under "Search for a particular name," and click "Search" to bring up a list of John Dewey's works available online.

Action research and action learning for community and organizational change site: http://www.aral.com.au. This site is maintained by an internationally known action researcher (Bob Dick). It has many links and resources.

Teacher action research resources page: http://gse.gmu.edu/research/tr/.

Educational Action Research: http://www.tandfonline.com/toc/reac20/current#.UZqibLWsh8F. This is a journal. You can browse the table of contents and receive an email message when each new issue is printed.

Action Research: http://arj.sagepub.com. This is a journal published by SAGE. You can browse the table of contents and receive an email message when each new issue is printed.

Action Research Special Interest Group of the American Educational Research Association: http://www.aera.net/SIG002/ActionResearchSIG2/tabid/11391/Default.aspx.

STUDENT STUDY SITE

Visit the Student Study Site at **edge.sagepub.com/rbjohnson6e** for these additional learning tools:

- Video links
- Self-quizzes
- eFlashcards
- Lecture Notes
- Full-text SAGE journal articles
- Interactive concept maps
- Web resources

RECOMMENDED READING

Dewey, J. (1938). *Experience and education*. New York, NY: Macmillan.

Reason, P., & Bradbury, H. (2008). *The SAGE handbook of action research: Participative inquiry and practice*. Thousand Oaks, CA: SAGE.

Sagor, R. D. (2011). *The action research guidebook: A four-stage process for educators and school teams*. Thousand Oaks, CA: Corwin.

NOTE

1. These are the five principles or disciplines of a learning organization: (a) *building shared vision* (i.e., about where the organization is going, what it is committed to for all employees, and how it can become better in a changing environment), (b) *mental models* (i.e., our deep assumptions and pictures that affect how we act; members become focused on growth, improvement, and positive change), (c) *personal mastery* (i.e., where every individual becomes a continual learner, takes pride in good work, and adapts and grows with the organization), (d) *team learning* (i.e., individuals frequently collaborate and work on shared goals, vision, and outcomes), and (e) *systems thinking* (i.e., the organization is a complex, adaptive, learning system with many subsystems working together to produce a better future for all organization members). Systems thinking is the "fifth discipline" that Senge believed could integrate the other four disciplines into a working whole.

PART II

Planning the Research Study

Chapter 4

How to Review the Literature and Develop Research Questions

LEARNING OBJECTIVES

After reading this chapter, you should be able to

- Identify research problems.
- Explain why it is necessary to conduct a literature search.
- Conduct a literature search.
- Explain the reason for stating the purpose of a research study and the research questions.
- Explain the difference between purpose statements and research questions in qualitative and quantitative studies.
- Explain the purpose and necessity of stating your research questions and hypotheses.
- Explain the difference between problem statements in qualitative and quantitative studies.
- State one or two research questions you would like to answer using empirical research.

Visit the Student Study Site for an interactive concept map.

RESEARCH IN REAL LIFE Studying School Success

istock/ majoros

One of the stereotypes that many people seem to harbor privately but few openly express is that poor students who attend the nation's worst public schools are a lost cause, regardless of how much money you throw at them or what innovative attempts are made to teach them, because they are inherently unteachable. This myth, however, is being exposed for exactly what it is in about two dozen schools statewide ("Our Opinions," 2002). Bethune Elementary School in Vine City, Georgia, is one of the schools that has achieved success, in spite of its location in one of Atlanta's most depressed in-town neighborhoods. About 86% of the fourth graders scored at or above the state average in math and reading tests in 2001.

Bethune has clearly defied the odds against poverty and has proved that children from poverty-stricken inner-city areas can perform well academically. The test scores vividly verify that Bethune has accomplished something that has eluded numerous other schools across the country. An educational researcher, however, would want to go beyond applauding the success of this school and learn why Bethune and other such schools have been successful when most schools in depressed inner-city areas are not. An educational researcher would look at the overall program instituted at Bethune and search for the primary reason for its success. It might be that all components are needed. However, it is also possible that one of the components, such as soliciting the help and cooperation of parents, was more important than the additional discipline, encouragement, and accountability implemented by the school staff. It is important to identify the most vital components of a successful program such as the one at Bethune because doing so identifies the primary way to transport the success to other programs.

This example illustrates how a real-life event can lead to a good research study, and it might suggest that research problems and questions are easy to generate. This is often true for the veteran researcher. However, beginning researchers frequently have difficulty identifying a research question that they can investigate. In this chapter, we try to minimize this difficulty by discussing the origin of most research questions and the way these research questions are converted to ones that can be investigated.

Up to this point in the text, we have discussed the basic characteristics of research, the three major research paradigms—quantitative, qualitative, and mixed—used in research, and the idea of becoming an action researcher. However, the research process begins when you have a problem in need of a solution, because a research study is conducted in an attempt to solve a problem.

Identifying a research problem should be relatively simple in the field of education because of the numerous problems that need to be solved and because of the exposure and experience we have all had in this arena. All of us have participated in the educational system, first as students and then perhaps as teachers, administrators, or parents. In one or both of these capacities, you have probably observed and discussed a host of problems with our current educational system and been exposed to the implementation of new techniques and methods of instruction. For example, you might think that certain instructional strategies such as computer-assisted instruction, team teaching, or cooperative learning enhance learning, or you might have questioned the value of activities such as field trips and extracurricular programs or some new approach to teaching biology, chemistry, or physics.

From a research perspective, each of these issues is a potential legitimate research problem. All you have to do is adjust your thinking a bit. For example, when George W. Bush was president of the United States, he advocated additional academic testing and spending for literacy on the assumption that these efforts would improve the education received by the youth of America. You, on the other hand, might think that the money spent on these programs should have been spent on reducing class size. You might even have gotten into arguments with your colleagues about the value of such alternatives and found that you could not change their opinions. Such an argument or disagreement is legitimate subject matter for a research study. All you have to do is convert your argument into a research question and ask, for example, "What benefits are derived from increasing academic testing?" or "What benefit is derived from reducing class size, and will this benefit be greater than doing more academic testing?"

Once you have converted the disagreement into a researchable question, you have taken the first step in developing a research study. Researchable questions are numerous in education. To identify them, all you have to do is develop an inquisitive attitude and ask questions.

SOURCES OF RESEARCH IDEAS

Where do ideas for research studies originate? Where should you look for a researchable idea? We discuss four major sources of ideas: everyday life, practical issues, past research, and theory. Regardless of where you look for your research ideas, you must develop a questioning and inquisitive approach to life when you are trying to come up with them.

Everyday Life

One fruitful source of ideas for beginning researchers is their own experience as educators. In the course of conducting your job as an educator, you continuously have to make decisions about such things as the best method of teaching students or how to maintain discipline in the classroom. You might observe that some students aggressively pursue their studies, whereas others procrastinate and do anything but schoolwork. Experiences such as these can be turned into research problems. For example, you could ask why some strategies of instruction work better with some students than with others. Or you might ask why some students use one method of study and others use another and whether there is any relationship between the method of study and the grades achieved.

Practical Issues

Many research ideas can arise from practical issues that require a solution. Educators are constantly faced with such problems as the instruction of our youth, disruptive behavior in the classroom, selection of textbooks, cheating, prejudice, and providing instruction for culturally diverse student populations, as well as issues such as salaries and burnout. A few controversial issues right now surround the usefulness of common core standards, the effects of school choice, the effects of poverty on children's achievement, how much math children should be required to know to graduate, what kind of technology should be incorporated into classrooms, and how to teach students with different backgrounds. You can think of many additional practical issues, especially the ones that you face!

Past Research

The research literature of previously conducted studies is an excellent source of ideas and might be the source of most research ideas. This might sound like a contradiction because a research study is designed to answer a research question. However, research tends to generate more questions than it answers. Furthermore, as you know from reviewing and critiquing journal articles in college classes you have taken, you often will find issues in an article that you believe are problematic; *the "problems" that you identify in your article critique can be an excellent starting point for proposing another, closely related study that builds on the research literature!*

Although each well-designed study advances knowledge in the field, phenomena are multidetermined. Any quantitative study can investigate only a limited number of variables,

TABLE 4.1 Ways in Which Prior Studies Can Provide Ideas for New Studies

Method	*Rationale*
Replication	You might decide that you want to repeat a study to see whether you can replicate the results because you think the author's results have significant educational importance and you want to verify them with different people.
Extension	You might read an empirical research article, that you like, but you realize that they excluded a variable that you would like to examine for theoretical significance, or you believe you have a better measure of one of the constructs, or you believe they didn't conduct the appropriate analysis, etc. In these cases, you could extend the article by conducting a similar study with your additional independent or predictor variable added, or using the superior measurement procedure, or conducting the more appropriate analysis with your data—in short, you would have built on or extended the original article in some way, thus improving the research literature.
Testing the external validity (i.e., generalizability) of a study	You might have read a laboratory-based study that has suggestions for important issues such as reading, control of aggression, or improving instruction. You want to find out whether the laboratory methods tested would work equally well in the classroom.
Improving a study's internal validity (i.e., accuracy of claims about causation)	In reading a study, you might realize that the study did not control one or more important variables and the lack of control of these variables led to an ambiguous interpretation of the results. For example, Gladue and Delaney (1990) thought that the Pennebaker et al. (1979) study that found that girls in bars "got prettier" at closing time did not answer the question of whether it was the time of night or alcohol consumption that contributed to perceptions of attractiveness.
Reconciling conflicting results	In reading the literature on a topic, you might find conflicting results and want to conduct a study to resolve the conflict. This conflict might be due to different ways in which the studies were conducted, the use of different measurement instruments, or the use of different participant populations. When studies conflict, you need to look for any differences in the studies because these differences might be the cause of the apparent conflict.
Generating a new theory	Especially in new areas of inquiry, one might use the grounded theory methodology to *generate* and construct a new theory that is grounded in empirical data to explain how and why some interesting phenomenon operates. One might also test additional implications of an existing theory.
Suggestions for future research	One of the easiest ways to get ideas from past research is to look for the author's suggestions for future research. Often, particularly in review articles, the author(s) of the article will make suggestions for the future direction of research. These suggestions are frequently valid and excellent sources of research ideas.
Theses and dissertations	Theses and dissertations often have a section devoted to future research that identifies subsequent studies the author believes need to be completed.

and the investigation of the variables that were selected can lead to hypotheses about the effects of other variables. Table 4.1 lists a variety of excellent ways in which past research can provide research ideas. Mining suggestions found in articles and coming up with your own suggestions through your article critiques are relatively easy ways to come up with a good research study.

Theory

■ **Theory** An explanation or explanatory system that discusses how a phenomenon operates and why it operates as it does

Theory, as defined in Chapter 1, is an explanation or explanatory system that discusses *how* a phenomenon operates and *why* it operates as it does. Theory serves the purpose of making sense out of current knowledge by integrating and summarizing this knowledge. This is referred to as the *goal function* of theory. Theory also guides research by making predictions. This is the *tool function* of theory. A good theory goes beyond the goal function of summarizing and integrating what is currently known to suggest new relationships and make new predictions. It is in this manner that theories guide research. Therefore, you should try to identify suggested relationships and new predictions based on theory that *you* can test in a new research study to confirm or disconfirm their authenticity.

Weiner's (1974) attributional theory of success and failure suggests a way of thinking about and explaining test anxiety. From this theory, Bandalos, Yates, and Thorndike-Christ (1995) hypothesized and confirmed the prediction that test anxiety was related to the type of attribution a student made for his or her good or bad grade on a test. Individuals who attributed failure on a test to a lack of effort on their part reported lower levels of test anxiety than did those who cited a lack of ability or some external cause, such as the difficulty of the test. Similarly, students who attributed successful performance on a test to some external factor, such as the test being easy or luck, reported higher levels of test anxiety. If there is little or no theory in the area of interest to you, then think about collecting data to help you generate a theory using the grounded theory method defined in Chapter 2.

These four sources of research ideas—everyday life, practical issues, past research, and theory—are the primary sources of research ideas. The important issue, however, is not the identification of sources of research ideas but the generation of researchable ideas from these sources. Generation of research ideas is the initial stage of a research project, and development of these ideas requires the development of a questioning and inquisitive way of thinking.

Identifying a research idea does not mean that it will be the exact focus of your research study, because the idea you have come up with might already have been investigated. The generation of a research idea really identifies the topic that you want to investigate. For example, assume you believe that teachers do a more effective job and the students learn more when they have a class size of 15 than when they have a class size of 30. You want to verify this belief in an empirical research study. However, this is a topic that others have likely thought of and investigated, so a considerable amount of past research probably exists on this issue. What you have done is to identify a **research topic**, or a broad subject matter area that you want to investigate. The research topic that you have identified is class size and its effect on academic performance. Identification of the research topic is the beginning of a sequential process that ends with the research question and research hypothesis, as illustrated in Figure 4.1.

■ **Research topic** The broad subject matter area to be investigated

■ **FIGURE 4.1** Flowchart of the development of a research idea

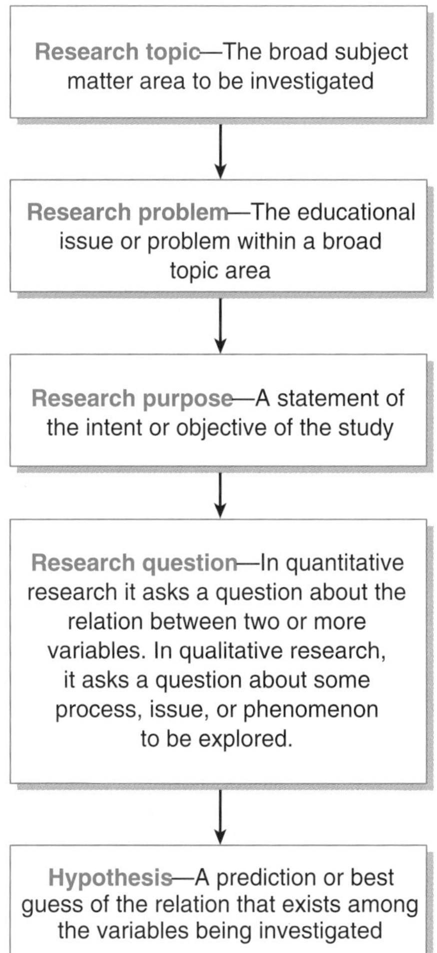

Ideas That Can't Be Resolved Through Empirical Research

Some ideas are very important, are debated vigorously, and consume large amounts of time and energy but cannot be resolved through empirical research study. These ideas typically involve making judgments about aesthetics, morality, and religion. Consider, for example, the issue of school prayer. It has been debated for years, has polarized segments of the US population, and has even been debated in the courts, ultimately resulting in the ruling that prayer should not be a regular part of public school activities. This ruling was based on the legal opinion of members of the judicial system and did not arise as a result of an empirical research study because the issue of school prayer is a moral issue. As such, it implies notions of what is morally right and wrong or proper or improper. Empirical research cannot provide answers to such questions, although it can provide useful data on opinions, attitudes, and behaviors of individuals and groups. The key point is that empirical research cannot resolve the issue of which value position is *morally* best.

REVIEW QUESTIONS

4.1 What sources of research ideas have been identified in this chapter?

4.2 How would you get a research idea from each of these sources?

4.3 What are some ideas and questions that cannot be resolved through empirical research?

Review of the Literature

See Journal Article 4.1 on the Student Study Site.

After you have identified a research idea, most investigators believe that your next step should be to conduct a full literature review to familiarize yourself with the available information on the topic. However, the use of the literature review can vary depending on whether one is conducting a qualitative or a quantitative study. We will therefore discuss the purpose of the literature review separately for quantitative and qualitative research studies.

Literature Review for Quantitative Research Studies

In quantitative research, an extensive literature review is done before the conduct of the study. For example, assume that you want to conduct research on the effect of students' self-concept on academic achievement. Before beginning to design this research project, you should first become familiar with the available information on the individual topics of self-concept and academic achievement.

The general purpose of the literature review is to gain an understanding of the current state of knowledge about your selected research topic. Specifically, a review of the literature

- will tell you whether the problem you have identified has already been researched. If it has, you should either revise the problem in light of the results of other studies to *build* on the previous literature or look for another problem, unless you think there is a need to replicate the study.
- will assist you in forming your research questions.
- might give you ideas as to how to proceed with and design your study so that you can obtain an answer to your research question(s).
- can point out methodological problems specific to the research question(s) you are studying. Are special groups or special pieces of equipment needed to conduct the research? If so, the literature can give clues as to where to find the equipment or how to identify the particular groups of participants needed.
- can identify appropriate data-collection instruments so that you will not need to construct a new instrument.

Familiarity with the literature will also help you after you have collected your data and analyzed your results. One of the last stages of a research project is to prepare a research report in which you communicate the results of the study to others. In doing so, you not only have to describe the study and the results you found but also must explain or interpret the results of your study. The literature can frequently provide clues as to why the effects occurred. If you are familiar with the literature, you can also discuss your results in terms of whether they support or contradict prior studies. If your study is at odds with other studies, you can speculate as to why this difference occurred, and this speculation then forms the basis for another study to attempt to resolve the contradictory findings.

Literature Review for Qualitative Research Studies

The literature review in qualitative research can be used in several ways. It can be used to explain the theoretical underpinnings of the research study, to assist in formulation of the research question and selection of the study population, or to stimulate new insights and concepts throughout the study. Qualitative researchers often integrate the literature review throughout their study, working back and forth between the literature and the research (LeCompte & Preissle, 1993). Still, there are two schools of thought about the use of literature reviews in qualitative research.

According to one school of thought, it is important to conduct a thorough literature review on your research topic *before* collecting data. According to the second school of thought, the researcher should set aside any preconceived notions (including published literature) and use a fully exploratory approach in which interpretations and additional research questions, hypotheses, and theory emerge from the data collected. From this perspective, you should initially familiarize yourself with the literature only enough to make sure that the study you are planning to conduct has not already been done. Only *after* you have collected your data do you conduct a thorough literature review to try to integrate what you have found with the literature.

For example, in Chapter 2 we introduced you briefly to grounded theory (a qualitative method in which the researcher develops a theory or explanation from qualitative data, such as interviews and observations). One camp of grounded theorists, led by Glaser (1978), recommends postponing the literature review until *after* data collection because of its potential "biasing" effects on the researcher. Glaser wanted researchers to use the grounded theory approach to discover or generate a set of constructs, relationships, and theory that are uncontaminated by any knowledge of prior research or theory. Glaser recommended that the literature be reviewed after the theory is sufficiently "grounded in the data" so that it fits the particular people in the study. Then the researcher can examine how the theory relates to the prior literature, checking to see if the grounded theory is similar to that put forward by other studies in the literature or if it suggests a different process operating for a particular kind of people in a particular context.

Although Glaser (1978) recommended postponing review of the literature until a theory was sufficiently grounded and developed, other grounded theorists believe that a literature review can be done earlier. Strauss and Corbin (1990) specified several different ways in which a literature review conducted before data collection can be of value:

- The literature review can be used to stimulate theoretical sensitivity toward concepts and relationships that prior literature has repeatedly identified and that therefore appear to be meaningful and significant. Because of their apparent significance, you might want to bring these concepts into the situation you are studying to identify the role they might play. For example, if the concept of isolation is repeatedly identified in the literature as being significantly related to creative achievement and you are studying creative achievement in underprivileged children, you might want to look for evidence of how isolation relates to creative achievement in your study.

- The literature can stimulate questions. The literature can assist you in deriving an initial list of pertinent questions to ask or behaviors to observe.
- Finally, the literature can provide some information about the situations and populations that you need to study so that you can uncover phenomena that are important to the development of your theory. For example, in a study of creativity, the literature might indicate that you should look at individuals who are experiencing various emotional states because mood might be an important variable in the development of your theory of creativity.

In sum, the current position among qualitative researchers seems to be that a literature review can be of value but the researcher must make sure that it does not constrain and stifle the discovery of new constructs, relationships, and theories.

Literature Review for Mixed Research Studies

In many cases a researcher will realize that the collection of both quantitative *and* qualitative data can best address the research questions(s) of interest. That is why the literature review should start as a full review of the published information on the research topic or problem or opportunity of interest. You should conduct a multidisciplinary literature review and be fully open to both quantitative and qualitative studies. In some cases there will also be published mixed research on your topic. Typically, the quantitative studies will show what theories and hypotheses have been tested and what findings resulted, and the qualitative studies will show what an exploratory study of the topic suggests is the case.

It will be important for you to determine during your literature review the state of the published research with regard to your topic. Is the research still in its infancy or has a lot of theory-testing research taken place? This will suggest to you what kind of mixed study you will want to conduct, such as a mixed study that starts with additional exploration and is followed with a quantitative testing phase or if you should conduct a mixed study that starts with a quantitative phase (putting together ideas found in the literature) and following that with a qualitative phase to further explore and explain your findings from the initial stage. The former is called a "qualitative–quantitative sequential design" and the latter is called a "quantitative–qualitative sequential design." Finally, you might decide that it would be wise to just see what different methods have to say about your topic to build on the literature, and in this case you could conduct a parallel or concurrent mixed design where you decide to collect qualitative and quantitative data at approximately the same time. Your decision about these issues will be based on (a) the state of the published research and (b) how you want to add to or contribute to the literature. During your literature search, you might ask the following questions: (a) Does the literature need further exploration followed by some quantitative testing? (b) Does the literature need a new instrument developed and tested/used? (c) Does the literature need theory testing with some follow-up in-depth explanation? In short, you need to understand the published literature before designing and conducting your own research study.

Sources of Information

The two primary sources for tracking down information relevant to any research topic are books and journals, although information can also be found in technical reports and academic theses and dissertations.

Books

Books are a good place to start your literature search because they provide an overview of the research topic and a summary of the literature published up to the time the book was written. Most books focus on a specific topic, such as team teaching or Head Start. If you have selected a research topic that focuses on one of these issues, then a book written about that topic will give you a good overview of the subject matter, as well as a bibliography of other works that might be of use to you. Remember, however, that the literature that is cited in books is generally several years old, so books do not provide the most current information.

Although books provide a good introduction to and overview of the issues of importance in your chosen research area, they do not give a comprehensive review of all the research conducted on any specific topic. Any book's author has to be selective and present only a small portion of the literature.

Journals

After you have examined several books and have become familiar with your research topic, your next step is to identify relevant journal articles. *Most of the current information about a research topic is usually found in journals.* If you already have some familiarity with your chosen research topic, you might forgo examining books and go directly to research journals. Numerous journals publish educational research or studies that are highly relevant for educational research. It would be impossible to go through each journal looking for relevant information. Therefore, you will use an automated search procedure, searching relevant computer databases (discussed next).

Computer Databases

With advances in computer technology and particularly the Internet, it has become possible to store and access large data sets electronically. Several comprehensive computerized information storage and retrieval systems, such as OVID, SilverPlatter, FirstSearch, and EBSCO, have been developed for this purpose. Information retrieval systems like these have access to many databases. The information that is of primary interest to educational researchers is available in EBSCO. When you use EBSCO, we strongly recommend that you search multiple databases, including, at a minimum, the following: **Educational Resources Information Center (ERIC)** (which includes all the entries for *Current Index to Journals in Education* or CIJE and *Resources in Education* or RIE), **PsycINFO** (which includes the entries for *Psychological Abstracts*), and **SocINDEX** (which includes the entries for *Sociological Abstracts*). If you are interested in leadership/management/supervision issues, you should also search a business database (e.g., **Business Source Premier**). Most universities give students access to many databases through use of an Internet connection. Check your

- **Educational Resources Information Center (ERIC)** A database containing information from *Current Index to Journals in Education* (CIJE) and *Resources in Education* (RIE)
- **PsycINFO** A database containing entries from *Psychological Abstracts*
- **SocINDEX** A database containing entries from *Sociological Abstracts*
- **Business Source Premier** A database containing entries from all areas of business

■ **Internet** A network-of-networks consisting of millions of computers and millions of users all over the world, interconnected to promote communication

library's home page or ask your reference librarian to tell you which databases your library subscribes to. Become familiar with your library's home page and the numerous information sources that are available to you through the library.

The Internet

Much information is available on the **Internet**, including some databases (e.g., see Google Scholar). We know that you already know how to use the Internet; therefore, we simply suggest that you are careful and be sure to judge the quality of what you find on the Internet. See Table 4.2 for some specific guidelines for judging what you find on the Internet.

REVIEW QUESTIONS

4.4 What is the purpose of conducting a review of the literature in a quantitative study?

4.5 What is the purpose of conducting a review of the literature in a qualitative study?

4.6 What information sources would you use in conducting a literature review, and what are the advantages of each source?

4.7 Why do you think it is important for educational researchers to search multiple databases?

4.8 How would you evaluate the validity of information obtained over the Internet?

Feasibility of the Study

After you have completed your literature review, you are ready to synthesize this wealth of material and not only identify the research problems within your chosen topic area but also formulate the specific research questions and research hypotheses to be investigated. As you develop your research questions and hypotheses, you must decide whether the study you want to conduct is feasible. Every research study that is conducted varies with respect to the amount of time required to gather the data, the type of research participants needed, expense, the expertise of the researcher, and ethical sensitivity. Studies that are too time-consuming, require skills you do not have, or are too expensive should not be initiated.

Statement of the Research Problem

After you have completed the literature review and have read and digested the literature, you should have a good idea of the problems in your topic area. Note that there is a difference between a research topic area and a research problem. A research topic is the broad area in which you are interested, such as distance education, mainstreaming, or self-esteem. A **research problem** is an education issue or problem within the broad topic area that you believe is important. For example, within the topic area of distance learning, there might be issues or problems relating to a lack of student interest or the accuracy of assessment of performance. However, the way in which the research problem is specified will differ depending on whether you are conducting a quantitative or a qualitative study.

■ **Research problem** An education issue or problem within a broad topic area

TABLE 4.2 How to Judge the Quality of Internet Resources

The main problem with the public Internet is determining the validity of the information provided because anyone can establish a website. The following criteria can help you differentiate good information from bad.

1. *Authority:* Authority exists if the web page lists the author and his or her credentials and the address has a preferred domain such as *.edu*, *.org*, or *.gov*. Therefore, to assess the site's authority, you should do the following:
   a. Find the source of the document. A URL ending with *.edu* is from an institution of higher education, with *.gov* is from a branch of the US federal government, with *.org* is from a nonprofit organization such as the American Psychological Association, with *.com* is from a commercial vendor, and with *.net* is from anyone who can afford to pay for space on a server.
   b. Identify the qualifications of the publisher of the web document. You can get some of this information from the website itself by reading the "about us," "mission," or "who we are" sections.
2. *Accuracy:* Accuracy is highest when the website lists the author of the content and the institution that publishes the page and provides a way of contacting the author. To assess accuracy, you should do the following:
   a. Look at the credentials of the person who wrote the website and check for a link or an email address that will permit you to contact this person.
   b. Identify the purpose of the information. Is it a public service announcement, advertisement, sales pitch, news release, or a published research study? The purpose may suggest that a certain bias exists in the information.
   c. Determine whether there is an acknowledgment of the limitations of the information, particularly if the information is the report of some study.
3. *Objectivity:* Objectivity is highest when the website has little or no advertising and provides accurate and objective information. Therefore, you should do the following:
   a. Identify any evidence of bias in the information presented.
      i. Is the information traceable to factual information presented in some bibliographic or Internet reference? Such information may be less biased.
      ii. Do the authors express their own opinions? Authors' opinions suggest bias.
4. *Currency:* Currency exists when the website and any links it provides are updated regularly. Determine the following information:
   a. When the website was created.
   b. When the website was updated and how up-to-date the links (if any) are.
5. *Coverage:* Coverage is good when you can view the information on the website without paying fees or installing additional software.

Stating a Quantitative Research Problem

In stating a quantitative research problem, the emphasis is on the need to explain, predict, or statistically describe some outcome or event. Look at this first paragraph of a quantitative study conducted by DeLaPaz (2001, p. 37):

> Difficulties with written language production have been well documented among students with learning disabilities (LD). Those students typically lack important knowledge of the writing process and demonstrate limited abilities to generate plans, organize text, or engage in substantive revision (Englert & Raphael, 1998; McCutchen, 1998; Thomas, Englert, & Gregg, 1987). Problems with mechanics, including spelling, capitalization, and punctuation, further interfere with composing. Consequently, the writing of students with LD is less polished, expansive, coherent, and effective than that of their peers (Englert & Raphael, 1998; Graham, 1990; Graham & Harris, 1989; Montague, Graves, & Leavelle, 1991; Newcomer & Barenbaum, 1991; Wong, Wong, & Blenkinsop, 1989).

DeLaPaz introduced the general topic area in the first sentence as "difficulties with written language production." She then identified the population in which this was a problem: students with learning disabilities. She continued by identifying the problems these students have, such as their limited ability to generate plans, organize text, and revise material. All of these are legitimate research problems because they represent educational issues that need a solution. Quantitative studies could be conducted to attempt to explain why the problems exist as well as how to ameliorate them.

Stating a Qualitative Research Problem

In a qualitative study, the research problem focuses on understanding the inner world of a particular group or exploring some process, event, or phenomenon. This is illustrated in Otieno's (2001, p. 3) introduction to her qualitative study of the educational experiences of seven African women:

> According to the late Dr. Kwegyir Aggrey of Ghana, educate a man and you have educated an individual, educate a woman and you have educated a nation. More than half of the population of Africa is made up of women. While this statement is true, female education in Africa has not developed at the same pace as that of males. There are many recent studies that examine problems African women encounter while attempting to pursue higher education (Yeboah, 1997, 2000; Namuddu, 1992; Lindasy, 1980; Bappa, 1985; and Eshwani, 1983). Most African countries have identified education as a key element in economic development. The linkage between female education and development in general cannot be overemphasized. Moreover, research has found that female education is highly correlated with better use of family planning, low fertility rates, and low infant mortality (Yehoah, 1997, 2000). The recognition by educators in the international community of the fact that female education is essential to national and global development is perhaps one reason why the education of women and girls is now a popular topic for many researchers. Returns on education are significant both for the individual and for society. Education is a particularly powerful achievement for women as it opens up the potential for wider participation in the economy. This increased awareness has raised questions as to what problems the female population face, what factors hold them back, and how these factors can be overcome to enable the majority of women to obtain higher education. It is through full inclusion in the process of obtaining higher education that women can participate fully in the process of the continent's development.

In this example, Otieno (2001) opened with a statement about the value of education, particularly for women, which is the general topic area of the study. She then pointed out the primary research problem: African women are less likely to receive an education than men are. She continued by pointing out that when women receive an education, many positive effects occur for both the individual and society, thus emphasizing the importance of studying this research problem. Otieno noted that awareness of the positive effects that result from an educated female population had raised questions regarding the problems these individuals face in getting a higher education. What holds them back from attaining a higher education, and how can these difficulties be overcome? She then stated that women can participate in the continent's development only by exploring the complete process by which women obtain a higher education.

Otieno proceeded to conduct a study to understand these women and explore this educational and cultural process.

Stating a Mixed Research Problem

In stating a mixed research problem, the emphasis is often on a combination of understanding insider's perspectives or exploration of some process (that's the qualitative part) *and* explanation, prediction, and statistical description (that's the quantitative part). In other words, the problem (of what is missing from the literature) is slightly larger in mixed methods research, and it often includes parts from quantitative and qualitative research problems. This should not be surprising because it makes a lot of sense to examine the world through the lenses of both quantitative and qualitative research in a research study.

A mixed research problem is illustrated below from an article titled "Understanding Black Make Student Athletes' Experiences at a Historically Black College/University: A Mixed Methods Approach" by Cooper and Hall (2016):

> A long-standing problem facing the NCAA and its member institutions has been the persistent academic underperformance of Black male student athletes (NCAA, 2013a, 2013b). The preponderance of scholarly research on this subgroup of student athletes has primarily applied positivistic approaches to measure and explain their academic achievement/cognitive outcomes (Sedlacek & Adams-Gaston, 1992; Sellers, 1992) and quality of overall college experiences (Eiche, Sedlacek, & Adams-Gaston, 1997; Gaston-Gayles, 2004; Potuto & O'Hanlon, 2006; Sellers, Kuperminc, & Waddell, 1991). Collectively, these studies revealed Black male student athletes encountered unique challenges related to their lack of academic preparation prior to college and differential treatment on campus based on their various identities (race/ethnicity, gender, sociocultural background, and athletic status). Despite identifying these alarming issues across different institutional settings, the aforementioned studies did not focus on the significant influence of contextual factors (e.g., institutional cultures) and socialization experiences (e.g., nature of faculty–student interactions, peer relationships, etc.). Therefore, a research approach that examines both the institutional context and subsequent experiences of Black male student athletes could provide vital insight into this phenomenon. In concert with this effort, a mixed methods approach was incorporated in this study.

In the above example, the state of the current literature is stated, noting that it is heavily quantitative in orientation with a lack of qualitative research. It also is noted that the current literature has neglected the importance of social/cultural context in understanding students' experiences. Qualitative research is especially helpful in providing contextual understanding. Therefore, the authors believed that a mixed research study, that gathered quantitative and qualitative data, was called for and justified.

Statement of the Purpose of the Study

The statement of the **purpose of a research study** expresses the researcher's intent or the study's objective. It might be the most important sentence in the proposal or research report. This statement follows logically from the identification of the research problem.

- **Purpose of a research study** The researcher's intent or objective of the study

Explicitly stating the purpose ensures that you have a good grasp of the specific problem you wish to investigate. A specific statement of the purpose of the study also enables you to communicate your research project clearly to others. Readers always appreciate a clearly stated purpose. Providing a specification of the study purpose at the outset of a study also has the advantage of guiding the research process by, for example, indicating how and by what methods the data will be collected. However, the nature of this statement will differ somewhat depending on whether you are conducting a qualitative or quantitative study. If the purpose statement appears in a proposal, it is written in present tense ("The purpose of the proposed study is to . . . "); if it appears in the final research report, it is written in past tense ("The purpose of the research was . . . ").

Statement of Purpose in a Quantitative Study

The purpose statement in a quantitative study is a declarative statement that identifies the type of relationship investigated between a set of variables. This relationship could be causal or descriptive. For example, if you wanted to investigate the causal connection that might exist between a treatment for a learning disability and spelling proficiency, your purpose statement could be written as follows:

> The purpose of this study is to investigate the effect that the learning disability treatment used in this study has on the spelling proficiency of children with a learning disability.

However, if the intent of your study is to describe the relationship between spelling proficiency and the extent of a person's learning disability, your purpose statement could be written as follows:

> The purpose of this study is to describe the direction and degree of relationship that might exist between spelling proficiency and the severity of a person's learning disability.

Both of these statements of purpose identify the intent of the study and the variables being investigated. The difference is that one study attempts to determine whether treatment for learning disability causes changes in academic achievement, whereas the other attempts only to describe the relationship that might exist between the two variables. These two illustrate the basic and essential characteristics that should exist in a statement of purpose: Both identify the variables being investigated and the intent of the study or way in which the variables will be investigated.

Statement of Purpose in a Qualitative Study

The statement of purpose in a qualitative study usually indicates that the study intent is to explore or understand some phenomenon experienced by individuals or a group at a specific place. This means that a qualitative study's statement of purpose should do the following:

- Convey a sense of an emerging design by stating that the purpose of the study is to describe, understand, develop, or discover something.
- State and define the central idea that you want to describe, understand, or discover.

- State the method by which you plan to collect and analyze the data by specifying whether you are conducting an ethnographic study, grounded theory study, case study, narrative, or phenomenological study.
- State the unit of analysis and/or the research site (e.g., fourth-grade students participating in a specific program in a particular school).

For example, N. Drew (1986) stated the following purpose of her study as follows:

> The focus of the present study was to explore distressing and nurturing encounters of patients with caregivers and to ascertain the meanings that are engendered by such encounters. The study was conducted on one of the surgical units and the obstetrical/gynecological unit of a 374-bed community hospital. (p. 40)

This purpose statement contains several of the essential ingredients characterizing a qualitative study. It conveys the sense of an emerging design and defines the central idea by stating that the researcher intended to "explore distressing and nurturing encounters." It also states that the research site will be a specific unit in a community hospital. Although this statement of purpose does not explicitly state the method used to collect and analyze the data, it does contain most of the elements of a statement of purpose for a qualitative study. This example also demonstrates that not every statement of purpose will contain all the fundamental characteristics of a good, qualitative purpose statement. However, good purpose statements will contain most of these characteristics.

Statement of Purpose in a Mixed Methods Study

Oftentimes, a mixed methods purpose statement will include a combination of elements found in quantitative and qualitative purpose statements. The purpose statement will suggest that the researchers want to obtain both quantitative and qualitative perspectives about the research phenomenon. For example, the purpose might be to survey a large group of people to understand the overall phenomenon, and follow this with in-depth interviews of a subset of the original sample to provide deeper insight into subjective and process-focused factors.

There are many possible purposes of mixed research. Here are some possibilities:

- To juxtapose and contrast quantitative and qualitative views of the research object.
- To produce a more comprehensive understanding than provided in a monomethod study.
- To add contextualized understanding to quantitative findings.
- To provide evidence of both descriptive and explanatory/process causation.
- To obtain deeper and more complex understanding of statistical findings.
- To show how a general theory can be made practical, that is, used in particular places and settings.
- To obtain multiple perspectives about the research phenomenon.
- To provide categories and constructs to be tested in the quantitative research phase.
- To show what works for whom, where, in what circumstances, in what respects, and how.
- To conduct a research study that overcomes the weaknesses of both quantitative and qualitative research through careful and strategic combination of quantitative and qualitative methods, methodologies, and paradigms.

The following is an example of a mixed methods purpose statement from an article titled "Profiles of Urban, Low SES, African American Girls' Attitudes Toward Science: A Sequential Explanatory Mixed Methods Study" (Buck, Cook, Quigley, Eastwood, & Lucas, 2009):

> The overall efforts of our collaborative action research group were guided by the identification and monitoring of the girls' engagement in science and how this engagement influences and was influenced by science teaching and learning. The purpose of this initial study was to explore the attitudes toward science of urban African American girls from low SES communities using a mixed methods sequential explanatory design. In the first phase, quantitative questions addressed what profiles emerged from the scores of 89 African American girls on the mATSI. Information from this first phase was explored further in a second [qualitative] phase. In this phase, interviews were used to probe significant themes by exploring aspects of the profiles with 30 of the girls at the academy. The reason for following up with qualitative research in the second phase was to better understand and explain the reasons for the differences in profiles. (pp. 390–391)

STATEMENT OF RESEARCH QUESTIONS

- **Research question** Statement of the specific question the researcher seeks to answer via empirical research

A **research question** is a statement of the specific question(s) the researcher seeks to answer using empirical research. Although research questions are found in both quantitative and qualitative studies, they differ somewhat in their structure. Quantitative research questions ask about the relationship being investigated between the target variables. Qualitative research questions are not as specific. Instead, qualitative research questions are more likely to ask a general question about a process or express the intent to explore or understand the participants' meanings of a particular phenomenon.

Statement of a Quantitative Research Question

- **Quantitative research question** A question about the relationship that exists between two or more variables

A **quantitative research question** asks about the relationship that might exist between two or more variables. Common forms are descriptive, predictive, and causal research questions, as illustrated in Table 4.3. Regardless of the type of research question, you should formulate it in very specific terms to ensure that you have a good understanding of the variables you are investigating. Doing so also aids in the design and conduct of your research study. To drive these points home, consider the difficulties you would encounter if you asked, "What is the effect of participation in extracurricular activities on academic performance?" This seems to ask an important question. However, it is worded so vaguely that it is difficult to pinpoint what is being investigated. What type of extracurricular activity and what type of academic performance? There are many types of extracurricular activity, and it would be inappropriate to assume that all types have similar effects. Similarly, academic performance could refer to overall average performance or to performance in specific subject areas.

Now contrast that question with the following:

> What effect does playing football have on students' overall grade point average during football season?

This question specifies exactly the variables that are to be investigated: the extracurricular activity of playing football and academic performance as measured by overall grade point average.

As you can see from this example, making a specific statement of the research question helps ensure that you understand the problem you are investigating. It also helps you to make decisions about such factors as who the research participants will be and what materials or measures you will need to conduct the study. A vaguely stated research question gives no such assistance. Remember that the purpose of formulating a specific research question is to ensure that you and your readers have a good grasp of the variables being investigated and to assist you in designing and completing your research study.

Statement of a Qualitative Research Question

A **qualitative research question** is question about some process, issue, or phenomenon that is to be explored. It is usually a general, open-ended, and overarching question that you would like to answer. From this overarching research question, you can frequently narrow the purpose of a qualitative study to more specific questions. It can be helpful to state the general

■ **Qualitative research question** A question about some process, issue, or phenomenon to be explored

TABLE 4.3 Scripts for Writing Quantitative Research Questions

Descriptive Questions

Descriptive research questions seek answers to such questions as "How much?" "How often?" or "What changes over time or over different situations?" The script for a descriptive research question would be as follows:

- (Description dimension) do(es) (participants) (variable stated in verb form) at (research site)?

This script could lead to the following descriptive question:

- How frequently do kindergarten children engage in aggressive acts on the playground?

Descriptive questions can seek to identify the degree of relationship that exists between two or more variables. The script for a descriptive relationship question would be as follows:

- What is the relationship between (variable 1) and (variable 2) for (participants)?

This script could lead to the following relationship question:

- What is the relationship between amount of time studied and grades for high school students?

Predictive Questions

Predictive questions ask whether one or more variables can be used to predict some future outcome. The script for a predictive question would be as follows:

- Does (predictor variable) predict (outcome variable) in (setting)?

This script could lead to the following predictive question:

- Does parental educational level predict students' propensity to drop out of high school?

Causal Questions

Causal questions compare different variations of some phenomenon to identify the cause of something. They usually involve the manipulation of an independent variable and the comparison of the outcome of this manipulation to no manipulation. The script for causal questions would be as follows:

- Does variation (or change) in (independent variable) produce changes (or an increase or decrease) in (a dependent variable)?

This script could lead to the following causal question:

- Does variation in amount of homework assigned produce a change in students' test performance?

purpose of the study and then state a number of subquestions that break the overall research question into components that will be investigated. For example, Bodycott, Walker, and Kin (2001) investigated the beliefs that preservice teachers held about their principals. Their statement of purpose was as follows:

> The purpose of this study was to explore how the social context of schools and schooling influenced preservice teachers' personal constructs of the principal. (p. 15)

The research question that followed from this purpose statement is this:

> How does the social context of a school influence preservice teachers' beliefs about the principal?

The overall research question, as you can see, is very similar to the statement of purpose and tends to restate the purpose statement in question form. Because the overarching research question is, to a great extent, a restatement of the purpose of the study, many researchers omit it. However, a number of subquestions or more specific questions are often asked. For example, Bodycott et al. (2001) implied the following two more specific subquestions:

1. What are preservice teachers' beliefs about principals?
2. What or who influenced these beliefs?

Statement of Research Questions in Mixed Research

There are three perspectives about mixed methods research questions. Perspectives two and three are the most common in mixed methods research. The first perspective states that one method is always primary in a mixed methods study and, therefore, one should have a set of primary and supplemental or secondary questions (Morgan, 2014; Morse & Niehaus, 2009). For example, if the study is largely a quantitative study with a supplemental qualitative component added, then the primary question will sound like a quantitative research question and the supplemental question(s) will sound like a qualitative research question. For example, a quantitative survey might be conducted and supplemented with a few open-ended questions. The core (quantitative) research question might be "What variables predict and explain undergraduate student success in introductory psychology courses?" The supplemental (qualitative) research question might be "What factors do students believe cause their success or lack of success in introductory psychology?"

According to the second perspective (Yin, 2006), the lenses of both qualitative and quantitative research can be used for virtually all research questions. The idea is that mixed research can almost always add something useful (i.e., provide an "added value") to answering each research question. In short, you should examine your question "both ways." You are advised to look at your "research object" quantitatively and quantitatively. For example, your research question might be "How do structure and agency affect decisions made by young people aged 18 to 25 years old?" Wooley (2009) answered this question using documents, a questionnaire, focus groups, and individual interviews. Wooley contended that

"Quantitative and qualitative methods provide differing perspectives on a subject and this is why the use of both may be viewed as complementary" (p. 8). Another example of a question that could be examined both quantitatively and qualitatively is "What kinds of online interactions occur in successful and unsuccessful online courses?"

According to the third perspective, a researcher should use separate quantitative and qualitative research questions, considered equally important, with both sets of questions addressing some aspect of the overall research topic (Creswell & Plano Clark, 2011). Then one can integrate the answers to the questions during data analysis and results interpretation. Here is an example from "A Mixed Methods Examination of the Influence of Dimensions of Support on Training Transfer" (Schindler & Burkholder, 2014):

Quantitative Research Questions in a Mixed Study

1. Is there a relationship between the dimensions of support (mentoring, coaching, social support, and task support) and training transfer?
2. Does transfer motivation mediate the relationship between the dimensions of support (mentoring, coaching, social support, and task support) and training transfer?

Qualitative Research Questions in a Mixed Study

1. How do participants experience specific dimensions of support (mentoring, coaching, task support, and social support), exhibited by their mentors, as they attempt to transfer learned knowledge and skills?
2. How do participants' experiences of specific dimensions of support (mentoring, coaching, task support, and social support) influence their motivation to transfer learned knowledge and skills and their attempts to transfer learned knowledge and skills?

Formulating Hypotheses

In quantitative research, after you have identified a research problem that you want to investigate and you have stated your research purpose and your research question(s), you are ready to formulate your hypotheses if you have predictions/expectations. Doing this leads to hypothesis- or theory-testing research. The research **hypothesis** is the formal statement of the researcher's prediction of the specific relationship that exists among the variables under investigation. For example, Butler and Neuman (1995) hypothesized or predicted the following:

- **Hypothesis** A prediction or educated guess; the formal statement of the researcher's prediction of the relationship that exists among the variables under investigation

Children in ego-involving settings will be less likely to request help than children in task-involving settings.

Note that this hypothesis includes two variables—help-seeking behaviors (the dependent variable) and type of setting (the independent variable)—and makes a prediction about how help-seeking behaviors will differ depending on the type of setting the children are in. You can use the following script for stating a research hypothesis:

(Group 1 participants) will (differ in some way—increase, decrease, improve) on (dependent variable) from (group 2 participants). (Note: Groups 1 and 2 are the levels of the independent variable.)

The hypothesis for the Butler and Newman study used this script in the following way:

Group 1 of independent variable = children in ego-involving settings.

Differ = be less likely.

Dependent variable = request help.

Group 2 of independent variable = children in task-involving settings.

Another example using this script might be as follows:

Children with learning disabilities who receive individualized instruction will show greater gains in academic achievement than children with learning disabilities who receive group instruction.

The stated hypothesis typically emerges from the literature review or from theory. As we stated earlier, one of the functions of theory is to guide research. One of the ways in which a theory accomplishes this function is to predict a relationship between variables. Similarly, the research literature might suggest that a relationship exists between the variables being investigated. However, hypotheses can also come from reasoning based on your observations of events. For example, you might have noticed that some children get very nervous when they take a test and that these children seem to get the poorest grades. From this observation, you might formulate the hypothesis that performance decreases as test anxiety increases.

Regardless of the source of your hypothesis, it must meet one criterion: *A hypothesis must be capable of being confirmed or not confirmed.* That is, the hypothesis must be about something for which one set of possible outcomes can be viewed as supporting the hypothesis and the other set of possible outcomes will be viewed as not supporting the hypothesis. A hypothesis that fails to meet this criterion is not *testable* and removes the hypothesis from the realm of empirical research. It is of no use to conduct empirical research if you plan to claim support for your hypothesis regardless of the outcome!

Hypotheses are important primarily in quantitative studies because their goal and purpose differ from those of qualitative research studies. Quantitative research has the goal of identifying the relationships that exist between sets of variables, whereas qualitative research attempts to discover, explore, or describe a given setting, event, situation, or set of meanings. In quantitative research, we usually conduct the study to determine whether the relation that we predict among the variables exists. This process is known as *hypothesis testing* (or theory testing). In a qualitative study, researchers are interested in describing and exploring phenomena, generating ideas, understanding participants' subjective perspectives, and obtaining particularistic findings about particular people and groups. This exploration is accomplished by asking very general, open-ended questions that permit a lot of latitude in participants' responses.

4.9 How does one determine whether it is possible to conduct a study?

4.10 How do research problems in qualitative and quantitative research differ?

4.11 How does the statement of the purpose of a study differ in qualitative and quantitative research?

4.12 How do research questions differ in qualitative and quantitative research?

4.13 Why should research questions in quantitative research be very specific?

4.14 What is a hypothesis, and what is the criterion that it must meet?

4.15 Why are hypotheses typically not formulated in qualitative research, and what is typically used instead?

Consumer Use of the Literature

See Journal Article 4.2 on the Student Study Site.

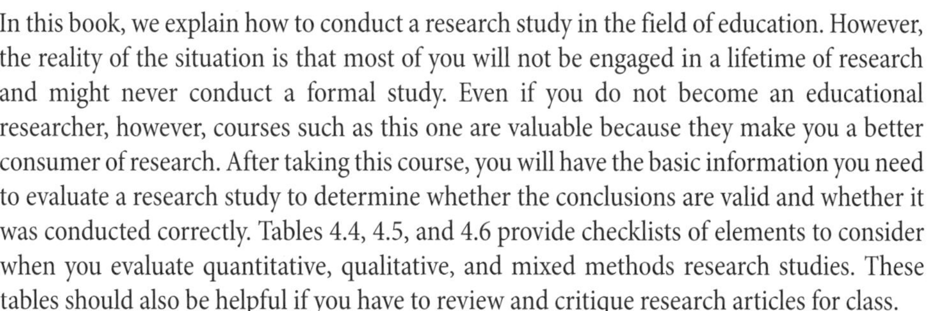

In this book, we explain how to conduct a research study in the field of education. However, the reality of the situation is that most of you will not be engaged in a lifetime of research and might never conduct a formal study. Even if you do not become an educational researcher, however, courses such as this one are valuable because they make you a better consumer of research. After taking this course, you will have the basic information you need to evaluate a research study to determine whether the conclusions are valid and whether it was conducted correctly. Tables 4.4, 4.5, and 4.6 provide checklists of elements to consider when you evaluate quantitative, qualitative, and mixed methods research studies. These tables should also be helpful if you have to review and critique research articles for class.

To be an effective consumer of research, you should not consider the results of any one study to be conclusive. You need to look across multiple studies to see whether the findings are repeatedly confirmed. For example, assume that you read a study demonstrating that computer-assisted instruction resulted in better performance than did instruction that did not have the aid of computers. Does this mean that you can conclude that computer-assisted instruction is always the superior mode of instruction? Of course not! One study does not produce a conclusive finding on which you can rely. For a conclusion to be reliable, the results must be replicated by other researchers on other populations in other locations because the phenomena that educational researchers investigate are too complex to be explained by a single study. Therefore, many studies are conducted on a given phenomenon, and each study is conducted in a slightly different way on a slightly different participant sample. The results will vary slightly from study to study, and you must somehow integrate them and relate them to your particular situation.

The technique that is used for summarizing the results of multiple quantitative studies of a given phenomenon is called meta-analysis. **Meta-analysis** is a term introduced by Glass (1976) to describe a quantitative approach that is used to integrate and describe the results of a large number of quantitative studies. Meta-analysis gets around the problem of making subjective judgments and preferences in summarizing the quantitative research literature because it uses a variety of quantitative techniques to analyze the results of studies conducted on a given topic (e.g., it provides the average size-of-effect of an independent variable across a large number of studies). Therefore, when you are conducting your literature review

- **Meta-analysis** A quantitative technique that is used to integrate and describe the results of a large number of studies

TABLE 4.4 Checklist for Evaluating a Quantitative Study

The following checklist can be used to help in evaluating the quality of a quantitative research study, although some of the questions apply only to experimental studies. If you are evaluating a nonexperimental study, you should disregard questions that focus on experimental studies.

Introduction

1. Is the research topic clearly stated in the first paragraph?
2. Is (are) the research problem(s) clearly stated?
3. Does the literature review accurately summarize the most important past research?
4. Does the literature review lead to the research purpose and/or research question(s)?
5. Is the purpose of the research clearly stated?
6. Are the research questions clearly stated?
7. Is each research hypothesis clearly stated, and does each state the expected relationship between the independent and dependent variables?
8. Is the theory from which the hypotheses came explained?

Method

9. Are the demographics of the participants accurately described, and are they appropriate to this study?
10. Was an appropriate method of sampling used, given the purpose of the study?
11. Were enough participants included in the study?
12. Are the research instruments reliable and valid for the participants used in the study?
13. For experimental research, did manipulation of the independent variable adequately represent the causal construct of interest? For experimental research, were the participants randomly assigned to conditions?
14. Are there elements in the procedure that might have biased the results?
15. Did the researchers take appropriate actions to control for extraneous variables?
16. Were the participants treated ethically?

Results

17. Were appropriate statistical tests and calculations of effect sizes used to analyze the data?
18. Are the results presented clearly?
19. Was any part of the data ignored, such as some participants being dropped?
20. Can the results be generalized to the populations and settings the researcher desires?

Discussion

21. Do the researchers clearly explain the meaning and significance of the results of the study?
22. Are the findings discussed in relation to the theoretical framework with which they began?
23. Are alternative explanations for the study results and conclusions examined?
24. Do the results conflict with prior research? If they do, has an explanation been provided for the conflicting data?
25. Are limitations of the study discussed?
26. Are future directions for research suggested?

and trying to reach some conclusion about a given phenomenon, pay particular attention to literature summaries that have made use of meta-analysis because these summaries provide more accurate conclusions.

To illustrate the use of meta-analysis, let us look at the meta-analysis conducted by Forness and Kavale (1996) on studies that investigated the efficacy of a social skills training program for children with learning disabilities. Fifty-three studies were identified from abstract and citation archives, reference lists from prior literature reviews, and bibliographies of research reports. Forness and Kavale applied standard meta-analytic statistical procedures to the results of these 53 studies to provide an overall integration and description of the findings. This analysis revealed that the social skills training

TABLE 4.5 Checklist for Evaluating a Qualitative Study

The following checklist can be used to help in evaluating the quality of a qualitative research study.

Introduction

1. Is the research topic specified at the outset of the article?
2. Is a research problem or important issue clearly identified?
3. Is there a sufficient review of the relevant research literature?
4. Is the purpose of the research clearly stated?
5. Are research questions identified and stated clearly?

Method

6. Are the characteristics of the participants, the research site, and the context accurately described?
7. Are the participants appropriate for the purpose of the study?
8. Is the number of participants large enough?
9. Was the amount of time spent with the participants sufficient?
10. Were adequate data collected to address the research question(s)?
11. Were triangulation and other validity-enhancing strategies used to help produce trustworthy evidence?
12. Were the participants treated ethically?

Results

13. Are the findings presented clearly and supported with evidence (e.g., quotes, content analysis)?
14. Were any potentially important data ignored by the researcher(s)?
15. Do the results provide a deep understanding of the inner views and meanings of the people studied?

Discussion

16. Is sufficient evidence provided to convince you of the trustworthiness of the conclusions?
17. Does the researcher fit the findings into the published literature?
18. Are limitations of the study discussed?
19. Did the researcher examine alternative explanations for the findings?
20. Are suggestions for future research provided?

TABLE 4.6 Checklist for Evaluating a Mixed Methods Research Study

The following checklist can be used to evaluate the quality of a mixed research study.

Introduction

1. Is the research topic specified at the outset of the article?
2. Is (are) the research problem(s) clearly stated?
3. Is there sufficient and integrated review of the relevant quantitative, qualitative, and mixed research literatures?
4. Is a mixed research purpose clearly stated?
5. Is it clear what the research question(s) is (are)?
6. Is it clear *why* a combination of quantitative and qualitative approaches was the best way to address the research topic or questions?

Method

7. Were the characteristics of the participants, the research sites, and the context carefully described?
8. Were appropriate participants used in the study?
9. Is the mixed research design clearly explained?
10. Were qualitative and quantitative data collected that allowed the researchers to address their research question(s) effectively?
11. Was a logical basis of mixed research (such as the fundamental principle of mixed research) used to design the study?
12. Were validity-enhancing strategies (such as those explained in Chapter 11) used for each part of the study?
13. If part of the study was a mixed methods experiment, was random assignment used and were the quantitative data supplemented with additional qualitative data?
14. If part of the study was a survey or if the goal was to generalize directly to a population, was a random sample used for the quantitative component?
15. Did the researchers have adequate strategies for understanding the participants' perspectives or the inside view of the group being studied?
16. Were the participants treated ethically?

Results

17. Were appropriate techniques of data analysis used for the qualitative, quantitative, and mixed analyses?
18. Were any potentially important data ignored by the researcher(s)?
19. Were the data merged, connected, or linked to show integration?
20. Was enough evidence provided to convince you of the validity, trustworthiness, and legitimacy of the findings?

Discussion

21. Do the researchers adequately integrate the results and explain what the results mean?
22. Do the researchers make clear the added value gained through the use of mixed research?
23. Did the researchers fit the results into the broader research literature?
24. Are limitations of the research offered?
25. Are future directions for research provided?

programs that were applied to children with learning deficits had a small but positive effect. This is the primary conclusion that you should retain from the currently available literature. If you looked at individual studies, you might find some that indicated that social skills training programs were totally ineffective and others that indicated that they were very effective. Without the benefit of a meta-analysis, you might be influenced more by one or several of these studies and reach an inappropriate conclusion. Meta-analysis eliminates this problem and provides an overall synopsis of the available quantitative literature. More advanced meta-analysis studies can also determine whether a finding varies according to the levels of a "moderator" variable; for example, perhaps the studies have different results because of different contexts. Meta-analysis is, thus, becoming more and more sophisticated.

In qualitative research, a study that attempts to summarize the findings of multiple qualitative studies is called a **meta-synthesis**, and some approximate synonyms are meta-study, meta-ethnography, grounded formal theory, and aggregated analysis (Onwuegbuzie & Frels, 2016). Here is a formal definition of meta-synthesis (from Zimmer, 2006):

■ **Meta-synthesis** The systematic review or integration of qualitative research findings into a literature summary article (i.e., a meta-synthesis is the qualitative version of a meta-analysis)

> a form of systematic review or integration of qualitative research findings in a target domain that are themselves interpretive syntheses of data, including phenomenologies, ethnographies, grounded theories, and other integrated and coherent descriptions or explanations of phenomena, events, or cases. (p. 227)

Because qualitative research is useful for showing both similarity and complex differences, a meta-synthesis will likely include some of both of these. Here is an example of a meta-synthesis from Pielstick (1998; also cited in Onwuegbuzie & Frels, 2016) that focused on what had been learned about transformational leadership over the past 20 years:

> The research findings clustered into seven major themes: (1) creating a shared vision, (2) communicating the vision, (3) building relationships, (4) developing a supporting organizational culture, (5) guiding implementation, (6) exhibiting character, and (7) achieving results. These have been reframed into the following model. A shared vision of the future is supported by the four pillars of leading: communicating regularly with followers, building a web of relationships with and among followers, creating a sense of community based on shared values and beliefs, and guiding achievement of the vision through empowerment and other actions. The pillars rest on a solid foundation of exceptional character. (pp. 20–31)

Mixed methods research uses both meta-analytic and meta-synthesis logics to produce comprehensive summaries of the research literature. These literature reviews include sections on quantitative and qualitative findings, which are then combined, with the goal of producing an integrated review of the literature. For more detail on mixed methods literature reviews, which is a cutting-edge technique, we recommend a recent book by Tony Onwuegbuzie and Rebecca Frels (2016) titled "7 Steps to a Comprehensive Literature Review."

See Journal Article 4.3 on the Student Study Site.

ACTION RESEARCH REFLECTION

Insight: Action researchers rely on multiple sources of information, listening to and learning from any source that might be helpful in improving their local situation.

1. As an action researcher (i.e., you are attempting to make something work better in your school or workplace), how can you get started; that is, where can you find information about an issue that interests you?
2. Think about a topic that interests you. Identify experts or knowledgeable people who might understand your workplace and talk to them about your issue, problems related to it, and possible solutions.
3. Connect to your library's website and access several databases covering multiple related disciplines (e.g., education, psychology, management, and sociology). Then, in the search box, enter your topic or terms related to your expected research problem. Try different search terms until you find what you are looking for. Read 15 or 20 journal article abstracts. If you are conducting a regular scientific research study, you would need to answer this question: What did the abstracts not address that you want to know? Your answer will probably be your *research question* or at least your *research problem*, which will lead to new knowledge that can be contributed to the research literature. If you are conducting an action research study, you will focus more on these questions: What is your local problem, and what solution do you think might be effective in your place of work? You can learn a lot from your literature review by answering this question: What practice has research shown to be effective elsewhere that I believe will be effective at my workplace?

SUMMARY

The first step in conducting a research study is to identify a research topic and then identify a research problem in need of a solution. Although the beginning researcher might have difficulty identifying a research problem, the field of education has numerous problems that are in need of solutions. To identify a research problem, you need to develop an inquisitive attitude and ask questions. Once you develop this mind-set, problem identification is relatively easy. Use of the research literature is especially helpful for identifying researchable problems.

Educational research problems arise from several traditional sources, such as theories, practical issues, and past research. Additionally, in education, we have our own experience to draw on, because we all have some experience with the field of education. Note that many problems dealing with moral, ethical, and religious issues cannot be resolved through empirical research.

Once a potential research problem has been identified, you must conduct a *comprehensive* literature search. This will reveal the state of knowledge about your topic, suggest specific ways that you can investigate the problem, and point out methodological issues. If you are conducting a *qualitative* research study rather than a quantitative study, you might want to familiarize yourself with the literature only sufficiently to make sure that the study you want to conduct has not been done. This approach assumes that the lack of knowledge of prior literature enables the researcher to take a fresh and uncontaminated perspective and develop a novel set of constructs, relationships, and theory from the data.

The most efficient means for conducting a literature review is to use one of the information retrieval systems available through your library, such as EBSCO, which has access to databases that have information relevant to educational research (e.g., ERIC, PsycINFO, and SocINDEX). Additionally, a wealth of information is available on the public Internet; we provided a set of guidelines that need to be followed for evaluating such information and separating the useful from the useless information. After you have conducted the literature review, have a preliminary research problem, and know the kind of study you want to conduct, you must determine whether the study you want to conduct is *feasible*. This means that you must assess the amount of time, research participant population, expertise, and expense requirements, as well as the ethical sensitivity, of the potential study. If this analysis indicates that a study will be feasible, then it's time to formally state your research problem(s). A quantitative research problem points to the need to explain, describe, or predict some variable(s). A qualitative research problem indicates the need to explore an important issue or group.

After formally stating your research problem(s), state the *purpose* of your study. In a qualitative study, the purpose statement should express the language, purpose, and methodology of the qualitative paradigm. In a quantitative study, the purpose statement should identify the intent of the study and the type of relationship (causal, descriptive, predictive) to be studied. A mixed purpose includes aspects from both qualitative and quantitative approaches. A statement of the *research question(s)* should follow the purpose statement. In some studies (especially qualitative), the purpose statement is followed by a series of subquestions that are more specific and inform the specific components of the study that will be conducted. In quantitative studies, the research question asks whether a relationship exists between two or more variables. This relationship must be capable of being empirically tested.

In quantitative research, the research question is usually followed by a *hypothesis,* typically derived from past research, which predicts the relationship between the variables being investigated. There is one criterion that any hypothesis must meet: It must be stated so that it is capable of being either "confirmed" or "not confirmed." Hypotheses frequently are not formulated in qualitative studies, at least not at the beginning of the study. Instead, qualitative studies focus on posing questions, some of which might emerge as the exploratory study progresses. In mixed research, there are three distinct approaches to the writing of research questions.

KEY TERMS

Business Source Premier (p. 89)
Educational Resources Information Center (ERIC) (p. 89)
hypothesis (p. 99)
Internet (p. 90)
meta-analysis (p. 101)
meta-synthesis (p. 105)
PsycINFO (p. 89)
purpose of a research study (p. 93)
qualitative research question (p. 97)
quantitative research question (p. 96)
research problem (p. 90)
research question (p. 96)
research topic (p. 84)
SocINDEX (p. 89)
theory (p. 84)

DISCUSSION QUESTIONS

1. In this chapter, we have listed several sources of research ideas.
   a. Which of these sources would produce the most ideas for research studies in education?
   b. If you had to produce an idea for a research study, which source would you use, and why would you use this source?
2. What is the best use of a literature review? Is it best to use it to assist in specifying the research question and hypothesis and designing the study, as is done in quantitative studies, or should the literature review be used only after much of the data have been collected to integrate the study findings with prior research, as some qualitative researchers recommend?
3. We constantly hear and read about the results of studies from television, radio, and newspaper reports. When you read the results of studies from these sources, what questions should you ask, and how should you evaluate the research reported?

PROPOSAL EXERCISES

1. Develop a quantitative research question by answering the following:
   a. My topic area is ______________________________

   ____

b. The research problems within this topic area are ____

____

c. The purpose of my study is ____

____

d. My research question is ____

____

e. My hypothesis is ____

____

2. For the quantitative research question you identified in Exercise 1, conduct a mini literature review by finding three empirical research studies related to your research question and supplying the following information for each study.
   a. Title
   b. Author
   c. Journal with volume and page number
   d. Abstract

RELEVANT INTERNET SITES

Information about searching and evaluating information on the World Wide Web
http://www.lib.berkeley.edu/TeachingLib/Guides/Internet/Evaluate.html

Checklists for evaluating websites
http://www.lib.unc.edu/instruct/evaluate/?section=websites
http://library.acphs.edu/PDFs/Website%20Evaluation%20Checklist.pdf

STUDENT STUDY SITE

Visit the Student Study Site at **edge.sagepub.com/rbjohnson6e** for these additional learning tools:

Video Links
Self-Quizzes
eFlashcards
Lecture Notes
Full-Text SAGE Journal Articles
Interactive Concept Maps
Web Resources

RECOMMEND READING

Onwuegbuzie, A. J., & Frels, R. K. (2016). *Seven steps to a comprehensive literature review: A multimodal and cultural approach.* London, England: SAGE.

Chapter 5

How to Write a Research Proposal

LEARNING OBJECTIVES

After reading this chapter, you should be able to

- Answer in some depth the question "What is a research proposal?"
- Specify the components that must be included in a research proposal.
- Specify the kind of content included in each of the major components of a research proposal.

Visit the Student Study Site for an interactive concept map.

RESEARCH IN REAL LIFE Preparing Proposals

istock/Steve Debenport

On November 1, 2006, the local newspaper reported that, in the past 6 weeks, students at the largest functioning high schools in New Orleans have assaulted guards, a teacher, and a police officer. The guard and teacher were beaten so badly that they were hospitalized. Educators in the New Orleans area have stated that this violence is one of the long-term effects of Hurricane Katrina because many of the teenagers in the city are separated from their parents and are living alone or with older siblings or relatives. Many of the students are fending for themselves, and they are angry. The principal of one high school has estimated that up to one fifth of the students live without parents or some other authority figure in the household.

Nossiter (2006) illustrated this point by reporting on one family whose son goes to that high school. The mother yielded to her son's and his cousin's pleas and sent them back to New Orleans to live with her older daughter while she stayed behind to work as a medical assistant in Houston. The mother sent a monthly check home to her children and nephew in New Orleans, who got jobs at a fast-food restaurant to make ends meet. However, there was no adult to supervise the children.

According to the authorities at that high school, such a lack of parental figures in the home has created a large cadre of belligerent students who are hostile to authority and do not have to worry about parental punishment at home. This group of very aggressive adolescents has created havoc. As a result, this high school has at least 25 security guards positioned at the entrance to the school, on the stairs, and outside classrooms. The school also has a metal detector, four police officers, and four police cruisers parked on the sidewalk.

If you were interested in checking the assumptions of the educators at this high school that the lack of parental control and presence in the home was the cause of these students' violent and aggressive behavior, you would naturally be interested in conducting a research study. If you are a graduate student, you might want to conduct this study for your doctoral dissertation. If you are a faculty member, you might want to write a grant to try to obtain funds to conduct such a research study. Regardless of the reason for wanting to conduct the study, the first step is to write a research proposal that outlines the rationale for wanting to conduct the study and specifies the method(s) of collecting the study data that will provide an answer to your research question. This chapter gives you information and guidelines to follow in preparing a research proposal.

Any good research study is preceded by the development of a good research idea and then careful planning of the way in which the study will be conducted to investigate the research idea. In the last chapter, we presented a variety of sources of research ideas. Good research ideas emerge from some combination of existing knowledge within a variety of domains. When this knowledge is mixed in the right proportions using some combination of inspiration, imagination, and luck, a good research idea emerges. As discussed in the last chapter, good ideas usually do not just pop out from sources such as everyday life or past research. Rather, ideas tend to go through a series of stages—from a vague notion that something is an interesting, researchable problem to the formulation of a specific idea and set of specific research questions that lead to a research study. Raw ideas brew in your mind, and, perhaps, you share them with others so that they can be sharpened and reshaped into good researchable ideas. Sometimes what you think is an excellent idea turns out not to be researchable or must be altered significantly. Regardless of where the research idea comes from or how much it changes, moving from the research idea to conducting the research study typically requires the development of a research proposal.

The preparation of a research proposal is a good first step in conducting a research study because it forces you not only to think about the rationale for the research study but also to think carefully through each step of the study. By writing the research proposal, you have the opportunity to try out various ideas and alternatives before actually conducting the study. This research proposal will then be read by either your professors or peers, who will give you feedback as to how to make the study even better. This means that any research proposal will probably go through several drafts, with each draft improving until the research proposal provides the details of a sound study.

See Journal Article 5.1 on the Student Study Site.

Framework of the Research Proposal

The **research proposal** is a written document that summarizes the prior literature, identifies the research topic area and the research questions to be answered, and specifies the procedure that will be followed in obtaining an answer to these research questions. If you are preparing a research proposal for a thesis project or your dissertation, you will submit this proposal to your committee members. They will read the proposal critically and provide suggestions for its improvement. At some point in your career, you might even be asked to prepare a grant proposal. The preparation of a grant proposal will have similar requirements as a thesis or dissertation proposal. Your completed research proposal also will be helpful if you are preparing an Institutional Review Board (IRB) protocol, which must be submitted for research with human participants and in many ways is similar to a research proposal. Writing a research proposal, therefore, is an important skill that needs to be mastered! Although the elements of most research proposals are similar, they may differ depending on the demands of your department, your college or university, or the funding agency—federal, state, or private—to which you will be sending the proposal. Table 5.1 gives two illustrations of what the major headings in a research proposal might look like. An example of a student proposal is provided in the bonus materials on the student companion website.

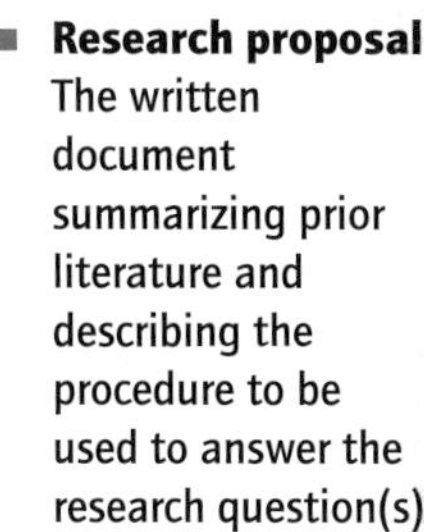

▪ **Research proposal** The written document summarizing prior literature and describing the procedure to be used to answer the research question(s)

See Tools and Tips 5.1 on the Student Study Site.

See Journal Articles 5.2 and 5.3 on the Student Study Site.

Strategies for Writing Each Section of the Research Proposal

The development of a research proposal generally takes place over some period of time. You have probably churned the idea you wish to research over in your mind for a while, thinking about its ramifications as well as the way in which you want to go about conducting the study. Once you have decided on your research idea and have read the relevant literature, it is time to get down to the business of writing the research proposal. Here are some guidelines to assist you.

See Tools and Tips 5.2 on the Student Study Site.

TABLE 5.1 Two Examples of the Major Headings of a Research Proposal*

Example A: Traditional Approach Headings

Title Page

Table of Contents

Abstract**

Introduction

1. Introduction to the research topic
2. Statement of the research problem
3. Summary of prior literature
4. Statement of the purpose of the study
5. Research question(s)
6. Research hypotheses (if a quantitative study is being proposed)

Method

1. Research participants
2. Apparatus and/or instruments
3. Research design***
4. Procedure

Data Analysis

References

Example B: "Three-Chapter" Approach Headings

Title Page

Table of Contents

Chapter 1: Introduction

1. Statement of the purpose of the research study
2. Statement of the research question(s)
3. Limitations of the proposed research
4. Key terms

Chapter 2: Review of the Literature

1. Insert major headings relevant to identifying the different segments of the literature review.
2. Statement of the research hypotheses

Chapter 3: Method

1. Participants
2. Instrumentation
3. Research design
4. Procedure
5. Data analysis

References

Appendixes

* To learn how to put headings into APA format, see Headings (I.2D) in Chapter 21.

**An abstract is *sometimes* included in a research proposal; you must check to see if one is needed in your context. A proposal abstract summarizes in 150–250 words what the study will be about, what you propose to do (data collection, design), and what kind of contribution the study should make to the literature.

***Research design is sometimes incorporated into the Procedure section; when this is done, the Procedure section is sometimes renamed Design and Procedure.

Introduction

The purpose of the **introduction** is to introduce your research idea to the reader and to establish its importance and its potential significance. This means that you should start out with a general introduction to the research topic that not only defines the topic but also demonstrates its importance. Mitchell and Jolley (2001) have identified several ways to demonstrate the importance of a research topic. The first is to show how the topic you are investigating is relevant to the lives of many individuals by quoting statistics or statements of influential people or organizations. For example, if you were studying teen violence, you might quote statistics revealing the incidence of violent acts in schools, or you might quote the concerns expressed by various organizations, such as the American Educational Research Association, the American Psychological Association, or the American Sociological Association. A second method for illustrating the importance of your research topic is to demonstrate its relevance to real life. For example, rather than citing statistics on teen violence, you might talk about a recent and widely publicized incident such as a school shooting. Giving a real-life example not only helps define the concept you are studying but also provides a vivid illustration of its importance.

- **Introduction** The section that introduces the research topic and establishes its importance and significance

After providing a clear discussion of the importance of your research topic, you should write the review of the relevant literature because this review sets up your study in two ways. First, it enables you to show how your research study fits in with existing work by building on the existing literature and existing knowledge. Second, it gives you the opportunity to sell your study. By "selling" your study, we mean presenting a logical argument telling the reader why it is important to conduct this particular study or why the research problem you want to study is important.

Selling a study or convincing the reader that the research problem is important is typically done by critically analyzing relevant studies to show how the study you are proposing either corrects some weakness in previous research or extends the work of other investigators. For example, Christensen and Pettijohn's (2001) review of the literature on carbohydrate craving revealed that all the studies supporting the connection between mood and carbohydrate cravings were confined to individuals with specific disorders, primarily psychiatric disorders. Their review revealed that a large portion of the general population experienced food cravings, so they proposed that the relationship found between cravings and a psychiatric population would also exist in the general population. Therefore, their study proposed extending the work of the prior investigators to individuals in the general population. The review of the literature should, therefore, lead directly into a statement of the purpose of the study because what you are investigating should have continuity with prior research. After stating the purpose of the study, qualitative researchers frequently state one or more study research questions. Quantitative researchers state one or more research questions along with research hypotheses proposed to be tested in the research. Mixed methods researchers sometimes include hypotheses, but sometimes they do not, depending on their purpose and questions.

Method

After you have reviewed the literature and developed a convincing case for your study, you must decide on the specific actions you will take to meet the study's stated purpose. This means that you must develop some plan or strategy that will give you the information needed to provide an answer to your research questions and test any hypotheses you might have stated. This plan or strategy specifies the procedures you propose to follow in collecting the data pertaining to your research questions. Specifying the procedures requires several actions, such as identifying the research participants who are to be included in your study, the instructions to the participants, what information will be obtained from them, and how you will get this information. You must thoroughly think through each step of your study and decide how you will conduct each one.

After you have thought through and decided on each step, you must provide a written narrative of these steps in your research proposal. In this written version, you should be sufficiently exact so that someone else could read the method section and conduct the same study that you are going to conduct. If another researcher can read your method section and replicate your study, then you have provided an adequate description. Although this section will vary slightly, depending on whether you are conducting a quantitative, qualitative, or mixed methods research study, it generally consists of a description of the research participants, any apparatus or instruments that are to be used in data collection, the design of the study, and the procedure to be followed in collecting the data. In mixed research, you sometimes will find it convenient (especially in sequential designs) to include separate subheadings and sections to discuss the qualitative and the quantitative components of the study.

Remember that the purpose of the introduction is to sell the reader on the importance and need to conduct your study. The **method** section not only focuses on telling the reader how you are going to collect the needed information but also sells the reader on the study design or plan that you have constructed. Basically, you are telling the reader what you are planning to do and trying to show that this is the correct and best way of gathering the needed information for obtaining an answer to your research question(s).

- **Method** The section in a research proposal or report that tells the reader about the research design and the method(s) of data collection

Research Participants

The **research participants** are the individuals who actually participate in the research study. In your research proposal, you should specify exactly who the research participants will be, how many will participate in the study, their characteristics (e.g., age, gender), and how they will be selected for inclusion in your study. Any other information relating to the research participants should also be included in this section. For example, you should mention whether you are going to give the research participants an inducement to participate or where the participants are located if you are conducting a qualitative or a mixed study. Often the method of obtaining participants—whether they are volunteers or are paid or if they come from an affluent or impoverished environment—can affect the data collected. When describing the participant sample, the general guideline you should follow is to provide sufficient detail to allow others to identify the population from which you are drawing your sample so that the appropriate generalization can be made. A description of the research participants might be as follows:

- **Research participants** The individuals who participate in the research study

> The research participants will be 140 randomly selected children from those attending Grades 2 and 6 in three Midwestern schools serving a primarily middle-class neighborhood. There will be an equal number of male and female children from each grade. Each child will be given a free ticket to a local theater when he or she completes the research study.

- **Design** The section in a research proposal or report that presents the plan or strategy used to investigate the research question(s)

Design

The **design** is the plan or strategy you will use to investigate your research question(s). Although a separate design section is frequently omitted in quantitative research, it should be included in your research proposal, especially if your study is at all complicated. For example, if you were conducting an experimental research study with several independent variables, each having several levels, you would need to provide a description of these variables and state which variables are *between-subjects* and/or *within-subjects* variables (see Glossary for definitions of these two terms, or wait to learn about them in Chapter 12). For example, you might state that the design is a *factorial design based on a mixed model* (this is explained in Chapter 12 on page 348) where the between-subjects variable is method of instruction (with three levels: cooperative learning, full-group discussion, traditional lecture) and the within-subjects variable is the school session (first, second, third, and fourth quarters) during the school year. The dependent variable might be the students' level of engagement measured at the end of each of the four quarters. In addition to describing the design, it is an excellent idea to include a figure that depicts the design visually (many examples are shown in Chapters 12 and 13).

A separate design section is often not needed in qualitative research because the designs are less structured and are more easily described in the procedure section. A design section is, however, strongly recommended for mixed research because (a) the quantitative component might have a structured design (which should be described separately) and (b) mixed research has identified a set of basic mixed designs that can be used as a starting point for constructing the design that you will be using to address your research questions.

It is helpful to draw a picture of your design to communicate to your reader what you propose to do and the order in which you will do it. An example is shown in Figure 5.1. The study purpose was to develop an explanatory model of how and why some students continue past the first year of foreign language study. The doctoral student labeled her design a "theory-development mixed methods design." In phase 1, she proposed to collect quantitative survey data about epistemological beliefs and other attitudes. In phase 2, which was to occur shortly after phase 1, she proposed to collect focus group and interview data. In phase 3, she planned to collect additional focus group and interview data as needed until theoretical saturation was reached. The final major outcome of the study was a tentative theory based on the quantitative and qualitative data.

Apparatus and/or Instruments

In this section, you describe the instruments (such as an intelligence test, achievement test, or a measure of self-concept or attitude), any materials (such as booklets or training manuals), apparatus (such as a computer or biofeedback equipment), interview procedures, or observational procedures you will be using to collect the data. If you are using specific measurement instruments, you should include information about their past reliability and validity, as well as where that information can be obtained and a thoughtful argument about why the instruments are appropriate to use with the particular kinds of people participating in your study. Any apparatus to be used should be described in sufficient detail to enable someone else to obtain comparable equipment. Following a description of the apparatus and/or instruments, you should explain and justify why each item is being used. If you are collecting data using an interview procedure, make sure that you provide information regarding the type of interview procedure (structured or semistructured) and the contents of the interview. If you are using an observational procedure, make sure that you

■ **FIGURE 5.1** Theory-development mixed methods design

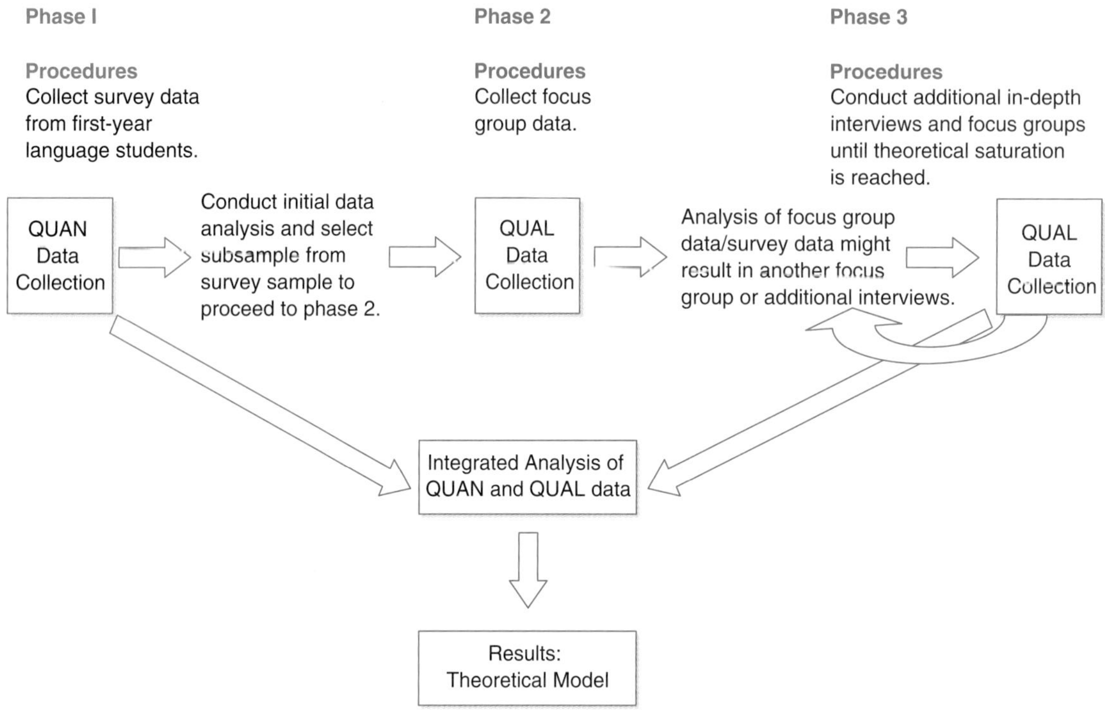

Dissertation Proposal, Sylvia E. Rogers, 2013, University of South Alabama, Mobile

provide information regarding the specific behaviors targeted, who will make the observations, when they will be made, and where they will be made. For example, this section might read as follows:

> The Information and Block Design subtests of the Wechsler Preschool and Primary Scale of Intelligence-Revised (WPPSI-R; Wechsler, 1989) will be used to estimate the research participants' general level of intellectual functioning. The Information subtest . . . [briefly explain what it is and what type of response is required of the child]. The Block Design subtest . . . [briefly explain what it is and what type of response is required of the child]. Test-retest reliability of the Information subtest ranges from .74 to .84 and of the Block Design subtest from .79 to .86. The subtests should be appropriate because the participants to be used in the study will be socially and demographically similar to the individuals in the norming group that was used to obtain the published reliability and validity data.

Procedure

■ **Procedure** The section in a research proposal or report that describes how the study will be executed

In the **procedure** section, you describe the design of the study, if you have not included a separate design section, and how you are going to implement the study design. You must describe how you are going to execute the study from the moment you meet the study participant to the moment when you terminate contact. Your step-by-step account of what both you and the research participant will do should include any instructions or conditions to be presented to the participants and the responses that are required of them, as well as any control techniques to be used, such as random assignment to groups. It is helpful to include a visual depiction (e.g., a Gantt chart) in a figure showing (a) when and how any groups are formed, (b) what kinds of data are to be collected, (c) when these data are to be collected, and (d) by whom the data are to be collected. Remember: The more clearly you explain and depict your proposed procedure, the happier your reviewer will be.

One criterion that you can use to determine whether you have adequately described the procedure section is to ask someone else to read it and then have that person explain to you how the study will be conducted. If your reader can read your procedure section and conduct the study you designed, you have adequately communicated the procedure you will use to collect the data. For example, a procedure section (from a study on diet and mood) might read as follows:

> Individuals responding to an advertisement asking for volunteers to participate in the research project will be interviewed over the telephone about their food cravings. Only individuals who indicate that they crave sweet, carbohydrate-rich foods will be invited to come to the research site for further evaluation. When they arrive at the research site, they will be given a "consent to participate" form to read, and when all questions have been answered and they have signed the form, they will be asked to complete a questionnaire asking about the intensity of their food cravings as well as demographic information such as their age and exercise habits.
>
> After completing the questionnaire, the research participants will be asked to complete a 3-day food record during the following week to assess their food intake. When they return with the food record, they will again rate their food cravings and complete several mood inventories, including the Profile of Mood States, the Symptom Checklist-90, and the Beck Depression Scale. Participants will then be randomly assigned to one of two groups. One randomly assigned group will be instructed to eliminate all added sugar from their diet for the next 2 weeks, and the other group will be instructed to eliminate all artificial sweeteners from their diet for the same period. Each group will be given a sample diet and instructions to follow that will assist them in eliminating either added sugar or artificial sweeteners. At the end of the first and second week, the participants will be asked to complete the mood scales to see if their mood has changed as a result of the dietary substance they have eliminated. At the end of the 2-week dietary alteration period, the research participants will be thanked for their participation, the study and hypotheses will be explained to them, and any questions they have will be answered.

In this procedure section, the researchers identified the way in which the research participants would be recruited and the inclusion criteria that had to be met to participate in the study. They then identified the type of questionnaire that would be administered, which determined the type of information they would receive, and specified when the questionnaire would be administered. The procedure described how the research participants would be assigned to groups and what would be done with each group. The procedure specified when and why response measures (i.e., the mood measures) would be taken. Last, the procedure stated that at the end of the study, all research participants would be debriefed prior to being released from the study. This is an example of the detail that must be included in the procedure section of a research proposal to allow reviewers to determine exactly what you are proposing to do.

Data Analysis

After you have provided a description of how you propose to collect the data for your study, you need to specify how you propose to analyze your data. In most instances, the nature of the data analysis will evolve directly from the study design. As you develop your study design, you should ask yourself, "How am I going to analyze the data collected to test the hypotheses I have formulated?" Asking this question is necessary to ensure that the data you collect can be analyzed appropriately. It also provides a check on the design of your study, because if you cannot identify a way of analyzing the data that are collected so that they provide information about the study hypothesis, you must redesign the study.

The appropriate method of analyzing your data depends on whether you are conducting a qualitative, a quantitative, or a mixed study and the specific components of each type of study. For example, if you were conducting a quantitative study in which the research participants were randomly assigned to one of three groups and each group of participants received a different method of instruction, you would probably use a one-way analysis of variance statistical test. Therefore, to specify the appropriate test for analyzing your data, you must have some knowledge of statistics. Only when you know something about both statistics and research methodology can you design a quantitative study from beginning to end.

Qualitative data analysis is much more eclectic, and there is no single "right" way of analyzing the data because of the nature of the data collected. The data that are collected from a qualitative study come from observations, interviews, documents, and audio-visual materials such as photographs, videotapes, and films. Analysis of the voluminous amount of information collected requires reduction to certain patterns, categories, or themes. These are then interpreted by using some schema. In general, qualitative data analysis requires coding and searching for relationships and patterns until a holistic picture emerges. If you are proposing a mixed methods research study, you will need to explain your proposed quantitative and qualitative analysis as well as any integrated analysis you might plan (e.g., putting qualitative and quantitative data into a single data set and analyzing the combined set of data).

Abstract

- **Abstract** A brief description of the essential characteristics of the study

The **abstract** is a brief description of the essential characteristics of the study. Inclusion of an abstract is required in a final research report, but it sometimes is and sometimes is not included in a research *proposal.* You will need to check with the person, group, or organization for which you are writing your proposal to determine whether an abstract is required.

Although the abstract comes before the introduction, it is generally easier to write the abstract *after* you have completed the research proposal. The abstract is a short summary of your research proposal, and it is easier to summarize the proposal after you have settled on and specified each component of the study.

The abstract in a research proposal should be a concise and precise statement of the research hypotheses or research questions and how they are to be addressed. It should contain a statement of the number of participants and their essential characteristics and how they will be treated or what they will be asked to do. You should also explain how you plan to collect the data and how you will analyze the results. In other words, the abstract should provide a concise summary of each of the components of the research proposal.

5.1 What is a research proposal, and what are some of the reasons for writing such a document?

5.2 What is the purpose and goal of the introduction?

5.3 Why should the introduction include a literature review?

5.4 What is the purpose of the method section, and what information should be included in this section?

5.5 What key information should be included regarding research participants?

5.6 What information should be included when preparing the apparatus and/or instruments section?

5.7 What is the purpose of the procedure section?

ACTION RESEARCH REFLECTION

Insight: Action researchers call their proposals action plans. An *action plan* focuses on how to solve a practitioner's local problem that needs attention. It occurs in the reflection and planning phases of the action research cycle. This chapter has taught you, as a reflective practitioner, how to write a formal proposal to conduct a research study. If you choose the route of action research, you now need to consider the following:

1. What is a situation or problem in your classroom, school, or workplace that you would like to change? Who are the people whom you want to help?
2. How can you make a change and improve yourself, your students, or whomever? What do the published research and professional literature have to say about the "problem" you identified in question 1? What do your day-to-day observations and reflections suggest? What does your theory suggest needs to be done?
3. Transform your problem and theory into two or three specific action research questions that you would like to answer in your study. They are a key part of your proposal because you will need to explain how you plan to answer these questions in your action research proposal or action plan.
4. What method(s) of data collection and research design do you think will help you to come up with a solution to the "problem" you identified in question 1? It is usually a good idea to collect multiple sources of evidence and obtain information from people in different roles to examine/observe your intervention from multiple perspectives and to obtain corroboration of information.

SUMMARY

A research proposal is developed before you conduct a research study. The preparation of a research proposal is a good exercise because it forces you to think through each step of the study you wish to conduct. When writing the introduction, you must establish the importance and potential significance of the research study by showing its relevance to real life. Additionally, writing the introduction gives you the opportunity to set up your research study by showing how it fits in with existing work and how it will build on existing work by either correcting some deficiency or extending the work of others.

After you have demonstrated the importance and significance of your study, you must describe how you will collect the data that will be used to answer the study's research question(s). This description constitutes the method section. In the method section, you will describe the essential characteristics of your research participants and how the participants are going to be selected for inclusion in the research study. You will also want to describe the various instruments you will use to collect your study data, as well as any apparatus or equipment, such as a computer, that is involved in data collection. Finally, you will want to describe the exact procedure you are going to use to execute the study from the moment you meet the first research participants to the moment you terminate contact with them.

After you have completed collecting the study data, you must analyze the data to provide an answer to your research question. The data analysis section presents a description of how you propose to analyze the study results.

KEY TERMS

abstract (p. 118)
design (p. 114)
introduction (p. 113)
method (p. 114)
procedure (p. 116)
research participants (p. 114)
research proposal (p. 111)

DISCUSSION QUESTIONS

1. What is the purpose of writing a research proposal, and what elements go into a good research proposal?
2. What type of information should be included in each component of a research proposal?

PROPOSAL EXERCISE

1. In the last chapter, the research exercise asked you to identify a research topic, a research question, and a hypothesis related to this research question. Now assume that you were going to prepare a research proposal specifying how you would conduct a study to answer the research question. Provide an answer to the following questions as a prelude to developing your research proposal:
   a. What characteristics of the research participants would you use in your study, and how would you recruit the participants?
   b. What instruments and/or apparatus would you use to collect your data?
   c. Detail the procedure you would use to collect the data.

RELEVANT INTERNET SITES

How to write an APA proposal
https://www.youtube.com/watch?v=4QlcSJeII40

Examples of an APA-style research proposal and additional information
http://www.vanguard.edu/psychology/wp-content/uploads/2010/12/proposal.pdf
http://www.people.vcu.edu/~jldavis/resources/apa/APA proposal.pdf
http://www.trinitydc.edu/sps/files/2010/09/APA-6-BGS-Quantitative-Research-Proposal-August-2014.pdf
http://dixie.edu/search/ (at this site search for "research proposal")

A non APA-style proposal
http://www.education.uwa.edu.au/students/research/?a=75347
http://uq.edu.au/student-services/pdf/learning/research-proposal-sample-v2.pdf

STUDENT STUDY SITE

Visit the Student Study Site at **edge.sagepub.com/rbjohnson6e** for these additional learning tools:

- Video Links
- Self-Quizzes
- eFlashcards
- Lecture Notes
- Full-Text SAGE Journal Articles
- Interactive Concept Maps
- Web Resources

RECOMMENDED READING

Bloomberg, L. D., & Volpe, M. F. (2012). *Completing your qualitative dissertation: A road map from beginning to end.* Thousand Oaks, CA: SAGE.

Onwuegbuzie, A. J., & Frels, R. K. (2016). *Seven steps to a comprehensive literature review: A multimodal and cultural approach.* London, England: SAGE.

Rudestam, K. E., & Newton, R. R. (2007). *Surviving your dissertation: A comprehensive guide to content and process.* Thousand Oaks, CA: SAGE.

Chapter 6

Research Ethics

LEARNING OBJECTIVES

After reading this chapter, you should be able to

- Explain why it is necessary to consider ethical issues when designing and conducting research.
- State the guidelines that must be followed in conducting research with humans.
- Explain the procedures that must be followed to obtain approval to conduct a study.
- Specify the issues involved in conducting research with minors.

Visit the Student Study Site for an interactive concept map.

RESEARCH IN REAL LIFE Ethical Issues

istock/keeweeboy

On April 26, 2002, Robert Steinhaeuser, a 19-year-old man dressed all in black, entered his former high school carrying a pump-action shotgun and a handgun and began shooting teachers in classrooms and corridors. Fourteen teachers and administrators, two female students, and a police officer were killed before hundreds of police commandos surrounded the four-story building and charged inside. Mr. Steinhaeuser retreated to a classroom, barricaded himself inside, and then fatally shot himself as the police closed in (Biehl, 2002).

Students described Steinhaeuser as an intelligent person who was not aggressive but was often late for classes and had difficulties with teachers. However, Mr. Steinhaeuser had been expelled for poor grades, and this had prevented him from taking university entrance exams. He apparently was angry over this expulsion, and this anger seemed to be the impetus for the shootings.

Teenage violence and mass murders, as illustrated in the case of Robert Steinhaeuser, are not isolated events. All we have to do is think back to the April 1999 shootings at Columbine High School in Littleton, Colorado, or to the 2013 shootings at Sandy Hook Elementary School in Newtown, Connecticut. Such violent expressions of anger always promote the questions "Why?" and "How could this have happened in our school?" These are questions that researchers are also asking and seeking to answer. However, conducting research on such questions generates a variety of ethical concerns. One of the most serious is the harmful effect it could have on the participants.

In the course of conducting the study, the researcher might identify a teenager who has severe anger and a tendency to vent anger in aggressive ways. The researcher has a responsibility to protect the research participant *and* the potential target of the anger by notifying the authorities about the participant's anger and his or her potential for engaging in violent behavior. Although the researcher would be acting appropriately, the privacy of the teenager would have been violated.

As you can see, a variety of ethical issues surround a research investigation. Thus, there is a need for a set of ethical guidelines for researchers to use when conducting educational research.

If you think about the potential good that can come out of an educational research study, it makes a lot of sense to interview or survey students and teachers or ask them to participate in an experiment. However, we live in a society in which we have the right to privacy and the right to expect freedom from surveillance of our behavior without our consent. We also have the right to know whether our behavior is being manipulated and, if so, why.

Unfortunately, these basic rights can be easily violated when a research study is conducted. This creates a problem for researchers because the public constantly demands to see improvements in the educational system. Whenever SAT scores decline or when results are publicized indicating that "Johnny can't read," the educational system is attacked, and demands are made for improving instruction. Improvements in education are a result, however, of well-designed and well-conducted research studies. In conducting these research studies, it is sometimes necessary to infringe on people's right to privacy and ask personal questions or observe their behavior, because this is the only way researchers can collect the information needed for improving the educational system as a whole. Additionally, for the educator who is trained in research techniques, a decision *not* to conduct research is a matter of ethical concern.

Consideration of research ethics is a necessary part of the development and implementation of any research study. Understanding ethical principles and procedures assists a researcher in preventing abuses that could occur and helps delineate his or her responsibilities as an investigator. For example, you will learn that maintaining participants' anonymity and obtaining their informed consent before conducting the study are important. In this chapter, we discuss the issues surrounding the ethics of educational research.

What Are Research Ethics?

- **Ethics** The principles and guidelines that help us uphold the things we value

See Journal Article 6.1 on the Student Study Site.

- **Deontological approach** An ethical approach that says ethical issues must be judged on the basis of some universal code

- **Ethical skepticism** An ethical approach that says concrete and inviolate moral codes cannot be formulated but are a matter of individual conscience

- **Utilitarianism** An ethical approach that says judgments of the ethics of a study depend on the consequences the study has for the research participants and the benefits that might arise from the study

Ethics are the principles and guidelines that help us uphold the things we value. When most people think of ethics, they first think of moralistic sermons and endless philosophical debates, but in fact ethics permeate our day-to-day lives. Whenever ethical issues are discussed, it is typical for individuals to differ about what does and what does not constitute ethical behavior. Most of the disagreements seem to arise because of the different approaches people take in attempting to resolve an ethical issue.

There are three basic approaches—deontology, ethical skepticism, and utilitarianism—that people tend to adopt when considering ethical issues in research. These approaches differ in terms of the criteria used to make decisions about what is right and wrong (Schlenker & Forsyth, 1977). The **deontological approach** takes the position that ethical issues must be judged on the basis of some universal code. (The root of the word is the Greek word *deon,* which means "duty" or "obligation.") Certain actions are inherently unethical and should never be performed regardless of the circumstances. For example, Baumrind (1985) used the deontological approach to argue that the use of deception in research is morally wrong and should not be used under any circumstances because it involves lying to research participants and precludes obtaining their informed consent.

A person using **ethical skepticism** would argue that concrete and inviolate moral codes such as those used by the deontologist cannot be formulated. Such a skeptic would not deny that ethical principles are important but would claim that ethical rules are relative to one's culture and time. According to this approach, an ethical decision must be a matter of the individual's conscience, and the researcher should do what he or she thinks is right and refrain from doing what he or she thinks is wrong. Research ethics are therefore a matter of the individual's conscience.

The third approach to assessing ethical issues is that of **utilitarianism**. This position, as applied in research, maintains that judgments regarding the ethics of a particular research study depend both on the consequences of that study for the individual research participant and the larger benefit that might arise from the study results. In this position, ethical decisions are based on weighing the potential benefits that might accrue from a research study against the potential costs, as illustrated in Figure 6.1. If the benefits are sufficiently large relative to the costs, then the study is determined to be ethically acceptable. *This is the primary approach used by the federal government, most professional organizations, and Institutional Review Boards* in reaching difficult ethical decisions about studies that place research participants at risk but also have the potential for yielding important knowledge and significant benefit to humans.

■ **FIGURE 6.1** Utilitarian approach to judging the ethical acceptability of a research study

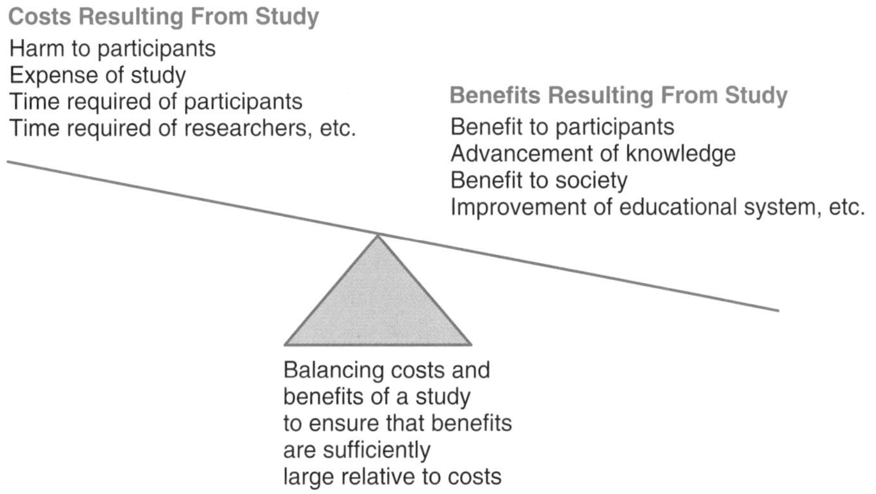

Ethical Concerns

If **research ethics** are a guiding set of principles developed to assist researchers in conducting ethical studies, it is important to identify the ethical issues that are of importance to researchers. Three areas of ethical concern for educational, social, and behavioral scientists are (1) the relationship between society and science, (2) professional issues, and (3) the treatment of research participants.

■ **Research ethics** A set of principles developed to guide and assist researchers in conducting ethical studies

Relationship Between Society and Science

See Journal Article 6.2 on the Student Study Site.

The ethical issue concerning the relationship between society and science revolves around the extent to which societal concerns and cultural values should direct the course of research. The society in which we live tends to dictate to a great extent the issues and research areas that are considered important and should be investigated. For example, the common cold is a condition that afflicts everyone at some point. However, little time is spent investigating ways to eliminate this affliction, probably because a cold is typically a temporary discomfort that is not life threatening. Many other issues have more far-reaching implications, such as the education of our children. Society considers such problems much more important, and it encourages research in areas that are considered important.

One of the ways in which these priorities are communicated to researchers is through the numerous funding agencies that exist. The largest funding agency is the federal government. The federal government spends millions of dollars every year on both basic and applied research, and it also sets priorities for how the money is to be spent. To increase the probability of obtaining a portion of these research funds, investigators must orient their research proposals toward these priorities, which means that the federal government at least partially dictates the type of research that is conducted. Every year these funding agencies announce "Requests for Proposals" in specific areas.

Professional Issues

▪ **Research misconduct** Fabrication, falsification, or plagiarism in proposing, performing, or reviewing research or reporting research results

The category of professional issues includes the expanding problem of research misconduct. In December 2000, the US Office of Science and Technology Policy defined **research misconduct** as "fabrication, falsification, or plagiarism (FFP) in proposing, performing, or reviewing research, or in reporting research results." The attention that fabrication, falsification, and plagiarism have received is understandable given that a scientist is trained to ask questions, to be skeptical, and to use the research process in the search for truth and social betterment.

This search for truth is completely antithetical to engaging in any form of deception. The most serious professional crime any researcher can commit is to cheat or present fraudulent results to the research community, such as the behavior described in Exhibit 6.1. Although there is an unwritten rule that scientists present uncontaminated results, there seems to be a disturbing increase in the tendency of some scientists to forge or falsify data, manipulate results to support a theory, or report data selectively (Woolf, 1988). For example, a 1987 study at George Mason University found that one third of the scientists interviewed suspected that a colleague had committed plagiarism. However, 54 percent of these did not report their suspicions to university officials (Brainard, 2000).

EXHIBIT 6.1 A Case of Fraudulent Research

Steven E. Breuning received his doctorate from the Illinois Institute of Technology in 1977. Several years later, he obtained a position at the Coldwater Regional Center in Michigan. At Coldwater, Breuning was invited to collaborate on a National Institute of Mental Health (NIMH)–funded study of the use of neuroleptics on institutionalized people who had intellectual disabilities. In January 1981, he was appointed director of the John Merck program at Pittsburgh's Western Psychiatric Institute and Clinic, where he continued to report on the results of the Coldwater research and even obtained his own NIMH grant to study the effects of stimulant medication on individuals with intellectual disabilities. During this time, Breuning gained considerable prominence and was considered one of the field's leading researchers. In 1983, however, questions were raised about the validity of Breuning's work. The individual who had initially taken on Breuning as an investigator started questioning a paper in which Breuning had reported results with an impossibly high reliability. This prompted a further review of Breuning's published work, and contacts were made with personnel at Coldwater, where the research had supposedly been conducted. Coldwater's director of psychology had never heard of the study and was not aware that Breuning had conducted any research while at Coldwater. NIMH was informed of the allegations in December 1983. Following a 3-year investigation, an NIMH team concluded that Breuning had "knowingly, willfully, and repeatedly engaged in misleading and deceptive practices in reporting his research." He reportedly had not carried out the research that was described, and only a few of the experimental participants had ever been studied. It was concluded that Breuning had engaged in serious scientific misconduct (Holden, 1987).

Both personal and nonpersonal factors seem to contribute to scientific misconduct (Knight, 1984). Personal factors focus on the psychological makeup of the individual (e.g., personality, value orientation). Nonpersonal factors include such things as the pressure to publish and the competition for research funding. Most research is conducted at research institutions, most of which are universities. These institutions evaluate professors on the basis of the grants they receive and the articles they publish. Receiving a promotion or even keeping one's position might be contingent on the number of articles published and grants obtained. This pressure is frequently reported by researchers who engage in fraudulent activities. Other nonpersonal factors include inadequate supervision of trainees, inadequate procedures for keeping records or retaining data, and the diffusion of responsibility for jointly authored studies.

Although personal and nonpersonal factors might contribute to a person's tendency to engage in fraudulent activity, there is never any justification for engaging in such behavior. The cost of fraudulent activity is enormous, both to the profession and to the researcher. Not only is the whole research enterprise discredited, but also the professional career of the individual is destroyed.

Although fraudulent activity is obviously the most serious form of scientific misconduct, several other, less serious issues also need attention. These include practices such as overlooking others' use of flawed data, failing to present data contradicting one's own work, or circumventing minor aspects of human-participant requirements. While these practices do not approach the seriousness of fabrication, falsification, or plagiarism, they are of concern to the profession, especially as Martinson, Anderson, and de Vries (2005) have revealed that more than a third of US scientists surveyed admitted to engaging in one or more of these practices in the past 3 years. These problems deserve attention as they also represent a form of research misconduct.

The increased frequency of and interest in scientific misconduct has stimulated discussion about its causes and what action needs to be taken to reduce its frequency (Hilgartner, 1990; Knight, 1984). One of the best deterrents is probably the development of an institutional culture in which key faculty members model ethical behavior, stress the importance of research integrity, and translate these beliefs into action (Gunsalus, 1993). Jane Steinberg, director of extramural activities and research integrity officer at NIMH, states that some specific strategies can be used to prevent fabrications of data. She advocates instituting prevention strategies (J. A. Steinberg, 2002), such as those listed in Table 6.1, that make it difficult to engage in scientific misconduct.

Additionally, the National Institutes of Health (NIH) requires that all investigators who receive funding from NIH, as well as other key personnel such as co-investigators and study coordinators, complete an education module on the protection of human participants. Most universities extend this requirement to all investigators, including other key personnel, such as graduate and undergraduate students who are conducting research with human participants whose research does not receive NIH funding.

TABLE 6.1 Strategies for Preventing Scientific Misconduct

- Have the researcher make it clear that he or she has checked and verified data that are collected and then make sure that some of the data are checked.
- Ask some of the research participants who should have been seen by each data collector if you can recontact them. Then recontact them to ensure that they participated in the study.
- Make sure there are no deviations from the approved study design.
- Watch for data collectors who complete data collection in record time. Make sure you review the work of every person who collects the study data.
- Teach ethical standards of conducting research in classes. Include reviews of cases of misconduct and discuss ethical issues and the ramifications of misconduct for the researcher, the field, and public trust.
- Provide guidelines for handling cases of suspected misconduct.

Treatment of Research Participants

Treatment of research participants is the most important and fundamental issue that researchers confront. Conduct of research with humans has the potential for creating physical and psychological harm. The grossly inhumane medical experiments conducted by Nazi scientists during World War II immediately come to mind as an extreme example. Among other atrocities, individuals were immersed in ice water to determine how long it would take them to freeze to death. Bones were broken and rebroken to see how many times they could be broken before healing was not possible. We seem to think that such studies could not possibly be performed in our culture. Before the 1960s, however, formal discussions about the ethics of research were virtually nonexistent. In the mid-1960s, ethical issues became a dominant concern, as it increasingly became clear that research did not invariably operate to benefit others and experiments were not always conducted in a manner that ensured the safety of participants. The most dramatic examples of unethical research have been located in the medical field; the Tuskegee experiment (Jones, 1981) described in Exhibit 6.2 represents the most blatant example of violation of human rights in the United States.

EXHIBIT 6.2 The Tuskegee Experiment

In July 1972, the Associated Press released a story that revealed that the US Public Health Service (PHS) had for 40 years (from 1932 to 1972) been conducting a study of the effects of untreated syphilis on African American men in Macon County, Alabama. The study consisted of conducting a variety of medical tests (including an examination) on 399 African American men who were in the late stages of the disease and on 200 controls. Physicians employed by the PHS administered a variety of blood tests and routine autopsies to learn about the serious complications that resulted from the final stages of the disease.

This was a study aimed strictly at compiling data on the effects of the disease and not on the treatment of syphilis. No drugs or alternative therapies were tested or ever used. The participants were never told the purpose of the study or what they were or were not being treated for. The PHS nurse monitoring the participants informed the local physicians of the individuals who were taking part in the study and that they were not to be treated for syphilis. Participants who were offered treatment by other physicians were advised that they would be dropped from the study if they took the treatment.

The participants were not aware of the purpose of the study or the danger it posed to them, and no attempt was ever made to explain the situation to them. In fact, participants were enticed with a variety of inducements, physical examinations, free rides to and from the clinic, hot meals, free treatment for other ailments, and a $50 burial stipend and were followed to ensure that they did not receive treatment from other physicians. This study violated almost every standard of ethics for research with humans, from informed consent to freedom from physical and/or psychological harm.

In December 1996, the Cleveland *Plain Dealer* reported on the results of its investigation of internal Food and Drug Administration records (Epstein & Sloat, 1996a–1996d). This analysis revealed that some research is still conducted on unknowing people and that, in other cases, the participants are not fully informed of the risks of their participation.

The Tuskegee experiment was clearly unethical and inflicted extensive physical harm and psychological pain on the research participants. Educational research does not appear to have the potential for inflicting a similar degree of physical or psychological harm on its research participants. Therefore, it would be easy to become complacent and conclude that consideration of ethical issues is something that other fields have to contend with but that educational research is spared. Reaching such a conclusion is wrong because ethical issues are part and parcel of educational research. However, the ethical issues that educational researchers must face are often not as dramatic or blatant as those that frequently exist in medical research. Consequently, educational researchers frequently must be *more* rather than less attuned to the ethical issues that surround their research.

Ethical issues in educational research can be subtle but, nonetheless, important. Consider a survey research study conducted by S. R. Phillips (1994). Phillips was interested in adolescents' attitudes and behaviors related to HIV/AIDS prevention. She collected data that would provide insight into adolescents' thoughts about using condoms during sexual intercourse and what influenced their decisions to use or not use condoms. Participants completed a questionnaire designed to measure sexually related attitudes and behavior. This research did not inject, expose, medicate, touch, deceive, or assign the participants to treatment or control groups, nor did it require them to reveal their identities. Although the study did investigate "sensitive" behavior, it did not seem to have the potential for violating the participants' rights.

Fortunately, S. R. Phillips (1994) met with various groups before conducting her study, and these meetings revealed several ethical concerns that led her to alter her questionnaire and her procedures. For example, she met with a student peer group and a combined parent-teacher group to discuss the objectives of the research and the content of the questionnaire. In addition to asking questions about sexual attitudes and behavior, the questionnaire inquired about the adolescents' drug use. In a parent-teacher group discussion, teachers and parents joked about how they would like to find out about the drug users because they had some children whom they suspected of using drugs. Although Phillips had told the schools that she would provide them with aggregate data only for each school, there was still the potential that a teacher, after learning that her school had, say, 10 drug users, would assume that she or he had guessed right and then treat the suspected student differently. To avoid such a possibility, Phillips decided to remove the questions about illicit drug use except one on alcohol and cigarette smoking. The same concern did not exist for sexual activity because many teachers seemed to assume that this was a widespread activity.

Another subtle ethical issue S. R. Phillips (1994) had to contend with was the issue of privacy. Because the survey instrument focused on sexual behavior, students who had not experienced sexual intercourse would find many of the questions not applicable. These students would skip most of the questions and finish more rapidly than their sexually active classmates. This more rapid completion could convey their sexual inexperience to their classmates. To avoid this possibility, Phillips constructed a second set of questions for the sexually inactive student that were designed to take about as long to complete as the sections for the sexually active student. This seemed to solve this problem. However, listening to students talk about completing surveys revealed that they would listen to or watch when their friends turned the page to branching questions to discern how they had answered the question. This is a sophisticated attempt to pry into another student's answers. To get around this privacy issue, Phillips reorganized the questionnaire to ensure that all branching questions were at the bottom of the page and that all students would have to turn a page at about the same time.

Although the survey study that S. R. Phillips (1994) conducted did not place the participants in any physical danger, there was the potential for emotional harm. Some of the students volunteered that they had been raped and/or were incest victims. This information was not requested in the survey, but it would have been unethical to disregard it because the questionnaire could create an environment in which these unpleasant events were recalled. The questionnaire also asked the adolescents to identify their sexual preference; this could result in the student having to confront homosexual tendencies, which could cause some emotional distress or discomfort. To deal with these issues, Phillips gave all the students her office phone number and told them that they could call her with any questions or concerns. During the administration of the questionnaire, students could ask questions in private, and any other questions they might have would be answered after completion of the questionnaire. Additionally, each student was given a pamphlet, published by the American Red Cross, that included telephone numbers for counseling referral services.

Ethical concerns are not limited to research about such sensitive issues as sexuality or drug use. Similar issues can arise in many other types of studies. For example, educational researchers conducting qualitative research sometimes make extensive use of in-depth interviews. During these interviews, research participants can, and often do, reveal sensitive information that is not part of the goal of the study. Research participants often view researchers as "experts" and frequently feel comfortable conveying confidential and sensitive information. For example, students might reveal that they are being abused, that they are having difficulty with a teacher, or that they are abusing drugs. When this information is revealed, the researcher must be prepared to address such issues rather than dismiss them as being outside the confines of the purpose of the study. These types of ethical issues can creep into a study, and the researcher must anticipate them and have a plan to conduct a study that is ethically sound.

REVIEW QUESTIONS

6.1 What is the definition of ethics, and how does this definition relate to research?

6.2 How do the three approaches that are used in considering ethical issues in research differ?

6.3 How do societal concerns relate to research ethics?

6.4 What are the professional issues involved in research ethics, and what is the appropriate ethical behavior related to each of these issues?

6.5 Why is treatment of the research participant an ethical issue to be considered in educational research when the potential for physical and psychological harm is minimal?

ETHICAL GUIDELINES FOR RESEARCH WITH HUMANS

We hope that we have convinced you of the necessity of considering the ethics of your research study before actually collecting any data. Even so, a novice researcher might not be sophisticated enough to know what types of issues to consider even if he or she is motivated to make the study as ethical as possible. To assist the researcher in conducting an ethically sound study, several organizations, such as the American Educational Research Association (AERA), the American Psychological Association, the Society for Research in Child Development, and the American Counseling Association, have prepared sets of ethical guidelines that can be used to assist in the conduct of an ethically acceptable study.

AERA (2011) has developed a set of standards designed specifically to guide the work of educational researchers. In developing this set of standards, AERA recognized that educational researchers come from many disciplines, each of which may have a set of ethical guidelines to guide its members. However, AERA recognizes that educational research is often directed at children and other vulnerable populations. Therefore, one key objective of the AERA standards is to remind researchers constantly to strive to protect these populations. The AERA standards also emphasize integrity in all other aspects of educational research. The standards can be accessed at http://www.aera.net/Portals/38/docs/About_AERA/CodeOfEthics(1).pdf. This website includes 5 aspirational or broad General Principles and 22 more specific Ethical Standards. Here are the five broad principles you should always follow:

1. Professional Competence. Act only in the areas in which you are competent and make sure you are up-to-date in your training.
2. Integrity. In all that you do, always be honest, trustworthy, and never jeopardize the welfare of others; this includes the ancient Greek idea of **nonmaleficence** or doing no harm to others.
3. Professional, Scientific, and Scholarly Responsibility. You must adhere to the AERA's 22 ethical standards found on its website (link provided in the previous paragraph) and discussed in the remainder of this chapter.
4. Respect for People's Rights, Dignity, and Diversity. Respect cultural and individual differences and work to eliminate bias and discrimination.
5. Social Responsibility. This includes **beneficence**, or striving to act for the benefit of others in our society and world.

- **Nonmaleficence** Doing no harm to others

- **Beneficence** Acting for the benefit of others

These AERA Guiding Principles and the related 22 Ethical Standards cover a multitude of issues that relate to the activities of educational researchers. We have discussed some of the issues, such as research misconduct, earlier in this chapter. Many others, such as authorship of research articles, are also important, and you should know about them if you are engaged in research. Therefore, we recommend that you read the material relating to each of the Ethical Standards. Other issues included in the various Ethical Standards are very important in the actual conduct of a research study and warrant additional attention here. These issues focus on informed consent; deception; freedom to withdraw; protection from physical and mental harm; confidentiality, anonymity, and privacy; and the ethics of research conducted over the Internet. We elaborate on these issues here because of their importance in conducting ethical research. They also must be addressed if one is to receive institutional approval to conduct a research study.

Informed Consent

Federal regulations as well as AERA guidelines state that research participants must give **informed consent** before they can participate in a study. Consent must also be given before a researcher can use individuals' existing records for research purposes. The Buckley Amendment, or the Family Education Rights and Privacy Act of 1974, protects the privacy of the records maintained by agencies such as a school system. This privacy act states that records maintained by an agency for one purpose cannot be released for another purpose without the consent of the individual. Records such as student grades that are collected and maintained for the purpose of recording student performance cannot be released to a researcher for research purposes without the student's consent or the parent's consent for minors.

- **Informed consent** Agreeing to participate in a study after being informed of its purpose, procedures, risks, benefits, alternative procedures, and limits of confidentiality

Before a person can participate in a research study, the researcher must give the prospective participant a description of all the features of the study that might reasonably influence his or her willingness to participate. For example, if you are planning to conduct a survey of sexual attitudes, you must inform the prospective participants about the nature of the survey and the type of questions to which they might have to respond, because some of the participants might not want to answer explicit sex-related questions. Similarly, if you are conducting a study pertaining to academic achievement and you are going to ask the students about their grades in other classes, you have to inform the students of this fact. In general, you must look at the tasks you are going to ask your research participants to complete and ask yourself whether this task could hurt, embarrass, or in some other way create a reaction in the participants that could make them not want to participate in the study. Table 6.2 specifies the information that should be included in a consent form.

Exhibit 6.3 provides an example of an informed consent form. Only when you have given the participant this information and he or she still volunteers to participate in the study have you obtained informed consent. Informed consent usually includes a brief summary of the general purpose of the study without providing information about the researcher's specific hypotheses. Again, what is most important is to include a description of anything that might affect a potential participant's willingness to participate.

TABLE 6.2 Information to Include in a Consent Form

Purpose of the research along with a description of the procedures to be followed and the length of time it will take the participant to complete the study
A description of any physical or psychological risks or discomforts the participant might encounter
A description of any benefits the participant or others might expect from the research
A description of any alternative procedure or treatment that might be advantageous to the participant
A statement of the extent to which the results will be kept confidential
Names of people the participant can contact with questions about the study or the research participant's rights
A statement indicating that participation is voluntary and the participant can withdraw and refuse to participate at any time with no penalty
A statement of the amount and schedule of payment if participants are to be paid for participation
The information should usually be written at an eighth-grade reading level; for studies targeting certain populations, a sixth-grade reading level might be appropriate.

For additional tips on preparation of the consent form, go to the US Department of Health and Human Services Office for Human Resource Protections website (http://www.hhs.gov/ohrp/policy/ictips.html).

EXHIBIT 6.3 Consent Form

Informed Consent

Title: Predictors of Speech Rate in Normally Fluent People
Principal Investigator: Sally Smith
Department: Education
Telephone Number: (111) 123-4567

You are invited to participate in a research study investigating the things that affect how fast normal people of different ages speak. If you volunteer to participate in this research study, we will test the clarity of your hearing, language, and speech.

The research will involve asking you to talk about different things such as telling what you see on picture cards, saying words and sounds as fast as you can, and repeating words and sentences. You will be asked to name animals, colors, letters, and numbers as fast as you can and to read a paragraph. If you get tired before the tests are finished, you can rest and finish the study later. Your speech will be recorded so we can study that later.

The study will take between 1.0 and 1.5 hours.

You might not get any benefit from participating in the study, but the tests we give you will help us understand how different things affect how fast people speak.

If you volunteer to participate in this study, you should always remember that you can withdraw and stop participating in the study at any time you wish. You will not be penalized in any way if you withdraw and stop participating in the study.

There are no risks from participating in this study other than, perhaps, you might get tired of doing the tests.

All information that you provide to us will be kept strictly confidential. At no time will we give any information to anyone outside the research staff. The recordings of your speech will be erased when the research is finished. The results of this study may be presented at professional meetings or published in a professional journal, but your name and any other identifying information will not be revealed.

If you have any questions about this study or if you have any questions regarding your rights as a research participant, you can call the Institutional Review Board of the university at (111) 123-5678. You can also contact Dr. Sally Smith at (111) 123-4567.

Agreement to Participate in Research

I have read, or have had read to me, the above study and have had an opportunity to ask questions, which have been answered to my satisfaction. I agree voluntarily to participate in the study as described.

____________	______________________________
Date	Participant's Name
____________	______________________________
Date	Signature of Consenting Party
____________	______________________________
Date	Signature of Investigator
____________	______________________________
Date	Signature of Witness

Federal as well as AERA ethical standards recognize the necessity of sometimes forgoing the requirement of informed consent. Whenever a judgment is made that informed consent would alter the outcome of a study or that the study could not be conducted if informed consent were required, the investigator incurs an added ethical obligation to ensure that the benefits of the research outweigh the risks. However, there are a number of limited circumstances where the requirement of informed consent will be waived. These circumstances include the following:

- When the identity of the research participant will be completely anonymous and the study involves minimal risk
- When it is not feasible to obtain informed consent due to the cultural norms of the population being studied and when the study involves minimal risk

- When signing the consent to participate form would subject the participant to possible legal, social, or economic risk (e.g., revealing the status of an undercover drug enforcement investigator)

Remember that it is the Institutional Review Board that must make the final determination of whether informed consent can be waived. If you think that it would be appropriate to waive consent in your study, you should request such a waiver from your Institutional Review Board.

Informed Consent and Minors as Research Participants

The principle of informed consent refers to the fact that a person, once given the pertinent information, is competent and legally free of the desire of others to decide whether to participate in a given research study. Minors, however, cannot make decisions about consent. Consent has to be obtained from parents (or the minor's legal guardian) after they have been informed of all features of the study that might affect their willingness to allow the child to participate (see Exhibit 6.4). Once consent has been obtained from the minor's parent or guardian, **assent** must be obtained from the minor. This means that the minor has to agree to participate in the research after being informed of all the features that could affect his or her willingness to participate.

- **Assent** Agreeing to participate after being informed of all the features of the study that could affect the participant's willingness to participate

Federal regulations state that the assent of the minor should be obtained when he or she is capable of providing assent. However, the age at which a person is capable of providing assent can differ among children. To provide assent, the child must be able to understand what is being asked, realize that permission is being sought, and make choices that are free from outside constraints. This depends on the cognitive capabilities of the child. Because the cognitive capabilities of children develop at different rates, it is difficult to state an age at which a child is capable of providing assent. Individuals older than the age of 9 generally have sufficient cognitive ability to make a decision concerning participation in research, and individuals older than 14 seem to make the same decisions as adults (Leikin, 1993). Most individuals (e.g., Leikin) and the ethical guidelines provided by the Society for Research in Child Development (2007) state that assent should be obtained from all children. This is the guideline that we also recommend. Not only is it more ethically acceptable to obtain the assent of minors, but doing so might also enhance the validity of the study. Insisting that minors participate when they clearly state that they do not want to can alter their behavioral responses and introduce a confounding influence on the data collected.

EXHIBIT 6.4 Example of a Parental Consent to Participate in Research for Use With Minors

Dear Parent or Legal Guardian:

I am doing research about children's ideas about effort. I would like to know whether ideas about effort are related to how children study and remember in learning and testing situations. I am asking for your permission to let your child be in this research.

There will be two 30-minute sessions alone with your child or in small groups. The sessions will be held in a room at your child's school during school hours. The time will be selected by your child's teacher. During the first session, your child will be asked to fill out two questionnaires. The Students' Perception of Control Questionnaire will be given to small groups.

The questionnaire has 60 questions about why things happen in school. It measures students' beliefs about whether they can make good grades if they try. The second questionnaire is a measure of self-esteem. It measures how a child feels about himself or herself in different situations such as at school and with friends.

In the second session, your child will be asked to put together a difficult puzzle. Each child will be shown the solution to the puzzle and then will be asked to study and remember some pictures. Some children will be told that the memory task is a test to see how well they remember, and others will be told it is a chance to learn how to remember better. Finally, children will be asked to rate how well they did, how they feel about what they just did, and whether they would like to do something like this again.

I would also like to look at your child's intelligence and achievement test scores. I am asking permission to use your child's records. Any personal information about you or your child will be confidential. The results from this research may be presented at a professional meeting or published in a professional journal, but your child's name and other identifying information will not be revealed.

You are under no obligation for your child to participate in this project. If you give your consent, you are free to change your mind and remove your child at any time without negative consequences. Also, your child is free to refuse to participate at any time without negative consequences.

If you are willing for your child to participate, and your child wants to participate, please sign below and return this form to school with your child. If you have any questions, please contact me at (111) 765-4321.

Sincerely,
Jane Doe, PhD
Assistant Professor

I give my permission for my child to be tested on the memory task described in this letter and to complete the questionnaires concerning beliefs about effort and self-esteem. I grant the County Public School System permission to release to Dr. Jane Doe or her assistant my child's test scores and/or access to my child's files.

________________________ ________________

Child's Name Birth Date

________________________ ________________

Signature of Parent/Legal Guardian Date

Passive Versus Active Consent

Our discussion of consent has, up to this point, focused on active consent. **Active consent** involves consenting to participate in a research study by signing a consent form. However, educational researchers conduct many studies using minors as the research participants. This means that consent must be obtained from the minors' parents or legal guardians. The typical way in which consent is obtained is to provide the parent or legal guardian with a consent form by some means, such as mailing the consent form or sending it home with the minor. Ideally, the parent would read the consent form, either give or refuse consent, and return the consent form to the researcher. However, studies (e.g., Ellickson, 1989) have revealed that only 50% to 60% of parents return the consent forms even when follow-up efforts are made. One interpretation of the failure to return the consent forms is that the parents are denying consent. However, there are other reasons why parents do not return consent forms. They might not have received the form, they might have forgotten to sign and return it, or they might not have taken enough time to read and consider the request. The existence of any of these possibilities would reduce the sample size and possibly bias the results.

▪ **Active consent** A process whereby consent is provided by signing a consent form

■ **Passive consent** A process whereby consent is given by not returning the consent form

To increase participation in research studies, Ellickson (1989) recommended the use of passive consent. **Passive consent** is a process whereby consent is given by not returning the consent form. Parents or legal guardians are told to return the consent form only if they do *not* want their child to participate in the research. Some investigators have promoted passive consent as a legitimate means of securing parental consent. Ethical concerns have been raised when passive consent procedures are used, however, because these studies might include children whose parents actually opposed their participation in the research but did not return the consent form or maybe did not receive it. Research (e.g., Ellickson & Hawes, 1989; Severson & Ary, 1983) has revealed that active and passive consent procedures yield comparable rates of participation when the active consent procedures include extensive follow-up techniques. This suggests that nonresponse to passive consent represents latent consent and that it might be an appropriate means of obtaining consent. Exhibit 6.5 provides an example of a passive consent form.

Although there is a place for passive consent, we recommend that you use active consent whenever possible. This is the best form of consent. Passive consent should be considered only when the integrity of the study would be seriously compromised by requiring active consent.

■ **EXHIBIT 6.5** Example of a Passive Consent Form

Dear Parent or Legal Guardian:

I am a faculty member in the Education Department at Excel University. I am interested in finding the best method of teaching mathematical concepts. To identify the best method, I am planning a study that will compare two different methods of teaching mathematical concepts. Both teaching methods are acceptable and standard methods of teaching these concepts, but we do not know which is the more effective method. My research will identify the more effective method.

To identify the more effective method, during the next 6 weeks I will be presenting material in two different ways to separate classes. To test the effectiveness of each method, I will measure students' performance by giving them a standard math test.

Your child's responses will remain confidential and will be seen only by myself and my research assistant.

No reports about this study will contain your child's name. I will not release any information about your child without your permission.

Participation in this study is completely voluntary. All students in the class will take the test. If you do not wish your child to be in this study, please fill out the form at the bottom of this letter and return it to me. Also, please tell your child to hand in a blank test sheet when the class is given the mathematics test so that your child will not be included in this study.

I will also ask the children to participate and tell them to hand in a blank test sheet if they do not want to be included in the study. Your child can choose to stop and not participate at any time.

If you have any questions about the study, please contact Professor John Doe, Excel University, Department of Education, Good Place, AL 12345, phone (251) 246-8102. You can also contact me at [provide address and phone number].

Thank you,
John Doe

Return this portion only if you do not want your child to participate in the study described above.

I do not wish for my child ______________________________ to be in the research study on the teaching of math concepts being conducted in his/her classroom.

______________________________ ______________
Parent's Signature Date

Additional Consent

Many educational research studies are conducted within the confines of a school system. These studies require the approval and cooperation of a variety of individuals such as the teacher, principal, and superintendent. Often a study cannot be legally conducted without approval from a particular office or administrator in the system. The researcher must not underemphasize the importance of this. You must identify the "gatekeepers" in your particular school or organization and deal with all questions that they might pose.

REVIEW QUESTIONS

6.6 What must a researcher do to ensure that his or her study is ethical?

6.7 What kinds of information does a consent form have to include?

6.8 Under what conditions can an investigator get a waiver of the requirement of informed consent?

6.9 What is the difference between consent from a minor's legal guardian and assent from the minor, and why are both important?

6.10 What is the difference between active and passive consent, and what are the advantages and disadvantages of each?

Deception

Under the principle of informed consent, research participants are supposed to receive information about the purpose and nature of the study in which they are being asked to participate so that they can evaluate the procedures to be followed and make an informed judgment as to whether they want to participate. Sometimes, however, providing full disclosure of the nature and purpose of a study will alter the outcome and invalidate the study. In such instances, it is necessary to mislead or withhold information from the research participants. It is often necessary to engage in some degree of **deception** to conduct a valid research study.

- **Deception** Misleading or withholding information from the research participant

Although the AERA Ethical Standards discourage the use of deception, these standards recognize that some research studies cannot be conducted without its use. For example, Butler and Neuman (1995) investigated some of the variables that influenced help-seeking behaviors among children. In conducting this study, the experimenters did not inform the children that they were studying the variables that influence whether they would seek help. Rather, the children were invited to try out some materials that consisted of completing several puzzles. They were not given any information suggesting that the variable of interest was help seeking but were given instructions as to how to seek help if they were so inclined. In this study, it was necessary to make use of deception in the form of withholding information because, if the true purpose of the study had been revealed, it could have altered the outcome and invalidated the results.

The form of deception used by Butler and Neuman (1995) consisted of withholding information. Withholding information is one of the milder forms of deception. However, even use of this mild form of deception might violate the principle of informed consent and therefore is of ethical concern. This is why the AERA Ethical Standards explicitly state that deception is discouraged unless it is necessary for the integrity of the study.

If deception is used, the reasons for the deception should be explained to the participants in the debriefing session held after the study has been completed. **Debriefing** refers to an interview conducted with each research participant after he or she has completed the study. In this interview, the experimenter and research participant talk about the study. It is an opportunity for each research participant to comment freely about any part of the study and express any concerns. S. R. Phillips (1994), for example, realized that her survey of adolescents' attitudes and behavior related to HIV/AIDS prevention was bound to raise questions not only about the survey but also about related issues. Consistent with Phillips's expectations, the student research participants asked numerous questions regarding HIV/AIDS specifically and sexuality more generally.

- **Debriefing** A poststudy interview in which all aspects of the study are revealed, any reasons for deception are explained, and any questions the participant has about the study are answered
- **Dehoaxing** Informing study participants about any deception that was used and the reasons for its use
- **Desensitizing** Helping study participants deal with and eliminate any stress or other undesirable feelings that the study might have created

Debriefing is also an opportunity for the researcher to reveal aspects of the study that were not disclosed at the outset. Holmes (1976a, 1976b) has pointed out that debriefing should meet the two goals of dehoaxing and desensitizing. **Dehoaxing** refers to informing the participants about any deception that was used and explaining the reasons for its use. The goal is to restore the participant's trust in the research process. **Desensitizing** refers to helping participants, during the debriefing interview, deal with and eliminate any stress or other undesirable feelings that the study might have created in them, as might exist if you are studying cheating behavior or failure. Desensitizing might be accomplished by suggesting that any undesirable behavior or feeling was the result of a situational variable, rather than a characteristic of the participant. Another tactic used by experimenters is to point out that the participant's behavior or feeling was normal and expected.

Freedom to Withdraw

AERA ethical standards explicitly state that research "participants have the right to withdraw from a study at any time, unless otherwise constrained by their official capacity or roles." This principle seems straightforward and easily accomplished: Merely inform the participant that he or she is free to withdraw from the study at any time. From the researcher's perspective, such a statement would seem to be sufficient to comply with the "freedom to withdraw" principle. However, from the participant's perspective, such a statement might not be sufficient because he or she might feel coercive pressure to participate. Such pressure could arise if a teacher requests students to participate or if a principal or superintendent asks teachers to participate in a study. Students might feel coercive pressure if they think that their grades might be affected if they don't participate, or teachers might believe that their jobs are in jeopardy if they refuse participation. In such instances, the participant is not completely free to withdraw, and the researcher must make a special effort to assure the research participants that refusing to participate or withdrawing from the study will have no adverse effect on them.

Protection From Mental and Physical Harm

The most important and fundamental ethical issue confronting the researcher is the treatment of research participants. Earlier, we provided examples of unethical medical studies that inflicted both physical and mental harm on participants. Fortunately, studies conducted by educational researchers seldom, if ever, run the risk of inflicting such severe mental and physical harm. Educational research has historically imposed either minimal or no risk to the participants and has enjoyed a special status with respect to formal ethical oversight. Much of this research has been singled out for exempt status in the Code of Federal Regulations for the Protection of Human Subjects (OPRR Reports, 1991). Paragraph 46.101(b)(1) of this code states that the following is exempt from oversight:

> research conducted in established or commonly accepted educational settings involving normal educational practices such as (i) research on regular and special educational instructional strategies, or (ii) research on the effectiveness of or the comparison among instructional techniques, curricula, or classroom management methods. (p. 5)

The problem with this statement lies in its ambiguity. It is worded so vaguely as to leave considerable room for competing interpretations as to what represents "commonly accepted educational settings involving normal educational practices." Additionally, educational research is not a static entity but one that is constantly changing. One of the more notable changes is the increased use of qualitative research methods.

Qualitative research, as Howe and Dougherty (1993) have pointed out, has two features, intimacy and open-endedness, that muddy the ethical waters and might exclude it from the special exempt status reserved for many educational research studies. Qualitative research is an ongoing and evolving process, with the data-collection process proceeding much like a friendship between the participant and the researcher. Interviewing, for example, requires one-to-one contact and removes the participant from his or her normal activities. Video- and audiotaping create permanent records that can pose a threat to confidentiality and anonymity. It is these activities as well as the ambiguity of the wording identifying "exempt" that indicate a need for some type of ethical oversight of educational research. The ethical oversight provided by virtually any institution that conducts research is the **Institutional Review Board (IRB)**. Unfortunately, some IRB members have demonstrated minimal understanding of qualitative research, and the relationship between IRB and qualitative research has been somewhat stormy (Lincoln, 2005).

- **Institutional Review Board (IRB)** The institutional review committee that assesses the ethical acceptability of research proposals

Confidentiality, Anonymity, and the Concept of Privacy

AERA ethical standards state that researchers are ethically required to protect the confidentiality of both the participants and the data. This component of the ethical standards relates to the concept of privacy. **Privacy** refers to controlling other people's access to information about a person. There are two aspects to this concept (Folkman, 2000). The first involves a person's freedom to identify the time and circumstances under which information is shared with or withheld from others. For example, people might not want information about their sexual behavior to be shared with others, or they might agree to share this information only if it is aggregated with others' information so that individuals cannot be identified. The second is the person's right to decline receiving information that he or she does not want. For example, a person might not want to know if he or she performed worse on a task than the average person.

- **Privacy** Having control of others' access to information about a person

Respecting the privacy of research participants is at the heart of the conduct of ethical research. Maintaining this privacy can be difficult at times because constitutional and federal laws have not been passed that would protect the privacy of information collected within the context of social and behavioral research. Researchers attempt to ensure the privacy of research participants by either collecting anonymous information or ensuring that the information collected is kept confidential. Anonymity is the best way to protect privacy because **anonymity** means that the identity of the participants is not known to the researcher. For example, anonymity could be achieved in a survey about cheating on examinations if the survey did not ask the students for any information that could be used to identify them (e.g., name, student number) and if the survey was administered in a manner (e.g., in a group setting) in which the researcher cannot attach a name to the completed survey instrument. Picou (1996) has revealed that removing all identifiers from data files might not be sufficient to maintain research participants' anonymity because a careful examination of participants' responses might allow a third party to deduce a participant's identity. This was a hard lesson Picou learned during a year in federal court.

- **Anonymity** Keeping the identity of the participant from everyone, including the researcher

Confidentiality is the other means that researchers use to protect the privacy of research participants. **Confidentiality**, in the context of a research study, is an agreement with the research investigators about what can be done with the information obtained about a research participant. Typically, this means that the participant's identity is not revealed to anyone other than the researcher and his or her staff. Confidentiality would be maintained, for example, if you were conducting a study on children with learning disabilities. Although the research staff would know which children were in the study and, therefore, had a learning disability, this information would not be revealed to anyone outside the research staff.

- **Confidentiality** Not revealing the identity of the participant to anyone other than the researcher and his or her staff

Although confidentiality is an important part of maintaining the privacy of research participants, researchers must be careful about what they promise. All states mandate reporting of child abuse or neglect. Researchers must be familiar with state and federal laws to determine what can and cannot be kept confidential, and this information should be included in the informed consent.

REVIEW QUESTIONS

6.11 What is deception, and when is it used in a research study?

6.12 What are the ethical obligations of a researcher who makes use of deception?

6.13 Why can participants still feel pressured to participate in a study even after the researcher has stated that they can withdraw or decline to participate?

6.14 What are the issues relating to freedom to withdraw with respect to minors?

6.15 Why do educational researchers have to be concerned with protecting participants from mental and physical harm in their studies?

6.16 What is the difference between confidentiality and anonymity, and how do each of these relate to the concept of privacy?

INSTITUTIONAL REVIEW BOARD

The legal requirement of having all human research reviewed by the IRB dates back to 1966. At that time, there was a serious concern for the way in which medical research was designed and conducted. The US surgeon general initiated an institutional review requirement at the

Department of Health, Education, and Welfare (DHEW). This policy was extended to all investigations funded by the Public Health Service that involved human participants, including those in the social and behavioral sciences. By 1973, DHEW regulations governing human research required a review by an IRB for all research organizations receiving Public Health Service funds. This meant that virtually all universities had to establish an IRB and file an assurance policy with the Office for Protection From Research Risks. This assurance policy articulates the responsibilities and purview of the IRB within that organization. Although the Public Health Service mandated only that federally funded projects be reviewed by the IRB, most organizations extended the scope of the IRB to include all research involving human participants, even those falling into the exempt category. Once an organization's assurance policy is approved, it becomes a legal document with which the organization and researchers must comply. If your university has such an assurance policy, you as an educational researcher must submit a proposal to the IRB to determine whether your study is exempt from ethical oversight. In this proposal, you should state whether you believe that it falls into the exempt category. A member of the IRB decides whether the study is exempt and can proceed as proposed or must be reviewed by the full IRB. The term **exempt studies** refers to research that is exempt from certain requirements and full committee review, not exempt from IRB oversight altogether.

■ **Exempt studies** Studies involving no risk to participants and not requiring full IRB review

In reviewing the research proposals, members of the IRB are required to make judgments regarding the ethical appropriateness of the proposed research and ensure that research protocols are explained to research participants and any risks of harm are reasonable in relation to the hoped-for benefits. To make this judgment, IRB members must have sufficient information about the specifics of the proposed research study. This means that the investigator must submit a **research protocol** that the IRB can review. Table 6.3 identifies the information that must be included in this protocol. A sample protocol excluding the consent form appears in Exhibit 6.6.

■ **Research protocol** The document submitted to the IRB by the researcher for review

TABLE 6.3 Information to Be Included in a Research Protocol

- Purpose of the research
- Relevant background and rationale for the research
- Participant population
- Experimental design and methodology
- Incentives offered, if any
- Risks and benefits to participants and precautions to be taken
- Privacy and confidentiality

Once the research protocol is submitted, the IRB administrators determine whether the protocol should be reviewed by the full board. There are three categories of review that a proposal might receive from the IRB. These categories relate to the potential risk of the study to participants. Studies can receive *exempt* status, *expedited* review, or *review by full board.* Exempt studies are those that appear to involve no risk to the participants and do not require review by the full IRB. Studies involving fetal participants and prisoners are never exempt unless the study involves observing these participants in the absence of any type of intervention. Also, studies with children involving survey or interview procedures

EXHIBIT 6.6 Example of a Research Protocol Submitted to the IRB

Title of Protocol The Relationship of Attributional Beliefs, Self-Esteem, and Ego Involvement to Performance on Cognitive Tasks in Students With Mental Retardation

Primary Investigator: Jane A. Donner, Department of Psychology, University of the Southeast, 460-6321

Co-Investigator: Carolyn L. Pickering, Graduate Student, Department of Psychology, University of the Southeast, 460-6321

Relevant Background and Purpose: Recent research suggests that the way in which a cognitive task is presented influences performance on the task. Nicholls (1984) suggested that ego involvement would often result in diminished task performance. He described ego involvement as a task orientation in which the goal is either to demonstrate one's ability relative to others or avoid demonstrating a lack of ability. This ego orientation is in contrast to task involvement, where the goal is simply to learn or improve a skill. In support of the Nicholls position, Graham and Golan (1991) found that ego-involving instructions resulted in poorer recall in a memory task than task-orienting instructions. Apparently, the focus on performance detracted from the necessary information processing.

The present investigation is designed to determine potential individual differences in the ego-involvement effect. It is possible that some persons are more at risk for the debilitating effects of ego-involving instructions than others. It is predicted that students with mental retardation who have low self-esteem and negative attributional beliefs will be influenced negatively by ego-involving instructions.

Participant Population: Forty students with mental retardation will be recruited from special education classrooms at approximately three elementary schools in the Mobile County Public School System. Students will be recruited from the intermediate classes (fourth through sixth grades). The students' participation will be voluntary, and they will have parental consent.

Materials and Procedure

Overview. The research will be conducted at the students' school and will include two sessions, each approximately a half hour long. In the first session, students will first complete attributional and self-esteem questionnaires, which will be read aloud to them, in small groups of about three. Students will be read pretraining exercises and provided guidance in answering the questions to be sure they understand how to answer the actual questionnaires.

In the next session, students will be tested individually. They will first work on a geometric puzzle task, which they will not have time to finish. The examiner will then show them how to finish the puzzle. Next, half the subjects will receive a categorization memory task with ego-orienting instructions, and the other half will receive the same task with task-orienting instructions.

Questionnaires. The attributional questionnaire (attached) is designed to assess the students' beliefs about the importance of different causal factors (e.g., effort, ability, luck, and powerful others) in academic performance. The self-esteem questionnaire (attached) is designed to measure global self-worth and self-esteem in four domains.

Experimental Tasks. The geometric puzzle task will use a difficult block design task from an intelligence test for children. One pattern on a card, which is not included in the intelligence test, will be shown to children for them to copy with their blocks, and they will be given 60 seconds to work on the design. It is not expected that the children will be able to finish the puzzle, and the examiner will then show the students how to finish the puzzle.

The categorization memory task will be used to assess students' performance. Each child will be presented with 16 pictures classifiable according to categories (e.g., clothes, vehicles, animals) with 4 items in each category. Relatively typical items (e.g., car, truck, boat, motorcycle) are used as stimuli. Children will first be given 60 seconds to arrange the pictures in any way that will help them remember. If a student does not touch the items, he or she will be reminded that he or she can arrange them in any way he or she would like. After 60 seconds, students will be given an additional 60 seconds to study their arrangement of the items, after which they will recall the items in any order. Students will be given three trials of the task. This task will yield three measures: (a) clustering (ARC) at organization (Roenker, Thompson, & Brown, 1971), (b) ARC at recall, and (c) recall accuracy. ARC scores indicate the amount of clustering relative to chance. An ARC score of 1 reflects perfect clustering, whereas an ARC score of 0 reflects the degree of clustering that would be expected by chance.

Instructional Formats. The categorization memory task will be presented in two instructional formats (adapted from Graham & Golan, 1991). Students will be randomly assigned to receive either the task-involvement format or the ego-involvement format. The instructions for the task-involvement format areas follow:

> You will probably make mistakes on this memory task at first, but you will probably get better as you go on. If you think about the task and try to see it as something you can learn from, you will have more fun doing it.

The instructions for the ego-involvement format are as follows:

> You are either good at this memory task compared to others or you are not. How well you do in this task will tell me something about your memory ability in this kind of activity.

After being read the instructions, the students will begin the task. At the end of the session, students will be asked to rate from 1 to 5 how well they think they did, how much fun they thought the task was, whether they would like to do the memory task again in the future, and whether they felt certain emotions (such as happy, sad, proud, and ashamed) during the task. Following this questionnaire, students will be told that since they performed so well on the tasks, they will receive a prize, such as a sticker or piece of candy.

Design and Methodology: Following approval by the appropriate school personnel, the attached consent form will be distributed by the classroom teacher. Students who return the consent form signed by their parent or guardian are then invited to participate in the research. Parental consent will also be requested to obtain students' IQ scores from their school files. These scores will be used to determine whether students' scores are within the range specified by the American Association on Mental Retardation and to obtain a group mean for the students. The data will be analyzed through multiple regression with attributions, self-esteem, and instructional format as predictors of performance.

Potential Benefit: The present literature on ego- and task-involvement indicates that ego instructions can negatively affect performance. It is important to determine the individual differences in this phenomenon. It is possible that children with mental retardation and with low self-esteem and with negative attributional beliefs are especially at risk for the debilitating effects of ego-involving instructions. If this is the case, one could reduce these individual differences in performance and support optimal learning by presenting tasks primarily in a task-involvement format.

Risks: The risks are minimal. It is possible that students will be discouraged by not having time to complete the puzzle and by not remembering all of the pictures. However, at the end of the session, we will make it clear to each student that the tasks were designed to be difficult for everyone. In addition, all students will be told at the end of the session that they did very well on the task.

Confidentiality: All personal information will remain confidential. All data will be stored securely in a locked laboratory on campus. Only the principal investigator and her assistants will have access to these data.

Signatures:

____________________________ ________________

Primary Investigator Date

____________________________ ________________

Department Chairperson Date

or observation of public behavior by the researchers are never exempt unless the study involves observing them in the absence of any type of intervention.

If the IRB staff reviews a protocol and places it in the exempt category, the protocol is typically returned to the investigator within a few days, and the investigator is free to begin his or her research project. Remember that *it is the IRB staff, not the researcher, that decides whether the protocol is exempt.* In making this decision, the IRB staff makes use of the exempt categories that are set forth in the OPRR Reports (1991) and listed in Table 6.4. These categories reveal that a large portion of educational research is exempt.

TABLE 6.4 Exempt Categories

1. Research conducted in established or commonly accepted educational settings, involving normal educational practices, such as (a) research on regular and special education instructional strategies or (b) research on the effectiveness of or the comparison among instructional techniques, curricula, or classroom management methods.
2. Research involving the use of educational tests (cognitive, diagnostic, aptitude, achievement), survey procedures, interview procedures, or observation of public behavior, unless:
   a. information obtained is recorded in such a manner that the participants can be identified, directly or through identifiers linked to the participants; and
   b. any disclosure of the participants' responses outside the research could reasonably place the participants at risk of criminal or civil liability or be damaging to the participants' financial standing, employability, or reputation.
3. Research involving the use of educational tests (cognitive, diagnostic, aptitude, achievement), survey procedures, interview procedures, or observation of public behavior that is not exempt under 2 above if
   a. the participants are elected or appointed public officials or candidates for public office, or
   b. federal statute(s) require(s) without exception that the confidentiality of the personally identifiable information will be maintained throughout the research and thereafter.
4. Research involving the collection or study of existing data, documents, records, pathological specimens, or diagnostic specimens if these sources are publicly available or if the information is recorded by the investigator in such a manner that participants cannot be identified, directly or through identifiers linked to the participants.
5. Research and demonstration projects that are conducted by or subject to the approval of department or agency heads and that are designed to study, evaluate, or otherwise examine:
   a. public benefit or service programs,
   b. procedures for obtaining benefits or services under those programs,
   c. possible changes in or alternatives to those programs or procedures, or
   d. possible changes in methods or levels of payment for benefits or services under those programs.

Source: From OPRR Reports. (1991). *Code of Federal Regulations 45* (Part 46, p. 5). Washington, DC: US Government Printing Office.

However, even if a study does fall into one of the exempt categories and receives approval from the IRB, there still are ethical issues to be considered. S. R. Phillips (1994) submitted her survey of adolescents' attitudes and behaviors related to HIV/AIDS prevention to the IRB and received approval pending only minor changes in the vocabulary of the consent form. She requested a full board review even though the study was an anonymous survey of adolescents' attitudes. Then, even with IRB approval, Phillips identified a number of ethical concerns ranging from privacy issues to potential harm to the participants. Again, the investigator must remain attuned to the ethics of his or her research and not become complacent just because IRB approval has been received.

If you submit a study that is exempt, you should not assume that this exempts you from the necessity of obtaining informed consent. The IRB might waive the requirement of informed consent under two conditions. First, if the consent document is the only record that could link the participant to the research and the primary harm arising from the research is a breach of confidentiality, informed consent might be waived. Second, if the research presents no more than minimal risk to participants and consent procedures are typically not required in the context of the study, informed consent might be waived. All other studies must obtain informed consent. Remember that it is the IRB that must provide the waiver of informed consent.

Some studies qualify for expedited review. **Expedited review** is a process whereby a study is rapidly reviewed by fewer members than constitute the full IRB board. Studies that receive expedited review are typically those involving no more than minimal risk, such as the following:

- **Expedited review** A process by which a study is rapidly reviewed by fewer members than constitute the full IRB board

- Research involving data, documents, records, or specimens that have been collected or will be collected solely for nonresearch purposes
- Research involving the collection of data from voice, video, digital, or image recordings made for research purposes
- Research on individual or group characteristics or behavior or research employing survey, interview, oral history, focus groups, program evaluation, human factors evaluation, or quality assurance methodologies when they present no more than minimal risk to participants

- **Full board review** Review by all members of the IRB

All other studies receive **full board review**, or review by all members of the IRB.

REVIEW QUESTIONS

6.17 What is the purpose of the IRB?

6.18 What kinds of information should be contained in a research protocol submitted to the IRB?

6.19 What are exempt studies, and what type of studies meet the exempt criterion?

6.20 What is expedited review, and what type of studies would receive expedited review?

Ethical Issues in Electronic Research

Over the past decade, researchers have increasingly turned to the Internet as a medium for conducting research. For example, Smucker, Earleywine, and Gordis (2005) made use of the Internet in their study examining the relationship between alcohol consumption and cannabis use. The increasing use of the Internet in the conduct of research is logical given the advantages it offers. Internet studies can access a large number of individuals in a short period of time, as well as individuals with diverse backgrounds. Conducting research through the Internet medium also raises ethical issues around topics such as informed consent, privacy, and debriefing. While these issues are recognized and discussed by such organizations as the American Association for the Advancement of Science (see http://www.aaas.org/spp/sfrl/projects/intres/report.pdf) and the Association of Internet Research (see http://www.aoir.org/reports/ethics.pdf), the development of a firm set of guidelines has not been achieved. Despite the absence of such guidelines, we want to elaborate on some of the ethical issues surrounding Internet research.

Informed Consent and Internet Research

Obtaining the informed consent of participants is a vital component of conducting ethical research because this component recognizes the autonomy of research participants. The issue of when informed consent should be obtained is complicated because it involves a determination of what is public and what is private behavior. Informed consent might not be needed with data collected from the public domain. For example, data collected from television or radio programs or from books or conferences are definitely within the public domain. However, are data obtained from newsgroups, email discussion lists, and chat rooms within the public or private domain? Some view these components of cyberspace as being in the public domain because the communications are there for anyone to read. Others disagree because, although the communications are public, the cyberspace participants might perceive and expect a degree of privacy in their communications. This issue has not yet been resolved.

If it is determined that a study requires informed consent, then the issue becomes how to obtain it. Informed consent has three components: providing the information to participants, ensuring that they comprehend it, and obtaining voluntary consent to participate. Obviously, a consent form can be placed online with a request that the participant read the form and check a box next to a statement such as "I agree to the above consent form." However, how do you ensure that the participant comprehends the information contained in the consent form, and how do you answer questions he or she might have? If a study is online, it is accessible 24 hours a day, but researchers are not. To try to deal with this issue, Nosek and Banaji (2002) have suggested that consent forms be accompanied by FAQs (frequently asked questions) that anticipate potential questions and concerns and address them.

Privacy and Internet Research

Maintaining the privacy of the data collected from research participants is essential to the conduct of an ethical study because participants can be harmed when their privacy is invaded or when their confidential information is inappropriately disseminated. This is important when conducting research over the Internet because one's ability to maintain the privacy and confidentiality of information is limited online. Privacy and confidentiality can be compromised during data transmission and storage in a multitude of ways from hackers to someone sending an email to the wrong address. However, Nosek and Banaji (2002) pointed out that it might be possible to guarantee a *greater* degree of privacy of research data collected over the Internet than in standard studies. This is because data transmitted over the Internet can be encrypted and, if no identifying information is collected, the only possible connection to a participant is the Internet Protocol (IP) address. Moreover, because IP addresses identify machines and not individuals, the only way an IP address could be connected to a participant is if the participant is the sole user of the machine or computer. If identifying data are obtained, then the guarantee of privacy and confidentiality is not as effective if the information is stored in a file that is on an Internet-connected server. Most of the data collected in educational studies are of little interest to hackers, so we suspect that there usually is little risk of the data being compromised by hackers. Nonetheless, individuals conducting Internet research must consider this possibility and take as many precautions as necessary to prevent it.

Debriefing and Internet Research

To conduct an ethical study, it is sometimes necessary to debrief participants following completion of the research. To be most effective, debriefing should be interactive, with the researcher providing a description of the study, including its purpose and the way in which the study was conducted. The researcher should also be available to answer any questions the participant might have and, more important, to ensure that the participant is adequately dehoaxed if deception was used or desensitized if the participant was made to feel uncomfortable. However, the Internet can create difficulties in effectively debriefing participants for a variety of reasons. The study might be terminated early through a computer or server crash caused by a broken Internet connection or a power outage. The participant might become irritated with the study or decide to terminate voluntarily because he or she is bored, is frustrated, is late for an appointment, or does not want to miss a television program. Nosek and Banaji (2002) have identified several options researchers can use to maximize the probability of a debriefing in the event that a study is terminated early, including the following:

- Require the participant to provide an email address so that a debriefing statement can be sent to him or her.
- Provide a "leave the study" radio button on every page that will direct the participant to a debriefing page.
- Incorporate a debriefing page into the program driving the study that directs the participant to this page if the study is terminated prior to completion.

As you can see, researchers conducting research on the Internet encounter a number of ethical issues that do not have a perfect solution. If you are going to conduct a study using the Internet, you must consider the issues of privacy, informed consent, and debriefing just discussed and identify the best way to accomplish each. In doing this, you must keep in mind both the ethical standards and the fact that data collected over the Internet are potentially available to anyone if they are not encrypted.

Ethical Issues in Preparing the Research Report

Throughout this chapter, we have concentrated on various ethical issues that must be considered in designing and conducting an ethical study. After you have completed the study, the last phase of the research process is to communicate the results of the study to others. Communication most frequently takes place through the professional journals in a field. This means that you must write a research report stating how the research was conducted and what was found. In writing the research report, several ethical issues must be considered.

Authorship

Authorship identifies the individual(s) who are responsible for the study. It is important because it is a record of a person's scholarly work, and, for the professional, it relates directly to decisions involving salary, hiring, promotion, and tenure. For the student, it can have implications for getting into a graduate program or for securing a job on completion of doctoral studies. Authorship, therefore, has serious implications for everyone involved. It is not necessarily true, however, that everyone who makes a contribution to the research study should receive authorship. Authorship should be confined to those individuals who made a substantial contribution to conceptualization, design, execution, analysis, or interpretation. The order of authorship of these individuals is typically such that the person who made the most substantial contribution is listed as the first author. Those who have made a contribution of a technical nature, such as collecting, coding, or entering data into a computer file or running a standard statistical analysis under the supervision of someone else, do not usually warrant authorship. These individuals' contributions are generally acknowledged in a footnote.

Writing the Research Report

The primary ethical guideline that must be followed in writing the research report is honesty and integrity. You should never fabricate or falsify any information presented, and you should report the methodology used in collecting and analyzing the data as accurately as possible and in a manner that allows others to replicate the study and draw reasonable conclusions about its validity. In writing a research report, it is necessary, especially with quantitative studies, to make use of the work of others both in the introduction section, where you set down the rationale for the study, and in the discussion section, where you discuss your study's findings and relate them to the findings of others.

When making use of the contributions of others, it is essential that you give credit to them. Making use of the contributions of others without giving them credit constitutes plagiarism. **Plagiarism** occurs when you use someone's idea or copy someone else's words but do not give that person credit. When you do not give credit, you are passing someone else's work off as yours. This is a type of scholarly thievery and is totally unethical.

- **Plagiarism** Using words or work produced by others and presenting it as your own

The type of plagiarism in which you steal someone's words occurs if you use a string of four or more words without using quotation marks and citing the author. If you have a **short quotation**, you must use quotation marks. If you are using 40 or more words, you are to display the quote as an *indented block* with quotation marks omitted and the page number provided at the end of the quote; the source must be provided in the lead-in sentence or at the end of the quotation. This type of quotation is called a **block quotation**.

- **Short quotation** Quotation of 4 or more words, but fewer than 40, around which quotation marks are used

For example, if you were using some of the material presented in the Nosek and Banaji (2002) article, you would put the brief material you were using in quotation marks and then give the authors credit as follows: Nosek and Banaji (2002) have stated, "The potential of the information highway to advance understanding of psychological science is immense" (p. 161). If you use a longer quotation (40 or more words), you would indent the quoted material as follows: Nosek and Banaji (2002) have stated:

- **Block quotation** Quotation of 40 or more words using indented format (including citation and page number)

> The potential of the information highway to advance understanding of psychological science is immense, and it is likely that the Internet will decisively shape the nature of psychological research. Yet as any researcher who has attempted to use the Internet to obtain data will have discovered, a host of methodological issues require consideration because of differences between standard laboratory research and Internet-based research concerning research methodology. (pp. 161–162)

If you do not use the author's words but do use his or her ideas or you have paraphrased something from the author, you must cite the source. For example, you might paraphrase the above quotation like this: The Internet has the potential to have a major effect on psychological research, but it brings with it many new methodological issues (Nosek & Banaji, 2002).

Another type of plagiarism is called **self-plagiarism**. This occurs if a researcher uses strings of words from one of his or her own published works in another publication without informing the reader. For the limited circumstances in which this is allowable, see the *Publication Manual of the American Psychological Association* (American Psychological Association, 2010).

- **Self-plagiarism** Presenting one's words as original when they have been used previously in another publication

While we have only addressed plagiarism with regard to published text, it is equally important that you give appropriate credit if you use tables or figures taken from someone else's work, including anything that you find on the Internet. The basic principle you must follow is that if you use something someone else has done, you must give him or her credit for that work.

See Journal Article 6.3 on the Student Study Site.

REVIEW QUESTIONS

6.21 What are the ethical issues involved in conducting research on the Internet?

6.22 What are the ethical issues involved in the preparation of the research report?

6.23 What constitutes plagiarism, and how do you give credit to another person when you use his or her work?

ACTION RESEARCH REFLECTION

Insight: Action researchers have ethics at the heart of their practice. They attempt to create a better world (their valued ethical ends) and they must act ethically (their valued ethical means). John Dewey's ethical/moral theory has been popular in action research. He emphasized that each situation can be complex (marked by competing goods and values). He argued that we should identify *problematic* situations, inquire into them, and attempt to continually improve them. Situations for Dewey included physical, social, and moral dimensions. Dewey's approach was an experimental or action research orientation that strives for growth and improvement (physical, social, and moral) in our communities and world. Dewey argued that local democracy or *democracy as a way of life* was important as we try to improve our world.

1. Think about a situation or problem that you would like to change. What is/are the negative value(s) in operation (i.e., underlying what you want to eliminate)? What is/are the positive value(s) (i.e., underlying what you want to help bring about, and why is that good)?

2. Continuing your thinking about a situation or problem you would like to change, what ethical principles and valued actions will you carry out if you conduct your action research?

3. Try to identify five major values that are near the core of your "self" (e.g., equality, tolerance, justice, love, freedom, democracy, reciprocity, fairness, justice). How do these relate to your goals and work practices?

4. How do your morals affect your actions in your profession?
5. What do you see as the strengths and weaknesses of Dewey's ethical or moral theory for action research? How might you improve his theory?

SUMMARY

Ethics are the principles and guidelines that help us to distinguish between right and wrong and to do the right thing. Research ethics assist researchers in conducting ethically sound research studies.

There are three major areas of ethical concern for the educational researcher:

1. *The relationship between society and science.* To what degree should society influence the research issues that we consider important and needing investigation? The most influential agency is the federal government because this agency not only provides most of the funds for research but also identifies priority areas.
2. *Professional issues.* The primary professional issue concerns research misconduct. In recent years, there has been an increase in the presentation of fraudulent results. Other, less serious professional issues include overlooking the use of flawed data by others.
3. *Treatment of research participants.* Treatment of research participants is the most fundamental ethical issue in research. Although most educational research does not run the risk of physical harm, many subtle ethical issues must be addressed relating to the potential for emotional harm, deception, and protecting the privacy of research participants.

The AERA has developed a set of ethical standards specifically directed toward the educational researcher, which need to be followed when conducting a research study. Some of the important points included in these standards are the following:

1. *The necessity of obtaining informed consent.* A person can participate in a research study only when he or she has agreed to participate after being given all information that would influence his or her willingness to participate. Providing full disclosure of the nature or purpose of the research will alter the outcome and invalidate the results of some studies. Therefore, the researcher usually does not disclose the exact hypothesis and, instead, provides a brief summary of the general purpose of the study.
2. *Assent and dissent with minors.* Minors cannot provide informed consent, but when they are capable of providing assent, it must be obtained.
3. *Passive versus active consent.* Although active consent is preferable and ensures that the participant has understood the demands and risks of the study, passive consent is sometimes used in educational research to increase participation and minimize bias. However, passive consent makes the assumption that nonresponse represents informed consent, which might or might not be the case.
4. *Deception.* Sometimes it is necessary to mislead or withhold information from research participants. When this is necessary, the researcher must use a debriefing session at the conclusion of the study; here you must explain that deception was used, explain the reason for the deception, and make sure that the deception did not cause any undue stress or other undesirable feelings. If such feelings were incurred, the researcher must incorporate procedures to eliminate the undesirable stress or feelings.
5. *Freedom to withdraw.* Research participants must be told that they are free to withdraw from the research study at any time without penalty. As a general rule, the dissent of a minor should be respected even if the guardian or parent has provided informed consent. Children below the age of being able to provide consent or infants should be excused from the research study if they seem to be disturbed by or uncomfortable with the procedures.

6. *Confidentiality, anonymity, and the concept of privacy.* Ideally, we should have control over who gets information about us. The best way to ensure privacy of information is to make sure that the research participant's identity is not known to anyone involved, including the researcher (anonymity). In cases in which it is not possible to maintain anonymity, the identity of the participant and his or her responses must not be revealed to anyone other than the research staff (confidentiality).

In all cases, it is necessary to present a research protocol to the IRB for approval, even if the guidelines presented by the AERA have been followed and the proposal seems to fall into the exempt category. Most organizational assurance policies state that *all* research involving humans is to be reviewed by the IRB, which means that it is the IRB that decides whether a study falls into the exempt category.

Ethical issues that have recently attracted the attention of researchers are those surrounding research conducted over the Internet. While the Internet offers many advantages, such as access to a large number of individuals over a short period of time, it raises many ethical issues: how to obtain informed consent, how to maintain the privacy of the research data collected, and how to debrief research participants once they have completed the study. No perfect solution currently exists for any of these issues, so when conducting an Internet study, you must identify the best way to accomplish each, keeping in mind the 5 Guiding Principles of the AERA and its 22 Ethical Standards.

After you have completed a research study, you should communicate the results to others, typically by publishing the results in a professional journal. When preparing the research report, you must make a decision as to the authorship, and when writing the report, you must ensure that it is written with honesty and integrity. This means that you must report everything as accurately as possible and always avoid plagiarism.

KEY TERMS

active consent (p. 135)
anonymity (p. 140)
assent (p. 134)
beneficence (p. 131)
block quotation (p. 148)
confidentiality (p. 140)
debriefing (p. 138)
deception (p. 137)
dehoaxing (p. 138)
deontological approach (p. 124)
desensitizing (p. 138)
ethical skepticism (p. 124)
ethics (p. 124)
exempt studies (p. 141)
expedited review (p. 145)
full board review (p. 145)
informed consent (p. 131)
Institutional Review Board (IRB) (p. 139)
nonmaleficence (p. 131)
passive consent (p. 136)
plagiarism (p. 148)
privacy (p. 139)
research ethics (p. 125)
research misconduct (p. 126)
research protocol (p. 141)
self-plagiarism (p. 149)
short quotation (p. 148)
utilitarianism (p. 124)

DISCUSSION QUESTIONS

1. Go to http://poynter.indiana.edu/mr/mr-banks.pdf. Read the sample case and then discuss whether Jessica Banks should photocopy the notebooks relating to her dissertation research.

2. Most of the research that educational researchers conduct falls into the exempt category. This means that requiring IRB review of educational research studies is an intrusion and a hurdle that accomplishes nothing. Therefore, IRB review of educational studies should be eliminated. Defend or refute this view.

3. Should passive consent be allowed, or does it violate ethical standards, meaning that active consent should always be obtained prior to participation in a research study?

RESEARCH EXERCISES

Find a published journal article on a topic area that interests you. Then get the article and complete the following exercises.

1. Using the published article you selected, construct a research protocol that might have been submitted to the IRB by providing the following information:

   Title of Protocol Primary Investigator

   Co-Investigator

   Relevant Background and Purpose

   Participant Population

   Materials and Procedure

   Design and Methodology

   Potential Benefit

   Risks

   Confidentiality

2. Using the published article you selected, construct an informed consent form that might be used in conjunction with this research study. Include the following:

   a. Statement of Invitation to Participate
   b. Statement of What the Study Will Ask the Participant to Do or Have Done to Him or Her
   c. Statement of the Benefits Derived From Participating in the Study
   d. Statement of the Risks Encountered From Participating in the Study
   e. Statement of How Confidentiality Will Be Maintained
   f. Identification of Person(s) Who Can Be Contacted if Questions Arise Regarding the Study

PROPOSAL EXERCISES

Assuming you are writing a research proposal this quarter/semester, please answer the following questions:

1. What specific ethical issues might come up in your proposed research study?
2. How will you deal with these issues?
3. What information will you put in your research protocol if you are to have the IRB (Institutional Review Board) evaluate your research proposal's ethical legitimacy?
4. What status do you think the IRB will consider appropriate for your research protocol: *exempt* status, *expedited* review, or *review by full board*? Why?
5. (Optional) Write a research protocol for submission to the IRB for your research study.

RELEVANT INTERNET SITES

Thinking About Research and Ethics (ethics of research in cyberspace)
http://jthomasniu.org/Papers/ethics.html

Office of Research Integrity of the US Department of Health and Human Services
http://ori.dhhs.gov

American Educational Research Association Code of Ethics
http://www.aera.net/Portals/38/docs/About_AERA/CodeOfEthics(1).pdf

American Psychological Association (ethics information)
http://www.apa.org/ethics/, also see http://www.apa.org/research/responsible/

STUDENT STUDY SITE

Visit the Student Study Site at **edge.sagepub.com/rbjohnson6e** for these additional learning tools:

- Video Links
- Self-Quizzes
- eFlashcards
- Lecture Notes
- Full-Text SAGE Journal Articles
- Interactive Concept Maps
- Web Resources

RECOMMENDED READING

Committee on Government Operations. (1990). *Are scientific misconduct and conflicts of interest hazardous to our health?* Washington, DC: US Government Printing Office.

Sales, B. D., & Folkman, S. (2002). *Ethics in research with human participants.* Washington, DC: American Psychological Association.

PART III

Foundations of Research

Chapter 7

Standardized Measurement and Assessment

LEARNING OBJECTIVES

After reading this chapter, you should be able to

- Explain the meaning of measurement.
- Explain the different scales of measurement, including the type of information communicated by each one.
- Articulate the seven assumptions underlying testing and assessment.
- Explain the meaning of reliability.
- Explain the characteristics of each of the methods for computing reliability.
- Explain the meaning of validity and validity evidence.
- Explain the different methods of collecting validity evidence.
- Identify the different types of standardized tests and the sources of information on these tests.

Visit the Student Study Site for an interactive concept map.

RESEARCH IN REAL LIFE Measuring Variables

istock/lisafx

In the 1990s, the National Center for Education Statistics published a report entitled *Adult Literacy in America* (Kaestle, Campbell, Finn, Johnson, & Mikulecky, 2001). This report stated that 47% of American adults scored in the two lowest levels of the 1992 National Adult Literacy Survey and that 21% scored at the lowest of the five literacy levels. It suggested that many Americans could not perform even the simplest tasks, such as understanding a simple news article or calculating the cost of movie tickets. Headlines of newspapers across the country stated that 50% of Americans were *functionally illiterate.* Politicians were alarmed, and many advocated increased testing and immediate school reform.

In February 2002, the *Chronicle of Higher Education* (Baron, 2002) reported that a new analysis of the 1992 survey data showed that less than 5% of the adult population was functionally illiterate. How can it be that a reanalysis of the same data dropped the illiteracy rate from 50% to less than 5%? Did the nation suddenly become more literate? In this case, the writers of the original report admitted that they had misread the data. They had used a single standard to evaluate the test results but later realized that literacy data should be viewed from multiple perspectives. Additionally, the more current 5% figure includes people with linguistic or physical problems that could have affected their performance. Of those scoring at the lowest proficiency level, 25% were immigrants, and many others were school dropouts, people older than 65, people who had significant physical or mental impairments, or people who had vision problems. Such problems would obviously affect the response to the survey.

As you can see, "literacy" is a complex issue, and it is difficult to assess. To make a statement about the literacy of the American people, we must collect data that will provide us with strong evidence that the inferences we make are defensible. Assessing literacy is not a simple matter of sorting people into those who "can read" and those who "can't read."

As educators or educational researchers, we are constantly faced with the question of how to measure the variables that are important to us. We want to measure various educational abilities and achievement levels such as mathematical performance. We want to measure constructs such as depression, stress, and self-esteem and be able to diagnose various problems such as learning disorders. In making these measurements, we collect data and then make inferences or assessments based on the data in a way very similar to what was done in the "literacy survey." In this chapter, we discuss many of the issues that must be considered to ensure that the inferences we make on the basis of our measurements are accurate, useful, and defensible.

Think for a moment about what you have learned about conducting an educational research study. You begin by formulating your research questions. Then you have to figure out how to answer each research question by collecting information, or data, that will give you an answer that is justified or warranted. Whenever you collect data, you are measuring or assessing something, and if your measurement is poor, your research will necessarily be poor. Here's a telling conversation: A new research methods student asks, "Why do we need to learn about measurement?" The professor replies, "Hmm . . . Have you heard of GIGO? In case you haven't, GIGO is the principle of garbage in, garbage out. It is a cardinal rule in research that *poor measurement results in GIGO*. Without good measurement, you don't have anything. Please remember that important point!"

DEFINING MEASUREMENT

- **Measurement** Assigning symbols or numbers to something according to a specific set of rules

Measurement refers to the act of measuring. When we measure, we identify the dimensions, quantity, capacity, or degree of something. **Measurement** operates by assigning symbols or numbers to objects, events, people, characteristics, and so forth according to a specific set of rules. Actually, this is something you do all the time. For example, when you determine how tall a person is or how much he or she weighs, you are engaged in measurement because you are assigning numbers according to a given set of rules. If you measure height in inches, you are using the rule of assigning the number 1 to a length that is exactly one inch on a standard ruler. Height is determined by counting the number of these one-inch lengths it takes to span the height of the person whom you are measuring. If you are measuring people's gender, you use the rule of assigning the symbol of *female* to individuals who have female characteristics and the symbol of *male* to individuals who have male characteristics. Stating that a person is 68 inches tall communicates the exact height of the person, just as the symbol of *female* communicates the gender dimension of the person.

Educational researchers might be interested in such variables as aggression, shyness, depression, dyslexia, gender, strategy use, and intelligence. To conduct a study investigating these variables, a procedure or technique is needed to represent the magnitude of quantitative variables (such as income and IQ) and the dimensions of categorical variables (such as gender and college major). Here are some examples: The number that is derived from an intelligence test provides an index of the magnitude of intellect. The number of times a child hits another has been used as an index of the magnitude of aggression. The biological makeup of a child is often used as an index of gender.

REVIEW QUESTION

7.1 What is measurement?

SCALES OF MEASUREMENT

Measurement can be categorized in terms of the type of information communicated by the symbols or numbers that are assigned. We now introduce you to a popular four-level classification scheme. This four-level scheme provides more information than the two-level (i.e., categorical versus quantitative variables) system used in earlier chapters. The earlier scheme works fine, and there is nothing wrong with it. Sometimes, however, researchers prefer to make the finer distinctions that are provided by the four-level system.

The four-level system, originally developed by Stevens (1946, 1951), includes four levels or "scales" of measurement: nominal, ordinal, interval, and ratio. As Table 7.1 illustrates, each of these levels conveys a different kind of information. To help you remember the order of the four levels, note that the first letters of the four scales spell the French word for "black": *noir*. (You didn't know you were going to learn French in your research methods course, did you?) It is important to know the level of measurement being employed because it suggests the type of statistical manipulations of the data that are appropriate and identifies the type of information being communicated.[1]

■ **TABLE 7.1** Scale of Measurement

Scale	*Characteristics*
Nominal	Categorizes, labels, classifies, names, or identifies types or kinds of things that can't be quantified.
Ordinal	Provides *rank order* of objects or individuals from first to last or best to worst.
Interval	Includes rank ordering and this additional characteristic: *equal intervals* or distances between adjacent numbers.
Ratio	Includes rank ordering, equal intervals, and this additional characteristic: a *true zero point*.

Nominal Scale

The first level of measurement, the nominal scale, is the simplest form of measurement. A **nominal scale** of measurement uses symbols, such as words or numbers, to label, classify, or identify people or objects. In Chapter 2, we called variables measured at this level *categorical variables*. Therefore, you are already familiar with this type of measurement. A few examples of nominal scales or nominal variables are gender, school type, race, political party, state of residence, college major, teaching method, counseling method, and personality type. The symbols that you attach to the levels of a nominal variable do little more than serve as markers. For the variable *school type,* you might use 1 for public school and 2 for private school, or you might use the full words (i.e., *public* and *private*) as your markers. For the variable *political party identification,* you might choose the markers 1 for Republican, 2 for Democrat, and 3 for other. The symbols that are used to mark the nominal variable categories cannot be added, subtracted, ranked, or averaged. However, you can count the frequency within each category, and you can relate a nominal variable to other variables.

■ **Nominal scale** A scale of measurement that uses symbols, such as words or numbers, to label, classify, or identify people or objects

Ordinal Scale

The **ordinal scale** of measurement is a rank-order scale. This scale of measurement is frequently used to determine which students will be accepted into graduate programs. Most graduate programs receive many more applicants than they can accept; therefore, applicants are rank ordered from the one with the most outstanding credentials to the one with the least outstanding credentials, and a specified number of students with the highest ranks are selected for admission. In another situation, students might be rank ordered in terms of their need for remedial instruction. In both examples, the key characteristic is that individuals are compared with others in terms of some ability or performance and assigned a rank, with 1 perhaps being assigned to the person with the most ability or the person who performs best, 2 to the next best, and so forth.

■ **Ordinal scale** A rank-order scale of measurement

You can see that an ordinal scale of measurement allows you to make ordinal judgments; that is, it allows you to determine which person is higher or lower than another person on a variable of interest. However, it does not give you any indication as to how much higher one person is than another. If you ranked 10 students in terms of their need for remedial instruction, as illustrated in Table 7.2, you would know that the person receiving a rank of 1 is the person who needs remedial instruction the most (i.e., he or she has the

TABLE 7.2 Ranking of Students on Need for Remedial Instruction

Student	*Ranking*	*Student*	*Ranking*
Tommy	1	William	6
Jerry	2	Joyce	7
Sally	3	Bob	8
Suzie	4	Pam	9
Nancy	5	Ben	10

highest or greatest need based on your measurement). However, you would not know how much more the person who was ranked first needed remedial instruction than the person who was ranked second. That's because an ordinal scale of measurement says nothing about *how much* greater one ranking is than another. All you can do with ordinal-level data is rank individuals on some characteristic according to their position on that characteristic.

Interval Scale

Interval scale A scale of measurement that has equal intervals of distances between adjacent numbers

The third level of measurement, the **interval scale**, includes the rank-order feature of ordinal scales, and it has the additional characteristic of *equal distances*, or equal intervals, between adjacent numbers on the scale. In other words, the difference between any two adjacent numbers on the scale is equal to the difference between any two other adjacent numbers.

Two examples of interval scales are the Celsius temperature scale (illustrated in Figure 7.1) and the Fahrenheit temperature scale, because all points on these scales are equally distant from one another. A difference in temperature between 0 and 20 degrees Fahrenheit is the same as the difference between 40 and 60 degrees Fahrenheit. However, you must remember that the zero point on an interval scale is arbitrary. The zero point on the Celsius scale is the point at which water freezes at sea level, not a complete absence of heat, which is what a true zero point would designate. Actually, the absence of heat is approximately –273 degrees Celsius, not the zero point on either a Celsius or a Fahrenheit temperature scale.

The absence of an absolute zero point restricts the type of information that is conveyed by interval-level measurements. Specifically, you cannot make "ratio statements." For example, it seems logical to say that 20 degrees Celsius is *twice* as warm as 10 degrees Celsius because the difference between 0 and 20 degrees is twice as great as the difference between 0 and 10 degrees, or 20/10 = 2. However, you cannot make this ratio statement because interval scales do not have absolute zero points. To illustrate this point further, consider the two temperatures 40 and 80 degrees Fahrenheit. If ratio statements could be made, 80 degrees Fahrenheit would be twice as warm as 40 degrees Fahrenheit. If this relationship were true, it would exist regardless of whether we were talking about temperature measured according to the Fahrenheit scale or the Celsius scale. However, 40 degrees Fahrenheit converts to approximately 5.4 degrees Celsius, and 80 degrees Fahrenheit converts to approximately 26.7 degrees Celsius. This paradox of an interval scale is a function of the absence of an absolute zero point.

■ **FIGURE 7.1** A Celsius temperature scale

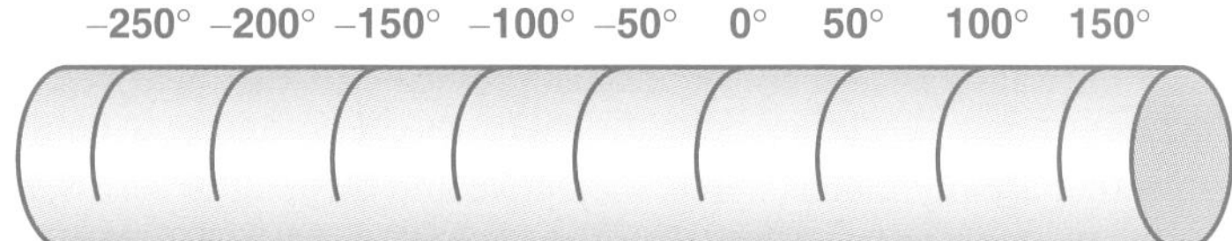

Once an interval level of measurement has been reached, it is possible to engage in arithmetic operations, such as computing an average and getting a meaningful result. Many of the scores (e.g., IQ, personality, attitude, aptitude, educational level, reading achievement) that we use in educational research are taken to be at the interval level of measurement. However, for most of the characteristics we investigate, remember that zero does not mean an absence of that characteristic. A science achievement score of zero would not necessarily mean that a person had a complete absence of science knowledge, just as an IQ score of zero would not necessarily mean a complete absence of intelligence.

Ratio Scale

The fourth level of measurement, the ratio scale, is the highest level of quantitative measurement. The **ratio scale** includes the properties of ordinal (rank order) and interval (equal distances between points) scales, plus it has a *true zero point.* The number zero represents an absence of the characteristic being measured. On the Kelvin temperature scale, zero refers to the complete absence of heat (and you thought zero degrees Fahrenheit was cold!). Most physical measurements are done at the ratio level (e.g., height, weight, age, distance, area). Something weighing zero pounds means that it is weightless. (If your weight is zero, you are in big trouble!) Similarly, if your annual income was zero dollars last year, you did not earn any money at all. Because the ratio scale of measurement has the characteristics of rank order, equal intervals, and a true or absolute zero point, all mathematical operations can meaningfully be performed.

■ **Ratio scale** A scale of measurement that has a true zero point

In education, ratio-level measurement is occasionally used. For example, if you are interested in the number of test items a student got correct or the amount of time taken to complete an assignment, you have ratio-level measurement. However, most of the characteristics that we measure in education are not at this level because educational researchers frequently deal with attributes such as educational attainment, learning disorders, personality, attitudes, opinions, and learning strategies. Such attributes and characteristics do not have all the characteristics of a ratio scale of measurement. Therefore, ratio-level measurement, desirable as it is, is not the level of measurement that is used in most educational research studies.

REVIEW QUESTION

7.2 What are the four different levels or scales of measurement, and what are the essential characteristics of each one?

ASSUMPTIONS UNDERLYING TESTING AND ASSESSMENT

As they conduct their research studies, educational researchers attempt to obtain measures of characteristics that are often considered subjective and difficult to assess, such as personality or teacher morale. Measuring these characteristics involves both testing and assessment. The distinction between testing and assessment is often somewhat ambiguous and has been slow in developing and becoming integrated into everyday parlance. However, there is a difference in spite of this overlap, and this difference needs to be made clear. For our purposes, we follow the lead of R. J. Cohen, Swerdlik, and Phillips (1996) and define **testing** as "the process of measuring . . . variables by means of devices or procedures designed to obtain a sample of behavior" and **assessment** as "the gathering and integration of . . . data for the purpose of making . . . an educational evaluation, accomplished through the use of tools such as tests, interviews, case studies, behavioral observation, and specially designed apparatus and measurement procedures" (p. 6).

- **Testing** Measurement of variables
- **Assessment** Gathering and integrating data to make educational evaluations

When assessing characteristics of interest, educational researchers use a variety of tools ranging from educational and psychological tests to interviews and behavioral observations. Educational researchers and psychometricians (i.e., professionals who specialize in test development) might devise a new assessment tool, use an existing tool, or adapt an existing tool previously used to measure a characteristic. It is important to note that virtually all measurement procedures involve some amount of error. **Error** is the difference between true scores and observed (i.e., measured) scores. It is the job of the psychometrician, or anyone else developing a test, to devise instruments that have small amounts of error when used in research and/or assessment.

- **Error** The difference between true scores and observed scores

In Table 7.3, we list seven assumptions that are commonly made by psychometricians and educational researchers who develop and use standardized tests (R. J. Cohen et al., 1996). Before looking at the table, you need to know the difference between traits and states. **Traits** are "any distinguishable, relatively enduring way in which one individual varies from another" (Guilford, 1959, p. 6); **states** are distinguishable ways in which individuals vary, but they differ from traits in that they are less enduring (Chaplin, John, & Goldberg, 1988) or are more transient characteristics. For example, trait anxiety is an enduring or constant level of anxiety that persists both over time and across situations; state anxiety is a more

- **Traits** Distinguishable, relatively enduring ways in which one individual differs from another
- **States** Distinguishable but less enduring ways in which individuals vary

TABLE 7.3 Assumptions Made by Professional Test Developers and Users

1. Psychological traits and states exist.
2. Traits and states can be quantified and measured.
3. A major decision about an individual should not be made on the basis of a single test score but, rather, from a variety of different data sources.
4. Various sources of error are always present in testing and assessment.
5. Test-related attitudes and behavior can be used to predict non–test-related attitudes and behavior.
6. With much work and continual updating, fair and unbiased tests can be developed.
7. Standardized testing and assessment can benefit society if the tests are developed by expert psychometricians and are properly administered and interpreted by trained professionals.

temporary anxiety condition, such as might exist if you were walking in the woods and saw a bear on the path in front of you. Now please examine Table 7.3.

7.3 What are the seven assumptions underlying testing and measurement?

REVIEW QUESTION

Identifying a Good Test or Assessment Procedure

When planning to conduct a research study, it is important to select measuring instruments that will provide the best and most accurate measure of the variables you intend to investigate. If you were investigating the usefulness of a reading program for teaching reading to children with dyslexia, you would need a good assessment of dyslexia to ensure that the children who are included in the study are truly dyslexic. You also would need a good measure of reading to document any change in reading achievement of the children with dyslexia as a result of having participated in the reading program. When selecting and using a measurement instrument (e.g., a test), you must always consider the issues of reliability and validity.

See Journal Article 7.1 on the Student Study Site.

Overview of Reliability and Validity

Reliability and validity are the two most important psychometric properties to consider in using a test or assessment procedure. *Reliability* is the consistency or stability of the test scores, and *validity* is the accuracy of the inferences or interpretations you make from the test scores. For example, let's say that you just got home from your local department store, where you bought a new scale for weighing yourself. It has an LCD readout that displays a number that indicates pounds. Assume that you weigh 125 pounds. You step on your new scale, and the readout says 130 pounds. You think this seems a little high, so you weigh yourself again, and this time the readout says 161. You think, "Wow! What's going on here?" You weigh yourself again, and this time the readout says 113. What is the problem with this scale? The problem is that the scores are not consistent: They are therefore *not reliable*. Because the scores are not reliable, the issue of validity is irrelevant, and you need to return your new scale to the store.

Now assume that you have a different kind of problem with your new LCD scale. Again assume that you weigh 125 pounds. You step on the scale for the first time, and the readout says 135. You know that's high, so you weigh yourself again, and the readout says 136. You weigh yourself five more times, and the readouts are 134, 135, 134, 135, and 135. This time your scale is reliable because you get approximately the same score each time. What is the problem with your new scale in this case? The problem is that there is a systematic error that occurs every time you use it. The scale is systematically high by about 10 pounds, so if you use it to infer your weight, you will be systematically wrong! In this example, the weights were reliable, but your inferences about your weight were *not valid* because the scale gave you the wrong weight. Just as in the case of unreliability, you need to return your new scale to the store.

- **Systematic error** An error that is present every time an instrument is used

In this third case, your new scale is going to work as promised. Again assume that you weigh 125 pounds. You step on the scale, and the readout says 125. You weigh yourself five more times, and the readouts are 124, 125, 125, 126, and 125. In this case, the scores are reliable (the scores are consistent), and you are also able to make a valid inference about your weight. In this case, the scores are both reliable *and* valid. You can keep your new scale because it works properly. If you think about it, you will see that *reliability is a necessary but not sufficient condition for validity,* which simply means that if you want validity, you must have reliability (Nunnally & Bernstein, 1994). On the other hand, reliability is no guarantee of validity. When judging the performance of a test and your interpretations based on that test, remember that reliability and validity are both important properties. You need both. Keep this point in mind as you read about how to obtain evidence of reliability and validity for testing and other measurements.

REVIEW QUESTION

7.4 What is the difference between reliability and validity? Which is more important?

Reliability

■ **Reliability** The consistency or stability of test scores

In psychological and educational testing, **reliability** refers to the consistency or stability of a set of test scores. If a test or assessment procedure provides reliable scores, the scores will be similar on every occasion. For example, if the scores from a test of intelligence are reliable, the same, or just about the same, IQ scores will be obtained every time the test is administered to a particular group of people.

The reliability of scores from a measure must be determined empirically. You can see a summary of the different ways of assessing reliability in Table 7.4. Each way provides a slightly different index of reliability. Researchers should select the method that provides the kind of information they need; often, several ways of computing reliability are used to demonstrate the different ways in which the scores are reliable to provide corroborating evidence of reliability. For example, test-retest and internal consistency reliability are usually reported in high-quality journal articles.

Reliability is often calculated by using some type of correlation coefficient. If you are a little rusty on the concept of correlation, you need to take a moment *right now* and reread

■ **TABLE 7.4** Summary of Methods for Computing Reliability

Type of Reliability	*Number of Testing Sessions*	*Number of Test Forms*	*Statistical Procedure*
Test-retest	2	1	Correlation coefficient
Equivalent-forms	1 or 2	2	Correlation coefficient
Internal consistency	1	1	Kuder-Richardson, coefficient alpha, or correlation coefficient
Interscorer	1	1	Correlation coefficient

the pages in Chapter 2 on correlation coefficients (i.e., see p. 44). When we calculate a correlation coefficient as our measure of reliability, we call it a **reliability coefficient.** A reliability coefficient of zero stands for no reliability at all. (If you get a negative correlation, treat it as meaning no reliability and that your test is faulty.) A reliability coefficient of +1.00 stands for perfect reliability. Researchers want reliability coefficients to be strong and positive (i.e., as close to +1.00 as possible) because this indicates high reliability. Now let's look at the different types of reliability.

- **Reliability coefficient** A correlation coefficient that is used as an index of reliability

REVIEW QUESTION

7.5 What are the definitions of reliability and reliability coefficient?

Test-Retest Reliability

Test-retest reliability is the consistency or stability of test scores over time. For example, if you were to assess the reliability of the scores from an intelligence test using the test-retest method, you would give the test to a group of, say, 100 individuals on one occasion, wait a period of time, and then give the same intelligence test to the same 100 individuals again. Then you would correlate the scores on the first testing occasion with the scores on the second testing occasion. If the individuals who received high IQ scores on the first testing occasion received high IQ scores on the second testing occasion and the individuals who received low IQ scores on the first testing occasion also received low IQ scores on the second testing occasion, the correlation between the scores on the two testing occasions would be high, indicating that the test scores were reliable. If these individuals received very different scores on the two testing occasions, the correlation between the two sets of scores would be low, indicating that the test scores were unreliable.

- **Test-retest reliability** A measure of the consistency of scores over time

Table 7.5 shows two sets of scores, one set that is reliable and another set that is unreliable. For the reliable intelligence test, the scores from the first and second testing period are about the same, which means that the test is providing about the same measure of intelligence on both testing occasions. The actual correlation (i.e., the reliability coefficient) is equal to .96, suggesting that the test-retest reliability is quite high. For the unreliable intelligence test, the scores and the rank order of the scores from the first and second testing periods are quite different. The correlation (i.e., the reliability coefficient) in this case is .23, which is extremely low for a reliability coefficient. In the first case, the scores were consistent over time; in the second case, the scores were not consistent. The assessment of intelligence would be very different in these two cases.

One of the problems with assessing test-retest reliability is knowing how much time should elapse between the two testing occasions. If the time interval is too short, the scores obtained from the second testing occasion might be similar to the first scores partially because individuals remember how they responded when they took the test the first time. In this case, the reliability of the test is artificially inflated. On the other hand, if the time interval is too long, the response to the second test might be due to changes in the individuals. As time passes, people change. They might, for example, learn new things, forget some things, or acquire new skills. Unfortunately, there does not seem to be an ideal time

■ **TABLE 7.5** Illustration of Reliable and Unreliable Intelligence Tests Using the Test-Retest Reliability Procedure

Reliable Test		*Unreliable Test*	
First Testing	*Second Testing*	*First Testing*	*Second Testing*
110	112	110	95
123	120	123	103
115	116	115	147
109	113	109	100
99	95	99	120
103	102	103	110
131	128	131	125
128	130	128	142
119	114	119	111
121	124	105	135

interval that works in all cases. The best time interval to use depends on the kind of test involved, the participants taking the test, and the specific circumstances surrounding the test that may affect participants' performance. It is safe to say that less than a week is usually too short an interval for most tests. Generally, as the length of time increases, the correlation between the scores obtained on each testing decreases. Because the time interval can have an effect on test-retest reliability, this information should always be provided in addition to the reliability coefficient when reporting results.

Equivalent-Forms Reliability

Have you ever taken an exam in which some people got one form of the test and other people got a different form of the test? If so, you have experienced the use of alternative forms. In constructing alternative forms, the tester attempts to make them equivalent in all respects. If you have ever wondered whether alternative forms are really equivalent, you have wondered about equivalent-forms reliability. **Equivalent-forms reliability** refers to the consistency of a group of individuals' scores on alternative forms of a test designed to measure the same characteristic. Two or more versions of a test are constructed so that they are identical in every way except for the specific items asked on the tests. This means that they have the same number of items; the items are of the same difficulty level; the items measure the same construct; and the test is administered, scored, and interpreted in the same way.

■ **Equivalent-forms reliability** The consistency of a group of individuals' scores on alternative forms of a test measuring the same thing

Once the two equivalent tests have been constructed, they are administered concurrently to a group of individuals, or the second test is administered shortly after the first test. Either way, each person takes both tests and has scores on both tests. The two sets of scores (participants' scores on each form) are then correlated. This correlation coefficient shows the consistency of the test scores obtained from the two forms of the test. We want this reliability coefficient to be very high and positive; that is, the individuals who do well on the first form of the test should also do well on the second form, and the individuals who perform poorly on the first form of the test should perform poorly on the second form.

Although the equivalent-forms reliability method is an excellent way of assessing reliability, the success of this method depends on the ability to construct two equivalent forms of the same test. It is difficult to construct two equivalent versions of the test because the two versions cannot include the same items. To the extent to which the versions are not equivalent, measurement error is introduced, which lowers the reliability of the test. In addition, the participants have to take essentially the same test twice in a short period of time. Sometimes this is difficult. Just think about the reaction you might have if you were told that you had to take the Graduate Record Examination (GRE) twice in the same day. Because of these problems, researchers seldom use this method of assessing reliability.

Internal Consistency Reliability

Internal consistency refers to how consistently the items on a test measure a single construct or concept. The test-retest and equivalent-forms methods of assessing reliability are general methods that can be used with just about any test. Many tests, however, are supposed to be homogeneous. A test is **homogeneous** or unidimensional when the items measure a single construct or a single dimension, such as reading comprehension or spelling ability. This is in contrast to a test that is heterogeneous or multidimensional, meaning that it measures more than one construct or dimension. For example, contrast a test that is constructed to measure academic performance of sixth-grade students with a test designed to measure just the reading comprehension of sixth-grade students. A test of academic performance would be more heterogeneous in content than a test of reading comprehension because academic performance involves many skills, one of which is reading comprehension.

- **Internal consistency** The consistency with which the items on a test measure a single construct
- **Homogeneous test** A unidimensional test in which all the items measure a single construct

Homogeneous tests have more interitem consistency (i.e., internal consistency) than do heterogeneous tests of equal length because the items focus on one construct and therefore sample a more narrow content area. Test homogeneity is generally desirable because it allows straightforward test score interpretation. If your test is multidimensional, then you should always check the internal consistency of each component of the test. For example, if your IQ test includes a reading component, a reasoning component, a mathematics component, and a creativity component, then you would need to check each of these components separately for internal consistency.

Internal consistency measures are convenient and are very popular with researchers because they only require a group of individuals to take the test one time. You do not have to wait for a period of time to elapse after administering the test before you can give it again (as in test-retest reliability), and you do not have to construct two equivalent forms of a test (as in equivalent-forms reliability). We now discuss two indexes of internal consistency: split-half reliability and coefficient alpha. Coefficient alpha is by far more popular with researchers, and you will commonly see it reported in journal articles. You will see both split-half and coefficient alpha coefficients reported in test manuals and in reviews of standardized tests.

- **Split-half reliability** A measure of the consistency of the scores obtained from two equivalent halves of the same test

Split-half reliability involves splitting a test into two equivalent halves and then assessing the consistency of scores across the two halves of the test, specifically by correlating the scores from the two halves. There are several ways of splitting a test into halves. The first procedure is to divide the test in the middle. This procedure is not recommended because factors such as different levels of fatigue influencing performance on the first versus the second half of the test, different amounts of test anxiety, and differences in item difficulty as a function of placement in the test could spuriously raise or lower the reliability coefficient. A more acceptable way to split a test is to use the odd-numbered items for one half of the test and the even-numbered items for the other half. Randomly assigning the items to one or the other half of the test is also acceptable. A fourth way is to divide the test by content so that each half contains an equal number of items that are equivalent in content and difficulty. In general, you want each half to be equal to the other in format, style, content, and other aspects. Once you have created the two halves, reliability of the scores is determined using the following steps:

1. Score each half of the test for every person to whom it was administered.
2. Compute the correlation between scores on the two halves of the test.
3. Adjust the computed correlation coefficient using the **Spearman-Brown formula** (the formula is provided at this book's companion website for interested readers).

- **Spearman-Brown formula** A statistical formula used for correcting the split-half reliability coefficient

The adjusted correlation is the split-half estimate of reliability. A low correlation indicates that the test was unreliable and contained considerable measurement error; a high correlation indicates that the test was reliable. Nunnally and Bernstein (1994) pointed out that before computers were commonly available, the split-half procedure was the most popular way used to estimate reliability. One of the problems with using the split-half procedure is that different results can be obtained from the different ways of subdividing the test. The next technique (coefficient alpha) is generally a better measure of internal consistency reliability.

The second approach to measuring internal consistency is known as coefficient alpha. Lee Cronbach (1951) developed coefficient alpha from an earlier internal consistency formula developed by G. Frederic Kuder and M. W. Richardson (1937). **Coefficient alpha** (also called **Cronbach's alpha**) provides a reliability estimate that can be thought of as the average of all possible split-half correlations, corrected by the Spearman-Brown formula. Another way of saying this is that *coefficient alpha tells you the degree to which the items are interrelated.*

- **Coefficient alpha** A formula that provides an estimate of the reliability of a homogeneous test or an estimate of the reliability of each dimension in a multidimensional test

A popular rule of thumb is that the size of coefficient alpha should generally be, at a minimum, greater than or equal to .70 for research purposes and somewhat greater than that value (e.g., $\geq .90$) for clinical testing purposes (i.e., for assessing single individuals). However, the size that is considered adequate will depend on the context and many other considerations (e.g., Nunnally & Bernstein, 1994).

- **Cronbach's alpha** A frequently used name for what Lee Cronbach called "coefficient alpha"

A strength of coefficient alpha is its versatility. It can be used for test items that allow for a range of responses. For example, on a 5-point agreement scale (*strongly disagree, disagree, neutral, agree, strongly agree*), respondents can select from a range of five answers. Coefficient alpha can also be used for dichotomous items. On a dichotomous item, either two choices are provided (e.g., true or false), or the item is scored as having only two answers (e.g., multiple-choice questions are scored as either right or wrong).

Now we examine a version of the formula for coefficient alpha that is instructive because it helps demonstrate two important points about coefficient alpha.[2]

$$r_\alpha = \frac{k\bar{r}}{1 + k\bar{r} - \bar{r}}$$

where

r_α is coefficient alpha;
k is the number of items; and
$\bar{r}$ is the average correlation between the items.

In the formula, k is the number of items on your test or subscale, and $\bar{r}$ is the average of the correlations between the items (i.e., every item is correlated with every other item, and the average of these is taken). You would not want to use this formula to compute coefficient alpha by hand because it would be cumbersome. For example, if there were 10 items on your test, you would have to get 45 correlations between the 10 items and then average them to obtain $\bar{r}$.[3] If your test had 20 items, you would have to calculate 190 correlations! Fortunately, researchers use computer packages to calculate coefficient alpha.

Now let's look at the formula and make two important points. First, the formula shows that coefficient alpha depends on the correlation among the items on the test. The stronger the correlations among the items (symbolized by $\bar{r}$ in the formula), the larger coefficient alpha will be. Because coefficient alpha measures internal consistency, one would expect the items to be correlated with one another. The second point is sometimes overlooked—coefficient alpha depends on the number of items in your test (symbolized by k in the formula). The more items you include in your test or subscale, the larger coefficient alpha will be. This means that *it is possible to get a large coefficient alpha even when the items are not very homogeneous or internally consistent; this can happen when many items are included on the test* (John & Benet-Martinez, 2000). Thus, the reader of a research report might be led to conclude falsely that a test is internally consistent because of a reported high coefficient alpha. Therefore, remember to be careful when interpreting coefficient alpha: Be sure to consider the number of items when interpreting coefficient alpha as a measure of internal consistency, and don't just assume that a large coefficient alpha means the items are strongly related.

Interscorer Reliability

Sometimes, an evaluation of a person's performance on a test is made by a committee or group of persons, such as a team of teachers, researchers, or other professionals. It is difficult for a single teacher or researcher to be a consistent rater. It is even more difficult for a team of raters to be consistent with each other in judging each person's performance, but once consistency of agreement is obtained, the result is more trustworthy and objective. The degree of agreement between two or more scorers, judges, or raters is referred to as **interscorer reliability** (also called judge reliability, interrater reliability, and observer reliability).

- **Interscorer reliability** The degree of agreement or consistency between two or more scorers, judges, or raters

The simplest way to determine the degree of consistency between two raters in the scoring of a test or some other performance measure is to have each rater independently rate the completed tests and then compute the correlation between the two raters' scores. For example, assume that you had each student in a class read a passage and had two "experts" rate the reading ability of each student. The scores provided by these two raters are then correlated, and the resulting correlation coefficient represents the interscorer reliability.

See Journal Articles 7.2 and 7.3 on the Student Study Site.

Frequently, the agreement between two or more raters is not very good unless training and practice precede the scoring. Fortunately, with training, the degree of agreement can improve. The important issues are that training is often required and that a measure of the reliability of an evaluation of performance by raters is necessary.

7.6 What are the different ways of assessing reliability?

7.7 Under what conditions should each of the different ways of assessing reliability be used?

Validity

■ **Validity** The accuracy of the inferences, interpretations, or actions made on the basis of test scores

When we select a test or other measure, we naturally want to select the one that will give us the information we want. If we want to measure a child's IQ, we obviously want some assessment that will provide us with a score that we can use to make a judgment about that particular child's intellectual level. This is the issue of **validity**, which is defined as the appropriateness of the interpretations, inferences, and actions that we make based on test scores (AERA, APA, & NCME, 1999; Messick, 1989b).[4] If the assessment procedure were a measure of intelligence, the score obtained from this test could be used to infer the person's intellectual level. On the basis of this interpretation of a person's intellectual level, we might also take some specific action such as placing the child in a special program for gifted children. Technically speaking, it is inaccurate to state that a test is valid or invalid, because this statement implies that validity is only a property of the test. Cronbach (1991) put it like this: "A test may be excellent in other respects, but if it is wrongly interpreted it is worthless in that time and place" (p. 150). What is important is to make sure that your test is measuring what you intend it to measure for the particular people in a particular context and that the interpretations you make on the basis of the test scores are correct.

■ **Validity evidence** Empirical evidence and theoretical rationales that support the inferences or interpretations made from test scores

When making inferences or taking some action on the basis of scores, we want our inferences to be accurate, and we want our actions to be appropriate. Whether the inferences and actions are accurate and appropriate is an empirical question. To validate the inferences that we make requires collecting validity evidence. **Validity evidence** is the empirical evidence and theoretical rationales that support the interpretations and actions that we take on the basis of the score or scores we get from an assessment procedure. For example, if we give a student an intelligence test and that student gets a score of 130, we would infer from that score that the student is bright and can master almost any academic skill attempted. To validate this inference, we would have to collect evidence indicating that a person obtaining a score of 130 on this test is a very bright person who can master subjects ranging from chemistry to philosophy.

Validation The process of gathering evidence that supports inferences made on the basis of test scores

Validation, therefore, is the inquiry process of gathering validity evidence that supports our score interpretations or inferences. It involves evaluating our interpretations or inferences for their soundness and relevance. Many different types of validity evidence can be collected, and in general, *the best rule is to collect multiple sources of evidence.* As we discuss how to collect validity evidence, remember that our discussion applies to any kind of measurement or assessment procedure and not just tests. It applies to the measurement of virtually anything that a researcher plans on empirically studying.

In recent years, our thinking about validity issues has moved from a discussion of types of validity (i.e., content validity, criterion validity, and construct validity) to a focus on obtaining evidence for a unitary validity.[5] The latest thinking is shown in the following quote from the authoritative *Standards for Educational and Psychological Testing* (AERA, APA, & NCME, 1999)[6,7]:

> These sources of evidence [content, criterion, and construct] may illuminate different aspects of validity, but they do not represent distinct types of validity. Validity is a unitary concept. It is the degree to which all the accumulated evidence supports the intended interpretation of test scores for the proposed purpose. (p. 11)

The primary sources of validity evidence are summarized in Table 7.6. Keep in mind that complete validation is never fully attained. Validation is very similar to theory development (you state your expectations or hypotheses, you collect data, you examine the results, and you refine the theory; then you go through this cycle again and again over time). Validation therefore should be viewed as a never-ending process (Messick, 1995). At the same time, the more validity evidence you have, the more confidence you can place in your interpretations. So let's see how educational researchers obtain evidence of the validity.

TABLE 7.6 Summary of Methods for Obtaining Validity Evidence

Type of Evidence	*Procedures*
Evidence based on content	Study the construct, examine the test content, and decide whether the test content adequately represents the construct. This is done by experts.
Evidence based on internal structure	First, determine how many dimensions or constructs the test measures using the technique called *factor analysis.* Second, examine the *homogeneity* of the items (for the whole test and for each of the subscales if the test measures more than one dimension). You can do this by calculating the *item-to-total correlation* (for a test measuring only one dimension) and by calculating *coefficient alpha* for the test and for each subscale for a test measuring more than one dimension.
Evidence based on relations to other variables	Relate the test scores to a known criterion by collecting *concurrent* and/or *predictive* evidence. Correlate the test scores with measures of the same construct and measures of different constructs to obtain *convergent* and *discriminant* evidence. Determine whether groups differ on the test in the way that would be expected (e.g., for a liberalism scale, determine whether Republican Party members differ from Democratic Party members).

REVIEW QUESTIONS

7.8 What are the definitions of validity and validation?

7.9 What is meant by the unified view of validity?

Evidence Based on Content

■ **Content-related evidence** Validity evidence based on a judgment of the degree to which the items, tasks, or questions on a test adequately represent the construct domain of interest

When you use **content-related evidence**, you evaluate the degree to which the evidence suggests that the items, tasks, or questions on your test represent the domain of interest (e.g., teacher burnout or student self-esteem). This representation is based on item content, but it is also based on the formatting, wording, administration, and scoring of the test. Judgments of content validity must be made by experts in the domain of interest.

Content validation follows three steps: (1) You must understand the construct that the test is supposed to measure (i.e., make sure that you understand how the construct is defined and understand the content domain the items should represent); (2) examine the content on the specific test; and (3) decide whether the content on the test adequately represents the content domain. If the answer is yes to step 3, you have evidence that you are measuring the construct you hope to be measuring. When making your decision, answer these three questions:

1. Do the items appear to represent the thing you are trying to measure?
2. Does the set of items underrepresent the construct's content (i.e., have you excluded any important content areas or topics)?
3. Do any of the items represent something other than what you are trying to measure (i.e., have you included any irrelevant items)?

As you can see, the process of content validation is basically a rational approach to judging a test's content. You define the content you want to represent, and then you determine whether the items represent the content adequately.

To illustrate content validation, let's assume that you are developing a measure to determine whether students have mastered a topic in introductory statistics. Statistical knowledge is typically measured by administering a statistics achievement test and using the test scores to infer students' mastery of statistics. If your instruction covered the theory, rationale, and computational procedure of Pearson product-moment correlation, *t* tests, and analysis of variance, then the items, questions, and tasks on the statistics test should also cover this material. The proportion of material covered on the test should match the proportion of material covered during the instructional period. If 20% of instruction time was spent covering correlation, 30% of the time was spent on *t* tests, and 50% of the time was spent on analysis of variance, then 20% of the test questions and tasks should be devoted to correlation, 30% to *t* tests, and 50% to analysis of variance. If all of the items were on analysis of variance, the test would not be valid because it would underrepresent the full content domain. Likewise, if the test had items from the areas listed plus the area of regression analysis, then the test would not be very valid because it would include measurement of an irrelevant content area. If your test questions, items, and tasks are formatted appropriately, are administered appropriately, and adequately represent the domain of information covered in the statistics instruction, then you will have good content-related evidence of validity.

See Journal Article 7.4 on the Student Study Site.

Evidence Based on Internal Structure

Some tests are designed to measure a single construct, but other tests are designed to measure several components or dimensions of a construct. The Rosenberg Self-Esteem

Scale is a 10-item scale designed to measure the construct of global self-esteem. (A copy of this test is shown in Figure 8.1 on page 192.) All 10 items on this test are intended to measure the same thing. You could check the internal structure of this self-esteem scale in several ways. Your goal in obtaining internal structure evidence for this self-esteem scale would be to make sure that the items in fact measure a single underlying construct (i.e., make sure it is unidimensional). In contrast, the Harter Self-Perception Profile for Children provides not only a measure of global self-esteem but also measures of five dimensions of self-esteem (i.e., scholastic competence, social acceptance, athletic competence, physical appearance, and behavioral conduct). So in the case of the Harter scale, when examining the internal structure, you would make sure that the different sets of items do indeed measure the separate dimensions.

A useful technique for examining the internal structure of tests is called factor analysis. **Factor analysis** is a statistical procedure that analyzes the relationships among items to determine whether a test is *unidimensional* (i.e., all of the items measure a single construct) or *multidimensional* (i.e., different sets of items tap different constructs or different components of a broader construct). You would run a factor analysis using a statistical software program (such as SPSS), and then you could see if your test items appear to measure one dimension or more than one dimension.

- **Factor analysis** A statistical procedure that analyzes correlations among test items and tells you the number of factors present. It tells you whether the test is unidimensional or multidimensional

An example will make the concept of factor analysis clear. Let's say that you did a factor analysis on the 10 items that make up the Rosenberg Self-Esteem Scale. Past research has shown that the Rosenberg Self-Esteem Scale is unidimensional, so your factor analysis should confirm that the items are indeed measuring a single dimension or "factor." Now let's add 10 new items to the original 10 and take these new items from a test that measures "introversion." When you run a factor analysis on these 20 items, what do you think you will get? The results should show that your 20 items measure *two* dimensions (a self-esteem dimension and an introversion dimension).

As another example, assume that you just did a factor analysis on the Harter scale we mentioned above. How many dimensions should this factor analysis show are present? We bet you said five (i.e., scholastic competence, social acceptance, athletic competence, physical appearance, and behavioral conduct). That's really all you need to know about factor analysis here. The technical details of factor analysis are beyond the scope of this text, but the basic idea is simply that a factor analysis tells you *how many dimensions or factors your test items represent.*

When examining the internal structure of a test, you can also obtain a measure of test **homogeneity** (i.e., the degree to which the different items measure the same construct or trait). One index of homogeneity is obtained by correlating the scores on each test item with the scores on the total test (i.e., the *item-to-total correlation*). For example, if you want to obtain evidence of the homogeneity of a test of student morale, you could give the test to a group of students and then correlate the scores on each test item with the total test scores. If all the items are correlated with the total test scores, you have evidence that the test is internally consistent and that it measures the construct of student morale. If a particular item correlates poorly with the total test score, it should be eliminated or revised because the low correlation indicates that item does not measure the same thing as the total test.

- **Homogeneity** In test validity, refers to how well the different items in a test measure the same construct or trait

A second index of homogeneity has already been discussed: coefficient alpha. You can have your computer calculate coefficient alpha for the test (or for each of the dimensions

See Tools and Tips 7.1 on the Student Study Site.

of the test if it is multidimensional, as the Harter test is). If the alpha is low (e.g., < .70), then some items might be measuring different constructs, or some items might be defective. When coefficient alpha is low, you should examine the items that are contributing to your low coefficient alpha and consider eliminating or revising them.

Evidence Based on Relations to Other Variables

- **Criterion-related evidence** Validity evidence based on the extent to which scores from a test can be used to predict or infer performance on some criterion such as a test or future performance
- **Criterion** The standard or benchmark that you want to predict accurately on the basis of the test scores
- **Validity coefficient** A correlation coefficient that is computed to provide validity evidence, such as the correlation between test scores and criterion scores
- **Concurrent evidence** Validity evidence based on the relationship between test scores and criterion scores obtained at the same time

Validity evidence is also obtained by relating your test scores to scores on other variables. The first form of evidence in this category, called **criterion-related evidence**, focuses on the usefulness of a test in predicting how people taking the test will perform on some criterion of interest. A **criterion** is the standard or benchmark that you want to predict accurately on the basis of the scores from your new test. You gain validity evidence when there is a strong correlation between your focal test (i.e., the test you are studying) and scores on a well-established criterion. Perhaps you have designed a test to give to middle school students to predict whether they will drop out of high school. An excellent criterion would be whether they eventually drop out of high school. You have selected a good criterion when your audience accepts it as important and when you have examined it for its relevance, completeness, and freedom from bias.

When you calculate correlation coefficients for the study of validity, you should call them **validity coefficients**. For example, if you are developing a test to predict student performance in advanced high school mathematics, you want a positive and high correlation (i.e., validity coefficient) between students' scores on the test and their mathematics performance scores. Specifically, the students who get low scores on the aptitude test should get low scores in the advanced high school mathematics class, and the students who get high scores on the aptitude test should get high scores in the advanced math class.

A distinction made with criterion-related evidence concerns *when* the tests are administered. You have **concurrent evidence** if you administer your focal test and the criterion test at approximately the same point in time (i.e., concurrently), correlate the two sets of scores, and find that the two sets of scores are highly correlated. You have **predictive evidence** of validity if you measure your participants' performance on your focal test at one point in time and measure them on the criterion measure at a future point in time and you find that these two sets of scores are highly correlated. As you can see, predictive evidence takes more time and effort than concurrent evidence because you have to wait before obtaining all of the data. However, predictive evidence is superior if your goal is to predict some future event or condition.

See Journal Article 7.5 on the Student Study Site.

Here is an example of the distinction. Assume that you have recently developed a new, shorter version of the Scholastic Aptitude Test (SAT). You hypothesize that your test, like the SAT, will predict college grade point average (GPA). Rather than waiting 4 years, however, you might administer your new test to high school students and see whether it is correlated with their high school GPA. Although you ultimately want to predict college GPA, you use high school GPA as a substitute or proxy variable because it is easy to obtain right now. This will provide concurrent evidence, but in this situation predictive evidence is preferred. To obtain predictive evidence, you would give your test to high school seniors and then wait 4 years to obtain their college GPA. Then you would correlate their scores on your test with their college GPA. If the correlation is high, you have good evidence that the test does what it is supposed to do: It accurately predicts students' performance in college.

Concurrent studies tend to be popular because they can be done quickly, but again, predictive studies are superior if your goal is to predict some future event or condition.

Validity evidence based on relations to other variables can also be obtained by collecting what is called convergent and discriminant evidence. The ideas of convergent and discriminant evidence come from a landmark work by Campbell and Fiske (1959). These kinds of evidence are used to demonstrate what your test measures and what it does not measure. **Convergent evidence** is based on the relationship between the focal test scores and other independent measures of the same construct. You get your participants to take both tests, and you correlate the two sets of scores. If the two measures are based on different modes of data collection (e.g., one is a paper-and-pencil test, and the other is based on observation or performance), that is fine because independent measures of the same thing should provide measures that are highly correlated. For example, you might collect evidence in support of the Rosenberg Self-Esteem Scale (which is based on a self-report measure) by showing that another self-esteem test based on peer ratings and one based on teacher observations are highly correlated with the Rosenberg scale. This kind of evidence would be important because it would show that your test is related to other measures of the same construct (as you would expect) and that your focal test measurement (in this case, the Rosenberg scale based on a self-report questionnaire) is not just an artifact of the method of measurement you have used (because you got similar results using peer ratings and observations).

- **Predictive evidence** Validity evidence based on the relationship between test scores collected at one point in time and criterion scores obtained at a later time

- **Convergent evidence** Validity evidence based on the relationship between the focal test scores and independent measures of the same construct

Discriminant evidence exists when test scores on your focal test are *not* highly related to scores from other tests that are designed to measure theoretically *different* constructs. This information is significant because it is also important to demonstrate what your test does *not* measure. In the words of Lee Cronbach (1991), "This principle of divergence of indicators keeps a science from becoming overloaded with many names for the same thing" (p. 182). For example, think about the Rosenberg Self-Esteem Scale again. First, the correlation between self-esteem and authoritarianism should be small or zero because these two constructs are not expected (for theoretical reasons) to be related. If you get a small or zero correlation, you will have some discriminant evidence that the Rosenberg scale measures something other than the construct of authoritarianism. Second, this discriminant correlation should be much smaller than the convergent validity correlations (i.e., the correlations between measures of the same construct). For example, you would expect the Rosenberg Self-Esteem Scale test to correlate more strongly with other measures of self-esteem than with measures of other constructs such as authoritarianism, attitudes toward contraception, and need for recognition. Basically, the goal is to show that your scale is correlated with what it should be correlated (convergent evidence) and that it is not correlated with different or theoretically unrelated constructs.

- **Discriminant evidence** Evidence that the scores on your focal test are *not* highly related to the scores from other tests that are designed to measure theoretically different constructs

The penultimate type of validity evidence is called **known groups evidence**. The idea here is to relate scores from the test you are studying with a grouping variable on which you would expect the members to differ. You would examine groups that are known to differ on your focal construct and see whether they differ in the hypothesized direction on the test you are using. For example, if you are developing a test measuring depression, you could administer your test to a group of participants who have been diagnosed with clinical depression and a group of participants who have not been diagnosed with clinical depression. The depressed participants should score higher on your depression test than the "normal" participants. For another example, you would expect members of the Democratic Party to score higher on a liberalism scale than members of the Republican Party.

- **Known groups evidence** Evidence that groups that are known to differ on the construct do differ on the test in the hypothesized direction

The final type of validity evidence is called consequential validity, and it refers to the psychological and social consequences of the use of the test. A test has **consequential validity** when it is used appropriately and works well and does not have negative or abnormal social and psychological consequences that are due to problems with the test. One needs evidence that the decisions and consequences that are made from the test are appropriate. Consequential validity answers the question of whether appropriate inferences are made from the test when it is used in society. If any problems occur, the researcher or assessment corporation that published the test must determine the problems and fix it. In the words of Messick (1989a), "adverse social consequences should not be attributable to any source of test invalidity such as construct-irrelevant variance [i.e., the test measures something in addition to or different from the construct of interest]" (p. 11). This is why tests undergo much modification before publication to make sure they are not biased against certain groups. Even after publication, many tests need additional revision if they are to be valid for multiple groups simultaneously.

- **Consequential validity** Degree to which the test is used appropriately, works well in practice, and does not have negative or abnormal social and psychological consequences

Using Reliability and Validity Information in Your Research

For you to use reliability and validity information (from a test manual or research article) legitimately, the participants on which the information was collected must be similar to the participants with which you are conducting your study. For example, if you are conducting a study investigating the academic achievement of fifth- and sixth-grade students with IQs below the normal range, the reliability and validity information provided with the academic achievement test that you select for this study must be based on norms from fifth- and sixth-grade students of below-normal intelligence. If the reliability and validity coefficients provided were derived from fifth- and sixth-grade students with normal or higher IQs, these coefficients would give little information about the reliability and validity of the scores of the students you are studying. Therefore, before you make use of any assessment procedure, you must look at the characteristics of the **norming group**, which is the group of people on which the reliability and validity coefficients were computed. These coefficients are typically reported in the manual that comes with the standardized test. If the characteristics of the participants in your study match the characteristics of the participants in the reliability and validity studies, you can use these coefficients to assess the quality of the assessment procedure. If they do not, you have no direct information by which to assess the quality of the assessment procedure. You can still get scores from using the assessment, but because you will not know what they mean, you essentially will be collecting data that you cannot interpret.

- **Norming group** The specific group for which the test publisher or researcher provides evidence for test validity and reliability

It is important to understand that it is *not* wise to rely solely on previously reported reliability and validity information, especially when the characteristics of your participants do not closely match the characteristics of the norming group. Therefore, you should attempt to collect additional empirical reliability and/or validity evidence demonstrating how well your selected test operates with your research participants or students. For example, reliability information, such as coefficient alpha and test-retest reliability, is usually reported in high-quality journals (such as the *Journal of Educational Psychology*). Validity information, such as convergent and discriminant evidence, is often reported when researchers need to justify the use of their measures. The point is that, when reading an empirical research report, you should be sure to look for any *direct* evidence that the researchers provide about reliability and validity and then upgrade your evaluation of the measurement component of the research to the degree that the authors provide this evidence. You will find this information in either the Method section or the Results section of an article. You will also find it in published reviews of tests.

7.10 What are the characteristics of the different ways of obtaining validity evidence?

REVIEW QUESTION

Educational and Psychological Tests

Whenever an educational researcher conducts a study, measurements must be taken on a number of variables. For example, if you are conducting an experimental study investigating the effect of exposure to a Head Start program on later academic achievement of disadvantaged children, you have to have some way of identifying children who are disadvantaged and some measure of academic achievement. One way of doing this is to administer a test that is designed to measure the extent to which a child is disadvantaged and a test that is designed to measure a child's level of academic achievement. Fortunately, educational and psychological tests have been developed to measure most situations, characteristics, and types of performance, and educational researchers make extensive use of these tests in their research projects. Although there are too many tests to mention in this textbook, we identify the primary areas in which tests have been developed, and we mention some of the more popular tests in each of these areas.

See Tools and Tips 7.2 on the Student Study Site.

Intelligence Tests

Intelligence tests have probably received the most attention and are the tests people are most familiar with because most of us have completed one at some time in our life. Intelligence, however, is an interesting construct because of the difficulty in coming up with an agreed-on definition. For example, what does intelligence mean to you? If you have difficulty answering this question, you are not alone. Sternberg, Conway, Ketron, and Bernstein (1981) asked 476 people, including students, commuters, and supermarket shoppers, to identify behaviors they considered intelligent and unintelligent. Behaviors that were most often associated with intelligence included "reasons logically and well," "reads widely," "displays common sense," "keeps an open mind," and "reads with high comprehension." Unintelligent behaviors mentioned most frequently included "does not tolerate diversity of views," "does not display curiosity," and "behaves with insufficient consideration of others." Do these examples fit your conception of intelligent and unintelligent behaviors? If they do not, don't be alarmed, because even the experts cannot agree on a definition.

One general definition is that **intelligence** is the ability to think abstractly and to learn readily from experience (Flynn, 1987). However, this is a general definition and not one that is universally accepted. Neisser (1979) has even concluded that intelligence, because of its nature, cannot be explicitly defined because for certain constructs, a single prototype

- **Intelligence** The ability to think abstractly and to learn readily from experience

does not exist. This is certainly true. However, just because a universally accepted definition of intelligence does not exist does not mean that the concept does not exist, that it lacks utility, or that it cannot be measured. Indeed, it is a multifaceted construct, and many tests have been developed to measure intelligence. A summary of some of the tests of intelligence that have been developed and used in educational research as well as other settings is provided at the book's companion website.

Personality Tests

- **Personality** The relatively permanent patterns that characterize and can be used to classify individuals

Personality is a construct that, like intelligence, has been defined in many different ways. A generally agreed-on definition is Mischel's (1999) statement that **personality** is "the distinctive patterns (including thoughts as well as feelings, emotions, and actions) that characterize each individual enduringly" (p. 4). Feist (1990) defined personality as "a global concept referring to all those relatively permanent traits, dispositions, or characteristics within the individual, which give some degree of consistency to that person's behavior" (p. 7). It is clear that personality is a multifaceted construct; as a result, many tests have been developed to measure different facets of personality (such as emotional, motivational, interpersonal, and attitudinal characteristics of individuals). A summary of some personality tests is provided at the book's companion website.

- **Self-report** A test-taking method in which participants check or rate the degree to which various characteristics are descriptive of themselves

Many personality tests are of the **self-report** variety (sometimes called *self-report inventories*), in which the test taker is asked to respond, either on a pencil-and-paper form or on a computer, to a series of questions about his or her motives and feelings. These self-reports provide a window into the test taker's behavioral tendencies, feelings, and motives, which are in turn summarized with a specific label. Some labels are clinical labels, such as neuroticism; others are trait labels, such as dominance or sociability. Still other labels refer to attitudes, interests, or the values a person holds. The numerous summary labels that are used to portray a person's "personality" and the numerous self-report inventories that have been developed to measure these further reflect the fact that personality is a multifaceted construct.

Although self-report measures of personality can be a valuable source of information, they are always subject to contamination. In some instances, to attain his or her goals, a person might be motivated to "fake good"; in other instances, a person might be motivated to "fake bad." For example, assume that you want your child to attend an elite private school that will not take children with negative attitudes on the assumption that they might be prone to violent behavior. If you are asked to report on your child's behavioral tendencies and attitudes, you might not tell the truth ("fake good") to enhance the probability of your child's being admitted into the school. Additionally, different individuals have different response styles that can influence the impression communicated by the responses to the personality test. For example, some people have a tendency to answer "yes" or "true" rather than "no" or "false" to short-answer items. Others may not have the insight into their own behavior or thinking needed to accurately communicate information about themselves. These limitations of self-report inventories always have to be considered when using them to collect information.

- **Performance measures** A test-taking method in which the participants perform some real-life behavior that is observed by the researcher

In addition to self-reports, personality dimensions are sometimes measured using **performance measures**. Here, the researcher provides the examinee with a task to perform and then makes an inference about the examinee's personality characteristics on the basis of the task performance. These kinds of testing situations are often designed to simulate everyday life or work situations. It is usually important to keep the precise nature or purpose of the performance testing disguised to help minimize faking or other types of reactive behaviors. An advantage of performance measures is that the researcher can directly observe the test taker's behavior, rather than relying only on self-report measures.

The last technique for tapping into personality is the use of **projective measures**. The major feature of projective measures or techniques is that the test taker has to respond to a relatively unstructured task using test stimuli that are usually vague or ambiguous. For example, the test taker might be asked to tell what he or she sees in a blot of ink on a piece of paper or to make up a story based on a card that shows an ambiguous picture of several people who are in a specific environment, such as what appears to be a surgical room. The underlying assumption is that the way in which the test taker structures and interprets the ambiguous test stimuli will reflect fundamental aspects of his or her personality or psychological functioning and in this way reveal his or her needs, anxieties, and conflicts. However, many projective techniques are inadequately standardized with respect to administration and scoring, which means that reliability and validity information might be hard to obtain.

- **Projective measures** A test-taking method in which the participants provide responses to ambiguous stimuli

See Tools and Tips 7.3 on the Student Study Site.

Educational Assessment Tests

One of the things many people associate with education is testing because it seems to be an inherent part of the educational process. The type of testing that many people think of is some type of performance or knowledge testing, because one of the most common ways of identifying whether a person has mastered a set of material is to measure whether he or she can answer questions about the material or measure his or her performance on activities that are indicative of mastery. However, many other types of tests are administered in schools: intelligence tests, personality tests, tests of physical and sensory abilities, diagnostic tests, learning styles tests, and so forth. In this section, we look at the major categories of educational assessment tests and mention some of the tests that fall into each of these categories.

Preschool Assessment Tests

Many tests that are used with preschool children are referred to as *screening tests* rather than intelligence tests or academic achievement tests, primarily because the predictive validity of many of the preschool tests is weak. During the preschool years, many factors other than children's cognitive capacity influence their later development and ability. A child's health, family environment, and temperament differences all influence the child's development. Therefore, testing at a young age typically fails to yield sufficient information about later performance in the classroom. When tests are used as screening tests, they are used to identify children who are "at risk" and in need of further evaluation. The term *at risk*, however, is not clearly defined. For example, it could refer to a child who is in danger of not being ready for the first grade, or it might describe a level of functioning that is not within normal limits. It might even refer to a child who has difficulties that might not have been identified were it not for routine screening. Preschool assessment tests do have a place. However, they must be used with caution and not be overinterpreted.

Preschool tests include the Early Screening Profile (Lasee & Smith, 1991) and the Miller Assessment for Preschoolers (P. G. W. Schouten & Kirkpatrick, 1993). The Early Screening Profile focuses on developmental functioning of children from age 2 to just under age 7 and includes cognitive/language, motor, and self-help/social subtests. The Miller Assessment for Preschoolers focuses on the detection of developmental problems in children aged 2.9 to 5.8 years by making use of verbal, coordination, and nonverbal foundations subtests. These are just two of many tests that assess the various behaviors and cognitive skills of young children.

Achievement Tests

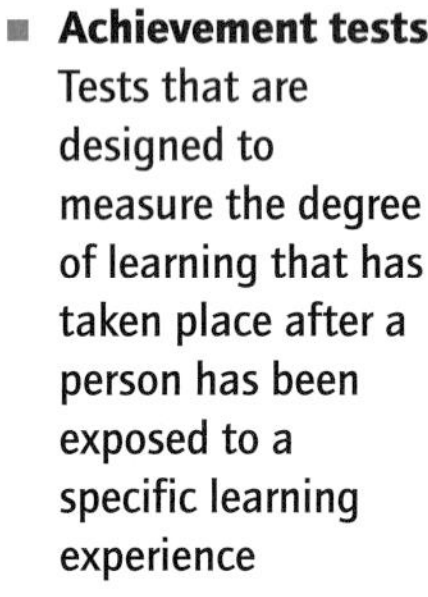

Achievement tests are designed to measure the degree of learning that has taken place after a person has been exposed to a specific learning experience. This learning experience can be virtually anything. In the context of education, the classroom learning experience is most frequently tested. After a teacher has covered a set of material in a course such as American history, he or she wants to measure how much of this material the students have learned. The typical way of doing this is to give a test covering the material. A summary of some standardized achievement tests is provided at the book's companion website.

Teacher-constructed tests such as a history test are not the only variety of achievement tests. Other achievement tests are the more standardized tests, such as the Metropolitan Achievement Test, which have been produced by a test publisher (e.g., Psychological Corporation) and contain normative data (data indicating how certain groups of individuals, such as sixth-grade white females, perform on the test). These tests might be given at the end of a school year so that the performance of the students who took the achievement test can be compared to the normative group. The comparison with the normative group is often used to measure accomplishment or achievement in various academic areas, such as biology, English, mathematics, and reading comprehension. These *standardized achievement tests* can be used for a variety of purposes, ranging from gauging the quality of instruction of a teacher, a school district, or even a state to screening for academic difficulties to identify areas in which remediation is needed.

The primary difference between teacher-constructed achievement tests and standardized achievement tests is their psychometric soundness. Reliability and validity studies are seldom, if ever, done on teacher-constructed tests. Teachers do not have the luxury of time to collect validity and reliability data. They must cover a given segment of material and then construct a test that seems to sample the content area and represent a reasonable measure of achievement. Reliability and validity data are collected on standardized achievement tests because these tests are developed and normed by psychometricians working for testing companies, who have to justify their tests before making them available for sale. Achievement tests can vary from measuring general achievement to measuring achievement in a specific subject area. Measures of general achievement cover a number of academic areas and are typically referred to as *achievement batteries* because they consist of several subtests. Each subtest typically focuses on a different academic area or skill. Measures of achievement in specific subject areas are tests that are designed to gauge achievement in specific areas, such as reading, arithmetic, and science. We provide a list of both general and specific standardized achievement tests on the book's companion website.

See Tools and Tips 7.4 on the Student Study Site.

Aptitude Tests

Aptitude tests focus on information acquired through the informal learning that goes on in life as opposed to the formal learning that exists in the educational system. Each individual's particular mental and physical abilities allow him or her to acquire different amounts of information through everyday life experiences, as well as through formal learning experiences such as course work in school. Achievement tests attempt to measure specific information that is acquired in a formal and relatively structured environment, such as a French or computer programming class. In contrast, aptitude tests attempt to measure the information people acquire under the uncontrolled and undefined conditions of life. Aptitude test performance, therefore, reflects the cumulative influence of all of our daily living experiences. There is an overlap and a sometimes blurry distinction between achievement and aptitude tests. A key idea is that achievement tests are more limited in scope and reflect the learning that takes place in definable conditions, such as a specific class designed to teach a specific subject, and aptitude tests reflect the learning that takes place in all of life's uncontrolled conditions.

■ **Aptitude tests** Tests that focus on information acquired through the informal learning that goes on in life

Another distinction between achievement and aptitude tests is that aptitude tests are typically used to make predictions, whereas achievement tests are used to measure accomplishment. This does not mean that achievement tests are never used to make predictions, because they can be used this way and sometimes are. For example, achievement test performance in a first-semester foreign language course might be considered predictive of achievement in subsequent foreign language courses. However, future predictions are more frequently made from aptitude tests.

Aptitude tests are used to make predictions about many things, ranging from readiness for school and aptitude for college-level work to aptitude for work in a given profession such as law or medicine. For example, the Metropolitan Readiness Tests are several group-administered tests that assess the development of reading and mathematics skills in kindergarten and first grade. The Scholastic Aptitude Test (SAT) is a group-administered test that is divided into verbal and mathematics sections. It is used in the college selection process and for advising high school students. Other aptitude tests consist of the Graduate Record Examination (GRE), used as a criterion for admission to many graduate schools; the Medical College Admission Test (MCAT), which is required of students applying to medical school; and the Law School Admission Test (LSAT), which is required of students applying to law school.

Diagnostic Tests

Diagnostic tests are designed to identify where a student is having difficulty with an academic skill. For example, a diagnostic mathematics test consists of subtests measuring the different types of knowledge and skills needed in mathematics. Poor performance on one or more subtests identifies the nature of the difficulty the student is having with mathematics, and attention can be directed to these areas to ameliorate the difficulty. These tests are usually administered to students who are suspected of having difficulty with a specific subject area because of poor performance either in the classroom or on an achievement test. For example, the Woodcock Reading Mastery Test is an individually administered test that is designed to measure skills inherent in reading. Its five subtests consist of letter identification, word

■ **Diagnostic tests** Tests that are designed to identify where a student is having difficulty with an academic skill

identification, word attack, word comprehension, and passage comprehension. The KeyMath Revised Test is an individually administered test for assessing difficulties with mathematical concepts, operations, and applications.

It is important to recognize that diagnostic tests are useful only in identifying where a student is having a problem with an academic skill. They do not give any information as to why the difficulty exists. The problem could stem from physical, psychological, or situational difficulties or some combination of these. Educators, psychologists, and physicians must help answer the question of why the student is struggling.

SOURCES OF INFORMATION ABOUT TESTS

We have focused on types of tests and the characteristics that a test or any other type of assessment measure must have to be considered a "good" test or assessment measure. For many years, educators, psychologists, and sociologists have been constructing tests to measure just about any construct you might be interested in. This means that if you are planning a research study investigating a construct such as teacher burnout, you do not have to worry about developing a measure of this construct because one probably exists. However, you have to know where to find such a measure. Fortunately, many reference sources provide information

TABLE 7.7 Sources of Information About Tests and Test Reviews

Source	*Description*
Mental Measurements Yearbook and *Tests in Print*	These are the most important information sources for test descriptions and reviews of educational and psychological tests.
Dictionary of Behavioral Assessment Techniques (Hersen & Bellack, 2002)	Presents description, purpose, development, psychometric characteristics, clinical use, and future directions of behavioral assessment techniques.
Test Critiques (Keyser & Sweetland, 1984–1994)	This series of 10 volumes provide a description, practical application, use, psychometric characteristics, and reviewer's critique of over 700 tests.
ETS Test Collection (available at ETS: http://www.ets.org/test_link/about/)	A collection of published and unpublished educational tests and measurement devices. A brief annotation including the scope, target audience, and availability of each test is provided.
Handbook of Individual Differences, Learning, and Instruction (Jonassen & Grabowski, 1993)	Includes descriptions and related research on tests in seven areas: learning and instruction, mapping mental abilities, cognitive controls, information gathering, learning styles, personality and learning, and prior knowledge.
Handbook of Research Design and Social Measurement (Miller & Salkind, 2002)	This source book presents many sociological and psychological tests as well as a discussion of the steps involved in conducting a social science research study.
Tests: A Comprehensive Reference for Assessment in Psychology, Education, and Business (Maddox, 2002)	Includes descriptions (not reviews) of over 2,000 assessment instruments.
Measures of Personality and Social Psychological Attitudes (Robinson, Shaver, & Wrightsman, 1991)	Reviews measures of personality and attitudes, including not only a brief description of each scale and its psychometric properties but also a brief presentation of its liabilities.

about both published and unpublished tests. Many of these resources are available online (so you can even find tests while you sit at home at your computer). Table 7.7 lists some useful reference books for locating tests, and some Internet sites to help you find the test you want to use are provided at the companion website (under Web Resources for this chapter). Remember that if a test is already available to measure the construct of interest to you, then it is usually a good idea to use it rather than constructing a new test.

Probably the most important sources of information about published tests are the *Mental Measurements Yearbook* (MMY) and *Tests in Print* (TIP), both of which are published by the Buros Institute of Mental Measurements at the Department of Educational Psychology of the University of Nebraska–Lincoln. If you are attempting to locate and learn about a test, you should consider consulting TIP first because it is a comprehensive volume that describes every test currently published as well as references to these tests. You can directly access MMY and TIP by going to your library. These and additional sources are shown in Table 7.7.

- ***Mental Measurements Yearbook*** A primary source of information about published tests
- ***Tests in Print*** A comprehensive primary source of information about published tests

Information about tests can also be obtained from catalogs distributed by test publishers and from the published literature. Remember that publishers are in the business of selling tests, and a critical review will be omitted. There are also several specialized journals in which researchers routinely publish test validation studies. Some important measurement journals include *Educational and Psychological Measurement*, *Applied Psychological Measurement*, *Applied Measurement in Education*, and the *Journal of Educational Measurement.* We highly recommend that you browse through these and related journals so that you see examples of how measurement research is conducted.

7.11 What are the purposes and key characteristics of the major types of tests discussed in this chapter?

7.12 What is a good example of each of the major types of tests that are discussed in this chapter?

ACTION RESEARCH REFLECTION

Insight: Action researchers are interested in standardized tests that help them diagnose, measure, and/or help solve their local problems. Standardized measurement also is helpful when you want to share your work with others, beyond your immediate setting.

1. Standardized measurement is helpful for measuring attitudes, beliefs, and constructs such as personal self-esteem and math self-efficacy. What are three constructs that you would like to measure in your classroom or workplace? Identify previously developed measures of these in the literature and evaluate their usability for your setting.
2. Look at our definition of validity again. How might you obtain valid measurement and inferences in relation to your action research project?

SUMMARY

Measurement is the act of assigning symbols or numbers to objects, events, people, and characteristics according to a specific set of rules. There are four different scales of measurement, which communicate different kinds of information. The *nominal* scale is a "name" scale that typically uses symbols to label, classify, or identify people or objects. The *ordinal* scale rank orders the people, objects, or characteristics being studied. The *interval* scale has the additional characteristic of equal distances between adjacent numbers. The *ratio* scale has the additional property of having a true zero point.

The two major characteristics of tests and assessments that must always be considered in using tests or other measures are reliability and validity. Reliability is the consistency or stability of the scores from a test. Reliability of a test or assessment procedure can be determined in several ways. *Test-retest* reliability is the consistency of scores over time. *Equivalent-forms* reliability is the consistency of scores on two equivalent forms of a test. *Internal consistency* refers to the homogeneity of the items on a test, and split-half correlations and coefficient alpha provide internal consistency reliability estimates. *Interscorer* reliability is the consistency of scores provided by two or more people scoring the same performance.

Validity refers to the appropriateness of the interpretations and actions we make on the basis of the scores we get from a test or assessment procedure. Validity evidence is based on the content of the test (Does the content adequately represent the construct?), the internal structure of the test (Does the test measure the number of dimensions it is purported to measure?), and the relationship between the test and other variables (Is the test related to other measures of the construct? Is it unrelated to different constructs? Can it be used to predict future performance on important criteria? Do groups that are known to differ on the construct get different scores on the test in the hypothesized direction?).

Reliability and validity evidence can be used to select the test or assessment procedure that will provide interpretable scores. The education researcher can consult a number of resource books and Internet sites to identify intelligence tests, personality tests, and educational assessment tests that can be used for his or her research study. Reliability and validity evidence should always be used in selecting the test or assessment procedure. In addition, researchers should collect additional reliability and validity evidence vis-á-vis the people in their studies to provide evidence that the testing instruments worked for their unique research participants.

KEY TERMS

achievement tests (p. 180)
aptitude tests (p. 181)
assessment (p. 162)
coefficient alpha (p. 168)
concurrent evidence (p. 174)
consequential validity (p. 176)
content-related evidence (p. 172)
convergent evidence (p. 175)
criterion (p. 174)
criterion-related evidence (p. 174)
Cronbach's alpha (p. 168)
diagnostic tests (p. 181)
discriminant evidence (p. 175)
equivalent-forms reliability (p. 166)
error (p. 162)
factor analysis (p. 173)
homogeneity (p. 173)
homogeneous test (p. 167)
intelligence (p. 177)
internal consistency (p. 167)
interscorer reliability (p. 169)
interval scale (p. 160)
known groups evidence (p. 175)
measurement (p. 158)
Mental Measurements Yearbook (p. 183)
nominal scale (p. 159)
norming group (p. 176)
ordinal scale (p. 159)
performance measures (p. 178)
personality (p. 178)
predictive evidence (p. 174)
projective measures (p. 179)
ratio scale (p. 161)
reliability (p. 164)
reliability coefficient (p. 165)
self-report (p. 178)
Spearman-Brown formula (p. 168)
split-half reliability (p. 167)
states (p. 162)
systematic error (p. 163)
test-retest reliability (p. 165)
testing (p. 162)
Tests in Print (p. 183)
traits (p. 162)
validation (p. 171)
validity (p. 170)
validity coefficient (p. 174)
validity evidence (p. 170)

DISCUSSION QUESTIONS

1. Assume that you have just finished developing a new test that you believe measures graduate education aptitude (you call it the GEA). How would you validate this instrument? (Ultimately, you hope that your university will use this new test rather than the test it currently requires of all applicants.)
2. What are some variables at each of the following levels of measurement: nominal, ordinal, interval, and ratio?
3. Your new bathroom scale provides the same weight each time you step on it. The problem is that the reported weight is wrong. What is the problem with your new scale?
4. Can a measurement procedure be reliable but not valid? Can it be valid but not reliable? Explain your answers.
5. What is your definition of measurement validity? How well does it match the definition provided in the chapter?

RESEARCH EXERCISES

1. To illustrate the type of research one would conduct in the field of testing and measurement, select one of the following articles. As you read your article, answer the following questions:
   a. What was measured?
   b. Were there any subscales? If so, what were they?
   c. How were the scales or measures constructed and scored?
   d. How were they validated?
   e. How was reliability assessed?
   f. Did the researchers follow the principles of test validation presented in this chapter? Be sure to explain your answers.
2. Review one of the following articles or a closely related article (i.e., a measurement article that empirically examines the properties of a test):

   Burney, D. M., & Kromery, J. (2001). Initial development and score validation of the Adolescent Anger Rating Scale. *Educational and Psychological Measurement*, *61*(3), 446–460.

   Copenhaver, M. M., & Eisler, R. M. (2000). The development and validation of the Attitude Toward Father Scale. *Behavior Modification*, *24*(5), 740–750.

   Kember, D., & Leung, Y. P. (2000). Development of a questionnaire to measure the level of reflective thinking. *Assessment and Evaluation in Higher Education*, *25*(4), 381–395.

   Shore, T. H., Tashchian, A., & Adams, J. S. (2000). Development and validation of a scale measuring attitudes toward smoking. *The Journal of Social Psychology*, *140*(5), 615–623.
3. Select the quantitative or the mixed research article from the companion website. Then answer, providing some detail, the following questions:
   a. What variables did the researcher study?
   b. How was each of these variables measured?
   c. Did the researcher present any evidence of reliability? What was the evidence?

d. Did the researcher present any evidence of validity? What was the evidence?

e. What is your evaluation of the measures used in the article?

4. If you are planning to propose or conduct a research study, fill out the following Proposal Exercise.

PROPOSAL EXERCISES

(If an item is not applicable to your study, then please write N/A.)

1. The variables in my research study are as follows:

____

____

2. Listed next, for each variable, are the variable types or functions (independent variable, dependent variable, intervening variable, moderator variable, control variable):

____

____

3. I plan on using an already existing instrument to measure the following variables (provide the name of the instrument and sample questions or items for each of these variables):

____

____

4. I plan on writing the new items to measure the following variables (provide sample questions or items for each variable):

____

____

5. Listed next is the level of measurement (nominal, ordinal, interval, ratio) for each of my variables:

____

____

6. Listed next, for each variable, is the reliability and validity evidence that is currently available and/or that I plan on obtaining during the conduct of my research:

____

____

RELEVANT INTERNET SITES

National Council on Measurement in Education
http://www.ncme.org

Glossaries of measurements and assessment terms
http://ericae.net/edo/ed315430.htm

https://www.ncme.org/ncme/NCME/Resource_Center/Glossary/NCME/Resource_Center/Glossary1.aspx?hkey=4bb87415-44dc-4088-9ed9-e8515326a061

http://www.cse.ucla.edu/products/glossary.php

http://www.apus.edu/community-scholars/learning-outcomes-assessment/university-assessment/glossary.htm
http://www.gallaudet.edu/Documents/AssessmentGlossary.pdf
http://edl.nova.edu/secure/mats/archives/eva13.pdf

Frequently asked questions about measurement theory and assessment
ftp://ftp.sas.com/pub/neural/measurement.html
http://assess.psu.edu/FAQ
https://www.utexas.edu/provost/iae/resources/pdfs/Outcomes%20Assessment%20Frequently%20Asked%20Questions.pdf

How to evaluate a test
http://ericae.net/seltips.txt
http://buros.org/questions-ask-when-evaluating-tests
http://pareonline.net/getvn.asp?v=4&n=2

STUDENT STUDY SITE

Visit the Student Study Site at **edge.sagepub.com/rbjohnson6e** for these additional learning tools:

- Video Links
- Self-Quizzes
- eFlashcards
- Lecture Notes
- Full-Text SAGE Journal Articles
- Interactive Concept Maps
- Web Resources

RECOMMENDED READING

American Educational Research Association, American Psychological Association, & National Council on Measurement in Education. (2014). *Standards for educational and psychological testing.* Washington, DC: Author.

Cronbach, L. J., & Meehl, P. E. (1955). Construct validity in psychological tests. *Psychological Bulletin*, *52*, 281–302.

John, O. P., & Benet-Martinez, V. (2000). Measurement: Reliability, construct validation, and scale construction. In H. T. Reis & C. M. Judd (Eds.), *Handbook of research methods in social and personality psychology* (pp. 339–369). Cambridge, England: Cambridge University Press.

Schultz, K. S., & Whitney, D. J. (2014). *Measurement theory in action: Case studies and exercises.* Los Angeles, CA: SAGE.

NOTES

1. Although Stevens's system is commonly used in selecting statistical procedures, there are some limitations to this usage. These limitations are discussed by Velleman and Wilkinson (1993).

2. This version of coefficient alpha assumes that the items are standardized to have the same variance.

3. The number of interitem correlations that would be calculated and then averaged to get the average interitem correlation (i.e.,) is equal to $[p(p - 1)]/2$, where p is the number of items in your test or subscale. For example, your test or subscale has 10 items on it, the number of interitem correlations is $[10(10 - 1)]/2 = 90/2 = 45$. Therefore, to get, you would have to take the average of the 45 interitem correlations.

4. According to the *Standards for Educational and Psychological Testing* (AERA, APA, & NCME, 1999), "Validity refers to the degree to which evidence and theory support the interpretations of test scores entailed by proposed uses of tests" (p. 9). In the words of Samuel Messick (1989b), the determination of validity is "an integrated evaluative judgment of the degree to which empirical evidence and theoretical rationales support the *adequacy* and *appropriateness* of *inferences* and *actions* based on test scores or other modes of assessment" (p. 13).

5. The current view is that construct validation is the unifying concept for validity evidence. In fact, we no longer say "construct validation" because the word *construct* would be redundant. A construct is the theoretical variable that you want to represent. It's what you want to measure. The idea of a construct is used broadly and refers both to abstract variables such as self-efficacy, intelligence, and self-esteem and to very concrete variables such as age, height, weight, and gender.

6. This book was written by a committee of experts approved by the following national associations: the American Educational Research Association, the American Psychological Association, and the National Council on Measurement in Education.

7. To study the evolution of thinking about validity, you can start by examining the following sources in chronological order: American Psychological Association (1954); Cronbach and Meehl (1955); Campbell and Fiske (1959); AERA, APA, and NCME (1985); Messick, 1989b; and AERA, APA, and NCME (1999).

Chapter 8

How to Construct a Questionnaire

LEARNING OBJECTIVES

After reading this chapter, you should be able to

- Explain each of the 15 principles of questionnaire construction.
- Know when open-ended questions and closed-ended questions should be used.
- Give multiple examples of response categories used for completely anchored rating scales.
- Explain how the different parts of a questionnaire are organized into a smoothly operating whole.
- List and explain the five major steps in questionnaire construction.
- Summarize and explain the content in the checklist for questionnaire development.

Visit the Student Study Site for an interactive concept map.

RESEARCH IN REAL LIFE Creating Questions That Work

istock/DeanDrobot

Rachel, a second-grade teacher, was excited by the prospect of offering her opinion by filling out a survey instrument (i.e., a questionnaire). The questionnaire was designed by a team of researchers investigating what needed to be done to improve student learning outcomes at her school. Rachel was happy to be asked to fill out the questionnaire. She knew that her opinions were valuable and could hardly wait to write them down. She had already discussed her thoughts with other teachers at her school about some of the topics that the questionnaire would probably address.

But as Rachel sat trying to fill out the questionnaire, she was dismayed. To begin with, the important questions weren't even asked. Nowhere was there a question about funding or afterschool programs. Even worse, there was nowhere to talk about any issues not specifically asked. As she worked through the questionnaire, she began to get more and more worried. The ordering and formatting of the questions was confusing to the extent that, at times, she wasn't sure if she was putting her answers in the proper place. Several questions asked about several issues all in *one* question, and she had different feelings about the issues. Some questions were so confusing that she didn't know whether she should say that she agreed or disagreed because she simply didn't know what the question was asking. She sat for almost 10 minutes wondering how to answer this question: "Do you not agree with letting students not do their homework on a daily basis?" She knew that homework was important, but did that mean she agreed or not? Even worse, what if she agreed with homework but not on a daily basis?

Further on in the questionnaire, she couldn't help but feel that the researchers had an agenda. She could tell that they believed in block scheduling of courses just by how the questions were phrased. Rachel worried about how she would look if she disagreed, even though she had never liked the block scheduling idea.

Finally, at the end of the questionnaire, Rachel decided to start randomly marking answers because the jargon used was so hard to understand. As Rachel turned in the questionnaire, she was saddened by the fact that the researchers would never know any of her well-thought-out opinions, and she decided never to waste her time by volunteering for a research project again.

The purpose of this chapter is to help you understand how to construct a questionnaire when you need this type of data-collection instrument for your research study and one is not already available from past research. The questionnaire might be the only data-collection instrument, or it might be used along with other data-collection methods in a research study. You will learn that if you follow the simple principles addressed in this chapter, your research participants will be less likely to face situations like the one faced by Rachel, our second-grade teacher, and your data will be more complete and useful as well.

What Is a Questionnaire?

- **Questionnaire** A self-report data-collection instrument filled out by research participants

A **questionnaire** is a self-report data-collection instrument that each research participant fills out as part of a research study. Researchers use questionnaires so that they can obtain information about the thoughts, feelings, attitudes, beliefs, values, perceptions, personality, and behavioral intentions of research participants. In other words, researchers measure many different kinds of characteristics using questionnaires.

We view the term *questionnaire* broadly. Questionnaires can be used to collect quantitative, qualitative, and mixed data. The content and organization of a questionnaire will correspond to the researcher's objectives. The key point is that the questionnaire is a versatile tool available to you and other educational researchers.

Questionnaires typically include many questions and statements. For example, a researcher might ask a question about the present (Do you support the use of corporal punishment in elementary schools?), the past (Have you ever used corporal punishment with one of your students?), or the future (Do you think that you will use corporal punishment sometime in the future?). See Table 8.1 for more examples. Questionnaires can also include statements that participants consider and respond to. For example, when filling out the Rosenberg Self-Esteem Scale shown in Figure 8.1, research participants must indicate their degree of agreement or disagreement with 10 statements measuring their attitudes toward themselves.

See Journal Article 8.1 on the Student Study Site.

TABLE 8.1 Type of Question Matrix With Examples

Question/Item Focus	*Time Dimension*		
	Past (Retrospective)	*Present (Current)*	*Future (Prospective)*
Behavior	When you were a teenager, did you use any illicit drugs?	Do you currently watch educational television?	Do you plan on moving to a new residence within the next calendar year?
Experiences	What was it like taking a class from your favorite teacher?	What is it like being interviewed about your childhood?	What do you think shopping for a new car will be like 10 years from now?
Attitudes, opinions, beliefs, and values	When you were a child, did you like school or church more?	Do you support school vouchers?	Do you think you will vote for the same political party in the next election?
Knowledge	Did you know the definition of *tabula rasa* when you first started college?	What is the definition of *tabula rasa*?	Do you think you will learn the definition of *tabula rasa* sometime in the future?
Process	Please describe how you chose your college major.	Please describe how you help your students develop an appreciation for literature.	Thinking about education 50 years in the future, please describe how you think students will learn math.
Background and demographics	How old were you when you entered the first grade?	What is your current age?	Where do you hope to live when you retire?

FIGURE 8.1 The Rosenberg Self-Esteem Scale

Circle one response for each of the following 10 items.

	Strongly Disagree	*Disagree*	*Agree*	*Strongly Agree*
1. I feel that I am a person of worth, at least on an equal basis with others.	1	2	3	4
2. I feel that I have a number of good qualities.	1	2	3	4
*3. All in all, I am inclined to feel that I am a failure.	1	2	3	4
4. I am able to do things as well as most other people.	1	2	3	4
*5. I feel I do not have much to be proud of.	1	2	3	4
6. I take a positive attitude toward myself.	1	2	3	4
7. On the whole, I am satisfied with myself.	1	2	3	4
*8. I wish I could have more respect for myself.	1	2	3	4
*9. I certainly feel useless at times.	1	2	3	4
*10. At times I think I am no good at all.	1	2	3	4

Source: Rosenberg, M. (1989). *Society and the adolescent self-image*. Revised edition. Middletown, CT: Wesleyan University Press.

*Items marked with an asterisk have reversed wording. The numbers on items with reversed wording should be reversed before summing the responses for the 10 items. For example, on item 3, "strongly agree" becomes 1, "agree" becomes 2, "disagree" becomes 3, and "strongly disagree" becomes 4.

PRINCIPLES OF QUESTIONNAIRE CONSTRUCTION

See Journal Article 8.2 on the Student Study Site.

The key principles of questionnaire construction are shown in Table 8.2. Take a moment to examine this list of 15 principles so that you will have an overview of what is important to consider when constructing a questionnaire. We will explain each of these principles in more detail. Remember that the goal of the questionnaire is to tap into and understand the opinions of your participants about variables related to your research objectives. As you construct your questionnaire, you must constantly ask yourself if your questions will provide clear data about what your participants think or feel.

Principle 1. Make sure the questionnaire items match your research objectives.

This cardinal principle should be obvious. You must always determine why you intend to conduct your research study before you can write a questionnaire. If you plan to conduct an exploratory research study (i.e., you want to collect original data to understand a group or examine some issue), your questionnaire will usually not need to be as detailed and specific as if you plan to conduct a confirmatory research study (i.e., when you intend to collect data that will enable you to test research hypotheses). That is, when your primary goal is to explore the topic, you want to be broad in your questions so that you do not miss an important concept that your research participants feel is relevant. In both exploratory

TABLE 8.2 Principles of Questionnaire Construction

Principle 1	Make sure the questionnaire items match your research objectives.
Principle 2	Understand your research participants.
Principle 3	Use natural and familiar language.
Principle 4	Write items that are clear, precise, and relatively short.
Principle 5	Do not use "leading" or "loaded" questions.
Principle 6	Avoid double-barreled questions.
Principle 7	Avoid double negatives.
Principle 8	Determine whether an open-ended or a closed-ended question is needed.
Principle 9	Use mutually exclusive and exhaustive response categories for closed-ended questions.
Principle 10	Consider the different types of response categories available for closed-ended questionnaire items.
Principle 11	Use multiple items to measure abstract constructs.
Principle 12	Consider using multiple methods when measuring abstract constructs.
Principle 13	Use caution if you reverse the wording in some of the items to prevent response sets in multi-item scales.
Principle 14	Develop a questionnaire that is properly organized and easy for the participant to use.
Principle 15	Always pilot test your questionnaire.

and confirmatory research, you should carefully review the existing research literature, as well as any related instruments that have already been used for your research objectives, before deciding to construct your own questionnaire. One of the worst things that can happen in questionnaire-based research is to realize that you should have asked a question or included a variable *after* your data have been collected.

Think back to Rachel, our second-grade teacher. She was upset that a question was not asked about afterschool programs. This omission of a question about an important issue could indicate that the designers of the questionnaire did not carefully consider the research on the topic before designing the questionnaire. As a result, a likely important variable was not measured fully, which will affect the research results as well as the researchers' understanding of Rachel's true opinion on the topic.

Principle 2. Understand your research participants.

A key to effective questionnaire construction is understanding your research participants. Remember that it is they, not you, who will be filling out the questionnaire. A very important strategy when you write a questionnaire is to develop an empathetic understanding or an ability to "think like" your potential research participants. If the questionnaire does not "make sense" to your participants, it will not work.

Principle 3. Use natural and familiar language.

You should use language that is understandable to the people who are going to fill out your questionnaire. Try to avoid the use of jargon or technical terms. This principle builds on the above principle of understanding your research participants. You must know enough about your participants to use language familiar to them. Consider the age of your participants, their educational level, and any of their relevant cultural characteristics when deciding on the kind of language to use. Remember that it is very possible that not everyone uses the same everyday language as you; if you are reading this book, you are probably a college graduate and are also working on a graduate degree. The use of natural and familiar language makes it easier for participants to fill out a questionnaire and helps participants feel more relaxed and less threatened by the task of filling it out.

One key issue related to both the principle of understanding your participants and that of using natural and familiar language is determining an appropriate reading level. It is important to use the reading level that is natural and appropriate for your research participants. Poorly constructed questionnaires are written at either too high or too low a reading level for the intended participants. If the reading level is too high for your participants, those filling out the questionnaire might skip questions simply because they do not understand what is asked, or, worse, they will "guess" an answer that might not reflect their true opinion. Almost as problematic is when the questionnaire is written significantly below the reading level of those for whom it is intended. When this occurs, participants are sometimes insulted by the low level and do not take the questionnaire seriously or refrain from participating in additional research. Further, a reading level that is too low can result in a more simplistic and less rich view of the topic than would have been possible if a higher level had been used. If you effectively consider how your research participants will interpret and react to each item on your questionnaire, then you likely will be able to write items that will provide useful information.

See Journal Article 8.3 on the Student Study Site.

8.1 Why is reading level important to consider when writing items and constructing a questionnaire? What else is important, regarding communication, in constructing a questionnaire?

Principle 4. Write items that are clear, precise, and relatively short.

Each item on your questionnaire should be understandable to you (the researcher) and to the participants (the people filling out the questionnaire). Because each item is measuring something, it is important for it to be clear and precise. The GIGO principle is relevant here: "Garbage in, garbage out." If the participants are not clear about what is being asked of them, their responses will result in data that cannot or should not be used in a research study. Your goal is for each research participant to interpret the meaning of each item in the questionnaire in exactly the same way. If you must use a technical term, remember to define it for the participants. Finally, try to keep most items relatively short because long items can be confusing and stressful for research participants.

Once again consider Rachel, our ill-fated research participant who reported being confused by the questions even though she was clear about the topics being studied. Although she could have offered valuable insights to the researchers, she got "lost" in the wording of the questions, the jargon used, and perhaps even the reading level. As a result, the researchers did not get a clear picture of her opinions, and Rachel became frustrated. This situation would have been avoided if the researchers had taken the time to understand their research participants and write clear, precise questions.

Principle 5. Do not use "leading" or "loaded" questions.

A leading or loaded question biases the response the participant gives to the question. A **loaded question** is one that contains emotionally charged words (words that create a positive or negative reaction). For example, the emotionally charged word *liberal* was often avoided by politicians with left-of-center leanings during the 1980s and 1990s because the word created a negative reaction in some people regardless of the content of the statement. Some other examples of loaded words are *politician*, *communist*, *welfare*, *drug czar*, *soccer mom*, *pro-life*, *pro-choice*, and *drug abuser.* A **leading question** is one that is phrased in such a way that it suggests a certain answer. Here is an example of a leading question:

- **Loaded question** A question containing emotionally charged words

- **Leading question** A question that suggests a certain answer

Don't you agree that teachers should earn more money than they currently earn?

- ☐ Yes, they should earn more.
- ☐ No, they should not earn more.
- ☐ Don't know/no opinion.

The phrase "Don't you agree" leads the participant. A more neutral wording of this question would be as follows:

Do you believe teacher salaries are lower than they should be, higher than they should be, or at the right amount?

- ☐ Teacher salaries are lower than they should be.
- ☐ Teacher salaries are higher than they should be.
- ☐ Teacher salaries are at the right amount.
- ☐ Don't know/no opinion.

Here is an entertaining example of a question that is leading and has loaded phrases in it (from Bonevac, 1999):

Do you believe that you should keep more of your hard-earned money or that the government should get more of your money for increasing bureaucratic government programs?

- ☐ Keep more of my hard-earned money.
- ☐ Give my money to increase bureaucratic government programs.
- ☐ Don't know/no opinion.

Always remember that your goal is to write questionnaire items that help participants feel free to provide their natural and honest answers. You want to obtain responses that are undistorted by the wording of the questions. Recall in our opening example that Rachel felt the researchers had an "agenda" and she was worried that she couldn't appropriately agree or disagree with certain questions. Have you ever felt that way when filling out a questionnaire? If so, you might have experienced leading or loaded questions.

REVIEW QUESTION

8.2 Think of an example of a leading or loaded question.

Principle 6. Avoid double-barreled questions.

▪ **Double-barreled question** A question that combines two or more issues or attitude objects

A **double-barreled question** combines two or more issues or attitude objects in a single item. Here's an example: Do you think that teachers should have more contact with parents and school administrators? As you can see, this single item asks about two different issues. The question is really asking, Do you think that teachers should have more contact with parents? *and* Do you think that teachers should have more contact with school administrators? Each of these two issues may elicit a different attitude, and combining them into one question makes it unclear which attitude or opinion is being measured. Once someone answers the question, it's impossible for the researcher to know which *barrel* of the question was answered.

Because it is impossible to know which part of the question the participant addressed or whether he or she addressed the union of the two, it is a good rule to avoid double-barreled questions. As a general rule, if the word *and* appears in a question or statement, you should check to see whether it is double-barreled or, rather, if the question is just getting at a very specific situation.

Principle 7. Avoid double negatives.

When participants are asked for their agreement with a statement, double negatives can easily occur. For example,

> Do you agree or disagree with the following statement?
>
> Teachers should not be required to supervise their students during library time.

▪ **Double negative** A sentence construction that includes two negatives

If you disagree with the statement, you must construct a **double negative** (a sentence construction that includes two negatives). If you disagree, you are saying that you do not think that teachers should not supervise students during library time (Converse & Presser, 1986). In other words, you probably believe that teachers should supervise students during library time.

Here is another example of a double negative:

Teachers should not be able to do the following things:

Spank children

❑ Yes

❑ No

Expel children from school

❑ Yes

❑ No

If you must use a negative item, you should underline the negative word or words to catch the participant's attention.

Principle 8. Determine whether an open-ended or a closed-ended question is needed.

An **open-ended question** enables participants to respond in any way that they please. Open-ended questions take you into the natural language and worlds of your research participants, and, therefore, open-ended questions provide primarily qualitative data. In contrast, a **closed-ended question** requires participants to choose from a limited number of responses that are predetermined by the researcher. Closed-ended questions provide primarily quantitative data. Although open-ended questions are typically analyzed qualitatively, the answers sometimes are analyzed quantitatively by counting the number of times a response was provided. Furthermore, a minimally open-ended question can provide quantitative information, as in this example: "How many times have you removed a student from your class for disciplinary reasons in the last year?"

- **Open-ended question** A question that allows participants to respond in their own words
- **Closed-ended question** A question that forces participants to choose from a set of predetermined responses

To determine someone's marital status, you could use the question "What is your current marital status?" and leave sufficient space for participants to write in their answer. In this case, the question would be an open-ended question because the participants would have to provide an answer in their own words. On the other hand, you could use a closed-ended question to determine someone's marital status, like this:

What is your current marital status? (Check one box.)

- ❑ Single
- ❑ Married
- ❑ Divorced
- ❑ Separated
- ❑ Widowed

In the question about marital status, notice that the **item stem** (the words forming the question or statement) was the same in the open-ended and the closed-ended question examples: Both ask, What is your current marital status? In short, the difference between an open-ended question and a closed-ended question is just the way participants are allowed to respond. In open-ended questions, participants must come up with their own answers; in closed-ended questions, participants must select from the predetermined responses provided by the researcher.

- **Item stem** The set of words forming a question or statement

Open-ended questions are usually used in exploratory research (i.e., when the researcher knows little about the topic), and closed-ended questions are usually used in confirmatory research (i.e., when the researcher wants to test specific hypotheses). Open-ended questions are valuable when the researcher needs to know what people are thinking and the dimensions of a variable are not well defined. Because the participants respond by writing their answers in their own words, open-ended questions can provide rich information. For example, the following open-ended question would provide some interesting information: What do you think teachers can do to keep students from using illicit drugs?

It is more difficult and more time-consuming to analyze the data obtained from open-ended questions than from closed-ended questions. Nonetheless, open-ended questions are at the heart of qualitative research, whose goal is to understand participants' inner worlds in their natural languages and categories.

A closed-ended question is appropriate when the dimensions of a variable are already known. Closed-ended questions expose all participants to the same response categories and allow standardized quantitative statistical analysis. Often, researchers will use the responses from open-ended questions to help design closed-ended questions for future questionnaires. For example, a researcher might group teachers' suggestions for keeping students off drugs into a set of categories (e.g., education, afterschool programs, discipline) and use these categories as response choices in a future closed-ended question.

- **Qualitative questionnaire** A questionnaire based on open-ended items and typically used in exploratory or qualitative research
- **Quantitative questionnaire** A questionnaire based on closed-ended items and typically used in confirmatory or quantitative research
- **Principle of standardization** Providing exactly the same stimulus to each research participant
- **Mixed questionnaire** A questionnaire that includes a mixture of open-ended and closed-ended items

Questionnaires can be classified by the type of questions that are used. Questionnaires that include mostly open-ended items are called **qualitative questionnaires**. These questionnaires are often used for exploratory research, such as when the researcher wants to know how participants think or feel or experience a phenomenon or when the researcher wants to know why participants believe something happens. An example of an open-ended questionnaire is provided in the bonus materials on the student companion website.

Questionnaires that include mostly closed-ended items are called **quantitative questionnaires**. These questionnaires are focused on getting participant responses to standardized items for the purpose of confirmatory research in which specific variables are measured and hypotheses are tested. The **principle of standardization** is very important in quantitative research; the goal is to provide a common stimulus (item stem, response categories, and any additional information) to each person in the research study (Dillman, 2007). This is done to ensure maximum comparability of responses. In practice, most questionnaires employ a mixture of open-ended and closed-ended items; these are called **mixed questionnaires** (Johnson & Turner, 2003). Although we have classified questionnaires into three types, note that questionnaires actually fall on a continuum with qualitative and quantitative as endpoints and mixed in the middle.

Consider, again, the frustration of our teacher in the opening example. A large part of this frustration was caused by the fact that the researchers failed to address a topic that she considered important. This frustration could have been avoided if the researchers had realized and acknowledged that they might not know *all* the important topics that their participants wanted to discuss. One way to deal with this potential limitation is to include an open-ended question such as "What topics do you feel are important to student learning outcomes?" The use of this open-ended question would allow participants to express their opinions more fully, especially opinions the researcher failed to anticipate, and it would provide the researchers with valuable information for their research studies.

See Tools and Tips 8.1 on the Student Study Site.

8.3 What is an item stem?

8.4 If you are conducting an exploratory research study, are you more likely to use closed-ended questions or open-ended questions?

Principle 9. Use mutually exclusive and exhaustive response categories for closed-ended questions.

Categories are **mutually exclusive** when they do not overlap. For example, the following response categories for a question about the participant's age are *not* mutually exclusive:

▪ **Mutually exclusive** Response categories that do not overlap

- ☐ 10 or less
- ☐ 10 to 20
- ☐ 20 to 30
- ☐ 30 to 40
- ☐ 40 to 50
- ☐ 50 to 60
- ☐ 60 to 70
- ☐ 70 to 80
- ☐ 80 or greater

Do you see the problem with these response categories? The problem is that they overlap. For example, a person who is 20 years old could be placed into two categories. In fact, persons aged 10, 20, 30, 40, 50, 60, 70, and 80 can all be placed into more than one category. In short, the response categories are not mutually exclusive. In a moment, we will show you how to fix this problem.

A set of response categories is **exhaustive** when there is a category available for all legitimate responses. For example, what is the problem with the following categories from a question asking for your current age?

▪ **Exhaustive** Response categories that include all possible responses

- ☐ 1 to 4
- ☐ 5 to 9
- ☐ 10 to 14

The problem is that these three categories are not exhaustive because there is no category available for anyone over the age of 14 or anyone younger than 1 year old. A set of categories is not exhaustive unless there is a category available for all potential responses.

Putting the ideas of mutually exclusive and exhaustive categories together, you can see that the following set of response categories is mutually exclusive and exhaustive:

Which of the following categories includes your current age? (Check one box.)

- ☐ Less than 18
- ☐ 18 to 29
- ☐ 30 to 39
- ☐ 40 to 49

- ❑ 50 to 59
- ❑ 60 to 69
- ❑ 70 to 79
- ❑ 80 or older

The principle of mutually exclusive categories applies because none of the categories overlap. The principle of exhaustive categories applies because a category is available for every possible age. Whenever you write a standard closed-ended question (a question with an item stem and a set of predetermined response categories), remember to make sure that your response categories are mutually exclusive and exhaustive!

Principle 10. Consider the different types of response categories available for closed-ended questionnaire items.

In this section, we introduce several popular types of closed-ended response categories by explaining the ideas of rating scales, rankings, semantic differentials, and checklists.

Rating Scales

Researchers often obtain data from research participants by providing questions or statements (the item stem) and rating scales (the response choices) with instructions to make judgments about each item stem using the rating scale that is provided. A **rating scale** is a continuum of response choices that participants are told to use in indicating their responses. Rating scales produce numerical (quantitative) data rather than qualitative data (nominal-level data). Rating scales have been used by researchers for quite a long time. In an early review of the history of rating scales, Guilford (1936) provided examples from as early as 1805 and many other examples from shortly after 1900. Some important early developers of rating scales were Sir Francis Galton (1822–1911), Karl Pearson (1857–1936), and Rensis Likert (1903–1981).

- **Rating scale** A continuum of response choices

A **numerical rating scale** consists of a set of numbers and "anchored" endpoints. When you **anchor** a point on a rating scale, you label the point with a written descriptor. Here is an example of an item stem and a numerical rating scale with anchored endpoints:

- **Numerical rating scale** A rating scale that includes a set of numbers with anchored endpoints
- **Anchor** A written descriptor for a point on a rating scale

How would you rate the overall job performance of your school principal?

1	2	3	4	5	6	7
Very Low						Very High

As you can see, the first endpoint (1) is anchored with the words *very low*. The other endpoint (7) is anchored with the words *very high*. This is a 7-point rating scale because there is a total of seven points on the scale. If you use a numerical rating scale that has only the endpoints anchored (as above), we recommend that you use an odd number of points rather than an even number of points. If you use an even number of points, a respondent might misinterpret *one* of the two centermost numbers as representing the center or neutral point (Dillman, 2007). If you choose to use an even number of points, you will need to anchor the two centermost numbers or clearly anchor the area between the two centermost numbers. For example, if you think you want to use a "10-point" rating scale, you should use the numbers 0 to 10 (which is 11 points); if you insist on using 1 to 10, you should place an anchor equally over the numbers 5 and 6 so that participants do not erroneously use the scale as if 5 is the center point.

A similar type of rating scale is called a fully anchored rating scale. A **fully anchored rating scale** has all points anchored with descriptors. Here is an example of an item stem followed by a fully anchored rating scale:

- **Fully anchored rating scale** A rating scale on which all points are anchored

My principal is an effective leader.

1	2	3	4	5
Strongly Disagree	Disagree	Neutral	Agree	Strongly Agree

This scale is called a *5-point scale* because there are five points on the scale. (We recommend that a single-item "scale" *not* be called a "Likert scale," as is sometimes done in research literature, because the term *Likert scale* has multiple meanings.[1,2]) Some researchers prefer to exclude the numbers and provide just the descriptors in a fully anchored rating scale. Regardless, you should attempt to make the words or anchors used for adjacent points an equal distance apart from each other. You must be very careful in your choice of anchors for both fully and partially anchored scales. Anchors provide *reference points* that participants will use to direct the expression of their opinions. If the reference points are one sided, are not clear, or are not spaced at equal distances, then you will not get an accurate measure of the participants' opinions. Consider the following *unbalanced* 5-point scale:

I enjoy my workplace environment.

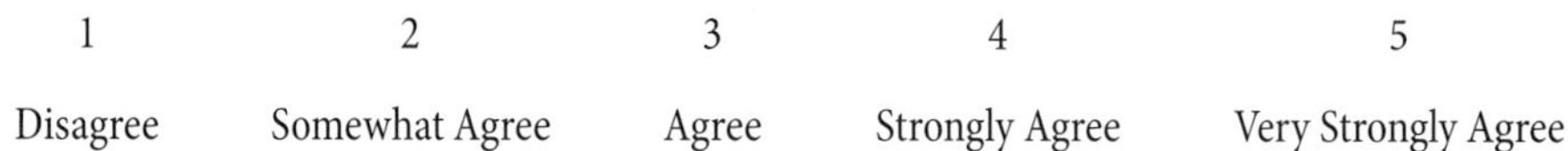

In the above example, there are four anchor or reference points for agreement and only one for disagreement. This looks like a scale that an unethical politician might try to use because he or she wants data showing that people agree with certain policies. These faulty response categories would make it easy for a respondent to agree but difficult for him or her to disagree. Remember: As you construct anchors for rating scales, always use a set of anchors that is balanced and place an equal distance between each pair of adjacent categories.

You might be wondering how many points a rating scale should have. Research suggests that you should use somewhere from 4 to 11 points on a rating scale (e.g., McKelvie, 1978; Nunnally, 1978). Rating scales with fewer than four points are not as reliable as rating scales with more points. Rating scales with more than 11 points can be confusing, because most participants have a limited ability to make fine distinctions among a great number of scale points.

When deciding how many points to include, consider how different the anchor points truly are. That is, what is the *real difference* between someone who indicates a 6 and someone who indicates a 7 on an 11-point scale? If you have more points than real differences, then you have too many points. Conversely, you must be sure to include enough points to see the real differences. Consider an extreme example of a 2-point scale: agree or disagree. While this might work on a simple issue, how many examples can you think of where a gray area exists that is neither full agreement nor full disagreement? In those cases, you would need more points to get an accurate picture of the issue. One thing to remember: You can always collapse categories during data analysis if you need to, but you cannot add extra categories after you have collected the data. As a result, some researchers err on the side of slightly more rather than fewer points on a scale. On the other hand, Dillman (2007) reported that he has, over the years, encouraged the use of fewer points (i.e., four or five points) for the sake of simplicity and easier comprehension by respondents. We recommend starting with the commonly used (i.e., "standard") rating scales, such as the ones provided in Exhibit 8.1, and adjusting them only if needed.

Empirical data can also inform your understanding of the number of response categories needed. For example, when pilot testing a questionnaire designed to measure researchers' methodological beliefs, I (Burke Johnson) found that the traditional 4-point agreement scale (*strongly disagree*, *disagree*, *agree*, *strongly agree*) was not working well. My participants sometimes complained that they didn't fully agree; at other times they complained that they didn't fully disagree. Therefore, I shifted to a 6-point scale (*strongly disagree*, *disagree*, *slightly disagree*, *slightly agree*, *agree*, *strongly agree*) to provide more gradated choices.

You might also wonder whether you should include a center or middle category in your rating scale. Research suggests that omitting the middle alternative (e.g., *neutral*, *about the same*, *average*, *no difference*) does not appreciably affect the overall pattern of results (Converse & Presser, 1986; Schuman & Presser, 1981/1996). As a result, some researchers choose to include a middle alternative, and others choose not to include it. Both practices can be defended. You can see in Figure 8.1 that Rosenberg used 4-point scales (i.e., he omitted the middle alternative) in his popular Self-Esteem Scale. Some researchers, such as Rosenberg, prefer to omit the middle alternative because doing so forces research participants to *lean* one way or the other; because it does not allow "fence-sitting," it provides less ambiguous data. On the other hand, omitting the middle alternative is more aggressive in style, it will occasionally irritate a participant, and some participants do hold a truly neutral attitude after carefully considering an issue.

Exhibit 8.1 shows some rating scales that researchers and practitioners commonly use. You can use these in your questionnaires. Although the ordering of categories (positive-to-negative, negative-to-positive) does not appear to affect response patterns (Barnette, 1999; Weng & Cheng, 2000), we generally recommend a negative-to-positive order because it might appear less leading. Note that both 4-point and 5-point rating scales are commonly used by survey research experts. As seen in Exhibit 8.1, you can construct rating scales for many dimensions, such as agreement, approval, importance, and satisfaction. When you construct your own rating scales, you will identify additional dimensions that you are interested in, and you will need to construct similar (i.e., analogous) response categories for those dimensions.

EXHIBIT 8.1 Examples of Commonly Used Response Categories for Rating Scales

Note: When you write response categories, make sure that the distance between each pair of anchors or response categories is the same. For example, the "distance" in meaning between *agree* and *strongly agree* is the same as between *disagree* and *strongly disagree.*

Agreement

(1) Strongly Disagree (2) Disagree (3) Agree (4) Strongly Agree
(1) Strongly Disagree (2) Disagree (3) Neutral (4) Agree (5) Strongly Agree
(1) Strongly Disagree (2) Moderately Disagree (3) Slightly Disagree (4) Slightly Agree (5) Moderately Agree (6) Strongly Agree

Amount

(1) Too Little (2) About the Right Amount (3) Too Much
(1) Not Enough (2) About the Right Amount (3) Too Many

Approval

(1) Strongly Disapprove (2) Disapprove (3) Approve (4) Strongly Approve
(1) Strongly Disapprove (2) Disapprove (3) Neutral (4) Approve (5) Strongly Approve

Belief

(1) Definitely False (2) Probably False (3) Probably True (4) Definitely True

Comparison

(1) Much Worse (2) Worse (3) About the Same (4) Better (5) Much Better
(1) Much Less (2) A Little Less (3) About the Same (4) A Little More (5) Much More
(1) Very Much Unlike Me (2) Somewhat Unlike Me (3) Somewhat Like Me (4) Very Much Like Me

Effectiveness

(1) Not at All Effective (2) Not Very Effective (3) Somewhat Effective (4) Very Effective

Evaluation

(1) Poor (2) Fair (3) Good (4) Excellent
(1) Very Poor (2) Poor (3) Fair (4) Good (5) Very Good
(1) Very Bad (2) Somewhat Bad (3) Somewhat Good (4) Very Good
(1) Very Poor (2) Below Average (3) Average (4) Above Average (5) Very Good

Frequency

(1) Never (2) Seldom (3) Sometimes (4) Often
(1) Almost Never (2) Seldom (3) About Half the Time (4) Often (5) Almost Always

Importance

(1) Not at All Important (2) Not Very Important (3) Fairly Important (4) Very Important
(1) Not at All Important (2) Not Very Important (3) Fairly Important (4) Very Important (5) Extremely Important

(Continued)

(Continued)

Knowledge

(1) Not at All Familiar (2) Not Very Familiar (3) Somewhat Familiar (4) Very Familiar

Performance

(1) Unsatisfactory (2) Fair (3) Good (4) Very Good

Probability

(1) A Lot Less Likely (2) Somewhat Less Likely (3) No Difference (4) Somewhat More Likely (5) A Lot More Likely

Satisfaction

(1) Very Dissatisfied (2) Somewhat Dissatisfied (3) Somewhat Satisfied (4) Very Satisfied

REVIEW QUESTIONS

8.5 How many points should a rating scale have?

8.6 Should all rating scales have a center point?

Rankings

▪ **Ranking** The ordering of responses in ascending or descending order

Sometimes you might want your research participants to rank order their responses. A **ranking** indicates the importance or priority assigned by a participant to an attitudinal object. Rankings can be used with open-ended and closed-ended questions. For example, you might first ask an open-ended question such as, In your opinion, who are the three top teachers in your school? Then you could follow up this question with a ranking item such as, Please rank order the teachers you just mentioned. Rankings can also be used with closed-ended items. For example, you might use the following closed-ended item:

> Please rank the importance of the following qualities in a school principal. (Fill in your rank order in the spaces provided using the numbers 1 through 5, with 1 indicating most important and 5 indicating least important.)
>
> _____ A principal who is sincere
>
> _____ A principal who gets resources for the school
>
> _____ A principal who is an advocate for teacher needs
>
> _____ A principal who is a strong disciplinarian
>
> _____ A principal who is a good motivator

As you can see, this is a closed-ended item because predetermined response categories are provided. As a general rule, you should *not* ask participants to rank more than three to five responses or response categories because ranking can be a difficult task for participants. Additionally, rank order items are difficult to analyze statistically and relate to other variables.

The use of a single item asking for a ranking is usually unnecessary. The recommended procedure is to have the participants rate each of the response categories using a rating scale. During data analysis, you obtain the average rating for each of the categories, and then you can rank order those averages. This way, you have data that are more easily analyzed for relationships with other variables, *and* you can obtain a ranking of the response categories.

Semantic Differential

The **semantic differential** is a scaling technique that is used to measure the meaning that participants give to various attitudinal objects or concepts (Osgood, Suci, & Tannenbaum, 1957). Participants are asked to rate each object or concept provided in the item stem on a series of 6- or 7-point, bipolar rating scales. The scales are "bipolar" because contrasting adjectives (antonyms) anchor the endpoints. You can see an example of a semantic differential in Exhibit 8.2.

■ **Semantic differential** A scaling technique in which participants rate a series of objects or concepts

■ **EXHIBIT 8.2** Example of Semantic Differential Scaling Technique

Please rate your school principal on each of the following descriptive scales. Place a checkmark on one of the blanks between each pair of words that best indicates how you feel.

Your School Principal

Sociable	____	____	____	____	____	____	____	Unsociable
Kind	____	____	____	____	____	____	____	Cruel
Successful	____	____	____	____	____	____	____	Unsuccessful
Wise	____	____	____	____	____	____	____	Foolish
Severe	____	____	____	____	____	____	____	Lenient
Masculine	____	____	____	____	____	____	____	Feminine
Active	____	____	____	____	____	____	____	Passive
Excitable	____	____	____	____	____	____	____	Calm
Fast	____	____	____	____	____	____	____	Slow
Predictable	____	____	____	____	____	____	____	Unpredictable
Clear	____	____	____	____	____	____	____	Confusing
Authoritarian	____	____	____	____	____	____	____	Democratic
Flexible	____	____	____	____	____	____	____	Rigid
Happy	____	____	____	____	____	____	____	Sad
Work	____	____	____	____	____	____	____	Fun

Semantic differentials are useful when you want to "profile" or describe the multiple characteristics associated with an attitudinal object. In Exhibit 8.2, you are asked to rate your school principal on 20 different bipolar rating scales. If you had all of the teachers in a school use this semantic differential, you could average the teachers' responses and profile their principal. You might find that different groups produce different profiles. For example, male and female teachers might view the principal differently. If you need to develop a semantic differential, it is helpful to look at an antonym dictionary for contrasting word pairs. You can also find some useful lists of semantic differential word pairs in Isaac and Michael (1995) and in Jenkins, Russell, and Suci (1958).

Checklists

- **Checklist** A list of response categories that respondents check if appropriate

Researchers sometimes provide a list of response categories (a **checklist**) and ask research participants to check the responses that apply. Multiple responses are allowed. Here is an example of a checklist:

Where do you get information about the most recent advances in teaching?

(Please check all categories that apply to you.)

- ❑ Other teachers
- ❑ Professors
- ❑ Principal
- ❑ Parents
- ❑ Superintendent
- ❑ Academic journals
- ❑ Professional journals
- ❑ Magazines
- ❑ Television
- ❑ Other. Please list: ______________________________

Checklists are occasionally useful for descriptive purposes. However, as a general rule, you should *avoid multiple-response items* such as checklists because they are difficult to analyze and because of primacy effects (i.e., respondents are more likely to check items placed earlier in the list; Dillman, 2007). The recommended alternative is to have respondents use a response scale for each of the categories.

- **Summated rating scale** A multi-item scale that has the responses for each person summed into a single score
- **Likert scale** A type of summated rating scale invented by Rensis Likert

Principle 11. Use multiple items to measure abstract constructs.

Multiple items designed to measure a single construct are used to increase the reliability and validity of the measure. Perhaps the most commonly used procedure for the measurement of abstract constructs is a **summated rating scale** (also called a **Likert scale**). Rather than being composed of a single item stem and a rating scale, *a summated rating scale is composed of multiple items* that are designed to measure the same construct. Each of the items is rated by each respondent using a rating scale (e.g., a 4- or 5-point scale), and these item ratings are summed by the researcher for each participant, providing a single score for each person.

The popular Rosenberg Self-Esteem Scale shown in Figure 8.1 is a summated rating scale. It consists of 10 items designed to measure self-esteem. The lowest possible total score on the full scale is 10, and the highest possible total score is 40. Participants will score somewhere between these two extremes (i.e., between the minimum and the maximum scores).

The summated rating scale procedure was originally developed by the famous social psychologist Rensis Likert (pronounced LICK-ert). Likert (1903–1981) published the results of his dissertation, which included the first known summated rating scale, in an article in 1932 (Likert, 1932). Since this time, researchers have used summated rating scales extensively, and construction of a Likert scale is one of the three traditional approaches to scale construction (the other two are Guttman and Thurstone scaling[3]).

The key advantages of multiple-item rating scales compared to single-item rating scales are that multiple-item scales provide more reliable (i.e., more consistent or stable) scores and they produce more variability, which helps the researcher make finer distinctions among the respondents. If you want to measure a complex construct (such as self-efficacy, locus of control, risk taking, test anxiety, dogmatism, or temperament), the use of a multiple-item scale is pretty much a necessity. When you want to measure constructs such as these, you should not, however, jump to develop your own scale. Rather, you should conduct a literature search to find already validated measures of your construct. If a measure is not available, only then would you need to consider developing your own measure. The development of a good summated rating scale takes a lot of time and expertise, and extensive validation is required before the scale should be used in a research study. The principles of test construction (reliability and validity) discussed in Chapter 7 must be followed when constructing a summated rating scale.

Principle 12. Consider using multiple methods when measuring abstract constructs.

This principle follows from the long-standing maxim in social research that our measurements are partially an artifact of our method of measurement. In fact, if you use one method of measurement for all of your variables, it is possible that your variables are correlated simply because you used the same measurement procedure (Cronbach & Meehl, 1955). The relationship between variables that you thought you were interpreting could be nothing but a measurement artifact! Think about this issue in your own life. Have you found that there is one type of measurement on which you do better than others? For instance, do you usually do well on essay tests, no matter the topic, but do worse on true/false tests? If you have experienced something like this, you have seen why Principle 12 is important.

The use of multiple measurement methods is so important today that more and more researchers are using "measurement models" based on two or even three measurement methods or procedures (e.g., questionnaires, interviews, observations, standardized tests). The resulting data are often analyzed by using advanced statistical software such as LISREL,

AMOS, mPlus, or EQS. The point is that the more methods a researcher uses to measure the relevant concepts or constructs, the more confidence you can place in the researcher's ability to tap into the characteristics of the concept, rather than the method.

Principle 13. Use caution if you reverse the wording in some of the items to prevent response sets in multi-item scales.

- **Response set** The tendency to respond in a specific direction regardless of content
- **Acquiescence response set** The tendency either to agree or disagree
- **Social desirability response set** The tendency to provide answers that are socially desirable

When participants rate multiple items using the same or similar rating scale, a "response set" might occur. A **response set** is the tendency for a research participant to respond to a series of items in a specific direction, regardless of the differences in item content. One type of response set is called the **acquiescence response set**, which is the tendency to say yes rather than no or to agree rather than to disagree on a whole series of items. Another response set, called the **social desirability response set**, is the tendency to provide answers that are socially desirable.

One technique used to help prevent response sets (especially the acquiescence response set) is to reverse the wording (and scoring) in some of the items. This technique is intended to encourage participants to read each item on the questionnaire more carefully. An example of reversed wording is shown in Figure 8.1. You can see that the wording for items 3, 5, 8, 9, and 10 of the Rosenberg Self-Esteem Scale is "reversed."

Whether one should use the reverse-wording technique has been debated in the questionnaire and test construction literature. One school of thought does not recommend reversing the wording because there is evidence that this practice can reduce the reliability and validity of multi-item scales (Barnette, 2000; Benson & Hocevar, 1985; Deemer & Minke, 1999; Weems & Onwuegbuzie, 2001; Wright & Masters, 1982). An opposing view holds that this reduction of reliability is attributable to a reduction in response sets and contends that the "benefit" of reducing the effects of response sets is greater than the "cost" of lower reliability. Dillman (2007) believed that reversing some items does not reduce response sets and that the reduction in reliability is due to respondents becoming confused because of the wording reversals. It is our recommendation that you use **reverse-worded items** only when response sets are a major concern. Furthermore, it is important for you to examine your data to try to "catch" when a response set occurs and eliminate those responses. Finally, do not use a reverse-worded item if it results in a double negative.

- **Reverse-worded item** An item on which a lower score indicates a higher level on a construct of interest (also called reverse-scored item)

Principle 14. Develop a questionnaire that is properly organized and easy for the participant to use.

Our checklist for questionnaire construction, shown in Table 8.3, lists what you should consider when designing your questionnaire. The ordering, or sequencing, of questionnaire items is one consideration. For example, Roberson and Sundstrom (1990) found that placing questions that respondents considered most important first and demographic questions (age, gender, etc.) last in an employee attitude survey resulted in the highest return rate. When constructing a questionnaire, you should begin the questionnaire with positive or nonthreatening items because doing so helps obtain commitment from participants as they fill out the questionnaire. Furthermore, as writers and professionals in survey research have pointed out for many years, *demographic questions should generally go last in a questionnaire,* with a lead-in such as "To finish this questionnaire, we have a few questions about you." The questionnaire should also not be overly long for the types of people in your target population. Otherwise, they might not fill out the questionnaire properly, or they might refuse to complete the entire questionnaire.

It also is a good idea to limit the number of contingency questions in a questionnaire because participants might become confused or agitated. A **contingency question** (also called a filter question) is an item that directs participants to different follow-up questions depending on their response. It allows the researcher to "filter out" participants from questions that these participants cannot or should not attempt to answer. Here is an example of an item operating as a contingency question:

- **Contingency question** An item that directs participants to different follow-up questions depending on their response

Question 1: What is your gender?

Male → (IF MALE, GO TO QUESTION 5.)

Female → (IF FEMALE, GO TO QUESTION 2.)

The use of contingency questions is usually not problematic for **web surveys** (i.e., those in which participants go to a website to complete a questionnaire), because in web surveys, the skip patterns associated with contingency questions can be programmed to take place automatically. The participants don't see the skips. The use of contingency questions also is less of a problem in interview protocols because the trained interviewer does the skipping rather than the research participant.

- **Web surveys** Participants read and complete a survey instrument that is developed for and located on the Internet

You should include clear instructions throughout your questionnaire and not put too many items on a page. If a questionnaire has several topical sections, you should provide transitional or "lead-in" statements to orient the participants to each new topic. Other important tips are to give your questionnaire a title (e.g., "School Culture Questionnaire"), number the items consecutively from the beginning to the end, list response categories vertically rather than horizontally (rating scales can be done horizontally or vertically), provide an open-ended question at the end of your questionnaire to give the participant a place to add any comments or additional insights (e.g., "Is there anything else that you would like to add?"), provide clear instructions throughout the instrument (e.g., "Please check one of the following categories."), and thank the participant for filling out your questionnaire (you can just put a "Thank You for Completing This Questionnaire" at the bottom of the last page). Finally, always try to make your questionnaire look professional, because participants are more likely to fill it out and they will go away with a better impression of you and your organization. By using font sizes and types that are clear and readable, you enhance the clarity of your questionnaire. Additionally, you should maximize the amount of white or blank space in the questionnaire. Novice questionnaire construction is most evident when there is little or no white space. It is better to have an extra page in a readable questionnaire than a compact questionnaire that is unclear. Remember that the appearance and quality of your questionnaire also reflect on you and your organization.

TABLE 8.3 Checklist for Questionnaire Construction

1. Follow the 15 principles of questionnaire construction discussed in this chapter.
2. Remember that appearance matters.
   - Make your questionnaire look professional. The overall look of your questionnaire should be presentable, readable, and clear. Several of the points below address specific appearance issues.
3. Use titles.
   - Always put a title on your questionnaire; it informs the participants about the topic of the questionnaire and gives the questionnaire an identity.
   - Consider using section titles within the questionnaire, especially with longer questionnaires. These help focus the participant on the topic or direction taken in the instrument.
   - Titles give a professional appearance to the overall document and show how it is organized.
4. Use short questions when possible.
   - Balance the length of the questions with that of the information to be gained. Although it is tempting to write long, detailed questions, short questions work better. The longer the question, the more likely the participant will misinterpret or simply not understand the item.
5. Carefully consider the placement of each question and set of related questions.
   - Where a question appears is important. Do not put sensitive questions, such as *demographic* questions, at the beginning of your questionnaire. *Always put sensitive questions at the end.* Participants are more likely to answer questions that may make them uncomfortable if they have already invested a great deal of time in filling out the other questions first.
   - Make use of warm-up questions, especially questions that participants find interesting, at the beginning of the questionnaire. Just as you do not want to put sensitive questions at the beginning of the questionnaire, it is a good idea *not* to start out with your most difficult or time-consuming question. This may "scare off" participants and reduce the response rate. Instead, ask interesting, easy, short, nonthreatening (i.e., warm-up) questions first.
   - Vary question types reasonably. Break up large sections of rating-scale items with an open-ended question and vice versa. Although you don't want to jump around too much, by breaking up question types, you can reduce participants' natural inclination to fall into a response set and reduce their fatigue.
6. Number the items consecutively from the beginning to the end.
7. Use plenty of white space.
   - This produces a less crowded, more easily read questionnaire. Do not crowd a questionnaire in an effort to reduce the number of pages.
8. Use a readable font size.
   - Stick to commonly used font types like Times New Roman or Arial. Cursive- or calligraphy-type fonts take away from the clean look of the questionnaire. Remember that your goal is a readable, professional-looking questionnaire, not a pretty one.
   - If your questionnaire is web based, be sure to use a TrueType font that appears on the Internet properly.
   - When considering the size of your font, be sure to consider your participants; however, a good rule of thumb is to stick to fonts no smaller than 12 point.
9. Consider different font styles but remember that "less is more."
   - Use different styles, such as underlining or bolding, to emphasize different sections and to aid in the flow of the questionnaire. Additionally, different styles can be used to emphasize specific words such as *not* and *always.*
   - Remember that "less is more." Too many style types can hinder the readability of the questionnaire. If everything is underlined or placed in a bold font, then the emphasis is lost.
10. Use lead-ins for new or lengthy sections to orient and guide the user.
    - Do not assume that participants can tell that you are switching topics or directions. Use clear transitions between the sections. Writing a questionnaire is like writing a story that flows easily and naturally.

11. Provide clear instructions.
    - When in doubt, add instructions to clarify the nature of a rating scale or whether a single response or multiple responses are allowed.
12. Direct the user exactly where to go in the questionnaire.
    - If you use screener and/or contingency questions, make sure the user knows where to go or what to do next. Writing a questionnaire is like writing a map; it must show the user exactly where to go within the instrument and show when and where to exit.
13. List response categories for closed-ended items vertically rather than horizontally. (Rating scales are the possible exception.)
14. Use matrix formatting for items using the same rating scale.
    - This is the exception to the previous rule.
    - If you have a series of questions with the same response choices or anchors, use a matrix design (see items 7–17 in Exhibit 8.3) rather than repeating the response choices for each item. This reduces redundancy and allows participants to work more quickly and easily through the questionnaire. Also, it allows researchers to spot response sets quickly in a particular questionnaire.
15. Avoid multiple-response questions.
16. Include some open-ended questions.
    - Even if your instrument is primarily a quantitative questionnaire, it is useful to provide participants places to insert their own thoughts, which might be missed by the closed-ended items.
17. Do not use lines with open-ended questions.
    - When using open-ended questions, do not supply lines in the response area. Simply leave that area as white space. White space adds to the clean look of the questionnaire and does not limit the amount of feedback you receive, as lines may do.
18. Do not "break" your questions.
    - Never carry a question or its response choices from one page to the next. This forces participants to flip between pages, which increases error. Additionally, many participants may miss a possible response alternative if it appears on the next page.
19. Include page numbers.
    - Using page numbers is a simple way to enhance the look and clarity of your questionnaire. This is even more important when you use contingency questions that require a participant to jump to different pages in the questionnaire.
20. Use closings.
    - Include a closing statement such as "Thank you for your time," or "We appreciate your participation." Closings allow a participant to be aware that he or she is finished, but more importantly, the use of a closing statement results in a more positive overall experience for the participant. This can result in a better response rate should you need to do any follow-up research with the participant.

REVIEW QUESTIONS

8.7 When should you use a contingency question?

8.8 What are some key ideas of Table 8.3: Checklist for Questionnaire Construction?

Principle 15. Always pilot test your questionnaire.

It is a cardinal rule in research that you must "try out," or **pilot test**, your questionnaire to determine whether it operates properly *before* using it in a research study. You should conduct your pilot test with a minimum of 5 to 10 people. You may want to start with colleagues or

- **Pilot test** The preliminary test of your questionnaire

friends, asking them to fill out the questionnaire and note any points of confusion. Then you will need to pilot test the questionnaire with several individuals similar to those who will be in your research study.

- **Think-aloud technique** Has participants verbalize their thoughts and perceptions while engaged in an activity

One useful technique to use during your pilot test is called the **think-aloud technique**, which requires research participants to verbalize their thoughts and perceptions while they engage in an activity. When this technique is used as part of a pilot test, you ask your participants to verbalize their thoughts and perceptions about the questionnaire, including why they chose a particular response choice, while they are filling it out. You must record or carefully write down exactly what they say. It is helpful to make audiotape or videotape recordings of the pilot test sessions for later review. The think-aloud technique is especially helpful for determining whether participants are interpreting the items the way you intended.

You will want to use the think-aloud technique with some of the participants in your pilot test, but you should have others in the pilot test fill out the questionnaire under circumstances that are as similar as possible to those of the actual research study. When you conduct a pilot test, you need to think about several issues. For example, be sure to check how long it takes participants to complete the questionnaire under circumstances similar to those of the actual research study. This will help you know whether the questionnaire is too long. You always can think of some additional items that you would like to add, but you must avoid writing overlong questionnaires. Other things being equal, the response rate and quality of responses are better for short and medium-length questionnaires than for long questionnaires.

Using the think-aloud technique, you should listen to what the participants think about the instructions and the items in your questionnaire. Try to determine whether any of the questionnaire items are confusing or threatening. Ask your participants to tell you when they reach an item that is difficult to understand and then ask them to paraphrase what they believe the problem item is stating or asking. Determine whether your participants understand the items in a consistent way. Check the veracity of the responses of your participants (i.e., whether their answers are true and accurate). These strategies will help you determine whether the items actually measure what they are intended to measure. Also, when the participants fill out your questionnaire, check to see whether they skip to the correct place if you have contingency questions in your questionnaire.

After participants finish filling out the questionnaire, you can discuss the questionnaire with them individually or in group sessions. Explain the purpose of your questionnaire to them and ask whether they believe anything important was left out, whether the instructions were clear, and whether any items stood out for any reason. Probe for explanations. If the questionnaire has an experimental manipulation embedded in it, be sure to check to see that the manipulation is working as intended. For example, if a statement or a vignette is supposed to increase empathy toward minority groups, ask your participants whether they understood it and whether they felt empathetic afterward. Ask participants to comment on the appearance and clarity of the presentation. Were there too many questions on a page? Was there not enough space to write responses? Was the questionnaire easily readable? Finally, check the responses and determine if too many "I don't know," or "Does not apply," answers are indicated. If so, you may be asking questions that are unclear or not applicable. After completing your pilot test, revise your questionnaire and then pilot test it again. Remember that you do not want to use a questionnaire in a research study until all of the kinks have been worked out.

8.9 What principles should you follow when constructing a questionnaire?

8.10 How does one pilot test a questionnaire or an interview protocol?

Putting It All Together

You now have the 15 principles of questionnaire construction and our checklist (Table 8.3) at your disposal. You should feel ready to start the construction of your own questionnaire! One good way to start your first questionnaire is to model it after an existing questionnaire that was properly constructed. Therefore, we now provide an example or model questionnaire in Exhibit 8.3; it is entitled the Research Methods Demonstration Questionnaire. Notice how the principles for questionnaire construction have been employed in this questionnaire. For example, take note of the appearance of the questionnaire and the ordering of the questions. This is an example of how a basic mixed questionnaire should look.

Okay, so now that you have all your information, what is the next step? Figure 8.2 is an outline to help guide you through the construction of your first—or ten thousandth—questionnaire. Questionnaire construction is not a straight path. It is an iterative process with many twists and turns. Even the most experienced researcher at questionnaire construction will find that he or she has to go back and revise the instrument at some point in the process. Remember, your goal is to design a questionnaire that works well! Questionnaire construction takes time, but when you get it right, your research participants and the readers of your research reports will thank you for it.

EXHIBIT 8.3 Example of a Mixed Questionnaire

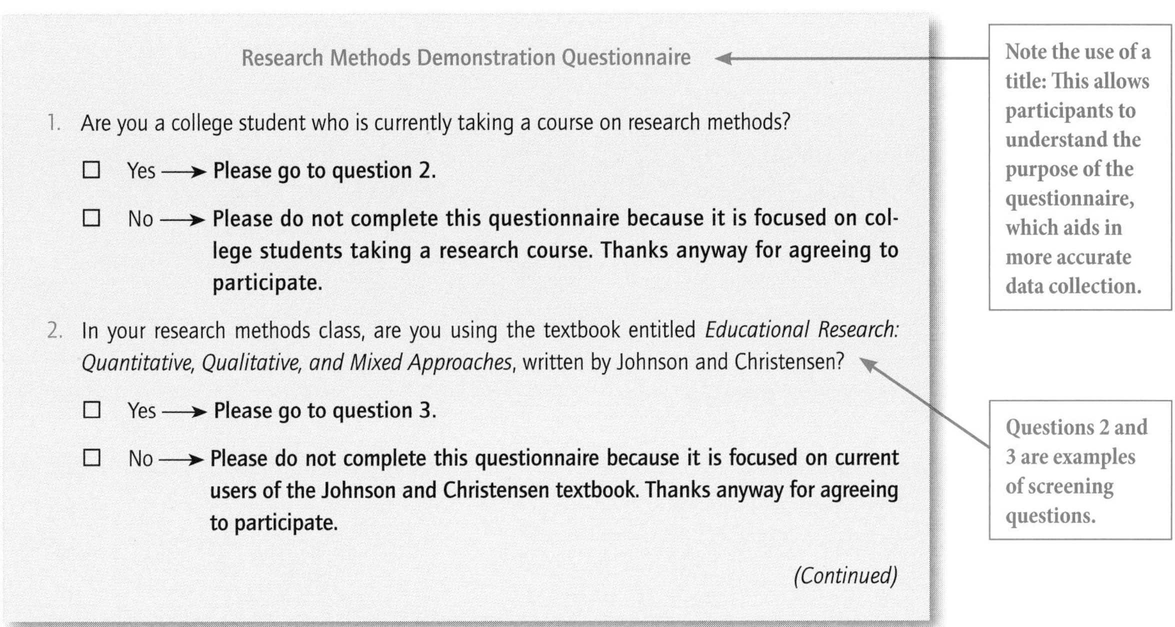

Research Methods Demonstration Questionnaire

1. Are you a college student who is currently taking a course on research methods?

 ☐ Yes ⟶ **Please go to question 2.**

 ☐ No ⟶ **Please do not complete this questionnaire because it is focused on college students taking a research course. Thanks anyway for agreeing to participate.**

2. In your research methods class, are you using the textbook entitled *Educational Research: Quantitative, Qualitative, and Mixed Approaches*, written by Johnson and Christensen?

 ☐ Yes ⟶ **Please go to question 3.**

 ☐ No ⟶ **Please do not complete this questionnaire because it is focused on current users of the Johnson and Christensen textbook. Thanks anyway for agreeing to participate.**

(Continued)

Note the use of white space with open-ended items.

Question about current opinions.

Use of the "don't know" option.

Lead-in instructions. Enhances both appearance and understanding of the set of items.

Matrix format for series of items using the same 4-point rating scale.

(Continued)

3. At what college or university are you currently taking this research methods class?

4. Is the Johnson and Christensen textbook the first book you have studied on research methods during the past 5 years?

- ☐ Yes
- ☐ No

5. How difficult do you find learning about research methods to be?

- ☐ Very difficult
- ☐ Somewhat difficult
- ☐ Not very difficult
- ☐ Not at all difficult
- ☐ Don't know

6. Which course do you think is more difficult, educational psychology or educational research methods?

- ☐ Educational psychology
- ☐ Educational research methods
- ☐ Don't know

Next, we want to know how *interesting* you find each of the following research method topics. Please respond with (1) not at all interesting, (2) not very interesting, (3) somewhat interesting, or (4) very interesting, or (DK) don't know. **(Circle one response for each item.)**

	Not at All Interesting	Not Very Interesting	Somewhat Interesting	Very Interesting	Don't Know
7. Developing research questions	1	2	3	4	DK
8. Writing proposals	1	2	3	4	DK
9. Research ethics	1	2	3	4	DK
10. Measurement	1	2	3	4	DK
11. Data collection	1	2	3	4	DK
12. Sampling	1	2	3	4	DK
13. Validity of research results	1	2	3	4	DK
14. Data analysis	1	2	3	4	DK
15. Quantitative research	1	2	3	4	DK
16. Qualitative research	1	2	3	4	DK
17. Mixed research	1	2	3	4	DK

18. Given sufficient study time, how much anxiety would you feel if you had to take a 100-item multiple-choice test on research methods?

- ☐ A great deal of anxiety----> **Go to question 19.**
- ☐ Some anxiety----> **Go to question 19.**
- ☐ A little anxiety----> **Go to question 21.**
- ☐ No anxiety----> **Go to question 21.**
- ☐ Don't know----> **Go to question 21.**

Contingency question.

19. What do you think are some reasons for your test anxiety?

20. What might be done by your teacher to help reduce your test anxiety?

Open-ended exploratory question.

<u>Next are three questions about the content of your research methods class.</u>

21. Which of the following research terms refers to "a technique for physically obtaining data to be analyzed in a research study"?

- ☐ Method of data collection
- ☐ Method of research
- ☐ Method of measurement
- ☐ Method of data analysis
- ☐ Don't know

Items 21–23 are designed to measure knowledge rather than opinions.

22. How many points should there generally be on a rating scale?

- ☐ 4 points
- ☐ 5 points
- ☐ 10 points
- ☐ Anywhere from 4 to 11 points is usually fine.
- ☐ Don't know

23. What is the problem with this potential questionnaire item: "Teachers should have extensive contact with parents and school administrators."

- ☐ It is too long
- ☐ It is a double-barreled question
- ☐ It has no item stem
- ☐ Don't know

24. How useful do you think your knowledge of research methods will be in your career?

- ☐ Not at all useful
- ☐ Not very useful
- ☐ Somewhat useful
- ☐ Very useful
- ☐ Don't know

Opinion-based question referring to future events.

(Continued)

Note: The change in font (i.e., underline) for the instructions. This aids in ease of use.

4-point agreement scale with Don't Know option.

(Continued)

The next three items refer to how you feel about yourself. Please indicate your degree of agreement or disagreement with each item using the following scale: (1) strongly disagree, (2) disagree, (3) agree, or (4) strongly agree. **(Circle one response for each item.)**

	Strongly Disagree	Disagree	Agree	Strongly Agree	Don't Know
25. I take a positive attitude toward myself.	1	2	3	4	DK
26. I am able to do things as well as most other people.	1	2	3	4	DK
27. I feel that I have a number of good qualities.	1	2	3	4	DK
28. On the whole, I am satisfied with myself.	1	2	3	4	DK

29. Realistically, what final letter grade do you expect to get in your research methods course?

- ☐ A
- ☐ B
- ☐ C
- ☐ D
- ☐ F
- ☐ Don't know

Sensitive or threatening information such as demographics should be placed at the end of the questionnaire.

Last are some demographic questions that will be used for classification purposes only.

30. What is your current college status?

- ☐ Undergraduate
- ☐ Graduate student
- ☐ Other (Please Specify): ____________________

Good use of a "catch-all" or Other option. This allows for categories that you may not have anticipated.

31. What is your gender?

- ☐ Female
- ☐ Male

32. Which of the following best describes your political party affiliation?

- ☐ Democrat
- ☐ Republican
- ☐ Independent
- ☐ Other (Please Specify): ____________________

33. Approximately what was your personal income last year?

_______ ← dollars

"Fill-in-the-blank" question. Researchers can classify responses into categories later if they so wish.

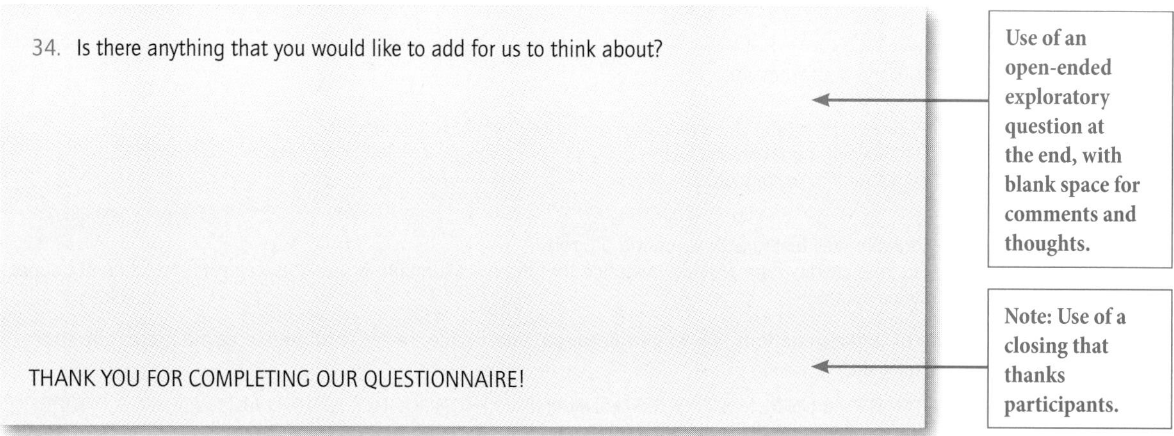

FIGURE 8.2 Outline of the steps in constructing a questionnaire

STEP 1. Review the relevant literature and begin planning the questionnaire.

Remember that if a questionnaire that fits your needs is already available, then there is no need to construct a new questionnaire.

Think about:
Do you understand the targeted participants?
Do you understand the issues to be examined?
What variables do you want to measure?
What do you want to know in the participants' own words?

Is the questionnaire to be self-administered, sent through the mail, or filled out on the Internet?

Decision:
Select the type of questionnaire you need to construct: qualitative, quantitative, or mixed.

(Continue with step 1 until you are ready to move to step 2.)

STEP 2. Write the items for the questionnaire.

Think about:
Have you examined other related questionnaires?
Have you examined items on other high-quality questionnaires that will be helpful models as you write yours?
Have you asked others (friends, family members, students) if your items are clear?

Decision:
Are my questions simple and clear?
Are all of the issues covered?
Does my draft questionnaire look good so far?

(If the answer is no to any of these questions, then continue working on step 2 or go back to step 1 if needed; otherwise, go to step 3.)

STEP 3. Design the layout and overall questionnaire.

Think about:
Does the questionnaire have a title, clear directions, section lead-ins, proper section ordering, demographics at the end, and a "thank you" at the conclusion?
Have you asked others (colleagues) to critique your questionnaire?

Decision:
Are the items and sections organized logically and clearly?
Do the skip patterns in the questionnaire clearly lead users exactly where they need to go through the questionnaire?

(If the answer is no to any of these questions, then continue working on step 3 or go back to step 1 or 2 as needed; otherwise, go to step 4.)

(Continued)

FIGURE 8.2 (Continued)

STEP 4. Conduct a pilot test of the questionnaire.

Think about:
What people can you administer the questionnaire to who are similar to the kinds of people to be used in your research study?
Have I collected reliability and validity data?

Decision:
Is your questionnaire well tested and operating properly?
Do the reliability and validity data provide evidence that the questionnaire is working well with the kinds of people to be used in your research?

(If the answer is no to any of these questions, go to earlier steps, and revise, revise, and revise some more, and then pilot test the questionnaire again.)

REMEMBER: DO NOT GO TO STEP 5 UNTIL YOUR QUESTIONNAIRE IS THOROUGHLY TESTED AND WORKING PROPERLY.

STEP 5. Administer your questionnaire in your research study.

Think about:
Does the questionnaire work properly with your research participants?
How good are the reliability and validity data with the real participants?
Do any items need improvement?

Decision: How can I improve my questionnaire?

(Continue to loop back to earlier steps as needed.)

REVIEW QUESTIONS

8.11 What principles, procedures, or specific ideas do you see "actualized" (i.e., applied) in the questionnaire shown in Exhibit 8.3?

8.12 Where were the demographic items placed in the Exhibit 8.3 questionnaire? Why were they placed there?

8.13 What are the steps in questionnaire construction? (Hint: See the outline in Figure 8.2.)

ACTION RESEARCH REFLECTION

Insight: Action researchers often use open-ended, closed-ended, and mixed questionnaires because questionnaires are an excellent way to determine and record what their clients, students, parents, administrators, and other participants believe. Action researchers use questionnaires to measure attitudes and, when using open-ended questions, they ask others to write down in their own words what they believe is helpful and not helpful.

1. Search the research literature for questionnaires on a topic of interest to you. Is a questionnaire already available that you would like to use? What is its name, and what does it measure?
2. What else would you like to find out that is not measured by the available questionnaire? Construct a short (e.g., 10–15 items) *mixed questionnaire* (i.e., combination of closed- and open-ended items) that you would like to administer to participants in your classroom or workplace. Do your items and questionnaire adequately follow the principles of good questionnaire construction explained in this chapter? If not, be sure to revise it and pilot test it again.

SUMMARY

This chapter explains how to write items and construct a questionnaire to be used in collecting data in a research study. This might seem like a simple task—and it is not overly difficult—but it is imperative that you take this process very seriously and that you follow the appropriate steps and procedures that we have provided. Remember that if your data-collection instrument (i.e., your questionnaire) does not work well, then your results will be meaningless. When developing a good questionnaire, you need to understand and use the 15 principles of questionnaire construction (Table 8.2) discussed in this chapter. We provided a checklist that you should use to make sure you have not forgotten any important points (Table 8.3). We also provided an example of a correctly written questionnaire that you can use as a model or example when you start constructing your own questionnaire (Exhibit 8.3). Over time, we recommend that you develop a collection of model questionnaires. When you add additional questionnaires to *your* collection, however, make sure that they come from professionals with many years of experience specifically in questionnaire construction or from a top-notch survey research organization (e.g., the University of Michigan Survey Research Center or the National Opinion Research Center in Chicago). Finally, we provided an outline showing you the cyclical steps in developing and continually improving your questionnaire (Figure 8.2).

KEY TERMS

acquiescence response set (p. 208)
anchor (p. 200)
checklist (p. 206)
closed-ended question (p. 197)
contingency question (p. 209)
double-barreled question (p. 196)
double negative (p. 196)
exhaustive (p. 199)
fully anchored rating scale (p. 201)
item stem (p. 197)
leading question (p. 195)
Likert scale (p. 206)
loaded question (p. 195)
mixed questionnaire (p. 198)
mutually exclusive (p. 199)
numerical rating scale (p. 200)
open-ended question (p. 197)
pilot test (p. 211)
principle of standardization (p. 198)
qualitative questionnaire (p. 198)
quantitative questionnaire (p. 198)
questionnaire (p. 190)
ranking (p. 204)
rating scale (p. 200)
response set (p. 208)
reverse-worded item (p. 208)
semantic differential (p. 205)
social desirability response set (p. 208)
summated rating scale (p. 206)
think-aloud technique (p. 212)
web surveys (p. 209)

DISCUSSION QUESTIONS

1. What do you think is the most important principle of questionnaire construction? Please be sure to give your reasons.
2. What are the key advantages of the following three types of questionnaires: a qualitative questionnaire (i.e., a fully open-ended questionnaire), a quantitative questionnaire (i.e., a fully closed-ended questionnaire), or a mixed questionnaire (i.e., a questionnaire composed of multiple open- and closed-ended items)?
3. If someone said "***All*** rating-scale questions must use 5 points," what would you say to them?
4. Why do you think professional survey researchers put the demographic questions at the end, rather than the beginning, of the questionnaire?
5. How, and with whom, should one pilot test a new questionnaire? Why?
6. If you are conducting a research study, should you construct your own questionnaire or attempt to find an already available questionnaire? Explain your reasoning.

RESEARCH EXERCISES

1. Fill out the Rosenberg Self-Esteem Scale shown in Figure 8.1. Then sum your responses to the 10 items to obtain your overall score (i.e., your summated score). Be sure that you “reverse-score” items 3, 5, 8, 9, and 10 (i.e., a 4 becomes a 1, a 3 becomes a 2, a 2 becomes a 3, and a 1 becomes a 4) before you add up your item scores to obtain your overall score. After doing this, you will know how to score a summated scale. Be sure that you are careful in interpreting your score!
2. Pick a topic and construct a 15-item questionnaire. Collect data from five of your classmates. Have them evaluate your data-collection instrument (i.e., your questionnaire) on the basis of what they have learned in this chapter. Revise your questionnaire.
3. Conduct a journal article search using the term *questionnaire.* List five questionnaires that you found interesting. What was the purpose of each of these?

PROPOSAL EXERCISE

In the previous chapter’s proposal exercise, you listed the variables you wanted to measure in your research proposal. Now, do the following: (a) locate questionnaires in the literature that measure some or all of your variables and (b) for variables not found in the literature, construct your own items. Note that you can also include open-ended items in your questionnaire! Finally, combine (a) and (b) into your final questionnaire for your research study.

RELEVANT INTERNET SITES

SPSS Survey Tips: This is a well-done (and free) guide on tips for constructing questionnaires and interview protocols
https://www.uic.edu/depts/accc/oldstats/spss/surveytips.pdf

“What Is a Survey?” This is a well-done (and free) guide on conducting survey research; Chapter 6 in the “Brochure” includes a few points about “designing a questionnaire.”

http://www.amstat.org/sections/srms/pamphlet.pdf
http://www.whatisasurvey.info (click download and follow directions)

STUDENT STUDY SITE

Visit the Student Study Site at **edge.sagepub.com/rbjohnson6e** for these additional learning tools:

Video Links
Self-Quizzes
eFlashcards
Lecture Notes
Full-text SAGE journal articles
Interactive Concept Maps
Web Resources

RECOMMENDED READING

Babbie, E. (1990). *Survey research methods* (9th ed.). Belmont, CA: Wadsworth.

Blackburn, N., Sudman, S., & Wansink, B. (2004). *Asking questions: The definitive guide to questionnaire design—For market research, political polls, and social and health questionnaires.* San Francisco, CA: Jossey-Bass.

Dillman, D. A., Smyth, J. D., & Christian, L. M. (2014). *Internet, mail, and mixed-mode surveys: The tailored design method* (4th ed.). Hoboken, NJ: Wiley.

NOTES

1. Rensis Likert is most famous for inventing a summated rating scale procedure (discussed later in this chapter). However, he also used a 5-point scale measuring "approval." Here are the anchors he used in the late 1920s: 1–*strongly approve*, 2–*approve*, 3–*undecided*, 4–*disapprove*, 5–*strongly disapprove*.

2. The term *rating scale* is flexible. You can vary the number of points, as in "5-point scale" and "7-point scale," and you can indicate the type of scale, as in "5-point agreement scale" or "5-point satisfaction scale."

3. You can learn more about these in Vogt and Johnson's (2016) *Dictionary of Statistics and Methodology*. You also can find useful information on the web.

Chapter 9

Methods of Data Collection

LEARNING OBJECTIVES

After reading this chapter, you should be able to

- List the six major methods of data collection.
- Explain the difference between method of data collection and research method.
- Define and explain the characteristics of each of the six methods of data collection.
- Explain the different modes of administration of the methods of data collection.
- Explain the concept of standardization.
- Explain the key characteristics of the four different types of interviews.
- Describe the four roles the researcher can take in qualitative interviewing.
- List at least five commonly used interviewing probes.
- Explain how the fundamental principle of mixed research can be applied to methods of data collection and provide an example.
- State the two "cardinal rules" of educational research mentioned in this chapter.

Visit the Student Study Site for an interactive concept map.

RESEARCH IN REAL LIFE Data Collecting and Research Questions

istock/Terraxplorer

September 11, 2001, is a day we will all remember. Our feelings of security and invulnerability to the attacks of terrorists were shattered. Before this time, terrorists' attacks were largely something that happened to people in other countries. As former President Bush stated, the terrorists' goal is to frighten us, not just kill, maim, and destroy. Indeed, the terrorists made progress in this regard.

After September 11, air traffic fell 20%. This didn't necessarily mean that people were traveling less; many people drove some of those unflown miles. Driving all of these additional miles would translate into 800 more highway deaths or 3 times the number of people that were killed on the four hijacked planes. Myers (2001) noted that data from the National Safety Council revealed that, in the last half of the 1990s, people were 37 times more likely to die in a vehicle crash than in a crash of a commercial plane. Crashing and dying while flying on a commercial flight were less likely than getting heads every time on 22 flips of a coin. The terrorists' attacks on September 11 were tragic and created a tremendous amount of grief for everyone involved, especially those who lost loved ones. And the fear they caused, particularly of flying, resulted in more rather than fewer deaths. Reports such as those of the National Safety Council provide much numerical information. Other reports include other types of information and data.

Collection of data is necessary to obtain information that will provide answers to important questions. In the above example, data were collected and converted to percentages to document the fact that flying is less dangerous than driving. Educational researchers also have to collect data to provide answers to their research questions. In this chapter, we review the six most common forms of data collection used by educational researchers. With your understanding of these forms of data collection, you will be armed with knowledge of the procedures needed to collect data that will provide answers to your own research questions.

In Chapter 7, we introduced you to the concept of measurement, and we discussed the different kinds of tests that are used for collecting data in educational research. If an already constructed test is available for the topics of interest to you, you should strongly consider using that test because reliability and validity information will usually be available for it. However, an already developed data-collection instrument might not be available for your particular research needs. In this case, you must construct a new test or another type of data-collection instrument, such as a questionnaire or an interview protocol, and doing this well takes time and effort. In the last chapter, you learned how to construct a questionnaire when one is needed for your research study.

This chapter builds on the last two chapters. It answers these four questions:

1. What are the six major methods of data collection?
2. What method or methods of data collection will allow me to obtain the information I need to answer my research questions?

3. What are the strengths and weaknesses of the different methods of data collection?
4. How do I use these methods of data collection in my research?

The following list shows the six most common methods of data collection used by educational researchers:

1. Tests
2. Questionnaires
3. Interviews
4. Focus groups
5. Observation
6. Constructed and secondary or existing data

- **Research method** Overall research design and strategy
- **Method of data collection** Technique for physically obtaining data to be analyzed in a research study
- **Fundamental principle of mixed research** Advises researchers to thoughtfully and strategically mix or combine qualitative and quantitative research methods, approaches, procedures, concepts, and other paradigm characteristics in a way that produces an overall design with multiple (divergent and convergent) and complementary (broadly viewed) strengths and nonoverlapping weaknesses

With these methods of data collection, researchers can have their participants fill out an instrument or perform a behavior designed to measure their ability or degree of skill (tests); researchers can have research participants fill out self-report instruments (questionnaires); researchers can talk to participants in person or over the telephone (interviews); researchers can discuss issues with multiple research participants at the same time in a small-group setting (focus groups); researchers can examine how research participants act in natural and structured environments (observation); and researchers can have participants construct new data during a study, such as drawings or recordings, or use data that came from an earlier time for a different purpose than the current research problem at hand (constructed and secondary or existing data). Some strengths and weaknesses of these methods of data collection are provided at the student companion website.

In a typical research study, researchers begin by identifying the important research problems and specific research questions that they want to address. Then they select the most appropriate **research method** or methods (experimental, correlational, ethnography, grounded theory, etc.) to help them decide on a research design and a research strategy that will allow them to answer their research questions. Researchers next decide how they are going to collect their empirical research data. That is, they decide what **methods of data collection** (i.e., tests, questionnaires, interviews, focus groups, observations, constructed and secondary/existing data) they will physically use to obtain the research data.

As you read this chapter, keep in mind the **fundamental principle of mixed research** defined in Chapter 2. According to this principle, thoughtful mixing of methods, procedures, and other paradigm characteristics is an excellent way to conduct high-quality research. Specifically, you should mix in a way that provides multiple (divergent and convergent) and complementary (broadly viewed) strengths and nonoverlapping weaknesses. The principle offers you one guiding "logic for mixing." In this chapter, think about how this principle can apply to the mixing of different *methods of data collection*. For example, you might collect standardized test data and then collect qualitative interview data to provide a fuller picture of a group of teachers' aptitude for teaching reading. As another example, a researcher might find a statistical relationship between parental social class and the likelihood of children joining the middle school band (e.g., perhaps higher social class is related to band membership). A researcher might mix into this study the collection of some focus group data from the parents and children from different social classes to explore the reasons and thinking that produce this quantitative relationship.

There are actually two kinds of mixing of the six major methods of data collection (Johnson & Turner, 2003). The first is **intermethod mixing**, which means *two or more* of the methods of data collection are used in a research study. This is seen in the two examples in the previous paragraph. In the first example, standardized test data and qualitative interview data were mixed/combined in the study. In the second example, a structured (quantitative) questionnaire and exploratory (qualitative) focus groups were mixed/combined.

- **Intermethod mixing** Use of more than one method of data collection in a research study

In the second kind of mixing, **intramethod mixing**, both quantitative and qualitative data are obtained through the creative use of a single method (i.e., using just *one* of the six major methods of data collection). For example, we previously described a *mixed questionnaire*. It includes both open-ended (exploratory) questions and standardized closed-ended items; the open-ended part provides qualitative data, and the closed-ended part provides quantitative data. One way to remember these two terms is to note their roots: *Inter-* means "between" and *intra-* means "within." Accordingly, intermethod mixing uses information from two (or more) data-collection methods, and intramethod mixing uses information collected by one method.

- **Intramethod mixing** Use of a single method of data collection to obtain a mixture of qualitative and quantitative data

Mixing methods of data collection is like putting together several flawed fishing nets—each of which has a hole, a torn part, or a weak point—to construct a "new," stronger net that works well despite the problem with each individual net. We highly recommend that you print out the six tables at the book's companion website that list the strengths and weaknesses of the six major methods of data collection. You will find these tables in the lecture notes for Chapter 9. Using these tables and what you learn in this chapter, you will be able to decide how to mix and match the methods in your own research study in a way that follows the fundamental principle of mixed research.

Although our focus in this chapter is on methods of data collection, the fundamental principle of mixed research also applies to the mixing of other research ingredients, such as research methods (e.g., experiments, ethnographies), sampling methods, and data analysis methods. Educational research is about providing solid evidence for your conclusions, and evidence is greater when you employ a logical mixing strategy. In fact, one cardinal rule in educational research is this: *Provide multiple sources of evidence.* Multiple sources of evidence will sometimes provide multiple-converging support for a single point, and at other times they will provide a fuller-diverging picture of what you are studying. In both cases, you will be glad that you used multiple methods. Here's another cardinal rule in educational research: *Rule out alternative explanations.* If you want to make a specific claim, following this rule is essential so that you can defend your claim. Carefully following these two rules, providing evidence from multiple perspectives and ruling out alternative explanations of your claims, will enable you to produce research reports that are convincing and defensible and will be taken seriously.

Remember that in this chapter we are concerned with how research data are collected from research participants, not with the different research methods. You will learn more about the different research methods in Chapters 12–17. Now we explain the different methods of data collection.

See Tools and Tips 9.1 on the Student Study Site.

REVIEW QUESTIONS

9.1 What is a method of data collection?

9.2 What are the six main methods of data collection? (Hint: The first letters make the rather awkward acronym TQIFOS.)

9.3 What are the two "cardinal rules" of educational research mentioned in this chapter?

TESTS

Tests are commonly used in quantitative research to measure attitudes, personality, self-perceptions, aptitude, and performance of research participants. Perhaps the most common type of test is the standardized test, which is developed by psychometricians and usually includes psychometric information on reliability, validity, and reference group norms. In fact, Chapter 7 was about standardized tests, so you already know a lot about this form of test (e.g., its characteristics, the different types, and where to find already developed tests). We emphasize again that if a relevant test is already available that measures the variables of interest to you, then you should seriously consider using that test.

Although many tests are available for use (e.g., standardized tests of intelligence and personality, achievement, preschool, aptitude, and diagnostic tests), experimental researchers often need to generate their own tests to measure very specific constructs that are operationalized in unique ways. An experimental researcher might design a test procedure to measure a cognitive or memory process or to measure participants' response time to a mental activity. For example, a researcher studying particular types of mathematics story problems might develop a test that deals specifically with those problem types. The point is that, when a researcher is looking at the manipulation of instructional content or context, tests usually need to be tailored to the content or task. Note that even though such "experimenter-constructed" tests are not normed for specific populations, the researcher is obliged to do his or her best to find ways to affirm the reliability and validity of the assessments.

Because you have already read a full chapter on tests, we do not elaborate more on tests here. Do keep in mind, however, that as with all methods of data collection, you may want to *mix* tests with other methods when you conduct a research study. For an example of mixing, you might take a look at a study by Mantzicopoulos and Knutson (2000) or another published study that interests you. These researchers used school records, parent interviews, teacher questionnaires, and standardized tests of achievement to determine the relationship of school and family mobility to children's academic achievement.

Technology and Tests

Some psychological tests have to be administered one-on-one by the researcher. However, most tests used in research can be administered in a group situation, and these tests are typically administered on computers by the researcher. A newer approach, sometimes used, is to administer the test online. For example, when all of the materials can be programmed, an experiment can be conducted over the Internet rather than in a laboratory. You should determine what mode of administration will work best and is most efficient in your research study. Advantages of computer testing are ease of administration and the ability to program complex sequences of questions. Internet testing also includes the advantage of lack of researcher effects because there is no researcher present. A key weakness of Internet testing is that you might not know, for sure, who is taking the test and what other activities the participant is engaging in that might affect his or her performance.

QUESTIONNAIRES

As discussed in Chapter 8, a **questionnaire** is a self-report data-collection instrument that each research participant completes as part of a research study. Researchers use questionnaires to obtain information about the thoughts, feelings, attitudes, beliefs, values, perceptions, personality, and behavioral intentions of research participants. In other words, researchers attempt to measure many different kinds of characteristics using questionnaires.

■ **Questionnaire** A self-report data-collection instrument filled out by research participants

Because you have already read a full chapter on questionnaire construction (Chapter 8), we do not elaborate more on questionnaires here. As with all of the methods of data collection, remember that you will often want to mix questionnaires with other methods when you conduct a research study. A table showing the strengths and weaknesses of questionnaires is provided in the lecture notes for Chapter 9 at the companion website. Be sure to consider these when you are considering using a questionnaire singularly or in combination with other methods of data collection.

Technology and Questionnaires

Survey research often is based on questionnaires as the survey instrument. The majority of the time the questionnaire is administered online because of the many advantages of *online survey research*. In Figure 9.1, you can see a screenshot from a *free* software package that you might want to use if you conduct an Internet survey—it is called Google Forms (https://docs.google.com/forms/u/0/). You can use the software in writing your questionnaire, sending it out to your participants in an email, and saving the results in your Google account.

■ **FIGURE 9.1** Free software called Google Forms. Use it to develop a questionnaire, email it to your recipients, and store the results in your Google account. Link: https://www.google.com/forms/about/

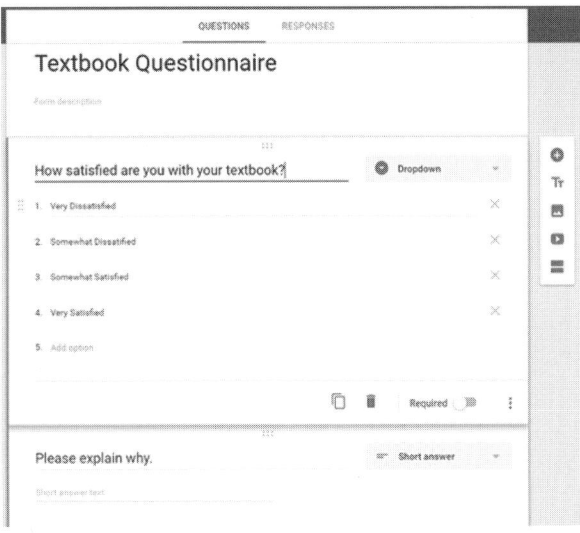

FIGURE 9.2 Modes of questionnaire and interview data collection

	Questionnaires			Interviews		
	In-Person Questionnaire	Mail Questionnaire	Internet Questionnaire	In-Person Interview	Telephone Interview	Internet Interview
Defining characteristics	• Questionnaire is completed by participants in group situation and given to the researcher upon completion	• Questionnaire is mailed to participants, who must complete it and mail it back to the researcher	• Participants click on an Internet link that takes them to the online questionnaire. Once they are finished, they click "end" and the session is finished	• A professionally trained interviewer goes to each participant's house (or other agreed-upon location) and interviews the participant face-to-face	• An interviewer reads the script from a single location and records the participants' responses into a Computer Assisted Telephone Interview (CATI) computer system	• A trained interviewer interviews the participant over the Internet using Internet software
How often used?	• Very common in experimental research	• Used in survey research, but less common than other survey methods (including in-person interviews) due to low response rate	• Most common of all survey methods used today	• Least common due to high cost	• Very popular in survey research in business and large grant-funded academic projects	• Less common than telephone interviews, but slowly becoming popular as researchers learn about software availability
Costs	• Inexpensive • Key costs are making copies of the instrument and data entry • Incentives often used for motivation	• Inexpensive • Only requires costs of materials, mailing, and data entry • Small incentives often used	• Inexpensive • Only requires software that is sometimes free for small-scale projects (e.g., Google Forms, Survey Monkey, SurveyGizmo, QUALTRICS, WebSurveyor, Google Consumer Surveys, QuestionPro, etc.)	• Most costly of the six modes compared here because requires extensive travel by professional interviewer • Key costs are for professional interviewers, copies of instruments, travel costs, sizable incentives, and data entry	• Less expensive than in-person survey; more expensive than mail survey • Start-up cost and software is expensive if conducting without a call center • Cost of using call center is considered high by many researchers without grant funding	• Inexpensive • Less expensive than telephone and mail surveys if researcher does the interviewing • Software not very expensive or free (e.g., GoToMeeting, Google Hangouts, WebEx, join.me, Adobe Connect, FreeConferenceCall.com, Highfive, and many more) • Key costs are data transcription and qualitative analysis of open-ended questions, which takes time

	Questionnaires			Interviews		
	In-Person Questionnaire	Mail Questionnaire	Internet Questionnaire	In-Person Interview	Telephone Interview	Internet Interview
Sampling	• Includes groups the researcher can identify and are willing to come to central location usually at a university	• Includes everyone in sampling frame with a home or work mailing address	• Can include everyone across the world that has access to the Internet. Excludes those without Internet	• Includes everyone willing to let the interviewer come to their house or other agreed-upon location	• Includes everyone that has a valid telephone number. (Random digit dialing locates unlisted numbers.) Excludes those without phones	• Can include everyone across the world that has access to the Internet. Excludes those without Internet
Response rate	• Depends on circumstance but within a subject pool, a high response rate is not uncommon	• Low rate of 10%–40% is typical • Higher rates are expected for topics of interest to respondents	• Moderate rate is typical (e.g., 25%–50%) • Higher rates for topics of interest to respondents	• Highest relative response rate (e.g., 75%–80% is not uncommon)	• Moderately high rate of 50%–60% is not uncommon for surveys from a respected source and when not selling anything	• Rate estimates not currently available. Moderately high rates are expected
Speed	• Quick turnaround if participants and research facility are available	• Takes several weeks to send reminders and wait for responses	• Quick turnaround	• Relatively slow, unless one has a large group of interviewers able to travel to diverse locations	• Quick turnaround when using a professional telephone call center	• Can more slowly (than Internet questionnaire and telephone call centers) gain responses when being done by the researcher and his or her small team
Additional advantages	• Researcher has control over the data collection setting	• Good for sensitive topics • Respondents can complete the questionnaire anytime they want to • It's the only way to reach certain people	• Can program complex question sequences • Respondents can complete the questionnaire anytime they want to • It's the only way to reach certain people	• Can probe for more information • Can develop rapport with respondents • Can conduct longer interviews • Can personalize the interview • Respondents can be at their home in their familiar environment and at a time that is highly convenient for them • It's the only way to reach certain people	• Can probe for more information • Can develop rapport with respondents • Can program complex sequences of items • Less interviewer bias than in-person interviews • It's the only way to reach certain people	• Can probe for more information • Can develop rapport with respondents • Can personalize the interview • Respondents can be at their home in their familiar environment and at a time that is convenient for them • It's the only way to reach certain people

(Continued)

FIGURE 9.2 (Continued)

	Questionnaires			Interviews		
	In-Person Questionnaire	Mail Questionnaire	Internet Questionnaire	In-Person Interview	Telephone Interview	Internet Interview
Disadvantages	• No probing	• No probing • No one present to help if a respondent has questions • Little control over who responds	• No probing	• Very expensive • Interviewer error/effects may occur	• Interview cannot effectively last more than 15 minutes • Interviewer error/effects may occur	• Takes a lot of time • Interviewee must have computer with webcam • Interviewer error/effects may occur
Special needs	• Need a participant pool that fits the research needs • Convenience samples often used in experiments • Requires training in questionnaire construction and delivery	• Need high-quality mailing list of population relevant to research study • Must send reminders • Requires training in questionnaire construction	• Need access to Internet addresses of population relevant to research study • Must send reminders • Requires training in questionnaire construction	• Need permission to visit • Need home addresses (or other place to meet) • Requires interviewer training	• Need high-quality phone number list of population of interest to research study • Might have to call back • Requires interviewer training	• Need access to relevant Internet addresses, and must set time to meet virtually • Requires interviewing expertise

Questionnaires are also used in laboratory research, and in those cases, they are usually computer administered (i.e., the participants sit at a computer and complete the battery of research instruments). Questionnaires can also be administered individually or in groups as paper-and-pencil tests—the printed-out questionnaires are completed by the participants and physically handed back to the researcher. Yet another mode of questionnaire administration is by mail—the researcher mails the survey instrument (i.e., the questionnaire) to the research participants, who fill out the questionnaires and return them in self-enclosed, addressed, stamped envelopes. Now, please take a moment to carefully examine Figure 9.2, which shows the relative strengths and limitations of mail, telephone, and Internet questionnaires. Figure 9.2 also provides names of various software packages available to help you in conducting your research.

INTERVIEWS

You learned in the last section that you can collect data from research participants by having them fill out a questionnaire. Another way to collect data is to interview research participants. An **interview** is a data-collection method in which an **interviewer** (the researcher or someone working for the researcher) asks questions of an **interviewee** (the research participant). That is, the interviewer collects the data from the interviewee, who provides the data. Interviews that are done face-to-face are called **in-person interviews**; interviews conducted over the telephone are called **telephone interviews**. A strength of interviews is that a researcher can freely use **probes** (prompts used to obtain response clarity or additional information). Some commonly used probes are given in Table 9.1.

- **Interview** A data-collection method in which an interviewer asks an interviewee questions
- **Interviewer** The person asking the questions
- **Interviewee** The person being asked questions
- **In-person interview** An interview conducted face-to-face
- **Telephone interview** An interview conducted over the phone
- **Probe** Prompt to obtain response clarity or additional information

An interview is an interpersonal encounter. It is important that you (the interviewer) establish rapport with the person you are interviewing (the interviewee). The interview should be friendly. At the same time, you must be impartial to whatever the interviewee says to you. If you react positively or negatively to the content of the interviewee's statements, you may bias the responses. It is also important that the interviewee trusts you, because without trust you are likely to obtain biased research data.

Some techniques for establishing trust and rapport are to explain who the sponsoring organization is, to explain why you are conducting the research, and to point out to the participant that his or her responses are either anonymous (no name or identification will be attached to the respondent's data) or confidential (the respondent's name or identification will be attached to the respondent's data, but the researcher will never divulge the respondent's name to anyone). You want each potential participant to understand that your research is important and that his or her participation is important for the integrity of your study. We have included in Table 9.2 a list of tips that you will find helpful if you ever need to conduct an interview.

In Table 9.3, you can see four types of interviews (Patton, 1987, 1990): the closed quantitative interview, the standardized open-ended interview, the interview guide approach, and the informal conversational interview. These four types can be grouped into quantitative interviews (which include the closed quantitative interview) and qualitative interviews (which include the standardized open-ended interview, the interview guide approach to interviewing, and the informal conversational interview). We first discuss quantitative interviews.

Technology and Interviews

Interviews are often conducted over the telephone using a Computer Assisted Telephone Interview (CATI) system, which is programmable software into which researchers input the interview protocol along with its skip sequences. The telephone interviewer simply reads the script and enters the answers provided by respondents. The system only allows valid entries (e.g., a 6 would not be allowed on a 1-to-5 response scale) and produces, as the output, a data file that can be input easily into standard statistical software (such as SPSS, Excel, and R) for data analysis. Some CATI systems also provide basic statistical output.

Interviews can also be conducted by the researcher over the Internet. Software such as GoToMeeting is very helpful, and the interviewer and interviewee can see each other and interact and develop rapport. The interviewer can share his or her computer screen with pictures, questions, and scales when needed. For a list of alternatives to GoToMeeting, go to https://www.g2crowd.com/products/gotomeeting/competitors/alternatives or simply conduct a Google search on your own to find the best alternatives. Although interviewing conducted over the Internet is just becoming popular in educational research, the Internet is an exciting form of data collection because (a) anyone with Internet access (anywhere in the world) can be interviewed, (b) you can see each other and develop rapport, and (c) you can record the interview sessions. Technology is making the world "smaller" because we can now communicate with people who were previously out of reach! Please see Figure 9.2 for more comparisons of the different modes of conducting interviews.

Quantitative Interviews

- **Interview protocol** Data-collection instrument used in an interview

When carrying out quantitative interviews, you must carefully read the words as they are provided in the interview protocol. The **interview protocol** is the data-collection instrument that includes the items, the response categories, the instructions, and so forth. The interview

TABLE 9.1 Commonly Used Probes and Abbreviations

Standard Interviewer's Probe	*Abbreviation Used on Interview Protocol*
Repeat question.	(RQ)
Anything else?	(AE or Else?)
Any other reason?	(AO?)
Any others?	(Other?)
How do you mean?	(How mean?)
Could you tell me more about your thinking on that?	(Tell more.)
Would you tell me what you have in mind?	(What in mind?)
What do you mean?	(What mean?)
Why do you feel that way?	(Why?)
Which would be closer to the way you feel?	(Which closer?)

Source: From University of Michigan Survey Research Center. (1976). *Interviewer's manual* (Rev. ed.). Ann Arbor: University of Michigan Survey Research Center.

TABLE 9.2 Tips for Conducting an Effective Interview

1. Make sure all interviewers are well trained.
2. Do background homework on the interviewees so that you will know a little about the people you will be interviewing.
3. Establish rapport and trust with your interviewee.
4. Be empathetic but remain neutral toward the content of what the interviewee says.
5. Use gentle nonverbal head nods and verbal "um-hms" to show your interest in what the interviewee says.
6. Be reflexive (i.e., monitor yourself).
7. Make sure the interviewee is doing most of the talking, not you.
8. Be sensitive to gender, age, and cultural differences between you and the interviewee.
9. Make sure the interviewee understands exactly what you are asking.
10. Provide sufficient time for the interviewee to answer each question.
11. Maintain control of the interview and keep the interview focused.
12. Utilize probes and follow-up questions to gain clarity and depth of responses.
13. Maintain a respect for the interviewee's valuable time.
14. Typically, you should tape-record the interview session.
15. After an interview is completed, check your notes and recordings for quality and completeness.

protocol in a quantitative interview is basically a script written by the researcher and read by the interviewer to the interviewees. The interviewer also records the interviewee's responses on the interview protocol. The interview protocol is usually written on paper for in-person interviews and shown on a computer screen for telephone interviews.

The goal of the quantitative interview is to standardize what is presented to the interviewees. **Standardization** has been achieved when what is said to all interviewees is the same or as similar as possible. The key idea here is that quantitative researchers want to expose each participant to the same stimulus so that the results will be comparable. Not surprisingly, quantitative interviews result in mostly quantitative data that are later analyzed using quantitative statistical procedures. The reason we say "mostly" is that quantitative interview protocols often include a few open-ended items. If an open-ended question is asked in a quantitative interview, however, it is asked in exactly the same way for each participant in the study.

■ **Standardization** Presenting the same stimulus to all participants

In Exhibit 9.1, you can see a section taken from an interview protocol. It includes five closed-ended items (items 25–30) from the 1998 Phi Delta Kappa/Gallup Education Poll. Note that DK stands for "don't know." Question 27 asks the participants to make their ratings using a 4-point scale. The instruction provided at the end of question 27 tells the interviewer to go to item 28 *if* the respondent has one or more children in a public, parochial, or private school. *Otherwise,* the interviewer is instructed to go directly to item 30 (skipping items 28 and 29). (The participants are asked early in the interview whether they have one or more children in a public, parochial, or private school.) As you can see, this instruction operates just like a filter question.

The interview protocol used in the quantitative interview looks very similar to a questionnaire. In fact, many researchers call their interview protocol a questionnaire (e.g., Babbie, 1998; Converse & Presser, 1986; Frankfort-Nachmias & Nachmias, 1992). Although the data-collection instruments are similar in interviews and questionnaires, there is a key difference in how they are used. When conducting an interview, an *interviewer* reads the questions or statements exactly as written on the interview protocol, and he or she records the interviewee's answers in the spaces that are provided. When using a questionnaire, the *research participant* reads and records his or her own answers in the spaces provided on the questionnaire.

The 15 principles of questionnaire construction discussed in the last chapter also apply to the construction of interview protocols. You might want to examine the list of principles shown in Table 8.2 again to convince yourself that those principles apply to interview protocols as well. When writing an interview protocol, the key point to remember is that the interviewer will read what you write and the research participant will hear what the interviewer reads. You will therefore need to make sure that your interview protocol operates properly for that purpose. You must also make sure that your interviewers are well trained in interviewing techniques and the proper use of an interview protocol.

EXHIBIT 9.1 Example of a Section of a Telephone Interview Protocol (Questions 25–30 Are From the Phi Delta Kappa/Gallup Poll Education Poll, 1998)

25. There is always a lot of discussion about the best way to finance the public schools. Which do you think is the best way to finance the public schools—by means of local property taxes, by state taxes, or by taxes from the federal government in Washington, D.C.?
    1. Local property taxes
    2. State taxes
    3. Federal taxes
    4. (DK)
    5. (Refused) __________
26. In your opinion, is the quality of the public schools related to the amount of money spent on students in those schools, or not?
    1. Yes
    2. No
    3. (DK)
    4. (Refused) __________
27. How serious a problem would you say each of the following is in the public schools in your community? Would you say **(read and rotate A–G)** (is/are) a very serious problem, fairly serious, not very serious, or not at all serious?

1. Very serious	A. Discipline	__________
2. Fairly serious	B. Drugs	__________
3. Not very serious	C. Alcohol	__________
4. Not at all serious	D. Smoking	__________
5. (DK)	E. Fighting	__________
6. (Refused)	F. Gangs	__________
	G. Teenage pregnancy	__________

(If code "1" in S4 or S5, continue; otherwise, skip to #30)

28. Thinking about your oldest child when he or she is at school, do you fear for his or her physical safety?
    1. Yes
    2. No
    3. (DK)
    4. (Refused) __________

29. When your oldest child is outside at play in your own neighborhood, do you fear for his or her physical safety?
    1. Yes
    2. No
    3. (DK)
    4. (Refused) __________

30. In your opinion, should children with learning problems be put in the same classrooms with other students, or should they be put in special classes of their own?
    1. Yes, same classrooms
    2. No, should be put in special classes
    3. (DK)
    4. (Refused) __________

Source: © Phi Delta Kappa International.

Qualitative Interviews

Qualitative interviews consist of open-ended questions and provide qualitative data. Qualitative interviews are also called *depth interviews* because they can be used to obtain in-depth information about a participant's thoughts, beliefs, knowledge, reasoning, motivations, and feelings about a topic. Qualitative interviewing allows a researcher to enter into the inner world of another person and to gain an understanding of that person's perspective (Patton, 1987). The interviewer must establish trust and rapport, making it easy for the interviewee to provide information about his or her inner world.

■ **Qualitative interview** An interview providing qualitative data

The interviewer should listen carefully and be the repository of detailed information. The interviewer should also be armed with probes or prompts to use when greater clarity or depth is needed from the person being interviewed. For example, the interviewer should freely use the probes shown in Table 9.1. The interviewer can also ask follow-up questions that may naturally emerge during the qualitative interview. A qualitative interview will typically last anywhere from 30 minutes to more than 1 hour.

Not surprisingly, qualitative interviews are very popular with qualitative researchers. It is not uncommon, however, for quantitative researchers also to conduct some qualitative interviews as part of their overall research study. The three types of qualitative interviews are shown in Table 9.3: the informal conversational interview, the interview guide approach, and the standardized open-ended interview. The key characteristics of these three types of qualitative interviews are also given in Table 9.3.

TABLE 9.3 Patton's Classification of Types of Interviews

Type of Interview	*Characteristics*	*Strengths*	*Weaknesses*
Informal conversational interview	Questions emerge from the immediate context and are asked in the natural course of things; there is no predetermination of question topics or wording.	Increases the salience and relevance of questions; interviews are built on and emerge from observations; the interview can be matched to individuals and circumstances.	Different information is collected from different people with different questions. Data are less systematic and comprehensive if certain questions do not arise "naturally." Data organization and analysis can be quite difficult.
Interview guide approach	Topics and issues to be covered are specified in advance, in outline form; interviewer decides sequence and wording of questions during the course of the interview.	The outline increases the comprehensiveness of the data and makes data collection somewhat systematic for each respondent. Logical gaps in data can be anticipated and closed. Interviews remain fairly conversational and situational.	Important and salient topics may be inadvertently omitted. Interviewer flexibility in sequencing and wording questions can result in substantially different responses from different perspectives, thus reducing the comparability of responses.
Standardized open-ended interview	The exact wording and sequence of questions are determined in advance. All interviewees are asked the same basic questions in the same order. Questions are worded in a completely open-ended format.	Respondents answer the same questions, thus increasing comparability of responses; data are complete for each person on the topics addressed in the interview. Reduces interviewer effects and bias when several interviewers are used. Permits evaluation users to see and review the instrumentation used in the evaluation. Facilitates organization and analysis of the data.	Offers less flexibility in relating the interview to particular individuals and circumstances; standardized wording of questions may constrain and limit naturalness and relevance of questions and answers.
Closed quantitative interview	Questions and response categories are determined in advance. Responses are fixed; respondent chooses from among these fixed responses.	Data analysis is simple; responses can be directly compared and easily aggregated; many questions can be asked in a short time.	Respondents must fit their experiences and feelings into the researcher's categories; may be perceived as impersonal, irrelevant, and mechanistic. Can distort what respondents really mean or experience by so completely limiting their response choices.

Source: Adapted from M. Q. Patton, *How to Use Qualitative Methods in Evaluation,* pp. 116–117, © 1987 by SAGE. Used by permission of SAGE.

- **Informal conversational interview** Spontaneous, loosely structured interview

- **Interview guide approach** Specific topics and/or open-ended questions are asked in any order

The **informal conversational interview** is the most spontaneous and loosely structured of the three types of qualitative interviews. The interviewer discusses the topics of interest and follows all leads that emerge during the discussion. Because the informal conversational interview does not use an interview protocol, it is a good idea to tape-record the interview so that no important information will be lost. Many times the interview will occur at an unexpected or unscheduled time, however, and recording it will not be possible. Therefore, you should always take some field notes during the informal conversational interview and/or immediately after conducting the interview.

In the next approach to qualitative interviewing, the **interview guide approach**, the interviewer enters the interview session with a plan to explore specific topics and to ask specific open-ended questions of the interviewee. These topics and questions are provided on an interview protocol written by the researcher before the interview session.

The interviewer, however, does not have to follow these topics and questions during the interview in any particular order. The interviewer can also change the wording of any questions listed in the interview protocol. In short, the interview session is still a relatively unstructured interaction between the interviewer and the interviewee. At the same time, because of the interview protocol, the interviewer will cover the same general topics and questions with all of the interviewees. The interviewer must try to keep the interview on track, bringing the respondent back when he or she goes off on a topic that is not relevant to the research purpose.

Cross and Stewart (1995) used the interview guide approach in their study of what it is like to be a gifted student attending a rural high school. They were interested in the experiences of gifted students attending rural high schools; gifted students attending urban schools had been examined in previous research. Here is Cross and Stewart's discussion of the qualitative interviewing process that they used in their research study followed by the open-ended questions that they used to elicit information about the students' experiences:

> To obtain highly elaborated descriptions, the researchers asked participants to situate their experiences in specific settings. The process attempted to get subjects to regress to the actual experience so that pure descriptions would emerge. The interviews consisted of a beginning question, which asked subjects:
>
> - When you think of your experience of being a student in your high school, what stands out in your mind?
>
> Follow-up questions included:
>
> - Can you think of a particular situation and describe it to me?
>
> After the subject described the situation, the researcher would follow up with prompts like:
>
> - Tell me more about that; or
> - What were you aware of at that time?
>
> When subjects exhausted their depictions, the researcher asked:
>
> - Can you think of another time when that happened?
>
> At this point, the aforementioned process would repeat. The researcher attended to the ideas conveyed by the subjects and tried not to lead the interviews in any direction. The interviews ranged in length from 40 to 90 minutes. All interviews were recorded on cassette tape and later transcribed. (p. 275)

In the third approach to qualitative interviewing, the **standardized open-ended interview**, the interviewer enters the interview session with a standardized interview protocol similar to the interview protocol used in quantitative interviewing. The key difference is that the interview protocol in the quantitative interview includes primarily closed-ended items, but the interview protocol in the standardized open-ended interview includes primarily open-ended items. The standardized open-ended interview, in which the interviewer does not vary from the interview protocol, is more structured than the interview guide approach to qualitative interviewing, in which the interviewer can vary from the protocol.

■ **Standardized open-ended interview** A set of open-ended questions are asked in a specific order and exactly as worded

In the standardized open-ended interview, the questions are all written out, and the interviewer reads the questions exactly as written and in the same order to all interviewees.

REVIEW QUESTION

9.4 What is the difference between a quantitative and a qualitative interview?

Focus Groups

▪ **Focus group** A moderator leads a discussion with a small group of people

A **focus group** is a type of group interview in which a moderator (working for the researcher) leads a discussion with a small group of individuals (e.g., students, teachers, teenagers) to examine, in detail, how the group members think and feel about a topic. It is called a "focus" group because the moderator keeps the individuals in the group focused on the topic being discussed. The moderator generates group discussion through the use of open-ended questions, and he or she acts as a facilitator of group process. Focus groups are used to collect qualitative data that are in the words of the group participants. The origin of focus groups is usually attributed to sociologist Robert K. Merton. He and his Columbia University students published the earliest works on focus groups (Merton, Fiske, & Kendall, 1956; Merton & Kendall, 1946).

See Journal Article 9.1 on the Student Study Site.

Focus groups can be used for multiple purposes. Here are seven of the many uses of focus groups identified by Stewart, Shamdasani, and Rook (2009):

1. Obtaining general background information about a topic of interest;
2. Generating research hypotheses that can be submitted to further research and testing using more quantitative approaches; . . .
3. Stimulating new ideas and creative concepts;
4. Diagnosing the potential for problems with a new program, service, or product;
5. Generating impressions of products, programs, services, institutions, or other objects of interest;
6. Learning how respondents talk about the phenomenon of interest (which may, in turn, facilitate the design of questionnaires, survey instruments, or other research tools that might be employed in more quantitative research); and
7. Interpreting previously obtained quantitative results. (p. 591)

A focus group is composed of 6 to 12 participants who are purposively selected because they can provide the kind of information of interest to the researcher. A focus group is usually homogeneous (composed of similar kinds of people) because the use of a homogeneous group promotes discussion. Homogeneous groups are less likely than heterogeneous groups to form cliques and coalitions. Using two to four focus groups as part of a single research study is quite common because it is unwise to rely too heavily on the information provided by a single focus group. Although each focus group is usually homogeneous, the set of focus groups used by the researcher may include some heterogeneity, depending on the purpose of the research.

The **group moderator** (the person leading the focus group discussion) must have good interpersonal skills, and he or she must know how to facilitate group discussion. He or she needs to get everyone involved in discussing the researcher's questions and not allow one or two people to dominate the discussion. If conflicts or power struggles occur, the moderator must skillfully bring the group back to the task. The moderator must know when to probe or ask for more information and know when the discussion about a particular topic has been exhausted. It is not uncommon for the moderator to have an assistant who observes the group process, provides information to the moderator when needed, and takes notes during the session. Some useful moderator roles (or metaphors) are the seeker of wisdom, the enlightened novice, the expert consultant, the challenger, the referee, the writer, the team member, the therapist, and the serial interviewer (Krueger, 1998).

■ **Group moderator** The person leading the focus group discussion

The focus group moderator needs to cover all the open-ended questions included in the focus group interview protocol. The interview protocol is basically an interview guide. It typically consists of a sheet of paper with approximately 10 open-ended questions on it. The more general questions are often placed early and the more specific questions placed later in the interview protocol. The moderator may have anywhere from 1 to 3 hours to complete the group session. The moderator does not have to take many notes during the session because focus groups are almost always recorded (using audio- and/or videotape) so that the data can be analyzed later.

Focus groups are especially useful as a complement to other methods of data collection. They are very useful for providing in-depth information in a relatively short period of time. In addition, the results are usually easy to understand. Researchers must, however, be very careful in making generalizations from focus groups because the sample size typically is too small and the participants are usually not randomly selected from any known population. If you need more information about focus groups, examine *The Focus Group Kit* (Morgan & Krueger, 1998).

Technology and Focus Groups

When appropriate, focus groups can now be conducted via the Internet if you have the required software. The respondents and the moderator see and hear each other (through webcams and microphones) in real time, directly over the Internet. Software used by marketing corporations can be expensive (e.g., QualMeeting, Channel M2, and Cisco TelePresence), but software already mentioned for online meetings is less expensive and in some cases it is free (e.g., GoToMeeting and its many competitors). Some key advantages of the Internet mode of focus group administration are that (a) members can be widely dispersed across a large geographic region, (b) rapport can be developed, and (c) participants can respond from the convenience of their computer screens in their homes. In addition, most meeting software also allows "instant messaging," allowing members to interact privately during the meeting. In sum, in-person focus groups are still the research standard, but Internet focus groups have much to offer as an alternative.

REVIEW QUESTION

9.5 Why would a researcher want to conduct a focus group?

OBSERVATION

The next method of data collection involves something that you do most of your waking hours: observing things. Researchers are also observers of things in the world. In research, **observation** is defined as the watching of behavioral patterns of people in certain situations to obtain information about the phenomenon of interest. The observer should attempt to be unobtrusive so as not to affect what is being observed. Observation is an important way of collecting information about people because people do not always do what they say they do. It is a maxim in the social and behavioral sciences that attitudes and behavior are not always congruent.

- **Observation** Watching the behavioral patterns of people

A classic study done by a social scientist named Richard LaPiere (1934) demonstrated many years ago that attitudes and behaviors are not always congruent. LaPiere traveled more than 10,000 miles in the United States over a 2-year period (1930–1931) with a Chinese couple. LaPiere usually had the Chinese male secure the lodging and restaurant accommodations so that he could observe behavior toward the Chinese. LaPiere reported that he and his friends were denied service only once. LaPiere later sent a questionnaire to the same establishments asking whether a Chinese person would be accepted as a guest. Fully 92 percent reported that they would *not* accept Chinese customers. This reported attitude was clearly at odds with the observed behavior.

Because of the potential incongruence between attitudes and behavior, it is helpful for researchers to collect observational data in addition to self-report data (e.g., tests, questionnaires, interviews, and focus groups). An advantage of observation over self-report methods is the researcher's ability to record actual behavior rather than obtain reports of preferences or intended behavior. Observation is not without weaknesses, however, some of which are that it generally takes more time than self-report approaches, it usually costs more money than self-report approaches, determining exactly why people behave as they do (i.e., determining their inner states) may not be possible through the use of observations, and people may act differently when they know they are being observed.

Observational data are collected in two different types of environments. **Laboratory observation** is carried out in settings that are set up by the researcher inside the confines of a research lab. An example would be observing the behavior of children through a one-way window in the researcher's laboratory. A one-way window is a mirror on one side and a window through which the researcher can observe on the other. **Naturalistic observation** is carried out in the real world. To make a naturalistic observation, you must go to wherever the behavior occurs naturally. For example, LaPiere (1934) made naturalistic observations because he observed the behavior of hotel and restaurant proprietors in their usual settings. Observing the behavior of children in their classrooms is another example of naturalistic observation. We now contrast how quantitative and qualitative researchers collect observational data.

- **Laboratory observation** Observation done in the lab or other setting set up by the researcher
- **Naturalistic observation** Observation done in real-world settings

Quantitative Observation

Quantitative (or structured) **observation** involves the standardization of all observational procedures in order to obtain reliable research data. It often involves the standardization of each of the following: who is observed (what kinds of people are to be studied, such as teachers or students), what is observed (what variables are to be observed by the researcher,

- **Quantitative observation** Standardized observation

such as time on task or out-of-seat behavior), when the observations are to take place (during the morning hour, during break time), where the observations are to be carried out (in the laboratory, in the classroom, in the lunchroom, in the library, on the playground), and how the observations are to be done (this involves the extensive training of observers so that they use the same procedures and so that high interrater reliability can be obtained). Quantitative observation usually results in quantitative data, such as counts or frequencies and percentages.

Different events may be of interest in quantitative observation (Weick, 1968). First, the researcher may observe nonverbal behavior (body movements, facial expressions, posture, eye contact, etc.). Second, the researcher may observe spatial behavior (the distance between different people and the distance between people and objects). Third, the researcher may observe extralinguistic behavior (characteristics of speech such as rate, tone, and volume). Fourth, the researcher may choose to observe linguistic behavior (what people say and what they write).

Quantitative observation might also involve observational sampling techniques. One technique is called **time-interval sampling**, which involves observing participants during time intervals specified in advance of the actual data collection (e.g., observing student behavior for the first 10 minutes of every hour). Another technique is called **event sampling**, which involves making observations during and directly after a specific event has occurred (e.g., observing the behavior of students in a classroom after the teacher sends a student to the principal's office). For more information on quantitative observation sampling, see Bakeman (2000), Dane (1990), and Suen and Ary (1989).

- **Time-interval sampling** Observing during specific time intervals
- **Event sampling** Observing during and directly after a specific event has occurred

Researchers conducting quantitative observation usually use checklists or other types of data-collection instruments, such as a laptop computer to record data or a videotape recorder to produce a record for later coding. The content of the data-collection instrument will depend on the research problem and objectives of interest to the researcher. Data-collection instruments in quantitative observation are usually more specific and detailed than those used in qualitative observation. Usually, data-collection instruments are closed ended in quantitative observation and open ended in qualitative observation because quantitative observation tends to be used for confirmatory purposes (i.e., to test hypotheses) and qualitative observation tends to be used for exploratory purposes (i.e., to generate new information).

Qualitative Observation

Qualitative observation involves observing all potentially relevant phenomena and taking extensive field notes without specifying in advance exactly what is to be observed. In other words, qualitative observation is usually done for exploratory purposes. It is also usually done in natural settings. In fact, the terms *qualitative observation* and *naturalistic observation* are frequently treated as synonyms in the research literature. Not surprisingly, qualitative observation is usually carried out by qualitative researchers.

- **Qualitative observation** Observing all potentially relevant phenomena

Whenever you conduct qualitative observations, you must remember exactly what you have observed. In fact, the researcher is said to be the data-collection instrument because it is the researcher who must decide what is important and what data are to be recorded. If you are wondering what to observe when you conduct a qualitative observation, you can consider the "Guidelines for Directing Qualitative Observation" in

Exhibit 9.2. Most importantly, you need to look for anything and everything to observe whatever may be relevant to your research questions.

■ **Field notes** Notes taken by an observer

Researchers record what they believe is important in their **field notes** (notes written down by the observer during and after making observations). It's a good idea to correct and edit any notes you write down during an observation as soon as possible after taking them because that is when your memory is best. If you wait too long, you might forget important details and not be able to make sense of your handwritten, scribbled field notes. In addition to taking field notes during your observations, consider audiotaping and videotaping important scenes.

The form of interaction or type of role taken by the researcher during the conduct of a qualitative observation (called "fieldwork") varies along the following continuum (Gold, 1958):

Although one role may be primary, the researcher may play all four roles at different times and in different situations during the conduct of a single qualitative research study. This is especially true when the researcher is in the field for an extended period of time.

■ **Complete participant** Researcher who becomes a member of the group being studied and does not tell members they are being studied

The **complete participant** takes on the role of an insider, essentially becoming a member of the group being studied and spending a great deal of time with the group. For example, you might spend a year teaching at a "model school" that you want to learn about. During the year, you would take extensive field notes, documenting what you observe and what you experience. Because the complete participant does not inform the group members that he or she is in a research study, many researchers question the use of this approach on ethical grounds. It is a cardinal rule in research ethics that research participants should know that they are involved in a research study, that they have the right *not* to participate, and that they are free to withdraw at any time during a research study if they do choose not to participate (see Chapter 6 on research ethics). You should therefore be very careful about doing "undercover" research except in legally open and accessible places such as a mall, a playground, or a sporting event.

■ **Participant-as-observer** Researcher who spends extended time with the group as an insider and tells members they are being studied

The **participant-as-observer** attempts to take on the role of an insider (a participant), similar to the complete participant. The participant-as-observer also spends a good deal of time in the field participating and observing. The participant-as-observer, however, explains to the people in the group being studied that he or she is a researcher and not a bona fide group member. The person in the previous example who spends a year teaching in a model school would be a participant-as-observer if the researcher informed the people in the school that he or she was conducting research and then participated in the school functions. An advantage of this approach is that, for ethical reasons, the researcher can request permission to collect and record data as needed. In addition, the researcher can obtain feedback about his or her observations and tentative conclusions from the people in the research study. A weakness is that the participants might not behave naturally because they are aware that they are being observed. Fortunately, this problem usually disappears as the people begin to trust the researcher and adjust to his or her presence.

The **observer-as-participant** takes on the role of observer much more than the role of participant. The participants are fully aware that they are part of a research study. The observer-as-participant does not spend much time in the field. Rather, the observer-as-participant has more limited and briefer interactions with the participants. For example, the researcher might negotiate entry to one faculty meeting, one PTA meeting, and one or two classes as part of a research study. Compared to the complete participant and participant-as-observer roles, a disadvantage of the observer-as-participant role is that obtaining an insider's view is more difficult. On the other hand, maintaining objectivity and neutrality is easier.

The **complete observer** fully takes on the role of outside observer. He or she does not inform the people in the group being studied that they are being observed, and they usually will not know that they are being observed. For example, the complete observer might view people through a one-way window or might sit in the back of the room at an open meeting. The advantage of this approach is that there is minimal **reactivity** (changes in the behavior of people because they know they are being observed). On the other hand, you can take the role of complete observer only in open settings because of ethical concerns.

Perhaps the most useful styles of observation are the participant-as-observer and the observer-as-participant. These roles are generally preferred because they allow voluntary consent by research participants. In addition, they allow the researcher to take on a mix of the insider's role and the outsider's role. The complete participant always runs the risk of losing his or her objectivity, and the complete observer always runs the risk of not understanding the insider's perspective. Not surprisingly, the participant-as-observer and observer-as-participant styles of observation are the most commonly used by researchers.

If you are going to enter the field and carry out qualitative observation, you should carry with you the general research question, a desire to learn, and an open mind. Good social skills are a must (Shaffir & Stebbins, 1991). Trust and rapport with the group being studied are essential if valid data are going to be obtained. Keep in mind, however, Erving Goffman's warning (1959) that much social behavior observed is **frontstage behavior** (what people want or allow us to see) rather than **backstage behavior** (what people say and do with their closest friends, when "acting" is at a minimum). After getting into the field, the researcher must learn the ropes, maintain relations with the people being studied, and, at the end of the study, leave and keep in touch (Shaffir & Stebbins). We provide a list of practical tips for conducting fieldwork in Table 9.4.

- **Observer-as-participant** Researcher who spends a limited amount of time observing group members and tells members they are being studied
- **Complete observer** Researcher who observes as an outsider and does not tell people they are being observed
- **Reactivity** Changes that occur in people because they know they are being observed
- **Frontstage behavior** What people want or allow us to see
- **Backstage behavior** What people say and do only with their closest friends

See Journal Article 9.2 on the Student Study Site.

EXHIBIT 9.2 Guidelines for Directing Qualitative Observation

1. *Who* is in the group or scene? How many people are there, and what are their kinds, identities, and relevant characteristics? How is membership in the group or scene acquired?
2. *What* is happening here? What are the people in the group or scene doing and saying to one another?
    a. What behaviors are repetitive, and which occur irregularly? In what events, activities, or routines are participants engaged? What resources are used in these activities, and how are they allocated? How are activities organized, labeled, explained, and justified? What differing social contexts can be identified?

(Continued)

(Continued)

b. How do the people in the group behave toward one another? What is the nature of this participation and interaction? How are the people connected or related to one another? What statuses and roles are evident in this interaction? Who makes what decisions for whom? How do the people organize themselves for interactions?

c. What is the content of participants' conversations? What subjects are common, and which are rare? What stories, anecdotes, and homilies do they exchange? What verbal and nonverbal languages do they use for communication? What beliefs do the content of their conversations demonstrate? What formats do the conversations follow? What processes do they reflect? Who talks and who listens?

3. *Where* is the group or scene located? What physical settings and environments form their contexts? What natural resources are evident, and what technologies are created or used? How does the group allocate and use space and physical objects? What is consumed, and what is produced? What sights, sounds, smells, tastes, and textures are found in the contexts that the group uses?

4. *When* does the group meet and interact? How often are these meetings, and how lengthy are they? How does the group conceptualize, use, and distribute time? How do participants view the past, present, and future?

5. *How* are the identified elements connected or interrelated, either from the participants' point of view or from the researcher's perspective? How is stability maintained? How does change originate, and how is it managed? How are the identified elements organized? What rules, norms, or mores govern this social organization? How is power conceptualized and distributed? How is this group related to other groups, organizations, or institutions?

6. *Why* does the group operate as it does? What meanings do participants attribute to what they do? What is the group's history? What goals are articulated in the group? What symbols, traditions, values, and world views can be found in the group?

Source: From M. D. LeCompte and J. Preissle, *Ethnography and Qualitative Design in Educational Research*, p. 294, © 1993 by Academic Press. Reprinted by permission of Elsevier and the authors.

TABLE 9.4 Tips for Conducting Fieldwork and Qualitative Observation

1. Make sure all observers are well trained, are good note takers, and know how to fit into diverse situations.
2. Do background homework on the people and cultural settings to be observed.
3. Be sensitive to gender, age, and cultural differences between you and the people being observed.
4. Establish rapport and trust, starting with gatekeepers and informants.
5. Don't promise anything to anyone in the setting that you cannot or should not deliver.
6. Be reflexive (i.e., monitor yourself).
7. Be unobtrusive (i.e., try to fit in and don't stand out).
8. Remain alert at all times and pay attention to anything that may be important.
9. Find an effective way to record what is being observed (i.e., by taking field notes or using audiovisual recorders).
10. Try to corroborate anything important that you see, hear, or learn about.
11. Conduct opportunistic interviews while you are in the field when possible.
12. Be empathetic, but also remain neutral to the content of what people say to you.
13. Make observations in multiple and disparate settings.

14. Include descriptive details in your field notes. Get direct quotes when possible. Include your own insights and interpretations when they arise, but keep them separate from the description and verbatims (i.e., quotes).
15. Observe and record characteristics of the setting and context, interpersonal interactions, significant behaviors, verbal and nonverbal communication, formal and informal interactions, what does not happen, power and status hierarchy in the group, and anything else that seems important to you at the time.
16. Spend sufficient time in the field to collect useful data and to allow corroboration of your findings.
17. When you leave the field, immediately write up your field notes so that you don't forget what you have seen, heard, and experienced.

9.6 What are the main differences between quantitative and qualitative observations?
9.7 What are the four main roles that a researcher can take during qualitative observation?
9.8 What is the difference between frontstage behavior and backstage behavior?

Visual Data

Because of the importance of photography in collecting observational data, we elaborate here on what is often called **visual data collection**. One of the richest methods of data collection is the image. The old adage "A picture is worth one thousand words" holds true in many research situations. One explanation is that the parts of the brain that process visual information are evolutionarily older than those that process verbal or numerical information. We see visual data concretely, whereas verbal and numerical data are more abstract. Visual data can be primarily qualitative, such as photographs, cartoons, drawings, videos, or carvings. Likewise, visual displays can reveal quantitative data by using graphs, charts, or pictographs in ways that numbers alone cannot communicate (see Photo 9.1).

- **Visual data collection** Process of collecting data using visual sources, such as photographs, drawings, graphics, paintings, film, and video

There are so many methods of visual data collection and visual restructuring that it is surprising that more studies do not incorporate visual perspectives. Many studies that do incorporate visual data use photography as a tool. Some researchers act as participant observers and record photographs as part of the group experience. Others take photographs as an "outside" observer viewing social rituals or documenting particular artifacts that might represent cultural symbolisms (Collier & Collier, 1986).

Some classic research studies using photography were conducted by Margaret Mead and her associates (Bateson & Mead, 1942; Mead, Bateson, & Macgregor, 1951) in studying child development using ethnography. In his classic book *The Hidden Dimension,* Edward Hall (1966) studied aspects of using space or "proxemics." Photographic data also are used in quantitative research. For example, beginning with the work of Eadweard Muybridge, researchers have used photography for many years to study motion. Beginning in 1872, Muybridge photographed horses galloping for 12 years to win a bet that at some point during a gallop a horse has all its hooves off the ground! His classic compilation of photos showing his evidence is shown in the accompanying pictures (see also http://www.eadweardmuybridge.co.uk).

Photographs sometimes are used as part of the interviewing process. **Photo interviewing** or photo elicitation (Dempsey & Tucker, 1994; Harper, 2002) uses visuals to

- **Photo interviewing** Process of eliciting data from a person using photographic or video imagery when conducting interviews

obtain additional information during interviews. The visual data (photographs, video) can be used to support alternate interpretations of the phenomenon being investigated. In some studies, the participants are given cameras and collect the initial photographic data themselves (Ziller, 1990). Research techniques such as these can expand the initial range of visual data enormously.

PHOTO 9.1

Constructed data Objects or things that are constructed by research participants during a research study

Secondary data Existing data originally collected or left behind at an earlier time by a different person for a different purpose

Personal documents Anything written, photographed, or recorded for private purposes

CONSTRUCTED AND SECONDARY OR EXISTING DATA

The last major method of data collection involves the collection of secondary or existing data for use in a research study or data/objects literally constructed by research participants during a research study. **Constructed data** are things *produced by your research participants during the research study* such as drawings, paintings, diaries, recordings, videos, and newly produced personal documents. **Secondary** or **existing data** are data that were collected, recorded, or left behind at an earlier time, usually by a different person and often for an entirely different purpose than the current research purpose at hand. In other words, the researcher uses what is already there. The researcher must, however, find these data or artifacts to use them in his or her research study. Secondary data may be used with other data for corroboration, or they may be the primary data to be used in a research study. Several types of secondary data that researchers commonly find are personal documents, official documents, physical data, and archived research data.

Documents are one major type of secondary data. **Personal documents** include anything that is written, photographed, or otherwise recorded for private purposes. Some examples of personal documents are letters, diaries, correspondence, family videos, and pictures. **Official documents** are written, photographed, or recorded by some type of public or private organization. Some examples are newspapers, educational journals and magazines, curriculum guides, annual reports, minutes of school board meetings, student records, student work, books, yearbooks, published articles, speeches, personnel files, and videos such as news programs and advertisements. Documents are frequently used by qualitative researchers and by historical researchers.

- **Official documents** Anything written, photographed, or recorded by an organization

Physical data include any physical traces left by people as they take part in various activities. Some examples of physical data that have been used by social scientists are wear on floor tiles in museums, wear on library books, soil from shoes and clothing, radio dial settings, fingerprints, suits of armor, and contents of people's trash (Webb, Campbell, Schwartz, & Sechrest, 2000). Physical data can also include instances of material culture (e.g., clothes, buildings, books, billboards, art).

- **Physical data** Any material thing created or left by humans that might provide information about a phenomenon of interest to a researcher

Archived research data were originally used for research purposes and then stored for possible later use. Archived research data may be in print form but are usually stored in a computer-usable form (floppy disks or CD-ROM). Some examples of archived research data are the census data and social science research data stored and kept by researchers or research-related organizations such as the US Census Bureau (www.census.gov), the Institute for Social Research at the University of Michigan (home.isr.umich.edu), the National Opinion Research Center (NORC) at the University of Chicago (www.norc.uchicago.edu), and Gallup (www.gallup.com). Archived research data are usually quantitative. We expect that qualitative research data will increasingly be archived for later access and reanalysis.

- **Archived research data** Data originally used for research purposes and then stored

The largest repository of archived social science data is kept by the Inter-university Consortium for Political and Social Research (ICPSR; http://www.icpsr.umich.edu). Based in Ann Arbor, Michigan, the ICPSR includes more than 500 colleges and universities in the United States and across the world. The ICPSR currently houses more than 20,000 computer-readable data files, and faculty at member institutions (such as your local university) can obtain the data sets at very modest costs. Typically, the data were part of a research study by an academic researcher. Many studies were grant funded. After a researcher has finished with the data, he or she provides a copy to the ICPSR, which makes it available to member institutions or anyone else who has a legitimate reason to use it. If you want to see some of the many data files that are available, visit the ICPSR website or go to your library and browse through the *ICPSR Guide to Resources and Services*, a book that includes descriptions of hundreds of research data files.

REVIEW QUESTION

9.9 What are some examples of constructed and secondary, or existing, data?

ACTION RESEARCH REFLECTION

Insight: Action researchers, at different times, creatively use all six of the major methods of data collection. They also use both qualitative and quantitative forms of the methods of data collection, and they often use a mixed version (e.g., a mixed questionnaire, an interview with both structured and unstructured components). That is, they often use *intramethod* mixing (mixing within a single method). An action researcher will rarely rely on a single method of data collection. The world is complex, and the multiple methods of data collection help us to see different parts of that complexity or see the same parts in different ways. Therefore, action researchers also often use *intermethod* mixing (mixing by using multiple methods).

1. How can you observe *your own* work practices (remember: self-development is an important part of action research)?
2. As an action researcher (e.g., attempting to make something work better in your school or workplace), what kinds of data would you like to collect about something that interests you? Be very specific.
3. Select three methods of data collection (your questionnaire from Chapter 8 can count as one). What might each of these help you to see and understand or learn about your targeted research participants?

SUMMARY

A method of data collection is the procedure that a researcher physically uses to obtain research data from research participants. The method of data collection that is used in a research study is discussed in the method section of a research report. There are six major methods of data collection. Researchers can have their participants fill out an instrument or perform a behavior designed to measure their ability or degree of a skill (*tests*); researchers can have research participants fill out self-report instruments (*questionnaires*); researchers can talk to participants in person or over the telephone (*interviews*); researchers can discuss issues with multiple research participants at the same time in a small-group setting (*focus groups*); researchers can examine how research participants act in natural and structured environments (*observations*); and researchers can use data that participants construct during a study and data that came from an earlier time for a different purpose than the current research problem at hand (*constructed* and *secondary* or *existing data*). One can use quantitative, qualitative, and mixed forms of the different major methods of data collection, although focus groups are usually used to collect qualitative data and tests are usually used to collect quantitative data. The mixed form of one method of data collection method is called *intra*method mixing (e.g., a mixed questionnaire), and the mixing or use of two or more methods of data collection is called *inter*method mixing. The researcher must pay particular attention to the construction of the data-collection instrument that is used to collect research data to make sure that it works well. Multiple modes of administration of data collection methods were provided for tests (in-person vs. online administration), questionnaires (mail, in-person, Internet), interviews, (in-person, telephone, Internet), and focus groups (in person vs. online) and were presented and compared in Figure 9.2. Finally, the fundamental principle of mixed research provides a logic for strengthening the evidence produced by a research study.

KEY TERMS

archived research data (p. 247)
backstage behavior (p. 243)
complete observer (p. 243)
complete participant (p. 242)
constructed data (p. 246)
event sampling (p. 241)
field notes (p. 242)
focus group (p. 238)
frontstage behavior (p. 243)
fundamental principle of mixed research (p. 224)
group moderator (p. 239)
in-person interview (p. 231)
informal conversational interview (p. 236)
intermethod mixing (p. 225)
interview (p. 231)
interview guide approach (p. 236)
interview protocol (p. 232)
interviewee (p. 231)
interviewer (p. 231)
intramethod mixing (p. 225)
laboratory observation (p. 240)
method of data collection (p. 224)
naturalistic observation (p. 240)
observation (p. 240)
observer-as-participant (p. 243)
official documents (p. 247)
participant-as-observer (p. 242)
personal documents (p. 246)
photo interviewing (p. 245)
physical data (p. 247)
probe (p. 231)
qualitative interview (p. 235)
qualitative observation (p. 241)

quantitative observation (p. 240)
questionnaire (p. 227)
reactivity (p. 243)
research method (p. 224)
secondary data (p. 246)
standardization (p. 233)
standardized open-ended interview (p. 237)
telephone interview (p. 231)
time-interval sampling (p. 241)
visual data collection (p. 245)

DISCUSSION QUESTIONS

1. We talked about six major methods of data collection in this chapter. Can you think of any method of data collection not mentioned in the chapter? What is it? Does it fit into one of the six major methods, or does it deserve a new category?
2. Which of the six methods of data collection do you think is most commonly used by educational researchers? Why?
3. Which of the six methods of data collection would you feel most comfortable using? Why?
4. What is the point of the fundamental principle of mixed research? Think of an example of its use to share with your classmates.
5. Should a researcher use a single item to measure an abstract concept, such as self-esteem, intelligence, or teaching self-efficacy? If not, how should the researcher measure such concepts?

RESEARCH EXERCISES

1. Construct a short interview protocol on a topic of interest to you. Go to the local shopping mall and interview five people who are demographically different. After interviewing the people, write up what you found out about the topic. Also write up your methodological observations about whether trust and rapport affected the interview process and how you could improve your interview procedure.
2. Go to a public place and observe interactions between couples. Use your observations to identify two research questions that you might later study in more depth.

RELEVANT INTERNET SITES

Methods data collection
http://www.nsf.gov/pubs/2002/nsf02057/nsf02057_1.pdf
https://cyfernetsearch.org/data-collection-techniques
http://www.cdc.gov/healthyyouth/evaluation/pdf/brief16.pdf
http://www.rand.org/content/dam/rand/pubs/technical_reports/2009/RAND_TR718.pdf
http://www.slideshare.net/priyansakthi/methods-of-data-collection-16037781

STUDENT STUDY SITE

Visit the Student Study Site at **edge.sagepub.com/rbjohnson6e** for these additional learning tools:

Video Links
Self-Quizzes
eFlashcards
Lecture Notes
Full-Text SAGE Journal Articles
Interactive Concept Maps
Web Resources

RECOMMENDED READING

Johnson, B., & Turner, L. A. (2003). Data collection strategies in mixed methods research. In A. Tashakkori & C. Teddlie (Eds.), *Handbook of mixed methods in social & behavioral research*. Thousand Oaks, CA: SAGE.

Krueger, R. A., & Casey, M. A. (2014). *Focus groups: A practical guide for applied research* (5th ed.). Thousand Oaks, CA: SAGE.

Wolcott, H. F. (2004). *The art of fieldwork.* Walnut Creek, CA: Altamira.

Chapter 10

Sampling in Quantitative, Qualitative, and Mixed Research

LEARNING OBJECTIVES

After reading this chapter, you should be able to

- Explain the difference between a sample and a census.
- Define the key terms used in sampling (*representative sample*, *generalize*, *element*, *statistic*, *parameter*, and so forth).
- Compare and contrast the different random sampling techniques.
- Know which sampling techniques are equal probability of selection methods.
- Draw a simple random sample.
- Draw a systematic sample.
- Explain the difference between proportional and disproportional stratified sampling.
- Explain the characteristics of one-stage and two-stage cluster sampling.
- List and explain the characteristics of the different nonrandom sampling techniques.
- Explain the difference between random selection and random assignment.
- List the factors that you should consider when determining the appropriate sample size to be selected when using random sampling.
- Discuss sampling in qualitative research and compare and contrast the different sampling techniques used in qualitative research.
- Explain the two criteria that produce the ten methods of sampling in mixed research.

Visit the Student Study Site for an interactive concept map.

RESEARCH IN REAL LIFE Representative Samples

istock/oztekinirfan

The concept of sampling has important applications in daily life. For example, most farm products that are grown in the United States are subject to inspection by the Federal-State Inspection Service. Because it is not possible for each apple, each ham, or each peanut to be inspected individually, the Inspection Service selects samples of each farm commodity for inspection. Analyses of these samples are used to infer the characteristics of large quantities of various farm products. Inspections of farm products by these government officials protect the general public by ensuring that the products in grocery stores are safe for public consumption.

Let's look more closely at the example of peanuts. Thousands of tons of peanuts are grown annually in the United States. As with other farm products, peanuts are subject to analysis by the Inspection Service before they can be put on the market. The inspectors need to know the percentages of specified components, such as whole peanut kernels, half kernels, shriveled kernels, hulls, and foreign material (e.g., hay, sand, and pebbles), in each load of peanuts, as well as the percentage of moisture in the peanuts.

A typical truckload of peanuts brought to market by a US farmer ranges in size from approximately 2,000 to 6,000 pounds. The Inspection Service inspectors draw a sample of peanuts from each load with the use of a special tool called a peanut auger, a hollow, stainless-steel cylinder approximately 4 inches in diameter and 7 feet long. The inspector pushes the auger into the peanuts from the top surface to the very bottom of the load. This procedure allows the auger to take a sample of peanuts from every level in the load. The inspector performs this procedure for each of several positions randomly selected by a computer that graphs the top surface of the load of peanuts. Theoretically, each peanut (and each other component of the load) has an equal chance of being included in the sample. This process produces samples that are *representative* of the loads of peanuts.

- **Sampling** The process of drawing a sample from a population
- **Generalize** To make statements about a population based on sample data
- **Census** A study based on data from the whole population rather than a sample

In this chapter, we examine the idea of sampling. **Sampling** is the process of drawing a sample from a population. When we sample, we study the characteristics of a subset (called the sample) selected from a larger group (called the population) to understand the characteristics of the larger group. After researchers determine the characteristics of the sample, they **generalize** from the sample to the population; that is, researchers make statements about the population based on their study of the sample. A sample is usually much smaller in size than a population; hence, sampling can save time and money.

If you study *every individual* in a population, you are actually conducting a census and not a survey. In a **census**, the whole population is studied, not just a sample, or subset, of the population. A well-known example of a census is the US Decennial Census conducted by the Census Bureau every 10 years. The purpose of this census is to determine the demographic characteristics (age, gender, race, income level), educational characteristics (educational attainment, school enrollment), family characteristics (number of children, age at marriage, family structure), and work characteristics (e.g., type of job, occupational prestige of job, number of hours worked per week) of *all* individual citizens of the United States. That's more than 300 million people! As you can probably imagine, a census is quite expensive and very difficult to conduct.

Researchers rarely study every individual in the population of interest. Instead, they study a sample of the population. The use of random sampling saves time and money compared to a census. Using the random sampling techniques discussed in this chapter, characteristics of the US population can be estimated within a small margin of error (plus or minus a few percentage points) using only 1,000 to 1,500 individuals. Conducting a census for large populations is generally too difficult and too expensive. On the other hand, if a population is very small (e.g., all 25 teachers at a single elementary school), including all of the individuals in your research study is your best bet. The real power of random sampling comes when you are studying large populations.

In this chapter, we discuss random (also called probability) sampling techniques and nonrandom (also called nonprobability) sampling techniques. Random sampling techniques are based on the theory of probability and usually produce "good" samples. A good sample is one that is representative of the population it came from. That is, *a **representative sample** resembles the population that it came from on all characteristics* (the proportions of males and females, teachers and nonteachers, young and old people, Democrats and Republicans, and so forth) *except total size. A representative sample is like the population except that it is smaller.* Although a random sample is rarely perfectly representative, random samples are almost always more representative than nonrandom samples. Nonrandom samples are said to be **biased samples** because they are almost always systematically different from the population on certain characteristics. In contrast, random samples are said to be unbiased samples because they tend to be representative of the populations from which they come.

Random sampling is frequently used in **survey research**, which is a nonexperimental research method in which questionnaires or interviews are used to gather information and the goal is to understand the characteristics of a population based on the sample data. Well-known examples of survey research include studies done to determine voter attitudes about political candidates and related issues of interest (e.g., education, family, crime, foreign affairs). Although the random sampling techniques discussed in this chapter are most commonly used in survey research, they are sometimes used in most other types of quantitative research as well.

As you read the rest of this chapter, remember that the main purpose of sampling in quantitative research is to enable the researcher to make accurate generalizations about a population using sample data. In short, obtaining a sample is a means to an end. After you learn about sampling in quantitative research (what it is and how it is conducted), we discuss sampling in qualitative research, where the goal is to select particular groups and to understand them. We conclude with a discussion of sampling in mixed methods research, which combines insights from the study of quantitative and qualitative sampling methods.

- **Representative sample** A sample that resembles the population
- **Biased sample** A sample that is systematically different from the population
- **Survey research** A nonexperimental research method based on questionnaires or interviews

See Journal Article 10.1 on the Student Study Site.

10.1 What type of sampling produces representative samples?

10.2 What is a representative sample, and when is it important to obtain a representative sample?

TERMINOLOGY USED IN SAMPLING

- **Sample** A set of elements taken from a larger population
- **Element** The basic unit that is selected from the population
- ***N*** The population size
- ***n*** The sample size
- **Population** The large group to which a researcher wants to generalize the sample results
- **Statistic** A numerical characteristic of a sample
- **Parameter** A numerical characteristic of a population
- **Sampling error** The difference between the value of a sample statistic and the population parameter
- **Sampling frame** A list of all the elements in a population
- **Response rate** The percentage of people in a sample who participate in a research study

To understand sampling better, it is helpful to know some specialized terms. A **sample** is a set of elements taken from a larger population according to certain rules. An **element** is the basic unit selected from the population. "Individuals" are the most common element sampled; however, other types of elements are possible such as "groups" (e.g., schools, classrooms, clinics) or "objects" (e.g., textbooks, school records, television commercials). A sample is always smaller than a population, and it is often much smaller. In sampling, the letter N stands for the population size (the total number of people or elements in a population), and n stands for the sample size (the number of people or elements in a sample). For example, if we selected a sample of 500 people from a population of 150,000, then n would be 500 and N would be 150,000. Sampling rules tell you how to select a sample. The methods of sampling discussed in this chapter follow different rules for selection.

A **population** (sometimes called a target population) is the set of all elements. It is the large group to which a researcher wants to generalize his or her sample results. In other words, it is the total group that you are interested in learning more about. A few possible populations are the citizens of the United States, all the students attending public and private schools in Portland, Oregon, and all counselors working at a mental health center in Austin, Texas.

A **statistic** is a numerical characteristic of a sample. For example, on the basis of the people included in a sample, a researcher might calculate the average reading performance or the correlation between two variables (e.g., test grades and study time). A **parameter** is a numerical characteristic of a total population. For example, it could be an average, a correlation, or a percentage that is based on the complete population rather than on a sample. We rarely know the values of the population parameters of interest. Therefore, we collect sample data so that we can estimate the probable values of the population parameters. A sample statistic will rarely be exactly the same as the population parameter, but most of the time it will not be very far off (assuming that the sample is a random sample of adequate size). The actual difference between a sample statistic value (let's say you calculated an average for the sample) and the population parameter (the actual average in the population) is called **sampling error**. Sampling error will fluctuate randomly over repeated sampling when a random sampling method is used. That is, a sample statistic (e.g., an average or a percentage) will sometimes be a little larger than a population parameter, and it will sometimes be a little smaller. However, it will *not* be consistently too large or too small. That is, it will not be biased if you use random sampling.

When we draw a sample, we typically begin by locating or constructing a **sampling frame**, which is a list of all the elements in the population. For example, if we are interested in drawing a sample of college students attending Ohio State University, then the sampling frame should be a list of all students attending Ohio State University. The researcher draws the sample from the sampling frame using one of the sampling methods discussed later. After the sample is selected, the members of the sample are contacted and asked if they will participate in the research study.

Typically, some of the people in a sample will refuse to participate in the research study. You can determine the percentage that actually participates by calculating the response rate. The **response rate** is the percentage of people in a sample that participates in the research study. The response rate will usually be less than 100%. If you select, for example, a sample size of 200 people and only 183 of the 200 individuals participate, then the response rate is 91.5% (183/200 × 100). The formula for the response rate is

$$\text{Response rate} = \frac{\text{Number of people in the sample who participate in the research}}{\text{Total number of people in the sample}} \times 100$$

If you want a sample to be representative of a population, then it is essential that the response rate be as high as possible. Response rates around 70% and higher are generally considered acceptable. However, the sample might still be *biased* (not representative of the population) even when the response rate is high because the kinds of people who drop out of the sample might be different from the kinds of people who remain in the sample. Researchers should discuss the issues of sample selection procedures, response rates, and sample integrity when they write up their reports. Generally, you should not trust research reports in which this information is not found.

REVIEW QUESTIONS

10.3 What is the difference between a statistic and a parameter?

10.4 What is a sampling frame?

Random Sampling Techniques

Simple Random Sampling

A simple random sample is what researchers are usually referring to when they say they have a random sample or a probability sample. Simple random sampling is the most basic form of random sampling, and it's the cornerstone of sampling theory. In fact, all the other random sampling methods use simple random sampling at some point during the sampling process. A simple random sample is formally defined as a sample drawn by a procedure in which every possible sample of a given size (e.g., size 100) has an equal chance of being selected from the population. More simply, a **simple random sample** is drawn by a procedure in which every member of the population has an equal chance of being selected for the study. When every member has an equal chance of being selected, the sampling method is called an **equal probability of selection method** (EPSEM).

- **Simple random sample** A sample drawn by a procedure in which every member of the population has an equal chance of being selected
- **Equal probability of selection method** Any sampling method in which each member of the population has an equal chance of being selected

One way to visualize the drawing of a simple random sample is to think about the "hat model." Here is how it works. First, go to a good hat store and buy a big top hat. Next, make one slip of paper for each individual in the population and place all of the slips in the hat. Make sure you use standard-sized slips of paper so that they will all be the same shape, size, and weight. If there are 1,000 people in the population of interest, you will need 1,000 slips of paper. Now, let's say you want to obtain a simple random sample of 100 people. To make sure all the pieces of paper are thoroughly mixed in the hat, cover the top of the hat and shake it up vigorously. Next, select one slip of paper from the hat. After selecting the slip of paper, shake the hat up again to be sure the remaining slips are well mixed and then select another slip of paper. After you have selected all 100 names, you will have a simple random sample size of 100 (n = 100) from a population size of 1,000 (N = 1,000). After you finish selecting the sample, you can look at the names to see who is included in the sample. These are the 100 people you will study.[1]

Drawing a Simple Random Sample

- **Table of random numbers** A list of numbers that fall in a random order

- **Random number generator** A computer program that produces random numbers used in random assignment and random selection

Now let's get a little more practical and see how researchers actually draw random samples. Although the hat model was a convenient metaphor for thinking about simple random sampling, it is rarely used in practice. Until relatively recently, a common approach was to use a **table of random numbers**, as shown in Table 10.1, which is a list of numbers that fall in a random order. In such a table, no number appears more often than any other number in the long run; all numbers have an equal chance of appearing. Furthermore, there will be no systematic pattern in the table. If you ever think you see a pattern in a table or that some number occurs more frequently than it should, you need only look farther in the table. The apparent pattern will disappear.

These days, practitioners usually use a **random number generator** for selecting their random samples. Here are links to two random number generators available for free on the Internet:

www.random.org

www.randomizer.org

If you use a random number generator, such as the ones just listed, you are actually randomly selecting a set of numbers. That means that all of the elements in the sampling frame must have a number attached to them. Remember, a sampling frame is just a list of all the people (elements) in a population. If you are sampling from a list of your students or your clients, then you need to give each person a unique number. These numbers serve

TABLE 10.1 Table of Random Numbers

Line/Column	*1*	*2*	*3*	*4*	*5*	*6*	*7*	*8*	*9*	*10*
1	10480	15011	01536	02011	81647	91646	69179	14194	62590	36207
2	22368	46573	25595	85393	30995	89198	27982	53402	93965	34095
3	24130	48360	22527	97265	76393	64809	15179	24830	49340	32081
4	42167	93093	06243	61680	07856	16376	39440	53537	71341	57004
5	37570	39975	81837	16656	06121	91782	60468	81305	49684	60672
6	77921	06907	11008	42751	27756	53498	18602	70659	90655	15053
7	99562	72905	56420	69994	98872	31016	71194	18738	44013	48840
8	96301	91977	05463	07972	18876	20922	94595	56869	69014	60045
9	89579	14342	63661	10281	17453	18103	57740	84378	25331	12565
10	85475	36857	53342	53988	53060	59533	38867	62300	08158	17983

as an index. An example of a sampling frame is shown in Table 10.2. This is a list of people in a small population with their associated identification numbers. The information on gender (a categorical variable) and age (a quantitative variable) is provided in the sampling frame because we want to be able to calculate later the average age and the percent male and female. With those calculations, we can see how well the sample that we draw compares with the actual population. Usually, you would have to collect this kind of information (data) before you would know how good the sample is. That is, a sampling frame usually contains only the names and the identification numbers.

Now let's draw a sample of size 10 from this population of size 60 in Table 10.2. You could use the table of random numbers. You can start anywhere in the table of random numbers, and then you can go in any direction (up, down, across, forward, or backward)

TABLE 10.2 A Sampling Frame With Information on Gender and Age Included[a]

Number	*Name*	*Age*	*Number*	*Name*	*Age*	*Number*	*Name*	*Age*
01	Johnny Adams (M)	64	21**	Scott House (M)	21	41	Beth Sanders (F)	63
02*	Fred Alexander (M)	18	22	Jan Hoffman (F)	60	42*	Lena Schmitt (F)	33
03**	Kathy Anderson (F)	57	23	Robert Johnson (M)	43	43	Cindy Scott (F)	31
04	Fred Baker (M)	30	24	John Jones (M)	18	44	Sam Shepherd (M)	20
05	Hasem Basaleh (M)	38	25	John Locke (M)	52	45**	Max Smart (M)	47
06*	Tom Baxter (M)	31	26	Carlton Lawless (M)	35	46	Rhonda Smith (F)	23
07*	Barry Biddlecomb (M)	52	27*,**	Pam Mackey (F)	35	47	Kin Sullivan (F)	29
08	Don Campbell (M)	42	28	Ronald May (M)	20	48	Jimmy Thompson (M)	42
09**	Martha Carr (F)	21	29	Mike McNuty (M)	64	49	Susan Tyler (F)	23
10*	Eugene Davis (M)	21	30*	John Mills (M)	19	50	Lisa Turner (F)	57
11	Marion Dunn (F)	55	31	Doug Morgan (M)	33	51**	Velma Vandenberg (F)	43
12	James East (M)	44	32	Jean Neal (F)	33	52	Richard Viatle (M)	20
13	Greg Ellis (M)	50	33**	Anh Nguyan (M)	40	53*	Larry Watson (M)	26
14	Alex Evans (M)	65	34	David Payne (M)	57	54	Melvin White (M)	29
15**	Donna Faircloth (F)	27	35	Susan Poole (F)	28	55	Mark Wiggens (M)	46
16*	Barbara Flowers (F)	37	36	Brenda Prine (F)	38	56	Leon Wilson (M)	31
17	Kirk Garner (M)	37	37	Andrea Quinn (F)	30	57**	Andrew Young (M)	39
18*	Marie Gaylord (F)	46	38	Mohamed Rashid (M)	64	58	Hun Yu (F)	51
19	William Gilder (M)	30	39**	Anneke Reeves (F)	32	59	Alex Zellars (F)	42
20	Mark Harris (M)	63	40	Charlie Rogers (M)	46	60	Ellen Zimmer (F)	46

[a]Data on variables such as age and gender are usually not included in a sampling frame. Data are obtained after they are collected from the sample respondents. To allow us to do a couple of calculations in this chapter, data on age and gender are provided in the columns and parentheses.

*Elements selected in the simple random sampling example discussed in the text.

**Elements selected in the systematic sampling example discussed in the text.

as long as you keep going in that direction. Rather than using the table of random numbers, however, we will use the newer approach. We will use the random number generator available for free at www.randomizer.org.

We need 10 numbers randomly selected from 1 to 60. To do this, we went to the randomizer.org website, clicked "Use the Randomizer form to instantly generate random numbers," and answered each of the following questions:

1. How many sets of numbers do you want to generate?
   - We inserted a 1 to indicate that we just wanted one set of numbers.
2. How many numbers per set?
   - We inserted a 10 to indicate that we wanted 10 numbers in our set.
3. Number range?
   - We inserted 1 and 60 to indicate the range of numbers in our sampling frame.
4. Do you wish each number in a set to remain unique?
   - We clicked "yes" to indicate that we wanted sampling *without replacement* (because this is a more efficient sampling method than sampling with replacement).
5. Do you wish to sort the numbers that are generated?
   - We clicked "yes" for convenience.
6. How do you wish to view your random numbers?
   - We left the program at its default value ("place markers off") because we were not interested in knowing the order in which the numbers happened to be selected.
7. Next, to obtain our set of random numbers, we clicked "Randomize Now!"

Our resulting set of numbers using the random number generator was 2, 16, 42, 7, 10, 53, 30, 6, 27, and 18. The next step is to see who these people are so you can find out whether they will participate in your research study. As you can see in Table 10.2, the sample is composed of Fred Alexander (element 2), Barbara Flowers (element 16), Lena Schmitt (element 42), Barry Biddlecomb (element 7), Eugene Davis (element 10), Larry Watson (element 53), John Mills (element 30), Tom Baxter (element 6), Pam Mackey (element 27), and Marie Gaylord (element 18). This is your sample of size 10. Single asterisks are placed by these names in Table 10.2.

After contacting and collecting data (e.g., age) from the individuals in the sample, you would conduct a statistical analysis. Let's do a very simple calculation. The age was given for each individual. (Generally, data would have been collected on many additional variables or characteristics besides age.) Now calculate the average age for the individuals in the sample. Just add the ages for the 10 people and divide that number by 10; that is, $(18 + 31 + 52 + 21 + 37 + 46 + 35 + 19 + 33 + 26)/10 = 31.8$. The average age of the individuals in the sample is 31.8, and this is our estimate of the average age of all of the individuals in the population shown in our sampling frame.

In this case, we know that the population average is 38.95 or about 39 years old. To get 38.95, just add up the ages for all 60 people in the population and divide that number by 60. The sample value of 31.8 is off by approximately 7 years. Don't be alarmed if this seems like a big sampling error; a sample size of 10 is actually quite small. The difference between the sample average and the population average occurred because of chance. That is how random sampling works. If you were to select another sample of size 10, the average age in the sample would probably also be different from the population average. Try it. Draw another sample of size 10 from the sampling frame and make sure you can draw a simple random sample on your own. Basically, sampling error follows a normal, bell-shaped curve. The vast majority of the time, the sample mean will be relatively near the population mean, but it is possible for it to be far from the population mean.

We conclude this section with an excerpt from a journal article that relied on simple random sampling (Lance, 1996):

> Participants were selected from the 1992 Membership Directory of the Association on Higher Education and Disability (AHEAD), a professional organization for service providers to students with disabilities at institutions of higher education. Entries in the directory were assigned numbers, excluding those members who were students, were specialists in only one type of disability, did not reside in the United States, or were not affiliated with an institution of higher education. A statistical computer program was used to select a random sample of 250 of the members deemed eligible for participation in the study. . . . The final sample included 190 members from 47 states and the District of Columbia. (p. 280)

As you can see in the above excerpt, the membership directory of AHEAD was the researcher's sampling frame. Also, the researcher used a computer program to generate the random numbers.

Systematic Sampling

Systematic sampling uses a different strategy for selecting the elements to be included in the sample.[2] A **systematic sample** is defined as a sample that is obtained by determining the **sampling interval** (i.e., the population size divided by the desired sample size, N/n, which is symbolized by k), selecting at random a **starting point** (a number between 1 and k, including 1 and k), and then selecting every kth element in the sampling frame. Systematic sampling is generally easier than simple random sampling when you are selecting from lists (e.g., lists of names, lists of schools).

- **Systematic sample** A sample obtained by determining the sampling interval, selecting a random starting point between 1 and k, and then selecting every kth element
- **Sampling interval** The population size divided by the desired sample size
- ***k*** The size of the sampling interval
- **Starting point** A randomly selected number between 1 and k

Let's hypothetically say that there are 50 teachers in your middle school and we have a list of these 50 middle school teachers, with the teachers numbered from 1 through 50. You have decided that you want to select five teachers to be on a PTA committee. We can select a systematic sample from our list of 50 teachers by following the three steps given in the definition of systematic sampling. First, determine the sampling interval (symbolized by the letter k). To obtain k, you need the population size and the desired sample size. Then just divide the population size by the desired sample size. In this case, the population size is 50, and we want a sample of size 5. If you divide 50 by 5, you will see that k is equal to 10 (i.e., $50/5 = 10$).[3]

Second, randomly select one number between 1 and k (including 1 and k). You should use a table of random numbers or a random number generator for this step because you want the sample to be a random sample. In our example, we want to randomly select a number between 1 and 10 because k equals 10. Using the same random number generator as before, we inserted a 1 for the question "How many numbers per set?" and changed the range to 1 to 10. We then clicked "Randomize now!" and found that our randomly selected number was 6. Therefore, the teacher with the ID number 6 is the first person selected to be in our sample. The number 6 also has a special name in our systematic sampling; it is called the *starting point*.

Third, after you have determined k (the sampling interval) and the starting point, you can select the rest of the systematic sample. In our example, we randomly selected the number 6, which is our starting point. This is also the first person to be included in the sample. We now need four more people so that we will have a sample of size 5. To get the rest of the elements in our sample, we need to select every kth element starting at the starting point. In this example, our starting point is 6 and $k = 10$; therefore, the second person to be included in the sample is person 16 because we start at 6 and we add 10 (i.e., $6 + 10 = 16$). To get the third person, we start with the second person's number (i.e., 16) and add k (i.e., 10). Therefore, the third person is person 26 ($16 + 10 = 26$). We continue adding k to get the other two people in the sample. The other two people in the sample will be person 36 ($26 + 10 = 36$) and person 46 ($36 + 10 = 46$). Summarizing, we started with 6 and continued adding 10 until we obtained our desired sample of size 5. The systematic random sample is composed of persons 6, 16, 26, 36, and 46. That is five people.

Now let's select a systematic sample from the sampling frame given in Table 10.2. Earlier, we selected a simple random sample from this sampling frame. Specifically, we selected a simple random sample of size 10 from the population of size 60 shown in Table 10.2. The 10 people chosen in the simple random sample are marked with single asterisks in the table. Now we will select a systematic sample of size 10 from this same population, and we will calculate the average age so that we can compare it to the average age in the simple random sample (31.9) and to the average age in the population (38.95).

What do we do first? Remember, there are three steps, and in the first step, we must find k. In this case, k is $60/10 = 6$. Now we select a random number between 1 and 6 (with 1 and 6 also being possible selections). To do this, go to the table of random numbers or use a random number generator. We used the random number generator, and our randomly selected number was 3. The number 3 is our starting point. What are the remaining nine numbers in our sample? Just keep adding 6, and you will see that they are 9, 15, 21, 27, 33, 39, 45, 51, and 57. The sample is therefore composed of persons 3, 9, 15, 21, 27, 33, 39, 45, 51, and 57. Specifically, it is composed of Kathy Anderson, Martha Carr, Donna Faircloth, Scott House, Pam Mackey, Anh Nguyan, Anneke Reeves, Max Smart, Velma Vandenberg, and Andrew Young. These 10 people are marked in Table 10.2 with double asterisks. Now calculate the average age for the 10 individuals in this systematic sample. It is $(57 + 21 + 27 + 21 + 35 + 40 + 32 + 47 + 43 + 39)/10$. That's 362 divided by 10, which is 36.2. Because the population value is 38.95, 36.2 is a pretty good estimate, especially with such a small sample size ($n = 10$).

In this case, the average age in our systematic sample (36.2) is a better estimate of the population average (i.e., it is closer to 38.95) than the average age in the simple random sample selected (31.8). This will not, however, always be the case. Sometimes simple random sampling will work better, and sometimes systematic sampling will work better. Basically, if a list (a sampling frame) is randomly ordered, then the results of a simple random sampling and systematic sampling will tend to be very similar (Tryfos, 1996). If the list is ordered (i.e., stratified) according to the levels of a categorical variable (e.g., females are listed and then males are listed) or according to the values of a quantitative variable (e.g., the list is ordered in ascending or descending order of age), then systematic sampling will tend to perform a little better than simple random sampling (Kalton, 1983; Scheaffer, Mendenhall, & Ott, 1996).[4] By "better," we mean it will tend to be a little more representative of the population, given a certain sample size. Systematic sampling produces representative samples in general because it is an equal probability of selection method; that is, each individual in the population has an equal chance of being included in the sample (Kalton).

However, if the list is ordered in such a way that there are cycles in the data that coincide with the sampling interval (k), then systematic sampling can fail dramatically. You must watch out for this potentially serious problem. Look at the sampling frame given in Table 10.3. The principal and assistant principals at 10 schools making up a hypothetical local school district are listed. Each school is assumed to have 1 principal and 1 assistant principal (i.e., there are 10 assistant principals and 10 principals). Let's say that we want to select a systematic sample of 5 of these 20 school administrators. Because the population size is 20 ($N = 20$) and we want a sample size of 5 ($n = 5$), the sampling interval k is 20/5, which is 4. Therefore we will select every fourth person (i.e., element) after randomly

TABLE 10.3 A Periodic or Cyclical Sampling Frame

Element 1	Principal 1
Element 2*	Assistant Principal 1
Element 3	Principal 2
Element 4	Assistant Principal 2
Element 5	Principal 3
Element 6*	Assistant Principal 3
Element 7	Principal 4
Element 8	Assistant Principal 4
Element 9	Principal 5
Element 10*	Assistant Principal 5
Element 11	Principal 6
Element 12	Assistant Principal 6
Element 13	Principal 7
Element 14*	Assistant Principal 7
Element 15	Principal 8
Element 16	Assistant Principal 8
Element 17	Principal 9
Element 18*	Assistant Principal 9
Element 19	Principal 10
Element 20	Assistant Principal 10

*Elements marked by an asterisk are in the example of systematic sampling with periodicity discussed in the text.

selecting a starting point between 1 and 4. Let the randomly selected starting point be 2; that is, assume that you used a random number generator and obtained the number 2. As a result, element 2 is included in the sample. Now select every fourth element after 2 until you have 5 elements. That would be 6, 10, 14, and 18. The sample is composed of elements 2, 6, 10, 14, and 18.

But look at what happened in Table 10.3. The sample included only assistant principals. All of the principals were excluded! This is obviously a major problem because the selected sample is not at all representative of the population; it is a biased sample that includes only assistant principals and no principals. The sampling frame in this case has a cyclical pattern; it is said to be "periodic." The cyclical pattern in the sampling frame is obvious because each assistant principal is directly preceded and followed by a principal. In this case, the **periodicity** (the presence of a cyclical pattern in a sampling frame) has caused a major problem. What should we learn from the bad experience we just had? Basically, always examine your sampling frame carefully. If you believe that there is a cyclical pattern in the list, then either reorder the list or do not use systematic sampling.

- **Periodicity** The presence of a cyclical pattern in the sampling frame

Stratified Random Sampling

Stratified sampling is a technique in which a population is divided into mutually exclusive groups (called strata) and then a simple random sample or a systematic sample is selected from each group (each stratum). For example, we could divide a population into males and females and take a random sample of males and a random sample of females. The variable that we divide the population on is called the **stratification variable**. In the case of males and females, the stratification variable is gender. If you are wondering why this approach is called stratified sampling, it is probably because the strata can be viewed metaphorically as being similar to the discrete levels or layers below our earth's surface. The word was probably borrowed from the field of geology.

- **Stratified sampling** Dividing the population into mutually exclusive groups and then selecting a random sample from each group
- **Stratification variable** The variable on which the population is divided

Proportional Stratified Sampling

The most commonly used form of stratified sampling is called **proportional stratified sampling**. If the stratification variable is gender, then the proportions of males and females in the sample are made to be the same as the proportions of males and females in the population. For example, if the population is composed of 70% females and 30% males, then 70% of the people in the sample will be randomly selected from the female subpopulation (i.e., all females in the total population), and 30% of the people in the sample will be randomly selected from the male subpopulation (i.e., all males in the total population). That is why it is called "proportional" stratified sampling. The proportions in the sample are made to be the same as the proportions in the total population on certain characteristics. (We tell you how to do this shortly.)

- **Proportional stratified sampling** Type of stratified sampling in which the sample proportions are made to be the same as the population proportions on the stratification variable

Proportional stratified sampling tends to be a little more efficient (it requires fewer people) than simple random sampling (Kalton, 1983). That's because when you draw a proportional stratified sample, the proportions in the sample on the stratification variable will be perfectly or almost perfectly representative of the proportions of that same stratification variable in the population. For example, if the stratification variable is gender, then the proportions of males and females in the sample will be the same as the proportions in the population. Other possible stratification variables can be used (e.g., grade level, intelligence, education), and you can use more than one stratification variable at the same time if you want (e.g., gender and education). A stratified random sample will also be representative of the population on all other variables that are not included as stratification variables because random samples are selected from each population stratum (i.e., from each subpopulation). Proportional stratified sampling is an equal probability of selection method, which means that every individual in the population has an equal chance of being included in the sample. That's why proportional stratified sampling produces representative samples.

As an example, suppose that you are interested in selecting a sample of students in Grades 1 through 3 in an elementary school. We will use grade level as our stratification variable. The levels of the stratification variable are Grade 1, Grade 2, and Grade 3. Because we are using proportional stratified sampling, we want to make sure that the percentages of students in Grades 1 through 3 in the sample are the same as the percentages in Grades 1 through 3 in the school, while making sure that our sample is random in every other respect. As you can see, you have to know the percentages of students in Grades 1 through 3 in the school *before drawing your sample* so that you can select the right number of students from each grade to be in your sample. Therefore, proportional stratified sampling requires that you know certain information before drawing a sample. If you have the required information, you can stratify your sampling frame and randomly select the right numbers of people so that your final sample will be proportional to the population on the stratification variable and random in every other way.

In our current example, assume that you know beforehand that 30% of the students in Grades 1 through 3 are in the first grade, 35% are in the second grade, and 35% are in the third grade. If you wanted a sample of size 100 in this example, you would divide your sampling frame into first-, second-, and third-grade strata, and then you would randomly select 30 first graders, 35 second graders, and 35 third graders. As you can see, your final sample of 100 people will include the correct proportions for each grade, and it is random in every other respect. Here's a check of your understanding: How many first, second, and third graders would you randomly select from their subgroups in the population sampling frame if you wanted a proportional stratified sample of *size 500* rather than 100? The answer is, you would randomly select 150 first graders (30% of 500), 175 second graders (35% of 500), and 175 third graders (35% of 500). As you can see, 150 plus 175 plus 175 is the 500 people you desire for your sample!

We have shown that once you determine the number of people to select in each stratum (group), you can take a simple random sample of the appropriate size from each group. There is, however, a way to select a proportional stratified sample without having to worry about the number of people to select from each group (strata). Here's what you do. First, make sure that your list (your sampling frame) is ordered by group (strata). If gender is your stratification variable, for example, then order your list by gender; that is, list all of the females first, and list all of the males second. Second, simply take a *systematic sample* from the entire list. Kalton (1983) showed that systematic sampling from ordered lists is often preferred to first determining the sample sizes and then taking simple random samples. We also recommend this procedure because when a list is ordered by a stratification variable, it is unlikely that the problem of periodicity (a cyclical pattern in the list) will be present.[5]

Disproportional Stratified Sampling

Disproportional stratified sampling A type of stratified sampling in which the sample proportions are made to be different from the population proportions on the stratification variable

So far, we have focused on proportional stratified sampling. Sometimes, however, you might need to select a **disproportional stratified sample.** That is, you might want to select a larger percentage of certain groups of people than you would obtain if you used proportional stratified sampling. For example, you might want 50% of your sample to be African Americans and 50% to be European Americans. Because only 12% of the general population in the United States is African American and because European Americans are a much larger percent than 50, you would definitely not get a 50/50 split using proportional stratified sampling. Therefore, you would oversample African Americans and undersample European Americans to obtain a 50/50 split. Notice that you would be selecting individuals disproportional to their occurrence in the population—that's why it is called disproportional stratified sampling. Disproportional stratified sampling is often used when the research interest lies more in comparing groups than in making generalizations about the total population. If you use disproportional stratified sampling and also want to generalize to the total population, subgroup-weighting procedures must be used. Disproportional stratified sampling is also sometimes used when certain groups in the population are very small; hence, you oversample these groups to ensure that you have adequate sample sizes.

Here is an example in which a disproportional stratified sample might be needed. Suppose you work at a traditionally female college of 5,000 students that recently started accepting males and the number of females still far outweighs the number of males. Assume that 90% of the students (4,500) are female and only 10% (500) are male. If you are mainly interested in comparing males and females or in obtaining large samples of both females and males, then you might wish to select the same number of males as females. That is, you might opt for a disproportional stratified sample. Let's say you have the resources to obtain a sample size of 300. In this case, you might decide to select an equal number of females and males (150 females and 150 males). This way, comparisons between females and males will be based on similar sample sizes for both groups. Furthermore, we have fully 150 males and 150 females, which might be considered adequate sample sizes given your monetary resources.

It is important to understand that when disproportional stratified sampling is used, statements cannot be made about the total population without weighting procedures because the relative sizes of the sample strata do not represent the relative sizes of the groups in the population. Weighting is something that statisticians do to provide less weight to the smaller strata so that they more accurately represent their sizes in the population. Without weighting, you can make statements only about separate groups and make comparisons between the groups. Sometimes this is all a researcher wants to do.

Cluster sampling Type of sampling in which clusters are randomly selected

Cluster A collective type of unit that includes multiple elements

Cluster Random Sampling

Cluster sampling is a form of sampling in which **clusters** (a collective type of unit that includes multiple elements, such as schools, churches, classrooms, universities, households, and city blocks) rather than single-unit elements (such as individual students, teachers, counselors, and administrators) are randomly selected. For example, a school is a cluster because it is composed of many individual students. At some point, cluster sampling always involves randomly selecting clusters (multiple-unit elements) rather than single-unit elements. For example, in cluster sampling one might randomly select classrooms. A classroom is a cluster because it is a collective unit composed of many single units (i.e., students). In the other sampling techniques discussed in this chapter, single units (individuals) were always the objects of selection rather than collective units (clusters). Basic cluster sampling is just like simple random sampling except that rather than taking a random sample of *individuals*, you take a random sample of *clusters*.

Cluster sampling requires a larger sample size than simple random sampling, systematic sampling, or stratified sampling. Although cluster sampling is less accurate for a given sample size, cluster sampling is preferred on some occasions. For example, cluster sampling is often used when the elements in the population are geographically spread out and you need to conduct in-person interviews. In this situation, cluster sampling will result in reduced travel costs, reduced interviewer costs, and a reduced time period needed to interview all the people in the sample. If a population is geographically dispersed (as in the United States), the physical act of driving to every person's house in a simple random sample to conduct an interview would be very difficult to carry out. On the other hand, if you are conducting telephone interviews, you will not need to use cluster sampling because you can easily call anywhere in the United States from a single location, such as your home or office.

An additional reason for cluster sampling is that sometimes a sampling frame of all the people in the population will not be available. When this is the case, you might be able to locate naturally occurring groups of sampling elements, such as classrooms, mental health agencies, census blocks, street maps, and voting districts. Lists of these clusters are often available, or they can be developed without too much effort. After a sample of clusters is randomly selected from the list of all the clusters in the population, you only need to develop detailed lists of the individual elements for the randomly selected clusters. There is no need to identify everyone in the entire population.

One-Stage Cluster Sampling

Now let's look at some examples of cluster sampling. In the simplest case of cluster sampling, **one-stage cluster sampling**, a set of clusters is randomly selected from the larger set of all clusters in the population. For example, you might take a random sample of 10 schools from all of the schools in a city. Typically, simple random sampling, systematic sampling, or stratified random sampling is used to select the clusters. After the clusters are selected, all the elements (e.g., people) in the selected clusters are included in the sample. Sampling is therefore conducted at only one stage.

■ **one-stage cluster sampling** A set of clusters is randomly selected, and all the cases in the selected clusters are included in the sample.

Here's an example of one-stage cluster sampling. Let's say you are interested in getting a sample of 250 fifth-grade students from a public school system composed of 80 classrooms. Assume that there are approximately 25 students in each classroom. To reduce interviewing and travel time, you might choose to randomly select 10 clusters (10 fifth-grade classrooms) and interview all the students in these classes. You will have to visit only 10 classrooms. This will result in a sample including approximately 250 fifth-grade students (depending on the response rate). If, on the other hand, you had taken a simple random sample of students (rather than classrooms), you would have needed to go to far more than 10 classrooms.

Two-Stage Cluster Sampling

- **Two-stage cluster sampling** A set of clusters is randomly selected, and then a random sample of elements is drawn from each of the clusters selected in stage one

In **two-stage cluster sampling**, sampling is done at two stages rather than at one. In stage one, a set of clusters is randomly selected from all of the clusters. In stage two, a random sample of elements is drawn from each of the clusters selected in stage one. For example, 25 classrooms (clusters) could be randomly sampled from the list of clusters. If all students in the 25 classrooms were included as in a one-stage cluster sample, the sample size would be 625 (25 classrooms × 25 students per classroom = 625). Just as before, however, we want to select a sample of size 250. Therefore, at stage two, 10 students could be randomly selected from each of the 25 classrooms. The outcome would be a two-stage cluster random sample of 250 students.

- **Probability proportional to size** A type of two-stage cluster sampling in which each cluster's chance of being selected in stage one depends on its population size

At this point, it is important to note that we have assumed that all the classrooms are composed of approximately 25 students. However, it is often *not* the case that clusters are of approximately equal sizes. As a result, in selecting clusters, a technique called **probability proportional to size** (PPS) is used frequently. Basically, this more advanced technique is used to give large clusters a larger chance of being selected and smaller clusters a smaller chance of being selected. Then a fixed number of individuals (e.g., 10) is randomly selected from each of the selected clusters. This approach, though more advanced, is the route that has to be taken when the clusters are unequal in size to ensure that all people in the population have an equal chance of being selected.

PPS is an equal probability of selection method technique. And remember, equal probability of selection methods produce representative samples. To use this advanced technique, you will need to go to a more advanced book on sampling or get help from a statistical consultant at your college or university. The important point for you to remember here is that if you want a representative sample, then probability proportional to size must be used when the clusters are unequal in size. For your convenience, we include a table with links to the websites of organizations that routinely use random sampling methods (Table 10.4).

TABLE 10.4 Survey Research Sites Providing Useful Sampling Information and Links

Address	*Name*
www.src.isr.umich.edu	Survey Research Center at University of Michigan's Institute for Social Research
www.norc.uchicago.edu	The National Opinion Research Center (NORC) at the University of Chicago
www.princeton.edu/~psrc/	Survey Research Center at Princeton University
http://csr.indiana.edu/	Center for Survey Research at Indiana University–Bloomington
www.irss.unc.edu/odum/	The Howard W. Odum Institute for Research in Social Science at the University of North Carolina
www.csr.vt.edu	Center for Survey Research at Virginia Tech
www.srl.uic.edu/srllink/srllink.htm#Survey-Related	This site published by the Survey Research Laboratory of the University of Illinois at Chicago provides some useful survey research links.
www.ropercenter.uconn.edu	Roper Center
www.gallup.com	Gallup Inc.
www.surveysampling.com	Survey Sampling International (SSI)
www.aapor.org	American Association for Public Opinion Research
www.ncpp.org	National Council on Public Polls

REVIEW QUESTIONS

10.5 How do you select a simple random sample?
10.6 What do all of the equal probability of selection methods have in common?
10.7 What are the three steps for selecting a systematic sample?
10.8 How do you select a stratified sample?
10.9 What is the difference between proportional and disproportional stratified sampling?
10.10 When might a researcher want to use cluster sampling?

NONRANDOM SAMPLING TECHNIQUES

Convenience Sampling

Researchers use **convenience sampling** when they include in their sample people who are available or volunteer or can be easily recruited and are willing to participate in the research study. That is, the researcher selects individuals who can be "conveniently selected." It should be noticed that technically speaking, we cannot generalize from a convenience sample to a population. First and most important, not everyone in a population has an equal chance of being included in the sample. Second, it is often not clear what specific population a convenience "sample" comes from.

■ **Convenience sampling** Including people who are available, volunteer, or can be easily recruited in the sample

When convenience samples are used, it is especially important that researchers describe the characteristics of the people participating in their research studies. Sometimes, researchers will even describe the "hypothetical population" that they believe most closely corresponds to their convenience sample. Ultimately, however, it is up to you, the reader of a research article, to examine the characteristics of a convenience sample and decide whom you believe the group of people may represent.

You might be surprised to learn that the majority of experimental researchers do *not* select random samples. Rather, they tend to use convenience samples. For example, some published research is conducted with undergraduate students enrolled in introductory psychology or educational psychology classes. Here is an example from a study by Turner, Johnson, and Pickering (1996):

> Seventy-nine college students (47 women and 32 men) were recruited from introductory psychology courses. Students participated in research as an option for course credit. The average of the sample was 23.7 yr. (Range = 17 to 52.) Seventy-three percent ($n = 58$) of the participants were Caucasian, 18% (or 14) were African American, and the remaining 9% (or 7) were of other ethnic origins. (p. 1053)

Convenience samples are not the optimal way to go, especially when the researcher wants to generalize to a population on the basis of a single study. Nonetheless, researchers are often forced to use convenience samples because of practical constraints.

■ **Quota sampling** The researcher determines the appropriate sample sizes or quotas for the groups identified as important and takes convenience samples from those groups

Quota Sampling

In **quota sampling**, the researcher identifies the major groups or subgroups of interest, determines the number of people to be included in each of these groups, and then selects a convenience sample of people for each group. Quota sampling is so named because once the researcher decides how many of certain types of people to include in the sample, he or she then tries to "meet the quotas"; that is, the researcher tries to get the right number of people. If the researcher decides to make the sample proportional to the population on certain characteristics (e.g., gender), then this method of quota sampling will have an apparent similarity to proportional stratified sampling. For example, if a school is composed of 60% females and 40% males, the researcher might decide to make sure that his or her sample is also 60% female and 40% male. However, an important difference between quota sampling and stratified random sampling is that once the researcher decides how many people to include in each group, random sampling is *not* used. Although a quota sample might look similar to a population on some characteristics (e.g., the percentage of females and males), it is not a probability sample, and as a result, one's ability to generalize is severely limited.

Purposive Sampling

- **Purposive sampling** The researcher specifies the characteristics of the population of interest and locates individuals with those characteristics

In **purposive sampling** (sometimes called judgmental sampling), the researcher specifies the characteristics of a population of interest and then tries to locate individuals who have those characteristics. For example, a researcher might be interested in adult females over the age of 65 who are enrolled in a continuing education program. Once the group is located, the researcher asks those who meet the inclusion criteria to participate in the research study. When enough participants are obtained, the researcher does not ask anyone else to participate. In short, purposive sampling is a nonrandom sampling technique in which the researcher solicits persons with specific characteristics to participate in a research study. Here is an example of purposive sampling from a published research article:

> Data were collected from 75 evaluation users and producers involved in a statewide Education Innovation Program in a southeastern state of the United States. The sample was purposive (Patton, 1987, p. 51) in that the goal was to find a group of experts who could make informed predictions about evaluation participation and utilization under different scenarios. The sample included internal and/or external project evaluators, project directors, local building administrators, teachers involved with the projects, and persons from external evaluation teams. Of the sample, 53% had doctorates, 33% had specialist degrees, and 14% had master's degrees. (Johnson, 1995, p. 318)

Purposive sampling has the same limitations as any nonrandom sampling method. Specifically, the ability to generalize from a sample to a population on the basis of a single research study is severely limited. The optimal situation would be for the researcher to specify the criteria that potential participants must meet to be included in a research study but then attempt to obtain a random sample of these people. However, this is not always possible or practical.

Snowball Sampling

- **Snowball sampling** Each research participant is asked to identify other potential research participants

In **snowball sampling**, each research participant who volunteers to be in a research study is asked to identify one or more additional people who meet certain characteristics and may be willing to participate in the research study. Tallerico, Burstyn, and Poole (1993) used snowball sampling to find 20 females who had once been school superintendents and

4 "informants" who had known a female superintendent so that they could study why females left this position. Only a few individuals might be identified in the beginning of a research study as being appropriate, willing, and able to participate. Over time, however, as each new participant suggests someone else who might participate, the sample becomes larger and larger. The sample can be viewed metaphorically as a snowball that is rolling down a hill, getting bigger and bigger. This sampling method can be especially useful when you need to locate members of hard-to-find populations or when no sampling frame is available.

10.11 Are convenience samples used very often by experimental researchers?

REVIEW QUESTION

Random Selection and Random Assignment

It is very important to understand the difference between *random selection* and *random assignment*. **Random selection** has been the focus of this chapter. Random selection is just another term that means random sampling. As you now know, simple random sampling is like pulling names from a hat. The names you pull out of the hat make up the random sample. We also discussed three specific methods of random sampling that are variations of simple random sampling: systematic sampling, stratified sampling, and cluster sampling. *The purpose of random selection is to allow you to make generalizations from a sample to a population.* Because random selection methods produce representative samples, you are able to generalize from the sample to the population. This form of generalization is sometimes called statistical generalization.

- **Random selection** Randomly selecting a group of people from a population

We briefly discussed **random assignment** in Chapter 2 when we described experimental research. Random assignment involves taking a particular set of people (usually a convenience or purposive sample) and randomly *assigning* them to the groups to be studied in an experiment. Random assignment is only used in experimental research, and it is the key factor that allows one to make a strong claim of cause and effect from the experiment. *The purpose of random assignment is to produce comparison groups that are similar on "all possible factors" at the beginning of the experiment.* Then, if these similar groups differ after they receive the different treatments, the researcher can attribute the difference to the independent variable because this was the only factor on which the groups systematically differed (e.g., one group may receive a pill and another group may receive a placebo). Experiments are rarely, if ever, based on random samples. Although you *can* make a strong statement about the causal effect of the independent variable on the dependent variable (e.g., the effect of the experimental pill on behavioral outbursts) in an experiment that has random assignment but does not have random selection, you will *not* be able to generalize directly from such an experiment. Fortunately, there is a way out of this problem in experimental research, and that is through the use of replication logic.

- **Random assignment** Randomly assigning a set of people to different groups

When experimental findings are *replicated* in different places at different times with different people, the findings about the causal effect of the independent variable on the dependent variable can be generalized to some degree, even when random selection is not used. That is because when we repeatedly see the same causal result (e.g., the experimental pill consistently reduces behavioral disorders), evidence that the causal relationship is real and that it applies to many people is obtained. Theoretically speaking, the strongest possible experimental design would be one in which the participants are randomly selected from a population *and* are randomly assigned to groups. This would allow one to make a strong claim about cause and effect (because of random assignment) and to generalize the findings to a known population (because of random selection).

See Tools and Tips 10.1 on the Student Study Site.

Earlier in this chapter, we showed how to use a random number generator for random selection. In the bonus materials at the student companion website, we show how to use a random number generator for random assignment.

10.12 If your goal is to generalize from a sample to a population, which is more important: random selection or random assignment?

Determining the Sample Size When Random Sampling Is Used

When you design a research study, you will inevitably ask how big your sample should be.[6] The simplest answer is that the larger the sample size, the better, because larger samples result in smaller sampling errors, which means that your sample values (the statistics) will be closer to the true population values (the parameters). In the extreme case, sampling error would be zero if you included the complete population in your study rather than drawing a sample. As a rule of thumb, we recommend using the whole population when the population numbers 100 or less. That way, without too much expense, you can be completely confident that you know about the total population. Our second answer to the question of sample size is that you may want to examine the research literature that is most similar to the research you hope to conduct and see how many research participants were used in those studies.

In Table 10.5, we have provided a list of recommended sample sizes for your convenience. The sample sizes provided here are usually adequate. The recommended sample sizes are given for populations ranging in size from very small (e.g., 10) to extremely large (e.g., 500 million). All you need to know to use the table is the approximate size of the population from which you plan on drawing your sample. You can see in Table 10.5 that if the population is composed of 500 people, you need to randomly select 217 people. Likewise, if the population is composed of 1,500 people, you need to randomly select 306 people.

We now make several additional points about random sampling from populations.

- If you examine the numbers in Table 10.5, you will notice that a researcher must randomly select a large percentage of the population when the population is small. However, *as the population becomes larger and larger, the percentage of the population needed becomes smaller and smaller.*
- *The more homogeneous a population, the smaller the sample size can be.* A homogeneous population is one that is composed of similar people. In fact, if everyone were exactly alike, you would need only one person in your sample. Conversely, the more heterogeneous a population (the more dissimilar the people are), the larger the sample size needs to be.

TABLE 10.5 Sample Sizes for Various Populations of Size 10 to 500 Million

N stands for the size of the population; *n* stands for the size of the recommended sample. The sample sizes are based on the 95% confidence level.

N	*n*	*N*	*n*	*N*	*n*	*N*	*n*	*N*	*n*
10	10	110	86	300	169	950	274	4,500	354
15	14	120	92	320	175	1,000	278	5,000	357
20	19	130	97	340	181	1,100	285	6,000	361
25	24	140	103	360	186	1,200	291	7,000	364
30	28	150	108	380	191	1,300	297	8,000	367
35	32	160	113	400	196	1,400	302	9,000	368
40	36	170	118	420	201	1,500	306	10,000	370
45	40	180	123	440	205	1,600	310	15,000	375
50	44	190	127	460	210	1,700	313	20,000	377
55	48	200	132	480	214	1,800	317	30,000	379
60	52	210	136	500	217	1,900	320	40,000	380
65	56	220	140	550	226	2,000	322	50,000	381
70	59	230	144	600	234	2,200	327	75,000	382
75	63	240	148	650	242	2,400	331	100,000	384
80	66	250	152	700	248	2,600	335	250,000	384
85	70	260	155	750	254	2,800	338	500,000	384
90	73	270	159	800	260	3,000	341	1,000,000	384
95	76	280	162	850	265	3,500	346	10,000,000	384
100	80	290	165	900	269	4,000	351	500,000,000	384

Source: Adapted from R. V. Krejecie and D. W. Morgan, "Determining Sample Size for Research Activities," *Educational and Psychological Measurement*, *30*(3), p. 608, copyright © 1970 by SAGE Publications, Inc. Reprinted by permission of SAGE Publications, Inc.

- *The more categories or breakdowns you want to examine in your data analysis, the larger the sample size needed.* For example, a researcher might be interested in determining the percentage of people in a city who plan on voting for a certain school superintendent candidate. But what if the researcher also wanted to know the percentages of females and males planning on voting for the candidate? The original population has now been divided into two subpopulations of interest, and the researcher would need an adequate sample size for each group.
- In our later chapter on inferential statistics (Chapter 19), we explain the idea of confidence intervals. For now, we note that sometimes researchers use a statistical procedure to estimate a population value and provide an interval of values that is likely to include the population value. For example, you might hear a news reporter say that 55% of the people in a city support the school superintendent's decision to adopt school uniforms, *plus or minus 5%,* and that the "level of confidence" is 95%. The statement is that the population value is probably (95% chance) somewhere between 50% and 60%. It turns out that the

more people are included in a sample, the smaller (narrower) the confidence interval will be. For example, if more people were included in the sample, one might be able to say that 55% of the people support the decision, *plus or minus 3%*. That is, the population value is probably somewhere between 52% and 58%. The rule is, *the larger the sample size, the greater the precision of statements about the population based on the sample.* Therefore, the bigger the sample, the better.

- Assume that you are planning to measure a relationship or the effect of an independent variable on a dependent variable. *If you expect the relationship or effect to be relatively* weak, *then you will need a* larger *sample size*. That's because there is less "noise" or "random error" in larger samples.
- *The more efficient the random sampling method, the smaller the sample size needs to be.* Stratified random sampling tends to need slightly fewer people than simple random sampling. On the other hand, cluster random sampling tends to require slightly more people than simple random sampling.
- The last consideration mentioned here is that some of the people in your original sample will refuse to participate in your research study. In other words, your final sample may end up being smaller than you had intended. *If you can guess approximately what percentage of the people will actually participate (the response rate), you can use the following formula to adjust your original sample size.* The numerator is the number of people you want to have in your research study. The denominator is the proportion of people you believe will agree to participate.

$$\frac{\text{Desired sample size}}{\text{Proportion likely to respond}} = \text{Number of people to include in your original sample}$$

For example, say that you want a sample size of 75 and you expect that only 80% of the people in your original sample will actually participate in your research study. All you need to do is to divide 75 by 0.80, and you will have the number of people you need to include in your sample. You will need 94 people. Let's check your understanding. Assume that you want a sample size of 50 people and you expect that 70% of them will participate. What is the number of people you need to include in your original sample? The numerator is 50, your desired sample size; the denominator is 0.70. And 50 divided by 0.70 is equal to 71. You will need 71 people. Using your calculator, this is a simple calculation, right?

See Journal Article 10.2 on the Student Study Site.

REVIEW QUESTION

10.13 If your population size is 250,000, how many participants will you need, at a minimum, for your research study? (Hint: Look at Table 10.5.)

SAMPLING IN QUALITATIVE RESEARCH

Qualitative researchers must first decide whom or what they want to study. (You will also want to decide the number of cases needed in your qualitative study; for some sample-size "rules of thumb," examine Table 15.2 on page 424.) This initial task is based on consideration of which populations or phenomena are relevant to the research focus being proposed or developed. The researcher typically defines a set of criteria or attributes that the people to be studied must possess and uses these criteria to distinguish the people of potential interest from those people who should be excluded from consideration. Once these inclusion boundaries are set, the researcher knows whom he or she wishes to study and can then attempt to locate and obtain the sample. It is important that you are perspicacious when thinking about sampling in qualitative research because of the following truism: "The cases you select affect the answers you get!" Don't forget this point.

Margaret LeCompte and Judith Preissle (1993) called the overall sampling strategy used in qualitative research *criterion-based selection*, because the researcher develops inclusion criteria to be used in selecting people or other units (e.g., schools). Another well-known qualitative researcher, Michael Patton (1987, 1990), used the term *purposeful sampling* to describe the same process, because individuals or cases are selected that provide the information needed to address the purpose of the research. The terms *criterion-based selection* and *purposeful sampling* are synonyms, and both describe what we earlier called *purposive sampling*. Purposive sampling is used in both quantitative and qualitative research. The other forms of nonprobability sampling previously discussed (snowball sampling, quota sampling, and convenience sampling) are also sometimes used in qualitative research.

Although the goal is always to locate information-rich individuals or cases, decisions about whom to study are also affected by logistical constraints, such as the accessibility of the potential participants and the costs of locating the people and enlisting their participation. Researchers virtually always face practical constraints such as these when they decide whom to include in their research studies. The key point is that a researcher should pick a sample that can be used to meet the purpose of the research study and answer research questions while meeting cost and other constraints. Trade-offs will always be present.

Many different types of sampling are used in qualitative research. We rely here mainly on the discussions by LeCompte and Preissle (1993) and Patton (1987, 1990). The first type is called **comprehensive sampling**, which means that all relevant cases (individuals, groups, settings, or other phenomena) are examined in the research study. This inclusion guarantees representativeness because everyone is included in the study. It can also be very expensive and quite impractical except for very small populations that are relatively easy to locate.

- **Comprehensive sampling** Including all cases in the research study

Another form of sampling that qualitative researchers sometimes use is called **maximum variation sampling**. In this form of sampling, a wide range of cases (individuals, groups, settings, or other phenomena) are purposively selected so that all types of cases along one or more dimensions are included in the research. One reason for using this approach is to help ensure that no one can claim that you excluded certain types of cases. During data analysis, the qualitative researcher can search for a central theme or pattern that occurs across the cases. Something all the cases have in common might be identified. For example, while studying the organizational culture of a local school, an ethnographic researcher might identify certain core values and beliefs common to most, if not all, of the teachers in the school. Here's an example from a journal article by Fisher (1993). Fisher was interested in describing the developmental changes experienced by older adults.

- **Maximum variation sampling** Purposively selecting a wide range of cases

> Initially five sites were selected at which to conduct interviews: two senior centers in an urban county and two senior centers and a nursing home located in adjacent counties which combined suburban and rural characteristics. These sites were selected in order to increase the probability that persons available for interviewing would represent a broad age spectrum with diverse backgrounds and experiences. (p. 78)

■ **Homogeneous sample selection** Selecting a small and homogeneous case or set of cases for intensive study

In **homogeneous sample selection**, a relatively small and homogeneous case or set of cases is selected for intensive study. Focus group researchers commonly use this procedure with small homogeneous groups of around six or seven participants. The focus group facilitator attempts to gain an in-depth understanding of how the people in the group think about a topic. The group discussion typically lasts about 2 hours. More generally, when specific subgroups are targeted for inclusion in a research study or as a component of a larger study, the researcher might have relied on homogeneous sample selection.

■ **Extreme-case sampling** Identifying the extremes or poles of some characteristic and then selecting cases representing these extremes for examination

In **extreme-case sampling**, the extremes, or poles, of some characteristic are identified, and then cases representing only the extremes are selected for examination. The strategy is to select cases from the extremes because they are potentially rich sources of information and then to compare them. You might locate and compare "outstanding cases" with "notable failures" and attempt to determine what circumstances led to these outcomes (Patton, 1990). For example, you might compare the teaching environment created by an outstanding teacher with that created by a notably ineffective teacher.

■ **Typical-case sampling** Selecting what are believed to be average cases

In **typical-case sampling**, the researcher lists the criteria that describe a typical or average case and then finds one or several to study. As the researcher, you should speak to several experts to try to gain consensus on what case(s) is typical of the phenomenon to be studied. If specific cases are not recommended, then the characteristics of a typical case should be identified, and then you would attempt to locate such a person. For example, a hypothetical teacher of interest might be described on characteristics such as age, gender, teaching style, and number of years of experience. Even in quantitative research, it is sometimes helpful to illustrate a typical case in the final report to help the reader make more sense of the findings.

■ **Critical-case sampling** Selecting what are believed to be particularly important cases

In **critical-case sampling**, cases that can be used to make a previously justified point particularly well or are known to be particularly important are selected for in-depth study. According to Patton (1990), "a clue to the existence of a critical case is a statement to the effect that 'if it happens there, it will happen anywhere,' or, vice versa, 'if it doesn't happen there, it won't happen anywhere.'" For example, perhaps a school superintendent wants to change a policy and expects that change to face resistance in the local schools. The superintendent might decide to select a school where he or she expects the greatest resistance to determine whether enacting the policy is feasible in practice.

■ **Negative-case sampling** Selecting cases that are expected to disconfirm the researcher's expectations and generalizations

In **negative-case sampling**, cases that are expected to disconfirm the researcher's expectations are purposively selected. For example, in the form of qualitative research called grounded theory, the qualitative researcher typically explores a phenomenon and attempts to build a theory inductively about it. As the researcher develops a tentative conclusion or generalization based on the data, however, it is important to search for instances in which the generalization might not hold in order to learn more about the boundaries of the generalization and about any potential problems that need to be addressed or qualifications that need to be made. If you are a careful and conscientious qualitative researcher, you must not overlook negative cases.

■ **Opportunistic sampling** Selecting cases when the opportunity occurs

In **opportunistic sampling**, the researcher takes advantage of opportunities during data collection to select important cases. These cases might be critical, negative, extreme, or even typical. The important point is that qualitative research is an ongoing and emergent process, and the researcher might not be able to state in advance of the research everyone and everything that will be included in the study. The focus might change, and opportunities that could not be foreseen might arise. The effective researcher is one who is quick to discern whom to talk to and what to focus on while collecting the data in the field. The term *opportunistic sampling* was coined to refer to this process.

The last form of sampling listed here is **mixed purposeful sampling**. Patton (1987) coined this term to refer to the mixing of more than one sampling strategy. A researcher might, for example, conduct a qualitative research study and start with maximum variation sampling, discover a general pattern or finding in the data, and then use negative-case selection to determine the boundaries and generality of the pattern. Mixed purposeful sampling is also likely to be used when a researcher uses data triangulation—examining multiple data sources, which might be selected according to different sampling methods.

- **Mixed purposeful sampling** The mixing of more than one sampling strategy

REVIEW QUESTION

10.14 Sampling in qualitative research is similar to which type of sampling in quantitative research?

SAMPLING IN MIXED RESEARCH[7]

Choosing a *mixed sampling design* involves choosing the sampling scheme and sample size for both the quantitative and qualitative components of a research study. We use the mixed sampling framework provided by Onwuegbuzie and Collins (2007). According to this framework, mixed sampling designs are classified according to two major criteria: (a) the time orientation of the components and (b) the relationship between the quantitative and qualitative samples (i.e., sample relationship). **Time orientation criterion** refers to whether quantitative and qualitative phases occur concurrently or sequentially. When using a *concurrent* time orientation, data are collected for the quantitative phase and qualitative phase of the study at the same or during approximately the same time period. Data from both samples (i.e., the quantitative sample and the qualitative sample) are combined and interpreted at the study's data interpretation stage. When the researcher uses a *sequential* time orientation, data obtained from the sample during the first phase of the study are used to shape or structure the sample selection of the next phase of the study (i.e., quantitative phase followed by qualitative phase, or vice versa).

- **Time orientation criterion** Refers to whether the samples are taken concurrently or sequentially

The **sample relationship criterion** of the quantitative and qualitative samples results in four major types: identical, parallel, nested, and multilevel. An *identical* sample relation means that the same people participate in both the quantitative and qualitative phases of the investigation. For example, the same participants could complete a questionnaire that contains both closed-ended items with rating scales (i.e., quantitative component) and open-ended items/questions (i.e., qualitative component). A *parallel* relation indicates that the samples for the quantitative and qualitative components of the research are different but are drawn from the same population. For example, you could select students from a fourth-grade class for the quantitative phase and select students from another fourth-grade class within the same school or even from another school for the qualitative phase. A *nonparallel* relation indicates that the samples are drawn from different populations. A *nested* relation means

- **Sample relationship criterion** Refers to whether the samples, taken in combination, are identical, parallel, nonparallel, nested, or multilevel

that the participants selected for one phase of the study represent a subset of those participants who were selected for the other phase of the study. As an example, if you are interested in studying the relationship between reading performance and reading attitudes, you could select a large number of students for the quantitative phase, then interview the three students with the most positive reading attitudes and the three students with the least positive reading attitudes for the qualitative phase. Finally, a *multilevel* relation involves the use of quantitative and qualitative samples that are obtained from different levels of the population under study. For example, for the same research on reading and attitudes, you could use students for the quantitative phase and their teachers or parents for the qualitative phase.

Mixed sampling designs The ten sampling designs that result from crossing the time orientation criterion and the sample relationship criterion

The two criteria just discussed—time orientation (which has two types) and sample relationship (which has five types)—result in ten **mixed sampling designs**: (1) identical concurrent, (2) identical sequential, (3) parallel concurrent, (4) parallel sequential, (5) nonparallel concurrent, (6) nonparallel sequential, (7) nested concurrent, (8) nested sequential, (9) multilevel concurrent, and (10) multilevel sequential. For example, in an *identical concurrent* mixed sampling design, quantitative and qualitative data are collected at approximately the same time (i.e., concurrently) on the same individuals who are participating in both the quantitative and qualitative phases of the study (i.e., identical relation). In a *parallel sequential* mixed sampling design, quantitative and qualitative data are collected one after the other (i.e., sequentially) on different participants who are selected to represent the same population under investigation (i.e., parallel relation). Now see if you can describe a mixed sampling design based on another time order and connective relationship: What does a *nested concurrent* design represent? The answer is that it involves quantitative and qualitative data being collected at approximately the same time (i.e., concurrently) but with the qualitative sample being a subset of the quantitative sample or vice versa (i.e., nested relation). Well done!

Once you have selected one of the ten mixed sampling designs, you must select the sampling method and sample size for both the quantitative and qualitative phases. For the quantitative sample, you would use one of the random or nonrandom sampling methods discussed earlier in this chapter. Ideally, for your quantitative sample, you would select a random sample that is large enough to represent your population of interest, and if hypotheses are being tested, your sample size should be large enough to be able to detect group differences or relationships (what researchers call having adequate *statistical power*). For the qualitative sample, you would use one of the qualitative sampling methods discussed earlier. A general rule in qualitative sampling is that you should use a sample size that is large enough to obtain *saturation* (i.e., where no new or relevant information seems to emerge as more data are collected) but small enough to conduct a deep, case-oriented analysis (Sandelowski, 1995). For additional discussions of sampling in mixed research, we recommend Collins, Onwuegbuzie, and Jiao (2007) and Teddlie and Yu (2007).

See Journal Article 10.3 on the Student Study Site.

REVIEW QUESTION

10.15 How many mixed sampling designs result if you make a matrix or table where you cross the time orientation criterion (two types) and the sample relationship criterion (four types)? (Hint: Draw that matrix, letting the two time orientation types be the rows and the four sample relationship types be the columns; how many cells did you get?)

ACTION RESEARCH REFLECTION

Insight: Action researchers decide whom they want to help and then creatively use quantitative, qualitative, and mixed sampling methods to obtain their research participants.

1. What are the strengths and weaknesses of each of the sampling paradigm(s) for research that you are interested in conducting—the quantitative, qualitative, and/or mixed approach?
2. Even though you might be most interested in studying a local problem or issue (rather than sampling from a large population), what are some ideas in this chapter that might be of use to you?

SUMMARY

Sampling is the process of drawing a sample from a population. When we sample, we study the characteristics of a subset (called the sample) selected from a larger group (called the population) in order to understand the characteristics of the larger group (the population). If the researcher selects a sample from a population by using a random sampling method, then the sample will be *representative* of the total population—it will be similar to the population. Therefore, after the researcher determines the characteristics of a randomly selected sample, he or she can generalize from the sample to the population. A sample is usually much smaller in size than a population; hence, sampling saves time and money.

The major random sampling methods are simple random sampling, systematic sampling, stratified random sampling, and cluster random sampling. Each of these random sampling methods is an equal probability of selection method (EPSEM), which means that each individual in the population has an equal chance of being included in the sample. Sampling methods that are "EPSEM" produce representative samples.

Researchers do not always, however, use the most powerful sampling methods. Frequently, nonrandom samples are drawn. The four types of nonrandom sampling discussed are convenience sampling, quota sampling, purposive sampling, and snowball sampling.

Qualitative research relies on a different set of approaches to sampling. Qualitative research sampling is *purposive* and relies on comprehensive sampling, maximum variation sampling, homogeneous sampling, extreme-case sampling, typical-case sampling, critical-case sampling, negative-case sampling, opportunistic sampling, or mixed purposeful sampling. Mixed research relies on quantitative *and* qualitative sampling methods and integrates these into ten *mixed sampling designs.*

KEY TERMS

biased sample (p. 253)
census (p. 252)
cluster (p. 264)
cluster sampling (p. 264)
comprehensive sampling (p. 273)
convenience sampling (p. 267)
critical-case sampling (p. 274)
disproportional stratified sampling (p. 264)
element (p. 254)
equal probability of selection method (p. 255)
extreme-case sampling (p. 274)
generalize (p. 252)
homogeneous sample selection (p. 274)
k (p. 259)
maximum variation sampling (p. 273)
mixed purposeful sampling (p. 275)
mixed sampling designs (p. 276)
N (p. 254)
n (p. 254)
negative-case sampling (p. 274)
one-stage cluster sampling (p. 265)
opportunistic sampling (p. 274)
parameter (p. 254)
periodicity (p. 262)
population (p. 254)
probability proportional to size (p. 266)

proportional stratified sampling (p. 262)
purposive sampling (p. 268)
quota sampling (p. 267)
random assignment (p. 269)
random number generator (p. 256)
random selection (p. 269)
representative sample (p. 253)
response rate (p. 254)
sample (p. 254)
sample relationship criterion (p. 275)
sampling (p. 252)
sampling error (p. 254)
sampling frame (p. 254)
sampling interval (p. 259)
simple random sample (p. 255)
snowball sampling (p. 268)
starting point (p. 259)
statistic (p. 254)
stratification variable (p. 262)
stratified sampling (p. 262)
survey research (p. 253)
systematic sample (p. 259)
table of random numbers (p. 256)
time orientation criterion (p. 275)
two-stage cluster sampling (p. 266)
typical-case sampling (p. 274)

DISCUSSION QUESTIONS

1. What is the difference between random selection and random assignment? Give an example of each.
2. Who do you think is more interested in using a random sampling method: a pollster running a political campaign or an experimental researcher who is studying a cause-and-effect relationship between two variables? Explain.
3. A local news radio station has people call in and voice their opinions on a local issue. Do you see any potential sources of bias resulting from this sampling approach?
4. Following are some examples of sampling. Identify the type of sample that is used in each.
   a. An educational psychology teacher asks all of her students to fill out her research questionnaire.
   b. An educational psychology teacher obtains a student directory that is supposed to include the students at your university. She determines the sampling interval, randomly selects a number from 1 to *k,* and includes every *k*th person in her sample.
   c. An educational researcher obtains a list of all the middle schools in your state. He then randomly selects a sample of 25 schools. Finally, he randomly selects 30 students from each of the selected schools. (That's a sample size of $25 \times 30 = 750$.) By the way, what are some potential problems with this procedure?
   d. A researcher takes a random sample of 100 males from a local high school and a random sample of 100 females from the same local high school. What are some potential problems with this procedure if the researcher wants to generalize from the 200 people to the high school population?
   e. Is simple random sampling the only equal probability of sampling method? If not, what are some other equal probability of sampling methods?

RESEARCH EXERCISES

1. Using one of the random number generators or using the table of random numbers in Table 10.1, draw a simple random sample of size 20 from the sampling frame in Table 10.2.
   a. What is the average age of the 20 people in your sample?
   b. Now draw a systematic sample of size 20 from the sampling frame in Table 10.2 and calculate the average age. What is the average age in your systematic sample?

c. Compare the two sample averages you just obtained. Which one is closer to the population mean?

d. Compare the sample averages you got above with the population parameter (i.e., the average age for all 60 people listed in Table 10.2). What was the sampling error for your simple random sample? (Hint: If you subtract the sample average from the population average, you obtain the sampling error.) Finally, what was the sampling error for your systematic sample?

2. Go to your library website and search the *New York Times* or another major newspaper. Find some articles on an issue involving sampling and write a short paper summarizing what you have found. Be sure to include your own position regarding the issue discussed in the newspaper article.

3. Congress and editorial writers have often discussed the pros and cons of eliminating the process of enumerating every single individual in the United States and instead using random sampling techniques. What side are you on: the side that says, "Do a census," or the side that says, "Do a survey"? For some useful information on this issue, go to this link at the American Statistical Association—www.amstat.org—and once there put in the search terms "sampling" and "census."

PROPOSAL EXERCISES

1. What kind of quantitative, qualitative, and/or mixed sampling approach do you propose to use in your research study? Please explain your reasoning.
2. How will you enact your sampling approach (i.e., with whom, how many participants, where, steps in the sampling process, and expected resulting sample[s])?
3. What kinds of generalizations would you be able to make from your sample(s) at the end of your study?

RELEVANT INTERNET SITES

A sample size calculator
http://www.surveysystem.com/sscalc.htm

Programs that can be used for random selection and random assignment
http://www.randomizer.org
http://www.random.org

Glossary of sampling terms from a sampling corporation
https://www.surveysampling.com/site/assets/files/1560/ssi-glossary-of-terms.pdf

Program for conducting random assignment
http://www.graphpad.com/quickcalcs/randomize1.cfm

STUDENT STUDY SITE

Visit the Student Study Site at **edge.sagepub.com/rbjohnson6e** for these additional learning tools:

Video Links
Self-Quizzes
eFlashcards
Lecture Notes
Full-Text SAGE Journal Articles
Interactive Concept Maps
Web Resources

RECOMMENDED READING

Daniel, J. (2012). *Sampling essentials: Practical guidelines for making sampling choices.* Los Angeles, CA: SAGE.

Henry, G. T. (1990). *Practical sampling.* Newbury Park, CA: SAGE.

Kalton, G. (1983). *Introduction to survey sampling.* Beverly Hills, CA: SAGE.

Schonlau, M., Fricker, R. D., & Elliott, M. N. (2002). *Conducting research surveys via e-mail and the web.* Santa Monica, CA: RAND.

NOTES

1. Sampling with replacement and sampling without replacement are both equal probability of selection methods (EPSEM; Cochran, 1977; Kish, 1965). Sampling without replacement, however, is slightly more efficient in practice.

2. Systematic sampling is included as a type of random sampling for three reasons. First, the starting point is randomly selected. Second, it is an EPSEM (Kalton, 1983). Third, it is typically as good as or better than a simple random sample of equal size (Scheaffer, Mendenhall, & Ott, 1996).

3. The sampling interval may not be a whole number in practice. A common solution is to round it off. If this does not work very well, see page 17 in Kalton (1983).

4. When lists are ordered in this way, they are said to be stratified. Often the researcher will stratify the list to improve the sampling results. Sometimes the list is already stratified without the researcher doing anything at all. This usually improves the sample because of a process called implicit stratification (Jaeger, 1984; Sudman, 1976).

5. The stratification variable has been categorical in our examples (e.g., grade level, gender). However, you can also select a proportional stratified sample with quantitative stratification variables (e.g., age, IQ). Just reorder the list by the quantitative stratification variable and take a systematic sample. In the case of age, for example, reorder the names in your original list from the youngest to the oldest person and take a systematic sample from your new list.

6. It has been erroneously suggested by some methodologists that researchers should sample 10% of a population or 10% of the people in each group in a population. You should avoid using this rule of thumb. Sampling experts make it clear that sample size should not be based on a percentage of a population. You can easily see the problem with the "10% rule" by applying it to a small population of 50 people and to a large population of 250 million people. In the former, the rule would say take a sample of size 5. In the latter, the rule would say take a sample of 25 million people!

7. This section was originally written by Anthony J. Onwuegbuzie and Burke Johnson.

Chapter 11

Validity of Research Results in Quantitative, Qualitative, and Mixed Research

LEARNING OBJECTIVES

After reading this chapter, you should be able to

- Explain the meaning of confounding variables.
- Explain the meaning of statistical conclusion validity, construct validity, internal validity, and external validity and their importance in the research process.
- Identify and explain the types of evidence that are needed to reach a causal conclusion.
- Explain the threats to internal validity and be able to identify when they might exist in a research study.
- Explain the threats to external validity and when they might exist in a research study.
- Explain the role of operationalization of constructs in research.
- Identify and explain the types of validity or trustworthiness used in qualitative research.
- Identify and explain the types of validity or legitimation used in mixed research.

Visit the Student Study Site for an interactive concept map.

RESEARCH IN REAL LIFE Identifying and Controlling Extraneous Variables

For generations, the road to becoming a teacher has required a college degree with a major in education. Traditionally, this academic training has required a 2- to 3-month internship in a classroom. After the completion of the internship and the degree requirements, the aspiring teacher applies for a position in a public school district or private school and reports for duty following the signing of a contract. In November 2001, the *Christian Science Monitor* (Savoye, 2001) reported that the Chicago public school district was going to try a different approach to the internship portion of the traditional training model. This change was spurred by a general belief that the traditional internship was not long enough, intense enough, or comprehensive enough.

In September 2001, the Chicago public school district opened the Chicago Academy with the objective of training prospective teachers over the course of a full school year. This training program encouraged student teachers to learn from many teachers at the school in addition to their master teacher. To implement the training, the academy was modified so that all classrooms have a small adjoining anteroom with mirrored, one-way glass that allows the master teacher to step out of the classroom and observe the student teacher working alone with the students. This observation phase was included to facilitate skill building that student teachers need but often do not receive, such as learning to pause so that students can absorb a concept, refraining from calling on the same child too frequently, and learning how to move around the class rather than remaining stationary.

The goals of the Chicago program are to be commended. However, just because such an initiative is implemented and seems to be a worthy endeavor does not mean that the stated goals will be accomplished. The only way one can determine whether the stated goals are being met is to conduct an empirical research study with the purpose of determining whether the quality of instruction is enhanced by providing the more intense, 10-month training program and whether students who participate in this program remain in the profession longer.

Let's assume that a study was conducted to test the benefit of providing prospective teachers with the more intensive 10-month internship program and the results of this study revealed that these students not only were better teachers but also stayed in the profession longer. Such results would suggest that other teacher education programs should incorporate a similar program. Before drawing such a conclusion, however, you must carefully examine all facets of the study, making sure it has no flaws and that no alternative explanations for the findings exist. For example, assume that the students who were selected to participate in the program were the brighter and more motivated students. This selective participation and not the intensive internship might have produced the more effective teachers. Similarly, if the students participating in the experimental program were students who were more dedicated to the profession of teaching, this factor could account for their greater longevity in the teaching profession. In research, these kinds of factors are called "extraneous variables," and these extraneous variables must be controlled if you hope to identify the effect of an independent variable. In this chapter, we discuss some of the extraneous variables that can creep into a study and compromise the validity of the inferences that we can make from the data we collected.

To conduct a research study that will provide an answer to your research question, you must develop a plan, outline, or strategy to use in data collection. You naturally want to develop a plan or strategy that will allow you to collect data that will lead to a valid conclusion. To accomplish this goal, you must have knowledge of the factors that will lead to both valid and invalid conclusions. These factors are different depending on whether you are conducting a quantitative study, a qualitative study, or a mixed study.

Validity Issues in the Design of Quantitative Research

In quantitative research, researchers usually want to identify the effect created by some independent variable and to be able to generalize the results beyond the confines of the study. We want the results of any study we conduct, regardless of whether it is experimental or nonexperimental, to be reliable, and we want the inferences we make from the result of any study to be valid. More formally stated, **research reliability** is present when the same results would be obtained if the study were conducted again (i.e., replicated), and **research validity** refers to the correctness or truthfulness of the inferences that are made from the results of the study. However, in every study, there is the possibility that some variable other than the independent variable influenced the dependent variable or limited the ability to generalize the results. For example, if you are investigating the effect of parents' involvement in their child's education (independent variable) on the child's achievement test scores (dependent variable), you probably want to conclude that greater parent involvement results in high achievement test scores. However, if the parents with the greater involvement also have the brightest children, the higher achievement test scores could be *due to* the child's greater intellect. In such an instance, intellect would be an **extraneous variable**, a variable other than the ones you are specifically studying that might have confounded the results of the study.

Extraneous variables might or might not introduce a confounding influence into your study. Extraneous variables are problematic when they systematically vary with the independent variable and also influence the dependent variable. These problematic extraneous variables are sometimes called **confounding variables**. Drawing clear and valid conclusions from the data you collect is impossible if an uncontrolled confounding variable is present. It is essential that you identify and control for all confounding variables that might threaten your study conclusions.

To illustrate how extraneous variables can confound the outcome of a study and produce ambiguous results, consider a hypothetical "Pepsi Challenge" study. Assume that Pepsi wants to conduct a study demonstrating that consumers prefer its product over Coke. In this study, research participants are given, in random order, Pepsi in a red cup and Coke in a black cup. The research participants are to drink the beverage in each cup and then identify the one they like more. Now assume that 80% of the participants indicate that they prefer the beverage in the red cup. Pepsi would take this as an indication that its product is preferred over Coke. However, if people are more likely to choose something in a red cup, this could influence their selection of the beverage of choice. If the cup color influences choice, the results are ambiguous because it is impossible to tell whether the choice was due to the beverage or to the color of the cup. This is the type of subtle extraneous variable that can systematically confound the outcome of a study and lead to ambiguous results. A key idea here is that an extraneous variable that varies systematically with the independent variable

- **Research reliability** The consistency, stability, or repeatability of the results of a study
- **Research validity** The correctness or truthfulness of an inference that is made from the results of a study
- **Extraneous variable** Any variable other than the independent variable that might influence the dependent variable
- **Confounding variable** An extraneous variable that systematically varies with the independent variable and also influences the dependent variable

might produce a confounding influence on the dependent variable. In the Pepsi Challenge, the problem could have been resolved by using a single cup color. To eliminate confounding extraneous variables and produce valid research results, you must be aware of the criteria that must be met to conduct an uncontaminated study and have some knowledge of the type of variables that can frequently be confounding extraneous variables. The problem illustrated in the Pepsi Challenge will later be called internal validity, which refers to the ability to make a claim of cause and effect.

In quantitative research, four major types of validity—internal, external, construct, and statistical conclusion—are used to evaluate the validity of the inferences that can be made from the results of a study. Please see Exhibit 11.1 to learn about the founder of this set of four major validity types and many of the threats to validity discussed in this chapter. We now discuss these four types of validity and present some of the threats to these validity types. In reading about these threats, you should realize that not all of them will occur in every study. The likelihood that any one will occur will depend on the context of the particular study. However, consideration of these threats serves the valuable function of increasing the probability that you will anticipate their existence and do something about it. If you can anticipate a threat before conducting a study, you can design the study in such a way as to rule it out. If you cannot institute design controls, maybe you can measure the threat directly to determine whether it actually operated in your study and then conduct statistical analysis to find out whether it can plausibly account for the observed relationship.

REVIEW QUESTIONS

11.1 What is a confounding variable, and why do confounding variables create problems in research studies?

11.2 What are the four different types of validity that are used to evaluate the inferences made from the results of quantitative studies?

EXHIBIT 11.1 Donald T. Campbell (1916–1996)

During the late 1950s until the early 1990s, Donald Campbell was perhaps the most prominent quantitative research methodologist in the behavioral and social sciences. We are showing you Campbell's picture in this chapter because he coined the terms *internal validity* and *external validity* and provided most of the threats to internal validity discussed in this chapter (Campbell, 1957; Campbell & Stanley, 1963). Campbell always emphasized the importance of *ruling out alternative explanations* of research findings. Campbell's legacy has been present in earlier chapters of this book, including Chapter 7 (Campbell & Fiske, 1959), which provided the ideas of convergent and discriminant evidence. Campbell (1988) provided the concept of multiple operationalism discussed in this chapter. Chapters 12 and 13 also draw heavily from Campbell's work, because Campbell coined the term *quasi-experimentation* and Campbell and Stanley provided the first systematic comparison of weak, quasi-, and strong or randomized experimental designs (Campbell & Stanley; Cook & Campbell, 1979). The third edition of Campbell's quasi-experimentation book came out after his death (Shadish, Cook, & Campbell, 2002), and it's currently the standard reference on the subject. Campbell also contributed to the philosophy of social science through his concept of *evolutionary epistemology*. To learn more about Donald Campbell, check him out on Google or another search engine.

Internal Validity (i.e., Causal Validity)

Internal validity is a term coined by Campbell and Stanley (1963). Cook and Campbell (1979) later refined the concept to refer to the "approximate validity with which we infer that a relationship between two variables is causal" (p. 37). It will help you to think of internal validity as also being called **causal validity** because that is exactly what it is about; it's about establishing evidence of *cause and effect*.

- **Internal (or causal) validity** The ability to infer that a causal relationship exists between two variables

Although research is conducted for the multiple purposes of description, exploration, explanation, prediction, and influence, a large amount of research focuses on the goal of attempting to determine whether a causal relationship exists between the independent and dependent variables being investigated.

Two Major Types of Causal Relationships

Shadish et al. (2002) have pointed out that there are two types of causal relationships: causal description and causal explanation. **Causal description** refers to describing the consequences of manipulating an independent variable. **Causal explanation** refers to explaining the mechanisms through which and the conditions under which a causal relationship holds. For example, assume that a study was conducted to investigate the benefit derived from incorporating a 10-month intensive internship program into the education of future teachers. Assume further that this study demonstrated that teachers who participated in the program were evaluated by their principals as being more effective than teachers who participated in the traditional 2- to 3-month internship. This study would provide evidence of causal description because it would have described the overall causal relationship that exists between the intensive internship program (compared to the traditional program) and later teaching effectiveness.

- **Causal description** Describing the consequences of manipulating an independent variable
- **Causal explanation** Explaining the mechanisms through which and the conditions under which a causal relationship holds

This study would not, however, explain exactly how or why this causal relationship exists. The teachers participating in the experimental program might be more effective for any of a number of reasons, such as the program giving them better skills to cope with difficult children, better organizational skills, better skills at presentation of material, more realistic expectations of the demands of the teaching profession, and so on. A full causal explanation of why the causal relationship exists "show[s] how the causally efficacious parts of the treatment influence the causally affected parts of the outcome through identified mediating processes" (Shadish et al., 2002, p. 9). In other words, causal explanation would require that you identify and show how the processes involved in the intensive internship program cause changes in the participants' later effectiveness as teachers. Generally speaking, once causal description is shown, much subsequent research is directed at explaining why and how the descriptive relationship exists (i.e., causal explanation research often follows causal description research).

The practical importance of causal explanation can be seen if a subsequent study does not replicate the beneficial effect previously demonstrated from the 10-month internship program. If explanatory studies had been conducted, this information could be used to show how to fix the program that did not produce the beneficial results. However, identifying how and why a causal relationship exists is more difficult than describing that overall relationship.

Criteria for Inferring Causation

Three types of evidence are needed to reach a conclusion of causation (i.e., that changes in your independent variable produce changes in your dependent variable).

Condition 1: the *relationship condition*. First, you need evidence that the independent and dependent variables are associated or correlated or *related*. Do changes in the independent variable correspond to changes in the dependent variable? For example, assume that you want to know whether being absent from school, the independent variable, has any effect on the grades students make, the dependent variable. If there is no relationship between these two variables, then one cannot directly affect the other; however, if there is a relationship between the variables, it is possible that they are causally related. Note that we used the word *possible* because evidence of association or covariation or correlation does *not* provide sufficient evidence of causation! *Evidence of association is necessary but not sufficient to infer causation.*

Condition 2: the *temporal antecedence condition*. The second type of evidence needed to infer causation is the correct temporal ordering of the variables being investigated, because *a cause must precede an effect*. This means that you need some knowledge of the time sequence of the events. If you cannot establish the correct temporal order, the problem is called **ambiguous temporal precedence** (i.e., you don't know if X causes Y or if Y causes X). This threat to internal validity is not a problem in experimental research because the researcher manipulates the independent variable (X) and then studies the effect (on dependent variable Y).

- **Ambiguous temporal precedence** The inability to specify which variable is the cause and which is the effect

In some nonexperimental studies, especially those that only investigate the degree of relationship between two variables with data collected at a single point in time, it is frequently unclear whether variable A precedes variable B or vice versa. For example, assume that you collected self-report data from a sample of 1,500 people at one point in time on two variables: criminal behavior and incarceration. Also assume that your analysis showed a positive correlation between the frequency of criminal behavior and the frequency of incarceration. On the surface, you might think the causal direction was from criminal behavior to incarceration. However, many individuals learn techniques for engaging in criminal behavior from association with other individuals while incarcerated, so being incarcerated might lead to more criminal behavior. In this nonexperimental study, it would be difficult to identify which variable was the cause and which was the effect because it is difficult to identify which variable came first. Remember this key point: If you want to make a claim of causation, you must have evidence of the temporal order of the relationship because *a cause must precede an effect*.

Condition 3: the *lack of alternative explanation condition*. The third type of evidence needed is that the variables being investigated are the ones that are causally related rather than being caused by some confounding extraneous variable. In other words, you should look for variables *other than* the independent variable that might explain the change observed in the dependent variable, and these competing explanations must be ruled out. In the "Pepsi Challenge" experiment, color of the cup was an alternative explanation for the participants' preference selections. In the example of student grades and attendance, it is possible that *both* the grades students get and their attendance at school are caused by parents monitoring their children. Children whose parents do not monitor their children's behavior might have poorer grades and lower school attendance, whereas children who are monitored by their parents might get better grades and have fewer absences. In this instance, there is still a relationship between grades and school attendance, but the cause of this relationship is the third variable: parent monitoring. **Third variable** is simply another term or name that researchers use to refer to a confounding

- **Third variable** A confounding extraneous variable

extraneous variable. *The "third-variable problem" means that two variables of interest might be correlated not because they are causally related but because they are both caused by or related to some third variable.*

It is very important to remember that researchers cannot automatically assume causality just because two or more variables are related (condition 1). Before you can reach the conclusion of causation, you must also meet the other two conditions, establishing correct temporal ordering (condition 2) and ruling out alternative explanations due to third variables (condition three). Establishing these conditions is easily accomplished in strong experimental designs because (a) the experimenter actively manipulates the presentation of the independent variable (the causal variable) and observes the effect on the dependent variable and (b) the experimenter randomly assigns participants to the treatment and control groups so that the groups are equated on all extraneous variables. Nonexperimental research studies also frequently attempt to infer causality. In nonexperimental research, condition 2 (showing direction of causation) is more difficult to establish because of the difficulty in showing the temporal sequencing of events. Ruling out the possible influence of confounding variables (i.e., "the third-variable problem") is especially problematic in nonexperimental research.

11.3 What is internal validity?

11.4 What are the two types of causal relationships, and how do these two types of causal relationships differ?

11.5 What type of evidence is needed to infer causality, and how does each type of evidence contribute to making a causal inference?

Threats to Internal Validity in Single-Group Designs

To infer that one variable caused an effect observed in another variable, we must control for all other possible causes. These other possible causes are threats to internal validity because they represent rival or competing or alternative explanations for the results. When alternative explanations exist, it is impossible to reach a solid causal explanation, leading to suspect results that cannot and should not be taken seriously. This is why it is necessary to control for and eliminate the systematic influence of these threats.

- **One-group pretest-posttest design** Administering a posttest to a single group of participants after they have been pretested and given an experimental treatment condition

Now we discuss the threats to internal validity in single-group research designs, such as the **one-group pretest-posttest design** shown in Figure 11.1. As Figure 11.1 illustrates, this is a research design in which one group of participants is pretested on some dependent variable; they are then administered a treatment condition; and, after this treatment is administered, they are posttested on the dependent variable.

FIGURE 11.1 One-group pretest-posttest design

Pretest	Treatment	Posttest measure
O_1	X	O_2

History

- **History** Any event, other than a planned treatment event, that occurs between the pretest and posttest measurements of the dependent variable and influences the postmeasurement of the dependent variable

History refers to any events, other than any planned treatment event, that occur between the first and second measurements of the dependent variable. In its basic form, it is a threat to single-group designs such as the one illustrated in Figure 11.2. These events, in addition to any treatment effect, can influence the postmeasurement of the dependent variable; therefore, these events are confounded with the treatment effect and are rival explanations for the change that occurs between pretest and posttest measurements in one-group designs.

Consider a study investigating the effect of a peer-tutoring procedure on spelling performance. In this procedure, one student serves as a tutor and the other as a tutee. Tutors dictate words to a tutee, provide feedback as to whether the tutee spells the word correctly, and then provide the correct spelling if the word is spelled wrong. After a given number of words, the students reverse roles and continue the tutoring procedure. The difficulty with this assumption is that a time interval elapsed between the pretest and posttest measurements. It is possible that some event other than just the tutoring system had an effect on the participants during this time and that this event influenced their performance on the spelling posttest. For example, during implementation of the peer-tutoring system, perhaps the principal was curious and entered the room and observed the instruction. This might have made the teacher and student nervous and led to lower scores that would have otherwise have occurred. In this case, the presence of the principal causes a history effect because the presence is confounded with the actual treatment (i.e., they occur together). History events are threats to the internal validity of studies when they are plausible rival explanations for the outcome of the study. The history threat is especially worrisome (a) when something in addition to the treatment occurs between the pretest and posttest measurements of the dependent variable and (b) when the time interval between pretest and posttest measurement is lengthy.

FIGURE 11.2 Illustration of extraneous history events

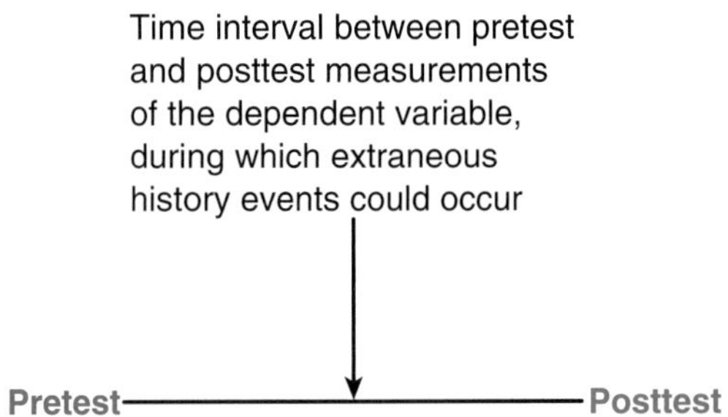

Maturation

- **Maturation** Any physical or mental change that occurs over time that affects performance on the dependent variable

Maturation refers to physical or mental changes that occur within individuals over time, such as aging, learning, boredom, hunger, and fatigue. Such changes can affect an individual's performance on some dependent variables. Because such changes might alter performance on the dependent variable, they are threats to the internal validity of a study (i.e., you don't know if the treatment or maturation is the real cause of change observed from pretest to posttest). If you use the one-group pretest-posttest design and you administer a treatment between the pretest and posttest, you might want to conclude that the change is due to your treatment, but any or all of the measured change from pretest to posttest could be due to maturation.

For example, assume that you want to assess the effect of a new program on the development of self-efficacy of children in the first grade. To test the effect of this program, you decide to pretest a group of first graders on self-efficacy before they enter your program and then test them a second time after they have been in your program for a year. At the end, perhaps you find that the children made significant advances in their self-efficacy. Although it might be tempting to attribute the improvement to your new program, all or part of the improvement might have been due to a maturation effect, or the improvement in self-efficacy that would have taken place without the program.

Testing

Testing refers to changes that may occur in participants' scores obtained on the second administration of a test as a result of previously having taken the test. In other words, the experience of having taken a pretest may alter the results obtained on the posttest, independent of any treatment effect or experimental manipulation intervening between the pretest and the posttest. Taking the pretest does a number of things that can alter a person's performance on a subsequent administration of the same test. Taking a test familiarizes you with the content of the test. After taking a test, you might think about errors you made that you could correct if you took the test again. When the test is administered a second time, you are already familiar with it and might remember some of your prior responses. This can lead to enhanced performance that is entirely tied to the initial or pretest administration. Any alteration in performance as a result of a testing effect threatens the internal validity of a one-group study because it serves as a rival hypothesis to the treatment effect. Whenever the same test is administered on multiple occasions, some control needs to be implemented to rule out the effect of testing as an alternative or rival hypothesis.

■ **Testing** Any change in scores obtained on the second administration of a test as a result of having previously taken the test

Instrumentation

Instrumentation refers to any change that occurs in the measuring instrument. An instrumentation threat occurs in two primary ways. First, it can occur when the measurement instrument that is used during pretesting is different from that used during posttesting. If the tests used during pretesting and posttesting are not equivalent, a difference between the two performance measures might be strictly due to the difference in the way the two tests assess performance. For example, assume that children with dyslexia are tested at time 1 with one test of rhyme sensitivity and are tested 2 years later with a different test of rhyme sensitivity. If a comparison is made of rhyme sensitivity from time 1 and 2 years later at time 2, any difference that is observed could be due to the children's enhanced development of rhyme sensitivity. However, the change could also be due to the differences in the way the two tests measure rhyme sensitivity, which would be an instrumentation effect that would represent a rival explanation for the change observed.

■ **Instrumentation** Any change that occurs in the way the dependent variable is measured

Second, instrumentation can occur when data are collected through observation. Many educational researchers use human observers to collect data. Human observers such as teachers are, unfortunately, subject to such influences as fatigue, boredom, and learning processes. For example, interviewers might gain additional skill with conducting an interview or with observing a particular type of behavior, producing changes in the data collected that cannot be attributed to either the participant or any experimental conditions being tested in the study. This is why studies that use human observers to collect data typically use more than one observer and have each observer go through a training program. In this way, some of the biases that are inherent in making observations can be minimized, and the various observers can serve as checks on one another to ensure that accurate data are being collected.

Regression Artifacts

- **Regression artifact** The tendency of very high pretest scores to become lower and very low pretest scores to become higher on posttesting

The concept of **regression artifact** (also called *regression toward the mean*) refers to the fact that *extreme (high or low) scores will tend to regress or move toward the mean of a distribution on a second testing or assessment.* Very low scores tend to become a little higher and very high scores tend to become a little lower. Many studies investigate special groups of individuals such as children with learning disabilities or people with a specific deficiency such as poor reading or low mathematical ability. These special groups of research participants are typically identified by having extreme scores such as low reading comprehension scores. After the research participants are selected based on low scores, they are given some experimental treatment condition to improve their deficiency or ameliorate the special condition, and then they are tested again to see if they have changed. Any positive change from pretesting to posttesting is frequently taken as evidence of the efficacy of the treatment program. However, the internal validity of such a study could be threatened because low-scoring research participants might tend to score higher on posttesting not because of any experimental treatment effect but simply because of a regression artifact. The key point to remember here is that whenever you select participants based on *very low or very high* scores, you need to worry about regression to the mean because that might be the reason for the change in test scores and not the treatment condition. (Time for a research joke: "What occurs when two highly intelligent professors have a child?" Answer: "Regression to the mean.")

See Journal Article 11.1 on the Student Study Site.

Threats to Internal Validity in Multigroup Designs

Before discussing the threats to validity in multigroup designs, we make a key point: *All of the basic (i.e., nondifferential) threats to internal validity for single-group designs just discussed would have been eliminated if a control group had been included.* Adding a control group to a single-group design produces a **multigroup research design**, such as the one shown in Figure 11.3. You are probably wondering, Why does inclusion of a control group eliminate so many threats? We will answer this in the next paragraph.

- **Multigroup research design** A research design that includes more than one group of participants

The addition of a control group (i.e., moving from a one-group design to a multigroup design) enables you to untangle the confounding effect of the previous basic threats from the influence of the independent variable. As long as the effect of a basic threat (e.g., history, maturation, testing, instrumentation, or regression artifact) occurs for both groups, it will not cause a problem in the multigroup design because you are determining the treatment effect by comparing the treatment group with a control group. None of the *difference* between the two groups can be due to the basic threat *as long as the basic threat affects both groups equally.* Conversely, in the one-group design, you determine the treatment effect by comparing the pretest scores of the individuals in the single group with their posttest scores, so you have no way of separating the effect of one of the basic threats from the effect of the treatment.

You will see in a moment that the basic threats can appear in a more complicated form in multigroup designs if the basic effect occurs for one group but not for the other group. These threats have different names to make this distinction. First, we discuss a *very serious threat* that affects only multigroup designs.

FIGURE 11.3 Two-group design comparing an experimental group that receives a treatment condition with a control group that does not receive the treatment condition

	Treatment	Posttest
Group A	X	O_2
Group B	—	O_2

Differential Selection

Differential selection (sometimes just called *selection*) is a threat to the internal validity of a multigroup study when a difference exists, at the outset of the research study, between the characteristics of the participants in the treatment and control groups. Participants in different groups can differ in many ways, as illustrated in Table 11.1. One common way in which this difference can occur is if you, the researcher, use nonequivalent groups of participants that are already formed (e.g., classes of students). Remember this: *it is a serious problem when the groups differ on variables other than the independent variable*, and this is called differential selection.

Differential selection Selecting participants who have different characteristics for the various treatment groups

For example, assume that you want to use the two-group design in Figure 11.3 to test a procedure for enhancing young children's motivation to learn. You want to administer a new procedure to one group of fourth-grade children and compare their motivation to learn, after this procedure has been implemented, with that of a group of fourth-grade children who have not experienced this procedure. In conducting this study, you obtain permission from your local school district. However, you find that you have to administer the experimental procedure to one fourth-grade class and compare its performance with that of another fourth-grade class (your control group). This might not seem to be a problem because both groups are fourth-grade students. However, there is no guarantee that the students in these two classes have the same motivation to learn before the study is conducted. If the class that receives the experimental procedure had a greater motivation to learn before conducting the study, they will naturally show up as having a greater motivation to learn after the experimental procedure is implemented. Any difference in motivation to learn between the two fourth-grade classes could therefore be due entirely to a selection bias.

Fortunately there is a general solution to differential selection that can sometimes be used by the researcher. The solution is to *randomly assign* participants to the groups. Random assignment equates your groups (when sample size is large enough), so there are no systematic initial differences. When this is the case, the treatment is the only difference between the groups, and you can claim that the treatment is the cause of the posttest differences. Random assignment thus "rules out" or eliminates the threat of differential selection.

TABLE 11.1 Characteristics on Which Research Participants Can Differ

Ability to do well on tests	Home environment	Reading ability
Age	Intelligence	Religious beliefs
Anxiety level	Language ability	Self-esteem
Attitudes toward research	Learning style	Socioeconomic status
Coordination	Maturity	Spelling ability
Curiosity	Motivation to learn	Stress level
Ethnicity	Personality type	Time spent on homework
Gender	Political beliefs	Vocabulary
Hearing ability	Quality of eyesight	

Additive and Interactive Effects

- **Additive and interactive effects** Occur when two or more basic threats to internal validity combine to produce a more complex bias

The term **additive and interactive effects** refers to the fact that the threats to internal validity can combine to produce complex biases *in multigroup designs*. We will briefly discuss some of these threats that have been identified by research methodologists. As we discuss these threats, keep in mind the key idea that *in a multigroup design your goal is for the comparison groups (e.g., treatment group and control group) to be similar on all variables except for the independent variable that delineates the different conditions for comparison.* We have mentioned in Chapters 2 and 10 that the best way to "equate the groups" on all extraneous variables at the start of an experiment is to use *random assignment.* Once your experiment begins, however, you must continue to treat the treatment and control groups in the same way, with the single exception being that the participants receive the different conditions defined by your independent variable.

- **Selection-history effect** Occurs when an event taking place between the pretest and posttest differentially affects comparison groups and obscures the treatment effect

Differential selection, or the fact that the comparison groups are composed of different kinds of people, can combine with any of the basic threats discussed above for single-group designs. For example, a **selection-history effect** occurs when the groups are exposed to the same history event but react differently to it. This can happen when the groups are composed of different kinds of people. A closely related effect is a *differential history* effect, where the groups are exposed to different history events and these produce differences between the groups on the dependent variable measure. For simplicity, we treat *selection-history* and *differential history* as synonyms because the key problem is the same—the groups become different because of a complex history factor.

- **Selection-maturation effect** Occurs when comparison groups mature at different rates, obscuring the treatment effect

A **selection-maturation effect** occurs if the groups mature at different rates. This can happen when the groups are composed of different people, specifically when the participants in one group (e.g., treatment) mature at a different rate than do the participants in the other group (e.g., control). For example, if you were comparing 6-year-olds and 10-year-olds, part of the difference on the dependent variable at the end of the study might be due to the groups maturing at different rates.

- **Attrition** Loss of people who do not complete the experiment

Attrition refers to the fact that some individuals do not complete the outcome measures. This can occur for any of a variety of reasons, such as failure to show up at the scheduled time and place or not participating in all phases of the study. Attrition becomes a problem to internal validity *when it causes the groups to become different.* **Differential attrition** (also called *selection-attrition*) refers to a bias that occurs in a multigroup study when the people who do *not* complete the outcome (i.e., the dropouts) makes the groups different (i.e., nonequivalent). Loss of participants is a problem when it causes the groups to become different in a way that produces differences on the dependent variable.

Similarly, the other three basic threats can also interact with selection. A **selection-testing effect** occurs if the groups react differently to taking the pretest, resulting in differences on the dependent variable. A **selection-instrumentation effect** occurs if the groups react differently to an instrumentation effect. Last, a **selection-regression effect** occurs if one group's scores regress to the mean more than another group's scores.

Fortunately, there is a general solution to the additive and interactive threats! What do you think it is? (Hint: What was the solution to differential selection?) If you said random assignment, you are correct! When the groups are composed of the same kinds of people (which is what random assignment does), additive and interactive threats are unlikely.

- **Differential attrition** A differential loss of participants from the various comparison groups that obscures the treatment effect
- **Selection-testing effect** Occurs when groups react to the pretest differently, obscuring the treatment effect

REVIEW QUESTIONS

11.6 What is an ambiguous temporal precedence threat, and why does it threaten internal validity?

11.7 What is a history threat, and how does it operate?

11.8 What is a maturation threat, and how does it operate?

11.9 What is a testing threat, and why does this threat exist?

11.10 What is an instrumentation threat, and when would this threat exist?

11.11 What is a regression artifact threat, and why does this threat exist?

11.12 What is a differential selection threat, and when would this threat exist?

11.13 What is meant by an additive and interactive effect as a threat to internal validity?

11.14 What is the key problem produced by additive and interactive effects?

External Validity (i.e., Generalizing Validity)

External validity is a term coined by Campbell and Stanley (1963) and extended by Shadish et al. (2002) to refer to the extent to which the results of a study can be generalized to and across populations of persons, settings, times, outcomes, and treatment variations. It will help you to *think of external validity as also being called* **generalizing validity** *because that is what it is about.* It's about generalizing! In Chapter 1, we state that one of the basic assumptions of science is that there are regularities in human behavior and these regularities can be discovered through systematic research. Whenever we conduct a research study, we are attempting to discover these regularities. However, each research study is conducted on a specific sample of individuals, in a specific setting, with a specific independent variable, with specific outcomes, and at a specific point in time.

To generalize the results from a single research study, you would have to identify a target group of individuals, settings, times, outcomes, and treatment variations and then

- **Selection-instrumentation effect** Occurs when groups react differently to changes in instrumentation, obscuring the treatment effect
- **Selection-regression effect** Occurs when groups regress to the mean, obscuring the treatment effect

- **External (or generalizing) validity** The extent to which the study results can be generalized to and across populations of persons, settings, times, outcomes, and treatment variations
- **Population validity** The ability to generalize the study results to individuals who were not included in the study
- **Target population** The larger population to whom the study results are to be generalized
- **Generalizing to a population** Applying a finding based on a research study sample (e.g., a sample average or correlation) to the target population (e.g., the population average or correlation)
- **Generalizing across subpopulations** Applying a finding based on a research study sample (e.g., a sample average or correlation) to all subgroups in the target population

randomly select from these populations so that you have a sample representative of these populations. Most studies cannot randomly sample from the populations of individuals, settings, times, outcomes, and treatment variations because of the expense, time, and effort involved. Therefore, all studies contain characteristics that threaten their external validity. We now discuss the different kinds of external validity and identify some factors that can limit the generalizability of a study.

Population Validity

Population validity is the ability to generalize from the sample of individuals on which a study was conducted to the larger target population of individuals and across different subpopulations within the larger target population. The **target population** is the larger population, such as all children with a learning disability, to whom the research study results are to be generalized. Within this larger target population, there are many subpopulations, such as male and female children with a learning disability. Population validity, therefore, has the two components of generalizing from a sample to a target population and generalizing from a sample across the types of persons in the target population.

Generalizing from a sample of individuals to the larger target population is a two-step process of defining the larger target population of individuals of interest and then randomly selecting a sample of individuals from this target population, as illustrated in Figure 11.4. Random sampling is required to obtain a representative sample. Random sampling is discussed in depth in Chapter 10 (the last chapter!) so we do not repeat that material here. Just remember that if you want to generalize from a single sample to a population, then you need to use one of the random sampling techniques discussed in that chapter.

Our discussion of external validity thus far has focused on **generalizing from a sample to a specific target population**. However, we should not forget that external validity also refers to the goal of **generalizing across subpopulations**. In any target population, there are many specific subpopulations (e.g., based on gender, age, grade level, religion, nation of origin, intelligence). When we talk about generalizing across populations, we are really asking whether the results hold for each of the subpopulations within the target population.

FIGURE 11.4 Two-step process involved in achieving external validity

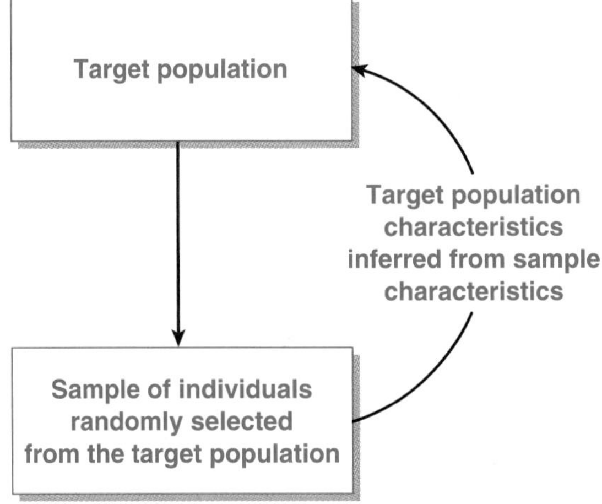

Assume that we conducted a study investigating a specific treatment enhancing the reading ability of children with dyslexia. Assume further that we randomly selected 500 children from the target population of children with dyslexia in the United States and found that the treatment was effective. Because we had randomly selected our sample (something that seldom occurs in this type of study), we could generalize back *to* the target population and conclude that children with dyslexia would, on the average, benefit from the treatment program. The results would not, however, say anything about the effectiveness of the treatment for the many subpopulations within the larger target population. You might ask: Can the results be generalized to both male and female children with dyslexia or to children with dyslexia of various socioeconomic groups, age groups, intellectual levels, and so forth? This is the issue of generalizing *across* subpopulations. In fact, many studies that are conducted to test the generalization of a specific treatment across subpopulations are attempting to identify the specific subpopulations to which a treatment can and cannot be generalized. In this type of research, the researcher determines whether a moderator variable is significant. (Please see Table 2.2 in Chapter 2 on page 38 for a definition of *moderator variable* because this is an important concept in quantitative research.)

Ecological Validity

Ecological validity is the ability to generalize the results of a study across settings. For example, one study might be conducted in a school whose computers are slow and antiquated. If the results obtained from this study can be generalized to other settings, such as a school well equipped with state-of-the-art technology, then the study possesses ecological validity. Ecological validity therefore exists to the extent that the study results are independent of the setting in which the study was conducted.

- **Ecological validity** The ability to generalize the study results across settings

One of the subtle setting factors that can affect the ability to generalize the results of a study is the participant's knowledge of the fact that he or she is participating in a study. This is known as a reactivity effect. **Reactivity** refers to the alteration in performance that can occur as a result of being aware that one is participating in a research study. It is similar to the effect many people feel when they are on television for the first time: Once you know the camera is on you, you might shift to your "television" behavior. A similar phenomenon can occur in research studies. Once you know you are in a research study, you might change your behavior. A reactivity effect can therefore threaten both the internal and external validity of a study.

- **Reactivity** An alteration in performance that occurs as a result of being aware of participating in a study

Temporal Validity

Temporal validity refers to the extent to which the results of a study can be generalized across time. Temporal validity is an issue because most educational research studies are conducted during one time period. For example, Thorkildsen, Nolen, and Fournier (1994) assessed children's views of several practices that teachers use to influence motivation to learn. The data for this study were collected by interviewing 7- to 12-year-old children at one point in time. Although the data are valid for the time period in which they were collected, there is no assurance that the same results would hold true 25 years later. Frequently, it is assumed that the results of studies are invariant across time. Although this might exist for the results of some studies (e.g., reinforcement theory), it almost certainly does not exist for the results of others (e.g., attitudinal studies). Failure to consider the time variable can lead one to form erroneous conclusions about the current external validity of the study.

- **Temporal validity** The extent to which the study results can be generalized across time

Treatment Variation Validity

- **Treatment variation validity** The ability to generalize across variations of the treatment

Treatment variation validity is the ability to generalize the results across variations of the treatment. Treatment variation validity is an issue because the administration of a treatment often varies from one time or situation to the next. For example, many studies have been conducted demonstrating that cognitive behavior therapy is effective in treating depression. However, these studies have typically been conducted in the context of a research study that has provided maximum assurance that the therapists were competent and delivered the therapy in the prescribed manner. Therapists who administer behavior therapy to the general public, in contrast, vary considerably in their competency and the extent to which they deliver the therapy in the prescribed manner. This means that there is considerable variation in the way in which cognitive behavior therapy is administered. If cognitive behavior therapy produces a beneficial effect for the treatment of depression across these different variations in the way it is delivered, treatment generalization exists. If the therapy is beneficial only when administered exactly as prescribed by a competently trained therapist, then there is limited treatment generalization.

Outcome Validity

- **Outcome validity** The ability to generalize across different but related dependent variables

Outcome validity is the ability to generalize research results across different but related dependent variables. Outcome validity refers to the extent to which the independent variable influences a number of related outcome measures. For example, a job-training program is expected to increase the likelihood of getting a job after graduation. This is probably the primary outcome measure of interest. However, an equally important issue is maintaining the job. This means that the person must arrive on time, not miss work, and follow orders as well as demonstrate an acceptable level of performance. The effectiveness of the job-training program might increase the probability of getting a job but might have no effect on job retention because it has little impact on these other essential adaptive job skills. Sometimes one outcome measure demonstrates that the treatment was effective. However, other outcome measures show no effect and maybe even a negative effect. Using several outcome measures is always desirable because this gives a more complete picture of the overall effect of the treatment. Fortunately, this is one of the easier design features to implement. You just need to include several related dependent variables in your study to answer questions about generalizability across outcomes.

REVIEW QUESTIONS

11.15 What is external validity, and why is it important?

11.16 What is population validity, and why is it difficult to achieve?

11.17 What is ecological validity?

11.18 What is temporal validity?

11.19 What is treatment variation validity, and why can this be a threat to external validity?

11.20 What is outcome validity?

Construct Validity

Up to this point in the chapter, we have discussed internal and external or causal and generalizing validity. Conducting a research study also requires that the variables be adequately measured or "operationalized." The educational researcher is therefore faced with the task of identifying or devising some way of measuring the constructs being investigated. This is a problem of construct validity. **Construct validity** is the extent to which a higher-order construct, such as help seeking, teacher stress, or dyslexia, is accurately "operationalized" and measured in a particular study. **Operationalizing a construct** involves identifying a specific instrument to be used to empirically measure the construct.

- **Construct validity** The extent to which a higher-order construct is accurately operationalized and measured in a particular study
- **Operationalizing a construct** Identifying a specific instrument to empirically measure the construct

So how do we achieve construct validity? Construct validity is fostered by having a good definition and explanation of the meaning of the construct of interest and then identifying effective items to measure the construct. To learn more about how to measure constructs, refer to Chapter 7 ("Standardized Measurement and Assessment"), especially the section on validity. One general rule to remember is that if an already developed measure for a construct is available with reliability and validity data, then use that measure. Make sure, however, that the measure is likely to work with the specific kind of participants that you will have in your study. Developing new measures requires a lot of work and is especially difficult for beginning researchers.

Treatment Diffusion

Even if you have operationalized a construct well, we need to mention a construct problem that sometimes occurs in experimental research conducted in field settings. Because the researcher cannot control who interacts with whom in a field study, **treatment diffusion** can occur if participants in the treatment group interact or share resources with participants in the control group. If this happens, what is thought to represent the control condition is no longer correct because it has become contaminated with something from the treatment condition. The point is that it can be difficult to keep the levels of your independent variable (e.g., treatment and control) truly separate in a field experiment, and this can be hard to detect.

- **Treatment diffusion** The participants in one treatment condition are exposed to all or some of the other treatment condition

REVIEW QUESTIONS

11.21 What is construct validity, and how is it achieved?

11.22 What is treatment diffusion, and what might you do to prevent it?

Statistical Conclusion Validity

- **Statistical conclusion validity** The ability to infer that the independent and dependent variables are related in the larger population of interest and the strength of that relationship

Statistical conclusion validity is the validity with which you can infer that two variables are related and the estimated strength of that relationship is accurate. Statistical conclusion validity is important when you are making statistical inferences from the sample data to the population of interest. The first statistical inference is whether a relationship exists between the independent and dependent variables in the population. The second statistical inference is an estimate of the magnitude of the relationship between the independent and dependent variables in the population. Both of these inferences rely on statistical tests with sample data. We will discuss inferential statistics in more detail in Chapter 19. Making an inference about the magnitude of the relationship between variables involves computing what is called an "**effect size**" estimate. Right now, our key point is for you to realize that the inferences to populations that you make from the results of statistical tests based on sample data might or might not be valid.

REVIEW QUESTION

11.23 What is the basic idea of statistical conclusion validity?

■ **Effect size indicator** A measure of the strength or magnitude of a relationship between the independent and dependent variables

RESEARCH VALIDITY (OR "TRUSTWORTHINESS") IN QUALITATIVE RESEARCH

Discussions of the term *validity* have traditionally been attached to the quantitative research tradition. Not surprisingly, reactions by qualitative researchers have been mixed regarding whether this concept should be applied to qualitative research. At the extreme, some qualitative researchers have suggested that the traditional quantitative criteria of reliability and validity are not relevant to qualitative research (e.g., J. K. Smith, 1984). Smith contended that the basic assumptions of quantitative and qualitative research are incompatible and that the concepts of reliability and validity should therefore be abandoned. Most qualitative researchers, however, do not hold this viewpoint, and neither do we.

Most qualitative researchers argue that some qualitative research studies are better than others, and they use the term *validity* or *trustworthiness* to refer to this difference in quality. When qualitative researchers speak of research validity, they are usually referring to qualitative research that is plausible, credible, trustworthy, and therefore defensible. We believe it is important to think about the issue of validity in qualitative research and to examine some strategies that have been developed to maximize validity. A list of these strategies is provided in Table 11.2. Keep in mind that most of these strategies can also be used in quantitative research.

See Journal Article 11.2 on the Student Study Site.

One general strategy that was popularized in qualitative research methodology several decades ago, called **triangulation**, is a validation approach based on the search for convergence of results obtained by using multiple investigators, methods, data sources, and/or theoretical perspectives. This approach builds into your study and research process systematic cross-checking of information and conclusions through the use of multiple procedures or sources. As an *outcome*, "triangulation" is said to occur when your results converge on the same conclusion. However, findings sometimes do not converge but are divergent. This is not necessarily a problem, because it can be quite useful and important to look at our objects of study in different ways and learn from the different methods and perspectives. It is an "empirical question" whether findings converge or diverge, and both convergent and divergent findings are important. You will find in Table 11.2 four strategies—the use of multiple data sources, multiple research methods, multiple investigators, and multiple theoretical perspectives—that are important for good research, and the findings might or might not converge or "triangulate."

■ **Triangulation** A validation approach using multiple investigators, methods, data sources, and/or theoretical perspectives in the search for convergence of results

TABLE 11.2 Strategies Used to Promote Qualitative Research Validity

Strategy	*Description*
Critical friend	A type of peer review in action research. A critical friend is useful throughout a research project (beginning, middle, and end).
Extended fieldwork	To provide for both discovery and validation, the collection of data in the field over an extended time period
External audit	Using outside experts to assess the study's quality
Low-inference descriptors	The use of description phrased very similarly to the participants' accounts and researchers' field notes. Verbatims (i.e., direct quotations) are a commonly used type of low-inference descriptors.
Multiple data sources	The use of multiple sources of data to help understand a phenomenon (e.g., interviewing different people, including those who might have different perspectives about the research object)
Multiple investigators	The use of multiple researchers and observers (including participant researchers in participatory research) in collecting, analyzing, and interpreting data
Multiple methods	The use of multiple research methods (e.g., ethnography and grounded theory) and methods of data collection (e.g., questionnaires, observations, and focus groups) to study a phenomenon
Multiple theoretical perspectives	The use of multiple theories, disciplines, and perspectives to help interpret and explain the data
Negative-case sampling	Attempting to identify cases that might disconfirm the researcher's expectations and generalizations
Participant feedback or member checking	The discussion of the researcher's interpretations and conclusions with the study participants and other members of the participant community for verification, insight, and deeper understanding
Pattern matching	Predicting a series of results that form a distinctive pattern and then determining the degree to which the actual results fit the predicted pattern or "fingerprint" or "signature"
Peer review	Discussion of the researcher's actions and interpretations during a study and conclusions at the end of the study with other people. This includes discussion with a disinterested peer (e.g., with another researcher not directly involved). This peer should be skeptical and play the devil's advocate, challenging the researcher to provide solid evidence for any interpretations or conclusions. Discussion with peers who are familiar with the research can also provide useful challenges and insights.
Reflexivity	Continual self-awareness and critical self-reflection by the researcher on his or her assumptions, biases, predispositions, and actions, and their impact on the research situation and evolving interpretations
Researcher-as-detective	A metaphor characterizing the qualitative researcher as he or she searches for evidence about causes and effects. The researcher develops an understanding of the data through careful consideration of potential causes and effects and by systematically eliminating rival explanations or hypotheses until the final case is made beyond a reasonable doubt. The detective can utilize any of the strategies listed here.
Ruling out alternative explanations	Making sure that you have carefully examined evidence for competing or rival explanations and that yours is the best explanation
Triangulation	Cross-checking information and conclusions through the use of multiple procedures or sources. When the different procedures or sources are in agreement, you have corroboration or convergence; when the procedures or sources are not in agreement, you have divergence.

One potential threat to validity that researchers must be careful to watch out for is called **researcher bias**. This problem is summed up in a statement a colleague of ours once made. She said, "The problem with qualitative research is that the researchers 'find' what they want to find, and then they write up their results." It is true that the problem of researcher bias is sometimes an issue in qualitative research because qualitative research

Researcher bias Obtaining results consistent with what the researcher wants to find

tends to be exploratory and is open-ended and less structured than quantitative research. (One would be remiss, however, to think that researcher bias is never a problem in quantitative research.) Researcher bias tends to result from selective observation and selective recording of information and also from allowing one's personal views and perspectives to affect how data are interpreted and how the research is conducted.

- **Reflexivity** Self-reflection by the researcher on his or her assumptions, biases, predispositions and actions, and their impact on the research situation and evolving interpretations

- **Negative-case sampling** Attempting to identify cases that are expected to disconfirm the researcher's expectations and generalizations

The key strategy that is used to understand researcher bias is called **reflexivity**, which means that the researcher actively engages in critical self-reflection about his or her potential biases and predispositions (Table 11.2). Through reflexivity, researchers become more self-aware, and they monitor and attempt to control their biases. Many qualitative researchers include a distinct section in their research proposals entitled "Researcher Bias," in which they discuss their personal background, how it might affect their research, and what strategies they will use to address the potential problem. Another strategy that researchers use to reduce the effect of researcher bias is called **negative-case sampling** (Table 11.2). This means that researchers attempt carefully and purposively to search for examples that disconfirm their expectations and explanations about what they are studying. If you use this approach, you will find it more difficult to ignore important information, and you will come up with more credible and defensible results.

Now let's look at some types of validity that are important in qualitative research. We start with three types of validity that are especially relevant to qualitative research (Maxwell, 1992, 1996): descriptive validity, interpretive validity, and theoretical validity. After discussing these three forms of validity, the traditional types of validity used in quantitative research, internal and external validity, are discussed.

Descriptive Validity

- **Descriptive validity** The factual accuracy of an account as reported by the researcher

Descriptive validity is the factual accuracy of the account as reported by the researchers. The key questions that are addressed in descriptive validity are these:

- Did what was reported as taking place in the group being studied actually happen?
- Did the researchers accurately report what they saw and heard?

- **Multiple investigators** The use of multiple researchers and observers in collecting and interpreting the data

In other words, descriptive validity refers to accuracy in reporting descriptive information (description of events, objects, behaviors, people, settings, and so forth). This form of validity is important because description is a major objective in nearly all qualitative research.

One effective strategy used to obtain descriptive validity is the use of **multiple investigators** (Table 11.2). In the case of descriptive validity, it is helpful to use multiple observers to record and describe the research participants' behavior and the context in which they were located. The use of multiple observers allows cross-checking of observations to make sure the investigators agree about what took place. When corroboration (agreement) of observations across multiple investigators is obtained, it is less likely that outside reviewers of the research will question whether something occurred. As a result, the research will be more credible and defensible.

- **Interpretive or emic validity** Accurately portraying the study participants' perspectives and meanings, providing the insider's viewpoint

Interpretive or Emic Validity

Interpretive or emic validity refers to portraying accurately the *meanings attached by participants* to what is being studied. More specifically, it is the degree to which the qualitative researcher accurately understands research *participants'* viewpoints, thoughts, feelings, intentions, and experiences, and successfully portrays them in the research report. It is also called emic (which means insider perspective) validity because it refers to understanding and portraying the "insider's meanings and perspectives." The most important skill required for conducting qualitative research is understanding the research participants' "inner worlds" (i.e., their subjective worlds), and *interpretive validity is the degree of accuracy in presenting these inner worlds.* Accurate interpretive validity requires that the researcher get inside the heads of the participants, look through their eyes, and see and feel what they see and feel. In this way, the qualitative researcher can understand things from the participants' perspectives and thus provide a valid account of these perspectives.

Participant feedback (or **member checking**) is perhaps the most important strategy (see Table 11.2). By sharing your interpretations of participants' viewpoints with the participants and other members of the group, you may clear up areas of miscommunication. Do the people being studied agree with what you have said about them? Although this strategy is not perfect, because some participants may attempt to put on a good face, it frequently obtains useful information and often identifies inaccuracies.

- **Participant feedback (or member checking)** Discussion of the researcher's conclusions with the study participants

When writing the research report, using many **low-inference descriptors** is also helpful so that the reader can experience the participants' actual language, dialect, and personal meanings (Table 11.2). In this way, the reader can hear how the participants think and feel about issues and experiences. A *verbatim* is the lowest-inference descriptor of all because the participants' exact words are provided in direct quotations. Here is an example of a verbatim from a high school dropout who was part of an ethnographic study of high school dropouts:

- **Low-inference descriptors** A description that is phrased very similarly to the participants' accounts and the researchers' field notes

> I wouldn't do the work. I didn't like the teacher and I didn't like my Mom and Dad. So, even if I did my work, I wouldn't turn it in. I completed it. I just didn't want to turn it in. I was angry with my Mom and Dad because they were talking about moving out of state at the time. (Okey & Cusick, 1995, p. 257)

This verbatim provides some description (i.e., what the participant did), but it also provides some information about the participant's interpretations and personal meanings (which is the topic of interpretive validity). The participant expresses his frustration and anger toward his parents and teacher and shares with us what homework meant to him at the time and why he acted as he did. By reading verbatims like this one, readers of a report can experience for themselves the participants' perspectives. Again, getting into the minds of research participants is a common goal in qualitative research, and Maxwell (1992, 1996) called our accuracy in portraying this "inner content" interpretive validity.

Theoretical Validity

Theoretical validity is the degree to which a theoretical explanation developed in a research study fits the data and is therefore credible and defensible. As we discuss in Chapter 1, theory usually refers to discussions of *how* a phenomenon operates and *why* it operates as it does. Theory is usually more abstract and less concrete than description and interpretation. Theory development moves beyond "just the facts" and provides an explanation of the phenomenon. In the words of Joseph Maxwell (1992),

- **Theoretical validity** The degree to which a theoretical explanation fits the data

> One could label the student's throwing of the eraser as an act of resistance, and connect this act to the repressive behavior or values of the teacher, the social structure of the school, and class relationships in U.S. society. The identification of the throwing as "resistance" constitutes the application of a theoretical construct. . . . The connection of this to other aspects of the participants, the school, or the community constitutes the postulation of theoretical relationships among these constructs. (p. 291)

In this example, the theoretical construct of resistance is used to explain the student's behavior. Maxwell points out that the construct of resistance may also be related to other theoretical constructs or variables. In fact, theories are often developed by relating multiple theoretical constructs.

A strategy for promoting theoretical validity is **extended fieldwork** (Table 11.2). This means spending a sufficient amount of time studying your research participants and their setting so that you can have confidence that the patterns of relationships you believe are operating are stable and so that you can understand why these relationships occur. As you spend more time in the field collecting data and generating and testing your interpretations, your theoretical explanation might become more detailed and intricate. You may decide to use the strategy called **multiple theoretical perspectives** (Table 11.2). This means that you would examine how the phenomenon being studied would be explained by different theories or different perspectives. The various theories/perspectives might provide you with insights and help you develop a more useful explanation. In a related way, you might also use multiple investigators and consider their ideas and explanations.

As you develop your theoretical explanation, you should make some predictions based on your theory and test the accuracy of your predictions. When doing this, you can use the **pattern-matching** strategy (Table 11.2). In pattern matching, the strategy is to make several predictions at once; then, if all of the predictions occur as predicted (i.e., if the pattern or "fingerprint" is found), you have good evidence supporting your explanation. As you develop your theoretical explanation, you should also use the negative-case sampling strategy mentioned earlier (Table 11.2). That is, you must always search for cases or examples that do not fit your explanation so that you do not simply locate data that support your developing theory. As a general rule, your final explanation should accurately reflect the majority of the people in your research study and you can build in contingency explanations for the other cases. Another useful strategy for promoting theoretical validity is called **peer review** (Table 11.2), which means that you spend time discussing your explanation with your colleagues so that they can identify any problems in it. In some cases, you will find that you will need to go back to the field and collect additional data. A related strategy is called **critical friend**. Used by action researchers, this is a type of peer review. A critical friend is someone you trust whom you interact with throughout your research project (beginning, middle, and end) to provide honest and open feedback about your actions. Finally, when developing a theoretical explanation, you must also think about the issues of internal (causal) validity and external (generalizing) validity, to which we now turn.

- **Extended fieldwork** Collecting data in the field over an extended period of time
- **Multiple theoretical perspectives** The use of multiple theories, disciplines, and perspectives to interpret and explain the data
- **Pattern matching** Predicting a pattern of results and determining whether the actual results fit the predicted fingerprint or signature pattern
- **Peer review** Discussing one's interpretations and conclusions with peers or colleagues
- **Critical friend** A type of peer review in which one trusted friend provides honest and open feedback about your actions throughout the study

Internal Validity

You are already familiar with internal validity (or causal validity) as it is used in quantitative research. As you know, internal validity is the degree to which a researcher is justified in concluding that an observed relationship is causal. Often qualitative researchers are not interested in cause-and-effect relationships among variables because they study particulars and are interested in description. Sometimes, however, qualitative researchers are interested in identifying local or singular causes and effects. Further, qualitative research can be very helpful in describing "how" and "why" phenomena operate (i.e., studying process and obtaining causal explanation) and in developing and testing preliminary causal hypotheses and theories (Blatter & Haverland, 2012; Campbell, 1979; Johnson, 1994; LeCompte & Preissle, 1993; Strauss, 1995; Yin, 2014). However, after potential causal relationships are studied using qualitative research, they should be tested and confirmed by using experimental methods when this is feasible. They also should be checked for generalizability versus situational or context boundedness of the causal conclusions.

When qualitative researchers identify potential cause-and-effect relationships, they must think about many of the same issues of internal validity and the strategies used to obtain theoretical validity discussed earlier in this chapter. The qualitative researcher takes on the role of the "detective" searching for cause(s) of a phenomenon, examining each possible "clue" and attempting to rule out each rival explanation generated (see **researcher-as-detective** and **ruling out alternative explanations** in Table 11.2). When trying to identify a causal relationship, the researcher makes mental comparisons. The researcher can think about what would have happened if the causal factor had not occurred. The researcher can sometimes rely on his or her expert opinion, as well as published research studies, in deciding what would have happened. If the event is something that should occur again, the researcher can check again to see whether the causal factor precedes the outcome. That is, when the causal factor occurs, does the effect follow, and when the causal factor does not occur, does the effect not follow?

- **Researcher-as-detective** A metaphor applied to the researcher who is searching for cause and effect
- **Ruling out alternative explanations** Making sure that other explanations of your conclusion are not better than the explanation you are using

When a researcher believes that an observed relationship is causal, he or she must also attempt to make sure that the observed change in the dependent variable or outcome is due to the independent variable or event and not to something else. The successful researcher will make a list of rival explanations that are possible reasons for the relationship other than the originally suspected cause. One way to identify rival explanations is to be a skeptic and think of reasons why the relationship should *not* be causal. After the list has been developed, each rival explanation must be examined. Sometimes you will be able to check a rival explanation against the data you have already collected through additional data analysis. At other times, you will need to collect additional data. One strategy would be to observe the relationship you believe to be causal under conditions in which the confounding factor is not present and compare this outcome with the original outcome. For example, if you concluded that a teacher effectively maintained classroom discipline on a given day but a critic maintained that this effect was the result of a parent visiting the classroom on that day, then you should try to observe the teacher again when the parent is not present. If the teacher is still successful, you have some evidence that the original finding was not due to the presence of the parent.

All the strategies shown in Table 11.2 are used to improve the internal validity of qualitative research. Now we explain the only two strategies not yet discussed: multiple methods and multiple data sources. When using **multiple methods** (Table 11.2), the researcher uses more than one method of research in a single research study. The word *methods* is used broadly here to refer to different methods of research (ethnography, correlational, experimental, and so forth) as well as to different methods of data collection (e.g., interviews, questionnaires, focus groups, observations). You can intermix any of these methods.

- **Multiple methods** The use of multiple research and data collection methods

Here is an example of multiple methods. Perhaps you are interested in why students in an elementary classroom stigmatize a certain student named Brian. A stigmatized student is an individual who is not well liked, has a lower status, and is seen as different from the "normal" students. Perhaps Brian has a different haircut than the other students, is dressed differently, or doesn't act like the other students. In this case, you might decide to observe how students treat Brian in various situations. In addition to *observing* the students, you will probably decide to conduct *interviews* with Brian and the other students to understand their beliefs and feelings about Brian. A strength of observational data is that you can see the students' behaviors. A weakness of interviews is that what the students say and what they actually do may be different. However, using interviews, you can delve into the students' thinking and reasoning, whereas you cannot do this using observational data. Therefore, the whole obtained from the use of observations and interviews will likely be better than the parts.

■ **Multiple data sources** The use of multiple sources of data within a single research or data collection method

When using **multiple data sources** (Table 11.2), the researcher uses multiple data sources in a single research study. Using multiple "data sources" does not mean using different research or data collection methods. Rather, it means *collecting data from multiple sources using a single method*. For example, the use of multiple interviews (especially from people with different perspectives) would provide multiple data sources while using only the interview method. Likewise, the use of multiple observations (especially from different vantage points) is another example of multiple data sources, because data would be provided via the observational method alone. An important part of multiple data sources involves collecting data at different times, at different places, and from different vantage points.

Here is an example of multiple data sources. Perhaps a researcher is interested in studying why certain students are apathetic. It would make sense to get the perspectives of several different kinds of people. The researcher might interview teachers, students identified by the teachers as being apathetic, and peers of apathetic students. Then the researcher could check to see whether the information obtained from these different data sources was in agreement. Each data source may provide additional reasons as well as a different perspective on the question of student apathy, resulting in a more complete understanding of the phenomenon. The researcher should also interview apathetic students during different class periods throughout the day and in different types of classes (e.g., math and social studies). Through the rich information gathered (from different people, at different times, at different places), the researcher can develop a better understanding of why students are apathetic than if the researcher used only one data source.

External Validity

As you know, external validity (or generalizing validity) is important when you want to generalize from a set of research findings to other people, settings, times, treatments, and outcomes. Traditionally, generalizability has *not* been a purpose of qualitative research, and, not surprisingly, external validity tends to be a weakness of qualitative research. There are at least two reasons for this view. First, the people and settings examined in qualitative research are rarely randomly selected and, as you know, random selection is the best way to generalize from a sample to a population. As a result, qualitative research is virtually always weak in the form of population validity focused on "generalizing to" populations.

Second, most qualitative researchers are interested in documenting "particularistic" findings rather than "universalistic" findings. In other words, in most qualitative research, the goal is to describe richly a certain group of people or a certain event in a specific context rather than to generate findings that are broadly applicable. At a fundamental level, many qualitative researchers do not believe in the presence of "general laws" or "universal laws." General laws apply to many people, and universal laws apply to everyone. When qualitative researchers are interested in causation, they tend to be more concerned about **idiographic or local or singular causation** (i.e., identifying the immediate, intentional, particular, complex, and local causes of specific attitudes, actions, and events) and less concerned with **nomothetic causation** (i.e., demonstrating universal or general scientific laws), which is important in quantitative research. As a result, qualitative research is frequently considered weak on external (i.e., generalizing) validity.

- **Idiographic causation** Local, singular, particularistic causes, including intentions, specific or local attitudes, conditions, contexts, and events

- **Nomothetic causation** The standard view of causation in science; refers to causation among variables at a general level of analysis and understanding

Perhaps the most reasonable stance toward the issue of generalizing is that we can generalize to other people, settings, times, and treatments to the degree to which they are similar to the people, settings, times, and treatments in the original study. Stake (1997) used the term **naturalistic generalization**[1] to refer to this process of generalizing on the basis of similarity. The bottom line is this: The more similar the people and circumstances in a particular research study are to the ones to which you want to generalize, the more defensible your generalization will be, and the more readily you should make such a generalization.

- **Naturalistic generalization** Generalizing on the basis of similarity

To help readers of a research report know when they can generalize, qualitative researchers should provide the following kinds of information: the number and kinds of people in the study, how they were selected to be in the study, contextual information, the nature of the researcher's relationship with the participants, information about any "informants" who provided information, the methods of data collection used, and the data analysis techniques used. This information is usually reported in the Method or Methodology section of the final research report. Using the information included in a well-written methodology section, readers will be able to make informed decisions about to whom the results may be generalized. They will also have the information they will need if they decide to replicate the research study with new participants.

Some experts show another way to generalize from qualitative research (e.g., Yin, 2014). Qualitative researchers can sometimes use **replication logic**, just like the replication logic that is commonly used by experimental researchers when they generalize beyond the people in their studies, even when they do not have random samples. According to replication logic, the more times a research finding is shown to be true with different sets of people, the more confidence we can place in the finding and in the conclusion that the finding generalizes beyond the people in the original research study (Cook & Campbell, 1979). In other words, if the finding is replicated with different kinds of people and in different places, then the evidence suggests that the finding applies very broadly. Yin's key point is that there is no reason why replication logic cannot be applied to qualitative research.[2]

- **Replication logic** The idea that the more times a research finding is shown to be true with different sets of people, the more confidence we can place in the finding and in generalizing beyond the original participants

Here is an example. Over the years, you might observe a certain pattern of interactions between boys and girls in a third-grade classroom. Now you decide to conduct a qualitative research study, and you find that the pattern of interaction occurs in your classroom and in two other third-grade classrooms you study. Because your research is interesting, you decide to publish it. Then other researchers replicate your study with other students, and they find that the same relationship holds in the third-grade classrooms they study.

See Journal Article 11.3 on the Student Study Site.

According to replication logic, the more times your theory or a research finding is replicated with other people, the greater the support for the generalizability of the theory or research finding. Now assume that other researchers find that the relationship holds in classrooms at several other grade levels. If this happens, the evidence suggests that the finding further generalizes to students in other grade levels.

REVIEW QUESTIONS

11.24 What is meant by research validity in qualitative research?

11.25 Why is researcher bias a threat to validity, and what strategies are used to reduce this effect?

11.26 What are the differences among descriptive validity, interpretive validity, and theoretical validity?

11.27 What strategies are used to promote descriptive, interpretative, and theoretical validity?

11.28 How is external validity assessed in qualitative research, and why is qualitative research typically weak on this type of validity?

- **Meta-inference** An inference or conclusion that builds on or integrates quantitative and qualitative findings
- **Inside-outside legitimation** The extent to which the researcher accurately understands, uses, and presents the participants' subjective insider or "native" views (also called the emic viewpoint) and the researcher's objective outsider view (also called the etic viewpoint)
- **Paradigmatic/philosophical legitimation** The degree to which the mixed researcher clearly explains his or her philosophical beliefs about research

RESEARCH VALIDITY (OR "LEGITIMATION") IN MIXED RESEARCH

As you know, mixed research involves the use of both quantitative and qualitative approaches in a single research study or set of closely related research studies. This means that all of the types of validity discussed in this chapter are important when conducting mixed research. Therefore, the first key point to remember is that you must design and conduct mixed research studies that have strong quantitative and qualitative validity.

Recently, several research methodologists have identified several types or dimensions of validity that are especially important in mixed research (cf. Onwuegbuzie & Johnson, 2006; Tashakkori & Teddlie, 2006). We focus here on Onwuegbuzie and Johnson's nine types of mixed research validity (also called types of legitimation). Onwuegbuzie and Johnson pointed out that the types can be viewed as types of validity or as types of legitimation for mixed research. We use the words *validity* and *legitimation* interchangeably here. In mixed research, inferences or conclusions are made based on the qualitative and quantitative components of the study. To be truly mixed, however, these inferences must be combined or integrated into larger **meta-inferences**.

The first type of validity in mixed research is called **inside-outside legitimation**. Inside-outside legitimation is the extent to which the researcher accurately understands, uses, and presents the participants' subjective insider or "native" views (also called the "emic" viewpoint) and the researcher's objective outsider view (also called the "etic" viewpoint). The idea is to enter fully the worlds of the participants and the world of the "objective" researcher, to move back and forth between these viewpoints, and to produce a viewpoint that is based on both of these carefully developed emic and etic perspectives. Understanding the phenomenon from both of these perspectives is important in producing fully informed descriptions and explanations.

Second, **paradigmatic/philosophical legitimation** is the extent to which the researcher reflects on, understands, and documents his or her "integrated" mixed research philosophical and methodological paradigm, including his or her epistemological, ontological, axiological, methodological, and rhetorical beliefs about mixed research. To obtain paradigmatic legitimation, the researcher's paradigm must make sense and enable the researcher to conduct a defensible mixed research study. To clarify some words just used, note that your *epistemological* beliefs are your beliefs about knowledge (e.g., What is knowledge? How can you gain knowledge? When do you consider results to be sufficient to claim that you have justified or warranted knowledge?). Your *ontological* beliefs are what you as a researcher assume to be real or true in the world as it exists (e.g., Do you believe there is one truth about what you are studying, or are there multiple truths about it?). Your *axiological* beliefs are about the place for values in research (e.g., Do you believe you are value neutral? Do you want to think about your values and address how they might affect your interpretation of results?). *Methodological* beliefs, in the narrow sense used here, are about how to conduct or practice research (e.g., Do you believe experiments are always the best research method? Do you believe that it is best to use multiple methods?). Your *rhetorical* beliefs are about the appropriate writing style to be used to describe your findings and to pose your arguments and the kind of language you prefer when writing research reports (e.g., Do you prefer an objective-sounding research report as in "The research found that . . . ," or do you like to include the researcher as a person as in "I found that . . . "?). Paradigmatic mixing occurs when the researcher demonstrates an understanding of the philosophical assumptions associated with quantitative and qualitative research and interrelates or "merges" these in a logical and defensible and practical way.

Commensurability approximation legitimation is the extent to which meta-inferences made in a mixed research study reflect a mixed worldview. This integrative worldview must be based on a deep understanding and appreciation of what a fully trained qualitative researcher would "see" in the world and what a fully trained quantitative researcher would "see" in the world, and it must move beyond these two basic lenses to see also what a fully trained mixed researcher is able to see. The idea is to become a qualitative researcher and a quantitative researcher and, by moving back and forth, to become a mixed researcher. Reaching some degree of commensurability requires an ability to switch between qualitative and quantitative viewpoints and create an "integrated," or broader or thoughtfully combined or multiple-lens, viewpoint that helps in understanding and explaining the phenomenon being studied. Some strategies to reach this difficult place include the cognitive and emotional processes of Gestalt switching, role reversal, and empathy. If a researcher is *not* able to escape one dominant approach to research, commensurability also can be gained through the use of a research team that includes a qualitative researcher, a quantitative researcher, and a mixed researcher who listens and helps mediate and integrate what is seen by the qualitative and quantitative researchers. For this strategy to work, sufficient time must be provided for joint discussions and integration of research interpretations into meta-inferences that reflect a mixed worldview.

- **Commensurability approximation legitimation** The degree to which a mixed researcher can make Gestalt switches between the lenses of a qualitative researcher and a quantitative researcher and integrate the two views into an "integrated" or broader viewpoint

Weakness minimization legitimation is the extent to which the weakness from one research approach is compensated for by the strengths from the other approach. The mixed methods researcher should combine qualitative and quantitative approaches that have nonoverlapping weaknesses. This is one component of the fundamental principle of mixed research discussed in Chapters 2, 9, and 17. For example, a highly structured measure of self-efficacy would provide precise numerical results, but it might miss out on many subjective nuances. In-depth interviews might be used to determine when and

- **Weakness minimization legitimation** The degree to which a mixed researcher combines qualitative and quantitative approaches that have nonoverlapping weaknesses

where the quantitative measure misrepresents individuals' thinking. This information would be especially important if the measure were used in a clinical setting with a particular student or client.

- **Sequential legitimation** The degree to which a mixed researcher appropriately addresses and/or builds on effects or findings from earlier qualitative and quantitative phases

In a sequential mixed research design in which one phase is followed by another, the researcher usually wants the latter phase to build purposively on the prior phase. **Sequential legitimation** is the extent to which one has appropriately built on the prior stage in a sequential design. For example, if you were developing a questionnaire, you might decide to conduct a qualitative phase to learn the language of the topic of interest and identify key concepts that might be useful. Then, you would follow-up with a quantitative phase in which you construct a structured questionnaire and test it to see if it works well (e.g., to see if it is reliable and allows valid claims about participants). The idea is for the second phase to appropriately build on the first phase, thereby achieving sequential validity. In a different situation, you might *not* want a later stage to be affected by a prior stage because the ordering was arbitrary. In this case, the idea is to try to understand whether the results would have been different had the phases been conducted in a different order. For example, if the qualitative part is done first and the quantitative part is done second, then one should ask what the results might have been if the quantitative part had been done first and the qualitative part second. Were participants changed in some way because of an earlier stage? If this issue is expected to be problematic, you might choose to use a multiple wave design (where you move back and forth between qualitative and quantitative phases).

- **Conversion legitimation** The degree to which quantitizing or qualitizing yields high-quality meta-inferences

Conversion legitimation is the extent to which a mixed researcher makes high-quality data transformations (quantitizing or qualitizing) and appropriate interpretations and meta-inferences based on the transformed data. These terms are discussed in Chapter 17, but briefly, *quantitizing* refers to quantifying qualitative data (e.g., counting words), and *qualitizing* refers to putting quantitative data into words, themes, or categories. This kind of legitimation is only relevant if you quantitize or qualitize some of your data. If you do, then you have conversion legitimation to the degree that you make accurate conversions and to the degree that you integrate the results of these conversions into meaningful meta-inferences.

- **Sample integration legitimation** The degree to which a mixed researcher makes appropriate conclusions, generalizations, and meta-inferences from mixed samples

Sample integration legitimation is the extent to which the relationship between the quantitative and qualitative sampling designs yields quality meta-inferences. For example, you might have a relatively large, randomly selected sample for a quantitative part of a survey research study. You might also have conducted a focus group, with a small convenience sample, to dig deeper into the issues examined in the survey study. The point is that you must be careful in how you combine these sets of people and how you make generalizations. You must be careful not to assume that the two groups would have the same beliefs.

- **Pragmatic legitimation** The extent to which the research purpose was met, research problem "solved," research questions sufficiently answered, and actionable results provided

A popular reason for conducting mixed methods research is its pragmatic function; hence, pragmatic validity/legitimation is important for many mixed studies. **Pragmatic legitimation** is the extent to which the research purpose was met, the research problem was "solved," the research questions were sufficiently answered, and actionable results were provided. Did the research pass the "so what?" test? This type of legitimation is especially important in applied research. When you read and evaluate the quality of mixed methods research, therefore, you should judge its pragmatic legitimation. You can do this by answering questions such as the following: Did the research help solve any practical problem? Did the research clearly provide and answer its research questions? Did the research motivate you to action in the sense that you believe you can use the findings?

An important goal in virtually all mixed research is integration. One can correctly state that if integration of the quantitative and qualitative aspects of the study is not present, then one does not have a mixed methods research study. This problem is one reason why many studies that claim to be mixed are rejected for publication (i.e., they are not truly mixed). Therefore, integration legitimation is the next type of validity or legitimation. **Integration legitimation** is the degree to which the researcher has achieved integration of quantitative and qualitative data, analysis, and conclusions. Integrated conclusions are supported by *meta-inferences*, which are inferences that show that a researcher has considered the quantitative and qualitative results and provided a combined or third viewpoint that gives added value beyond just the separate quantitative and qualitative findings. That is, the mixed methods findings should be more than the sum of its parts. For an example, see Buck et al. (2009). In the "Mixed Methods Finding and Implications" section of the article, they stated the following:

- **Integration legitimation** The degree to which the researcher achieved integration of quantitative and qualitative data, analysis, and conclusions

> By combining these data sets, it provided us with an insightful look into this seemingly homogeneous group to demonstrate the vast differences and similarities in these urban African American girls' profiles and understanding how these girls orient themselves as learners of science . . . Figure 3 illustrates the emergence of the personal orientations toward science as a result of the linking of the quantitative survey results with the qualitative interview data. (pp. 402–403)

If that quote piqued your interest, we recommend that you read this exemplary mixed methods article.

Sociopolitical legitimation or legitimation is the extent to which a mixed researcher appropriately addresses the interests, values, and standpoints of multiple stakeholders. The way to reach this kind of legitimation is to understand fully the politics, interests, and viewpoints involved with your research topic and to respect and represent these viewpoints. For example, in an evaluation study, you would need to understand the key stakeholder groups, to examine the issues of concern to each group, and to provide data with sufficient explanation to be defensible and responsive to their needs. You should be extra sensitive to the needs of stakeholders with minimal power and voice and attempt to "give them voice."

- **Sociopolitical legitimation** The degree to which a mixed researcher addresses the interests, values, and viewpoints of multiple stakeholders in the research process

The last (and most important) type of validity or legitimation in mixed research is **multiple validities legitimation**. This term refers to the extent to which the mixed methods researcher successfully addresses and resolves all relevant validity types, including the quantitative and qualitative validity types discussed earlier in this chapter as well as the mixed validity dimensions. In other words, the researcher must identify and address all of the relevant validity/legitimation/trustworthiness issues facing a particular research study. Successfully addressing the pertinent "validity" issues will help researchers produce the kinds of inferences and meta-inferences that should be made in mixed research.

- **Multiple validities legitimation** The extent to which all of the pertinent "validities" (quantitative, qualitative, and mixed) are addressed and resolved successfully

REVIEW QUESTIONS

11.29 What is meant by research validity or legitimation in mixed research?

11.30 How is validity or legitimation obtained in mixed research?

11.31 What is the implication of the type of validity/legitimation known as "multiple validities" according to mixed research?

ACTION RESEARCH REFLECTION

Insight: Action researchers are *reflective practitioners*. One important part of this reflexivity is considering how to obtain results that are defensible and trustworthy not only to the researcher but also to insiders (the people studied) and "objective outsiders" who might have the power to make decisions about sanctioned practices. Keeping track of evidence of success and effectiveness is very important to successful action researchers.

1. Which "validity paradigm" do you think most closely fits an action researcher's position on research validity—the quantitative, qualitative, or mixed approach? (Yes, that was a leading question because it assumes a simple answer.)
2. What specific validity strategies do you think will be most useful and important for the kinds of conclusions you want to draw?
3. How exactly can you use the validity strategies just listed in your place of study?

SUMMARY

Four types of validity are used to evaluate the accuracy of the inferences made from quantitative study results: construct validity, statistical conclusion validity, internal validity, and external validity. When we conduct a research study, we need to select good measures of the variables we are investigating. Construct validity is the extent to which a higher-order construct is correctly represented in the study. It answers the question: Did I have good measurement in my study? Statistical conclusion validity is the validity with which we infer that two variables are related and the strength of that relationship.

Internal (i.e., causal) validity is the validity with which we infer that the relationship between two variables is causal. To make a causal connection between independent and dependent variables, we need evidence that (1) they are related, (2) the direction of effect is from the independent variable (the cause) to the dependent variable (the effect), and (3) the observed effect on the dependent variable is due to the independent variable and not to some extraneous variable. Internal validity is especially related to the ability to rule out the influence of extraneous variables. The influence of extraneous variables must be controlled or eliminated if you are to make a defensible claim that changes in one variable *cause* changes in another variable. We discussed one threat that is controlled for in all experimental research but not in nonexperimental research; this threat is ambiguous temporal precedence—the inability to specify which variable preceded which other variable.

Next we discussed some threats that threaten one-group designs such as the one-group pretest-posttest design. Those threats are the following:

- History—specific events, other than the independent variable, that occur between the first and second measurements of the dependent variable
- Maturation—the physical or mental changes that may occur in individuals over time such as aging, learning, boredom, hunger, and fatigue
- Testing—changes in the score a person makes on the second administration of a test that can be attributed entirely to the effect of having previously taken the test
- Instrumentation—any change that occurs in the measuring instrument between the pretesting and posttesting
- Regression artifact—the tendency of extreme scores to regress or move toward the mean of the distribution on a second testing

Next we discussed some threats that threaten designs comparing two or more groups. Those threats are the following:

- Differential selection—differences that exist in the comparison groups at the outset of the research study and are not due to the independent variable

- Additive or interactive effects—differences that exist in the comparison groups because one of the threats, such as maturation or history, affects the groups differently
- Differential attrition—difference that exists in the comparison groups because the participants who drop out of the various comparison groups have different characteristics

In most studies, we want to be able to generalize the results and state that they hold true for other individuals in other settings and at different points in time. This ability to generalize is called external validity or generalizing validity. External/generalizing validity is achieved if we can generalize the results of our study to the larger target population, at other points in time, in other settings, across different treatment variations, and across different outcomes. Threats to external validity include a lack of population validity, ecological validity, temporal validity, treatment variation validity, and outcome validity. Population validity is to the ability to generalize to and across subpopulations in the target population. Ecology validity is the ability to generalize the results of a study across different settings. Temporal validity is to the extent to which the results of a study can be generalized across time. Treatment variation validity is the extent to which the results of the study can be generalized across variations of the treatment condition. Outcome validity is the extent to which the results of the study can be generalized across different but related dependent variables that should be influenced by the treatment condition.

The majority of this chapter focused on validity in traditional quantitative research, especially experimental research. However, validity is also important issue in qualitative and mixed research. Three types of validity in qualitative research are descriptive validity, interpretive/emic validity, and theoretical validity. Descriptive validity is the factual accuracy of the account as reported by the qualitative researcher. Interpretive/emic validity is obtained to the degree that the participants' viewpoints, thoughts, intentions, and experiences are accurately understood and reported. Theoretical validity is obtained to the degree to which a theory or theoretical explanation developed from a research study fits the data and is therefore credible and defensible. Internal validity and external validity are also important to qualitative research when the researcher is interested in making cause-and-effect statements and generalizing, respectively. Sixteen strategies that are used to promote validity/trustworthiness in qualitative research were discussed. Last, 11 types of validity/legitimation that are used in mixed methods research were listed and briefly discussed.

KEY TERMS

additive and interactive effects (p. 292)
ambiguous temporal precedence (p. 286)
attrition (p. 292)
causal description (p. 285)
causal explanation (p. 285)
causal validity (p. 285)
commensurability approximation legitimation (p. 307)
confounding variable (p. 283)
construct validity (p. 297)
conversion legitimation (p. 308)
critical friend (p. 302)
descriptive validity (p. 300)
differential attrition (p. 293)
differential selection (p. 291)
ecological validity (p. 295)
effect size indicator (p. 298)
extended fieldwork (p. 302)
external validity (p. 293)
extraneous variable (p. 283)
generalizing across subpopulations (p. 294)
generalizing to a population (p. 294)
generalizing validity (p. 293)
history (p. 288)
idiographic causation (p. 305)
inside-outside legitimation (p. 306)
instrumentation (p. 289)
integrative legitimation (p. 309)
internal validity (p. 285)
interpretive or emic validity (p. 300)
low-inference descriptors (p. 301)
maturation (p. 288)
member checking (p. 301)
meta-inference (p. 306)
multigroup research design (p. 290)
multiple data sources (p. 304)
multiple investigators (p. 300)
multiple methods (p. 303)
multiple theoretical perspectives (p. 302)
multiple validities legitimation (p. 309)
naturalistic generalization (p. 305)
negative-case sampling (p. 300)
nomothetic causation (p. 305)
one-group pretest-posttest design (p. 287)
operationalizing a construct (p. 297)
outcome validity (p. 296)
paradigmatic/philosophical legitimation (p. 306)
participant feedback (p. 301)
pattern matching (p. 302)
peer review (p. 302)

population validity (p. 294)
pragmatic legitimation (p. 308)
reactivity (p. 295)
reflexivity (p. 300)
regression artifact (p. 290)
replication logic (p. 305)
research reliability (p. 283)
research validity (p. 283)
researcher-as-detective (p. 303)
researcher bias (p. 299)
ruling out alternative explanations (p. 303)
sample integration legitimation (p. 308)
selection-history effect (p. 292)
selection-instrumentation effect (p. 293)
selection-maturation effect (p. 292)
selection-regression effect (p. 293)
selection-testing effect (p. 293)
sequential legitimation (p. 308)
sociopolitical legitimation (p. 309)
statistical conclusion validity (p. 297)
target population (p. 294)
temporal validity (p. 295)
testing (p. 289)
theoretical validity (p. 301)
triangulation (p. 298)
third variable (p. 286)
treatment diffusion (p. 297)
treatment variation validity (p. 296)
weakness minimization legitimation (p. 307)

DISCUSSION QUESTIONS

1. In this chapter, we listed and discussed four different types of validity in quantitative research. We also stated that it is unlikely that a researcher will be able to attain all four types in a single study. If only three of the different types of validity can be achieved, which three should the researcher strive for? Does this mean that the one type that is disregarded is less important?
2. In this chapter, we have discussed several criteria for inferring causation. Can we ever be sure that we have met these criteria? What type of evidence is needed to ensure that each of the criteria has been met?
3. In what research designs would each of the various threats to internal validity be most prevalent?
4. Why do qualitative and quantitative researchers refer to different concepts when referring to research validity?
5. Is it ever possible to attain interpretive validity in a qualitative research study?

RESEARCH EXERCISES

Using ERIC or another electronic database, find a quantitative or qualitative research article in an area in which you are interested, such as teacher burnout. When selecting an article, make sure it is about a cause-and-effect issue. Read the article, and then answer questions 1 through 4. If you selected a qualitative article, also answer questions 5 and 6.

1. Is the study a causal descriptive or causal explanatory study? Explain why it is one and not the other.
2. Identify the threats to internal validity that might exist in this study.
3. Identify the constructs that are used in this study and the operations used to define these constructs.
4. What problems might exist in trying to generalize the results of the study, and to whom and what conditions might the results be generalized?
5. Does the study have descriptive validity, interpretive validity, or theoretical validity? If it has any of these, how does the author demonstrate this type of validity?
6. Is internal or external validity an issue in the study, and how are these handled?

RELEVANT INTERNET SITES

Workshops focusing on research methods: To get to the one on reliability and validity, click on the "Research Methods Workshop" link on the left side of the page. Then click on the "Reliability and Validity" workshop link.
http://wadsworth.cengage.com/psychology_d/templates/student_resources/workshops/index.html

An extended discussion of validity as applied to drawing conclusions from data
http://www.statisticalassociates.com/validityandreliability.htm
https://www.youtube.com/watch?v=msrVDB7YGqg
https://www.youtube.com/watch?v=mZafK0VPpeY

Validity in mixed methods research
http://videolectures.net/site/normal_dl/tag=48066/MixedMethodsaandValidity.RITS.pdf

Validity in qualitative research
http://www.fctl.ucf.edu/ResearchAndScholarship/SoTL/creatingSoTLProjects/implementingmanaging/qualitativeresearchvalidity.php
http://www.socialresearchmethods.net/kb/qualval.php
http://ebn.bmj.com/content/18/2/34.full
http://www.medscape.com/viewarticle/731165_2

STUDENT STUDY SITE

Visit the Student Study Site at **edge.sagepub.com/rbjohnson6e** for these additional learning tools:

Video Links
Self-Quizzes
eFlashcards
Lecture Notes
Full-Text SAGE Journal Articles
Interactive Concept Maps
Web Resources

RECOMMENDED READING

Campbell, D. T. (1988). Definitional versus multiple operationism. In E. S. Overman (Ed.), *Methodology and epistemology for social science: Selected papers* (pp. 31–36). Chicago, IL: University of Chicago Press.
Maxwell, J. A. (1992). Understanding and validity in qualitative research. *Harvard Educational Review*, *62*, 279–299.
Onwuegbuzie, A. J., & Johnson, R. B. (2006). The validity issue in mixed research. *Research in the Schools*, *13*(1), 48–63.
Shadish, W. R., Cook, T. D., & Campbell, D. T. (2002). *Experimental and quasi-experimental designs for generalized causal inference*. Boston, MA: Houghton Mifflin. (Chapters 2 and 3 discuss the various types of validity and threats to these types of validity.)

NOTES

1. Donald Campbell (1988) made a similar point, and he used the term *proximal similarity* to refer to the degree of similarity between the people and circumstances in the original research study and the people and circumstances to which you wish to apply the findings. Your goal, using Campbell's term, is to check for proximal similarity.

2. The late Donald Campbell, perhaps the most important research methodologist over the past 50 years, approved of Robert Yin's case study work.

PART IV

Selecting a Research Method

Section A: Quantitative Research Methods: Five Major Approaches

Chapter 12
Experimental Research: Weak and Strong Designs

Chapter 13
Experimental Research: Quasi and Single-Case Designs

Chapter 14
Nonexperimental Quantitative Research

Section B: Qualitative Research Methods: Five Major Approaches

Chapter 15
Narrative Inquiry and Case Study Research
by D. Jean Clandinin and R. Burke Johnson

Chapter 16
Phenomenology, Ethnography, and Grounded Theory

Section C: Mixed Methods Research: Many Approaches

Chapter 17
Mixed Research

Chapter 12

Section A: Quantitative Research Methods: Five Major Approaches

Experimental Research: Weak and Strong Designs

LEARNING OBJECTIVES

After reading this chapter, you should be able to

- Explain how experiments produce evidence of causality.
- Describe the different ways an independent variable can be manipulated.
- Explain the importance of control in experimental research and how control is achieved.
- Explain the different ways of controlling the influence of potentially confounding variables.
- Explain why some experimental research designs are weak designs and others are strong designs.
- Compare and contrast factorial and repeated-measures designs.
- Explain the concept of an interaction effect.

Visit the Student Study Site for an interactive concept map.

RESEARCH IN REAL LIFE Experiments and Causation

istock/PeopleImages

One of the rituals that seems to be performed every 10 to 15 years in the hallowed halls of academia is curriculum reform. Seldom, if ever, is there complete agreement about the curriculum that undergraduates should complete. This lack of agreement initiates a movement to reform a current curriculum. For example, Richard R. Beeman, the dean of the University of Pennsylvania's School of Arts and Sciences, has stated that the university's current curriculum "isn't perfect." Others at the university have described the current curriculum as "a shambles" and "a Hodgepodge" in serious need of overhaul (Bartlett, 2002).

When curriculum reform is initiated, it is frequently hashed out in committees. This approach is often hamstrung by poor management and a failure to build consensus. For example, when the University of Pennsylvania started discussing reform in the undergraduate curriculum in 1998, almost everyone had a vision. The problem was that everyone's vision was different. The result is frequently a half-hearted compromise, with idealism giving way to political horse-trading that typically results in another revision in another 10 to 15 years.

Curriculum reform is a task for which the educational researcher should be well suited because educational researchers are the experts in conducting research on educational issues. Curriculum reform should be just as amenable to a research study as any other educational issue. This is exactly the approach taken by the University of Pennsylvania. The university's president, Judith Rodin, has stated that these important changes should be approached in the same manner and with the same seriousness as any other scholarly activity (Bartlett, 2002).

As a result, the University of Pennsylvania decided to conduct an experimental study to investigate the outcome of students' taking different curricula. To conduct this experimental study, the investigators had to design research that would provide knowledge of the effects of following different curricula. This means that they had to make decisions about the independent and dependent variables, and they had to identify the control techniques to be used. The independent variable in this study was the different curricula followed by the students. The students in the control group were to follow the standard curriculum, and the students in the experimental group were allowed more freedom in selecting their courses but were also required to take a series of interdisciplinary courses, many of which were team taught.

The dependent variables in this study involved the results of focus groups, interviews, questionnaires, grades achieved, and skills tests, as well as the courses selected by students in the experimental group. Control over many extraneous variables was accomplished by randomly assigning the volunteer students to either a control or an experimental group. These are the types of decisions that have to be made to construct a research design that will provide information to help answer your research question. In this chapter, we discuss the decisions that must be made in developing a good research design and present the most basic research designs used in experimental studies.

The experiment is the research method that provides the strongest evidence of cause-and-effect relationships. Causal relationships can be established because experiments allow us to observe, under controlled conditions, the effect of systematically changing one or more variables. The experimental approach permits greater control over confounding extraneous variables than any other method. The greater the degree of control, the greater the degree of internal (i.e., causal) validity of the study and the greater our confidence in our claims about causality. However, the more control that is exerted over confounding extraneous variables, the more unnatural the study becomes, threatening the external (i.e., generalizing) validity of the study. Experimental research therefore frequently sacrifices external validity for enhanced internal validity. In spite of this disadvantage, experimental research is an extremely valuable methodology for the educational researcher.

THE EXPERIMENT

- **Experiment** An environment in which the researcher attempts to "objectively" observe phenomena that are made to occur in a strictly controlled situation in which one or more variables are varied and the others are kept constant

An **experiment** is defined as the development of an environment in which the researcher, typically called the experimenter, attempts to objectively observe "phenomena which are made to occur in strictly controlled situations in which one or more variables are varied and the others are kept constant" (Zimney, 1961, p. 18). This seems to be one of the better definitions, so let's take a closer look at what it is saying. First, it is saying that we must attempt to make impartial and unbiased observations. This is not always possible because experimenters can unintentionally influence the outcome of an experiment. However, we must realize that we are capable of some unintentional influence and strive to make observations that are free of this bias.

In conducting experiments, we make observations of "phenomena which are made to occur." The term *phenomena* refers to some observable event. These phenomena are "made to occur" because we present a set of conditions to the research participants and record the effect of these conditions on their behavior. We present a set of stimulus conditions—the independent variable—and then observe the effect of this independent variable presentation on the dependent variable.

The observations are made in "controlled situations." This means that we must eliminate the influence of confounding extraneous variables. Controlling for variables confounded with the independent variable is necessary to achieve internal validity.

The last component of the definition of experiment is that "one or more variables are varied and the others are kept constant." This means that we deliberately vary (i.e., "manipulate") the independent variable(s) along a defined range and attempt to *make sure that all other variables do not vary*. For example, if you want to test the effect of eating breakfast on the ability to solve math problems, you might want to vary the independent variable by assigning participants to a group that gets to eat breakfast and a group that does not get to eat breakfast. You might also want to vary the type of breakfast that the participants eat. You might feed some participants a high-carbohydrate, low-protein breakfast and feed others a high-protein, low-carbohydrate breakfast. The point is that you must vary the independent variable in some way, but the nature of the variation will depend on your research question and hypothesis. Regardless of the type of variation produced, you must keep all variables other than the independent variable constant. In other words, you must make sure that variables other than the independent variable do not vary along with the independent variable. This is in effect saying that when you conduct an experiment, you must create a set of conditions in which extraneous variables are controlled and not confounded with the independent variable.

EXPERIMENTAL RESEARCH SETTINGS

Experimental research studies can be conducted in a variety of settings. These include the field, the laboratory, and the Internet. Each of these settings has slightly different attributes that deserve mention.

Field Experiment

A **field experiment** is an experimental research study that is conducted in a real-life setting. The study (Bartlett, 2002) described in the introduction to this chapter is an excellent example of a field research study because it was conducted in the real-life setting of a college campus with actual students. It is also an example of an experiment, because there was a manipulation of the type of college curriculum that different students took and control techniques such as random assignment were used to eliminate the influence of confounding extraneous variables.

■ **Field experiment** An experimental study that is conducted in a real-life setting

The advantage of field experiments is that they are excellent for determining whether a manipulation works in a real-world setting. The primary disadvantage of field experiments is that they do not control for the influence of extraneous variables as well as do laboratory experiments. In the Bartlett (2002) study, even though students were randomly assigned to different curricula, different instructors taught the different courses, so there was no control over the effectiveness of the instructional process. Also, the different curricula might have consisted of different courses that were of different interest and difficulty levels. Although exercising control over many extraneous variables in field experiments is difficult, such experiments are necessary to determine whether some effect will work in a real-life setting where maximum control over extraneous variables cannot be exercised.

See Journal Article 12.1 on the Student Study Site.

Laboratory Experiment

A **laboratory experiment** is a study that is conducted in the controlled environment of a laboratory where the researcher precisely manipulates one or more variables and controls for the influence of all or nearly all extraneous variables. Where the field experiment is strong, the laboratory experiment is weak, and where the laboratory experiment is strong, the field experiment is weak. The laboratory experiment is strong in terms of its ability to control for the influence of extraneous variables. When a study is conducted in a laboratory environment, outside influences, such as the presence of other students, noise, or other distracting influences, can be eliminated or controlled. However, the price of this increase in control is that the experiment takes place in an artificial environment.

■ **Laboratory experiment** A study conducted in a controlled environment where one or more variables are precisely manipulated and all or nearly all extraneous variables are controlled

For example, Verhallen, Bus, and de Jong (2006) tested kindergarten children in a spare room that contained a computer, a table, two chairs, and a digital video camera. The researchers' goal was to determine whether book-based animated stories would have a positive effect on young children's comprehension and language skills. This obviously is not a real-life setting in which children would typically hear or read stories. The artificiality of the setting is why the results of laboratory experiments must be verified by experiments conducted in a real-life setting.

Internet Experiment

An **Internet experiment** is an experimental study that is conducted over the Internet. Internet experiments have the same characteristics as either a field or laboratory experiment in that the researcher manipulates one or more independent variables and controls for as many extraneous variables as possible. Since about 2000, the number of studies conducted via the Internet has grown considerably, and this growth rate is expected to continue given

■ **Internet experiment** An experimental study that is conducted over the Internet

the advantages an Internet study has over the typical laboratory study (Birnbaum, 2001; Reips, 2000). The advantages of conducting experiments over the Internet include (1) ease of access to demographically and culturally diverse participant populations; (2) the ability to bring the experiment to the participant, rather than the participant to the experiment; (3) high statistical power by enabling access to large samples; and (4) cost savings of laboratory space, person-hours, equipment, and administration. The disadvantages include issues "such as (1) multiple submissions, (2) lack of experimental control, (3) self-selection, and (4) dropout" (Reips, p. 89).

INDEPENDENT VARIABLE MANIPULATION

In an experiment, the researcher *manipulates* the independent variable. This manipulation is expected to cause a change in the dependent variable. In any given study, many possible independent variables can be used. The independent variable or variables used are specified by the research question(s). For example, one of the research questions Breznitz (1997) asked was "Does accelerated reading among dyslexic children partially account for changes in their short-term memory processing?" Breznitz wanted to determine the effect that increasing reading speed has on short-term memory, so reading speed had to be the independent variable. This meant that reading speed had to be varied in some way. Breznitz hypothesized that readers with dyslexia who engaged in fast-paced reading relative to self-paced reading would show significant improvement in short-term memory. This hypothesis specified the variation that had to be created in the independent variable. There had to be at least two levels of the independent variable of reading speed: fast-paced and self-paced reading. Although the research question identified the independent variable, it was not always easy to create the needed variation. For example, Breznitz had to develop a procedure that would allow for the manipulation of reading speed and do so in such a way that the experimenter could increase the speed of reading over that of the children's self-paced reading.

From this brief discussion, you can see that many decisions must be made regarding the manipulation of the independent variable. You must identify the independent variable, and then you must decide how to manipulate the independent variable to provide an answer to your research question.

- **Presence or absence technique** Manipulating the independent variable by presenting one group the treatment condition and withholding it from the other group

Ways to Manipulate an Independent Variable

The research question identifies the independent variable. However, it does not specify how the independent variable is to be manipulated. There are at least three different ways, illustrated in Figure 12.1, in which you can manipulate an independent variable. The first is by a **presence or absence technique**. This technique is exactly what the name implies: One group of research participants receives a treatment condition (treatment group), and the other group does not (control group). For example, assume that you want to determine whether a review session will improve the mathematics test grades of high school students taking algebra. You can manipulate the independent variable using the presence or absence technique by having one group of algebra students take the examination after participating in a review session and the other group take the same examination without the aid of a review session.

- **Amount technique** Manipulating the independent variable by giving the various comparison groups different amounts of the independent variable

A second way in which you can manipulate the independent variable is by the **amount technique**. This technique involves administering different amounts of the independent

FIGURE 12.1 Three ways of manipulating the independent variable

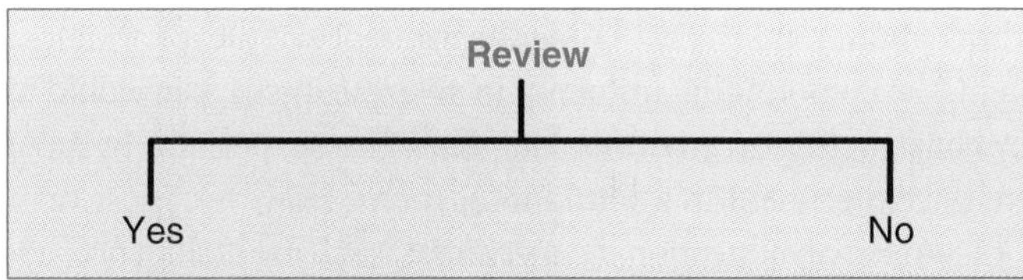

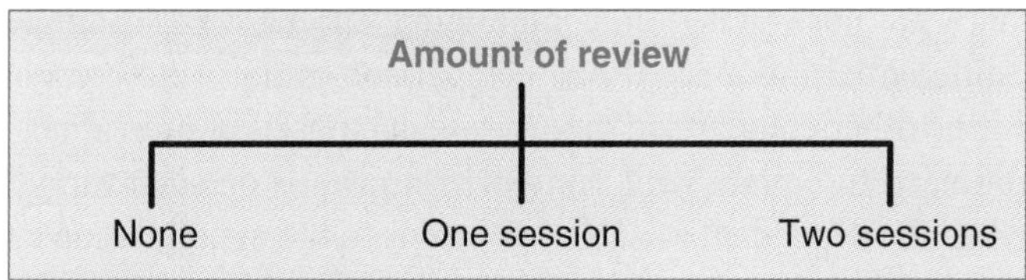

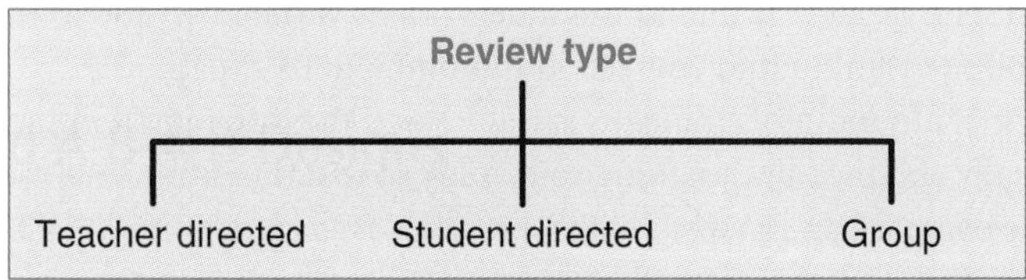

variable to several groups of participants. For example, you might think that if one review session is good, several review sessions would be better. This manipulation would essentially involve varying the amount of review the students receive. You could manipulate the amount of review by having one group of students take the algebra examination without the aid of a review session, a second group take the examination after one review session, a third group after two review sessions, and a fourth group after three review sessions.

A third way of manipulating the independent variable is by a **type technique**. Using this technique involves varying the type of condition presented to the participants. For example, rather than varying the amount of review the participants received, you might think that the type of review is the important variable. You could, for example, have a teacher-directed review session, a student-directed review session, and a group review session. Once you have identified the types of review sessions you want to investigate, you would expose a different group of research participants to each type of review session before they took the examination.

- **Type technique** Manipulating the independent variable by varying the type of condition presented to the different comparison groups

Control of Confounding Variables

In Chapter 11 we discussed a number of the more obvious extraneous variables that can threaten the internal (i.e., causal) validity of an experiment. These are the types of extraneous variables that must be controlled within an experiment to enable us to reach causal conclusions. Confounding extraneous variables can be controlled in a number of ways. Before we discuss these control techniques, we want to discuss briefly the meaning

- **Experimental control** Eliminating any differential influence of extraneous variables

- **Differential influence** The influence of an extraneous variable that is different for the various comparison groups

- **Equating the groups** Experimenter's goal of constructing comparison groups that are similar on all confounding extraneous variables and different only on the independent variable

of **experimental control** (i.e., controlling for confounding variables through the design and conduct of your experiment).

When you first consider controlling for potentially confounding extraneous variables, you probably think about totally eliminating the influence of these variables. For example, if noise is a potentially confounding influence in an experiment, you would naturally try to control for it by constructing an environment void of noise, perhaps by having the participants complete the experiment in a soundproof room. However, most variables that can influence the outcome of an educational experiment, such as intelligence, age, motivation, and stress, cannot be eliminated that way. Control of these variables comes through the elimination of any **differential influence** that they may have. Differential influence occurs when your groups are not equated on confounding variables. For example, intelligence would have a differential influence if one comparison group were composed of bright individuals and the other comparison group were composed of individuals with average intelligence. You need to **equate your comparison groups** on such variables; then, any *difference* noted on the dependent variable will be due to the manipulation of the independent variable. Remember: If the groups forming the levels of your independent variable differ on an extraneous variable, then you will not know whether the difference in outcome on your dependent variable is due to the independent variable or due to the extraneous variable. You do not want to find yourself in this ambiguous situation!

Control for confounding extraneous variables and the differential influence that they produce is usually obtained by designing your study so that the extraneous variables do not vary across the comparison groups. That is, *your goal is to equate your groups on all extraneous variables.* Then, any difference observed on the dependent variable will be attributable to the independent variable. The differential influence of the extraneous variable will be "controlled." *Control*, as you can see, generally refers to achieving constancy across the groups. The question that must be answered is how to achieve this constancy. We now turn our attention to some of the more general techniques for achieving constancy of effect of potentially confounding variables.

12.1 What is an experiment, and what are the significant components of this definition?

12.2 What are the different settings in which researchers conduct experiments?

12.3 What are the different ways a researcher could use to manipulate an independent variable?

12.4 What is meant by the term *experimental control*, and how is experimental control related to differential influence within the experiment?

Random Assignment

Random assignment is a control procedure that makes assignments to conditions on the basis of chance. Random assignment maximizes the probability that potentially confounding extraneous variables, known and unknown, will not systematically bias the results of the study. Stated differently, random assignment is the best technique for *equating the comparison* *groups* on all variables at the start of an experiment. As discussed above, the key idea of an experiment is to equate all comparison groups on all variables and then systematically vary only the independent variable. When this is done, the researcher can claim that changes on the dependent variable are *caused* by the independent variable that was systematically manipulated by the researcher. Because random assignment controls for both known and unknown variables, this procedure should be used whenever and wherever possible—it is the best control technique for equating groups.

▪ **Random assignment** A procedure that makes assignments to conditions on the basis of chance and in this way maximizes the probability that comparison groups will be equated on all extraneous variables

When research participants are randomly assigned to various comparison groups, each research participant has an equal probability of being assigned to each group. This means that chance determines which person gets assigned to each comparison group. Remember that each person brings with him or her certain variables, such as intelligence. If we want to control for a variable such as intelligence, we want individuals with approximately the same intelligence levels in each comparison group. This is exactly what random assignment accomplishes. When participants are randomly assigned, the variables they bring with them are also randomly assigned. Therefore, the comparison groups are similar on these variables, and any differences that exist will be due to chance. Random assignment produces control because levels of extraneous variables are distributed in approximately the same manner in all comparison groups at the beginning of the experiment. If the comparison groups are similar on the extraneous variables, the groups are expected to perform approximately the same on the dependent variable *when* the independent variable has no effect on the participants. If the participants respond differently on the dependent variable, this difference can be attributed to the independent variable.

Although random assignment is the most important control technique, it does not always work. It is possible that the comparison groups will not be similar even with random assignment because chance determines the way in which the variables are distributed. For example, it is possible that random assignment would result in the brightest individuals being assigned to one comparison group and individuals with average intelligence being assigned to another comparison group. The smaller the number of research participants, the greater the risk that this problem will happen. However, random assignment minimizes the probability of this problem happening. The vast majority of the time, random assignment will work well (given a sample size that allows at least 20 participants per group), but *occasionally* it will fail to equate the groups. Since the probability of the groups being equal is so much greater with than without random assignment, this strategy is the most powerful method for generating similar groups and eliminating the threat of confounding variables. Furthermore, because random assignment is the only method for controlling for the influence of unknown variables, you should randomize whenever and wherever possible, even when other control techniques are used.

Do not confuse *random assignment* with *random sampling*! Random sampling produces a sample. Specifically, random sampling (also called random selection) involves the selection of units from a population by chance so that the sample selected is similar to the population. Therefore, from this sample you can generalize to the population. Random assignment *starts* with a sample, usually a convenience or purposive sample, and then makes assignments to groups on the basis of chance to maximize the probability that the groups generated will be similar. Random assignment produces comparison groups that are similar on all variables so that you can manipulate the independent variable and determine its causal effect.

In a perfect research world, in any research study, you should select participants randomly from the population, because this method of selection provides maximum assurance that a systematic bias does not exist in the selection process and that the selected participants are representative of the population. If the average IQ in the population is 110, then the average IQ in the randomly selected sample should be about 110. The sample can say something about the population only when it is representative of the population.

Once participants have been randomly *selected* from the population, they should be randomly *assigned* to the comparison groups, as illustrated in Figure 12.2. Unfortunately, it is usually not possible to randomly select research participants from the target population. Just think of the difficulty of randomly selecting a sample of children with attention-deficit/hyperactivity disorder (ADHD) from the population of all children in the United States (or the world) with ADHD. Consequently, random selection of participants from the population is an ideal that is seldom achieved. Fortunately, however, random selection of participants is *not* the crucial element needed to achieve high internal (i.e., causal) validity. Achieving high internal validity (to allow strong conclusions about cause and effect) is the *raison d'être* of experimental research. Therefore, please remember this key point: *Random assignment is the most powerful technique for equating groups in experimental research and, thereby, increasing the study's internal validity.*

FIGURE 12.2 The ideal procedure for obtaining participants for an experiment

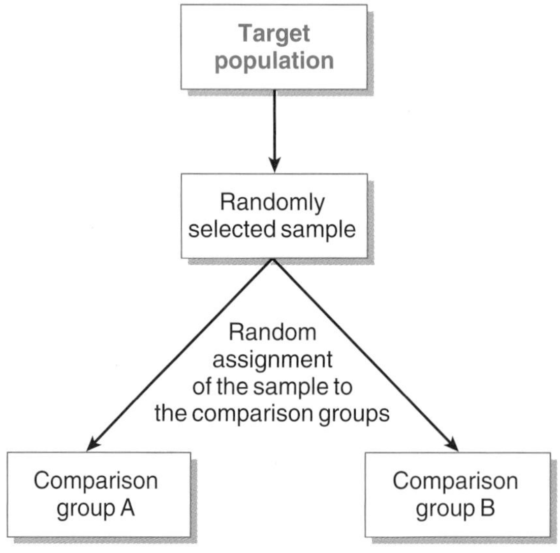

See Journal Articles 12.2 and 12.3 on the Student Study Site.

Random sampling using a random number generator is demonstrated in Chapter 10. That same random number generator (randomizer.org) can easily be used for random assignment or you can use a table of random numbers as illustrated on the companion website for this book.

Matching

Matching Equating comparison groups on one or more variables that are correlated with the dependent variable

Matching is a control technique for equating the comparison groups on one or more specific variables that are expected to be correlated with the dependent variable. The most commonly used matching procedure is to match participants in the comparison groups on a case-by-case basis on each of the selected extraneous variables. For example, assume that you want to conduct an experiment testing the effectiveness of three different methods of instruction in algebra on algebra test performance. You know that variables such as IQ and math anxiety probably affect test performance, so you want to control for the influence of these two variables. One way to obtain the needed control is to match individual participants in the three comparison groups so that each group contains individuals with about the same IQ and math anxiety. In other words, if the first participant who volunteers for the study is a male with an IQ of 118 and a low level of math anxiety, then we have to find two other males with IQs very close to 118 and low levels of math anxiety. It would be very difficult to find individuals with exactly the same IQ, so the criterion is that the participants have to be very similar on the variables on which they are matched. Once these individuals have been matched, you will match another set of three individuals on another level of IQ and continue this process until you have a sufficient number of participants with different levels of IQ. The key point is that the three *groups will not differ on the matching variable* (IQ), that is, the groups will be equated on IQ. You can match on as many variables as you like, although it gets more difficult as the number of matching variables increases.

The matching technique just described is an *individual* matching approach because individuals are matched. It is also possible to engage in *group* matching. Group matching

FIGURE 12.3 The matching control technique (for three matched groups)

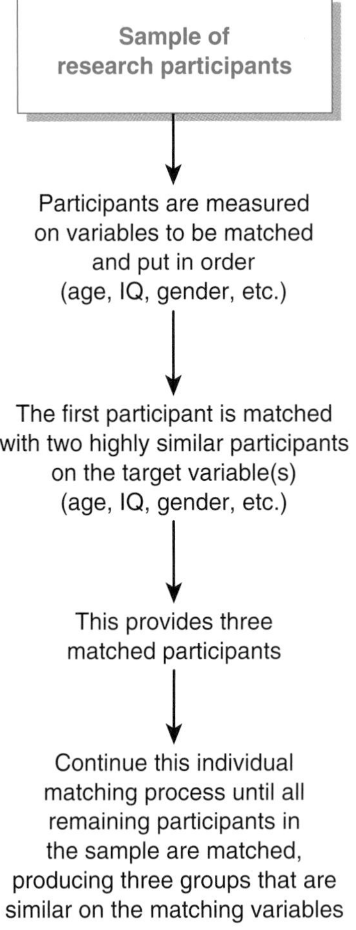

involves selecting groups of individuals that have similar average scores and a similar distribution of scores. In other words, if you were matching the three groups on intelligence and one group of participants had an average IQ of 118 and a standard deviation of IQ scores of 6, you would want to select participants for the other two groups such that each group had an average IQ of about 118 and a standard deviation of IQ scores of about 6. The key limitation of matching (individual or group matching) is that the groups will be equated *only* on the matching variables identified by the researcher. Remember, random assignment is stronger because it equates the groups on all known and unknown variables. Matching is a good way to transform a weak experimental design into a **quasi-experimental design** (i.e., a medium level experiment that falls between weak and strong experiments), but random assignment is required of a strong, randomized experiment. These middle-of-the-road designs (i.e., quasi-experimental designs) are explained in the next chapter. The current chapter only covers the weak and the strong designs.

- **Quasi-experimental design** A design that is stronger than the weak designs but not as strong as the strong or randomized designs

Holding the Extraneous Variable Constant

Another frequently used control technique is to hold the extraneous variable constant across the comparison groups by limiting it to a single value or type. This means that the participants in each comparison group will have the same type or amount of the extraneous variable. For example, assume that you want to test the efficacy of a new physical education program at promoting strength and endurance. Strength and endurance might be influenced by gender, so you might decide first to include only one gender, such as females. In this case, the groups will not differ on gender. After selecting a sample of only female students, if it is possible you should also use the control technique of randomly assigning these students to the comparison groups. This approach of holding the extraneous variable constant combined with random assignment is illustrated in Figure 12.4. Although holding the extraneous variable constant equates the groups on the extraneous variable and thus improves the internal validity of the study, the technique simultaneously reduces the external validity of the study because an entire category of participants (males) is excluded!

FIGURE 12.4 Control exercised by holding the extraneous variable constant

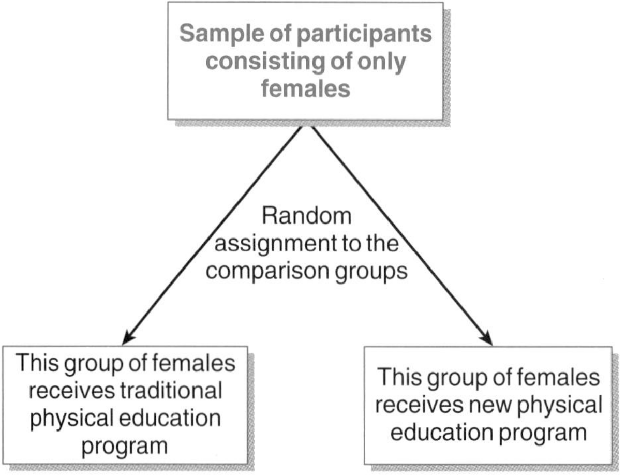

Building the Extraneous Variable Into the Research Design

Extraneous variables can be controlled by being built into the research design. When this is done, the extraneous variable becomes another independent variable. For example, in the hypothetical study investigating the use of the new physical education program, you want to control for the effects of gender. Instead of holding gender constant, you could use gender as an additional variable. By including both males and females in the study, you could determine whether the new program is equally effective for males and females, as illustrated in Figure 12.5. Building the extraneous variable into the research design is especially attractive when you also have a theoretical interest in the additional variable. In addition, this technique overcomes the external validity problem of the previous technique (holding the extraneous variable constant) because when you build the variable into your design, no group of participants is systematically excluded from your study. Building the extraneous variable into the design takes an extraneous variable that could bias your experiment and makes it focal as an independent variable.

Analysis of covariance A control method that can be used to statistically equate groups that differ on a pretest or some other variable; also called ANCOVA

Analysis of Covariance

Analysis of covariance (ANCOVA) is a control method used to equate comparison groups that differ on a pretest or some other variable or variables. It is useful when the participants

FIGURE 12.5 Control of an extraneous variable by building it into the research design

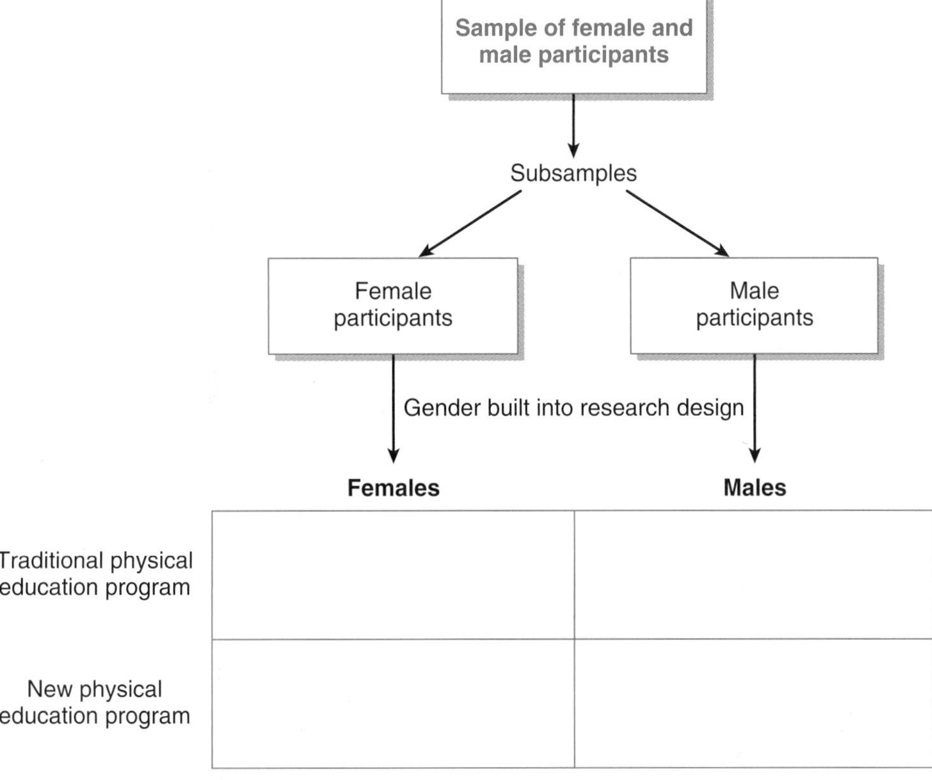

in the various comparison groups differ on a pretest variable that is related to the dependent variable. If the pretest variable is related to the dependent variable, differences observed on the dependent variable at the posttest might be due to differences on the pretest variable. Analysis of covariance adjusts the posttest scores for differences on the pretest variable, and in this way it *statistically equates* the participants in the comparison groups. For example, if you are conducting a study on gender differences in solving mathematics problems, you will want to make sure that the male and female students are of equal ability level. If you measure the IQ of the participants and find that the male students are brighter than the female students, any difference in mathematics performance found could be due to this difference in ability and not gender. You could use analysis of covariance to adjust the mathematics scores for this difference in intelligence and in this way create two groups of participants that are *equated* on this variable.

Counterbalancing

The previous control techniques were used when the comparison groups defined by the independent variable were composed of different research participants. Our last technique, counterbalancing, is only used with a different type of research design: *repeated-measures* research designs (discussed in more detail later in this chapter). The distinguishing characteristic of a repeated-measures design is that *all participants receive all treatments.* The control technique of **counterbalancing** refers to administering the experimental conditions to all participants but in different orders.

- **Counterbalancing** Administering all experimental conditions to all participants but in different orders
- **Sequencing effects** Biasing effects that can occur when each participant must participate in each experimental treatment condition
- **Order effect** A sequencing effect that occurs due to the order in which the treatment conditions are administered

Counterbalancing is used to control for **sequencing effects**, which can occur when each participant participates in more than one comparison group, as illustrated in Figure 12.6. Two types of sequencing effects can occur when every person participates in each comparison group.

The first type of sequencing effect is an **order effect**, which arises from the order in which the treatment conditions are administered. Suppose you are interested in the effect of caffeine on learning to spell based on the fact that caffeine is assumed to increase attention and alertness. To test the effect of caffeine, you might administer caffeine on one day to all of the participants and a placebo on the second day to all of the participants. This means that the research participants would get one of two possible *orders of the treatment conditions*: caffeine on the first day and placebo on the second day or placebo on the first day and caffeine on the second day.

In a study such as this, on the first experimental day, the research participants might be unfamiliar with the experimental procedure, participating in an educational experiment, or the surroundings of the experiment. If they are administered the placebo condition on the first day, the participants might not perform effectively because their attention is not focused totally on the spelling task. On the second day, when they are administered caffeine, familiarity will exist, increasing the chances that the participants can focus more on the spelling task, thereby enhancing performance. The result is that the participants might perform better under the caffeine treatment condition administered on the second day not because it is more effective but because the participants are more familiar with the experiment and the experimental surroundings. This type of effect is an order effect because it occurs strictly due to the order of presentation of the experimental treatment conditions.

The second type of sequencing effect is a carryover effect. A **carryover effect** occurs when performance in one treatment condition depends partially on the conditions that precede it. For example, if caffeine were administered on the first day, it is possible that the caffeine would not be completely metabolized and cleared from the body before the participants consumed the placebo on the next day. Any effect of the prior day's dose of caffeine would therefore carry over to the next day and affect performance. Therefore, the performance on the day that participants consumed the placebo would be influenced by any placebo effect plus any carryover from the prior day's consumption of caffeine.

■ **Carryover effect** A sequencing effect that occurs when performance in one treatment condition is influenced by participation in a prior treatment condition(s)

The primary way to control for carryover and order effects is to counterbalance (i.e., vary) the order in which the experimental conditions are administered to the participants. One way to counterbalance is to randomize the order across participants (i.e., let a random number generator randomly assign a sequence order to each participant). Another popular technique is to administer each experimental condition to sets of research participants in a different order. For example, in the caffeine experiment, assume that we wanted to test the effect of three different doses of caffeine (100, 200, and 300 mg of caffeine) against no caffeine or a placebo group. One way of counterbalancing would be to have sets of participants equal to the number of levels of the independent variable. In this caffeine experiment, there are four levels of caffeine, ranging from no caffeine to 300 mg, so there are four experimental conditions. If you had 40 participants, you could divide them into four sets of 10 and administer the four experimental conditions in a different order for each set, as follows:

Set 1 (participants 1–10) order of conditions: placebo, 100 mg, 300 mg, 200 mg

Set 2 (participants 11–20) order of conditions: 100 mg, 200 mg, placebo, 300 mg

Set 3 (participants 21–30) order of conditions: 200 mg, 300 mg, 100 mg, placebo

Set 4 (participants 31–40) order of conditions: 300 mg, placebo, 200 mg, 100 mg

As you can see, each set of participants receives all experimental conditions but in a different order or sequence. After administering the conditions, you can compare the

■ **FIGURE 12.6** Type of design that can include sequencing effects

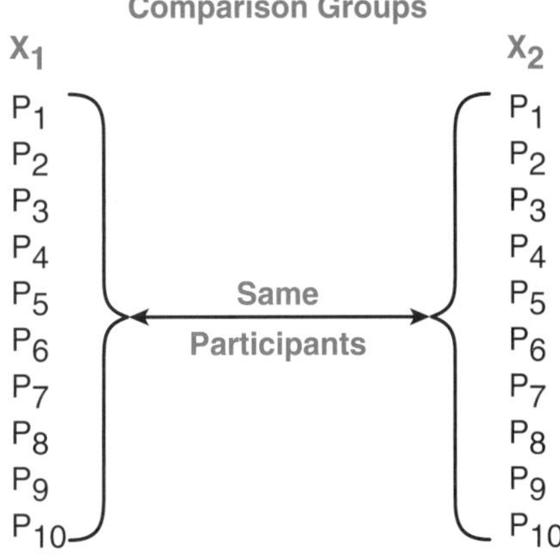

mean/average of all 40 participants in each of the four conditions and look for significant differences. Counterbalancing operates by averaging out the order and sequencing effects. To learn how to logically establish counterbalanced sequences, see Christensen, Johnson, and Turner (2014, pp. 205–206) or see this book's companion website.

REVIEW QUESTIONS

12.5 What is random assignment, and what is the difference between random assignment and random selection?

12.6 How does random assignment accomplish the goal of controlling for the influence of confounding variables?

12.7 How would you implement the control technique of matching, and how does this technique control for the influence of confounding variables?

12.8 How would you use the control technique of holding the extraneous variable constant?

12.9 When would you want to build the extraneous variable into the research design?

12.10 What is analysis of covariance, and when would you use it?

12.11 What is counterbalancing, and when would you use it?

12.12 What is the difference between a carryover effect and an order effect?

EXPERIMENTAL RESEARCH DESIGNS

■ **Research design** The outline, plan, or strategy that is used to answer a research question

Research design refers to the outline, plan, or strategy you are going to use to seek an answer to your research question(s). In other words, when you get to the stage of designing your experiment, you have to identify the plan or strategy to be used in collecting the data that will adequately test your hypotheses. Planning a research design means that you must specify how the participants will be assigned to the comparison groups, how you will control for potentially confounding extraneous variables, and how you will collect and analyze the data.

How do you go about designing an experiment that will test your hypotheses and provide an answer to your research questions? This is no simple task, and there is no set way to tell others how to do it. Designing a research study requires thought about which components to include and pitfalls to avoid. However, it helps to have some knowledge of the general types of research designs that can be used. Some of these research designs are weak in the sense that they do not provide for maximum control of potentially confounding variables. Others are strong in that they provide for the maximum control. Yet others are in between weak and strong designs; these are called "quasi-experimental designs," which are discussed in the next chapter. Now, we first discuss the weak designs and point out their deficiencies. We then discuss strong (i.e., the best) experimental designs that you can use as models when designing your research study.

See Tools and Tips 12.1 on the Student Study Site.

Weak Experimental Research Designs

We present three experimental research designs that are designated weak designs because they do not control for many potentially confounding extraneous variables. Remember that, in an experimental research study, we want to identify the causal effect produced by the independent variable on the dependent variable. Any uncontrolled confounding variables threaten our ability to do this and can render the experiment useless in the worst case and, even in the best of circumstances, jeopardize our ability to reach a valid conclusion. This is not to say that these weak experimental designs do not provide any valuable information. They can provide useful information. However, whenever a researcher uses one of them, he or she must be alert to the influence of potentially confounding extraneous variables that can threaten the internal validity of the study. Table 12.1 provides a summary of some of the threats to internal (i.e., causal) validity that may operate in each of these three designs.

TABLE 12.1 Summary of the Threats to Internal Validity of Weak Experimental Designs

Designs	*Ambiguous Temporal Precedence*	*History*	*Maturation*	*Testing*	*Instrumentation*	*Regression Artifact*	*Differential Selection*	*Differential Attrition*	*Additive and Interactive Effects*
One-group posttest-only design $X_T\ O_2$	+	–	–	NA	NA	NA	NA	NA	NA
One-group pretest-posttest design $O_1\ X_T\ O_2$	+	–	–	–	–	–	NA	NA	NA
Posttest-only design with nonequivalent groups $X_T\ O_2$ / $X_C\ O_2$ (dashed line between)	+	+	+	NA	NA	+	–	–	–

A negative sign (–) indicates a potential threat to internal validity, a positive sign (+) indicates that the threat is controlled, and *NA* indicates that the threat does not apply to that design. X_T designates a treatment condition, X_C designates a control or standard treatment condition, O_1 designates a pretest, O_2 designates a posttest, and a dashed line indicates no random assignment to groups.

One-Group Posttest-Only Design

In the **one-group posttest-only design**,[1] a single group of research participants is exposed to an experimental treatment and then measured on the dependent variable to assess the effect of the treatment condition, as illustrated in Figure 12.7. This design might be used if a school system wanted to find out whether implementation of a new reading program enhances students' desire to read. After implementation of the program for an entire school year, a questionnaire is given to all students in the program to assess their attitude toward reading. If the results indicate that the students' attitude is positive, the program is assumed to produce a positive attitude toward reading.

One-group posttest-only design Administering a posttest to a single group of participants after they have been given an experimental treatment condition

The problem with reaching such a conclusion is that you cannot attribute the students' attitudes toward reading to the new reading program. It is possible that the students had a positive attitude toward reading before participating in the program and that the program actually had no impact on their attitude. Because the students were not pretested, the researcher does not know anything about what the students were like prior to implementation of the reading program. The important point is that it is impossible to determine whether the new reading program had any effect or what that effect was without some sort of comparison. From a scientific point of view, this design is of almost no value because, without pretesting or comparing the students in the program to students who did not participate in the reading program, it is impossible to determine whether the treatment produced any effect. You could improve this design by adding a pretest and a control group.

FIGURE 12.7 One-group posttest-only design in which X_T is the treatment and O_2 is the posttest assessment

Treatment	Posttest Measure
X_T	O_2

One-Group Pretest-Posttest Design

One-group pretest-posttest design Administering a posttest to a single group of participants after they have been pretested and given an experimental treatment condition

Most individuals quickly recognize that the one-group posttest-only design is ineffective because of the lack of some type of comparison. The first response in many instances is to state that a pretest is needed so that the pretreatment response can be compared with the posttreatment response. This design, called the **one-group pretest-posttest design** and illustrated in Figure 12.8, is an improvement over the one-group posttest-only design. A group of research participants is measured on the dependent variable, O, prior to administration of the treatment condition. The independent variable, X, is then administered, and the dependent variable, O, is again measured. The difference between the pretest and posttest scores is taken as an index of the effectiveness of the treatment condition.

Although the one-group pretest-posttest design is an improvement over the one-group posttest-only design, any observed change in the posttest scores over the pretest scores cannot automatically be taken as an index of an effect produced by the independent variable. Many potentially confounding extraneous variables, such as history, maturation, testing, instrumentation, and regression artifacts, could also influence the posttest results. To the extent that they do, these extraneous variables represent rival hypotheses to explain any difference between the pretest and posttest scores.

Consider a hypothetical study in which an educational researcher wants to test a new instructional program for teaching reading to slow learners in the fifth grade. At the beginning of the school year, slow learners are identified by administering the Metropolitan Achievement Tests to all fifth-grade students in the New Approach elementary school. Those fifth-grade students who score at least 2 years below the fifth-grade level are considered slow learners and placed in an experimental classroom, where the new reading instructional program is administered. At the end of 2 years, the Metropolitan Achievement Tests are again administered, and the average reading grade placement score received by the students at this time (posttest-O) is compared with their average pretest-O score. Now let's assume that this comparison indicates that the slow learners have improved an average of 2.2 years in reading grade placement, suggesting that they advanced significantly during the 2 years that they were in the experimental classroom. It is tempting to attribute this improvement to the experimental reading program. However, if you think about it for a moment, you can probably identify several rival hypotheses that could account for this change in performance.

History is a very real possibility. The students were placed in an experimental classroom, which means that they were singled out and given special attention (beyond just receiving the treatment). The special effort made by the school system might have motivated the parents of these children to encourage them to read and perform their homework assignments. This parental encouragement, in addition to the experimental program, could have enhanced the students' reading performance. Similarly, 2 years elapsed between the pretest and posttest assessments. The students were 2 years older, and maturation would predict that some of the improvement would occur just because the students were older and thus had matured during the intervening 2 years. A testing effect could exist because the students took the Metropolitan Achievement Tests as the pretest and posttest, which means that the tests might have been more familiar on the second testing occasion. However, a testing effect would be more likely if a shorter amount of time had elapsed between the pretesting and posttesting. Finally, a regression artifact is a very real possibility because the students selected for the experimental classroom were those who scored lowest on the initial pretest. A regression artifact effect would predict that some of these students would improve on posttesting because their low scores on the pretest were in part due to chance.

As you can see, the one-group pretest-posttest design can be problematic in that many potentially confounding extraneous variables, in addition to the independent variable, can reasonably account for the change in behavior, making it a relatively weak design. Although the one-group pretest-posttest design is weak, it does provide some information in that it lets you know whether a change occurred between pretesting and posttesting. However, it might not provide a reasonable explanation of the cause of this change because of the many factors that could also account for the behavioral change. When using this design, you should be cautious about interpreting any effect as being due to the independent variable and try to seek evidence that would rule out the existence of each of the possible threats to the internal validity of the design.

FIGURE 12.8 One-group pretest-posttest design in which X_T is the treatment and 0_1 and 0_2 represent the pretest and posttest assessments

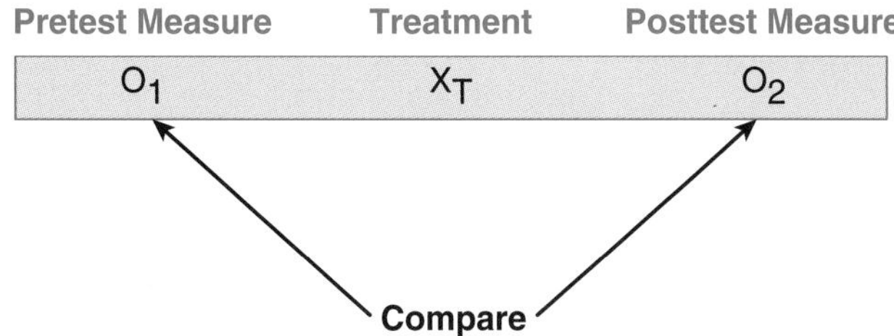

Posttest-Only Design With Nonequivalent Groups

The **posttest-only design with nonequivalent groups** is a design in which one group of research participants is administered a treatment and is then compared, on the dependent

- **Posttest-only design with nonequivalent groups** Comparing posttest performance of a group of participants who have been given an experimental treatment condition with that of a group that has not been given the experimental treatment condition

variable, with another group of research participants that did not receive the experimental treatment, as illustrated in Figure 12.9. The dashed line in Figure 12.9 indicates that intact or nonrandomly assigned groups are formed, X_T indicates the experimental treatment condition, and X_C indicates the control comparison condition. For example, if you want to determine whether including a computer-assisted drill and practice lab enhances learning and performance of students taking an educational statistics course, you might have one class take the statistics course without the computer laboratory (X_C) and the other class take statistics with the computer laboratory (X_T). Both classes would be taught by the same instructor, so there would not be an effect of different instructors. At the end of the course, you would compare the two classes in terms of their statistics performance (O). If the class that includes the computer laboratory performs better than the class that does not have computer laboratory practice, this should indicate that the addition of the computer laboratory enhanced statistics performance. In fact, examination of Table 12.1 shows that many threats to internal validity have been eliminated because of the addition of a control group! Unfortunately, Table 12.1 also shows that this design has other threats to internal validity. Therefore, it might not be true that the computer laboratory enhanced statistics performance. Some potentially confounding extraneous variables can easily creep into this design and severely threaten its internal validity.

The posttest-only design with nonequivalent groups might seem on the surface to be adequate because a comparison group is included. This group provides for a comparison of the performance of participants who were and were not exposed to the computer laboratory. Additionally, the same instructor taught the two courses, so there should be little difference in instructional quality. Why, then, is the design included as an example of a weak design? The reason is that the two classes of research participants were not equated on variables other than the independent variable. The two classes were formed on the basis of the students who signed up for them at the two times offered rather than being randomly assigned to the comparison groups, as the dashed line in Figure 12.9 illustrates. This problem is called *differential selection,* and the word *nonequivalent* in the title of the design highlights this serious threat. (Note: Selection also can combine or interact with any of the basic threats to internal validity, as discussed in the last chapter.) The difference in performance could have resulted because the students in the two classes were very different on many variables other than the independent variable. For example,

FIGURE 12.9 The posttest-only design with nonequivalent groups in which X_T represents the experimental treatment, X_C represents the control or standard treatment, and O_2 represents the posttest assessment

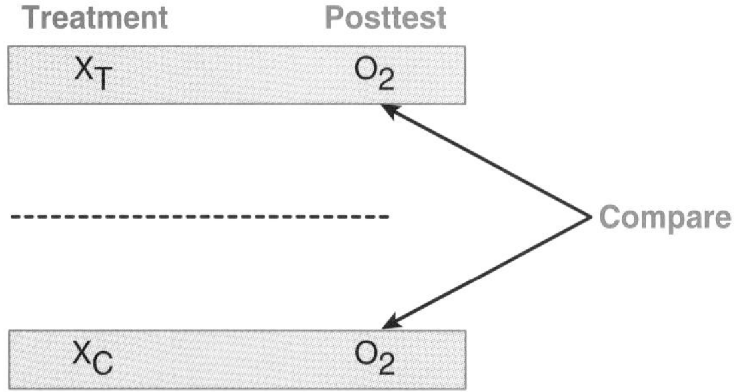

the students taking the course that included the computer laboratory might have been brighter or older or more motivated to do well than the students in the comparison group that did not have exposure to the computer laboratory. Any of those differences could serve as rival hypotheses to explain the outcome. To achieve maximum assurance that two or more comparison groups are equated, participants must be randomly assigned, and in this design they are not. The use of matching could also improve this design because you could equate the groups on a few worrisome variables. Finally, the inclusion of a pretest also would improve this design.

REVIEW QUESTIONS

12.13 What is a research design, and what are the elements that go into developing a research design?

12.14 When would the one-group posttest-only design be used, and what problems are encountered in using this design?

12.15 When would you use the one-group pretest-posttest design, and what potential rival hypotheses can operate in this design?

12.16 What potential rival hypotheses can operate in the posttest-only design with nonequivalent groups?

Strong Experimental Research Designs

The designs just presented are considered weak because they do not provide a way of isolating the effect of the independent variable from the influence of potentially confounding variables. A strong experimental research design is one in which the influence of confounding extraneous variables is controlled. Table 12.2 summarizes the threats to internal (i.e., causal) validity that are controlled by strong experimental designs. A strong experimental research design therefore is one that has high internal validity (i.e., you can be confident about your conclusion of cause and effect).

In most experimental research designs, the most effective way to achieve internal validity and eliminate rival hypotheses is to include one or more of the control techniques discussed earlier in this chapter and to include a control group. Once again, of the many control techniques that are available to the researcher, *random assignment is the most important!* Its importance cannot be overemphasized because it is the only means by which unknown variables can be controlled.

Control of several threats to internal validity is achieved by including a control group. You will see this clearly if you take a moment, right now, to compare (in Table 12.1) the threats to the one-group pretest-posttest design and the posttest-only design with nonequivalent groups. (Notice that five minus signs changed to positive signs.) Now, shift to Table 12.2 and notice that all strong experimental research designs include at least two comparison groups: an experimental group and a control group. They control for all of the standard threats to internal validity because they have random assignment to these groups (except for the repeated-measures design, which requires counterbalancing rather than random assignment).

- **Experimental group** The group that receives the experimental treatment condition
- **Control group** The group that does not receive the experimental treatment condition

The experimental group is the group that receives the experimental treatment condition. The control group is the group that does not receive the experimental treatment condition. This might mean that nothing was done to the control group or that the control group got what might be viewed as a standard or typical condition. If you were investigating the efficacy of a new method of teaching reading, the experimental group would be exposed to the new reading method, and the control group would be exposed to the typical or standard way of teaching reading. If you were testing a new drug on children with ADHD based on the hypothesis that it would reduce their level of ADHD and permit them to learn more effectively, the experimental group would receive the drug, and the control group would receive either a placebo or the standard or commonly administered drug for treating ADHD. In this type of study, you might even have three groups: a group that received the placebo, another that received the standard drug, and a third that received the new experimental drug.

A control group is necessary because of the functions it serves. It serves as a comparison and a control for rival hypotheses. To determine whether some treatment condition or independent variable had an effect, we need a comparison or control group that did not receive the treatment. Consider a situation in which certain students in your classroom are repeatedly talking to each other. This is disruptive not only to these children but also to others in the classroom. To control this behavior, you keep these students in during recess and also move them to different areas in the classroom. To your delight, your interventions stop them from talking and allow you to teach without this disruption. You attribute this change in behavior to having kept these students inside during recess. However, you also changed their seating location, and perhaps being seated together promoted their talking. When you moved their locations in the classroom, you might have placed each student in a spot surrounded by people who were not the student's friends, so a rival hypothesis is that the talking was prompted by being surrounded by friends. To determine whether keeping the students in during recess or moving them to other locations produced the change in behavior, a control group—who would be moved to other locations in the classroom but not be kept in during recess—would have to be included. If both groups stopped talking to other students, we would know that being kept in during recess was probably not the variable causing the elimination of talking behavior.

As mentioned above, just including a control group is not enough, however, to construct a strong experimental design. For example, one of the weak designs included a control group, but it did not have random assignment. Be sure to notice the three minus signs associated with that design in Table 12.1 (i.e., the posttest-only design with nonequivalent groups). Those threats will be transformed into strengths once random assignment is added! Random assignment is present only in strong experimental designs. If you have different participants in different comparison groups (see the first three designs in Table 12.2), you must *randomly assign* participants to the comparison groups to achieve the status of "strong experimental design." To emphasize the inclusion of random assignment, these very strong designs are sometimes called *randomized designs.*

- **RCT** A popular term for experimental designs with random assignment of participants to experimental and control groups and, if possible, use of double-blind procedures

Because of the importance of random assignment and the use of a true control group for much experimental research, the term *RCT* has become popular in education and medical research. *RCT* stands for *randomized controlled trial* or, in medicine, *randomized clinical trial.* An RCT is any experimental design with random assignment to experimental and control groups. In medicine, an additional requirement is often added: double-blind

TABLE 12.2 Summary of the Threats to Internal Validity for Strong Experimental Designs

Designs	*Ambiguous Temporal Precedence*	*History*	*Maturation*	*Testing*	*Instrumentation*	*Regression Artifact*	*Differential Selection*	*Differential Attrition*	*Additive and Interactive Effects*	*Sequencing*
Pretest-posttest control-group design R → $O_1\ X_c\ O_2$ R → $O_1\ X_T\ O_2$	+	+	+	+	+	+	+	+	+	NA
Posttest-only control-group design R → $X_c\ O_2$ R → $X_T\ O_2$	+	+	+	+	+	+	+	+	+	NA
Factorial design R → $X_{T1}\ Z_{T1}\ O_2$ R → $X_{T1}\ Z_{T2}\ O_2$ R → $X_{T2}\ Z_{T1}\ O_2$ R → $X_{T2}\ Z_{T2}\ O_2$	+	+	+	+	+	+	+	+	+	NA
Repeated-measures design* $\lvert X_{T1}\ O_2 \rvert\ X_{T2}\ O_2 \rvert\ X_{T3}\ O_2 \rvert$ Same participants take every level of the treatment condition in a repeated-measures design.	+	+	+	+	+	+	NA	+	NA	+
Factorial design based on a mixed model** $\lvert X_{T1}\ Z_{T1}\ O_2 \rvert\ X_{T2}\ Z_{T1}\ O_2 \rvert\ X_{T3}\ Z_{T1}\ O_2 \rvert$ $\lvert X_{T1}\ Z_{T2}\ O_2 \rvert\ X_{T2}\ Z_{T2}\ O_2 \rvert\ X_{T3}\ Z_{T2}\ O_2 \rvert$ All participants receive all three levels of the within-subjects IV labeled "X" and the participants are randomly assigned to the two levels of the between-subjects IV labeled Z. This is a 3 by 2 factorial design.	+	+	+	+	+	+	+	+	+	+

A positive sign (+) indicates that the threat is controlled and NA indicates that the threat does not apply to that design. X_T designates a treatment condition; X_C designates a control or standard treatment condition; O_1 designates a pretest; O_2 designates a posttest; X_{T1}, X_{T2}, and X_{T3} designate the three levels of one independent variable; Z_{T1} and Z_{T2} designate the two levels of a second independent variable; and R designates random assignment to groups.

* The "+" marks are based on the assumption that counterbalancing is used. When counterbalancing is used, this design controls for all applicable threats except possibly a **differential carryover effect** (a complex but possible type of carryover effect; see Glossary for a full definition).

**This design needs counterbalancing for the within-subjects IV and random assignment for the between-subjects IV.

- **Double-blind procedure** Design in which neither the researcher nor the participant knows the specific condition (experimental or control) that the participant is in
- **Single-blind procedure** Design in which the participant does not know the specific condition he or she is in
- **Pretest-posttest control-group design** A research design that administers a posttest to two randomly assigned groups of participants after both have been pretested and one of the groups has been administered the experimental treatment condition

procedures. A study is **double-blind** when the researcher does not know what treatment any particular participant receives and the participants do not know whether they are in the active experimental condition or in the control/placebo condition. Double-blind procedures also are helpful in educational research and should be used when feasible. Often, however, educational experiments are only **single-blind**; that is, the participants do not know what group they are in, but the researcher does know. Now let's carefully examine each of the strong designs summarized in Table 12.2.

Pretest-Posttest Control-Group Design

The **pretest-posttest control-group design** is illustrated in Figure 12.10. In this design, a group of research participants is randomly assigned to experimental and control groups and is pretested on the dependent variable, O. Next, the independent variable, X, is administered, and, last, the experimental and control groups are posttested on the dependent variable, O. Figure 12.10 reveals that the basic pretest-posttest control-group design is a two-group design containing one control and one experimental group. However, this design can be, and frequently is, expanded to include more than one experimental group, as illustrated in Figure 12.11. For example, if you want to determine which of four different ways of teaching reading—the standard way or three recently introduced ways—is most effective, you would randomly assign participants to four groups and then pretest each before administering the different reading programs. After the reading programs are administered, the participants would be posttested, and the data would be analyzed by one of the appropriate statistical techniques, such as analysis of covariance, to determine whether the different reading programs produced different results.

The pretest-posttest control-group design is an excellent experimental design because it effectively controls for rival hypotheses that would threaten the internal validity of the experiment. History and maturation are controlled because any history event or maturation effect that occurs in the experimental group also occurs in the control group, unless the history event occurred for only one of the two groups (in this case, the history event would not be controlled because it would not affect both groups equally). Instrumentation and testing are controlled because both the experimental and control groups are exposed to the pretest, so any effect of the pretest should exist in both groups. Regression and differential attrition variables are controlled because participants are randomly assigned to the experimental and control groups. The key idea is that random assignment provides maximum assurance that the two groups

FIGURE 12.10 Pretest-posttest control-group design in which X_T represents the treatment condition, X_C represents the control or standard treatment condition, and O_1 and O_2 represent the pretest and posttest assessments of the dependent variable

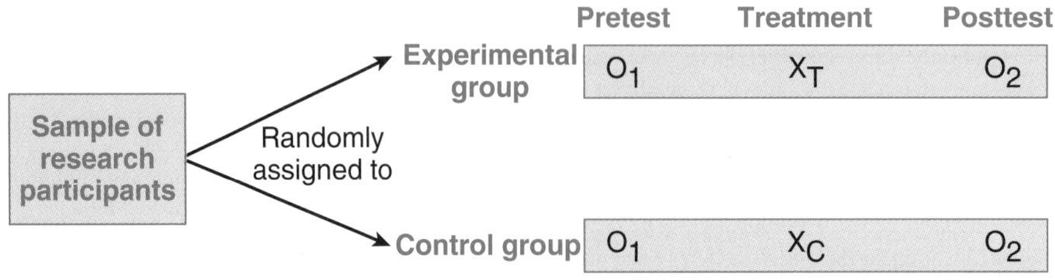

FIGURE 12.11 Pretest-posttest control-group design with more than one experimental group in which O_1 and O_2 represent the pretest and posttest assessments, X_C is the control or standard condition, and X_{T1}–X_{T3} represent three experimental treatment conditions

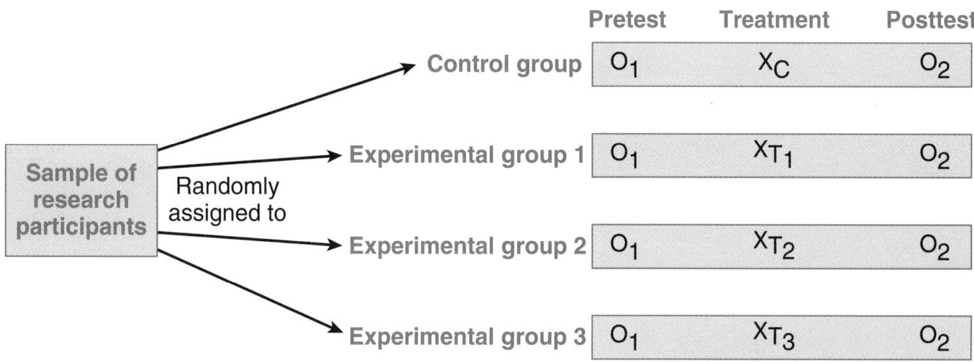

are equated on all extraneous variables at the outset of the experiment and is the key reason for strong internal validity. Although random assignment does not provide 100% assurance of initial equality of the experimental and control groups, it is the *best* technique available for equating groups in experimental research. It works well most of the time.

Posttest-Only Control-Group Design

The **posttest-only control-group design**, illustrated in Figure 12.12, is an experimental design in which the research participants are randomly assigned to an experimental group and a control group. The independent variable is administered, and then the experimental and control groups are measured on the dependent variable. The posttest scores of the experimental and control groups are statistically compared to determine whether the independent variable produced an effect.

- **Posttest-only control-group design** Research design in which a posttest is administered to two randomly assigned groups of participants after one group has been administered the experimental treatment condition

This is a strong experimental design because of the control it provides for the threats to internal validity. Because the posttest-only control-group design includes a control group and randomly assigned participants in the experimental and control groups, it controls for all potential threats to internal validity in the same way the pretest-posttest control-group design did. Although differential attrition—that is, the differential loss of participants from the two comparison groups—is unlikely (because the groups are composed of similar kinds of people), it is still possible. If one group loses participants with characteristics that are different from those of people who are lost from the other comparison group, a difference could be found on posttesting because the differential loss would produce two groups of participants who are no longer equivalent on all variables other than the independent variable.

The two-group posttest-only control-group design presented in Figure 12.12 is only one variation of this design. Many times more than two groups are needed for comparison in a study, and the posttest-only control-group design can be expanded to include as many comparison groups as are needed. As illustrated in Figure 12.13, the same design structure is maintained with more than two groups in that participants are randomly assigned to groups. After the experimental treatment is administered, the participants are posttested and compared, using a statistical technique called analysis of variance, to determine whether a statistically significant difference exists among the groups.

FIGURE 12.12 Posttest-only control-group design in which X_C is the control condition, X_T is the treatment condition, and O_2 is the posttest assessment

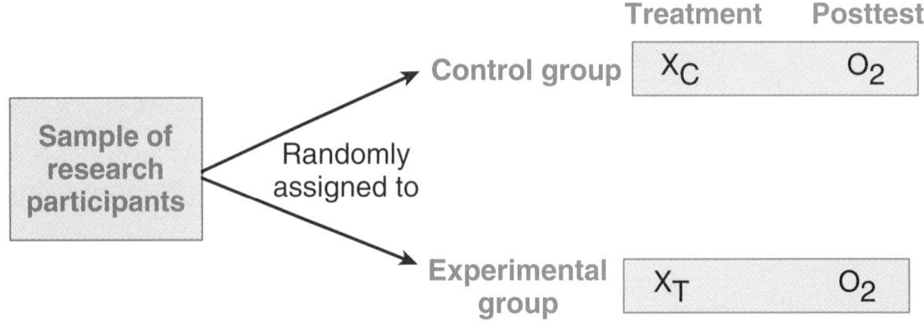

FIGURE 12.13 Posttest-only control-group design with more than one experimental group in which X_C is the control or standard treatment condition, X_{T1}–X_{T3} represent three treatment conditions, and O_2 is the posttest assessment

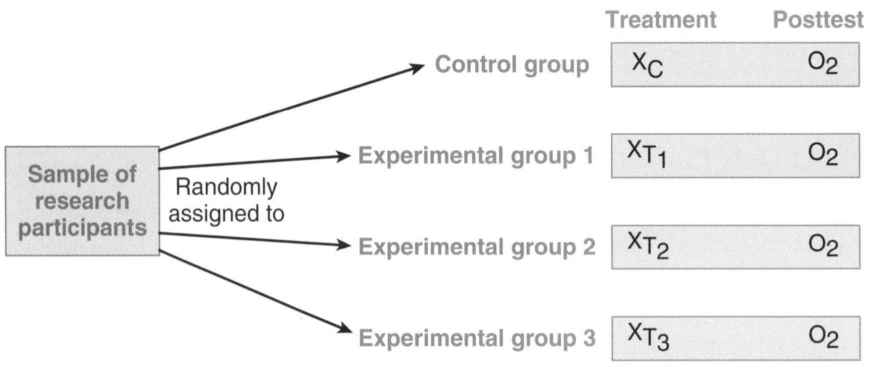

REVIEW QUESTIONS

12.17 What makes a design a strong experimental design?

12.18 What is the difference between an experimental group and a control group?

12.19 What functions are served by including a control group in a research design?

12.20 What potentially confounding extraneous variables are controlled in the pretest-posttest control-group design, and how does the design control for them?

12.21 What potentially confounding extraneous variables are controlled in the posttest-only control-group design, and how does the design control for them?

Factorial Designs

A **factorial design** is a strong experimental design in which two or more independent variables, at least one of which is manipulated, are simultaneously studied to determine their independent and interactive effects on the dependent variable. The experimental designs we have discussed up to this point have all been limited to investigating only *one* independent variable. For example, assume that you want to identify the most effective way of teaching mathematics and have identified three types of instruction: computer-assisted, lecture, and discussion. In designing this study, you have one independent variable—method of instruction—and three levels of that independent variable—the three types of instruction. Because there is only one independent variable, either the pretest-posttest control-group design or the posttest-only control-group design could be used. The design selected would depend on whether a pretest was included.

▪ **Factorial design** A design in which two or more independent variables, at least one of which is manipulated, are simultaneously studied to determine their independent and interactive effects on the dependent variable

In educational research, however, we are often interested in the effect of several independent variables acting in concert. Most variables of significance to educators do not act independently. For example, one type of instruction might be more effective for large classes and another type for small classes. Similarly, a student's anxiety level might hinder effective performance when a discussion format is used, whereas a computer-assisted format might allow the student to relax and perform better. This is where factorial designs come in because they *allow us to investigate simultaneously several independent variables and the interaction among those independent variables.*

If you are interested in investigating the effect of anxiety level *and* type of instruction on mathematics performance, you are obviously investigating two independent variables. Let's assume that you want to investigate the effect of two levels of anxiety—high and low—and three types of instruction—computer-assisted, lecture, and discussion. This means that you have two independent variables: anxiety level and type of instruction. The anxiety variable has two levels of variation—high and low—and the type of instruction variable has three levels of variation corresponding to the three types of instruction. Figure 12.14 depicts this design, which reveals that there are six combinations of the two independent variables: high anxiety and computer-assisted instruction, low anxiety and computer-assisted instruction, high anxiety and lecture, low anxiety and lecture, high anxiety and discussion, and low anxiety and discussion.

Each of the independent variable combinations is referred to as a **cell**. In the 2×3 design layout shown in Figure 12.14, participants would be randomly assigned to the six cells. (We are assuming that both type of instruction and anxiety are manipulated in the experiment.) If you had 90 participants, then after random assignment, there would be 15 participants in each of the six cells. The participants randomly assigned to a given cell receive the combination of independent variables corresponding to that cell. After the research participants have received their appropriate combination of independent variables and responded to the dependent variable, their dependent variable responses would be analyzed to check for two types of effects: main effects and interaction effects.

▪ **Cell** A combination of two or more independent variables in a factorial design

▪ **Main effect** The effect of one independent variable on the dependent variable

A **main effect** refers to the influence of a single independent variable. The design depicted in Figure 12.14 has two independent variables and can therefore have two main effects: anxiety level and type of instruction. The presence of an *anxiety main effect* would mean that there was a statistically significant difference in performance depending on whether a person experienced high or low anxiety. The presence of an *instruction main effect* would mean that there was a statistically significant difference in performance depending on the type of mathematics instruction the research participant received.

▪ **Interaction effect** The effect of one independent variable on the dependent variable depends on the level of another independent variable

A factorial design also allows us to investigate interaction effects. An **interaction effect** exists when the effect of one independent variable on the dependent variable is different or varies across the levels of another independent variable. The concept of interaction is rather difficult for most students to grasp, so we will spend some time on this issue. First, we

■ FIGURE 12.14 Factorial design with two independent variables

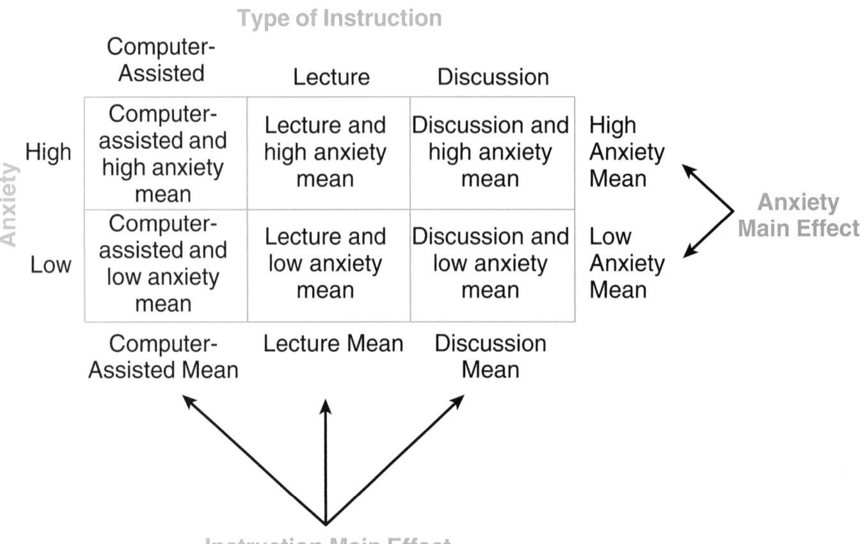

demonstrate in Figures 12.15a and b an outcome in which the two main effects of anxiety level and type of instruction are present but there is *no interaction effect.*

Look at Figure 12.15a. The scores in the cells show the mean, or average, posttest score for each group of participants (e.g., the high-anxiety participants who received computer-assisted instruction had a mean score of 10). The hypothetical posttest cell scores represent the mean dependent variable scores, such as number of mathematics problems correctly answered. The marginal mean, or the mean of the scores in the cells of a column or row, shown outside the cells, is the mean posttest score across the cells (e.g., the mean score of 15 for the high-anxiety participants is the average of the scores in the three cells of the high-anxiety participants). In this example, the marginal mean for the high-anxiety individuals is 15, and the marginal mean for the low-anxiety participants is 25, indicating that there is a main effect of anxiety level on performance. Similarly, there is a difference between the type of instruction marginal means, indicating that there is a main effect of type of instruction on performance.

■ **Marginal mean** The mean of scores in the cells of a column or a row of a table representing factorial design outcomes

Now look at the corresponding graph in Figure 12.15b. Take note of the fact that the two lines are parallel. Whenever the lines are parallel, an interaction is *not* present, because an interaction means that the effect of one variable, such as anxiety level, depends on the level of the other variable being considered, such as the three types of instruction, and this would produce nonparallel lines. In this example, individuals with low anxiety levels always performed better than those with high anxiety levels regardless of the type of instruction received, indicating an anxiety main effect. Similarly, discussion instruction resulted in the best performance regardless of the participants' anxiety level, again indicating a main effect but no interaction effect. In this example, we had two main effects and no interaction.

Let us now look at an example with an interaction effect. First, look at Figure 12.15c: You will see that there is no difference between the marginal means for the two anxiety

FIGURE 12.15A Tabular representation of data showing a main effect for both independent variables but not their interaction

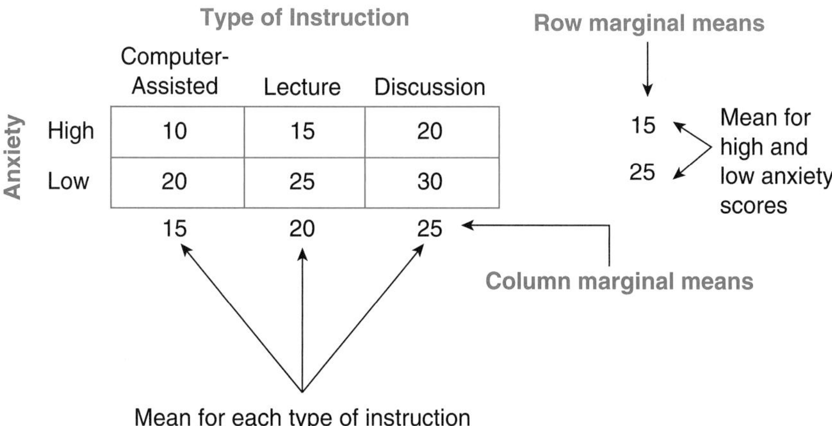

FIGURE 12.15B Graphic illustration of a main effect for both independent variables but no interaction effect

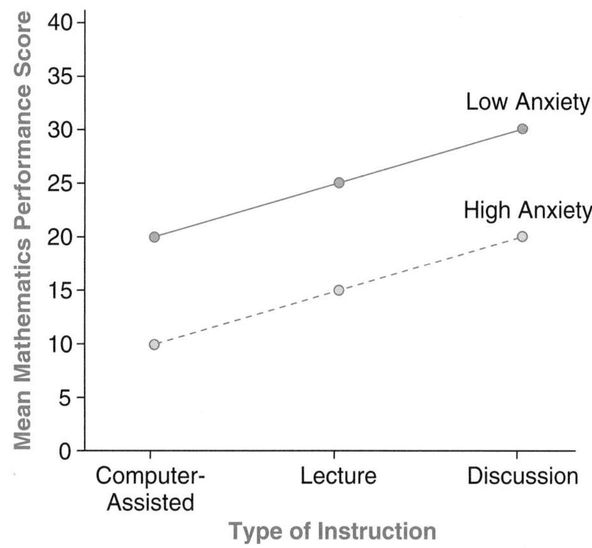

levels or for the different types of instruction, indicating that there are no main effects influencing mathematics performance. If you had conducted a study just on anxiety levels or just on type of instruction, you would have concluded that neither variable was important, but that is wrong. The cell means tell a very different story; they show that high-anxiety participants received the highest scores when receiving computer-assisted instruction and the lowest scores when receiving discussion instruction. Low-anxiety participants, on the other hand, got the lowest scores under computer-assisted instruction and the highest scores when receiving discussion instruction. In other words, the effect of type of instruction was quite important, but it depended on the participants' anxiety level—an interaction existed between the type of instruction and participant anxiety level.

- **Disordinal interaction effect** An interaction effect represented graphically by crossed lines on a graph plotting the effect

Now please examine Figure 12.15d: You will see that the lines for high- and low-anxiety individuals cross. Whenever the lines *cross* like this, you have a **disordinal interaction effect**. Performance increases under low anxiety levels and decreases under high anxiety levels as you move from computer-assisted instruction to discussion. Therefore, the effectiveness of the type of instruction depends on whether a person has a high or low level of anxiety, which is an interaction effect.

Before leaving this section on interaction, we need to point out that a possible interaction exists whenever the lines on the graph are not parallel even if they do *not* cross. Now

FIGURE 12.15C Tabular representation of data showing no main effects but the presence of an interaction effect

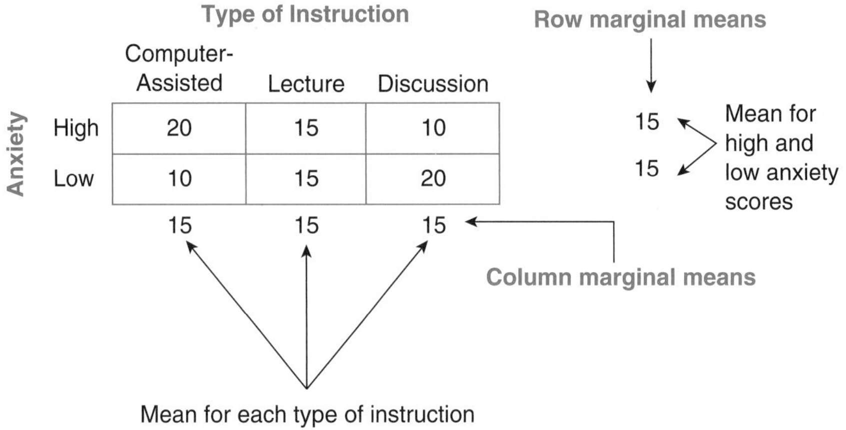

FIGURE 12.15D Graphic illustration of a disordinal interaction effect

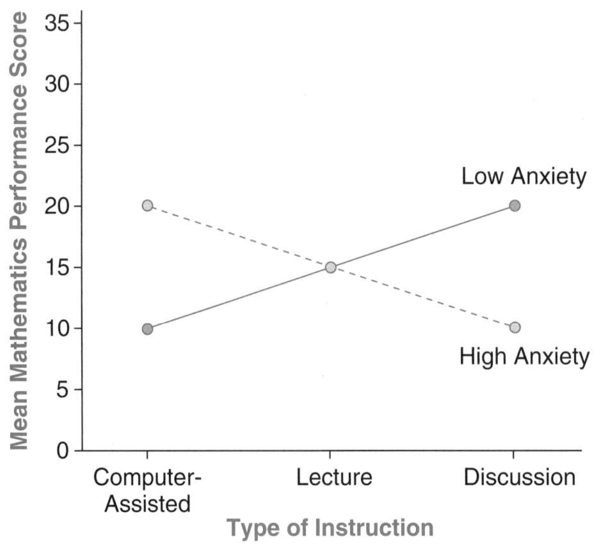

FIGURE 12.15E Graphic illustration of an ordinal interaction

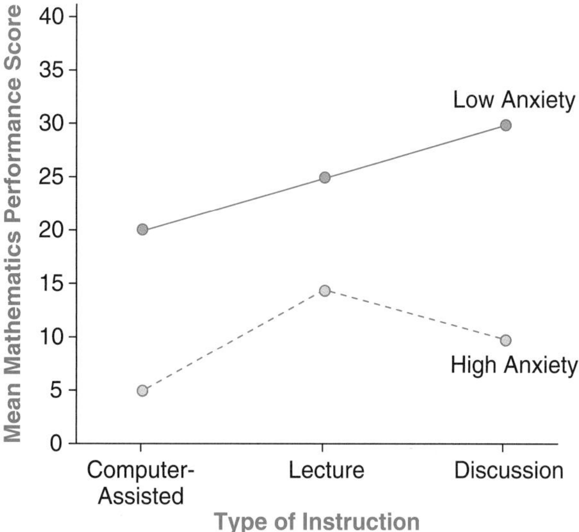

look at Figure 12.15e to see a graph in which the lines do not cross but are also not parallel. This is an **ordinal interaction effect**. Performance increases under low anxiety levels and decreases under high anxiety levels as we move from computer-assisted instruction to discussion. Again, the effectiveness of type of instruction depends on the level of anxiety a person has, which is an interaction effect.

Ordinal interaction effect An interaction effect represented graphically by nonparallel lines plotting the effect that do not cross

So far, our discussion of factorial designs has been limited to those with two independent variables. Sometimes it is advantageous to include three or more independent variables in a study. Factorial designs enable us to include as many independent variables as we consider important. Mathematically or statistically, there is almost no limit to the number of independent variables that can be included in a study. Practically speaking, however, several difficulties are associated with increasing the number of variables. First, there is an associated increase in the number of research participants required. In an experiment with two independent variables, each of which has two levels of variation, a 2×2 arrangement is generated, yielding four cells. If 15 participants are required for each cell, the experiment requires a total of 60 participants. In a three-variable design, with two levels of variation per independent variable, a $2 \times 2 \times 2$ arrangement exists, yielding eight cells, and 120 participants are required to have 15 participants per cell. Four variables and two levels of variation mean that 16 cells and 240 participants are required. As you can see, the required number of cells and participants increases rapidly with an increase in the number of independent variables.

A second difficulty with factorial designs incorporating more than two independent variables arises when higher-order interactions are statistically significant. In a design with three independent variables, it is possible to have an interaction among the three variables. Consider a study that investigates the effect of the independent variables of type of instruction, anxiety level, and participant gender on performance in mathematics. A three-variable interaction is complex and means that the effect of type of instruction on mathematics performance depends on people's anxiety level and whether they are male or female. In other words, the two-way interaction between type of instruction and anxiety level is different for males and females. If you conduct this study, you must look at this triple interaction and interpret its meaning, deciphering what combinations produce which effect and why. Triple interactions can be difficult to interpret, and interactions of an even higher order tend to become unwieldy. Therefore, it is advisable to restrict a research design to no more than three variables. In spite of these problems, factorial designs are very important and popular because they permit the investigation of more than one independent variable and of the interactions that might exist among these variables.

See Journal Article 12.4 on the Student Study Site.

Repeated-Measures Designs

- **Repeated-measures design** A design in which all participants participate in all experimental conditions
- **Within-subjects independent variable** An independent variable of which all participants receive all levels
- **Between-subjects independent variable** An independent variable of which each participant receives only one level

In a **repeated-measures design**, as shown in Figure 12.16, the same research participants participate in all experimental conditions. Another way of stating this is that all participants are repeatedly measured (i.e., under each experimental condition). For example, if the independent variable has two levels, then all participants participate in both of these levels or conditions; if the independent variable has three levels, then all participants participate in three levels or conditions; and so forth. This design feature is in direct contrast to the other designs in this chapter in which the different experimental conditions are administered to different research participants. Here's some convenient terminology for making this distinction: If all participants receive all levels of the independent variable, we call it a **within-subjects independent variable** (also called a repeated-measures variable); if the participants are separated so that any particular participant receives only *one* level of the independent variable, we call it a **between-subjects independent variable**.

For example, Carr and Jessup (1997) used the repeated-measures design in one part of their study investigating variables that contributed to gender differences in first graders' mathematics strategy use. First-grade children were interviewed individually outside the classroom in October, January, and May of the school year to determine the strategies they used when solving addition and subtraction problems. The researchers were interested in the independent variable of "time"; therefore, the strategies used by the participants (the dependent variable) were repeatedly investigated at three different times (the within-subjects independent variable) during the school year to determine whether strategy use changed over the course of the school year.

The repeated-measures design has the benefit of requiring fewer participants than the other strong designs based on between-subjects independent variables because in the repeated-measures design, all participants participate in all experimental conditions. Remember that in the factorial design that we just discussed, the number of participants needed is equal to the number needed in a one-cell or experimental condition times the number of experimental conditions or cells. In the repeated-measures design, the number of participants needed is equal to the number needed in one experimental condition because all participants participate in all experimental conditions, just as all the children in the Carr and Jessup (1997) study participated in the interviews conducted in October, January, and May.

With the repeated-measures design, the investigator does not have to worry about the participants in the different groups being equated because the same participants participate in all experimental conditions. The participants are said to "serve as their own control," which means that the participants in the various experimental conditions are perfectly

FIGURE 12.16 Repeated-measures design

	Experimental treatment conditions	
A	B	C
P_1	P_1	P_1
P_2	P_2	P_2
P_3	P_3	P_3
P_4	P_4	P_4
.	.	.
.	.	.
.	.	.
P_n	P_n	P_n

Note: All research participants are in all conditions; n = total number of participants in the study.

FIGURE 12.17 Repeated-measures design with counterbalancing in which levels X_1–X_3 of the single independent variable represent three treatment conditions administered to all groups of participants in a different counterbalanced order and O represents the dependent variable measured after each treatment condition

Group I	X_1	O	X_2	O	X_3	O
Group II	X_2	O	X_3	O	X_1	O
Group III	X_3	O	X_1	O	X_2	O

matched. Note, however, that in order to rule out all key threats to internal validity the *counterbalancing* control technique must be used with the repeated-measures design. Counterbalancing is discussed earlier in the chapter and is demonstrated in Figure 12.17. The key idea is that different participants receive the treatments in different orders. All participants receive all treatments (making it a repeated-measures design) but they receive the treatments in different orders. Counterbalancing therefore "averages out" sequencing and order effects so that these problems are not present in the final, combined results.

Factorial Designs Based on a Mixed Model

There are times in educational research when one or more of the variables of interest fit into a repeated-measures design and the other variable(s) of interest fits into a posttest-only control-group design. These variables can be combined into one study by using a factorial design based on a mixed model. The simplest form of this design involves an experiment using two independent variables. One independent variable has a comparison group for each level of the independent variable. These levels of the independent variable include different people. The other independent variable is constructed in such a way that all participants have to take each level the independent variable at separate times. The first independent variable (the between-subjects IV) requires a posttest-only control-group design, and the second independent variable (the within-subjects IV) requires a repeated-measures design. When the two independent variables are included in the same scheme, it becomes a factorial design based on a mixed model, as illustrated in Figure 12.18.[2]

Factorial design based on a mixed model A factorial design in which different participants are randomly assigned to the different levels of one independent variable but all participants take all levels of another independent variable

In this design, participants are randomly assigned to the different comparison groups required by the between-subjects independent variable, and all participants then take each level of variation of the repeated-measures/within-subjects independent variable. This combination gives us a strong experimental design with the advantage of being able to test for the effects produced by each of the two independent variables as well as for the interaction between the two independent variables. Additionally, we have the advantage of needing fewer participants because all participants take all levels of variation of one of the independent variables.

We have limited our discussion of the factorial design based on a mixed model to two independent variables. This does not mean that the design cannot be extended to include more than two independent variables. As with the standard factorial design, we can include as many independent variables as are considered necessary.

FIGURE 12.18 Factorial design based on a mixed model

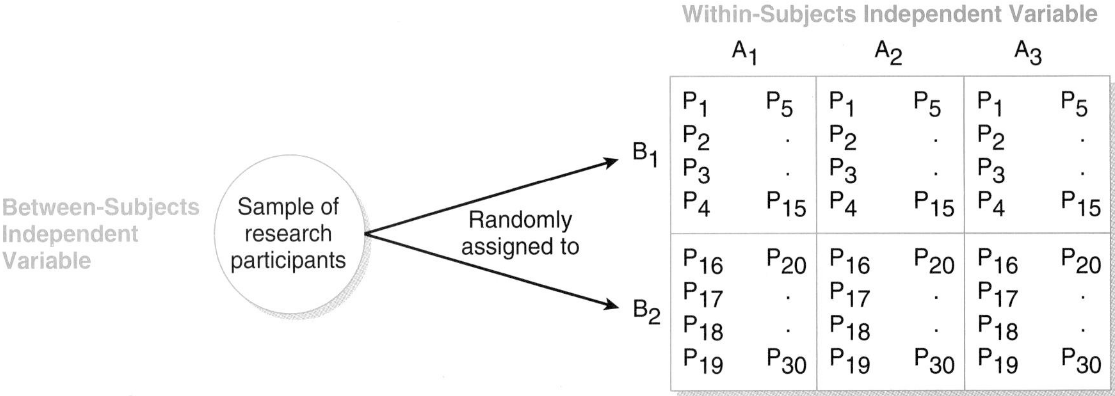

REVIEW QUESTIONS

12.22 What is a factorial design, and what is the advantage of this design over the two-group posttest-only design?

12.23 What is a main effect?

12.24 What is an interaction effect, and what is the difference between an ordinal and a disordinal interaction?

12.25 What is the difference between a factorial and a repeated-measures design?

12.26 What are the advantages and disadvantages of factorial and repeated-measures designs?

12.27 What is a factorial design based on a mixed model, and when would it be used?

ACTION RESEARCH REFLECTION

Insight: Action researchers tend to be more interested in *idiographic* (i.e., local, particularistic, contextual, intentional) causation than *nomothetic* (i.e., scientific, highly generalizable, lawful) causation. However, broadly viewed, *all action researchers are experimental researchers* because they want to cause good things to happen with their students and participants; they continually try new things to see if they work. They actively introduce experimental conditions and observe what happens. They inquire in the Deweyan sense of inquiry discussed earlier. One very popular design in action research is the one-group pretest-posttest design, but other designs discussed in this and in the next chapter also are used.

1. Conduct a means-ends analysis or MEA (A. P. Johnson, 2008). That is, (a) identify a problem you want to change, (b) brainstorm and generate a list of solutions to the problem, (c) select the solution that you think has the best chance of solving the problem, (d) decide exactly how you will conduct this manipulation, (e) implement your "solution," and (f) determine how well it worked (using multiple sources and eliminating alternative explanations).
2. Can you use or adapt one of the experimental designs discussed in this chapter to help you solve your action research problem? Explain.

SUMMARY

The key purpose of experimental research is to identify cause-and-effect relationships. This research is conducted within the context of an experiment, which is an environment in which the experimenter attempts to objectively observe phenomena that are made to occur in a strictly controlled environment in which one or more variables are varied and the others are kept constant. The environments or settings in which educational experiments are conducted include field settings, laboratory settings, and the Internet.

Conducting an educational experiment involves manipulating the independent variable so that the effect of this manipulation can be observed on the dependent variable. The independent variable can be manipulated by using a presence or absence technique, varying the amount of the independent variable that is administered, or varying the type of the independent variable condition administered to participants.

Conducting an educational experiment necessitates control of the effect of potentially confounding extraneous variables. Control is achieved in most studies by eliminating any differential influence of the extraneous variables across the comparison groups. *The most effective method for controlling the differential influence of extraneous variables is to randomly assign the research participants to the various comparison groups.*

In addition to random assignment, control of potentially confounding extraneous variables is achieved by matching individual participants, holding extraneous variables constant, building the extraneous variable into the research design, counterbalancing, and using analysis of covariance. However, none of these control techniques takes the place of random assignment. Even if one or more of these other control techniques are used, you should still randomly assign whenever and wherever possible.

The next step in conducting a research study is to design the study. Research design is the outline, plan, or strategy used in conducting the study. A number of experimental research designs can be used. Some are weak designs because they do not control for the effect of many potentially confounding extraneous variables. These designs include the one-group posttest-only design, the one-group pretest-posttest design, and the posttest-only design with nonequivalent groups. Other designs—such as the pretest-posttest control-group design and the posttest-only control-group design—are strong experimental designs because they control for the effect of potentially confounding extraneous variables. This control is achieved primarily through the inclusion of a control comparison group and random assignment of participants to the comparison groups.

Factorial designs are frequently used in education research because they permit the simultaneous assessment of two or more independent variables. Use of a factorial design has the advantage of permitting us to investigate simultaneously the effect of more than one independent variable and the interaction between these independent variables. Investigation of the interaction allows us to determine whether the effect that one independent variable has on the dependent variable depends on the level of the other independent variable. Thus, we can investigate more complex relationships.

A repeated-measures design is used when the same research participants must participate in all experimental treatment conditions. Although the repeated-measures design has the advantage of needing fewer research participants and ensures that participants are equated across treatment conditions, it has the potentially major disadvantage of including sequencing effects. Counterbalancing can be used to control for sequencing effects in some but not all studies.

There are times when one of the independent variables of interest would fit into a repeated-measures design and the other independent variable would fit into a posttest-only control-group design. When such an instance exists, a factorial design based on a mixed model is appropriate. When using this design, participants are randomly assigned to the different comparison groups required by the one independent variable (the between-subjects IV). All participants then take each level of variation of the second independent variable (the within-subjects IV).

KEY TERMS

amount technique (p. 320)
analysis of covariance (p. 327)
between-subjects independent variable (p. 346)
carryover effect (p. 329)
cell (p. 341)
control group (p. 336)
counterbalancing (p. 328)
differential influence (p. 322)
disordinal interaction effect (p. 344)
double-blind procedure (p. 338)
equating the comparison groups (p. 322)
experiment (p. 318)
experimental control (p. 322)
experimental group (p. 336)
factorial design (p. 340)
factorial design based on a mixed model (p. 348)
field experiment (p. 319)
interaction effect (p. 341)
Internet experiment (p. 319)
laboratory experiment (p. 319)
main effect (p. 341)
marginal mean (p. 342)
matching (p. 324)
one-group posttest-only design (p. 331)
one-group pretest-posttest design (p. 332)
order effect (p. 328)
ordinal interaction effect (p. 345)
posttest-only control-group design (p. 339)
posttest-only design with nonequivalent groups (p. 333)
presence or absence technique (p. 320)
pretest-posttest control-group design (p. 338)
quasi-experimental design (p. 326)
random assignment (p. 322)
RCT (p. 336)
repeated-measures design (p. 346)
research design (p. 330)
sequencing effects (p. 328)
single-blind procedure (p. 338)
type technique (p. 321)
within-subjects independent variable (p. 346)

DISCUSSION QUESTIONS

1. What are you trying to do when you incorporate control techniques such as matching and random assignment, and how do these control techniques accomplish this?
2. What are the strengths and weaknesses of matching?
3. Shouldn't the control group used in the posttest-only design with nonequivalent groups control for most extraneous variables and enable a researcher using this design to test the effect of an independent variable effectively?
4. Why is a factorial design more powerful than the posttest-only control-group design?
5. Why is the posttest-only control-group design used more frequently than the repeated-measures design?

RESEARCH EXERCISES

1. To give you some experience in identifying the elements that go into conducting an experimental research study, use ERIC (http://eric.ed.gov) to identify an experimental study in any area such as teacher stress, distance education, violence in schools, or burnout among teachers.

Read the article and then answer the following questions:

   a. What makes this study an experimental research study?
   b. Is this a field experiment, laboratory experiment, or an Internet experiment?
   c. What research questions and hypotheses were posed by the researchers?
   d. What are the independent and dependent variables?
   e. What control techniques were used?
   f. What research design did the researchers use?

2. Using the six questions in the previous exercise, review the experimental study on the companion website.
3. Read the following research brief and identify the type of research design used.

   To examine the relationship between problem behavior and classroom atmosphere, Kato and Okubo (2006) first identified junior high school classrooms that had high levels of problem behaviors and classrooms that had low levels of problem behaviors. Within each of these classrooms, they identified students with and without problem behaviors. Then they assessed the students' image of the individuals exhibiting the problem behaviors. They found that students in the classrooms with high levels of problem behavior viewed the students who engaged in problem behaviors more positively and school life more negatively than did students in the classrooms with low levels of problem behaviors.

   a. How many independent variables are in this design, and what are they?
   b. What are the dependent variables in this design?
   c. What type of design did the researchers use to conduct this study?

RELEVANT INTERNET SITES

This site has several tutorials maintained by Wadsworth. Click on Research Methods Workshops and then on the links for True Experiments and Between Versus Within Designs.
http://www.wadsworth.com/psychology_d/templates/student_resources/workshops/index.html

Instruction on factorial designs and interactions
http://www.socialresearchmethods.net/kb/expfact.htm
http://web.mst.edu/~psyworld/experimental.htm

STUDENT STUDY SITE

Visit the Student Study Site at **edge.sagepub.com/rbjohnson6e** for these additional learning tools:

Video Links
Self-Quizzes
eFlashcards
Lecture Notes
Full-Text SAGE Journal Articles
Interactive Concept Maps
Web Resources

RECOMMENDED READING

Campbell, D., & Stanley, J. (1963). *Experimental and quasi-experimental designs for research*. Chicago, IL: Rand McNally. This is the original classic that discussed primary experimental research designs.

Shadish, W. R., Cook, T. D., & Campbell, D. T. (2002). *Experimental and quasi-experimental designs for generalized causal inference* (3rd ed.). Boston, MA: Houghton Mifflin. Read Chapter 8, which discusses randomized experiments. This is the third edition of Campbell and Stanley (1963) and includes advances not discussed in the earlier book.

NOTES

1. In some texts, this design is called the "one-shot case study," which is incorrect.
2. This design is sometimes called a "split-plot design."

Chapter 13

Experimental Research: Quasi and Single-Case Designs

LEARNING OBJECTIVES

After reading this chapter, you should be able to

- Explain the difference between strong experimental research designs and quasi-experimental research designs.
- Explain the limitations of quasi-experimental designs in making causal inferences compared to strong designs.
- Explain the characteristics of the nonequivalent comparison-group quasi-experimental design and how to search for rival hypotheses that might explain the obtained results.
- Explain the characteristics of the interrupted time-series designs.
- Explain how the regression-discontinuity design assesses the effect of a treatment.
- Explain how time-series and single-case research designs attempt to rule out confounding variables.
- Explain how a treatment effect is demonstrated in single-case research designs.
- Explain the limitations of each of the single-case research designs.
- Recognize and understand the methodological issues in single-case research designs.

Visit the Student Study Site for an interactive concept map.

RESEARCH IN REAL LIFE Quasi-Experimental Design

istock/ZargonDesign

In 1995, Zipora Jacob took a day trip to Disneyland, where she hopped on the Indiana Jones Adventure, a roller coaster that was slower than most but had high-tech hydraulics that made it seem speedier and jerkier. When the ride stopped, Jacob said she felt as though her head was exploding. "By the next morning, she was in a coma from a massive brain bleed. She endured surgeries and memory loss, and still has a permanent shunt draining fluid from her brain" (Rosenberg, 2002, p. 49).

Although Jacob has settled a lawsuit with Disney, the roller coaster industry denies the fact that a roller coaster is a risky thrill ride. Instead, the industry states that it is "one of the safest family activities you can engage in" and that millions of people enjoy rides on roller coasters every year without incident. Yet some scientists are concerned that the g-forces and the rapid jerking of the head incurred during a roller coaster ride can cause serious injury. Although the link between g-forces and injuries has not been supported with scientific evidence, there is a movement to regulate the g-force permitted on roller coasters in the belief that excessive g-force experienced on a roller coaster can place a person at risk.

Rather than being based on individual cases such as Zipora Jacob's, laws and regulations should be based on sound scientific evidence. However, conducting a randomized experimental study to determine whether a given g-force in combination with rapid jerking of the head causes head injury would mean that some individuals would have to suffer the g-force and rapid head jerking thought to be potentially dangerous. Others would experience lower levels of g-force and head jerking to determine not only whether the amount experienced on roller coasters causes head injury but also, if head injuries occur, how much force can be tolerated before they occur.

Conducting such experiments would place the individuals in the experiment at potential serious risk and would therefore be unethical and not permitted. Recall from Chapter 6 on ethics that the potential benefit derived from a study must be greater than the risk to the participants for the study to be permitted. The possibility of serious and permanent brain injury is a risk that definitely exceeds the benefit that could be derived. In cases such as this, however, researchers need not throw up their hands and abandon their research program. Rather, they must turn to the use of quasi-experimental designs—designs that enable researchers to investigate problems that preclude the use of some of the procedures required by a strong or randomized experiment. We discuss this type of design in this chapter, along with single-case designs, which can be used when you have only one or a couple of participants or a single intact group on which to test your research question.

In the previous chapter, we discussed the characteristics of experimental research and presented a number of strong experimental research designs that can be used to test causal hypotheses. However, as the vignette at the beginning of this chapter reveals, there are times when researchers are confronted with situations in which not all of the demands of experimental research can be met. For example, sometimes it is not possible to randomly assign participants to groups, a requirement of strong experimental research. On other occasions, a researcher might have access to only a single intact group, such as a classroom of individuals with learning disabilities, or to only one or two participants, such as a student with school phobia. In these instances, it would be impossible to use one of the strong research designs discussed in Chapter 12 because these designs require the random assignment of participants to at least two groups (or participation in all experimental conditions). In such situations, researchers should use quasi-experimental and single-case research designs.

Quasi-Experimental Research Designs

A **quasi-experimental research design** is an experimental research design that does not provide for full control of potential confounding variables. The primary reason why full control is not achieved is that participants cannot be randomly assigned to groups. For example, assume that you want to investigate the efficacy of several ways of teaching reading to third-grade students. To control for confounding variables, you ideally want to randomly assign the students to the classrooms in which the different reading techniques will be taught. Usually, it is not possible to randomly assign students to classrooms because the school year might have already begun and the school system is not willing to allow you to reassign students to classrooms. This means that you will have to conduct a study making use of existing classes of students.

- **Quasi-experimental research design** An experimental research design that does not provide for full control of potential confounding variables primarily because it does not randomly assign participants to comparison groups

Quasi-experimental designs are superior to the weak designs but inferior to the strong designs provided in Chapter 12. When random assignment is not possible, you should make use of a quasi-experimental research design rather than a weak experimental research design. Because random assignment is *not* used with quasi-experimental designs, threats to the internal validity of the study might exist. Table 13.1 provides a list of the threats that are controlled as well as the threats that are not controlled when using the quasi-experimental designs discussed in this chapter. The important issue that must be considered is whether it is possible to reach a valid causal conclusion using a quasi-experimental design, because it does not rule out the influence of all confounding variables. To make a causal inference from a quasi-experiment, you must meet the same basic requirements that are needed for any causal relationship: *Cause must covary with effect, cause must precede effect, and rival hypotheses or alternative explanations must be implausible.* The first two of these requirements are easy to handle because quasi-experiments, like strong or randomized experiments, manipulate conditions so that the cause is forced to precede the effect and covariation between cause and effect is tested, typically through statistical analysis. The third requirement, ruling out rival hypotheses, is frequently difficult to meet because quasi-experiments do not use random assignment.

Causal inferences can be made using quasi-experimental designs, but these inferences are made only when data are collected that make rival explanations or the threats to internal validity implausible. For example, assume that you have a son who scored a perfect 100 on a multiple-choice history test. If he had studied diligently for several days before taking the test, you would probably attribute the good grade to the diligent study. He could also have obtained the perfect score in a number of other ways (sheer luck in selecting the correct answer for each question, for example), but such alternative explanations might not be accepted because they are not plausible, given their unlikely occurrence and the fact that your son had spent so much time studying. In like manner, causal interpretations are made from quasi-experiments only when rival explanations have been shown to be implausible. The difficulty is identifying the *plausible* rival explanations. There are several ways to

TABLE 13.1 Summary of Threats to Internal Validity of Quasi-Experimental Designs

Designs	*History*	*Maturation*	*Testing*	*Instrumentation*	*Regression Artifact*	*Differential Selection*	*Differential Attrition*	**Additive and Interactive Effects*
Nonequivalent comparison-group design $O_1 X_1 O_2$ - - - - - - - - - $O_1 X_2 O_2$	+	+	+	+	+	–	–	–
Interrupted time-series design $O_1O_2O_3O_4O_5\ X_1\ O_6O_7O_8O_9O_{10}$	–	+	+	+	+	NA	NA	NA
Regression-discontinuity design* O_P C X O_2 O_P C O_2	+	+	+	+	+	+	?	–

*The possibility of differential history, differential maturation, and differential instrumentation occurring between the participants below and above the cutoff score is the reason for the minus sign for additive and interactive effects under the regression-discontinuity design.

A (+) sign indicates that the threat is controlled; a (–) sign indicates that the threat is not controlled; a (?) indicates that the threat may occur under specific and limited circumstances.

address rival explanations and demonstrate that they are implausible. We focus attention on the identification and study of plausible threats to internal validity in this chapter.

13.1 What is a quasi-experimental design, and when would you use such a design?

13.2 What requirements must be met to reach a valid causal inference when using a quasi-experimental design?

▪ **Nonequivalent comparison-group design** A design consisting of an experimental group and a nonequivalent untreated comparison group, both of which are administered pretest and posttest measures

Nonequivalent Comparison-Group Design

Shadish et al. (2002) identified several quasi-experimental designs. Probably the most commonly used quasi-experimental design is the **nonequivalent comparison-group design**, depicted in Figure 13.1. This design consists of giving an experimental and a comparison/control group a pretest and then, after the experimental treatment condition has been administered to the experimental group, administering a posttest. There are several ways to analyze the data from this design. In the most popular approach, you compare the experimental and control groups' posttest scores after they have been adjusted for any differences that exist on their pretest scores using analysis of covariance (ANCOVA). Although ANCOVA is the analytic method most frequently recommended, there are several other approaches (and two of them are quite good).[1]

Consider the study conducted by R. Brown, Pressley, Van Meter, and Schuder (1996), which investigated the effect of using a specific type of instruction, called transactional strategies, on enhancing students' comprehension of the text that they read. In conducting this study, the investigators identified a group of accomplished teachers who used the transactional-strategies instructional method in their classrooms and a group of teachers in the same school district with reputations as excellent reading teachers who taught reading using the regular literacy curriculum. The investigators did not randomly assign the teachers to type of reading instruction, as they felt that it was inappropriate to ask teachers to alter their instructional strategy for a year. Additionally, the students who participated in the study (those reading below grade level at the beginning of the school year) were not randomly assigned to classes that taught the transactional strategies or regular literacy curriculum. The researchers did, however, select students from the various classes who were matched on reading comprehension at the beginning of the study. However, doing so equated the students only on initial reading comprehension. Because many teachers were used in the study and they, as well as the students, were not randomly assigned to groups, a quasi-experimental design had to be used.

See Journal Article 13.1 on the Student Study Site.

R. Brown et al. (1996) selected the nonequivalent comparison-group research design with matching of participants in the two groups, as illustrated in Figure 13.2. Both groups, each consisting of several classes, were interviewed at the beginning of the academic year to identify the strategy the students used in reading and were pretested on several outcome measures, including reading comprehension. After matched samples of students (students who had similar reading comprehension scores) were identified, one group was taught reading by using the transactional strategy, and the other group was taught by using the regular literacy curriculum. At the end of the academic year, the students in each group were posttested on the outcome measures. Analysis of the results revealed that the students who received transactional-strategies instruction improved in reading comprehension more than the students taught by the conventional reading method.

The results of the R. Brown et al. study (1996) demonstrated that the performance of the students receiving transactional-strategy instruction was superior to that of the students receiving conventional reading instruction. Because a nonequivalent comparison-group quasi-experimental design was used, the groups were potentially nonequivalent on extraneous variables other than the one matched variable of reading comprehension. Therefore, biases might be present that would threaten the validity of the study. Table 13.2 identifies the type of biases that can exist in this design.

FIGURE 13.1 Nonequivalent comparison-group design. The dashed line indicates nonrandom assignment to comparison groups.

	Pretest Measure	Treatment	Posttest Measure
Experimental Group	O_1	X_1	O_2
Control Group	O_1	X_2	O_2

FIGURE 13.2 Design of the R. Brown, Pressley, Van Meter, and Schuder study (1996)

		Pretest measure	*Treatment conditioning*	*Posttest measure*
Classes in the experimental condition	⟶	Reading comprehension	Teach reading using transactional strategies.	Reading comprehension
↑				
Matched on initial reading comprehension				
↓				
Classes in the control condition	⟶	Reading comprehension	Teach reading using the regular literacy curriculum.	Reading comprehension

The students in the two groups were matched in terms of initial reading comprehension, so it is reasonable to assume that the results were not due to any differences in initial reading comprehension. However, the teachers were not randomly assigned to the two groups, nor was there an attempt to equate the teachers in terms of teaching effectiveness. The authors state that the teachers who used the transactional-strategies method were excellent teachers who offered rich language arts experiences for their students. Consequently, these teachers would seem to represent very effective teachers.

TABLE 13.2 Potential Biases in the Nonequivalent Comparison-Group Design

- *Selection Bias*—Because there is no random assignment, there will always be potential *differential selection*. However, the pretest allows exploration of the possible size and direction of the bias on the variables that you measure at pretesting.
- *Selection-Maturation*—Exists if participants in one group become more experienced, tired, or bored than participants in the other group.
- *Selection-Instrumentation*—Exists if the nature of the dependent variable or the way it is measured varies across the nonequivalent groups.
- *Selection-Testing*—Exists if one group of participants reacts differently to taking the pretest.
- *Selection-Regression*—Exists if the two groups are from different populations, such as the experimental treatment group being from a population of individuals with low reading scores and the comparison group being from a population of individuals with high reading scores.
- *Selection-History*—Exists if an event occurring between the pretest and posttest affects one group more than the other group.
- *Differential Attrition*—Exists if the dropping out of participants from either group produces group differences on the posttest scores.

The investigators selected comparison teachers who were recommended by school principals and district reading specialists on the basis of four criteria, such as fostering student involvement in reading and providing motivating learning activities. However, no attempt was made to ensure that the teachers providing instruction in the two methods were equated in their ability to teach reading. Therefore, there could be a difference in the ability of these teachers to motivate and/or provide instruction in reading, and the events occurring between the pretest and posttest could be different for the two groups of students, creating a selection-history bias. Such differences could have accounted for some or all of the observed differences in reading comprehension of the two groups of students.

Shadish et al. (2002) have pointed out that rival explanations arising from the use of designs such as the nonequivalent comparison-group design are "dependent on the joint characteristics of the design, on extra study knowledge about the threats, and on the pattern of observed results" (p. 139). Therefore, just because a threat is possible does not mean that it is plausible. The primary way to determine whether a threat is plausible is to look at the pattern produced by the results, because the plausibility of a threat tends to be related to the results obtained.

For example, look at Figure 13.3, which illustrates hypothetical results that might have been obtained from using the nonequivalent comparison-group design without matching on the pretest. This figure reveals that the control group did not change from pretesting to posttesting. The experimental group, however, started at a higher level and showed a significant positive change. This outcome would seem to suggest that the experimental treatment was effective. However, this outcome could also have been due to a selection-maturation effect.

In the R. Brown et al. study (1996), a selection-maturation effect would have been present if the participants in the experimental condition were developing intellectually and motivationally more rapidly than the participants in the control group and therefore increased their reading comprehension from pretesting to posttesting because of these maturational factors and not because of the type of instruction they received. If this were the case, the posttest improvement in reading comprehension of the experimental group would be due to maturational factors and not to the experimental treatment effect.

FIGURE 13.3 Hypothetical results that might be obtained from a study using a nonequivalent comparison-group design

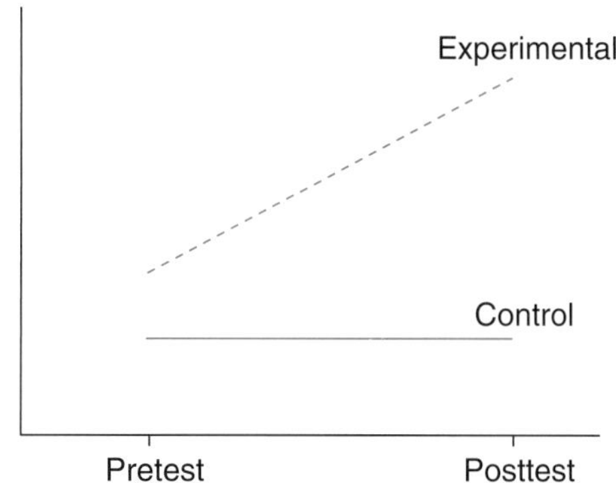

Many investigators attempt to eliminate threat of bias from the selection-maturation effect by matching experimental and control participants on important variables. R. Brown et al. (1996) matched participants on initial reading comprehension, equating the groups on this variable. Ideally, this equality would persist over time, so any difference observed during a posttest could be attributed to the experimental treatment condition. However, Campbell and Boruch (1975) have shown that this assumption can be erroneous because a statistical regression phenomenon can occur in the groups of matched participants, accounting for part or all of the difference observed between the two groups on posttesting. This difference could be misinterpreted as being due to a treatment effect. If you conduct a study using a nonequivalent comparison-group design with matching during pretesting, you should consult Campbell and Boruch's article (or see Figure 10.7 in Christensen, Johnson, & Turner, 2011).

The nonequivalent comparison-group design, as we have just discussed, is susceptible to producing biased results because of the potential for a number of threats to internal validity. The existence of these potential threats suggests that the results obtained from this quasi-experimental design are likely to be biased and different from those that would be obtained from one of the strong experimental designs. Heinsman and Shadish (1996) conducted a meta-analysis comparing the effect size estimates from experiments that included random assignment (i.e., strong designs) with effect size estimates from experiments that lacked random assignment (i.e., nonequivalent comparison-group designs). The purpose was to determine the extent to which similar results would be obtained from these two kinds of studies. This analysis suggested that if the strong experimental design and the nonequivalent comparison-group design were equally well designed and executed, they would yield about the same effect size. In other words, the nonequivalent comparison-group design would give about the same results as the strong experimental design. However, other studies comparing results from experimental and quasi-experimental designs have not supported this conclusion. Glazerman, Levy, and Myers (2003) found that experimental and quasi-experimental designs produced different results, favoring true experiments, and Rosenbaum (2002) found that quasi-experimental designs produced results of unknown accuracy.

These studies suggest that the results obtained from quasi-experimental designs should not be given the same degree of credibility as results from strong experimental studies, which makes it even more imperative that a nonequivalent comparison-group design is well designed and executed. As Heinsman and Shadish (1996) have pointed out, it is probably very difficult, in many studies, to design and execute the nonequivalent comparison-group design as well as a strong experimental design. Therefore, in many studies, the nonequivalent comparison-group design will give biased results.

There seem to be two design components on which researchers must focus when designing and conducting quasi-experiments to maximize the probability that results are not biased. The first component deals with the way in which participants are assigned to groups. To obtain unbiased results, you must not let the participants self-select into groups or conditions. The more they self-select into the treatment conditions, the more biased the results will be. The second component concerns pretest differences. Big differences at the pretest will lead to big differences at the posttest. This means that the researcher should try to reduce any pretest differences by matching the comparison groups on variables that are correlated with the dependent variable. When it is not possible to match, you should consider statistically adjusting the posttest scores for any pretest differences (e.g., using ANCOVA) as well as statistically adjusting for differences on other extraneous variables that you had the foresight to measure (because you had expected your groups to differ on those extraneous variables). Focusing on these two design characteristics will mean that the results obtained from your nonequivalent comparison-group design will be a closer approximation to those of a strong experimental research design.

See Journal Article 13.1 on the Student Study Site.

13.3 What is a nonequivalent comparison-group design, and what are its essential features?

13.4 How are rival explanations addressed when using the nonequivalent comparison-group design?

13.5 What types of biases can exist when using the nonequivalent comparison-group design?

13.6 What is the best way to determine whether a threat is plausible when using the nonequivalent comparison-group design?

Interrupted Time-Series Design

In educational research, there are times when it is difficult to find an equivalent group of participants to serve as a control group. When only one group of participants is available, you could use the *one-group pretest-posttest design*. However, as we discussed in the last chapter, many confounding variables may threaten the internal validity of this *weak* design. To control for these potentially confounding variables in situations in which we have only one group of research participants, we must think of mechanisms other than the use of a control group. The use of other control mechanisms is part of the interrupted time-series design—specifically, this design uses multiple pretests and multiple posttests.

In the **interrupted time-series design**, a single group of participants is pretested a number of times during the A, or baseline, phase; exposed to a treatment condition; and then posttested a number of times during the B, or treatment, phase, as depicted in Figure 13.4. *Baseline* refers to the observation of a given behavior before the presentation of any treatment designed to alter behavior. The baseline phase is therefore the period during which the participants' behavior is recorded in its freely occurring state. After the baseline behavior is recorded, a treatment is implemented, and behavior is recorded during the application of the treatment or after it is applied. The treatment effect is demonstrated by discontinuity in the pretest versus the posttest responses. Discontinuity could be represented by a change in the level of the pretest and posttest responses. For example, pretest responses might consist of a group of children committing an average of 8 to 10 disruptive behaviors during a given class period, and the posttest responses might consist of an average of only 3 to 5 disruptive behaviors, indicating a change, or decline, in the level of response. Discontinuity could also be demonstrated by a change in the slope of the pretest and posttest responses. A change in the slope would occur if the pretest responses demonstrated a change in one direction, such as a gradual increase in the number of disruptive behaviors during a class period, and the posttest responses demonstrated a change in the opposite direction, such as a gradual decrease in these behaviors.

- **Interrupted time-series design** A design in which a treatment condition is assessed by comparing the pattern of pretest responses with the pattern of posttest responses obtained from a single group of participants

FIGURE 13.4 Interrupted time-series design

Multiple Pretests	Treatment	Multiple Posttests
O_1 O_2 O_3 O_4 O_5	X_1	O_6 O_7 O_8 O_9 O_{10}

To illustrate this design, consider a study conducted by Mayer, Mitchell, Clementi, Clement-Robertson, and Myatt (1993). They investigated whether making the classroom environment more positive affected the percentage of at-risk students who were engaged in their assigned activities. They identified ninth-grade students who had low grade point averages and were frequently absent from school. All these students were assigned to attend the experimental classroom for at least one period each school day. Thus, there was a single group of participants available for experimentation, which meant that some form of a time-series design had to be used. In this experimental classroom, emphasis was placed on the positive. For example, classroom rules were stated positively (e.g., show courtesy and respect to others), and points and praise were given to students when they followed the rules. While in this experimental classroom, the experimenters assessed the percentage of students who were engaged in their assigned activities, defined as being "on-task," at 10 and 40 minutes into the class period. The percentage of students who were on-task was repeatedly measured before and after the teachers focused on making the classroom more positive.

Figure 13.5 illustrates the percentage of students who were on-task at both 10 and 40 minutes into the class period. From this figure, you can see that the percentage was assessed multiple times before and after implementation of the positive classroom environment, making it an interrupted time-series design. The results reveal that the percentage of students who were on-task remained rather constant during the first seven baseline class sessions, or the class sessions before implementation of the positive classroom environment. After implementation of the positive classroom environment starts, the percentage of on-task students consistently rose over the next six class sessions, suggesting that the implementation of the positive approach had a beneficial effect on the students' behavior.

In the interrupted time-series design, visual inspection of the pattern of preintervention and postintervention behavior can be very helpful in ruling out some potentially confounding variables and in determining whether an experimental treatment had an effect. Figure 13.6 illustrates a number of possible patterns that might be obtained from time-series data. Look at the first three patterns: 1, 2, and 3. Pattern 1 reveals a continuous increase in response before intervention, and this pattern of continuous increase is maintained during posttesting. Such a response pattern could reflect an instrumentation or a maturation effect rather than a treatment effect. Similarly, response patterns 2 and 3 reveal that the pattern of responses established during pretesting continued during posttesting. Response patterns 1, 2, and 3, therefore, do not reveal a treatment effect because the postintervention pattern of responses is a *continuation* of the preintervention pattern of responses. However, if several pretests and posttests had not been obtained, it would have been tempting to infer that a treatment effect had occurred. Look at the response immediately preceding and immediately following the intervention in patterns 1 and 3. In these patterns, you can see that the preintervention response was lower than the postintervention response, seeming to indicate an improvement in behavior. In pattern 2, the postintervention response was lower than the preintervention response, seeming to indicate a decline in response. Without taking repeated assessments before and after intervention, you would not know that the postintervention response represented a continuation of the preintervention pattern of response, and you would have drawn an erroneous conclusion if you had used the one-group pretest-posttest design (which has only a single pretest and a single posttest).

See Journal Article 13.2 on the Student Study Site.

Response patterns 4, 5, and 6 in Figure 13.6 appear to represent true changes in behavior because the posttest response pattern was different from the pretest response pattern. Additionally, the change in the response pattern continued, with the exception of pattern 4, during the entire posttesting period. It is this change in the posttest pattern of responses, particularly if it is a continuous change, that gives some assurance that a change in response occurred.

Even with this visual inspection of the data, it is important to determine whether the change in response pattern is statistically significant by conducting a test of significance. The most widely used and appropriate significance test seems to be the autoregression moving average model (Box & Jenkins, 1970; Glass, Willson, & Gottman, 1975). Basically, this method consists of determining whether the pattern of postresponse measures differs from the pattern of preresponse measures. Use of this statistical method requires obtaining at least 50 data points (Glass et al.), which frequently cannot be accomplished. Fortunately, Tryon (1982) and Cosbie (1993) have developed statistical procedures that can be used with as few as 10 data points so that valid statistical analysis can be conducted on the data collected in most time-series studies.

FIGURE 13.5 Percentage of students who are on-task at 10 minutes and 40 minutes into the class period. The figure presented here depicts the results of one of five classrooms investigated by Mayer et al. (1993). Only one classroom is presented here to illustrate a time-series design, whereas Mayer et al. used five classrooms and a multiple-baseline design. "PLA" refers to planned activity.

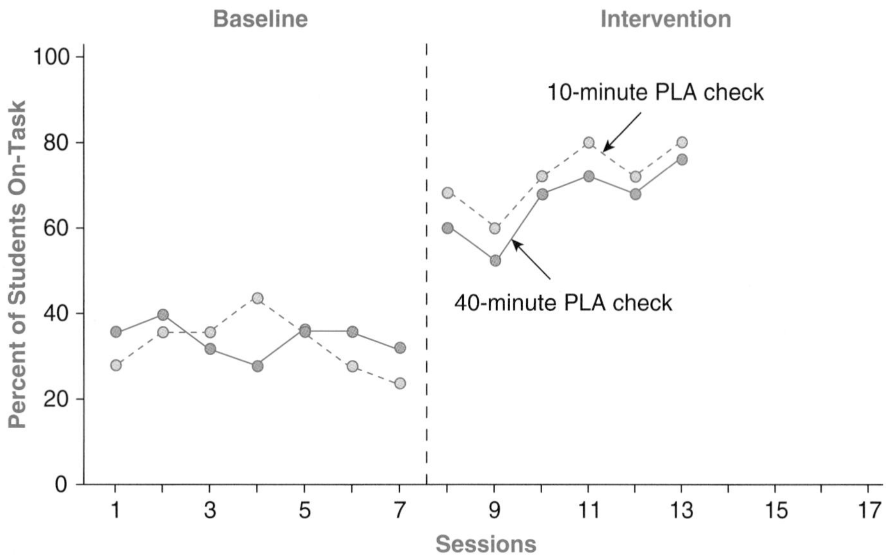

Source: Adapted from G. R. Mayer, L. K. Mitchell, T. Clementi, E. Clement-Robertson, & R. Myatt. (1993). A dropout prevention program for at-risk high school students: Emphasizing consulting to promote positive classroom climates. *Education and Treatment of Children, 16*, 135–146.

FIGURE 13.6 Possible patterns of data in a time-series design

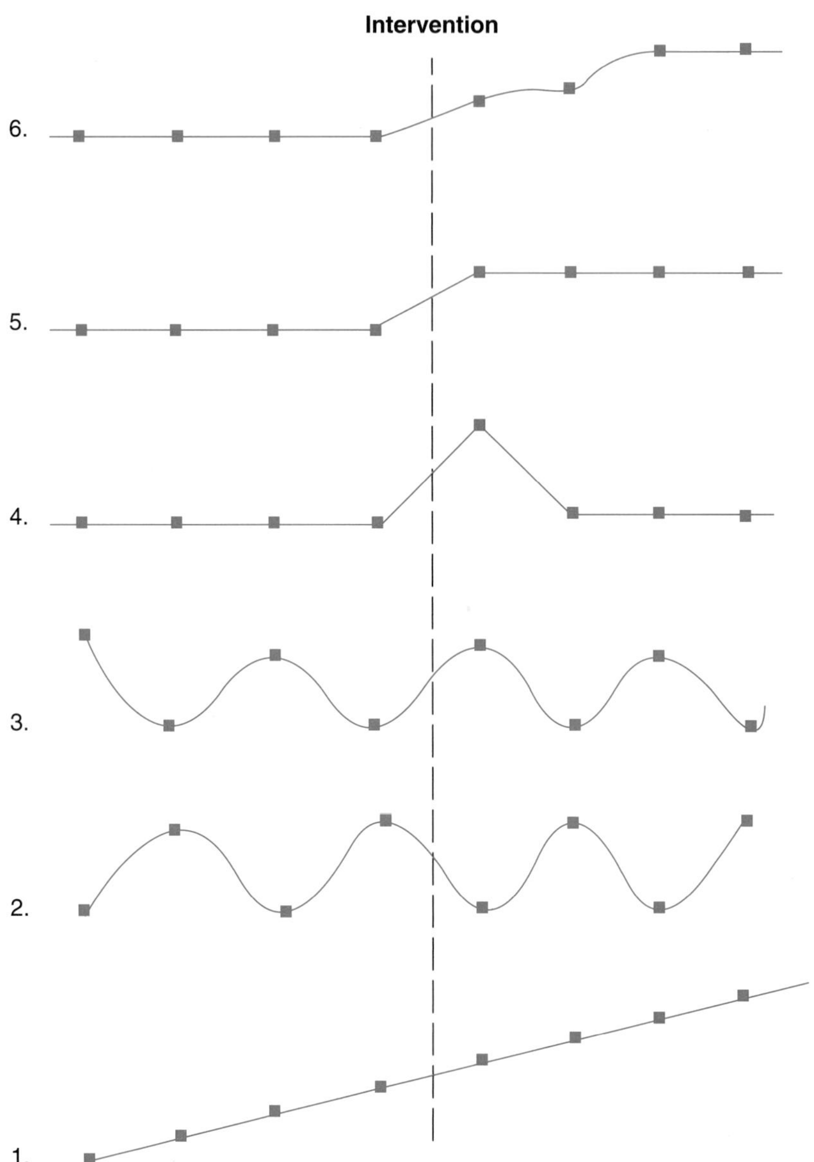

Source: From J. A. Caporaso & L. L. Roos., Jr. (Eds.), *Quasi-Experimental Approaches: Testing Theory and Evaluation Policy.* Copyright 1973 Northwestern University Press.

After the data are analyzed and an assessment is made as to whether the preresponse pattern differs from the postresponse pattern, it is important to determine whether the change was due to the experimental intervention or to some confounding variable. For example, Mayer et al. (1993) had to determine whether the implementation of the positive classroom environment led to the increase in on-task behavior or whether some extraneous variable was responsible. This means that you have to look at the data and identify the possible confounding variables that could have produced the behavioral change.

The primary threat to internal validity that exists in the interrupted time-series design is a *history effect*. If some extraneous variable that increased the percentage of students engaged in on-task behaviors occurred at the same time as the implementation of the positive classroom environment, this extraneous variable would serve as a rival explanation for the change in the students' behavior. A researcher using the interrupted time-series design must consider all other events taking place at the time of implementation of the experimental treatment and determine whether they might be rival explanations.

See Journal Article 13.3 on the Student Study Site.

REVIEW QUESTIONS

13.7 What are the essential design characteristics of an interrupted time-series design?

13.8 How is a treatment effect demonstrated when using an interrupted time-series design?

13.9 How are potential confounding variables ruled out when using the interrupted time-series design?

Regression-Discontinuity Design

The **regression-discontinuity design** is used to determine whether a group of individuals meeting some predetermined criterion profit from receiving a treatment condition. This design, depicted in Figure 13.7, consists of measuring all participants on a preassignment measure and then selecting a cutoff score on this measure. This provides two groups of potential participants—those scoring above the cutoff and those scoring below the cutoff. Then you administer the treatment condition to one of the two groups. For example, the participants who score above the cutoff score receive the treatment, and the participants who score below the cutoff score do not receive the treatment. After the treatment condition is administered, the posttest measure is obtained, and the two groups are compared on this measure to determine whether the treatment was effective. However, the way in which the two groups are compared in the regression-discontinuity design is different from that in any other design we have considered so far. A treatment effect is demonstrated by a discontinuity in the regression line that would have been formed had no treatment effect existed.

■ **Regression-discontinuity design** A design that assesses the effect of a treatment condition by looking for a discontinuity in regression lines between individuals who score lower and higher than some predetermined cutoff score

■ **FIGURE 13.7** Structure of the regression-discontinuity design in which O_p is the preassignment measure, C indicates the preassignment measure cutoff score used to assign participants to conditions such that participants with scores above the cutoff are assigned to the treatment condition and participants with scores below the cutoff are assigned to the control condition, X refers to a treatment condition, and O_2 refers to the posttest measure or the outcome or dependent variable

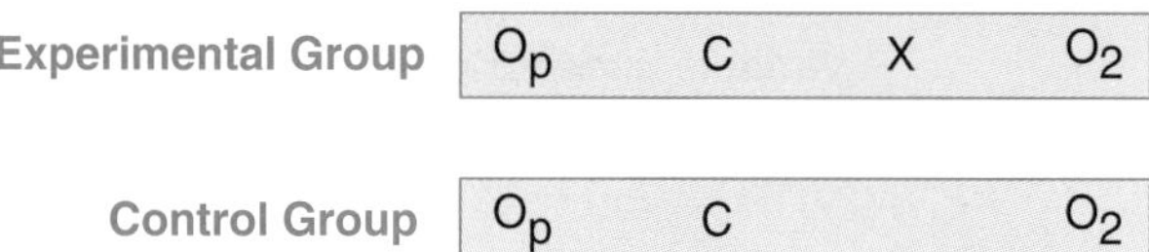

To illustrate what we mean by "discontinuity in the regression line," Figure 13.8 shows a continuous increase of scores from a low of about 30 to a high of about 50 and a cutoff score of 40 separating the control group from the treatment group. The straight line pushed through these scores is the regression line. Note that this regression line is continuous and that the individuals who received the treatment made a score of higher than 40 on the preassignment variable. The continuous regression line indicates that there was *no* effect of the treatment because the scores of the people above the cutoff of 40 and receiving the treatment continued the pattern of scores of people below the cutoff of 40 who did not receive the treatment.

FIGURE 13.8 Regression-discontinuity design with no treatment effect

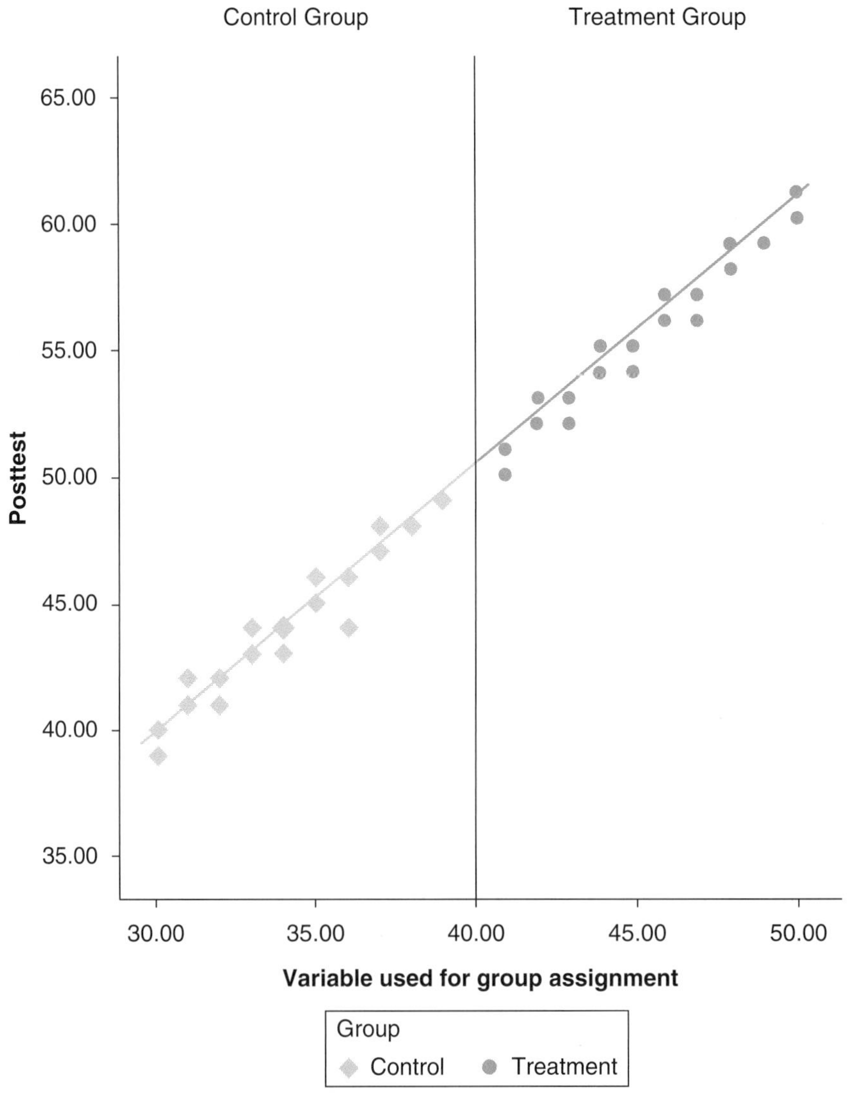

FIGURE 13.9 Regression-discontinuity design with an effective treatment

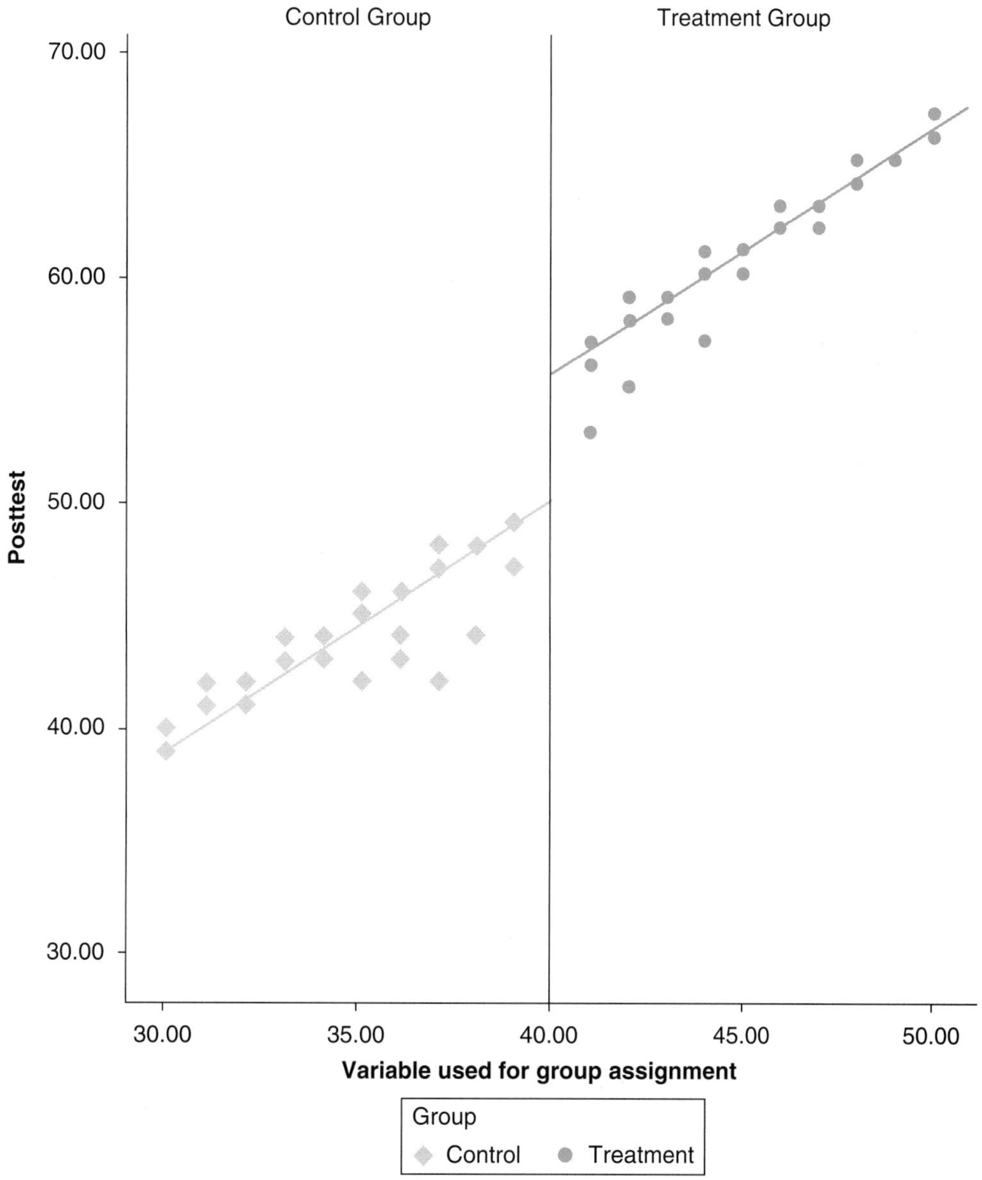

Now look at Figure 13.9. This figure reveals that the regression line for the people above the cutoff score of 40 is not a continuation of the regression line established for the people with a cutoff score below 40. In other words, there is a *discontinuity* of the regression line for the people with a cutoff score below and above 40. This discontinuity indicates that the treatment had an effect because if no treatment effect had existed, there would be no discontinuity of the regression line (as illustrated in Figure 13.8).

Braden and Bryant (1990) used the regression-discontinuity design to determine whether a program for gifted students enhanced their achievement more than regular school placement. The cutoff score to be admitted into the gifted program was set at two or more standard deviations above the mean on the Stanford-Binet or WISC-R intelligence test. Students who met or exceeded this cutoff score were admitted to the gifted program, and students who were referred to the program but did not meet the cutoff score were the control group and remained in the regular classroom. Three years after initiation of the gifted program, outcome data were collected by using the California Achievement Test. Statistical analysis of the outcome data demonstrated that a significant discontinuity of the regression lines for the two groups of students did not exist, indicating that the gifted program did not enhance the bright students' academic achievement.

The regression-discontinuity design is an excellent design that can be used when researchers want to investigate the efficacy of some program or treatment but cannot randomly assign participants to comparison groups. However, the design must adhere to a number of criteria, listed in Table 13.3, for it to assess the effectiveness of a treatment condition. When these criteria are met, the regression-discontinuity design typically is more powerful than all other quasi-experimental designs.

TABLE 13.3 Requirements of the Regression-Discontinuity Design

- Assignment to comparison groups must be based only on the cutoff score.
- The assignment variable must be at least an ordinal variable and is best if it is a continuous variable. It cannot be a nominal variable such as sex, ethnicity, religious preference, or status as a drug user or nonuser.
- The cutoff score ideally should be located at the mean of the distribution of scores. The closer the cutoff score is to the extremes, the lower the statistical power of the design.
- Assignment to comparison groups must be under the control of the experimenter to avoid a selection bias. This requirement rules out most retrospective uses of the design.
- The relationship between the assignment and outcome variables (whether it is linear, curvilinear, etc.) must be known to avoid a biased assessment of the treatment effect.
- All participants must be from the same population. With respect to the regression-discontinuity design, this means that it must have been possible for all participants to receive the treatment condition. Therefore, the design would not be appropriate if, for example, the experimental participants are selected from one school and control participants are selected from another school.

Any threat to the validity of the regression-discontinuity design would have to cause a sudden discontinuity in the regression line that coincides with the cutoff. As Shadish et al. (2002) have pointed out, this is improbable, though possible. The primary threat that could produce such an effect is a differential history effect, which is a type of additive and interactive effect. This history effect would have to be one that affected only participants on only one side of the cutoff, which makes it unlikely. Of the other threats to internal validity that we discussed in Chapter 11, differential effects (e.g., differential attrition) are possible but unlikely because the researcher is able to statistically control for the group assignment mechanism.

- **Single-case experimental design** Design that uses a single participant to investigate the effect of an experimental treatment condition

Single-Case Experimental Designs

Single-case experimental designs use a single participant in the experimental design to investigate the efficacy of an experimental treatment condition. Conducting a study that investigates a single individual can be necessary anytime you want to investigate some phenomenon but have access to only one or two individuals who demonstrate that phenomenon. For example, assume that you have an unusually bright student in your class and you want to study this person's learning strategies. Because only one student with this ability level is in your class, you have to use a single-case design.

All single-case experimental designs are some form of a time-series design, because these designs require repeated measurement on the dependent variable before and after implementation of the experimental treatment condition. The pretreatment responses are used as the comparison responses for assessing the effect of the independent variable. Additionally, the multiple pretreatment and posttreatment responses permit us to rule out many extraneous variables, such as history and maturation, that could confound the results. The way in which this is accomplished is identical to that presented under the topic of interrupted time-series design earlier in this chapter.

As we discuss the single-case experimental research designs, you should realize that these designs can be, and frequently are, used with an intact group of participants, as well as with single participants. There are times when you cannot break a group of participants, such as a class, into a control and experimental group but still want to investigate the efficacy of an independent variable. In these instances, you can treat the class as a single case and use one of the single-case experimental designs.

A-B-A and A-B-A-B Designs

The **A-B-A design** is a single-case design involving three phases, as illustrated in Figure 13.10. The first phase, the first A of this design, is the baseline condition during which the target response is repeatedly recorded before any experimental intervention. The second phase, the B part of this design, is the experimental treatment condition. During this phase, some treatment condition is deliberately imposed to try to change the response of the participant. This treatment phase is typically continued for the same length of time as the original baseline phase or until some substantial and stable change occurs in the behaviors being observed. After the treatment condition has been introduced and the desired behavioral change has occurred, the second A phase is introduced. The second A phase of this design is a return to the baseline conditions. In other words, the treatment condition is withdrawn, and whatever conditions existed during baseline are reinstated. This second A phase is reinstated to determine whether the behavior will *revert* to its original pretreatment level. This reverting to the original pretreatment level is very important for demonstrating that the treatment condition, and not some other extraneous variable, produced the behavioral change observed during the B phase. If the response reverts to the original baseline level when the treatment condition is withdrawn, rival hypotheses such as history become less plausible.

■ **A-B-A design** A single-case experimental design in which the response to the experimental treatment condition is compared to baseline responses taken before and after administering the treatment condition

As an illustration of the use of this design, consider the study conducted by Gunter, Shores, Jack, Denny, and DePaepe (1994). These researchers investigated the effect of a

■ **FIGURE 13.10** A-B-A time-series design

Baseline (A)	Treatment (B)	Baseline (A)
O_1 O_2 O_3 O_4 O_5	O_6 O_7 O_8 O_9 O_{10}	O_{11} O_{12} O_{13} O_{14} O_{15}

teaching method that involved ensuring correct responses on an assigned task. Tom was selected to participate in the study because of his high rate of disruptive behavior during academic instruction. A baseline rate of disruptive behaviors (defined as making inappropriate noises, talking without permission, walking away from the instructional area without permission, and making nondirected negative verbalizations) was recorded for 10 class periods. Baseline recording for each class began when the teacher gave Tom his math assignment and ended with the completion of the math activity or the expiration of 30 minutes of continuous observation.

Intervention was then implemented that consisted of the teachers providing Tom with the information that would ensure his getting a correct response. For example, during intervention the teacher would say, "Tom, 6 times 4 is 24. What is 6 times 4?" After Tom had completed 17 class periods under intervention conditions, the teacher reverted to her baseline behavior of not providing information that would ensure a correct response.

You can see a display of the per-minute rate of disruptive behaviors Tom displayed for each session in Figure 13.11. Tom displayed a number of disruptive behaviors during every session of the first baseline (A) condition. When the treatment condition (B) of giving Tom information that ensured his giving a correct response was implemented, the disruptive behaviors declined, and during several of the sessions, Tom did not display any disruptive behaviors. When baseline conditions (A) were reinstated and Tom no longer

FIGURE 13.11 Rate of Tom's disruptive behaviors during baseline and intervention. This figure depicts the first three phases of the design used by Gunter et al. (1994) to illustrate the A-B-A design.

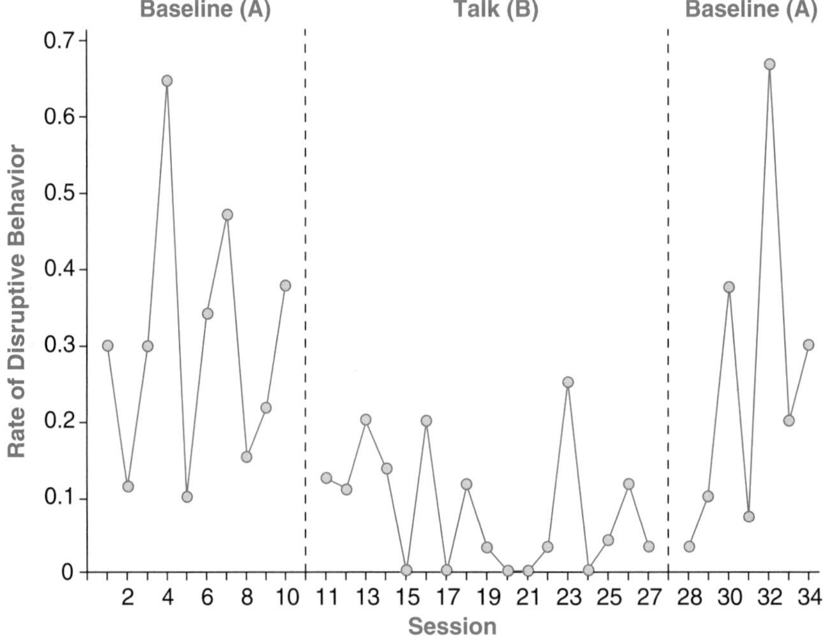

Source: Adapted from P. L. Gunter, R. E. Shores, S. L. Jack, R. K. Denny, and P. A. DePaepe, 1994, "A case study of the effects of altering instructional interactions on the disruptive behavior of a child identified with severe behavior disorders," *Education and Treatment of Children, 17,* 435–444.

received the information he needed to provide a correct response, disruptive behaviors became more frequent.

In looking at the results of this study, it appears that the use of the A-B-A design provides a rather dramatic illustration of the influence of the experimental treatment condition. However, there are some problems with this design (Hersen & Barlow, 1976). The first problem is that the design ends with the baseline condition. From the standpoint of an educator who desires a positive behavioral change, this might be unacceptable because the benefits of the treatment condition are denied. Fortunately, this limitation can be handled easily by adding a fourth phase to the A-B-A design in which the treatment condition is reintroduced. This makes it an **A-B-A-B design**, as illustrated in Figure 13.12. In the A-B-A-B design, the participant ends the experiment with the full benefit of the treatment condition. Actually, Gunter et al. (1994) used the A-B-A-B design. In Figure 13.12 you can see that they reinstated the treatment conditions. When the treatment condition was reinstated a second time, the disruptive behaviors declined once again. Tom, their experimental participant, did therefore end the study with the positive effects of the experimental treatment condition.

■ **A-B-A-B design** An A-B-A design that is extended to include the reintroduction of the treatment condition

A second problem with using the A-B-A or A-B-A-B design is that it is necessary for the dependent variable response to *revert* to baseline conditions when the experimental treatment condition is withdrawn to rule out rival explanations such as history. If Tom's disruptive behavior did not revert to its baseline level when the treatment condition was withdrawn, it would have been impossible to determine whether the behavioral change was

FIGURE 13.12 Rate of Tom's disruptive behaviors during baseline and intervention

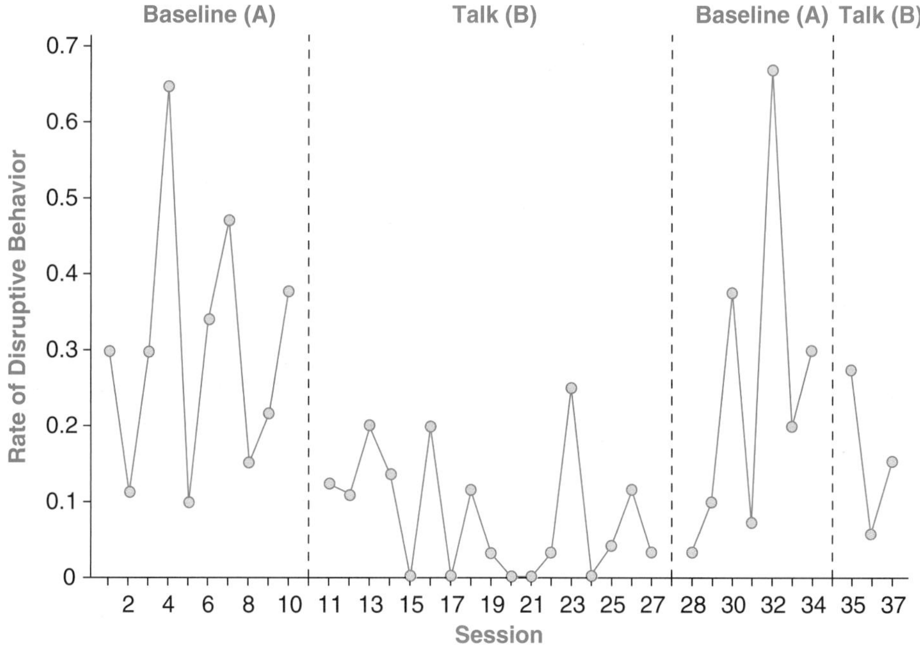

Source: From P. L. Gunter, R. E. Shores, S. L. Jack, R. K. Denny, and P. A. DePaepe, 1994, "A case study of the effects of altering instructional interactions on the disruptive behavior of a child identified with severe behavior disorders," *Education and Treatment of Children, 17,* 435–444.

due to the treatment condition or to a history variable that occurred at the same time that the treatment condition was introduced. A key point to remember is that *reversal is essential to rule out rival hypotheses with A-B-A and A-B-A-B designs.*

The key problem with A-B-A or A-B-A-B designs is that a reversal to baseline does not occur with all dependent variable responses. Failure to reverse might be due to a carryover effect across phases, whereby the treatment condition was maintained so long that a relatively permanent change in behavior took place. For example, if you were investigating the effect of reinforcing students every time they correctly completed their mathematics homework, either by giving them praise, granting them additional recess time, or allowing them to chat with their friends for 10 minutes during class time, the reinforcer might work so well that the students find that successful completion of their homework and receiving a good grade were reinforcing by themselves. This would sustain the behavior of completing homework without any intervention. In such a case, the intervention could be removed and the students' behavior of completing their homework would continue, which would mean that the students' behavior would not reverse. Because of the possibility of such a carryover effect, Bijou, Peterson, Harris, Allen, and Johnston (1969) recommended that short experimental periods be used to facilitate obtaining a reversal effect. Once the influence of the experimental treatment has been demonstrated, attention can be placed on its persistence.

REVIEW QUESTIONS

13.10 What are the essential characteristics of the A-B-A and A-B-A-B designs?

13.11 How do the A-B-A and A-B-A-B designs rule out rival hypotheses and demonstrate the effect of an experimental treatment condition?

13.12 What are the primary problems that can arise from using the A-B-A and A-B-A-B designs, and how can they be solved?

Multiple-Baseline Design

- **Multiple-baseline design** A single-case experimental design in which the treatment condition is successively administered to different participants or to the same participant in several settings after baseline behaviors have been recorded for different periods of time

The primary limiting component of the A-B-A and the A-B-A-B designs is their inability to eliminate the rival hypothesis of history when the target behavior does not revert to baseline following withdrawal of the treatment condition. If you suspect that such a situation exists, you should select a design that does control for the history threat to internal validity. In this situation, the multiple-baseline design is a logical alternative because it does not entail withdrawing the treatment condition. Therefore, its effectiveness does not hinge on a reversal of behavior to baseline level.

The **multiple-baseline design**, as depicted in Figure 13.13, focuses on two or more different behaviors in the same individual, on the same behavior exhibited by two or more individuals, or on the same behavior exhibited by one individual but in different settings.

Let's focus on the same behavior exhibited by four individuals. With this focus, the first phase of this design involves collecting baseline behavior on all four individuals. During the second phase, the treatment condition is administered to the first individual, and baseline behavior continues to be collected on the other three individuals. For each subsequent phase, the treatment condition is successively administered to another individual. If the

FIGURE 13.13 Multiple-baseline design

		Phase 1	*Phase 2*	*Phase 3*	*Phase 4*	*Phase 5*
Different people, different behaviors, or different settings	A	Baseline	Treatment	Treatment	Treatment	Treatment
	B	Baseline	Baseline	Treatment	Treatment	Treatment
	C	Baseline	Baseline	Baseline	Treatment	Treatment
	D	Baseline	Baseline	Baseline	Baseline	Treatment

individual who is exposed to the treatment condition demonstrates a change in behavior and no behavioral change occurs for those who continue the baseline phase, evidence exists supporting the efficacy of the treatment condition.

Gilbert, Williams, and McLaughlin (1996) used this design to investigate the effect of an assisted reading program on correct oral reading rates of three elementary school children with learning disabilities. These investigators collected baseline reading rates of the children by having them read independently for 4 minutes into a tape recorder after having practiced silently reading a designated passage over a 45-minute period. The assisted reading treatment program consisted of having the students listen to recorded passages using earphones while they followed the lines of print with their fingers and then reading the passage three times aloud while listening to the tape recorder. While reading the passage, the students were praised and encouraged for their effort. The morning after the assisted reading, the students read the passage independently for 4 minutes into a tape recorder. The number of words that were read correctly for each minute of the 4-minute tape recordings represented the dependent variable.

From Figure 13.14, it can be seen that baseline was maintained for 14 days for the first student, after which the assisted reading program was implemented. The assisted reading program was introduced for the second student after 16 baseline days and after 19 baseline days for the third student. Figure 13.14 reveals that the number of correct words read for each student remained stable or declined slightly during all baseline days. However, immediately after the introduction of the assisted reading program, the number of words that were correctly read increased over baseline for all three individuals. The important point is that the change in number of correct words read did not occur until the assisted reading program was implemented, providing evidence that it was the assisted reading program that caused the improvement in reading.

Although the multiple-baseline design can provide convincing evidence for the efficacy of a treatment and avoids the problem of reversibility, it has another basic difficulty. For this design to be effective in evaluating the efficacy of a treatment, the target behaviors (e.g., talking out and being out of seat) or participants must not be highly interrelated. This means that the behaviors or participants must not be interdependent such that a change in one behavior or participant alters the other behaviors or participants. Borden, Bruce, Mitchell, Carter, and Hall (1970), for example, used a multiple-baseline design and found that reinforcement not only changed the inattentive behavior of the target participant but also changed that of an adjacent peer. When interdependence exists, it destroys much of the power of this design because its power depends on the ability to demonstrate change

FIGURE 13.14 The correct reading rates during baseline and assisted reading for each participant in a multiple-baseline design study. Solid horizontal lines indicate condition means. The assisted reading treatment is staggered, first being provided to participant 1, second to participant 2, and third to participant 3. Notice the change in behavior in all three cases after the introduction of the treatment condition.

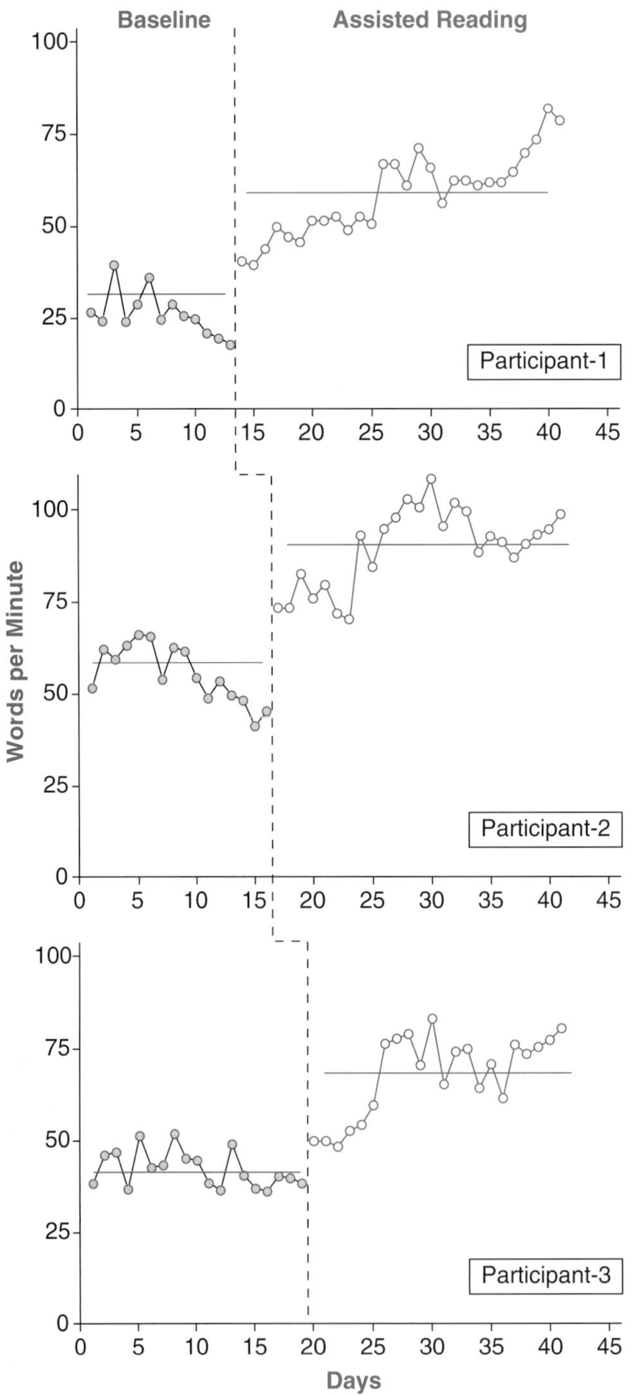

Source: From L. M. Gilbert, R. L. Williams, and T. F. McLaughlin. (1996). Use of assisted reading to increase reading rates and decrease error rates of students with learning disabilities. *Journal of Applied Behavior Analysis, 29*, 255–257.

when the treatment condition is administered to each behavior, individual, or setting. This means that when considering the use of a multiple-baseline design, you must determine whether the behaviors, individuals, or settings are independent. Different behaviors of the same individual are probably the most likely to be interdependent and problematic. If you have information suggesting that the behaviors you want to change are interdependent for the individual, then you should attempt to produce each behavior change with a different individual, or you might attempt to produce the behavior change with the individual in different settings.

See Journal Article 13.4 on the Student Study Site.

Changing-Criterion Design

The changing-criterion design is presented because it is particularly useful for investigating educational problems that require shaping of behavior over a period of time or in cases where a step-by-step increase in accuracy, frequency, or amount is the goal of the research. The **changing-criterion design**, depicted in Figure 13.15, starts with an initial baseline measure on a single target behavior. A treatment condition is then implemented and continued across a series of intervention phases. During the first intervention or treatment phase, an initial or starting criterion of "successful performance" is set. If the participant successfully achieves this level of performance, the experiment moves to the second phase, in which a new and more difficult criterion level is set, and the treatment condition is continued. If the participant successfully reaches this new criterion level of performance and it is maintained, the next phase, with its more difficult criterion level, is introduced. In this manner, each successive phase of the experiment requires a step-by-step increase in the level of performance on the dependent or outcome variable. Experimental control and elimination of alternative explanations are demonstrated by the successive change in the target behavior with each stepwise change in the criterion.

- **Changing-criterion design** A single-case experimental design in which a participant's behavior is gradually altered by changing the criterion for success over successive treatment periods

The changing-criterion design is illustrated well by the study conducted by Himadi, Osteen, Kaiser, and Daniel (1991). These investigators attempted to reduce the delusional verbalizations engaged in by a male patient with schizophrenia. The content of this patient's verbalizations included the delusional beliefs that he was the son of Jesus and Mary; that he controlled the US government; that he owned the US Mint; and that, during infancy, his brain had been surgically removed. Changing these delusional verbalizations involved first recording the frequency, over five baseline sessions, of the answers he provided to 10 questions that consistently elicited delusional answers. After obtaining these baseline data, the treatment condition was administered. The treatment consisted of eliciting a delusional response to a question and then instructing the patient to answer the question again "so that other people would agree with your answers." If the patient gave a delusional answer, the experimenter provided a nondelusional answer and had the patient echo or model the

FIGURE 13.15 Changing-criterion design. After baseline, the criterion level is incremented in each subsequent stage of the design.

Phase A	*Phase B*	*Phase C*	*Phase D*
Baseline	Treatment and initial criterion	Treatment and new (incremented) criterion (compared to Phase B criterion)	Treatment and new (incremented) criterion (compared to Phase C criterion)

answer until the patient provided a nondelusional answer. Each time the patient gave a nondelusional answer, he was given a cup of coffee, which was a reinforcer for this patient.

The changing-criterion component of this design can be seen in that the treatment was first applied to *two* questions and the criterion that had to be met to receive reinforcement was to provide nondelusional answers to both questions over five sessions. Once this criterion was met, the criterion was changed to requiring nondelusional responses to *four* questions over five sessions. Once this criterion was met, nondelusional answers had to be provided to *six* questions over five sessions. This incremental procedure was followed until the patient provided nondelusional responses to all 10 questions. You can see the results of this study in Figure 13.16—each time the criterion changed, there was a corresponding change in the patient's performance. When such correspondence exists, the efficacy of the treatment condition is rather effectively demonstrated. The pattern shown in Figure 13.16 is the signature of a successful changing-criterion study.

Successful use of the changing-criterion design requires attention to three issues. First is the length of the baseline and treatment phases. The treatment phases should be of different lengths, but if they are the same length, the baseline phase should be longer than the treatment phases. This helps to ensure that the step-by-step changes in behavior are caused by the experimental treatment and not by a history or maturational variable that occurs simultaneously with the criterion change. Each treatment phase should be long enough to allow the behavior to change to its new criterion level and stabilize. If the behavior fluctuates between the new and old criterion levels, stability has not been achieved. The second issue is the amount of change in criterion. The change in the criterion should be large enough for you to detect a behavioral change but small enough that it can be achieved by your participant. The third issue is the number of changes in the treatment criterion, with two to four changes in the criterion usually being adequate.

FIGURE 13.16 Number of delusional responses in study using a changing-criterion design

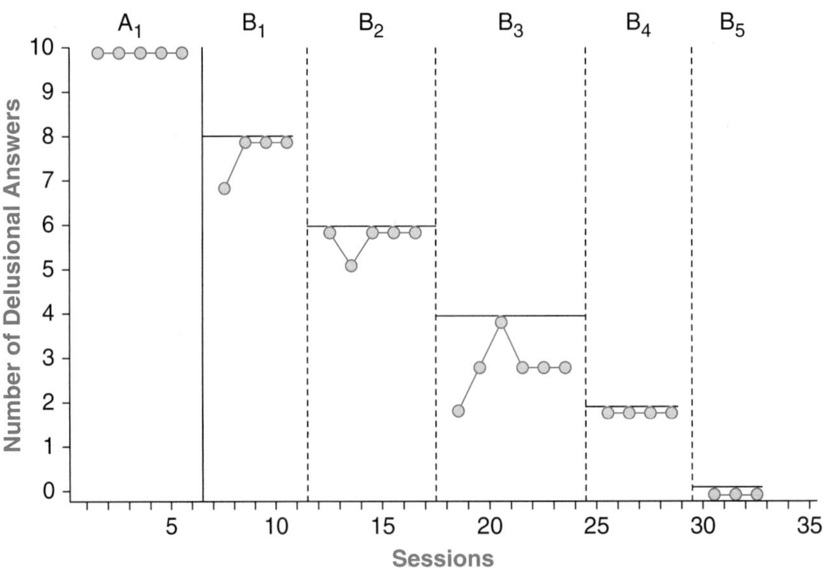

Source: From B. Himadi, F. Osteen, A. J. Kaiser, and K. Daniel. (1991). A record of a behavioral training program of delusional beliefs during the modification of delusional verbalizations. *Behavioral Residential Treatment, 6*, 355–366.

13.13 How does the multiple-baseline design demonstrate a treatment effect?

13.14 What is the primary problem that can be encountered in using the multiple-baseline design?

13.15 When would you use the changing-criterion design?

13.16 What are the essential characteristics of the changing-criterion design?

Methodological Considerations in Using Single-Case Designs

Our discussion of single-case experimental designs is not an exhaustive survey, but it shows the most basic and commonly used designs. If you are interested in other single-case designs, you should consult Barlow, Nock, and Hersen's (2009) excellent book. Regardless of the design used, several methodological issues must be considered in attempting to conduct a single-case study. These issues are summarized in Table 13.4.

TABLE 13.4 Methodological Issues in Single-Case Studies

1. *Baseline*—The behavior of the participant before the administration of the experimental treatment condition. Baseline serves as the benchmark for assessing change induced by the experimental treatment condition, and to serve this purpose, it must be stable. A stable baseline is characterized by (a) an absence of trend (no increase or decrease) over time and (b) little variability (e.g., 5% variation or less).
2. *Changing One Variable at a Time*—Only one variable should be changed from one phase of the experiment to the next. This is necessary to isolate the effect produced by that variable.
3. *Length of Phases*—Agreement does not exist regarding the length of phases. Some researchers state that the various phases should be of equal length, but others emphasize that each phase should be continued until stability has been achieved.
4. *Assessment of Treatment Effect*—There are two approaches to assessing treatment effects:
    a. *Visual inspection*—Looking at the pattern of outcomes across the phases is sufficient to identify a treatment effect if the baseline and intervention levels do not overlap or if the trend of the data in the baseline phase is different from the pattern in the intervention phase.
    b. *Statistical analysis*—A statistical analysis such as a time-series analysis is necessary if there is a great deal of variability in the data. In general, the statistical analysis is not needed if there is little variability in the data and the baseline pattern is very stable. When these two conditions do not exist, however, a statistical analysis should be used.

ACTION RESEARCH REFLECTION

Insight: Action researchers might use a weak, quasi-, or strong experimental design, or they might use a single-case design, but they will always, like a good detective, do their best to check and rule out all plausible alternative explanations for their claims.

1. Look back at your means-ends analysis from Chapter 12. How might you use one of the designs in this chapter?
2. Think about your action research goal: Would a group design (with two or more groups), an interrupted time-series design, or a single-case design best help you reach your research goal? What specific design best fits your needs?

SUMMARY

Quasi-experimental designs are used when all the demands of experimental research cannot be met. Quasi-experimental designs are superior to the weak experimental designs but inferior to the strong experimental designs provided in Chapter 12. For example, use these designs when you cannot randomly assign research participants to the comparison groups. Confounding variables might be present that will make the interpretation of results ambiguous. Therefore, whenever you use a quasi-experimental design, you must be alert for the influence of extraneous variables that could confound the results.

Many designs, such as the nonequivalent comparison-group design and the interrupted time-series design, fall under the rubric of quasi-experimental designs. The most frequently used design is the *nonequivalent comparison-group design,* which consists of pretesting an experimental group and a control group, administering the treatment to the experimental group, and then posttesting the experimental and control groups. The *interrupted time-series design* consists of taking multiple pretests, introducing a treatment condition, and then taking multiple posttests. The *regression-discontinuity design* consists of administering an experimental treatment condition to participants who score above some preset cutoff score. A treatment effect is assumed to exist if there is a discontinuity of the regression lines representing the participants above and below the cutoff score.

Single-case designs are all some type of a time-series design. Two of the most frequently used single-case designs are the A-B-A and A-B-A-B designs and the multiple-baseline design. The A-B-A and A-B-A-B designs assess the effect of an independent variable by determining whether the dependent variable responses differ from baseline following implementation of the experimental treatment and whether they revert to baseline level when the independent variable is removed. The A-B-A and A-B-A-B designs rule out history by demonstrating that the dependent variable response *reverts* to baseline when the treatment condition is withdrawn. The *multiple-baseline design* assesses the effect of an independent variable by demonstrating that a change in behavior occurs only when the treatment effect is successively administered to different individuals, different behaviors, or the same behavior in different settings.

The *changing-criterion design* can be used when your goal is to increase the amount, accuracy, or frequency of some behavior. After a baseline is established, a treatment condition is administered following attainment of a specific criterion of initial successful performance. When this performance criterion has been achieved, the criterion of required performance on the dependent variable is progressively increased until the desired behavioral level is attained. The treatment condition is administered only after the criterion of successful performance is attained.

A number of methodological issues must be considered in designing a single-case study. These include establishing the baseline, changing one variable at a time, determining the length of phases, and assessing the treatment effect.

KEY TERMS

A-B-A design (p. 369)
A-B-A-B design (p. 371)
changing-criterion design (p. 375)
interrupted time-series design (p. 361)
multiple-baseline design (p. 372)
nonequivalent comparison-group design (p. 356)
quasi-experimental research design (p. 355)
regression-discontinuity design (p. 365)
single-case experimental designs (p. 368)

DISCUSSION QUESTIONS

1. Reread the definitions of the various selection effects in Chapter 11. Is selection a problem in the nonequivalent comparison-group design? If so, what can a researcher do to minimize the problem of selection?
2. What type of design from this chapter would you select for each of the following hypothetical studies? Briefly list the strengths and weaknesses of the design.
   a. You want to compare two different ways of teaching college algebra to college students. One group uses calculators, and the other group carries out hand calculations.
   b. You want to study the effect of a new training program, and you are able to divide people rigidly into two groups based on a cutoff score on the quantitative variable called *achievement pretest.*
   c. You want to study the effect of a curriculum implemented a few years ago. You have located baseline data (on the dependent variable) before implementation of the new curriculum and continue to record data after the intervention.
   d. You want to determine the usefulness of a behavioral reinforcement technique for keeping a student on-task.
   e. You have only three or four people to study, and you want to determine the impact of a new technique for teaching students how to perform multiplication.
3. List any problems you identify for each of the following hypothetical studies:
   a. A researcher uses the nonequivalent comparison-group design. She compares the achievement scores of a third-period high school English class taught by Ms. Turner using the discussion method with the scores obtained by the students in a different third-period high school English class that is taught by Mr. Newman using the lecture method.
   b. A researcher uses the nonequivalent comparison-group design. The researcher compares the achievement scores of a third-period high school English class taught by an instructional computer program with a class taught by the lecture method. The instructional period is equal for both the computer and lecture treatments.
   c. A school financial officer uses the interrupted time-series design to study the impact of a new program aimed at increasing donations to the PTA. The program was implemented in January 2008. The financial officer has 5 years of pretest data and will collect annual data for the next 5 years. (Hint: Note that in 2008, the stock market took a major downturn.)
   d. A teacher uses the A-B-A design to study the impact of her new strategy for teaching multiplication.
   e. The Baker Elementary School uses the regression-discontinuity design to investigate the effect of a new reading program aimed at increasing the reading skills of students reading below grade level. The reading program is to be administered to students reading two grade levels below their current grade level. To ensure that enough students are administered the reading program to get a good measure of its effectiveness, students with reading deficiencies at two other schools who also meet the established criteria are allowed to participate in the reading program.

RESEARCH EXERCISES

1. To gain some experience in reading and identifying quasi-experimental and single-case designs, use ERIC (http://eric.ed.gov) to find one of the following articles:

   Copland, M. A. (2000). Problem-based learning and prospective principals' problem-framing ability. *Educational Administration Quarterly, 36*, 585–607.

Hitendra, P. (1998). An investigation of the effect of individual cognitive preferences on learning through computer-based instruction. *Educational Psychology*, *18*, 171–182.

Moore, D. W., Prebble, S., Robertson, J., Waetford, R., & Anderson, A. (2001). Self-recording with goal setting: A self-management programme for the classroom. *Educational Psychology*, *21*, 255–265.

Once you have selected your article, read it carefully and answer the following questions:

a. What is the primary research question that the study addresses?

b. What are the independent and dependent variables in the research design?

c. What type of design was used in the study to answer the research question?

d. Why do you think the researchers used the design they selected?

e. What limitations exist for the design used in the research study?

f. What could the researchers have done to improve the research design?

2. Using the criteria just provided, review and critique the quasi-experimental research article at the companion website.

3. Identify the type of research design that would be used to investigate the following research problems:

a. A college wants to identify the effect of making the dean's list on academic performance in subsequent terms.

b. A teacher wants to investigate the effect of praise on getting a student in her classroom to focus on assigned work rather than bothering students seated at nearby desks.

c. A university tracked the graduation rate of its athletes for 10 years and found that only 53% of them completed their bachelor's degree. The university wanted to increase the graduation rate of its athletes, so a program was implemented that restricted athletes from participating in any sports activity if they had less than a C average in their classes. The program also provided academic tutoring for students with less than a C average.

RELEVANT INTERNET SITES

Brief discussion of quasi-experimental design and links to other designs, such as the nonequivalent groups design and the regression-discontinuity design, as well as other issues relevant to this topic
http://www.socialresearchmethods.net/kb/quasiexp.htm

Discussion of the basic single-case designs and other methodological issues, such as the characteristics of single-case evaluation, including how to determine whether a treatment is effective
http://www.msu.edu/user/sw/ssd/issd01.htm

STUDENT STUDY SITE

Visit the Student Study Site at **edge.sagepub.com/rbjohnson6e** for these additional learning tools:

Video Links
Self-Quizzes
eFlashcards
Lecture Notes
Full-Text SAGE Journal Articles
Interactive Concept Maps
Web Resources

RECOMMENDED READING

Braden, J. P., & Bryant, T. J. (1990). Regression discontinuity designs: Applications for school psychologists. *School Psychology Review*, *19*, 232–239.

Campbell, D. T., & Russo, M. J. (1999). *Social experimentation.* Thousand Oaks, CA: SAGE.

Eckert, T. L., Ardoin, S. P., Daiesy, D. M., & Scarola, M. D. (2000). Empirically evaluating the effectiveness of reading interventions: The use of brief experimental analysis and single case designs. *Psychology in the Schools*, *37*, 463–473.

Mark, M. M., & Reichardt, C. S. (2009). Quasi-experimentation. In L. Bickman & D. J. Rog (Eds.), *The SAGE handbook of applied social research methods* (2nd ed., pp. 182–213). Thousand Oaks, CA: SAGE.

Shadish, W. R., Cook, T. D., & Campbell, D. T. (2002). *Experimental and quasi-experimental designs for generalized causal inference.* New York, NY: Houghton Mifflin.

NOTE

1. Additional analysis approaches are available. One approach that is usually *not* recommended because of reliability issues is using ANOVA to compare the pretest to posttest change scores for the groups; that is, "Is the average change of one group greater than the average change for another group?" Another, more popular approach is to look for an interaction between time (pretest, posttest) and group in a mixed ANOVA. Time is a within-subjects independent variable, and group is a between-subjects independent variable. Another recommended approach is reliability-corrected ANCOVA (for details, see Trochim & Donnelly, 2008).

Chapter 14

Nonexperimental Quantitative Research

LEARNING OBJECTIVES

After reading this chapter, you should be able to

- State the definition of nonexperimental quantitative research.
- List categorical and quantitative independent variables that cannot be manipulated by a researcher.
- Evaluate evidence for cause and effect using the three required conditions for cause-and-effect relationships.
- Explain the "third-variable problem."
- List and briefly describe the three major techniques of control that are used in nonexperimental research.
- Compare and contrast cross-sectional research, longitudinal research, and retrospective research.
- Compare and contrast the two types of longitudinal research.
- Identify descriptive research studies, predictive research studies, and explanatory research studies when examining published research.
- Explain the difference between a direct effect and an indirect effect in causal modeling.
- Draw the typology of nonexperimental quantitative research formed by crossing the time dimension with the research objective dimension.

Visit the Student Study Site for an interactive concept map.

RESEARCH IN REAL LIFE Nonexperimental Research Design and Causation

istock/alexandrumagurean

In 1962, Surgeon General Dr. Luther Terry assembled the US Surgeon General's Advisory Committee. The mission for this group of experts was to examine all of the research on the association between smoking and cancer. Their job was clear. They were to provide the nation with an answer to this question: Does smoking cause cancer of the lungs? Because it was not possible to study smoking and cancer experimentally with humans, most of the research was nonexperimental research, which is more controversial when researchers are trying to make statements about causes and effects. Over the next 2 years, the Advisory Committee reviewed the vast research literature, and it examined all known plausible alternative explanations for the association between smoking and lung cancer.

In 1964, the committee's landmark conclusion was made public: "Cigarette smoking is causally related to lung cancer in men; the magnitude of the effect of cigarette smoking far outweighs all other factors. The data for women, though less extensive, point in the same direction" (US Office of the Surgeon General, 1964, p. 37).

Despite the Surgeon General's report, scientists working for the tobacco industry did not give up. They repeatedly espoused the view that you can "prove" that smoking causes lung cancer *only* through the conduct of experimental research. They argued that the association between smoking and cancer was an artifact due to some hidden and unknown factor. They argued that smokers and nonsmokers probably differed on some genetic factor that caused smokers to smoke and also caused lung cancer. The "scientists" working for the tobacco industry were exploiting the limitation of nonexperimental research: This type of research does not eliminate the influence of extraneous variables as easily and as successfully as does experimental research. However, over time, the nonexperimental research studies continued to demonstrate a relationship between lung cancer and smoking when all other plausible extraneous variables were taken into account. The evidence for a causal relationship became so strong that it revealed that the critics working for the tobacco industry were wrong. Smoking did and does cause lung cancer.

In March 1997, the cigarette company Liggett Group became the first to admit that the wealth of evidence, including decades of its own research, supported the conclusion that smoking is addictive and does indeed cause lung cancer. As of now (2016), most cigarette companies have admitted that smoking causes lung cancer. Legal battles continue, however, over who is to be held responsible for the effects of smoking, what companies must legally admit, what information must appear on a package of cigarettes, and more.

In this chapter, we discuss a number of nonexperimental research designs and show you why these designs are not as effective as experimental designs in demonstrating a causal relationship. We also show you what needs to be done to arrive at a causal conclusion when using these designs.

Researchers are interested in the issue of causation because they want to learn how the world operates and to obtain information about how to make it work better. You have learned in earlier chapters that experimental research is the strongest research method for providing evidence of a causal relationship between two variables. Sometimes, however, researchers are interested in causality, but they cannot conduct an experiment, either because the independent variable cannot be manipulated or because it would be unethical to manipulate it. For example, let's say that you want to determine whether cigarette smoking causes lung cancer. What kind of research would you choose? Would you set up the following experiment? Select 500 newborn babies and randomly assign them to two groups, an experimental group (n = 250) that would be forced to smoke cigarettes and a control group (n = 250) that would not be allowed to smoke cigarettes. Then you would measure the rates of lung cancer in the two groups many years later. Obviously, you should never conduct this experiment because it would be highly unethical. So what must you do instead? Should you give up on scientific research because you can't manipulate the independent variable? Of course not. The research problem is much too important. What you have to do in cases like this is use a *non*experimental research method and attempt to establish the best evidence that you can, given your practical constraints.

- **Nonexperimental research** Research in which the independent variable is not manipulated and there is no random assignment to groups

Here is the formal definition of **nonexperimental research** used in this chapter (Kerlinger, 1986):

> Nonexperimental research is systematic empirical inquiry in which the scientist does not have direct control of independent variables because their manifestations have already occurred or because they are inherently not manipulable. Inferences about relations among variables are made, without direct intervention, from concomitant variation of independent and dependent variables. (p. 348)

You can see in Kerlinger's definition that the researcher does not manipulate the independent variable in nonexperimental research (i.e., "the scientist does not have direct control of independent variables"); the researcher can look back at what naturally happened in the past, or he or she can move forward and observe what happens over time (i.e., "because their manifestations have already occurred or because they are inherently not manipulable"); and the researcher observes how variables relate to one another (i.e., "Inferences about relations among variables are made . . . from concomitant variation of independent and dependent variables"). The independent and dependent variables can be categorical and/or quantitative in nonexperimental research. In this chapter, you should assume that the dependent variable is quantitative unless we tell you otherwise. However, the logic that is explained in this chapter equally applies to a research study with a categorical dependent variable.[1]

Both manipulation of an independent variable and random assignment to groups are missing in *non*experimental research studies. This means that nonexperimental researchers must study the world as it naturally occurs. Because nonexperimental researchers cannot directly manipulate their independent variables or randomly assign research participants to experimental and control groups, a red flag should always pop up in your mind reminding you that nonexperimental research cannot provide evidence for causality that is as strong as the evidence obtained in experimental research. Evidence for causality in nonexperimental research is more tentative, more exploratory, and less conclusive.

Despite its limitations, nonexperimental research is very important to the field of education because many important educational variables cannot be manipulated or created in the laboratory and it is difficult, if not impossible, to create many real-life settings using experiments. Here is the way one leading research methodologist put it:

> It can even be said that nonexperimental research is more important than experimental research. This is, of course, not a methodological observation. It means, rather, that most social scientific and educational research problems do not lend themselves to experimentation,

> although many of them do lend themselves to controlled inquiry of the nonexperimental kind. Consider Piaget's studies of children's thinking, the authoritarianism studies of Adorno et al., the highly important study *Equality of Educational Opportunity,* and McClelland's studies of need for achievement. If a tally of sound and important studies in the behavioral sciences and education were made, it is possible that nonexperimental studies would outnumber and outrank experimental studies. (Kerlinger, 1986, pp. 359–360)

Kerlinger was emphasizing the importance of nonexperimental research in this quote, despite the fact that he actually preferred experimental to nonexperimental research. He was careful to point out that his reasoning was not based on a methodological observation because, again, other things being equal, you should prefer an experiment when you are interested in studying causality. It is a cardinal rule in research, however, that *your research questions should drive your research.* This means that you first determine your research questions and then select the strongest research method available to address those questions. In education, this often means that we have to conduct nonexperimental research to address important questions.

Steps in Nonexperimental Research

The typical steps in nonexperimental research are similar to the steps in experimental research: (1) The researcher determines the research problem and hypotheses to be tested. (2) The researcher selects the variables to be used in the study. (3) The researcher collects the data. (4) The researcher analyzes the data. (5) The researcher interprets the results of the study. The researcher specifically determines whether the hypotheses are supported. The researcher also typically explores the data to generate additional hypotheses to be tested in future studies. It is important that the researcher follow these steps when conducting nonexperimental research in order to avoid the post hoc fallacy.

The **post hoc fallacy** reads "*Post hoc, ergo propter hoc.*" In English, this says, "After this, therefore because of this." (Now you know a little Latin!) We engage in the post hoc fallacy if we argue after the fact that because A preceded B, A must have caused B. For example, you get the flu and attribute it to your friend's sniffling child, who visited your home yesterday. This kind of reasoning is more informally known as "twenty-twenty hindsight." We are all pretty good at explaining, after the fact, why something happened. Although this kind of reasoning is fine for generating ideas, it is far from conclusive scientific evidence. An especially egregious form of the post hoc fallacy would occur if a researcher analyzed some data, found some statistically significant correlations or group differences, and then acted as if he or she had predicted those relationships. The point is that in explanatory research, you must *test* your hypotheses with new empirical data to make sure that they work.

- **Post hoc fallacy** Making the argument that because A preceded B, A must have caused B

Independent Variables in Nonexperimental Research

Independent variables used in nonexperimental research frequently cannot be manipulated because it is either impossible or unethical to manipulate them. Nonexperimental research is also sometimes done on independent variables that could be manipulated but are not, either because the researcher wants to explore how the independent variable is related to other variables before doing an experiment or because the researcher wants to examine relationships to determine whether findings established in laboratory experiments generalize to real-world settings. All these forms of nonexperimental research can make a contribution to the educational research literature.

Now let's look at some examples of categorical and quantitative independent variables that might be used in nonexperimental research because they cannot be manipulated. Some *categorical* independent variables that cannot be manipulated by the researcher are gender, parenting style, student learning style, ethnicity, retention in grade (i.e., retained or not retained), drug or tobacco use, and any enduring personality trait that is operationalized as a categorical variable (e.g., high extroversion versus low extroversion). If you try, you can probably think of some additional categorical independent variables that cannot be manipulated by the researcher. Some *quantitative* independent variables that cannot be manipulated by the researcher are intelligence, aptitude, age, GPA, any enduring personality trait that is operationalized as a quantitative variable (e.g., degree of extroversion varying from a low value of 1 to a high value of 100), and so forth. Again, if you take a moment or so, you can probably think of some additional quantitative independent variables that can't be manipulated by the researcher.

Researchers sometimes turn inherently quantitative independent variables into categorical independent variables. For example, you could take the quantitative variable *aptitude* and categorize it into three groups (high, medium, and low). Another example is in the previous paragraph, where we pointed out that extroversion could be operationalized as either a categorical variable or a quantitative variable. Categorizing an independent variable makes the research study look like an experiment because the independent variable in experimental research studies is usually categorical. Do *not* be misled, however. If the independent variable is not manipulated, then the research study is not an experiment. Most experts contend that categorizing quantitative independent variables is a poor practice that should be discontinued (e.g., Kerlinger, 1986, p. 558; Pedhazur & Schmelkin, 1991, p. 308). The problem is that you lose some information about the relationship between the independent and dependent variables when you categorize a quantitative variable. Also, if only two categories are used (e.g., high vs. low), then only linear (straight-line) relationships can be examined. You can solve this last problem by simply using three categories rather than two categories. However, the problem of loss of information cannot be avoided if you categorize your quantitative variable. In short, we recommend that researchers generally avoid turning quantitative variables into categorical variables.

- **Simple case** Nonexperimental research design with one independent variable, one dependent variable, and no control for any extraneous variables

- **First simple case of nonexperimental quantitative research** Design with one categorical independent variable and one quantitative dependent variable

SIMPLE CASES OF NONEXPERIMENTAL QUANTITATIVE RESEARCH

When you are first learning about research, it is helpful to start with the weakest and most basic forms of nonexperimental quantitative research. These are called the **simple cases** (or simple designs), which means you have one independent or predictor variable and one dependent variable *and you have not taken steps to control for any extraneous variables.*

In the **first simple case of nonexperimental quantitative research**, you have one categorical independent variable and one quantitative dependent variable. For example, perhaps a researcher examined the relationship between gender and math performance and found out that, on average, the males did slightly better than the females. In this example, there is one categorical independent variable (gender) and one quantitative dependent variable (math performance). In this situation, the researcher would compare the two group means (males vs. females) to see whether the groups differed on the dependent variable (math performance). The researcher would also use a statistical test to determine whether the relationship between the independent and dependent variables was statistically significant. The researcher would specifically use either a *t* test or an ANOVA to determine whether the difference between the two group means is **statistically significant**. Statistical significance simply means that you can conclude that the difference between the group means is greater than what you would expect to see by chance alone. Group means that are very different are usually statistically significant (i.e., we don't think the difference between them is just a chance occurrence). If you determine that the difference between the means is statistically significant, you will draw the conclusion that a real relationship exists between the independent and dependent variables. (We explain the ideas of *t* test, ANOVA, and statistical significance in Chapter 19, so don't worry about knowing more than the basic definitions for now! We just want to start using these terms here to show you where they fit into the overall research process.)

■ **Statistically significant** Describes a research finding that is probably not attributable to chance alone; we believe it is a real relationship

In the **second simple case of nonexperimental quantitative research**, you have one quantitative independent variable and one quantitative dependent variable. For example, perhaps a researcher examined the relationship between students' level of motivation and their math performance and found out that lower levels of motivation predicted lower math performance and higher levels of motivation predicted higher math performance (i.e., there was a positive correlation). In this simple case, the researcher would plot the data to determine whether the relationship was linear or curvilinear. Examples of linear and curvilinear relationships are shown in Figure 14.1. As you can see, a linear relationship follows a straight-line pattern, and a curvilinear relationship follows a curved-line pattern. If the relationship between the variables is linear, then the researcher computes the Pearson product-moment correlation coefficient. This is the most commonly used correlation coefficient (discussed in Chapters 2 and 18), and it is the one that researchers are usually referring to if they say they computed the "correlation." If the relationship is curvilinear, the researcher must rely on an alternative measure of the relationship between two variables such as η (Greek *eta*; for details, see Howell, 2002, pp. 351–353) or use curvilinear regression (for details, see Pedhazur & Schmelkin, 1991, pp. 451–458).

■ **Second simple case of nonexperimental quantitative research** Design with one quantitative independent variable and one quantitative dependent variable

After determining the correlation between the single independent variable and the single dependent variable in the second simple case of nonexperimental research, the researcher conducts a statistical test to determine whether the correlation is statistically significant. A correlation coefficient is said to be statistically significant when it is larger than would be expected by chance. Correlation coefficients that are much different from zero are usually statistically significant.

Assume now that a researcher found that the relationship between the two variables was statistically significant (i.e., it is a real relationship and not just due to chance factors) in our examples of the two simple cases. *It is important for you to remember that both of these simple cases of nonexperimental research are seriously flawed if you want to make a causal attribution* (i.e., if you want to conclude that gender causes math performance or if you want to conclude that level of motivation causes math performance). The biggest

■ **FIGURE 14.1** Linear and curvilinear relationships

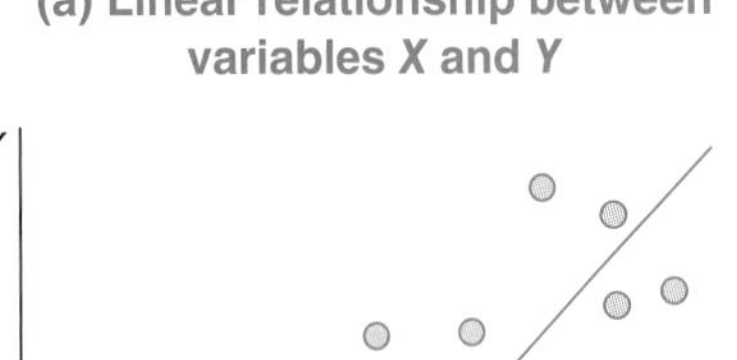

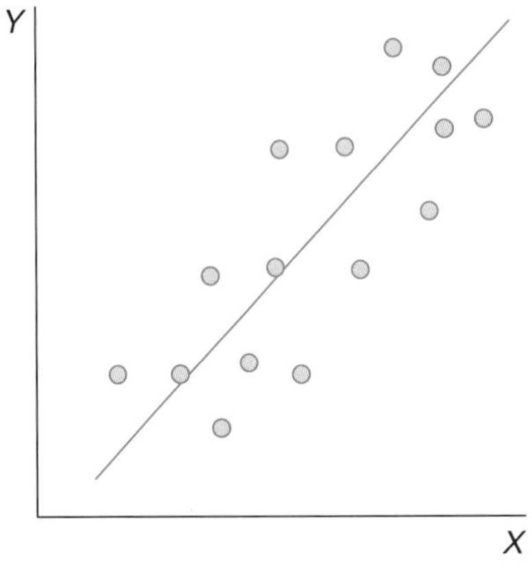

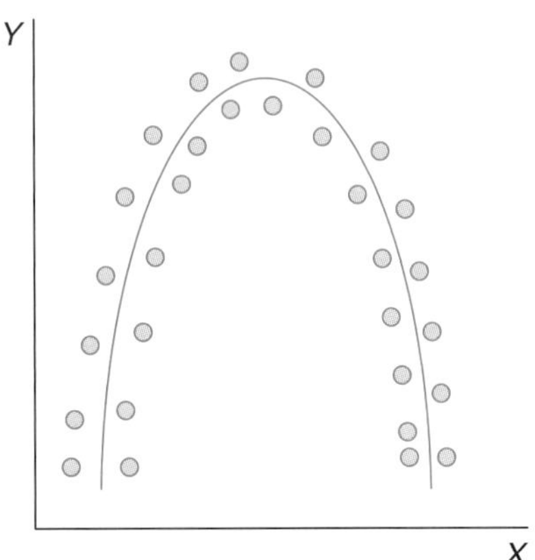

problem is that there are too many uncontrolled extraneous variables that might be the reason for the observed relationship. For example, can you think of some alternative explanations for an observed relationship between gender and math achievement (e.g., perhaps females are socialized to deemphasize mathematics and males are socialized to emphasize mathematics)? Can you think of some reasons why level of motivation might not be causally related to math achievement (e.g., perhaps math achievement is due to the amount of time spent studying and ability)?

The key point is that you cannot draw a conclusion about *cause and effect* from either of the simple cases because *observing a relationship between two variables is not enough evidence to conclude that the relationship is causal.* In the next sections, we explain how you can establish some evidence of causation by looking at the two-variable relationship *while controlling for worrisome confounding variables*. Remember this: we can improve the simple cases by controlling for confounding variables.

In practice, you should always avoid the simple cases when you are interested in studying cause and effect. Our goal in the rest of this chapter is to show you how to design and conduct *high-quality* nonexperimental research studies when your research situation demands that you use nonexperimental research techniques.

■ **Three required conditions** Three things that must be present if you are to contend that causation has occurred

■ **Probabilistic cause** Changes in variable *A* tend to produce changes in variable *B*

THREE REQUIRED CONDITIONS FOR CAUSE-AND-EFFECT RELATIONSHIPS

Whenever you want to claim that changes in variable *A* tend to produce (i.e., cause) changes in variable *B*, you must check for the presence of the **three required conditions** (Asher, 1983; Cook & Campbell, 1979; Shadish et al., 2002). Notice that we said "tend to" in the previous sentence. We used those words to remind you that educational researchers are interested in **probabilistic cause** (i.e., changes in variable *A* tend to cause changes in variable *B*), not perfect causation (i.e., changes in variable *A* always produce the same changes in variable *B*). The idea of probabilistic cause should make sense to you because you know that, for example, a technique of teaching might work quite well for many students but not work well for a few of your students. Counselors know that a certain type of therapy might work well for many clients but not for a few of their clients. It is also true that the same individual might not always react the same way to the same stimulus. For these reasons, when educational researchers talk about causation, they are almost always talking about probabilistic causation rather than about perfect or absolute causation.

The three required conditions that you must always consider if you want to establish that changes in variable *A* tend to *cause* changes in variable *B* were outlined in Chapter 11. They are shown again in Table 14.1. As you can see in the table, condition 1 states that variable *A* and variable *B* must be related. This is the *relationship* condition: If there is no relationship whatsoever between two variables, then one variable cannot directly affect the other variable. Condition 2 states that the proper *time order* must be established. This condition should be obvious, because if changes in variable *A* are to cause changes in variable *B*, the changes in variable *A* must precede the changes in variable *B*.

Condition 3 says that the relationship between variable *A* and variable *B* must not be due to a confounding extraneous or third variable. This means that alternative or *rival explanations* must be eliminated. A common rival explanation states that an observed relationship was due to an extraneous variable (i.e., a third variable) that was not "controlled for" in the research study where the causal claim was made. This rival explanation is called the **third-variable problem** because it states that the relationship between *A* and *B* is actually due to *C*. The key point is that, because you want to conduct a strong nonexperimental research study, you must identify all extraneous variables that might offer rival explanations. Furthermore, you should identify those variables during the planning and designing phases of your study so that you can attempt to prevent this problem from happening. After your study has been completed, it will be too late to do anything about an unmeasured extraneous variable.

- **Third-variable problem** An observed relationship between two variables that may be due to an extraneous variable

Some terminology in nonexperimental research is potentially confusing. First, the terms *confounding variables* and *third variables* are used interchangeably because they are synonyms. Both terms refer to extraneous variables that researchers need to identify before they collect data so that they can attempt to eliminate these variables as rival explanations for an observed relationship between two other variables. You can eliminate or minimize the influence of third (i.e., confounding) variables by using one of the approaches discussed in the subsequent section on techniques of control in nonexperimental research. Second, the terms *alternative explanation*, *rival explanation*, and *rival hypothesis* also are synonyms. These terms are used to refer to reasons for an observed relationship other than the reason originally stated by a researcher (i.e., the new reasons operate as alternatives or rivals).

A useful technique for identifying rival explanations is called the **method of working multiple hypotheses** (Chamberlin, 1890/1965). Chamberlin explained the method of working multiple hypotheses this way:

- **Method of working multiple hypotheses** Attempting to identify rival explanations

> The effort is to bring up into view every rational explanation of new phenomena, and to develop every tenable hypothesis respecting their cause and history. The investigator thus becomes the parent of a family of hypotheses; and, by his parental relation to all, he is forbidden to fasten his affections unduly upon any one. (p. 756)

If you conduct a research study, remember to use the method of working multiple hypotheses when you are *planning* the study, not after you have completed it and someone

TABLE 14.1 The Three Required Conditions for Causation

Researchers must establish three conditions if they are to conclude that changes in variable A cause changes in variable B.

Condition 1:	Variable A and variable B must be related (the relationship condition).
Condition 2:	Proper time order must be established (the temporal antecedence condition).
Condition 3:	The relationship between variable A and variable B must not be due to some confounding extraneous or "third" variable (the lack of alternative or rival explanation condition).

has identified a flaw. This way you can plan and conduct a research study that will provide defensible conclusions.

The three required conditions for cause and effect that we just discussed are truly general. They apply to both experimental and nonexperimental research. In fact, the criteria apply whenever you want to establish evidence that a relationship is causal, regardless of your research method (e.g., the conditions apply in qualitative research if you are interested in causality). You learned in previous chapters that strong experimental research designs (i.e., designs with manipulation and random assignment) perform extremely well on the three conditions for causation. Now we examine how well (or poorly) nonexperimental research performs on the three required conditions for causality.

APPLYING THE THREE REQUIRED CONDITIONS FOR CAUSATION IN NONEXPERIMENTAL RESEARCH

Neither manipulation nor random assignment is present in nonexperimental research. Let's examine the implications this fact has for establishing evidence of cause and effect. We start with the two simple cases of nonexperimental research discussed earlier. Recall that in the simple cases, there is a single independent variable and a single dependent variable. In an earlier example, we saw that a relationship was observed between gender and math performance and a relationship was observed between level of motivation and math performance. *The problem that we run into with the two simple cases is that just observing a relationship is not sufficient grounds for concluding that a relationship is causal.* Let's apply the three required conditions for causation to the two simple cases.

In the case of gender and math performance, a relationship was observed. This means that causal condition 1 is met (i.e., a relationship between the two variables must be observed). We can also assume that gender occurs before math performance as measured in the research study if we assume that gender is a measure of one's biological sex, which is fixed at birth. In this case, causal condition 2 also is met (i.e., gender comes before math performance). Note that one might argue that gender is much more than biological sex. If one made this argument, it would be wise to measure specifically the important aspects of gender and study how they relate to the dependent variable. One would then have to consider the issue of time order for each new aspect studied.

Our biggest problem, based on the three conditions, is with condition 3. There are many alternative explanations for an observed relationship between gender and math performance. As we pointed out earlier, perhaps males and females are socialized differently regarding mathematics. Or perhaps females are just as good at math as males but tend to have higher math anxiety than males, which lowers their math performance in a test condition. Socialization and math anxiety, and possibly many other factors you can think of, represent uncontrolled third variables that are confounded (entangled) with the independent variable gender. Therefore, we cannot know for sure whether math performance is due to gender or whether it is due to socialization or to math anxiety (or to some other unnamed third variable). This problem is an example of the *third-variable problem* that is omnipresent in nonexperimental research. The third-variable problem is present whenever uncontrolled and therefore potentially confounding extraneous variables are present. To strengthen this study you would need to control for these third variables.

Now let's move to the case of level of motivation and math performance. Once again, a relationship was observed (the higher the motivation, the higher the math performance). Therefore, condition 1 is met. We can't know for sure whether level of motivation or math performance occurred first, since we assume that the researchers measured both variables at the same time in this example. (Later in this chapter, we discuss some nonexperimental designs in which participants are studied at more than one time point.) We might assume on theoretical grounds that the level of motivation was to some degree present before the students took the test measuring their math performance. It is reasonable to assume, for example, that students who are more motivated will attend class regularly and study harder and that attending class and studying for exams occur before the exams. On the other hand, we cannot know time ordering for sure because it is also reasonable to believe that math performance has some impact on level of motivation. In short, causal condition 2 (proper time order) is only partially met because the proper time order is only assumed or hypothesized to occur—no direct evidence exists that it did occur.

As was the case in the gender study example, causal condition 3 is a major problem. There are alternative explanations for the observed relationship between level of motivation and math performance. We listed two rival explanations earlier: Perhaps the students' math performance was due to the amount of time spent studying or to ability rather than to level of motivation. To strengthen this study you would need to control for these third variables. The problem of alternative or rival explanations is omnipresent in nonexperimental research. In a nonexperimental study, the researcher can never know for sure whether an observed relationship can be explained away by some uncontrolled extraneous or third variable that the researcher failed to identify.

Here is a key point to remember: *The most serious problem that we run into in the simple cases of nonexperimental research is that the observed relationship might be due to an extraneous variable (causal condition 3), and this problem is widespread in nonexperimental research.* We have called this the third-variable problem. Fortunately, one can control for third variables identified by the researcher using the control techniques discussed later in this chapter (e.g., matching and statistical control). One can never know, however, that all third variables have been identified.

- **Spurious relationship** A relationship between two variables that is due to a third variable

When the relationship between two variables is due to another variable, researchers sometimes call it a **spurious relationship**. A spurious relationship is a completely *non*causal relationship. When the relationship between two variables is only partially due to another variable, we sometimes call it a **partially spurious relationship** (Davis, 1985). If an extraneous variable causes the third-variable problem to occur, it must be related to both the independent and the dependent variable.

- **Partially spurious relationship** A relationship between two variables that is partially due to a third variable

Here is an example of a spurious correlation: Did you know that the amount of fire damage to houses and the number of fire trucks responding to fires is positively related? Should we conclude based on this observed relationship that calling more fire trucks to a fire will cause more fire damage to occur? Of course not! The real cause of the relationship between fire damage and the number of trucks responding is the *size of the fire.* More fire trucks respond to larger fires, and more damage results from larger fires. However, if you examined only the relationship between the number of fire trucks and amount of fire damage without considering the size of fire, you would find a clear, positive relationship between the number of fire trucks responding and the amount of fire damage (see Figure 14.2a).

Researchers check to see whether relationships are due to third variables by *controlling for* these variables. You have controlled for a third variable when you have provided evidence that the relationship between two variables is not due to a third variable. In particular, *the original relationship between two variables will disappear when controlling for the third variable if the relationship is totally spurious,* as in the case of fire damage and fire trucks.[2] In part (b) of Figure 14.2, we controlled for the size of fire by examining the original relationship separately for small, medium, and large fires (i.e., we examined the relationship within levels of the extraneous variable). As you can see, there is no relationship between fire damage and

FIGURE 14.2 Relationship between amount of fire damage and number of trucks responding before and after controlling for size of fire. We controlled for size of fire by examining the original relationship at different levels of size of fire. The original relationship disappears.

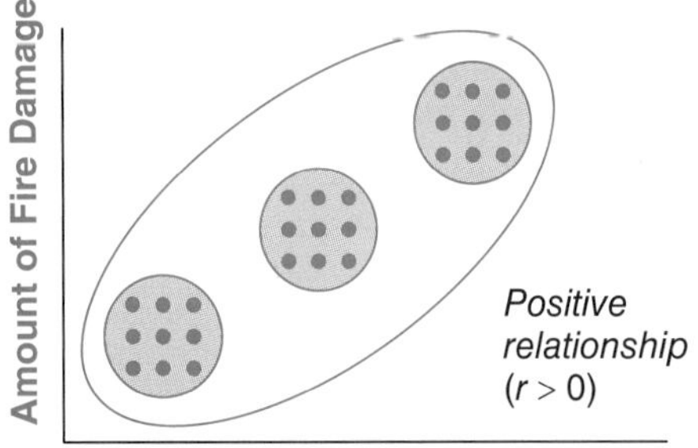

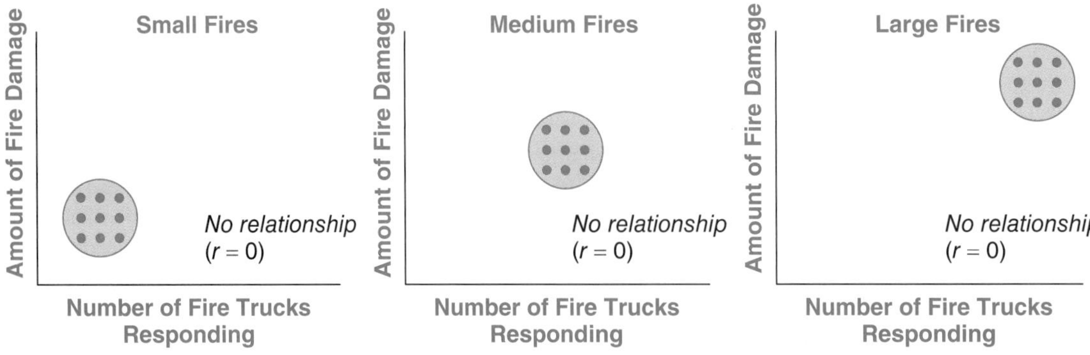

the number of trucks when you look only at small fires. There is also no relationship when you look only at medium fires. And finally, there is no relationship when you look only at large fires. Therefore, the original relationship seen between the variables fire damage and the number of fire trucks responding disappears when you control for the size of the fire. In other words, there is no longer a relationship between the variables fire damage and number of fire trucks responding after you control for the third variable, the size of the fire. Examining a relationship within the different levels of a third variable such as we just did is an important strategy of controlling for an extraneous variable. This strategy is a type of what we refer to as *statistical control.*

We have provided a list of some additional spurious relationships in Table 14.2. We think that you will find the list quite entertaining! For example, did you know that there is a positive relationship (i.e., a positive correlation) between the number of police officers in an area and the number of crimes in the area? Obviously, we cannot conclude on the basis

TABLE 14.2 Examples of Spurious Relationships

*Observed Spurious Relationship**	*Reason for the Relationship (the Third Variable)*
Amount of ice cream sold and deaths by drownings (Moore, 1993)	Season: Ice cream sales and drownings tend to be high during the warm months of the year.
Size of left hand and size of right hand	Genetics: The size of both hands is due to genetic makeup.
Height of sons and height of daughters (Davis, 1985)	Genetics: Heights of sons and daughters are both due to their parents' genetic makeup.
Ministers' salaries and price of vodka	Area (i.e., urban or rural): In urban areas, prices and salaries tend to be higher.
Shoe size and reading performance for elementary school children	Age: Older children have larger shoe sizes and read better.
Number of doctors in region and number of people dying from disease	Population density: In highly dense areas, there are more doctors and more people die.
Number of police officers and number of crimes (Glass & Hopkins, 1996)	Population density: In highly dense areas, there are more police officers and more crimes.
Number of homicides and number of churches	Population density: In highly dense areas, there are more homicides and more churches.
Number of storks sighted and the population of Oldenburg, Germany, over a 6-year period (Box, Hunter, & Hunter, 1978)	Time: Both variables were increasing over time.
Number of public libraries and the amount of drug use	Time: Both were increasing during the 1970s.
Teachers' salaries and the price of liquor (Moore & McCabe, 1993)	Time: Both tend to increase over time.
Tea drinking and lung cancer	Smoking: Tea drinkers have a lower risk only because they smoke less.

*All but one of the spurious relationships in the first column shows a positive relationship. That is, as one of the variables increases, the other variable also increases. The one negative relationship is the relationship between tea drinking and lung cancer.

of this observed relationship that having more police officers causes crime. The completely spurious relationship is due to the third variable, population density. There are more crimes and more police officers in areas with many people, and there are fewer crimes and fewer police officers in areas with fewer people. Once the researcher controls for the third variable (population density), the original relationship will disappear. For example, if the researcher examines the relationship between police officers and crime within the different levels of population density (low, medium, and high population density), the relationship will no longer exist. Each of the spurious relationships shown in Table 14.2 will vanish if the researcher *controls for the third variable* causing the relationship. None of the relationships is causal.

REVIEW QUESTIONS

14.1 Why is experimental research much stronger than nonexperimental research when the researcher is interested in making cause-and-effect statements?

14.2 Why must a researcher sometimes conduct nonexperimental research rather than experimental research?

14.3 Why must researchers watch out for the post hoc fallacy?

14.4 Name a potential independent variable that cannot be manipulated.

14.5 Explain the problems with the simple cases of nonexperimental research. Why is a researcher not justified in making a cause-and-effect claim from these two cases?

14.6 Explain exactly how strong experimental research fulfills each of the three required conditions for cause and effect.

14.7 On which of the three required conditions for cause and effect is nonexperimental research especially weak? On which one of the three required conditions is nonexperimental research strong?

14.8 Explain why you cannot make a defensible causal claim based on an observed relationship between two variables (e.g., gender and achievement) in nonexperimental research.

TECHNIQUES OF CONTROL IN NONEXPERIMENTAL RESEARCH (I.E., HOW TO DESIGN STRONG NONEXPERIMENTAL RESEARCH)

You learned in the previous section that the third-variable problem is usually present in nonexperimental research. This means that the threat of confounding extraneous variables is virtually always present in this kind of research. Now we discuss the major techniques that researchers use to control for extraneous variables in nonexperimental research. You have already been introduced to most of these techniques in earlier chapters (e.g., Chapters 11 and 12). The appropriate use of these control techniques helps improve the rigor and credibility of nonexperimental research. You should upgrade your evaluation of nonexperimental research studies that use these techniques, and if you are planning to conduct a nonexperimental study, you should include one or more of the techniques as part of your study's research design.

Matching

As was discussed in earlier chapters, one way to control for extraneous variables is to use matching. To perform matching, you must first select one or more **matching variables**. The matching variable(s) are extraneous variable(s) that you want to eliminate as rival explanations of the presumed causal relationship between your independent and dependent variables. The second step in matching is to select participants to be in your study in such a way that your independent and matching variables will be unrelated (i.e., uncorrelated, or unconfounded). If your independent variable is categorical, this second step simply involves constructing your comparison groups to be similar on the matching variable but still different on the independent variable. This is exactly the same goal that you had in experimental research: You want your comparison groups or categories to be the same on all extraneous variables and different *only* on the levels of the independent variable so that you can attribute the causal effect uniquely to the independent variable.

■ **Matching variable** The variable the researcher matches on to eliminate it as an alternative explanation

For example, assume that your independent variable is gender and your dependent variable is math performance. Also assume that you want to match the male and female groups on interest in mathematics because you think the relationship that is sometimes observed between gender and math performance is due to the fact that boys are socialized to be interested in mathematics. That is, perhaps boys are more interested in mathematics because of gender socialization and, as a result, boys try harder and perform better in mathematics. To match on interest in mathematics, you could give an interest-in-mathematics test to all the students in your local high school. You could find 25 boys whose interest levels varied from low to high. Then, for each of these 25 boys, you would locate a girl with a similar score on the interest-in-mathematics test. When you were done, you would have 25 boys and 25 girls who were matched on interest in mathematics (for a total of 50 research participants). The two groups would be similar on the variable *interest in mathematics* (the extraneous variable you were worried about), but they would differ on gender (the independent variable). To complete this *comparative* nonexperimental research study, you would measure the dependent variable *math performance* for the 25 boys and 25 girls to see whether they differed. If they did differ, it would not be because of interest in mathematics because the groups were similar on interest in mathematics.

Matching can also be used when the independent variable is quantitative. Assume that your independent variable is level of mathematics motivation (a quantitative variable varying from a low value of 1 to a high value of 10), your dependent variable is actual math performance, and the extraneous variable you want to eliminate as a rival explanation is grade point average (i.e., GPA is a proxy for overall academic achievement). Your research hypothesis is that higher motivation leads to higher math performance. In this example, you could match on the extraneous variable (GPA) by finding students with high, medium, and low GPAs at each of the 10 levels of mathematics motivation. That is, for low-motivation students, you would locate students with high, medium, and low GPAs. Then for the next higher level of motivation, you would locate students with high, medium, and low GPAs. You would continue this process for all 10 levels of motivation.[3] After completing this process, you would have your research participants. Furthermore, your independent variable (motivation) and your matching variable (GPA) would be uncorrelated and therefore unconfounded. If you still observed a relationship between motivation and math performance, you would conclude that it is not due to GPA because you eliminated GPA as a threat through the matching technique.

The key idea is that matching is used to strengthen nonexperimental research studies on condition 3 of the required conditions for causation (Table 14.1). That is, it is used to eliminate alternative explanations due to extraneous variables. Matching unfortunately has a number of weaknesses that limit its use. We conclude our discussion by listing its seven major limitations:

1. Matching can be cumbersome because you must search for individuals who meet the criteria for inclusion in the research study. This is a serious limitation unless you have a very large pool of potential participants to select from and you have access to information about them.
2. Researchers frequently cannot find matches for many potential research participants. These potential participants are eliminated or excluded from the research study.
3. There is usually more than one alternative explanation for the relationship of interest, so you need to match on more than one variable.
4. You must know what the relevant extraneous variables are in order to match on them.
5. You never know for sure that you have matched on all of the appropriate variables.
6. Matching can create an unrepresentative sample because the participants are selected for the purpose of matching rather than for the purpose of being representative of a population. Therefore, generalizability might be compromised.
7. If you match groups from different populations (e.g., disadvantaged and advantaged groups matched on pretest achievement based on extreme scores), then the threat to internal validity called regression to the mean can sometimes be a problem in studies occurring over time.

Holding the Extraneous Variable Constant

When using this technique of control, researchers turn the extraneous variable into a constant. They do this by restricting the research study to a particular subgroup. For example, if you are concerned that gender might operate as a confounding extraneous variable, then you can turn gender into a constant by including only female participants in your research study. If everyone is a female, then gender does not vary (it is a constant). Most important, if all participants are of one gender, then gender cannot possibly confound the relationship between the independent and dependent variables. If you were concerned that age is a confounding extraneous variable, you could limit your research study to young people, middle-aged people, or older people. You could even limit the study to 16-year-olds. Unfortunately, there is a serious problem with this technique of restricting your research study to a certain subpopulation. The researcher cannot generalize to the kinds of people who are excluded from the study. In other words, the generalizability (the external validity) of the study is restricted. For example, if the study were done only with 16-year-olds, then the researcher could generalize only to 16-year-olds.

Statistical Control

Statistical control is the most commonly used technique for controlling for extraneous variables in nonexperimental research. When statistically controlling for one or more extraneous variables, the researcher uses a statistical technique to remove the influence of the extraneous variable(s). Most techniques of statistical control are spinoffs of a mathematical procedure called the **general linear model**, or the GLM (Knapp, 1978; Tabachnick & Fidell, 1996; Thompson, 1998). All you need to know about the general linear model is that it is the "parent" of many statistical techniques (i.e., the "children") that are used in education. (See the student companion website for more on the GLM.) More formally, many statistical procedures commonly used to control for extraneous variables are called special cases of the general linear model.

- **General linear model** A mathematical procedure that is the "parent" of many statistical analysis techniques

One **special case of the general linear model**, called **partial correlation**, is used to examine the relationship between two quantitative variables, controlling for one or more quantitative extraneous variables (Cohen, 1968; Cohen & Cohen, 1983). It is called a partial correlation because the effect of the third variable is "partialed out" or removed from the original relationship. Typically, all the variables used in partial correlation analysis must be quantitative rather than categorical. Here's a relatively easy way to think about partial correlation. If you determine the regular correlation between your independent variable and your dependent variable *at each of the levels* of your extraneous variable, you will have several correlations (e.g., if your extraneous variable had 10 levels, then you would have 10 correlations; if your extraneous variable had 100 levels, then you would have 100 correlations). The partial correlation coefficient is simply the weighted average of those correlations (Pedhazur, 1997). The range of a partial correlation coefficient is the same as a regular correlation coefficient (i.e., –1.00 to +1.00, with zero signifying no relationship at all). As a general rule, if a researcher used a regular correlation coefficient (the correlation between two variables) rather than a partial correlation coefficient (the correlation between two variables controlling for one or more additional variables), then you can be pretty sure that he or she was not thinking about extraneous variables. On the other hand, if a researcher used a partial correlation coefficient (or another control technique), you can be pretty sure that he or she was thinking about controlling for extraneous variables. As a general rule, you should upgrade your evaluations of research articles when the authors controlled for extraneous variables.

- **Special case of the general linear model** One of the "children" of a broader statistical procedure known as the general linear model (GLM)
- **Partial correlation** Used to examine the relationship between two quantitative variables, controlling for one or more quantitative extraneous variables

Another special case of the general linear model is called **analysis of covariance** (ANCOVA), which was discussed in earlier chapters. ANCOVA is used to determine the relationship between one categorical independent variable and one quantitative dependent variable, controlling for one or more quantitative extraneous variables (Pedhazur & Schmelkin, 1991). For example, there is a relationship between gender (a categorical variable) and income (a quantitative variable) in the United States. Men earn more money, on average, than do women. You might decide, however, that you want to control for education; that is, you want to make sure that the difference is not due to education. You could eliminate education as a rival explanation (i.e., you could control for it) by comparing the average income levels of males and females at each of the levels of education in your data. You could also have the computer analyze your data using the ANCOVA technique to tell you whether gender and income are still related after controlling for education. If gender and income are still related, then the researcher can conclude that education has been eliminated as a rival hypothesis. The details of ANCOVA and partial correlation are beyond the scope of this book. *The important point here is that ANCOVA shows the relationship between a categorical independent variable (e.g., gender) and a quantitative dependent variable (e.g., income level), controlling for a quantitative extraneous variable (e.g., level of education).*

- **Analysis of covariance** Used to examine the relationship between one categorical independent variable and one quantitative dependent variable, controlling for one or more quantitative extraneous variables

See Tools and Tips 14.1 on the Student Study Site.

An advantage of statistical control (compared to matching) is that researchers can base their research on samples of participants who are randomly selected from a population (Pedhazur & Schmelkin, 1991). (You don't have to throw out cases from the data as you do in matching when you can't find a match for an individual.) To control statistically for one or more extraneous variables, the researcher must collect data on the extraneous variables in addition to data on the independent and dependent variables (i.e., collect data on all the important variables). In effect, the researcher incorporates the extraneous variables into the design of the research study. Then, after collecting the data, the researcher controls for the extraneous variables during data analysis (using ANCOVA, partial correlation, or another technique). The most serious limitation to statistical control techniques is that you must make certain statistical assumptions that frequently are not met in practice (e.g., random selection of cases, normality of residuals, reliable and valid measurement).

REVIEW QUESTION

14.9 What is the purpose of the techniques of control in nonexperimental research?

INTERLUDE (THE STUDY OF CAUSAL RELATIONSHIPS IN EPIDEMIOLOGY)

So far in this chapter we have outlined the three conditions required for making claims about cause and effect and the ways to "control for" rival explanations. Remember that it also is important that research is based on good theory and that researchers *test* their hypotheses. Because the issue of establishing some evidence of causation in nonexperimental research is so important, and so controversial, we provide a short summary of how causation has long been established in the field of epidemiology. Take a moment now to read about this in Exhibit 14.1. You can use the ideas provided in Exhibit 14.1 to supplement the three required conditions as you attempt to obtain evidence of cause and effect in your research. Once you finish examining the exhibit, you can move on to the last part of this chapter, where we identify a useful way to classify nonexperimental research along two dimensions: time and research objective.

EXHIBIT 14.1 How Do Epidemiologists Determine Causality?

Epidemiology is the branch of medical science that studies the incidence, distribution, cause, and control of disease in a population. You often hear the results of epidemiological research on the news. Although epidemiologists prefer to conduct strong experimental research when possible, often their research questions and variables do not lend themselves to experimental research. It is constructive to look at epidemiology to learn how to conduct high-quality nonexperimental research.

Perhaps the single most important individual in the development of research methods and analysis in epidemiology is Sir Austin Bradford Hill (1897–1991). Bradford Hill developed a list of criteria that continues to be used today. When using them, don't forget Hill's advice:

> None of these nine viewpoints can bring indisputable evidence for or against a cause and effect hypothesis and equally none can be required as a *sine qua non*. What they can do, with greater or less strength, is to help answer the fundamental question—is there any other way of explaining the set of facts before us, is there any other answer equally, or more, likely than cause and effect? (cited in Doll, 1992, p. 1523)

The Bradford Hill Criteria

1. Strength of Association. The stronger the relationship between the independent variable and the dependent variable, the less likely it is that the relationship is due to an extraneous variable.
2. Temporality. It is logically necessary for a cause to precede an effect in time.
3. Consistency. Multiple observations, of an association, with different people under different circumstances and with different measurement instruments increase the credibility of a finding.
4. Theoretical Plausibility. It is easier to accept an association as causal when there is a rational and theoretical basis for such a conclusion.
5. Coherence. A cause-and-effect interpretation for an association is clearest when it does not conflict with what is known about the variables under study and when there are no plausible competing theories or rival hypotheses. In other words, the association must be coherent with other knowledge.
6. Specificity in the Causes. In the ideal situation, the effect has only one cause. In other words, showing that an outcome is best predicted by one primary factor adds credibility to a causal claim.
7. Dose-Response Relationship. There should be a direct relationship between the risk factor (i.e., the independent variable) and people's status on the disease variable (i.e., the dependent variable).
8. Experimental Evidence. Any related research that is based on experiments will make a causal inference more plausible.
9. Analogy. Sometimes a commonly accepted phenomenon in one area can be applied to another area.

In the following example, we apply Hill's criteria to the classic case of smoking and lung cancer.

1. Strength of Association. The lung cancer rate for smokers was quite a bit higher than for nonsmokers (e.g., one study estimated that smokers are about 35% more likely than nonsmokers to get lung cancer).
2. Temporality. Smoking in the vast majority of cases preceded the onset of lung cancer.
3. Consistency. Different methods (e.g., prospective and retrospective studies) produced the same result. The relationship also appeared for different kinds of people (e.g., males and females).
4. Theoretical Plausibility. The biological theory that smoking causes tissue damage that over time results in cancer in the cells was a highly plausible explanation.
5. Coherence. The conclusion (that smoking causes lung cancer) "made sense" given the current knowledge about the biology and history of the disease.
6. Specificity in the Causes. Lung cancer is best predicted from the incidence of smoking.
7. Dose-Response Relationship. Data showed a positive, linear relationship between the amount smoked and the incidence of lung cancer.

(Continued)

(Continued)

8. Experimental Evidence. Tar painted on laboratory rabbits' ears was shown to produce cancer in the ear tissue over time. Hence, it was clear that carcinogens were present in tobacco tar.

9. Analogy. Induced smoking with laboratory rats showed a causal relationship. It, therefore, was not a great jump for scientists to apply this to humans.

References

Doll, R. (1992). Sir Austin Bradford Hill and the progress of medical science. *British Medical Journal, 305*, 1521–1526.

Hill, B. A. (1965). The environment and disease: Association or causation? *Proceedings of the Royal Society of Medicine, 58*, 295–300.

Susser, M. (1977). Judgement and causal inference: Criteria in epidemiologic studies. *American Journal of Epidemiology, 105*, 1–15.

CLASSIFYING NONEXPERIMENTAL RESEARCH BY TIME AND RESEARCH OBJECTIVE

Two major dimensions that should be used to classify nonexperimental research are the *time* dimension and the *research objective* dimension. We discuss these in some detail presently, but first note that if you cross these two dimensions in a matrix (shown in Table 14.3), a typology of nine types of nonexperimental research is obtained (Johnson, 2001).

To use this classification, all you have to do is answer these two questions:

1. How are the data collected in relation to time (i.e., are the data retrospective, cross-sectional, or longitudinal)?
2. What is the primary research objective (i.e., description, prediction, or explanation)?

TABLE 14.3 Types of Research Obtained by Crossing Research Objective and Time Dimension

	Time Dimension		
Research Objective	*Retrospective*	*Cross-Sectional*	*Longitudinal*
Descriptive	retrospective, descriptive study (type 1)	cross-sectional, descriptive study (type 2)	longitudinal, descriptive study (type 3)
Predictive	retrospective, predictive study (type 4)	cross-sectional, predictive study (type 5)	longitudinal, predictive study (type 6)
Explanatory	retrospective, explanatory study (type 7)	cross-sectional, explanatory study (type 8)	longitudinal, explanatory study (type 9)

Source: Johnson, R. B. (2001). Toward a new classification of nonexperimental quantitative research. *Educational Researcher, 30*, 3–13.

Your answer to these two questions will lead you to one of the nine cells shown in Table 14.3. There is no need to memorize the names of the nine cells (e.g., retrospective descriptive or cross-sectional explanatory) because as soon as you answer the two questions, you will have the name! When writing about your nonexperimental design, you will need to inform your reader of your study's characteristics on these two dimensions so that the reader will be in a position to evaluate your assertions.

We now explain these two dimensions in more depth.

The Time Dimension in Nonexperimental Research

The first dimension used in our typology of nonexperimental research methods (Table 14.3) is the time dimension. It is important to have an understanding of the time dimension for at least two reasons. First, researchers often want to know how variables change over time (e.g., What happens to children as they get older?). Second, when studying cause and effect, researchers must establish the proper time order. This means that we are concerned about the time dimension whenever we talk about a cause and effect. Nonexperimental research is classified into three types of research that address the time dimension issue quite differently: cross-sectional research, longitudinal research, and retrospective research (see Table 14.4).

TABLE 14.4 Summary of Cross-Sectional, Longitudinal, and Retrospective Research

Design Type	*Description*
Cross-sectional	Data are collected at one point in time on several variables such as gender, income, and education.
Longitudinal	Data are collected in a forward direction over time on one or more variables such as gender, IQ, discipline problems in middle school, high school GPA, and dropout status.
Retrospective*	Data are collected that represent present and past status on variables such as dropout, use of drugs, and GPA.

*If data from the past are located and combined with current data, then you have constructed a retrospective longitudinal time configuration; if survey data are collected at one time and participants are simply asked about their status on variables in their past, then you have a retrospective cross-sectional time configuration.

Cross-Sectional Research

In **cross-sectional research**, data are collected from the research participants at a single point in time or during a single, relatively brief time period (i.e., a period long enough to collect data from all of the participants selected to be in the study). The data are typically collected from multiple groups or types of people in cross-sectional research. For example, data in a cross-sectional study might be collected from males and females, from people in different socioeconomic classes, from multiple age groups, and from people with different abilities and accomplishments. The major advantage of cross-sectional research is that data can be collected on many different kinds of people in a relatively short period of time.

Cross-sectional research Data are collected at a single point in time

Cross-sectional research has several weaknesses. One disadvantage is that it is difficult to establish time order (condition 2 of the required conditions for causality). If you collect data from research participants at a single time point only, you can't directly measure changes that are occurring over time. Time order can be partially established in cross-sectional research through theory, through past research findings, and through an understanding of the independent variable (e.g., you can safely assume that adults' biological sex occurs before the amount of education completed because biological sex is set at birth). However, these techniques for establishing time order are weaker than actually observing people over time. A related disadvantage is that the study of developmental trends (changes in people as they get older) can be misleading when using cross-sectional data.

Suppose that you collected cross-sectional data from 1,000 adults who were age 18 or older. When analyzing the data, suppose that you found that age and political conservatism were positively correlated (the older the participants were, the more conservative they tended to be). You could not safely conclude in this case that aging causes conservatism because you would not have established proper time order (causal condition 2) or ruled out rival explanations (causal condition 3). Remember this important point: In a cross-sectional study, people at different ages are not the same people. Therefore, you are not able to observe your participants change over time and properly establish time order. In addition, the older and younger people may differ on important extraneous variables (e.g., they might differ on education and experience of certain historical events). An alternative explanation for the relationship between age and political conservatism is that the people in the earlier generations of your data (the older people) have always been more conservative than the more recent generations (the younger people), perhaps because of some historical effect. The younger people lived in different historical times during their formative years, and they may turn out differently when they are older. Thus, you can't make a strong conclusion that age causes people to become more conservative.

Longitudinal Research

- **Longitudinal research** Data are collected at multiple time points, and comparisons are made across time

The term *longitudinal research* refers to research that occurs over time. In **longitudinal research**, the data are collected at more than one time point or during more than one data-collection period, and the researcher is interested in making comparisons across time. Although longitudinal research requires a minimum of two distinct time periods, data can be collected over as many time periods as needed to address the research questions. There are two major variations of longitudinal research: trend studies and panel studies. For examples of longitudinal research, some of which are still ongoing, see Young, Savola, and Phelps's book *Inventory of Longitudinal Studies in the Social Sciences* (1991). Although not discussed in this chapter, longitudinal research can also be done in qualitative research (e.g., see Huber & Van de Ven, 1995).

- **Trend study** Independent samples are taken from a population over time, and the same questions are asked

A **trend study** is the form of longitudinal research in which independent samples (samples composed of different people) are taken from a general population over time and the same questions are asked of the samples of participants. In a trend study, you might, for example, take a new sample each year for 5 consecutive years of US citizens who are 18 years or older (i.e., adults). An example of a survey that has been used in many trend studies is the General Social Survey (GSS), which has been conducted annually since 1972 by interviewers working for NORC (National Opinion Research Center), based in Chicago. The interviewers document the status of approximately 1,500 randomly selected adult (18 years or older) participants on an extensive number of variables each year (Davis & Smith, 1992).

The second major type of longitudinal research is a **panel study**.[4] The defining characteristic of a panel study is that the *same individuals* are studied at successive points over time. The researcher's goal is to understand why the panel members change over time. Because the researcher starts in the present and moves forward in time, the term **prospective study** is also applied. For example, if you select 200 beginning teachers and follow them over the next 10 years (e.g., interviewing them every other year), you have a panel, or prospective, study. You would be studying the same people over time. The individuals in a panel study are often selected from multiple age cohorts to strengthen the design. A **cohort** is defined as any group of people with a common classification or characteristic. For example, a researcher might follow individuals from three age cohorts for 3 consecutive years. If the children in the study were ages 5, 7, and 9 in the first year of the study, they would be ages 6, 8, and 10 in the second year of the study (assuming the study was conducted at the same time of year), and they would be ages 7, 9, and 11 in the third year, or "third wave" of the study. Clearly, individuals in panel studies grow older over time. This means that the average age of the people in the study will increase over time, and at some point it will be impossible to continue a panel study because all of the participants will have died of old age!

- **Panel study** Study in which the same individuals are studied at successive points over time
- **Prospective study** Another term applied to a panel study
- **Cohort** Any group of people with a common classification or characteristic

Let's say that you interview 1,500 randomly selected participants who are representative of the United States in the year 2015. This group of people will become more and more unrepresentative of the United States at later dates (e.g., in 2025, 2035, and 2045) because the US population is constantly changing (e.g., people are constantly born into and move into and out of the United States) while no new people are added to the panel study over time.[5] The point is that, even if no one ever drops out of your panel study, the panel and the current population can become very different over time. This is a threat to external validity because it limits your ability to generalize from the panel to the current population.

Perhaps an even greater problem is **differential attrition**, which occurs when participants do not drop out of the study randomly (i.e., when the people who drop out do not resemble the people who remain). In other words, this problem occurs when only certain types of people drop out of the research study. Differential attrition can reduce external validity because after certain types of people drop out of the panel, the panel no longer resembles the population. Differential attrition can also reduce internal validity (the ability to establish firmly evidence of cause and effect). Assume, for example, that you are studying children's use of effective study strategies as they age. Your hypothesis is that age has a causal influence on effective strategy use (i.e., older children will use more effective study strategies than younger children). A problem might occur, however, if the less motivated and less effective strategy users (i.e., children who use immature or inefficient strategies) drop out of your panel. You might erroneously conclude that effective strategy use increases with age simply because the users of less effective strategies dropped out over time and the users of effective strategies remained. Because of the problems caused by differential attrition, researchers should provide information about the kinds of people who dropped out of their research study and the potential implications this has for their conclusions.

- **Differential attrition** Participants who drop out are different from those who stay

Panel studies have a major strength. You are better able to establish causal condition 2 (proper time order) because you actually study the people over a period of time. Therefore, *for studying cause and effect, panel studies are superior to cross-sectional studies. Panel studies are also more powerful than trend studies* because changes can be measured at the level they occur (within the individuals who change). Remember that in a trend study, you are limited to comparing different sets of people at different times, but in a panel study, you can study the same individuals over time. One strategy in panel studies is to divide the original sample into groups based on the independent variable, follow the participants over time, and document what happens to them. Another strategy is to identify participants who change on a variable and the participants who do not change on the variable and then investigate the factors that help explain this change or lack of change.

You might, for example, decide to test the research hypothesis that students who begin using drugs in the 10th grade are more likely to drop out of high school than are students who have not used drugs by the end of the 10th grade. To test this hypothesis, you could select a sample of ninth-grade students and then interview them each year for the next 5 years. You could identify the students who begin drug use during the 10th grade and compare them with the other students over the next several years, looking for differences between the two groups. You might also want to test the hypothesis that students who start drug use earlier in high school (e.g., the 9th or 10th grade) are more likely to drop out than students who start drug use later in high school or students who never use drugs at all during the high school years. You would divide your sample during data analysis as before, this time to see whether the early users were more likely to drop out than the later users or the nonusers to determine whether the hypotheses are supported. You could also analyze the data to test additional hypotheses or to locate additional behaviors and attitudes that are associated with drug use (e.g., peers who use drugs, poor grades, low self-esteem, family problems).

Medical researchers have effectively used prospective panel studies to help establish that smoking causes lung cancer (Gail, 1996). In a typical study, two groups of individuals (smokers and nonsmokers) are matched on multiple extraneous variables and are then followed forward in time. Researchers use matching to make the two groups as similar as possible, with the ultimate (but probably unattainable) goal being that the only important difference between the two groups is the participants' status on the independent variable. Then the researchers follow these two groups over time, documenting their relative rates of lung cancer. The researchers also check for a **dose-response relationship**; that is, they check to see whether there is a positive correlation between the number of cigarettes smoked and the likelihood of lung cancer.

- **Dose-response relationship** Present when increased amounts, or greater strength, of the treatment results in increased amounts of response on the dependent variable

Prospective studies such as this cancer study are strong on the first two conditions of causation. The relationship between smoking and lung cancer can be clearly established because different rates of lung cancer are found in the two groups and because a dose-response relationship is found. Time order is fairly well established because individuals are observed before and after the onset of cancer. Researchers use a variety of control techniques to help establish condition 3 (i.e., to rule out alternative explanations). As noted earlier, matching is used to create similar groups. Then, during data analysis, statistical control is used to further control for extraneous variables. Although prospective studies can be used to rule out many alternative explanations, they cannot rule out all of them. The key is that no *plausible* alternative explanation exists for the relationship between smoking and lung cancer.

The scientific opinion that smoking causes lung cancer (Gail, 1996) is based on the evidence obtained from a multitude of research studies. The most important human studies used in establishing this causal relationship have been prospective panel studies. Remember that *the panel study is a relatively powerful nonexperimental method for examining causality.* Unfortunately, prospective research is usually expensive and can take a long time to complete.

Therefore, it should not be surprising that longitudinal studies are less common than cross-sectional studies. Prospective studies are often done at large universities by faculty members with federal funding and large staffs to help them conduct their research.

Retrospective Research

In **retrospective research**, the researcher typically starts with the dependent variable (i.e., with an observed result or outcome) and then "moves backward in time," locating information on variables that help explain individuals' current status on the dependent variable. Retrospective research was one of the earliest kinds of research used to suggest that smoking led to lung cancer (Gail, 1996). Medical researchers compared the smoking habits of people who currently had lung cancer with people who did not currently have lung cancer and found that smokers had higher rates of cancer than nonsmokers (Wynder & Graham, 1950). Retrospective research may be based on actual data collected in the past, or, frequently, researchers use retrospective questions to learn about the participants' pasts. **Retrospective questions** ask people to recall something from an earlier time in their life. In a smoking study, a retrospective question might ask current smokers how old they were when they first started smoking cigarettes. Another question might ask what type of cigarettes they smoked when they first started smoking.

- **Retrospective research** The researcher starts with the dependent variable and moves backward in time

- **Retrospective questions** Questions asking people to recall something from an earlier time

Here are some retrospective questions you might ask if you were studying drug use among high school students: Did you use drugs when you were in high school? What drug did you use most often? How frequently did you use that drug? Who first introduced you to the drug? Did your grades decline after you began using drugs? What grade were you in when your grades started declining? You must be careful when using retrospective questions because individuals' accounts of their past are not always entirely accurate. If possible, you should try to verify retrospective accounts by collecting additional corroborative information. For example, if someone said that his or her grades started declining in the 10th grade, you could check the student's school records for corroboration. Obviously, researchers cannot always corroborate each finding. You should, however, upgrade your evaluation of research studies in which corroboration was done for some or many of the research findings.

See Journal Article 14.1 on the Student Study Site.

The Research Objective Dimension in Nonexperimental Research

The second dimension used in our typology of nonexperimental research (Table 14.3) is the primary purpose or research objective. After determining that your research study is nonexperimental (because there is no manipulation or random assignment), you must determine your primary research objective.[6] We discussed six major research objectives in Chapter 1: exploration, subjective understanding, description, prediction, explanation, and influence. Nonexperimental quantitative research often takes one of three forms: descriptive research, predictive research, or explanatory nonexperimental research. Your decision about the research objective will affect your thinking about other issues as well. For example, if you want to conduct an explanatory study and obtain evidence of cause and effect, you should form theoretical hypotheses to be tested, use control techniques (e.g., statistical control, matching), and, if possible, collect longitudinal data, because these strengthen nonexperimental designs for this purpose. We now explain each of the three kinds of nonexperimental research in relation to purpose and provide some examples.

Descriptive Nonexperimental Research

- **Descriptive research** Research focused on providing an accurate description or picture of the status or characteristics of a situation or phenomenon

The primary purpose of **descriptive research** is to provide an accurate description or picture of the status or characteristics of a situation or phenomenon. The focus is not on ferreting out cause-and-effect relationships but rather on describing the variables that exist in a given situation and, sometimes, on describing the relationships that exist among those variables. An examination of the research questions or the author's stated purpose in each research article you look at will help you know when you should apply the label *descriptive research.* Researchers doing descriptive research commonly follow these three steps: (1) randomly select a sample from a defined population, (2) determine the sample characteristics, and (3) infer the characteristics of the population based on the sample.

Educators sometimes conduct descriptive research to learn about the attitudes, opinions, beliefs, behaviors, and demographics (e.g., age, gender, ethnicity, education) of people. Although the survey method of data collection is commonly used in descriptive research, keep in mind that this method (i.e., the use of questionnaires and/or interview protocols, as discussed in Chapter 8) can also be used in predictive and explanatory research (see Babbie, 1990; Finkel, 1995; Kerlinger, 1986; Kiecolt & Nathan, 1985; Rosenberg, 1968; Stolzenberg & Land, 1983). Another research area that is primarily descriptive is in the field of tests and measurement. Test developers are constantly developing and refining tests and other measurement instruments, and they base many decisions on validity and reliability coefficients. On the basis of this descriptive information, they establish evidence about how well their tests operate with different kinds of people under a variety of circumstances.

An example of a published descriptive research study is "Myers-Briggs Personality Profiles of Prospective Educators" by Sears, Kennedy, and Kaye (1997). These researchers administered the Myers-Briggs personality test to 4,483 undergraduate university students who were considering majoring in education. Their primary purpose was to provide descriptive information about prospective teachers based on the popular Myers-Briggs personality test. They also checked student records several years later to see which of the students graduated and what area of education they selected as their major.

Sears and colleagues (1997) found that the predominant personality profile of the prospective educators who later graduated with degrees in elementary education was SFJ (sensing, feeling, and judging). They described SFJs as "warm, sociable, responsible, and caring about people" (Sears et al., p. 201). In contrast, the personality profile of the students who graduated with degrees in secondary education was NTJ (intuitive, thinking, and judging). The researchers described NTJs as "oriented to the theoretical, disposed to investigate possibilities and relationships; and drawn to complexity, innovation, and change" (Sears et al., p. 201). Because of these personality traits, the researchers predicted that the secondary education majors would be more likely than the elementary majors to advance educational innovation and reform once they became teachers. If the researchers tested this prediction in a future research study, they would produce an example of predictive research, which we discuss next. Remember, the key to descriptive research is that the researchers collect data used for description.

See Journal Article 14.2 on the Student Study Site.

Predictive Nonexperimental Research

Predictive research is done so that we can predict the future status of one or more dependent (or criterion) variables on the basis of one or more independent (or predictor) variables (Pedhazur, 1997). For example, college admissions officers might be interested in predicting student performance based on such variables as high school GPA, scores on admissions tests, gender, and type of school attended (e.g., public, private). Insurance companies are interested in predicting who will have auto accidents, who will get sick, who will be injured, and who will die of old age. (That's why auto insurance rates are higher for males and for adolescents.) Employers are interested in predicting who will be a happy and productive employee. An economist might want to predict the performance of the US economy using "leading indicators." Educators are often interested in predicting who is at risk for problems like poor academic performance, drug use, dropping out of high school, and skipping class. The key point is that if a researcher wants to see how well he or she can predict some outcome based on one or more independent or predictor variables, then the research study is labeled predictive research.

- **Predictive research** Research focused on predicting the future status of one or more dependent variables based on one or more independent variables

Dykeman, Daehlin, Doyle, and Flamer (1996) produced an example of predictive research that was published in a journal article titled "Psychological Predictors of School-Based Violence: Implications for School Counselors." The researchers wanted to find out whether three psychological constructs could be used to predict violence among students in Grades 5 through 10. The first psychological predictor was a measure of impulsivity. The researchers' hypothesis was that the more impulsive children are, the more prone to violence they will be. The second predictor was a measure of empathy. Their hypothesis was that there would be a negative relationship between empathy and violence (i.e., the more empathy students have, the less prone they are to violence). The third psychological predictor variable was locus of control. People with an internal locus of control tend to view their own experiences as resulting from their own actions and decisions. The researchers hypothesized that people with internal locus of control would be less prone to violence than people who had more external locus of control.

The researchers used a special case of the general linear model called multiple regression to determine how well the three variables predicted violence. It turned out that all three of the predictive hypotheses were supported. Impulsivity was the most important of the three predictor variables. The authors concluded that the aim of a violence prevention program might be

> (a) to change group norms about violence, (b) to enhance family relationship characteristics, (c) to improve peer relationship skills, (d) to decrease substance abuse, (e) to lessen impulsivity, (f) to increase empathy, and (g) to engender internal locus of control. (Dykeman et al., 1996, p. 44)

See Journal Articles 14.3 and 14.4 on the Student Study Site.

The last three points were directly based on the data from this research study.

Explanatory Nonexperimental Research

- **Explanatory research** Testing hypotheses and theories that explain how and why a phenomenon operates as it does

In **explanatory research**, researchers are interested in testing hypotheses and theories that explain how and why a phenomenon operates as it does (Pedhazur, 1997). The researcher's goal is to understand the phenomenon being studied. The researcher is also interested in establishing evidence for cause-and-effect relationships. Although experimental research is the strongest form of explanatory research for providing evidence of cause and effect, you have learned in this chapter that many important independent variables cannot be manipulated, which means that these variables must be investigated using nonexperimental explanatory research.

A good example of explanatory nonexperimental research is "A Prospective, Longitudinal Study of the Correlates and Consequences of Early Grade Retention" by Jimerson, Carlson, Rotert, Egeland, and Sroufe (1997). It is important to understand the effects of early grade retention (not promoting a child). However, it would be unethical to manipulate this independent variable (i.e., you cannot randomly assign students to be either retained in their grade or promoted). Therefore, nonexperimental explanatory research must be used to study the effects of grade retention.

In the Jimerson et al. (1997) study, a retained group was identified from the participants in a larger, long-term study of at-risk children and their parents. A group of similar low-achieving promoted students (the nonretained group) was also identified from the project participants as a comparison group. The retained and nonretained groups were matched on academic ability and academic performance because the researchers wanted to compare retained students who are low achieving with promoted students who are low achieving to learn about the effects of retention/promotion. The researchers also used the control technique called statistical control (discussed earlier in this chapter) when making some of their comparisons to equate the groups on additional variables. The practical question driving the research was whether a low-achieving student should be retained or promoted.

Key results from the research study include the following. The retained students showed a short-term improvement in math achievement. However, that improvement disappeared once new material was taught. The retained and nonretained students did not differ on most measures of social and personal adjustment or on a measure of behavior problems. The one difference found was that the promoted students were more emotionally adjusted several years after being promoted. The researchers concluded, "Essentially, the retained and low-achieving promoted students did not differ . . . despite an extra year, and [they] continued to remain comparable years after the promotion or retention" (Jimerson et al., 1997, p. 18). In short, this research study confirmed the results of many additional studies suggesting that elementary grade retention produces few, if any, of its promised effects. In general, retention appears to be an ineffective strategy for improving the achievement levels or psychological adjustment of children or for reducing behavior problems.

Another form of explanatory research increasing in popularity is called causal modeling (Asher, 1983; Maruyama, 1998; Pedhazur, 1997; Schumacker & Lomax, 2004). Although many of the details of causal modeling are beyond the scope of this book, we cover some of the basic conceptual ideas here. **Causal modeling** is a procedure in which a researcher hypothesizes a causal model and then empirically tests the model to determine how well it fits the data. The researcher develops or constructs the causal model based on past research findings and on theoretical considerations. Causal models depict the interrelationships among several variables and are used to explain how some theoretical process operates. Some synonyms for the term *causal model* are *path model, structural model,* and *theoretical model.* Many researchers use these terms interchangeably.

- **Causal modeling** A form of explanatory research in which the researcher hypothesizes a causal model and then empirically tests it

A hypothetical causal model with four variables is shown in Figure 14.3. The four variables in the causal model are parental involvement, student motivation, teaching quality (of the schoolteachers), and student achievement. You can understand this model by realizing that each of the arrows stands for a hypothesized causal relationship. The type of causal relationship between any two variables connected by an arrow is known as a **direct effect**; as depicted, this is the effect of the variable at the origin of an arrow on the variable at the receiving end of the arrow. For example, look at Figure 14.3 and you will see that an arrow goes from parental involvement to student motivation (parental involvement → student motivation). This means that parental involvement is hypothesized to have a direct effect on student motivation. It is important to realize that the assumption that parental involvement affects student motivation (rather than student motivation affecting parental involvement) is based on theory. In the absence of experimental research data, assumptions like this will always be tentative.

- **Direct effect** In a causal model, the effect of the variable at the origin of an arrow on the variable at the receiving end of the arrow

The numbers on the arrows are called **path coefficients**; they provide quantitative information about the direct effects based on the data collected in a research study. If the coefficient is positive, then the relationship between the two variables is positive (i.e., as one variable increases, the other variable increases). If the coefficient is negative, then the relationship is negative (i.e., as one variable increases, the second variable decreases). You can interpret the strength of the relationship by looking at the size of the coefficient, just as with correlation coefficients (i.e., coefficients that are close to +1.00 or –1.00 are very strong, and coefficients that are near zero are very weak). Looking at Figure 14.3, you see the number .76 on the path from student motivation to student achievement. This suggests that a strong positive relationship exists between student motivation and student achievement.

- **Path coefficient** A quantitative index providing information about a direct effect

Take a moment now to look at the other arrows in the causal model. Try to answer these questions: (1) What two variables are hypothesized to have direct effects on student motivation? (2) What variable is hypothesized to have a direct effect on teaching quality? (3) What three variables are hypothesized in the model to have direct effects on student achievement? [The answers are that (1) student motivation is shown to be influenced by parental involvement and teaching quality; (2) teaching quality is influenced by parental involvement; and (3) student achievement is influenced by parental involvement, teaching quality, and student motivation.]

In addition to showing hypothesized direct effects, causal models also show hypothesized indirect effects. An **indirect effect** occurs when one variable affects another variable indirectly, that is, when a variable affects another variable by way of an **intervening variable**. We defined intervening variables (which are also called **mediating variables**) in Chapter 2. According to the causal path A → B → C, variable *B* is an intervening variable (it occurs between *A* and *C*). Furthermore, variable *A* has an indirect effect on variable *C* by way of the intervening variable *B*. Whenever a variable falls between two other variables in a causal chain, it is called an intervening variable. (See bonus material at the student companion website for more on this topic.)

- **Indirect effect** An effect occurring through an intervening variable
- **Intervening or mediating variable** A variable occurring between two other variables in a causal chain

Now that you know what an indirect effect is, see whether you can find some indirect effects in the causal model shown in Figure 14.3. You might have noticed that teaching quality has an indirect effect on student achievement through student motivation. In this case, student motivation is the intervening variable. You can see that teaching quality also has a direct effect on student achievement because an arrow goes from teaching quality to student achievement. In other words, a variable can have both a direct effect and an indirect

See Tools and Tips 14.2 on the Student Study Site.

effect. Also, parental involvement indirectly influences student achievement through teaching quality and through student motivation. There are quite a few relationships (indirect and direct) in even a relatively small causal model.

FIGURE 14.3 A causal model of student achievement

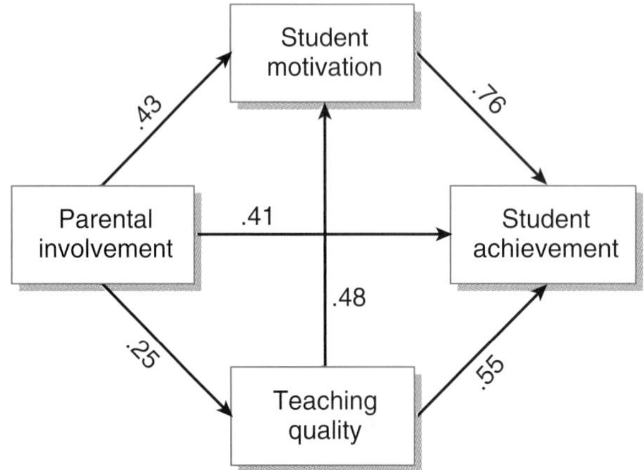

Figure 14.4 shows another example of a causal model. This model was developed and tested by Karabenick and Sharma (1994) and was reported in the *Journal of Educational Psychology*. It shows the effects of several variables on the likelihood of students asking questions during lectures. The researchers collected data to test their model from 1,327 undergraduate college students. After collecting the data, they used a statistical program called LISREL to calculate the path coefficients (the numbers on the arrows). Look at the model and see whether you think the researchers have done a good job explaining what factors cause students to ask or not ask questions.

FIGURE 14.4 A causal model of question asking

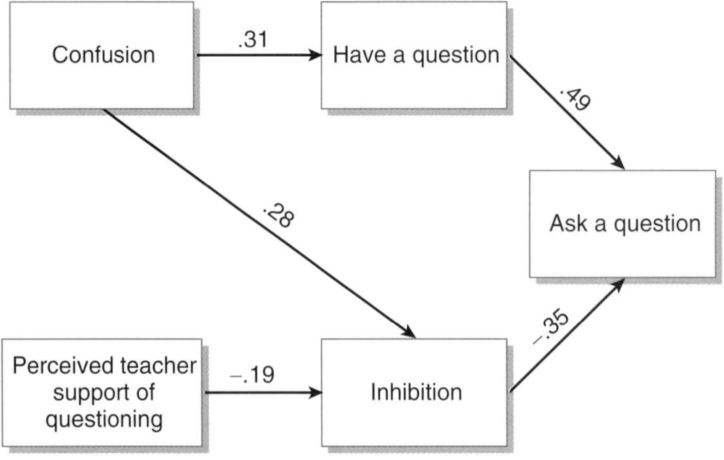

Source: From S. A. Karabenick and R. Sharma. (1994). Perceived teacher support of student questioning in the college classroom: Its relation to student characteristics and role in the classroom questioning process. *Journal of Educational Psychology*, *86*(1), 90–103. Copyright by the American Psychological Association. Adapted with permission of the author.

The original theoretical model developed by the researchers looked like the model shown in Figure 14.4, except that it included an arrow from "Perceived teacher support of questioning" to "Ask a question." Because this particular path turned out to be unimportant on the basis of the data collected in the research study (it was not statistically significant), the researchers eliminated it from the final model shown in Figure 14.4. It is a common practice in the field of causal modeling to exclude arrows that turn out to be unimportant based on the data. This process of eliminating arrows is called *theory trimming.* The other arrows in the model in Figure 14.4 were correctly predicted by the researchers to be important.

You can determine the strength and direction of the direct effects by looking at the path coefficients on the arrows. For example, the path coefficient from inhibition to asking a question is −.35. This means that the effect of inhibition on asking a question (controlling for having a question) is small to moderate in size and the relationship operates in the negative direction. Recall from your study of correlation that a negative relationship exists when two variables move in opposite directions. In this case, the more inhibition students feel, the less likely they are to ask questions. Not surprisingly, the relationship between confusion and having a question (+.31) is moderately small, and the relationship is positive (i.e., the more confusion students have, the more likely they are to have questions). You can interpret the other path coefficients in the model in a similar way.

You can also find the indirect effects in Figure 14.4 by noting when variables affect other variables through intervening variables. For example, perceived teacher support of questioning does not affect students asking questions directly (i.e., there is no direct arrow). However, it does affect asking questions indirectly by way of the intervening variable called inhibition. Likewise, confusion indirectly affects asking questions through having a question and through inhibition. In other words, confusion has two indirect effects on asking questions. This model is complex, but its complexity is a strength because it more closely approximates how a small part of the real world actually operates. Also, researchers can communicate all of the relationships suggested by their theory in a picture.

We discussed causal modeling in this chapter because these complex models are usually used in nonexperimental research, although they are occasionally tested in experimental research. Note also that although causal models are most frequently based on cross-sectional data (data collected at a single time), they are more and more frequently being based on longitudinal data (data collected at two or more time points). As a general rule, causal models based on experiments provide the most solid evidence for cause and effect, causal models based on longitudinal data are second best, and causal models based on cross-sectional data are the weakest. Even when based on cross-sectional data, however, causal models represent drastic improvements over the simple cases of nonexperimental research.

REVIEW QUESTIONS

14.10 Which form of nonexperimental research tends to be the best for inferring cause and effect: cross-sectional research, trend studies, cohort studies, panel studies (i.e., prospective studies), or retrospective research studies? Why?

14.11 Explain the difference between a direct effect and an indirect effect.

14.12 List an advantage and a disadvantage of causal modeling.

ACTION RESEARCH REFLECTION

Insight: When action researchers are not conducting experimental research, they are informally conducting nonexperimental research—they constantly observe potential antecedents and consequences in their worlds and think about how they might later try to reproduce these relationships in their places of practice.

1. Can you think of any nonexperimental quantitative data that you might want to collect to understand your students or participants better?
2. Why is the third required condition (ruling out alternative explanations) important when you are going to claim that one thing caused another?

SUMMARY

The researcher does not manipulate independent variables in nonexperimental research but does compare groups and study relationships among variables. If the researcher's questions concern independent variables that cannot be manipulated, nonexperimental research is the logical choice. A few independent variables that cannot be manipulated are gender, parenting style, grade retention, ethnicity, and intelligence. Researchers must be very careful when using the nonexperimental research method, however, if they wish to obtain evidence of cause-and-effect relationships. The three required conditions for concluding that the relationship between variable *A* and variable *B* is causal are that (1) there must be a relationship between variable *A* and variable *B*, (2) variable *A* must occur before variable *B*, and (3) alternative explanations must be eliminated. Unfortunately, the third condition is virtually always a problem in nonexperimental research. Researchers must attempt to control for any extraneous, or third, variables that might potentially explain the relationship between two variables when they want to obtain evidence that the relationship is causal. The three key techniques of control that are used in nonexperimental research are (1) matching, (2) restricting the study to a subpopulation, and (3) statistical control.

Nonexperimental research is sometimes classified on the basis of the time dimension. If the data are collected at a single time point or during a single data-collection period, the research is a cross-sectional study. If the data are collected at multiple time points over time, it is a longitudinal study. If the data are collected backward in time, it is a retrospective study. Nonexperimental research is also classified on the basis of the researcher's primary research objective. The purpose of descriptive research is to provide an accurate description or picture of the status or characteristics of a situation or phenomenon. The purpose of predictive research is to predict the future status of one or more dependent or outcome variables on the basis of one or more independent or predictor variables. The purpose of explanatory nonexperimental research is to test hypotheses and theories explaining how and why a phenomenon operates as it does. Causal modeling is a form of explanatory research in which the researcher develops a causal model and empirically tests it to determine how well the model fits the data.

KEY TERMS

analysis of covariance (p. 397)
causal modeling (p. 408)
cohort (p. 403)
cross-sectional research (p. 401)
descriptive research (p. 406)
differential attrition (p. 403)
direct effect (p. 409)
dose-response relationship (p. 404)
explanatory research (p. 407)
first simple case of nonexperimental quantitative research (p. 386)
general linear model (GLM) (p. 397)
indirect effect (p. 409)
intervening or mediating variable (p. 409)
longitudinal research (p. 402)
matching variable (p. 395)
method of working multiple hypotheses (p. 389)
nonexperimental research (p. 384)

panel study (p. 403)
partial correlation (p. 397)
partially spurious relationship (p. 391)
path coefficient (p. 409)
post hoc fallacy (p. 385)
predictive research (p. 407)
probabilistic cause (p. 388)
prospective study (p. 403)
retrospective questions (p. 405)
retrospective research (p. 405)
second simple case of nonexperimental quantitative research (p. 387)
simple case (p. 386)
special case of the general linear model (p. 397)
spurious relationship (p. 391)
statistically significant (p. 387)
third-variable problem (p. 389)
three required conditions (p. 388)
trend study (p. 402)

DISCUSSION QUESTIONS

1. What kind of nonexperimental quantitative study would you find most interesting: a descriptive study, a predictive study, or an explanatory study? Why?
2. Why do methodologists and researchers emphasize the point that association does not prove causation?
3. How should researchers approach the issue of cause and effect in nonexperimental quantitative research? How do researchers attempt to meet each of the three required conditions for cause and effect? How do they strengthen their designs to move beyond the simple cases of nonexperimental research? Note that you do need to tell your reader the nature of the study according to the time dimension of the data (i.e., retrospective, cross-sectional, longitudinal) and the research objective dimension (i.e., descriptive, predictive, explanatory).
4. Can you think of two variables that are associated but are not causally related? (Hint: You might want to take a look at Table 14.2 to get started.)
5. Which kind of data do you think provides the most solid evidence of causal condition 2 (proper time order): retrospective, cross-sectional, or longitudinal?
6. Carefully examine Exhibit 14.1: How Do Epidemiologists Determine Causality? Then answer these questions: What do you think about this list? Which criteria do you believe are most important? How do you think these criteria add to the three required conditions that also are discussed in this chapter?

RESEARCH EXERCISES

1. Think of a hypothetical example of a nonexperimental educational research study that would be interesting to you for each of the following research objectives. Be sure to explain why it is nonexperimental rather than experimental:
   a. Explanatory
   b. Predictive
   c. Descriptive
2. Search a database at your library. Find and then list the titles of several nonexperimental articles that appear to be based primarily on each of the following research objectives.
   a. Prediction
   b. Explanation
   c. Description

Also provide an annotated bibliography of the three articles in which you briefly explain why you think each article is of a certain type.

3. It is helpful to examine published examples of nonexperimental research so that you can see more concretely how to carry it out. As an exercise, read and write up a two-page review of the article provided on the companion website.

   When you write up your article review, organize it into the following general sections:

   1. Purpose
   2. Methods
   3. Results
   4. Strengths and weaknesses of the research

PROPOSAL EXERCISES

Are you using one of the following kinds of design in your proposed research study: weak, quasi, or strong experimental design, nonexperimental quantitative design, or a single case design? If yes, look back to the proposal outline on page 112 (Table 5.1) and notice the section labeled "Design."

Make sure you include a Design section in your research proposal. In doing this, (a) draw a picture of your design layout, (b) clearly describe your independent, dependent, and control variables for your reader, and (c) list the threats to internal and external validity of your design and explain how you will control for the threats.

RELEVANT INTERNET SITES

Program evaluation links
http://www.eval.org/p/cm/ld/fid=98

Many discussions of causality issues when using nonexperimental data are found in these archives of this popular academic discussion group:
https://listserv.ua.edu/archives/evaltalk.html

More information
http://onlinestatbook.com/2/research_design/causation.html
http://www.ncbi.nlm.nih.gov/pubmed/18063905
http://core.ecu.edu/psyc/wuenschk/stathelp/Correlation-Causation.htm
http://serious-science.org/causal-analysis-of-non-experimental-data-5279
http://bolt.mph.ufl.edu/6050-6052/unit-2/causation-and-observational-studies/

STUDENT STUDY SITE

Visit the Student Study Site at **edge.sagepub.com/rbjohnson6e** for these additional learning tools:

Video Links
Self-Quizzes
eFlashcards
Lecture Notes
Full-Text SAGE Journal Articles
Interactive Concept Maps
Web Resources

RECOMMENDED READING

Berk, R. A. (1988). Causal inference for sociological data. In N. J. Smelser (Ed.), *Handbook of sociology* (pp. 155–172). Newbury Park, CA: SAGE.

Bullock, H. E., Harlo, L. L., & Mulaik, S. A. (1994). Causation issues in structural equation modeling research. *Structural Equation Modeling, 1*, 253–257.

Johnson, R. B. (2001). Toward a new classification of non-experimental quantitative research. *Educational Researcher*, 30(2), 3–13.

Kaufman, J. S., & Poole, C. (2000). Looking back on "causal thinking in the health sciences." *Annual Review of Public Health, 21*, 101–119.

Reynolds, A. J. (1998). Confirmatory program evaluation: A method for strengthening causal inference. *American Journal of Evaluation, 19*, 203–221.

Susser, M. (1991). What is a cause and how do we know one? A grammar for pragmatic epidemiology. *American Journal of Epidemiology, 133*, 635–648.

NOTES

1. The only thing that changes is the type of statistical analysis used after the data are collected.
2. The relationship also will disappear when the variable is an intervening variable. Therefore, the use of theory is very important in determining whether the variable is a confounding variable or an intervening variable.
3. If the quantitative independent variable has more than 10 levels, then we recommend that you collapse it into fewer categories for the purposes of matching.
4. Panel studies can also be used in experimental research. A panel study with manipulation is more powerful than a panel study without manipulation when you are interested in studying cause and effect.
5. There is a type of panel study, called the revolving panel design, in which new people are added to the panel (see Menard, 1991).
6. When you examine published research articles, keep in mind that some research studies may have more than one objective.

Chapter 15

Section B: Qualitative Research Methods: Five Major Approaches

Narrative Inquiry and Case Study Research

By D. Jean Clandinin and R. Burke Johnson

LEARNING OBJECTIVES

After reading this chapter, you should be able to

- List and define Patton's (2002) 12 major characteristics of qualitative research.
- Compare and contrast the two major approaches to qualitative research discussed in this chapter: narrative inquiry and case study research.
- Define and compare poststructuralism and postmodernism.
- Define and explain how to conduct a narrative inquiry research study.
- Define and explain how to conduct case study research.

Visit the Student Study Site for an interactive concept map.

RESEARCH IN REAL LIFE Qualitative Research Approaches

istock/Steve Debenport

The following is from a narrative account of Truong.

> I first met Truong when Sean, who knew Truong from working with him in junior high school, brought him to the university. As Sean, Truong, and I stood in the doorway of my office, I knew that Truong was deciding whether or not he wanted to talk with me. Was I someone who he could trust? I knew his relationship with Sean had enabled Sean to interest him in the study but now Truong wanted to check me out. After all, I was the one with whom he would have the conversations. I was careful to maintain eye contact as I sensed there was much to learn from Truong's story. I could not help but notice, though, the tattoos on his arm.
>
> Truong let Sean know that he would participate after meeting me. We met about a week after that first encounter on October 15, 2008, and again a week later on October 22, 2008. Three weeks later, Sean arranged for Truong, Vera, and another study participant, and Sean and me to meet up at Hamilton School so Truong could show us around the school. I knew from our first meeting that Hamilton School was a home place for Truong, a place where he felt he belonged.
>
> It was as we began our second conversation that I asked Truong about the tattoos engraved on his arm. Truong described the first tattoo, the tiger, as his "Chinese Zodiac animal." He described the second tattoo, the dragon, by saying "in the Chinese tradition, it's like protection." He began to have the tattoos engraved on his body when he was 16 and, over the next 4 years or so, he added a Koi fish that "represents prosperity." One artist did all the tattoos except for a Japanese demon mask that he now regrets having done. In response to my wonder about whether having the tattoos done hurt, he said it was "a burning sensation and a cutting at the same time. So almost like a knife and a lighter at the same time." The pain he described helped me realize how important these tattoos were for Truong. (Clandinin, 2013b, pp 153–154)

This story is an example of what you would write if you use the qualitative approach known as narrative inquiry. Does it sound like something you would find interesting? You will learn about narrative inquiry and case study research in this chapter. But first, we will talk a little more about qualitative research more generally.

In Chapter 2, we defined **qualitative research** as research relying primarily on the collection of qualitative data (nonnumerical data, such as words and pictures). Qualitative researchers tend to rely on the inductive mode of the scientific method, and the major objective of this type of research is exploration or discovery. This means that qualitative researchers generally study a phenomenon in an open-ended way, without prior expectations, and they develop hypotheses and theoretical explanations that are based on their interpretations of what they observe. Qualitative researchers prefer to study the world as it naturally occurs, without manipulating it. While observing, qualitative researchers try

- **Qualitative research** Research that relies primarily on the collection of qualitative data

not to draw attention to themselves. That is, they try to be unobtrusive so that they will have little influence on the naturally occurring behavior being studied. Qualitative researchers view human behavior as dynamic and changing, and they advocate studying phenomena in depth and over an extended period of time. The product of qualitative research is usually a narrative report with rich description (vivid and detailed writing) rather than a statistical report (with a lot of numbers and statistical test results).

In Figure 15.1, we list the eight common steps in a qualitative research study. In a simple qualitative research study, the researcher might move directly through the steps. Much more frequently, however, the qualitative researcher does not follow the eight steps in a linear fashion (i.e., step 1, then step 2, then step 3, and so on). Typically, the qualitative researcher selects a topic and generates preliminary questions at the start of a research study. The questions can be changed or modified, however, during data collection and analysis if any are found to be naive or less important than other questions. This is one reason why qualitative research is often said to be an *emergent* or fluid type of research. During the conduct of a qualitative research study, the researcher acts like a detective or novelist and goes wherever interesting and enlightening information may be.

Data collection and analysis (steps 4 and 5 in Figure 15.1) in qualitative research have a longitudinal character because qualitative research often takes place over an extended period of time. The researcher purposely selects people to interview and/or observe at early

FIGURE 15.1 Steps in a qualitative research study. The steps are not always linear or sequential.

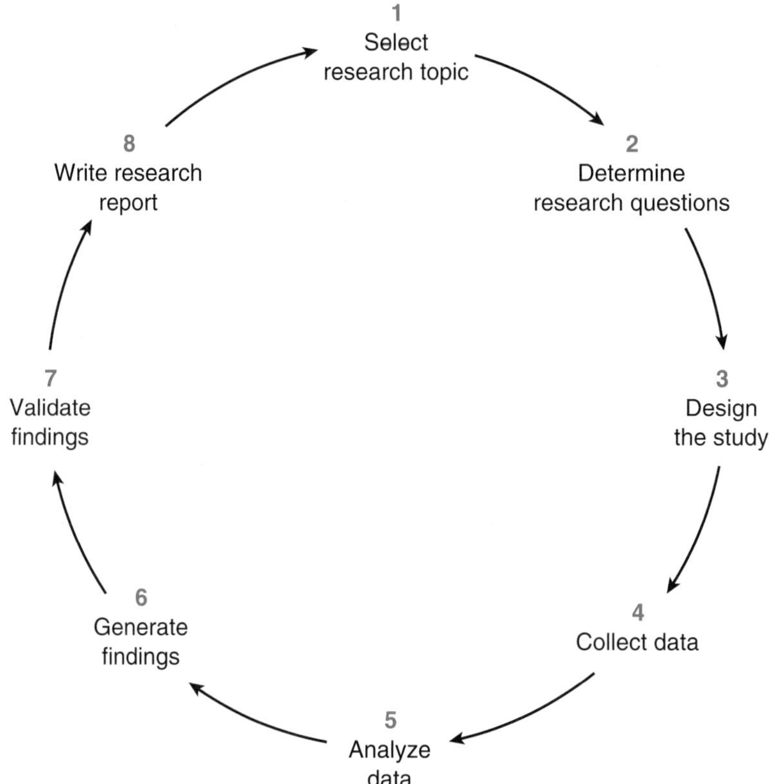

points as well as at later points in a research study. Data collection and data analysis are often done concurrently or in cycles in qualitative research (e.g., the researchers collect some data, analyze those data, collect more data, analyze those data, and so on). The researcher also attempts to validate the data and his or her interpretations throughout the research study (steps 6 and 7). For example, the researcher should attempt to establish the kinds of qualitative research validity you learned about in Chapter 11 (descriptive validity, interpretative validity, theoretical validity, internal validity, and external validity). At the end of the research study, the researcher finishes the research report (step 8).

For further extension of your knowledge about general qualitative research, we include Patton's (2002) list of 12 major characteristics of qualitative research in Table 15.1. Patton did a good job of succinctly summarizing the key characteristics of qualitative research, and his list should be helpful as you learn about qualitative research. Although not all qualitative research studies have all of the characteristics mentioned by us and by Patton, these characteristics are very typical of qualitative research.

Next, many qualitative researchers today are heavily influenced by what are called poststructuralism and postmodernism, and researchers rely on these rather complex ideas. We explain these ideas in Exhibit 15.1. Take a moment now and examine Patton's description of the key ideas of qualitative research in Table 15.1 and read Exhibit 15.1 for an introduction to the concepts of poststructuralism and postmodernism.

Although you already understand much about qualitative research, *qualitative research* is actually a relatively general term because there are five big or major approaches to qualitative research and many additional smaller types of qualitative research. Because the five major approaches all fall under the heading of qualitative research, the characteristics of qualitative research reviewed earlier usually apply to each approach, meaning that the five approaches have much in common. At the same time, each approach is different and distinct from the others in important ways. Table 15.2 provides a quick comparison of the five approaches discussed in this and the following chapter. If you have any difficulty distinguishing the approaches, realize that each has a different core idea or *emphasis* and each has its unique set of key terms, which is the "language" it uses. Also note that each of the qualitative approaches is sometimes flavored with the assumptions and ideas of poststructuralism and postmodernism.

In the remainder of this chapter, we introduce you to narrative inquiry and case study research. In the next chapter, Chapter 16, we introduce you to the other major approaches: phenomenology, ethnography, and grounded theory.

TABLE 15.1 Twelve Major Characteristics of Qualitative Research

Design Strategies
1. *Naturalistic inquiry*—The researcher studies real-world situations as they unfold naturally in a nonmanipulative and noncontrolling way, being open to whatever emerges (lack of predetermined constraints on findings).
2. *Emergent design flexibility*—With openness to adapting the inquiry as understanding deepens and/or situations change, the researcher avoids getting locked into rigid designs that eliminate responsiveness and pursues new paths of discovery as they emerge.
3. *Purposeful sampling*—Cases for study (e.g., people, organizations, communities, cultures, events, critical incidences) are selected because they are "information rich" and illuminative; that is, they offer useful manifestations of the phenomenon of interest. Sampling, then, is aimed at insight about the phenomenon, not empirical generalization from a sample to a population.

(Continued)

TABLE 15.1 (Continued)

Data-Collection and Fieldwork Strategies

4. *Qualitative data*—Consist of observations that yield detailed, thick description; inquiry in depth; interviews that capture direct quotations about people's personal perspectives and experiences; case studies; and careful document review.
5. *Personal experience and engagement*—The researcher has direct contact with and gets close to the people, situation, and phenomenon under study. The researcher's personal experiences and insights are an important part of the inquiry and critical to understanding the phenomenon.
6. *Empathic neutrality and mindfulness*—Researcher adopts an empathic stance in interviewing and seeks vicarious understanding without judgment (neutrality) by showing openness, sensitivity, respect, awareness, and responsiveness. In observation this means being fully present (mindful).
7. *Dynamic systems*—Attention is paid to process. Researcher assumes change is ongoing whether the focus is on an individual, an organization, a community, or an entire culture; therefore, the researcher is mindful of—and attentive to—system and situation dynamics.

Analysis Strategies

8. *Unique case orientation*—The researcher assumes that each case is special and unique. The first level of analysis is being true to, respecting, and capturing the details of the individual cases being studied; cross-case analysis follows from—and depends on—the quality of individual case studies.
9. *Inductive analysis and creative synthesis*—Researcher seeks immersion in the details and specifics of the data to discover important patterns, themes, and interrelationships. Begins by exploring, then confirming; is guided by analytical principles rather than rules. Study ends with a creative synthesis.
10. *Holistic perspective*—The whole phenomenon under study is understood as a complex system that is more than the sum of its parts. The focus is on complex interdependencies and system dynamics that cannot meaningfully be reduced to a few discrete variables and linear, cause-effect relationships.
11. *Context sensitivity*—Researcher places findings in a social, historical, and temporal context and is careful about, even dubious of, the possibility or meaningfulness of generalizations across time and space. Emphasizes instead careful comparative case analyses and extrapolating patterns for possible transferability to and adaptation in new settings.
12. *Voice, perspective, and reflexivity*—The qualitative analyst owns and is reflective about her or his own voice and perspective; a credible voice conveys authenticity and trustworthiness. Complete objectivity being impossible and pure subjectivity undermining credibility, the researcher's focus is on balance—understanding and depicting the world authentically in all its complexity while being self-analytical, politically aware, and reflexive in consciousness.

Source: Based on M. Q. Patton, *Qualitative Research and Evaluation Methods* (3rd ed.), pp. 40–41. Copyright © 2002 by SAGE Publications, Inc., Thousand Oaks, CA. Reproduced with permission of the publisher.

EXHIBIT 15.1 A Historical Introduction to Poststructuralism and Postmodernism

Poststructural and postmodern ideas offer a critique of what is commonly seen as "science." These ideas are an important part of the qualitative research paradigm. Therefore, it is important to gain a clear understanding of what these words are about, but first you will need to learn about some background concepts. The first background concept is **structuralism**.

Looking back at the 20th century, the idea of structure (and structuralism) was a common theoretical concept used to explain human behavior in anthropology, sociology, and psychology. The basic idea of structuralism is that there is a deep reality or "structure" that exists beyond the individual. This structure is the "scientific" basis of social reality in society; it exerts a causal force on people; and most of what we call social, cultural, and even psychological reality is due to deep structures. Some structures found in all societies are family structure, rites of passage, religion, power, and language. The content of structures can vary, but the same structures exist and operate similarly in all societies. We can't "touch" these structures, but they are said to exist.

According to structuralism, individuals are born into social/cultural structures that strongly influence what they will become and what they view as real, important, and good. An interesting structuralist concept is the *Sapir-Whorf hypothesis* (also called linguistic relativity hypothesis), which states that people's thoughts are bound by their language. If a word does not exist for something, you literally are not able to see that thing; the concept would not exist in your mental world. Another interesting structural idea is that of binary oppositions, which appear to exist in every society; for example, male/female, nature/culture, rationality/emotion, normality/madness, public/private, we/them, and legitimate/illegitimate. Structuralism is a deterministic theory because individuals are seen as becoming what the larger social, cultural, and linguistic structures provide; people follow accepted rules and practices as defined through their socialization and based on what they see in their day-to-day lives. Structuralism is scientific in the sense that it claims that structure causes behavior and it de-emphasizes the place of free will. Some intellectual "giants" in this line of thought, whom you can look up on the Internet to learn more about, are Émile Durkheim (sociology), Ferdinand de Saussure (linguistics), and Claude Levi-Strauss (anthropology). (Note: We include their names here because you might want to learn more about these important historical figures sometime.) Structuralism continues to be an important element of much social and educational theory.

- **Structuralism** A broad or grand theory that emphasizes the importance of cultural, structural, institutional, and functional relations as constituting a large part of the social world in which humans live and holds that this structure is key in determining meaning and influencing human behavior

Before moving to poststructuralism and postmodernism, we also need to think about a second background concept, modernism. The idea of **modernism** goes back to Renaissance humanism, which expressed faith in the positive qualities, capabilities, learning, and accomplishments of humans in contrast to the previous supremacy of religion in all matters. Modernism evolved during the Scientific Revolution of the 16th and 17th centuries (e.g., Nicolaus Copernicus, René Descartes, Galileo Galilei, Isaac Newton) and the Enlightenment of the 17th and 18th centuries (e.g., Denis Diderot, David Hume, John Locke, Voltaire). The theme of the Scientific Revolution was that the natural world was understandable in natural terms, it followed deterministic laws, and over time natural philosophers would be able to delineate fully the laws of nature. (It was not until the 1840s that the word *scientist*, in its modern usage, was coined by William Whewell.)

- **Modernism** A term used by postmodernists to refer to an earlier and outdated period in the history of science that viewed the world as a static (i.e., unchanging) machine where everyone follows the same laws of behavior

The Enlightenment built on the expectations and promises of the Scientific Revolution, taking them further by suggesting that laws of *human* behavior would also be forthcoming; it was just a matter of time before individual, social, and societal problems would be solved through the application of rational thought and the development of the psychological and social sciences. The Enlightenment idea of rationality was that it was universal, which meant that rational people would ultimately agree on what is true, important, and good.

An important countermovement that emerged in reaction to the Scientific Revolution and Enlightenment rationalism was 19th-century *romanticism* (e.g., Jean-Jacques Rousseau, F. W. Schelling), which emphasized the importance of individualism and human feelings, passions, creativity, spirituality, and change. Another important movement was German idealism (e.g., G. W. F. Hegel, Johann Herder, and Johann Gottlieb Fichte), which shifted focus from the scientific or physical world to an

(Continued)

- **Positivism** A term used by qualitative researchers to refer to what might be better labeled "scientism," which is the belief that all true knowledge must be based on science; the term is used by qualitative researchers, not quantitative researchers

- **Poststructuralism** A historical intellectual movement that rejects universal truth and emphasizes differences, deconstruction, interpretation, and the power of ideas over people's behavior

(Continued)

emphasis on reality and meaning as provided in language and culture; writers on idealism stressed the dominance of ideas as providing knowledge and as shaping history.

Also during the 19th century, the famous movement known as positivism started with Auguste Comte. Positivism is the idea that only what we can empirically observe is important and that science is the only true source of knowledge. Positivism got a boost during the early 20th century (e.g., A. J. Ayer, Moritz Schlick), and its influence in the social and psychological sciences remained dominant until approximately 1950. These are the most important historical predecessors to poststructuralism and postmodernism. Now we jump forward to the 1960s when poststructuralism was born.

During the 1960s, poststructuralism began as an intellectual movement in social and literary theory, especially in the works of two French writers, Michel Foucault and Jacques Derrida. Michel Foucault (1926–1984) developed a critique of Western knowledge and its history. He argued that social concepts, such as madness, illness, criminality, and sexuality, are historically defined by those with power in society and that those kinds of ideas change over time. He went further by arguing that what we consider to be knowledge is not constant; rather, knowledge is little more than a set of ideas that are historically situated in society and change as knowledge-power relationships change in societies. Knowledge is indexed (i.e., connected to) specific social-cultural contexts; this is one reason why different writers often have different positions about what is true and good. They construct social reality differently, and they interpret events differently.

You can see the structural part of Foucault's position in his emphasis on culture and historically situated ideas as influencing our thoughts. But Foucault often is considered to be a poststructuralist because he rejects the structuralist claim that universal structures and universal truths exist. Poststructuralism is antiscientific in this sense because it focuses on differences among people rather than on regular or predictable patterns of thought and behavior. Foucault recognized the influence of structures, but he saw them not as universal or true. That is why he is part of the movement known as poststructuralism, which is an attempt to use some ideas of structuralism but also to move beyond traditional structuralism. For Foucault, what was labeled "knowledge" constantly changed through dynamic, power-laden discourses.

Jacques Derrida (1930–2004) also critiqued Enlightenment rationalism, science, and positivism. He focused on the importance of language and built on Ferdinand de Saussure's idea that meaning comes from relations within language rather than from the connection of language to the external world. Words and their meaning are viewed as arbitrary, as can be seen by the multiple definitions of the same word, the varying meaning of the same word (or other symbol) across cultures, and the very different ways in which words are spelled (i.e., the correct spelling of a word is "correct" only because it is defined to be the correct or true spelling within a particular language). Derrida (and Foucault) argued that there is no single, correct meaning to text. Hence, the question "But what does that text really mean?" has no single answer. The answer will depend on how you are viewing it. In fact, Derrida generalized the idea of "text" by suggesting that most of what we see in the world can be viewed as text and narrative. The houses in your neighborhood are "texts," the lectures your professors give orally are "texts," and political campaign images and messages are "texts." In short, Derrida generalized or broadened the meaning of the word *text*, using it as a metaphor for any set of symbols that we observe or give meaning to in our worlds. Knowledge is viewed as coming in the form of stories or narratives rather than in scientific truths. Derrida shifted the source of meaning from universal structures to local, multiple narratives. He also rejected the idea of pure binary oppositions, claiming that each pole includes an element of the other in itself (e.g., each woman has some "man" in her and vice versa).

An important part of Derrida's approach to research and interpretation is what is called *deconstructionism*. This means that any truth that you or anyone else can provide can be deconstructed or broken down, revealing that it rests on a specific history, requires many particular assumptions, and is in many ways arbitrary. Derrida believed that there is no center or foundation for truth, and he wanted to demonstrate this point continually. Both Derrida and Foucault emphasized difference over similarity, and this has led many qualitative researchers to focus on parts of reality that might have otherwise been overlooked by traditional social science.

Postmodernism is an intellectual movement, closely related to poststructuralism, that became popular concurrently or very shortly after poststructuralist thought, especially in literature, art, architecture, and cultural theory. Two prominent writers are Jean Baudrillard (1929–2007) and Jacques Lacan (1901–1981). During the 1980s and 1990s, many qualitatively oriented writers appear to have been influenced by postmodern ideas. The word **postmodern** suggests that one has moved beyond modernism; in fact, postmodern writers to a significant degree define their movement in *opposition* to what they call modernism. Therefore, as you read through the following word pairs, note that the first word is said by postmodernists to describe modernism, and the second word is said to describe postmodernism: presence versus absence, center versus periphery, hierarchy versus anarchy, design versus chance, stability versus change, type versus hybrid, determinacy versus indeterminacy, similarity versus difference, universalism versus relativism, universal versus local, general versus particular, clarity versus blurriness, objective versus subjective, and reality versus hyperreality.

- **Postmodernism** A historical intellectual movement that constructs its self-image in opposition to modernism. Emphasizes the primacy of individuality, difference, fragmentation, flux, constant change, lack of foundations for thought, and interpretation

Jean Baudrillard viewed the culture of the United States as an example of a postmodern culture because of its focus on cities, consumerism, anonymity, visual images, and constant change. To a significant degree, image becomes reality. Television, Disney, and Internet worlds (e.g., Internet game worlds as well as other interactions) are as real as anything else and are called by Baudrillard *hyperrealities*. Jacques Lacan incorporated the idea of the unconscious (from Freud), with its focus on desires, nonrational motivations, sexuality, and the body, into his explanation of postmodernism. There is no single self; each person has multiple selves, and those are constantly in flux. Who you are changes from day to day, from moment to moment.

We have separated poststructuralism and postmodernism in this short introduction, but these terms often are used interchangeably, which is fine. The terms also overlap with the ideas of relativism and constructivism. As you have seen, these sets of ideas attack traditional science, as well as traditional views of humanity and many of our commonsense views of our world. This attack was a full assault, and it left in its wake no foundation, no center, no grand idea, nothing to hold on to for stability. As a result, many other writers thought the movement went too far, and they counterattacked poststructuralism and postmodernism, claiming that those movements had no positive message (only the negative message of what is *not* true) and that the ideas represented intellectual anarchy and scientific despair.

On the whole, the movements of poststructuralism and postmodernism have resulted in a healthy and important re-examination and much growth in intellectual thought. Many qualitative research methodologists appear to be influenced by poststructuralism and postmodernism, especially the prominent editors and many of the contributors to the landmark book that currently is in its fourth edition, the *SAGE Handbook of Qualitative Research* (2011), edited by Norman Denzin and Yvonna Lincoln. This handbook is on the shelves of virtually all qualitative and most mixed methods researchers. The impact of this movement continues today, and we view qualitative research as one of the three major research or methodological paradigms in educational research. As you know, our position is that each of these three paradigms has much to offer as we consider how to go about studying our world.

TABLE 15.2 Characteristics of the Five Major Approaches to Qualitative Research (Discussed in Chapters 15 and 16)

	Qualitative Research Approach				
Dimension	*Phenomenology*	*Ethnography*	*Case Study*	*Grounded Theory*	*Narrative Inquiry*
Research purpose	To describe one or more individuals' experiences of a phenomenon (e.g., the experience of the death of a loved one)	To describe the cultural characteristics of a group of people and to describe cultural scenes	To describe one or more cases in depth and address the research questions and issues	To inductively generate a grounded theory describing and explaining a phenomenon	To inquire into people's lived and told stories that can add to our understanding of people's experiences
Disciplinary origin	Philosophy	Anthropology	Multidisciplinary roots, including business, law, social sciences, medicine, and education	Sociology	Historically found in multiple human storytelling disciplines, but the form discussed in Chapter 15 originated in education
Primary data-collection method	In-depth interviews with 10–15 people	Participant observation over an extended period of time (e.g., 1 month to 1 year); interviews with informants	Multiple methods (e.g., interviews, observations, documents)	Interviews with 20–30 people or collect data until theoretical saturation is reached. Observations also frequently used	Multiple conversations (e.g., 3–5) with a participant and inquiry into related artifacts and documents as researcher gains understanding and retells stories of experience
Data analysis approach	List significant statements, determine meaning of statements, and identify the essence of the phenomenon	Use holistic description and search for cultural themes in data	Use holistic description and search for themes shedding light on the case. May also include cross-case analysis	Begin with open coding, then use axial coding, and end with selective coding	Attending to place, time, and relationships, researcher and participant co-construct stories using narrative threads, tensions, and plotlines
Narrative report focus	Rich description of the essential or invariant structures (i.e., the common characteristics, or essences) of the experience	Rich description of context and cultural themes	Rich description of the context and operation of the case or cases; discussion of themes, issues, and implications	Description of topic and people being studied; end with a presentation of the grounded theory. May also list propositions	Showing participants' evolving and complex stories over time, relationships, and place

15.1 What are the key characteristics of qualitative research?

15.2 Why is it said that qualitative research does not follow a series of steps in a linear fashion?

15.3 Why is qualitative research important for educational research?

15.4 What is poststructuralism, and what is postmodernism?

REVIEW QUESTIONS

NARRATIVE INQUIRY

I. Introduction: The Importance of Coming to Terms and Definitions

Foundational question: What understandings can we gain from people's storied experiences?

See Journal Article 15.1 on the Student Study Site.

Narrative inquiry (or NI) has become increasingly popular in the field of social science research since approximately the year 2000. With an explosion of interest in narrative inquiry, it is important that we clearly differentiate definitions and terms. It is commonly known that people have lived and told stories about their experiences for as long as we could talk. As MacIntyre (2007) and many others noted, humans are storytelling animals. Clandinin and Rosiek (2007) wrote that "lived and told stories and the talk about the stories are one of the ways that we fill our world with meaning and enlist one another's assistance in building lives and communities" (p. 35).

While story living and telling is not new, what is new is the emergence of narrative inquiry or narrative research in social science research. While there is a history of narrative work within the traditions of narratology (theory and study of narrative), it was in 1990 that Connelly and Clandinin named, and articulated, narrative inquiry as a social science research methodology. Here is the most well-accepted definition of **narrative inquiry**:

> People shape their daily lives by stories of who they and others are and as they interpret their past in terms of these stories. Story, in the current idiom, is a portal through which a person enters the world and by which their experience of the world is made personally meaningful. Narrative inquiry, the study of experience as story, then, is first and foremost a way of thinking about experience. Narrative inquiry as a methodology entails a view of the phenomenon. To use narrative inquiry methodology is to adopt a particular view of experience as phenomenon under study. (Connelly & Clandinin, 2006, p. 375)

- **Narrative inquiry** Study of experience when experience is understood as lived and told stories. It is a collaboration between researcher and participants, over time, in a place or series of places and in social interaction with their social milieus

There is now a well-established view of narrative inquiry as a methodology through which researchers inquire into the phenomenon of experience when experience is understood as a narrative phenomenon (Clandinin, 2007). The philosophic underpinning of narrative inquiry is Dewey's theory of experience (1938a; also discussed in Chapter 3) and his two criteria of experience: (a) *continuity* of experience (i.e., each person's experience can be understood temporally in that it grows out of earlier experiences and influences or shapes subsequent experiences) and (b) *interaction between each person and his or her situation*. The narrative inquiry conception of experience builds on Dewey's philosophy of experience. Clandinin and Rosiek (2007) explained this as follows:

> Framed within this view of experience, the focus of narrative inquiry is not only on an individual's experience but also on the social, cultural, and institutional narratives within which individuals' experiences are constituted, shaped, expressed, and enacted. Narrative inquirers study the individual's experience in the world, an experience that is storied both in the living and telling and that can be studied by listening, observing, living alongside another, and writing, and interpreting texts. (pp. 42–43)

In sum, the view of experience underlying narrative inquiry flows from the above definitions in that experience is understood as relational, continuous, and both personal and social. While stories are personal and unique to each person, larger cultural, social, familial, and institutional narratives shape a person's experiences. The term *relational* draws attention to the ways in which people are in temporal and social interaction when telling and living out their stories. People are always in the making; that is, they are always in the process of composing their lives. Stories of experience are not already there, waiting to be told, but are composed and told in the relational space between inquirer and participant. Stories are shaped by, and occur in, the contexts of their living and telling. Because of this co-compositional aspect, both the stories of researchers and participants are under study.

II. Designing a Narrative Study

Narrative inquiry is a fluid kind of research inquiry. It is not a set of procedures or steps to be followed but a relational inquiry methodology that is open to where participants' stories take a researcher. In the sections that follow, we introduce the elements of narrative inquiry that must be considered in designing and carrying out a narrative inquiry.

In a recent study, Clandinin, Steeves, and Caine (2013) engaged in a narrative inquiry with youth who left school before graduating. The research puzzle explored was around how the youths' experiences of school shaped their leaving of school and how their experiences of leaving school early shaped their lives. The research puzzle that guided the inquiry is quite different from a research question such as what are the factors that influence a person's decision to leave school. We use this study to illustrate the design features of narrative inquiry.

- **Living and telling stories** In narrative inquiry, people are seen to live out stories in their experiences and tell stories of those experiences to others
- **Retelling stories** When researchers inquire into stories, they move beyond regarding a story as a fixed entity and begin to retell stories
- **Reliving stories** As researchers come alongside research participants, both may begin to relive their stories

1. Four Key Terms to Structure a Narrative Inquiry

Four key terms emerge from the definition of narrative inquiry: **living stories**, **telling stories**, retelling stories, and reliving stories. Narrative inquirers understand that people live out stories and tell stories of that living. Narrative inquirers come alongside participants and begin to engage in narrative inquiry into participants' lived and told stories. Of necessity, researchers also engage in narrative inquiry into their own lived and told stories as part of the process of coming alongside research participants. This process of coming alongside participants and inquiring into lived and told stories is called **retelling stories**. Because both participants and researchers are changed in this process of coming alongside each other as they retell their lived and told stories, they may begin to relive their stories. Hence, we have the fourth key term, **reliving stories**.

As narrative inquirers retell stories, that is, inquire into participants' and their own stories, they move beyond regarding stories as fixed entities and begin to retell participants' stories. However, in narrative inquiry, this retelling includes both the participants' stories as well as the stories of the inquirer that are called forth by the experience of hearing the participants' stories. For example, as Caine (Clandinin et al., 2013) attended to the experience of a youth who came as a refugee to Canada, Caine's experiences of coming as a young woman to Canada were called forward. Her stories of coming to understand each person's stories as situated in a particular geography became part of the narrative inquiry. As Clandinin attended to the stories of one participant with whom she worked, that participant began to make more visible to Clandinin how a deep religious faith shaped the ways he lived his own life.

In the inquiry process, narrative inquirers work within the three-dimensional inquiry space of (a) temporality (movement in time and experience of time), (b) sociality (interaction of the personal and social), and (c) place (particular situation and geographical location). In this space they "unpack" the lived and told stories. In retelling, that is, engaging in inquiring narratively into the lived and told stories, inquirers and participants may begin to relive the retold stories. Put another way, they restory themselves and perhaps begin to shift the institutional, social, and cultural narratives in which they are embedded. Our human world is constructed and continually reconstructed through the processes of story living and storytelling.

2. Inquiry Starting Points

There are two starting points for narrative inquiry. The first is asking participants to tell stories of their experiences. In the study with the early school leavers (Clandinin et al., 2013), the starting point was telling stories. The researchers asked youth to tell stories of their experiences of schooling and leaving school. The second starting point is coming alongside participants as they live their lives. For example, in a narrative inquiry with children, their families, and their teachers into their experiences of schooling in a time of increased achievement testing, J. Huber, Murphy, and Clandinin (2011) worked alongside children and their teachers in their classrooms.

The processes of attending to the living, telling, retelling, and reliving of stories is narrative inquiry, regardless of the starting point. In all narrative inquiries, researchers situate themselves in more or less relational ways with participants to come to understand the participants' stories. While it might seem that stories are waiting to be told and gathered or collected by researchers, narrative inquirers work from the assumption that stories of experience are always being made, and that the living and telling of stories is a process of life composing in particular times, places, and relationships. Indeed, relationships are central to the work of narrative inquirers. Rather than trying to "bracket" themselves as researchers who live outside of an inquiry (a common approach in other kinds of research), narrative inquirers bracket themselves within the inquiry. That is, they understand that the stories that are lived and told within a narrative inquiry are a co-composition that attends to both participants' and researchers' lived and told stories. Not only is the relational space between researchers and participants integral to understanding the composition of field texts and research texts, but also relationships are a central way of making sense of the temporal and contextual aspects of narrative inquiry.

3. Attending to Justifications at the Inquiry Outset and Throughout the Inquiry

There are three kinds of justifications that narrative inquirers attend to in order to be able to respond to the questions of "So what?" and "Who cares?" that all social science researchers must be able to address. Researchers cannot engage in a narrative inquiry without addressing all three justifications at the outset of the inquiry, throughout the inquiry, and at the end of the inquiry.

- **Personal justifications** A researcher's reasons for undertaking a particular narrative inquiry, that is, why this inquiry matters to the researcher as a person

Personal justifications allow researchers to justify a particular narrative inquiry in the context of their own life experiences and personal inquiry puzzles. This is best achieved through a kind of autobiographical narrative inquiry by the researcher. There are three reasons for this justification: Researchers understand who they see themselves as being, and becoming, within the inquiry; researchers are more fully awake to the stories they are living and telling in the research relationship alongside participants; and researchers are more fully awake to the ways in which they attend to the experiences of participants. For example, in the study with the early school leavers (Clandinin et al., 2013), Clandinin intentionally inquired into her stories of experiences around early school leaving to understand how she worked initially from an assumption that school completion was something to be desired for all students.

- **Practical justifications** The ways in which the research can make a difference to practice

Practical justifications allow researchers to justify any particular narrative inquiry in practical terms, that is, to attend to the importance of considering the possibility of shifting or changing current practices. In the study with the early school leavers, the practical justification was around the need for policy makers to attend to the lives of the 20 to 25 percent of students who do not complete high school. As Lessard (Caine, Lessard, Steeves, & Clandinin, 2013) in the early school-leaving study showed, through designing and implementing a particular form of summer school for high school students of Aboriginal heritage, it is necessary to imagine new ways of engaging students in school to help them achieve high school completion.

- **Social/theoretical justifications** The contribution the research can make to theoretical understandings or to making situations more socially just

Social and/or theoretical justifications allow researchers to attend to justifying the work in terms of new methodological and disciplinary or interdisciplinary knowledge. Social action and policy justifications come in terms of social action, usually focused on social justice concerns. In the study with the early school leavers, Clandinin and colleagues (2013) developed a conceptualization of transition, not centered on the event of transition out of school but adopting a view of youth as living in and through transitions as they compose their lives.

See Journal Article 15.2 on the Student Study Site.

4. Research Puzzles Rather Than Research Questions

- **Research puzzle** What guides the study by pointing toward the experiences of participants that a researcher wants to understand more deeply

Framing or composing a **research puzzle** is part of the design process in a narrative inquiry. Each narrative inquiry is composed around a particular wonder and, rather than framing a research question with a precise definition or expectation of an answer, narrative inquirers frame a research puzzle that carries with it a sense of a "re-search"—a searching again—that suggests "a sense of continual reformulation" (Clandinin & Connelly, 2000, p. 124). For an example of a research puzzle, see the study of the experiences of early school leavers. This shift from research question to research puzzle opens up the possibilities of change over time in the inquiry as researchers and participants live out the inquiry. This shift

> creates reverberations as it bumps against dominant research narratives. The shift from question to puzzle is one that allows narrative inquirers to make explicit that narrative inquiry is different from other methodologies. We begin in the midst, and end in the midst of experience. (Clandinin, 2013a, p. 43)

In the narrative inquiry into the experiences of the youth who left school early, researchers were attentive to the ways youths' lives shifted as they engaged in the narrative inquiry: For example, they moved residences, they found other ways to live out life dreams, and they became parents. Subsequently, the researchers awakened to the importance of designing another study of students who were still in junior high school as they learned from the youth who left that, for many of them, junior high school was their last experience of being engaged in schooling in educative ways. The researchers also realized that they had left the participants in the midst of their lives. They proposed to undertake a further inquiry to see how the participants' experiences of early school leaving and experiences of becoming parents may have shifted the stories they live and tell in relation to schooling.

5. Entering Into the Midst

Narrative inquirers enter into research relationships with research participants in the midst of their own ongoing personal and professional lives—in the midst of lives enacted within particular institutional narratives such as funded projects, graduate student research, and other organizational narratives and in the midst of social, political, linguistic, cultural, and familial narratives. Participants are also always in the midst of their lives. So too are the places or sites of inquiry where researchers live alongside and/or meet with participants. When lives come together in an inquiry relationship, they find themselves in the midst of many midsts. In short, **being in the midst** means attending to the temporal midst of the past, present, and future; to the place midst as participants move to new locations; and to the relational midst as the participants enter into new relationships, sustain old relationships, and engage in different work and social situations.

- **Being in the midst** Attending to temporal, place, and relational aspects of reality

Understanding that researchers and participants are meeting in the midst of their lives reverberates throughout the designing, living out, and representing the narrative inquiry findings. There are reverberations for how we think of (a) negotiating entry, for example, the times and number of times of meeting; (b) negotiating or co-composing living alongside or spaces for telling stories, for example, places of meeting and the presence of friends, siblings, or family members during conversations; (c) negotiating kinds of field texts, for example, whether photographs or school/life artifacts are shared; (d) negotiating or co-composing research texts, for example, whether some stories are included and whether **pseudonyms** are used; (e) and eventually negotiating exit, for example, whether there will be further meetings after the research is completed. What is also important to recognize, as part of this design feature, is that everyone participating in the research study must continually hold before them the idea that their lives are always on the way, in the making.

- **Pseudonyms** New names researchers construct to hide the identity of individual research participants

6. From Field to Field Texts

The **field** in a narrative inquiry can be the ongoing conversations with participants in which participants tell stories or the living alongside participants in a particular place or places.

- **Field** The inquiry space created between researchers and participants during conduct of the research

Being in the field involves settling into the temporal unfolding of lives in place or places. In narrative inquiry, we negotiate and compose and/or construct with participants "an ongoing relational inquiry space" (Clandinin & Caine, 2012), that is, a relational space that we call the field. For example, in the narrative inquiry with the early school leavers, the field, for the most part, was the ongoing space for conversations. However, for some participants who wanted to take researchers to meet with family members, to visit their former junior high school, or to visit other places of importance to them, the field became more than the conversational spaces. In narrative inquiry, researchers must follow where participants want to take them as they work together to inquire into the participants' experiences.

- **Field texts** The term narrative inquirers use for data

There are many ways to gather, compose, and create **field texts** as we enter the field with participants. Field texts can be field notes of activities and events, transcripts of conversations or interviews, artifacts such as memory box or keepsake items, photographs, work samples, documents, plans, policies, annals, and chronicles (Clandinin & Connelly, 2000). Connelly and Clandinin began to use the term *field texts* many years ago rather than the term *data* in order to signal that texts composed in narrative inquiry are experiential, intersubjective texts rather than objective texts. Field texts are composed and/or co-composed by researcher and participants, and they reflect the relationship between researcher and participants.

As narrative inquirers negotiate relational spaces with participants, including places and times to meet, researchers and participants also negotiate and produce a diversity of field texts. It is important to stay awake to the possibility of what could be field texts because they will enable you, as the researcher, to see how others make meaning from their experience and help you to see possibilities for final research texts, that is, ways you can represent the retold stories. For example, in the early school leavers' study, some participants were gifted artists and shared their drawings with the researchers. When they shared the drawings with the researchers and then explained the times when, the places where, and the purposes they had for making the drawings, the drawings became field texts. As the researchers composed narrative accounts with each participant, sometimes the drawings were included in the final research texts.

7. From Field Texts to Interim and Final Research Texts

Field texts are always embedded within research relationships. Working alone or within the relational three-dimensional narrative inquiry space, researchers shape field texts first into interim research texts and then into final research texts (the narrative way of thinking of data analysis and interpretation). This move from field texts to research texts is always marked by tensions and uncertainties.

> Although interpretation is always underway as the inquiry is lived out with participants in the field, at some point there is a move away from the close intensive contact with participants to begin work with the field texts. Given the quantity of field texts, including transcripts, artifacts, documents, photographs, and field notes, all composed with attention to temporality, sociality, and place, the task is often daunting. (Clandinin, 2013a, p. 47)

In Clandinin (2013a) there is a detailed description of how Clandinin moved from field texts to research texts with one participant. These are processes that are often called analyses and interpretations. The process of moving from field texts to interim and final research texts focused on identifying narrative threads that wove through the participant's life and that shaped how he experienced his leaving of school early.

As narrative inquirers work to inquire into the field texts, they continue to think narratively, that is, to inquire into the texts with attentiveness to the three-dimensional narrative inquiry space—to temporality, sociality, and place. Moving from field texts to interim and final research texts is not a straightforward, linear process. Rather it is marked by reflexivity as researchers continue to live in relational ways with participants and as they negotiate and co-compose interim and final research texts with them.

As part of composing **interim research texts**, researchers—or researchers and participants together—may write narrative accounts of the retold experience as it relates to the research puzzle. When researchers move from the interim research texts to final research texts, both researchers and participants become acutely aware that texts will be visible to public audiences. At this point, narrative inquirers become aware of the relational ethics that guide narrative inquiries, reminding themselves that their first ethical responsibility is to participants. As they compose final research texts, they return to the personal, practical, and social/theoretical justifications of the inquiry, reminding themselves why they have undertaken the inquiry and attending closely to how they are responding to the "So what?" and "Who cares?" questions.

- **Interim research texts** The evolving research reports or texts that are continually written and revised during the research project as researchers move from field texts to final research texts

Final research texts include academic publications such as books and articles, dissertations, theses, and presentations for academic and nonacademic audiences. All research texts need to reflect temporality, sociality, and place. As narrative inquirers attend simultaneously to all three dimensions, they understand in deeper and more complex ways the experiences relevant to their research puzzles. As they make visible narrative thinking through the three-dimensional narrative inquiry space, they make the complexity of storied lives visible. By not smoothing over complexity or writing stories with a distinct beginning, middle, and end, they allow people's experiences to open up the possibilities of imagining otherwise, to seeing something that was unseen before. "Final research texts do not have final answers, because narrative inquirers do not come with questions. These texts are intended to engage audiences to rethink and reimagine the ways in which they practice and engage with others" (Clandinin, 2013a, p. 51).

- **Final research texts** Final representations of a narrative inquiry, such as books and articles, dissertations, theses, and presentations for academic and nonacademic audiences, that are made public for a wider audience

Composing Lives in Transition (Clandinin et al., 2013) is a final research text of the narrative inquiry with the youth who left school early. In the final research text, there is a description of the research purposes; the methodology; the methods; and a series of 11 narrative accounts, the interim research texts that were negotiated with each participant and researcher. There are also chapters that provide new theories of narrative conceptions of identity and of transition that emerged from looking across the experiences of the participants. The researchers also provide examples of how the research impacted them both practically and personally.

8. Relational Ethics at the Heart of Narrative Inquiry—Relational Responsibilities

As Clandinin and Connelly (2000) noted, ethical matters need to be attended to over the entire narrative inquiry process. Ethical matters are not dealt with once at the outset of a study, as frequently is seen to happen when ethical review forms are completed and submitted

■ **Relational ethics** Caring for and attending to participants' experiences in responsible and responsive ways

to Institutional Review Boards for approval. "Ethical matters shift and change as we move through an inquiry. They are never far from the heart of our inquiries no matter where we are in the inquiry process" (Clandinin & Connelly, 2000, p. 170). What we term **relational ethics**, that is, the ethics of living in relational ways with participants, need to be continually at the heart of narrative inquiries (J. Huber & Clandinin, 2002). Relational ethics are founded in an ethic of care.

Narrative inquirers comply with the legal and procedural aspects of ethics held by Institutional Research Boards. However, "the requirement to obtain ethical approval of our research proposals prior to beginning to negotiate our inquiries works against the relational negotiation that is part of narrative inquiry" (Clandinin & Connelly, 2000, p. 170). Issues that narrative inquirers face with ethics boards are around the timing of obtaining ethical approval, what it means to obtain informed consent in institutional settings, and who researchers are in relation with those in the research. Thinking about who narrative inquirers are helps them think in relational ways about issues of informed consent, particularly about with whom they need to engage in conversations about gaining consent.

Working within "fidelity to relationships" (Noddings, 1984), the ethical considerations in narrative inquiries are responsibilities negotiated by participants and narrative inquirers at all phases of an inquiry (Clandinin & Connelly, 1988, 2000). These ethical matters need to be lived out throughout the inquiry. These relational responsibilities are responsibilities in the short and long term (M. Huber, Clandinin, & Huber, 2006). As researchers move from field texts and to co-composing or negotiating interim and final research texts, relational ethics become even more sharply defined, as each move must be carefully and respectfully negotiated. Issues of anonymity and confidentiality take on added importance as the complexity of lives are made visible in research texts.

The relational aspects of narrative inquiries compel narrative inquirers to pay attention to particular ethical matters as research texts are written. Narrative inquirers understand that a person's lived and told stories are who they are and who they are becoming and that a person's stories sustain that person. This understanding shapes the necessity of negotiating research texts that respectfully represent participants' lived and told stories. When participants are uncertain about being too visible or too vulnerable as interim research texts are negotiated, sometimes strategies such as fictionalizing and blurring times, places, and identities (e.g., pseudonyms) become part of the process of negotiation.

While the move from field texts to interim research texts to final research texts is part of the analysis and interpretive processes of narrative inquiry as a methodology, it remains, at its heart, an ethical undertaking. Narrative inquiry reminds us that who researchers are, and are becoming, in relationships with participants means they need to attend to their own storied lives, to participants' lives, and, perhaps, to the lives of others in changed ways. No one leaves a narrative inquiry unchanged.

III. Narrative Inquiry: So Much More Than Telling Stories

But don't all qualitative researchers use stories? Don't we all tell stories with our data? Isn't narrative inquiry just telling stories? These questions are some of those often asked by those new to narrative inquiry.

Stories or narratives are often seen as the data collected by many qualitative researchers. People tell their stories to researchers in response to interview questions, in oral histories, in open-ended interview studies, and even in open-ended sections of questionnaires. There is usually an assumption that the stories are waiting to be told and, when asked, people tell them, usually in the Western tradition of a beginning, middle, and end with a plot line, characters, and resolution. Sometimes these stories and narratives follow other cultural formats, but the underlying assumptions are the same. However, not all studies that use stories as data are narrative inquiries. In phenomenology, discussed in the next chapter, the intent is to be able to understand the essence of a common experience across multiple research participants. For example, what is the essence of the experience of being a single parent? There is an intention to leave the experiences of each person aside to be able to speak to the essence of the experience of a particular phenomenon. Stories are also sometimes told in grounded theory studies where interviews are used. However, the intent in grounded theory is to look across the stories to discern categories and themes that will allow the development of a midlevel theory or description of a process. A key point is that the use of stories as data does not necessarily make a study a narrative inquiry. In the same way that not all studies that use story as data are narrative inquiry, neither are all research reports that convey findings in a story format narrative inquiry.

In sum, narrative inquiry requires more than just telling stories. Narrative inquiry is a research approach for studying the experience of lived and told stories, such as the phenomenon of experiences of youth dropping out of school. Narrative inquiry is a way to understand human experience. In many ways, human experience is fundamentally narrative. Narrative inquiry helps us to see and understand that who we are and the stories we live by are fundamentally narrative in nature. It asks us to share and publish our stories and inquiries into our stories that might enlighten or help others.

REVIEW QUESTIONS

15.5 What are the key characteristics of narrative inquiry?

15.6 What are the key terms used in narrative inquiry?

Case Study Research

Foundational question: What are the characteristics of this single case or of these comparison cases?

Merriam (1988) told us that "case study research is nothing new" (p. xi), pointing out that the idea of studying cases has been around for a long time and used across many different disciplines (e.g., medicine, law, business, the social sciences). During the late 1970s and the 1980s, however, authors such as Robert Stake (1978), Robert Yin (1981), and Sharan Merriam delineated case study research as a specific type of research. Although Stake and Merriam have a qualitative orientation toward case study research (preferring an inductive or generative approach) and Yin has a more quantitative orientation (preferring a more deductive or testing approach), what these case study researchers have in common is that they choose to call their objects of study "cases," they collect primarily qualitative data, and

- **Case study research** A form of qualitative research that is focused on providing a detailed account of the characteristics and dynamics present in one or more cases
- **Case** A bounded system

they organize their research efforts around the study of those cases (e.g., Merriam; Stake, 1995; Yin, 1998). We define **case study research** simply as research that provides a detailed account and analysis of the characteristics and dynamics present in one or more cases.[1]

What Is a Case?

A **case** is defined as a bounded system. In the words of one prominent case study researcher, Robert Stake (1997), "Lou Smith used a fancy name, 'bounded system,' to indicate that we are going to try to figure out what complex things go on within that system. The case study tells a story about a bounded system" (p. 256). Note that a *system* is a set of interrelated elements that form an organized whole. Using the system metaphor, cases are seen as holistic entities that have parts and that act or operate in their environments. *Bounded* is added to emphasize that you should identify the outline or boundaries of the system—you must determine what the case is and what it is not.

Typical cases are a child with a learning disability, a pupil with a special need, a language arts classroom, a charter school, and a national program (e.g., the Head Start Program). Some case study researchers are very inclusive in what they call cases (e.g., Creswell, 1998; Merriam, 1988; Yin, 2009). For them, a case not only is an object or entity with a clear identity (e.g., a group, a person, a classroom, or an organization) but can also include an event (e.g., a campus protest), an activity (e.g., learning to play softball), or a process (e.g., becoming a professional teacher during one's first year of teaching). When you read case study articles, you should check early on to see what kind of case the authors are examining.

For example, Gallo and Horton (1994) conducted a case study of one high school in East Central Florida. Here the high school was the case. The research focused on the process and results of having access to the Internet at the high school. The authors concluded that Internet access could have many positive effects on teachers (e.g., incorporation of technology into the classroom, increased self-esteem, development of positive attitudes toward computers), especially if the teachers were given adequate training in how to use the Internet and how to incorporate it into their classrooms. Valentine and McIntosh (1990) examined the characteristics of an organization (the case) in which women held all the positions of power. They found that the organization took on a *gemeinschaft* (a local community) type of character rather than a *gesellschaft* (city-like, impersonal) character. Van Haneghan and Stofflett (1995) conducted case studies of four fifth-grade teachers (four cases). They determined how each teacher implemented an innovative videodisc curriculum focused on problem solving. These authors developed a heuristic model based on their observations that could be used to train teachers to implement the new curriculum in their classrooms.

Because case study researchers define a case as a bounded system, it should not be surprising that they study how the system operates. As a result, they are interested in holistic description. Almost all systems are made up of components or parts, and it is important to understand how the parts operate together in order to understand the system (i.e., the case). For example, a high school is made up of teachers, buildings, students, classrooms, and books (among many other things). You can also view an individual as being composed of many different components or parts (e.g., cognitive, emotional, physiological). How the parts come together (i.e., their synergism) is of utmost interest to a case study researcher.

Case study researchers also view each case as having an internal and an external context. Take a school as an example. Internally, a researcher might examine the organizational climate at a school, the leadership style used by the principal, and the condition of the physical and instructional facilities. Externally, the school is situated in a geographical area with specific social, economic, and demographic characteristics. If the school is a public school, it is situated within a public school system with additional characteristics. The point is that case study researchers carefully examine the contexts of the case to describe and explain better the functioning of the case.

See Journal Article 15.3 on the Student Study Site.

Types of Case Study Research Designs

There are three kinds of case studies according to Stake (1995): intrinsic case studies, instrumental case studies, and collective case studies. In an **intrinsic case study** the researcher's primary interest is in understanding a specific case. This design is the classic, single-case design. Here the researcher describes, in depth, the particulars of the case to shed light on it. For example, a researcher might want to understand a student who is having difficulty in class, or a researcher might want to understand how the local PTA operates. The goal is to understand the case as a holistic entity, as well as to understand its inner workings. A secondary goal is to understand a more general process based on an analysis of the single case.

- **Intrinsic case study** Interest is in understanding a specific case

The intrinsic case study is very popular in education. It is also popular with program evaluators, whose goal is to describe a program and to evaluate how effectively it is operating (e.g., an evaluator might evaluate a local drug education program for at-risk middle and high school students). Finally, the intrinsic case study is often used in exploratory research in which the researcher attempts to learn about a little-known phenomenon by studying a single case in depth. The advantage of the intrinsic case study is that researchers can put all their time and resources into the study of a single case and can therefore develop an in-depth understanding of it. A weakness is that generalizing from a single case can be very risky.

In an **instrumental case study**, the researcher's primary interest is in understanding something other than the particular case. The case is seen as important only as a means to an end. In other words, the researcher studies the case to learn about something more general (e.g., teenage drug use in general rather than teenage drug use at a particular high school, or discipline in general rather than discipline in a particular teacher's classroom). The goal tends to be less particularistic and more universalistic. That is, researchers doing instrumental case studies are less interested in making conclusions that are specific to the case and its particular setting than they are in making conclusions that apply beyond a particular case.

- **Instrumental case study** Interest is in understanding something more general than the particular case

In the instrumental case study design, the researcher is usually interested in how and why a phenomenon operates as it does. That is, the researcher chooses the case to develop and/or test a theory or to understand some important issue better. Explanation is a key goal. The specific case can be selected because it is extreme or unique in some way (and can be used to test theoretical predictions) or because it is typical (and can be used to understand the general case). The instrumental case study is popular with many academic researchers when they are interested in generalizing and extending the findings in research literatures on various topics.

In the **collective case study**, the researcher believes that he or she can gain greater insight into a research topic by concurrently studying multiple cases in one overall research study. The collective case study is also called the multiple-case design (e.g., Yin, 1994). Several cases

- **Collective case study** Studying multiple cases in one research study

are usually studied in a collective case study. For example, two or three cases might be studied when a relatively in-depth analysis of each case is required and when resources are limited. When less depth is required and when greater resources are available, collective case studies of around 10 cases are common. The cases in the collective case study are usually studied instrumentally rather than intrinsically. For example, a researcher might select several cases to study because he or she is interested in studying the effects of inclusion of children with mild mental retardation in general education classes. Rather than studying the outcomes in a single classroom, the researcher studies the impact in several different classrooms.

There are several advantages to studying more than one case. First, a comparative type of study can be conducted in which several cases are compared for similarities and differences. For example, a public school might be studied and compared with a private school. Second, one can more effectively test a theory by observing the results of multiple cases. Third, one is more likely to be able to generalize the results from multiple cases than from a single case. Yin (1994) pointed out that replication logic can be used when one has multiple cases. In experimental research, we have more confidence in a finding when it has been replicated many times. Here is what Yin said about this idea and its relevance for case study research:

> Thus, if one has access only to three cases of a rare, clinical syndrome in psychology or medical science, the appropriate research design is one in which the same results are predicted for each of the three cases, thereby producing evidence that the three cases did indeed involve the same syndrome. If similar results are obtained from all three cases, replication is said to have taken place. (p. 45)

In Yin's example mentioned in this quote, the theory that predicted the same result for each case was supported. Therefore, compared to a single case study, the researcher would have greater confidence that a similar result would happen in a new case.

A disadvantage of studying multiple cases is that depth of analysis will usually have to be sacrificed because of the breadth of analysis obtained from studying more than one case. This is the classic depth-versus-breadth trade-off, and it is a common trade-off in case study research. In other words, because of limited resources (e.g., money and time) available in most research studies, you will be forced to make a choice between "depth and detail" and "breadth and comparative information." It takes considerable time to study one case in depth, but you end up with a deep understanding of the case. On the other hand, if you are going to study multiple cases, you will have to reduce the amount of time spent on each case, but you will get important comparative information. As you can see, there are advantages and disadvantages to both sides of this trade-off. You will ultimately have to make the final judgment about how to deal with this trade-off if you conduct a research study.

Data Collection, Analysis, and Report Writing

Case study research methodologists (those researchers who write books about doing case study research) tend to be pragmatic and advocate the use of multiple methods and multiple data sources (i.e., methods and data triangulation). These methodologists recommend that you take an eclectic approach and rely on any data that will help you understand your case and answer your research questions. Any of the methods of data collection (observation, interviews, questionnaires, focus groups, tests, and secondary data such as documents) discussed in Chapter 9 can be used when they help answer your research questions. Qualitative versions of these methods (such as participant observations, in-depth interviews, open-ended questionnaires) do, however, tend to be the most popular in educational case studies.

In the final report, research questions (or research "issues," according to Stake, 1995) and the relevant findings are presented for each question. During analysis and writing, the researcher will always examine and report on the case (e.g., a school) because the case is always the primary unit of analysis in case study research. Other units of analysis that are embedded in the case might also be examined (e.g., within a school, some embedded units of analysis could be the classrooms, the teachers, and the students). If multiple cases are used, then each case is usually first examined as a separate entity (called **within-case analysis**), and then the different cases are compared in a **cross-case analysis** for similarities (patterns that cut across the cases) as well as differences. When people or groups of people are studied, an attempt is usually made to reconstruct the participants' realities and portray the multiple viewpoints existing in the case (e.g., you might portray the different viewpoints of the teachers in a school).

- **Within-case analysis** Searching for themes and patterns within a single case
- **Cross-case analysis** Searching for similarities and differences across multiple cases

The final report is usually written to address the research questions (or "research issues" according to Stake, 1995), provide the relevant findings, and present a rich (vivid and detailed) and holistic (i.e., describes the whole and its parts) description of the case and its context. An example of rich description is given in Exhibit 15.2. The findings should be related to similar findings in the research literature when possible. When people or groups of people are studied, an attempt is usually made to reconstruct the participants' realities and portray the multiple viewpoints existing in the case (e.g., you might portray the different viewpoints of the teachers in a school). When a collective case study is conducted (i.e., studying multiple cases), the report might be organized case by case, with a separate section integrating the findings from all of the cases. Through data collection, analysis, and report writing, the researcher should use the validity strategies discussed in Chapter 11, such as the different types of triangulation, to help increase the validity or trustworthiness of the case study findings.

EXHIBIT 15.2 An Example of Rich Description in a Case Study

That first morning, I reached Harper [School] a few minutes after 8 A.M., in time to see most of the students arriving. It was a nippy morning, the day following Martin Luther King's birthday. Many youngsters were bundled in Chicago Bulls gear. All were walking, almost all from the adjacent high-rise housing. Residents called it "The Place."

A middle-school youngster wearing a crossing-guard sash courteously escorted me to an unmarked door. Also unmarked—by graffiti or weather—was the white brick face of the building, lettered simply Frances Harper School. Just inside the door, Mr. Carter, the security captain, pointed the way to the office. A janitor and several kids took notice of my arrival.

The office clerk, with a large smile, introduced me to "the boss." Principal Lyda Hawkins's greeting also was warm. We moved into her room for a lengthy conversation—in spite of mounting traffic. First we commented on yesterday's Denver confrontation between King marchers and Klansmen. I said, "How could it be?" She said, "Some things don't change."

Lyda Hawkins had taught in this part of Chicago since the 1950s and had been principal of this school for over 16 years. She knew her neighborhood. We talked about change, about the Chicago school reform plan, about its orientation to governance

(Continued)

(Continued)

more than to teaching and learning. "To many, it was license to get the principal," she said with feeling. She spoke of Local School Councils, noting that she had a good council. She spoke of unrealistic expectations of reform groups about readiness of parents to assume school governance responsibilities, the lack of experience before election, the insufficiency of orientation after. One of her council members had said, "How do you expect us to understand a $2 million budget? I can't manage $460 a month!"

Community involvement in Harper School was not high. Only a few parent volunteers worked with teachers. It was even difficult to get Local School Council members to come to council meetings. In the words of Mattie Mitchell, teacher and school community representative, "Who wants to make decisions? Who is ready to make decisions? Not many."

Source: Reprinted from R. E. Stake, *The Art of Case Study Research*, pp. 138–139, copyright © 1995 by SAGE Publications, Inc. Reprinted by permission of SAGE Publications, Inc.

REVIEW QUESTIONS

15.7 What are the key characteristics of case study research?

15.8 What is a case?

15.9 Define intrinsic case study, instrumental case study, and collective case study.

ACTION RESEARCH REFLECTION

Insight: Action researchers like qualitative research methods because these methods help them to understand the world from their students' or participants' perspectives.

1. What qualitative method(s) discussed in this chapter would you want to use to learn about your students or participants? Why and how?
2. What information might narrative inquiry and case study research provide you with in relation to your action research project?
3. Conduct a literature search for interesting narrative inquiry and case study research examples that are relevant to your needs at your workplace. Would you want to conduct or extend one of these studies in your place of work?

SUMMARY

We show in Figure 15.1 that qualitative research follows eight steps, although researchers often cycle within these steps and cycle through the set (i.e., the steps are not fully linear). In Table 15.1 we show Patton's 12 characteristics of qualitative research. This is a good set to remember if you are ever asked the general question, "What is qualitative research?" Next we, in Exhibit 15.1, explain in simple language and simple definitions the somewhat complicated concepts of structuralism, modernism, positivism, poststructuralism, and postmodernism. Next we point out that there are five major traditions or approaches to qualitative research, and each has a different *emphasis* and set of concepts and preferred "language." The five major approaches are narrative inquiry, case study, phenomenology, ethnography, and grounded theory. In the remainder of the chapter we explain the first two of these. In the next chapter we explain the other three.

Briefly, *narrative inquiry* or NI research provides us with understanding of the phenomena of experience by studying people's lived and told stories. One begins with the participants' stories, but the stories are jointly produced and *restoried* through relational inquiry with a narrative researcher. NI validity or quality is based on *personal justification* (researcher states why he or she views the story as important), *practical justification* (the researcher states why the story should contribute to practice), and *social/theoretical justification* (the researcher states what contribution the research will make to theory or to making situations in society more just). During NI, the researcher enters the *field* and pays attention to temporal/time, place, and relational aspects of people's experiences; this is called *being in the midst*. While in the field, the researcher creates *field texts* such as notes of activities, events, conversations, and photos. According to *relational ethics*, the NI researcher must care for and attend to participants' experiences in a responsible and caring way. The result of an NI study is called a *research text* that provides a representation to be shared publically.

Next, *case study research* is a general and inclusive approach to qualitative research. What case study researchers have in common is that they choose to call their objects of study "cases" and they organize their research efforts around the study of those cases. The focus is usually on describing the characteristics of one or more cases, describing how the case or cases operate, and answering specific research questions about the case(s). The major types of case study research are *intrinsic case study* (the researcher is interested in a specific case), *instrumental case study* (the researcher studies a case for a broader purpose), and *collective case study* (the researcher studies multiple cases for comparison). When there is more than one case, *cross-case analysis* is used to identify similarities and differences across the cases.

KEY TERMS

being in the midst (p. 429)
case (p. 434)
case study research (p. 434)
collective case study (p. 435)
cross-case analysis (p. 437)
field (p. 429)
field texts (p. 430)
final research texts (p. 431)
instrumental case study (p. 435)
interim research texts (p. 431)
intrinsic case study (p. 435)
living and telling stories (p. 426)
modernism (p. 421)
narrative inquiry (p. 425)
personal justifications (p. 428)
positivism (p. 422)
postmodernism (p. 423)
poststructuralism (p. 422)
practical justifications (p. 428)
pseudonyms (p. 429)
qualitative research (p. 417)
relational ethics (p. 432)
reliving stories (p. 426)
research puzzle (p. 428)
retelling stories (p. 426)
social/theoretical justifications (p. 428)
structuralism (p. 420)
within-case analysis (p. 437)

DISCUSSION QUESTIONS

1. Which qualitative method or methods discussed in this chapter do you think would be most appropriate for studying a teacher who constantly excels above all others in a school?
2. What could we learn from a narrative inquiry into the experiences of students who leave school early that would enrich a larger research study of schools where there is a high attrition rate?
3. Why do you think it is important to study the experiences of teachers, children, and parents through narrative inquiries?
4. When would use of the case study method be appropriate?

RESEARCH EXERCISES

1. Review and critique the qualitative research article at the companion website.
2. Think of a hypothetical example of a qualitative research study that would interest you for each of the following qualitative research methods. Write a paragraph or two about each example.
   a. Narrative inquiry
   b. Case study research
3. Search a database at your library. Find and then list the titles of a narrative inquiry and a case study. Also provide a brief (one-paragraph) summary of each article.
4. This exercise will help you experience narrative inquiry and think narratively about experience. Think about an experience that you have had with a child and then write about the experience. Then try to think about what happened before the experience and what happened during the experience. Who else was present in the situation? How did you feel in the experience?
5. We have pointed out repeatedly that one of the best ways to learn about research is to read published research articles. Here are several good examples of narrative and case study research articles. Select one article to review.

Narrative inquiry example

Christensen, E. (2012). Micropolitical staffroom stories: Beginning health and physical education teachers' experiences of the staffroom. *Teaching and Teacher Education, 30,* 74–83.

Schaefer, L. (2013). Beginning teacher attrition: A question of identity making and identity shifting. *Teachers and Teaching: Theory and Practice, 19,* 260–274.

Case study example

Abell, S. K., & Roth, M. (1994). Constructing science teaching in the elementary school: The socialization of a science enthusiast student teacher. *Journal of Research in Science Teaching, 31,* 77–90.

PROPOSAL EXERCISES

Propose a qualitative study that you would like to conduct and answer the following questions:

1. What is the tentative title of your study?
2. What do you hope to learn in your study?
3. Will you use a generic approach to qualitative or will you use one of the following specific qualitative research methods/methodologies: narrative inquiry, case study research, phenomenology, ethnography, or grounded theory? Be sure to explain your selection of approach.
4. What are your research questions or, if it is a narrative inquiry, what are your research puzzles?
5. Whom will you study? Where will you study them? How many people will you study? How long will you study them?
6. What data-collection methods will you use?
7. What validity/trustworthiness strategies will you use to help ensure the trustworthiness of your data and conclusions? (Hint: See the strategies discussed in Chapter 11.)

RELEVANT INTERNET SITES

Visit this site for good materials on qualitative research.
http://www.nova.edu/ssss/QR/qualres.html

Case study research links
http://writing.colostate.edu/guides/guide.cfm?guideid=60
http://www.sagepub.com/sites/default/files/upm-binaries/41407_1.pdf
http://isites.harvard.edu/icb/icb.do?keyword=qualitative&pageid=icb.page340344
http://scholarworks.umass.edu/cgi/viewcontent.cgi?article=1001&context=nursing_faculty_pubs

Narrative research links
http://www.tc.umn.edu/~dillon/CI%208148%20Qual%20Research/Session%2012/Narrative-Clandinin%20ER%20article.pdf
https://www.youtube.com/watch?v=RnaTBqapMrE
https://www.ualberta.ca/~iiqm/backissues/5_4/HTML/moen.htm
http://web.ics.purdue.edu/~cumming3/Portfolio/pdf/ENE695_Inquiry_Narrative_Research_final.pdf

STUDENT STUDY SITE

Visit the Student Study Site **edge.sagepub.com/rbjohnson6e** for these additional learning tools:

Video Links
Self-Quizzes
eFlashcards
Lecture Notes
Full-Text SAGE Journal Articles
Interactive Concept Maps
Web Resources

RECOMMENDED READING

Clandinin, D. J. (2013). *Engaging in narrative inquiry*. Walnut Creek, CA: Left Coast Press.

Clandinin, D. J., & Connelly, F. M. (2000). *Narrative inquiry: Experience and story in qualitative research*. San Francisco, CA: Jossey-Bass.

Johnson, R. B. (2008). Knowledge. In L. M. Given (Ed.), *The SAGE encyclopedia of qualitative research methods* (Vol. 1, pp. 478–482). Thousand Oaks, CA: SAGE.

Schwandt, T. A. (2007). *Qualitative inquiry: A dictionary of terms* (3rd ed.). Thousand Oaks, CA: SAGE.

Stake, R. E. (1995). *The art of case study research*. Thousand Oaks, CA: SAGE.

Yin, R. K. (2013). *Case study research: Design and methods*. Newbury Park, CA: SAGE.

NOTE

1. Don't be surprised if you see journal articles in which the authors claim to be performing case study research as well as using another research method. The term *case study* is not used consistently. For example, it is not uncommon for ethnographers to refer to their groups as "cases" (LeCompte & Preissle, 1993). Similarly, other qualitative researchers may call the individuals or groups in their study "cases."

Chapter 16

Phenomenology, Ethnography, and Grounded Theory

LEARNING OBJECTIVES

After reading this chapter, you should be able to

- Compare and contrast the three major approaches to qualitative research discussed in this chapter: phenomenology, ethnography, and grounded theory.
- Define and explain phenomenology.
- Define and explain ethnography.
- Define and explain grounded theory.

Visit the Student Study Site for an interactive concept map.

RESEARCH IN REAL LIFE Qualitative Research Approaches

istock/BanksPhotos

On April 20, 1999, Denver police officer John Lietz received a phone call shortly after 11:00 a.m. that will stay with him for the rest of his life. He picked up the phone to hear Matthew Depew, the son of a fellow police officer, say that he and 17 other Columbine High School students were trapped in a storage room off the school cafeteria, hiding from kids with guns. Bursts of gunfire could be heard in the background as Lietz told the kids to barricade the door with chairs and sacks of food. As Lietz and Depew spoke, Lietz could hear the shooters trying to break in on several occasions. At one point, they pounded on the door, prompting Depew to tell Lietz calmly that he was sure he was going to die.

The shooters, Eric Harris and Dylan Klebold, had started their day as they always did, attending a bowling class at 6:15 A.M. When either of them hit a strike or spare, they shouted "Sieg Heil!" in celebration, something they had done in the past. By 11:00 A.M., Harris and Klebold were walking toward the Columbine cafeteria wearing their trademark black trench coats and wraparound shades. Denny Rowe, sitting on a knoll not far from the cafeteria's entrance, watched one of them take off his coat, revealing something that looked like grenades. The other lit some firecrackers and threw them toward the school entrance. One of the boys then brandished a semiautomatic rifle, pointed it toward a 17-year-old freshman male, and shot the freshman in the thigh and then in the back as he tried to run away. The killers then turned toward Rowe and his friends, shooting one of them in the knee and another in the chest as they proceeded toward the cafeteria, where there were some 500 students. By the time the terror ended with the killers committing suicide, 12 students and a teacher were dead, and 23 students were wounded, several critically.

Following such a tragic incident, the overarching question in the minds of many Americans is "Why?" Eric Harris and Dylan Klebold were bright kids who came from seemingly stable, affluent homes. Almost immediately, a variety of possible explanations emerged. Violence on network television and in cartoons, comic books, music, video games, and movies might have been a contributor. The availability of information on the Internet about such things as how to make bombs may have contributed. The access that teenagers have to guns in our society is also seen as a potential contributor (Dority, 1999).

With so many possibilities, how can one identify the most likely causes of Eric Harris and Dylan Klebold's killing spree? Although we might never know all of the causes, psychologists would conduct extensive qualitative interviewing of the killers; study their life histories; and interview the killers' friends, classmates, teachers, and family members to obtain some evidence. One day, through the study of multiple cases, perhaps psychologists and educators will come up with a viable theory about why such events occur and what parents, teachers, and students can do to prevent future outbreaks of violence. Qualitative research approaches are very useful in exploring situations like this and in developing explanations that can be further developed over time. The previous chapter introduced you to two of the major types of qualitative research, narrative inquiry and case study. This chapter acquaints you with three others.

The purpose of this chapter is to introduce you to phenomenology, ethnography, and grounded theory. This chapter, in combination with the previous chapter, provides you with an overview of the five major approaches to qualitative research. A summary of all five approaches is shown in Table 15.2 in the previous chapter. As was the case with the two approaches discussed in Chapter 15 (narrative inquiry and case study), the three approaches in this chapter share many common characteristics of qualitative research, but each approach has its own emphasis and set of concepts.

PHENOMENOLOGY

Foundational question: What is the meaning, structure, and essence of the lived experience of this phenomenon by an individual or by many individuals?

- **Phenomenology** The description of one or more individuals' consciousness and experience of a phenomenon

- **Life-world** An individual's inner world of immediate experience

Phenomenology refers to the description of one or more individuals' consciousness and experience of a phenomenon, such as the death of a loved one, viewing oneself as a teacher, the act of teaching, the experience of being a minority group member, or the experience of winning a soccer game. The purpose of phenomenological research is to obtain a view into your research participants' life-worlds and to understand their personal meanings (i.e., what something means to them) constructed from their "lived experiences." **Life-world** is the translation of the German term *Lebenswelt* used by the founder of phenomenology, philosopher Edmund Husserl (1859–1938), to refer to the individual's "world of immediate experience." It is the individual's inner world of consciousness and experience. You are in your life-world right now as you read this chapter and as you exist wherever you are. In other words, your life-world is in your mind. It is your combination of feelings, thoughts, and self-awareness at any moment in time. The purpose of phenomenology is to gain access to individuals' life-worlds and to describe their experiences of a phenomenon.

To experience phenomenology firsthand, try describing your own personal experience of a phenomenon. To do this effectively, you must give it your full attention—the following poem by Moffitt[1] makes this point quite eloquently (cited in Moustakas, 1990):

> To look at any thing
> If you would know that thing,
> You must look at it long:
> To look at this green and say
> "I have seen spring in these
> Woods," will not do—you must
> Be the thing you see:
> You must be the dark snakes of
> Stems and ferny plumes of leaves,
> You must enter in
> To the small silences between
> The leaves,
> You must take your time
> And touch the very place
> They issue from.

When you want to experience something to its fullest, you must stop what you are doing; focus on what you are experiencing at that meaningful moment; and experience the thoughts, sensations, and feelings associated with that experience. Traditional phenomenologists point out that, to experience something in its purest form, you need to **bracket**, or suspend, any preconceptions or learned feelings that you have about the phenomenon. This is because they want you to experience the phenomenon "as it is." When you bracket your preconceptions, you set aside your taken-for-granted orientation toward the phenomenon, and your experience of it becomes part of your consciousness.

See Journal Article 16.1 on the Student Study Site.

- **Bracket** To suspend your preconceptions or learned feelings about a phenomenon to experience its essence

Examples of Phenomenology

Here are brief descriptions of a few phenomenological research studies, any of which you can look up and read if you need to learn more about phenomenological research. Only one of these articles was based on a single individual's experiences (Green, 1995). First, Cross and Stewart (1995) studied what it is like to be a gifted student in a rural high school in an article entitled "A Phenomenological Investigation of the *Lebenswelt* of Gifted Students in Rural High Schools." Cross and Stewart also compared rural students' experiences with the experiences of urban school students based on previous research. If you want to read just one phenomenological research article, this one is exemplary. Green, in an article entitled "Experiential Learning and Teaching," studied a teacher's meaning for and experience of using an experiential learning approach with her students. T. Brown (1996), in an article entitled "The Phenomenology of the Mathematics Classroom," examined children's experiences of being in a mathematics classroom. Finally, Muller (1994) studied the meaning and experience of empowering other people from the perspective of the person doing the empowering, in this case six women who had been identified as leaders; the article is entitled "Toward an Understanding of Empowerment: A Study of Six Women Leaders." Again, we remind you that one of the best ways to learn about qualitative research is to read qualitative research journal articles.

Types of Phenomenology

Phenomenology can be used to focus on the unique characteristics of an individual's experience of something. We all know that events, objects, and experiences can mean different things to different people. For example, different individuals may view a single event differently. The hiring of a new principal at a school might mean the school is moving in the right direction and offer solace to one teacher, while to another teacher, the change might arouse anger and result in restlessness because of the uncertainty it brings. In counseling, the phenomenological method is often used to understand each client's unique perspective on some life event or personal condition. The counselor assumes that each client's perspective is unique to that individual and attempts to understand that perspective empathetically. In education, a tenet of constructivist teaching is that teachers need to understand the unique perspective of each student in order to be in touch with and better understand each individual student and his or her needs. Thus, there is a phenomenological component to this theory.

Phenomenological researchers do not, however, generally assume that individuals are completely unique. More technically speaking, phenomenological researchers do not study just the variant structures of an experience (the unique part of an individual's experience that varies from person to person). Instead, phenomenologists generally assume that there is some commonality in human experience, and they seek to understand this commonality. This commonality of experience is called an **essence**, or invariant structure, of the experience (a part of the experience that is common or consistent across the research participants). An essence is an essential characteristic of an experience. It is universal and is present in particular instances of a phenomenon (van Manen, 1990). Consider the experience of the death of a loved one. Certainly, each of us reacts to and experiences this event somewhat differently (i.e., the idiosyncratic or variant structure). However, there are probably essences of this experience that are common to everyone (i.e., the common or invariant structures). For example, in the case of the death of a loved one, grief and sorrow would probably be elements of the common experience. You can search for the essential structures of a phenomenon by studying multiple examples of it and finding what experiences different people have in common. An essence will often be more abstract than literal descriptions of the particular experiences (e.g., general sorrow is more abstract than being "sad that your Uncle Bob is no longer around to provide love and friendship").

- **Essence** An invariant structure of an experience

The search for the essences of a phenomenon is probably the defining characteristic of phenomenology as a research technique. Exhibit 16.1 gives an example of a rich description of the essences of the experience of guilt. Are your experiences of guilt similar to the ones described in the exhibit? The description is from Yoder's (1990) doctoral dissertation.

In contrast to traditional or classical phenomenology (founded by Husserl and discussed above), a newer type of phenomenology has recently come onto the scene. It is called **interpretative phenomenological analysis** or IPA (J. A. Smith, Flowers, & Larkin, 2009). IPA also tries to get at individuals' experiences, but it critically questions the concept of participants bracketing out their demographic, cultural, and personal characteristics. IPA is interested in how particular people in particular contexts make meaning and interpret their experiences. Different people might experience phenomena differently. IPA is interested in research participants' perspectives on their experiences and in their somewhat distinctive experiences rather than attempting to describe their *transcendental experience* (i.e., experience that cuts across all people, universally). IPA starts with and is interested in the particular (particular people's experiences at particular places and times) and works up to understanding different group's shared experiences, in contrast to searching for universal experiences that cut across all individuals and groups. We believe that both traditional Husserlian phenomenology and IPA are useful, and it is an empirical question as to which is most applicable for your data. For example, experiences might vary along the following continuum:

- **Interpretative phenomenological analysis (IPA)** New type of phenomenology more focused on situated, interpreted, and particular lived experiences than on transcendental experiences

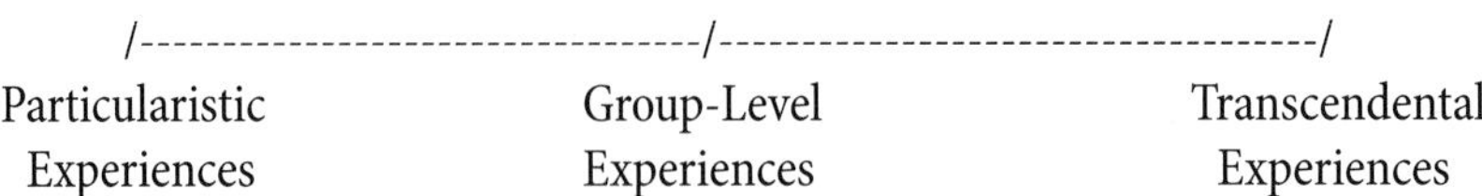

Data Collection, Analysis, and Report Writing

In a typical phenomenological research study, the researcher collects data from several individuals and depicts their experience of something. The data are usually collected through in-depth interviews. Using the interview data, the researcher attempts to reduce the statements to the common core or essence of the experience as described by the research

■ **EXHIBIT 16.1** The Essence of Guilt

Feelings of guilt are signs of significant turbulence, flaring up within the person. They come like a storm with lightning and cold winds. "It felt like mists, cold wind, dark streets, uncomfortable things. Stormy clouds in the sky. Occasional flashes of lightning. Empty beaches on a cold day. A cold wind from the water."

Guilt feelings close in. They are an imprisonment in which there is no way out. "You feel closed in when you are really feeling guilty. You feel cramped, very claustrophobic, limited, constricted, walled in."

The feeling of guilt is sharp and jagged. It is "being on the hook," a "knife," a pain as sharp as a surgical incision. The feeling of guilt is fast. "I'm thinking of lightning because it is a jab."

Guilt feelings are "a heavy weight." They are experienced as a "crushing blow." The feeling of guilt pushes, removes, evokes withdrawal, a sinking enormously heavy feeling. It comes in waves. "This intense push that jolts me back." "I'm gonna sink down. It's like this weight is on me."

Feeling guilty is "being in a shell," an invisible agent in a "world of strangers." Guilt feelings send one adrift into space where time is unending and the link with others is severed and closed. There is no hope of repair, renewal, belonging, no chance of even recognizing a genuine self.

The experience of feeling guilty is the experience of being forcibly removed from the flow of everyday life, from the world of ordinary human sharing and warmth. When we feel guilty, we are cast into a painful, frozen, inner-focused world that takes over the self and creates a reality of its own. Guilt feelings sever our sense of connectedness with everyday things, with other people and with ourselves. In the experience of feeling guilty, time stands still. All exits are closed. We are isolated and trapped within ourselves.

In guilt feelings, self-respect deteriorates, a sense of physical ugliness often awakens. Real emotions are hidden. Masked ways of being show themselves in pleasing others. In everyday and in ultimate moments, "The real me is not good enough. Not ever."

Time is experienced as slowed down and unchangeable. Clock time goes haywire. Everything churns and then freezes. Only the crystallized moment of guilt endures. The past is relived over and over again, an endless recycling, a movie that repeats itself without any genuine change or realization.

In guilt feelings, the relationship to the body is also affected. The body becomes distant, moves like a robot. It is in pain, anxious to move somehow, yet, at the same time, fearful that any action will reawaken the scenes of guilt.

In spite of the torturous feelings and helpless, endless, sense of guilt, there is still within the self, the possibility of recovering oneself and regaining the sense of harmonious flow with life. There is the potential to come to terms with the guilt, accept it, share it with another and, in this acceptance, find a way to peace. What is required is the courage to take the first step and risk scornful judgment and the pain of acknowledging one's limitations. There is no guarantee that if one freely and honestly expresses the guilt, and recognizes the vulnerability and limitedness of the self, that the guilty feelings will be excised permanently, but for some of my co-researchers this acceptance and sharing enabled them to reclaim themselves and reestablish inner tranquility.

Source: Reprinted with permission from Yoder (1990).

participants. For research participants to explore their experience, they must be able to relive it in their minds, and they must be able to focus on the experience and nothing else. This is what you must get your research participants to do if you conduct a phenomenological research study.

One effective strategy for eliciting data from participants is to tell each participant to recall a specific experience he or she has had, to think about that specific experience carefully, and then to describe that experience to you. You might use the following general question to get participants talking about their experience: "Please carefully describe your experience with ________." You might also say, "When you think of your experience with ________, what comes into your mind?" You might find that you need to prompt the respondent during the interview for greater detail, and you should do so. Remember that your goal is to get your participants to think about their specific experience and to describe it in rich detail. Rather than having research participants describe the meaning and structure of their experiences to you in an in-person interview, you can also have them write about their experiences and then give you their written narratives. Both approaches work, but interviews are usually better.

During data analysis, the researcher searches for *significant statements*. These are statements (a few words or a phrase, a sentence, or a few sentences) that have particular relevance to the phenomenon being studied. For example, perhaps you asked a kindergarten student to describe what school is like and one of her statements was that "We are all like a family at my school." If this statement seemed to fit her other statements, then the statement is probably a significant statement. In general, to determine whether a statement is significant, you should ask yourself, "Does the statement seem to have meaning to the participant in describing his or her experience? Is the statement descriptive of the experience? Does the statement tap into the participant's experience?" Many researchers like to record the significant statements verbatim (i.e., in the actual words of the participants). Some researchers also like to interpret and describe the meanings of the significant statements at this point by making a list of the *meanings*. For example, in the case of the kindergarten student's statement, you might conclude that the child sees school as being like a family because there is a teacher (the head of the family) and other students (family members) at school and the family does things together as a unit (plays, eats, takes naps). This interpretative process done by the researcher should be verified by the participants (i.e., use the member-checking technique discussed in Chapter 11).

After constructing the lists of significant statements and meanings, the researcher searches for *themes* in the data. In other words, what kinds of things did the participants tend to mention as being important to them? The researcher might find that certain individuals or groups (e.g., males and females) tend to describe an experience somewhat differently. This information is useful in understanding individual and group differences. However, the phenomenological researcher is usually most interested in describing the fundamental structure of the experience (the essence) for the total group. It is here that the researcher describes the fundamental features of the experience that are experienced in common by virtually all the participants. Finally, researchers should use member checking as a validity check whenever possible in this process. This means that *the researcher should have the original participants review the interpretations and descriptions of the experience, especially the statement of the fundamental structure of the experience.*

In a dissertation entitled "The Essential Structure of a Caring Interaction: Doing Phenomenology," Riemen (1983) reported hospital patients' experiences of "caring" and "noncaring" nurses. We have included Riemen's description of the "essential structure" of her hospital patients' experiences of caring and noncaring nurses in Exhibits 16.2 and 16.3. Riemen also compared males' and females' significant statements and meanings. This is an excellent example of phenomenological research and a good model to follow.

The final report in a typical phenomenological study is a narrative that includes a description of the participants in the study and the methods used to obtain the information from the participants (usually interviews), a rich description of the fundamental structure of the experience, and a discussion of the findings. The researcher might also describe any interesting individual or group differences. A well-written report is highly descriptive of the participants' experience of the phenomenon, and it will elicit in the readers a feeling that they understand what it would be like to experience the phenomenon themselves. This kind of feeling is called a vicarious experience.

EXHIBIT 16.2 Description of a Caring Nurse

In a caring interaction, the nurse's existential presence is perceived by the client as more than just a physical presence. There is the aspect of the nurse giving of oneself to the client. This giving of oneself may be in response to the client's request, but it is more often a voluntary effort and is unsolicited by the client. The nurse's willingness to give of oneself is primarily perceived by the client as an attitude and behavior of sitting down and really listening and responding to the unique concerns of the individual as a person of value. The relaxation, comfort, and security that the client experiences both physically and mentally are an immediate and direct result of the client's stated and unstated needs being heard and responded to by the nurse.

Source: Riemen (1983). The essential structure of a caring nurse: A phenomenological study. Retrieved from ProQuest Dissertations and Theses databases (UMI No. 8401214).

EXHIBIT 16.3 Description of a Noncaring Nurse

The nurse's presence with the client is perceived by the client as a minimal presence of the nurse being physically present only. The nurse is viewed as being there only because it is a job and not to assist the client or answer his or her needs. Any response by the nurse is done with a minimal amount of energy expenditure and bound by the rules. The client perceives the nurse who does not respond to this request for assistance as being noncaring. Therefore, an interaction that never happened is labeled as a noncaring interaction. The nurse is too busy and hurried to spend time with the client and therefore does not sit down and really listen to the client's individual concerns. The client is further devalued as a unique person because he or she is scolded, treated as a child, or treated as a nonhuman being or an object. Because of the devaluing and lack of concern, the client's needs are not met and the client has negative feelings, that is, he or she is frustrated, scared, depressed, angry, afraid, and upset.

Source: Riemen (1983). The essential structure of a caring nurse: A phenomenological study. Retrieved from ProQuest Dissertations and Theses databases (UMI No. 8401214).

REVIEW QUESTIONS

16.1 What are the key characteristics of phenomenology?

16.2 How does the researcher analyze the data collected in a phenomenology?

Ethnography

Foundational question: What are the cultural characteristics of this group of people or of this cultural scene?

Ethnography is an approach to qualitative research that originated in the discipline of anthropology around the turn of the 20th century. *Ethnography* literally means "writing about people" (*ethnos* means "people, race, or cultural group," and *graphia* means "writing or representing"; LeCompte & Preissle, 1993). Because of the importance of the concept of culture to the discipline of anthropology, **ethnography** is traditionally or classically defined as the discovery and comprehensive description of the culture of a group of people. Educational ethnographers also focus on cultural description, as is done in classical ethnography. The main difference is that anthropologists usually describe small cultures across the world (especially in less developed nations), whereas educational ethnographers usually study the cultural characteristics of small groups of people or other cultural scenes as they relate to educational issues.

- **Ethnography** A form of qualitative research focused on discovering and describing the culture of a group of people

The Idea of Culture

Culture is a system of shared beliefs, values, practices, perspectives, folk knowledge, language, norms, rituals, and material objects and artifacts that members of a group use in understanding their world and in relating to others. So that you can better understand this definition, here are the definitions of several important words in it. **Shared beliefs** are the specific cultural conventions or statements that people who share a culture hold to be true or false. **Shared values** are the culturally defined standards about what is good or bad or desirable or undesirable. **Norms** are the written and unwritten rules that specify appropriate group behavior (e.g., "Raise your hand when you have a question" is a common norm in a classroom).

- **Culture** A system of shared beliefs, values, practices, perspectives, folk knowledge, language, norms, rituals, and material objects and artifacts that members of a group use in understanding their world and in relating to others
- **Shared beliefs** The specific cultural conventions or statements that people who share a culture hold to be true or false
- **Shared values** The culturally defined standards about what is good or bad or desirable or undesirable
- **Norms** The written and unwritten rules that specify appropriate group behavior

If you look at the definition of *culture*, you will notice it includes a nonmaterial component (the shared beliefs, values, norms, and so forth of the members of a group) and a material component (the material things produced by group members, such as buildings, books, classroom bulletin boards, and art). Ethnographers sometimes refer to these two components as *material culture* and *nonmaterial culture*. Although ethnographers do not usually specify whether they are referring to the material or nonmaterial component of culture or both, the intention is usually clear from the context of the statement. When one is attempting to understand and explain human behavior, the nonmaterial component is usually the focus of attention.

Individuals become members of a culture through the socialization process by which they learn and are trained about the features of the culture. During socialization, they usually internalize the culture; that is, they take the values and beliefs to be their own. Over time, people identify so strongly with their culture that the ways of doing things in their own culture might seem natural to them and the ways of doing things in other cultures might seem strange. You might have heard the term *culture shock*, which is an experience people have when they observe different cultural practices. Cultures are maintained over time through socialization and a social-sanctioning process through which members of a culture stigmatize people who break group norms and praise and associate with the people who follow the appropriate cultural norms. In general, as people become members of any new group, they learn the culture of that group so that they can become fully functioning and accepted members of the group. The people who follow the norms of a group or society are often called normal, and those who deviate from the cultural norms are called deviant.

Although we often think of a culture as being associated with a very large group such as a society (e.g., the culture of the United States), the concept of culture can be used on a much smaller scale. In fact, culture can be viewed as varying on a continuum, with macro culture on one end and micro culture on the other end. At the macro level, we might study the cultural characteristics (the shared values, beliefs, and norms) of US citizens, Japanese adolescents, or the Ohio Amish. On a more micro level, we might study the cultural characteristics of a group of American high school students whose families immigrated from the Punjab state in India and practice Sikhism. Other micro-level groups we might study include the members of the Chicago Bears football team, the band members at a local high school, Spanish-speaking students at a local middle school, or the students in Ms. Smith's first-grade classroom. Educational ethnographers are most likely to study cultures or the cultural characteristics of groups much smaller than an entire nation like the United States or Japan. That is, they usually (but not always) study relatively small or micro cultures.

In an educational ethnography conducted at a clearly micro level, a researcher might choose to study a classroom culture. For example, the researcher might want to study the culture of one elementary school teacher's homeroom students to find out how and why the teacher has been successful in helping these students learn to read. Ethnographic concepts (shared values, beliefs, group norms, etc.) and procedures (observations and interviews) will be very useful in understanding this classroom. You might ask questions such as, What norms do the students follow while they are in this classroom? What values do they adopt while they are in the classroom? How does the teacher interact with the students? How do the students interact with one another? Are all of the students usually doing the same thing, or are there several clusters of interacting students at a time? What seems to motivate the students to work so hard? What classroom values have the students internalized? What teaching practices and strategies does the teacher use to teach? This list of questions is unlimited because an ethnography should be a relatively comprehensive description of the group's culture and the important cultural scenes.

Sometimes the term **subculture** is used to refer to a culture that is embedded within a larger culture. For example, a high school can be viewed as containing several subcultures (e.g., a teacher culture and various student group cultures). However, researchers usually continue to use the more general term *culture* even for these smaller groups (i.e., they say the school is composed of several cultures), rather than using the more specific term *subculture.* If you want to make the point that a group of people is composed of two or more smaller but distinct groups, then you may use the term *subculture.* Otherwise, using the more general term *culture* is fine. In general, humans are members of and are affected by multiple cultures or subcultures simultaneously. For example, the members of the school band at a suburban high school are probably affected by the overall US culture, by the adolescent culture within the United States, by a suburban culture, by their school's culture, and by any cultural characteristics they share by virtue of their membership in the band.

■ **Subculture** A culture embedded within a larger culture

Examples of Ethnographic Research

Now that you know what ethnography and culture are, we briefly describe several published research articles that use ethnographic techniques. As with all of the qualitative research approaches discussed in this chapter, the best way to learn more about them is to read some published articles or book-length examples. In "An Ethnographic Study of Norms of Inclusion and Cooperation in a Multiethnic Middle School," Deering (1996) studied the culture in a middle school that was known to be supportive of inclusion. Deering defined *inclusion* as "the degree to which all persons and their aspirations and interests are incorporated into a given social context" (p. 22). Deering studied the school over a 2-year period by observing and talking to teachers, administrators, students, parents, and other community members. He described the school culture, the peer culture, and parent and community involvement. It was remarkable how well students from different groups got along at this particular school. Some reasons were the leadership provided by the principal, a norm of respect applied to everyone in the school, and an expectation of positive involvement by all groups in the school.

In "The Content of Conversations About the Body Parts and Behaviors of Animals During Elementary School Visits to a Zoo and the Implications for Teachers Organizing Field Trips," Tunnicliffe (1995) observed and listened to children while they were at a zoo. She provided a description of what the children said, she classified those statements by topic, and she provided some quotes from the children (e.g., "It's showing its teeth." "Miss Wicks, look! Their hands are like ours!" "There's a baby one."). This study took the reader into a small part of the children's culture and described it to the reader. It is an example of a cultural scene.

In "An Ethnographic Study of Cross-Cultural Communication With Puerto Rican–American Families in the Special Education System," Harry (1992) observed and interviewed parents from 12 Spanish-speaking Puerto Rican American families who had children in the special education system. She also interviewed several educators. She found that cultural differences seemed to lead to communication breakdowns between the educators and the Puerto Rican American parents. For example, the parents expected the educational professionals to treat them as friends (i.e., as "*mi amiga*" or "my friend") as in Puerto Rico, but they did not perceive this to be happening. They felt that the American school system was impersonal, and they did not trust it. Much of the communication about their children, as well as the Individual Education Plan (IEP), was in written form, which tended to alienate the parents further. Sometimes the parents didn't understand the language and jargon used by the educators (e.g., the term *IEP* was sometimes misunderstood). Feeling a lack of power, the parents often withdrew from the communication process and deferred to the professionals, who, as a result, felt the parents were apathetic. In sum, the educators and the parents tended to come from different cultures, and they often misunderstood one another.

See Journal Article 16.2 on the Student Study Site.

Types of Ethnographic Research

- **Ethnology** The comparative study of cultural groups

Two other types of ethnographic work are closely related to classical ethnography: ethnology and ethnohistory. An **ethnology** is the comparative study of cultural groups. It involves conducting or comparing a series of separate ethnographic studies of the same or different cultural groups to uncover general patterns and rules of social behavior. For example, ethnology might involve the comparison of family practices or educational practices in several different cultures. The ethnologist would look for similarities and differences among the groups. As an example, sociologists and anthropologists have found that all societies have some form of the family institution. However, the extended family pattern, in which parents, children, and other kin such as grandparents and aunts and uncles interact a great deal, is more common in traditional agrarian societies (e.g., El Salvador and Bangladesh); the nuclear family pattern, in which one or two parents and their children interact the most, is more common in modern industrial societies (e.g., the United States and Sweden). Because there is greater interest in general patterns (what many people have in common) in ethnology than in particular patterns (the unique characteristics of each group), this form of research tends to have greater external validity than a single ethnography.

An example of an educational ethnology is LeCompte and Preissle's (1992) chapter entitled "Toward an Ethnology of Student Life in Schools and Classrooms: Synthesizing the Qualitative Research Tradition." LeCompte and Preissle had been conducting educational ethnographies for over two decades, and in this ethnology, they compared the findings from a large number of ethnographic studies over that time period. Their goal was to find some common themes across the educational ethnographies. We mention only three of their findings. First, they found that children's focus of attention changes over time (e.g., from kindergarten to high school): "Younger children conceptualize school experience as types of activity [e.g., work and play] and the structures that support them. Older students shift their attention from structures, tasks, and schedules to relationships with people" (p. 823). Not surprisingly, students' and teachers' perspectives about what is important tended to be different. Second, they also found that teacher expectations for different kinds of students tended to affect student behavior. Third, they found that "students who are better integrated into their home culture achieve higher success in school, even if they are members of stigmatized minority groups" (p. 846).

Another form of ethnographic research is **ethnohistory**, which is the study of the cultural past of a group of people. An ethnohistory is often done during the early stages of an ethnography to uncover the group members' cultural roots and to study how the group has changed (or not changed) over time. This information provides the researcher with a deeper sense of the people being studied. The researcher relies on data such as official documents, oral histories, journals, and newspapers and on information gathered from talking with the older people in the group to learn about how things used to be and how things are different now. The ethnohistory can be the end purpose of a research study, but it is usually part of a larger ethnographic study. A last type of ethnographic research is called **autoethnography**. This is like an autobiography written by a qualitative researcher. The writer engages in extensive self-examination and self-reflection, and purposively thinks about and includes extensive cultural and contextual description of his or her life. It would be like you writing your personal and cultural history.

- **Ethnohistory** The study of the cultural past of a group of people

- **Autoethnography** Like an autobiography written by a qualitative researcher; focuses on self-examination, self-reflection, and purposive inclusion of extensive cultural and contextual description and detail of one's life

Data Collection, Analysis, and Report Writing

Ethnography relies on extended fieldwork. This means that the researcher spends a long time in the field with the people being studied. The researcher typically becomes a participant or nonparticipant observer. In fact, extended fieldwork and participant observation are the distinguishing characteristics of a classical or ideal type ethnography. Spending 6 months to 1 year in the field is not at all uncommon. As you can see, this type of research can be quite demanding!

Data collection and data analysis in ethnography are said to be concurrent or alternating. This means ethnographers typically collect some data and analyze those data, then return to the field to collect more data and analyze those data, and so on. This process cycles during most of the time spent in the field. The researcher needs to look at the data and analyze them while he or she is still fresh out of the field and also to know what kinds of data need to be collected next and from where.

Ethnography is an emergent, fluid, and responsive approach to qualitative research because the original research questions sometimes change. For example, Holland and Eisenhart (1990) spent several years studying females attending college. They were originally interested in the influence of peer groups on females' role identities and how peer groups affected the women's choices of college majors. They realized over time that the women's peers knew very little about how or why their friends chose their college major. The researchers decided that the more important questions emerging from their study were how the women responded to their college culture, how they specifically responded to the patriarchal conditions that they faced, and what important subcultural differences existed among the women. Although an ethnographer might think he or she knows exactly what to study in the field, it is always possible that extended fieldwork will show the original research questions to be naive, unimportant, or not researchable or that other issues and questions will emerge as more important.

The researcher collects data during fieldwork that might help in understanding the group of people. Ethnographers talk to people, observe their behavior in their natural day-to-day environments, and examine documents kept by the group members. They also take extensive field notes of what they see on an ongoing basis, and they write memos to themselves, recording their thoughts and interpretations about the developing ethnographic description. Video- and audio-recording devices are frequently helpful because of their accuracy and because the tapes can be reviewed later.

- **Ethnocentrism** Judging people from a different culture according to the standards of your own culture

One of the cardinal rules in doing ethnographic research is not to be ethnocentric toward the people you are studying. **Ethnocentrism** means judging people from a different culture or group according to the standards of your own culture or group. An example of ethnocentric behavior would be going to another country and being judgmental about what the people there eat (e.g., "Why would anyone eat snails?!"). When we are being ethnocentric, we don't try to understand people who are different from us. Therefore, when doing ethnographic research, you must take a nonjudgmental stance toward the people you are studying to gain useful information.

- **Emic perspective** The insider's perspective
- **Emic terms** Special words or terms used by people in their social and cultural groups
- **Etic perspective** An external, social scientific view of reality
- **Etic terms** "Objective" outsiders' words or special terms used by social scientists to describe a group

Ethnographers also try to take on the emic and etic perspectives during data collection and analysis. The **emic perspective** is the insider's perspective. It includes the meanings and views of the people in the group being studied. Taking the emic perspective also means considering questions and issues for study that are important to insiders. The researcher documenting the emic perspective must try to get inside of the heads of the group members. Therefore, this aspect of ethnography is very phenomenological in approach. For you to understand the emic perspective, it is very important to learn the local language and forms of expression used by the people being studied. Special words or terms used by the study participants in their natural settings in their social groups are called **emic terms**. Some emic terms used by high school students in a middle-sized Southern city to refer to the more academic-type students were *brains*, *advanced*, *intellectuals*, *nerds*, *geeks*, *dorks*, and *smarties* (H. J. Smith, 1997). A larger list of emic terms identified by Smith for various groups in high schools is shown in Table 16.1.

Ethnographers use the term **etic perspective** to refer to an external, social scientific view of reality (Fetterman, 2009). This is the perspective of the objective researcher studying a group of people. The goal is to move beyond the perspectives of the people being studied and use social science concepts, terms (i.e., **etic terms**), and procedures to describe the people and explain their behavior. Researchers using the etic perspective also bring their research questions from the outside (e.g., issues are considered important on the basis of a review of the research literature). They tend to take an instrumental view, wanting to study the participants to answer a specific question or to produce a specific product.

Effective ethnographers are able to use both perspectives. If a researcher only took the emic perspective, he or she would risk what is called **going native**, which means that the researcher identifies so completely with the group that he or she can no longer step back and take an objective perspective. Someone who goes native has basically become an insider. That person overidentifies with the group and can view things only from the viewpoint of the insiders. On the other hand, if researchers took only the etic viewpoint, they would risk not understanding the people from the native perspective. They would also risk imposing their own predetermined beliefs and categories on their interpretations about the participants. We believe that effective researchers walk the fine line between the emic and etic perspectives and periodically delve into the world of each perspective (*strategically moving back and forth* over time) to gather useful insights and produce a good ethnography.

- **Going native** Identifying so completely with the group being studied that you can no longer provide an "objective outsider" or etic perspective

Because of the reliance on observational and interview data, ethnographers should constantly triangulate their observations and data sources to corroborate their research findings. For example, if a participant or informant says that some event took place, the ethnographer does not take that single participant's account at face value. Instead, the ethnographer searches for other participants who experienced (or observed or heard about) the same event and listens to their accounts and interpretations. In this way, evidence for descriptive validity is improved. During the later months in the field, ethnographers frequently begin composing and writing their final report. This way, the written description and interpretation can be shown to the participants for their review and validation. Recall that this process is called *participant review* or *member checking.*

When writing the final report, ethnographers contextualize their study. That is, they carefully examine the context in which the group is situated, and they write this up in the report. For example, ethnographers describe the particulars of the physical and social settings, including the time, the place, and the situation in which a study was conducted. Contextualization helps make the ethnographer more aware of the relationship between the context and the observed behavior, and it helps readers of the research report know where and to whom they can apply the research results.

When describing a group, ethnographers also try to be holistic. **Holism**, or holistic description, was discussed briefly in Chapter 2 and also in Table 15.1 (characteristic 10). Although the concept of holism is summed up in the statement "The whole is greater than its parts," holistic description does not ignore the parts of the whole because an analysis of the parts is essential to understanding the whole. The ethnographer consciously works back and forth between the parts and the whole, ultimately creating a picture of the cultural group or scene. For example, a high school band is composed of individuals who come together as a unit and create a holistic product (music). In a typical ethnography, holistic description involves examining the characteristics of the individuals in a group (e.g., what the individuals are like), it involves examining how the individuals in the group interact with one another (e.g., when they interact and what they do), and it involves examining how the individuals come together to form the group (e.g., what they have in common, what their group norms and rituals are, and what the group identity is). In short, when composing a holistic description, you must study the parts of the whole in addition to describing the whole. The final ethnographic report typically includes a rich and holistic description of the group. It also usually includes many verbatims (direct quotations from group members).

- **Holism** The idea that the whole is greater than the sum of its parts

TABLE 16.1 Selected Emic Terms Used by High School Students

Losers	Rebels	Skanks	Jocks	Prep	Holy Rollers
Retards	Rednecks	Bubbas	Mechanics	Vo Techs	Goody-Goodies
Hippies	Peacers	Gangsters	Druggies	Burnouts	Clowns
Grubbies	Loners	Roaches	Wannabes	Woodies	Azalea Trail Maids
Surfers	Whammers	Punks	Airheads	Rockers	Brains
Geeks	Dorks	Duds	Bookworms	Grunge	Band

Source: From Smith, H. J., 1997, *The Role of Symbolism in the Structure, Maintenance, and Interaction of High School Social Groupings.* Master's thesis, University of South Alabama Department of Sociology and Anthropology, Mobile.

REVIEW QUESTIONS

16.3 What are the key characteristics of ethnography?

16.4 What is the difference between a macro culture and a micro culture?

16.5 How do people become members of cultures?

16.6 What is the difference between the emic perspective and the etic perspective?

GROUNDED THEORY

▪ **Grounded theory** A general methodology for developing theory that is grounded in data systematically gathered and analyzed

Foundational question: What theory or explanation emerges from an analysis of the data collected about this phenomenon?

Barney Glaser and Anselm Strauss wrote a book in 1967 on what they called **grounded theory**. These two sociologists contended that theory should emerge inductively from empirical data. They said we need to "discover theory from data" (p. 1). Although this was not an entirely new idea in the field of research, Glaser and Strauss wanted to counter what they saw as a tendency in their field to focus on *theory confirmation* (testing hypotheses developed from previous theories) rather than on *theory generation* and construction (developing new theories grounded in new data). They thought that the discipline of sociology had stagnated because of a reliance on older theories. They also thought that current research was too quantitative and had become too far removed from the empirical reality that it sought to explain. They believed that many of the popular theories at that time were not grounded in real data but were, instead, based on the thinking of a few famous theorists. Since publication of Glaser and Strauss's important book in 1967, grounded theory has become a popular approach to qualitative research in many different disciplines, including education, counseling, and nursing.

"Grounded theory is a *general methodology* for developing theory that is grounded in data systematically gathered and analyzed" (Strauss & Corbin, 1994, p. 273). The product of the grounded theory methodology is frequently called a grounded theory. Therefore, when you do grounded theory research, your goal is to construct a grounded theory. It is important to understand that *a grounded theory is not generated a priori* (i.e., based only on reasoning). Rather, a grounded theory is based on concepts that are generated directly from the data that are collected in one or more research studies. This is another way of saying that the theory is inductively derived. Figuratively speaking, you can think of inductive analysis as "getting into your data" (during data collection and analysis), "living there" or "hanging out there for a while," and developing an understanding of the phenomenon based on the data. For example, if someone outside of education wanted to learn about teaching, this person could go to a real classroom, observe a teacher for several weeks, and then draw some tentative, data-based conclusions about teaching. Induction is a bottom-up approach based on original data (i.e., you start with the data and then make your generalizations after looking at your data). Strauss and Corbin (1990) pointed out the inductive nature of grounded theory research when they wrote, "One does not begin with a theory, then prove it. Rather, one begins with an area of study and what is relevant to that area is allowed to emerge" (p. 23). During a particular grounded theory research study, some data are collected and analyzed, and as the theory is being developed, additional data are collected and analyzed to clarify, develop, and validate the theory.

Characteristics of a Grounded Theory

Glaser and Strauss (1967) listed four important characteristics of a grounded theory: fit, understanding, generality, and control. First, the theory must *fit* the data if it is to be useful. Glaser and Strauss made an important point when they said that a researcher

> often develops a theory that embodies, without his realizing it, his own ideals and the values of his occupation and social class, as well as popular views and myths, along with his deliberate efforts at making logical deductions from some formal theory to which he became committed as a graduate student. (p. 238)

The point is that theory must correspond closely to the real-world data, not to our personal wishes or biases or predetermined categories.

Second, the theory should be clearly stated and readily *understandable* to people working in the substantive area, even to nonresearch types. One reason for this is that practitioners might need to use the theory or employ someone else to use the theory one day. If the theory is not understandable to them, it might never be used. Glaser and Strauss (1967) pointed out, "Their understanding the theory tends to engender a readiness to use it, for it sharpens their sensitivity to the problems that they face and gives them an image of how they can potentially make matters better" (p. 240).

Third, the theory should have *generality*. This means that the scope of the theory and its conceptual level should not be so specific that the theory only applies to one small set of people or to only one specific situation. Such a theory would rarely be of use. Furthermore, it would be practically impossible to develop a new theory for every single person and situation. A strategy for avoiding such specificity is to conceptualize the concepts in the theory at a level abstract enough to move beyond the specifics in the original research study.

The fourth characteristic of a good grounded theory as discussed by Glaser and Strauss is *control*. If someone uses the theory, he or she should have some control over the phenomenon that is explained by the theory. In the words of Glaser and Strauss (1967), "The substantive theory must enable the person who uses it to have enough control in everyday situations to make its application worth trying" (p. 245). As a result, it is a good idea to identify controllable variables and build them into your grounded theory.

As you can see, meeting the criteria of fit, understanding, generality, and control is a lot to expect from a grounded theory, especially if the theory is developed from a single research study. That is why the development of a grounded theory is a never-ending process. In a single research study, the researcher should try to collect as extensive data as is feasible. During the study, the researcher will interact with the data and collect additional data when questions arise and need answering. A grounded theory should be elaborated and modified further in future research studies; the key strategy, again, is that the developing theory should be grounded in the data. Practitioners who attempt to use the theory should also be involved in making suggestions for theory modifications. As Glaser and Strauss (1967) said, "The person who applies the theory becomes, in effect, a generator of theory" (p. 242).

Example of a Grounded Theory

To give you a better idea of what a real grounded theory research study looks like, we now describe a study conducted by Creswell and Brown (1992) entitled "How Chairpersons Enhance Faculty Research: A Grounded Theory Study." The article is easy to read, and it is a good example of a grounded theory based on a single research study.

Creswell and Brown (1992) studied how college and university department chairpersons interact with their faculty members. They conducted "semi-structured telephone interviews with thirty-three chairpersons" (p. 42). They found that the chairpersons performed many different roles. Seven roles were identified in the data: provider, enabler, advocate, mentor, encourager, collaborator, and challenger. Creswell and Brown also found that the chairpersons performed different roles at different times, depending on the level of the faculty member with whom they were interacting. The important levels identified in the study were beginning faculty (faculty who had been in the department from 1 to 3 years), pretenured faculty (faculty who had been in the department from 3 to 5 years), posttenured faculty (faculty who had not yet been promoted to full professor), and senior faculty (faculty who were full professors). They found, for example, that beginning faculty needed extra time for writing and publishing, and the chairperson would provide additional resources and try to enable the faculty member by providing a favorable schedule and a reduction in committee work. If this strategy were successful, the outcome would be more publications by the faculty member, which would improve the faculty member's chance of getting tenure. You can see Creswell and Brown's depiction of their grounded theory in Figure 16.1. As shown there, the type of faculty issue that a chairperson is concerned with depends on the career stage of the faculty member and other signs such as a lack of productivity. Given a faculty member who is at a specific stage and the presence of certain signs, the department chairperson performs certain roles (strategies) to help the faculty member develop. These actions result in specific outcomes (e.g., improved productivity, an improved attitude toward the department). Finally, the general process operates within a context, which can also affect how the chairperson works with the faculty member.

See Journal Article 16.3 on the Student Study Site.

Data Collection, Analysis, and Report Writing

Data analysis in grounded theory starts at the moment of initial contact with the phenomenon being studied, and it continues throughout the development of a grounded theory. In other words, data collection and analysis in grounded theory are concurrent and continual

FIGURE 16.1 Creswell and Brown's model for chairpersons' role in enhancing faculty research performance

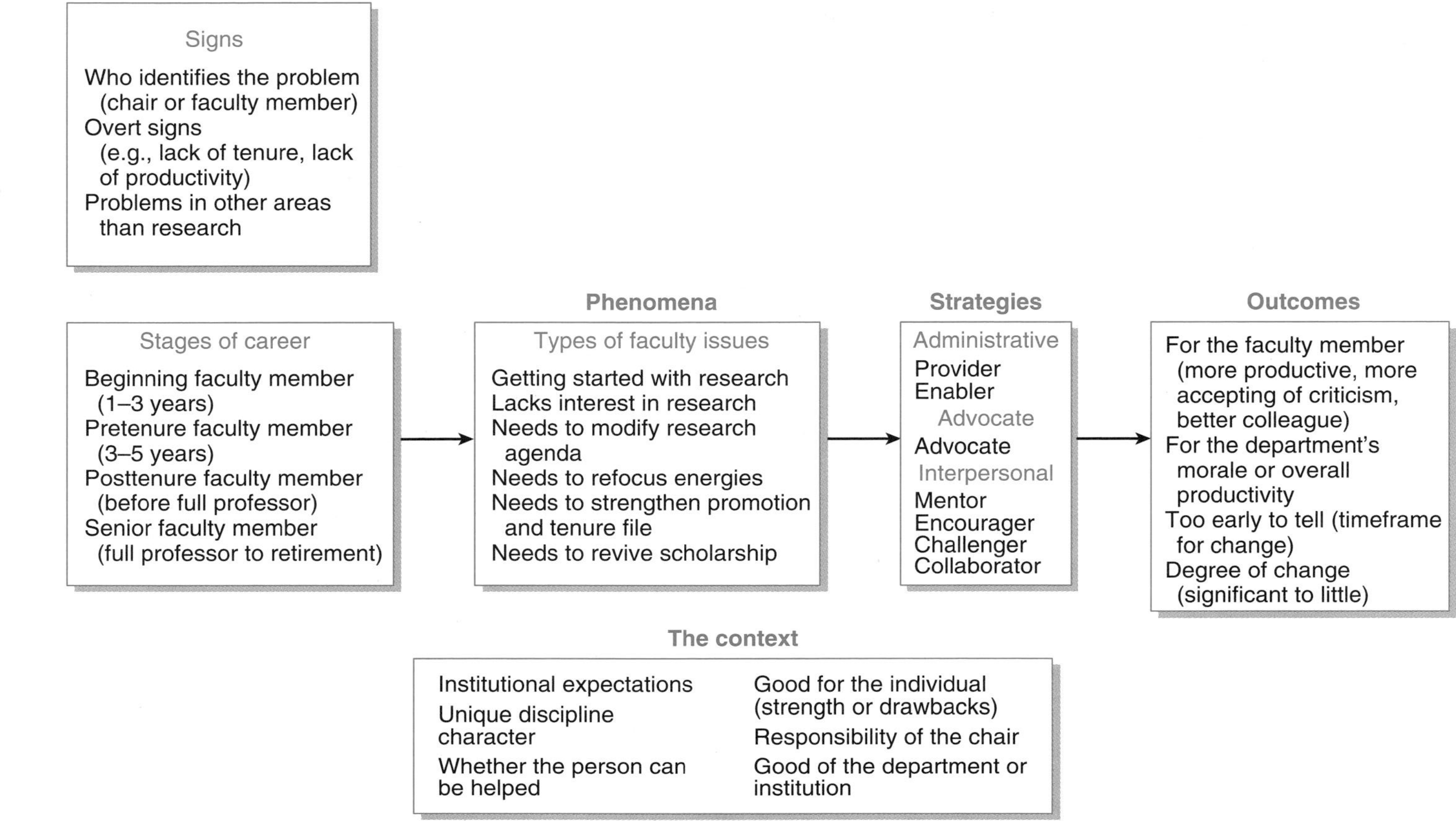

Source: From Creswell, J. W., and M. L. Brown. "How Chairpersons Enhance Faculty Research: A Grounded Theory Study," 1992, *Review of Higher Education*, *16*(1), 41–62. Copyright © The Johns Hopkins University Press. Reprinted by permission of Johns Hopkins University Press.

activities. The most popular data-collection method in grounded theory is the open-ended interview, although other strategies, especially direct observations, are often used to collect original data. Technically, any data-collection method is allowed in developing a grounded theory. Remember that what is always required in a grounded theory research study is that the theory be grounded in the data.

- **Constant comparative method** Data analysis in grounded theory research

- **Theoretical sensitivity** Thinking effectively about what kinds of data need to be collected and what aspects of already-collected data are the most important for the grounded theory

Data analysis in grounded theory is called the **constant comparative method**, and it involves constant interplay among the researcher, the data, the categories, and the developing theory. Because of the active role of the researcher in this process, it is important that the researcher have **theoretical sensitivity**, thinking effectively about what kinds of data need to be collected and what aspects of the already-collected data are the most important for the grounded theory. It involves a mixture of analytic thinking ability, curiosity, and creativity. The theoretically sensitive researcher is able to ask questions continually of the data to develop a deeper and deeper understanding of the phenomenon. Over time, the theoretically sensitive researcher will be able to develop a grounded theory that meets the criteria discussed earlier (i.e., fit, understanding, generality, and control). The more research experience you get, the more theoretically sensitive you will become. If you like to ask questions, then it is very possible that you have what it takes!

The theoretically sensitive researcher attempts continually to learn by observing and listening to research participants and by examining and thinking about the data. As was just mentioned, the researcher must constantly ask questions of the data to learn what the data are saying. During analysis, ideas and hypotheses are generated and then provisionally tested, either with additional data that have already been collected or by collecting more data. When a grounded theory study involves extended fieldwork (spending many months in the field), there will be plenty of time to collect additional data to fill in gaps in the developing grounded theory. There will also be time to verify and test propositions based on the theory. As you can see, extended fieldwork is an optimal situation because you can continue to collect important data. If all the data have to be collected in one short period of time, then the conditions for developing a convincing grounded theory are not nearly as favorable. Nonetheless, you still may be able to develop a tentative grounded theory that can be further developed in later research.

- **Open coding** The first stage in grounded theory data analysis

One of the unique parts of the grounded theory research approach is its approach to data analysis. The three types or stages of data analysis are called open coding, axial coding, and selective coding (Strauss & Corbin, 1990). **Open coding** is the first stage in grounded theory data analysis. It begins after some initial data have been collected, and it involves examining the data (usually reading transcripts line by line) and naming and categorizing discrete elements in the data. In other words, it involves labeling important words and phrases in the transcribed data. For example, let's say that you have collected interview data from 20 participants. You are reading an interview transcript, and it says, "I believe that two important properties of a good teacher are caring about your students and motivating them to learn." From this phrase, you might generate the concepts *teaching techniques*, *caring about students*, and *motivating students*. Open coding means finding the concepts like this in your data. As you continue open coding, you would continue to see whether teaching techniques are reflected again in future comments by the same person or by another person in another interview.

- **Axial coding** The second stage in grounded theory data analysis

Axial coding follows open coding. During **axial coding**, the researcher develops the concepts into categories (i.e., slightly more abstract concepts) and organizes the categories. The researcher then looks to see what kinds of things the participants mentioned many times (i.e., what themes appeared across the interviews). The researcher also looks for possible relationships among the categories in the data. A goal is to show how the phenomenon operates (i.e., showing its process). The researcher also asks questions like, How is the phenomenon manifested? What are its key features? What conditions bring about the phenomenon? What strategies do participants use to deal with the phenomenon? What are the consequences of those strategies? Creswell and Brown (1992) addressed many of these questions in their grounded theory. For example, looking at Figure 16.1, you will see that the characteristics of the phenomenon are listed under the title "Phenomena." The conditions that bring about the phenomenon are listed under "Causal conditions." Strategies are listed under "Strategies," and the consequences of the strategies are listed under "Outcomes."

Selective coding is the stage of data analysis in which the researcher puts the finishing touches on the grounded theory for the current research study. In particular, this is where the grounded theorist looks for the story line of the theory (i.e., the main idea) by reflecting on the data and the results that were produced during open coding and axial coding. The researcher will usually need to continue to analyze the data but with more focus on the central idea of the developing theory. Ultimately, it is during selective coding that the researcher writes the story, explaining the grounded theory. Here the researcher fleshes out the details of the theory. Selective coding also involves rechecking the theory with the data to make sure that no mistakes were made. The researcher also goes to the published literature during selective coding for additional ideas to consider in developing the grounded theory and in understanding its broader significance. The grounded theorist has finished analyzing the data when **theoretical saturation** occurs, that is, when no new information or concepts are emerging from the data and when the grounded theory has been thoroughly validated with the collected data.

- **Selective coding** The final stage in grounded theory data analysis

- **Theoretical saturation** Occurs when no new information or concepts are emerging from the data and the grounded theory has been validated

A grounded theory research report reflects the process of generating a grounded theory. The major research question or topic is discussed first. The participants who were selected for the study and why they were selected are also discussed early in the report. Then the methods of data collection are discussed. As you know, interviews and observations are the most popular data-collection methods in grounded theory research. The results section is the most lengthy section in the report because a grounded theory is usually based on extensive information learned in a research study. Ultimately, the final grounded theory is discussed. Glaser and Strauss, the founders of grounded theory, usually wrote book-length expositions of their grounded theories. Today, grounded theories are commonly reported in journal articles. By way of summary, we have provided an example of a grounded theory in Exhibit 16.4.

See Journal Article 16.4 on the Student Study Site.

EXHIBIT 16.4 A Grounded Theory of Instructional Leadership

Harchar and Hyle (1996) were interested in the process of instructional leadership by administrators in elementary schools. They studied known leaders (most were principals who were nominated because of their leadership abilities), and they determined what these leaders did when they were leading. Although there is much more to this journal article, we first provide a quote in which they discussed their procedures, and then we provide a quote in which they summarized their grounded theory:

> Grounded Theory served as both the theoretical structure and research design. Data collection, analysis and theory development followed Strauss and Corbin's Grounded Theory. Loosely-structured, open-ended interviews served as the primary data

(Continued)

(Continued)

> collection strategy. Following transcription, we subjected the data to three coding procedures: open, axial and selective. In open coding, the information was labeled, classified, and named, and categories developed in terms of their properties and dimensions, simultaneously and, at times, randomly. Through axial coding, the researcher arranged the data in new ways through the exploration of elements of context, intervening conditions, action/interaction strategies and consequences to those strategies. Selective coding, the last analytic process, resulted in the development of a story line, the gist of the phenomenon under study. On the basis of these related concepts, a theory was developed which described elementary instructional leadership. (p. 16)

Here is Harchar and Hyle's final description of their grounded theory.

> Through collaborative power, instructional leaders balance power inequities in the school and school community. . . . School environments are fraught with power inequities, both experiential and knowledge-based, ranging from educational and district/building experience to knowledge and preparation expertise. Within this environment, the elementary instructional leader works to develop a common vision across staff and throughout the community. Through visioning, each organizational and community supporter is empowered with direction and purpose. The principal recognizes and supports positive behaviors and confronts and defuses negative behaviors. Trust, respect and collegiality form the foundation of the school environment as all work for the development of a quality school where staff, students and community share and work toward common, dynamic goals. The importance of all organizational members is recognized and an even playing field developed from which all can and must contribute. Consistency, honesty, and visibility are key constants. The principal must demand that all teachers voice their opinions and ideas, thus fostering problem solving, constructive discourse and ownership in an equitable school environment. Even though all principals did not use the same strategies, there were general tactics used to balance power. The strategies are not linear; they occur both simultaneously and at varying times, building on each other. (pp. 26–27)

REVIEW QUESTIONS

16.7 What are the key characteristics of grounded theory?

16.8 What are the four important characteristics of grounded theory according to Glaser and Strauss?

16.9 When does the researcher stop collecting data in grounded theory research?

ACTION RESEARCH REFLECTION

Insight: Action researchers especially like qualitative research methods because these methods help them to understand the world from their students' or participants' perspectives.

1. What qualitative method(s) discussed in this chapter (phenomenology, ethnography, grounded theory) would you most want to use to learn about your students or participants?
2. What information might each of these three major methods provide you with in relation to something you might like to study?
3. Think about the distinction we made earlier about nomothetic versus idiographic causation (e.g., see Chapter 12 action research journaling insight on page 349). How might a broadened view and use of grounded theory help connect these two levels of general and local causation and help produce a "practical theory"? (Hint: How would a mixed researcher use grounded theory?)

SUMMARY

In this chapter we discussed three major approaches to qualitative research, specifically phenomenology, ethnography, and grounded theory. Although each approach follows the qualitative research paradigm, the focus of each approach is different from the others in its particular emphasis and language. In a phenomenology, the researcher is interested in obtaining a vivid description of individuals' experiences of some phenomenon. In ethnography, the researcher is also interested in getting into the heads of the people being studied. However, ethnographers are specifically interested in studying cultural groups, and they focus on cultural description and on relating cultural characteristics to human behavior. In grounded theory, the researcher focuses on inductively generating a theory grounded in the data to explain how and why some phenomenon operates. Important characteristics of a good grounded theory are fit, understanding, generality, and control.

KEY TERMS

autoethnography (p. 453)
axial coding (p. 460)
bracket (p. 445)
constant comparative method (p. 460)
culture (p. 450)
emic perspective (p. 454)
emic terms (p. 454)
essence (p. 446)
ethnocentrism (p. 454)
ethnography (p. 450)
ethnohistory (p. 453)
ethnology (p. 452)
etic perspective (p. 454)
etic terms (p. 454)
going native (p. 455)
grounded theory (p. 456)
holism (p. 455)
interpretative phenomenological analysis (IPA) (p. 446)
life-world (p. 444)
norms (p. 450)
open coding (p. 460)
phenomenology (p. 444)
selective coding (p. 461)
shared beliefs (p. 450)
shared values (p. 450)
subculture (p. 451)
theoretical saturation (p. 461)
theoretical sensitivity (p. 460)

DISCUSSION QUESTIONS

1. Which qualitative method or methods discussed in this chapter do you think would be most appropriate for studying a teacher who constantly excels above all others in a school?
2. What are some examples of a macro culture? What are some examples of a micro culture?
3. Do you think you have any tendency toward ethnocentrism? Can you think of an example?
4. If you are a teacher, what are some emic terms used by students at your school?
5. If you were interested in conducting an explanatory qualitative research study and you wanted to probe the issue of cause and effect, which qualitative method would you select? Why?

RESEARCH EXERCISES

1. Review and critique the qualitative research article at the companion website.
2. Think of a hypothetical example of a qualitative research study that would interest you in using each of the following qualitative research methods. Write a paragraph or two about each example.

a. Phenomenology
b. Ethnography
c. Grounded theory

3. Search a database at your library. Find and then list the titles of a phenomenology, an ethnography, and a grounded theory study. Also provide a brief (one-paragraph) summary of each article.
4. This exercise will help you experience phenomenology. Think about a time in your past when you were afraid. For example, you might have been afraid of the dark when you were a child. You might have been accosted by a stranger. You might have been in an accident. Try to remember how you felt and write this down in rich detail. Compare your description with some others and search for the essential characteristics of the phenomenon of being afraid.
5. We have pointed out repeatedly that one of the best ways to learn about research is to read published research articles. Here are several good examples of qualitative research articles. Go to the library and look at each article. Then choose *one* article to review.

Ethnography example

Deering, P. D. (1996). An ethnographic study of norms of inclusion and cooperation in a multiethnic middle school. *The Urban Review*, *28*(1), 21–39.

Phenomenology example

Cross, T. L., & Stewart, R. A. (1995). A phenomenological investigation of the *Lebenswelt* of gifted students in rural high schools. *Journal of Secondary Gifted Education*, *6*(4), 273–280.

Grounded theory example

Neufeldt, S. A., Karno, M. P., & Nelson, M. L. (1996). A qualitative study of experts' conceptualization of supervisee reflectivity. *Journal of Counseling Psychology*, *43*(1), 3–9.

PROPOSAL EXERCISES

If you are proposing or conducting a qualitative study, answer the following questions.

1. What is the tentative title of your study?
2. What do you hope to learn in your study?
3. What qualitative research method/methodology (or combination) will you use in your proposed study?
4. What are your research questions?
5. Who will you study? Where will you conduct your study? How many people will you study? How long will you study them?
6. What data-collection methods will you use?
7. What validity strategies will you use to help ensure the trustworthiness of your data and conclusions? (Hint: See Table 11.2 and the types of validity/trustworthiness in qualitative research discussed in Chapter 11.)

RELEVANT INTERNET SITES

Visit this site for good materials on qualitative research.
http://www.nova.edu/ssss/QR/qualres.html

Website of the Grounded Theory Institute and more
http://www.groundedtheory.com
http://www.groundedtheoryonline.com/what-is-grounded-theory
http://www.qualres.org/HomeGrou-3589.html
https://www.youtube.com/watch?v=D5AHmHQS6WQ
https://www.youtube.com/watch?v=zY1h3387txo
https://www.youtube.com/watch?v=OcpxaLQDnLk
https://www.youtube.com/watch?v=Cva4xWYquA0

Library of Congress Folklife Sourcebook, a database of ethnographic resources related to folklore, anthropology, ethnomusicology, and the humanities
http://www.afsnet.org/?page=FolkloreWiki
http://www.afsnet.org

Web page of an important writer in phenomenology, Max Van Manen, and more
http://www.maxvanmanen.com
http://www.slideshare.net/RalphBawalan/qualitative-research-phenomenology
http://plato.stanford.edu/entries/phenomenology/
http://www.iep.utm.edu/phen-psy/
https://www.sonoma.edu/users/d/daniels/phenomlect.html
https://www.ualberta.ca/~iiqm/backissues/3_1/pdf/groenewald.pdf

STUDENT STUDY SITE

Visit the Student Study Site at **edge.sagepub.com/rbjohnson6e** for these additional learning tools:

Video Links
Self-Quizzes
eFlashcards
Lecture Notes
Full-Text SAGE Journal Articles
Interactive Concept Maps
Web Resources

RECOMMENDED READING

Corbin, J., & Strauss, A. L. (2014). *Basics of qualitative research: Techniques and procedures for developing grounded theory*. Newbury Park, CA: SAGE.

LeCompte, M. D., & Preissle, J. (1993). *Ethnography and qualitative design in educational research*. New York, NY: Academic Press.

Moustakas, C. (1994). *Phenomenological research methods*. Thousand Oaks, CA: SAGE.

Schwandt, T. A. (2007). *Qualitative inquiry: A dictionary of terms*. Thousand Oaks, CA: SAGE.

Van Manen, M. (1990). *Researching the lived experience*. London, Canada: University of Western Ontario.

NOTE

1. Reprinted by permission of John Moffitt Papers, Special Collections, University of Virginia Library.

Chapter 17

Section C: Mixed Methods Research: Many Approaches

Mixed Research

LEARNING OBJECTIVES

After reading this chapter, you should be able to

- List the major strengths and limitations of qualitative research.
- List the major strengths and limitations of quantitative research.
- Define mixed research (also called mixed methods research).
- List several synonyms for the term *mixed research.*
- Explain how to use the notational system that is used to depict mixed research designs.
- Compare and contrast the nine mixed methods research designs.
- List and explain Greene, Caracelli, and Graham's (1989) five purposes or rationales for conducting mixed research.
- Describe the eight major steps in the mixed research process.
- Explain the strengths and limitations of mixed research.

Visit the Student Study Site for an interactive concept map.

RESEARCH IN REAL LIFE Improving Research With Mixed Methods

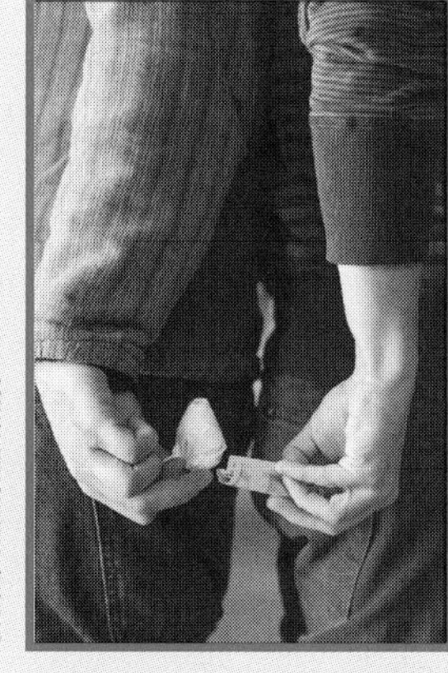
istock/MrKornFlakes

One evening in December 2001, Garmzaban was with two of his friends in a mall food court in Baltimore, Maryland, when they were approached by 16-year-old Christopher Williams and 18-year-old Richard Rodriguez. Williams and Rodriguez told Garmzaban that they wanted to purchase some marijuana. Although Garmzaban did not know either of them, he agreed to sell Williams and Rodriguez some marijuana. Williams said that his car was on the south side of the mall and the money he needed to pay for the marijuana was in the car. Garmzaban agreed to drive Williams to his car. When they arrived at his car, Williams pulled out a gun and told Garmzaban to hand over the marijuana he was carrying. Garmzaban, a former high school wrestler, started to fight with Williams. However, Williams had the gun, and he fatally shot Garmzaban in the chest (O'Brien, 2002).

Drug-related deaths such as this one are not uncommon, as Thomasina Piercy knows firsthand. Her oldest son died of a heroin overdose, stimulating her to action. In 2001, she started a drug awareness program, the Piercy Drug Program, at all of the schools in the county where she lives (McMenamin, 2002). She set up a 24-hour crisis hotline for students and an ambitious program of parent presentations; she also amassed an encyclopedic volume of substance abuse information and publishes excerpts in school newsletters each month. She and her team of community leaders also prepared skits designed to shock complacent parents who thought that drug abuse would never afflict their children. As you can see, the Piercy Drug Program has several components.

As of 2002, the Piercy Drug Program had not been formally examined for its effectiveness. Some evidence of effectiveness had come from participants who had seen the skits (which brought tears to the eyes of some parents), letters from parents, and counting the number of parents who had picked up *Not My Kid* brochures (McMenamin, 2002). This information, though useful, was limited.

If you wanted some evidence that this program was working, you could take several approaches. For example, if you were lucky, you might find secondary data that provide estimates of the percentage of students at the county schools who were involved with drugs before and after the introduction of the program (i.e., quantitative approach). You could have children and parents rate the program using rating scales (i.e., quantitative approach). You could interview parents to find out how their lives have changed and what changes they have made in their relationships with their children after being involved in the program (i.e., qualitative approach). You could interview children to determine their awareness of the risks of substance abuse and ask them about the program and their relationship with their parents (i.e., qualitative approach). Although you could take either a qualitative or a quantitative approach to assessing the effect of the program, it would be wise to take a combined (i.e., mixed) approach by collecting qualitative *and* quantitative data. Often, as you will learn in this chapter, the use of both qualitative and quantitative approaches is a more complete way to learn about phenomena in which we are interested, such as the Piercy Drug Program.

In Chapter 2, we introduced you to the three major research paradigms that are currently used in education: quantitative research, qualitative research, and mixed research. In the previous chapters, we extensively discussed the two major methods of quantitative research (experimental and nonexperimental research) and the five major methods of qualitative research (phenomenology, ethnography, case study, grounded theory, and historical research).

We now move to the mixed research paradigm, a paradigm that systematically combines or mixes ideas from both quantitative and qualitative research. To get you oriented, take a moment (yes, right now please) and review Table 2.1 (on page 34). You need to review the main characteristics of quantitative and qualitative research so that you can begin to think about mixing the different research approaches. By the way, so that you don't get confused when you read published research articles, note that various authors refer to mixed research as *mixed methods research*, *mixed method research*, *mixed methodology*, *multimethod research*, *methodological pluralism*, and *multiplism*. You will be glad to know that you can treat all of these terms as synonyms. The most commonly used term today is *mixed methods research*, which we use interchangeably with *mixed research* in this book.

As Tables 17.1 and 17.2 show, both quantitative and qualitative research have strengths and limitations. For example, quantitative research, especially experimental research, is very useful for establishing cause-and-effect relationships (strength). When based on random samples (such as in survey research), quantitative research is very useful for making statistical generalizations about populations (strength). Quantitative research is less useful for exploring new phenomena or for documenting participants' personal perspectives and personal meanings about phenomena in their lives (limitation). On the other hand, qualitative research studies behavior in naturalistic settings, which helps yield more holistic insights into educational processes that occur in particular settings (strength). Qualitative research provides in-depth and rich information about participants' worldviews and their personal perspectives and subjective meanings (strength). Qualitative research also can provide detailed information about why a phenomenon occurs (strength). However, qualitative research is typically based on small, nonrandom (i.e., purposive) samples and often is used more for exploratory or discovery purposes than for hypothesis testing and validation purposes, which means that qualitative research findings are often not very generalizable beyond the local research participants (limitation).

- **Mixed research** Research that involves the mixing of quantitative and qualitative methods or other paradigm characteristics
- **Compatibility thesis** The idea that quantitative and qualitative approaches can be thoughtfully combined in a research study
- **Pragmatist philosophy** A philosophy that says to use what works in particular situations and contexts
- **Dialectical pragmatism** The version of pragmatism specifically focused on listening to multiple paradigms and interdisciplinary perspectives

Because of the strengths and limitations of both quantitative and qualitative research, more and more researchers are advocating that studies be conducted that combine these research traditions within the same investigation. These integrated studies represent what is called mixed research. **Mixed research** is the class of research studies in which a researcher mixes or combines quantitative and qualitative research ideas, approaches, and techniques in a single research study. Proponents believe that mixed research helps improve the overall quality of research. Proponents advocate a **compatibility thesis**, which says that quantitative and qualitative approaches *can* be used together in a single research study as long as you respect the assumptions associated with quantitative and qualitative research (Table 2.1) and construct a thoughtful combination that will help you to address your research question(s) (e.g., Brewer & Hunter, 1989; Morgan, 1998; Onwuegbuzie & Johnson, 2006; Pring, 2000; Reichardt & Cook, 1979; Reichardt & Rallis, 1994; Teddlie & Tashakkori, 2009).

Researchers who conduct mixed research studies often adhere to the philosophy of pragmatism. A summary of the tenets of the philosophy of pragmatism according to its three founders—Charles Sanders Peirce, William James, and John Dewey—is provided in Table 17.3. Applied to research, the **pragmatist philosophy** is to mix research components in a way that you believe will work for your research problem, research question, and research circumstance. The pragmatist researcher carefully thinks about the perspectives provided by qualitative and quantitative research, and then he or she constructs a combined or mixed approach to address the research question or questions. I call the version of pragmatism specifically focused on listening to multiple paradigms and interdisciplinary perspectives **dialectical pragmatism** (Johnson, 2009; Johnson & Gray, 2010). The adjective

TABLE 17.1 Strengths and Limitations of Quantitative Research

Strengths

- Is useful for testing and validating already constructed theories about how and why phenomena occur.
- Is useful for testing hypotheses that are constructed before the data are collected.
- One can generalize research findings when the data are based on random samples of sufficient size.
- One can generalize a research finding when it has been replicated on many different populations and subpopulations.
- Is useful for obtaining data that allow quantitative predictions to be made.
- Is useful for determining nomothetic causation (i.e., general scientific causal relationships or scientific laws).
- The researcher may construct a situation that eliminates the confounding influence of many variables, allowing one more credibly to establish cause-and-effect relationships.
- Data collection using some quantitative methods is relatively quick (e.g., telephone interviews).
- Provides precise, quantitative, numerical data.
- Data analysis is relatively less time-consuming (using statistical software).
- The research results are relatively independent of the researcher (e.g., statistical significance).
- Study may have more credibility with many people in power (e.g., administrators, politicians, people who fund programs).
- Is useful for studying large numbers of people.

Limitations

- The researcher's categories might not reflect local constituencies' understandings.
- The researcher's theories might not reflect local constituencies' understandings.
- The researcher might miss observing phenomena because of a focus on theory or hypothesis testing rather than on theory or hypothesis generation (called the confirmation bias).
- Knowledge produced might be too abstract and general for direct application to specific local situations, contexts, and individuals.

dialectical should remind you of the importance of a back-and-forth listening and synthesis of multiple perspectives. According to a pragmatic philosophy, you also need to make your value positions and desired outcomes explicit.

See Journal Article 17.1 on the Student Study Site.

For example, you might state that you will consider the research good if it leads to explanation, prediction, rich description, social justice, and/or fewer inequalities (e.g., based on gender, class, or ethnicity). We contend that dialectical pragmatism (henceforth called pragmatism) offers the philosophy that best supports mixed research.

Recently, Johnson and colleagues have extended and transformed dialectical pragmatism into a full philosophy/theory known as *dialectical pluralism* (Johnson, 2012, 2013, 2016; Johnson & Stefurak, 2013). **Dialectical pluralism** is a fully developed philosophy and metaparadigm that (a) assumes reality in our world is multifaceted and plural (cf. subjective, intersubjective, objective reality; different disciplinary realities; different levels of reality; etc.) and (b) relies on dialectical, dialogical, and hermeneutical/interpretative approaches to discussion, learning from differences, and working together to produce shared team-based products. If you ever work in a research team, you should examine this philosophy in more depth, share it with your colleagues, and use it to guide your team process. The following references explain the social psychological strategies used with dialectical pluralism: (a) Johnson, 2016 and (b) Johnson, Onwuegbuzie, Tucker, & Icenogle, 2014.

Dialectical pluralism A metaparadigm and philosophy that assumes reality is plural and relies on dialectical, dialogical, and hermeneutical approaches to learn from others and produce team-based research products

The pragmatist takes seriously but is not *overly* concerned about many long-standing philosophical divides that exist among some researchers who consider themselves either quantitative or qualitative researchers. The pragmatist is much more concerned about doing

TABLE 17.2 Strengths and Limitations of Qualitative Research

Strengths

- Data are based on the participants' own categories of meaning.
- Is useful for studying a limited number of cases in depth.
- Is useful for describing complex phenomena.
- Provides individual case information.
- One can conduct cross-case comparisons and analysis.
- Provides understanding and description of people's personal experiences of phenomena (i.e., the emic or insider's viewpoint).
- Can describe in rich detail phenomena as they are situated and embedded in local contexts.
- The researcher almost always identifies contextual and setting factors as they relate to the phenomenon of interest.
- The researcher can study dynamic processes (i.e., documenting sequential patterns and change).
- The researcher can use the primarily qualitative method of grounded theory to generate inductively a tentative but explanatory theory about a phenomenon.
- Can determine how participants interpret constructs (e.g., self-esteem, IQ).
- Data are usually collected in naturalistic settings in qualitative research.
- Qualitative approaches are especially responsive to local situations, conditions, and stakeholders' needs.
- Qualitative researchers are especially responsive to changes that occur during the conduct of a study (especially during extended fieldwork) and may shift the focus of their studies as a result.
- Qualitative data in the words and categories of participants lend themselves to exploring how and why phenomena occur.
- One can use an important case to demonstrate a phenomenon vividly to the readers of a report.
- Is useful for determining idiographic causation (i.e., causes that we see, experience, and intentionally produce in our lives; causes of particular events).

Limitations

- Knowledge produced might not generalize to other people or other settings (i.e., findings might be unique to the relatively few people included in the research study).
- It is difficult to make quantitative predictions.
- It is more difficult to test hypotheses and theories with large participant pools.
- The study might have less credibility with some administrators and commissioners of programs.
- Collecting data generally takes more time than with quantitative research.
- Data analysis is often time-consuming.
- The results are more easily influenced by the researcher's personal biases and idiosyncrasies.

"what works" (i.e., conducting research that provides useful answers to important research questions and provides "practical theory" that works locally). Rather than expecting to find final proof (which we can't obtain anyway in empirical research, as seen in Chapter 1), the pragmatist researcher attempts to provide evidence that meets the epistemological standard of what John Dewey called **warranted assertability**. If an educational researcher provides strong evidence for his or her claims about what practices are effective, then the researcher has met this standard.

▪ **Warranted assertability** The standard you meet when you provide very good evidence

Mixed researchers view the use of multiple perspectives, theories, and research methods as a strength in educational research. This fits well with what is a cardinal rule in virtually all kinds of research: *Use multiple sources of evidence to warrant or justify your claims.* Mixed researchers believe that mixed research can usually produce a study that is superior to one produced by either quantitative research or qualitative research alone. As was noted in Chapter 2, when you mix research or when you read and evaluate research that involves mixing, you should always be sure to consider the **fundamental principle of mixed research**.

TABLE 17.3 General Characteristics of Pragmatism

- The project of pragmatism is to find a middle ground between philosophical dogmatisms and skepticism and to find a workable solution (sometimes including outright rejection) to many long-standing philosophical dualisms about which agreement has not been historically forthcoming.
- Rejects traditional dualisms (e.g., rationalism vs. empiricism, realism vs. antirealism, free will vs. determinism, Platonic appearance vs. reality, facts vs. values, subjectivism vs. objectivism) and generally prefers more moderate and commonsense versions of philosophical dualisms based on how well they work to solve problems.
- Recognizes the existence and importance of the natural or physical world as well as the emergent social and psychological world, which includes language, culture, human institutions, and subjective thoughts.
- Holds in high regard the reality and influence of the inner world of human experience in action.
- Knowledge is viewed as being both constructed *and* based on the reality of the world we experience and live in.
- Replaces the historically popular epistemic distinction between subject and external object with the naturalistic and process-oriented organism-environment transaction.
- Endorses fallibilism; that is, current beliefs and research conclusions are rarely, if ever, viewed as perfect, certain, or absolute.
- Justification comes in the form of what Dewey called "warranted assertability."
- According to Peirce, "reasoning should not form a chain which is no stronger than its weakest link, but a cable whose fibers may be ever so slender, provided they are sufficiently numerous and intimately connected" (1868/1997, pp. 5–6).
- Theories are viewed instrumentally. They become true and they are true to different degrees based on how well they currently work; workability is judged especially on the criteria of predictability and applicability.
- Endorses eclecticism and pluralism. For example, different, even conflicting, theories and perspectives can be useful and true: Observation, experience, and experiments are all useful ways to gain an understanding of people and the world.
- Human inquiry (i.e., what we do in our day-to-day lives as we interact with our environments) is viewed as being analogous to experimental and scientific inquiry. We all try out things to see what works, what solves problems, and what helps us to survive. We obtain warranted evidence that provides us with answers that are ultimately tentative (i.e., inquiry provides the best answers we can currently muster), but in the long run, use of this "scientific" or evolutionary or practical epistemology moves us toward some larger Truths.
- Endorses a strong and practical empiricism as the path to determine what works.
- Views current truth, meaning, and knowledge as tentative and as changing over time. What we obtain on a daily basis in our lives and in our research should be viewed as provisional truths.
- Capital *T* Truth (i.e., absolute Truth) is what will be the "final opinion," perhaps at the end of history. Lowercase *t* truths (i.e., the instrumental and provisional truths that we obtain and live by in the meantime) are given through experience and experimenting.
- Instrumental truths are a matter of degree (i.e., some estimates are more true than others). Instrumental truth is not "stagnant," and therefore James (1907/1910) stated that we must "be ready to-morrow to call it falsehood" (p. 223).
- Prefers action to philosophizing (pragmatism is, in a sense, an anti-philosophy).
- Takes an explicitly value-oriented approach to research that is derived from cultural values; specifically endorses shared values such as democracy, freedom, equality, and progress.
- Endorses practical theory (theory that informs effective practice; praxis).
- Organisms are constantly adapting to new situations and environments. Our thinking follows a dynamic homeostatic process of belief, doubt, inquiry, modified belief, new doubt, new inquiry, . . . in an infinite loop, in which the person or researcher (and research community) constantly tries to improve upon past understandings in a way that fits and works in the world in which he or she operates. The present is always a new starting point.
- Generally rejects reductionism (e.g., reducing culture, thoughts, and beliefs to nothing more than neurobiological processes).
- Offers the "pragmatic method" for solving traditional philosophical dualisms as well as for making methodological choices.

According to this principle, researchers should thoughtfully and strategically mix or combine qualitative and quantitative methods, approaches, procedures, concepts, and other paradigm characteristics in a way that produces an overall design with multiple (divergent and convergent) and complementary (broadly viewed) strengths and nonoverlapping weaknesses (Brewer & Hunter, 1989; Johnson & Turner, 2003; Webb, Campbell, Schwartz, Sechrest, &

Fundamental principle of mixed research Advises researchers to thoughtfully and strategically mix or combine qualitative and quantitative research methods, approaches, procedures, concepts, and other paradigm characteristics in a way that produces an overall design with multiple (divergent and convergent) and complementary (broadly viewed) strengths and nonoverlapping weaknesses

Grove, 1981). The fundamental principle offers a "logic" for mixed research; it should help you think about how you should mix or combine qualitative and quantitative approaches in a single research study to answer your research question(s) (Johnson, Onwuegbuzie, & Turner, 2007). To get started, use Table 17.1 (strengths and limitations of quantitative research) along with Table 17.2 (strengths and limitations of qualitative research) as you think about how you want to combine qualitative and quantitative research in your research study so that you meet the requirements of the fundamental principle.

For example, you have learned that experiments can provide very strong conclusions about the presence of a cause-and-effect relationship. Experiments, however, are usually based on convenience (i.e., nonrandom) samples. They tend to be strong on internal validity (i.e., causal validity) but weaker on external validity (generalizing validity). You might decide to check your experimental research finding using a survey based on a probability sample (if the research question can be studied this way). If the finding is corroborated (i.e., the same research finding is obtained in both the experimental data and the survey data), then you will have increased the generalizability of the research finding. You can often improve experiments even further by conducting in-depth interviews and focus groups (i.e., collecting some qualitative data) to get at the research participants' perspectives and meanings that lie behind the experimental research findings and numbers. We have provided a list of the strengths and limitations of mixed research in Table 17.4. In addition, in Exhibit 17.1 we show how mixed research can improve the traditional gold standard for establishing cause and effect in experimental research.

TABLE 17.4 Strengths and Limitations of Mixed Research

Strengths

- Words, pictures, and narrative can be used to add meaning to numbers.
- Numbers can be used to add precision to words, pictures, and narrative.
- Can strategically combine quantitative and qualitative research strengths in a single study to cover a single purpose better or to cover multiple purposes well in a single study. (This is the principle of complementary strengths.)
- One can increase generalizability of qualitative research by including a quantitative, "large-n" component in the study.
- One can understand the mean (e.g., average effects) *and* the variance (i.e., important variation that characterizes humans).
- Researcher can generate and test a mixed methods grounded theory.
- Can answer a broader and more complete range of research questions because the researcher is not confined to a single method or research approach.
- Can provide fuller, deeper, more meaningful answers to a single research question.
- Can concurrently study and link nomothetic (general) *and* idiographic (particularistic) causation, link theory and practice, and produce "practical theory."
- The mixed research designs discussed in this chapter have specific strengths and limitations that should be considered. For example, in a two-phase sequential design, the phase 1 results can be used to develop and inform the purpose and design of the phase 2 component.
- A researcher can use the strengths of an additional method to overcome the limitations of another method by using both in a research study. (This is the principle of nonoverlapping weaknesses.)
- Can provide validation and stronger evidence for a conclusion through convergence and corroboration of findings. (This is the principle of triangulation.)
- One can document generalities *and* the complexity and mechanisms explaining them.
- One can obtain multiple stakeholders' perspectives on reality.
- Can add insights and understanding that might be missed when only a single method is used.
- Qualitative data can identify quantitative measurement problems and help the researcher rectify such problems.

- Qualitative components can insert an exploratory and feedback loop into otherwise quantitative studies.
- Quantitative data can insert understanding of amount and frequency into otherwise qualitative studies.
- Quantitative sampling approaches can be used to increase the generalizability of qualitative results.
- Combining qualitative and quantitative research produces integrated knowledge that best informs theory and practice.

Limitations

- It can be difficult for a single researcher to carry out both qualitative and quantitative research, especially if two or more approaches are expected to be done concurrently (i.e., the study might require a research team).
- The researcher has to learn about multiple methods and approaches and understand how to mix them appropriately.
- Methodological purists contend that one should always work within either a qualitative or quantitative paradigm.
- It is more expensive.
- It is more time-consuming.
- Some of the details of mixed research remain to be worked out fully by research methodologists (e.g., problems of paradigm mixing, techniques for qualitatively analyzing quantitative data, how to integrate data and inferences, and how to interpret conflicting results).

EXHIBIT 17.1 The Benefits of the Mixed Research Approach to Improve the "Gold Standard" for Causation

Many research methodologists argue that the RCT (randomized controlled/clinical trial) is the "gold standard" for establishing evidence of cause and effect. As stated in Chapter 12, an RCT is an experimental design with random assignment of participants to two groups: a treatment group that receives what is expected to produce the desired outcome (such as a new medicine, an educational program, etc.) and a no-treatment control group (that receives the "placebo" or does not participate in the educational program). When possible, double-blind procedures also should be used so that neither the researcher nor the participant knows the specific condition (experimental or control) that the participant is in. As you learned in Chapter 12, this kind of strong experimental design meets the three required conditions for causation quite well (relationship between the independent variable [IV] and dependent variable [DV]; proper time order, with changes in the IV coming before changes in the DV; and ruling out of all plausible alternative explanations or rival hypotheses).

Mixed methods researchers have made a strong argument that this traditional "gold standard" design *can be made even better through the use of a mixed research approach.* The following strategies outline when and how mixed research can provide an advantage and improve the RCT. We label this approach the *MM-RCT approach* (where MM-RCT stands for mixed methods, randomized controlled trial).

I. Strategies to Use Before the RCT

Make decisions about conceptual, cultural, and contextual factors:

- Determine fit of conceptual framework (theory) for population and setting.
- Determine program need/fit and factors needing measurement.
- Determine the nature of the context (e.g., social, political, cultural) environment, program (e.g., resources, staffing), and participants.
- Determine relevance of constructs (consider cultural relevance and social validity) and underlying theory that will guide program development.
- Begin checking auxiliary and background assumptions that will be necessary to conduct the planned RCT and interpret the results.

(Continued)

(Continued)

Make decisions about data-collection instruments/outcome measurement:

- Develop data-collection instruments that are meaningful to participants.
- Make sure the constructs of interest will be measured and will be measured appropriately; consider both proximal and distal measures.
- Obtain thick, "meaningful" qualitative data at baseline to supplement quantitative data.

Engage stakeholders:

- Facilitate participatory process for engaging stakeholders in identifying foci for change.
- Determine how to promote the evaluation and obtain participation.

II. Strategies to Use During the RCT

Examine acceptability and control group perceptions:

- Determine acceptability of program to stakeholders.
- Use insider knowledge to help explain reasons for attrition; this can help inform diagnoses of missing data patterns, support corrective statistical procedures, and help determine whether sample loss is directly related to treatment condition (i.e., acceptability as it relates to treatment condition).

Document integrity:

- Determine whether and how well the educational program is being implemented in the field and identify potential problems as they arise.
- Provide data for decision making about needed adaptations to environmental conditions/situations and contexts.
- Identify challenges encountered during implementation.

Strengthen internal (causation) validity:

- Obtain additional case data to help rule out rival hypotheses and strengthen internal validity (e.g., intensely examine cases where the intervention worked well and those that did not to supplement nomological causality with idiographic causality).
- Identify "other" factors/variables operating in the field that may influence outcomes.
- Identify threats to internal validity such as potential history effects, whether maturation appears to occur, potential ceiling and floor effects, differential selection, and other selection interactions.

Explore causal hypotheses/theory generation:

- Identify new/additional moderating variables that were not identified at the outset of the study.
- Identify intervening or mediating variables operating between the independent and dependent variables.
- Describe the process of change as it occurs in context and attempt to observe temporal ordering of variables in causal chains of outcomes.
- Generate grounded theories.
- Add understanding of explanatory causation in addition to traditional descriptive causation.
- Collect hard-to-quantify data on contexts, cultures, and changing conditions that appear to facilitate or inhibit program impact.
- Collect data about motives, emotions, and reasons that often are neglected in traditional measurement and analyses of human/social causation.

- Explore success cases and non-success cases to explore causal factors in operation.
- Identify unintended outcomes (what Michael Scriven calls *goal-free evaluation*).
- Identify omitted variables to improve specificity of the theoretical and model to be tested statistically.
- Add a discovery/generative dimension to an otherwise testing/justification approach to research.
- Study individuals (in addition to groups) to learn what happens for each individual.

Facilitate transferability/external (generalizing) validity:

- Collect "meaningful, thick, contextual" data to help consumers understand the subtleties of the intervention-context interaction and aid in generalizing the report findings.
- Document complexity through individual case analyses to facilitate understanding of what occurs in real time at an individual level, in contrast to comparing aggregate means.

III. Strategies to Use After the RCT

Explore acceptability and social-cultural validity:

- Gain better understanding of practical and clinical significance by seeing what a program means in individuals' lives (i.e., social validity); consider taking the impact estimate into account (e.g., strong effect, no effect, negative effect) during this process.
- Retrospectively explore the acceptability of the program from participants' perspectives.

Examine integrity and internal validity:

- Collect data from participation as a manipulation check: How do participants describe the intervention?
- Determine which ways used to tailor the intervention worked.
- Collect open-ended retrospective data from participants about process and implementation.
- Have multiple participants tell their stories about what happened.
- Use traditional qualitative strategies for promoting validity (or trustworthiness or legitimation), including researcher-as-detective, triangulation, peer review or interpretations, member checking, and negative case sampling.

Examine transferability and external validity:

- Continue to document the meanings, the characteristics of the participants, and the context to improve external (generalizing) validity.
- Determine participants' views about useful future directions for improving program and evaluation procedures.

Strengthen outcome-evidence and process-outcome links:

- Collect open-ended retrospective data from participants about the program's impact, unintended influences, and outcomes.
- Conduct measurement checks: Did the measures mean what the researchers assumed they meant? Were important outcomes and nuances missed by the quantitative measures?
- Have participants react to conclusions about them and offer their emic interpretations.
- Make pre-to-post comparisons on qualitative data as well as experimental-to-control group comparisons.
- Explore process-outcome links.
- Compare dropouts to non-dropouts.
- Explore data or collect additional in-depth qualitative data with an eye toward understanding null results.

Note: Ideas in this exhibit are adapted from Hitchcock, J., Johnson, R. B., & Nastasi, B. K. (2009, November). RCT-MM designs: An attempt to improve upon the causal "gold standard." Paper presented at the American Evaluation Association Conference, Orlando, FL.

REVIEW QUESTIONS

17.1 What position does the mixed researcher take on the compatibility thesis and pragmatist philosophy?

17.2 Why is the fundamental principle of mixed research important?

THE RESEARCH CONTINUUM

Mixed research provides a framework for conducting a study that incorporates quantitative and qualitative research approaches. Typically, in each mixed research study, a combination of quantitative and qualitative data is collected, analyzed, validated, and interpreted using systematic principles. As shown in Figure 17.1, mixed research takes most of the space on the research continuum that varies from not mixed (i.e., what is called *monomethod*) to fully mixed. A monomethod research study, at the far left of the continuum, involves the exclusive use of either a quantitative or qualitative research approach. As long as both quantitative and qualitative research approaches are used within the same investigation, the study moves from being monomethod to at least a partially mixed method, even if one of the research approaches is used only minimally. As you move to the right on the research continuum, the mixing or integration of elements of quantitative and qualitative research becomes greater and greater.

For example, the following study would be situated relatively far to the left on the research continuum (i.e., not strongly mixed): The researcher conducts a primarily quantitative research study using a questionnaire in which the participants use 5-point scales to show agreement with many statements measuring several factors, but the researcher also includes one open-ended question on that questionnaire to provide some limited qualitative data. For instance, at the end of the structured questionnaire based on rating scales, it is common for survey researchers to include an open-ended question that says, "Please list any additional thoughts that you have here." In contrast, more strongly mixed research involves more extensive mixing of qualitative and quantitative approaches (e.g., inductive and deductive), research methods (e.g., experiments and grounded theory), data analysis (e.g., combining the qualitative and quantitative data into one overall set of data), and interpretation (e.g., considering the findings from the perspective of a qualitative researcher and from the perspective of a quantitative researcher). In short, mixing can take place in many different ways and to varying degrees.

In mixed research, the researcher should, at a minimum, integrate the results during data analysis and interpretation to provide a full picture of the phenomenon being studied. There are probably an infinite number of ways in which qualitative and quantitative techniques can be mixed, but each single study can be placed on the research continuum showing the degree of mixing. In the next section, we introduce you to some specific mixed methods research *designs*.

See Journal Article 17.2 on the Student Study Site.

FIGURE 17.1 The research continuum

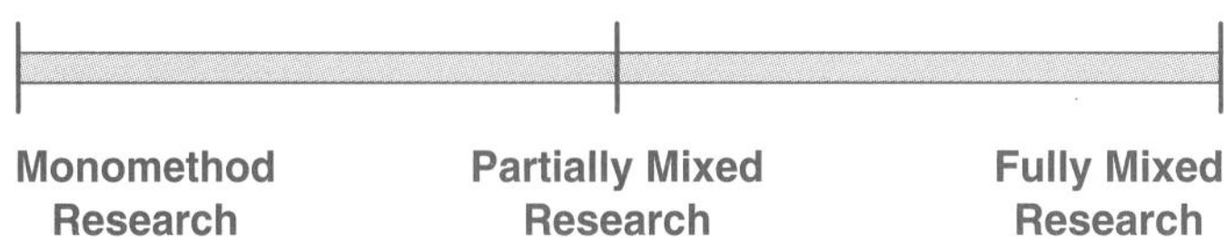

Types of Mixed Research Designs

Mixed research is a rapidly developing field. As such, many mixed research designs are still being developed. There are several competing typologies of mixed research (i.e., lists of types of designs). We provide what we consider to be the best introductory typology in this chapter.

In our basic and practical typology of mixed designs, we conceptualize mixed methods research as a function of two fundamental dimensions: (1) time orientation of the qualitative and quantitative components (concurrent vs. sequential) and (2) paradigm/research-approach emphasis (equal emphasis vs. primary/core-component emphasis with a supplemental component added; cf. Morse, 1991; Morgan, 1998, 2014). *Time orientation* refers to whether the qualitative and quantitative components or phases of the study occur at approximately the same time (i.e., concurrently) or whether they are organized into phases over time (i.e., sequentially). *Paradigm emphasis* refers to whether the qualitative and quantitative components are given approximately equal emphasis in the research study (i.e., equal-status/interactive design) or whether one component is primary and the other is secondary (i.e., as in a qualitatively driven design or a quantitatively driven design). If you use our typology to select a design, you make two major decisions: First, decide whether your study will operate largely within one primary paradigm or not and, second, decide whether you want to conduct the qualitative and quantitative components concurrently or sequentially.

Crossing the two dimensions we just mentioned (i.e., paradigm emphasis and time order) produces a 2 (equal emphasis vs. primary/core emphasis) by 2 (concurrent vs. sequential) matrix with 4 cells. This matrix is shown in Figure 17.2. To understand the specific designs shown in these four cells, however, you must become familiar with some notation that is commonly used in mixed methods research (Morse, 1991). The symbol system works like this:

- The letters *qual* or *QUAL* stand for qualitative research.
- The letters *quan* or *QUAN* stand for quantitative research.
- Capital letters denote priority or increased weight or a core role in the study.
- Lowercase letters denote lower priority or weight or supplemental role in the study.
- A plus sign (+) represents a concurrent collection of data.
- An arrow (→) represents a sequential collection of data.

For example, the combination of symbols QUAL + QUAN indicates a design in which the qualitative and quantitative paradigms are given equal weight or equal priority (both are in caps) and are conducted concurrently (see the plus sign). The combination of the symbols QUAL → quan indicates that the qualitative paradigm is emphasized in the research study (*QUAL* is in capital letters, and *quan* is lowercase) and a follow-up quantitative component is included to supplement the study (see the arrow between *QUAL* and *quan*). Now you try it. What would this set of symbols indicate: qual → QUAN? (Answer: It indicates that the quantitative paradigm is emphasized and that a qualitative phase is followed sequentially by the quantitative phase.) Now you know a new symbol system. Don't forget to share it with your friends!

Now take a moment to examine the nine designs shown in Figure 17.2. As you can see, some of the cells include more designs than others (e.g., there is only one equal-emphasis concurrent design, but there are four primary-emphasis sequential designs). In actual

- **Qualitatively driven design** Mixed research design in which the qualitative perspective or way of thinking is emphasized and some quantitative data are added to the study
- **Quantitatively driven design** Mixed research design in which the quantitative perspective or way of thinking is emphasized and some qualitative data are added to the study

research practice, some designs are more commonly used than others. For example, many researchers are trained in a single research paradigm, and if they conduct mixed research, they tend to use one core approach (either QUAL or QUAN) and supplement it with the other approach (quan or qual), producing a **qualitatively driven design** or a **quantitatively driven design**. For example, predominantly qualitative researchers often will include a supplementary quantitative component in their research without changing their overall paradigm or approach to research. Likewise, predominantly quantitative researchers often will include a supplementary qualitative component without changing their overall paradigm or approach to research. As mixed research grows over time as a research paradigm, we expect to see more and more equal-emphasis or fully interactive designs. Such designs are most easily carried out through the use of a research team composed of researchers with different strengths (Johnson et al., 2014).

In addition to *selecting* one of the nine mixed designs in our 2 × 2 matrix, you also can start thinking about how to *construct your own design*. Please remember this point: Research questions come before research methods—methods are the tools you use to help obtain answers to your research questions. Therefore, if a standard design is not available that fits your research questions and needs, you can use the components provided above to construct your own design (for additional components, see Exhibit 17.2 shown on page 489). You can indicate several characteristics of your mixed research study using the symbols in the notation system provided above. First, you can indicate if your study is *concurrent* (e.g., QUAL + quan), *sequential* (e.g., QUAL → quan), or a combination of concurrent and sequential (e.g., [QUAL + quan] → QUAL). Second, in sequential designs, you can indicate the order of qualitative and quantitative parts; for example, in a QUAL → QUAN → QUAL design, a qualitative phase is conducted first, a quantitative phase is conducted second (building on the prior phase), and a second qualitative phase is conducted last (building on the prior phases). Third, you can indicate whether your study is qualitatively driven or is quantitatively driven or whether both types of research are given equal priority. Finally, for the interested reader, we have included some additional design dimensions for your consideration in Exhibit 17.2 at the end of this chapter (p. 489).

FIGURE 17.2 Mixed methods design matrix

Paradigm Emphasis Decision	Time Order Decision: Concurrent	Time Order Decision: Sequential
Equal Status	QUAL + QUAN	QUAL→QUAN QUAN→QUAL
Dominant Status	QUAL + quan QUAN + qual	QUAL→quan qual→QUAN QUAN→qual quan→QUAL

Examples of Qualitatively Driven, Quantitatively Driven, and Equal-Status or Interactive Studies

An example of a study based on a *qualitatively driven concurrent design* was conducted by McVea et al. (1996); the title of this article is "An Ounce of Prevention? Evaluation of 'Put Prevention Into Practice' Program." The researchers evaluated the effectiveness of the Put Prevention Into Practice program by examining how well it worked with family physicians, their staff, and patients in eight private-practice settings. The specific design was a QUAL + quan design. The quantitative component (the component with less weight) involved collection of office environment and clinical encounters checklist data. The qualitative component, which took place concurrently, had the primary emphasis because more qualitative data were collected than quantitative data and the qualitative data were collected for a longer period of time than were the quantitative data. The qualitative phase involved participant observations of clinic operations and patient encounters, in-depth interviews with physicians and staff members, and encounters with patients after their care. Obtaining the insiders' views was a key part of the study. The quantitative and qualitative data were analyzed separately before being compared near the end of the study.

An example of a study based on a *quantitatively driven sequential design* was conducted by Way, Stauber, Nakkula, and London (1994) and published with the title "Depression and Substance Use in Two Divergent High School Cultures: A Quantitative and Qualitative Analysis." They specifically used a QUAN → qual design. First, a structured questionnaire was administered to students in suburban and urban high schools. The questionnaires measured student depression, substance abuse, and several demographic variables. During data analysis, the researchers found a positive correlation between depression and substance abuse (i.e., the higher the depression, the higher the substance abuse) for students in the suburban high schools but not for students in the urban high schools. In the second phase, the researchers conducted follow-up qualitative interviews with the most depressed students from both urban and suburban high schools to explore why the relationship was present only for suburban students. They found that suburban students saw drugs as a way to escape problems. In contrast, the urban students saw drugs more as a cause of their problems. Phase 2 was used in a complementary way; specifically, phase 2 data and results helped clarify the phase 1 finding about the relationship between depression and substance abuse.

Up to this point, the examples of mixed research that we have provided were carried out in a single research study. Although usually a mixed design requires that your study be a single research study, the word *study* can be viewed broadly because you might have to publish the qualitative and quantitative results in separate publications and/or your research program might purposively shift from one approach to another because of the need for qualitative and quantitative approaches to help achieve your research aims. Therefore, we view the word *study* broadly in this example. For the following evaluative study of an antipoverty program, the researchers formed a team, but they published the results of their *equal-status sequential design* (QUAN → QUAL) in two reports. The first part of this study was published by Bos et al. (1999) with the title *New Hope for People With Low Incomes: Two-Year Results of a Program to Reduce Poverty and Reform Welfare*. These researchers conducted phase 1 of an evaluation of the New Hope program.

New Hope was a 2-year voluntary antipoverty initiative that took place in selected inner-city neighborhoods in Milwaukee, Wisconsin. In this program, residents from these neighborhoods who worked for 30 hours a week received, when appropriate, a wage subsidy, health insurance, and child care benefits. Bos et al. (1999) evaluated this first phase of the project using quantitative research techniques. Specifically, they used a randomized experiment, focusing on causal explanations of targeted program outcomes. These targeted outcomes included poverty reduction, full-time employment, and child and family well-being. Bos et al. collected administrative records and family and teacher surveys both at baseline and at the end of the 2-year program. The experimental and control groups were compared on the quantitative data.

The qualitative phase of this study was started at the 2-year point of the New Hope program (after the quantitative phase just described). This part consisted of an ethnographic study with the goal of obtaining an in-depth understanding of the meaningfulness of the participants' experiences over the first 2 years of the program (Weisner, 2000). Approximately one half of the treatment and control group members were interviewed, and their responses were compared. In this sequential study (i.e., phases 1 and 2), the quantitative and qualitative data sets were analyzed separately, and mixing took place in interpreting the final results. In this study, published with the title "Understanding Better the Lives of Poor Families: Ethnographic and Survey Studies in the New Hope Experiment," the quantitative data and design provided evidence that the New Hope program was working. The qualitative, ethnographic data provided insights into how members of the different groups viewed their participation and their circumstances, both complementing and corroborating the quantitative data.

REVIEW QUESTIONS

17.3 What is mixed methods research?

17.4 What kind of study does this notation imply: qual → QUAN + qual. Can you think of why a researcher might use such a design?

17.5 What is the difference between a sequential and a concurrent design feature?

STAGES OF THE MIXED RESEARCH PROCESS

The mixed research process discussed in this chapter follows eight iterative steps:

1. Determine whether a mixed design is appropriate.
2. Determine the rationale for using a mixed design.
3. Select or construct a mixed research design and mixed sampling design.
4. Collect data.
5. Analyze the data.
6. Continually validate the data.
7. Continually interpret the data and findings.
8. Write the research report.

These steps are shown in Figure 17.3. Although all research starts with one or more research questions, the rest of the steps can vary in order (i.e., they are not necessarily linear as implied by the figure). For example, interpretation and validation are ongoing processes. Also, writing the research report is shown as the last step in the research process, although some preliminary writing or the writing of some sections of a report often occurs before the end of a research project. The arrow leading back to the first step shows that the research question(s) or objective(s) can even be reformulated during a single research study or subsequent studies. Each of these steps is discussed in more detail below.

FIGURE 17.3 Important steps in a mixed research study with your research questions at the core of the study.

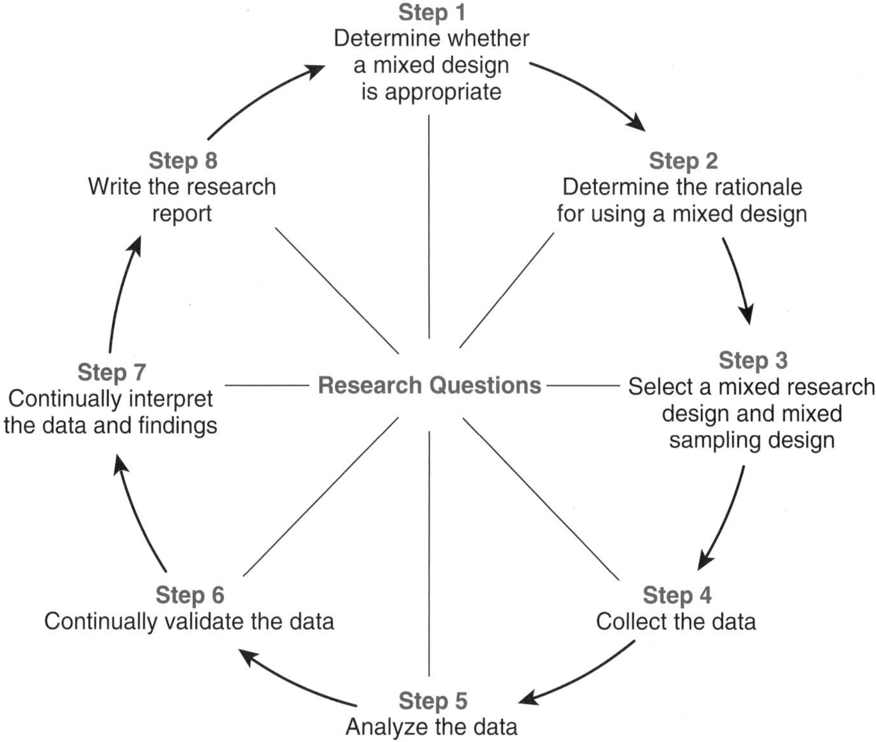

Note: Although the steps are numbered, researchers often move around in the circle in multiple directions (especially in steps 4 through 7). Feedback loops can occur at any place.

Step 1. Determine Whether a Mixed Design Is Appropriate

You learned in Chapter 4 that all empirical research starts by selecting a research topic (i.e., the broad subject matter area to be investigated), identifying a research problem (i.e., the educational issue or problem within a broad topic area), determining the research purpose (i.e., a statement of the intent or objective of the study), and finally coming up with the research question(s) (i.e., the very specific question that you have determined needs to be answered). Sometimes, especially in quantitative research, a statement of the hypothesis is also made (i.e., the researcher makes a prediction about the research outcome).

Once you have identified your research questions, it is helpful to determine the objective of your research. As we discussed in Chapter 1, there are five major research objectives in educational research: exploration, description, explanation, prediction, and influence. These five objectives are just as relevant when conducting mixed research as they are when using monomethods. Furthermore, it is common in mixed research to have more than one objective for your research study.

What is unique in mixed research is that the research problem and your research question or set of questions suggest to you that a mixed design is appropriate. For example, you might need to explore the language of a group of people and then develop a standardized questionnaire that will work for them. Or perhaps you want to develop a grounded theory, but after developing it, you want to test the theory empirically on an independent group of people to assess the emergent theory's generalizability or transferability. Both of these examples imply a mixed research study.

If you are willing to go the route of mixed research, this means that you are willing to take a pragmatic position toward your research and that you do not view any single method dogmatically. You are open-minded, flexible in a thoughtful way, and creative. You probably adhere to the compatibility thesis rather than the incompatibility thesis. Although you might feel that one paradigm tends to have the best overall approach for studying educational problems, if you use a mixed design, it is apparent that you are open to collecting both quantitative and qualitative data to help answer your research question(s).

An important consideration, before making the final decision to design a mixed study, is to make sure that the study you are planning is feasible. Mixed designs might be new in the research literature on your topic and might not yet be well established in practice. Mixed methods studies are typically more expensive, so if expense is a major issue, you might decide to do just one part of your study now and wait until later to do another part (i.e., you might decide to mix methods across your research program, rather than mixing methods in a single study).

Step 2. Determine the Rationale for Using a Mixed Design

Once you have decided that a mixed design is needed for your research, the next step is to determine your rationale for using a mixed design. What do you want to achieve by mixing quantitative and qualitative approaches? How will mixing approaches help you in answering your research questions? In answering these questions, we recommend that you consider Greene and colleagues' (1989) framework (see Table 17.5). Their framework is based on using one of the following five broad rationales for a mixed research study: (1) triangulation, (2) complementarity, (3) development, (4) initiation, and (5) expansion.

1. *Triangulation* is the term given when the researcher hopes for convergence, correspondence, and corroboration of results from different methods studying the same phenomenon. When you want to make a statement with confidence, you want your pieces of evidence to lead to the same overall conclusion or inferences. Triangulation can substantially increase the credibility or trustworthiness of a research finding.

2. The purpose is said to be *complementarity* when the investigator seeks elaboration, enhancement, illustration, and clarification of the results from one method with results from the

other method. This helps you in understanding the overlapping and different facets of a phenomenon.

3. *Development* is the name given when the researcher uses the results from one method to help inform the other method.
4. *Initiation* refers to discovering paradoxes and contradictions as well as providing different perspectives that may lead to a reframing of the research question or results.
5. Finally, the purpose of research is called *expansion* when the investigator attempts to expand the breadth and range of inquiry by using different methods for different inquiry components. For example, you might use qualitative research to study an educational program's process (i.e., how it works) and use quantitative research to study the program's outcomes.

Determining the mixed research purpose using Greene and colleagues' (1989) framework helps further to form or select a mixed research design. For example, if the purpose and empirical outcome of the research are triangulation, then, at the very least, mixing should occur during data interpretation and report writing. If the purpose is development, then a sequential design is needed. (For an additional set of rationales for mixed research, see Collins, Onwuegbuzie, & Sutton, 2006.)

TABLE 17.5 Greene, Caracelli, and Graham's List of Purposes for Mixed Research

Purpose	*Explanation*
Complementarity	Seeks elaboration, enhancement, illustration, and clarification of the results from one method with the results from the other method.
Triangulation	Seeks convergence, correspondence, and corroboration of results from different methods.
Development	Seeks to use the results from one method to develop or inform the other method, where development is broadly construed to include sampling and implementation as well as measurement decisions.
Initiation	Seeks the discovery of paradox and contradiction, new perspectives and new frameworks, and the recasting of questions or results from one method with questions or results from the other method.
Expansion	Seeks to extend the breadth and range of inquiry by using different methods for different inquiry components.

Source: Based on Greene, Caracelli, and Graham (1989).

Step 3. Select or Construct the Mixed Research Design and Mixed Sampling Design

When selecting or constructing a mixed design, researchers have all the research methods, research designs, and research strategies at their disposal that are discussed in the other chapters of this book. That's part of the beauty of mixing. You are not bound by any particular philosophy, style, or method. You are free to be creative, as long as the design that you create is useful and is appropriate for your research questions. For example, an experimental approach in a quantitative phase of a mixed research study could be followed up with qualitative interviews to get at the participants' insights and experiences regarding their participation in the experiment (as a manipulation check or validity check). In the mixed research world, one could even conduct an experiment (a quantitative research method) by collecting qualitative data, although such a study might be difficult and time-consuming in practice (and it would be better to collect both quantitative and qualitative data).

Once you have decided that a mixed research design is needed, you need to craft your specific mixed design. If you are using the design typology in Figure 17.2, then you will need to answer these two questions:

1. Is the qualitative or quantitative paradigm going to be given priority, or will both be given equal status in your study?
2. Should the qualitative and quantitative components be carried out concurrently or sequentially?

Your answer to those two questions leads you to one of the four cells shown in Figure 17.2. You can check to see whether one of the mixed methods designs in Figure 17.2 is appropriate for your study. If your study requires a more complex design, then you can still use the designs shown in Figure 17.2 as a starting point for configuring your design. For example, you might decide that you first need to collect some exploratory qualitative data, then conduct an explanatory and confirmatory quantitative stage, and then follow this phase with additional qualitative interviews to explore and help interpret the earlier findings. In this case, you would use a qual → QUAN → qual design.

To further aid you in the design construction process, read Exhibit 17.2 which is located at the end of this chapter on page 489 (and is considered optional, for the more advanced student). In contrast to our design typology in Figure 17.2 (which is based on two key dimensions), the multidimensional approach provided in Exhibit 17.2 includes multiple dimensions for your consideration. The two key ideas emphasized in Exhibit 17.2 are (a) oftentimes you will need to *construct* rather than *select* your mixed methods research design, and (b) in order to construct a strong design, you should consider the multiple dimensions provided in the Exhibit.

In addition to selecting/constructing the mixed research design, you will need to determine which mixed *sampling* design fits your research needs. We showed how to construct ten mixed sampling designs in the last section in Chapter 10. The overall design of the qualitative and quantitative parts of your study also should follow good qualitative and quantitative design principles (e.g., the quantitative component might use a randomized experiment). You can also modify part of your study design, if needed, during the conduct of a mixed research study. For example, perhaps your early findings provide a serendipitous insight and suggest a change in the kind of data you need to collect or the sequence of your activities.

Step 4. Collect Data

Data in mixed research designs can be collected on the same sample or on different samples. You can use any of the various ways of selecting samples in quantitative and qualitative research, which are classified (see Chapter 10) as random sampling (i.e., simple, stratified, systematic, and cluster) and nonrandom sampling (i.e., convenience, quota, purposive, snowball/network, comprehensive, maximum variation, homogenous sample, extreme-case, typical-case, critical-case, negative-case, opportunistic) techniques. Any combination of random sampling and nonrandom sampling can be used in mixed research. For example, random sampling can be used in the quantitative phase and nonrandom sampling in the qualitative phase.

Mixed researchers also have the full complement of data-collection methods at their disposal. Specifically, as presented in Chapter 9, all six major methods of data collection (i.e., tests, questionnaires, focus groups, observations, interviews, and secondary or existing data) should be considered. You must determine the most appropriate combination of data-collection methods depending on your research questions, your research objective(s), and your rationale for using mixed research.

Step 5. Analyze the Data

When analyzing quantitative data, mixed researchers can select from the whole range of techniques available. Mixed researchers can use quantitative data analysis procedures, which you will learn about in Chapters 18 and 19, as well as qualitative data analysis procedures, discussed in Chapter 20. The combination of approaches usually will fit into one of the types of mixed data analysis discussed in Chapter 20. Your choice of analysis should be driven by the research objective(s), research purpose, research questions/hypotheses, and type of data collected.

In mixed research, researchers sometimes conduct quantitative analyses of qualitative data and/or perform qualitative analyses of quantitative data. The former can be accomplished by undertaking what Tashakkori and Teddlie (1998) called quantitizing data. **Quantitizing** data involves converting qualitative data into numerical codes and then using statistical analysis techniques with the data. This typically involves some form of counting or numerical representation. For example, a researcher who is interviewing students to find out their experiences in an educational research class could construct a frequency distribution that shows the number of times words such as *anxiety* and *fun* are used during the interviews. Thus, words or themes are converted to numbers. You might also determine the percentage of participants who contribute to a theme you see in your data; the idea is to give some evidence of amount or how often qualitative statements or results occur.

- **Quantitizing** Converting qualitative data into quantitative data

Conversely, qualitative analyses of quantitative data can be undertaken by converting quantitative data into narrative representations that can be analyzed qualitatively, or **qualitizing** (Tashakkori & Teddlie, 1998). For instance, quantitative scales can be converted to categories based on the numeric scores. You might take scores based on a 4-point scale—(1) *strongly disagree*, (2) *somewhat disagree*, (3) *somewhat agree*, (4) *strongly agree*—and decide to merge options 1 and 2 and merge options 3 and 4, categorizing participants' responses into "disagree" or "agree." Another popular way of qualitizing data is through narrative profile formation (e.g., modal profiles, average profiles, comparative profiles, holistic profiles, normative profiles). The idea is to create narrative descriptions from numeric data. For example, Teddlie and Stringfield (1993) studied effective schools and qualitized numeric performance data into the following qualitatively defined school profiles: (a) stable more effective, (b) stable less effective, (c) improving, and (d) declining. The profiles were used to add meaning to evolving perspectives on the schools. For additional information on conducting mixed research data analysis, see Onwuegbuzie and Teddlie (2003).

- **Qualitizing** Converting quantitative data into qualitative data

Step 6. Continually Validate the Data

In Chapter 11, we introduced you to the key validity issues in quantitative, qualitative, and mixed research. As discussed in that chapter, the primary mixed research types of legitimation or validity are sample integration, inside-outside, weakness minimization, sequential, conversion, paradigmatic mixing, commensurability, political, and multiple validities. The last type of legitimation or validity for mixed research (i.e., multiple validities) tells you to identify and use a combination of the relevant quantitative and qualitative validity types for your mixed study. As a reminder, the primary quantitative research types of validity are internal, external, construct, and statistical conclusion validity, and the primary qualitative research types of validity are descriptive, interpretative, and theoretical validity. In mixed research, establishing and assessing research validity is a cyclical and ongoing process. An initial assessment of data and conclusion validity may lead to more data being collected (e.g., extended fieldwork and participant feedback).

Step 7. Continually Interpret the Data and Findings

It is important to remember that data interpretation begins as soon as the very first data are collected and it continues throughout a research study. Once most or all of the data have been collected, analyzed, and validated, the mixed researcher is in a position to begin the formal process of interpreting the data. In a sequential study, the data collected in phase 1 are interpreted before the researcher moves on to phase 2. For example, interpretations made here might be used developmentally to help inform phase 2 data collection and interpretation. Phase 2 data collection and interpretations in a sequential design may also be undertaken for one of the additional rationales discussed earlier, such as collecting more data for the purpose of triangulation, complementarity, initiation, and/or expansion.

See Journal Article 17.3 on the Student Study Site.

In a concurrent mixed research study, the qualitative and quantitative data can be interpreted separately or together, depending on the research purpose and rationale. However, more often than not, some integration or comparison occurs during data interpretation. This integration produces meta-inferences because this type of mixing can help the researcher identify convergence, inconsistency, and contradiction in the data. The ultimate goal of the mixed researcher, as with monomethod researchers, is to form trustworthy conclusions after ruling out as many rival hypotheses as possible. Therefore, data validation and data interpretation are extremely interactive, reciprocal, and important to forming accurate and defensible conclusions.

Step 8. Write the Research Report

Once conclusions have been formulated and assessed for validity, the mixed researcher is ready to write the final report. The researcher can write separate reports for the quantitative and qualitative phases. For example, in the New Hope study, the quantitative data (Bos et al., 1999) and qualitative data (Weisner, 2000) were written up separately. However, the two phases are more likely to be integrated in one report, either by presenting the two sets of findings and interpretations in separate sections or by fully integrating them in the same section. In any case, mixed research reports contain the same features as do most monomethod reports, including review of the related literature, methods, results, and discussion. Typically, the Results section is the longest section in the report because it contains both the quantitative and qualitative findings. A well-written report will be highly descriptive of all eight phases of the mixed research process. Even when the quantitative phase is emphasized, mixed researchers should always contextualize their reports; that is, they should carefully communicate the context in which the mixed research study took place. Contextualization not only helps the mixed researcher examine how the quantitative and qualitative findings relate to one another but also helps readers know the extent to which they can generalize the findings. Also, where possible, mixed research reports should be holistic, with both the parts of the whole and the whole being described adequately.

In writing a report, the mixed researcher should always be aware of and address four potential problems. The first problem stems from the fact that quantitative research and qualitative research traditionally have yielded different styles of writing. In particular, quantitative reports have traditionally been relatively impersonal and formal, whereas qualitative reports tend to be more personal and informal. Thus, a challenge to mixed researchers is to strike a balance between the two forms of writing without compromising the integrity of either the quantitative or the qualitative sections of the report.

A second problem is that of writing to audiences that likely are not sufficiently versed in both qualitative and quantitative techniques. Therefore, the mixed researcher should not take highly specialized quantitative, qualitative, or mixed research terms for granted and should define any research terms that are likely to be unknown to the audience; the researcher should provide useful references for readers who want to expand their understanding of the related concepts. Endnotes can play a useful role here.

A third problem pertains to the length of mixed research studies. Because mixed studies involve two or more components or phases, the reports tend to be longer than those stemming from monomethod studies. This is a problem when mixed researchers attempt to publish their reports because most journals have strict page limits. Fortunately, more and more reputable online journals are emerging, which often are more liberal in the number of pages allowed. Mixed researchers also should consider publishing their reports as monographs, book chapters, and books to have more page space available. Additionally, it might be appropriate for mixed researchers to publish the different phases of their studies separately, especially if the phases are sequential over a long period of time, as was the case in the New Hope evaluation study (Bos et al., 1999; Weisner, 2000).

The final problem that mixed researchers may face is the fact that mixed research is still an emerging field. Mixed research now appears to be accepted by most as the third major research or methodological paradigm, and mixed research studies are increasing dramatically in the literature. However, occasionally, some readers, especially pure qualitative or pure quantitative researchers, might not be very open to mixed research reports and might read them with negative biases. This is a particular problem with manuscripts that are being read by skeptical journal editors and reviewers, who might reject them because of their philosophical orientation, regardless of their quality. Encouragingly, many journals that routinely publish mixed research are now available (e.g., *Field Methods*, *Quality and Quantity*, *Evaluation*, *Evaluation Practice*, *Educational Evaluation and Policy Analysis*, *Research in Nursing & Health*, and *Research in the Schools*), and the list is growing. Also, several special issues on mixed methods have been published (i.e., *International Journal of Social Research Methodology: Theory & Practice*, *Evaluation & Research in Education*, *Journal of Research in Nursing*, and *Research in the Schools*) or planned for publication (i.e., *Quality & Quantity: International Journal of Methodology*). In fact, two relatively new journals have been founded that focus on mixed research; they are the *Journal of Mixed Methods Research* and the *International Journal of Multiple Research Approaches.*

In an effort to gain more credibility, it is essential that mixed researchers show the highest degree of organization and rigor. We believe that using mixed research frameworks such as those outlined in this chapter will help in this quest.

17.6 What are the eight stages of the mixed research process?

17.7 Explain each of Greene, Caracelli, and Graham's (1989) five rationales for conducting a mixed research study.

17.8 What is the difference between quantitizing and qualitizing?

17.9 What kinds of validity might be relevant in a mixed design?

LIMITATIONS OF MIXED RESEARCH

Although mixed research studies have great potential for enhancing understanding of the issues facing educational research, there are several limitations. First and foremost, because they use more complex designs than do monomethod studies, they tend to require more time and resources to undertake.

Second, mixed methods research requires expertise in designing and implementing both qualitative and quantitative phases. For this reason, several pragmatist researchers (e.g., Rossman & Wilson, 1994) recommend that more than one researcher be engaged in a mixed research study, each bringing a unique methodological expertise to the team.

Third, some mixed research studies yield contradictory findings, especially between the quantitative and qualitative phases. Although sometimes viewed as a weakness, this also is a very important strength because with the use of a single approach, the researcher would be blind to the different ways the phenomenon can be understood. Conflicting findings can motivate additional data collection in the original study or new studies in which the research objective, purpose, and/or questions are reframed to reflect better the current state of knowledge. However, such extensions require additional investment of time, expertise, resources, and effort. Moreover, when stakeholders and policymakers are dependent on a single mixed research study to set policy, conflicting findings not only make it difficult to form firm recommendations but also can potentially promote division among interested parties. Therefore, mixed researchers must deliberate carefully about how to report contradictory findings to users of the results.

Fourth, little is known about the relative merits of the different types of mixed research designs proposed in this chapter and elsewhere. Research methodologists need to systematize this knowledge and make it readily available to other researchers. Such information is needed so that researchers will be in a position to choose a design that has the most potential to address their mixed research objective(s). Nevertheless, as the number of mixed research studies increases, this information will become available.

17.10 What are the four potential problems involved in writing and attempting to publish a mixed research report?

REVIEW
QUESTION

EXHIBIT 17.2 A Multiple-Dimension Approach to Mixed Design (Optional)

In this chapter (e.g., see Figure 17.2), we provide a basic two-dimension typology for getting you started with designing your mixed research study. The text asks you to think about

a. whether you want to emphasize one primary approach (QUAL or QUAN) with the other approach acting as a supplement to the core approach or if you want to give equal priority to qualitative and quantitative research approaches (often this requires a research team); and

b. if you need a concurrent design to answer your questions (i.e., qualitative and quantitative approaches used at approximately the same time), a sequential design (i.e., qualitative first or quantitative first, with the second stage building on and/or supplementing the first stage), or a more complex design based on the pieces provided (e.g., a concurrent design with prior or subsequent sequential components added).

Figure 17.2 specifically showed nine designs (resulting from the two dimensions) and pointed out that they can also be put together in more complex arrangements. We believe this approach to design is helpful for beginning researchers but, ultimately, falls short in more advanced research. For readers interested in building on their knowledge and learning a more advanced and more flexible approach to design, we recommend that you consider multiple key dimensions and *construct* your own design (Schoonenboom & Johnson, in press). All current design typologies (ours included) are based on a small number of dimensions (typically two to four dimensions) and are, therefore, limited. To help you remember our more advanced approach, we call it the multiple-dimension process approach (MDPA) to mixed design.

As with our two-dimension approach, the first key point of the MDPA approach is to start with your research questions. Using MDPA, however, asks you to think next about what combination of data, methods, and multiple additional dimensions will provide you with the best chance of obtaining accurate, relatively complete, and useful answers to your research questions. MDPA fills a void in the current mixed methods literature by showing that there are multiple dimensions to consider when designing your study.

Before examining the dimensions, it is important that you understand that the following list is not exhaustive, you will likely never use all of the dimensions, and the list is fluid in the sense that other researchers should continually build additional dimensions into the "multiple-dimension process approach." Nonetheless, you should examine and think about our dimensions before you start your study and carefully address the dimensions that you will need to build into your design and study.

List of Primary and Secondary Mixed Methods Research Design Dimensions

Primary Dimensions

1. *Purpose for mixing.* Why are you mixing? Here are a few purposes: complementarity; triangulation; development; initiation; expansion; credibility; incorporation of context; incorporation of illustration; utility; discover-*and*-confirm; include diversity of views; achieving multiple participation, social justice, and action; determining what works for whom; producing interdisciplinary substantive theory; juxtaposition-dialogue/comparison *and* synthesis; breaking down binaries/dualisms; explaining interaction between/among natural and human systems; and explaining generality *and* complexity and mechanisms.

2. *Theoretical drive.* Will the study have (a) an inductive/qualitative drive (with quantitative data as supplementary), (b) a deductive/quantitative drive (with qualitative data as supplementary), or (c) equal status drive (where quantitative and qualitative data and approaches equally drive the study)?

3. *Timing.* Will you use a sequential design, a concurrent design, or a combination design (e.g., a "concurrent-sequential design" that is concurrent in one or more stages that is/are preceded or followed by another stage or stages)?

4. *Point of integration.* Where will the quantitative and qualitative approaches be brought together, interrelated, and integrated (e.g., conceptualization, data set, analysis, results)?

5. *Typological vs. constructed design.* Will the researcher *select* an a priori design from a known design typology or will the researcher *construct* a new, nuanced design tailored to his or her specific research questions?
6. *Planned vs. emergent design.* Will the research design be fixed before data collection or will parts of the design be allowed to emerge during the study (e.g., additional or modified research questions, new sources of data, etc.), or will a combination design be used?

Secondary Dimensions

1. *Phenomenon.* If the ontological object of study is multidimensional, then the design must be tailored to address each dimension.
2. *Social scientific theory.* If a substantive theory is to be used to generate hypotheses or aid in scientific explanation, then the design must address the objects and processes identified by the theory.
3. *Ideological drive.* If the researcher plans to use an explicit ideology (e.g., feminism, critical race theory, class stratification theory, etc.), then the design must provide the needed information and type of knowledge.
4. *Combination of sampling methods.* What combination of quantitative and qualitative sampling methods will be used to obtain the research group(s) and participants?
5. *Degree to which the research participants will be similar or different.* Will only one kind of research participant be studied, resulting in a homogeneous sample, or do the research questions require multiple kinds of people and perspectives to be examined?
6. *Degree to which the researchers on the research team will be similar or different.* Do the research purpose and research questions suggest a need to use researchers from different philosophical paradigms and/or different research disciplines?
7. *Type of implementation setting.* Will the study be conducted in the laboratory or naturalistically in the field, or is a combination of these needed?
8. *Degree to which the methods similar or different.* Greene (2007) recommends that many mixed methods studies should include research methods that are likely to provide different or divergent information and perspectives (e.g., tests, observations, and interviews).
9. *Validity criteria and strategies.* How will the researcher design the study so that the issue of *multiple validities legitimation* is achieved (i.e., using the pertinent package of qualitative, quantitative, and mixed validities for the particular research study)?
10. *Full study vs. multiple studies.* Will the mixing occur within one study or across multiple, closely related studies on a single topic?

ACTION RESEARCH REFLECTION

Insight: Mixed research is the action researcher's favorite research approach.

1. Why do action researchers tend to favor mixed research approaches?
2. Whom can you draw upon for different but worthwhile perspectives on your action research procedures and results?
3. If you were to conduct an equal-status mixed methods study, do you think you could do it by yourself, or would you use a team of researchers with different perspectives? If you need a team, whom would you choose to work with? Why?
4. What mixed design best fits your action research plan?

SUMMARY

This chapter has provided a framework for conducting mixed research. We briefly summarized the philosophy of pragmatism, which says to use any combination of method or research techniques that works in answering your research question(s). Also, we reviewed the fundamental principle of mixed research, which prescribes that you use a mixture or combination that has complementary strengths and nonoverlapping weaknesses. To help you in using the fundamental principle, you can use Tables 17.1 and 17.2, which show the strengths and limitations of quantitative and qualitative research, respectively. You should also use the tables showing the strengths and limitations of the different methods of data collection that are provided in the Chapter 9 lecture at the companion website.

We pointed out that in mixed research, a combination of quantitative and qualitative data is collected, analyzed, validated, and interpreted using systematic techniques. We noted that using some combination of both quantitative and qualitative research approaches within the same inquiry makes that inquiry a mixed research investigation. Next, we described our typology of mixed research designs. This typology (shown in Figure 17.2) is based on consideration of time orientation (i.e., concurrent vs. sequential) and paradigm emphasis (i.e., equal-status design vs. either a qualitatively driven design or a quantitatively driven design status), yielding nine distinct mixed research designs. We showed you how to use basic notation to symbolize each of these designs, and we provided some examples of mixed designs from the published literature. In Exhibit 17.2 at the end of the chapter, we provide a more advanced approach for constructing mixed designs.

We next specified and described the eight steps in the mixed research process: determine whether a mixed design is appropriate, determine the rationale for using a mixed design, select or construct a mixed research design and mixed sampling design, collect data, analyze the data, continually validate the data, continually interpret the data and findings, and write the research report.

The final section of the chapter presented the major limitations of mixed research. In this section, we noted that mixed researchers must be cognizant of these limitations, especially those that pertain to time, expertise, resources, and effort expended. Clearly, a number of methodological issues must be considered before conducting a mixed research study. Nevertheless, the potential gains achieved by mixing methods are great: greater diversity and collaboration among researchers with different orientations, more comprehensive findings, increased confidence in results, increased conclusion validity, more insightful understanding of the underlying phenomenon, promotion of more creative ways of collecting data, and increased synthesis or integration of theories. Therefore, the limitations of mixed research should be weighed against the numerous potential benefits of this approach.

KEY TERMS

compatibility thesis (p. 468)
dialectical pluralism (p. 469)
dialectical pragmatism (p. 468)
fundamental principle of mixed research (p. 470)
mixed research (p. 468)
pragmatist philosophy (p. 468)
qualitatively driven design (p. 478)
qualitizing (p. 485)
quantitatively driven design (p. 478)
quantitizing (p. 485)
warranted assertability (p. 470)

DISCUSSION QUESTIONS

1. Which of the following do you tend to like the best: qualitative research, quantitative research, or mixed research? Why?
2. How could you apply the fundamental principle of mixed research? Give an example.

3. Which of the rationales for conducting mixed research do you think is the most important in the area of research that is most important to you (triangulation, complementarity, development, initiation, or expansion)? Why?

4. Try to think of a hypothetical study design that includes quantitative and qualitative components. What would you call the design?

RESEARCH EXERCISES

1. If you are proposing or conducting a mixed methods research study, answer the following questions to help clarify your thinking.
   a. What are your research questions and/or hypotheses?
   b. What is the rationale for using a mixed design in your research study?
   c. What mixed research design will you use?
   d. What methods of data collection will you use? If there is an ordering (i.e., sequence) to your data collection, please explain it.
   e. How will you analyze your data?
   f. How will you validate your data?
   g. How and when will you interpret your data?
   h. Write out your anticipated table of contents (i.e., the important headings you expect to use in your report).

2. Locate a published article that is based on mixed methods research. Explain how the study relates to each of the eight steps of mixed research:
   a. Was a mixed design appropriate, given the research questions and objectives?
   b. Which of the five rationales for using a mixed design (shown in Table 17.5) best fits your research article?
   c. What mixed research design did the researcher use?
   d. What kind of data were collected?
   e. How did the researchers analyze the data?
   f. How did the researchers validate the data?
   g. When and how do you suspect the researchers interpreted the data?
   h. How was the journal article organized and written?

3. Using the criteria in the previous question, review and critique the mixed research article at the companion website.

4. Write a three-page paper comparing and contrasting the two major typologies of mixed methods research discussed in this chapter. One is shown in Figure 17.2, and the other is shown in Exhibit 17.2.

PROPOSAL EXERCISES

If you are proposing to use a mixed methods research design, please answer the following questions and integrate your answers into your written research proposal:

1. What are your qualitative and quantitative research questions, or questions to be addressed both qualitatively and quantitatively (see Chapter 4)?
2. What is your mixed research purpose (see Chapter 4)?
3. What is your purpose for mixing (see Exhibit 17.2, Primary Dimension 1)?
4. What qualitative and quantitative "methods of data collection" will you use (see Chapter 9)? Explain why.
5. What "research method(s)"/methodology(ies) will you use (see Chapters 12–16)? Explain why.
6. What combination of sampling methods will you use, and what "mixed sampling method" results (see Chapter 10)?
7. What is your mixed methods research design? Did you select a design (is so, from where) or did you construct your design? What are the characteristics of your design (see primary and secondary design characteristics in Exhibit 17.2)? Be sure to draw a picture of your design and utilize the notation provided in this chapter (e.g., [Qual + QUAN] → QUAL).

RELEVANT INTERNET SITES

Mixed Methods International Research Association
http://mmira.org

Journal of Mixed Methods Research
http://mmr.sagepub.com/

Bridges: Mixed Methods Network for Behavioral, Social, and Health Sciences
https://www.linkedin.com/groups/1888486

A free book entitled *The 2002 User-Friendly Handbook for Project Evaluation*
http://www.nsf.gov/pubs/2002/nsf02057/nsf02057_1.pdf

More
https://www.youtube.com/watch?v=1OaNiTlpyX8
https://www.youtube.com/watch?v=L8Usq_TPfko
https://www.youtube.com/watch?v=oO3cspRrq4E

STUDENT STUDY SITE

Visit the Student Study Site at **edge.sagepub.com/rbjohnson6e** for these additional learning tools:

Video Links
Self-Quizzes
eFlashcards
Lecture Notes
Full-Text SAGE Journal Articles
Interactive Concept Maps
Web Resources

RECOMMENDED READING

Greene, J. C., & Caracelli, V. J. (Eds.). (1997). *Advances in mixed-method evaluation: The challenges and benefits of integrating diverse paradigms* (New Directions for Evaluation, no. 74). San Francisco, CA: Jossey-Bass.

Hesse-Biber, S. N., & Johnson, R. B. (Eds.). (2015). *Oxford handbook of multimethod and mixed methods research inquiry*. New York, NY: Oxford.

Johnson, R. B., Onwuegbuzie, A. J., & Turner, L. A. (2007). Toward a definition of mixed methods research. *Journal of Mixed Methods Research*, *1*(2), 1–22.

Tashakkori, A., & Teddlie, C. (Eds.). (2010). *Handbook of mixed methods in social and behavioral research* (2nd ed.). Thousand Oaks, CA: SAGE.

PART V

Analyzing the Data

Chapter 18

Descriptive Statistics

LEARNING OBJECTIVES

After reading this chapter, you should be able to

- Explain the purpose of descriptive statistics.
- Distinguish between inferential and descriptive statistics.
- Explain the difference between a frequency distribution and a grouped frequency distribution.
- Read and interpret bar graphs, line graphs, and scatter plots.
- Calculate the mode, median, and mean.
- List the strengths and weaknesses of the mode, median, and mean.
- Explain positive skew and negative skew.
- Explain the impact of skewness on the measures of central tendency.
- Describe and interpret the different measures of variability.
- Calculate the range, variance, and standard deviation.
- Explain percentile ranks and *z* scores.
- Explain how to construct and interpret a contingency table.
- Explain the difference between simple and multiple regression.
- Explain the difference between the *y*-intercept and the regression coefficient.

Visit the Student Study Site for an interactive concept map.

RESEARCH IN REAL LIFE Describing Data Accurately

istock/skynesher

During the 1960s and 1970s and continuing into this century, there has been concern about discrimination and ensuring that it does not occur. The following vignette is a simplified version of what happened at the University of California–Berkeley in 1973. The admissions data suggested that there was gender discrimination in admissions to graduate programs at Berkeley, but when the data were examined more carefully, it was clear that discrimination did not exist. In this example, we show you the kind of data that suggested discrimination and the kind that did not. This case was written up in *Science* (Bickel, 1975), and the results are due to what is called Simpson's paradox.

Assume that you work in the College of Education admissions office at your local university. You find that the acceptance rate for men is 55% (i.e., 55% of the men who apply to your school are accepted) and the acceptance rate for women is 44%. What would you conclude? Would you conclude that gender discrimination might be occurring? After all, men are being accepted at a significantly higher rate than are women.

Let's say that the numbers for your university are shown in the following table:

	Number Applied	*Number Admitted*	*Percentage Admitted*
Men	360	198	55%
Women	200	88	44%

You, however, know a little bit about statistics and decide to delve further into the data. There only are two departments in your College of Education, so you decide to look at the admissions rates for each of the two departments. These results are shown below. Here is what you find when you look at the acceptance rate for both departments: Women (not men) are more likely to be admitted in both departments!

	DEPARTMENT A				*DEPARTMENT B*		
	Number Applied	*Number Admitted*	*Percentage Admitted*		*Number Applied*	*Number Admitted*	*Percentage Admitted*
Men	120	18	15%	Men	240	180	75%
Women	120	24	20%	Women	80	64	80%

In other words, when you look at your data more carefully, you find out that women are more likely to be admitted, and it is clear now that the claim of discrimination against women is unlikely. In this example, the overall data suggested one thing, but when the data were examined more carefully, a completely different conclusion was apparent. One reason for the surprising result is that men were more likely to apply to the department that was easy to get into while women were more likely to apply to the department that was harder to get into. Our purpose for this chapter is to show how to describe your data accurately so that you can inform your audience and not mislead them.

- **Descriptive statistics** Statistics that focus on describing, summarizing, or explaining data
- **Inferential statistics** Statistics that go beyond the immediate data and infer the characteristics of populations based on samples
- **Data set** A set of data

The field of statistics is a branch of mathematics that deals with the analysis of numerical data. It can be divided into two broad categories called descriptive statistics and inferential statistics. In **descriptive statistics**, the goal is to describe, summarize, or make sense of a particular set of data. The goal of **inferential statistics** is to go beyond the immediate data and to infer the characteristics of populations based on samples. As you can see in Figure 18.1, inferential statistics may be subdivided into estimation and hypothesis testing, and estimation may be divided into point and interval estimation. In this chapter, we focus on descriptive statistics, and in the next chapter, we focus on inferential statistics. Our discussion requires very little mathematical background, so don't worry! We focus more on interpretation than on calculation. We do, however, show you how to perform a few basic calculations, so get your calculator handy.

DESCRIPTIVE STATISTICS

Descriptive statistics starts with a set of data, sometimes called a **data set**. The researcher attempts to convey the essential characteristics of the data by arranging the data into a more interpretable form (e.g., by forming frequency distributions and generating graphical displays) and by calculating numerical indexes, such as averages, percentile ranks, and measures of spread. The researcher can summarize the variables in a data set one at a time. He or she can also examine how the variables are interrelated (e.g., by examining correlations). The

FIGURE 18.1 Major divisions in the field of statistics

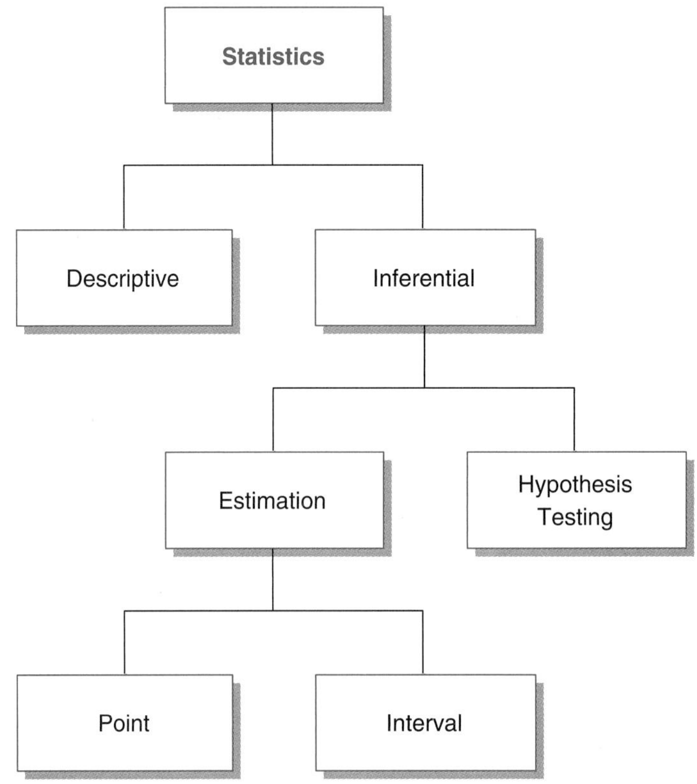

key question in descriptive statistics is how we can communicate the essential characteristics of the data. An obvious way would be to supply a printout of the complete set of data. However, we can do much better than that!

See Tools and Tips 18.1 on the Student Study Site.

We have included a data set in Table 18.1 that we will use in several of our examples in this chapter and the next. We refer to this data set as the "college student data set." The hypothetical data are for 25 recent college graduates. Data values are provided for three quantitative variables—starting salary, grade point average, and GRE Verbal scores—and for two categorical variables—college major and gender. Take a look at Table 18.1 now to see what a data set looks like. Notice that the data set is structured so that the cases (i.e., individuals) are represented in rows and the variables are represented in columns. This cases-by-variables arrangement is the standard way of organizing data after data collection has been completed. (The SPSS file for our data set is provided at the student companion website.)

TABLE 18.1 Hypothetical Set of Data for 25 Recent College Graduates

Person	*Starting Salary*	*GPA*	*College Major*	*Gender*	*GRE Verbal Score*
1	31,000	2.9	2	1	154
2	32,000	3.6	1	1	160
3	33,000	3.7	1	1	160
4	28,000	2.4	2	0	150
5	37,000	3.4	3	0	153
6	32,000	3.0	3	0	153
7	33,000	3.1	2	0	154
8	25,000	2.5	1	1	150
9	38,000	3.0	3	0	163
10	33,000	2.7	2	0	152
11	30,000	3.0	2	1	153
12	32,000	2.6	1	0	158
13	32,000	3.1	2	1	152
14	31,000	3.1	1	1	155
15	24,000	2.5	1	1	151
16	40,000	3.3	3	0	162
17	31,000	3.3	1	1	154
18	38,000	3.2	2	1	161
19	35,000	3.1	3	1	165
20	32,000	3.2	2	0	156
21	41,000	3.5	3	0	165
22	34,000	3.0	3	1	159
23	28,000	3.0	1	1	163
24	30,000	2.9	2	0	152
25	36,000	3.5	2	0	158

Note: For the categorical variable *college major*, the value labels are 1 = education, 2 = arts and sciences, and 3 = business. For the categorical variable *gender*, the value labels are 0 = male and 1 = female.

REVIEW QUESTION

18.1 What is the difference between descriptive statistics and inferential statistics?

FREQUENCY DISTRIBUTIONS

■ **Frequency distribution** Arrangement in which the frequencies of each unique data value are shown

One of the most basic ways to describe the data values of a variable is to construct a frequency distribution. A **frequency distribution** is a systematic arrangement of data values in which the data are rank ordered and the frequencies of each unique data value are shown. Just follow these steps, and you can construct a frequency distribution for the data values of any variable:

1. List each unique number in ascending or descending order in column 1. If a particular number appears more than once, remember to list it only once. For example, even if the number 3 appears five times, list it only once. If a number does not appear in the data, do not list it.
2. Count the number of times each number listed in column 1 occurs and place the results in column 2.
3. (Optional) Construct a third column by converting column 2 into percentages by dividing each number in column 2 by the total number of numbers.

Thus, the first column shows the unique data values, the second column shows the frequencies, and the third column shows the percentages.

TABLE 18.2 Frequency Distribution of Starting Salary

(1) *Starting salary (X)*	*(2)* *Frequency (f)*	*(3)* *Percentage (%)*
24,000	1	4.0
25,000	1	4.0
28,000	2	8.0
30,000	2	8.0
31,000	3	12.0
32,000	5	20.0
33,000	3	12.0
34,000	1	4.0
35,000	1	4.0
36,000	1	4.0
37,000	1	4.0
38,000	2	8.0
40,000	1	4.0
41,000	1	4.0
	$n = 25$	100.0%

Note: Column 2 shows the frequency distribution. Column 3 shows the percentage distribution.

For example, look at Table 18.2. This frequency distribution is for the variable *starting salary* from the college student data set provided in Table 18.1. You can see in column 1 that the lowest starting income is $24,000 and the highest starting income is $41,000. The frequencies are shown in column 2. For example, the most frequently occurring starting income for our recent college graduates was $32,000. Percentages are shown in column 3. For example, 20% of the students started at $32,000 per year, and 4% started at $41,000 per year.

When a variable has a wide range of data values, interpretation may be facilitated by collapsing the values of the variable into intervals. The result is called a **grouped frequency distribution** because the data values are clustered, or grouped, into intervals. Researchers typically construct around five to eight equal-sized intervals. We constructed a grouped frequency distribution for starting income, which you can see in Table 18.3. Column 1 shows the intervals. As before, the frequencies are shown in column 2, and the percentages are shown in column 3. You can see that the most frequent interval is $30,000–$34,999. This interval includes 14 of the data values, which make up 56% of all starting income data values.

In constructing a grouped frequency distribution, it is important that the intervals be **mutually exclusive**. This means that there is no overlap among the intervals. (The intervals $20,000–$25,000 and $25,000–$30,000 are not mutually exclusive because a person earning $25,000 can be placed into two intervals.) It is also important that the intervals be **exhaustive**. A set of intervals is exhaustive when it covers the complete range of data values. If all the data values fall into the set of intervals, the intervals are exhaustive.

- **Grouped frequency distribution** The data values are clustered or grouped into intervals, and the frequencies of each interval are given
- **Mutually exclusive** The property that intervals do not overlap
- **Exhaustive** The property that a set of intervals covers the complete range of data values

TABLE 18.3 Grouped Frequency Distribution of Starting Salary

Starting Salary (X)	*Frequency (f)*	*Percentage (%)*
20,000–24,999	1	4.0
25,000–29,999	3	12.0
30,000–34,999	14	56.0
35,000–39,999	5	20.0
40,000–44,999	2	8.0
	$n = 25$	100.0%

Graphic Representations of Data

Graphs are pictorial representations of data in two-dimensional space. Many graphs display the data on two dimensions or *axes*. These two axes are the x- and y-axes, where the x-axis (also called the abscissa) is the horizontal dimension and the y-axis (also called the ordinate) is the vertical dimension. If you are graphing the data for a single variable, the values of this variable are represented on the x-axis, and the frequencies or percentages are represented on the y-axis. If you are examining two variables, the values of the independent variable are put on the x-axis, and the values of the dependent variable are put on the y-axis. Graphs can also be constructed for more than two variables.

Bar Graphs

■ **Bar graph** A graph that uses vertical bars to represent the data

A **bar graph** is a graph that uses vertical bars to represent the data. You can see a bar graph of college major in Figure 18.2. The data are from Table 18.1, our college student data set. Notice that the *x*-axis represents the variable called college major and the *y*-axis represents frequency of occurrence. The bars provide graphical representations of the frequencies of the three different college majors. Arts and sciences was the most common major ($n = 10$), education was the second most common ($n = 8$), and business was the least common ($n = 7$).

FIGURE 18.2 A bar graph of college major

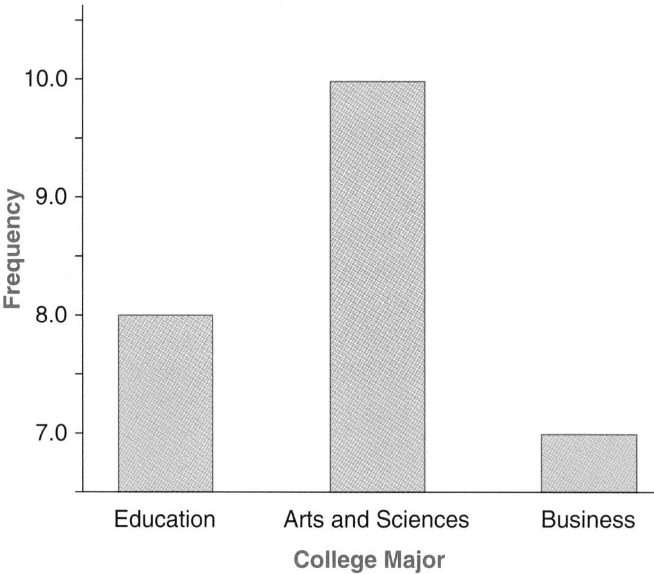

Histograms

■ **Histogram** A graphic that shows the frequencies and shape that characterize a quantitative variable

Bar graphs are used when your variable is a categorical variable. However, if your variable is a quantitative variable, a histogram is preferred. A **histogram** is a graphic presentation of a frequency distribution. It is especially useful (compared to a frequency distribution) because it shows the shape of the distribution of values. We used the computer program called SPSS to generate the histogram of starting salary (shown in Figure 18.3). Notice that, in contrast to bar graphs, the bars in histograms are set next to each other with no space in between.

Line Graphs

■ **Line graph** A graph that relies on the drawing of one or more lines

One useful way to draw a graphical picture of the distribution of a variable is to construct a **line graph**. A line graph is a format for illustrating data that relies on the drawing of one or more lines. You can see a line graph of grade point average (from the college student data set) in Figure 18.4. GPA data values around 3.0 are near the center of the distribution, and they occur the most frequently (i.e., low B grades occur the most frequently). You can also see that quite a few GPA data values are higher and lower than 3.0. In other words, the GPA data values are somewhat spread out.

■ **FIGURE 18.3** A histogram of starting salary

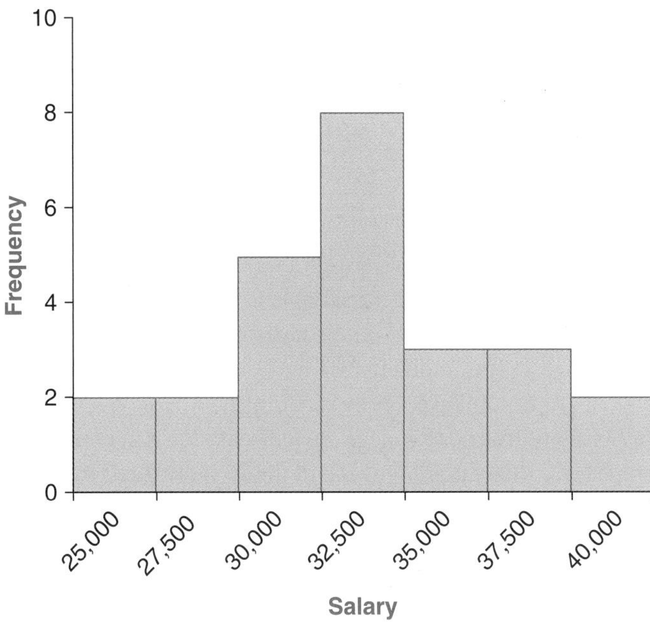

In the previous example, the line graph was given for a single variable: grade point average. Line graphs can also be used with more than one variable. For example, look back at Figure 12.15b (page 343), and you will see the type of line graph that is commonly constructed in factorial research designs. The dependent variable is placed on the vertical axis,

■ **FIGURE 18.4** A line graph of grade point average

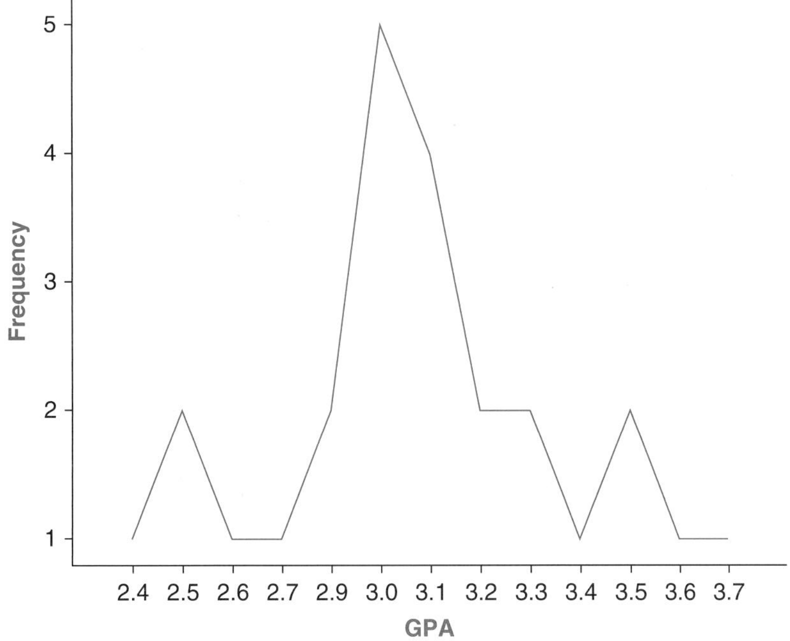

one of the independent variables is placed on the horizontal axis, and the categories of a second independent variable are represented by separate lines.

Another common use of line graphs is to show trends over time. In this case, the variable that you wish to observe changing over time is placed on the vertical axis, and time is placed on the horizontal axis. The key point is that there is not just one type of line graph. Line graphing is a versatile tool that you might want to use in the future.

Scatter Plots

■ **Scatter plot** A graph used to depict the relationship between two quantitative variables

A **scatter plot**, or scatter diagram, is a very useful way to visualize the relationship between two quantitative variables. The dependent variable is represented on the vertical axis, and the independent variable is represented on the horizontal axis. Dots are plotted within the graph to represent the cases (i.e., individuals).

A scatter plot of grade point average by starting salary is shown in Figure 18.5. These quantitative variables are from our college student data set. There are a total of 25 data points in the graph (i.e., 1 data point for each of the 25 individuals in the data set). If you examine the graph in Figure 18.5, you will clearly see that there is a positive relationship between GPA and starting salary. We calculated the correlation coefficient and found that it is equal to +.628. This moderately strong, positive correlation coefficient confirms our observation that as GPA increases, starting salary also tends to increase. In short, there is a clear linear relationship between GPA and starting salary.

When you examine a scatter plot, it is helpful to consider the following questions:

- Does there appear to be a relationship between the two variables?
- Is it a linear relationship (a straight line) or a curvilinear relationship (a curved line)? (Linear relationships are much more common than curvilinear relationships.)

■ **FIGURE 18.5** A scatter plot of starting salary by grade point average

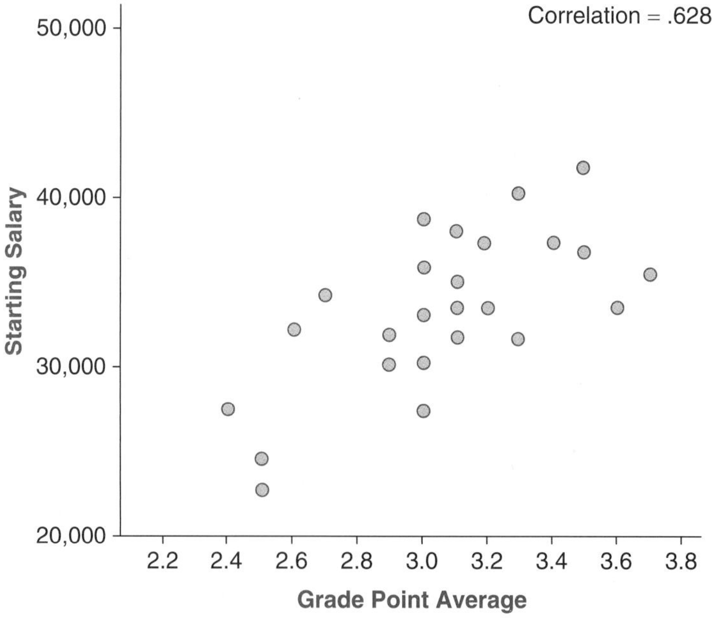

- If a linear relationship is present, is it a positive relationship or a negative relationship? The relationship is positive if the data points move in a southwest-to-northeast direction. The relationship is negative if the data points move in a northwest-to-southeast direction.
- If there is a relationship, how strong does it appear to be? The more the data points look like a straight line, the stronger is the relationship. The more they look like a circle or the more dispersed the data are, the weaker is the relationship.

18.2 List the three steps in constructing a frequency distribution.

18.3 What types of graphical representations of data were discussed in this section?

18.4 Which graphical representation is used to examine the correlation between two quantitative variables?

Measures of Central Tendency

A **measure of central tendency** is the single numerical value that is considered the most typical of the values of a quantitative variable. For example, if someone asked a teacher how well his or her students did on their last exam, a measure of central tendency would provide an indication of what score was typical. If someone wanted to know how much money people tend to earn annually in the United States, a measure of central tendency would again be called for. Finally, in an experiment, a researcher might be interested in comparing the average performance (which is a measure of central tendency) of the experimental group with the average performance of the control group. We now discuss the three most commonly used measures of central tendency: the mode, the median, and the mean.

- **Measure of central tendency** The single numerical value considered most typical of the values of a quantitative variable

Mode

The **mode** is the most frequently occurring number. For example, if you had the numbers

- **Mode** The most frequently occurring number

1, 2, 3, 3, 4

the mode is 3 because the number 3 occurs twice and the other numbers only occur once. Therefore, the number 3 is the most frequently occurring number. Suppose you had this set of numbers:

1, 1, 3, 3, 4

In this case, you have two modes: 1 and 3. When you have two modes like this, you can use the term *bimodal* to describe the data. (If you have three or more modes, some researchers use the term *multimodal* as a descriptor.) If you had this set of numbers,

1, 3, 5, 8

you could conclude that you have multiple modes because all the numbers occur an equal number of times; alternatively, you could conclude that you have no mode. For practice, determine the mode in this set of numbers:

1, 4, 6, 7, 7, 7, 9, 9, 11, 11, 30

The mode is 7 because 7 is the most frequently occurring number. For a more challenging exercise, find the mode of the variable called starting salary in our data set in Table 18.1. You will see that the mode is equal to $32,000.

Median

■ **Median** The 50th percentile

The **median**, or 50th percentile, is the middle point in a set of numbers that has been arranged in order of magnitude (either ascending order or descending order). If you have an odd number of numbers, the median is defined as the middle number. Here is a simple example. If you had the numbers

2, 9, 1, 7, 10

you would first put them in ascending order of magnitude as follows:

1, 2, 7, 9, 10

Now you can easily see that the median is equal to 7 because 7 is the middle number. (If you "slice" the number 7 down the center, you have the middle point.)

If you have an even number of numbers, the median is defined as the average of the two innermost numbers. For example, if you had the numbers

3, 4, 1, 10

you would first put them in ascending order:

1, 3, 4, 10

Because there is no center number, you take the average of the two innermost numbers (i.e., take the average of the numbers 3 and 4). You can see that the median is 3.5 because that is the average of the two innermost numbers [i.e., $(3 + 4)/2 = 3.5$].

Before moving on, check to make sure that you can find the median in a set of numbers. Here is an easy one: What is the median of 1 and 2? Right, it is 1.5. Now find the median for this set of numbers: 1, 5, 7, 8, 9. The median is 7, because 7 is the middle number. As a more challenging check on your understanding, find the median of starting salary in the college student data set (Table 18.1). The median is equal to $32,000.

Mean

■ **Mean** The arithmetic average

The **mean** is the arithmetic average, or what most people call the average. You probably already know how to get the average. For example, find the average of these three numbers:

1, 2, and 3. The average is 2. That wasn't hard, was it? Here is what you did, according to the formula for the mean:

$$\text{Mean} = \frac{\Sigma X}{n}$$

This formula is not hard to use once you learn what the symbols stand for. The symbol X stands for the variable whose observed values are 1, 2, and 3 in our example. The symbol (the Greek letter sigma) means "sum what follows." Therefore, the numerator (the top part) in the formula says "sum the X values." The n in the formula stands for the number of numbers. You get the average by summing the observed values of your variable and dividing that sum by the number of numbers. If the numbers are 1, 2, and 3, you would use the formula as follows:

$$\text{Mean} = \frac{\Sigma X}{n} = \frac{1+2+3}{3} = \frac{6}{3} = 2$$

Now don't say that you can't do this because you already know how to get the average of these three numbers. You do need to note carefully the symbols that are used, however, since they are probably new to you. For practice, use the formula now to get the average of 2, 3, 6, 7, and 2. (The average is 4.) You could also calculate the mean of the starting salary from the college student data set (Table 18.1). If you add up all the numbers and divide by the total number of numbers, you will find that the mean starting salary is equal to $32,640.

A Comparison of the Mean, Median, and Mode

In this section, we are going to introduce the normal distribution and the concept called skewness. Afterward we show the impact that the shape of a distribution of scores has on the mean, median, and mode. We also provide some commentary on the properties of the mean, median, and mode. Let's start with the idea of the normal curve.

The **normal distribution**, or normal curve, is a unimodal, symmetrical, bell-shaped distribution that is the theoretical model used to describe many physical, psychological, and educational variables. You can see an example in Figure 18.6b. The normal distribution is unimodal because it has only one mode. It is symmetrical because the two sides of the distribution are mirror images. It is said to be bell shaped because it is shaped somewhat like a bell (i.e., the curve is highest at the center and tapers off as you move away from the center). The height of the curve shows the frequency or density of the data values. Now, remember this important characteristic of the normal distribution: *The mean, the median, and the mode are the same number.*

- **Normal distribution** A unimodal, symmetrical, bell-shaped distribution that is the theoretical model of many variables

The other two distributions shown in Figure 18.6 are not normally distributed [see the distributions in parts (a) and (c)]. These two distributions are **skewed**, which means that they are not symmetrical. A distribution is skewed when one tail is stretched out longer than the other tail, making the distribution asymmetrical. The numbers in the longer tail occur less frequently than the numbers in the "mound" of the distribution. If one tail appears to be stretched or pulled toward the left, the distribution is said to be skewed to the left, or **negatively skewed** (i.e., stretched in the negative direction, where numbers are decreasing in numerical value). The scores on an easy test will tend to be negatively skewed.

- **Skewed** Not symmetrical

- **Negatively skewed** Skewed to the left

■ **Positively skewed** Skewed to the right

If a tail appears to be stretched or pulled toward the right, the distribution is said to be skewed to the right, or **positively skewed** (i.e., stretched in the positive direction, where numbers are increasing in numerical value). The scores on a very difficult test will tend to be positively skewed.

Something interesting happens when a distribution is skewed. In particular, the mean, the median, and the mode are different when a distribution is skewed. In the negatively skewed distribution shown in Figure 18.6a, the numerical value of the mean is less than the median, and the numerical value of the median is less than the mode (i.e., mean < median < mode). In the positively skewed distribution shown in Figure 18.6c, the numerical value of the mean is greater than the median, which is greater than the mode (i.e., mean > median > mode).

Why does the mean change more than the other measures of central tendency in the presence of a skewed distribution? The answer is that the mean takes into account the magnitude of all of the scores. In contrast, the median takes into account only the number of scores and the values of the middle scores.

■ **FIGURE 18.6** Examples of normal and skewed distributions

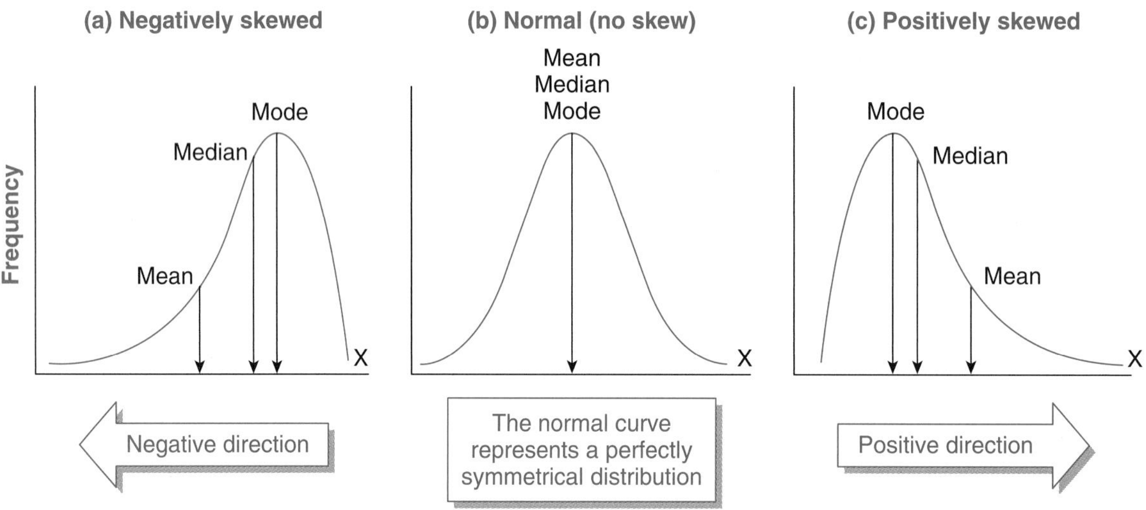

Here is a demonstration. If you have these five numbers,

1, 2, 3, 4, 5

you can see that the median and the mean are both equal to 3. However, look at what happens if the last number is changed from 5 to 1,000. Here are the new numbers:

1, 2, 3, 4, 1,000

This time, the mean is 202 rather than 3. That is a dramatic change. The median, however, is unchanged. The median is still 3. The point is that the mean uses the magnitude of all the scores and is affected by the scores in the tails of a distribution (i.e., by the large numbers and by the small numbers), whereas the median is affected only by the middlemost scores. This means that the mean is pulled more to the left in a negatively skewed distribution (the small values pull the mean down), and the mean is pulled more to the right in a positively skewed distribution (the large values pull the mean up). Because of this pattern, you should remember this general rule:

- If the mean is less than the median, the data are skewed to the left.
- If the mean is greater than the median, the data are skewed to the right.

This rule is helpful because it allows you to obtain a rough indication of skewness simply by comparing the mean and the median. If they are very different, the data are probably skewed.[1]

You might wonder which measure of central tendency is the best. As a general rule, the mean is the best measure because it is the most precise. The mean takes into account the magnitude of all scores. The median and the mode do not do this. The mean is also the most stable from sample to sample. As you know, the median takes into account only the number of scores and the values of the middle scores. The mode is usually the least desirable because it provides information only about what data value occurs the most often. Therefore, you should use the mode only when you believe that it is important to express which single number or category occurs the most frequently. Otherwise, the mean or the median is usually the preferred measure of central tendency.

There is one situation in which the median is preferred over the mean. The median is usually preferred when your data are highly skewed. This is because the median is less affected by extreme scores and we want our measure of central tendency to describe what is *typical* for a set of numbers.

Here is an example in which the median would be preferred. Assume that the annual incomes for the 10 families living in a small residential neighborhood are as follows:

$16,000

$18,000

$18,000

$18,000

$19,000

$19,000

$20,000

$21,000

$21,000

$500,000

Nine of the families earn somewhere between $16,000 and $21,000. There is, however, an **outlier,** a number that is very atypical of the other numbers in a distribution. One family in the neighborhood earns $500,000. (Think of it like this: If Bill Gates lived in your neighborhood, his income would certainly be an outlier!) The median income in this example is

- **Outlier** A number that is very atypical of the other numbers in a distribution

$19,000, and the mean income is $67,000. Which of these two numbers do you believe best describes the "typical family income"? Many would argue that the median better represents these 10 families. The median is much closer than is the mean to the actual incomes of 90% of the people in this example. Ninety percent of these families are under some financial constraints because of low income levels. The mean provides an overly optimistic assessment of the income levels by suggesting that the average or typical family income is $67,000. This is why researchers usually use the median rather than the mean when they are reporting annual income and, more important, why they often use the median when their data are highly skewed. (See bonus material at the student companion website for another comparison of the mean and median.)

See Tools and Tips 18.2 on the Student Study Site.

REVIEW QUESTIONS

18.5 What is a measure of central tendency, and what are the common measures of central tendency?

18.6 When is the median preferred over the mean?

18.7 If the mean is much greater than the median, are the data skewed to the right or skewed to the left?

MEASURES OF VARIABILITY

- **Measure of variability** A numerical index that provides information about how spread out the data values are or how much variation is present

A **measure of variability** is a numerical index that provides information about how spread out or dispersed the data values are or how much variation is present. In other words, measures of variability tell you how similar or different people are with respect to a variable. For example, do the individuals in our earlier data set tend to have very similar or very different grade point averages? The variability in grade point average in our data set was visually shown by the line plot in Figure 18.4. Measures of variability provide a numerical indication of the amount of variation and therefore provide another type of information you can use to describe a set of numbers.

If all the numbers were the same, there would be no variability at all. For example, if the set of numbers was

7, 7, 7, 7, 7, 7, 7, 7

you would conclude that there was no variability for the simple reason that there is no variation in the data. On the other hand, the following set of numbers does have some variability:

1, 3, 7, 10, 12, 15, 17, 20

- **Homogeneous** A set of numbers with little variability
- **Heterogeneous** A set of numbers with a great deal of variability

When there is very little variability in a set of numbers, we sometimes say that the numbers are **homogeneous**. If, on the other hand, there is a great deal of variability, we describe the numbers as being **heterogeneous**. When a set of numbers is relatively homogeneous, you can place more trust in the measure of central tendency (mean, median, or mode) as being typical. Conversely, when a set of numbers is relatively heterogeneous, you should view the measure of central tendency as being less typical or representative of the data values.

Following are examples of relatively low variability and relatively high variability:

Data for group A: 53, 54, 55, 55, 56, 56, 57, 57, 58, 59

Data for group B: 4, 8, 23, 41, 57, 72, 78, 83, 94, 100

You can see that the numbers for group B are more spread out (and have higher variability) than the numbers for group A. You might be surprised to learn that the mean is actually the same in both of these sets of data! The mean is 56 for both. When the numbers are not very spread out, the mean is more representative of the set of numbers than when the numbers are quite spread out. Therefore, a measure of variability should usually accompany measures of central tendency. We now discuss the three most commonly used indexes of variability: the range, the variance, and the standard deviation.

Range

The **range** is simply the difference between the highest and lowest numbers. In the following formula, the range is the highest (i.e., largest) number minus the lowest (i.e., smallest) number in a set of numbers:

Range The difference between the highest and lowest numbers

Range $= H - L$

where

H is the highest number, and

L is the lowest number.

Find the range for the distributions for group A and group B shown in the previous section. The range in distribution A is 6 (i.e., 59 – 53 = 6). The range in distribution B is 96 (i.e., 100 – 4 = 96). The range works to convey variability in this case because distribution B has more variability than distribution A. Although the range is very easy to calculate, its use is limited. In fact, researchers do not use the range very often. One problem with the range is that it takes into account only the two most extreme numbers. A related problem is that it is severely affected by the presence of a single extreme number. To see this problem, change the highest number in distribution A from 59 to 101. The range changes from 6 to 48; it becomes 8 times larger on the basis of changing a single number.

Variance and Standard Deviation

The two most popular measures of variability among researchers are the variance and standard deviation because these measures are the most stable and are the foundations of more advanced statistical analysis. These measures are also based on all the data values of a variable and not just the highest and lowest numbers, as is the case with the range. They are essentially measures of the amount of dispersion or variation around the mean of a variable.

- **Variance** A measure of the average deviation of data points from the mean in squared units
- **Standard deviation** The square root of the variance

The **variance** is a measure of the average deviation of all the numbers from the mean in squared units. To turn the variance into more appealing units, you just take the square root. When you take the square root of the variance, you obtain the standard deviation. You can view the **standard deviation** as an approximate indicator of how far the numbers tend to vary from the mean. The variance and standard deviation will be larger when the data are spread out (heterogeneous) and smaller when the data are not very spread out (homogeneous).

We show you how to calculate the variance and standard deviation in Table 18.4. We also explain it to you in words here. To calculate the variance and standard deviation, follow these five steps:

1. Find the mean of a set of numbers. As illustrated in Table 18.4, add the numbers in column 1 and divide by the number of numbers. (Note that we use the symbol "X-bar" (i.e., $\bar{X}$) to stand for the mean.)
2. Subtract the mean from each number. As illustrated in Table 18.4, subtract the mean from each number in column 1 and place the result in column 2.
3. Square each of the numbers you obtained in the last step. As illustrated in Table 18.4, square each number in column 2 and place the result in column 3. (To square a number, multiply the number by itself. For example, 2 squared is 2 × 2, which is equal to 4.)
4. Put the appropriate numbers into the variance formula. As illustrated in Table 18.4, insert the sum of the numbers in column 3 into the numerator (the top part) of the variance formula. The denominator (the bottom part) of the variance formula is the number of numbers in column 1. Now divide the numerator by the denominator, and you have the *variance.*
5. You obtained the variance in the previous step. Now take the square root of the variance, and you have the *standard deviation.* (To get the square root, type the number into your calculator and press the square root [√] key.)

TABLE 18.4 Calculating the Variance and Standard Deviation

	(1) *X	(2) $(X - \bar{X})$	(3) $(X - \bar{X})^2$
	1	−2	4
	2	−1	1
	3	0	0
	4	1	1
	5	2	4
	15	0	10
	↑	↑	↑
Sums	ΣX	$\Sigma(X - \bar{X})$	$\Sigma(X - \bar{X})^2$

(4)** Variance $= \dfrac{\Sigma(X-\bar{X})^2}{n} = \dfrac{10}{5} = \dfrac{2}{1} = 2.$

(5) Standard deviation $= \sqrt{\text{Variance}} = \sqrt{2} = 1.14$

*The mean of column 1 = $\bar{X} = \dfrac{\Sigma X}{n} = \dfrac{15}{5} = \dfrac{3}{1} = 3.$

**If the variance is used in inferential statistics (i.e., where the sample variance is used as the estimate of the population variance), then you need to use $n - 1$ rather than n in the denominator for technical reasons. When you use $n - 1$, the variance is referred to as the *sample variance.*

Standard Deviation and the Normal Distribution

Now that you understand the idea of standard deviation, we can point out another important characteristic of the normal distribution that we did not mention earlier. The following will always be true *if* the data fully follow a normal distribution:

- 68.26% of the cases fall within 1 standard deviation.
- 95.00% fall within 1.96 standard deviations.
- 95.44% fall within 2 standard deviations.
- 99.74% fall within 3 standard deviations.

A good rule for approximating the area within 1, 2, and 3 standard deviations is what we call the "68, 95, 99.7 percent rule" (Figure 18.7). Don't forget, however, that you can *only* use this rule when you know that the data are normally distributed. The rule is a useful approximation, for example, when you are talking about things like height, weight, and IQ. You should be careful, however, when you have collected your own data, because a distribution usually does not become normally distributed (even if the underlying population distribution is normal) until many, many cases have been collected. If you want to apply the 68, 95, 99.7 percent rule, check to see that the data are normally distributed. Do not automatically assume that the rule is applicable.

FIGURE 18.7 Areas under the normal curve. *SD* = standard deviation.

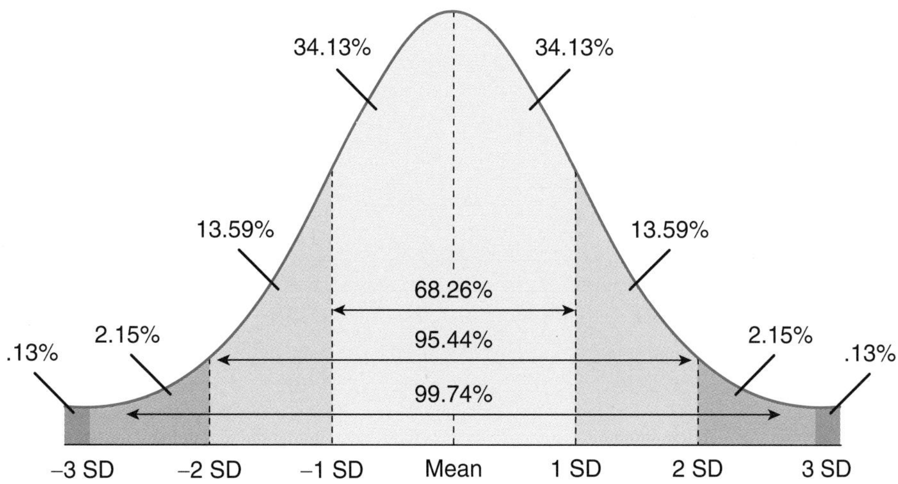

REVIEW QUESTIONS

18.8 What is a measure of variability, and what are the common measures of variability?

18.9 How are the variance and standard deviation mathematically related?

18.10 If a set of data is normally distributed, how many of the cases fall within 1 standard deviation? How many fall within 2 standard deviations? How many fall within 3 standard deviations?

- **Measures of relative standing** Provide information about where a score falls in relation to the other scores in the distribution of data
- **Percentile ranks** Scores that divide a distribution into 100 equal parts
- **Standard scores** Scores that have been converted from one scale to another to have a particular mean and standard deviation

MEASURES OF RELATIVE STANDING

The raw scores of many research and assessment instruments are not inherently meaningful. How would you feel, for example, if someone told you that your raw scholastic aptitude score was 134? Likewise, how would you compare your score to a score of 119? Without more information, you obviously would not know exactly how to interpret your raw score of 134. This is why standardized test makers rarely report raw scores. Instead, they report various **measures of relative standing**, which provide information about where a score falls in relation to the other scores in the distribution of data. We focus on two types of relative standing: **percentile ranks** (scores that divide a distribution into 100 equal parts) and **standard scores** (scores that have been converted from one scale to another so that they have a particular mean and standard deviation that are believed to be more interpretable). Our following discussion of standard scores focuses on *z* scores, although two additional types of standard scores are shown in Figure 18.8. We have included IQ scores (which usually have a mean of 100 and a standard deviation of 15) and SAT scores (which have a mean of 500 and a standard deviation of 100) for your comparison.

FIGURE 18.8 Percentile ranks and standard scores in relation to the normal curve. *SD* = standard deviation.

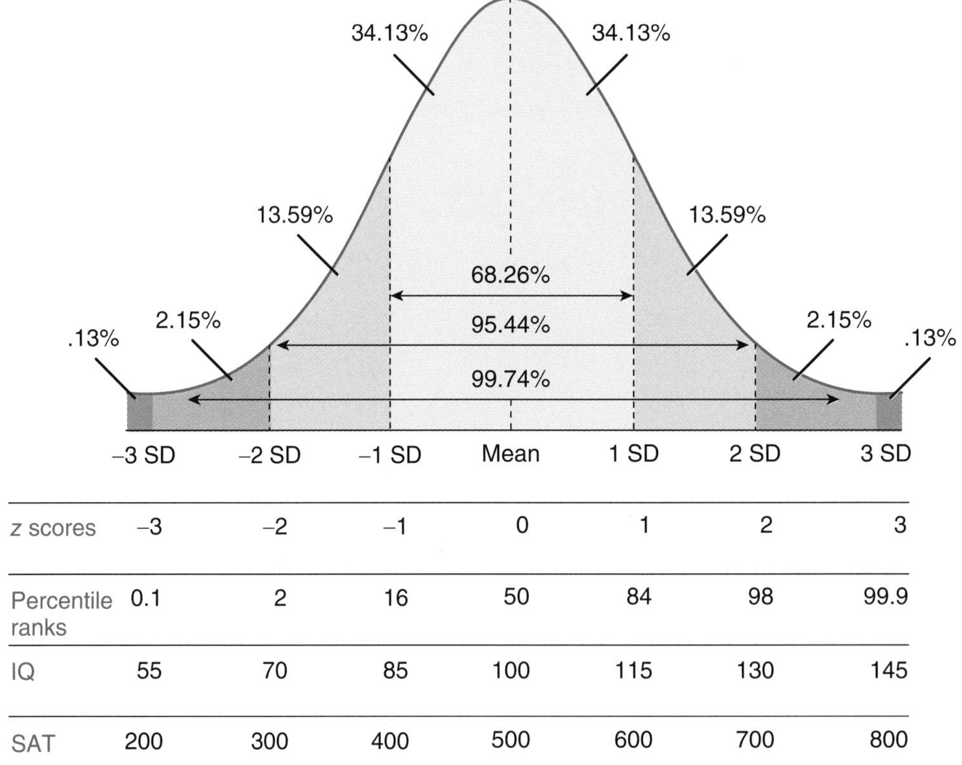

z scores	–3	–2	–1	0	1	2	3
Percentile ranks	0.1	2	16	50	84	98	99.9
IQ	55	70	85	100	115	130	145
SAT	200	300	400	500	600	700	800

Percentile Ranks

A **percentile rank** is interpreted as the percentage of scores in a reference group that fall below a particular raw score (Crocker & Algina, 1986; Cronbach, 1984; Educational Testing

Service, 2013). Percentile ranks help individuals interpret their test scores in comparison to those of others. A **reference group** is the group of people that is used to determine the percentile ranks. The reference group is often referred to as the norm group or the standardization sample. A reference group might be a national sample, a sample of children of a particular age, or all of the students in a school district. As a general rule, percentile ranks should be used when the reference group is quite large and representative of a group of interest to you.

- **Percentile rank** The percentage of scores in a reference group that fall below a particular raw score
- **Reference group** The norm group that is used to determine the percentile ranks

To interpret the meaning of a score using a percentile rank, let's say that you made a raw score of 166 on the Graduate Record Examination Verbal Reasoning Test. This score of 166 corresponds to a percentile rank of 96, which means that 96% of the individuals in the norm group made scores lower than your score. For another example, assume that a friend of yours got a Verbal score of 149. Because this score corresponds to a percentile rank of 40, only 40% of the individuals got a score lower than that of your friend. You can see the list of other GRE Verbal test standard scores and the corresponding percentile ranks in Table 18.5. As a final example, how would you interpret a Verbal score of 159? As you can see in Table 18.5, this score corresponds to the percentile rank of 81.

TABLE 18.5 GRE General Test Interpretive Data

Scaled Score	*Verbal Reasoning*	*Quantitative Reasoning*
170	99	98
169	99	97
168	98	96
167	97	95
166	96	93
165	95	91
164	93	89
163	91	87
162	89	84
161	87	81
160	84	78
159	81	75
158	78	72
157	73	69
156	70	65
155	66	61
154	62	57
153	58	53
152	53	49

(Continued)

■ **TABLE 18.5** (Continued)

Scaled Score	*Verbal Reasoning*	*Quantitative Reasoning*
151	49	45
150	44	41
149	40	37
148	36	33
147	32	29
146	28	25
145	24	22
144	21	18
143	18	15
142	15	13
141	12	11
140	10	8
139	7	6
138	6	5
137	5	3
136	3	2
135	2	2
134	2	1
133	1	1
132	1	—
131	1	—
130	—	—
Mean	150.75	151.91
Standard deviation	8.40	8.79
Number of examinees	952,816	953,916

*Based on the performance of all GRE examinees who were tested between August 1, 2011, and April 30, 2013. Percentile ranks are updated yearly.

z Scores

■ ***z* score** A raw score that has been transformed into standard deviation units

A *z* **score** is defined as a raw score that has been transformed into standard deviation units. This means that *a z score tells you how many standard deviations a raw score is from the mean.* If a raw score is above the mean, the *z* score will be positive; if a raw score is below the mean, the *z* score will be negative; and if a raw score is equal to the mean, the *z* score will equal zero (because the mean of a set of *z* scores will always be zero).

The z score standardization transforms any set of raw scores into a new set of scores that has a mean of 0 and a standard deviation of 1. *The z score transformation does not affect the overall shape of the data distribution.* If the data are normal (not skewed) before the z score transformation, then they will still be normal after the z score transformation, and if the data are skewed before the z score transformation, then they will still be skewed after the z score transformation. The new, transformed scores are called "z scores."

For example, let's say that Jenny has a z score of +2.00 on some standardized test (e.g., the GRE, the MAT, or the SAT). This means that Jenny scored 2 standard deviations above the mean. Remember, z scores tell you where a person's score stands in relation to the mean. Jenny obviously did better than the average person. Let's say that Jay has a z score of −2.00; therefore, Jay scored 2 standard deviations below the mean. In other words, Jay did worse than the average person. John's z score is 0; therefore, John's raw score is equal to the mean (i.e., the overall average). John was exactly average. Jean's z score is +3.50. Jean's raw score falls 3½ deviations above the mean, which is far above the average and better than Jenny's score, which was 2 standard deviations above the mean.

If the underlying data are normally distributed, then z scores communicate additional information. In Figure 18.8, we show the normal distribution along with percentile ranks and several standard scores (z scores, IQ scores, and SAT scores). Because we are now assuming that the scores are normally distributed, we have additional information about Jenny's score of +2.00. Because a z score of +2.00 has a percentile rank of 98 when the data are normally distributed, we know that Jenny's score is better than the scores of 98% of the people taking the standardized test. Jay's score has a percentile rank of 2, which means that he did better than only 2% of the people. John was right at the median (i.e., the 50th percentile). Jean did better than virtually everybody, including Jenny.

You can compute a z score by taking the difference between a particular raw score and the overall mean and then dividing by the standard deviation. You would use this formula:

$$z\,\text{score} = \frac{\text{raw score} - \text{mean}}{\text{standard deviation}} = \frac{X - \overline{X}}{SD}$$

To use this formula, you need the raw score that you wish to transform into a z score, and you need to know the mean and standard deviation of all of the scores. Most IQ tests have a mean of 100 and a standard deviation of 15. Therefore, the z score for Maria, who scored 115 on an IQ test, would be determined as follows:

$$z\,\text{score} = \frac{115 - 100}{15} = \frac{15}{15} = 1$$

We put Maria's IQ of 115 into the formula, along with the IQ mean (100) and standard deviation (15). The resulting z score is equal to 1 (+1.00), which means Maria's IQ is 1 standard deviation above the mean. That's all you do if you want to use the z score formula!

An advantage of z scores is that they can be used to compare raw scores between two different tests that have different means and standard deviations. To compare a person's scores on two different tests, you simply convert the two raw scores into z scores and compare them. For example, assume that Maria got an SAT score of 700. Did Maria do better on the SAT or on the IQ test? You already know that Maria's IQ score results in a z score of +1.00. An SAT score of 700 results in a z score of +2.00. (If you want to calculate the z score for an SAT score of 700, put these values into the formula: raw score = 700, mean = 500, and standard deviation = 100. The result will be a z score of +2.00.) Obviously, a z score of +2.00 is better than a z score of +1.00, which means that Maria did better on the SAT than she did on the IQ test.

REVIEW QUESTIONS

18.11 What is a measure of relative standing, and what are the common measures of relative standing?

18.12 How do you calculate a z score?

EXAMINING RELATIONSHIPS AMONG VARIABLES

Throughout this book, we have been talking about relationships among variables. This is because researchers are seldom satisfied with describing the characteristics of single variables. Research becomes much more interesting when the relationships among variables are also described. We have already talked about comparing means in earlier chapters (e.g., in Chapters 11, 12, and 13 means are compared for the different treatment conditions in an experiment) and about interpreting correlation coefficients (e.g., see discussion of correlation coefficients in Chapter 2). There are two more topics, however, that you need to know about. These topics are contingency tables and regression.

Contingency Tables

■ **Contingency table** A table displaying information in cells formed by the intersection of two or more categorical variables

A **contingency table** (also called a cross-tabulation) displays information in cells formed by the intersection of two or more categorical variables. In a two-dimensional contingency table, the rows represent the categories of one variable, and the columns represent the categories of the other variable. Various kinds of information can be put into the cells of a contingency table (e.g., observed cell frequencies, row percentages, column percentages). You can see a contingency table with cell frequencies in Table 18.6a. You can see a contingency table with column percentages in Table 18.6b.

Look at the contingency table in Table 18.6a. You can see that the row variable is *political party identification* and the column variable is *gender*. The numbers in the cells are the observed cell frequencies, which indicate the number of people in each cell. For example, 92 people in the hypothetical set of data were Democratic and male, and 390 were Democratic and female. A table with cell frequencies is a good starting point in constructing a contingency table, but you should not stop there because it is very difficult to detect a relationship between the variables when you examine only the cell frequencies.

Look at the contingency table in Table 18.6b. This table was constructed in the following way: We made the independent or predictor variable the column variable, we made the dependent variable the row variable, and we obtained column percentages by calculating

TABLE 18.6 Party Identification by Gender Contingency Tables

(a) Contingency Table Showing Cell Frequencies (Hypothetical Data)

	Gender		
Political Party Identification	*Males*	*Females*	*Total*
Democrat	92	390	482
Republican	16	169	185
Total	108	559	667

(b) Contingency Table Showing Column Percentages [based on the data in Part (a)]*

	Gender	
Political Party Identification	*Males*	*Females*
Democrat	85.2%	69.8%
Republican	14.8%	30.2%
Total Column %	100%	100%

*The column percentage 85.2% was obtained by dividing 92 by 108 (and multiplying by 100 to get a percentage); 14.8% was obtained by dividing 16 by 108; 69.8% was obtained by dividing 390 by 559; 30.2% was obtained by dividing 169 by 559. Note that both columns in part (b) sum to 100%. [If you want to obtain row percentages, just divide the number of cases in each cell in part (a) by the corresponding row total. Then each row will sum to 100%.]

the percentages down the columns. This is an appropriate table construction because it allows us to make our comparisons across the levels of the independent variable (*gender*). We explain exactly where the numbers came from in a footnote to the table. Whenever you obtain *column* percentages, each column will sum to 100 percent, just as the columns do in part (b). After you construct your table in this way, you should make your comparisons across the rows.

When you convert your data to column percentages like this, the table is composed of rates, which you should use for comparison purposes. A **rate** shows the percentage (or proportion) of people in a group who have a specific characteristic. For example, in Table 18.6b, you can see that the rate of membership in the Democratic Party for males is 85.2% and that for females is 69.8%. In short, males have a higher rate of membership in the Democratic Party than do females. (Remember that our data are hypothetical!)

Rate The percentage of people in a group who have a specific characteristic

When group comparisons are presented in the news, they are usually calculated in this way; that is, you will often hear that members of one group are more likely than members of another group to have some characteristic. For example, the poverty rate is higher for unwed mothers than for mothers who are married, the rate of lung cancer is higher for smokers than for nonsmokers, the rate of cirrhosis of the liver is higher for heavy drinkers than for light drinkers, and so forth. Comparing across cells helps the researcher determine whether a relationship exists between the two categorical variables in the contingency table (e.g., marriage status is related to poverty, smoking is related to cancer, getting cirrhosis of the liver is related to the amount people drink, and, in our hypothetical example, gender is related to political party).[2] If there is no relationship between the variables, the rates will be the same.

Here is a simple rule for you to use whenever you want to determine whether the variables in a contingency table are related:

- If the percentages are calculated down the columns, compare across the rows.
- If the percentages are calculated across the rows, compare down the columns.

This simple rule will help you see very quickly whether there is a relationship between two variables in a contingency table. It is also easy to memorize.

You can extend the ideas presented here by adding more categorical variables to the mix. If you have three categorical variables, the appropriate strategy is to examine the original two-dimensional table separately for each level of the third categorical variable. If you want to see an example of this process or learn more about higher-level contingency tables (i.e., tables based on three or more variables), we recommend reading Babbie (1998, pp. 378–383 and Chapter 18) and Frankfort-Nachmias and Nachmias (1992, pp. 403–412). We also have an example at the book's companion website. Now we introduce a technique called regression analysis.

- **Regression analysis** A set of statistical procedures that are used to explain or predict the values of a dependent variable on the basis of the values of one or more independent variables

Regression Analysis

Regression analysis is a set of statistical procedures used to explain or predict the values of a dependent variable based on the values of one or more independent variables. In regression analysis, there is always a single quantitative dependent variable. Although the independent variables can be either categorical or quantitative, we discuss only the case in which the independent variables are quantitative. The two main types of regression are called **simple regression**, in which there is a single independent variable, and **multiple regression**, in which there are two or more independent variables.

- **Simple regression** Regression based on one dependent variable and one independent variable
- **Multiple regression** Regression based on one dependent variable and two or more independent variables
- **Regression equation** The equation that defines the regression line
- **Regression line** The line that best fits a pattern of observations

Simple Regression

The basic idea of simple regression is that you obtain a **regression equation**. The regression equation defines the **regression line** that best fits a pattern of observations. The two important characteristics of any line (including a regression line) are the slope of the line and the *y*-intercept of the line. The slope of a line basically tells you how steep the line is. The *y*-intercept tells you where the line crosses the *y*-axis.

Here is the simple regression equation formula:

$$\hat{Y} = a + bX$$

where

$\hat{Y}$ (called *Y*-hat) is the predicted value of the dependent variable,

a is the *y*-intercept,

b is the regression coefficient or slope, and

X is the single independent variable.

Researchers rarely calculate regression equations by hand. Most researchers use a computer program such as SPSS or SAS. All of this might seem complicated, but it will become clearer with an example. Let's use our college student data set (Table 18.1) to see whether we can predict starting salary using our knowledge of grade point average. If you look at Figure 18.9, you can see the regression line that resulted when we used the computer program SPSS to fit the regression line to the data. The regression line shows that the relationship is positive (i.e., as grade point average increases, starting salary increases).

FIGURE 18.9 The regression line showing the relationship between starting salary and GPA

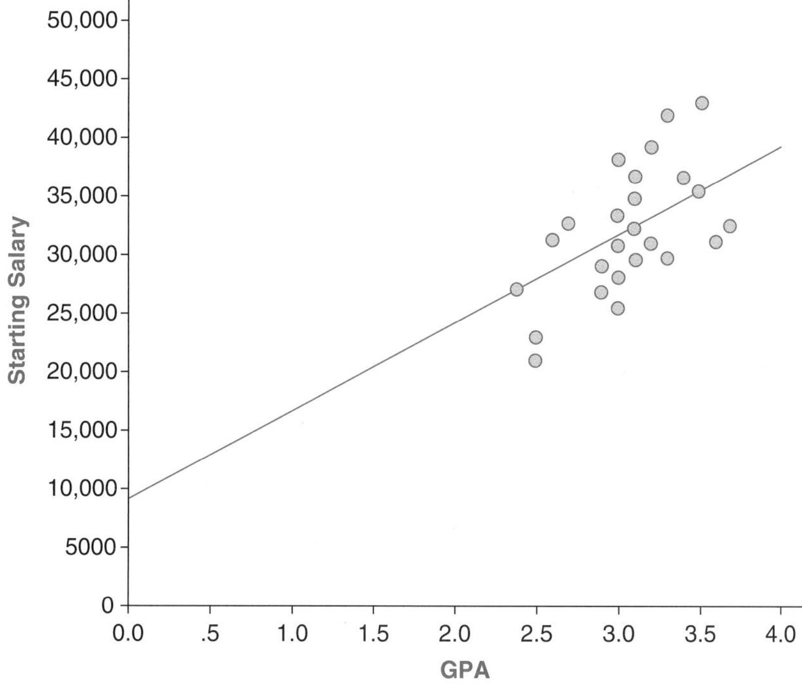

You can also use the regression line to make approximate predictions. Here is how to do this. You can visually examine the regression line to see what value of Y (the dependent variable) corresponds to a particular value of X (the independent variable). For example, first find the value 3.00 for grade point average on the horizontal axis. Then mark the point on the regression line that corresponds to this grade point average of 3.00. Third, determine what starting salary (i.e., what point on the vertical axis) corresponds to this point on the regression line. It looks as though the predicted starting salary is about halfway between $30,000 and $35,000, so our guess is that the predicted starting salary is about $32,000.

Rather than making predictions by visually examining the regression line, we usually obtain the regression equation and *insert values of* X *and obtain the predicted values of* Y. We will show you how to insert values in a moment. Now look at the regression equation that was provided by the computer program:

$$\hat{Y} = 9{,}234.56 + 7{,}638.85(X)$$

- ***y*-intercept** The point where the regression line crosses the *y*-axis

The *y*-intercept is equal to $9,234.56. The ***y*-intercept** is defined as the point where the regression line crosses the *y*-axis. In Figure 18.9, the *x*-axis is grade point average, and the *y*-axis is starting salary. The value of *Y* at the point where the regression line touches the *y*-axis is $9,234.56. It is the value of the *Y* variable (the dependent variable) that would be predicted if the independent variable (*X*) were equal to zero.

- **Regression coefficient** The predicted change in *Y* given a 1-unit change in *X*

The regression coefficient in the regression equation is equal to $7,638.85. The regression coefficient, or slope, tells you how steep the regression line is. The **regression coefficient** is more formally defined as the predicted change in *Y* given a 1-unit change in *X*. A large regression coefficient implies a steep line, and if a line is very steep, *Y* will change quite a lot given a 1-unit change in *X*. A small regression coefficient implies a line that is not very steep, and if a line is not very steep, *Y* will not change much given a 1-unit change in *X*. In our example, the regression equation tells us that if someone's GPA increased by 1 full unit (it went from a C to a B or it went from a B to an A), then we would expect his or her starting salary to increase by $7,638.85. In sum, you can see in Figure 18.9 that the variables starting salary and grade point average are related, and the regression coefficient tells you how much, on average, starting salary increases given a 1-unit increase in grade point average.

Now we will show you something you will probably find interesting: You can use a simple regression equation to make predictions. In our example, the dependent variable *Y* is starting salary. We can obtain a predicted value of starting salary by inserting a value for grade point average into the equation and solving for it. Let's find the predicted starting salary for someone who has a B grade point average (for someone whose grade point average is 3.00). First we write down the equation:

$$\hat{Y} = 9{,}234.56 + 7{,}638.85(X)$$

Now we insert the value for *X* (grade point average) and see what predicted value for *Y*, we obtain:

$\hat{Y} = 9{,}234.56 + 7{,}638.85(300)$	We inserted the GPA value of 3.00.
$\hat{Y} = 9{,}234.56 + 22{,}916.55$	We multiplied $7,638.85 by 3.00.
$\hat{Y} = 32{,}151.11$	We added $9,234.56 and $22,916.55.

Our predicted value of starting salary is $32,151.11 when grade point average is a 3.00 (i.e., B). In short, on the basis of our hypothetical college student data, we expect B students to have a starting salary of $32,151.11. We have now used our regression equation to make a prediction.

You should try to make a prediction now. Determine what starting salary you would predict college students with a grade point average of 3.8 to have on the basis of our data. All you need to do is take the equation = 9,234.56 + 7,638.85(*X*) and insert the value of 3.8 where it says *X*. Then do the arithmetic and find the result. You will find that the predicted value is $38,262.19. You can insert other grade point averages into the equation to find other predicted starting salaries.

When you use a regression equation such as the one we just used from our college student data set, you need to remember that you should use it only for values of *X* that are in the range of the X values in your data set. In our case, we should *not* use our equation for grade point averages that are below a C or higher than an A because we do not have any data on these grade levels. All the students in our data set had grades in the C to A range. In fact, it is impossible for a student to get a grade higher than an A, so you would never insert a value greater than 4.00 into the equation. Researchers must be very careful when using a regression equation to make predictions.

Multiple Regression

Multiple regression is similar to simple regression except that there are two or more independent variables. The main difference is that the regression coefficients in multiple regression are called **partial regression coefficients**, and they show the predicted change in Y given a 1-unit change in the independent variable *while controlling for the other independent variable(s) in the equation.* The regression coefficients still show the relationship between an independent variable and the dependent variable. However, the multiple regression coefficients also take into account the fact that other independent variables are included in the regression equation. Multiple regression coefficients are similar to partial correlation coefficients, discussed in Chapter 14.

■ **Partial regression coefficient** A regression coefficient obtained in multiple regression

Let's use our college student data set again. We let starting salary be our dependent variable, and we use two independent variables: grade point average and GRE Verbal scores. Here is the multiple regression equation that was provided by our statistical program, SPSS:

$$\hat{Y} = -42{,}809.11 + 4{,}734.26(X_1) + 389.37(X_2)$$

where

X_1 is grade point average, and

X_2 is the GRE Verbal score.

According to this equation, starting salary increases by $4,734.26 for a 1-unit increase in grade point average when you control for GRE Verbal performance. Also, starting salary increases by $389.37 for a 1-unit increase in GRE Verbal performance when you control for grade point average.

You can also use the multiple regression equation to find the predicted starting salary for a set of values for the two independent variables that you choose. Let's say you want to know the predicted starting salary when a student is a B student (i.e., the student's GPA is 3.00) and the student earned a 150 on the GRE Verbal test. All you have to do is insert 3.00 for GPA and 150 for GRE Verbal and then find the predicted value for Y, the predicted starting income:

$$\hat{Y} = -42{,}809.11 + 4{,}734.26(3) + 389.37(150)$$ We inserted the two values.

$$\hat{Y} = -42{,}809.11 + 14{,}202.78 + 389.37(150)$$ We multiplied 4,734.26 by 3.00.

$$\hat{Y} = -42{,}809.11 + 14{,}202.78 + 58{,}405.50$$ We multiplied 389.36 by 150.

$$\hat{Y} = 29{,}799.17$$

If a recent college graduate has a grade point average of 3.00 and a GRE Verbal score of 150, we predict that his or her starting salary will be $29,799.17. You can put any other valid values into the regression equation and obtain the predicted starting salary. For example, you might want to know the predicted starting salary for someone with a GPA of 3.8 and a GRE Verbal score of 165. All you need to do is insert these two values into the equation and get the predicted salary.

REVIEW QUESTIONS

18.13 What are some of the different ways to examine the relationships among variables?

18.14 If you calculate percentages down a contingency table, then should you make your comparisons down the columns or across the rows?

18.15 What is the difference between simple regression and multiple regression?

18.16 How is the regression coefficient interpreted in simple regression?

18.17 How is the regression coefficient interpreted in multiple regression?

ACTION RESEARCH REFLECTION

Insight: Action researchers believe in counting what counts as they attempt to implement change and produce desired outcomes.

1. How might a measure of central tendency be useful in action research? Which measure(s) (mode, median, mean) do you prefer and why?
2. What can you gain by using a measure of variability (in addition to measures of central tendency) as you attempt to understand and describe your students or participants?
3. Why is it important to understand both similarity and difference within your data and across participants?
4. How can you use the idea of rates (e.g., seen in the column percentages in a contingency table), and why are rates useful?

SUMMARY

The goal of descriptive statistics is to describe or summarize a set of data. Typically, variables are summarized one at a time. Some common ways to describe the values of a variable are to construct a frequency distribution or a grouped frequency distribution. Graphical representations—such as bar graphs, histograms, and line graphs—are also useful in describing data. Scatter plots are useful when you want to examine the relationship between two quantitative variables. Measures of central tendency (mean, median, and mode) provide the numerical value that is considered most typical of the values of a quantitative variable. The mean takes into account the magnitude of the scores and is usually considered the best measure of central tendency. However, the median is sometimes the preferred measure of central tendency if the data are severely skewed (not symmetrical). Measures of variability tell you how spread out or dispersed the data values are. The most useful measures are the variance and the standard deviation. When data are normally distributed, you can apply the following approximate rule:

68% of the cases will fall within 1 standard deviation, 95% of the cases will fall within 2 standard deviations, and 99.7% of the cases will fall within 3 standard deviations. Measures of relative standing tell you where a score falls in relation to other scores. The most important measures of relative standing are percentile ranks and *z* scores. Some important ways to examine and describe the relationships among variables are scatter plots, contingency tables, and regression analysis.

KEY TERMS

bar graph (p. 502)
contingency table (p. 518)
data set (p. 498)
descriptive statistics (p. 498)
exhaustive (p. 501)
frequency distribution (p. 500)
grouped frequency distribution (p. 501)
heterogeneous (p. 510)
histogram (p. 502)
homogeneous (p. 510)
inferential statistics (p. 498)
line graph (p. 502)
mean (p. 506)
measure of central tendency (p. 505)
measure of variability (p. 510)
measures of relative standing (p. 514)
median (p. 506)
mode (p. 505)
multiple regression (p. 520)
mutually exclusive (p. 501)
negatively skewed (p. 507)
normal distribution (p. 507)
outlier (p. 509)
partial regression coefficient (p. 523)
percentile rank (p. 514)
percentile ranks (p. 514)
positively skewed (p. 508)
range (p. 511)
rate (p. 519)
reference group (p. 515)
regression analysis (p. 520)
regression coefficient (p. 522)
regression equation (p. 520)
regression line (p. 520)
scatter plot (p. 504)
simple regression (p. 520)
skewed (p. 507)
standard deviation (p. 512)
standard scores (p. 514)
variance (p. 512)
y-intercept (p. 522)
z score (p. 516)

DISCUSSION QUESTIONS

1. When do you think the use of descriptive statistics is important?
2. Some statisticians say that a measure of central tendency such as the mean should be accompanied by a measure of variability. Why do you think they say this?
3. Which measure (or measures) of relative standing should teachers use when communicating students' test scores to parents? Why?
4. Name a variable that you think is normally distributed. Does it have all the characteristics of the normal curve? For example, does it precisely follow the 68, 95, 99.7 percent rule? Do the tails of the curve ever completely touch the bottom axis (which is also a characteristic of a normal curve)?
5. For each of the following cases, list the procedure shown in this chapter that is used to examine the relationship between two variables:
    a. You have two categorical variables.
    b. You have two quantitative variables.
    c. You have a quantitative dependent variable and one or more quantitative independent variables.
    d. To foreshadow what is coming up in the next chapter, note the following: When you have a quantitative dependent variable and one categorical independent variable, the procedure is called a *one-way analysis of variance.* When you have one quantitative dependent variable and two categorical independent variables, it is called a *two-way analysis of variance.*

RESEARCH EXERCISES

1. Determine the mean, median, and mode of the following numbers: 1, 2, 2, 2, 3, 3, 3, 3, 4, 4, 4, 9, 1,650. Are these data skewed to the left (negatively skewed) or skewed to the right (positively skewed)? Which measure of central tendency do you think best represents the central tendency of the data?
2. In Table 18.4, we calculated the standard deviation of the following set of numbers: 1, 2, 3, 4, 5. Now calculate the z score for each of the five numbers. You will recall that we claimed that the mean is zero and the standard deviation is 1 for any complete set of z scores. Is this true for your set of z scores?
3. If someone tells you that his or her IQ is 145, how rare is this event? (Hint: Calculate the z score and interpret it in relation to the normal curve.)
4. In the chapter, we provided a simple regression equation showing the relationship between grade point average and starting salary. The regression equation is $\hat{Y} = 9{,}234.56 + 7{,}638.85(X)$. What starting salary would you predict (using the regression equation) for someone who has a GPA of 4.00 (a student who has all A's)?
5. In Table 18.6a, we showed a contingency table with cell frequencies. In Table 18.6b, we showed a contingency table in which percentages had been calculated in each column. The table that follows shows a new set of cell frequencies.

	Gender		
Party Identification	*Males*	*Females*	*Total*
Democrat	390	920	1,310
Republican	569	160	729
Total	959	1,080	2,039

Calculate percentages in this new table down the columns and interpret the results.

PROPOSAL EXERCISES

Please go to the next chapter for the quantitative analysis proposal exercises.

RELEVANT INTERNET SITES

Online statistics textbooks
http://davidmlane.com/hyperstat/
http://www.psychstat.missouristate.edu/sbk00.htm

Statistical applets useful for explaining and learning about statistical analysis
http://www.math.hope.edu/swanson/statlabs/stat_applets.html
http://bcs.whfreeman.com/sris/#730892__926949__
http://www.amstat.org/sections/educ/applets.html
http://www.stat.berkeley.edu/~stark/Java/Html/

Lots of statistics-related learning materials that demonstrate statistics
http://wise.cgu.edu

STUDENT STUDY SITE

Visit the Student Study Site at **edge.sagepub.com/rbjohnson6e** for these additional learning tools:

Video Links
Self-Quizzes
eFlashcards
Lecture Notes
SPSS Data Set
Full-Text SAGE Journal Articles
Interactive Concept Maps
Web Resources

RECOMMENDED READING

Henry, G. T. (1995). *Applied social research methods series: Vol. 36. Graphing data: Techniques for display and analysis.* Thousand Oaks, CA: SAGE.

Huff, D., & Geis, I. (1993). *How to lie with statistics.* New York, NY: Norton. (Original work published 1954)

Koomey, J. G. (2008). *Turning numbers into knowledge: Mastering the art of problem solving.* Oakland, CA: Analytics Press.

Vogt, W. P., & Johnson, R. B. (2016). *Dictionary of statistics and methodology: A nontechnical guide for the social sciences* (5th ed.). Thousand Oaks, CA: SAGE.

NOTES

1. You cannot necessarily conclude that the data are normal when the mean and the median are the same.
2. If you form the ratio of the rates, you can obtain what is called the relative risk, which is also frequently given on the national news. In our example, the relative rate is 85.2/69.8 = 1.22. This rate of 1.22 means that males are 22% more likely than females to be Democrats. If the relative rate were 2.00, then males would be twice as likely to be Democrats; if the rate were 15.00, males would be 15 times as likely to be Democrats.

Chapter 19

Inferential Statistics

LEARNING OBJECTIVES

After reading this chapter, you should be able to

- Define inferential statistics.
- Explain the difference between a sample and a population.
- Explain the difference between a statistic and a parameter.
- Recognize the symbols used for the mean, variance, standard deviation, correlation coefficient, proportion, and regression coefficient.
- Provide the definition of sampling distribution.
- Compare and contrast point estimation and interval estimation.
- Explain how confidence intervals work over repeated sampling.
- List and explain the steps in hypothesis testing.
- Explain the difference between the null hypothesis and the alternative hypothesis.

Visit the Student Study Site for an interactive concept map.

RESEARCH IN REAL LIFE Making Generalizations With Inferential Statistics

istock/monkeybusinessimages

Over the past 10 to 15 years, many studies have compared smaller schools with larger schools and found that students in smaller schools "come to class more often, drop out less, earn better grades, participate more often in extracurricular activities, feel safer, and show fewer behavior problems" (Viadero, 2001). One of the studies contributing to this conclusion was funded by the Chicago-based Joyce Foundation (Wasley et al., 2000). In this 2-year study, the Chicago public schools were classified into different types, the primary distinction being small schools with fewer than 350 students versus larger schools with more than 350 students. The researchers collected data on a variety of indicators of school performance, such as dropout rates, attendance rates, retention rates, school grades, and standardized test scores. Following completion of the study, the researchers had to analyze this large data set in a way that would provide answers to the research questions that directed the study. One of the questions was whether a relationship existed between school size and student achievement. They also wanted to find out whether the effect of school size differed between elementary schools and high schools.

How did these researchers go about analyzing their data to answer their research questions? To analyze any set of quantitative data appropriately requires knowledge of statistics. Note that these researchers were not just interested in the particular schools that they studied but were also asking a general question regarding the effect of school size. In other words, they wanted to be able to generalize from the results of their study to other schools in similar circumstances. To be able to make such statements requires the use of inferential statistical techniques, and this is the type of statistical analysis that Wasley et al. (2000) used when they analyzed the results of their study. We discuss these statistical techniques in this chapter.

- Explain the difference between a nondirectional and a directional alternative hypothesis.
- Explain the difference between a probability value and the significance level.
- Draw the hypothesis-testing decision matrix and explain the contents.
- State how to decrease the probability of Type I and Type II errors.
- Explain the purpose of hypothesis testing.
- Explain the basic logic of significance testing.
- Explain the different significance tests discussed in the chapter.
- Explain the difference between statistical and practical significance.
- Explain what an effect size indicator is.

- **Inferential statistics** Use of the laws of probability to make inferences and draw statistical conclusions about populations based on sample data

- **Sample** A set of cases taken from a larger population

- **Population** The complete set of cases

- **Statistic** A numerical characteristic of a sample

- **Parameter** A numerical characteristic of a population

In descriptive statistics, researchers attempt to describe the numerical characteristics of their data. In **inferential statistics**, researchers attempt to go beyond their data. In particular, they use the laws of probability to make inferences about populations based on sample data. In the branch of inferential statistics known as *estimation*, researchers want to estimate the characteristics of populations based on their sample data. To make valid statistical estimations about populations, they use random samples (i.e., "probability" samples). In the branch of inferential statistics known as *hypothesis testing*, researchers test specific hypotheses about populations based on their sample data. You can see the major divisions of the field of statistics by reviewing Figure 18.1 (page 498).

Let's start with four important points about inferential statistics. First, the distinction between samples and populations is essential. You will recall that a **sample** is a subset of cases drawn from a population and a **population** is the complete set of cases. A population might be all first-grade students in the city of Ann Arbor, Michigan, and a sample might consist of 200 first-grade students selected from this population. The researcher should always define the population of interest.

Second, a **statistic** (also called a sample statistic) is a numerical characteristic of a sample, and a **parameter** (also called a population parameter) is a numerical characteristic of a population. Some examples of numerical characteristics that interest researchers are means (averages), proportions (or percentages), variances, standard deviations, correlations, and regression coefficients. Here is the main idea: If a mean or a correlation (or any other numerical characteristic) is calculated from sample data, it is called a statistic; if it is based on all the cases in the entire population (such as in a census), it is called a parameter.

Third, in inferential statistics, we study samples when we are actually much more interested in populations. We don't study populations directly because it would be cost prohibitive and logistically impossible to study everyone in most populations that are the focus of research studies. However, because we study samples rather than populations, our conclusions will sometimes be wrong. The solution provided by inferential statistics is that we can assign probabilities to our statements and we can draw conclusions that are very likely to be correct.

Fourth, random sampling is assumed in inferential statistics. You will recall from Chapter 10 that random sampling produces *representative* samples (i.e., samples that are similar to the populations from which they are selected). The assumption of random sampling is important in inferential statistics because it allows researchers to use the probability theory that underlies inferential statistics. Basically, statisticians have studied and come to understand the behavior of statistics based on random samples.

Now you need to become familiar with some symbols that are used to represent several commonly used statistics and parameters. Researchers and statisticians use different symbols for *statistics* and *parameters* because they want to communicate whether their research is based on sample or population data. Statisticians usually use Greek letters to symbolize population parameters and Roman letters (i.e., English letters) to symbolize sample statistics. (This is probably why some students say, "Statistics is like Greek to me!") This convention goes quite far back in the history of statistics. Please take a moment now and examine the symbols shown in Table 19.1. In the next paragraph, we are going to ask you a few questions about the symbols shown in the table.

Let's say that you have calculated the average reading performance of a sample of 100 fifth-grade students. What symbol would you use for this sample mean? The most

TABLE 19.1 A List of Symbols Used for Statistics and Parameters

Name	*Sample Statistic*	*Population Parameter*
Mean	$\bar{X}$	μ (mu)
Variance	SD^2	σ^2 (sigma squared)
Standard deviation	*SD*	σ (sigma)
Correlation	*r*	ρ (rho)
Proportion	*p*	π (pi)
Regression coefficient	*b*	β (beta)

Note: Statistics are usually symbolized with Roman letters and parameters with Greek letters.

commonly used symbol is $\bar{X}$ (it's called "*X*-bar"). Now assume that you have conducted a census of all fifth-grade students in the United States and you have calculated the average reading performance of all these students. What symbol would you use? As you can see in Table 19.1, the correct symbol for the population mean is μ (mu). The average is calculated in exactly the same way for both a sample and a population. The only difference is the symbol that is used to stand for the mean.

Now assume that you also calculated the correlation between math performance and reading performance for the 100 students in your sample of fifth-graders. What symbol would you use? The correct symbol for the sample correlation coefficient is *r*. If you conducted a census of all the fifth-grade students in the US population and calculated the correlation between math performance and reading performance, what symbol would you use? The appropriate symbol is ρ (rho). The important point is that when you calculate numerical indexes such as means, percentages, and correlations, you should use the appropriate symbol, and the correct symbol depends on whether you are analyzing sample data or population data. Statistics and parameters are *usually* calculated in exactly the same way. For example, the mean is calculated the same way for sample and population data. The key exception to this rule is that researchers use $n - 1$ rather than n in the denominator of the variance and standard deviation formulas when they are analyzing sample data. (You don't need to worry about the technical reason for this exception to the rule.[1])

- **Sampling distribution** The theoretical probability distribution of the values of a statistic that results when all possible random sam ples of a particular size are drawn from a population

REVIEW QUESTIONS

19.1 What is the difference between a statistic and a parameter?

19.2 What is the symbol for the population mean?

19.3 What is the symbol for the population correlation coefficient?

SAMPLING DISTRIBUTIONS

The theoretical notion of sampling distribution is what allows researchers to make probability statements about population parameters based on sample statistics. The **sampling distribution** of a statistic is defined as the theoretical probability distribution of the values of a statistic that results when all possible random samples of a particular size are drawn from a population. More simply, a sampling distribution is the distribution of a sample statistic that comes from **repeated sampling** (i.e., drawing a sample, calculating the statistic, drawing *another* sample, calculating the statistic, drawing *another* sample, and so forth, until *all* possible samples have been selected). If you actually did this process of *repeated sampling*, you would find that every time you select a new sample from the population and calculate the value of the statistic, the value is a little different. That's because of the role of *chance* in inferential statistics. The sample values are rarely exactly equal to the true population value—they vary randomly around that true value in a sampling distribution. The key idea here is that in inferential statistics, we never have full certainty about population parameters and must make our decisions based on the known rules of probability. The sampling distribution is an important idea to know about because it explains how sample statistics operate during repeated sampling.

- **Repeated sampling** Drawing many or all possible samples from a population

The idea of a sampling distribution is broadly applicable because a sampling distribution can be constructed for any sample statistic. For example, a sampling distribution can be constructed for the mean (the sampling distribution of the mean), a percentage (the sampling distribution of the percentage or proportion), a correlation (the sampling distribution of the correlation coefficient), a variance (the sampling distribution of the variance), and even the difference between two means. Can you guess what this last type of sampling distribution is called? (It's called the sampling distribution of the difference between two means.) You will be glad to know that you will never actually have to construct a sampling distribution! Statisticians have already constructed the sampling distributions for every common statistic that educational researchers use. You need to understand the *concept* of sampling distributions as expressed by the definition above.

It is important that you remember the following point: Researchers do *not* actually construct sampling distributions when they conduct their research. A researcher typically selects only *one* sample, not all possible samples, from a population, and then uses a computer program such as SPSS or SAS to analyze the data collected from the people in the sample. Remember that a sampling distribution is based on all possible samples, not the single sample that the researcher studies. The computer program does, however, use sampling distributions. In particular, the computer uses the idea of a sampling distribution to determine certain probabilities, which we will discuss shortly. You should therefore think of a sampling distribution as a theoretical distribution because there is a sampling distribution underlying each inferential statistical procedure that a researcher uses.

A sampling distribution demonstrates that *the value of any sample statistic* (such as a mean or a correlation coefficient) *varies from sample to sample.* Think of it like this: If you selected several random samples from a population and calculated the value of a statistic (such as a mean) for each of the samples, wouldn't you expect the sample values to be a little different from one another? You would *not* expect all of your sample values to be *exactly* the same number. This chance variation from sample to sample results in sampling error.

- **Sampling error** The difference between the value of a sample statistic and the corresponding population parameter

Sampling error is the difference between a sample statistic and the corresponding population parameter, and it is virtually always present in research because researchers rarely study everyone in a population. The presence of sampling error does not mean that random sampling doesn't work or that a researcher has made a mistake. It simply means that the values of statistics calculated from random samples will tend to vary because of chance fluctuations.

Researchers sometimes need an indicator of the amount of sampling error (i.e., variation) present in a sampling distribution. That is, they need to know what is called the standard error of a sampling distribution. The **standard error** is nothing more than the standard deviation of a sampling distribution. Recall from Chapter 18 that the standard deviation tells you how much variation there is in a distribution of data. The variation of a sampling distribution can also be described by determining the standard deviation. However, statisticians like to call this special type of standard deviation (the standard deviation of a *sampling distribution*) the standard error. It tells you how much variation there is in the scores that make up a sampling distribution. Whenever you hear the term *standard error*, you should therefore think of the variation in a sampling distribution.

■ **Standard error** The standard deviation of a sampling distribution

When there is a lot of sampling error in a sampling distribution, the standard error will be large, and when there is not much sampling error, the standard error will be small. For example, if a sampling distribution is based on large random samples (e.g., all possible samples of size 1,500), the standard error will be smaller than if the sampling distribution is based on small random samples (e.g., all possible samples of size 20). That's because, on average, large samples provide values closer to the population parameter than small samples do. In short, researchers prefer a small standard error, and a good way to get a small standard error is to select a large sample.

There is one more characteristic of sampling distributions to remember: If you construct a sampling distribution, you see that *the average of the values of the sample statistic is equal to the population parameter.* For example, if you took all possible samples from a population and calculated the correlation for each sample, the average of all those sample correlations would equal the correlation in the entire population. The reason is that while a sample statistic value will sometimes overestimate the population value and will sometimes underestimate the population value, it will not be consistently too large or too small. As a result, the average of all the possible sample statistic values is equal to the population parameter.

Sampling Distribution of the Mean

Now let's make things a little more concrete by considering the sampling distribution of a particular statistic. Let's think about the sampling distribution of the mean. Let's say that you just drew a random sample of 100 people from the population of a city. *For the purpose of this example, we are telling you that the average income of the population is $50,000.* (In practice you would *not* know the population mean.) What value would you expect to obtain if you calculated the mean income of the 100 people in your randomly selected sample? You would expect the sample mean to be around $50,000 (since you happen to know that the population mean is $50,000). Let's say, however, that your sample mean turns out to be $45,600. Your sample mean is a little less than the population mean, and the amount of sampling error is $4,400 (i.e., $50,000 – $45,600 = $4,400). Your sample mean is not exactly the same as the population mean.

Now assume that you select another random sample of 100 people from the same city population. What value would you expect for the sample mean this time? Again, you would expect the sample mean to be about $50,000. This time, however, the sample mean is equal to $52,000. Now draw *another* random sample of 100 people. Let's say this sample mean is $49,800. Now let's say, hypothetically speaking, that you continue this process (of selecting a random sample of a specified size and calculating the sample mean on each sample) until all possible samples have been examined. You would obviously have a lot of sample means! The line graph constructed from all of these means would form a normal curve, and the overall average of this sampling distribution would be $50,000 (the same as the population parameter). The name of this theoretical distribution of sample means is the **sampling distribution of the mean.**

- **Sampling distribution of the mean** The theoretical probability distribution of the means of all possible random samples of a particular size drawn from a population

You can see a picture of our hypothetical sampling distribution of the mean in Figure 19.1. We assume that the standard error is $10,000. That is, the standard deviation of our hypothetical sampling distribution of the mean is $10,000. If you look at the line graph in Figure 19.1, you see that the sampling distribution of the mean is normally distributed. Because the distribution is normally distributed, we know that most of the randomly selected sample means will be close to the population mean but a few of them will be farther away. Basically, random sampling works well most of the time but not all of the time.

The mean of the sampling distribution of the mean is equal to the true population mean because random sampling is an unbiased sampling process (i.e., random sampling does not produce sample statistics that are systematically larger or smaller than the population parameter). If you take all possible random samples and calculate the mean of each sample, the means will fluctuate randomly around the population mean, and they will form a normal distribution. Some of these means will fall above the population mean, and some will fall below the population mean, but the average of all of these sample means will equal the true population mean. That's how random sampling operates. It is a chance process. You now have the important ideas of sampling distributions. Sampling distributions are important in estimation and hypothesis testing, the major divisions of inferential statistics.

FIGURE 19.1 The sampling distribution of the mean. *SEM* stands for standard error of the mean (i.e., the standard deviation of the sampling distribution of the mean).

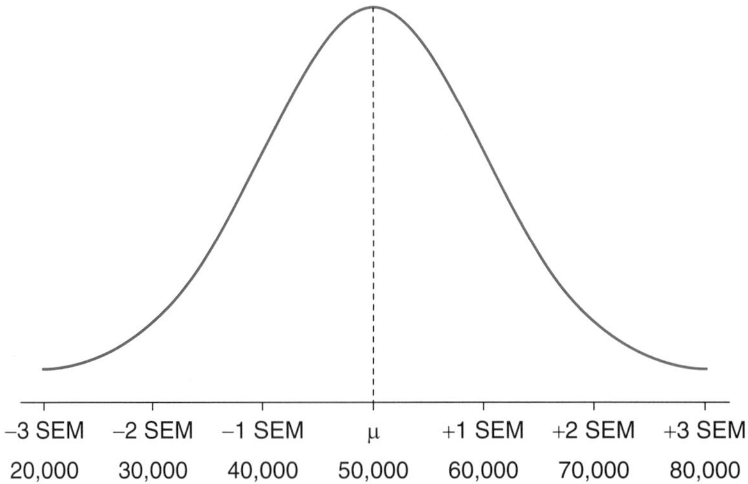

REVIEW QUESTIONS

19.4 What is the definition of a sampling distribution?

19.5 How does the idea of repeated sampling relate to the concept of a sampling distribution?

Estimation

People often make estimations. For example, if your best friend asks you what time you're coming to his house Sunday for a visit, you will provide an estimate. You might say, "I'll probably come over about two o'clock." In other words, your estimate is "two o'clock." Researchers use inferential statistics to make an estimation of a population parameter. The key question in the field of statistical estimation is,

- Based on my random sample, what is my estimate of the population parameter?

There are two kinds of estimation procedures in inferential statistics. If you use a single number (the value of your sample statistic) as your estimate (your best guess) of the population parameter, then you are engaged in point estimation. If you use a range of numbers that you believe includes the population parameter, then you are engaged in interval estimation. As an analogy, let's say that you take your car in for a repair and the service manager gives you an estimate of how much the repair will cost. If the manager says that the cost will probably be $300, then the manager has provided a point estimate (a single number). If the manager says that the cost will probably be "somewhere between $250 and $350," then the manager has provided an interval estimate (a range of numbers that is likely to include the true cost). That's the basic idea. Now we explain these two kinds of estimation a little further.

Point Estimation

Point estimation is defined as the use of the value of a sample statistic as the estimate of the value of a population parameter. You might use the sample mean to estimate the population mean, the sample percentage to estimate the population percentage, or the sample correlation to estimate the population correlation. The specific value of the statistic is called the **point estimate**, and it is the estimated value of the population parameter. The point estimate is your best guess about the likely value of the unknown population parameter.

- **Point estimation** The use of the value of a sample statistic as the estimate of the value of a population parameter
- **Point estimate** The estimated value of a population parameter

Let's see whether you can now engage in point estimation. Say that the average income of the people in a random sample of 350 teachers from San Antonio, Texas, USA, is $39,000. What is your point estimate of the population mean? You would estimate the value in the population of teachers in San Antonio to be $39,000 because that was the mean of your random sample. Now let's say that 59% of the 350 teachers in your sample say that they support bilingual education. What is the point estimate of the population percentage? You would estimate the percentage in the population of teachers in San Antonio to be 59% because that was the percentage in your random sample. In sum, your point estimates are $39,000 (for income) and 59% (for supporting bilingual education).

Point estimation is used whenever a researcher uses the value of the sample statistic as the estimate of the population parameter. Because of the presence of sampling error, however, a point estimate will rarely be exactly the same value as the population parameter. Think of it like this. If the average income in a population is $35,000, would you expect your sample value to be exactly $35,000, or would you expect it to be some number near $35,000? You should expect that it would be a number near but not exactly equal to $35,000. An insight from our earlier study of sampling distributions is that *the value of a statistic varies*

See Journal Article 19.1 on the Student Study Site.

from sample to sample. That's why a point estimate is usually wrong. Because of the presence of sampling error, many researchers recommend the use of interval estimation.

Interval Estimation

- **Confidence interval** A range of numbers inferred from the sample that has a certain probability or chance of including the population parameter
- **Confidence limits** The endpoints of a confidence interval
- **Lower limit** The smallest number of a confidence interval
- **Upper limit** The largest number of a confidence interval
- **Level of confidence** The probability that a confidence interval to be constructed from a random sample will include the population parameter

When researchers use interval estimation, they construct confidence intervals. A **confidence interval** is a range of numbers inferred from the sample that has a certain probability or chance of including the population parameter. The endpoints of a confidence interval are called **confidence limits**; the smallest number is called the **lower limit**, and the largest number is called the **upper limit**. In other words, rather than using a point estimate (which is a single number), the researcher uses a range of numbers, bounded by the lower and upper limits, as the interval estimate. This way, researchers can increase their chances of capturing the true population parameter.

Researchers are able to state the probability (called the **level of confidence**) that a confidence interval to be constructed from a random sample will include the population parameter. We use the future tense because our confidence is actually in the long-term process of constructing confidence intervals. For example, 95% confidence intervals will capture the population parameter 95% of the time (the probability is 95%), and 99% confidence intervals will capture the population parameter 99% of the time (the probability is 99%). This idea is demonstrated in Figure 19.2.

In the top part of Figure 19.2, you see a hypothetical sampling distribution of the mean. Recall from our earlier discussion that the sampling distribution of the mean is normally distributed and its mean is equal to the population mean. Also, a key idea of the sampling distribution of the mean is that the values of individual sample means vary from sample to sample because of sampling error. Now look at the 20 sample means (the dots) surrounded by their confidence intervals below the sampling distribution in Figure 19.2. These 20 means randomly jump around the population mean, just as you would expect. Notice, however, that 19 of the 20 confidence intervals covered the population mean. Only one of the confidence intervals missed the true population mean. The process worked as we would expect for these 20 samples.

Most of the time, confidence intervals will include the population parameter, but occasionally, they will miss it. In Figure 19.2, the process worked 19 times out of 20. Because the intervals were 95% confidence intervals, that is exactly what we expected would happen. We expected to be right about 95% of the time, and we were (19 out of 20 is 95%). The bottom line is that if you construct 95% confidence intervals, then you will capture the population parameter 95% of the time in the long run.

You are probably wondering why a researcher would use 95% confidence intervals rather than 99% confidence intervals. After all, the researcher will make a mistake 5% of the time with 95% confidence intervals but only 1% of the time with 99% confidence intervals. The reason is that 99% confidence intervals are wider than 95% confidence intervals and wider intervals are less precise (e.g., the interval from 20 to 80 is wider and less precise than the interval from 45 to 55). That is the trade-off. Fortunately, there is a way out of it. *An effective way to achieve both a higher level of confidence and a more narrow (i.e., more precise) interval is to increase the sample size.* Bigger samples are therefore better than smaller samples. As a general rule, most researchers use 95% confidence intervals, and as

■ **FIGURE 19.2** A sampling distribution of the mean (based on all possible samples of size 100) and an illustration of the 95% confidence intervals for 20 possible samples. The width of the intervals will be slightly different because they are estimated from different random samples. In the long run, 95% of confidence intervals will capture the population mean.

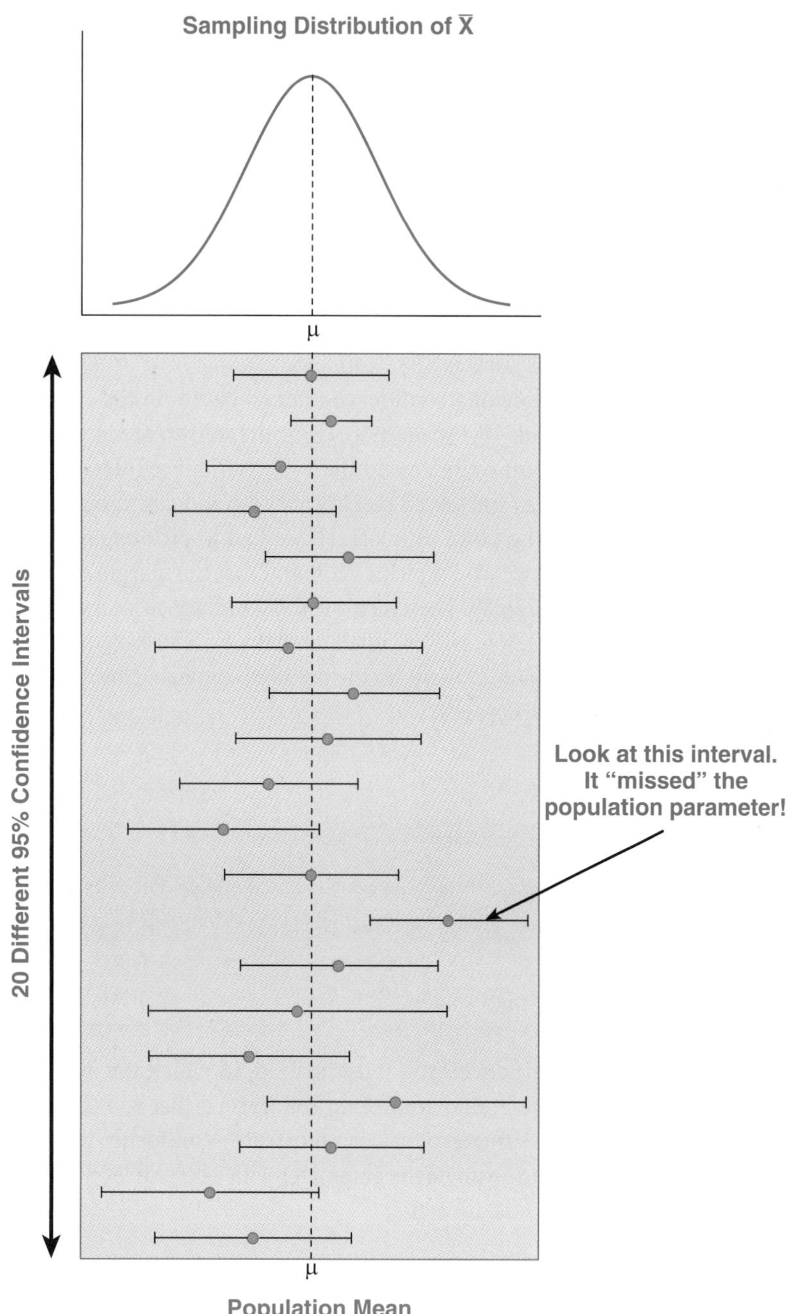

a result, they make a mistake about 5% of the time. Researchers also attempt to select sample sizes that produce intervals that are narrow (i.e., precise) enough for their needs.

Now we want to give you an intuitive explanation of how a confidence interval is constructed. Here is the general formula for a confidence interval:

$$\text{Confidence interval} = \text{point estimate} \pm \text{margin of error}$$

where the symbol ± means plus or minus. As you can see, a confidence interval is a point estimate (a sample mean, a sample percentage, a sample correlation, and so forth) plus or minus the margin of error. The **margin of error** is simply one half the width of the confidence interval. A confidence interval is constructed by taking a point estimate and surrounding it by the margin of error. For example, if you wanted a confidence interval for the mean, you could find the sample mean and surround it on each side by the margin of error.

- **Margin of error** One half the width of a confidence interval

To find out how to calculate the margin of error, you will need to consult a statistics book (e.g., Howell, 2013a). Fortunately, researchers rarely need to calculate their confidence intervals by hand because confidence intervals are easily obtained through the use of statistical computer programs such as SPSS and SAS.

Now we show you an example of a confidence interval based on the college student data set that we introduced in Table 18.1 (page 499). Using the statistical computer program called SPSS, we obtained the point estimate and the 95% confidence interval for starting salary. The average starting salary for the 25 recent college graduates in our data set was $32,640. Therefore, $32,640 is the point estimate. (If we had to pick *one* number as our estimate, $32,640 is the number we would pick.) We found that the margin of error for the 95% confidence interval was $1,726.29. Therefore, the 95% confidence interval is the range of values from $30,913.71 to $34,366.29. We conclude that we are 95% confident that the interval from $30,913.71 to $34,366.29 includes the population mean. Now you know how to interpret a confidence interval correctly!

REVIEW QUESTIONS

19.6 Which of the two types of estimation do you like the most? Why?

19.7 What are the advantages of using interval estimation rather than point estimation?

HYPOTHESIS TESTING

In the preceding section, we introduced you to estimation, in which the goal was to use sample statistics to estimate population parameters. You learned that you can use a single number as the estimate (a point estimate) or you can construct a confidence interval around the point estimate, allowing you to estimate the parameter with a certain level of confidence. The key question in estimation is the following:

- Based on my random sample, what is my (point or interval) estimate of the true population parameter?

- **Hypothesis testing** The branch of inferential statistics that is concerned with how well the sample data support a null hypothesis and when the null hypothesis can be rejected

In this section, we introduce **hypothesis testing**, the branch of inferential statistics that is concerned with how well the sample data support a particular hypothesis, called the null hypothesis, and when the null hypothesis can be rejected. Unlike estimation, in which the researcher usually has no clear hypothesis about the population parameter, in hypothesis testing, the researcher states his or her null and alternative hypotheses and then uses inferential statistics on a new set of data to determine what decision needs to be made about these hypotheses. For now, just think of the null hypothesis as the hypothesis that states, "There is no effect present," and the alternative hypothesis as the hypothesis that states, "There is an effect present." Here is another way to say this: In hypothesis testing, the researcher hopes to "nullify" the null hypothesis (i.e., we hope to find relationships or patterns in the world, which means that we want to reject the null hypothesis).

This is the key question that is answered in hypothesis testing:

- Is the value of my sample statistic unlikely enough (*assuming that the null hypothesis is true*) for me to reject the null hypothesis and tentatively accept the alternative hypothesis?

For example, a researcher might do an experiment to compare a new method of counseling (given to the experimental group) to no counseling at all (the control group). In this case, the null hypothesis says that there is no effect (i.e., the treatment group is *not* any better than the control group after the treatment), and the alternative hypothesis says that there is an effect (i.e., the treatment and control groups do differ after the treatment). If the two groups are very dissimilar after the treatment, the researcher might be able to reject the null hypothesis and accept the alternative hypothesis.[2] The goal of hypothesis testing is to help a researcher make a probabilistic decision about the truth of the null and alternative hypotheses. Ultimately, the researcher hopes the research data will allow him or her to reject the null hypothesis and support the alternative hypothesis.

In the next section, we carefully explain the null hypothesis and the alternative hypothesis because these two hypotheses are the foundation of hypothesis testing. In Exhibit 19.1, we provide an illustrative preview of the material that follows by showing that hypothesis testing has some similarities to what takes place in the courtroom.

EXHIBIT 19.1 An Analogy From Jurisprudence

The US criminal justice system operates on the assumption that the defendant is innocent until proven guilty beyond a reasonable doubt. In hypothesis testing, this assumption is called the null hypothesis. That is, researchers assume that the null hypothesis is true until the evidence suggests that it is not likely to be true.

The researcher's null hypothesis might be that a technique of counseling does not work any better than no counseling. The researcher is somewhat like a prosecuting attorney, who brings someone to trial when he or she believes that there is some evidence against the accused; the researcher brings a null hypothesis to "trial" when he or she believes that there is some evidence against the null hypothesis (i.e., the researcher actually believes that the counseling technique does work better than no counseling). In the courtroom, the jury decides what constitutes reasonable doubt, and it makes a decision about guilt or innocence. The researcher uses inferential statistics to determine the probability of the evidence under the assumption that the null hypothesis is true. If this probability is low, the researcher is able to reject the null hypothesis and accept the alternative hypothesis. If this probability is not low, the researcher is not able to reject the null hypothesis.

No matter what decision is made, things are still not completely settled because a mistake could have been made. In the courtroom, decisions of guilt or innocence are sometimes overturned or found to be incorrect. Similarly, in research, the decision to reject or not reject the null hypothesis is based on probability, so researchers sometimes make a mistake. Inferential statistics shows researchers how likely it is that they have made a mistake.

Null and Alternative Hypotheses

In earlier chapters, you learned about "research hypotheses" or predictions researchers make and test through the collection of new empirical data. During hypothesis testing, two new hypotheses come into focus: the null hypothesis and the alternative hypothesis. The starting point for hypothesis testing is to state the null and the alternative hypotheses. The **null hypothesis**, represented by the symbol H_0, is a statement about a population parameter and states that some condition concerning the population parameter is true. In most educational research studies, the null hypothesis (H_0) predicts no difference or no relationship in the population. The null hypothesis is the hypothesis tested directly using probability theory; that's why hypothesis testing sometimes is called "null hypothesis significance testing" or NHST. Please remember this key point: Hypothesis testing operates under the *assumption* that the null hypothesis is true. Then, if the results obtained from the research study are very different from those expected under the assumption that the null hypothesis is true, the researcher rejects the null hypothesis and tentatively accepts the alternative hypothesis. Again, the null hypothesis is the focal point in hypothesis testing because it is the null hypothesis, not the alternative hypothesis, that is tested directly.

- **Null hypothesis** A statement about a population parameter

The **alternative hypothesis**, represented by the symbol H_1, states that the population parameter is some value other than the value stated by H_0. The alternative hypothesis asserts the opposite of the H_0 and usually is a statement of a difference between means or a relationship between variables. The null and alternative hypotheses are logically contradictory because they cannot both be true at the same time. If hypothesis testing allows the researcher to reject the null hypothesis, then the researcher can tentatively accept the alternative hypothesis. The alternative hypothesis is almost always more consistent with the researcher's research hypothesis; therefore, the researcher hopes to support the alternative hypothesis, not the null hypothesis. The null hypothesis is like a "means to an end." The researcher has to use the null hypothesis because that is what must be stated and tested directly in statistics.

- **Alternative hypothesis** Statement that the population parameter is some value other than the value stated by the null hypothesis

You can see several examples of research questions, null hypotheses, and alternative hypotheses in Table 19.2. Later in this chapter, we will test several of these null hypotheses using our college student data set from Table 18.1 (page 499).

Many students are curious why researchers use the term *null hypothesis.* It was developed by a famous statistician, Sir Ronald Fisher (1890–1962), who invented the procedure of hypothesis testing. The idea is to set up a hypothesis to be "knocked down" or rejected. Researchers do this because the convention is to assume no effect or no difference from the hypothesized null value until sufficient evidence to the contrary is provided. You can therefore view the null hypothesis as the no-change or the no-effect hypothesis. You can also view it as the status quo or the "nothing new" or the "business as usual" hypothesis. The key point once again is that *the null hypothesis is what researchers assume until they can demonstrate otherwise.*

Here is how Harnett (1982) explained the null hypothesis:

> The term "null hypothesis" developed from early work in the theory of hypothesis testing, in which this hypothesis corresponded to a theory about a population parameter that the researcher thought did not represent the true value of the parameter (hence the word "null," which means invalid, void, or amounting to nothing). The alternative hypothesis generally specified those values of the parameter that the researcher believed did hold true. (p. 346)

According to the logic of hypothesis testing, you should assume that an effect is *not* present until you have good evidence to conclude otherwise. The researcher states a null hypothesis but hopes ultimately to be able to reject it. In other words, the null hypothesis is the hypothesis that the researcher hopes to be able to nullify by conducting the hypothesis test.

As an example, let's assume that we are interested in knowing which teaching method works better: the discussion teaching method or the lecture teaching method. Here are the null and alternative hypotheses:

Null hypothesis: H_0: $\mu_D = \mu_L$

Alternative hypothesis: H_1: $\mu_D \neq \mu_L$

where

μ_D is the symbol for the discussion group population mean, and

μ_L is the symbol for the lecture group population mean.

This null hypothesis says that the average performance of students in discussion classes is equal to the average performance of students in lecture classes. This null hypothesis is called a point or exact hypothesis because it contains an equal sign (=). As you can see, the

TABLE 19.2 Examples of Null and Alternative Hypotheses in Inferential Statistics

Research Question	*Verbal Null* (H_0) *Hypothesis*	*Symbolic* H_0 *Hypothesis*	*Verbal Alternative* (H_1) *Hypothesis*	*Symbolic* H_1 *Hypothesis*
Do teachers score higher on the GRE Verbal than the national average?	The teacher population GRE Verbal mean is equal to the national average of 476.	H_0: $\mu_{\text{GRE V}} = 476$	The teacher population GRE Verbal mean is different from the national average of 476.	H_1: $\mu_{\text{GRE V}} \neq 476$
Do males or females tend to score better on the GRE Verbal?	The male and female population means are not different.	H_0: $\mu_M = \mu_F$	The male and female population means are different.	H_1: $\mu_M \neq \mu_F$
Do education, arts and sciences, and business students have different starting incomes?	The education, arts and sciences, and business student populations have the same mean starting incomes.	H_0: $\mu_E = \mu_{A\&S} = \mu_B$	At least two of the three population means are different.	H_1: Not all equal
Is there a correlation between GPA (X) and starting salary (Y)?	The population correlation between GPA and starting salary is equal to zero.	H_0: $\rho_{XY} = 0$	The population correlation between GPA and starting salary is not equal to zero.	H_1: $\rho_{XY} \neq 0$
Is there a relationship between GRE Verbal (X_1) and starting salary (Y), controlling for GPA (X_2)?	The population regression coefficient is equal to zero.	H_0: $\beta_{YX1.X2} = 0$	The population regression coefficient is not equal to zero.	H_1: $\beta_{YX1.X2} \neq 0$

alternative hypothesis states the opposite of the null hypothesis (i.e., that the discussion and lecture population means are *not* equal).

It is a good idea to remember the following three points about hypothesis testing. First, the alternative hypothesis can never include an equal sign (=). Second, the alternative hypothesis is based on one of these three signs: ≠ (not equal to), < (less than), or > (greater than). Third, the null hypothesis is based on one of these three signs: = (equal to), ≤ (less than or equal to), or ≥ (greater than or equal to). As you can see, the equality sign is always a part of the null hypothesis.

Directional Alternative Hypotheses

- **Nondirectional alternative hypothesis** An alternative hypothesis that includes the not equal (≠) sign
- **Directional alternative hypothesis** An alternative hypothesis that contains either a greater than sign (>) or a less than sign (<)

Sometimes the researcher will state an alternative hypothesis in a directional form rather than in a nondirectional form. A **nondirectional alternative hypothesis** includes a not equal to sign (≠). A **directional alternative hypothesis** contains either a greater than sign (>) or a less than sign (<).

For example, the researcher in our previous example could have stated this set of hypotheses:

Null hypothesis: $H_0: \mu_D \leq \mu_L$

Alternative hypothesis: $H_1: \mu_D > \mu_L$

You can see that the alternative hypothesis in this case states that the discussion group population mean is greater than the lecture group population mean. In other words, a directional alternative hypothesis is stated. Depiction of the null hypothesis was also changed so that all possible outcomes were included in the two hypotheses (i.e., to make them complementary). Note that the null hypothesis still has the equality sign in it (i.e., the sign ≤ means less than or *equal* to).

The researcher could have also stated this set of hypotheses:

Null hypothesis: $H_0: \mu_D \geq \mu_L$

Alternative hypothesis: $H_1: \mu_D < \mu_L$

Once again, a directional alternative hypothesis is given. This time, however, the alternative hypothesis states that the discussion group population mean is less than the lecture group population mean. In other words, it is hypothesized that students learning by lecture do better, on average, than do students learning by discussion.

Although the use of directional alternative hypotheses for the purpose of statistical analysis might seem attractive, there is a major drawback. If a researcher uses a directional alternative hypothesis and a large difference in the *opposite* direction is found, the researcher must conclude that *no* relationship exists in the population. That is the rule of hypothesis testing when using a directional alternative hypothesis. However, this conclusion of no relationship would operate against the *discovery* function of science. Because of this, most practicing researchers state directional research hypotheses (i.e., they make a directional prediction), but they test nondirectional alternative hypotheses so that they can leave open this discovery function of science. This process results in a slight loss of statistical power, but that minor drawback can be offset simply by including a few more participants in your research study. Therefore, when you read journal articles, the vast majority of the alternative hypotheses will be nondirectional (even if the researcher's "research hypothesis" or actual prediction is directional). In fact, if a researcher has used a *directional* alternative hypothesis, he or she is obliged to tell you (Pillemer, 1991). If a researcher does not state the type of alternative hypothesis used in the statistical analysis procedure, you can assume that it was a nondirectional alternative hypothesis.

Examining the Probability Value and Making a Decision

Now you are going to learn how the researcher decides to reject or fail to reject the null hypothesis. As we told you earlier, it is the null hypothesis that is tested directly in the hypothesis-testing procedure. When a researcher states a null hypothesis, the researcher is able to use the principles of inferential statistics to construct a probability model about what would happen *if the null hypothesis were true.*[3] This probability model is nothing but the sampling distribution that would result for the sample statistic (mean, percentage, correlation) over repeated sampling if the null hypothesis were true. In practice, the researcher uses a computer package, such as SPSS or SAS, that automatically selects the correct sampling distribution for the particular statistical test. For example, if you tested a null hypothesis about the mean, SPSS would use information about the sampling distribution of the mean for your statistical test. All you have to do is know what null hypothesis you want to test and then select the appropriate statistical test; the software package does the rest.

After the researcher states the null hypothesis, collects the research data, and selects a statistical test using SPSS, the computer program analyzes the research data and provides something called a probability value as part of the computer output. The **probability value** (also called the ***p* value**) is the probability of the observed result of your research study (or a more extreme result) under the assumption that the null hypothesis is true. As an aside, the probability value is a conditional probability because it tells you the probability of the observed value of your test statistic (or a more extreme value) *if the null hypothesis is true.* The probability value is *not* the probability that the null hypothesis is true, it is *not* the probability that the null hypothesis is false, it is *not* the probability that the alternative hypothesis is true, and it is *not* the probability that the alternative hypothesis is false. It *is* the long-run frequency (through repeated sampling) that the particular observed value of your sample statistic or a more extreme value would occur simply due to chance fluctuations, when the null hypothesis is true. We mention these possible mistakes concerning the meaning of the term *probability value* so that you will not make one of these mistakes. Please remember that the term *probability value* (or *p* value for short) has a very precise meaning, and you need to place its definition in your long-term memory right now. The probability value is the probability of the observed outcome if the null hypothesis were true.

- **Probability value or *p* value** The probability of the observed result of your research study or a more extreme result if the null hypothesis were true

Obtaining the probability value is the key idea in hypothesis testing because the researcher uses this value to make a decision about the null hypothesis. In particular, the researcher uses the probability value that is based on his or her research results to determine whether the observed value of the sample statistic (mean, percentage, correlation, and so forth) is probable or improbable, assuming that the null hypothesis is true. If the probability value is very small, the researcher is allowed to reject the null hypothesis.

For example, suppose a researcher wants to determine who has the higher starting salary: recent male college graduates or recent female college graduates. Let's say that you construct these two statistical hypotheses for your research study:

Null hypothesis: H_0: $\mu_{\text{Males}} = \mu_{\text{Females}}$

Alternative hypothesis: H_1: $\mu_{\text{Males}} \neq \mu_{\text{Females}}$

As you can see, you want to test the null hypothesis that the average starting salaries for the males and females are the same in their respective populations. The alternative hypothesis says the average starting salaries are *not* the same. You have randomly selected samples of males and females, and you have calculated the starting salaries for these individuals in your research study.

If the average starting salary was $43,000 for the males and $27,000 for the females in your research study, the probability value would be small because such a large difference would be unlikely if the null hypothesis were true. When the probability value is small, the researcher rejects the null hypothesis because the research results call into question the null hypothesis. (We will explain in a moment when you should consider a probability value to be "small.") When the researcher rejects the null hypothesis, the researcher decides to accept the alternative hypothesis. If you did reject the null hypothesis and therefore tentatively accepted the alternative hypothesis, you would also make the claim that the finding is **statistically significant**. Researchers claim their finding is statistically significant when they do *not* believe (based on the evidence of their data) that their observed result was due only to chance or sampling error.

- **Statistically significant** Claim made when the evidence suggests an observed result was probably not due to chance

On the other hand, if the average starting salary was $33,000 for the males in your study and $31,000 for the females in your study, the difference between $33,000 and $31,000 could simply be due to chance (i.e., sampling error). In this case, the probability value would be larger than that in the previous example because this time the difference is not so unlikely under the assumption that the null hypothesis is true. If the probability value is large, the researcher will fail to reject the null hypothesis. The researcher will also make the claim that the research finding is not statistically significant (i.e., the observed difference between the two means may simply be a random or chance fluctuation).

We told you that you can use a computer program such as SPSS to find out how likely or unlikely your sample result is, *assuming that the null hypothesis is true.* You make this determination using the probability value that you get from the computer printout. If the probability value is small, then your sample result is unlikely (assuming that the null hypothesis is true). If the probability value is large, then your sample result is not unlikely (assuming that the null hypothesis is true). You are probably wondering, "When do I consider a probability value to be small?" and "When do I consider a probability value to be large?" The answer is that most researchers consider a probability value that is less than or equal to .05 to be small and a probability value that is greater than .05 to be relatively large.

For example, assume that the probability value (based on your computer analysis of the research data) was .03 when the male and female incomes were very different ($43,000 versus $27,000). Because this probability value is less than .05, the researcher would reject the *null hypothesis* that the two population means are the same (H_0: $\mu_{\text{Males}} = \mu_{\text{Females}}$), and the researcher would accept the alternative hypothesis that the two population means are different ($H_1: \mu_{\text{Males}} \neq \mu_{\text{Females}}$). The researcher would also claim that the difference between the two sample means is statistically significant.

On the other hand, assume that the probability value (based on your computer analysis of the data) was .45 when the male and female incomes were similar ($33,000 versus $31,000). In this case, the probability value is greater than .05. Therefore, the researcher would *fail to reject the null hypothesis.* The researcher would also claim that the difference between the two sample means is not statistically significant. Note that the researcher cannot claim that the two population means are the same. The researcher can only claim that he or she has failed to reject the null hypothesis. Basically, whenever the researcher is unable to reject the null hypothesis, he or she is left in an ambiguous situation.

This number .05 that we just used is the significance level that we chose to help us decide when the probability value was small or large. In other words, a researcher selects a significance level to aid in making the decision about the size of the probability value obtained from the analysis of the research data. The **significance level** (also called the **alpha level**) is the cutoff that the researcher uses to decide when to reject the null hypothesis: (1) When the *probability value* is less than or equal to the *significance level*, the researcher rejects the null hypothesis, and (2) when the probability value is greater than the significance level, the researcher fails to reject the null hypothesis. It is important to understand that a significance level does not have to be .05. The researcher can select any significance level to use in a research study as long as he or she can justify why a particular significance level was used.

- **Significance level or alpha level** The cutoff the researcher uses to decide when to reject the null hypothesis

You might wonder why educational researchers usually select a significance level of .05 and why they believe that a probability value that is less than or equal to .05 is small enough to reject the null hypothesis and that a probability value greater than .05 is not small enough (is too large) to reject the null hypothesis. There are no ultimate answers to these questions, but the significance level of .05 has become a widespread convention among researchers in education and every other social and behavioral science. In other words, it is the significance level that researchers have decided to adopt. Historically, Sir Ronald Fisher originally used the .05 significance level, and ever since then, the .05 significance level has been popular with many researchers. Remember, however, that the .05 significance level is not used by all researchers; it is only the most commonly used significance level.

What exactly does a significance level of .05 mean? Choosing a significance level of .05 means that if your sample result would occur only 5% of the time or less (when the null hypothesis is true, as indicated by the probability value), then you are going to question the veracity of the null hypothesis, and you will reject the null hypothesis. Remember, the researcher hopes to reject the null hypothesis. When the researcher rejects the null hypothesis, he or she "tentatively accepts" the alternative hypothesis. Using a term to be discussed later, the significance level is the maximum risk that a researcher is willing to take of committing a *Type I error* (i.e., incorrectly rejecting the null hypothesis when it is true). Remember this key point: The *significance level* is the value with which the researcher compares the *probability value.*

First, the researcher selects a significance level that he or she wants to use in the research study. The significance level is cutoff value (such as .05) that the researcher chooses to use in deciding when the probability value is small enough to call into question the null hypothesis. Be careful not to get the *probability value* and the *significance level* mixed up! You should carefully compare the definitions and memorize them. Second, the researcher runs the computer program and gets the probability value from the computer printout. The probability value is based on the statistical analysis of the research data. It tells the researcher how likely the observed value of the sample statistic is, under the assumption that the null hypothesis is true. Remember that the probability value is based on the empirical research data collected by the researcher.

When you engage in hypothesis testing, you follow these two rules:

- *Rule 1.* If the probability value (which is a number obtained from the computer printout and is based on your research results) is less than or equal to the significance level (the researcher usually uses .05), then the researcher rejects the null hypothesis and tentatively accepts the alternative hypothesis. The researcher also concludes that the observed relationship is statistically significant (i.e., the observed difference between the groups is not just due to chance fluctuations).
- *Rule 2.* If the probability value is greater than the significance level, then the researcher cannot reject the null hypothesis. The researcher can only claim to fail to reject the null hypothesis and conclude that the relationship is not statistically significant (i.e., any observed difference between the groups is probably nothing but a reflection of chance fluctuations).

If you memorize rules 1 and 2, the rest of the material in this chapter is going to be easier than you might expect! These two rules are stated more concisely in Table 19.3. At this point, you should review the steps in hypothesis testing summarized in Table 19.3 so that you can remember the *logic of hypothesis testing* (also called the logic of significance testing). Because of the importance of the concepts of probability value and significance level, we also explain them in an intuitive way in Exhibit 19.2.

TABLE 19.3 Steps in Hypothesis Testing

1. State the null and alternative hypotheses.
2. Set the *significance level* before analyzing the data. (Most educational researchers use .05 as the significance level. Note that the significance level is also called the *alpha level* or, more simply, *alpha.*)
3. Obtain the *probability value* based on the analysis of your empirical data using a computer program such as SPSS. (Note that the probability value is also called the *p* value.)
4. Compare the probability value to the significance level and make the statistical decision.

Step 4 includes two decision-making rules:

Rule 1:

If:	Probability value ≤ significance level (i.e., probability value ≤ alpha).
Then:	Reject the null hypothesis.
And:	Conclude that the research finding is statistically significant.

In practice, this usually means the following:

If:	Probability value ≤ .05.*
Then:	Reject the null hypothesis.
And:	Conclude that the research finding is statistically significant.

Rule 2:

If:	Probability value > significance level (i.e., probability value > alpha).
Then:	Fail to reject the null hypothesis.
And:	Conclude that the research finding is not statistically significant.

In practice, this usually means the following:

If:	Probability value > .05.
Then:	Fail to reject the null hypothesis.
And:	Conclude that the research finding is not statistically significant.

5. Compute effect size, interpret the results, and make a substantive, real-world judgment about practical significance.
This means that you must decide what the results of your research study actually mean. Statistics are only a tool for determining statistical significance. If you have obtained statistical significance, you must now interpret your results in terms of the variables used in your research study. For example, you might decide that females perform better, on average, than males on the GRE Verbal test or that client-centered therapy works better than rational emotive therapy or that phonics and whole language in combination work better than phonics only.

You must also determine the *practical significance* of your findings. A finding is practically significant when the difference between the means or the size of the relationship is big enough, in your opinion, to be of practical use. For example, a correlation of .15 would probably not be practically significant, even if it were statistically significant. On the other hand, a correlation of .85 would probably be practically significant. *Effect size indicators* (p. 551) are important aids when you are making a judgment about practical significance.

*When should one consider the probability value (i.e., the p value) approximately equal to .05? We use a convention provided by the late Jacob Cohen that a p value of .00 to .05 is sufficiently small to reject the null, but one rounding to a number in the range .051 to 1.00 is not sufficiently small. Using this convention, a p value of .0504 is statistically significant because it rounds to .05, but .0505 is not because it rounds to .051. Note that some professors and journals do not consider .05 to be statistically significant when your significance level is set at .05 because they require that the p value be *less than* the alpha level; in this case, the largest statistically significant p value is .049, with the 9 repeating as many places as your printout might show.

EXHIBIT 19.2 Understanding Probability Value and Significance Level

The ideas of probability value and significance level are extremely important. A coin-tossing example might help you to gain a deeper understanding of the ideas of significance level and probability value.

Let's suppose that your research teacher decides to test the null hypothesis that a particular coin is fair. A fair coin has an equal chance of coming up heads or tails on a given toss. The coin that your teacher is using looks like a normal coin, but you can see it only from a distance. Next, your research teacher tells you that she is going to check to see whether the assumption that the coin is fair seems to be justified. The two hypotheses in this example are as follows:

Null hypothesis:	H_0: The coin is fair.
Alternative hypothesis:	H_1: The coin is biased.

Your teacher tells you that she is going to flip the coin 10 times and record the number of heads. Obviously, if the coin is fair, you would expect to get about as many heads as tails over the 10 flips of the coin. Your teacher flips the coin for the first time, looks at it, and says, "It was heads." She puts a check on the board to record the result. She flips the coin again, looks at it, and says, "It was heads." She puts another check on the board. Once again, your teacher flips the coin, looks at it, and says, "It was heads." She puts yet another check on the board. Your teacher continues this coin-flipping exercise seven more times, and each time she tells you that the coin flip resulted in heads! Is this coin fair? The teacher flipped the coin 10 times, and it came up heads every single time. That is 10 heads in a row. Does this seem like a likely or an unlikely result?

Most students reject the null hypothesis that the coin in this exercise is fair, and they claim that the coin must be biased. Some students will start questioning the assumption that the coin is fair after only three or four heads have come up in a row. By the time heads has come up 10 times in a row, virtually everyone rejects the null hypothesis that the coin is fair. Basically, each student has the concepts of significance level and probability in his or her head. The cutoff point (the point at which the student decides the coin is not fair) is the student's significance level. The student's perception of how likely the particular

(Continued)

(Continued)

observed result would be, assuming the coin is fair, is the probability value. Students compare this probability value to the significance level. When the probability value reaches the student's significance level (the point where the student decides that the fair-coin hypothesis appears too improbable to believe), the student rejects the null hypothesis—the student rejects the original assumption that the coin is fair.

In Table 19.4, you can see the actual probability values of getting heads under the assumption that the coin is fair. The probability of getting 10 heads in a row is .00098. What this probability value means is that if the coin is fair, the rules of probability inform us that we will get 10 heads in a row only about 1 every 1,000 times. In other words, getting 10 heads in a row is quite unlikely. Formal hypothesis testing works a lot like this coin-tossing example. Researchers compare the actual probability value (which they get from the computer printout) to the significance level that they choose to use. As you know, researchers usually use a significance level of .05. In our coin-tossing example, we would have rejected the null hypothesis (that the coin is fair) because the probability value (.00098) is clearly less than the significance level (.05). Remember that the *probability value* is the mathematical probability of an observed result, under the assumption that the null hypothesis is true. The *significance level* is the cutoff point that the researcher chooses to use when deciding how unlikely an event must be in order to reject the null hypothesis.

TABLE 19.4 Coin Toss Probabilities

Number of Tosses	*Probability*	*Value of Consecutive Heads*
1	.50000	Probability of heads
2	.25000	Probability of 2 heads in a row
3	.12500	Probability of 3 heads in a row
4	.06250	Probability of 4 heads in a row
5	.03125	Probability of 5 heads in a row
6	.01563	Probability of 6 heads in a row
7	.00781	Probability of 7 heads in a row
8	.00391	Probability of 8 heads in a row
9	.00195	Probability of 9 heads in a row
10	.00098	Probability of 10 heads in a row

The Hypothesis-Testing Decision Matrix

Because samples rather than complete populations are studied in inferential statistics, hypothesis testing is based on incomplete data. Because hypothesis testing is based on sample data, it relies on probability theory to inform the decision-making process. As a result, decision-making errors will inevitably be made some of the time. The four possible hypothesis-testing outcomes are illustrated in Table 19.5.

Across the top of Table 19.5 are the two possible conditions that can exist in the population: The null hypothesis is true, or the null hypothesis is false. Across the rows of the table are the two possible decisions that a researcher can make: A researcher can reject the null hypothesis, or a researcher can fail to reject the null hypothesis. You will see in Table 19.5 that these two sets of conditions result in four possible outcomes. Two of the outcomes are good (they are correct decisions), and two of the outcomes are bad (they are incorrect decisions).

Can you locate the two correct decisions in Table 19.5? Type A correct decisions occur when the null hypothesis is true and you do not reject it (i.e., you fail to reject the null hypothesis). This is exactly what you hope to do when the null hypothesis is true. Type B correct decisions occur when the null hypothesis is false and you reject it. Again, this is exactly what you hope to do when the null hypothesis is false. If the null hypothesis is false, you always want to reject it. Researchers hope for a Type B correct decision; that is, they hope their null hypothesis is false and that they will be able to reject it and claim that their research findings are statistically significant.

Now look at the two "errors" in Table 19.5. These errors are called Type I errors and Type II errors. A **Type I error** occurs when the researcher rejects a true null hypothesis. Remember: If the null hypothesis is true, it should *not* be rejected. Type I errors are called *false positives* because the researcher has falsely concluded that there is a relationship in the population. The researcher has erroneously claimed statistical significance. Here is an analogy. In medicine, the null hypothesis is "The patient is not ill." Therefore, a false positive occurs when a medical test says that you have a disease but you really don't. As another analogy, in the criminal justice system, the defendant is presumed to be innocent until found guilty by a judge or jury. Hence, a Type I error occurs when an innocent person is found guilty.

- **Type I error** Rejecting a true null hypothesis

A **Type II error** occurs when the researcher fails to reject a false null hypothesis. Remember, if the null hypothesis is false, it is supposed to be rejected. Type II errors are also called *false negatives* because the researcher has falsely concluded that there is no relationship in the population. That is, the researcher has claimed it to be not statistically significant in error. In a medical analogy, a false negative occurs when a medical test says that you do not have a disease but you really do. In the courtroom, a Type II error occurs when a guilty person is found to be not guilty.

- **Type II error** Failing to reject a false null hypothesis

Traditionally, researchers have been more concerned with avoiding Type I errors than Type II errors. In fact, the significance level that we have been discussing is defined as the probability of making a Type I error that the researcher is willing to tolerate. If a researcher

TABLE 19.5 The Four Possible Outcomes in Hypothesis Testing

		The True (But Unknown) Status of the Null Hypothesis	
		The null hypothesis is true. (It should not be rejected.)	The null hypothesis is false. (It should be rejected.)
Your Decision*	Fail to reject the null hypothesis	Type A correct decision!	**Type II error** (false negative)
	Reject the null hypothesis	**Type I error** (false positive)	Type B correct decision!

*Remember that if the null hypothesis is true, it should *not* be rejected, but if the null hypothesis is false, it *should* be rejected. The problem is that you will not know whether the null hypothesis is true or false. You only have the probabilistic evidence obtained from your sample data.

uses .05 as the significance level, the researcher is saying that he or she is only willing to tolerate making a Type I error 5% of the time. In other words, the researcher is willing to tolerate making false positives (claiming there is an effect when there is none) only 5% of the time. This attitude suggests that researchers are conservative people when it comes to making claims from their research data. They are willing to claim *incorrectly* that they have an effect only 5% of the time.

Controlling the Risk of Errors

We pointed out in the previous section that the significance level used by a researcher is the probability of making a Type I error that a researcher is willing to accept. When a researcher uses the .05 significance level, for example, the researcher is willing to make Type I errors only 5% of the time. You might wonder, therefore, why researchers don't just use a smaller significance level. For example, why don't researchers just use a significance level equal to .01 rather than a significance level equal to .05? After all, a researcher who uses this smaller level will make fewer Type I errors.

The problem with using a smaller significance level is that Type I errors and Type II errors tend to be inversely related. In other words, when you try to *decrease* the likelihood of making a Type I error, you usually *increase* the likelihood of making a Type II error. In particular, if you use a smaller significance level—say, .01 rather than .05—you will make it harder to reject the null hypothesis. This reduces the frequency of Type I errors, but it increases the risk of making Type II errors. That is, you are more likely to fail to reject the null hypothesis when you should have rejected it. That is the trade-off. In short, when you try to make a false positive less likely, you tend to make a false negative more likely.

▪ **Power** The likelihood of rejecting the null hypothesis when it is false

You will be glad to know that there is a solution. The solution is to include more participants in your research study. In other words, you need to increase your sample size. Larger samples provide a test that is more sensitive or has more **power**. If you increase the sample size, you are less likely to make a hypothesis-testing error, and that is exactly what we all want! So remember, "The bigger the sample size, the better."[4] Larger sample sizes are better than smaller sample sizes because you will be more likely to draw the correct conclusion.

▪ **Practical significance** A conclusion made when a relationship is strong enough to be of practical importance

If you are able to use large sample sizes and you also happen to obtain statistical significance (you reject the null hypothesis), you must also make sure that your finding has **practical significance** (the difference between the means is large enough or the correlation is strong enough to be of practical importance). This is because even small deviations from the null hypothesis are sometimes found to be statistically significant when large sample sizes are used. Scriven (1991) made this point when he quoted a Harvard statistician as follows: "Fred Mosteller, the great applied statistician, was fond of saying that he did not care much for statistically significant differences; he was more interested in interocular differences, the differences that hit us between the eyes" (p. 198).

For example, perhaps you compared two techniques for teaching spelling, and the means of the two groups in your study turned out to be 86% and 85% correct on the spelling test after the intervention. The difference between these two means is quite small and is probably not practically significant; however, this difference might end up being statistically significant if you have a very large number of people in each of the two treatment groups. Likewise, a small correlation might be statistically significant but not practically significant if there is a very large number of people in the research study you conduct or that you read about and evaluate. This does *not* mean that larger samples are bad. The rule—the bigger the sample size, the better—still applies. It simply means that you must always make sure that a finding is practically significant in addition to being statistically significant.

A useful tool for helping you determine when a finding is practically significant is to examine an effect size indicator. An **effect size indicator** is a statistical measure of the strength of a relationship. It tells you how big an effect is present. Some effect size indicators are Cohen's standardized effect size, eta squared, omega squared, Cramer's *V*, and the correlation coefficient squared. We will use some effect size indicators in the last section of this chapter. (If you want to learn more about effect size indicators, you can refer to a statistics book such as Howell, 2013b; or Huck, 2012; or see Vogt & Johnson, 2011.) All you need to know now is that effect size indicators tell you how big or how strong a relationship or an effect is. You also need to understand that hypothesis testing is only a tool that the researcher uses to determine whether the null or the alternative hypothesis provides a better explanation for the data. *Knowing that a finding is statistically significant does not tell you anything about the effect size or the practical importance of a research finding.* Statistical significance only tells you that a finding is probably not just a chance occurrence. That's why it is so important to determine whether a finding has a large effect size and whether it is practically significant (see step 5 in Table 19.3).

- **Effect size indicator** A measure of the strength or magnitude of a relationship between the independent and dependent variables

REVIEW QUESTIONS

19.8 What is a null hypothesis?

19.9 To whom is the researcher similar in hypothesis testing: the defense attorney or the prosecuting attorney? Why?

19.10 What is the difference between a probability value and the significance level?

19.11 Why do educational researchers usually use .05 as their significance level?

19.12 State the two decision-making rules of hypothesis testing.

19.13 Do the following statements sound like typical null or alternative hypotheses? (a) The coin is fair. (b) There is no difference between male and female incomes in the population. (c) There is no correlation in the population. (d) The patient is not sick (i.e., is well). (e) The defendant is innocent.

19.14 What is a Type I error? What is a Type II error? How can you minimize the risk of both types of errors?

19.15 If a finding is statistically significant, why is it also important to consider its practical significance?

Hypothesis Testing in Practice

When you read educational journal articles, you will quickly notice that researchers frequently test hypotheses and therefore report on the statistical significance of their findings. You will recall that when a null hypothesis is rejected, the finding is said to be statistically significant, and when a null hypothesis is not rejected, the finding is said to be not statistically significant. Researchers report statistical significance to add credibility to their conclusions. Researchers do not want to interpret findings that are not statistically significant because these findings are probably nothing but a reflection of sampling error (i.e., chance fluctuations). On the other hand, researchers do want to interpret research findings that are statistically significant. A commonly used synonym for the term *hypothesis testing* is the term **significance testing**, because when you engage in hypothesis testing, you are also checking for statistical significance.

- **Significance testing** A commonly used synonym for *hypothesis testing*

We now show some examples of several commonly used significance tests. Keep in mind that we use the .05 significance level for all of our statistical tests. For a more exhaustive introduction to significance testing, you will need to examine a statistics textbook (e.g., Glass & Hopkins, 2008; Howell, 2013b; Huck, 2012; Knoke & Bohrnstedt, 2002; Moore, McCabe, & Craig, 2012).

Before we get started, you need to review the two hypothesis testing rules discussed earlier and shown in Table 19.3.

- *Rule 1.* If the probability value is less than or equal to your significance level, then reject the null hypothesis, tentatively accept the alternative hypothesis, and conclude that the finding is statistically significant.
- *Rule 2.* If the probability value is greater than your significance level, then you must fail to reject the null hypothesis and conclude that the finding is not statistically significant.

The key to conducting a significance test is to set your significance level, obtain the probability value, and determine if rule 1 or rule 2 applies. The significance level is set by the researcher (usually at .05). The probability value is based on the computer analysis of the data from your research study, and the researcher gets the probability value from the computer printout. Finally, you compare the probability value to the significance level and determine whether rule 1 or rule 2 applies. In all of the following examples, we follow these two rules.

We use the same college student data set that we used in Table 18.1 (page 499). The data set includes the hypothetical data for 25 recent college graduates on several variables (starting salary, gender, GRE Verbal score, GPA, and college major). Because we will use these data for inferential statistics in this chapter, we *assume* that the 25 individuals are a random sample from a larger population of recent college graduates. In practice, a sample of only 25 people would be quite small. However, our data set is for illustration only.

See Journal Article 19.2 on the Student Study Site.

t Test for Independent Samples

- ***t* test for independent samples** Statistical test used to determine whether the difference between the means of two groups is statistically significant

One of the most common statistical significance tests is called the *t* test for independent samples. The ***t* test for independent samples** is used with a quantitative dependent variable and a dichotomous (i.e., composed of two levels or groups) independent variable. The purpose of this test is to see whether the difference between the means of two groups is statistically significant. The reason this test is called a *t* test is that the sampling distribution used to determine the probability value is known as the *t* distribution. The *t* distributions (there is a separate *t* distribution for each sample size) look quite a bit like the normal curve shown in Chapter 18. The main difference is that for relatively small sample sizes, the *t* distribution is a little flatter and a little more spread out than the normal curve. The mean of the *t* distribution is equal to zero. Just like the normal curve, the t distribution is symmetrical, is higher at the center, and has a "right tail" and a "left tail" that represent extreme events.

The t distribution used in significance testing is the sampling distribution *under the assumption that the null hypothesis is true*. Therefore, the researcher rejects the null hypothesis when the value of t is large (i.e., when it falls in one of the two tails of the t distribution). Typically, t values that are greater than +2.00 (e.g., +2.15) or less than −2.00 (e.g., −2.15) are considered to be large t values.

When we say *large*, we mean that the value is not near the center of the distribution; instead, the value is in a tail of the distribution. As an analogy, think about the normal curve. Values that are more than two standard deviations away from the center of the normal curve are considered to be extreme because fewer than 5% of the cases fall beyond these points. It is exactly the same way with the t distribution. That is, when the t value of the sample result falls in one of the two tails of the t distribution (i.e., in the left tail or in the right tail), it is considered to be an unlikely event (under the assumption that the null hypothesis is true). Therefore, the researcher rejects the null hypothesis and claims that the alternative hypothesis is the better explanation of the results.

We used the sample data in our college student data set (Table 17.1) to examine the following research question: Is the difference between the average starting salary for males and the average starting salary for females statistically significant? The dependent variable is starting salary, and the independent variable is gender. The two statistical hypotheses are

Null hypothesis: $H_0: \mu_M = \mu_F$

Alternative hypothesis: $H_1: \mu_M \neq \mu_F$

As you can see, the null hypothesis states that the male and female population means are the same. The alternative hypothesis states that the male and female population means are different (i.e., they are not equal). Assuming that our male and female data were randomly selected, we can legitimately test the null hypothesis.

The average starting salary for the males in our data set was $34,333.33, and the average starting salary for the females in our data set was $31,076.92. Obviously, these two sample means are different. Remember, however, that whenever sample data are used, sampling error is present. This means that the observed difference in the sample means could be due to chance. The key question is whether the sample means are different enough for us to conclude that the difference is probably not due to random sampling error (i.e., chance) and that there is a real difference between male and female starting salaries in the population from which the data came.

Using SPSS, we conducted the t test for independent samples on our student data. The t value was 2.08, and because this t value falls in the right tail of the t distribution, it is an unlikely value. (If the t value had been −2.08, then it would have fallen in the left tail of the t distribution, which would have also been an unlikely value.) Because the t value is relatively unlikely, assuming that the null hypothesis is true, the probability value is small. We got the probability value from the computer printout based on the analysis of our data. *The probability value is equal to .049*. Because this probability value (.049) is less than the significance level (.05), we reject the null hypothesis and we accept the alternative hypothesis (using rule 1 from Table 19.3).

We conclude that the observed difference between the male and female means is statistically significant. We do not believe that the observed difference between our sample means is due to chance. Rather, we believe that there is a real difference between the starting salaries of males and females in the population. The male mean is higher than the female mean, and the effect size eta squared is .16, which means that gender explains 16% of the variance in salary. We conclude that males have a higher starting salary, on average, than females. We further conclude that this is important for policymakers to know. It is practically significant.

One-Way Analysis of Variance

■ **One-way analysis of variance** Statistical test used to compare two or more group means

One-way analysis of variance (one-way ANOVA) is used to compare two or more group means. It is appropriate whenever you have one quantitative dependent variable and one categorical independent variable. (Two-way analysis of variance is used when you have two categorical independent variables, three-way analysis of variance is used when you have three categorical independent variables, and so forth.) Analysis of variance techniques use what is called the *F* distribution. Don't be surprised if you sometimes hear analysis of variance techniques referred to as *F* tests. The *F* distribution looks like the distribution shown in Figure 18.6c, which is skewed to the right (i.e., the tail is pulled or stretched out to the right) (see page 508). You don't have to worry much about the *F* distribution because the statistical computer programs will take care of that for you.

Here is the research question that we were interested in for our example: Is there a statistically significant difference in the starting salaries of education majors, arts and sciences majors, and business majors? The dependent variable is starting salary, and the independent variable is college major.

The two statistical hypotheses are these:

Null hypothesis:	$H_0\colon \mu_E = \mu_{A\&S} = \mu_B$
Alternative hypothesis:	H_1: Not all equal

The null hypothesis states that the education, the arts and sciences, and the business student populations all have the same mean starting income. The alternative hypothesis states that at least two of the population means are different from one another. The alternative hypothesis does *not* state which two of the population means are different from one another.

Once again we used SPSS to obtain our results. The *F* value is equal to 9.66, which is quite an extreme value. When there is no relationship, the *F* value is theoretically equal to 1.0. Our *F* value of 9.66 is quite a bit bigger than 1.0, which means our sample result falls in the right tail of the *F* distribution. Therefore, the probability value is small (i.e., the sample result is unlikely, assuming the null hypothesis is true). *The probability value, which we got from the SPSS printout, is equal to .001.* Because we are using a significance level of .05, we reject the null hypothesis and conclude that the relationship between college major and starting income is statistically significant. That's because, from rule 1, our probability value (.001) is less than our significance level (.05). The effect size indicator eta squared is .47, which means that college major explains 47% of the variance in salary. We can conclude that at least two of the college major means are significantly different and that follow-up tests are needed to determine which means are significantly different.

Post Hoc Tests in Analysis of Variance

One-way analysis of variance tells the researcher whether the relationship between the independent and dependent variables is statistically significant. In our example, college major and starting income are significantly related. We therefore concluded that at least two of the means are significantly different. If you want to know which means are significantly different, you have to use what is called a **post hoc test**, a follow-up test to analysis of variance that is used to determine which means are significantly different. If an independent variable has only two levels, you don't need a post hoc test. You just need to look to see which mean is bigger. If an independent variable has three or more levels, you will need to conduct post hoc testing.

- **Post hoc test** A follow-up test to the analysis of variance

Many different post hoc tests are available to a researcher. All of them provide appropriate probability values for a researcher to use in determining statistical significance. Some of the popular post hoc tests are the Newman-Keuls test, the Tukey test, and the Bonferroni test. We used the Bonferroni procedure to see which of the means in our previous example were significantly different.[5]

Here are the mean incomes for our example:

- Average starting salary for education majors is \$29,500.
- Average starting salary for arts and sciences majors is \$32,300.
- Average starting salary for business majors is \$36,714.29.

These are the sample means. The question is, Which of these means are significantly different from each other? We must check for statistical significance because the differences between our sample means *could* be due to chance (i.e., sampling error).

First, we check to see whether the education and the arts and sciences means are significantly different. *The Bonferroni-adjusted probability value (obtained from the SPSS printout) is .233*. Our significance level is .05. As you can see, our probability value (.233) is greater than the significance level (.05). Therefore, we use rule 2: We fail to reject the null hypothesis (that the population means are the same), and we conclude that the difference between the two means is *not* statistically significant. We can't really say whether the education or the arts and sciences mean is larger in the population.

Second, we check to see whether the education and the business majors' means are significantly different. *The Bonferroni-adjusted probability value is .001*. Our significance level is .05. You can see that our probability value (.001) is less than the significance level (.05). Therefore, we use rule 1: We reject the null hypothesis (that the population means are the same), and we conclude that the difference between the two means is statistically significant. We believe that business majors have a higher starting salary than education majors, and because this difference is so large, it also appears to be practically significant.

Third, we check to see whether the arts and sciences and the business majors' means are significantly different. *The Bonferroni-adjusted probability value is .031*. Our significance level is .05. Therefore, we use rule 1: We reject the null hypothesis (that the population means are the same), and we conclude that the difference between the two means is statistically significant. We conclude that the starting salary for business majors is greater than the starting salary for arts and sciences in the population. This difference is sizable and would be practically significant.[6]

t Test for Correlation Coefficients

Correlation coefficients are usually used to show the relationship between a quantitative dependent variable and a quantitative independent variable. In inferential statistics, the researcher wants to know whether an observed correlation coefficient is statistically significant. The **t test for correlation coefficients** is the statistical test that is used to determine whether a correlation coefficient is statistically significant. We call this procedure a *t* test for correlation coefficients because the sampling distribution used to test the null hypothesis (that the population correlation coefficient is zero) is the same *t* distribution that we used earlier. The *t* distribution is used for many different statistical tests.

■ ***t* test for correlation coefficients** Statistical test used to determine whether a correlation coefficient is statistically significant

Using our college student data set, we decided to answer this research question: Is there a statistically significant correlation between GPA (X) and starting salary (Y)? The statistical hypotheses are as follows:

Null hypothesis: $H_0: \rho_{XY} = 0$

Alternative hypothesis: $H_1: \rho_{XY} \neq 0$

The null hypothesis says that there is no correlation between GPA and starting salary in the population from which the data were selected. The alternative hypothesis says that there is a correlation between these variables in the population.

Our sample correlation between GPA and starting salary is +.63, which suggests that there is a moderately strong positive correlation between GPA and starting salary. However, we want to know whether this correlation is statistically significant. *Our probability value (based on the analysis of our data and obtained from the SPSS printout) is equal to .001.* Once again, we are using a significance level of .05. Because the probability value is less than the significance level, our correlation is statistically significant. We conclude that GPA and starting salary are correlated in the population. We also conclude that this correlation is practically significant because of its relatively large magnitude (i.e., .63). A correlation of .63 means that almost 40% of the variance in salary is accounted for by GPA. (That's because, with a simple correlation, you obtain the percentage of variance in a dependent variable that is explained by the independent variable by squaring the correlation coefficient and converting it to a percentage: $.63 \times .63 = .397 = 39.7\%$.)

t Test for Regression Coefficients

We pointed out in Chapter 18 that simple regression is used to test the relationship between one quantitative dependent variable and one independent variable. We also pointed out that multiple regression is used to test the relationship between one quantitative dependent variable and two or more independent variables. The **t test for regression coefficients** uses the *t* distribution (sampling distribution) to test each regression coefficient for statistical significance.

■ ***t* test for regression coefficients** Statistical test used to determine whether a regression coefficient is statistically significant

Because we introduced you to simple and multiple regression in Chapter 18, we do not repeat that material here. Rather, we take the multiple regression equation discussed in Chapter 18 and now test the two regression coefficients in that equation for statistical significance. Look at the equation from Chapter 18 once again. (The only difference is that we use lowercase x and y here to denote that the equation is now viewed as based on sample data, rather than population data as in the previous chapter on descriptive statistics.)

$$\hat{Y} = -42{,}809.11 + 4{,}734.26(x_1) + 389.37(x_2)$$

where

$\hat{Y}$ is predicted starting salary,

x_1 is grade point average,

x_2 is GRE Verbal score,

−42,809.11 is the y-intercept,

4,734.26 is the value of the regression coefficient for x_1—it shows the relationship between starting salary and GPA (controlling for GRE Verbal score), and

389.37 is the value of the "regression coefficient" for x_2—it shows the relationship between starting salary and GRE Verbal score (controlling for GPA).

The key point for you to understand is that researchers usually test their regression coefficients for statistical significance. A researcher will not trust a coefficient that is not statistically significant because the coefficient might simply be due to chance (sampling error). On the other hand, if a coefficient is statistically significant, a researcher can conclude that there is a real relationship in the population from which the data came.

Our first research question relates to the first regression coefficient (4,734.26):

Research question 1. Is there a statistically significant relationship between starting salary (y) and GPA (x_1) [controlling for GRE Verbal score (x_2)]?

The two statistical hypotheses for this first research question are as follows:

Null hypothesis: $H_0: \beta_{yx1.x2} = 0$

Alternative hypothesis: $H_1: \beta_{yx1.x2} \neq 0$

The null hypothesis says that the population regression coefficient is equal to zero (i.e., there is no relationship). The alternative hypothesis says that the population regression coefficient is not zero (i.e., there is a relationship).

Using SPSS, we computed the t test and obtained the probability value corresponding to the regression coefficient, showing the relationship between starting salary and GPA. *The probability value is equal to .034.* Because this probability value (.034) is less than our significance level (.05), we reject the null hypothesis and accept the alternative hypothesis. The semipartial correlation squared (sr^2) is equal to.11, which says that 11% of the variance in starting salary is uniquely explained by GPA. We conclude that the relationship between starting salary and GPA (controlling for GRE Verbal score) is statistically and practically significant.

This is the research question for the second regression coefficient (389.37):

Research question 2. Is there a statistically significant relationship between starting salary (y) and GRE Verbal score (x_2) [controlling for GPA (x_1)]?

The two statistical hypotheses for research question 2 are

Null hypothesis: $H_0: \beta_{yx2.x1} = 0$

Alternative hypothesis: $H_1: \beta_{yx2.x1} \neq 0$

Using SPSS, we computed the t test and obtained the probability value corresponding to the regression coefficient showing the relationship between starting salary and GRE Verbal. *The probability value is equal to .017.* Because this probability value (.017) is less than our significance level (.05), we reject the null hypothesis and accept the alternative hypothesis. The semipartial correlation squared is .14, which says that 14% of the starting salary variance is uniquely explained by the GRE Verbal score. We conclude that the relationship between starting salary and GRE Verbal score (controlling for GPA) is statistically and practically significant.

Chi-Square Test for Contingency Tables

- **Chi-square test for contingency tables** Statistical test used to determine whether a relationship observed in a contingency table is statistically significant

The **chi-square test for contingency tables** is used to determine whether a relationship observed in a contingency table is statistically significant. In Chapter 18, we taught you how to construct and interpret the numbers in contingency tables. We told you that contingency tables are used when both variables are categorical. The two categorical variables in our college student data set are gender and college major. Therefore, let's see whether these two variables are significantly related. We used the computer package called SPSS to produce the contingency table shown in Table 19.6. The row variable is college major, and the column variable is gender. Within the body of the table are the counts (the number of people in each cell), the expected counts (the number of people that would be expected to be in each cell if the variables were not related), and the "percent of gender" (the column percentages).

How can you determine whether the variables in this contingency table are related? These are the rules from the last chapter:

- If the percentages are calculated down the columns, compare across the rows.
- If the percentages are calculated across the rows, compare down the columns.

You can see that we calculated the percentages down the columns in Table 19.6. Therefore, you can determine whether college major and gender are related by reading across the rows. If you do this, you will see that the variables appear to be related. Looking at the first row, you can see that 53.8% of the females were education majors but only 8.3% of the males were education majors. Obviously, females have the higher rate. Also, fully 50% of the males were arts and sciences majors, but only 30.8% of the females were arts and sciences majors. Finally, 41.7% of the males were business majors, and only 15.4% of the females were business majors. College major and gender are clearly related.

The inferential statistics question is, Is the observed relationship between college major and gender in the contingency table statistically significant? The null hypothesis says that college major and gender are *not* related in the population from which the data were selected. The alternative hypothesis says that college major and gender *are* related in the population. The sampling distribution used for contingency tables is called the chi-square distribution. The computed value of chi-square in our example is 6.16. *The probability value is .046*. Our probability value of .046 is less than our significance level of .05. Therefore, we reject the null hypothesis (there is no relationship) and accept the alternative hypothesis (there is a relationship). The effect size indicator for contingency tables that we used is called Cramer's *V*. We can interpret the size of Cramer's *V* just as we can the size of a correlation coefficient. Cramer's *V* is .496, which suggests that the relationship between college major and gender is moderately large. We conclude that there is a relationship between college major and gender, that the relationship is statistically significant, and that the relationship appears to be practically significant.

TABLE 19.6 Contingency Table of College Major by Gender*

			Gender		
			Male	*Female*	*Total*
College Major	Education	Count	1	7	8
		Expected count	3.8	4.25	8.0
		% of gender	8.3%	53.8%	32.0%
	Arts and sciences	Count	6	4	10
		Expected count	4.8	5.2	10.0
		% of gender	50.0%	30.8%	40.0%
	Business	Count	5	2	7
		Expected count	3.4	3.6	7.0
		% of gender	41.7%	15.4%	28.0%
Total		Count	12	13	25
		Expected count	12.0	13.0	25.0
		% of gender	100.0%	100.0%	100.0%

*Because the percentages are calculated down, you should compare across the rows. Our convention is to make the predictor variable the column variable and make the outcome variable the row variable. Then, one percentages down and compares the percentages/rates across each row.

Other Significance Tests

Believe it or not, you have come a long way! There are many additional significance tests that we could discuss. In fact, we mentioned several other statistical analyses in earlier chapters. For example, we briefly discussed analysis of covariance (ANCOVA) in Chapter 12 and in Chapter 14, and we briefly discussed partial correlation coefficients in Chapter 14. If you ever need to refresh yourself on any of these procedures, you can review that material. If you run across a significance test that is not discussed in this book, go to our book's companion website, where we have an extensive listing of statistical tests. The key point is that the ideas that you have learned in this chapter apply to any significance test (including ANCOVA and partial correlation). In other words, you can determine whether the observed relationship is statistically significant.

■ **Logic of significance testing** Understanding and following the steps shown in Table 19.3

Here is some good news. You now understand the fundamental **logic of significance testing**. You state the null and alternative hypotheses. Then you determine the probability value and compare it to the significance level. You decide whether the finding is statistically significant or not statistically significant using the two rules shown in Table 19.3. Finally you obtain a measure of effect size, interpret the results, and determine practical significance. This fundamental logic will carry you a long way when you read journal articles or begin conducting your own research. If you run across a significance test that is not mentioned in this book, you can consult a textbook focused on statistics (e.g., Glass & Hopkins, 2008; Hays, 1994; Howell, 2013b; Huck, 2012; Knoke & Bohrnstedt, 2002; Moore et al., 2012). However, the idea of statistical significance will remain the same across the various tests for it.

REVIEW QUESTION

19.16 How do you write the null and alternative hypotheses for each of the following?

a. The *t* test for independent samples

b. One-way analysis of variance

c. The *t* test for correlation coefficients

d. The *t* test for a regression coefficient

ACTION RESEARCH REFLECTION

Insight: Action researchers sometimes are interested in using inferential statistics to make generalizations beyond their immediate research participants or to test hypotheses about relationships and differences between groups. They often do this when they want to inform the scientific community about the world from the bottom up. It is very important that traditional education science carefully listen to practitioners' action research findings.

1. Try to think of a situation in which you would use statistical estimation (point and interval) in your action research.
2. Try to think of a situation in which you would use statistical hypothesis testing in your action research.

SUMMARY

The purpose of inferential statistics is to estimate the characteristics of populations and to test hypotheses about population parameters. Randomization (random sampling or random assignment) is required when using the probability theory underlying inferential statistics, which is based on the idea of sampling distributions. A sampling distribution is the theoretical probability distribution of the values of a statistic that results when all possible random samples of a particular size (e.g., all possible samples of size 100 or all possible samples of size 500) are drawn from a defined population. Sampling distributions make it clear that the value of a sample statistic varies from sample to sample. The sampling distribution constructed for the sample mean is called the sampling distribution of the mean. It shows the distribution of the sample mean when many samples are taken. Other sample statistics (e.g., proportions, correlation coefficients) have their own sampling distributions.

There are two types of estimation. In point estimation, the researcher uses the value of a sample statistic as the estimate of the population parameter. In interval estimation, the researcher constructs a confidence interval (a range of numbers) that will include the population parameter a certain percentage of the time over the long run. For example, 95% confidence intervals will capture the population parameter 95% of the time.

Hypothesis testing is the branch of inferential statistics concerned with testing hypotheses about population parameters. Hypothesis testing follows a very specific logic, called the logic of significance testing. Basically, the researcher sets up a null hypothesis that he or she hopes to ultimately reject in order to accept the alternative hypothesis. It is the null hypothesis (not the alternative hypothesis) that is tested directly using probability theory. To engage in hypothesis testing, you must understand the difference between the probability value and the significance level. The *probability value* is the probability of the sample results under the assumption that the null hypothesis is true. The *significance level* is the cutoff point that the researcher believes represents an unlikely event. Using these ideas, the researcher follows these decision-making rules:

- *Rule 1.* If the probability value is less than or equal to the significance level, then reject the null hypothesis, tentatively accept the alternative hypothesis, and conclude that the finding is statistically significant.
- *Rule 2.* If the probability value is greater than the significance level, then you must fail to reject the null hypothesis and conclude that the finding is not statistically significant.

A statistically significant finding is a finding that the researcher does *not* believe is due to chance. A finding is statistically significant when the evidence supports the alternative hypothesis rather than the null hypothesis. The logic of significance testing will carry you a long way because the basic logic applies to all significance tests and significance tests are frequently reported in published research.

KEY TERMS

alternative hypothesis (p. 540)
chi-square test for contingency tables (p. 558)
confidence interval (p. 536)
confidence limits (p. 536)
directional alternative hypothesis (p. 542)
effect size indicator (p. 551)
hypothesis testing (p. 538)
inferential statistics (p. 530)
level of confidence (p. 536)
logic of significance testing (p. 560)
lower limit (p. 536)
margin of error (p. 538)
nondirectional alternative hypothesis (p. 542)
null hypothesis (p. 540)
one-way analysis of variance (p. 554)
parameter (p. 530)
point estimate (p. 535)
point estimation (p. 535)
population (p. 530)
post hoc test (p. 555)
power (p. 550)
practical significance (p. 550)
probability value or *p* value (p. 543)
repeated sampling (p. 532)
sample (p. 530)
sampling distribution (p. 531)
sampling distribution of the mean (p. 534)
sampling error (p. 532)
significance level or alpha level (p. 545)
significance testing (p. 552)
standard error (p. 533)
statistic (p. 530)
statistically significant (p. 544)
t test for correlation coefficients (p. 556)
t test for independent samples (p. 552)
t test for regression coefficients (p. 556)
Type I error (p. 549)
Type II error (p. 549)
upper limit (p. 536)

DISCUSSION QUESTIONS

1. What exactly does it mean when a researcher reports that a finding is statistically significant?
2. What do you think is more important: statistical significance or practical significance?

3. How does one determine practical significance?
4. What is the difference between null and alternative hypotheses?
5. The p value is at the core of hypothesis testing. What exactly is the p value, and what is it sometimes incorrectly thought to be? (Hint: See section entitled "Examining the Probability Value and Making a Decision.")

RESEARCH EXERCISES

1. Some quantitative research articles in education still do not provide the exact probability values (e.g., $p = .036$). Rather, they include statements of probability values such as $p < .05$, $p < .01$, $p < .03$, $p < .001$, and so forth. Remember that the significance level used in most articles is .05. For each of the following possible probability values, indicate whether the result would be statistically significant or not statistically significant. *Assume that the significance level is set at .05.* (Hint: If a probability value is less than or equal to the significance level, the result is statistically significant. Otherwise, it is not statistically significant.) Place a check in the box to the left of each of your answers.

Probability Value	Your Statistical Decision	
$p > .05$	❐ Statistically significant	❐ Not statistically significant
$p < .05$	❐ Statistically significant	❐ Not statistically significant
$p < .03$	❐ Statistically significant	❐ Not statistically significant
$p < .01$	❐ Statistically significant	❐ Not statistically significant
$p < .001$	❐ Statistically significant	❐ Not statistically significant
$p < .0001$	❐ Statistically significant	❐ Not statistically significant

2. Let's now assume that the researcher is using a more conservative significance level; specifically, the researcher is using the .01 significance level rather than the .05 significance level. For each of the following probability values, indicate whether the result would be statistically significant or not statistically significant.

Probability Value	Your Statistical Decision	
$p > .05$	❐ Statistically significant	❐ Not statistically significant
$p < .05$	❐ Statistically significant	❐ Not statistically significant
$p < .03$	❐ Statistically significant	❐ Not statistically significant
$p < .01$	❐ Statistically significant	❐ Not statistically significant
$p < .001$	❐ Statistically significant	❐ Not statistically significant
$p < .0001$	❐ Statistically significant	❐ Not statistically significant

3. Find a quantitative journal article (you can use one from the companion website if you want to) and note where the authors talk about statistical significance. (*Note:* Some researchers still say "significant" when they actually mean "statistically significant.") Did the authors report exact probability values when they claimed that a finding was statistically significant? Were any of the findings in the research article you examined *not* statistically significant? For any findings that were statistically significant, did the authors adequately address the issue of practical significance in addition to statistical significance?
4. There has been a widespread debate among researchers about the importance or lack of importance of statistical significance testing. One side in this debate is that if researchers report effect sizes (which show the magnitude or size of a relationship),

then statistical significance testing (i.e., the use of p values to rule out chance as an explanation of the result) is not needed. Another group says that significance testing is essential because if a finding is not statistically significant, then we might simply be observing a chance event. Do you think we need significance testing? Do you think we need to report effect sizes (which indicate the strength of a relationship or effect)? Do we need both? Explain your reasoning. You will find some discussion of these issues here: http://www.personal.psu.edu/users/d/m/dmr/sigtest/Cover.pdf. You can find additional discussion, as needed, using your preferred search engine.

PROPOSAL EXERCISES

If you are proposing to conduct a quantitative research study, please answer the following questions, and integrate your answers into your research proposal:

1. What are your independent/predictor, control, and dependent variables?
2. How do you think these variables will be related? That is, what are your "research hypotheses"?
3. For each variable, what is its level of measurement (i.e., nominal, ordinal, interval, or ratio [see Chapter 7])?
4. What specific statistical techniques do you propose to use when analyzing your data?
5. What results do you expect to find when your data are collected and analyzed?

RELEVANT INTERNET SITES

An excellent free online statistics textbook and related materials
http://davidmlane.com/hyperstat/index.html

Statistics concepts demonstrated
http://onlinestatbook.com/rvls/index.html

A special issue of the journal *Research in the Schools* that was devoted to the controversy over using significance testing
http://www.personal.psu.edu/users/d/m/dmr/sigtest/Cover.pdf

Brief definitions and explanations of most of the concepts discussed in this chapter
http://www.animatedsoftware.com/statglos/statglos.htm#index
http://www.stats.gla.ac.uk/steps/glossary/
http://www.statsoft.com/textbook/statistics-glossary
http://www.stat.berkeley.edu/~stark/SticiGui/Text/gloss.htm
http://bobhall.tamu.edu/FiniteMath/Module8/Introduction.html

Applets demonstrating statistical ideas

- These are listed under relevant Internet sites for the previous chapter (Chapter 18) and on the student companion website

STUDENT STUDY SITE

Visit the Student Study Site at **edge.sagepub.com/rbjohnson6e** for these additional learning tools:

Video Links
Self-Quizzes
eFlashcards
Lecture Notes
SPSS Data Set
Full-Text SAGE Journal Articles
Interactive Concept Maps
Web Resources

RECOMMENDED READING

Grimm, L. G., & Yarnold, P. R. (1995). *Reading and understanding multivariate statistics.* Washington, DC: American Psychological Association.

Harlow, L. L., Mulaik, S. A., & Steiger, J. H. (Eds.). (1997). *What if there were no significance tests?* Mahwah, NJ: Erlbaum.

Huck, S. W. (2012). *Reading statistics and research* (6th ed.). Boston, MA: Pearson.

Kirk, R. E. (2001). Promoting good statistical practices: Some suggestions. *Educational and Psychological Measurement, 61*(2), 213–218.

Vogt, W. P., & Johnson, R. B. (2016). *Dictionary of statistics and methodology: A nontechnical guide for the social sciences* (5th ed.). Thousand Oaks, CA: SAGE.

NOTES

1. In case you are curious, researchers use $n - 1$ because statisticians have shown that the use of n provides an underestimate of the population parameter.

2. Although we sometimes say that you "accept" the alternative hypothesis, remember that whenever you reject the null hypothesis, you can only *tentatively accept* the alternative hypothesis. This is because even though you were able to reject the null and tentatively accept the alternative, you could have made a mistake; specifically, you could have made a Type I error (rejecting the null when it is true).

3. Don't forget that the research participants must be randomly selected or randomly assigned whenever one uses inferential statistics. That is, without randomization, the probability model will have no meaning.

4. At some point, a sample size becomes large enough. In other words, it would become wasteful to include more participants in the research study. You might want to review our discussion in Chapter 10 on how big a sample is big enough.

5. When you only have three groups and you reject the overall null hypothesis, the most powerful post hoc adjustment approach is the least significant difference (LSD) approach, rather than the Bonferroni (or any other adjustment approach). However, when you have four or more groups you cannot use the LSD procedure.

6. Some statisticians suggest *not* following the procedure we just explained (i.e., conducting an analysis of variance and following it up with post hoc tests). Instead, they suggest that researchers should conduct what are called *planned comparisons.* That is, they suggest that researchers plan, before they collect their data, the exact hypotheses that they want to test.

Chapter 20

Data Analysis in Qualitative and Mixed Research

LEARNING OBJECTIVES

After reading this chapter, you should be able to

- Understand the terminology surrounding qualitative data analysis.
- Describe the process of coding.
- List the different types of codes.
- Know what it means to analyze data inductively.
- Code some text data.
- Know some of the common types of relationships found in qualitative data.
- Describe the procedures used to analyze qualitative data.
- List the three most popular computer programs that are used to analyze qualitative data.
- Know the advantages and disadvantages of using computer programs for qualitative data analysis.
- Describe the cells of the mixed research data analysis matrix.
- Describe the seven analytical procedures used in mixed analysis.

Visit the Student Study Site for an interactive concept map.

RESEARCH IN REAL LIFE Making Sense of Data

istock/Winterzz

In the latter half of 2002, Josh Max got one of the nicest experiences of his life. He was allowed to test drive that year's hottest bike, a Harley-Davidson V-Rod. As he climbed on the bike and took off, he had what he said was "a moment of pure mechanical joy" (Max, 2002). Not only did the bike carve every twist and turn, but it looked great doing it. He had the bike for a total of 8 hours and rode it for all but 15 minutes of that time, sailing for miles past the Pacific Ocean, winding up and down deserted side roads. This was the most fun he had had in a long time, taking all day to go nowhere.

Obviously, for motorcycle riders, the new Harley-Davidson V-Rod is a great bike. However, there seems to be a mystique associated with owning a Harley-Davidson motorcycle that goes beyond the quality of the bike or the experience of riding a motorcycle. For example, every year in August, a bike rally is held in Sturgis, South Dakota, USA, that is attended by about 250,000 motorcyclists, most of whom are Harley-Davidson owners. At this rally and at many other places where you find Harley-Davidson riders, you will see that they tend to wear a similar biker "uniform" consisting of some combination of jeans, black boots, T-shirt, black leather jacket, and a vest that might carry insignias of club affiliation. Wearing anything else would cast you as someone other than a member of the Harley-Davidson club. The rally and ownership of a Harley-Davidson attract people from all walks of life. For example, not only was the late Malcolm Forbes of *Forbes* magazine a Harley enthusiast, but the whole Forbes clan is replete with riders (Forbes Family, 2002).

To John Schouten, professor of marketing at University of Portland, and James McAlexander, professor of marketing at Oregon State University, this tremendous identification with Harley-Davidson objects and activities suggested that a subculture of consumption had been created. They decided to document this subculture (Schouten & McAlexander, 1995) by conducting an ethnographic analysis specifically of "new bikers," defined as Harley-Davidson owners who did not belong to known outlaw organizations.

Over a 3-year period, Schouten and McAlexander attended the rally in Sturgis, South Dakota; attended the Daytona bike week; bought BMW and Honda motorcycles initially and later purchased Harley-Davidson motorcycles; attended the Iowa BMW rally, the ABATE rally, and the western HOG rally; conducted interviews with individuals at Harley-Davidson headquarters; and became active HOG members. They also went to dealerships, club meetings, bars, and restaurants where there were other Harley-Davidson owners. While appearing at these events and riding with other Harley-Davidson motorcycle owners, Schouten and McAlexander observed the behavior of these "other" owners and jotted down their observations; they also interviewed many Harley-Davidson motorcycle owners and took pictures of many of these individuals in a variety of situations. The result was that, over the 3 years, Schouten and McAlexander accumulated a mass of diverse information. At the end of the data-collection period, they had to decide how to synthesize and summarize this wealth of information so that it made sense and, in this case, presented a picture of the subculture of consumption that exists among Harley-Davidson motorcycle owners. The process of summarizing and making sense of qualitative data such as that collected by Schouten and McAlexander is difficult and time-consuming. However, specific techniques and recommendations can make it manageable. The purpose of the present chapter is to acquaint you with these techniques.

Formal qualitative research has been conducted since the early 20th century. Qualitative data analysis, however, is still a relatively new and rapidly developing branch of research methodology. Writing in 1984, in the first edition of their book entitled *Qualitative Data Analysis*, pioneers in qualitative data analysis Matthew Miles and Michael Huberman noted that "we have few agreed-on canons for qualitative data analysis" (p. 16).

In 1994, in the second edition of their book, they noted, "Today, we have come far from that state of affairs. . . . Still, much remains to be done" (Miles & Huberman, p. 428). Over recent years, many qualitative researchers have realized the need for more systematic data analysis procedures, and they have started to write more about how to conduct qualitative research data analysis (e.g., Bazeley, 2013; Bernard & Ryan, 2010; Bryman & Burgess, 1994; Dey, 1993; Huberman & Miles, 1994; LeCompte & Preissle, 1993; Lofland & Lofland, 1995; Miles & Huberman, 1994; Miles, Huberman, & Saldaña, 2014; Patton, 1990; Silverman, 1993; Strauss & Corbin, 1990). In this chapter, we introduce you to the terminology surrounding qualitative data analysis, show you the basics of qualitative data analysis, and briefly discuss the use of computer software in the analysis of qualitative data.

See Journal Article 20.1 on the Student Study Site.

Interim Analysis

Data analysis begins early in a qualitative research study, and during a single research study, qualitative researchers alternate between data collection (e.g., interviews, observations, focus groups, documents, physical artifacts, field notes) and data analysis (creating meaning from raw data). This cyclical or recursive process of collecting data, analyzing the data, collecting additional data, analyzing those data, and so on throughout the research project is called **interim analysis** (Miles & Huberman, 1994).

Interim analysis The cyclical process of collecting and analyzing data during a single research study

Interim analysis is used in qualitative research because qualitative researchers usually collect data over an extended time period and they continually need to learn more and more about what they are studying during this time frame. In other words, qualitative researchers use interim analysis to develop a successively deeper understanding of their research topic and to guide each round of data collection. This is a strength of qualitative research. By collecting data at more than one time, qualitative researchers are able to get data that help refine their developing theories and test their inductively generated hypotheses (i.e., hypotheses developed from examining their data or developed when they are in the field). Qualitative researchers basically act like detectives when they carefully examine and ask questions of their data and then re-enter the field to collect more data to help answer their questions. Interim analysis continues until the process or topic the researcher is studying is understood (or until the researcher runs out of resources!). Grounded theorists use the term *theoretical saturation* to describe the situation in which understanding has been reached and there is no current need for more data. We have summarized the qualitative data-collection process in Figure 20.1.

20.1 What is interim analysis?

REVIEW QUESTION

Memoing

A helpful tool for recording ideas generated during data analysis is **memoing** (writing memos). Memos are reflective notes that researchers write to themselves about what they are learning from their data. Memos can include notes about anything, including thoughts

Memoing Recording reflective notes about what you are learning from the data

FIGURE 20.1 Data analysis in qualitative research

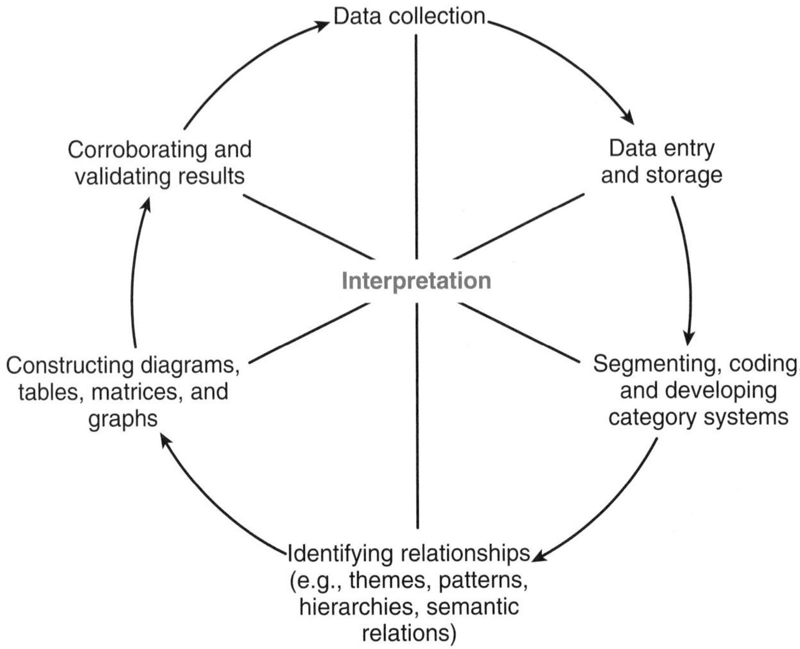

on emerging *concepts*, *themes*, and *patterns* found in the data; the need for further data collection; a comparison that needs to be made in the data; and virtually anything else. Memos written early in a project tend to be more speculative, and memos written later in a project tend to be more focused and conclusive. Memoing is an important tool to use during a research project to record insights gained from reflecting on data. Because qualitative data analysis is an interpretative process, it is important that you keep track of your ideas. You should try to record your insights as they occur so that you do not have to rely on your memory later.

REVIEW QUESTION

20.2 What is memoing?

ANALYSIS OF VISUAL DATA

As you read about visual data, think about the old adage that "a picture is worth a thousand words." We will change the adage to "an image might be worth a thousand words" because visual data can include any type of image, such as photographs, art, pictures in books, video images, nonverbal expressions shown to you by your research participants, and any "signs" that are in the field for you to see. Researchers who rely on extensive visual data argue that it is a myth that it is necessary to present findings in written form, or what Collier (2002) called "the deceptive world of words" (p. 59). In many fields, such as cultural anthropology and media studies, visual data are primary sources of evidence. We mention here three approaches to visual data analysis: photo interviewing analysis, semiotic visual analysis, and visual content analysis.

Photo interviewing is a method of data collection (described in Chapter 9) in which researchers show images to research participants during formal or informal interviews. What is unique in this approach is that the researcher has the participant "analyze" the pictures shown to him or her; the researcher records the participant's thoughts, memories, and reactions as "results." In this approach, the pictures are the stimulus, and the participant is the analyst. The researcher reports these descriptive findings as the primary results. In addition to this **photo interviewing analysis**, the researcher can interpret the results further. In the remainder of this chapter, data analysis is considered to be conducted by the qualitative researcher or the qualitative researcher in combination with the participants after the initial data have been collected.

- **Photo interviewing analysis** Analysis is done by the participant, who examines and "analyzes" a set of visual images

Semiotic visual analysis is based on the theory of semiotics. **Semiotics** is the study of signs and what they stand for in a human culture. A *sign* is something that stands for something else and may mean something different to people in different capacities. A researcher who conducts semiotic analysis is therefore very concerned with what the signs in visual images mean. Semiotic researchers are not concerned with finding images that are statistically representative of a large set of images. Rather, they are concerned with individual images that have conceptual meaning or with how meaning is produced by images.

- **Semiotic visual analysis** The identification and interpretation of symbolic meaning of visual data
- **Semiotics** The study of signs and what they stand for in human culture

Images often have layered meanings. From a semiotic perspective, images are denotative and connotative (Barthes, 1973). In the first layer, called *denotative* meaning, researchers simply want to know what is being depicted in the images. This layer assumes that we can only recognize what we already know, and this knowledge can be affected by verbal captions placed under photographs, for example, or by visual stereotypes in our cultures. The second semiotic layer, *connotative* meaning, builds on what researchers and participants know and explores the ways in which ideas and values are expressed and represented in images. This is what is so exciting and so exasperating about semiotic research. *Semiotics* explores myths, and nowhere is mythology as evident as in visual imagery.

Visual content analysis is different from semiotic analysis. Visual content analysis is based on what is directly visible to the researcher in an image or set of images. It differs from other methods of visual analysis in that it is more quantitative. For example, with visual content analysis, researchers might examine the relative frequencies of women or minorities in school texts or on websites that recruit college professors. Unlike more qualitative visual data analysis methods, visual content analysis concentrates on studying a representative sample rather than individual instances of images. It is less concerned with deep meaning and more concerned with prevalence. Visual content analysis begins with assertions or hypotheses that categorize and compare visual content. The categories are observable. The corpus (sample size or domain) of the study is decided ahead of time based on the research questions, how important it is to generalize the findings, and the statistical procedures to be employed. Visual content analysis is often limited to isolated content that represents particular variables under study. The variables are limited by clearly defined values that coders can classify consistently (reliably). For example, the variable *setting* takes on one or more of the values of office, domestic, public, religious, school, outside, or other.

- **Visual content analysis** The identification and counting of events, characteristics, or other phenomena in visual data

There are numerous methods of visual analysis, using both qualitative (interpreting) and quantitative (counting) data analysis approaches. The visual data analyzed can include single images, such as a photograph or a drawing, or multiple images, such as time-sequenced images or videos. Visual data can be "analyzed" by participants (group members, informants) during data collection to report events and construct meaning, by expert coders to count the occurrence of particular concrete phenomena, and by individuals adept at interpreting cultural meaning as well as through a number of other approaches. Visual data also can be included in qualitative software, and they can be in their original form (e.g., pictures, photographs, video images). You can write up theoretical memos (i.e., your and your participants' interpretations and thoughts about your visual data) and include these memos along with your other transcribed materials in your qualitative research data set. In qualitative research, you often will have a set of multiple kinds of materials to analyze in order to learn about what you are studying.

REVIEW QUESTION

20.3 What are visual data, and how might they be analyzed?

Data Entry and Storage

- **Transcription** Transforming qualitative data into typed text

To analyze qualitative data carefully, we recommend that you transcribe most of your data. **Transcription** is the process of transforming qualitative research data, such as audio recordings of interviews or field notes written from observations, into typed text. The typed text is called a transcript. If the original data source is an audio recording, transcription involves sitting down, listening to the tape recording, and typing what was said into a word processing file. If the data are memos, open-ended questionnaires, or observational field notes, transcription involves typing the handwritten text into a word processing file. In short, transcription involves transferring data from a less usable to a more usable form. After you transcribe your data, you should put your original data somewhere for safekeeping.

Some qualitative researchers use a voice recognition computer program, which can make transcribing relatively easy. These programs create transcriptions of data while you read the words and sentences into a microphone attached to your computer. Two popular programs are IBM's ViaVoice and Dragon's Naturally Speaking. The main advantage of voice recognition software is that it is easier to talk into a microphone than it is to type. Time savings are not currently large in comparison with typing, but the efficiency of these programs will continue to improve over time.

The principles discussed in this chapter also apply when your qualitative data do not directly lend themselves to text (e.g., videotapes of observations, still pictures, and artifacts). You cannot directly transcribe these kinds of data sources. What you can do, however, is use the principles of coding (discussed in the next section) and put the codes and your comments into text files for further qualitative data analysis.

REVIEW QUESTION

20.4 Why is it important to transcribe qualitative data when possible?

Segmenting, Coding, and Developing Category Systems

Segmenting involves dividing the data into meaningful analytical units. When you segment text data, you read the text line by line and continually ask yourself the following kinds of questions: Do I see a segment of text that has a specific meaning that might be important for my research study? Is this segment different in some way from the text coming before and after it? Where does this segment start and end? A meaningful unit (i.e., segment) of text can be a word, a single sentence, or several sentences, or it might include a larger passage such as a paragraph or even a complete document. The segment of text must have meaning that the researcher thinks should be documented.

■ **Segmenting** Dividing data into meaningful analytical units

Coding is the process of marking segments of data (usually text data) with symbols, descriptive words, or category names. Here is how Miles and Huberman (1994) explained it:

■ **Coding** Marking segments of data with symbols, descriptive words, or category names

> Codes are tags or labels for assigning units of meaning to the descriptive or inferential information compiled during a study. Codes usually are attached to "chunks" of varying size—words, phrases, sentences, or whole paragraphs. . . . They can take the form of a straightforward category label or a more complex one. (p. 56)

When a researcher finds a meaningful segment of text in a transcript, he or she assigns a code or category name to signify or identify that particular segment. As you can see, segmenting and coding go hand in hand because segmenting involves locating meaningful segments of data and coding involves marking or labeling those segments with codes or categories.

An example of a coded interview transcript is shown in Table 20.1. The narrative in the transcript is from an interview with a college teacher (CT) by a researcher (R). You can see that the researcher read the text line by line and placed descriptive words or phrases in the left-hand margin next to the segments of text. The researcher also placed brackets around the segments of data to make it clear where each segment started and ended. (Some other ways to mark segments are to use line numbers or to underline the relevant text.) In this example, a college teacher was asked about the experiences her students had when they visited elementary school classrooms as a course requirement in an educational psychology course. The teacher believed that the visitation experiences provided experiential learning by giving her students (potential future teachers) information that helped them make career choices.

As new codes are developed during coding, they must be added to the master list of codes if they are not already on the list. A **master list** is simply a list of all the codes used in the research study. The master list should include each code followed by the full code name and a brief description or definition of the code. A well-structured master list will enable other researchers working on the project to use the list readily.

■ **Master list** A list of all the codes used in a research study

During coding, the codes on the master list should be reapplied to new segments of text each time an appropriate segment is encountered. For example, one category from the master list for the data in Table 20.1 would be "career choice." Therefore, when the data analyst for this research study encountered another segment of data in which the same or a different person being interviewed made a comment about career choice, the researcher would reapply the label "career choice." Every time a segment of text was about career choice, the researcher would use the code "career choice" to refer to that segment.

See Journal Article 20.2 on the Student Study Site.

TABLE 20.1 Example of Coded Text Data

	R: Well, let's start with the impact of early field experiences in the schools for undergraduate education majors. What kind of an impact do you see these experiences having on your students?
Book learning Experiential learning	CT: I think it gives them a needed view into the classroom in the real world. [It's one thing to read about teaching in books;] [it is another to actually go into a real classroom, with real students, and actually try to teach them something. Basically, I think that there is something to learning by experience.]
Classroom management Teaching strategies	[My students can try out the classroom management principles] and the [teaching strategies] I teach them about in my educational psychology course. My students can also learn that all elementary students are not alike.
Common student needs Individual student needs	[The kids have a set of common needs], but [they also have a set of needs unique to each individual in the classroom].
	R: Are there any other results from going into the classroom?
Career choice Timing of vocational learning	CT: Yes. Most of my students have not been in a real classroom since they were in school themselves. Things have changed in the schools in many ways since then. [The vocational experience of going into the classroom has helped some of my students decide that teaching really was not for them.] I hate to lose potential teachers, but [it is probably better that they decide now than wait until they have completed four years of education learning to be a teacher and then decide they don't want to be in a classroom.]

Here is an example of coding based on data from a consulting project done by one of this book's authors. The members of a public organization filled out an open-ended questionnaire in which one of the questions asked was, What are some specific problems needing action in your organization? The participants' responses are shown in Table 20.2. Take a look at the responses for a moment and decide whether you notice any meaningful categories of information. Then look at Table 20.3 and see how the data were coded. As you can see, the answers to the open-ended question are segmented into six categories. The codes are shown in the left-hand margin. The members of the organization listed a number of problems in their organization, and these problems fell into the categories of management issues, physical environment, personnel practices, employee development, intergroup and interpersonal relations, and work structure. These six categories were determined by examining the responses and sorting them into these inductive categories.

- **Intercoder reliability** Consistency among different coders
- **Intracoder reliability** Consistency within a single individual

If you think that you or someone else might have coded the responses from the previous example differently, you are probably right. When you have high consistency among different coders about the appropriate codes, you have **intercoder reliability**. Intercoder reliability is a type of interrater reliability (discussed in Chapter 7; also see Miles & Huberman, 1994, p. 64). Intercoder reliability adds to the objectivity of the research, and it reduces errors due to inconsistencies among coders. Achieving high consistency requires training and a good deal of practice. **Intracoder reliability** is also important. That is, it is also important that each individual coder be consistent. To help you remember the difference between intercoder reliability and intracoder reliability, remember that the prefix *inter-* means "between" and the prefix *intra-* means "within." Therefore, intercoder reliability means reliability, or consistency, between or across coders, and intracoder reliability means reliability within a single coder. If the authors of qualitative research articles that you read address the issues of intercoder and intracoder reliability, you should upgrade your evaluation of their research.

TABLE 20.2 Unordered List of Responses to the Open-Ended Question, What are some specific problems needing action in your organization?

Participant Responses
There is not enough space for everyone.
Our office furniture is dated and needs replacing.
We need a better cleaning service for the office.
We need more objective recruitment and hiring standards.
We need objective performance appraisal and reward systems.
We need consistent application of policy.
There are leadership problems.
Nonproductive staff members should not be retained.
Each department has stereotypes of the other departments.
Decisions are often based on inaccurate information.
We need more opportunities for advancement here.
Our product is not consistent because there are too many styles.
There is too much gossiping and criticizing.
Responsibilities at various levels are unclear.
We need a suggestion box.
We need more computer terminals.
There is a lot of "us and them" sentiment here.
There is a lack of attention to individual needs.
There is favoritism and preferential treatment of staff.
More training is needed at all levels.
There needs to be better assessment of employee ability and performance so that promotions can be more objectively based.
Training is needed for new employees.
Many employees are carrying the weight of other untrained employees.
This office is "turf" oriented.
There is a pecking order at every level and within every level.
Communication needs improving.
Certain departments are put on a pedestal.
There are too many review levels for our product.
Too many signatures are required.
There is a lot of overlap and redundancy.
The components of our office work against one another rather than as a team.

If you want to code your own data and develop category names, you should start with words that describe the content of the segments of data. You will often want the category name to be more abstract than the literal text so that the same category name can be applied to other, similar instances of the phenomenon that you encounter as you read more text. For example, in Table 20.3, the category name "physical environment" was used rather than "office furniture" so that other aspects of the physical environment, in addition to office

TABLE 20.3 Categorization of Responses to the Open-Ended Question, What are some specific problems needing action in your organization?

Inductive Categories	*Participant Responses*
Management issues	There are leadership problems.
	We need a suggestion box.
	There is a lack of attention to individual needs.
	There is favoritism and preferential treatment of staff.
	Decisions are often based on inaccurate information.
	We need consistent application of policy.
Physical environment	We need a better cleaning service for the office.
	Our office furniture is dated and needs replacing.
	We need more computer terminals.
	There is not enough space for everyone.
Personnel practices	We need more objective recruitment and hiring standards.
	We need objective performance appraisal and reward systems.
	Nonproductive staff members should not be retained.
	There needs to be better assessment of employee ability and performance so that promotions can be more objectively based.
Employee development	More training is needed at all levels.
	Training is needed for new employees.
	Many employees are carrying the weight of other untrained employees.
	We need more opportunities for advancement here.
Intergroup and interpersonal relations	This office is "turf" oriented.
	There is a lot of "us and them" sentiment here.
	There is a pecking order at every level and within every level.
	Communication needs improving.
	There is too much gossiping and criticizing.
	Certain departments are put on a pedestal.
	Each department has stereotypes of the other departments.
Work structure	There are too many review levels for our product.
	Too many signatures are required.
	Responsibilities at various levels are unclear.
	The components of our office work against one another rather than as a team.
	There is a lot of overlap and redundancy.
	Our product is not consistent because there are too many styles.

furniture, could be included in the category. This ability to develop category names comes with practice. You might not get the best category name on your first try. If you don't, all you have to do is generate a new category name and use the new category name on the transcripts. When you actually code some written text, you will find that this process of coding is easier than you might think.

Full descriptive words or phrases are not always used in coding. Some researchers prefer to use abbreviations of category names as their codes. Using abbreviations can save time compared to writing out full category names every time a category appears in the data. Other researchers develop complex symbol systems for coding their data. When you code some data for yourself, you must decide whether you want to use full words, phrases, abbreviations, or a complex symbolic coding system.

An example of data coded using a symbolic coding system is shown in Table 20.4. The transcript is an excerpt from an observational study done by educational ethnographer Margaret LeCompte, who was studying norms in the elementary school classroom. LeCompte placed the time in the left column every 5 minutes or when an activity changed. She placed teacher talk in quotes and placed student talk and information recorded by the researcher in parentheses. The type of activity is indicated in the left margin. The code *R* stands for teacher talk that establishes rules, the code *T* stands for teacher talk focused on organizing a time schedule for the students, and the code *W* stands for teacher talk that is

TABLE 20.4 Symbolic Coding System Used on Field Note Transcript

<table>
<tr><td colspan="4">(Children are playing outside the classroom; a few are standing on the porch. The teacher arrives.)</td></tr>
<tr><td>8:55
8:57</td><td>Getting
settled</td><td>T2A
R1A
R2B
R1A
R4B
R4A
R4B</td><td>"Come in, girls first." (There's some messing around before they line up.) (They come in and move toward their seats.) (T2A) "Mrs. Smith is ready to start." (She's sitting on the desk in the front of the room.) (R1A) "Mrs. Smith is waiting." (R2B) "I like the way Bernie is sitting down, and Atocha." (R1A) "Please, people, do not throw snowballs at one another." (R4B) "There isn't enough snow on the ground and you pick up rocks with it. If we have a lot of snow we'll have a snowball fight, but please don't throw the snow when there isn't much . . ." (R4A) "If you go along with me and don't throw now, as soon as there's good stuff we'll have a snowball fight." (R4B) "It isn't just that you hurt people, but you'll get in trouble too."</td></tr>
<tr><td>9:03</td><td></td><td>T2A
W1B</td><td>(T2A) "All right, the girls will go to bake cookies at recess." (W1B) "Boys, come back here if you aren't done; if you can't work alone you can go into Mrs. Dvorak's game</td></tr>
<tr><td></td><td>Getting
organized</td><td>W2B
R1A</td><td>room." (W2B) "I expect if you come in here to work
I expect you to work." (R1A) "I want everybody to bring a nickel by Monday." (Is it for the girl's surprise?) "No, it's for everybody"."</td></tr>
</table>

Source: From M. D. LeCompte and J. Preissle, *Ethnography and Qualitative Design in Educational Research,* p. 294, copyright © 1993 Academic Press. Reprinted by permission of Elsevier and the authors.

Note: Teacher talk is recorded in quotations; pupil talk and locational description are enclosed in parentheses.

focused on student tasks or student work. Although the codes that are used in the table are not very clear to the outside reader, they had very precise meaning to LeCompte. LeCompte inductively developed her coding system early in her research study, and she used it in her later data analysis.

Inductive and A Priori Codes

Because of the inductive nature of most qualitative research, qualitative researchers traditionally generate their codes or category names directly from their data. When you develop codes this way, you are actually generating **inductive codes**, which are defined as codes that are generated by the researcher by directly examining the data during the coding process. Inductive codes can be based on emic terms (terms that are used by the participants themselves). Codes that use the language and words of the participants are called **in vivo codes**. For example, high school students might use the emic term *jocks* to refer to students who play sports. Inductive codes can also be based on social science terms that a researcher is familiar with. For example, a social science term for *jocks* might be *athletic role*. Finally, inductive codes might be good, clear, descriptive words that most people would agree characterize a segment of data (e.g., we might agree that the segment of data refers to athletes).

- **Inductive codes** Codes that are generated by a researcher by directly examining the data
- **In vivo codes** Codes that use the words of the research participants
- **A priori codes** Codes that were developed before examining the current data

Sometimes researchers bring an already developed coding scheme to the research project. These codes are called **a priori codes** or preexisting codes because they were developed before or at the very beginning of the current research study. A priori codes are used when a researcher is trying to replicate or extend a certain line of previous research. Researchers may also establish some a priori codes before data collection based on their relevance to the research questions. When researchers bring a priori codes to a research study, they come in with a start list of codes—an already developed master list that they can use for coding. During coding, however, the researcher should apply these codes only when they clearly fit segments of data. The codes should not be forced onto the data, and new codes should be generated when data segments are found that do not fit any of the codes on the list. In practice, many researchers employ both preexisting and inductive codes.

Co-Occurring and Facesheet Codes

In our discussion so far, we have used just one descriptive category for any given segment of data. If you code transcripts, however, it is very possible that the codes will overlap. In other words, more than one topic or category might be applied to the same set of data. If the categories are intertwined, you simply allow the codes to overlap naturally, and the result is what is called co-occurring codes. **Co-occurring codes** are sets of codes (i.e., two or more codes) that overlap partially or completely. Co-occurring codes might merely show conceptual redundancy in coding (i.e., the two codes mean basically the same thing). More interestingly, co-occurring codes might suggest a relationship among categories within a set of text for a single individual (e.g., an interview transcript) or across multiple sets of text for different individuals (i.e., across several interview transcripts).

- **Co-occurring codes** Codes that overlap partially or completely

An example of co-occurring codes within an individual's transcript is shown in Table 20.5. If you look at the text in the table, you will see that "mood" is the category marking lines 8–13, "positive" is the category for lines 11–20, "like" is the category for lines 16–20, "don't like" is the category for lines 21–29, "miss" is the category for lines 30–40,

TABLE 20.5 Text With Overlapping Codes

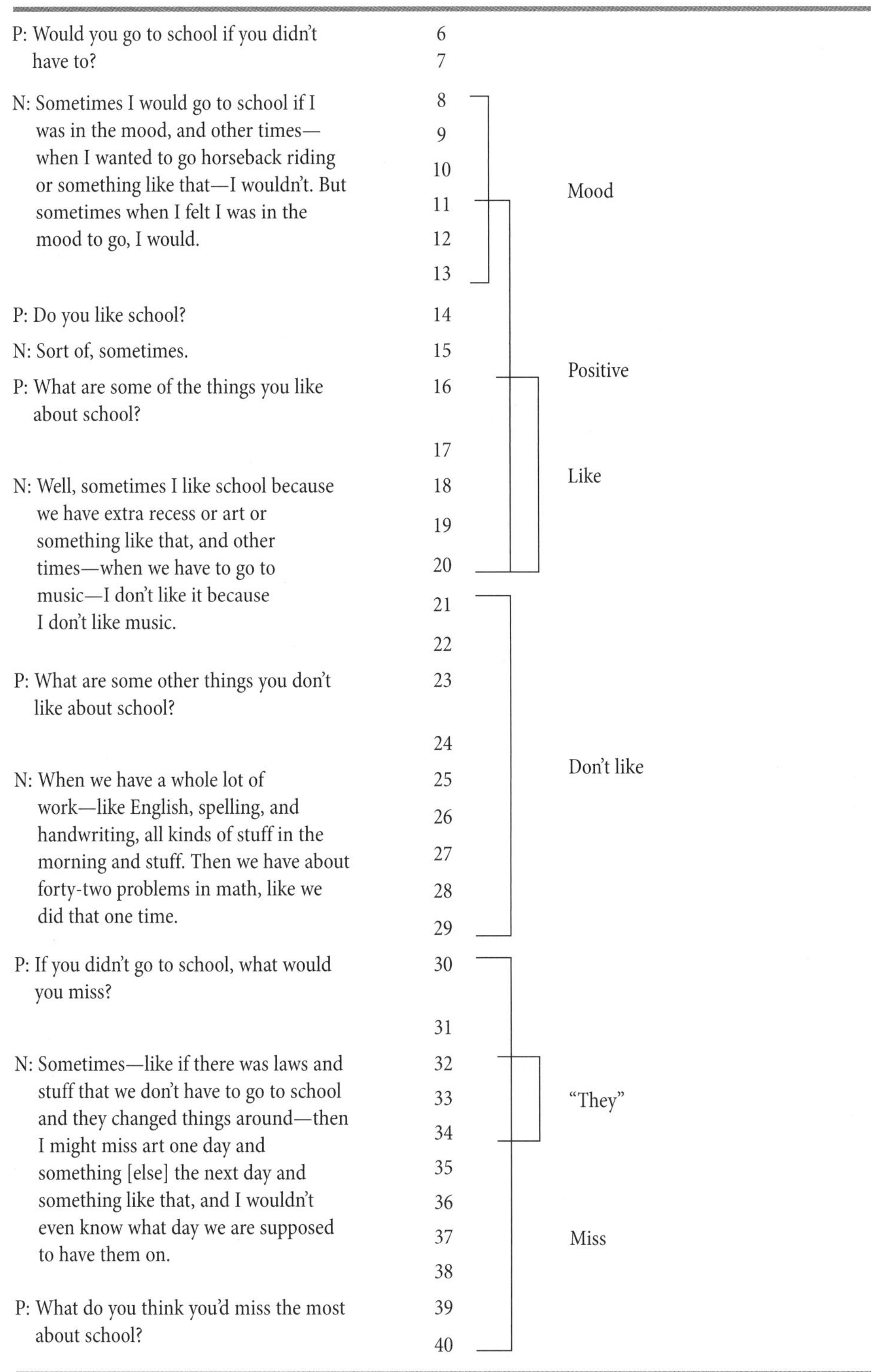

P: Would you go to school if you didn't have to?

N: Sometimes I would go to school if I was in the mood, and other times—when I wanted to go horseback riding or something like that—I wouldn't. But sometimes when I felt I was in the mood to go, I would.

P: Do you like school?

N: Sort of, sometimes.

P: What are some of the things you like about school?

N: Well, sometimes I like school because we have extra recess or art or something like that, and other times—when we have to go to music—I don't like it because I don't like music.

P: What are some other things you don't like about school?

N: When we have a whole lot of work—like English, spelling, and handwriting, all kinds of stuff in the morning and stuff. Then we have about forty-two problems in math, like we did that one time.

P: If you didn't go to school, what would you miss?

N: Sometimes—like if there was laws and stuff that we don't have to go to school and they changed things around—then I might miss art one day and something [else] the next day and something like that, and I wouldn't even know what day we are supposed to have them on.

P: What do you think you'd miss the most about school?

Source: From M. D. LeCompte and J. Preissle, *Ethnography and Qualitative Design in Educational Research*, p. 294, copyright © 1993 Academic Press. Reprinted by permission of Elsevier and the authors.

and "they" is the category for lines 32–34. As you can see, some of these categories overlap. More specifically, lines 32–34 are coded with two co-occurring codes. The two codes "miss" and "they" co-occur for these three lines. Also, lines 16–20 are coded with the codes "like" and "positive." Therefore, these are also co-occurring codes. The key point to remember is that you can allow codes to overlap when coding data.

A researcher can also attach codes to an entire document, interview, or set of lines. For example, lines 6–40 in Table 20.5 (i.e., all the given lines) could have been given a code such as "school" because that was the topic of discussion in all of the lines. If you had several interview transcripts, you might decide to attach the code "female" or "male" to each transcript to signify the participant's gender. Codes that apply to a complete document or case (e.g., to an interview) are called **facesheet codes**. The origin of the term *facesheet* probably comes from researchers attaching a sheet of paper to each transcript with codes listed that apply to the whole transcript. Demographic variables are frequently used as facesheet codes (e.g., gender, age, race, occupation, school). Researchers might later decide to sort their data files by facesheet codes to search for group differences (e.g., differences between older and younger teachers) or other relationships in the data.

- **Facesheet codes** Codes that apply to a complete document or case

FIRST-STAGE AND SECOND-STAGE CODING

We have now provided you with the basics of what can be called first-stage coding. It is similar to what grounded theorists call open coding. In **first-stage coding** you inductively and/or deductively code and categorize your transcribed data and show the results. It is called first-stage coding because it is the initial or first stage of your qualitative analysis. You should *not* end with first stage coding. After this process, you need to do something more with your codes, categories, and text. That is, you need to look for themes, enumerate them, and you should look for relationships among the codes/categories/themes. This later step is called **second-stage coding**, and it is where you make sense of your codes and complete the analysis. Before moving to the next section, we recommend that you browse the Chapter 20 Appendix (titled "Additional Types of Codes for Qualitative Research"). This appendix includes 13 additional kinds of codes that will add to your analytic repertoire and help you to become a better coder. We put the material in an appendix because it is not something to memorize but, instead, is a helpful resource for your research.

- **First-stage coding** Initial coding of qualitative research data
- **Second-stage coding** Follow-up coding to organize codes/categories and determine their interrelationships for the research report

REVIEW QUESTIONS

20.5 What is the difference between segmenting and coding?

20.6 What is the difference between inductive codes and a priori codes?

20.7 What is the difference between co-occurring codes and facesheet codes?

ENUMERATION

We have talked about the importance of transcribing data, and we have shown you the basics of assigning codes to qualitative data. At this point, a data analyst might decide to determine how frequently words or coded categories appear in the data. This process of quantifying data is called **enumeration**. Enumeration helps qualitative researchers communicate concepts such as "amount" or "frequency" when writing up the results. Often a reader needs to know how much or how often, in addition to knowing that something happened. Weber (1990), for example, reported the word frequencies used in the 1980 Democratic and Republican platforms. The five most common words in the Democratic platform were *our* (430 occurrences), *must* (321), *Democratic* (226), *federal* (177), and *support* (144). The most common words in the Republican platform were *our* (347), *their* (161), *administration* (131), *government* (128), and *Republican* (126). Word or code frequencies can help researchers determine the importance of words and ideas. Listing frequencies can also help in identifying prominent themes in the data (e.g., What kinds of things did the participants say many times?).

- **Enumeration** The process of quantifying data

When numbers are reported in qualitative research reports, you must always be sure to check the basis of the numbers being used, or you could be misled. For example, in the Democratic and Republican platform example, the basis was all words in the document (e.g., 144 of the words in the Democratic platform were *support*). A number such as this simply points out the emphasis placed on a word by the writer of the document. If several interview transcripts are analyzed, the basis of a reported number might be the number of words mentioned by all of the participants. If a word had a high frequency in this case, you might be inclined to believe that most of the participants used the word frequently. However, a high frequency of a particular word could also mean that a single participant used the particular word many times. In other words, a word might have a large frequency simply because one or two research participants used the word many times, not because a large number of different participants used the word. Enumeration can be helpful in qualitative data analysis, but always be careful to recognize the kinds of numbers that are being reported.

REVIEW QUESTION

20.8 Explain the process of enumeration.

"Themeing the Data" and Creating Hierarchical Category Systems

Categories are the basic building blocks of qualitative data analysis because qualitative researchers make sense of their data by identifying and studying the categories that appear in their data. You can think of the set of categories for a collection of data as forming a classification system characterizing those data. Rather than having to think about each sentence or each word in the data, the researcher will, after coding the data, be able to focus on the themes and relationships suggested by the classification system. You learned earlier how to find categories in qualitative data, and you learned that you may want to count these categories for suggestive **themes**. Themes are frequently occurring codes/categories/words that occur frequently in your data and help summarize the findings. Themeing the data or **thematic analysis** is perhaps the most popular type of qualitative data analysis, and it is quite important. However, we recommend that you do not stop after identifying themes because this may result in your missing many important nuances and relationships in your data.

- **Theme** A word, or more typically, a set of words denoting an important idea that occurs multiple times in your data
- **Thematic analysis** Identification of themes in the research findings

- **Hierarchical analysis** Search for potential hierarchical arrangement of inductively generated categories in qualitative data analysis

Another kind of analysis is hierarchical analysis. In **hierarchical analysis**, categories are organized into different levels, typologies, and hierarchical systems. A set of subcategories might fall beneath a certain category, and that certain category might itself fall under an even higher-level category. Think about the category called *fruit.* In this case, some possible subcategories are oranges, grapefruit, kiwi, apples, and bananas. These are subcategories of fruit because they are "part of" or "types of" the higher-level category called *fruit.* The category fruit may itself be a subcategory of yet a higher category called *food group.* Systems of categories like this are called hierarchies because they are layered or fall into different levels.

An example of a hierarchical classification system can be found in a research article by Frontman and Kunkel (1994). These researchers were interested in when and how counselors believed a session with a client was successful. They interviewed 69 mental health workers from various mental health fields, including counseling psychology, clinical psychology, marriage and family therapy, social work, and school psychology. After an initial session with a client, the participants filled out an open-ended questionnaire asking them to describe what they felt was successful in the session. A team of researchers analyzed the transcripts and came up with a rather elaborate hierarchical classification system. Frontman and Kunkel reported that they developed their hierarchy in a bottom-up fashion, which means that the lowest-level categories are the closest to the actual data collected in the study. This bottom-up, or inductive, strategy is the most common approach used by qualitative researchers (Weitzman & Miles, 1995).

We have reproduced a small part of Frontman and Kunkel's (1994) classification system in Figure 20.2 to give you a feel for hierarchical coding. When looking at the figure, be sure to realize that many of the categories in Frontman and Kunkel's hierarchical system are left out; the downward arrows indicate where additional levels and categories were excluded. All 44 categories in their full hierarchical classification system are given in the published article.

You can see that the higher levels of the hierarchy shown in Figure 20.2 are more general than the lower levels. That is, a higher-level category includes or subsumes the categories falling under it. The highest level of the hierarchy in Figure 20.2 includes the very general categories called positive awareness and collaboration. Frontman and Kunkel (1994) decided near the conclusion of their research project that these two general categories subsumed the sets of categories falling below them. At the second-highest level of the hierarchy in Figure 20.2, you can see that the researchers categorized counselors' construal of success into five categories. The five categories with brief explanations are as follows:

1. Client display of strengths ("The skills, actions, and characteristics expressed by the client that the counselor connotes as indication of success.")
2. Counselor self-evaluation of performance ("Counselor assesses success through evaluating the quality of his or her performance during the session.")
3. Adherence to desired interactional norms ("Success is determined by the presence of particular interactional patterns in the session.")
4. Establishment of rapport ("Success is defined as indication that rapport between counselor and client is being established.")
5. Progress in problem solving ("Success is attributed to client making progress toward establishing and implementing direct steps in solving a problem"; Frontman & Kunkel, pp. 498–499.)

FIGURE 20.2 Hierarchical categorization of counselors' construal of success in the initial session. The vertical ellipses show where we have left out some of Frontman and Kunkel's subcategories.

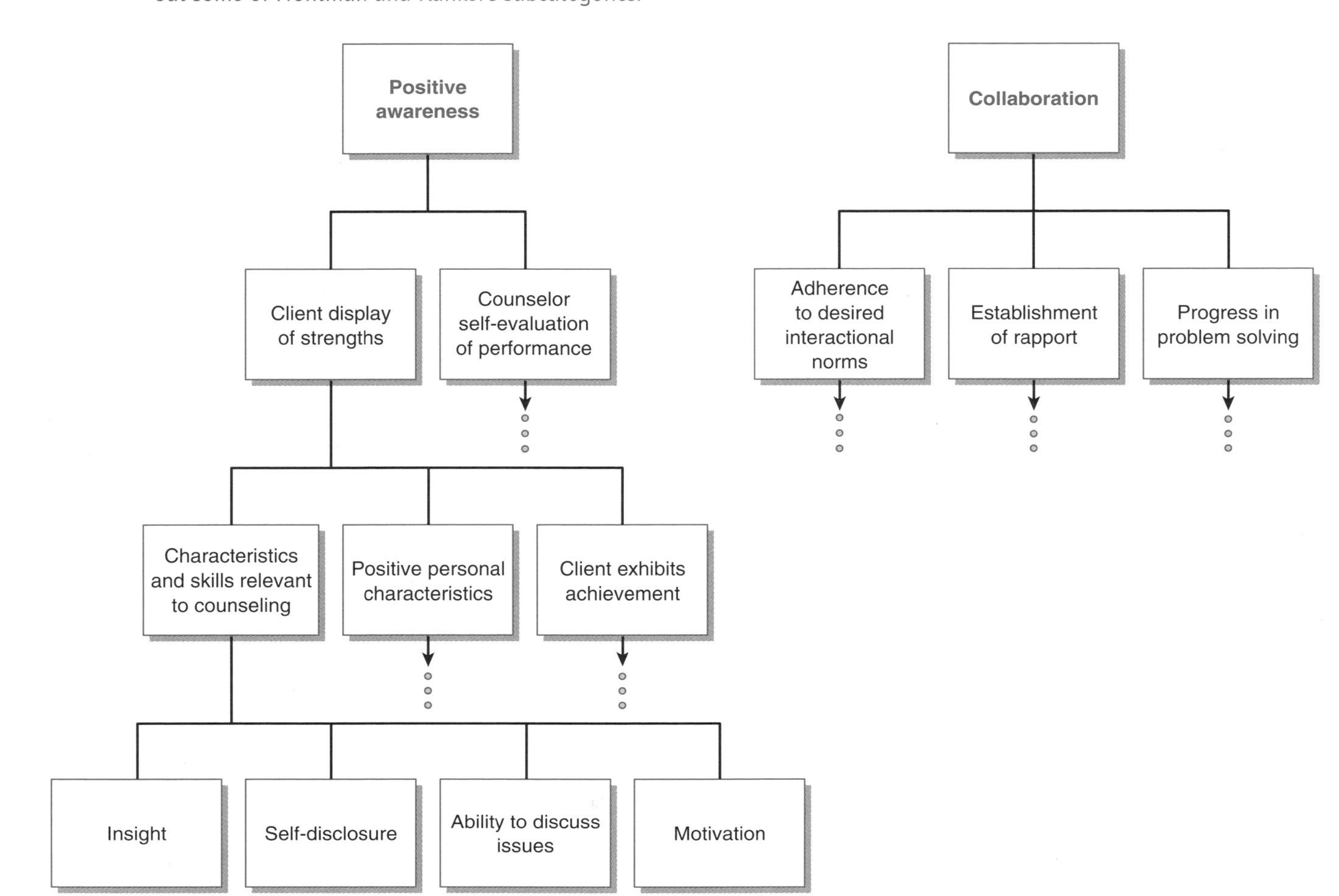

Source: From K. C. Frontman and M. A. Kunkel. A grounded theory of counselors' construal of success in the initial session. *Journal of Counseling Psychology*, *41*(4), 492–499. Copyright © by the American Psychological Association. Reproduced with permission.

The first two of the five categories we just listed are part of positive awareness, and the last three are part of collaboration. At the second-lowest level of the hierarchy, we provide the categories falling under "client display of strengths." At the lowest level of the hierarchy, we show the categories falling under "characteristics and skills relevant to counseling." As you can see, there is a total of four levels in the hierarchy shown in Figure 20.2. We find Frontman and Kunkel's (1994) hierarchy interesting because it provides a direct picture of the hierarchical structure of their data. It is also interesting to see what counselors believe makes therapy successful.

REVIEW QUESTION

20.9 What is a hierarchical category system, and why can it be useful to construct hierarchical systems?

IDENTIFYING RELATIONSHIPS AMONG CATEGORIES

In this section, we show you some ways to explore relationships in qualitative research data. *When qualitative researchers use the term* relationship, *it has a slightly different meaning than when quantitative researchers use the term*. You learned in earlier chapters that quantitative researchers focus their efforts on examining the relationships among variables. Qualitative researchers, however, attach a much broader meaning to the term *relationship*. The hierarchical system just shown in Figure 20.2 is one type of relationship. Another important type of relationship is potentially found when you check to see if your categories or themes *vary* by demographic or other grouping factors. For example, do males and females or different ethnic groups interpret the phenomenon (e.g., teaching math) differently and therefore act differently? This adds nuance and greater understanding to your general themes. We call this **qualitative subgroup analysis**.

- **Qualitative subgroup analysis** Looking for relationships between categories/themes and demographic or other grouping factors

In short, qualitative researchers use the term *relationship* to refer to many different kinds of relations or connections between things, including but not limited to variables. This is not better or worse than quantitative analysis; it is just different. A summary of several additional kinds of relationships identified by one well-known qualitative researcher named James Spradley (1979) is given in Table 20.6. Take a moment to examine the nine relationships because you might identify some of these relationships when you are reading transcripts or when you are examining categories generated from your data. Spradley's list is not exhaustive, but it is suggestive. You will undoubtedly find additional kinds of relationships if you analyze some transcribed data.

Suppose you were reading an interview transcript and you came across the following text: "When I just ignore Johnny's acting out, he becomes more aggressive toward the other students in my classroom. But if I walk over and stand beside him, he will usually quiet down for a little while." This text suggests a possible causal process operating among several categories. (In Table 20.6, this is called a cause-effect relationship.) It is suggested, in particular, that ignoring Johnny's behavioral outbursts results in aggressive behavior and proximity results in less aggressive behavior. Obviously, two sentences like this in a transcript do not provide solid evidence of a general cause-and-effect relationship; however,

TABLE 20.6 Spradley's Universal Semantic Relationships

Title	*Form of Relationship*
1. Strict inclusion	*X* is a kind of *Y*.
2. Spatial	*X* is a place in *Y*; *X* is a part of *Y*.
3. Cause-effect	*X* is a cause of *Y*; *Y* is a result of *X*.
4. Rationale	*X* is a reason for doing *Y*.
5. Location for action	*X* is a place for doing *Y*.
6. Function	*X* is used for *Y*.
7. Means-end	*X* is a way to do *Y*.
8. Sequence	*X* is a step (stage) in *Y*.
9. Attribution	*X* is an attribute (characteristic) of *Y*.

Source: Adapted from J. P. Spradley, 1979, p. 111.

statements like this do have a causal form, and they might suggest that you do additional analysis and data collection to explore the relationship further.

Now recall the hierarchical categorization that we showed you in Figure 20.2. If you look at the figure again, you will see that one of the categories was "characteristics and skills relevant to counseling." That category has four characteristics falling under it: insight, self-disclosure, ability to discuss issues, and motivation. You can view these four subcategories as following Spradley's strict inclusion relationship because they are "kinds of" characteristics or skills. Strict inclusion is a very common form of relationship in qualitative data analysis.

Educational researchers often use the term *typology* to refer to categories that follow Spradley's strict inclusion form of relationship. A **typology** is a classification system that breaks something down into its different types or kinds. A typology is basically the same thing as a taxonomy. You might remember what a taxonomy is from your high school or college biology class. (Okay, I know it has been a long time!) In biology, the levels of the animal taxonomy are kingdom, phylum, class, order, family, genus, and species. (Here's a memory aid: **K**ings **P**lay **C**hess **O**n **F**iber **G**lass **S**tools.) Bailey (1994) pointed out that "the term *taxonomy* is more generally used in the biological sciences, while *typology* is used in the social sciences" (p. 6). Typologies are useful because they help make sense out of qualitative data.

- **Typology** A classification system that breaks something down into different types or kinds

Typologies can be simple or complex. You might, for example, be interested in the types of cliques in schools, types of teaching strategies used by teachers, or types of student lifestyles. These would be fairly simple, one-dimensional typologies. At a more complex level, you could view the hierarchical classification in Figure 20.2 as one big typology, showing the types of counselors' construals of success. To construct a typology, it is helpful to construct mutually exclusive and exhaustive categories. **Mutually exclusive categories** are clearly separate or distinct; they do not overlap. **Exhaustive categories** classify all the relevant cases in your data. Exhaustiveness of categories can be difficult in qualitative research because some cases simply don't fit into a typology. However, the more cases there are that fit into your typology, the better.

- **Mutually exclusive categories** A set of categories that are separate or distinct
- **Exhaustive categories** A set of categories that classify all of the relevant cases in the data

Another interesting typology was constructed by Patton (1990) when he was helping a group of high school teachers develop a student dropout prevention program. Patton observed and interviewed teachers, and here is what he found:

> The inductive analysis of the data suggested that teachers' behaviors toward dropouts could be conceptualized along a continuum according to the extent to which teachers were willing to take direct responsibility for doing something about the problem. This dimension varied from taking responsibility to shifting responsibility to others. The second dimension concerned the teachers' views about the effective intervention strategies. The inductive analysis revealed three perspectives among the teachers. Some teachers believed that a rehabilitation effort was needed to help kids with their problems; some teachers preferred a maintenance or caretaking effort aimed at just keeping the school running, that is, maintaining the system; and still other teachers favored finding some way of punishing students for their unacceptable and inappropriate behaviors, no longer letting them get away with the infractions they had been committing in the past. (pp. 411–412)

You can see from this quote that Patton found two simple or one-dimensional typologies that were related to dropout prevention: (1) teachers' beliefs about how to deal with dropouts and (2) teachers' behaviors toward dropouts.

Patton then decided to cross these two simple typologies in a two-dimensional matrix. When he did this, he found a typology that made a lot of sense to the teachers in the research study. The typology included six types of teacher roles in dealing with the high school dropout problem. The roles are shown in the six cells of the matrix in Figure 20.3.

FIGURE 20.3 Patton's typology of teacher roles in dealing with high school dropouts

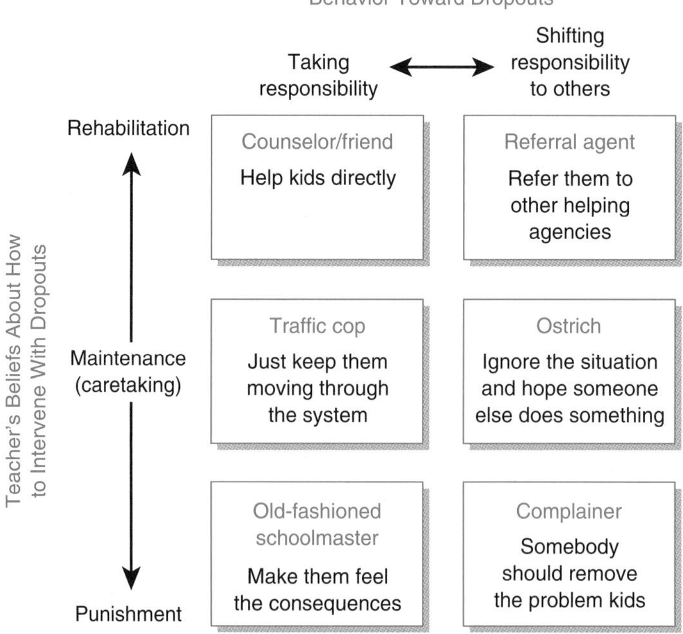

Source: Adapted from M. Q. Patton, *How to Use Qualitative Methods in Evaluation,* p. 413, copyright © 1990 by SAGE, Thousand Oaks, CA. Reprinted by permission of SAGE.

The different types of teacher roles shown in the figure are counselor/friend, traffic cop, old-fashioned schoolmaster, referral agent, ostrich, and complainer. You might know some of these kinds of teachers at your own school. Remember, when analyzing qualitative data, you can sometimes find new and interesting information by cross-classifying two or more dimensions.

Now let's look at an example of Spradley's "sequence" type of relationship (Table 20.6). This example comes from an article titled "A Framework for Describing Developmental Change Among Older Adults" by Fisher (1993). Fisher pursued this research because he was interested in determining whether older adulthood could be categorized into a set of meaningful stages. He decided not to rely on the stages presented in popular developmental psychology books because many of these lists were dated. Also, some of these lists lumped all older people into a single developmental stage called *old age.* Fisher decided that he wanted to explore the concept of old age using qualitative research.

Fisher conducted in-depth interviews with 74 adults whose ages ranged from 61 to 94 years. Using in-depth, open-ended interviews, he asked his participants what kinds of experiences they had in their lives. An interesting theme in his research findings was a tendency by all of the older adults toward adaptation to their life circumstances, no

TABLE 20.7 Categories Ordered by Time

Category I: Continuity With Middle Age	
Characteristics:	Retirement plans pursued
	Middle-age lifestyle continued
	Other activities substituted for work
Category II: Early Transition	
Characteristics:	Involuntary transitional events
	Voluntary transitional events
	End of continuity with middle age
Category III: Revised Lifestyle	
Characteristics:	Adaptation to changes of early transition
	Stable lifestyle appropriate to older adulthood
	Socialization realized through age-group affiliation
Category IV: Later Transition	
Characteristics:	Loss of health and mobility
	Need for assistance and/or care
	Loss of autonomy
Category V: Final Period	
Characteristics:	Adaptation to changes of later transition
	Stable lifestyle appropriate to level of dependency
	Sense of finitude, mortality

Source: Adapted from Fisher, J. C. (1993). A framework for describing developmental change among older adults. *Adult Education Quarterly*, *43*(2), 81.

matter what the circumstances were. Fisher also generated five core categories from his data that could be ordered by time. These categories resulted in the following sequence of old age: (1) continuity with middle age, (2) early transition, (3) revised lifestyle, (4) later transition, and (5) final period. You can see the defining characteristics of each of these five stages in Table 20.7.

Drawing Diagrams

■ **Diagramming** Making a sketch, drawing, or outline to show how something works or to clarify the relationship between the parts of a whole

A useful tool for showing the relationships among categories is called **diagramming** (i.e., making diagrams). A diagram is "a plan, sketch, drawing, or outline designed to demonstrate or explain how something works or to clarify the relationship between the parts of a whole" (*The American Heritage Dictionary*, 2010). Figures 20.2 and 20.3, which we discussed in the previous section, are examples of diagrams. Diagrams are very popular with visually oriented learners and can be used to demonstrate relationships effectively for the readers of reports. The use of diagrams can also be helpful during data analysis when you are trying to make sense out of your data.

An easily understood example of a diagram showing a complex process appears in Figure 16.1 (page 459). This diagram depicts a grounded theory about how departmental chairpersons at universities facilitate the growth and development of their faculty members. The diagram shows that the career stage of the faculty member determines the type of faculty issue chairpersons are concerned with, and the faculty issue determines the specific strategy a chairperson uses in working with a faculty member. The diagram also lists the outcomes resulting from applying the strategies.

■ **Network diagram** A diagram showing the direct links between variables or events over time

A similar type of diagram is called a network diagram. A **network diagram** shows the direct links between variables or events over time (Miles & Huberman, 1994). An example of a network diagram is the path analysis diagram that appears in Figure 14.4 (page 410). The path analysis diagram was based on quantitative research. However, network diagrams can also be based on qualitative data. Qualitative researchers often use these diagrams to depict their thinking about potential causal relationships. We have included an example of a part of a network diagram based on qualitative data in Figure 20.4. This diagram is based on a school innovation and improvement study by Miles and Huberman. According to the diagram, low internal funds in school districts resulted in high environmental turbulence in those districts (e.g., a shortage of money resulted in uncertain operating conditions for principals). This resulted in low stability for the leaders of the various school improvement programs and in low stability for the program staff. As a result of this instability, job mobility was high.

To learn more about causal network diagrams, you should take a look at the work of Miles and Huberman (1994). They provide an extensive discussion of the issues surrounding causal analysis in qualitative research, and they discuss how to develop causal networks based on a single case or on multiple cases. If you are interested in cause-and-effect relationships with qualitative data, you should also review Chapter 11 on research validity in this book, especially the sections on internal validity. Miles and Huberman also discussed how to construct many different kinds of interesting matrices (i.e., classifications of two or more dimensions) to aid in the analysis and presentation of qualitative research data.

FIGURE 20.4 Network diagram for job mobility

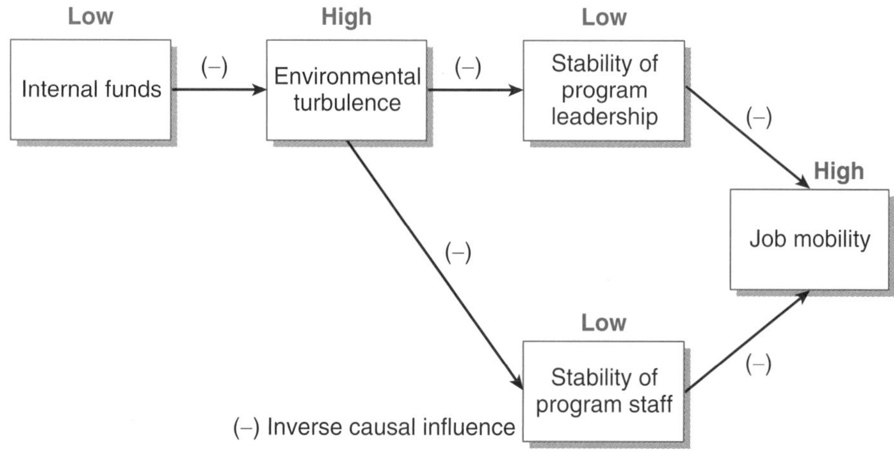

Source: From M. B. Miles and A. M. Huberman, *Qualitative Data Analysis: An Expanded Source Book,* p. 231, copyright © 1994 by SAGE, Thousand Oaks, CA. Reprinted by permission of SAGE.

20.10 How do qualitative researchers show relationships among categories?

20.11 How are network diagrams used in qualitative research?

Corroborating and Validating Results

In Chapter 11, we discussed how to assess and promote the validity or trustworthiness of your qualitative research data (in the last section of the chapter). We recommend that you take a moment right now and review the five types of validity and the strategies that are used to promote qualitative research validity (they are shown in Table 11.2). It is essential that you think about validity and use the strategies throughout the qualitative data-collection, analysis, and write-up process whenever possible.

20.12 What are the five types of validity that are of potential importance in qualitative research, and what are their definitions?

20.13 What are the 16 strategies that are used to promote validity in qualitative research, and what are their definitions?

Computer Programs for Qualitative Data Analysis

Qualitative researchers are just beginning to capitalize on the possibilities for computer use in the analysis of qualitative data. Although qualitative researchers have been using word processors for transcribing and editing their data for quite some time, only during the last decade have a number of qualitative data analysis computer programs become readily available. The developers of these programs examined the procedures that qualitative researchers follow when making sense of their data and then developed programs that help automate these procedures. Before we examine the potential of using qualitative data analysis programs, we look at how qualitative researchers have traditionally made sense of their data without these programs.

Qualitative researchers traditionally use a filing system approach to data analysis. They begin their data analysis by transcribing their data and making copies of the various data documents. Then they hand-code the data in the left margin of these copies. After this, researchers make copies of the coded data and cut the data into segments of text with the marked codes. A filing system is created, with one folder for each code, and the segments of text are placed into their appropriate folders. If a segment of text has more than one code, then more than one copy of the segment is made, and a copy of the segment is placed in all the relevant folders. This way, all the folders contain all the appropriate data segments. At this point, researchers can reread the segments of text in each folder, looking for themes in the data.

More complex analyses require even more work when done by hand. For example, searching for two co-occurring codes typically requires making a folder with the two codes as its title, locating the two individual code folders, and then checking the text segments in those folders to see whether they include both codes in the left margin. If both codes are present, the segment of text is copied and placed into the new two-code folder.

As you can see, doing complex data analysis by hand can be time-consuming and quite difficult. Perhaps this is one reason why qualitative data analysis has not advanced as rapidly as has quantitative data analysis. Because of the increasing use of computer programs, however, we predict that the analysis of qualitative data will take a giant step forward during the next decade. One reason for our prediction is that procedures that are highly time-consuming when done by hand can be done with just a few keystrokes on the computer. So that you have a basic idea about the potential of computer data analysis, we list a few of the capabilities of qualitative data analysis programs.

Qualitative data analysis programs can be used to do virtually everything we have discussed in this chapter. They can, for example, be used to store and code your data. During coding, most programs allow complex hierarchical classification systems such as the one shown in Figure 20.2 to be developed. Most programs allow the use of many different kinds of codes, including co-occurring and facesheet codes. Enumeration is easily done with just a few clicks of the computer mouse. Many programs allow you to attach memos or annotations to the codes or data documents so that you can record the important thoughts you have during analysis. Some programs will produce graphics that can be used in presenting the data. Finally, the heart and soul of most qualitative data analysis programs are their searching capabilities, the topic to which we now turn.

- **Boolean operators** Words such as *and* and *or* that create logical combinations

You can perform simple or complex searches with computer packages that use Boolean operators. **Boolean operators** are words used to create logical combinations based on basic laws of thought. We all use Boolean operators every day when we think and talk about things. Some common Boolean operators we all use are AND, OR, NOT, IF, THEN, and EXCEPT. Qualitative data analysis computer programs are written so that you can search your data or a set of codes using these and many other operators.

You might, for example, search the codes or text in a set of interview transcripts concerning teacher satisfaction using the following string of words: "male AND satisfied AND first grade." The Boolean operator AND is called the intersection operator because it finds all intersections of the words or codes. This search would locate all instances of male, first-grade teachers who were satisfied. Similarly, you could search for female teachers using this string of words: "female AND teacher." You can find disconfirming cases (instances that do not have any of the characteristics) by adding the word NOT to the search command (e.g., "NOT teacher" will find all nonteacher instances).

Another operator is OR, also called the union operator. This operator finds all instances that take on any one of the provided words or codes. For example, if you searched a document with the command "female OR first grade" you would come up with instances that are either "female" or "first grade" or both. Another kind of search command is called FOLLOWED-BY in one popular program. Using this you can find instances in which two codes occur in a specific order in the data (e.g., punishment FOLLOWED-BY quiet behavior). As you can see, you can do a lot of different kinds of searches using Boolean operators.

Many qualitative and mixed research data analysis computer programs are available. The most popular programs are MAXQDA (http://www.maxqda.com), QDA Miner (http://provalisresearch.com/products/qualitative-data-analysis-software/), NVivo (http://www.qsrinternational.com/products_nvivo.aspx), and HyperRESEARCH (http://www.researchware.com/products/hyperresearch.html). Many others also work well, such as the new package Dedoose (http://www.dedoose.com) and older packages such as Ethnograph (http://www.qualisresearch.com) and ATLAS (http://www.atlasti.com/qualitative-analysis-software.html). These and some additional links also are provided at the end of this chapter. Most of the companies will allow you to download a demonstration copy from their Internet site free of charge. If you decide that you are interested in a qualitative data analysis program, testing out a demonstration copy is an excellent way to find out which program best suits your particular needs.

We conclude by listing some of the advantages and disadvantages of using computer programs for the analysis of qualitative data. The advantages are that qualitative data analysis computer programs can help in storing and organizing data, they can be used for all of the analyses discussed in this chapter plus many more, they can reduce the time required to analyze data (e.g., an analysis procedure that takes a lot of time by hand may take virtually no time with a computer program), and they can make procedures available to you that are rarely done by hand because they are either too time-consuming or too complex. Some disadvantages are that computer programs can take time to learn, they cost money and require computer availability, and they can become outdated. The biggest disadvantage is startup time. Nonetheless, if you are planning on doing a lot of qualitative data analysis for an extended period of time, we recommend the use of computer programs.

See Journal Articles 20.3 and 20.4 on the Student Study Site.

REVIEW QUESTIONS

20.14 What are some of the capabilities of computer programs for data analysis?

20.15 What are some of the leading qualitative data analysis computer programs?

DATA ANALYSIS IN MIXED RESEARCH[1]

Collecting quantitative and qualitative data within the same study has been done for many decades. However, formal techniques for analyzing both quantitative and qualitative data within the same framework, a process known as mixed methods data analysis or, even more simply, mixed analysis, have emerged only recently. Although mixed analysis techniques have not yet been fully developed, in recent years an increasing number of published works have focused primarily or exclusively on mixed analyses (e.g., Bazeley, 2003; Caracelli & Greene, 1993; Chi, 1997; Greene et al., 1989; Li, Marquart, & Zercher, 2000; Onwuegbuzie & Leech, 2004, 2006; Onwuegbuzie & Teddlie, 2003; Sandelowski, 2000, 2001). We now introduce a few current concepts and techniques discussed in the recent literature on mixed analysis.

In a mixed research study, after you have collected qualitative and/or quantitative data, you will be in a position to analyze the data. That is, you will be ready to conduct a mixed analysis. The term **mixed data analysis** simply means that a researcher uses both quantitative and qualitative analytical techniques in a single research study. The researcher might use quantitative and qualitative techniques at approximately the same time (concurrently). For example, the qualitative and quantitative data might be merged into a single data set and analyzed concurrently. On the other hand, the researcher might use quantitative and qualitative techniques at different times (i.e., sequentially or iteratively). For example, initial qualitative data might be analyzed, interpreted, and used to inform a quantitative phase of the study, after which quantitative data are analyzed. More complex possibilities also exist. For example, during each phase of a research study, both types of data might be collected, analyzed, and used in multiple ways. The key idea is that in mixed data analysis, quantitative and qualitative data and/or quantitative and qualitative data analytic approaches are used in the same research study.

- **Mixed data analysis** The use of both quantitative and qualitative analytical procedures in a research study

See Journal Article 20.5 on the Student Study Site.

Mixed Analysis Matrix

Before conducting a mixed analysis, you need to make two decisions. First, you should determine the number of data types that you intend to analyze. Of course, this depends on the number of data types obtained during data collection. Data types are classified as either quantitative data or qualitative data. For example, quantitative data include measurements based on standardized tests, rating scales, self-reports, symptom checklists, or personality inventories. Qualitative data include open-ended interview responses, open-ended questionnaire responses, observations and field notes, personal journals, diaries, permanent records, transcription of meetings, social and ethnographic histories, and photographs. If only one data type (i.e., quantitative only *or* qualitative only) is used, then we refer to this as *mono*data. Conversely, if both qualitative *and* quantitative data types are used, then we refer to this as *multi*data.

Second, you should determine how many data analysis types you intend to use. These data analysis types can be either quantitative (i.e., statistical) or qualitative. Quantitative analysis is presented in the previous two chapters, and qualitative analysis is presented earlier in this chapter. If you only use one type of data analysis (i.e., quantitative analysis only or qualitative analysis only), then it is called *mono*analysis. Conversely, if you use both types of data analysis, then it is called *multi*analysis.

The two considerations just mentioned generate what is called the *mixed analysis matrix.* (Our matrix is a simplified version of the one found in Onwuegbuzie, Slate, Leech, & Collins, 2007.) Crossing the two types of data (monodata and multidata) with the two types of analysis (monoanalysis and multianalysis) produces a 2 × 2 matrix with four cells. You can examine the mixed analysis matrix in Table 20.8, and each of the cells is described in the following paragraphs.

Cell 1. The first cell represents analysis of one data type using its standard analysis type. As such, this cell contains traditional *monodata-monoanalysis,* which involves either a quantitative (i.e., statistical) analysis of quantitative data *or* a qualitative analysis of qualitative data. Such analysis indicates that the underlying study is either a quantitative or a qualitative study in nature, respectively—neither of which represents mixed research. Therefore, the mixed analysis matrix presented in Table 20.8 includes analyses involved in all three research paradigms (i.e., quantitative research only or qualitative research only is in cell 1, and mixed research is in the other cells). We are interested here in the mixed analysis approaches.

Cell 2. The second cell represents analysis of one data type (e.g., quantitative only or qualitative only) using both analysis types (i.e., qualitative and quantitative). This class of analysis is called *monodata-multianalysis.* Because both quantitative and qualitative analytical techniques are used, this type of analysis is mixed. The first analysis employed in this cell should directly match the data type. Thus, if the data type is

TABLE 20.8 The Mixed Research Data Analysis Matrix

Analysis Types[a]		
Data Types[b]	*One Type of Analysis: Monoanalysis*	*Both Types of Analysis: Multianalysis*
One Type of Data: Monodata	Cell 1 **Monodata-monoanalysis** This is *not* a type of mixed data analysis.	Cell 2 **Monodata-multianalysis** (a) For quantitative data: Quantitative analysis (QUAN) and qualitative analysis of quantitative data (QUALITIZE). OR (b) For qualitative data: Qualitative analysis (QUAL) and quantitative analysis of qualitative data (QUANTITIZE)
Both Types of Data: Multidata	Cell 3 **Multidata-monoanalysis** This type is not frequently used. Only quantitative analysis of both quantitative and qualitative data OR Only qualitative analysis of both qualitative and quantitative data	Cell 4 **Multidata-multianalysis** This is a combination of "(a)" AND "(b)" from cell 2. This is the type of analysis typically conducted in mixed methods research.

[a] An analysis type is either quantitative (i.e., statistical) or qualitative.

[b] A data type is either quantitative or qualitative.

Notation: "QUAL" stands for qualitative analysis; "QUAN" stands for quantitative analysis.

quantitative, then the first phase of the mixed analysis should be quantitative (i.e., statistical). Similarly, if the data type is qualitative, then the first phase of the mixed analysis should be qualitative. The data stemming from the initial analyses then are converted into the other data type. That is, the quantitative data are transformed into data that can be analyzed qualitatively or what is known as *qualitizing* data (Tashakkori & Teddlie, 1998), or the qualitative data are transformed into numerical codes that can be analyzed statistically or what is known as *quantitizing* data (Tashakkori & Teddlie).

- *Qualitizing data.* One way of qualitizing data is by forming narrative profiles (e.g., modal profiles, average profiles, holistic profiles, comparative profiles, normative profiles), in which narrative descriptions are constructed from statistical data. For example, Teddlie and Stringfield (1993) conducted a longitudinal study of eight matched pairs of schools that were initially classified as either effective or ineffective with regard to baseline data. Five years after the study was initiated, these researchers used eight empirical criteria to reclassify the schools' effectiveness status. These criteria were (a) norm-referenced test scores, (b) criterion-referenced test scores, (c) time-on-task in classrooms, (d) scores on quality of classroom instruction measures, (e) faculty stability, (f) student attendance, (g) changes in socioeconomic status of the schools' student bodies, and (h) measures of school "climate." Teddlie and Stringfield converted these quantitative data (i.e., qualitized them) into the following four qualitatively defined school profiles: (a) stable–more effective, (b) stable–less effective, (c) improving, and (d) declining. These school profiles were used to add greater understanding to the researchers' evolving perspectives on the schools.

- *Quantitizing data.* When researchers quantitize data, "qualitative 'themes' are numerically represented, in scores, scales, or clusters, in order more fully to describe and/or interpret a target phenomenon" (Sandelowski, 2001, p. 231). This allows researchers to understand how often various categories or statements occurred in qualitative data, rather than only knowing what categories or statements occurred. Quantitizing sometimes involves reporting "effect sizes" associated with qualitative observations (Onwuegbuzie, 2003; Sandelowski & Barroso, 2003), which can range from manifest effect sizes (i.e., counting qualitative data to determine the prevalence rates of codes, observations, words, or themes) to latent effect sizes (i.e., quantifying nonobservable content, for example, by factor-analyzing emergent themes).

Cell 3. The third cell represents analysis of two data types (i.e., qualitative *and* quantitative) using only one data analysis type—that is, *multidata-monoanalysis.* This combination is uncommon in research. In fact, this cell generally should be avoided because it would entail one of the types of data being analyzed using a nonstandard analysis (e.g., only analyzing qualitative data using quantitative analysis or only analyzing quantitative data using qualitative analysis).

Cell 4. The fourth cell represents the analysis of both data types (e.g., quantitative and qualitative) using both analysis types (i.e., qualitative and quantitative). This class of analysis is called *multidata-multianalysis.* Because both quantitative and qualitative analytical techniques are used, the analysis is mixed. Multidata-multianalysis might be done concurrently, involving a statistical analysis of the quantitative data combined with a qualitative analysis of the qualitative data, followed by meta-inferences being made in which interpretations stemming from the quantitative and qualitative findings are integrated some way into a coherent whole (Tashakkori & Teddlie, 2003). Alternatively, multidata-multianalysis could be sequential in nature such that findings from the qualitative analysis inform the subsequent quantitative analysis, or vice versa. Cell 4 can accommodate rather complex analytical designs. For example, Li et al. (2000) used what they called cross-tracks analysis. This was characterized by a concurrent analysis of both qualitative and quantitative data such that the data analysis oscillated continually between both sets of data types throughout various stages of the data analysis process.

Analytical Procedures in Mixed Data Analysis

The conduct of mixed analysis potentially can involve many analytical strategies and procedures (Onwuegbuzie & Teddlie, 2003). Although Onwuegbuzie and Teddlie viewed the following as mixed data analysis stages, we prefer to view these as mixed data analysis strategies or procedures, some of which you will use and some of which you will not use in a particular research study:

1. *Data reduction* involves reducing the number of dimensions in the quantitative data (e.g., via descriptive statistics, exploratory factor analysis) and/or in the qualitative data (e.g., via thematic analysis, memoing).
2. *Data display* refers to describing visually your quantitative data (e.g., using tables and graphs) and/or your qualitative data (e.g., using graphs, charts, matrices, checklists, rubrics, networks, and Venn diagrams).
3. *Data transformation* involves quantitizing and/or qualitizing data.
4. *Data correlation* involves correlating or cross-classifying different data types, such as transforming qualitative data into categorical variables and examining their relationships with quantitative variables.
5. In *data consolidation*, the quantitative and qualitative data are combined to create new or consolidated codes, variables, or data sets.

The next two procedures are important for virtually all mixed research studies.

6. In *data comparison*, the findings from the qualitative and quantitative data sources or analyses are compared.
7. In *data integration* (typically done last), the qualitative and quantitative findings are integrated into a coherent whole.

Constructing Joint Displays in Mixed Data Analysis

Constructing visual joint displays in mixed analysis is an excellent way to organize and make sense of your qualitative and quantitative data. A **joint display** is a matrix juxtaposing qualitative and quantitative results for cases, research questions, variables, outcomes, times, locations, or any other dimension of interest. For example, Table 20.9 provides a template for a case-by-outcome joint display. For the quantitative and qualitative outcome columns, you fill the cells in with statements of the quantitative and qualitative outcomes for each person. Next, in the difference/similarity column, you note if the results converged or diverged. Finally, in the last column, you provide your integrated statement(s) about the outcomes, their theoretical relevance, reasons for differences or similarities, and/or your meta-inference(s). Table 20.9 will be quite detailed, in that it provides information for every person in your data set. This table will not be feasible if you have a large number of participants.

- **Joint display** Matrix juxtaposing qualitative and quantitative results for cases, research questions, variables, outcomes, times, locations, or any other dimension of interest

TABLE 20.9 Case-by-Outcome "Joint Display"

Case	*Quantitative Outcome*	*Qualitative Outcome*	*Difference/Similarity*	*Integrated Statement*
Person 1				
Person 2				
Person 3				
.				
.				
.				
Person *n*				

Table 20.10 shows a variable-by-outcome joint display (also called an input-output matrix). Here, the quantitative and qualitative outcomes are placed in the cells for each independent variable. Then, similar to the previous joint display, you would note whether the results were similar or different. Finally, you would provide your integrated statement(s) in the last column. A variable-by-outcome joint display will have fewer rows than a case-by-outcome joint display if there are fewer variables than cases, which is often the case.

TABLE 20.10 Variable-by-Outcome "Joint Display"

Independent Variable	*Quantitative Outcome*	*Qualitative Outcome*	*Difference/ Similarity*	*Integrated Statement*
Variable 1				
Variable 2				
Variable 3				
.				
.				
.				
Variable *n*				

TABLE 20.11 Research Question-by-Outcome "Joint Display"

Research Question	*Quantitative Outcome*	*Qualitative Outcome*	*Difference/ Similarity*	*Integrated Statement*
RQ1				
RQ2				
RQ3				
.				
.				
.				
RQ-*n*				

Another very useful display is shown above in Table 20.11. This is a research question-by-outcome joint display. The difference between this joint display and the previous two is that the first column displays the research questions. The other columns are the same. The three joint displays just shown are not the only possible joint displays in mixed methods research. In fact, you are encouraged to be creative in constructing any display that facilitates your analysis, interpretative process, and communication of results for your reader. Here are a few additional possibilities:

- Let rows equal qualitative themes, and let columns equal relevant quantitative statistical results such as on a 5-point scale (this is a themes-by-statistics display). Cells include quotes and frequency counts (Creswell, 2015).
- Let rows equal issues, locations, events, and situations, and let columns equal stakeholder group results on quantitative and qualitative measures (e.g., students, teachers, parents, administrators).
- Let rows equal independent variables, location, or whatever you like, and let columns equal time-ordered outcomes.
- Let rows equal cases, and let columns equal time-ordered outcomes (time 1, time 2, time 3, time 4).
- For a QUAL → QUAN design, let rows equal qualitative results, and let columns equal quantitative follow-up results showing how the quantitative data build upon (or add value to) the qualitative results.
- For a QUAN → QUAL design, let rows equal quantitative results, and let columns equal qualitative follow-up results showing how qualitative findings build upon and explain the qualitative findings.

An example of this last possibility is shown in Table 20.12.

TABLE 20.12 Integration in a Joint Display for a QUAN → QUAL Sequential Design

See Tools and Tips 20.1 on the Student Study Site.

Quantitative Results	*Qualitative Follow-Up Interviews Explaining Quantitative Findings*	*How Qualitative Findings Helped to Explain Quantitative Results*
The more experienced the teachers, and the greater the use of the program materials, the higher the students' scores.	Themes: More experienced teachers were willing to use the materials. More experienced teachers were able to blend the materials into their own approach. More experienced teachers were more willing to follow the school's approach.	Motivation and willingness surfaced as explanations. How the teachers blended the materials was highlighted in the explanations.

Note: More rows can be added to this display for additional quantitative results.

Source: Used with permission, Creswell, J. W. *A Concise Introduction to Mixed Methods Research*, (p. 86). Los Angeles, CA: SAGE, 2015.

The number of possibilities of joint displays or matrices in your analysis is large. It is up to you to include the joint display(s) that most effectively communicates the key ideas and results of your study. For more information on creatively constructing matrices for your data, see Miles, Huberman, and Saldaña (2014). Remember: Be creative!

20.16 What are the four types of analysis corresponding to the four cells in the mixed research data analysis matrix?

20.17 What are some of the strategies or procedures that are used in mixed data analysis?

ACTION RESEARCH REFLECTION

Insight: Action researchers typically collect quantitative *and* qualitative data. Therefore, they rely on quantitative, qualitative, and mixed data analysis techniques.

1. What do you find to be the advantages and disadvantages of transcribing your various qualitative data (e.g., theoretical memos, field notes, interviews, open-ended questionnaires) versus just reading and rereading them?
2. What major themes and relationships have you found in qualitative data that you have collected?
3. How can you merge qualitative and quantitative data and findings to produce larger conclusions ("meta-inferences")?

SUMMARY

Qualitative data analysis typically involves the analysis of text from interview or field note transcripts. Some basic procedures in qualitative data analysis are transcribing data, reading and rereading transcripts (i.e., immersing yourself in your data to understand what is going on), segmenting and coding the data, counting words and coded categories (enumeration), searching for relationships and themes in the data, and generating diagrams to help in interpreting the data. The goal of data analysis is to be able to summarize your data clearly and generate inductive theories based on the data. Some questions you might ask of your data are, What themes occurred in your interviews or field notes? What topics were mentioned most often? What issues were most important to the people in your study? What are the cultural characteristics of the people in your research study? How do your participants view the topic of your research? What kinds of relationships (e.g., strict inclusion, cause-effect, function, sequence) are apparent in your data? How can the categories you have identified in the data be ordered into meaningful grounded theories? The questions you can ask are virtually unlimited, and they will vary depending on your research problem, the type of qualitative research you are conducting (e.g., phenomenology, ethnography, case study, grounded theory, historical), and your own theoretical perspective based on your disciplinary training. Qualitative data analysis computer programs can aid in the analysis of qualitative data, but they do take quite a bit of time to learn.

KEY TERMS

a priori codes (p. 576)
Boolean operators (p. 588)
coding (p. 571)
co-occurring codes (p. 576)
diagramming (p. 586)
enumeration (p. 579)
exhaustive categories (p. 583)
facesheet codes (p. 578)
first-stage coding (p. 578)
hierarchical analysis (p. 580)
inductive codes (p. 576)
intercoder reliability (p. 572)
interim analysis (p. 567)
intracoder reliability (p. 572)
in vivo codes (p. 576)
joint display (p. 593)
master list (p. 571)
memoing (p. 567)
mixed data analysis (p. 590)
mutually exclusive categories (p. 583)

network diagram (p. 586)
photo interviewing analysis (p. 569)
qualitative subgroup analysis (p. 582)
second-stage coding (p. 578)
segmenting (p. 571)
semiotic visual analysis (p. 569)
semiotics (p. 569)
thematic analysis (p. 579)
theme (p. 579)
transcription (p. 570)
typology (p. 583)
visual content analysis (p. 569)

DISCUSSION QUESTIONS

1. In quantitative research, data analysis provides information on statistical significance and size of effects. How would you determine whether something was important or practically significant in qualitative research?
2. Table 20.6 lists nine kinds of relationships. Think of an example of one of these and share it with the class.
3. What are the advantages and disadvantages of having more than one data analyst in a qualitative study?
4. Why is traditional qualitative data analysis said to be inductive? How might you also make it more deductive in your approach?

RESEARCH EXERCISES

1. Analyze the following data. The data are transcribed field notes from a classroom observation done in Mexico City by Robert Stake. As you code the data, be on the lookout for answers to the following questions: What topics appeared in the text? What was the context of the classroom like? What teaching style did the instructor use? Explain this teaching style. What were some of the norms of the classroom (e.g., arrival to class, speaking out in class)? What was the content of the lesson? What was the political persuasion of the students and/or teacher? What kinds of instructional materials were used in the classroom? After you finish coding the text, write a brief summary report on the observation, answering the questions just posed and adding any additional insights that emerge as you code the data.

Class Notes, October 23[2]

The temperature will climb into the 70's today, but now it is chilly in this white tile and terrazzo classroom. Eleven students (of 29 still on the roster) are here, each in a jacket or sweater. No doubt it was cooler still when they left home. The instructor, Señor Pretelin, reminds them of the topic, the Origins of Capitalism, and selects a question for which they have prepared answers. An answer from the back row is ventured. Two more students arrive—it is ten past the hour—now four more.—Señor Pretelin undertakes a correction of the answer, but asks for still more of an answer. His style is casual. He draws long on a cigarette. His audience is alert.—Marx is a presence, spoken in name, and looming from the cover of the textbook. Two books only are in sight. Several students have photocopies of the chapter assigned.—The chalkboard remains filled with last class's logic symbols, now unnoticed. Some students read through their answers, most concentrate on what Pretelin says about answers that are offered.—The first answers had been volunteered by males, now one from a female. The instructor draws her out, more of her idea, then improves upon the explanation himself.

—The coolness of the space is warmed by the exchanges.—Outside a power mower sputters, struggling with a thickness of grass for which it probably was not designed.—It is 20 past the hour. Another student arrives. Most are around 20, all have black hair. These are incoming freshmen in the social studies and humanities program, enrolled in a sociology course

(Continued)

(Continued)

on political doctrines. Still another arrives. She pushes the door closed, and jams it with a chair, to thwart the breeze from the squared-out plaza.—Señor Pretelin is expanding an answer at length. He then turns to another question, lights another cigarette while awaiting a volunteer—again he asks for improvement, gets a couple of tries; then answers the question to his satisfaction. Another question. He patiently awaits student initiative. The students appear to think or read to themselves what they had written earlier.

—The haze of Mexico City shrouds the city-center several miles to the southeast. Yesterday's downpour did not long cleanse the sky.—Quiet again while awaiting a volunteer. The first young woman offers her answer. She is the only female of the seven or so students who have ventured forth. Heads nod to her reference to the camposinos, and to Pretelin's amplification. There seems to be an empathy for these abstract, at least distant, camposinos. If capitalistic advocacy exists in this classroom it does not speak out. A half hour has passed. The recital continues. Only a few students are correcting their notes (or creating them belatedly), most try to read or listen. Minds are mobilized, not idling. Finally a small wedge of humor.

—The air may relax a bit.—Four observers are dispersed about the room, little noticed even as they write. The instructor maintains his task, not ever stopping to take roll. Pretelin is a slight man, perhaps 40. He wears a smart jacket, a dark shirt buttoned high, a gold neck-chain. His fingers are long and expressive.—For several minutes, the dragging of heavy objects outside the room interferes.—For a last time the students are sent to their answers, even asked to look further. Few have books. Then the students are invited to pose questions. The exchange becomes more good natured, but business-like still. The engagement goes on, minds "full on," provoked sociably, heads nodding agreement.—More immediate camposinos, now drawn 17 million strong to the streets below, make the noises of the city. A poster admonishes: "Admon. Vota. Platestda." Near the door the graffiti begins "La ignorancia mata. . . ." The hour draws to a close, a final cigarette, a summary, a warm smile.

PROPOSAL EXERCISES

1. What are the research questions (RQs), and hypotheses (if you have any), for your proposed research study? (See Chapter 4 for more information on writing RQs and hypotheses.)
2. For each research question, list the kind(s) of data you intend to collect. (For more information on data collection, see Chapters 7, 8, and 9.)
3. For each research question, list the kind(s) of analysis you plan to conduct. (See current chapter.)
4. How will you validate your findings for each research question? (For more information on validity, see Chapter 11.)
5. How will you decide whether your qualitative and/or quantitative findings are practically significant?
6. If you are conducting a mixed methods study, where and when will you engage in *integration* (e.g., questions, theory, methods, methodology[ies], analysis, interpretation, writing of results, integration cross stages, etc.). (For more information on integration, see Chapter 17.)

RELEVANT INTERNET SITES

Qualitative data analysis software links
http://www.researchware.com
http://www.unige.ch/ses/sococ/aqual/links/qual.html

Specific popular qualitative and mixed data analysis programs
MAXQDA, http://www.maxqda.com
QDA Miner, http://provalisresearch.com/products/qualitative-data-analysis-software/

HyperRESEARCH, http://www.researchware.com/products/hyperresearch.html
NVivo, http://www.qsrinternational.com/products_nvivo.aspx

Dedoose, http://www.dedoose.com
Ethnograph, http://www.qualisresearch.com
ATLAS, http://www.atlasti.com/qualitative-analysis-software.html

Many links to qualitative data analysis sites

http://caqdas.soc.surrey.ac.uk
http://www.nova.edu/ssss/QR/web.html
http://toolkit.pellinstitute.org/evaluation-guide/analyze/analyze-qualitative-data/
http://onlineqda.hud.ac.uk/Intro_QDA/what_is_qda.php
https://www.youtube.com/user/MAXQDA
https://www.youtube.com/watch?v=ziCxFIU0yZY

(There are many additional tutorials on QDA software on YouTube.)

STUDENT STUDY SITE

Visit the Student Study Site at **edge.sagepub.com/rbjohnson6e** for these additional learning tools:

Video Links
Self-Quizzes
eFlashcards
Lecture Notes
Full-Text SAGE Journal Articles
Interactive Concept Maps
Web Resources

RECOMMENDED READING

Bazeley, P. (2013). *Qualitative data analysis: Practical strategies.* Los Angeles, CA: SAGE.
Buckley, C. A., & Waring, M. J. (2013). Using diagrams to support the research process: Examples from grounded theory. *Qualitative Research, 13*(2), 146–172.
Miles, M. B., Huberman, A. M., & Saldaña, J. (2014). *Qualitative data analysis: A methods sourcebook* (3rd ed.). Los Angeles, CA: SAGE.
Patton, M. Q. (2014). *Qualitative research and evaluation methods.* Thousand Oaks, CA: SAGE.
van Leeuwen, T., & Jewitt, C. (Eds.). (2001). *Handbook of visual analysis.* London, England: SAGE.

NOTES

1. This section was originally written by Anthony J. Onwuegbuzie and Burke Johnson.
2. Reprinted from Robert E. Stake, "Class Notes, October 23," *The Art of Case Study Research*, pp. 88–90, copyright © 1995 by SAGE, Thousand Oaks, CA. Reprinted by permission of SAGE, and the author.

Chapter 20 Appendix

Additional Types of Codes for Qualitative Research*

A currently popular book about qualitative data analysis is Johnny Saldaña's (2016) book entitled *The Coding Manual for Qualitative Researchers*. In this excellent and cutting-edge book, the author explains 8 major styles of coding and 32 particular types of codes/coding. Here, we have abstracted the 13 types of codes/coding (and their definitions) that especially enhance the coding process explained in this chapter. Please read and reread the following, and then use them in your qualitative data analysis when the need arises. We suspect you will find some of the types quite useful and eye-opening.

13 Additional Types of Coding

1. Causation Coding. Extracts attributions or causal beliefs from participant data about not just how but why particular outcomes came about. Searches for combinations of antecedent conditions and mediating variables that lead toward certain pathways. Attempts to map a three-part process as a CODE 1 → CODE 2 → CODE 3 sequence. Appropriate for discerning motives, belief systems, worldviews, processes, recent histories, interrelationships, and the complexity of influences and affects on human actions and phenomena. May serve grounded theorists in searches for causes, conditions, contexts, and consequences. Also appropriate to evaluate the efficacy of a particular program, or as preparatory work before diagramming or modeling a process through visual means such as decision modeling and causation networks. Examples: SPEECH TRAINING → CONFIDENCE → COLLEGE PREP; COMPETITION → WINNING → SELF-ESTEEM; SUCCESS + HARD WORK REWARDS + GOOD COACH → CONFIDENCE.

2. Dramaturgical Coding. Applies the terms and conventions of character, play script, and production analysis to qualitative data. For character, these terms include such items as participant objectives (OBJ), conflicts (CON), tactics (TAC), attitudes (ATT), emotions (EMO), and subtexts (SUB). Appropriate for exploring intrapersonal and interpersonal participant experiences and actions in case studies, power relationships, and the processes of human motives and agency. Examples: OBJ: CONFRONT; TAC: ADMONISH; ATT: IRONIC.

3. Emotion Coding. Labels the emotions recalled and/or experienced by the participant, or inferred by the researcher about the participant. Appropriate for virtually all qualitative studies, but particularly for those that explore intrapersonal and interpersonal participant experiences and actions. Provides insight into the participants' perspectives, worldviews, and life conditions. Examples: "TEARING ME APART"; MILD SURPRISE; RELIEF.

4. Hypothesis Coding. Application of a research-generated, predetermined list of codes to qualitative data specifically to assess a researcher-generated hypothesis. The codes are developed from

Adapted from Saldana, J., *The Coding Manual for Qualitative Researchers*, SAGE Publications, (2016.

a theory/prediction about what will be found in the data before they have been collected or analyzed. Statistical applications, if needed, can range from simple frequency counts to more complex multivariate analyses. Appropriate for hypothesis testing, content analysis, and analytic induction of the qualitative data set, particularly the search for rules, causes, and explanations in the data. Can also be applied midway or later in a qualitative study's data collection or analysis to confirm or to disconfirm any assertions or theories developed thus far. Example: It is hypothesized that the responses to a particular question about language issues in the United States will generate one of four answers from participants: RIGHT, We have the right to speak whatever language we want in America; SAME, We need to speak the same language in America—English; MORE, We need to know how to speak more than one language; and NR, no response or "I don't know."

5. Longitudinal Coding. The attribution of selected change processes to qualitative data collected and compared across time. Matrices organize data from fieldwork observations, interview transcripts, and document excerpts into similar temporal categories that permit researcher analysis and reflection on their similarities and differences from one time period through another to generate inferences of change, if any. Appropriate for studies that explore identity, change, and development in individuals, groups, and organizations through extended periods of time. Examples of change processes: INCREASE AND EMERGE; CONSTANT AND CONSISTENT; CUMULATIVE.

6. Magnitude Coding. Consists of and adds a supplemental alphanumeric or symbolic code or subcode to an existing coded datum or category to indicate its intensity, frequency, direction, presence, or evaluative content. Magnitude codes can be qualitative, quantitative, and/or nominal indicators to enhance description. Appropriate for mixed methods and qualitative studies in social science and health care disciplines that also support quantitative measures as evidence of outcomes. Examples: STRONGLY (STR); 1 = LOW; + = PRESENT.

7. Pattern Coding. A category label ("meta code") that identifies similarly coded data. Organizes the corpus into sets, themes, or constructs and attributes meaning to that organization. Appropriate for second cycle coding; development of major themes from the data; the search for rules, causes, and explanations in the data; examining social networks and patterns of human relationships; or the formation of theoretical constructs and processes. Example: DYSFUNCTIONAL DIRECTION as the pattern code for the related codes UNCLEAR INSTRUCTIONS, RUSHED DIRECTIONS, "YOU NEVER TOLD ME," and so forth.

8. Process Coding. Uses gerunds ("-ing" words) exclusively to connote observable and conceptual action in the data. Processes also imply actions intertwined with the dynamics of time, such as things that emerge, change, occur in particular sequences, or become strategically implemented. Appropriate for virtually all qualitative studies, but particularly for grounded theory research that extracts participant action/interaction and consequences, and the documentation of routines and rituals. Part of and employed in other grounded theory methods (Initial, Focused, Axial, and Theoretical Coding). Examples: TELLING OTHERS; REJECTING RUMORS; STICKING BY FRIENDS.

9. Protocol Coding. The coding of qualitative data according to a pre-established, recommended, standardized, or prescribed system. The generally comprehensive lists of codes and categories provided to the researcher that are applied after his or her own data collection. Some protocols also recommend specific qualitative (and quantitative) data analytic techniques with the coded data. Appropriate for qualitative studies in disciplines with previously developed and field-tested coding systems. Examples: ALCOH = alcoholism or drinking; DRUG = drug use; MONEY = lack of money or financial problems.

10. Provisional Coding. Begins with a "start list" of researcher-generated codes based on what preparatory investigation suggests might appear in the data before they are collected and analyzed. Provisional codes can be revised, modified, deleted, or expanded to include new codes. Appropriate for qualitative studies that build on or corroborate previous research and investigations. Example: Language arts and drama research suggests that the following may be observed in child participants during classroom work: VOCABULARY DEVELOPMENT; ORAL LANGUAGE FLUENCY; STORY COMPREHENSION; DISCUSSION SKILLS.

11. Structural Coding. Applies a content-based or conceptual phrase to a segment of data that relates to a specific research question to both code and categorize the data corpus. Similarly coded segments are then collected together for more detailed coding and analysis. Appropriate for virtually all qualitative studies, but particularly for those employing multiple participants, standardized or semi-structured data-gathering protocols, hypothesis testing, or exploratory investigations to gather topics lists or indexes of major categories or themes. Example: Research question: What types of smoking cessation techniques (if any) have participants attempted in the past? Structural Code: UNSUCCESSFUL SMOKING CESSATION TECHNIQUES.

12. Values Coding. The application of codes to qualitative data that reflect a participant's values, attitudes, and beliefs, representing his or her perspectives or worldview. A value (V:) is the importance we attribute to oneself, another person, thing, or idea. An attitude (A:) is the way we think and feel about ourselves, another person, thing, or idea. A belief (B:) is part of a system that includes values and attitudes, plus personal knowledge, experiences, opinions, prejudices, morals, and their interpretive perceptions of the social world. Appropriate for virtually all qualitative studies, but particularly for those that explore cultural values, identity, intrapersonal and interpersonal participant experiences and actions in case studies, appreciative inquiry, oral history, and critical ethnography. Examples: V: RESPECT; A: DISLIKES "LAME EXCUSES"; B: THE IDEAL IS POSSIBLE.

13. Versus Coding. Identifies in dichotomous or binary terms the individuals, groups, social systems, organizations, phenomena, processes, concepts, and so forth in direct conflict with each other, a duality that manifests itself as an X vs. Y code. Appropriate for policy studies, discourse analysis, critical ethnography, action and practitioner research, and qualitative data sets that suggest strong conflicts, injustice, power imbalances, or competing goals within, among, and between participants. Examples: "IMPOSSIBLE" vs. REALISTIC; CUSTOM vs. COMPARISON; STANDARDIZATION vs. "VARIANCES."

NOTE

* Adapted from Saldana, J., *The Coding Manual for Qualitative Researchers*, pp 291–298, copyright © 2016 by SAGE, Thousand Oaks, CA.

PART VI

Writing the Research Report

Chapter 21

How to Prepare a Research Report and Use APA Style Guidelines

Chapter 21

How to Prepare a Research Report and Use APA Style Guidelines

LEARNING OBJECTIVES

After reading this chapter, you should be able to

- Explain the different principles used in writing an APA style research report (e.g., language, specificity, labels, etc.).
- Describe the five levels of APA headings.
- List the seven sections of an APA style quantitative research report and describe what goes in each section.
- Explain how one might use the example of an APA-style manuscript provided in the chapter.
- Explain how to write a qualitative research report.
- Explain how to write a mixed methods research report, especially the Results section.

Visit the Student Study Site for an interactive concept map.

After you have conducted a research study, you should consider preparing a research report to present at a conference and then submit to a journal for publication. Before preparing the research report, you should critically review it and ask yourself whether the study is free from flaws and important enough to justify conference presentation and then publication. Would others be interested in the results, and would it influence their work or have some educational impact? As a general rule, you should never conduct a study that you do not think is publishable. If the study is important and free from flaws, you should proceed with the preparation of a research report because this is the mechanism for communicating the results of research studies. Table 21.1 lists some of the journals in which educational researchers publish.

TABLE 21.1 Some Journals That Publish the Results of Educational Research

American Educational Research Journal	Journal of Education
American Journal of Education	Journal of Education for Students Placed at Risk
Anthropology and Education Quarterly	Journal of Educational and Behavioral Statistics
Applied Measurement in Education	Journal of Educational Psychology
Art Education	Journal of Educational Research
Cambridge Journal of Education	Journal of Information Technology for Teacher Education
Child Development	Journal of In-service Education
Cognition and Instruction	Journal of Literacy Research
Creativity Research Journal	Journal of Negro Education
Curriculum/Technology Quarterly	Journal of Research in Science Teaching
Early Childhood Education Journal	Journal of Vocational Education and Training
Education and Urban Society	Kappa Delta Pi Record
Educational Action Research	New Teacher Advocate
Educational Assessment	Oxford Studies in Comparative Education
Educational Evaluation and Policy Analysis	Phi Delta Kappan
The Educational Forum	PROSPERO
Educational Policy	Reading Research Quarterly
Educational Psychologist	Research in Post-Compulsory Education
Educational Psychology Review	Research in the Teaching of English
Educational Research and Evaluation	Review of Educational Research
Educational Researcher	School Leadership and Management
Elementary School Journal	Teacher Development
Harvard Educational Review	Teacher Education Quarterly
International Studies in Sociology of Education	Teachers and Teaching: Theory and Practice
Journal for Research in Mathematics Education	Teachers College Record
Journal of Classroom Interaction	Teaching and Teacher Education
Journal of Cross-Cultural Psychology	Theory Into Practice
Journal of Curriculum and Supervision	Urban Education
Journal of Curriculum Studies	The Urban Review

Most journals of interest to educational researchers specify that authors follow the style specified in the *Publication Manual of the American Psychological Association* (American Psychological Association, 2010). We refer to this manual as the *APA Publication Manual.* We explain this style here because it is so prevalent among the journals of interest to educational researchers.

The preparation of research reports differs somewhat depending on whether you conducted a quantitative or a qualitative research study. Remember that quantitative studies focus on hypothesis testing and are epitomized by experimental research studies, whereas qualitative studies are more often exploratory and bridge a variety of approaches or methods from ethnography to historical research. Because of the different goals and approaches of quantitative and qualitative research, the approaches to writing quantitative and qualitative research reports differ. We focus first on quantitative research report writing and then on qualitative research report writing. However, before this discussion, we want to cover several general principles that must be adhered to in writing either type of research report.

See Journal Article 21.1 on the Student Study Site.

GENERAL PRINCIPLES RELATED TO WRITING THE RESEARCH REPORT (I)

Perhaps the overriding general principle of writing the research report is that it must be prepared in a manner that communicates clearly to the reader. Good writing is a craft that requires thoughtful concern for the presentation and language used. Good writing is usually a developmental process that is acquired over time. Instruction in developing good writing is obviously not the purpose of this textbook or the course you are taking. However, because good writing is so important, we discuss some of the general principles to which you should adhere when preparing a research report, which are elaborated on in the *APA Publication Manual* (2010). In order to learn quickly about some common mistakes that you can avoid, see the bonus item Burke's Writing Tips at the student companion website.

If you have difficulty with writing, there are several books, in addition to the *APA Publication Manual*, that can be very helpful. W. Strunk Jr. and E. B. White's *The Elements of Style* (1918/2000) is a classic and has the virtue of being short. Gage's *The Shape of Reason* (2006) and Rosnow and Rosnow's *Writing Papers in Psychology* (2012) are excellent resources and can be of assistance in writing clearly. Hult's book *Researching and Writing in the Social Sciences* (1996) and Becker's book *Writing for Social Scientists* (1986) are also excellent references.

Clear communication requires an orderly presentation of ideas. There must be a continuity of words, concepts, and thematic development from the beginning to the end of the report. This continuity can be achieved by the use of punctuation marks to show the relationship between ideas and by the use of transitional words, such as *then*, *next*, *therefore*, and *however.* Because you are so familiar with the material you are reporting, objectivity is frequently lost, and problems in clarity of communication might not be immediately apparent. One good technique is to write the research report and then put it aside for several days before reading it again. A later reading of the report can uncover difficulties in clarity of communication.

Writing the research report requires a smoothness and economy of expression. Smoothness of expression is achieved by avoiding ambiguity, or shifting topics, tense, or person, all of which might confuse the reader. For example, consistency of verb tenses enhances the clarity of expression. Economy of expression is achieved by being frugal with words. This means eliminating redundancy, wordiness, jargon, evasiveness, overuse of the passive voice, circumlocution, and clumsy prose as well as overly detailed descriptions in any part of the research report, such as of participants or procedures. For example, rather than using *at the present time*, use *now.* The phrase *absolutely essential* is redundant and should be reduced to *essential.* You should make certain the words you use convey their intended meaning. This means that you must avoid the use of colloquial expressions, jargon, or ambiguous comparisons. According to APA guidelines, you should use the personal pronouns *I* or *we* when describing the steps you have taken in completing your study. All of the guidelines we now present are based on the most recent version of the *APA Publication Manual* (2010).

See Tools and Tips 21.1 on the Student Study Site.

See Journal Article 21.2 on the Student Study Site.

Language (I.1)

The language that is used to communicate the results of research should be free of demeaning attitudes and biased assumptions. There are three guidelines that should be followed to achieve this goal: specificity, sensitivity to labels, and acknowledgment of participation.

Specificity (I.1A)

When referring to a person or persons, you should choose accurate and clear words that are free from bias. When in doubt, err in the direction of being more rather than less specific. For example, if you are describing age groups, it is better to provide a specific age range (for example, *ages 8 to 12*) instead of a broad category (such as *under 12*). *People at risk* is also too broad. Instead, identify the risk and the people involved (e.g., *children at risk for sexual abuse*). Similarly, *gender* is preferred when referring to men and women as a social group rather than *sex,* as *sex* can be confused with sexual behavior.

Labels (I.1B)

The preferences of the participants in any study must be respected, and participants should be called what they prefer to be called. This means avoiding labels when possible or, as has been common in science, categorizing participants as objects (e.g., the elderly) or equating participants with their conditions (e.g., depressives, stroke victims). An effective solution is to place the person first, followed by a descriptive phrase (e.g., *children with a diagnosis of attention-deficit/hyperactivity disorder*). Similarly, sensitivity should be given to any suggestion that one group is better than another or is the standard against which another is to be judged. For example, it would be inappropriate to contrast *abused children* with *normal children,* thus stigmatizing the abused children. A more appropriate contrast would be between *children who have been abused* and *children who have no history of abuse.*

Participation (I.1C)

You should write about the participants in your study in a way that acknowledges their participation. The fifth edition of the *APA Publication Manual* (2001) recommended using the general term *participants* to refer to the individuals who participated in a study. In the current sixth edition, this recommendation has been changed to using either the general term *participants* or *subjects*. In general, you should be specific when describing your research participants, using descriptive terms such as *children with ADHD* and *middle school teachers*. You should also use the active voice when writing your research report (e.g., "the students completed," not "the assessment was completed by the students"). In general, tell what the research participants did in a way that acknowledges their participation. These guidelines need to be followed to avoid writing in a way that reflects demeaning attitudes and biased assumptions. Keeping these guidelines in mind, specific attention should be given to the following issues.

Gender. Participants should be described in a way that avoids ambiguity in sex identity or sex role. This means that you should never use *he* to refer to both sexes or *man* or *mankind* to refer to people in general. The words *people*, *individuals*, and *persons* can be substituted without losing meaning or clarity of expression.

Sexual Orientation. When referring to the enduring pattern of sexual emotion, attraction, and behavior, you should use the term *sexual orientation* and avoid the term *sexual preference*. Also, you should replace less accurate terms such as *homosexual* with terms such as *gay men*, *bisexual men*, *lesbians*, and *bisexual women* when referring to individuals who identify this way. In general, you should avoid terms that have become loaded or are reflective of stereotypes because doing so is denigrating to individual people.

Racial and Ethnic Identity. Remember that ethnic and racial designations often change and can become dated and negative. When referring to a person's ethnic or racial group, keep in mind the guidelines of specificity and sensitivity and the research participants' preferred designations. Some individuals of African ancestry might prefer the term *Black* whereas many others will prefer *African American*. At present, when referring to people indigenous to North America, *Native American*, *American Indian*, and *Native North American* are all accepted terms. Because there are hundreds of indigenous groups of people, you should usually try to be more specific (e.g., *Samoans*, *Inuit*, *Dine*).

Disabilities. When describing individuals with handicaps, it is important to maintain their integrity and dignity as human beings. Avoid language equating them with their condition, such as describing participants as *cancer victims*, or that gives a pictorial metaphor, such as *wheelchair bound*. Instead, describe a participant as *a person who has cancer* or *a person who is confined to a wheelchair.* Similarly, avoid condescending euphemisms such as "special or physically challenged."

Age. The general rule to follow regarding age is to be specific in describing the age of participants and avoid open-ended definitions, such as *over 65*. People under the age of 12 can be referred to as *boys* and *girls*, and individuals aged 13 to 17 can be referred to as *young men or women* or as *female or male adolescents*. Call people 18 and older *men* and *women*. *Older adults* is preferred to *elderly*.

For information about unbiased language, you can consult the full *APA Publication Manual*, and you should go to http://www.apastyle.org and search for the most recent documents about the topics we have discussed here.

Editorial Style (I.2)

Editorial style refers to the rules or guidelines a publisher uses to ensure a clear, consistent presentation of published material. These rules specify the basic rules and guidelines to be followed when writing the research report. Below we list and discuss some of these rules based on the *APA Publication Manual*; this manual is used in most social, behavioral, and educational research. If you require additional information, you should consult that manual.

Punctuation (I.2A)

The primary rule change with regard to punctuation is that you are to space twice after the end of a sentence. The *APA Publication Manual* has recommendations regarding virtually all punctuation issues. If you are uncertain about a particular punctuation issue, consult the *APA Publication Manual.* Also, some of the more common punctuation mistakes are explained in the document "Burke's Writing Tips" at this book's companion website. Here are four rules where mistakes are often made:

1. Always include a comma before the *and* in a series (e.g., apples, oranges, and pears).
2. Commas and periods are included inside the quote marks (e.g., Popular terms in high school are "geeks," "dorks," and "jocks.").
3. Separate two independent clauses with a semicolon, not a comma.
4. Precede a colon with an independent clause. An independent clause is a set of words that could stand alone as a sentence.

Italics (I.2B)

As a general rule, use italics infrequently. Use the italics function of your word processing software for words that are to appear in italics. Italics are required for some written items, including titles (e.g., of books, journals), initial introduction of a new technical term, many statistical symbols, and words that might easily be misread. Do not use italics for foreign words that appear in English dictionaries (e.g., a priori, per se, et al.) or for Greek letters. Use italics for emphasis rarely, if at all.

Abbreviations (I.2C)

You should use abbreviations sparingly. Abbreviate only when the abbreviations are conventional and likely to be familiar to the reader or when you can save considerable space and avoid cumbersome repetition. A general rule to follow is to abbreviate only when the abbreviation will help you communicate with your reader. The following Latin abbreviations are to be used only in parenthetical material: cf. (compare), e.g. (for example), etc. (and so forth), i.e. (that is), viz. (namely), and vs. (versus, against). The exception to this rule is the Latin abbreviation et al. (and others), which is used in the text of the manuscript. Some units of time, such as second, hour, minute, millisecond, and nanosecond, are abbreviated with s, hr, min, ms, and ns. Day, week, month, and year are not abbreviated. Abbreviations and symbols are used for many measurement units, such as m (meter), N (newton), P.M. (post meridiem), and V (volt). These abbreviations are not italicized or underlined. Some abbreviations are now accepted as words (e.g., AIDS, HIV, IQ, ESP). Many other abbreviations, identified in the *APA Publication Manual*, can be used in a research report, and this manual should be consulted prior to using abbreviations not mentioned here.

Headings (I.2D)

Headings indicate the organization of your manuscript. There are five levels of headings in a manuscript, and they have the following top-down progression (APA, 2010, p. 62):

Level of heading	*Format of heading*
1	**Centered, Boldface, Uppercase and Lowercase Heading**
2	**Flush Left, Boldface, Uppercase and Lowercase Heading**
3	**Indented, boldface, lowercase paragraph heading with a period.**
4	***Indented, boldface, italicized, lowercase paragraph heading with a period.***
5	*Indented, italicized, lowercase paragraph heading with a period.*

Note that lowercase paragraph headings (i.e., levels 3, 4, and 5) begin with a capital letter and all remaining letters are lowercase. Also, written text begins on the same line as the lowercase paragraph headings.

All headings are not used in every manuscript. The logic of APA style headings use is simple. If only one level of heading is needed in an article, use level 1. If two levels are needed, use levels 1 and 2, and so forth. The following illustrates the use of several levels of headings.

Level of heading	*Format of heading*
Two levels of heading would appear as follows:	**Method** **Selection of Research Participants**
Three levels of heading would appear as follows:	**Experiment 1** **Method** **Selection of research participants.**
Four levels of headings would appear as follows:	**Experiment 1** **Method** **Selection of research participants.** ***Experimental and control participants.***
Five levels of headings would appear as follows:	**Experiment 1** **Method** **Selection of research participants.** ***Experimental and control participants.*** *Strategies used with participants.*

Do not use letters or numbers to mark your headings (e.g., I, II, III).

Quotation (I.2E)

In Chapter 6 we discussed *plagiarism* and defined it as using work produced by others and presenting it as your own. When using authors' exact words (i.e., a string of four or more words), you must always follow the two primary quotation rules. Quotation rule 1 states that a quotation of fewer than 40 words is inserted into the text and enclosed with double quotation marks. Quotation rule 2 states that a quotation of 40 or more words is displayed in a freestanding block of lines without quotation marks but indented about a half inch and started on a new line. In both cases, you must include the author and year of publication of the quotation and include the full citation of the work in the reference section of your manuscript. With both block quotations and quotations inserted into the text, you must include the specific page from which the quote is taken.

Numbers (I.2F)

Use words to express numbers that begin a sentence as well as any number below 10. Use numerals to express all other numbers. Exceptions to this rule are specified in the *APA Publication Manual.* When you express numerals, make sure that you use Arabic (1, 2, 3) and not Roman (I, II, III) numerals.

Physical Measurements (I.2G)

State all physical measurements in metric units. If a measurement is expressed in nonmetric units, put its metric equivalent in parentheses.

Presentation of Statistical Results (I.2H)

When presenting the results of inferential statistical tests in the text, provide enough information to allow the reader to understand fully the analysis that was conducted. When reporting statistical tests, you should provide the test statistic value, degrees of freedom, probability value, and an effect size indicator of the magnitude of relationship or an effect-size confidence interval. For example, t and F tests could be reported as follows:

$t(28) = 4.67$, $p = .04$, $d = 0.55$, 95% CI [0.30, 0.95]

$F(3, 32) = 8.79$, $p = .02$, est $\omega^2 = .08$

When reporting confidence intervals, you should put the lower and upper limit in brackets preceded by its designation, such as in the following example:

95% CI [−2.36, 4.75]

Reference Citations in the Text (I.2I)

When you cite the work of others in the text of the research report, you must give them credit by referencing the work you have used. Use the author-date citation method, which involves inserting the author's surname and the publication date at the appropriate point, as follows:

Smith (2009) reported that education and income were positively correlated for all groups.

or

It has been demonstrated (Smith, 2009) that education and income are positively correlated.

or

> Research has shown that education and income are positively correlated (Smith, 2009).

With this information, the reader can turn to the reference list of your manuscript and locate complete information regarding the source. Multiple citations involving the same author are arranged in chronological order:

> Smith (1987, 1993, 1998, 1999)

Multiple citations involving different authors are arranged alphabetically:

> Several studies (Adams, 1997; Cox, 1994; Smith, 1998; Thomas, 1999) have revealed that the developmental changes . . .

If a citation includes more than two but fewer than six authors, all authors should be cited the first time the reference is used. Subsequent citations include only the surname of the first author, followed by the abbreviation *et al.* and the year the article was published as follows:

> Smith et al. (1998)

If six or more authors are associated with a citation, only the surname of the first author followed by *et al.* is used for all citations. You will need to consult the *APA Publication Manual* if you encounter references from sources not explained here.

Reference List (I.3)

All citations in the text of the research report must be cited accurately and completely in the reference list so that it is possible for readers to locate the works. This means that each entry should include the name of the author, year of publication, title, publishing data, and any other information necessary to identify the reference. All references are to appear in alphabetical order by the surname of the first author and typed double-spaced with a hanging indent and on a separate page with the word *References* centered at the top of the page in uppercase and lowercase letters.

The general form of a reference is as follows for a periodical, book, and book chapter, respectively:

Canned, I. B., & Had, U. B. (2009). Moderating violence in a violent society. *Journal of Violence and Peace Making, 32*, 231–243.

Breeze, C. (2013). *Why children kill.* New York, NY: Academic.

Good, I. M. (2011). Moral development in violent children. In A. Writer & N. Author (Eds.), *The anatomy of violent children* (pp. 134–187). Washington, DC: Killer Books.

For electronic sources and locator information, some of the models used in the past for referencing do not apply because sometimes it is difficult to tell whether an online version of an article is an advanced version or the version of record. The general recommendation is to use the same elements when referencing an electronic source as you would a fixed-media source and then add as much electronic retrieval information as necessary to allow others to locate the source you cited. In the past, if you cited information obtained from the Internet, you included the home page uniform resource locator (URL) of the journal, book, or report publisher, as shown in the following examples of (a) an article published in a journal that appeared only on the Internet and (b) a document appearing on the Internet.

Van Camp, R., & Roth, C. (2002). Role of parental discipline on classroom behavior. *Journal of Child and Adolescent Behavior, 21,* 121–132. Retrieved from http://www.esciencecentral.org/journals/child-and-adolescent-behavior.php

Task Force on Teen Pregnancy in the Southeastern Region. (n.d.). *Methods for reducing teen pregnancy.* Retrieved from http://www.reduceteenpregnancy.org

However, content on the Internet is frequently moved or deleted, which results in nonworking URLs. To overcome this difficulty, a group of international publishers developed the digital object identifier (DOI) system to provide a stable means of identifying information on digital networks. This system assigns a unique identifier to each article that directs you to the article regardless of where it resides on the Internet. Publishers assign a DOI to an article when it is published and made available in an electronic format. The DOI is located on the first page of the article. A reference to a journal article with a DOI would take the following form:

Johnson, B. (2010). The advantages of doing a grounded-theory study. *Journal of Advanced Qualitative Methods, 43,* 154–163. doi:10.1276/j.aqm.2009.34.108

You will need to consult the *APA Publication Manual* if you need to reference items not discussed here.

Typing (I.4)

When typing your manuscript, double-space all material and select a uniform typeface. Times New Roman with a 12-point font size is the preferred typeface for APA publications. There should be 1-inch margins (2.54 centimeters) at the top, bottom, left, and right of every page. Use the italic and bold functions of your word processing software as well as other special fonts or styles of type as specified in the *APA Publication Manual.*

Writing an APA-Style Quantitative Research Report (II)

There are seven major sections in the research report:

1. Title page
2. Abstract
3. Introduction

4. Method
5. Results
6. Discussion
7. References

In Chapter 5 we discussed several of these sections as they are used in a research proposal. In this chapter we focus on writing the final research report. When looking above at the seven sections, note that the Results section and the Discussion section are not included in a research proposal because the research has not yet been conducted. These two major sections are included in the research report, however, because the research report is where you write up your completed research study. We now present the material to be included in each of these seven sections.

See Journal Article 21.3 on the Student Study Site.

Title Page (II.1)

The title page contains a running head, title, author(s) and institutional affiliation(s) of the author(s), and author note. The running head, which is a shortened version of the title, is typed flush left in uppercase letters at the top of the title page and on all subsequent pages. The title is centered on the page and typed in uppercase and lowercase letters. It should clearly summarize the main topic of the paper and concisely identify the variables or theoretical issues under investigation and the relationship between them that is examined. The length of the title should be 12 words or fewer.

The names of authors who have made a substantial contribution to the study should appear immediately below the title typed in uppercase and lowercase letters, centered on the page and in the order of their contribution to the study. The preferred form is to use the author's first name, middle initial, and last name with titles and degrees omitted. The institutional affiliation where the author(s) conducted the study is centered under the author(s) name.

The label "Author Note" is centered and placed below the author's institutional affiliation. The Author Note should provide information about each author's departmental affiliation; any acknowledgments, disclaimers, or conflicts of interest; and how to contact the author. Each bit of information is provided in a separate paragraph, and each paragraph is started with an indent. The first paragraph identifies the departmental affiliation of each author at the time the study was conducted. The second paragraph identifies any change in author affiliation since the completion of the study. The third paragraph provides acknowledgment of any financial support for the study or assistance in completing the study. This paragraph also includes information about any special circumstances surrounding the research needing disclosure (e.g., disclaimers or perceived conflicts of interest). The fourth paragraph provides contact information for the primary person with whom readers should correspond regarding the report. This includes a complete mailing and email address of the contact person. If any of the four paragraphs is not relevant for your study, that paragraph is disregarded. Therefore, some "Author Note" information will have only two or three paragraphs. Our sample APA-style research report provided later in this chapter (starting on page 620) has three author note paragraphs.

All pages of the manuscript are to be numbered consecutively, at the top right of the page, beginning with the title page.

Abstract (II.2)

The abstract is a comprehensive summary of the contents of the research report. Word limits vary from journal to journal, but typically the abstract ranges from 150 to 250 words. The abstract should be typed on a separate page with the word Abstract centered at the top of the page in uppercase and lowercase letters. The abstract should be a single paragraph with no paragraph indentation, and it should be accurate, concise, and coherent. An abstract of an empirical study should summarize the problem, the research participants, the method used, the basic findings or results of the study (including statistical significance levels, effect size, and confidence levels), and any important conclusions and their applications or implications.

Introduction (II.3)

The research report begins with the introduction, which is not labeled with a heading because of its position in the paper. Type the title of the paper in upper and lowercase letters and center it at the top of the page. The introduction presents the specific problem being investigated in the context of prior research and describes the research strategy. You should usually begin with a general introduction to the problem area and perhaps a statement of the point of the study. The introduction continues with a review of prior studies that have been conducted in the area and relate to the specific issue being investigated. This literature review is not exhaustive; it cites only studies that are directly pertinent to place the current study in the context of prior work and gives an appropriate history and recognition of the work of others. An exhaustive review of the literature is more appropriate for a thesis or dissertation.

After introducing the research problem and reviewing prior literature, you should tell what you did in the study you are reporting. This might take the form of stating the purpose of the study and any hypotheses that would give clarity to the paper. Overall, the introduction should specify the purpose of the study, show how it relates to prior work in the area, and identify hypotheses to be tested.

Method (II.4)

The Method section follows the introduction. It does not start on a separate page. The purpose of the Method section is to tell your reader exactly how the study was conducted. It enables the reader to evaluate the appropriateness of the design of the study and make an assessment of the reliability and validity of the results. If the method is presented well, another researcher can replicate your study.

To facilitate communication, the Method section is typically divided into subsections: participants or subjects, apparatus or instruments, and procedure. Additional subsections may be included, if the research design is complex, to help communicate specific information.

Participants (II.4A)

The participants subsection should identify the major demographic characteristics of the participants such as their age and gender. You must include a description of the sampling method used to select the participants, the sample size, and the response rate. Any other pertinent information should also be included, such as how they were assigned to the experimental treatment conditions, the number of participants that were selected for the study but did not complete it (and why), eligibility and exclusion criteria, and any inducements given to encourage participation.

Apparatus or Instruments (II.4B)

This subsection describes the apparatus or instruments used to collect the data and why they were used. Any methods that were used to improve the reliability and quality of the measures should be described. The psychometric and biometric properties of the instruments used should be provided.

Procedure (II.4C)

The procedure subsection tells the reader exactly how the study was executed, from the moment the participant and the researcher came into contact to the time the participant left the study. This subsection includes a step-by-step account of what the experimenter and participant did during the study, including any instructions; stimulus conditions that were presented to the participants and the responses they were to make; and any control techniques that were used, such as randomization or counterbalancing. In other words, in the procedure subsection, you are to tell exactly what both you and the participants did and how you did it.

Results (II.5)

The Results section follows the Method section. It does not start on a separate page. The purpose of the Results section is to summarize the data that were collected and their statistical treatment. In making this presentation, remember that any discussion of the results takes place in the Discussion section. The Results section should tell the reader how the data were analyzed and the results of this analysis. In presenting the results of statistical analysis, remember to state all relevant results, including the alpha level, effect size, and confidence intervals. Treatment of missing data should be reported along with the frequency or percentage of missing data and any explanation of the cause of the missing data. If multiple significance tests were conducted, it is convenient to state the significance level used once, such as in the following:

> The .05 alpha level was used for all statistical tests.

Results of any inferential tests (e.g., *t* tests, *F* tests, and chi-square) should be accompanied by the numerical value of the test statistic along with the accompanying degrees of freedom, the exact probability level, and an indicator of the size and direction of the effect. Be sure to include sufficient descriptive statistics, such as cell sample size, means, correlations, and standard deviations, so that the nature of the effect can be understood. You should also provide evidence that your study has sufficient a priori power to detect an effect.

In reporting and illustrating the direction of a statistically significant effect (nonsignificant effects are not elaborated on for obvious reasons), you should decide which medium will most clearly and economically serve your purpose. Generally, tables are preferred for presenting detailed quantitative data and illustrating main effects on multiple variables. Figures can illustrate interactions effectively, if space allows. If you use a figure or table, make sure that you tell the reader, in the text of the report, what it depicts. Then give sufficient explanation to make sure that the reader is able to interpret it correctly. For example, when means are reported, always include an associated measure of variability, such as standard deviation or mean square error.

Discussion (II.6)

The Discussion section has the purpose of interpreting and evaluating the study results, giving primary emphasis to the relationships between the results and the hypotheses of the study. Begin your discussion by stating whether the hypotheses of the study were or were not supported. Follow this statement with an interpretation of the results, telling the reader what you think they mean. In doing so, you should attempt to integrate your research findings with the results of prior research so that the results of your study are placed in the context of the literature in the field; this approach should also clarify any conclusions you reach. When interpreting the study results, you should take into consideration any limitations or weaknesses inherent in the study such as possible bias or threats to internal validity, imprecise measuring instruments, and effect size. In general, you should acknowledge any limitations of the study as well the extent to which the results can be generalized.

The Discussion section should end with commentary on the importance of the findings. This can be a brief or somewhat lengthy discussion as long as the commentary is not overstated. The Discussion might also end with a statement of the new or unresolved problems that emerged as a result of the study. This will include suggestions for future research in the area.

References (II.7)

The References section provides a list of all citations in the text of the research report. This section provides both an acknowledgment of the scholarly work of others and a way to locate their work. In preparing the list of references, you should begin on a new page with the word References typed at the top center of the page in upper- and lowercase bold letters. All entries are double-spaced, although the guidelines for some theses and dissertations specify that the reference list be single-spaced. Type references using a hanging indent format; set the first line of each reference flush left with subsequent lines indented.

Footnotes (II.8)

Footnotes are numbered consecutively, with a superscript Arabic numeral, in the order in which they appear in the text of the report. Most footnotes are content footnotes, containing material needed to supplement or amplify the information provided in the text, but footnotes are also used to acknowledge copyright permission. Content footnotes should be included only if they strengthen a discussion, because they can be distracting. Footnotes can be placed either at the bottom of the page on which their referent is discussed or placed in consecutive order on a separate page after the references.

Tables (II.9)

Tables are expensive to publish and therefore should be reserved for use only when they can convey and summarize data more economically and clearly than can a lengthy discussion. Tables should be viewed as informative supplements to the text. Although each table should be intelligible by itself, it should also be an integral part of the text and should be referred to somewhere in the text. When referring to a table, identify it by name (e.g., Table 5) and do not use a reference such as "the table above" or "the table on page 6." In the text, only the table's highlights should be discussed. If you decide to use tables, number them with Arabic numerals in the order in which they are mentioned in the text.

Each table should have a brief title that clearly explains the data it contains. This title and the word Table and its number are typed flush with the left margin at the top of the table. Each column and row of data within the table should be given a label that identifies, as briefly as possible, the data contained in that row or column. You have the option of either single- or double-spacing the table content; the spacing used should be guided by the readability of the table content. Numerical values listed in the table should be carried to the number of decimal places needed to express the precision of the measurement. A dash should be used to indicate missing data.

Many different types of tables are used to present data. The *APA Publication Manual* provides a discussion of the construction of almost any type of table you might want to use and illustrates many of these tables. If you are constructing a table, you should consult the *APA Publication Manual* for additional details to be used in its preparation.

The following checklist should be used to help ensure that the table you have constructed meets the specifications listed in the *APA Publication Manual*:

- Is the table necessary?
- Should the table be presented in a print version, or can it be placed in an online supplemental file?
- Is there consistency between tables that present comparable data?
- Is the title brief, and does it indicate the table's contents?
- Does a column heading exist for each column?
- Are all abbreviations, special italics, dashes, boldface, and special symbols explained?
- Do notes have the appropriate order of (a) general note, (b) special note, (c) probability note?
- Have all vertical lines between columns been eliminated?
- Do all tables use the same confidence levels, and do all major point estimates have confidence intervals?
- Have the correct probability levels been identified for the statistical significance tests conducted?
- Has full credit been given to the reproduction of a copyrighted table, and has permission to reproduce the table been obtained?
- Is there a reference to the table in the text?

Figures (II.10)

Figures represent any illustration other than a table such as a chart, graph, or drawing. Figures provide an overall view of the pattern of results but provide less precise information than tables because they require the reader to estimate values. There are times when figures are a more appropriate way than tables to present information. If the figure will contribute substantially to the understanding of the manuscript and will most efficiently present the information, you should include the figure. A figure is typically included in a manuscript when it is needed to illustrate some complex theoretical formulation or represent the empirical result of a complex interaction.

The focus should be on simplicity, clarity, continuity, and information value when constructing a figure. Figures, therefore, should be used only when they augment the text and can present the essential facts in a way that is clear and easy to understand.

Figure Captions and Legends (II.10A)

Each figure has a caption and a legend. The figure caption explains the figure contents, and it serves as the title of the figure. It is placed below the figure. A figure legend explains any symbols used in the figure. It is placed within the figure.

Figure Preparation (II.10B)

Figures should be computer generated using professional-grade software. The resolution used should be sufficient to produce a high-quality image with letters typically no smaller than 8 points and no larger than 14 points. When preparing a figure, the primary guideline is to ensure that the presentation is clear and complete. The following checklist can be used to assist in the preparation of a figure:

- Is the figure necessary?
- Has the figure been presented in a clear and simple format with no extraneous detail?
- Does the title describe the contents?
- Have all parts of the figure been labeled clearly?
- Is there a reference to all figures in the manuscript?
- Is the resolution high enough to permit accurate reproduction?

Example of an APA-Style Manuscript

To assist you in the preparation of a research report, we now provide a sample research report that was prepared according to the guidelines we have presented. It conforms to the guidelines specified in the *APA Publication Manual.* Each part of this research report includes a brief comment regarding its content and a numeral reference to the specific section in this chapter that discusses that part. We expect that you will find this sample APA style to be helpful as you write your own quantitative report. If you are wondering how to construct your title page or how to cite a reference in text (and so forth), you can quickly look at this article to see how it is done. We have modeled our article after the one included in the latest *APA Publication Manual.* After this manuscript, we explain in the last two sections of this chapter how to write up qualitative and mixed research reports.

Running head: EFFECTS OF SHAME ON FORGIVENESS 1

Effects of Shame on Forgiveness
Among College Students

Danny L. McCarty
University of South Alabama

Author Note

Danny L. McCarty, Department of Psychology, University of South Alabama.

Danny L. McCarty is now pursuing a graduate degree at the Department of Pr

This research

conducted at the

Corresponder

Danny McCarty,

South Alabama,

edu

Manuscript title—See section II.1.

Author name, and Institutional affiliation—See section II.1.

Information to include in the author note is discussed in section II.1.

Information to include when writing the abstract is discussed in section II.2.

Double space the entire manuscript and use a Times Roman Typeface with a 12 point font size as discussed in section I.4.

EFFECTS OF SHAME ON FORGIVENESS 2

Abstract

Trait shame and trait forgiveness have been correlated with many social, psychological, and physical problems. The current study was designed to experimentally test the impact of shame on forgiveness. College students were recruited through introductory psychology courses and were exposed to one of three scenarios: shame, guilt, or neutral. Ages of the 119 students in the study sample ranged from 17 to 30 ($M = 18.3$). Following the scenarios, shame and forgiveness were measured. Results indicated that students exposed to the shame scenario reported significantly more shame than students exposed to the guilt scenario ($p = .03$) or students exposed to the neutral scenario ($p = .04$). Similarly, students exposed to the shame scenario reported less forgiveness than students exposed to the guilt ($p = .04$) or neutral scenario ($p = .02$). It appears that in this experimental context, shame had a negative impact on the tendency to forgive.

Keywords: forgiveness, shame, state forgiveness, revenge

EFFECTS OF SHAME ON FORGIVENESS 3

Effects of Shame on Forgiveness among College Students

Forgiveness is an important cognitive, emotional, and behavioral construct. According to Thompson et al. (2005), "forgiveness is the framing of a perceived transgression such that one's responses to the transgressor . . . are transformed from negative to neutral or positive" (p. 318). There must be a perceived wrong before a person can forgive. First, the person who has been wronged develops negative thoughts, feeling[s]
through the proce[ss]
are transformed f[rom]

When the pro[cess]
psychological dist[ress]
forgiveness also r[e]
& Chickering, 20[0]
forgiveness has be[en]
and anger (Berry &
et al., 2008). In co[ntrast]
reported higher ov[erall]
forgiveness was al[so]
and positive emoti[ons]
Kraft & Witvliet, [
Ludwig, and Vand[er]
pressure, while in[c]

Given the pos[itive]
understand factor[s]
of this study is to
shame on the ten[dency]

Information to include when writing the introduction is in section II.3.

EFFECTS OF SHAME ON FORGIVENESS 4

Shame

Tracy and Robins (2004) reported that shame involves making negative assessments about the self that are global and stable, as opposed to specific and changeable. Individuals who experience shame will attribute a fault to an innate lack of ability as opposed to a lack of practice or a lack of experience. Shame reflects no clear difference between a person's actions and a person's self (Tangney, 1991). Instead, with shame, a person considers wrong behavior as a representation that the self is generally a defective person (Konstam, Chernoff, & Deveney, 2001).

Tangney (1991) showed that shame is negatively correlated with empathy and perspective taking. Dost and Yagmurlu (2008) reported that shame has been connected with "resentment, irritability, symptoms of somatization, obsessive-compulsive behavior disorder, psychoticism, depression, and personal distress" (p. 112). The experience of shame, however, is not limited to adults. Luby et al. (2009) found that children in preschool can experience shame, and this shame, according to those researchers, is connected with higher levels of depression and early disruptive behavior in children.

Shame can al
embarrassment, c
unfortunately, ca
head. In fact, peo
from their reflect

Tracy and Rob
manipulating locu
attribute a failure t
shame increased. I
guilt increased—tl
controllable, and tl

What relation
Studies show that
common construc
depression, anger
Worthington, 200
Webb et al., 2008
forgiveness also l

Webb et al. (2
relationship betw
experience shame
the whole self. In
action as represen
individuals who e
possible. Individu

believe the offender also cannot change; this likely causes individuals who feel shame to be less willing to forgive.

Another hypothesis proposed by Webb et al. (2008) was that, just as shame is experienced as an attack on the whole self, offenses are also perceived as an attack on the whole self. This makes every offense seem more personal and damaging, thus more difficult to forgive. Finally, individuals prone to shame show less empathy; and less empathy is related to lower levels of forgiveness. For future research, Webb et al. (2008) suggested focusing on "the healing of shame as a facilitative process for forgiveness" (p. 2513).

Konstam, Chernoff, and Deveney (2001) suggested that experiences with shame might affect the ability to forgive. Thus, individuals prone to shame most likely have difficulty forgiving others. But little, if any, empirical research has been done in order to explain how shame might affect forgiveness. Several studies examined the relation of shame and forgiveness, but the results were conflicting. Konstam et al. (2001) found no significant correlation between shame and forgiveness. However, Tangney et al., in 1999 (as cited in Konstam et al., 2001), showed a negative correlation between the two constructs. Also, Webb et al. (2008) reported a negative correlation between shame and forgiveness.

Current Study

Several studies show a negative relationship between the constructs of shame and forgiveness. Webb et al. (2008) point out

EFFECTS OF SHAME ON FORGIVENESS 7

that "Empirical research to date has not clarified the mechanisms by which these negative correlations between shame and forgiveness exist" (Webb et al., 2008, p. 2509). Given the implications that shame and forgiveness have for individuals and for society, it is important to determine whether a causal relationship exists between shame and forgiveness. In this study, I attempted to influence the amount of shame that participants experienced in response to a hypothetical scenario. I hypothesized that the shame scenario would result in greater shame and lower forgiveness than in the guilt or neutral scenarios.

Method

Participants

One hundred

Alabama were re

research system.

Use the correct order of headings as presented in section I.2D.

Information to be included describing participants is disscussed in section II.4A.

The Information to be included when describing the materials, apparatus, or instruments used in the study appears in section II.4B.

EFFECTS OF SHAME ON FORGIVENESS 8

SD = 0.9). The sample was 70% women. Participants reported their race/ethnicity as Caucasian (50%), African American (28%), Asian American (14%), and other (8%).

Materials and Procedure

Participants completed a number of self-report measures through an on-line data collection system. Trait measures of shame and forgiveness were competed first. Following the trait measures, students read a scenario designed to increase either state shame or state guilt; the students received a shame, guilt, or neutral manipulation taken from Tracy and Robins (2006).

Shame, guilt, and neutral scenarios. The shame scenario from Tracy and Robins (2006) read, "You have never had much natural talent (i.e., been smart) in English. You recently had an important English exam, and you studied hard for it, but it still seemed very difficult to you. You just found out that you did badly on the exam" (p. 1346). The guilt scenario read, "You recently had an important English exam, but you didn't bother to study for it.

Express numbers correctly as described in section I.2F.

Acknowledge the subjects' active participation as discussed in section II.4A.

The information to include when presenting the study procedure appears in section II.4C.

EFFECTS OF SHAME ON FORGIVENESS 9

You just found out that you did badly on the exam" (Tracy & Robins, 2006, p. 1346). The neutral scenario read, "You recently had an important Englis
exam" (Tracy &
participants com
Dearing, 2002) i

Next, studen
situation, where
scenario for the
"Imagine that y
poor grade. In fr
specifically poin
your grade was
exam, and you s
participants assi
professor just in
front of the who
you out, and yo
poor. Remember
bother to study f
assigned to the n
just informed th
whole classroom
your grade—par
Remember, this
completed a me
professor's trans

Measures. F
participants com

Use abbreviations sparingly and only under limited conditions as discussed in section I.2C.

EFFECTS OF SHAME ON FORGIVENESS 10

(SSGS; Tangney & Dearing, 2002) that measured state shame and state guilt. Participants were prompted by reading this statement: "The following are some statements which may or may not describe how you are feeling *right now*. Please rate each statement using the 5-point scale below. Remember to rate each statement based on how you are feeling *right at this moment*." According to Tangney and Dearing, the SSGS has an internal consistency of .89 for state shame and .82 for state guilt; Cronbach's alpha for the present study was .88 and .74 for state shame and state guilt, respectively.

Following the perceived transgression of the professor, participants completed an adapted version of the Transgression-Related Interpersonal Motivations Inventory (TRIM; McCullough et al., 1998). The TRIM is a 12-item scale used to measure state forgiveness in response to the professor's transgression. The TRIM consists of two subscales: one subscale measures state avoidance and the other measures state revenge. To interpret forgiveness scores from the TRIM, it is necessary to reverse the TRIM score. High scores on state avoidance or state revenge indicate low state forgiveness. Low scores on state avoidance or state revenge indicate high state forgiveness. Responses were provided using a 5-point scale ranging from 1 (*strongly disagree*) to 5 (*strongly agree*). According to McCullough et al., the TRIM has an internal consistency ranging from .86 for avoidance to .93 for revenge. In the present study, Cronbach's alpha was .90 and .89 for avoidance and revenge, respectively.

EFFECTS OF SHAME ON FORGIVENESS 11

Results

It was important to determine the effectiveness of the exam scenario in inducing state shame. Therefore, as a manipulation check, an ANOVA was conducted with Exam Scenario (shame, guilt, or neutral) as the independent variable and state shame score as the dependent variable. The exam scenario effect was statistically significant, $F(2, 115) = 6.25$, $p = .02$, $\eta^2 = .034$. The Tukey HSD method was used to identify the groups that were significantly different. This analysis revealed that the shame group differed significantly fron
from the neutral g
the sample means
state guilt scores
To test the hy
state forgiveness t
conducted. The in
guilt, or neutral) a
forgiveness measu
As predicted, ther
$= .04$, $\eta^2 = .028$. T
groups that were s
shame group diffe
groups ($p = .02$). I
To further inve
forgiveness scores
significantly positi
.43, $p < .001$, indic

The information to include in presenting the study results appears in secion II.5.

See presentation of statistical results in section II.5.

The elements that need to be included when writing the Discussion section appear in section II.6.

EFFECTS OF SHAME ON FORGIVENESS 12

also scored higher on the TRIM. Shame was also statistically significantly positively correlated with scores on the revenge subscale of the TRIM, $r(117) = .53$, $p < .001$, and with scores on the avoidance subscale of the TRIM, $r(117) = .37$, $p = .004$, indicating that participants who reported greater shame also reported greater revenge motivations and avoidance motivations toward the offending professor.

Discussion

The current study demonstrated that shame can be manipulated by reading a hypothetical scenario and that the shame inducing scenario resulted in lower levels of forgiveness. This is an important contribution to our understanding of forgiveness. It suggests that we need a deeper understanding of shame and how shame operates to fully understand the process of forgiveness.

Evidence from the forgiveness literature indicates a number of contextual factors that are related to the tendency to forgive (Fehr, Gelfand, & Nag, 2010).

EFFECTS OF SHAME ON FORGIVENESS 13

It is important to recognize the role that shame may play in the process of forgiveness. When offenses induce shame, it appears that the offended party may have greater difficulty forgiving the transgressor. Offenses that induce shame are typically those that suggest some flaw in the other person that is not easily changed or controlled (Tracy & Robins, 2006).

In the current investigation, shame was manipulated within the context of the transgression. It is also possible that given an identical transgression, individuals may differ in their experience of shame in response to the offense. If this is the case, it is important to investigate whether individuals who are prone to experiencing shame also have difficulty forgiving others. Luby et al. (2009) reported that individual differe young as prescho

Therapists w investigate the el offenses that clie necessary to addr addition to the pr

The current s could address. Fi within the acade was selected bec because the parti However, it is ve teacher evaluatio scenario may hav

The correct way to cite others in the text of the research report is discussed in section I.21.

EFFECTS OF SHAME ON FORGIVENESS 14

than others. It would be interesting to investigate shame induction within other scenarios that may be very important to the participants.

The current study is also limited by the use of only self-report measures. Although, in measuring shame and forgiveness, self-report is an important approach, the current study would be strengthened by the addition of observations or more in-depth interviews. Both of these measures would advance our understanding of the relationships reported.

In sum, the current study provides an important first step in our understanding of the relation of shame and forgiveness. Shame was induced with a relatively weak manipulation and resulted in differences in self-reported forgiveness. These findings suggest that offenses which induce shame may be particularly difficult. Understanding these difficulties may help us understand long-standing disputes where individuals have difficulty forgiving each other.

EFFECTS OF SHAME ON FORGIVENESS 15

The style in which the references are to be presented appears in section II.7 and in section I.3.

References

Berry, J. W., & Worthington, Jr., E. L. (2001). Forgivingness, relationship quality, stress while imagining relationship events, and physical and mental health. *Journal of Counseling Psychology, 48*, 447–455. doi:10.1037/0022.0167.48.4.447

Dost, A., & Yagm

essential featu

Theory of Soc

Exline, J. J., Baum

(2008). Not s

wrongdoing p

Psychology, 9

Fehr, R., Gelfand

analytic synth

Bulletin, 136,

Konstam, V., Che

role of shame

26–39.

Lewis, H. B. (198

In H. B. Lewi

Hillsdale, NJ:

Luby, J., Belden,

(2009). Sham

in self-consci

Child Psycho

doi:10.1111/j.

EFFECTS OF SHAME ON FORGIVENESS 16

McCullough, M. E., Rachal, K. C., Sandage, S. J., Worthington, Jr., E. L., Brown, S. W., & Hight, T. L. (1998). Interpersonal forgiving in close relationships: II. Theoretical elaboration and measurement. *Journal of Personality and Social Psychology, 75*, 1586–1603. doi:10.1037/0022-3514.75.6.1586

Retzinger, S. R. (1987). Resentment and laughter: Video studies of the shame-rage spiral. In H. B. Lewis (Ed.), *The role of shame in symptom formation* (pp. 151–182). Hillsdale, NJ: Lawrence Erlbaum.

Tangney, J. P. (1991). Moral affect: The good, the bad, and the ugly. *Journal of Personality and Social Psychology, 61*, 598–607.

Tangney, J. P., & Dearing, R. L. (2002). *Shame and guilt*. New York, NY: Guilford Press.

Thompson, L. Y., Snyder, C. R., Hoffman, L., Michael, S. T., Rasmussen, H. N., Billings, L. S., Neufeld, J. E., . . . , Roberts, D. E. (2005). Dispositional forgiveness of self, others, and situations. *Journal of Personality, 73*, 313–359.doi:10.1111/j.1467-6494.2005.00311.x

Tracy, J. L., & Robins, R. W. (2004). Putting the self into self-conscious emotions: A theoretical model. *Psychological Inquiry,15*, 103–125.

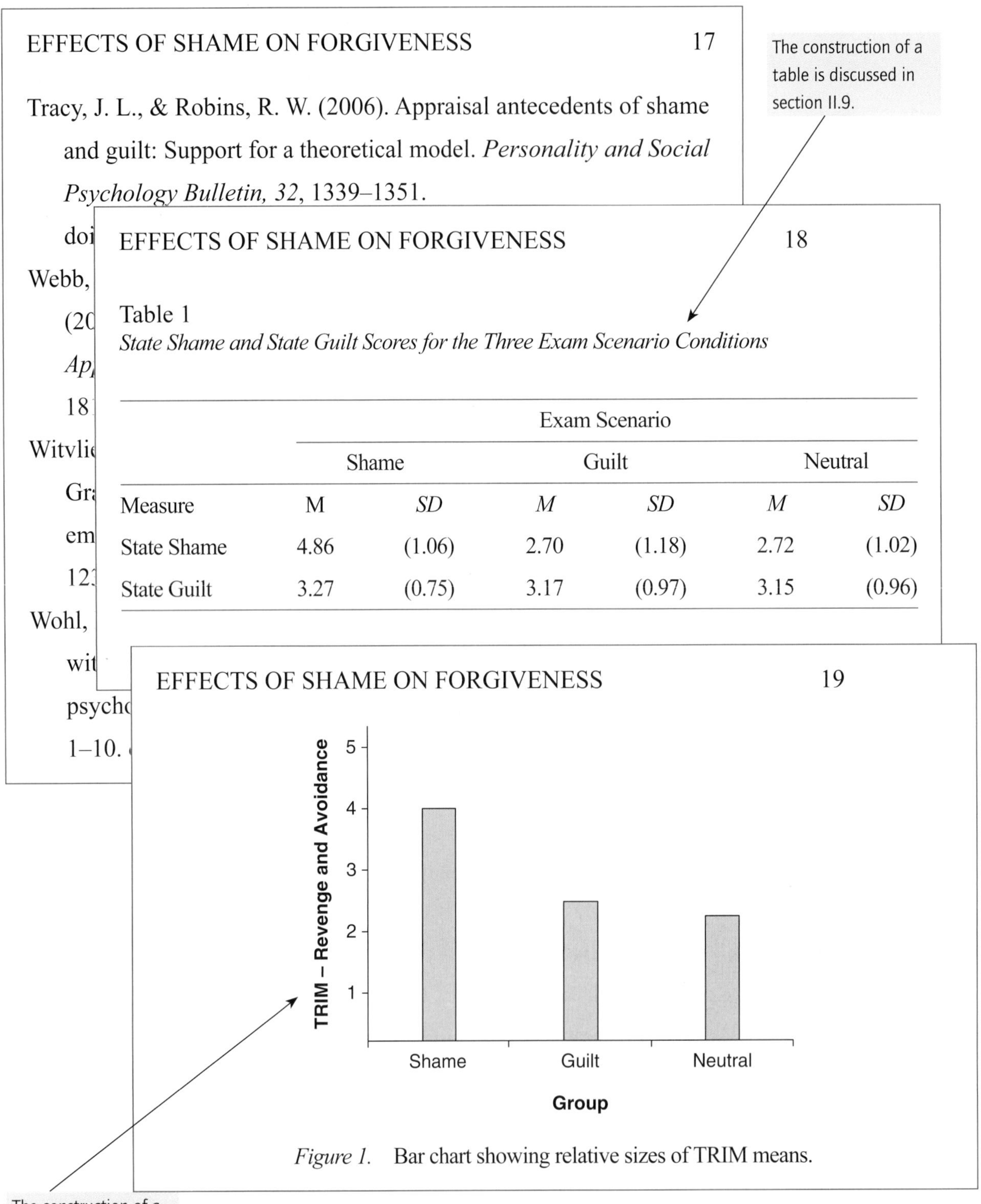

EFFECTS OF SHAME ON FORGIVENESS 17

Tracy, J. L., & Robins, R. W. (2006). Appraisal antecedents of shame and guilt: Support for a theoretical model. *Personality and Social Psychology Bulletin, 32*, 1339–1351. doi

Webb, (20 *Ap* 18

Witvli Gr em 12

Wohl, wi psych 1–10.

The construction of a table is discussed in section II.9.

EFFECTS OF SHAME ON FORGIVENESS 18

Table 1

State Shame and State Guilt Scores for the Three Exam Scenario Conditions

	Exam Scenario					
	Shame		Guilt		Neutral	
Measure	M	*SD*	*M*	*SD*	*M*	*SD*
State Shame	4.86	(1.06)	2.70	(1.18)	2.72	(1.02)
State Guilt	3.27	(0.75)	3.17	(0.97)	3.15	(0.96)

EFFECTS OF SHAME ON FORGIVENESS 19

Figure 1. Bar chart showing relative sizes of TRIM means.

The construction of a figure is discussed in section II.10.

Writing Qualitative Research Reports

We agree with Sharon Merriam (2009) that "there is no standard format for reporting qualitative research" (p. 245). Lofland (1971) stated three decades ago that diversity in style was rampant in qualitative research, and diversity is still somewhat common today. For example, qualitative researchers use many nontraditional and creative styles, such as incorporating stories, poems, essays, drawings, and photographs in qualitative reports. At the same time, we and a growing number of scholars (e.g., Berg & Lune, 2012; Merriam) believe that writing qualitative journal articles with a relatively systematic structure can be helpful because it lets readers know what information to expect and where that information will be located and can aid in the comparison of qualitative research reports. In short, when you write a qualitative research article, you need to find a balance between the creative end of writing and the structured end of writing that works well for you and for the outlet in which you plan to disseminate your qualitative research (e.g., journal, dissertation, thesis, evaluation report).

A good way to learn how to write the qualitative research report is to examine published examples and to use ideas learned there to aid in writing your own manuscript. We have included an ethnographic study at the companion website for this textbook to illustrate a qualitative research report.

Earlier in this chapter, we discussed some general principles related to writing the research report. These principles apply to quantitative research, qualitative research, and mixed research. However, we would like to add to that discussion two points that are especially relevant in qualitative research. First, qualitative researchers tend to view the use of the first person (i.e., *I* rather than *the researcher*) and the active voice ("I interviewed the teachers" rather than "the teachers were interviewed by the researcher") very positively. Qualitative researchers believe that this style situates the qualitative researcher in his or her research and encourages qualitative researchers to take responsibility for their active role in their research. This makes sense because of the central role that the qualitative researcher must play in virtually every step of conducting a qualitative research study (e.g., the researcher is the "data-collection instrument" because the researcher must make on-the-spot decisions about what is important and what should be noted and recorded, the researcher must manually code transcripts rather than using a statistical analysis program to provide an output of standard statistical results, the researcher must make interpretations throughout the research study, and so on).

Second, pseudonyms (i.e., fictitious names) are commonly used in qualitative research. Because of the small number of participants common to qualitative research and the in-depth information obtained about these individuals, qualitative researchers must be cautious to ensure that the identities of their research participants are adequately concealed. The guarantee of confidentiality may not be sufficient if the readers of a report are able to identify individuals based on descriptive information given about them in the report. For example, if you are conducting an ethnography of an elementary school, everyone in the school will know the principal, the librarian, and so forth. It might not be enough to use pseudonyms just for the individuals. You might also need to give a pseudonym to the school or city in the published version of the report. A last-resort strategy is to withhold certain revealing information about an individual to make him or her less identifiable. In most cases, you will be able to obtain written permission from the participants in your study to use pseudonyms and not make any additional effort to conceal their identities. These ethical issues are especially critical in qualitative research.

Earlier in this chapter, we discussed the seven major parts of the quantitative research report as recommended in the *APA Publication Manual* (the title page, abstract, introduction, method, results, discussion, and references). These seven sections can also be used quite effectively with qualitative research reports. Most of the earlier comments about these seven sections also apply to the qualitative research report. We do not repeat those ideas here; however, we highlight several important issues surrounding these seven sections in relation to writing a qualitative research report.

The title page, from a technical standpoint, is similar for quantitative and qualitative research reports. Always try to write a title that is clear and descriptive, regardless of the type of report. The abstract is also very similar for quantitative and qualitative research reports. When writing an abstract, your goal is always to describe succinctly the key focus of the article, its key methodological features, and its most important findings.

In the introduction (sometimes called *background*), clearly explain the purpose of your research and then report any research literature that is relevant to your study. For example, if you are hoping to fit your study into a larger body of research, much of this material should be placed in the introduction. The qualitative research report introduction does, however, differ somewhat from the quantitative research introduction. For example, the qualitative report usually does not include any deductive hypotheses (tentative predictions about the relationships between variables based on prior literature and theory) because qualitative research is usually done for exploratory rather than confirmatory reasons. Although research questions and issues are often reported in the qualitative report introduction, they are usually stated in open-ended and general forms (e.g., the researcher hopes to "discover," "explore a process," "explain or to understand," or "describe the experiences") rather than in the form of highly specific questions, as is more common in quantitative research.

The Methods section is sometimes incorporated into the introduction of the qualitative research report. However, it is becoming more common for qualitative research authors to include a separate section on their methods. We believe that a separate Methods section should be included in qualitative journal articles. The author might wish to relegate the methods to an appendix in a more popularized version of a report, but even here it is important that the researcher describes the methods that were used to carry out the research study. Otherwise, the reader lacks sufficient information to evaluate the quality of the research study.

The Methods section needs to include information telling how the study was done, where it was done, with whom it was done, why the study was designed as it was, how the data were collected and analyzed, and, most important, what procedures were carried out to ensure the validity of the arguments and conclusions. It is common today for qualitative researchers also to include a section in the report in which they reflect on their personal standpoints, their disciplinary backgrounds, their theoretical and paradigmatic perspectives, and how these characteristics might affect their research. Researchers should discuss what strategies they used to ensure qualitative research validity (e.g., see our discussion of triangulation, low-inference descriptors, extended fieldwork, and reflexivity in Chapter 11). When you read the Methods section of a qualitative research report, a key question will be, Did the authors convince you that they conducted their study effectively and appropriately?

Perhaps the most important section in a qualitative research report is the Results section (sometimes called the Findings section in qualitative research reports). This is where the researcher provides the bulk of the evidence supporting his or her arguments. The overriding issue when writing your Results section is to provide sufficient and convincing evidence. Your assertions must be backed up with empirical data (e.g., quotations, grounded theories). Basically, you do not want the reader to go away saying, "I'm not sure that I agree with this writer's contentions." Researchers should try to minimize the situation in which readers must take the researchers' word for their arguments without any evidence. We should all keep in mind the following point when we work on our Results sections: "It's about evidence!" As Bogdan and Biklen (1998) pointed out, "The qualitative researcher, in effect, says to the reader, 'Here is what I found and here are the details to support that view'" (p. 195). If we follow this advice, we are likely to produce a Results section that is convincing, trustworthy, and defensible.

You will need to find an appropriate balance between description and interpretation to write a convincing Results section. On the one hand, you don't need to overkill with extensive descriptive detail and little interpretative commentary. For example, you don't want to provide pages and pages of interviews and field notes with no interpretation. Keep in mind that such information might very well seem important to you because you are immersed in your research data; however, such detailed information is probably not important to your reader, and in journal articles, space is limited. On the other hand, you do need to provide sufficient descriptive detail to support your conclusions and interpretative commentary. If you don't provide sufficient descriptive detail, the reader will be forced to rely too heavily on your word without supportive evidence, and if you don't provide enough interpretative commentary, your reader will end up lost in the details. Finding the best balance between description and interpretative commentary takes time and practice in writing qualitative research reports. It also depends on the audience and the outlet for your report. For example, space is more plentiful in a book or a dissertation than in a journal. Also, the readers of journal articles are usually less willing to take your word for your interpretations than are readers of a best-selling nonfiction book version of your qualitative research.

One important strategy for writing a Results section is to provide quotes from your research participants and to include short sections from your field notes and other data to bring your reader close to your research participants and to the real-world situations described in your report. You should provide some rich and vivid description of the context, setting, participants, cultural scenes, and interactions among the participants. This way, the reader can vicariously experience what it is like to be in the same situation as the research participants. The use of vignettes (e.g., detailed examples) and low-inference descriptors (e.g., quotes from the participants) is helpful for this purpose. Another way to present your data is to make interpretative statements and follow each statement with one or more illustrative examples. Interweaving your descriptive data with interpretative commentary throughout your Results section helps your reader follow your line of reasoning. Regardless of the specific format of your Results section, remember that you must always provide data (descriptions, quotes, data from multiple sources, and so forth) that back up your assertions.

The Results section of a qualitative report often includes more subheadings than the Results section of a quantitative report. The particular organization identified by the subheadings will vary depending on the type of qualitative research conducted and the results of the data analysis. For example, qualitative research results may be organized around (a) the research questions or research issues examined in the research, (b) an a priori literature-based conceptual scheme applied to the research data, (c) a typology that is developed during data analysis, (d) the key themes found in the data, or (e) a conceptual scheme based on a grounded theory generated from the research data. Regardless of the exact format, remember that you must convince your reader of your arguments. That is the key to effective report writing.

In the Discussion section (sometimes called the Conclusion), the qualitative researcher should state the overall conclusions and offer additional interpretation of the findings. The researcher should also determine whether the results are consistent with other results published in the research literature about the particular topic or group. Even if the research is exploratory, it is important to fit your findings into the relevant research literature in your Discussion section. It is also helpful to provide suggestions for further research, because research is rarely done in a vacuum. Virtually all research can and should be related to the big picture of where we have been and where we are going in our efforts to increase research-based knowledge of humans and their conditions.

The References section is the same in a quantitative and qualitative report. If the APA referencing style is used, the references should follow the APA format described earlier in this chapter and demonstrated in the sample report. Finally, the ancillary components discussed earlier (charts, tables, figures, and so forth) also have an important place in qualitative research reports. For example, a data chart or matrix is very helpful when a great deal of narrative text would be needed to convey the same information. An excellent source for learning more about displaying qualitative research data is Miles and Huberman's (1994) book entitled *Qualitative Data Analysis: An Expanded Source Book.*

See Journal Articles 21.4 and 21.5 on the Student Study Site.

WRITING MIXED RESEARCH REPORTS

We have explained, in some depth, how to write a quantitative research report and how to write a qualitative research report. When your report is based on both quantitative and qualitative research, however, what should you do? Our advice is, first and foremost, to know your audience and write in a manner that clearly communicates to that audience. Second, consider briefly articulating your mixed research philosophy/paradigm and your synthesis of these (Johnson, 2016); this is a component of *paradigmatic/philosophical legitimation*, discussed in Chapter 11. Third, we think it is important that a mixed research report demonstrate multiple perspectives on the research phenomena studied. One creative style (that we have not seen used) would be to alternate between the emic and etic perspectives in the Results and Discussion sections of your report. Another would be to use the judicial metaphor and have protagonists defend conflicting qualitative and quantitative positions, followed by an attempt to provide a broader and/or more complex integrative, mixed perspective. Another creative style would use a dialectical logic (i.e., thesis, antithesis, synthesis) such that each approach is written, then followed by a critique by its rival paradigm (qualitative critiquing the quantitative first draft, quantitative critiquing the qualitative first draft), and, finally, the mixed perspective would complete the report with a synthesis.

Next, we emphasize that there is no single writing technique that is appropriate for mixed research in all cases, and you can be creative in your presentation style as long as you sufficiently warrant your assertions with data and evidence. Fifth, if you are attempting to write a report of an equal-status mixed design, you will need to respect fully the thinking styles of each approach when writing about them and merging them in your mixed report. Sixth, make sure that you integrate ideas from the qualitative and quantitative data, findings, and perspectives into warranted **meta-inferences** (i.e., integrative inferences or conclusions based on qualitative and quantitative data and findings). This integrative viewpoint is required if you are to have *commensurability approximation legitimation*, as discussed in Chapter 11 (p. 307). Your meta-inferences also should be cognizant of social and political needs and how your research findings can contribute to both knowledge and social justice. This is *sociopolitical legitimation* in mixed research, as discussed in Chapter 11.

■ **Meta-inference** An inference or conclusion that builds on or integrates quantitative and qualitative insights and findings

As a starting point and for ease of communication, in many cases you can structure your report around the same seven generic parts of an APA report discussed earlier in this chapter (i.e., title page, abstract, introduction, method, results, discussion, and references). The primary modification for mixed reports is the need to organize the qualitative, quantitative, and integrated parts within one or more of these sections and to do this in a way that works for your readers.

The biggest change occurs in the Results section because you now have multiple kinds of results. If you address each research question quantitatively and qualitatively as recommended by Yin (2006) then an effective organization style is to organize the Results section first by your research questions and organize within each research question by method/paradigm—you tell your reader what the quantitative, qualitative (or qualitative then quantitative), and integrated/mixed viewpoints have to say about each research question as follows:

Results

Research Question One

Quantitative findings.

Qualitative findings.

Integrated findings.

Research Question Two

Quantitative findings.

Qualitative findings.

Integrated findings.

Cumulative Integration

Creswell and Plano Clark (2011) recommend that one can/should have separate qualitative, quantitative (and sometimes mixed methods) questions. In this case, you would organize your Results section as shown below:

Results

Quantitative (or qualitative) Research Question(s)

Qualitative (or quantitative) Research Question(s)

Integration of Results

Design also can be the key consideration in report writing. For example, in a sequential design, a popular reporting style is to organize the results by research stages or phases, followed by additional integration of findings as follows:

Results

Phase One Findings

(Start by listing the relevant research questions.)

Phase Two Findings

(Start by listing the relevant research questions.)

Cumulative Integration of Findings

Another writing style approach (which can work quite well) is to integrate seamlessly the qualitative, quantitative, and mixed findings in a single narrative instead of separating the narrative by method/paradigm subsections. This approach is recommended by Bazeley (2015). In this approach, integration is ongoing, rather than being separated into its own final section in the Results chapter. These would be the Results headings:

Results

(Continuous integrated narrative starts here. Often, there will be separate narrative for each research question.)

Yet another style (e.g., in multi-article dissertations that are becoming popular) is to write essentially separate subreports (one for the qualitative part and one for the quantitative part), followed by a third, mixed report that synthesizes these. The subreports can be published separately. If you take this last approach, the mixed methods publication should usually occur last so that it can integrate findings from the previous two articles.

As you can see, writing a mixed research report is different from writing a traditional monomethod research report. However, it also is similar to writing any other kind of research report. In all research reports, the key is to address clearly each of your research questions; to make your report highly descriptive and readable; and to provide your reader with sufficient, convincing, and defensible evidence for each of your research findings, claims, and recommendations.

See Journal Articles 21.6 and 21.7 on the Student Study Site.

ACTION RESEARCH REFLECTION

Insight: Action researchers should share what they learn with others in their setting and add their knowledge to the broader scientific knowledge base. We mentioned earlier that it is essential that education science listen carefully to practitioners' action research findings. Therefore, action researchers must write up their findings and share them with others via outlets such as professional and scholarly conferences and publications (local, regional, and national). Interpersonal communication mechanisms also are important, such as sharing your findings and ideas with colleagues, participants, administrators, and parents. Always remember that communication must be two-way (or multiway) for the participants to engage in continual and lifelong learning.

1. How should you specifically communicate and disseminate your insights gained from your action research project?
2. What is your communication and dissemination plan?
3. How have you already communicated your findings? Did others find it useful? What insights did they have about your project? With whom do you want to continue your "action communication and learning"? Should you organize a learning community to continue focusing on a particular action research issue?
4. What follow-up questions do you have, if you are to continue your action research project?
5. What specifically are your next action research questions and your action plan?

SUMMARY

At some point in your career, you probably will be asked to write a research report. In this chapter, we explained the seven parts of a typical APA-style research report: Title page, Abstract, Introduction, Method, Results, Discussion, and References. We provided a summary of some of the most important ideas found in the *APA Publication Manual*. In addition to explaining key APA style practices, we provided a manuscript that is formatted using APA style, which you can quickly examine for examples of APA style when you are writing your papers. Our manuscript and explanations are modeled on those found in the *APA Publication Manual*, currently in the sixth edition. Last, we provided suggestions for writing and structuring quantitative research reports, qualitative research reports, and mixed methods research reports.

KEY TERM

meta-inferences (p. 633)

DISCUSSION QUESTIONS

1. What writing errors or writing problems do you think are most common among beginning research methods students?
2. What section of a research report do you believe is the most difficult to write?
3. What type of research do you think is the most demanding of a writer: quantitative research, qualitative research, or mixed research?
4. What are the similarities and key differences between quantitative, qualitative, and mixed research reports?
5. What is the best organization for the Results section in a mixed research report?

RESEARCH EXERCISES

1. Using one of the article reviews you conducted this semester, critique your writing.
2. Using ERIC, find a qualitative research article, read this article, and then answer the following questions:
   a. What are the various sections of the article?
   b. What did the authors attempt to accomplish in each section?
   c. What evidence did the authors use to support the conclusions or interpretations?
   d. How do the format and style of this report differ from the way in which a quantitative study would be reported?

PROPOSAL EXERCISES

It is essential that you write your proposal well! Note that the key difference between a research proposal and a research report is that the latter includes Results and Discussion sections. Also, a proposal is written in future sense, explaining what you propose to do (not what you have already done). As you write your research proposal, please answer the following questions:

1. Have you met APA recommendations regarding each of the following: language, specificity, labels, participation, editorial style, punctuation, italics, abbreviations, headings, quotations, numbers, physical measurements, reference citations in the text, and your reference list?
2. Does your proposal include the correct material on the title page, and in these sections: introduction (and literature review), method, and references? (Remember, a proposal does not have Results or Discussion.)
3. Are you using the major headings shown in Table 5.1 (on page 112)? (You are offered two possibilities in Table 5.1, either of which is fine.)
4. Does your research proposal include APA style headers and page numbering?
5. Have you edited and *reedited* your proposal until it is without mistakes, follows APA style, and is written exactly as it should be for clear, professional communication?

RELEVANT INTERNET SITES

William Strunk's famous and very useful *Elements of Style*
http://www.bartleby.com/141/

Discusses plagiarism
http://www.indiana.edu/~wts/pamphlets/plagiarism.shtml
http://www.plagiarism.org/plagiarism-101/what-is-plagiarism/
http://writingcenter.unc.edu/handouts/plagiarism/

APA Style Blog of the American Psychological Association
http://blog.apastyle.org/apastyle/2011/01/have-you-found-some-apa-style-rules-more-challenging-to-learn-than-others.html

Several useful links for APA writing style
http://www.apastyle.org
http://www.msera.org/old-site/download/RITS_16_2_APAErrors6th.pdf
https://owl.english.purdue.edu/owl/resource/560/01/
https://owl.english.purdue.edu/owl/section/2/10/

Examples of APA style report
http://www.radford.edu/~jaspelme/Writing_Guides/Vol_6_Revised/Whats_new_with_APA_Vol6_revised.pdf
https://owl.english.purdue.edu/media/pdf/20090212013008_560.pdf

STUDENT STUDY SITE

Visit the Student Study Site at **edge.sagepub.com/rbjohnson6e** for these additional learning tools:

Video Links
Self-Quizzes
eFlashcards
Lecture Notes
Full-Text SAGE Journal Articles
Interactive Concept Maps
Web Resources

RECOMMENDED READING

American Psychological Association. (2010). *Publication manual of the American Psychological Association* (6th ed.). Washington, DC: American Psychological Association.

Becker, H. S. (2007). *Writing for social scientists.* Chicago, IL: University of Chicago Press.

Manhard, S. J. (2000). *The goof-proofer: How to avoid the 41 most embarrassing errors in your speaking and writing.* New York, NY: Fireside.

Rosnow, R. L., & Rosnow, M. (1992). *Writing papers in psychology.* New York, NY: Wiley.

Rudestam, K. E., & Newton, R. R. (2014). *Surviving your dissertation: A comprehensive guide to content and process.* Thousand Oaks, CA: SAGE.

Strunk, W., & White, E. B. (2000). *The elements of style.* Boston, MA: Allyn & Bacon.

APPENDIX

CITATIONS FOR JOURNAL ARTICLES NOTED IN THE MARGINS

Chapter 1. Introduction to Educational Research

Journal Article 1.1: Mercier, C., Piat, M., Peladeau, N., & Dagenais, C. (2000). An application of theory-driven evaluation to a drop-in youth center. *Evaluation Review, 24*(1), 73–91.

Journal Article 1.2: DeBlase, G. L. (2003). Missing stories, missing lives: Urban girls (re) constructing race and gender in the literacy classroom. *Urban Education, 38*(3), 279–329.

Journal Article 1.3: Renzulli, J. S., & Park, S. (2000). Gifted dropouts: The who and the why. *Gifted Child Quarterly, 44*(4), 261–271.

Chapter 2. Quantitative, Qualitative, and Mixed Research

Journal Article 2.1: Wong, C. S. (2013). A play and joint attention intervention for teachers of young children with autism: A randomized controlled pilot study. *Autism, 17*(3), 340–357.

Journal Article 2.2: Finn, K. V., & Frone, M. R. (2003). Predictors of aggression at school: The effect of school-related alcohol use. *NASSP Bulletin, 87*(636), 38–54.

Journal Article 2.3: Davis, R. E. (2002). "The strongest women": Exploration of the inner resources of abused women. *Qualitative Health Research, 12*(9), 1248–1263.

Journal Article 2.4: Johnson, R. B., Onwuegbuzie, A. J., & Turner, L. A. (2007). Toward a definition of mixed methods research. *Journal of Mixed Methods Research, 1*(2), 112–133.

Chapter 3. Action Research for Lifelong Learning

Journal Article 3.1: Brydon-Miller, M., Greenwood, D., & Maguire, P. (2003). Why action research? *Action Research, 1*(1), 9–28.

Journal Article 3.2: Bradbury-Huang, H. (2010). What is good action research?: Why the resurgent interest? *Action Research, 8*(1), 93–109.

Journal Article 3.3: Burgess, J. (2006). Participatory action research: First-person perspectives of a graduate student. *Action Research, 4*(4), 419–437.

Chapter 4. How to Review the Literature and Develop Research Questions

Journal Article 4.1: Boote, D. N., & Beile, P. (2005). Scholars before researchers: On the centrality of the dissertation literature review in research preparation. *Educational Researcher*, *34*(6), 3–15.

Journal Article 4.2: Lauer, P. A., Akiba, M., Wilkerson, S. B., Apthorp, H. S., Snow, D., & Martin-Glenn, M. L. (2006). Out-of-School-Time programs: A meta-analysis of effects for at-risk students. *Review of Educational Research*, *76*(2), 275–313.

Journal Article 4.3: Kitchen, J., & Stevens, D. (2008). Action research in teacher education: Two teacher-educators practice action research as they introduce action research to preservice teachers. *Action Research*, 6(1), 7–28.

Chapter 5. How to Write a Research Proposal

Journal Article 5.1: Rawnsley, D. E. (1979). Proposal writing made palatable. *NASSP Bulletin*, *63*(426), 60–66.

Journal Article 5.2: Morse, J. M. (2003). A review committee's guide for evaluating qualitative proposals. *Qualitative Health Research*, *13*(6), 833–851.

Journal Article 5.3: Sandelowski, M., & Barroso, J. (2003). Writing the proposal for a qualitative research methodology project. *Qualitative Health Research*, *13*(6), 781–820.

Chapter 6. Research Ethics

Journal Article 6.1: Gordon, W., & Sork, T. J. (2001). Ethical issues and codes of ethics: Views of adult education practitioners in Canada and the United States. *Adult Education Quarterly*, *51*(3), 202–218.

Journal Article 6.2: Moon, T. R. (2011). A primer on research ethics in the field of gifted education. *Gifted Child Quarterly*, *55*(3), 223–229.

Journal Article 6.3: Brydon-Miller, M., Greenwood, D., & Eikeland, O. (2006). Conclusion: Strategies for addressing ethical concerns in action research. *Action Research*, *4*(1), 129–131.

Chapter 7. Standardized Measurement and Assessment

Journal Article 7.1: Watkins, K. E., & O'Neal, J. (2013). The dimensions of the Learning Organization Questionnaire (the DLOQ): A nontechnical manual. *Advances in Developing Human Resources*, *15*(2), 133–147.

Journal Article 7.2: Munroe, A., & Pearson, C. (2006). The Munroe multicultural attitude scale questionnaire: A new instrument for multicultural studies. *Educational and Psychological Measurement*, *66*(55), 819–834.

Journal Article 7.3: Johnson, B., Stevens, J. J., & Zvoch, K. (2007). Teachers' perceptions of school climate: A validity study of scores from the revised school level environment questionnaire. *Educational and Psychological Measurement*, *67*(5), 833–844.

Journal Article 7.4: Harris, S.M., & Halpin, G. (2002). Development and validation of the factors influencing pursuit of higher education questionnaire. *Educational and Psychological Measurement*, *62*(1), 79–96.

Journal Article 7.5: Beyers, W., & Goossens, L. (2002). Concurrent and predictive validity of the student adaptation to college questionnaire in a sample of European freshman students. *Educational and Psychological Measurement*, *62*(3), 527–538.

Chapter 8. How to Construct a Questionnaire

Journal Article 8.1: Edwards, J. E., & Thomas, M. D. (1993). The organizational survey process: General steps and practical considerations. *American Behavioral Scientist*, *36*(4), 419–442.

Journal Article 8.2: Schwarz, N., & Oyserman, D. (2001). Asking questions about behavior: Cognition, communication, and questionnaire construction. *American Journal of Evaluation*, *22*(2), 127–10.

Journal Article 8.3: Forsyth, B. H., Kudela, M. S., Levin, K., Lawrence, D., & Willis, G. D. (2007). Methods for translating an English-language survey questionnaire on tobacco use into Mandarin, Cantonese, Korean, and Vietnamese. *Field Methods*, *19*(3), 264–283.

Chapter 9. Methods of Data Collection

Journal Article 9.1: DuBois, D. L., Lockerd, E. M., Reach, K., & Parra, G. R. (2003). Effective strategies for esteem-enhancement: What do young adolescents have to say? *Journal of Early Adolescence*, *23*(4), 405–434.

Journal Article 9.2: Walshe, C., Ewing, G., & Griffiths, J. (2011). Using observation as a data collection method to help understand patient and professional roles and actions in palliative care settings. *Palliative Medicine*, *26*(8), 1048–1054.

Chapter 10. Sampling in Quantitative, Qualitative, and Mixed Research

Journal Article 10.1: O'Connell, A.A. (2000). Sampling for evaluation: Issues and strategies for community-based HIV prevention programs. *Evaluation and the Health Professions*, *23*(2), 212–234.

Journal Article 10.2: Luborsky, M.R., & Rubinstein, R.L. (1995). Sampling in qualitative research: Rationale, issues, and methods. *Research on Aging*, *17*(1), 89–113.

Journal Article 10.3: Teddlie, C., & Yu, F. (2007). Mixed methods sampling: A typology with examples. *Journal of Mixed Methods Research*, *1*(1), 77–100.

Chapter 11: Validity of Research Results in Quantitative, Qualitative, and Mixed Research

Journal Article 11.1: Reynolds, K. D., & West, S. G. (1987). A multiplist strategy for strengthening nonequivalent control group designs. *Evaluation Review*, *11*(6), 691–71.

Journal Article 11.2: Cho, J., & Trent, A. (2006). Validity in qualitative research revisited. *Qualitative Research*, *6*(3), 319–340.

Journal Article 11.3: Dellinger, A. B., & Leech N. L. (2007). Toward a unified validation framework in mixed methods research. *Journal of Mixed Methods Research, 1*(4), 309–332.

Chapter 12. Experimental Research: Weak and Strong Designs

Journal Article 12.1: Kiernan, N. E., Kiernan, M., Oyler, M. A., & Gilles, C. (2006). Is a web survey as effective as a mail survey? *American Journal of Evaluation, 26*(2), 245–252.

Journal Article 12.2: Jones, L. P., Harris, R., & Finnegan, D. (2002). School attendance demonstration project: An evaluation of a program to motivate public assistance teens to attend and complete school in an urban school district. *Research on Social Work Practice, 12*(2), 222–237.

Journal Article 12.3: Batchelder, J. S., & Rachal, J. R. (2000). Efficacy of a computer-assisted instruction program in a prison setting: An experimental study. *Adult Education Quarterly, 50*(2), 120–133.

Journal Article 12.4: Greifeneder, R. Alt, A., Bottenberg, K., Seele, T., Zelt, S., & Wagener, D., (2010). On writing legibly: Processing fluency systematically biases evaluations of handwritten material. *Social Psychological and Personality Science, 1*(3), 230–237.

Chapter 13. Quasi-Experimental and Single-Case Designs

Journal Article 13.1: Conyers, L. M., Reynolds, A. J., & Ou, S. (2003). The effect of early childhood intervention and subsequent special education services: Findings from the Chicago child-parent centers. *Educational Evaluation and Policy Analysis, 25*(1), 75–95.

Journal Article 13.2: Fraser, K., Wallis, M., & St. John, W. (2004). Improving children's problem eating and mealtime behaviours: An evaluative study of a single session parent education programme. *Health Education Journal, 63*(3), 229–241.

Journal Article 13.3: Mathews, M. S., Peters, S. J., & Housand, A. M. (2012). Regression discontinuity design in gifted and talented education research. *Gifted Child Quarterly, 56*(2), 105–112.

Journal Article 13.4: Reinke, W. M., Lewis-Palmer, T., & Martin, E. (2007). The effect of visual performance feedback on teacher use of behavior-specific praise. *Behavior Modification, 31*(3), 247–263.

Chapter 14. Nonexperimental Quantitative Research

Journal Article 14.1: Darling-Hammond, L., Chung, R., & Frelow, F. (2002). Variation in teacher preparation: How well do different pathways prepare teachers to teach? *Journal of Teacher Education, 53*(4), 286–302.

Journal Article 14.2: Lopez, F. G., & Ann-Yi, S. (2006). Predictors of career indecision in three racial/ethnic groups of college women. *Journal of Career Development, 33*(1), 29–46.

Journal Article 14.3: Peltier, J. W., Schibrowsky, J. A., & Drago, W. (2007). The interdependence of the factors influencing the perceived quality of the online learning experience: A causal model. *Journal of Marketing Education, 29*(2), 140–153.

Journal Article 14.4: Bogler, R. (2001). The influence of leadership style on teacher job satisfaction. *Educational Administration Quarterly*, *37*(5), 662–683.

Chapter 15. Narrative Inquiry and Case Study Research (by D. Jean Clandinin and Burke Johnson)

Journal Article 15.1: Huber, J., Craine, V., Huber, M., & Steeves, P. (2013). Narrative inquiry as pedagogy in education: The extraordinary potential of living, telling, retelling, and reliving stories of experience. *Review of Research in Education*, *37*(1), 212–242.

Journal Article 15.2: Polkinghorne D. E. (2007). Validity issues in narrative research. *Qualitative Inquiry*, *13*(4), 471–486.

Journal Article 15.3: Terry, A.W. (2003). Effects of service learning on young, gifted adolescents and their community. *Gifted Child Quarterly*, *47*(4), 295–308.

Chapter 16. Phenomenology, Ethnography, and Grounded Theory

Journal Article 16.1: Lee, I., & Koro-Ljungberg, M. (2007). A phenomenological study of Korean students' acculturation in middle schools in the USA. *Journal of Research in International Education*, *6*(1), 95–117.

Journal Article 16.2: Reisinger, H. S. (2004). Counting apples as oranges: Epidemiology and ethnography in adolescent substance abuse treatment. *Qualitative Health Research*, *14*(2), 241–258.

Journal Article 16.3: Cranton, P., & Carusetta, E. (2004). Perspectives on authenticity in teaching. *Adult Education Quarterly*, *55*(1), 5–22.

Journal Article 16.4: Coghlan, D., & Holian, R. (2007). Editorial: Insider action research. *Action Research*, *5*(1), 5–10.

Chapter 17. Mixed Research

Journal Article 17.1: Johnson, R. B., & Onwuegbuzie, A. J. (2004). Mixed methods research: A research paradigm whose time has come. *Educational Researcher*, *33*(7), 14–26.

Journal Article 17.2: Bryman, A. (2006). Integrating quantitative and qualitative research: How is it done? *Qualitative Research*, *6*(1), 97.

Journal Article 17.3: Leech, N. L. (2012). Writing mixed research reports. *American Behavioral Scientist*, *56*(6), 866–881.

Chapter 19. Inferential Statistics

Journal Article 19.1: Thompson, B. (2002). What future quantitative social science research could look like: Confidence intervals for effect sizes. *Educational Researcher*, *31*(3), 25–32.

Journal Article 19.2: Fidler, F. (2002). The fifth edition of the APA publication manual: Why its statistics recommendations are so controversial. *Educational and Psychological Measurement*, *62*(5), 749–770.

Chapter 20. Data Analysis in Qualitative and Mixed Research

Journal Article 20.1: Li, S., & Seale, C. (2007). Learning to do qualitative data analysis: An observational study of doctoral work. *Qualitative Health Research, 17*(10), 1442–1452.

Journal Article 20.2: Yeh, C. J., & Inman, A. G. (2007). Qualitative data analysis and interpretation in counseling psychology: Strategies for best practices. *Counseling Psychologist, 35*(3), 369–403.

Journal Article 20.3: Moret, M., Reuzel, R., van der Wilt, G. J., & Grin, J. (2007). Validity and reliability of qualitative data analysis: Interobserver agreement in reconstructing interpretative frames. *Field Methods, 19*(1), 24–39.

Journal Article 20.4: Caracelli, V. J., & Greene, J. C. (1993). Data analysis strategies for mixed method evaluation designs. *Educational Evaluation and Policy Analysis, 15*(2), 195–207.

Journal Article 20.5: Bazeley, P., & Kemp, L. (2012). Mosaics, triangles, and DNA: Metaphors for integrated analysis in mixed methods research. *Journal of Mixed Methods Research, 6*(1), 55–72.

Chapter 21. How to Prepare a Research Report and Use APA Style Guidelines

Journal Article 21.1: Statements of purpose for the different journals published by the American Educational Research Association. (2004). Statements of purpose for AERA journals. *Educational Researcher, 32*(2), 42–53.

Journal Article 21.2: Greenberg, K. P. (2012). A reliable and valid weighted scoring instrument for use in grading APA-style empirical research report. *Teaching of Psychology, 39*(1), 17–23.

Journal Article 21.3: Zientek, L. R., Capraro, M. M., & Capraro, R. M. (2008). Reporting practices in quantitative teacher education research: One look at the evidence cited in the AERA panel report. *Educational Researcher, 37*(4), 208–216.

Journal Article 21.4: Sandelowski, M., & Leeman, J. (2012). Writing usable qualitative health research findings. *Qualitative Health Research, 22*(10), 1404–1413.

Journal Article 21.5: Wolcott, H. F. (2002). Writing up qualitative research . . . better. *Qualitative Health Research, 12*(1), 91–103.

Journal Article 21.6: Marshall, J. (2004). Living systemic thinking: Exploring quality in first-person action research. *Action Research, 2*(3), 305–325.

Journal Article 21.7: Sommer, R. (2009). Dissemination in action research. *Action Research, 7*(2), 227–236.

Glossary

A priori codes—codes that were developed before examining the current data

A-B-A design—a single-case experimental design in which the response to the experimental treatment condition is compared to baseline responses taken before and after administering the treatment condition

A-B-A-B design—an A-B-A design that is extended to include the reintroduction of the treatment condition

Abstract—a summary of what is in an article; a brief description of the essential characteristics of the study

Accessible population—the research participants who are available for participation in the research

Achievement tests—tests that are designed to measure the degree of learning that has taken place after a person has been exposed to a specific learning experience

Acquiescence response set—the tendency either to agree or disagree

Action phase—a step in the action research cycle in which one conducts an exploratory-descriptive study or an experimental-intervention study

Action plan—a synonym for the research proposal that is used by action researchers

Action research—applied research focused on solving practitioners' local problems

Action research attitude—valuing and thinking like a practitioner and researcher in your job and life

Action research journal—a place where one records learnings and reflections

Action science—the science of practice, with the aims of making theories in use explicit and producing a learning organization

Active consent—a process whereby consent is provided by signing a consent form

Additive and interactive effects—occur when threats to internal validity combine to produce an additive or multiplicative bias

Alpha level—see **Significance level**

Alternative hypothesis—a statement that the population parameter is some value other than the value stated by the null hypothesis; it is the complement of the null hypothesis. For example, if the null hypothesis states that two population means are *equal*, then the alternative hypothesis would state that the two means are *not equal*

Ambiguous temporal precedence—the inability to specify which variable is the cause and which is the effect

Amount technique—manipulating the independent variable by giving the various comparison groups different amounts of the independent variable

Analysis of covariance—a control method that can be used to statistically equate groups that differ on a pretest or some other variable; used to examine the relationship between one categorical independent variable and one quantitative dependent variable, controlling for one or more extraneous variables (also called ANCOVA)

Anchor—a written descriptor for a point on a rating scale

Anonymity—keeping the identity of the participant from everyone, including the researcher

Applied research—research focused on answering practical questions to provide relatively immediate solutions

Appreciative inquiry—finding the best in organization members and working with them to achieve a jointly constructed and shared purpose, vision, and goal

Aptitude tests—tests that focus on information acquired through the informal learning that goes on in life

Archived research data—data originally used for research purposes and then stored

Assent—agreeing to participate after being informed of all the features of the study that could affect the participant's willingness to participate

Assessment—gathering and integrating data to make educational evaluations

Attrition—loss of people who do not complete the experiment

Autoethnography—like an autobiography written by a qualitative researcher; focuses on self-examination, self-reflection, and purposive inclusion of extensive cultural and contextual description and detail of one's life

Axial coding—the second stage in grounded theory data analysis

Axiology—the branch of philosophy dealing with values and ethics

Backstage behavior—what people say and do only with their closest friends

Bar graph—a graph that uses vertical bars to represent the data

Basic research—research aimed at generating fundamental knowledge and theoretical understanding about basic human and other natural processes

Being in the midst—attending to temporal, place, and relational aspects of reality

Beneficence—acting for the benefit of others

Between-subjects independent variable—each participant receives only one level of the independent variable

Biased sample—a sample that is systematically different from the population

Block quotation—a quotation of 40 or more words using indented format (including citation and page number)

Boolean operators—words such as *and* and *or* that create logical combinations

Bracket—to suspend your preconceptions or learned feelings about a phenomenon to experience its essence

Business Source Premier—a database containing entries from all areas of business

Carryover effect—a sequencing effect that occurs when performance in one treatment condition is influenced by participation in a prior treatment condition(s)

Case—a bounded system

Case study research—a form of qualitative research that is focused on providing a detailed account of the characteristics and dynamics present in one or more cases

Categorical variable—a variable that varies in type or kind

Causal-comparative research—a form of nonexperimental research in which the primary independent variable of interest is a categorical variable

Causal description—describing the consequences of manipulating an independent variable

Causal explanation—explaining the mechanisms through which and the conditions under which a causal relationship holds

Causal modeling—a form of explanatory research in which the researcher hypothesizes a causal model and then empirically tests the model

Causal validity—the ability to infer that a causal relationship exists between two variables; it's a synonym for internal validity

Causation coding—defined on page 600 in Chapter 20

Cause-and-effect relationship—relationship in which one variable affects another variable

Cell—a combination of two or more independent variables in a factorial design

Census—a study based on data from the whole population rather than a sample

Changing-criterion design—a single-case experimental design in which a participant's behavior is gradually altered by changing the criterion for success during successive treatment periods

Checklist—a list of response categories that respondents check if appropriate

Chi-square test for contingency tables—a statistical test used to determine whether a relationship observed in a contingency table is statistically significant

Closed-ended question—a question that forces participants to choose from a set of predetermined responses

Cluster—a collective type of unit that includes multiple elements

Cluster sampling—a type of sampling in which clusters are randomly selected

Coding—marking segments of data with symbols, descriptive words, or category names

Coefficient alpha—a formula that provides an estimate of the reliability of a homogeneous test or an estimate of the reliability of each dimension in a multidimensional test

Cohort—any group of people with a common classification or characteristic

Collaborative action research—an action research study in which a team designs and enacts research on one part of an organization

Collective case study—studying multiple cases in one research study

Commensurability approximation legitimation—the degree to which a mixed researcher can make Gestalt switches between the lenses of a qualitative researcher and a quantitative researcher and integrate the two views into an "integrated" or broader viewpoint

Compatibility thesis—the idea that quantitative and qualitative approaches can be used together in a single research study as long as you respect the assumptions associated with quantitative and qualitative research and construct a thoughtful combination that will help you to address your research question(s)

Complementary strengths—the whole is greater than the sum of its parts

Complete observer—the researcher observes as an outsider and does not tell people they are being observed

Complete participant—the researcher becomes a member of the group being studied and does not tell members they are being studied

Comprehensive sampling—including all cases in the research study

Concurrent evidence—validity evidence based on the relationship between test scores and criterion scores obtained at the same time

Confidence interval—a range of numbers inferred from the sample that has a certain probability or chance of including the population parameter

Confidence limits—the endpoints of a confidence interval

Confidentiality—not revealing the identity of the participant to anyone other than the researcher and his or her staff

Confirmatory method—a top-down or theory-testing approach to research

Confounding variable—an extraneous variable that was not controlled for and is the reason a particular "confounded" result is observed; an extraneous variable that systematically varies with the independent variable and also influences the dependent variable

Consequential validity—degree to which the test works well in practice and does not have negative or abnormal social and psychological consequences

Constant—a single value or category of a variable

Constant comparative method—data analysis in grounded theory research

Construct validity—the extent to which a higher-order construct is accurately represented in a particular study

Constructed data—objects or things that are constructed by research participants during a research study

Content-related evidence—validity evidence based on a judgment of the degree to which the items, tasks, or questions on a test adequately represent the construct domain of interest

Contextualization—the identification of when and where an event took place

Contingency question—an item that directs participants to different follow-up questions depending on their response

Contingency table—a table displaying information in cells formed by the intersection of two or more categorical variables

Control group—the group that does not receive the experimental treatment condition

Convenience sampling—people who are available, volunteer, or can be easily recruited are included in the sample

Convergent evidence—validity evidence based on the relationship between the focal test scores and independent measures of the same construct

Conversion legitimation—the degree to which quantitizing or qualitizing yields high-quality meta-inferences

Co-occurring codes—codes that overlap partially or completely

Correlation coefficient—a numerical index that indicates the strength and direction of the relationship between two variables

Correlational research—a form of nonexperimental research in which the primary independent variable of interest is a quantitative variable

Corroboration—comparing documents to each other to determine whether they provide the same information or reach the same conclusion

Counterbalancing—administering all experimental treatment conditions to all participants but in different orders; it is used with within-subjects independent variables

Criterion—the standard or benchmark that you want to predict accurately on the basis of the test scores

Criterion of falsifiability—the property that statements and theories should be testable and refutable

Criterion-related evidence—validity evidence based on the extent to which scores from a test can be used to predict or infer performance on some criterion such as a test or future performance

Critical action research—an openly transparent form of ideology-driven research designed to emancipate and reduce oppression of disadvantaged groups in society

Critical-case sampling—selecting what are believed to be particularly important cases

Critical friend—a person whom you trust to be open, honest, and constructively critical of your work

Cronbach's alpha—a frequently used name for what Lee Cronbach called "coefficient alpha"

Cross-case analysis—searching for similarities and differences across multiple cases; contrasted with within-case analysis

Cross-sectional research—data are collected at a single point in time

Culture—a system of shared beliefs, values, practices, perspectives, folk knowledge, language, norms, rituals, and material objects and artifacts that members of a group use in understanding their world and in relating to others

Data set—a set of data

Debriefing—a poststudy interview in which all aspects of the study are revealed, any reasons for deception are explained, and any questions the participant has about the study are answered

Deception—misleading or withholding information from the research participant

Deductive reasoning—the process of drawing a conclusion that is necessarily true if the premises are true

Dehoaxing—informing study participants about any deception that was used and the reasons for its use

Deontological approach—an ethical approach that says ethical issues must be judged on the basis of some universal code

Dependent variable—a variable that is presumed to be influenced by one or more independent variables

Description—attempting to describe the characteristics of a phenomenon

Descriptive research—research focused on providing an accurate description or picture of the status or characteristics of a situation or phenomenon

Descriptive statistics—statistics that focus on describing, summarizing, or explaining data

Descriptive validity—the factual accuracy of an account as reported by the researcher

Desensitizing—helping study participants deal with and eliminate any stress or other undesirable feelings that the study might have created

Design—the section in a research proposal or report that presents the plan or strategy used to investigate the research question

Determinism—assumption that all events have causes

Deweyan inquiry—problem solving that relies on reflection, observation, and experimentation

Diagnostic tests—tests that are designed to identify where a student is having difficulty with an academic skill

Diagramming—making a sketch, drawing, or outline to show how something works or to clarify the relationship between the parts of a whole

Dialectical pluralism—a metaparadigm and philosophy that assumes reality is plural and that relies on dialectical, dialogical, and hermeneutical approaches to learn from others and produce team-based research products

Dialectical pragmatism—the version of pragmatism specifically focused on listening to multiple paradigms and interdisciplinary perspectives

Differential attrition—in a single-group design, participants who drop out are different from those who stay, causing the sample composition to change; in a multigroup design, refers to a differential loss of participants from the various comparison groups that causes the groups to become nonequivalent

Differential carryover effect—a complex carryover effect, such as when a particular treatment affects participants' performance in a later condition in one way but in another way when followed by a different condition; counterbalancing does not neutralize (i.e., control for) *differential* carryover effects

Differential influence—when the influence of an extraneous variable is different for the various comparison groups

Differential selection—selection of participants who have different characteristics for the various treatment groups; it produces "nonequivalent groups"

Direct effect—the effect of the variable at the origin of an arrow on the variable at the receiving end of the arrow

Directional alternative hypothesis—an alternative hypothesis that contains either a greater-than sign (>) or a less-than sign (<)

Discriminant evidence—evidence that the scores on your focal test are *not* highly related to the scores from other tests that are designed to measure theoretically different constructs

Disordinal interaction effect—an interaction effect that occurs when the lines on a graph plotting the effect cross

Disproportional stratified sampling—a type of stratified sampling in which the sample proportions are made to be different from the population proportions on the stratification variable

Dose-response relationship—this is present when increased amounts, or greater strength, of the treatment results in increased amounts of response on the dependent variable

Double-barreled question—a question that combines two or more issues or attitude objects

Double-blind procedure—a design in which neither the researcher nor the participant knows the specific condition (experimental or control) that the participant is in

Double-loop learning—learning how a problem relates to the system it resides in so that a more satisfying solution can be found

Double negative—a sentence construction that includes two negatives

Dramaturgical coding—defined on page 600 in Chapter 20

Driving forces—forces pushing for changes from the current state

Ecological validity—the ability to generalize the study results across settings

Educational Resources Information Center (ERIC)—a database containing information from *Current Index to Journals in Education* (CIJE) and *Resources in Education* (RIE)

Effect size indicator—a measure of the strength or magnitude of a relationship between the independent and dependent variables

Element—the basic unit that is selected from the population

Emic perspective—the insider's perspective

Emic terms—special words or terms used by the people in a group

Emotion coding—defined on page 600 in Chapter 20

Empirical statement—a statement based on observation, experiment, or experience

Empiricism—the idea that knowledge comes from experience

Enumeration—the process of quantifying data

Epistemology—the theory of knowledge and its justification; the branch of philosophy dealing with knowledge and its justification

Equal probability of selection method—any sampling method in which each member has an equal chance of being selected

Equating the groups—experimenter's goal of constructing comparison groups that are similar on all confounding extraneous variables and different only on the independent variable

Equivalent-forms reliability—the consistency of a group of individuals' scores on alternative forms of a test measuring the same thing

Error—the difference between true scores and observed scores

Essence—an invariant structure of the experience

Espoused theory—the theory or explanation we provide for our actions

Ethical skepticism—an ethical approach that says concrete and inviolate moral codes cannot be formulated but are a matter of individual conscience

Ethics—the principles and guidelines that help us uphold the things we value

Ethnocentrism—judging people from a different culture according to the standards of your own culture

Ethnography—a form of qualitative research focused on discovering and describing the culture of a group of people

Ethnohistory—the study of the cultural past of a group of people

Ethnology—the comparative study of cultural groups

Etic perspective—an external, social-scientific view of reality

Etic terms—"objective" outsiders' words or special terms used by social scientists to describe a group

Evaluation—determining the worth, merit, or quality of an evaluation object

Event sampling—observing during and directly after a specific event has occurred

Exempt studies—studies involving no risk to participants and not requiring full IRB review

Exhaustive—on a questionnaire or interview protocol, *exhaustive* refers to response categories that include all possible responses; in descriptive statistics, *exhaustive* refers to a set of intervals that cover the complete range of data

Exhaustive categories—a set of categories that classify all of the relevant cases in the data

Expedited review—a process by which a study is rapidly reviewed by fewer members than constitute the full IRB board

Experiment—an environment in which the researcher attempts to objectively observe phenomena that are made to occur in a strictly controlled situation in which one or more variables are varied and the others are kept constant

Experimental control—eliminating any differential influence of extraneous variables

Experimental group—the group that receives the experimental treatment condition

Experimental research—research in which the researcher manipulates the independent variable and is interested in showing cause and effect

Explanation—attempting to show how and why a phenomenon operates as it does

Explanatory research—testing hypotheses and theories that explain how and why a phenomenon operates as it does

Exploration—attempting to generate ideas about phenomena

Exploratory method—a bottom-up or theory-generation approach to research

Extended fieldwork—collecting data in the field over an extended period of time

External criticism—the validity, trustworthiness, or authenticity of the source

External validity—the extent to which the study results can be generalized to and across populations of persons, settings, times, outcomes, and treatment variations; also called "generalizing validity"

Extraneous variable—a variable that may compete with the independent variable in explaining the outcome; any variable other than the independent variable that might influence the dependent variable; a variable that you need to "control for" to eliminate it as a competing explanation for the observed relationship between an independent and a dependent variable

Extreme-case sampling—identifying the extremes or poles of some characteristic and then selecting for examination cases representing these extremes

Facesheet codes—codes that apply to a complete document or case

Factor analysis—a statistical procedure that analyzes correlations among test items and tells you the number of factors present. It tells you whether the test is unidimensional or multidimensional

Factorial design—a design in which two or more independent variables, at least one of which is manipulated, are simultaneously studied to determine their independent and interactive effects on the dependent variable

Factorial design based on a mixed model—a factorial design in which different participants are randomly assigned to the different levels of one independent variable, but all participants take all levels of another independent variable

Feminist action research—studies that provide a feminist lens to help eliminate various forms of sexism and empower women in society

Field—the inquiry space created between researchers and participants during conduct of the research

Field experiment—an experimental study that is conducted in a real-life setting

Field notes—notes taken by an observer

Field texts—the term narrative inquirers use for data

Final research texts—final representations of a narrative inquiry, such as books and articles, dissertations, theses, and presentations for academic and nonacademic audiences, that are made public for a wider audience

First simple case of nonexperimental quantitative research—design with one categorical independent variable and one quantitative dependent variable

First-stage coding—initial coding of qualitative research data

Focus group—a moderator leads a discussion with a small group of people

Force field analysis—identifying and understanding the driving and restraining forces present in a situation

Force field theory—explanation of action and inaction as resulting from driving and restraining forces

Formative evaluation—evaluation focused on improving the evaluation object

Frequency distribution—an arrangement in which the frequencies of each unique data value are shown

Frontstage behavior—what people want or allow us to see

Full board review—review by all members of the IRB

Fully anchored rating scale—a rating scale on which all points are anchored

Fundamental principle of mixed research—advises researchers to thoughtfully and strategically mix or combine qualitative and quantitative research methods, approaches, procedures, concepts, and other paradigm characteristics in a way that produces an overall design with multiple (divergent and convergent) and complementary (broadly viewed) strengths and nonoverlapping weaknesses

General linear model (GLM)—a mathematical procedure that is the "parent" of many statistical techniques

Generalize—to make statements about a population based on sample data

Generalizing across subpopulations—applying a finding based on a research study sample (e.g., a sample average or correlation) to all subgroups in the target population

Generalizing to a population—applying a finding based on a research study sample (e.g., a sample average or correlation) to the target population (e.g., the population average or correlation)

Generalizing validity—the extent to which the study results can be generalized to and across populations of persons, settings, times, outcomes, and treatment variations; it's a synonym for internal validity

Going native—identifying so completely with the group being studied that you can no longer remain objective

Grounded theory—a general methodology for developing theory that is grounded in data systematically gathered and analyzed

Grounded theory research—a qualitative approach to generating and developing a theory from the data that the researcher collects

Group moderator—the person leading the focus group discussion

Grouped frequency distribution—the data values are clustered or grouped into separate intervals, and the frequencies of each interval are given

Heterogeneous—a set of numbers with a great deal of variability

Hierarchical analysis—search for potential hierarchical arrangement of inductively generated categories in qualitative data analysis

Histogram—a graphic that shows the frequencies and shape that characterize a quantitative variable

Historical research—research about people, places, and events in the past; the process of systematically examining past events or combinations of events to arrive at an account of what happened in the past

History—any event, other than a planned treatment event, that occurs between the pretest and posttest measurement of the dependent variable and influences the postmeasurement of the dependent variable

Holism—the idea that the whole is greater than the sum of its parts

Holistic description—the description of how members of a group interact and how they come together to make up the group as a whole

Homogeneity—in test validity, refers to how well the different items in a test measure the same construct or trait

Homogeneous—a set of numbers with little variability

Homogeneous sample selection—selecting a small and homogeneous case or set of cases for intensive study

Homogeneous test—a unidimensional test in which all the items measure a single construct

Hypothesis—a prediction or educated guess; the formal statement of the researcher's prediction of the relationship that exists among the variables under investigation

Hypothesis coding—defined on page 600 in Chapter 20

Hypothesis testing—the branch of inferential statistics that is concerned with how well the sample data support a null hypothesis and when the null hypothesis can be rejected

Idiographic causation—particular causes, including intentions, of specific or local attitudes, conditions, and events

Idiographic knowledge—understanding of particular events, people, and groups

In-person interview—an interview conducted face-to-face

Incompatibility thesis—the proposition that one cannot mix quantitative and qualitative research

Independent variable—a variable that is presumed to cause a change in another variable

Individual action research—action research that is planned, designed, and conducted by one primary person, such as a teacher

Indirect effect—an effect occurring through an intervening variable

Inductive codes—codes that are generated by a researcher by directly examining the data

Inductive reasoning—the process of drawing a conclusion that is "probably" true

Inferential statistics—statistics that go beyond the immediate data and infer the characteristics of populations based on samples; use of the laws of probability to make inferences and draw statistical conclusions about populations based on sample data

Influence—attempting to apply research to make certain outcomes occur

Informal conversational interview—a spontaneous, loosely structured interview

Informed consent—agreeing to participate in a study after being informed of its purpose, procedures, risks, benefits, alternative procedures, and limits of confidentiality

Inside-outside legitimation—the extent to which the researcher accurately understands, uses, and presents the participants' subjective insider or "native" views (also called the emic viewpoint) and the researcher's objective outsider view (also called the etic viewpoint)

Institutional Review Board (IRB)—the institutional review committee that assesses the ethical acceptability of research proposals

Instrumental case study—interest is in understanding something more general than the particular case

Instrumentation—any change that occurs in the way the dependent variable is measured

Integration legitimation—the degree to which the researcher achieved integration of quantitative and qualitative data, analysis, and conclusions

Intelligence—the ability to think abstractly and learn readily from experience

Interaction effect—when the effect of one independent variable on the dependent variable varies across or depends on the level of another independent variable

Intercoder reliability—consistency among different coders

Interim analysis—the cyclical process of collecting and analyzing data during a single research study

Interim research texts—the evolving research reports or texts that are continually written and revised during the research project

Intermethod mixing—use of more than one method of data collection in a research study

Internal consistency—the consistency with which the items on a test measure a single construct

Internal criticism—the reliability or accuracy of the information contained in the sources collected

Internal validity—the ability to infer that a causal relationship exists between two variables; also called "causal validity"

Internet—a "network of networks" consisting of millions of computers and tens of millions of users all over the world, all of which are interconnected to promote communication

Internet experiment—an experimental study that is conducted over the Internet

Interpretative phenomenological analysis (IPA)—a new type of phenomenology more focused on situated, interpreted, and particular lived experiences than on transcendental experiences

Interpretive or emic validity—accurately portraying the participants' perspectives and meanings, and providing the insider's viewpoint

Interrupted time-series design—a design in which a treatment condition is assessed by comparing the pattern of pretest responses with the pattern of posttest responses obtained from a single group of participants

Interscorer reliability—the degree of agreement or consistency between two or more scorers, judges, or raters

Interval scale—a scale of measurement that has equal intervals of distances between adjacent numbers

Intervening variable—a variable occurring between two other variables in a causal chain (also known as a mediating variable)

Interview—a data-collection method in which an interviewer asks an interviewee questions

Interview guide approach—specific topics and/or open-ended questions are asked in any order

Interview protocol—a data-collection instrument used in an interview

Interviewee—the person being asked questions

Interviewer—the person asking the questions

Intracoder reliability—consistency within a single individual

Intramethod mixing—use of a single method of data collection to obtain a mixture of qualitative and quantitative data

Intrinsic case study—interest is in understanding a specific case

Introduction—the section that introduces the research topic and establishes its importance and significance

In vivo codes—codes that use the words of the research participants

Item stem—the set of words forming a question or statement

Joint display—matrix juxtaposing qualitative and quantitative results for cases, research questions, variables, outcomes, times, locations, or any other dimension of interest

k—the size of the sampling interval

Known groups evidence—evidence that groups that are known to differ on the construct do differ on the test in the hypothesized direction

Laboratory experiment—a study conducted in a controlled environment where one or more variables are precisely manipulated and all or nearly all extraneous variables are controlled

Laboratory observation—observation done in the lab or other setting set up by the researcher

Leading question—a question that suggests a certain answer

Learning organization—organization in which members work together and grow over time, continually improving the organization as a whole

Level of confidence—the probability that a confidence interval to be constructed from a random sample will include the population parameter

Lewin's change theory—a theory of change that includes a three-step process for planned changes in human settings

Life-world—an individual's inner world of immediate experience

Likert scale—a type of summated rating scale invented by Rensis Likert

Line graph—a graph that relies on the drawing of one or more lines

Linguistic-relativity hypothesis—the idea that people see and understand the world through the lens of their local language; people's thoughts are bound by their language (also called the Sapir-Whorf hypothesis)

Living and telling stories—in narrative inquiry, people are seen to live out stories in their experiences and tell stories of those experiences to others

Loaded question—a question containing emotionally charged words

Logic of significance testing—understanding and following the steps shown in Table 19.3

Longitudinal coding—defined on page 601 in Chapter 20

Longitudinal research—data are collected at multiple time points, and comparisons are made across time

Low-inference descriptors—a description that is phrased very similarly to the participants' accounts and the researchers' field notes

Lower limit—the smallest number on a confidence interval

Magnitude coding—defined on page 601 in Chapter 20

Main effect—the effect of one independent variable

Manipulation—an intervention studied by an experimenter

Margin of error—one half the width of a confidence interval

Marginal mean—the mean of scores in the cells of a column or a row

Master list—a list of all the codes used in a research study

Matching—equating the comparison groups on one or more variables that are correlated with the dependent variable

Matching variable—the variable the researcher matches on to eliminate it as an alternative explanation

Maturation—any physical or mental change that occurs over time that affects performance on the dependent variable

Maximum variation sampling—purposively selecting a wide range of cases

Mean—the arithmetic average

Measure of central tendency—the single numerical value considered most typical of the values of a quantitative variable

Measure of variability—a numerical index that provides information about how spread out the data values are or how much variation is present

Measurement—assigning symbols or numbers to something according to a specific set of rules

Measures of relative standing—provide information about where a score falls in relation to the other scores in the distribution of data

Median—the 50th percentile

Mediating variable—see **Intervening variable**

Member checking—discussion of the researcher's conclusions with the study participants

Memoing—recording reflective notes about what you are learning from the data

Mental Measurements Yearbook—one of the primary sources of information about published tests

Meta-analysis—a quantitative technique that is used to integrate and describe the results of a large number of studies

Meta-inference—an inference or conclusion that builds on or integrates quantitative and qualitative insights and findings

Meta-synthesis—the systematic review or integration of qualitative research findings into a literature summary article; it's the qualitative version of a meta-analysis

Method—the section in a research proposal or report that tells the reader about the research design, participants, instruments, and the method(s) of data collection

Method of data collection—a technique for physically obtaining data to be analyzed in a research study

Method of working multiple hypotheses—attempting to identify rival explanations

Methodology—the identification, study, and justification of research methods

Mixed data analysis—the use of both quantitative and qualitative analytical procedures in a research study

Mixed purposeful sampling—the mixing of more than one sampling strategy

Mixed questionnaire—a questionnaire that includes a mixture of open-ended and closed-ended items

Mixed research—(also called **mixed methods research**) research that involves the mixing of quantitative and qualitative methods or other paradigm characteristics

Mixed sampling designs—the eight sampling designs that result from crossing the time orientation criterion and the sample relationship criterion

Mode—the most frequently occurring number

Moderator variable—a variable that changes the relationship between other variables

Modernism—a term used by postmodernists to refer to an earlier and outdated period in the history of science that viewed the world as a static (i.e., unchanging) machine in which everyone follows the same laws of behavior

Multigroup research design—a research design that includes more than one group of participants

Multiple-baseline design—a single-case experimental design in which the treatment condition is successively administered to different participants or to the same participant in several settings after baseline behaviors have been recorded for different periods of time

Multiple data sources—the use of multiple sources of data within a single research or data-collection method

Multiple investigators—the use of multiple researchers and observers in collecting and interpreting the data

Multiple methods—the use of multiple research and data-collection methods

Multiple operationalism—the use of several measures of a construct

Multiple theoretical perspectives—the use of multiple theories, disciplines, and perspectives to interpret and explain the data

Multiple regression—regression based on one dependent variable and two or more independent variables

Multiple validities legitimation—the extent to which all of the pertinent validities (quantitative, qualitative, and mixed) are addressed and resolved successfully

Mutually exclusive—on a questionnaire or interview protocol, *mutually exclusive* refers to response categories that do not overlap (i.e., they are separate or distinct); in descriptive statistics, it's the property that intervals do not overlap at any point

Mutually exclusive categories—a set of categories that are separate or distinct

N—the population size

n—the sample size

Narrative inquiry—the study of experience when experience is understood as lived and told stories; it is a collaboration between researcher and participants, over time, in a place or series of places and in social interaction with their social milieus

Naturalistic generalization—generalizing on the basis of similarity

Naturalistic observation—observation done in real-world settings

Negative-case sampling—selecting cases that are expected to disconfirm the researcher's expectations and generalizations

Negative correlation—the situation when scores on two variables tend to move in opposite directions

Negative criticism—establishing the reliability or authenticity and accuracy of the content of the documents and other sources used by the researcher

Negatively skewed—skewed to the left

Network diagram—a diagram showing the direct links between variables or events over time

Nominal scale—a scale of measurement that uses symbols, such as words or numbers, to label, classify, or identify people or objects

Nomothetic causation—the standard view of causation in science; it refers to causation among variables

Nomothetic knowledge—understanding of general scientific or causal laws

Nondirectional alternative hypothesis—an alternative hypothesis that includes the not equal ($\neq$) sign

Nonequivalent comparison-group design—a design consisting of an experimental group and a nonequivalent untreated comparison group, both of which are administered pretest and posttest measures

Nonexperimental research—research in which the independent variable is not manipulated and there is no random assignment to groups

Nonmaleficence—doing no harm to others

Normal distribution—a unimodal, symmetrical, bell-shaped distribution that is the theoretical model of many variables

Norming group—the specific group for which the test publisher or researcher provides evidence for test validity and reliability

Norms—the written and unwritten rules that specify appropriate group behavior

Null hypothesis—a statement about a population parameter

Numerical rating scale—a rating scale that includes a set of numbers with anchored endpoints

Observation—watching the behavioral patterns of people

Observe phase—a step in the action research cycle in which one collects data and obtains evidence about the success of actions

Observer-as-participant—the researcher spends a limited amount of time observing group members and tells members they are being studied

Official documents—anything written, photographed, or recorded by an organization

One-group posttest-only design—administering a posttest to a single group of participants after they have been given an experimental treatment condition

One-group pretest-posttest design—administering a posttest to a single group of participants after they have been pretested and given an experimental treatment condition

One-stage cluster sampling—a set of clusters is randomly selected, and all the cases in the selected clusters are included in the sample.

One-way analysis of variance—a statistical test used to compare two or more group means (also called one-way ANOVA)

Ontology—the branch of philosophy dealing with the nature of reality and truth

Open coding—the first stage in grounded theory data analysis

Open-ended question—a question that allows participants to respond in their own words

Operationalism—representing constructs by a specific set of steps or operations

Operationalizing a construct—identifying a specific instrument to empirically measure the construct

Opportunistic sampling—selecting cases when the opportunity occurs

Oral histories—interviews with a person who has had direct or indirect experience with or knowledge of the chosen topic

Order effect—a sequencing effect that occurs from the order in which the treatment conditions are administered

Ordinal interaction effect—an interaction effect that occurs when the lines on a graph plotting the effect do not cross

Ordinal scale—a rank-order scale of measurement

Orientational research—research explicitly done for the purpose of advancing an ideological position or orientation

Outcome validity—the ability to generalize across different but related dependent variables

Outlier—a number that is very atypical of the other numbers in a distribution

Panel study—a study in which the same individuals are studied at successive points over time

Paradigm—see **Research paradigm**

Paradigmatic/philosophical legitimation—the degree to which the mixed researcher clearly explains his or her philosophical beliefs about research

Parameter—a numerical characteristic of a population

Partial correlation—used to examine the relationship between two quantitative variables controlling for one or more quantitative extraneous variables

Partial regression coefficient—the regression coefficient obtained in multiple regression

Partially spurious relationship—when the relationship between two variables is partially due to one or more third variables

Participant feedback—discussion of the researcher's conclusions with the actual participants

Participant-as-observer—the researcher spends extended time with the group as an insider and tells members they are being studied

Participatory action research—studies in which team members jointly frame and conduct research, producing knowledge about a shared problem

Passive consent—a process whereby consent is given by not returning the consent form

Path coefficient—the quantitative index providing information about a direct effect

Pattern coding—defined on page 601 in Chapter 20

Pattern matching—predicting a pattern of results and determining whether the actual results fit the predicted pattern

Peer review—discussing one's interpretations and conclusions with one's peers or colleagues

Percentile rank—the percentage of scores in a reference group that fall below a particular raw score

Percentile ranks—scores that divide a distribution into 100 equal parts

Performance measures—a test-taking method in which the participants perform some real-life behavior that is observed by the researcher

Periodicity—the presence of a cyclical pattern in the sampling frame

Personal documents—anything written, photographed, or recorded for private purposes

Personal justifications—a researcher's reasons for undertaking a particular narrative inquiry, that is, why this inquiry matters to the researcher as a person

Personality—the relatively permanent patterns that characterize and can be used to classify individuals

Phenomenology—a form of qualitative research in which the researcher attempts to understand how one or more individuals experience a phenomenon

Photo interviewing—the process of eliciting data from a person using photographic or video imagery when conducting interviews

Photo interviewing analysis—analysis is done by the participant, who examines and "analyzes" a set of visual images

Physical data—any material thing created or left by humans that might provide information about a phenomenon of interest to a researcher

Pilot test—the preliminary test of your questionnaire

Plagiarism—using words or work produced by others and presenting it as your own

Planning phase—articulation of the action research project plan

Point estimate—the estimated value of a population parameter

Point estimation—the use of the value of a sample statistic as the estimate of the value of a population parameter

Population—the large group to which a researcher wants to generalize the sample results; the complete set of cases

Population validity—the ability to generalize the study results to individuals who were not included in the study

Positive correlation—the situation when scores on two variables tend to move in the same direction

Positive criticism—ensuring that the statements made or the meaning conveyed in the various sources is correct

Positively skewed—skewed to the right

Positivism—a term used by qualitative researchers to refer to what might better be labeled "scientism," which is the belief that all true knowledge must be based on science; the term is used by qualitative researchers, not quantitative researchers

Post hoc fallacy—making the argument that because A preceded B, A must have caused B

Post hoc test—a follow-up test to the analysis of variance

Postmodernism—a historical intellectual movement that constructs its self-image as in opposition to modernism; postmodernism emphasizes the primacy of individuality, difference, fragmentation, flux, constant change, lack of foundations for thought, and interpretation

Poststructuralism—a historical intellectual movement that rejects universal truth and emphasizes differences, deconstruction, interpretation, and the power of ideas over people's behavior

Posttest-only control-group design—administering a posttest to two randomly assigned groups of participants after one group has been administered the experimental treatment condition

Posttest-only design with nonequivalent groups—comparing the posttest performance of a group of participants who have been given an experimental treatment condition with that of a group that has not been given the experimental treatment condition

Power—the likelihood of rejecting the null hypothesis when it is false

Practical justifications—the ways in which the research can make a difference to practice

Practical significance—a conclusion made when a relationship is strong enough to be of practical importance

Pragmatic legitimation—the extent to which the research purpose was met, research problem "solved," research questions sufficiently answered, and actionable results provided

Pragmatism—the philosophical position that what works in particular situations is what is important and justified or "valid"

Pragmatist philosophy—a philosophy focused on identifying and relying on what works in particular situations and contexts

Prediction—attempting to predict or forecast a phenomenon

Predictive evidence—validity evidence based on the relationship between test scores collected at one point in time and criterion scores obtained at a later time

Predictive research—research focused on predicting the future status of one or more dependent variables based on one or more independent variables

Presence or absence technique—manipulating the independent variable by presenting one group the treatment condition and withholding it from the other group

Presentism—the assumption that the present-day connotations of terms also existed in the past

Pretest-posttest control-group design—a research design that administers a posttest to two randomly assigned groups of participants after both have been pretested and one of the groups has been administered the experimental treatment condition

Primary source—a source in which the creator was a direct witness or in some other way directly involved with or related to the event

Principle of evidence—the philosophical idea that empirical research provides evidence, not proof

Principle of standardization—providing exactly the same stimulus to each research participant

Privacy—having control of others' access to information about you

Probabilistic—stating what is likely to occur, not what will necessarily occur

Probabilistic cause—a cause that usually produces an outcome; changes in variable *A* tend to produce changes in variable *B*

Probability proportional to size—a type of two-stage cluster sampling in which each cluster's chance of being selected in stage one depends on its population size

Probability value—the probability of the observed result of your research study or a more extreme result, if the null hypothesis were true (also called *p* value)

Probes—prompts to obtain response clarity or additional information

Problem of induction—the future might not resemble the past

Procedure—the section in a research report that describes how the study will be executed

Process coding—defined on page 601 in Chapter 20

Projective measures—a test-taking method in which the participants provide responses to ambiguous stimuli

Proportional stratified sampling—a type of stratified sampling in which the sample proportions are made to be the same as the population proportions on the stratification variable

Prospective study—another term applied to a panel study

Protocol coding—defined on page 601 in Chapter 20

Provisional coding—defined on page 602 in Chapter 20

Pseudonyms—new names researchers construct to hide the identity of individual research participants

Psychological factors—individual-level factors or variables

PsycINFO—a database containing entries from *Psychological Abstracts*

Purpose of a research study—a statement of the researcher's intent or objective of the study

Purposive sampling—the researcher specifies the characteristics of the population of interest and locates individuals with those characteristics

Qualitative interview—an interview providing qualitative data

Qualitative observation—observing all potentially relevant phenomena

Qualitative questionnaire—a questionnaire based on open-ended items and typically used in exploratory or qualitative research

Qualitative research—research that relies primarily on the collection of qualitative data

Qualitative research question—a question about some process, issue, or phenomenon to be explored

Qualitative researcher—a researcher who focuses on exploration, description, and understanding of subjective meanings and sometimes the generation and construction of theories using qualitative data

Qualitative subgroup analysis—looking for relationships between categories/themes and demographic or other grouping factors

Qualitatively driven design—a mixed research design in which the qualitative perspective or way of thinking is emphasized and some quantitative data are added to the study

Qualitizing—converting quantitative data into qualitative data

Quantitative observation—standardized observation

Quantitative questionnaire—a questionnaire based on closed-ended items and typically used in confirmatory or quantitative research

Quantitative research—research that relies primarily on the collection of quantitative data

Quantitative research question—a question about the relationship that exists between two or more variables

Quantitative researcher—a researcher who focuses on testing theories and hypotheses using quantitative data to see if they are confirmed or not

Quantitative variable—a variable that varies in degree or amount

Quantitatively driven design—a mixed research design in which the quantitative perspective or way of thinking is emphasized and some qualitative data are added to the study

Quantitizing—converting qualitative data into quantitative data

Quasi-experimental research design—an experimental research design that does not provide for full control of potential confounding variables primarily because it does not randomly assign participants to comparison groups; it is superior to a weak but inferior to a strong experimental design

Questionnaire—a self-report data-collection instrument filled out by research participants

Quota sampling—the researcher determines the appropriate sample sizes or quotas for the groups identified as important and takes convenience samples from those groups

Random assignment—a procedure that makes assignments to conditions on the basis of chance and in this way maximizes the probability that the comparison groups will be equated on all extraneous variables; randomly assigning a set of people to different groups

Random number generator—a computer program that produces random numbers used in random assignment and random selection

Random selection—randomly selecting a group of people from a population

Range—the difference between the highest and lowest numbers

Ranking—the ordering of responses in ascending or descending order

Rate—the percentage of people in a group who have a specific characteristic

Rating scale—a continuum of response choices

Ratio scale—a scale of measurement that has a true zero point

Rationalism—the philosophical idea that reason is the primary source of knowledge

RCT—a popular term for experimental designs with random assignment of participants to experimental and control groups and, if possible, the use of double-blind procedures

Reactivity—changes that occur in people because they know they are being observed; an alteration in performance that occurs as a result of being aware of participating in a study

Reference group—the norm group that is used to determine the percentile ranks

Reflection phase—a step in the action research cycle in which one thinks about the results, considers strategies for improvement, and begins future planning

Reflexivity—self-reflection by the researcher on his or her assumptions, biases, predispositions, and actions, and their impact on the research situation and evolving interpretations

Regression analysis—a set of statistical procedures that are used to explain or predict the values of a dependent variable on the basis of the values of one or more independent variables

Regression artifact—the tendency of very high pretest scores to become lower and very low pretest scores to become higher on posttesting

Regression coefficient—the predicted change in Y given a 1-unit change in X

Regression-discontinuity design—a design that assesses the effect of a treatment condition by looking for a discontinuity in regression lines between individuals who score lower and higher than some predetermined cutoff score

Regression equation—the equation that defines the regression line

Regression line—the line that best fits a pattern of observations

Relational ethics—caring for and attending to participants' experiences in responsible and responsive ways

Reliability—the consistency or stability of test scores

Reliability coefficient—a correlation coefficient that is used as an index of reliability

Reliving stories—as researchers come alongside research participants, both may begin to relive their stories

Repeated-measures design—a design in which all participants participate in all experimental treatment conditions

Repeated sampling—drawing many or all possible samples from a population

Replication—research examining the same variables with different people

Replication logic—the idea that the more times a research finding is shown to be true with different sets of people, the more confidence we can place in the finding and in generalizing beyond the original participants

Representative sample—a sample that resembles the population

Research design—the outline, plan, or strategy that is used to answer a research question

Research ethics—a set of principles to guide and assist researchers in conducting ethical studies

Research literature—a set of published research studies on a particular topic

Research method—the overall research design and strategy

Research misconduct—fabrication, falsification, or plagiarism in proposing, performing, or reviewing research or reporting research results

Research paradigm—a worldview or perspective held by a community of researchers that is based on a set of shared assumptions, concepts, values, and practices

Research participants—the individuals who participate in the research study

Research problem—an education issue or problem within a broad topic area

Research proposal—the written document summarizing prior literature and describing the procedure to be used to answer the research question(s)

Research protocol—the document submitted to the IRB by the researcher for review

Research puzzle—what guides the study by pointing toward the experiences of participants that a researcher wants to understand more deeply

Research question—statement of the specific question the researcher seeks to answer via empirical research

Research reliability—the consistency, stability, or repeatability of the results of a study

Research topic—the broad subject matter area to be investigated

Research validity—the correctness or truthfulness of an inference that is made from the results of a study

Researcher-as-detective—a metaphor applied to the researcher when searching for cause and effect

Researcher bias—obtaining results consistent with what the researcher wants to find

Response rate—the percentage of people in a sample who participate in a research study

Response set—the tendency to respond in a specific direction regardless of content

Restraining forces—forces resisting change and supporting the status quo

Retelling stories—when researchers inquire into stories, they move beyond regarding a story as a fixed entity and begin to retell stories

Retrospective questions—questions asking people to recall something from an earlier time

Retrospective research—the researcher starts with the dependent variable and moves backward in time

Reverse-worded item—an item on which a lower score indicates a higher level on a construct of interest (also called a reverse-scored item)

Rhetoric—the art or science of language and oral and written communication and argument

Rule of parsimony—preferring the most simple theory that works

Ruling out alternative explanations—making sure that other explanations of your conclusion are not better than the explanation you are using

Sample—a set of elements or cases taken from a larger population

Sample integration legitimation—the degree to which a mixed researcher makes appropriate conclusions, generalizations, and meta-inferences from mixed samples

Sample relationship criterion—says the samples, taken in combination, are identical, parallel, nested, or multilevel

Sampling—the process of drawing a sample from a population

Sampling distribution—the theoretical probability distribution of the values of a statistic that results when all possible random samples of a particular size are drawn from a population

Sampling distribution of the mean—the theoretical probability distribution of the means of all possible random samples of a particular size drawn from a population

Sampling error—the difference between the value of a sample statistic and the population parameter

Sampling frame—a list of all the elements in a population

Sampling interval—the population size divided by the desired sample size

Sapir-Whorf hypothesis—see **Linguistic-relativity hypothesis**

Scatter plot—a graph used to depict the relationship between two quantitative variables

Science—an approach for the generation of knowledge

Second simple case of nonexperimental quantitative research—a design with one quantitative independent variable and one quantitative dependent variable

Second-stage coding—follow-up coding to organize codes/categories and determine their interrelationships for the research report

Secondary data—existing data originally collected or left behind at an earlier time by a different person for a different purpose

Secondary source—a source that was created from primary sources, secondary sources, or some combination of the two

Segmenting—dividing data into meaningful analytical units

Selection-history effect—occurs when an event taking place between the pretest and posttest differentially affects the comparison groups

Selection-instrumentation effect—occurs when the groups react differently to changes in instrumentation

Selection-maturation effect—occurs when the comparison groups mature at different rates

Selection-regression effect—occurs when the groups regress to the mean in a way that obscures the treatment effect

Selection-testing effect—occurs when the groups react to the pretest differently

Selective coding—the final stage in grounded theory data analysis

Self-plagiarism—presenting one's words as original when they have been used previously in another publication

Self-report—a test-taking method in which the participants check or rate the degree to which various characteristics are descriptive of themselves

Semantic differential—a scaling technique in which participants rate a series of objects or concepts

Semiotic visual analysis—the identification and interpretation of symbolic meaning of visual data

Semiotics—the study of signs and what they mean in human cultures

Sequencing effects—biasing effects that can occur when each participant must participate in each experimental treatment condition

Sequential legitimation—the degree to which a mixed researcher appropriately addresses and/or builds on effects or findings from earlier qualitative and quantitative phases

Shared beliefs—the specific cultural conventions or statements that people who share a culture hold to be true or false

Shared values—the culturally defined standards about what is good or bad or desirable or undesirable

Short quotation—quotation of 4 or more words, but fewer than 40, around which quotation marks are used

Significance level—the cutoff the researcher uses to decide when to reject the null hypothesis (also called alpha level); the researcher hopes the p value will be less than the significance level

Significance testing—a commonly used synonym for *hypothesis testing*

Simple cases—when there is only one independent variable and one dependent variable

Simple random sample—a sample drawn by a procedure in which every member of the population has an equal chance of being selected

Simple regression—regression based on one dependent variable and one independent variable

Single-blind procedure—design in which the participant does not know the specific condition he or she is in

Single-case experimental designs—designs that use a single participant to investigate the effect of an experimental treatment condition

Single-loop learning—"fixing" a small problem to get the immediately desired result

Skewed—not symmetrical

Snowball sampling—each research participant is asked to identify other potential research participants

Social desirability response set—the tendency to provide answers that are socially desirable

Social psychological factors—factors relating individuals to other individuals and to social groups

Social/theoretical justifications—the contribution the research can make to theoretical understandings or to making situations more socially just

SocINDEX—a database containing entries from *Sociological Abstracts*

Sociological factors—group- and society-level factors

Sociopolitical legitimation—the degree to which a mixed researcher addresses the interests, values, and viewpoints of multiple stakeholders in the research process

Sourcing—information that identifies the source or attribution of the document

Spearman-Brown formula—a statistical formula used for correcting the split-half reliability coefficient

Special case of the general linear model—one of the "children" of a broader statistical procedure known as the general linear model (GLM)

Split-half reliability—a measure of the consistency of the scores obtained from two equivalent halves of the same test

Spurious relationship—when the relationship between two variables is due to a third variable

Standard deviation—the square root of the variance

Standard error—the standard deviation of a sampling distribution

Standard scores—scores that have been converted from one scale to another to have a particular mean and standard deviation

Standardization—presenting the same stimulus to all participants

Standardized open-ended interview—a set of open-ended questions are asked in a specific order and exactly as worded

Starting point—a randomly selected number between 1 and k

States—distinguishable but less enduring ways in which individuals vary

Statistic—a numerical characteristic of a sample

Statistical conclusion validity—the ability to infer that the independent and dependent variables are related and the strength of that relationship

Statistically significant—a research finding that is probably not attributable to chance alone; a real relationship; the claim made in significance testing when the evidence suggests that the observed result was probably *not* due to chance

Stratification variable—the variable on which the population is divided

Stratified sampling—dividing the population into mutually exclusive groups and then selecting a random sample from each group

Structural coding—defined on page 602 in Chapter 20

Structuralism—a broad or grand theory that emphasizes the importance of cultural, structural, institutional, and functional relations as constituting a large part of the social world in which humans live and holds that this structure is key in determining meaning and influencing human behavior

Subculture—a culture embedded within a larger culture

Summated rating scale—a multi-item scale that has the responses for each person summed into a single score

Summative evaluation—evaluation focused on determining the overall effectiveness and usefulness of the evaluation object

Survey research—a nonexperimental research method based on questionnaires or interviews

Systematic error—an error that is present every time an instrument is used

Systematic sample—a sample obtained by determining the sampling interval, selecting a random starting point between 1 and *k*, and then selecting every *k*th element

Systemwide action research—an action research study in which all organization members work to produce system wide change

Synthesis—the selection, organization, and analysis of the materials collected

***t* test for correlation coefficients**—statistical test used to determine whether a correlation coefficient is statistically significant

***t* test for independent samples**—statistical test used to determine whether the difference between the means of two groups is statistically significant

***t* test for regression coefficients**—statistical test used to determine whether a regression coefficient is statistically significant

Table of random numbers—a list of numbers that fall in a random order

Target population—the larger population to whom the study results are to be generalized

Telephone interview—an interview conducted over the phone

Temporal validity—the extent to which the study results can be generalized across time

Test-retest reliability—a measure of the consistency of test scores over time

Testing—in measurement, testing refers to the measurement of variables; in research design, the testing effect is any change in scores obtained on the second administration of a test as a result of having previously taken the test

Tests in Print—a primary source of information about published tests

Thematic analysis—identification of themes in the research findings

Theme—a word, or more typically, a set of words denoting an important idea that occurs multiple times in your data

Theoretical saturation—occurs when no new information or concepts are emerging from the data and the grounded theory has been validated

Theoretical sensitivity—when a researcher is effective at thinking about what kinds of data need to be collected and what aspects of already collected data are the most important for the grounded theory

Theoretical validity—the degree to which a theoretical explanation fits the data

Theory—an explanation or explanatory system that discusses how a phenomenon operates and why it operates as it does

Theory in use—the theory or explanation that explains what we actually do

Think-aloud technique—has participants verbalize their thoughts and perceptions while engaged in an activity

Third variable—a confounding extraneous variable

Third-variable problem—an observed relationship between two variables that may be due to an extraneous variable

Three required conditions—three things that must be present if you are to contend that causation has occurred

Time-interval sampling—checking for events during specific time intervals

Time orientation criterion—says the samples are either concurrent or sequential

Traits—distinguishable, relatively enduring ways in which one individual differs from another

Transcription—transforming qualitative data into typed text

Translational research—studies focused on converting scientific research into easily understood language and procedures

Treatment diffusion—the participants in one treatment condition are exposed to all or some of the other treatment condition

Treatment variation validity—the ability to generalize across variations of the treatment

Trend study—independent samples are taken from a population over time, and the same questions are asked

Triangulation—a validation approach based on the convergence of results obtained by using multiple investigators, methods, data sources, and/or theoretical perspectives

Two-stage cluster sampling—a set of clusters is randomly selected and then a random sample of elements is drawn from each of the clusters selected in stage one

Type I error—rejecting a true null hypothesis

Type II error—failing to reject a false null hypothesis

Type technique—manipulating the independent variable by varying the type of condition presented to the different comparison groups

Typical-case sampling—selecting what are believed to be average cases

Typology—a classification system that breaks something down into different types or kinds

Understanding—the objective of educational research that attempts to understand the subjective viewpoints of particular people and particular groups

Upper limit—the largest number on a confidence interval

Utilitarianism—an ethical approach that says judgments of the ethics of a study depend on the consequences the study has for the research participants and the benefits that might arise from the study

Vagueness—uncertainty in the meaning of words or phrases

Validation—the process of gathering evidence that supports inferences made on the basis of test scores

Validity—the accuracy of the inferences, interpretations, or actions made on the basis of test scores

Validity coefficient—a correlation coefficient that is computed to provide validity evidence, such as the correlation between test scores and criterion scores

Validity evidence—empirical evidence and theoretical rationales that support the inferences or interpretations made from test scores

Values coding—defined on page 602 in Chapter 20

Variable—a condition or characteristic that can take on different values or categories

Variance—a measure of the average deviation from the mean in squared units

Verstehen—a method of empathetic understanding of others' viewpoints, meanings, intentions, and cultural beliefs

Versus coding—defined on page 602 in Chapter 20

Visual content analysis—the identification and counting of events, characteristics, or other phenomena in visual data

Visual data collection—a process of collecting data using visual sources, such as photographs, drawings, graphics, paintings, film, and video

Warranted assertability—the standard you meet when you provide very good evidence

Weakness minimization legitimation—the degree to which a mixed researcher combines qualitative and quantitative approaches to have nonoverlapping weaknesses

Web surveys—participants read and complete a survey instrument that is developed for and located on the Internet

Who does what, when chart—a useful chart showing what is to occur during the study

Within-case analysis—searching for themes and patterns within a single case; contrasted with cross-case analysis

Within-subjects independent variable—all participants receive all levels of the independent variable

y-intercept—the point where the regression line crosses the y-axis

z score—a raw score that has been transformed into standard deviation units

References

Adams-Price, C. E., Henley, T. B., & Hale, M. (1998). Phenomenology and the meaning of aging for young and old adults. *International Journal of Aging and Human Development, 47*, 263–277.

American Association for the Advancement of Science. (1990). *Science for all Americans: Project 2061*. New York, NY: Oxford University Press.

American Educational Research Association (AERA). (2011). *Code of ethics*. Retrieved from http://www.aera.net/Portals/38/docs/About_AERA/CodeOfEthics(1).pdf

American Educational Research Association, American Psychological Association, & National Council on Measurement in Education (AERA, APA, & NCME). (1985). *Standards for educational and psychological testing*. Washington, DC: American Psychological Association.

American Educational Research Association, American Psychological Association & National Council on Measurement in Education (AERA, APA, & NCME). (1999). *Standards for educational and psychological testing* (2nd ed.). Washington, DC: American Psychological Association.

American Heritage Dictionary of the English Language (4th ed.). (2010). Boston, MA: Houghton Mifflin Harcourt. Retrieved from http://www.yourdictionary.com

American Psychological Association (APA). (1954). Technical recommendations for psychological tests and diagnosis techniques. *Psychological Bulletin, 51*, 201–238.

American Psychological Association (APA). (2001). *Publication manual of the American Psychological Association* (5th ed.). Washington, DC: American Psychological Association.

American Psychological Association (APA). (2010). *Publication manual of the American Psychological Association* (6th ed.). Washington, DC: American Psychological Association.

Anderson, J. R. (1995). *Cognitive psychology and its implications*. New York, NY: W. H. Freeman.

Anguiano, P. (2001). A first-year teacher's plan to reduce misbehavior in the classroom. *Teaching Exceptional Children, 33*, 52–55.

Anyon, J. (2009). *Theory and educational research: Toward critical social explanation*. New York, NY: Routledge.

Argyris, C., Putnam, R., & McLain Smith, D. (1985). *Action science*. San Francisco, CA: Jossey-Bass.

Argyris, C., & Schön, D. (1978). *Organizational learning: A theory of action perspective*. Reading, MA: Addison Wesley.

Argyris, C., & Schön, D. (1996). *Organizational learning II: Theory, method, and practice*. Reading, MA: Addison-Wesley.

Asher, H. B. (1983). *Causal modeling*. Beverly Hills, CA: SAGE.

Babbie, E. (1998). *The practice of social research* (8th ed.). Belmont, CA: Wadsworth.

Babbie, E. R. (1990). *Survey research methods*. Belmont, CA: Wadsworth.

Bailey, K. D. (1994). *Typologies and taxonomies: An introduction to classification techniques*. Thousand Oaks, CA: SAGE.

Bailley, S. E., Dunham, K., & Kral, M. J. (2000). Factor structure of the grief experience questionnaire (GEQ). *Death Studies, 24*, 721–738.

Bakeman, R. (2000). Behavioral observation and coding. In H. T. Reis & C. M. Judd (Eds.), *Handbook of research methods in social and personality psychology* (pp. 138–159). Cambridge, England: Cambridge University Press.

Bandalos, D. L., Yates, K., & Thorndike-Christ, T. (1995). Effects of math self-concept, perceived self-efficacy, and attributions for failure and success on test anxiety. *Journal of Educational Psychology, 87*, 611–623.

Barlow, D. H., Nock, M. K., & Hersen, M. (2009). *Single case experimental designs: Strategies for studying behavior change* (3rd ed.). Boston, MA: Allyn & Bacon.

Barnette, J. J. (1999, April). *Likert response alternative direction: SA to SD or SD to SA: Does it make a difference?* Paper presented at the annual meeting of the American Educational Research Association, Montreal, Canada.

Barnette, J. J. (2000). Effects of stem and Likert response option reversals on survey internal consistency: If you feel the need, there is a better alternative to using those negatively worded stems. *Educational and Psychological Measurement, 60*, 361–370.

Baron, D. (2002, February 1). Will anyone accept the good news on literacy? *Chronicle of Higher Education*, p. 10.

Barthes, R. (1973). *Mythologies*. London, England: Paladin.

Bartlett, T. (2002, May 10). Students become curricular guinea pigs. *Chronicle of Higher Education*, pp. A12–A14.

Bateson, G., & Mead, M. (1942). *Balinese character: A photographic analysis*. New York, NY: Academy of Sciences.

Baumrind, D. (1985). Research using intentional deception: Ethical issues revisited. *American Psychologist, 40,* 165–174.

Bazeley, P. (2003). Computerized data analysis for mixed methods research. In A. Tashakkori & C. Teddlie (Eds.), *Handbook of mixed methods in social and behavioral research* (pp. 385–422). Thousand Oaks, CA: SAGE.

Bazeley, P. (2013). *Qualitative data analysis: Practical strategies.* London, England: SAGE.

Bazeley, P. (2015). Writing up multimethod and mixed methods research for diverse audiences. In S. Hesse-Biber & R. B. Johnson, *The Oxford handbook of multimethod and mixed methods research inquiry* (pp. 296–313). New York, NY: Oxford University Press.

Becker, H. S. (with Richards, P.). (1986). *Writing for social scientists: How to start and finish your thesis, book, or article.* Chicago, IL: University of Chicago Press.

Benson, J., & Hocevar, D. (1985). The impact of item phrasing on the validity of attitude for elementary school children. *Journal of Educational Measurement, 22,* 231–240.

Berg, B. L., & Lune, H. (2012). *Qualitative research methods for the social sciences* (8th ed.). Boston, MA: Pearson.

Berkowitz, A., & Padavic, I. (1999). Getting a man or getting ahead: A comparison of white and black sororities. *Journal of Contemporary Ethnography, 27*(4), 530–557.

Bernard, H. R., & Ryan, G. W. (2010). *Analyzing qualitative data: Systematic approaches.* Thousand Oaks, CA: SAGE.

Bickel, J. (1975). Sex bias in graduate admissions: Data from Berkeley. *Science, 187,* 398–404.

Biehl, J. K. (2002, April 27). 18 die in German high school shooting: Ex-student targets teachers, kills self. *Boston Globe,* p. A1.

Bijou, S. W., Peterson, R. F., Harris, F. R., Allen, K. E., & Johnston, M. S. (1969). Methodology for experimental studies of young children in natural settings. *Psychological Record, 19,* 177–210.

Birnbaum, M. H. (2001). *Introduction to behavioral research in the Internet.* Upper Saddle River, NJ: Prentice Hall.

Blackburn, S. (1994). *The Oxford dictionary of philosophy.* Oxford, England: Oxford University Press.

Blatter, J., & Haverland, M. (2012). *Designing case studies: Explanatory approaches in small-N research.* Basingstoke, England: Palgrave Macmillan.

Bodycott, P., Walker, A., & Kin, J. L. C. (2001). More than heroes and villains: Pre-service teacher beliefs about principals. *Educational Research, 43,* 15–31.

Bogdan, R. C., & Biklen, S. K. (1998). *Qualitative research education: An introduction to theory and methods.* Boston, MA: Allyn & Bacon.

Bollen, K. A., & Lennox, R. (1991). Conventional wisdom on measurement: A structural equation perspective. *Psychological Bulletin, 110,* 305–314.

Bonevac, D. (1999). *Simple logic.* Fort Worth, TX: Harcourt Brace.

Borden, M., Bruce, C., Mitchell, M. A., Carter, V., & Hall, R. V. (1970). Effects of teacher attention on attending behavior of two boys at adjacent desks. *Journal of Applied Behavior Analysis, 3,* 199–203.

Bos, J., Huston, A. C., Granger, R., Duncan, G., Brock, T., & McLoyd, W. C. (1999). *New Hope for people with low incomes: Two-year results of a program to reduce poverty and reform welfare.* New York, NY: Manpower Research Demonstration Corporation.

Bourke, R. T. (2008). First graders and fairy tales: One teacher's action research of critical literacy. *The Reading Teacher, 62,* 304–312.

Box, G. E. P., Hunter, W. G., & Hunter, J. S. (1978). *Statistics for experimenters.* New York, NY: Wiley.

Box, G. E. P., & Jenkins, G. M. (1970). *Time-series analysis: Forecasting and control.* San Francisco, CA: Holden-Day.

Braden, J. P., & Bryant, T. J. (1990). Regression discontinuity designs: Applications for school psychologists. *School Psychology Review, 19,* 232–239.

Brainard, J. (2000, December 8). As U.S. releases new rules on scientific fraud, scholars debate how much and why it occurs. *Chronicle of Higher Education,* p. A26.

Brewer, J., & Hunter, A. (1989). *Multimethod research: A synthesis of styles.* Newbury Park, CA: SAGE.

Breznitz, Z. (1997). Effects of accelerated reading rate on memory for text among dyslexic readers. *Journal of Educational Psychology, 89,* 289–297.

Brown, R., Pressley, M., Van Meter, P., & Schuder, T. (1996). A quasi-experimental validation of transactional strategies instruction with low-achieving second-grade readers. *Journal of Educational Psychology, 88,* 18–37.

Brown, T. (1996). The phenomenology of the mathematics classroom. *Educational Studies in Mathematics, 31,* 115–150.

Bryman, A., & Burgess, R. G. (1994). *Analyzing qualitative data.* London, England: Routledge.

Buck, G., Cook, K., Quigley, C., Eastwood, J., & Lucas, Y. (2009). Profiles of urban, low SES, African American girls' attitudes toward science: A sequential explanatory mixed methods study. *Journal of Mixed Methods Research, 3,* 386–410.

Butler, R., & Neuman, O. (1995). Effects of task and ego achievement goals on help-seeking behaviors. *Journal of Educational Psychology, 87,* 261–271.

Caine, V., Lessard, S., Steeves, P. & Clandinin, D. J. (2013). A reflective turn: Looking backward, looking forward. In Clandinin, D. J., Steeves, P., Caine, V. (Eds.), *Composing lives in transition: A narrative inquiry into the lives of early school leavers.* London, England: Emerald.

Calabrese, R. L., Hester, M., Friesen, S., & Burkhalter, K. (2010). Using appreciative inquiry to create a sustainable rural school district and community. *International Journal of Educational Management, 24,* 250–265.

Campbell, D. T. (1957). Factors relevant to the validity of experiments in social settings. *Psychological Bulletin, 54,* 297–312.

Campbell, D. T. (1969). Reforms as experiments. *American Psychologist, 24,* 409–429.

Campbell, D. T. (1979). Degrees of freedom and the case study. In T. D. Cook & C. S. Reichardt (Eds.), *Qualitative and quantitative methods in evaluation research* (pp. 49–67). Beverly Hills, CA: SAGE.

Campbell, D. T. (1988). Definitional versus multiple operationism. In E. S. Overman (Ed.), *Methodology and epistemology for social science: Selected papers* (pp. 31–36). Chicago, IL: University of Chicago Press.

Campbell, D. T., & Boruch, R. F. (1975). Making the case for randomized assignments to treatments by considering the alternatives: Six ways in which quasi-experimental evaluations in compensatory education tend to underestimate effects. In C. A. Bennett & A. A. Lunsdaine (Eds.), *Evaluation and experiment: Some critical issues in assessing social programs* (pp. 195–275). New York, NY: Academic Press.

Campbell, D. T., & Fiske, D. W. (1959). Convergent and discriminant validation by the multitrait-multimethod matrix. *Psychological Bulletin, 56*, 81–105.

Campbell, D. T., & Stanley, J. C. (1963). *Experimental and quasi-experimental designs for research.* Chicago, IL: Rand McNally.

Capobianco, B. M., & Lehman, J. D. (2006). Integrating technology to foster inquiry in an elementary science methods course: An action research study of one teacher educator's initiatives in a PT3 project. *Journal of Computers, Mathematics, and Science Teaching, 25*, 123–146.

Caracelli, V. W., & Greene, J. C. (1993). Data analysis strategies for mixed-method evaluation designs. *Educational Evaluation and Policy Analysis, 15*, 195–207.

Carr, E. H. (1963). *What is history?* New York, NY: Knopf.

Carr, M., & Jessup, D. L. (1997). Gender differences in first-grade mathematics strategy use: Social and metacognitive influences. *Journal of Educational Psychology, 89*, 318–328.

Cartwright, D. (1978). Theory and practice. *Journal of Social Issues, 34*, 168–180.

Chamberlin, T. (1965). The method of multiple working hypotheses. *Science, 147*, 754–759. (Originally published in 1890 in *Science* (old series), *15*(92))

Chaplin, W. F., John, O. P., & Goldberg, L. R. (1988). Conceptions of state and traits: Dimensional attributes with ideals as prototypes. *Journal of Personality and Social Psychology, 54*, 541–557.

Chi, M. T. H. (1997). Quantifying qualitative analyses of verbal data: A practical guide. *Journal of the Learning Sciences, 6*, 271–315.

Chicago Manual of Style (16th ed.). (2010). Chicago, IL: University of Chicago Press.

Christensen, L., & Pettijohn, L. (2001). Mood and carbohydrate cravings. *Appetite, 36*, 137–145.

Christensen, L. B., Johnson, R. B., & Turner, L. A. (2011). *Research methods, design, and analysis* (11th ed.). Boston, MA: Allyn & Bacon.

Christensen, L. B., Johnson, R. B., & Turner, L. A. (2014). *Research methods, design, and analysis* (12th ed.). New York, NY: Pearson.

Christy, T. E. (1975). The methodology of historical research: A brief introduction. *Nursing Research, 24*, 189–192.

Clandinin, D. J. (Ed.). (2007). *Handbook of narrative inquiry: Mapping a methodology.* Thousand Oaks, CA: SAGE.

Clandinin, D. J. (2013a). *Engaging in narrative inquiry*. Walnut Creek, CA: Left Coast Press.

Clandinin, D. J. (2013b). A narrative account of Truong. In Clandinin, D. J., Steeves, P., Caine, V. (Eds.), *Composing lives in transition: A narrative inquiry into the lives of early school leavers* (pp. 153–166). London, England: Emerald.

Clandinin, D. J., & Caine, V. (2012). Narrative inquiry. In A. A. Trainor & E. Graue (Eds.), *Reviewing qualitative research in the social sciences* (pp. 166–179). New York, NY: Routledge.

Clandinin, D. J., & Connelly, F. M. (2000). *Narrative inquiry: Experience and story in qualitative research.* San Francisco, CA: Jossey-Bass.

Clandinin, D. J., & Rosiek, J. (2007). Mapping a landscape of narrative inquiry: Borderland spaces and tensions. In D. J. Clandinin (Ed.), *Handbook of narrative inquiry: Mapping a methodology* (pp. 35–75). Thousand Oaks, CA: SAGE.

Clandinin, D. J., Steeves, P., & Caine, V. (Eds.). (2013). *Composing lives in transition: A narrative inquiry into the experiences of early school leavers.* Bingley, England: Emerald.

Clark, M. A., Lee, S. M., Goodman, W., & Yacco, S. (2008). Examining male underachievement in public education: Action research at a district level. *NASSP Bulletin, 92*(2), 111–132.

Cochran, W. G. (1977). *Sampling techniques.* New York, NY: Wiley.

Cohen, J. (1968). Multiple regression as a general data-analytic system. *Psychological Bulletin, 70*, 426–443.

Cohen, J., & Cohen, P. (1983). *Applied multiple regression/correlation analysis for the behavioral sciences.* Hillsdale, NJ: Erlbaum.

Cohen, R. J., Swerdlik, M. E., & Phillips, S. M. (1996). *Psychological testing and assessment: An introduction to tests and measurements* (3rd ed.). Mountain View, CA: Mayfield.

Coles, A. P. (2002). How the mayor should fix the schools. *City Journal, 12*(3), 44–51. Retrieved from http://www.city-journal.org/html/how-mayor-should-fix-schools-12354.html

Collier, J., & Collier, M. (1986). *Visual anthropology: Photography as a research method*. Albuquerque: University of New Mexico Press.

Collier, M. (2002). Approaches to analysis in visual anthropology. In T. van Leeuwen & J. Carey (Eds.), *Handbook of visual analysis* (pp. 35–60). London, England: SAGE.

Collingwood, R. G. (1940). *An essay on metaphysics.* Oxford, England: Clarendon.

Collins, K. M. T., Onwuegbuzie, A. J., & Jiao, Q. G. (2007). A mixed methods investigation of mixed methods sampling designs in social and health science research. *Journal of Mixed Methods Research, 1*, 267–294.

Collins, K. M. T., Onwuegbuzie, A. J., & Sutton, I. L. (2006). A model incorporating the rationale and purpose for conducting mixed methods research in special education and beyond. *Learning Disabilities: A Contemporary Journal, 4*, 67–100.

Connelly, F. M., & Clandinin, D. J. (1988). Studying teachers' knowledge of classrooms: Collaborative research, ethics, and the negotiation of narrative. *Journal of Educational Thought, 22*(2A), 269–282.

Connelly, F. M., & Clandinin, D. J. (1990). The cyclic temporal structure of schooling. In M. Ben-Peretz & R. Bromme (Eds.),

Time for teachers: Time in school from the practitioners' perspective (pp. 36–63). New York, NY: Teachers College Press.

Connelly, F. M., & Clandinin, D. J. (2006). Narrative inquiry. In J. Green, G. Camilli, & P. Elmore (Eds.), *Handbook of complementary methods in education research* (3rd ed., pp. 477–487). Mahwah, NJ: Lawrence Erlbaum.

Converse, J. M., & Presser, S. (1986). *Survey questions: Handcrafting the standardized questionnaire.* Newbury Park, CA: SAGE.

Cook, T. D., & Campbell, D. T. (1979). *Quasi-experimentation. Design and analysis issues for field settings.* Chicago, IL: Rand McNally.

Cook, T. D., & Shadish, W. R. (1994). Social experiments: Some developments over the past fifteen years. *Annual Review of Psychology, 45,* 545–580.

Cooper, J. N., & Hall, J. (2016). Understanding black make student athletes' experiences at a historically black college/university: A mixed methods approach. *Journal of Mixed Methods Research, 10,* 46–63.

Cooperrider, D. L., & Whitney, D. (2005). *Appreciative inquiry: A positive revolution in change.* San Francisco, CA: Berrett-Koehler.

Cooperrider, D. L., Whitney, D., & Stavros, J. M. (2008). *Appreciative inquiry handbook* (2nd ed.). Brunswick, OH: Crown Custom.

Cosbie, J. (1993). Interrupted time-series analysis with brief single-subject data. *Journal of Consulting and Clinical Psychology, 61,* 966–974.

Creswell, J. W. (1994). *Research design: Qualitative and quantitative approaches.* Thousand Oaks, CA: SAGE.

Creswell, J. W. (1998). *Qualitative inquiry and research design: Choosing among five traditions.* Thousand Oaks, CA: SAGE.

Creswell, J. W.. (2015). *A concise introduction to mixed methods research.* Los Angeles, CA: SAGE.

Creswell, J. W., & Brown, M. L. (1992). How chairpersons enhance faculty research: A grounded theory study. *Review of Higher Education, 16,* 41–62.

Creswell, J. W., & Plano Clark, V. L. (2011). *Designing and conducting mixed methods research* (2nd ed.). Thousand Oaks, CA: SAGE.

Crocker, L., & Algina, J. (1986). *Introduction to classical and modern test theory.* Fort Worth, TX: Holt, Rinehart, and Winston.

Croft, S. E. (1999). Creating locales through storytelling: An ethnography of a group home for men with mental retardation. *Western Journal of Communication, 63,* 329–347.

Cronbach, L. J. (1951). Coefficient alpha and the internal structure of tests. *Psychometrika, 16,* 297–334.

Cronbach, L. J. (1984). *Essentials of psychological testing* (4th ed.). New York, NY: Harper & Row.

Cronbach, L. J. (1991). *Essentials of psychological testing.* New York, NY: Harper & Row.

Cronbach, L. J., & Meehl, P. E. (1955). Construct validity in psychological tests. *Psychological Bulletin, 52,* 281–302.

Cross, T. L., & Stewart, R. A. (1995). A phenomenological investigation of the *Lebenswelt* of gifted students in rural high schools. *Journal of Secondary Gifted Education, 6,* 273–280.

Dane, F. C. (1990). *Research methods.* Pacific Grove, CA: Brooks/Cole.

Davis, J. A. (1985). *The logic of causal order:* Beverly Hills, CA: SAGE.

Davis, J. A., & Smith, T. W. (1992). *The NORC General Social Survey: A user's guide.* Newbury Park, CA: SAGE.

Deemer, S. A., & Minke, K. M. (1999). An investigation of the factor structure of the Teacher Efficacy Scale. *Journal of Educational Research, 93,* 3–10.

Deering, P. D. (1996). An ethnographic study of norms of inclusion and cooperation in a multiethnic middle school. *Urban Review, 28,* 21–39.

Dempsey, J. V., & Tucker, S. A. (1994). Using photo-interviewing as a tool for research and evaluation. *Educational Technology (Research Section), 34*(4), 55–62.

DeLaPaz, S. (2001). Teaching writing to students with attention deficit disorders and specific language impairment. *Journal of Educational Research, 95,* 37–47.

Denzin, N. K., & Lincoln, Y. S. (Eds.). (2011). *The SAGE handbook of qualitative research* (4th ed.). Thousand Oaks, CA: SAGE.

Devries, P. (2000). Learning how to be a music teacher: An autobiographical case study. *Music Education Research, 2,* 165–179.

Dewey, J. (1896). The reflex arc concept in psychology. *Psychological Review, 3,* 357–370

Dewey, J. (1916). *Democracy and education.* New York, NY: Macmillan.

Dewey, J. (1933). *How we think* (2nd ed.). Boston, MA: D. C. Heath.

Dewey, J. (1938a). *Experience and education.* New York, NY: Macmillan.

Dewey, J. (1938b). *Logic: The theory of inquiry.* New York, NY: H. Holt.

Dey, I. (1993). *Qualitative data analysis: A user-friendly guide for social scientists.* London, England: Routledge.

Deyhle, D. M. (1992, January). Constructing failure and maintaining cultural identity: Navajo and Ute school leavers. *Journal of American Indian Education, 31*(2), 24–47.

Dillman, D. A. (2007). *Mail and internet surveys: The tailored design method.* Hoboken, NJ: John Wiley & Sons.

Doll, R. (1992). Sir Austin Bradford Hill and the progress of medical science. *British Medical Journal, 305,* 1521–1526.

Dority, B. (1999). The Columbine tragedy: Countering the hysteria. *The Humanist, 59*(4), 7.

Draper, R. J., Adair, M., Broomhead, P., Gray, S., Grierson, S., Hendrickson, S., . . . Wright, G. (2011). Seeking renewal, finding community: Participatory action research in teacher education. *Teacher Development, 15*(1), 1–18.

Drew, N. (1986). Exclusion and confirmation: A phenomenology of patients' experiences with caregivers. *IMAGE: Journal of Nursing Scholarship, 18,* 39–43.

Drew, R. S. (1997). Embracing the role of amateur. *Journal of Contemporary Ethnography, 25,* 449–469.

Dykeman, C., Daehlin, W., Doyle, S., & Flamer, H. S. (1996). Psychological predictors of school-based violence: Implications for school counselors. *The School Counselor, 44,* 35–44.

Educational Testing Service. (2013). *GRE Guide to the Use of Scores: 2013–2014.* Princeton, NJ: Educational Testing Service.

Ellickson, P. L. (1989). *Limiting nonresponse in longitudinal research: Three strategies for school-based studies* (Rand Note N-2912-CHF). Santa Monica, CA: RAND.

Ellickson, P. L., & Hawes, J. A. (1989). An assessment of active versus passive methods for obtaining parental consent. *Evaluation Review, 13*, 45–55.

Epstein, K. C., & Sloat, B. (1996a, December 15). In the name of healing: Unwitting test subjects in clinical trials often kept in the dark. (Cleveland, OH) *Plain Dealer*. Retrieved from http://www.kepstein.com/2009/07/31/in-the-name-of-healing/

Epstein, K. C., & Sloat, B. (1996b, December 18). Overseers operate in the dark: Ethics panels only manage cursory reviews of research. (Cleveland, OH) *Plain Dealer*. Retrieved from http://www.kepstein.com/2008/08/05/overseers-operate-in-the-dark/

Epstein, K. C., & Sloat, B. (1996c, December 17). Research standards overseas vary greatly: Europeans worry about fraud, sloppy drug experiments. (Cleveland, OH) *Plain Dealer*. Retrieved from http://www.kepstein.com/2008/08/05/research-standards-overseas-vary-greatly/

Epstein, K. C., & Sloat, B. (1996d, December 16). "Used our kids as guinea pigs": U.S. conducts, pays for experiments on unsuspecting Americans. (Cleveland, OH) *Plain Dealer*. Retrieved from http://www.kepstein.com/2009/07/30/%E2%80%9Cthey-used-our-kids-as-guinea-pigs/

Farrell, E., Peguero, G., Lindsey, R., & White, R. (1988). Giving voice to high school students: Pressure and boredom, ya know what I'm sayin'? *American Education Research Journal, 25*, 489–502.

Feist, J. (1990). *Theories of personality.* Fort Worth, TX: Holt, Rinehart, and Winston.

Fetterman, D. M. (2009). Ethnography. In L. Bickman & D. J. Rog (Eds.), *Handbook of applied social research methods* (2nd ed., pp. 543–588). Thousand Oaks, CA: SAGE.

Finkel, S. E. (1995). *Causal analysis with panel data.* Thousand Oaks, CA: SAGE.

Fisher, J. C. (1993). A framework for describing developmental change among older adults. *Adult Education Quarterly, 43*(2), 76–89.

Flynn, J. R. (1987). Massive IQ gains in 14 nations: What IQ tests really measure. *Psychological Bulletin, 101*, 171–191.

Folkman, S. (2000). Privacy and confidentiality. In B. D. Sales & S. Folkman (Eds.), *Ethics in research with human participants* (pp. 49–58). Washington, DC: American Psychological Association.

Forbes Family. (2002, September 9). The Forbes family (and "Forbes") continues to ride Harleys. *Min Media Newsletter.* Retrieved from Lexis-Nexis.

Ford, D. N., Voyer, J. J., & Wilkinson, J. M. G. (2000). Building learning organizations in engineering cultures: Case study. *Journal of Management in Engineering, 16*(4), 72–83.

Forness, S. R., & Kavale, K. A. (1996). Treating social skill deficits in children with learning disabilities: A meta-analysis of the research. *Learning Disability Quarterly, 19*, 2–9.

Frankfort-Nachmias, C., & Nachmias, D. (1992). *Research methods in the social sciences* (4th ed.). New York, NY: St. Martin's Press.

Freire, P. (1970). *Pedagogy of the oppressed* (M. Bergman Ramos, Trans.). New York, NY: Seabury Press. (Originally published in Portuguese as *Pedagogia do oprimido* in 1968)

Fritze, R. H., Coutts, B. E., & Vyhnanek, L. A. (1990). *Reference sources in history: An introductory guide.* Santa Barbara, CA: ABC-CLIO.

Frontman, K. C., & Kunkel, M. A. (1994). A grounded theory of counselors' construal of success in the initial session. *Journal of Counseling Psychology, 41*, 492–499.

Fuertes, J. N., Sedlacek, W. E., & Liu, W. M. (1994). Using the SAT and noncognitive variables to predict the grades and retention of Asian American university students. *Measurement and Evaluation in Counseling and Development, 27*, 74–84.

Fultz, M. (1995). African American teachers in the South, 1890–1940: Powerlessness and the ironies of expectation and protest. *History of Education Quarterly, 35*, 401–422.

Gage, J. T. (2006). *The shape of reason: Argumentative writing in college* (4th ed.). New York, NY: Pearson/Longman.

Gail, M. H. (1996). Statistics in action. *Journal of the American Statistical Association, 91*(433), 1–13.

Gallo, M. A., & Horton, P. B. (1994). Assessing the effect on high school teachers of direct and unrestricted access to the Internet: A case study of an East Central Florida High School. *Educational Technology Research and Development, 42*(4), 17–39.

Gilbert, L. M., Williams, R. L., & McLaughlin, T. F. (1996). Use of assisted reading to increase correct reading rates and decrease error rates of students with learning disabilities. *Journal of Applied Behavior Analysis, 29*, 255–257.

Gladue, B. A., & Delaney, H. J. (1990). Gender differences in perception of attractiveness of men and women in bars. *Personality and Social Psychology Bulletin, 16*, 378–391.

Glaser, B. G. (1978). *Theoretical sensitivity.* Mill Valley, CA: Sociology Press.

Glaser, B. G., & Strauss, A. L. (1967). *The discovery of grounded theory: Strategies for qualitative research.* New York, NY: Aldine De Gruyter.

Glass, G. V. (1976). Primary, secondary, and meta-analysis of research. *Educational Research, 5*, 3–8.

Glass, G. V., & Hopkins, K. D. (2008). *Statistical methods in education and psychology* (3rd ed.). Boston, MA: Allyn & Bacon.

Glass, G. V., Willson, V. L., & Gottman, J. M. (1975). *Design and analysis of time series.* Boulder, CO: Laboratory of Educational Research Press.

Glazerman, S., Levy, D., & Myers, D. (2003). *Nonexperimental replications of social experiments: A systematic review.* Princeton, NJ: Mathematica Policy Research.

Goffman, E. (1959). *The presentation of self in everyday life.* Garden City, NY: Anchor Books.

Gold, R. (1958). Roles in sociological field observations. *Social Forces, 36*, 217–223.

Goldenberg, C. (1992). The limits of expectations: A case for case knowledge about teacher expectancy effects. *American Educational Research Journal, 29*, 517–544.

Graham, S., & Golan, S. (1991). Motivational influences on cognition: Task involvement, ego involvement, and depth of processing. *Journal of Educational Psychology, 83*, 187–194.

Grant, D. F. (2000). The journey through college of seven gifted females: Influences on their career related decisions. *Roeper Review, 22*, 251–261.

Green, A. J. (1995). Experiential learning and teaching: A critical evaluation of an enquiry which used phenomenological method. *Nurse Education Today, 15*, 420–426.

Greene, J. C. (2007). *Mixed methods in social inquiry*. San Francisco, CA: Jossey-Bass.

Greene, J. C., Caracelli, V. J., & Graham, W. F. (1989). Toward a conceptual framework for mixed-method evaluation designs. *Educational Evaluation and Policy Analysis, 11*, 255–274.

Guba, E. G. (1990). *The paradigm dialog*. Newbury Park, CA: SAGE.

Guba, E. G., & Lincoln, Y. S. (1981). *Effective evaluation*. San Francisco, CA: Jossey-Bass.

Guba, E. G., & Lincoln, Y. S. (1989). *Fourth generation evaluation*. Newbury Park, CA: SAGE.

Guba, E. G., & Lincoln, Y. S. (1992). *Effective evaluation: Improving the usefulness of evaluation results through responsive and naturalistic approaches* (Paperback ed.). San Francisco, CA: Jossey Bass.

Guilford, J. P. (1936). *Psychometric methods*. New York, NY: McGraw-Hill.

Guilford, J. P. (1959). *Personality*. New York, NY: McGraw-Hill.

Gunsalus, C. K. (1993). Institutional structure to ensure research integrity. *Academic Medicine, 68* (Sept. Suppl.), 533–538.

Gunter, P. L., Shores, R. E., Jack, S. L., Denny, R. K., & DePaepe, P. A. (1994). A case study of the effects of altering instructional interactions on the disruptive behavior of a child identified with severe behavior disorders. *Education and Treatment of Children, 17*, 435–444.

Hall, E. (1966). *The hidden dimension*. Garden City, NY: Anchor Books.

Harchar, R. L., & Hyle, A. E. (1996). Collaborative power: A grounded theory of administrative instructional leadership in the elementary school. *Journal of Educational Administration, 34*(3), 15–29.

Harnett, D. L. (1982). *Statistical methods* (3rd ed.). Reading, MA: Addison Wesley.

Harper, D. (2002). Talking about pictures: A case for photo elicitation. *Visual Studies, 17*(1), 13–26.

Harry, B. (1992). An ethnographic study of cross-cultural communication with Puerto Rican–American families in the special education system. *American Educational Research Journal, 29*, 471–494.

Hays, W. L. (1994). *Statistics*. New York, NY: Holt, Rinehart, and Winston.

Heinsman, D. T., & Shadish, W. R. (1996). Assignment methods in experimentation: When do nonrandomized experiments approximate answers from randomized experiments. *Psychological Methods, 1*, 154–169.

Hersen, M., & Barlow, D. H. (1976). *Single case experimental designs: Strategies for studying behavioral change*. New York, NY: Pergamon.

Hersen, M., & Bellack, A. S. (2002). *Dictionary of behavioral assessment techniques*. Clinton Corners, NY: Percheron Press.

Hesse-Biber, S. N. (2010). *Mixed methods research: Merging theory with practice*. New York, NY: Guilford Press.

Hildebrand, D. (2008). *John Dewey: A beginner's guide*. Oxford, England: Oneworld Press.

Hilgartner, S. (1990). Research fraud, misconduct, and the IRB. *IRB: A Review of Human Subjects Research, 12*, 1–4.

Himadi, B., Osteen, P., Kaiser, A. J., & Daniel, K. (1991). Assessment of delusional beliefs during the modification of delusional verbalizations. *Behavioral Residential Treatment, 6*, 355–366.

Hitchcock, J., Johnson, R. B., & Nastasi, B. K. (2009, November). RCT-MM designs: An attempt to improve upon the causal "gold standard." Paper presented at the American Evaluation Association Conference, Orlando, FL.

Holden, C. (1987). NIMH finds a case of "serious misconduct." *Science, 235*, 1566–1567.

Holland, D. C., & Eisenhart, M. A. (1990). *Educated in romance: Women, achievement, and college culture*. Chicago, IL: University of Chicago Press.

Holmes, D. S. (1976a). Debriefing after psychological experiments: I. Effectiveness of postexperimental desensitizing. *American Psychologist, 31*, 868–875.

Holmes, D. S. (1976b). Debriefing after psychological experiments: II. Effectiveness of postdeception dehoaxing. *American Psychologist, 31*, 858–867.

Holy Horatio! (1974, June 10). *Time, 103*, 18.

Howard, J. (2006, November 10). Oral history under review. *Chronicle of Higher Education*, pp. A14–A17.

Howe, K. R., & Dougherty, K. C. (1993). Ethics, institutional review boards, and the changing face of educational research. *Educational Researcher, 22*, 16–21.

Howell, D. C. (2002). *Statistical methods for psychology* (5th ed.). Pacific Grove, CA: Wadsworth.

Howell, D. C. (2013a). *Fundamental statistics for the behavioral sciences*. Belmont, CA: Wadsworth.

Howell, D. C. (2013b). *Statistical methods for psychology* (8th ed.). Belmont, CA: Wadsworth.

Huber, G. P., & Van de Ven, A. H. (1995). *Longitudinal field research methods: Studying processes of organizational change*. Thousand Oaks, CA: SAGE.

Huber, J., & Clandinin, D. J. (2002). Ethical dilemmas in relational narrative inquiry with children. *Qualitative Inquiry, 8*, 785–803.

Huber, J., Murphy, M. S., & Clandinin, D. J. (2011). *Places of curriculum making: Narrative inquiries into children's lives in motion*. London, England: Emerald.

Huber, M., Clandinin, D. J., & Huber, J. (2006). Relational responsibilities of narrative inquirers. *Curriculum and Teaching Dialogue, 8*(1/2), 209–223.

Huberman, A. M., & Miles, M. B. (1994). Data management and analysis methods. In N. K. Denzin & Y. S. Lincoln (Eds.), *Handbook of qualitative research* (pp. 428–445). Newbury Park, CA: SAGE.

Huck, S. W. (2012). *Reading statistics and research* (6th ed.). Boston, MA: Pearson.

Hult, C. A. (1996). *Researching and writing in the social sciences.* Boston, MA: Allyn & Bacon.

Humphreys, P. (1989). *The chances of explanation: Causal explanation in the social, medical, and physical sciences.* Princeton, NJ: Princeton University Press.

Isaac, S., & Michael, W. B. (1995). *Handbook in research and evaluation: For education and the behavioral sciences.* San Diego, CA: Educational and Industrial Testing Services.

Jacob, B. A. (2001). Getting tough? The impact of high school graduation exams. *Educational Evaluation and Policy Analysis, 23*(3), 99–121.

Jaeger, R. M. (1984). *Sampling in education and the social sciences.* New York, NY: Longman.

James, W. (1910). *Pragmatism, a new name for some old ways of thinking: Popular lectures on philosophy.* New York, NY: Longmans, Green. (Originally published in 1907)

Jenkins, J. J., Russell, W. A., & Suci, G. J. (1958). An atlas of semantic profiles for 360 words. *American Journal of Psychology, 71,* 688–699.

Jimerson, S., Carlson, E., Rotert, M., Egeland, B., & Sroufe, L. A. (1997). A prospective, longitudinal study of the correlates and consequences of early grade retention. *Journal of School Psychology, 35,* 3–25.

John, O. P., & Benet-Martinez, V. (2000). Measurement: Reliability, construct validation, and scale construction. In H. T. Reis & C. M. Judd (Eds.), *Handbook of research methods in social and personality psychology* (pp. 339–369). Cambridge, England: Cambridge University Press.

Johnson, A. P. (2008). *A short guide to action research.* Boston, MA: Pearson.

Johnson, R. B. (1994). Qualitative research in education. *SRATE Journal, 4,* 3–7.

Johnson, R. B. (1995). Estimating an evaluation utilization model using conjoint measurement and analysis. *Evaluation Review, 19*(3), 313–338.

Johnson, R. B. (2001). Toward a new classification of nonexperimental quantitative research. *Educational Researcher, 30*(2), 3–13.

Johnson, R. B. (2008). Knowledge. In *The SAGE encyclopedia of qualitative research methods.* Thousand Oaks, CA: SAGE.

Johnson, R. B. (2009). Toward a more inclusive "scientific research in education." *Educational Researcher, 38,* 449–457.

Johnson, R. B. (2012). Guest editor's editorial: Dialectical pluralism and mixed research. *American Behavioral Scientist, 56,* 751–754.

Johnson, R. B. (2016). Dialectical pluralism: A metaparadigm whose time has come. *Journal of Mixed Methods Research,* 1–18. doi: 10.1177/1558689815607692

Johnson, R. B., & Gray, R. (2010). A history of philosophical and theoretical issues for mixed methods research. In A. Tashakkori & C. Teddlie (Eds.), *SAGE handbook of mixed methods in social & behavioral research* (2nd ed., pp. 69–94). Thousand Oaks, CA: SAGE.

Johnson, R. B., & Onwuegbuzie, A. J. (2004). Mixed methods research: A research paradigm whose time has come. *Educational Researcher, 33,* 14–26.

Johnson, R. B., Onwuegbuzie, A. J., Tucker, S., & Icenogle, M. L. (2014). Conducting mixed methods research using dialectical pluralism and social psychological strategies. In P. Leavy (Ed.), *The Oxford handbook of qualitative research.* New York, NY: Oxford.

Johnson, R. B., Onwuegbuzie, A. J., & Turner, L. A. (2007). Toward a definition of mixed methods research. *Journal of Mixed Methods Research, 1*(2), 1–22.

Johnson, R. B., & Stefurak, T. (2013). Considering the evidence-and-credibility discussion in evaluation through the lens of dialectical pluralism. *New Directions for Evaluation, 2013*(138), 37–48.

Johnson, R. B., & Turner, L. A. (2003). Data collection strategies in mixed methods research. In A. Tashakkori & C. Teddlie (Eds.), *Handbook of mixed methods in social and behavioral research* (pp. 297–319). Thousand Oaks, CA: SAGE.

Jonassen, D. H., & Grabowski, B. L. (1993). *Handbook of individual differences, learning, and instruction.* Hillsdale, NJ: Erlbaum.

Jones, J. H. (1981). *Bad blood: The Tuskegee syphilis experiment.* New York, NY: Free Press.

Kaestle, C. F. (1992). Standards of evidence in historical research. *History of Education Quarterly, 32,* 361–366.

Kaestle, C. F. (1997). Recent methodological developments in the history of American education. In R. M. Jaeger (Ed.), *Complementary methods for research in education* (pp. 119–132). Washington, DC: American Educational Research Association.

Kaestle, C. F., Campbell, A., Finn, J. D., Johnson, S. T., & Mikulecky, L. J. (2001). *Adult literacy and education in America: Four studies based on the National Adult Literacy Survey* (NCES 2001-534). Washington, DC: U.S. Department of Education, Office of Educational Research and Improvement, National Center for Education Statistics.

Kalton, G. (1983). *Introduction to survey sampling.* Newbury Park, CA: SAGE.

Karabenick, S. A., & Sharma, R. (1994). Perceived teacher support of student questioning in the college classroom: Its relation to student characteristics and role in the classroom questioning process. *Journal of Educational Psychology, 86,* 90–103.

Kato, H., & Okubo, T. (2006). Problem behavior and classroom atmosphere: A comparison of classes with high and low levels of problem behavior. *Japanese Journal of Educational Psychology, 54,* 34–44.

Keedy, J. L., Fleming, T. G., Gentry, R. B., & Wheat, D. L. (1998). Students as meaning makers and the quest for the common school: A micro-ethnography of a US history classroom. *Journal of Curriculum Studies, 36,* 619–645.

Kenny, D. A., Kashy, D. A., & Bolger, N. (1998). Data analysis in social psychology. In D. Gilbert, S. Fiske, & G. Lindzey (Eds.), *The handbook of social psychology* (Vol. 1, 4th ed., pp. 233–265). Boston, MA: McGraw-Hill.

Kerlinger, F. N. (1986). *Foundations of behavioral research*. Fort Worth, TX: Harcourt Brace Jovanovich.

Keyser, D. J., & Sweetland, R. C. (1984–1994). *Test critiques* (Vols. 1–10). Austin, TX: Pro-Ed.

Kiecolt, K. J., & Nathan, L. E. (1985). *Secondary analysis of survey data*. Newbury Park, CA: SAGE.

Kish, L. (1965). *Survey sampling*. New York, NY: Wiley.

Knapp, T. R. (1978). Canonical correlation analysis: A general parametric significance testing system. *Psychological Bulletin, 85*, 410–416.

Knight, J. A. (1984). Exploring the compromise of ethical principles in science. *Perspectives in Biology and Medicine, 27*, 432–441.

Knoke, D., & Bohrnstedt, G. W. (2002). *Statistics for social data analysis* (4th ed.). Itasca, IL: F. E. Peacock.

Krueger, R. A. (1998). *Moderating focus groups*. Thousand Oaks, CA: SAGE.

Kuder, G. F., & Richardson, M. W. (1937). The theory of the estimation of reliability. *Psychometrika, 2*, 151–160.

Kuhn, T. S. (1962). *The structure of scientific revolutions*. Chicago, IL: University of Chicago Press.

Lake, J. F., & Billingsley, B. S. (2000). An analysis of factors that contribute to parent-school conflict in special education. *Remedial and Special Education, 21*, 240–251.

Lance, G. D. (1996). Computer access in higher education: A national survey of service providers for students with disabilities. *Journal of College Student Development, 37*, 279–288.

Lankenau, S. E. (1999). Stronger than dirt. *Journal of Contemporary Ethnography, 28*, 288–319.

LaPiere, R. T. (1934). Attitudes vs. actions. *Social Forces, 13*, 230–237.

Lasee, M. J., & Smith, D. K. (1991). *Relationships between the KABC and the early screening profiles*. Paper presented at the annual meeting of the National Association of School Psychologists, Dallas, TX.

LeCompte, M. D., & Preissle, J. (1992). Toward an ethnology of student life in schools and classrooms: Synthesizing the qualitative research tradition. In M. D. LeCompte, W. L. Millroy, & J. Preissle (Eds.), *The handbook of qualitative research in education* (pp. 815–859). San Diego, CA: Academic Press.

LeCompte, M. D., & Preissle, J. (1993). *Ethnography and qualitative design in educational research* (2nd ed.). San Diego, CA: Academic Press.

Leikin, S. (1993). Minors' assent, consent, or dissent to medical research. *IRB: A Review of Human Subjects Research, 15*, 1–7.

Lessard. (2013). A narrative account of Skye. In D. J. Clandinin, P. Steeves, & V. Caine (Eds.), *Composing lives in transition: A narrative inquiry into the experiences of early school leavers* (pp. 191–206). Bingley, England: Emerald Group.

Lewin, K. (1946). Action research and minority problems. *Journal of Social Issues, 2*(4), 34–46.

Li, S., Marquart, J. M., & Zercher, C. (2000). Conceptual issues and analytical strategies in mixed-method studies of preschool inclusion. *Journal of Early Intervention, 23*, 116–132.

Likert, R. (1932). A technique for the measurement of attitudes. *Archives of Psychology, 140*, 5–53.

Lincoln, Y. S. (2005). Institutional review boards and methodological conservatism: The challenge to and from phenomenological paradigms. In N. K. Denzin & Y. S. Lincoln (Eds.), *The SAGE handbook of qualitative research* (3rd ed., pp. 165–181). Thousand Oaks, CA: SAGE.

Lincoln, Y. S., & Guba, E. G. (1985). *Naturalistic inquiry*. Newbury Park, CA: SAGE.

Lincoln, Y. S., & Guba, E. G. (2000). Paradigmatic controversies, contradictions, and emerging confluences. In N. K. Denzin & Y. S. Lincoln (Eds.), *Handbook of qualitative research* (pp. 163–188). Thousand Oaks, CA: SAGE.

Lofland, J. (1971). *Analyzing social settings: A guide to qualitative observation and analysis*. Belmont, CA: Wadsworth.

Lofland, J., & Lofland, L. H. (1995). *Analyzing social settings: A guide to qualitative observation and analysis* (2nd ed.). Belmont, CA: Wadsworth.

Losen, D. J., & Skiba, R. J. (2010). *Suspended education: Urban middle schools in crisis*. Montgomery, AL: Southern Poverty Law Center. Retrieved from http://www.splcenter.org/sites/default/files/downloads/publication/Suspended_Education.pdf

Mack, L. (2012). Does every student have a voice? Critical action research on equitable classroom participation practices. *Language Teaching Research, 16*, 417–434.

Maddox, T. (Ed.). (2002). *A comprehensive reference for assessment in psychology, education, and business* (5th ed.). Austin, TX: Pro Ed.

Manthei, R., & Gilmore, A. (1996). Teacher stress in intermediate schools. *Educational Research, 38*, 3–18.

Mantzicopoulos, P., & Knutson, D. J. (2000). Head Start children: School mobility and achievement in the early grades. *Journal of Educational Research, 93*, 305–311.

Markham, J. M. (1985, January 6). Hitler diaries trial stirs judge to disbelief and ire. *New York Times*, p. A14.

Martinson, B. C., Anderson, M. S., & de Vries, R. (2005). Scientists behaving badly. *Nature, 420*, 739–740.

Maruyama, G. M. (1998). *Basics of structural equation modeling*. Thousand Oaks, CA: SAGE.

Max, J. (2002, October 28). Vroom, vroom. *Newsweek*, p. 79.

Maxwell, J. A. (1992). Understanding and validity in qualitative research. *Harvard Educational Review, 62*(3), 279–299.

Maxwell, J. A. (1996). *Qualitative research design*. Newbury Park, CA: SAGE.

Mayer, G. R., Mitchell, L. K., Clementi, T., Clement-Robertson, E., & Myatt, R. (1993). A dropout prevention program for at risk high school students: Emphasizing consulting to promote positive classroom climates. *Education and Treatment of Children, 16*, 135–146.

MacIntyre, A. (2007). *After virtue: A study in moral theory* (3rd ed.). Notre Dame, IN: University of Notre Dame Press.

McKelvie, S. (1978). Graphic rating scales: How many categories? *British Journal of Psychology, 69*, 185–202.

McMenamin, J. (2002, September 20). Schools step up anti-drug efforts with crisis hot line, skits in Carroll: Principal leads campaign after son's fatal overdose. *Baltimore Sun*, p. 6B.

McVea, K., Crabtree, B. F., Medder, J. D., Susman, J. L., Lukas, L., McIlvain, H. E.,. . . Hawver, M. (1996). An ounce of prevention? Evaluation of "Put Prevention into Practice" program. *Journal of Family Practitioners, 43*, 361–369.

Mead, M., Bateson, G., & Macgregor, F. (1951). *Growth and culture: A photographic study of Balinese childhood*. New York, NY: Putnam.

Menard, S. (1991). *Longitudinal research*. Newbury Park, CA: SAGE.

Merriam, S. B. (1988). *Case study research in education: A qualitative approach*. San Francisco, CA: Jossey-Bass.

Merriam, S. B. (2009). *Qualitative research: A guide to design and implementation*. San Francisco, CA: Jossey-Bass.

Merton, R. K. (1948). The self-fulfilling prophecy. *Antioch Review, 8*, 193–210.

Merton, R. K., Fiske, M., & Kendall, P. L. (1956). *The focused interview*. New York, NY: Free Press.

Merton, R. K., & Kendall, P. L. (1946). The focused interview. *American Journal of Sociology, 51*, 541–557.

Messerli, J. (1972). *Horace Mann*. New York, NY: Knopf.

Messick, S. (1989a). Meaning and values in test validation: The science and ethics of assessment. *Educational Researcher, 18*, 5–11.

Messick, S. (1989b). Validity. In R. L. Linn (Ed.), *Educational measurement* (3rd ed., pp. 13–103). New York, NY: Macmillan.

Messick, S. (1995). Validity of psychological assessment: Validation of inferences from persons' responses and performances as scientific inquiry into score meaning. *American Psychologist, 50*, 741–749.

Miles, M. B., & Huberman, A. M. (1984). *Qualitative data analysis*. Beverly Hills, CA: SAGE.

Miles, M. B., & Huberman, A. M. (1994). *Qualitative data analysis: An expanded source book*. Thousand Oaks, CA: SAGE.

Miles, M. B., Huberman, A. M., & Saldaña, J. (2014). *Qualitative data analysis: A methods sourcebook* (3rd ed.). Thousand Oaks, CA: SAGE.

Miller, D. C., & Salkind, N. J. (Eds.). (2002). *Handbook of research design and social measurement* (6th ed.). Thousand Oaks, CA: SAGE.

Mischel, W. (1999). *Introduction to personality*. New York, NY: Holt, Rinehart, and Winston.

Mitchell, M., & Jolley, J. (2001). *Research design explained*. New York, NY: Harcourt College.

Moore, D. S. (1993). *Telecourse study guide for against all odds: Inside statistics and introduction to the practice of statistics*. New York, NY: W. H. Freeman.

Moore, D. S., McCabe, G. P., & Craig, B. (2012). *Introduction to the practice of statistics* (7th ed.). New York, NY: W. H. Freeman.

Morgan, D. L. (1998). Practical strategies for combining qualitative and quantitative methods: Applications to health research. *Qualitative Health Research, 8*, 362–376.

Morgan, D. L. (2014). *Integrating qualitative and quantitative methods: A pragmatic approach*. Thousand Oaks, CA: SAGE.

Morgan, D. L., & Krueger, R. A. (1998). *The focus group kit*. Newbury Park, CA: SAGE.

Morse, J. M. (1991). Approaches to qualitative-quantitative methodological triangulation. *Nursing Research, 40*, 120–123.

Morse, J. M., & Niehaus, L. (2009). *Mixed method design: Principles and procedures*. Walnut Creek, CA: Left Coast Press.

Moustakas, C. (1990). *Heuristic research: Design, methodology, and applications*. Newbury Park, CA: SAGE.

Muller, L. E. (1994). Toward an understanding of empowerment: A study of six women leaders. *Journal of Humanistic Education and Development, 33*, 75–82.

Myers, D. G. (2001). Do we fear the right things? *American Psychological Society Observer, 14*(10). Retrieved from http://www.psychologicalscience.org/observer/1201/prescol.html

National Historical Publications and Records Commission. (1988). *Directory of Archives and Manuscript Repositories in the United States*. Washington, DC: National Historical Publications and Records Commission.

Neisser, U. (1979). The concept of intelligence. *Intelligence, 3*, 217–227.

Nicholls, J. G. (1984). Achievement motivation: Conceptions of ability, subjective experience, task choice and performance. *Psychological Review, 91*, 328–346.

Noddings, N. (1984). *Caring: A feminine approach to ethics and moral education*. Berkeley: University of California Press.

Norton, M. B. (1995). *The American Historical Association's guide to historical literature* (3rd ed.). New York, NY: Oxford University Press.

Nosek, B. A., & Banaji, M. R. (2002). E-research: Ethics, security, design, and control in psychological research on the Internet. *Journal of Social Issues, 58*, 161–176.

Nossiter, A. (2006, November 1). Post-Katrina anger boils over in school. *Mobile Register*, p. 7B.

Nunnally, J. (1978). *Psychometric theory*. New York, NY: McGraw-Hill.

Nunnally, J. C., & Bernstein, L. H. (1994). *Psychometric theory*. New York, NY: McGraw-Hill.

Nye, B., Hedges, L. V., & Konstantopoulos, S. (2001). Are effects of small classes cumulative? Evidence from a Tennessee experiment. *Journal of Educational Research, 94*, 336–345.

O'Brien, D. (2002, July 11). Boy, 16, gets 25 years in killing: Ex high school wrestler fatally shot on mall lot. *Baltimore Sun*, p. 3B.

Ohles, J. F. (Ed.). (1978). *Biographical dictionary of American educators*. Westport, CT: Greenwood.

Okey, T. N., & Cusick, P. A. (1995). Dropping out: Another side of the story. *Educational Administration Quarterly, 31*(2), 244–267.

Omizo, M. M., & Omizo, S. A. (1990). Children and stress: Using a phenomenology approach. *Elementary School Guidance and Counseling, 25*, 30–36.

Onwuegbuzie, A. J. (2003). Effect sizes in qualitative research: A prolegomenon. *Quality & Quantity: International Journal of Methodology, 37*, 393–409.

Onwuegbuzie, A. J., & Collins, K. M. T. (2007). A typology of mixed methods sampling designs in social science research. *The Qualitative Report, 12*, 281–316. Retrieved from http://eric.ed.gov/?id=EJ800183

Onwuegbuzie, A. J., & Johnson, R. B. (2006). The validity issue in mixed research. *Research in the Schools, 13*(1), 48–63.

Onwuegbuzie, A. J., & Leech, N. L. (2004). Enhancing the interpretation of "significant" findings: The role of mixed methods research. *The Qualitative Report, 9*, 770–792.

Onwuegbuzie, A. J., & Leech, N. L. (2006). Linking research questions to mixed methods data analysis procedures. *The Qualitative Report, 11*, 474–498.

Onwuegbuzie, A. J., Slate, J. R., Leech, N. L., & Collins, K. M. T. (2007). Conducting mixed analyses: A general typology. *International Journal of Multiple Research Approaches, 1*, 4–17.

Onwuegbuzie, A. J., & Teddlie, C. (2003). A framework for analyzing data in mixed methods research. In A. Tashakkori & C. Teddlie (Eds.), *Handbook of mixed methods in social and behavioral research* (pp. 351–383). Thousand Oaks, CA: SAGE.

OPRR Reports. (1991). *Code of federal regulations* 45 (Part 46, p. 5). Washington, DC: US Government Printing Office.

Osgood, C. E., Suci, G. J., & Tannenbaum, P. H. (1957). *The measurement of meaning.* Urbana: University of Illinois Press.

Otieno, T. N. (2001). *Higher education: A qualitative inquiry into the educational experiences of seven African women.* Retrieved from http://eric.ed.gov/?id=ED453773

Our opinions: Without excuses, schools succeed [Editorial]. (2002, May 8). *Atlanta Journal-Constitution*, p. 15A.

Patton, M. Q. (1987). *How to use qualitative methods in evaluation.* Newbury Park, CA: SAGE.

Patton, M. Q. (1990). *Qualitative evaluation and research methods.* Newbury Park, CA: SAGE.

Patton, M. Q. (2002). *Qualitative research and evaluation methods* (3rd ed.). Thousand Oaks, CA: SAGE.

Pedhazur, E. J. (1997). *Multiple regression in behavioral research: Explanation and prediction.* Fort Worth, TX: Harcourt Brace.

Pedhazur, E. J., & Schmelkin, L. P. (1991). *Measurement, design, and analysis: An integrated approach.* Hillsdale, NJ: Lawrence Erlbaum.

Peirce, C. S. (1997). Some consequences of four incapacities. In L. Menand (Ed.), *Pragmatism: A reader* (pp. 4–6). New York, NY: Vintage Books. (Originally published in 1868)

Pennebaker, J. W., Dyer, M. A., Caulkins, R. S., Litowitz, D. L., Ackreman, P. L., Anderson, D. B., & McGraw, K. M. (1979). Don't the girls' get prettier at closing time: A country and western application to psychology. *Personality and Social Psychology Bulletin, 5*, 122–125.

Phi Delta Kappa. (1996, September). The 28th annual Phi Delta Kappa/Gallup poll. *Phi Delta Kappan.*

Phillips, D. C., & Burbules, N. C. (2000). *Postpositivism and educational research.* New York, NY: Rowman & Littlefield.

Phillips, S. R. (1994). Asking the sensitive question: The ethics of survey research and teen sex. *IRB: A Review of Human Subjects Research, 16*, 1–6.

Picou, J. S. (1996). Compelled disclosure of scholarly research: Some comments on "high stakes litigation." *Law and Contemporary Problems, 59*, 149–157.

Pielstick, C. (1998). The transforming leader: A meta-ethnography analysis. *Community College Review, 26*, 15–34.

Pillemer, D. B. (1991). One- versus two-tailed hypothesis tests in contemporary educational research. *Educational Researcher, 20*(9), 13–17.

Popper, K. R. (1965). *Conjectures and refutations* (2nd ed.). New York: Basic Books.

Popper, K. R. (1974). Replies to my critics. In P. A. Schilpp (Ed.), *The philosophy of Karl Popper* (pp. 963–1197). La Salle, IL: Open Court.

Popper, K. R. (1985). Falsificationism versus conventionalism. In D. Miller (Ed.), *Popper selections* (pp. 143–151). Princeton, NJ: Princeton University Press. (Originally published in 1934)

Pring, R. (2000). The "false dualism" of educational research. *Journal of Philosophy of Education, 34*, 247–260.

Rech, J. F. (1996, Winter). Gender differences in mathematics achievement and other variables among university students. *Journal of Research and Development in Education, 29*, 73–76.

Reichardt, C. S., & Cook, T. D. (1979). Beyond qualitative versus quantitative methods. In T. D. Cook & C. S. Reichardt (Eds.), *Qualitative and quantitative methods in evaluation research* (pp. 7–32). Beverly Hills, CA: SAGE.

Reichardt, C. S., & Rallis, S. F. (1994). Qualitative and quantitative inquiries are not incompatible: A call for a new partnership. In C. S. Reichardt & S. F. Rallis (Eds.), *The qualitative-quantitative debate: New perspectives* (pp. 85–91). San Francisco, CA: Jossey-Bass.

Reips, U. (2000). The web experiment method: Advantages, disadvantages, and solutions. In M. H. Birnbaum (Ed.), *Psychology experiments on the Internet* (pp. 89–117). New York, NY: Academic Press.

Riemen, D. J. (1983). *The essential structure of a caring interaction: A phenomenological study.* Retrieved from ProQuest Dissertations and theses database (UMI No. 8401214)

Roberson, M. T., & Sundstrom, E. (1990). Questionnaire design, return rates, and response favorableness in an employee attitude questionnaire. *Journal of Applied Psychology, 75*, 354–357.

Robinson, J. P., Shaver, P. R., & Wrightsman, L. S. (1991). *Measures of personality and social psychological attitudes.* New York, NY: Academic.

Roenker, D. L., Thompson, C. P., & Brown, S. C. (1971). Comparison of measures for the estimation of clustering in free recall. *Psychological Bulletin, 76*, 45–48.

Rosenbaum, P. R. (2002). *Observational studies* (2nd ed.). New York, NY: Springer-Verlag.

Rosenberg, D. (2002, June 10). Fighting G-force. *Newsweek*, p. 49.

Rosenberg, M. (1968). *The logic of survey analysis.* New York, NY: Basic Books.

Rosenthal, R. (1991). Teacher expectancy effects: A brief update 25 years after the Pygmalion experiment. *Journal of Research in Education, 1*, 3–12.

Rosenthal, R., & Jacobson, L. (1968). *Pygmalion in the classroom.* New York, NY: Holt, Rinehart, and Winston.

Rosnow, R. L., & Rosnow, M. (2012). *Writing papers in psychology* (9th ed.). Belmont, CA: Wadsworth.

Rossi, P. H., Lipsey, M. W., & Freeman, H. E. (2004). *Evaluation: A systematic approach.* Thousand Oaks, CA: SAGE.

Rossman, G. B., & Wilson, B. L. (1994). Numbers and words revisited: Being "shamelessly eclectic." *Quality and Quantity, 28*, 315–327.

Salmon, M. H. (2007). *Introduction to logic and critical thinking.* Belmont, CA: Thomson Higher Education.

Sandelowski, M. (1995). Focus on qualitative methods: Sample sizes in qualitative research. *Research in Nursing & Health, 18*, 179–183.

Sandelowski, M. (2000). Combining qualitative and quantitative sampling, data collection, and analysis techniques in mixed-method studies. *Research in Nursing Health, 23*, 246–255.

Sandelowski, M. (2001). Real qualitative researchers don't count: The use of numbers in qualitative research. *Research in Nursing and Health, 24*, 230–240.

Sandelowski, M., & Barroso, J. (2003). Creating metasummaries of qualitative findings. *Nursing Research, 52*, 226–233.

Sandoval, C. (2000). *Methodology of the oppressed.* Minneapolis: University of Minnesota Press.

Savoye, C. (2001, November 13). First stop for urban teachers-in-training. *Christian Science Monitor*, p. 14.

Schafer, M., & Smith, P. K. (1996). Teachers' perceptions of play fighting and real fighting in primary school. *Educational Research, 38*, 173–180.

Scheaffer, R. L., Mendenhall, W., & Ott, R. L. (1996). *Elementary survey sampling* (5th ed.). Belmont, CA: Duxbury Press.

Schindler, L. A., & Burkholder, G. J. (2014). A mixed methods examination of the influence of dimensions of support on training transfer. *Journal of Mixed Methods Research*, 1–19. doi: 10.1177/1558689814557132

Schlenker, B. R., & Forsyth, D. R. (1977). On the ethics of psychological research. *Journal of Experimental Social Psychology, 13*, 369–396.

Schön, D. A. (1983). *The reflective practitioner: How professionals think in action.* New York, NY: Basic Books.

Schön, D. A. (1987). *Educating the reflective practitioner.* San Francisco, CA: Jossey-Bass.

Schoonenboom, J., & Johnson, R. B. (in press). How to construct a mixed methods research design. *Cologne Journal for Sociology and Social Psychology.*

Schouten, J. W., & McAlexander, J. H. (1995). Subcultures of consumption: An ethnography of the new bikers. *Journal of Consumer Research, 22*, 43–60.

Schouten, P. G. W., & Kirkpatrick, L. A. (1993). Questions and concerns about the Miller Assessment for Preschoolers. *Occupational Therapy Journal of Research, 13*, 7–28.

Schultz, K. S., & Whitney, D. J. (2014). *Measurement theory in action: Case studies and exercises.* Los Angeles, CA: SAGE.

Schumacker, R. E., & Lomax, R. G. (2004). *A beginner's guide to structural equation modeling* (2nd ed.). Mahwah, NJ: Erlbaum.

Schuman, H., & Presser, S. (1996). *Questions and answers in attitude surveys: Experiments on question form, wording, and content.* Thousand Oaks, CA: SAGE. (Originally published in 1981)

Schutz, P., Croder, K. C., & White, V. E. (2001). The development of a goal to become a teacher. *Journal of Educational Psychology, 93*, 299–308.

Science and Technology Policy Office. (2000, December 6). Executive Office of the President: Federal policy on research misconduct; preamble for research misconduct policy. *Federal Register, 65*, 76260–76264.

Scriven, M. (1967). The methodology of evaluation. In R. E. Stake (Ed.), *Perspectives of curriculum evaluation* (pp. 39–83). Chicago, IL: Rand McNally.

Scriven, M. (1991). *Evaluation thesaurus* (4th ed.). Newbury Park, CA: SAGE.

Sears, S. J., Kennedy, J. J., & Kaye, G. L. (1997). Myers-Briggs personality profiles of prospective educators. *Journal of Education Research, 90*, 195–202.

Senge, P. M. (2006). *The fifth discipline: The art and practice of the learning organization* (Rev. & updated ed.). New York, NY: Doubleday.

Senge, P. M., Cambron-McCabe, N., Lucas, T., Smith, B., Dutton, J., & Kleiner, A. (2012). *Schools that learn: A fifth discipline fieldbook for educators, parents, and everyone who cares about education* (Rev. & updated ed.). New York, NY: Crown.

Severson, H. H., & Ary, D. V. (1983). Sampling bias due to consent procedures with adolescents. *Addictive Behaviors, 8*, 433–437.

Shadish, W. R., Cook, T. D., & Campbell, D. T. (2002). *Experimental and quasi-experimental designs for generalized causal inference.* Boston, MA: Houghton Mifflin.

Shaffir, W. B., & Stebbins, R. A. (Eds.). (1991). *Experiencing fieldwork: An inside view of qualitative research.* Newbury Park, CA: SAGE.

Silverman, D. (1993). *Interpreting qualitative data: Methods for analyzing talk, text and interaction.* London, England: SAGE.

Smith, B. A. (1998). The problem drinker's lived experience of suffering: An exploration using hermeneutic phenomenology. *Journal of Advanced Nursing, 27*, 213–222.

Smith, H. J. (1997). *The role of symbolism in the structure, maintenance, and interactions of high school groupings.* Unpublished master's thesis, University of South Alabama, Mobile.

Smith, J. A., Flowers, P., & Larkin, M. (2009). *Interpretative phenomenological analysis: Theory, method, and research.* London, England: SAGE.

Smith, J. K. (1984). The problem of criteria for judging interpretive inquiry. *Educational Evaluation and Policy Analysis, 6*, 379–391.

Smith, L. T. (2008). *Decolonizing methodologies: Research and indigenous peoples.* New York, NY: Zed Books.

Smucker, B.S., Earleywine, M., & Gordis, E.B. (2005). Alcohol consumption moderates the link between cannabis use and cannabis dependence in the Internet survey. *Psychology of Addictive Behaviors, 19*, 212–216.

Snowling, M. J., Goulandris, N., & Defty, N. (1996). A longitudinal study of reading development in dyslexic children. *Journal of Educational Psychology, 88*, 653–659.

Society for Research in Child Development. (2007). *Ethical standards in research.* Retrieved from http://www.srcd.org/about-us/ethical-standards-research

Solot, D., & Arluke, A. (1997). Learning the scientist's role: Animal dissection in middle school. *Journal of Contemporary Ethnography, 26*, 28–54.

Spradley, J. P. (1979). *The ethnographic interview.* Fort Worth, TX: Holt, Rinehart, and Winston.

Stake, R. E. (1978). The case study method in social inquiry. *Educational Researcher, 7*(2), 5–9.

Stake, R. E. (1995). *The art of case study research.* Thousand Oaks, CA: SAGE.

Stake, R. E. (1997). Case study methods in educational research. In R. M. Jaeger (Ed.), *Complementary methods for research in education* (2nd ed., pp. 253–300). Washington, DC: American Educational Research Association.

Steinberg, J. A. (2002). Misconduct of others: Prevention techniques for researchers. *Observer, 15*, 11, 40.

Sternberg, R. J., Conway, B. E., Ketron, J. L., & Bernstein, M. (1981). People's conception of intelligence. *Journal of Personality and Social Psychology, 41*, 37–55.

Stevens, S. S. (1946). On the theory of scales of measurement. *Science, 103*, 677–680.

Stevens, S. S. (1951). Mathematics, measurement, and psychophysics. In S. S. Stevens (Ed.), *Handbook of experimental psychology* (pp. 1–49). New York, NY: Wiley.

Stewart, D. W., Shamdasani, P. N., & Rook, D. W. (2009). Group depth interviews: Focus group research. In L. Bickman & D. J. Rog (Eds.), *The SAGE handbook of applied social research methods* (2nd ed., pp. 589–616). Thousand Oaks, CA: SAGE.

Stolzenberg, R. M., & Land, K. C. (1983). Causal modeling and survey research. In P. H. Rossi, J. D. Wright, & A. B. Anderson (Eds.), *Handbook of survey research* (pp. 613–675). Orlando, FL: Academic.

Strauss, A. (1995). Notes on the nature and development of general theories. *Qualitative Inquiry, 1*(1), 7–18.

Strauss, A., & Corbin, J. (1990). *Basics of qualitative research: Grounded theory procedures and techniques.* Newbury Park, CA: SAGE.

Strauss, A., & Corbin, J. (1994). Grounded theory methodology: An overview. In N. K. Denzin & Y. S. Lincoln (Eds.), *Handbook of qualitative research* (pp. 273–285). Thousand Oaks, CA: SAGE.

Stringer, E. T. (2013). *Action research* (4th ed.). Thousand Oaks, CA: SAGE.

Strunk, W., Jr., & White, E. B. (2000). *The elements of style* (4th ed.). New York, NY: Longman.

Sudman, S. (1976). *Applied sampling.* New York, NY: Academic.

Suen, H. K., & Ary, D. (1989). *Analyzing quantitative behavioral observation data.* Hillsdale, NJ: Erlbaum.

Tabachnick, B. G., & Fidell, L. S. (1996). *Using multivariate statistics.* New York, NY: HarperCollins.

Tallerico, M., Burstyn, J. N., & Poole, W. (1993). *Gender and politics at work: Why women exit the superintendency.* Fairfax, VA: National Policy Board for Educational Administration.

Tashakkori, A., & Teddlie, C. (1998). *Mixed methodology: Combining qualitative and quantitative approaches.* Thousand Oaks, CA: SAGE.

Tashakkori, A., & Teddlie, C. (2006, April). *Validity issues in mixed methods research: Calling for an integrative framework.* Paper presented at the annual meeting of the American Educational Research Association, San Francisco, CA.

Teddlie, C., & Stringfield, S. (1993). *Schools make a difference: Lessons learned from a 10-year study of school effects.* New York, NY: Teachers College Press.

Teddlie, C., & Tashakkori, A. (2006). A general typology of research designs featuring mixed methods. *Research in the Schools, 13*, 12–28. Retrieved from http://www.msera.org/Rits_131/Teddlie_ Tashakkori_131.pdf

Teddlie, C., & Tashakkori, A. (2009). *Foundations of mixed methods research: Integrating qualitative and quantitative approaches in the social and behavioral sciences.* Thousand Oaks, CA: SAGE.

Teddlie, C., & Yu, F. (2007). Mixed methods sampling: A typology with examples. *Journal of Mixed Methods Research, 1*, 77–100.

Thompson, B. (1998, April 15). *Five methodology errors in educational research: The pantheon of statistical significance and other faux pas.* Invited address presented at the annual meeting of the American Educational Research Association, San Diego, CA.

Thorkildsen, T. A., Nolen, S. B., & Fournier, J. (1994). What is fair? Children's critiques of practices that influence motivation. *Journal of Educational Psychology, 86*, 475–486.

Trochim, W. M. K., & Donnelly, J. P. (2008). *The research methods knowledge base.* Mason, OH: Atomic Dog/Cengage Learning.

Tryfos, P. (1996). *Sampling methods for applied research: Text and cases.* New York, NY: Wiley.

Tryon, W. W. (1982). A simplified time-series analysis for evaluating treatment interventions. *Journal of Applied Behavior Analysis, 15*, 423–429.

Tunnicliffe, S. D. (1995). The content of conversations about the body parts and behaviors of animals during elementary school visits to a zoo and the implications for teachers organizing field trips. *Journal of Elementary Science Education, 7*, 29–46.

Turner, L. A., Johnson, R. B., & Pickering, S. (1996). Effect of ego and task instructions on cognitive performance. *Psychological Reports, 78*, 1051–1058.

University of Michigan Survey Research Center. (1976). *Interviewer's manual* (Rev. ed.). Ann Arbor, MI: Institute for Social Research.

US Office of the Surgeon General. (1964). *Smoking and health: Report of the Advisory Committee to the Surgeon General of the Public Health Service.* Washington, DC: Public Health Service, Office of the Surgeon General.

Valentine, P., & McIntosh, G. (1990). Food for thought: Realities of a women-dominated organization. *Alberta Journal of Educational Research, 36*, 353–369.

Van Haneghan, J. P., & Stofflett, R. T. (1995). Implementing problem solving technology into classrooms: Four case studies of teachers. *Journal of Technology and Teacher Education, 3*(1), 57–80.

Van Manen, M. (1990). *Researching lived experience: Human science for an action sensitive pedagogy.* London, Ontario, Canada: State University of New York Press.

Velleman, P. F., & Wilkinson, L. (1993). Nominal, ordinal, interval, and ratio typologies are misleading. *The American Statistician, 47*, 65–72.

Verhallen, M., Bus, A. G., & de Jong, M. T. (2006). The promise of multimedia stories for kindergarten children at risk. *Journal of Educational Psychology, 98*, 410–419.

Viadero, D. (2001, November 28). Research: Smaller is better. *Education Week.* Retrieved from http://www.edweek.org

Vogt, W. P., & Johnson, R. B. (2011). *Dictionary of statistics and methodology: A nontechnical guide for the social sciences* (4th ed.). Thousand Oaks, CA: SAGE.

Wasley, P. A., Fine, M., King, S. P., Powell, L. C., Holland, N. E., Gladden, R. M., & Mosak, E. (2000). *Small schools: Great strides.* New York, NY: Bank Street College of Education.

Way, N., Stauber, H. Y., Nakkula, M. J., & London, P. (1994). Depression and substance use in two divergent high school cultures: A quantitative and qualitative analysis. *Journal of Youth and Adolescence, 23*(33), 1–357.

Webb, E. J., Campbell, D. T., Schwartz, R. D., & Sechrest, L. (2000). *Unobtrusive measures.* Thousand Oaks, CA: SAGE.

Webb, E. J., Campbell, D. T., Schwartz, R. D., Sechrest, L., & Grove, J. B. (1981). *Nonreactive measures in the social sciences* (2nd ed.). Boston, MA: Houghton Mifflin.

Weber, M. (1968). *Economy and society.* New York, NY: Bedminster.

Weber, R. P. (1990). *Basic content analysis* (2nd ed.). Newbury Park, CA: SAGE.

Wechsler, D. (1989). *Wechsler preschool and primary scale of intelligence—revised.* San Antonio, TX: Psychological Corporation.

Weems, G. H., & Onwuegbuzie, A. J. (2001). The impact of midpoint responses and reverse coding on survey data. *Measurement and Evaluation in Counseling and Development, 34*, 166–176.

Weick, K. E. (1968). Systematic observational methods. In G. Lindzey & E. Aronson (Eds.), *The handbook of social psychology* (Vol. 2, pp. 357–451). Reading, MA: Addison Wesley.

Weiner, B. (Ed.). (1974). *Achievement motivation and attribution theory.* Morristown, NJ: General Learning Press.

Weisner, T. (2000). Understanding better the lives of poor families: Ethnographic and survey studies in the New Hope experiment. *Poverty Research News, 4*(1), 10–12.

Weitzman, E. A., & Miles, M. B. (1995). *Computer programs for qualitative data analysis.* Thousand Oaks, CA: SAGE.

Weng, L., & Cheng, C. (2000). Effects of response order on Likert type scales. *Educational and Psychological Measurement, 60*, 908–924.

Williamson, W. P., Pollio, H. W., & Hood, R. W. (2000). A phenomenological analysis of the anointing among religious serpent handlers. *International Journal for the Psychology of Religion, 10*, 221–240.

Wineburg, S. S. (1991). Historical problem solving: A study of the cognitive processes used in the evaluation of documentary and pictorial evidence. *Journal of Educational Psychology, 33*, 73–87.

Wooley, C. M. (2009). Meeting the mixed methods challenge of integration in a sociological study of structure and agency. *Journal of Mixed Methods Research, 3*, 7–25.

Woolf, P. K. (1988). Deception in science. In American Association for the Advancement of Science and American Bar Association Conference of Lawyers and Scientists, *Project on Scientific Fraud and Misconduct: Report on Workshop Number One.* Washington, DC: American Association for the Advancement of Science.

Worthen, B. R., Sanders, J. R., & Fitzpatrick, J. L. (1997). *Program evaluation.* New York, NY: Longman.

Wright, B. E., & Masters, G. N. (1982). *Rating scale analysis.* Chicago, IL: Mesa Press.

Wynder, E. L., & Graham, E. A. (1950). Tobacco smoking as a possible etiologic factor in bronchogenic carcinoma. *Journal of the American Medical Association, 143*, 329–336.

Yin, R. K. (1981). The case study as a serious research strategy. *Knowledge: Creation, Diffusion, Utilization, 3*, 84–100.

Yin, R. K. (1994). *Case study research: Design and methods.* Thousand Oaks, CA: SAGE.

Yin, R. K. (1998). The abridged version of case study research: Design and method. In L. Bickman & D. J. Rog (Eds.), *Handbook of applied social research methods* (pp. 229–259). Thousand Oaks, CA: SAGE.

Yin, R. K. (2006). Mixed methods research: Are the methods genuinely integrated or merely parallel. *Research in the Schools, 13*, 41–47.

Yin, R. K. (2009). How to do better case studies (with illustrations from 20 exemplary cases). In L. Bickman & D. J. Rog (Eds.), *Handbook of applied social research methods* (2nd ed., pp. 254–282). Thousand Oaks, CA: SAGE.

Yin, R. K. (2014). *Case study research: Design and methods.* Los Angeles, CA: SAGE.

Yoder, P. (1990). Guilt, the feeling and the force: A phenomenological study of the experience of feeling guilty. *Dissertation Abstracts International, 50*, 5341B.

Yow, V. (1994). *Recording oral history: A practical guide for social scientists.* Thousand Oaks, CA: SAGE.

Young, C. H., Savola, K. L., & Phelps, E. (1991). *Inventory of longitudinal studies in the social sciences.* Newbury Park, CA: SAGE.

Ziller, R. C. (1990). *Photographing the self: Methods for observing personal orientations.* Newbury Park, CA: SAGE.

Zimmer, L. (2006). Qualitative meta-synthesis: A question of dialoguing with texts. Journal of Advanced Nursing, 53, 311–318. doi:10.1111/j.1365-2648.2006.03721.x

Zimney, G. H. (1961). *Method in experimental psychology.* New York, NY: Ronald Press.

Author Index

SUBJECT INDEX

About the Authors

R. Burke Johnson (PhD, College of Education, University of Georgia) is a Professor in the Professional Studies Department at the University of South Alabama. He also has graduate degrees in psychology, sociology, and public administration, which give him a multidisciplinary perspective on research methodology. He has published in journals such as the *Educational Researcher*, *Evaluation and Program Planning*, *Evaluation Review*, *Journal of Mixed Methods Research*, *Journal of Educational Psychology*, and *Quantity and Quality.* He was guest editor for a special issue of *Research in the Schools* and a special issue of *American Behavioral Scientist*, both focusing on mixed methods research. He was on the editorial board of the *Educational Researcher* and was an Associate Editor of the *Journal of Mixed Methods Research.* Burke is also coauthor of *Research Methods, Design, and Analysis*; *Dictionary of Statistics and Methodology: A Nontechnical Guide for the Social Sciences*; and the *Oxford Handbook of Multimethod and Mixed Methods Research Inquiry.* Burke also is Executive Director of the Mixed Methods International Research Association (MMIRA) (http://mmira.org).

Larry Christensen (PhD, University of Southern Mississippi) is Professor and Chair of the Department of Psychology at the University of South Alabama. Larry is the author of several successful textbooks and has published more than 70 journal articles.